THE OXFORD DICTIONARY OF
AMERICAN LEGAL QUOTATIONS

THE OXFORD DICTIONARY OF

American
Legal
Quotations

Fred R. Shapiro

New York   Oxford
OXFORD UNIVERSITY PRESS
1993

OXFORD UNIVERSITY PRESS

Oxford   New York   Toronto
Delhi   Bombay   Calcutta   Madras   Karachi
Kuala Lumpur   Singapore   Hong Kong   Tokyo
Nairobi   Dar es Salaam   Cape Town
Melbourne   Auckland   Madrid
and associated companies in
Berlin   Ibadan

Published by Oxford University Press, Inc.
200 Madison Avenue, New York, New York 10016

Oxford is a registered trademark of Oxford University Press

Library of Congress Cataloging-in-Publication Data
Shapiro, Fred R.
The Oxford dictionary of American legal quotations /
Fred R. Shapiro.
p.   cm.
Includes bibliographical references and index.
ISBN 0–19–505859–3
1. Law—United States—Quotations.   I. Title.
KF159.S53   1993
349.73—dc20   92–37829
[347.3]

Permission to use the following quotations is gratefully acknowledged.

DIVORCE 3. Reprinted by permission of Sony Music Publishing, from "D-I-V-O-R-C-E" by
Bobby Braddock and Curly Putman. Copyright © 1968 Tree Publishing Co., Inc. (All rights
administered by Sony Music Publishing, Nashville, TN 37203)
LAWLESSNESS 14. Reprinted by permission of Dwarf Music from "Absolutely Sweet Marie,"
words and music by Bob Dylan. Copyright © 1966 Dwarf Music. All rights reserved.
International copyright secured.
TRIALS, FAMOUS 15, 16. Reprinted by permission of Brandt & Brandt Literary Agents, Inc.,
from Stephen Vincent Benét, *John Brown's Body* (1931), 55, 58.
WEALTH AND POVERTY 20. Reprinted by permission of Ticknor & Fields, a Houghton
Mifflin Company imprint, from "The Grown-Ups," *Old and New Poems* by Donald Hall.
Copyright © 1990 by Donald Hall.

9 8 7 6 5 4 3 2

PRINTED IN THE UNITED STATES OF AMERICA
on acid-free paper

To Jane, Jamie, and Andy

Contents

Preface

Law is the intersection of language and power. Lawyers use words to persuade, to justify, and to govern. Although law produces some of the worst writing to be found anywhere, the best legal writers, such as Oliver Wendell Holmes, Jr., and Abraham Lincoln, have been masters of English prose. Imaginative writers such as Herman Melville have produced a substantial literature addressing legal themes, and humorists such as Mark Twain, Ambrose Bierce, Will Rogers, and Finley Peter Dunne have focused some of their sharpest verbal sword-thrusts on the foibles of the legal system. Reflecting the importance of legal writing and of legal concerns in fiction and drama, a rapidly growing "law and literature" movement commands scholarly and professional attention.

This book brings together for convenient reference and browsing the most famous, the wittiest, and the most insightful words about American law. Lawyers and law students who require material for their legal writing or who are interested in the rich cultural and historical dimensions of their profession, as well as anyone interested in the legal system so pervasive in modern life or in the vital American constitutional legacy, will find here not only a source for locating specific, well-known passages but also a distillation of the best thought on legal issues.

The Oxford Dictionary of American Legal Quotations differs from previous legal quotation dictionaries in two important respects. First, this is the most complete legal compilation ever published, with over 3,500 quotations. It includes a comprehensive collection of the most famous passages of American judges and legal commentators, assembled with the aid of computerized research methods, and the core of the American heritage of constitutional history. Also included are sayings from literature, humor, motion pictures, and even some song lyrics relating to American law. The coverage extends from the earliest to the most contemporary, from the Mayflower Compact to Clarence Thomas.

Second, this is the most scholarly legal quotation dictionary yet published. Most quotation dictionaries are, in reality, works of fiction. By this I mean that there is little relationship between the words printed and words actually written or uttered by the person to whom they are attributed. Paraphrases, misidentifications, and apocryphal sayings are passed along from one book to another. In the legal area only one or two previous books are at all reliable as reference works for quotations.

In the present book all quotations were verified, to the extent possible, from their original source. Where I had to use a later, secondary source, I made every effort to use the most reliable source available, and such source is precisely identified. Citations are exact down to the page number, in keeping with the requirements of legal citation form. In all instances (subject, of course, to inevitable human error) I preserved the wording of the original. As a result, the text and citations of the quotations here are authentic records and are suitable for use in legal writing.

Errors do creep into even the most meticulously prepared reference work. I would welcome corrections from readers, and contributions of additional quotations, for inclusion in future editions. Please address correspondence to Fred R. Shapiro, Yale Law Library, Box 401A Yale Station, New Haven, CT 06520.

S C O P E

What is an "American legal quotation"? This book includes quotations by Americans about law, or by foreigners about American law. Thus, comments on American legal subjects by the Frenchman Alexis de Tocqueville and the Russian Aleksandr Solzhenitsyn are interspersed among remarks by American men and women.

Much harder than defining "American" is defining "legal." I had to draw a line between law and politics, excluding many quotations that could conceivably be called law-related. My principal rule was to include items pertaining to the Constitution, the courts, or the Justice Department. Quotes pertaining to legislation or regulation were included if they focus on aspects likely to be of specific concern to lawyers rather than on general policy issues. Somewhat arbitrarily, I decided to encompass all aspects, whether legal or political, of the following important topics: abortion, capital punishment, censorship, and taxation.

Another borderline area is crime. Here I included quotations about trials or the legal and constitutional standards governing the criminal law. I excluded passages solely about the commission or investigation of crime.

This dictionary includes primarily passages of writing or speech ranging from a sentence to a paragraph in length. Because legal prose is often long-winded and often presents complex ideas requiring exposition, many of the sentences and paragraphs here are longer than is typical in quotation dictionaries. Some passages longer than a paragraph are included because of their great interest or importance. At the other extreme are quotations notable for their brevity: famous phrases, epithets, slogans, and proverbs.

Most quotations were selected because they are well known in law or literature. I made great efforts to include all the most famous law-related quotations. Of the many methods I pursued to achieve this goal, perhaps the most interesting was extensive searching on Mead Data Central's full-text online legal database, LEXIS, which enabled me to retrieve thousands of instances where a judge or law review author referred to something as a "famous quotation" or the like.

This is not, however, a dictionary containing only familiar passages. I supplemented well-known passages with many others that are not famous but that deserve to be because of their wit, eloquence, or insight. The judgment of deservingness is of course a subjective one on my part, but it is my hope that my choices added spice and provocativeness to this compilation. I also put in some quotes solely because of their historical importance.

I cast the widest possible net to encompass quotations from all types of relevant sources. In these pages will be found passages from judicial opinions, legal treatises, law review articles, arguments before courts, constitutions, statutes, legislative materials, ethics rules, presidential documents, and speeches. The colonial documents that underlie our constitutional heritage are fully represented. Nonlegal sources range from fiction, drama, poetry, and other literary works to philosophical, historical, political, and social-scientific writings to humor, folklore, and popular music. A sizable collection of the most memorable law-related lines from motion pictures is also included. Although I preferred the wit of great writers and judges over anonymous humor, I did not neglect the best-known "lawyer jokes," anecdotes, and proverbs, generally recording the earliest version I was able to discover.

It will come as no surprise to students of legal literature that the most often quoted author in *The Oxford Dictionary of American Legal Quotations* is that peerless stylist and aphorist Oliver Wendell Holmes, Jr. More of a revelation is the second-ranked contributor, Robert H. Jackson, who packed more eloquence into his thirteen years on the Supreme Court than any of the longer-serving and more famous justices save Holmes. Third is the great rhetorician Benjamin N. Cardozo. The list of people most often quoted is shaped in part by nonliterary factors, such as historical importance, but it seems to ring pretty true as a ranking of the most eloquent commentators on American law and may therefore be of some interest. Here it is, down to the level of ten quotations (the number in the right-hand column is the number of quotations included):

Oliver Wendell Holmes, Jr.	255	George Sutherland	21
Robert H. Jackson	134	Logan E. Bleckley	20
Benjamin N. Cardozo	127	Finley Peter Dunne	20
Thomas Jefferson	102	Theodore Roosevelt	20
Learned Hand	89	Jerome N. Frank	19
John Marshall	84	Karl N. Llewellyn	19
William O. Douglas	79	Fred Rodell	19
Felix Frankfurter	70	Warren E. Burger	18
Louis D. Brandeis	53	John M. Harlan (1899–1971)	18
William J. Brennan, Jr.	53	Thurgood Marshall	18
Mark Twain	53	Harlan F. Stone	18
Ambrose Bierce	52	James Fenimore Cooper	17
Hugo L. Black	52	Woodrow Wilson	17
Abraham Lincoln	51	Herman Melville	16
Joseph Story	41	Byron R. White	16
H. L. Mencken	37	John Adams	15
Clarence S. Darrow	35	Alexander M. Bickel	15
Earl Warren	35	Lewis F. Powell, Jr.	15
Potter Stewart	32	John M. Harlan (1833–1911)	14
Benjamin Franklin	31	Frank Murphy	14
Alexander Hamilton	31	Franklin D. Roosevelt	14
Charles Evans Hughes	30	Owen J. Roberts	13
Ralph Waldo Emerson	29	William Howard Taft	13
James Madison	27	Arthur Train	12
Alexis de Tocqueville	26	David J. Brewer	11
Harry A. Blackmun	23	John Chipman Gray	11
Henry David Thoreau	23	Roger B. Taney	10
Daniel Webster	23	Robert Traver	10
Will Rogers	21	George Washington	10

ACKNOWLEDGMENTS

Although this book is more the product of an individual's scholarship than are most major reference works, its compilation was greatly aided by some splendid people. Bonnie Turner was my principal research assistant, verifying and inputting the great majority of the quotations. Her accuracy and productivity were exceptional and indispensable to the book's completion. In addition, she contributed many quotations found in the course of research verifying other quotes. Jane Garry performed excellent work of verification and research and also contributed quotations.

A number of volunteers responded helpfully to my appeals for contributions printed in the *New York Times* and other publications. The foremost such contributor was Mary Whisner, who sent me many fine quotations of various types, including invaluable materials from statutory sources. Other substantial contributors were Edward J. Bander, who furnished a collection of one hundred quotes; Bryan A. Garner, who focused on quotations about legal writing; Geoffrey C. Hazard, Jr., who gave me much-needed items on legal ethics; and Michael J. Lynch, who helped with copyright and other areas. Other correspondents who supplied more than one usable contribution were Philip H. DeTurk, David W. Farrar, Jo-Anne Giammattei, Ann Greenfield, Thomas G. Hungar, Seth Kaplan, Jeffrey H. Orleans, Rebecca R. Pressman, S. Victor Tipton, Bernard Weissman, and Carl A. Yirka. It is unfortunately not possible to thank the many people who provided a single quotation each.

I am also indebted to the compilers of previous dictionaries of quotations. Every quotation dictionary stands on the shoulders of its predecessors. Although this work embodies voluminous original research, verification, and editing, I drew upon many previous collections to ensure that all famous passages were included. The most helpful such collections are listed below:

Tony Augarde, *The Oxford Dictionary of Modern Quotations* (1991)
Daniel B. Baker, *Political Quotations* (1990)
John Bartlett, *Familiar Quotations* (various editions)
Gorton Carruth and Eugene Ehrlich, *Harper Book of American Quotations* (1988)
Lester E. Denonn, *The Wit and Wisdom of Oliver Wendell Holmes, Father and Son* (1953)
Mayo DuBasky, *The Gist of Mencken* (1990)
H. H. Emmons, *Light of Emerson* (1930)
John P. Foley, *Jeffersonian Cyclopedia* (1900)
Eugene C. Gerhart, *Quote It!* (1969)
Caroline T. Harnsberger, *Treasury of Presidential Quotations* (1964)
Harry Haun, *The Movie Quote Book* (1980)
Jane E. Horning, *The Mystery Lover's Book of Quotations* (1988)
Percival E. Jackson, *The Wisdom of the Supreme Court* (1962)
Fred Kerner, *A Treasury of Lincoln Quotations* (1965)
M. Frances McNamara, *Ragbag of Legal Quotations* (1960)
M. Frances McNamara, *2,000 Famous Legal Quotations* (1967)
H. L. Mencken, *A New Dictionary of Quotations* (1942)
Elaine Partnow, *The Quotable Woman, 1800–1981* (1982)
Suzy Platt, *Respectfully Quoted* (1989)
George Seldes, *The Great Thoughts* (1985)
Archer H. Shaw, *The Lincoln Encyclopedia* (1950)
David S. Shrager and Elizabeth Frost, *The Quotable Lawyer* (1986)
David L. Sills and Robert K. Merton, *Social Science Quotations* (1991)
Burton E. Stevenson, *Home Book of Proverbs, Maxims, and Familiar Phrases* (1948)
Burton E. Stevenson, *Home Book of Quotations* (various editions)
Ralph L. Woods, *The Businessman's Book of Quotations* (1951)

At Oxford University Press, both former and current staff members were helpful. I thank William Mitchell for first suggesting this work to me, Linda Halvorson Morse for getting it off the ground, and Claude Conyers for providing outstanding editorial guidance. Catherine Guldner superbly set up the database that transformed thousands of index cards into a book, saved my sanity during hard-disk glitches and other crises large and small, and through her hard work and intelligence accomplished myriad computer and editorial aspects of the project.

I acknowledge my deep debts to Morris L. Cohen and Diana Vincent-Daviss, successive directors of the Yale Law Library, for their supportiveness, particularly in granting me a one-month research leave. I thank my other colleagues at the Yale Law Library as well for their encouragement throughout the preparation of this work. My wife, Jane Garry, and my sons Andy and Jamie bore the real brunt of putting up with a husband and father "caught in the web of quotations"; hence the dedication of this book to them.

Fred R. Shapiro
New Haven, Connecticut
October 1992

How to Use This Book

Quotations in this book are arranged by topic, with the topics ordered alphabetically. There are cross-references from topics to other topics. Within each topic, quotes are in chronological order and numbered sequentially. The Constitution of the United States is printed in its entirety as an appendix.

Supplementing the subject arrangement of the body of the dictionary, there is an extensive index by key word at the back of the book to enable the reader to find quotations about highly specific concepts and to locate quotations whose important words are remembered or partially remembered. An index by author is also provided.

Quotations. The text of each quotation is presented as faithfully as possible to the original. Wording and punctuation have been preserved, as have emphasis and capitalization, with the exception that the first letter of the first word is capitalized even when in the original the word is in the middle of a sentence. Archaic spellings have not been modernized.

Citations: Judicial Opinions. This dictionary follows a modified version of the legal citation form prescribed by *The Bluebook* (15th ed. 1991). For quotations from judicial opinions, the citation looks like this:

John M. Woolsey, *United States v. One Book Called "Ulysses,"* 5 F. Supp. 182, 184 (S.D.N.Y. 1933)

This means that the quotation is taken from an opinion by Judge John M. Woolsey in the case titled *United States v. One Book Called "Ulysses."* The case was published in volume 5 of the reporter called the *Federal Supplement* (F. Supp.). The case begins on page 182 of that volume; the quotation is taken from page 184. The court Woolsey sat on was the United States District Court for the Southern District of New York (S.D.N.Y.). The year of the decision was 1933. If the opinion was a dissenting or concurring opinion, "(dissenting)" or "(concur-

ring)" would appear at the end of the citation.

The following are the more common abbreviations used for judicial reporters:

A., A.2d	*Atlantic Reporter*
F., F.2d	*Federal Reporter*
F. Cas.	*Federal Cases*
F. Supp.	*Federal Supplement*
Ga.	*Georgia Reports*
Mass.	*Massachusetts Reports*
N.E., N.E.2d	*North Eastern Reporter*
N.W., N.W.2d	*North Western Reporter*
N.Y., N.Y.2d	*New York Reports*
P., P.2d	*Pacific Reporter*
S. Ct.	*Supreme Court Reporter*
S.E., S.E.2d	*South Eastern Reporter*
So., So.2d	*Southern Reporter*
S.W., S.W.2d	*South Western Reporter*
U.S.	*United States Reports*

State abbreviations, such as "N.J" or "Cal.," represent the official state reporter (*New Jersey Reports* or *California Reports*, in these examples).

Citations: Books. The basic form for citations from books is as follows:

Oliver Wendell Holmes, Jr., *The Common Law* 38 (1881)

Here the quotation is taken from Oliver Wendell Holmes, Jr.'s book *The Common Law*, at page 38. The book was published in 1881. A page number such as 2:143 would mean page 143 of volume 2.

For legal books, every effort has been made to trace and verify quotations from the first edition of the book in question or the earliest edition in which the quote appears. If the edition quoted is not the first, the edition will be indicated before the date, such as "(3d ed. 1895)." If the book has an editor, this will be indicated before the date, as in "(Max Lerner ed. 1943)."

For literary works published after 1900, I have tried where possible to quote from the first edition of the book. For pre-1900 literary works, however, I have generally quoted from the most authoritative modern edition available. The original date of publication of a book quoted from a modern edition is indicated in parentheses, as follows:

> James Fenimore Cooper, *The American Democrat* 167 (1956) (1838)

Citations: Articles. Quotations from law review or other periodical articles are cited with this form:

> Charles A. Reich, "Police Questioning of Law Abiding Citizens," 75 *Yale Law Journal* 1161, 1172 (1966)

The quotation appears in Charles A. Reich's article titled "Police Questioning of Law Abiding Citizens," published in volume 75 of the *Yale Law Journal*. The article begins on page 1161 of that volume, with the quote on page 1172. The article was published in 1966.

If the periodical is separately paginated within each issue, the citation will look like this:

> Derek C. Bok, "A Flawed System," *Harvard Magazine*, May-June 1983, at 38, 41

This article begins on page 38, with the quotation on page 41.

Citations: Reprinted Works. Many quotations in this book are taken from articles, arguments, documents, speeches, short stories, poems, essays, letters, and other works reprinted in collections. Citations for such reprinted works have this form:

> Martin Luther King, Jr., "The Time for Freedom Has Come," 1961, in *A Testament of Hope: The Essential Writings of Martin Luther King, Jr.* 160, 164 (James M. Washington ed. 1986)
>
> Clarence S. Darrow, Speech at Scopes Trial, Dayton, Tenn., 13 July 1925, in *The World's Most Famous Court Trial* 87 (1925)
>
> Thomas Jefferson, Letter to Samuel Kercheval, 12 July 1816, in *Writings of Thomas Jefferson* 10:42–43 (Paul L. Ford ed. 1899)

Note that the author is indicated, followed by the title or description of the reprinted work and its original date. Then the source in which the work is reprinted is cited in the same format outlined above under "Citations: Books." The sources cited are generally authoritative modern editions.

Citations: "Quoted in." Some citations take this form:

> Thomas Reed Powell, quoted in Thurman W. Arnold, *The Symbols of Government* 101 (1935)
>
> Leona Helmsley, quoted in *New York Times*, 12 July 1989, at B2

This kind of citation indicates that the original source is a spoken remark or a published passage that could not be verified in the original source. The secondary source cited is generally the earliest source that could be traced.

Citations: Statutes. A citation to a statute will look like this:

> National Environmental Policy Act of 1969, Pub. L. No. 91–190, § 101(c), 83 Stat. 852, 853 (1970)

This cites to the National Environmental Policy Act of 1969, which was Public Law Number 91–190. The quotation is from section 101(c) of the original act. The act was published in volume 83 of the *Statutes at Large*, beginning at page 852, with the quotation appearing at page 853. The act was passed by Congress in 1970.

Citations: Other Forms. Other citation forms besides the above are either self-explanatory or may be interpreted by consulting the legal citation manual, *The Bluebook* (15th ed. 1991).

Annotations. For selected quotations, I have provided an annotation (in a footnote) supplying further information. Annotations may be editorial comments or other quotations. Editorial comments illuminate the context or significance of the quotation or otherwise add clarification. For example, the annotation to Samuel Goldwyn's attributed remark, "A verbal contract isn't worth the paper it's written on," explains:

> According to Norman Zierold, *The Moguls* 128 (1969), Goldwyn actually said, in praise of the trustworthiness of motion picture executive Joseph M. Schenck, that "His verbal contract is worth more than the paper it's written on." The sentence was then "improved," like many other Goldwynisms, and became famous in the form above.

If a quotation is printed as a footnote, this means that the footnote quotation is a precursor of or a commentary on the quotation footnoted. Joseph Story's renowned 1829 saying "The Law . . . is a jealous mistress" is footnoted with two earlier quotes that foreshadow Story's words: William Jones writing in a 1774 letter that "the law is a jealous science" and an anonymous "Member of the Inner Temple" stating in 1824 that "the law is not so jealous a mistress as to exclude every other object from the mind of her devotee." As is clear from this example, the footnote quotations may be non-

American; I have attempted to track the backgrounds of American quotations wherever the path might lead.

Cross-References. Cross-references, appearing immediately after the citation, direct the reader from the quotation in view to other, related quotations. Thus Alexander Bickel's "The least dangerous branch of the American government is the most extraordinarily powerful court of law the world has ever known" has a cross-reference, "JUDICIARY 3." This refers to the third quotation under the topic JUDICIARY, a passage from the *Federalist* in which Alexander Hamilton writes that "The judiciary, from the nature of its functions, will always be the least dangerous to the political rights of the constitution" (Bickel was alluding to Hamilton's words here).

Index by Key Word. An index by key word is provided in the back of this dictionary to give the reader additional help, beyond the topical arrangement of the quotations themselves, in finding desired quotes. The most important words in the text of the quotations, as many as eight per quote, have been indexed here.

To discover passages about footnotes, for example, you could look up "footnote" alphabetically in the Index by Key Word. There you would see:

footnote: a fat f. is a mother lode, a vein of
LEGAL WRITING 17
The f. foible breeds nothing but sloppy
LEGAL WRITING 15

This tells you that two quotations containing the word "footnote" have been indexed under that key word. For each one, a phrase of several words of context around the key word in the quotation is printed. The phrases are arranged alphabetically. The key word itself is abbreviated (to just the first letter) in its correct position. The absence of an abbreviated word in a phrase means that the key word is the first word of the phrase. If you wished to look up the first phrase above, the notation "LEGAL WRITING 17" on the right tells you that you would find the full quote in this dictionary under the topic LEGAL WRITING, numbered seventeenth within that topic.

The Index by Key Word is especially helpful when you remember or vaguely remember the significant words of a quotation. If you remembered, for example, that a Supreme Court justice had said something about courts not entering a "political thicket," you could look up "political" in the Index by Key Word. Scanning the phrases under that key word, you would come across:

ought not to enter this p. thicket
VOTING 7

Under the topic VOTING in this dictionary, you would find the statement "Courts ought not to enter this political thicket," cited to Felix Frankfurter's opinion in the 1946 case *Colegrove v. Green*.

Index by Author. The Index by Author in the back of this book allows you to find all the items in *The Oxford Dictionary of American Legal Quotations* by a given author. A notation such as "TREASON 2" under an author's name tells you that a passage by that author is the second quotation under the topic TREASON in the dictionary. Each author's name in the Index by Author is followed by his or her birth and death dates, occupation, and, if the person was born in a country other than the United States, his or her nation of birth.

American Legal Quotations

See also PRIVACY

1 This right of privacy, whether it be founded in the Fourteenth Amendment's concept of personal liberty and restrictions upon state action, as we feel it is, or . . . in the Ninth Amendment's reservation of rights to the people, is broad enough to encompass a woman's decision whether or not to terminate her pregnancy.

> **Harry A. Blackmun,** *Roe v. Wade,* 410 U.S. 113, 153 (1973)

2 A State may properly assert important interests in safeguarding health, in maintaining medical standards, and in protecting potential life. At some point in pregnancy, these respective interests become sufficiently compelling to sustain regulation of the factors that govern the abortion decision.

> **Harry A. Blackmun,** *Roe v. Wade,* 410 U.S. 113, 154 (1973)

3 We, therefore, conclude that the right of personal privacy includes the abortion decision, but that this right is not unqualified and must be considered against important state interests in regulation.

> **Harry A. Blackmun,** *Roe v. Wade,* 410 U.S. 113, 154 (1973)

4 Texas urges that, apart from the Fourteenth Amendment, life begins at conception and is present throughout pregnancy, and that, therefore, the State has a compelling interest in protecting that life from and after conception. We need not resolve the difficult question of when life begins. When those trained in the respective disciplines of medicine, philosophy, and theology are unable to arrive at any consensus, the judiciary, at this point in the development of man's knowledge, is not in a position to speculate as to the answer.

> **Harry A. Blackmun,** *Roe v. Wade,* 410 U.S. 113, 159 (1973)

5 (a) For the stage prior to approximately the end of the first trimester, the abortion decision and its effectuation must be left to the medical judgment of the pregnant woman's attending physician.

(b) For the stage subsequent to approximately the end of the first trimester, the State, in promoting its interest in the health of the mother, may, if it chooses, regulate the abortion procedure in ways that are reasonably related to maternal health.

(c) For the stage subsequent to viability, the State in promoting its interest in the potentiality of human life may, if it chooses, regulate, and even proscribe, abortion except where it is necessary, in appropriate medical judgment, for the preservation of the life or health of the mother.

> **Harry A. Blackmun,** *Roe v. Wade,* 410 U.S. 113, 164–65 (1973)

6 *Roe v. Wade* seems like a durable decision. It is, nevertheless, a very bad decision. . . . It is bad because it is bad constitutional law, or rather because it is *not* constitutional law and gives almost no sense of an obligation to try to be.

> **John Hart Ely,** "The Wages of Crying Wolf: A Comment on *Roe v. Wade,*" 82 *Yale Law Journal* 920, 947 (1973)

7 A neutral and durable principle may be a thing of beauty and a joy forever. But if it lacks connection with any value the Constitution marks as special, it is not a constitutional principle and the Court has no business imposing it.

> **John Hart Ely,** "The Wages of Crying Wolf: A Comment on *Roe v. Wade,*" 82 *Yale Law Journal* 920, 949 (1973)

8 If men could get pregnant, abortion would be a sacrament.

> **Florynce Kennedy,** quoted in "The Verbal Karate of Florynce R. Kennedy," *Ms.,* Mar. 1973, at 89

9 The Court's opinion will accomplish the seemingly impossible feat of leaving this area of the law more confused than it found it.

> **William H. Rehnquist,** *Roe v. Wade,* 410 U.S. 113, 173 (1973) (dissenting)

10 The upshot is that the people and the legislatures of the 50 States are constitutionally disentitled to weigh the relative importance of the continued existence and development of the fetus, on the one hand, against a spectrum of possible impacts on the mother, on the other hand. As an exercise of raw judicial power, the Court perhaps has authority to do what it does today; but in my view its judgment is an improvident and extravagant exercise of the power of judicial review that the Constitution extends to this Court.

> **Byron R. White,** *Doe v. Bolton,* 410 U.S. 179, 222 (1973) (dissenting)

11 [In response to the question, "How fair do you believe it is then, that women who can afford to get an abortion can go ahead and have one, and women who cannot afford to are precluded?":] There are many things in life that are not fair,* that wealthy people can afford and poor people can't.

> **Jimmy Carter,** News conference, 12 July 1977, in *Public Papers of the Presidents: Jimmy Carter, 1977,* at 1231, 1237

12 Affirmative sponsorship of particular ethical, religious, or political beliefs is something we expect the State *not* to attempt in a society constitutionally committed to the ideal of individual liberty and freedom of choice.

> **Lewis F. Powell, Jr.,** *Bellotti v. Baird,* 443 U.S. 622, 638 (1979) (plurality)

13 I've noticed that everybody that is for abortion has already been born.

> **Ronald W. Reagan,** Presidential campaign debate, Baltimore, 21 Sept. 1980, quoted in *New York Times,* 22 Sept. 1980, at B7

---

* Some men are killed in a war and some men are wounded, and some men never leave the country, and some men are stationed in the Antarctic and some are stationed in San Francisco. It's very hard in military or in personal life to assure complete equality. Life is unfair.—John F. Kennedy, News Conference, 21 Mar. 1962, in *Public Papers of the Presidents: John F. Kennedy, 1962,* at 254, 259 (1962)

Carter's statement is usually misquoted as "Life is unfair."

14 Neither sound constitutional theory nor our need to decide cases based on the application of neutral principles can accommodate an analytical framework that varies according to the "stages" of pregnancy, where those stages, and their concomitant standards of review, differ according to the level of medical technology available when a particular challenge to state regulation occurs. . . . Our recent cases indicate that a regulation imposed on "a lawful abortion 'is not unconstitutional unless it unduly burdens the right to seek an abortion.'" . . . In my view, this "unduly burdensome" standard should be applied to the challenged regulations throughout the entire pregnancy without reference to the particular "stage" of pregnancy involved.

> **Sandra Day O'Connor,** *City of Akron v. Akron Center for Reproductive Health,* 462 U.S. 416, 452–53 (1983) (dissenting)

15 The Roe framework, then, is clearly on a collision course with itself. As the medical risks of various abortion procedures decrease, the point at which the State may regulate for reasons of maternal health is moved further forward to actual childbirth. As medical science becomes better able to provide for the separate existence of the fetus, the point of viability is moved further back toward conception.

> **Sandra Day O'Connor,** *City of Akron v. Akron Center for Reproductive Health, Inc.,* 462 U.S. 416, 458 (1983) (dissenting)

16 The States are not free, under the guise of protecting maternal health or potential life, to intimidate women into continuing pregnancies.

> **Harry A. Blackmun,** *Thornburgh v. American College of Obstetricians & Gynecologists,* 476 U.S. 747, 759 (1986)

17 Few decisions are more personal and intimate, more properly private, or more basic to individual dignity and autonomy, than a woman's decision . . . whether to end her pregnancy. A woman's right to make that choice freely is fundamental.

> **Harry A. Blackmun,** *Thornburgh v. American College of Obstetricians & Gynecologists,* 476 U.S. 747, 772 (1986)

18 Thus, "not with a bang, but a whimper," the plurality discards a landmark case of

the last generation, and casts into darkness the hopes and visions of every woman in this country who had come to believe that the Constitution guaranteed her the right to exercise some control over her unique ability to bear children. The plurality does so either oblivious or insensitive to the fact that millions of women, and their families, have ordered their lives around the right to reproductive choice, and that this right has become vital to the full participation of women in the economic and political walks of American life.

> Harry A. Blackmun, *Webster v. Reproductive Health Services*, 109 S. Ct. 3040, 3077 (1989) (concurring in part and dissenting in part)

19 For today, at least, the law of abortion stands undisturbed. For today, the women of this Nation still retain the liberty to control their destinies. But the signs are evident and very ominous, and a chill wind blows.

I dissent.

> Harry A. Blackmun, *Webster v. Reproductive Health Services*, 109 S. Ct. 3040, 3079 (1989) (concurring in part and dissenting in part)

20 We are not asking the Court to unravel the fabric of unenumerated and privacy rights . . . which this Court has woven in cases like Meyer and Pierce and Moore and Griswold. Rather, we are asking the Court to pull this one thread.

> Charles Fried, Oral argument before Supreme Court in *Webster v. Reproductive Health Services*, 26 Apr. 1989, quoted in *New York Times*, 27 Apr. 1989, at B12

21 I think the Solicitor General's [Charles Fried's] submission . . . is somewhat disingenuous when he suggests to this Court that he does not seek to unravel the whole cloth of procreational rights, but merely to pull a thread. It has always been my personal experience that when I pull a thread, my sleeve falls off. There is no stopping.

> Frank Susman, Oral argument before Supreme Court in *Webster v. Reproductive Health Services*, 26 Apr. 1989, quoted in *New York Times*, 27 Apr. 1989, at B13

22 Three years ago . . . four Members of this Court appeared poised to "cas[t] into darkness the hopes and visions of every woman in this country" who had come to believe

that the Constitution guaranteed her the right to reproductive choice. . . . All that remained between the promise of *Roe* and the darkness of the plurality was a single, flickering flame. . . . But now, just when so many expected the darkness to fall, the flame has grown bright.

> Harry A. Blackmun, *Planned Parenthood v. Casey*, 112 S. Ct. 2791, 2844 (1992) (concurring in part and dissenting in part)

23 In one sense, the Court's approach is worlds apart from that of THE CHIEF JUSTICE and Justice SCALIA. And yet, in another sense, the distance between the two approaches is short—the distance is but a single vote.

I am 83 years old. I cannot remain on this Court forever, and when I do step down, the confirmation process for my successor well may focus on the issue before us today. That, I regret, may be exactly where the choice between the two worlds will be made.

> Harry A. Blackmun, *Planned Parenthood v. Casey*, 112 S. Ct. 2791, 2854–55 (1992) (concurring in part and dissenting in part)

24 Liberty finds no refuge in a jurisprudence of doubt. Yet 19 years after our holding that the Constitution protects a woman's right to terminate her pregnancy in its early stages, *Roe v. Wade*, . . . that definition of liberty is still questioned.

> Sandra Day O'Connor, Anthony M. Kennedy, and David H. Souter, *Planned Parenthood v. Casey*, 112 S. Ct. 2791, 2803 (1992) (joint opinion)

25 A decision to overrule [*Roe v. Wade*'s] essential holding under the existing circumstances would address error, if error there was, at the cost of both profound and unnecessary damage to the Court's legitimacy, and to the Nation's commitment to the rule of law. It is therefore imperative to adhere to the essence of *Roe* 's original decision, and we do so today.

> Sandra Day O'Connor, Anthony M. Kennedy, and David H. Souter, *Planned Parenthood v. Casey*, 112 S. Ct. 2791, 2816 (1992) (joint opinion)

26 An undue burden exists, and therefore a provision of law is invalid, if its purpose or effect is to place a substantial obstacle in

the path of a woman seeking an abortion before the fetus attains viability.

Sandra Day O'Connor, Anthony M. Kennedy, and David H. Souter, *Planned Parenthood v. Casey,* 112 S. Ct. 2791, 2821 (1992) (joint opinion)

27 The sum of the joint opinion's labors in the name of *stare decisis* and "legitimacy" is this: *Roe v. Wade* stands as a sort of judicial Potemkin Village, which may be pointed out to passers by as a monument to the importance of adhering to precedent.

William H. Rehnquist, *Planned Parenthood v. Casey,* 112 S. Ct. 2791, 2866–67 (1992) (concurring in part and dissenting in part)

28 That is, quite simply, the issue in this case: not whether the power of a woman to abort her unborn child is a "liberty" in the absolute sense; or even whether it is a liberty of great importance to many women. Of course it is both. The issue is whether it is a liberty protected by the Constitution of the United States. I am sure it is not.

Antonin Scalia, *Planned Parenthood v. Casey,* 112 S. Ct. 2791, 2874 (1992) (concurring in part and dissenting in part)

ADMINISTRATIVE LAW

See also REGULATION

1 The legislature cannot delegate its power to make a law; but it can make a law to delegate a power to determine some fact or state of things upon which the law makes, or intends to make, its own action depend. To deny this would be to stop the wheels of government. There are many things upon which wise and useful legislation must depend, which cannot be known to the law-making power, and must, therefore, be a subject of inquiry and determination outside of the halls of legislation.

Daniel Agnew, *Locke's Appeal,* 72 Pa. 491, 498–99 (1873)

2 In determining these mixed questions of law and fact, the court confines itself to the ultimate question as to whether the Commission acted within its power. It will not consider the expediency or wisdom of the order, or whether, on like testimony, it would have made a similar ruling. . . . Its conclusion, of course, is subject to review, but when supported by evidence is ac-

cepted as final; not that its decision, involving as it does so many and such vast public interests, can be supported by a mere scintilla of proof—but the courts will not examine the facts further than to determine whether there was substantial evidence to sustain the order.

Joseph R. Lamar, *ICC v. Union Pacific R.R.,* 222 U.S. 541, 547–48 (1912)

3 Before these agencies [federal administrative agencies] the old doctrine prohibiting the delegation of legislative power has virtually retired from the field and given up the fight. There will be no withdrawal from these experiments. We shall go on; we shall expand them, whether we approve theoretically or not, because such agencies furnish protection to rights and obstacles to wrong doing which under our new social and industrial conditions cannot be practically accomplished by the old and simple procedures of legislatures and courts as in the last generation.

Elihu Root, "Public Service by the Bar" (address), Chicago, 30 Aug. 1916, in 41 *American Bar Association Report* 355, 368–69 (1916)

4 In recent years we have been trying some dangerous experiments in autocracy in this country, in passing numerous laws under which administrative officers are given extraordinary powers over the liberty and property of individuals without those safeguards afforded by judicial review and by our traditional legal procedure.

Harlan F. Stone, Address to New Jersey State Bar Association, Newark, N.J., 26 Feb. 1921, in *New Jersey State Bar Association Yearbook, 1921–1922,* at 49, 60

5 The power of administrative bodies to make findings of fact which may be treated as conclusive, if there is evidence both ways, is a power of enormous consequence. An unscrupulous administrator might be tempted to say "Let me find the facts for the people of my country, and I care little who lays down the general principles."

Charles Evans Hughes, "Important Work of Uncle Sam's Lawyers," 17 *American Bar Association Journal* 237, 238 (1931)

6 Where the regulation is within the scope of authority legally delegated, the presump-

tion of the existence of facts justifying its specific exercise attaches alike to statutes . . . and to [rules] of administrative bodies.

Louis D. Brandeis, *Pacific States Box & Basket Co. v. White,* 296 U.S. 176, 186 (1935)

7 The difficulty is that it has not said so with the simplicity and clearness through which a halting impression ripens into reasonable certitude. In the end we are left to spell out, to argue, to choose between conflicting inferences. Something more precise is requisite in the quasi-jurisdictional findings of an administrative agency. . . . We must know what a decision means before the duty becomes ours to say whether it is right or wrong.

Benjamin N. Cardozo, *United States v. Chicago, Milwaukee, St. Paul & Pac. R.R.,* 294 U.S. 499, 510–11 (1935)

8 The supremacy of law demands that there shall be opportunity to have some court decide whether an erroneous rule of law was applied; and whether the proceeding in which facts were adjudicated was conducted regularly. To that extent, the person asserting a right, whatever its source, should be entitled to the independent judgment of a court on the ultimate question of constitutionality. But supremacy of law does not demand that the correctness of every finding of fact to which the rule of law is to be applied shall be subject to review by a court. If it did, the power of courts to set aside findings of fact by an administrative tribunal would be broader than their power to set aside a jury's verdict. The Constitution contains no such command.

Louis D. Brandeis, *St. Joseph Stock Yards Co. v. United States,* 298 U.S. 38, 84 (1936) (concurring)

9 Arbitrary power and the rule of the Constitution cannot both exist. They are antagonistic and incompatible forces. . . . To escape assumptions of such power on the part of the three primary departments of the government, is not enough. Our institutions must be kept free from the appropriation of unauthorized power by lesser agencies as well. And if the various administrative bureaus and commissions . . . are permitted gradually to extend their powers by encroachments—even petty encroachments—upon the fundamental rights, privileges and immunities of the people, we shall in the end . . . become submerged by a multitude of minor invasions of personal rights, less destructive but no less violative of constitutional guaranties.

George Sutherland, *Jones v. SEC,* 298 U.S. 1, 24–25 (1936)

10 These independent commissions have been given broad powers to explore, formulate, and administer policies of regulation; they have been given the task of investigating and prosecuting business misconduct; they have been given powers, similar to those exercised by courts of law, to pass in concrete cases upon the rights and liabilities of individuals under the statutes. They are in reality miniature independent governments. . . . They constitute a headless "fourth branch" of the Government, a haphazard deposit of irresponsible agencies and uncoordinated powers. They do violence to the basic theory of the American Constitution.

President's Committee on Administrative Management, *Report of the Committee* 39–40 (1937)

11 The vast expansion of this field of administrative regulation in response to the pressure of social needs is made possible under our system by adherence to the basic principles that the legislature shall appropriately determine the standards of administrative action and that in administrative proceedings of a quasi-judicial character the liberty and property of the citizen shall be protected by the rudimentary requirements of fair play.

Charles Evans Hughes, *Morgan v. United States,* 304 U.S. 1, 14–15 (1938)

12 Court and agency are not to be regarded as wholly independent and unrelated instrumentalities of justice, each acting in the performance of its prescribed statutory duty without regard to the appropriate function of the other in securing the plainly indicated objects of the statute. Court and agency are the means adopted to attain the prescribed end, and so far as their duties are defined by the words of the statute, those words should be construed so as to attain that end through coördinated action. Neither body should repeat in this day the mistake made by the courts of law when equity was struggling for recognition as an

ameliorating system of justice; neither can rightly be regarded by the other as an alien intruder, to be tolerated if must be, but never to be encouraged or aided by the other in the attainment of the common aim.

> Harlan F. Stone, *United States v. Morgan*, 307 U.S. 183, 191 (1939)

13 Our Administrative Law has largely "growed" like Topsy.

> Felix Frankfurter, "Foreword," 41 *Columbia Law Review* 585, 586 (1941)

14 If upon the coming down of the order litigants might demand rehearings as a matter of law because some new circumstance has arisen, some new trend has been observed, or some new fact discovered, there would be little hope that the administrative process could ever be consummated in an order that would not be subject to reopening. It has been almost a rule of necessity that rehearings were not matters of right, but were pleas to discretion. And likewise it has been considered that the discretion to be invoked was that of the body making the order, and not that of a reviewing body.

> Robert H. Jackson, *ICC v. City of Jersey City*, 322 U.S. 503, 514–15 (1944)

15 Rulings, interpretations and opinions of the [responsible agency] . . . , while not controlling upon the courts by reason of their authority, do constitute a body of experience and informed judgment to which courts and litigants may properly resort for guidance. The weight of such a judgment in a particular case will depend upon the thoroughness evident in its consideration, the validity of its reasoning, its consistency with earlier and later pronouncements, and all those factors which give it power to persuade, if lacking power to control.

> Robert H. Jackson, *Skidmore v. Swift & Co.*, 323 U.S. 134, 140 (1944)

16 Since the Commission, unlike a court, does have the ability to make new law prospectively through the exercise of its rule-making powers, it has less reason to rely upon *ad hoc* adjudication to formulate new standards of conduct. . . . The function of filling in the interstices of the Act should be performed, as much as possible, through this quasi-legislative promulgation of rules to be applied in the future. But any rigid requirement to that effect would make the administrative process inflexible and incapable of dealing with many of the specialized problems which arise. . . . Not every principle essential to the effective administration of a statute can or should be cast immediately into the mold of a general rule.

> Frank Murphy, *SEC v. Chenery Corp.*, 332 U.S. 194, 202 (1947)

17 Law has reached its finest moments when it has freed man from the unlimited discretion of some ruler, some civil or military official, some bureaucrat. Where discretion is absolute, man has always suffered. At times it has been his property that has been invaded; at times, his privacy; at times, his liberty of movement; at times his freedom of thought; at times, his life. Absolute discretion is a ruthless master. It is more destructive of freedom than any of man's other inventions. But the rule we announce has wide application and a devastating effect. It makes a tyrant out of every contracting officer. He is granted the power of a tyrant even though he is stubborn, perverse or captious. He is allowed the power of a tyrant though he is incompetent or negligent. He has the power of life and death over a private business even though his decision is grossly erroneous. Power granted is seldom neglected.

> William O. Douglas, *United States v. Wunderlich*, 342 U.S. 98, 101 (1951) (dissenting)

18 Whether or not it was ever permissible for courts to determine substantiality of evidence . . . merely on the basis of evidence which in and of itself justified it, without taking into account contradictory evidence or evidence from which conflicting inferences could be drawn, . . . new legislation definitively precludes such a theory of review and bars its practice. The substantiality of evidence must take into account whatever in the record fairly detracts from its weight.

> Felix Frankfurter, *Universal Camera Corp. v. NLRB*, 340 U.S. 474, 487–88 (1951)

19 The rise of administrative bodies probably has been the most significant legal trend of the last century and perhaps more values today are affected by their decisions than by those of all the courts. . . . They have be-

come a veritable fourth branch of the Government, which has deranged our three-branch legal theories much as the concept of a fourth dimension unsettles our three-dimensional thinking.

Robert H. Jackson, *Federal Trade Comm'n v. Ruberoid Co.*, 343 U.S. 470, 487 (1952) (dissenting)

20 In a society where a significant portion of the population is dependent on social welfare, decisions about eligibility for benefits are among the most important that a government can make. By one set of values the granting of a license to broadcast over a television channel, or to build a hydroelectric project on a river, might seem of more far-reaching significance. But in a society that considers the individual as its basic unit a decision affecting the life of a person or a family should not be taken by means that would be unfair for a television station or power company. Indeed, full adjudicatory procedures are far more appropriate in welfare cases than in most of the areas of administrative procedure.

Charles A. Reich, "Individual Rights and Social Welfare: The Emerging Legal Issues," 74 *Yale Law Journal* 1245, 1253 (1965)

21 A person suffering legal wrong because of agency action, or adversely affected or aggrieved by agency action within the meaning of a relevant statute, is entitled to judicial review thereof.

Administrative Procedure Act, Pub. L. No. 89–554, § 702, 80 Stat. 378, 392 (1966)

22 The reviewing court shall—...
(2) hold unlawful and set aside agency action, findings, and conclusions found to be—
(A) arbitrary, capricious, an abuse of discretion, or otherwise not in accordance with law.

Administrative Procedure Act, Pub. L. No. 89–554, § 706, 80 Stat. 378, 393 (1966)

23 Without undertaking to survey the intricacies of the ripeness doctrine it is fair to say that its basic rationale is to prevent the courts, through avoidance of premature adjudication, from entangling themselves in abstract disagreements over administrative policies, and also to protect the agencies from judicial interference until an administrative decision has been formalized

and its effects felt in a concrete way by the challenging parties.

John M. Harlan (1899–1971), *Abbott Laboratories v. Gardner*, 387 U.S. 136, 148–49 (1967)

24 To make this finding [that a decision is arbitrary] the court must consider whether the decision was based on a consideration of the relevant factors and whether there has been a clear error of judgment. . . . Although this inquiry into the facts is to be searching and careful, the ultimate standard of review is a narrow one. The court is not empowered to substitute its judgment for that of the agency.

Thurgood Marshall, *Citizens to Preserve Overton Park, Inc. v. Volpe*, 401 U.S. 402, 416 (1971)

25 Resolution of the issue whether the administrative procedures provided here are constitutionally sufficient requires analysis of the governmental and private interests that are affected. . . . More precisely, our prior decisions indicate that identification of the specific dictates of due process generally requires consideration of three distinct factors: First, the private interest that will be affected by the official action; second, the risk of an erroneous deprivation of such interest through the procedures used, and the probable value, if any, of additional or substitute procedural safeguards; and finally, the Government's interest, including the function involved and the fiscal and administrative burdens that the additional or substitute procedural requirement would entail.

Lewis F. Powell, Jr., *Mathews v. Eldridge*, 424 U.S. 319, 334–35 (1976)

ADMIRALTY

1 The most bigotted idolizers of state authority have not thus far shewn a disposition to deny the national judiciary the cognizance of maritime causes.

Alexander Hamilton, *The Federalist* No. 80, at 2:306-07 (1788)

2 The delegation of cognizance of "all civil cases of admiralty and maritime jurisdiction" to the courts of the United States comprehends all maritime contracts, torts, and injuries. . . . the former extends over all

contracts, (wheresoever they may be made or executed, or whatsoever may be the form of the stipulations,) which relate to the navigation, business or commerce of the sea.

> **Joseph Story**, *De Lovio v. Boit,* 7 F. Cas. 418, 444 (C.C.D. Mass. 1815) (No. 3,776)

3 As at sea no appeal lies beyond the captain, he too often makes unscrupulous use of his power. And as for going to law with him at the end of the voyage, you might as well go to law with the Czar of Russia.

> **Herman Melville**, *Redburn* 288 (G. Thomas Tanselle ed. 1983) (1849)

4 The notorious lawlessness of the Commander has passed into a proverb, familiar to man-of-war's men, *the law was not made for the Captain!*

> **Herman Melville**, *White Jacket,* 1850, in *Writings of Herman Melville* 5:301 (Harrison Hayford ed. 1970)

5 Perhaps the only formal whaling code authorized by legislative enactment, was that of Holland. It was decreed by the States-General in A.D. 1695. But though no other nation has ever had any written whaling law, yet the American fishermen have been their own legislators and lawyers in this matter. They have provided a system which for terse comprehensiveness surpasses Justinian's Pandects and the By-laws of the Chinese Society for the Suppression of Meddling with other People's Business. Yes; these laws might be engraven on a Queen Anne's farthing, or the barb of a harpoon, and worn round the neck, so small are they.

I. A Fast-Fish belongs to the party fast to it.

II. A Loose-Fish is fair game for anybody who can soonest catch it.

> **Herman Melville**, *Moby Dick,* 1851, in *Writings of Herman Melville* 6:395–96 (Harrison Hayford ed. 1988)

6 These two laws touching Fast-Fish and Loose-Fish, I say, will, on reflection, be found the fundamentals of all human jurisprudence; for notwithstanding its complicated tracery of sculpture, the Temple of the Law, like the Temple of the Philistines, has but two props to stand on.

Is it not a saying in every one's mouth, Possession is half of the law: that is, regardless of how the thing came into possession? But often possession is the whole of the law. What are the sinews and souls of Russian serfs and Republican slaves but Fast-Fish, whereof possession is the whole of the law? What to the rapacious landlord is the widow's last mite but a Fast-Fish? What is yonder undetected villain's marble mansion with a door-plate for a waif; what is that but a Fast-Fish? What is the ruinous discount which Mordecai, the broker, gets from poor Woebegone, the bankrupt, on a loan to keep Woebegone's family from starvation; what is that ruinous discount but a Fast-Fish? What is the Archbishop of Savesoul's income of £100,000 seized from the scant bread and cheese of hundreds of thousands of broken-backed laborers (all sure of heaven without any of Savesoul's help); what is that globular £100,000 but a Fast-Fish? What are the Duke of Dunder's hereditary towns and hamlets but Fast-Fish? What to that redoubted harpooneer, John Bull, is poor Ireland, but a Fast-Fish? What to that apostolic lancer, Brother Jonathan, is Texas but a Fast-Fish? And concerning all these, is not Possession the whole of the law?

> **Herman Melville**, *Moby Dick,* 1851, in *Writings of Herman Melville* 6:397–98 (Harrison Hayford ed. 1988)

7 But if the doctrine of Fast-Fish be pretty generally applicable, the kindred doctrine of Loose-Fish is still more widely so. That is internationally and universally applicable.

What was America in 1492 but a Loose-Fish, in which Columbus struck the Spanish standard by way of waifing it for his royal master and mistress? What was Poland to the Czar? What Greece to the Turk? What India to England? What at last will Mexico be to the United States? All Loose-Fish.

What are the Rights of Man and the Liberties of the World but Loose-Fish? What all men's minds and opinions but Loose-Fish? What is the principle of religious belief in them but a Loose-Fish? What to the ostentatious smuggling verbalists are the thoughts of thinkers but Loose-Fish? What is the great globe itself but a Loose-Fish! And what are you, reader, but a Loose-Fish and a Fast-Fish, too?

> **Herman Melville**, *Moby Dick,* 1851, in *Writings of Herman Melville* 6:398 (Harrison Hayford ed. 1988)

8 There are two royal fish so styled by the English law writers—the whale and the sturgeon; both royal property under certain limitations, and nominally supplying the tenth branch of the crown's ordinary revenue. I know not that any other author has hinted of the matter; but by inference it seems to me that the sturgeon must be divided in the same way as the whale, the King receiving the highly dense and elastic head peculiar to that fish, which, symbolically regarded, may possibly be humorously grounded upon some presumed congeniality. And thus there seems a reason in all things, even in law.

> Herman Melville, *Moby Dick*, 1851, in *Writings of Herman Melville* 6:401 (Harrison Hayford ed. 1988)

9 A fiction is not a satisfactory ground for taking one man's property to satisfy another man's wrong.

> Oliver Wendell Holmes, Jr., *The Eugene F. Moran*, 212 U.S. 466, 474 (1909)

10 In deciding this question we must realize that however ancient may be the traditions of maritime law, however diverse the sources from which it has been drawn, it derives its whole and only power in this country from its having been accepted and adopted by the United States. There is no mystic over-law to which even the United States must bow. When a case is said to be governed by foreign law or by general maritime law that is only a short way of saying that for this purpose the sovereign power takes up a rule suggested from without and makes it part of its own rules.

> Oliver Wendell Holmes, Jr., *The Western Maid*, 257 U.S. 419, 432 (1922)

ADVOCACY

1 With a pencil dipped in the most vivid colours, and guided by the hand of a master, a splendid portrait has been drawn exhibiting this vessel and her freighter as forming a single figure, composed of the most discordant materials, of peace and war. So exquisite was the skill of the artist, so dazzling the garb in which the figure was presented, that it required the exercise of that cold investigating faculty which ought always to belong to those who sit on this bench, to discover its only imperfection; its want of resemblance.

> John Marshall, *The Nereide,* 13 U.S. (9 Cranch) 388, 430 (1815)

2 Be brief, be pointed; let your matter stand
Lucid in order, solid, and at hand;
Spend not your words on trifles, but condense;
Strike with the mass of thought, not drops of sense;
Press to the close with vigor, once begun,
And leave, (how hard the task!) leave off, when done.
. . . Victory in law is gain'd, as battles fought,
Not by the numbers, but the forces brought.

> Joseph Story, "Advice to a Young Lawyer," 1831, in *Life and Letters of Joseph Story* 2:88 (William W. Story ed. 1851)

3 Whene'er you speak, remember every cause
Stands not on eloquence, but stands on laws.
Pregnant in matter, in expression brief,
Let every sentence stand in bold relief!
On trifling points, nor time, nor talents waste,
A sad offence to learning and to taste;
Nor deal with pompous phrase; nor e'er suppose
Poetic flights belong to reasoning prose.

> Joseph Story, "Advice to a Young Lawyer," 1832, in *Life and Letters of Joseph Story* 2:88–89 (William W. Story ed. 1851)

4 Who's a great lawyer? He, who aims to say
The least his cause requires, not all he may.

> Joseph Story, Memorandum-book of arguments before the Supreme Court, 1831–32, in *Life and Letters of Joseph Story* 2:90 (William W. Story ed. 1851)

5 I have heard an experienced counsellor [Samuel Hoar] say that he never feared the effect upon a jury of a lawyer who does not believe in his heart that his client ought to have a verdict. If he does not believe it, his unbelief will appear to the jury, despite all his protestations, and will become their unbelief.

> Ralph Waldo Emerson, "Spiritual Laws," *Essays: First Series*, 1841, in *Complete Works*

of *Ralph Waldo Emerson* 2:131, 156–57
(1903)

6 Come, you of the law, who can talk, if
you please,
Till the man in the moon will allow it's a
cheese.

Oliver Wendell Holmes, Sr., "Lines," 1844,
in *Poetical Works of Oliver Wendell Holmes*
1:82, 82 (1892)

7 I find speaking here [in Congress] and elsewhere about the same thing. I was about
as badly scared, and no worse, as I am
when I speak in court.

Abraham Lincoln, Letter to William H.
Herndon, 8 Jan. 1848, in *Collected Works of
Abraham Lincoln* 1:430 (Roy P. Basler ed.
1953)

8 The power of clear statement is the great
power at the bar.

Daniel Webster, Letter to R. M. Blatchford,
1849, in Peter Harvey, *Reminiscences and
Anecdotes of Daniel Webster* 118 (1878)

9 Extemporaneous speaking should be practised and cultivated. It is the lawyer's avenue to the public. However able and faithful he may be in other respects, people are
slow to bring him business if he cannot
make a speech. And yet there is not a more
fatal error to young lawyers than relying
too much on speech-making. If any one,
upon his rare powers of speaking, shall
claim an exemption from the drudgery of
the law, his case is a failure in advance.

Abraham Lincoln, "Notes for a Law
Lecture," 1 July 1850?, in *Collected Works of
Abraham Lincoln* 2:81 (Roy P. Basler ed.
1953)

10 Law is whatever is boldly asserted and
plausibly maintained.

Aaron Burr, quoted in James Parton, *Life
and Times of Aaron Burr* 149 (7th ed. 1858)

11 A man's opinions, look you, are generally
of much more value than his arguments.
These last are made by his brain, and perhaps he does not believe the proposition
they tend to prove,—as is often the case
with paid lawyers.

Oliver Wendell Holmes, Sr., *The Professor at
the Breakfast-Table,* 1859, in *Works of Oliver
Wendell Holmes* 2:118 (1892)

12 The one absolutely unselfish friend that
man can have in this selfish world, the one
that never deserts him, the one that never
proves ungrateful or treacherous, is his
dog. A man's dog stands by him in prosperity and poverty, in health and sickness.
He will sleep on the cold ground where the
wintry winds blow and the snow drives
fiercely, if only he may be near his master's
side. He will kiss the hand that has no food
to offer; he will lick the wounds and sores
that come in encounter with the roughness
of the world. He guards the sleep of his
pauper master as if he were a prince. When
all other friends desert he remains. When
riches take wings and reputation falls to
pieces, he is as constant in his love as the
sun in its journey through the heavens.*

George Graham Vest, Address to jury,
Burden v. Hornsby, Warrensburg, Mo., 1870,
in Edwin M. C. French, *Senator Vest:
Champion of the Dog* 34 (1930)

13 There is no enjoyment so keen to certain
minds as that of looking upon the slow torture of a human being on trial for life, except it be an execution; there is no display
of human ingenuity, wit, and power so fascinating as that made by trained lawyers in
the trial of an important case, nowhere else
is exhibited such subtlety, acumen, address, eloquence.

Mark Twain and Charles Dudley Warner,
The Gilded Age, 1873, in *Writings of Mark
Twain* 6:223 (1929)

14 Tears have always been considered legitimate arguments before a jury. . . . It would
appear to be one of the natural rights of
counsel, which no Court or constitution
could take away. It is certainly, if no more,
a matter of the highest personal privilege.
Indeed, if counsel has them at command,
it may be seriously questioned whether it
is not his professional duty to shed them
whenever proper occasion arises, and the
trial Judge would not feel constrained to
interfere unless they were indulged in to
such excess as to impede or delay the business of the Court.

John S. Wilkes, *Ferguson v. Moore,* 98 Tenn.
342, 351–52 (1897)

---

* This case was a suit for damages by a farmer against
his neighbor for the unlawful killing of the farmer's
hound dog. Vest's closing argument for the plaintiff Burden is said to have originated the saying, "A man's best
friend is his dog."

15 Never was there a better court manner; the Justices, who had been anticipating an opportunity to demonstrate, at his expense, the exceeding dignity of the Supreme Court, could only admire and approve. As for his speech, it was a straightway argument; not a superfluous or a sophomoric word, not an attempt at rhetoric. . . . There is the logic that is potent but answerable; there is the logic that is unanswerable, that gives no opportunity to any sane mind, however prejudiced by association with dispensers of luxurious hospitality, of vintage wines and dollar cigars, however enamored of fog-fighting and hair-splitting, to refuse the unqualified assent of conviction absolute. That was the kind of argument Josh Craig made. And the faces of the opposing lawyers, the questions the Justices asked him plainly showed that he had won.

David Graham Phillips, *The Fashionable Adventures of Joshua Craig* 75 (1909)

16 A traditional story of Marshal Wright's was that when Jeremiah—otherwise "Jerry"—Wilson began an elaborate opening by citing many of the fundamental authorities, he was interrupted by an Associate Justice who said that Mr. Wilson ought to take it for granted that the Court knew some elementary law. To this "Jerry" Wilson replied:

"Your Honors, that was the mistake I made in the Court below."

Charles Henry Butler, *A Century at the Bar of the Supreme Court of the United States* 88–89 (1942)

17 He was troubled by the problem of how to phrase and arrange the few things he could say to give himself every chance, no matter how remote or small, of getting at just one juror, of giving just one man or woman some scruple or sentiment that, catching in the simple or the over-complicated mind, would stay there, resisting the consensus, immune to sense or reason, only hardened in obstinacy by the arguments or expostulations of the others.

James Gould Cozzens, *The Just and the Unjust* 342 (1942)

18 After all, advocates . . . are like managers of pugilistic and election contestants in that they have a propensity for claiming everything.

Felix Frankfurter, *First Iowa Hydro-Electric Coop. v. Federal Power Comm'n*, 328 U.S. 152, 187 (1946) (dissenting)

19 On your first appearance before the Court, do not waste your time or ours telling us so. We are likely to discover for ourselves that you are a novice but will think none the less of you for it. Every famous lawyer had his first day at our bar, and perhaps a sad one. It is not ingratiating to tell us you think it is an overwhelming honor to appear, for we think of the case as the important thing before us, not the counsel. Some attorneys use time to thank us for granting the review, or for listening to their argument. Those are not intended as favors and it is good taste to accept them as routine performance of duty. Be respectful, of course, but also be self-respectful, and neither disparage yourself nor flatter the Justices. We think well enough of ourselves already.

Robert H. Jackson, "Advocacy before the Supreme Court: Suggestions for Effective Case Presentations," 37 *American Bar Association Journal* 801, 802 (1951)

20 I used to say that, as Solicitor General, I made three arguments of every case. First came the one that I planned—as I thought, logical, coherent, complete. Second was the one actually presented—interrupted, incoherent, disjointed, disappointing. The third was the utterly devastating argument that I thought of after going to bed that night.

Robert H. Jackson, "Advocacy before the Supreme Court: Suggestions for Effective Case Presentations," 37 *American Bar Association Journal* 801, 803 (1951)

21 I always feel that there should be some comfort derived from any question from the bench. It is clear proof that the inquiring Justice is not asleep.

Robert H. Jackson, "Advocacy Before the Supreme Court: Suggestions for Effective Presentation," 37 *American Bar Association Journal* 801, 862 (1951)

22 The old lawyer said, "If the evidence is against you, talk about the law. If the law is against you, talk about the evidence."

The young lawyer asked, "But what do you do when both the law and the evidence are against you?"

"In that case," replied the old lawyer, "give somebody hell. That'll distract the judge and the jury from the weakness of your case."*

A Treasury of American Anecdotes 10 (B. A. Botkin ed. 1957)

23 As the docket of the [Supreme] Court became more crowded, necessarily the time allowed for argument had to shrink.... Time is usually rigidly controlled; the legend is that Chief Justice Hughes once cut off an attorney in the middle of the word "if."

John P. Frank, *Marble Palace* 92 (1958)

24 Gambling on what a jury will do is like playing the horses. The notorious undependability of juries, the chance involved, is one of the absorbing features of the law. That's what makes the practice of law, like prostitution, one of the last of the unpredictable professions—both employ the seductive arts, both try to display their wares to the best advantage, and both must pretend enthusiastically to woo total strangers.

Robert Traver, *Anatomy of a Murder* 39–40 (1958)

25 It seemed that Professor Scott had just finished presenting his deliberations to the Court and had seated himself when opposing counsel stood up with Scott's work on Trusts in one hand and said, "May it please the Court, Professor Scott has just argued the last hour and it seems he is taking a contrary position to that which he takes in his works." Whereupon Professor Scott rose and said, "May it please the Court, I am in the process now of revising my editions, and I can assure you that when I come to this chapter I will conform it to the position I just argued."

Austin W. Scott, reported in Willard H. Linscott, Address, Augusta, Maine, 17 Jan. 1963, in 52 *Report of the Maine State Bar Association* 78–79 (1963)

---

* The same joke, with the punchline "pound on the table and yell like hell," appears in Carl Sandburg's poem, *The People, Yes,* 1936, in *Complete Poems of Carl Sandburg* 439, 551 (1970).

26 "Young Mr. Mack, like too many of our idle aristocrats, is, I fear, a blue blood with a Red heart."

I believe it was this final metaphor that won Froebel [opposing counsel] the judgment. I saw the newspaper people virtually doff their hats in tribute, and scribble words for the next editions of their papers. Even the Judge smiled benignly upon the trope: I could see that it struck him square in the prejudices, and found a welcome there.

... How could mere justice cope with poetry? Men, I think, are ever attracted to the *bon mot* rather than the *mot juste,* and judges, no less than other men, are often moved by considerations more aesthetic than judicial.

John Barth, *The Floating Opera* 94–95 (1967)

27 Oral argument is the absolutely indispensable ingredient of appellate advocacy.... often my whole notion of what a case is about crystallizes at oral argument.

William J. Brennan, Jr., quoted in *Harvard Law School Occasional Pamphlet Number Nine* 22 (1967)

28 [On his experience as a lawyer:] I'll tell you what my daddy told me after my first trial. I thought I was just great. I asked him, "How did I do?" He paused and said, "You've got to guard against speaking more clearly than you think."

Howard H. Baker, Jr., quoted in *Washington Post,* 24 June 1973, at K2

29 The trial lawyer does what Socrates was executed for: making the worse argument appear the stronger.

Irving R. Kaufman, quoted in Rodney R. Jones, Charles M. Sevilla, and Gerald F. Uelmen, *Disorderly Conduct* 57 (1987)

30 Most of the great trial lawyers I know are very, very scared. Fear, for an actor, stirs you to a greater performance.

Arthur Liman, quoted in *What They Said in 1989,* at 150 (1989)

AFFIRMATIVE ACTION

See also CIVIL RIGHTS

1 The Constitution is both color blind and color conscious. To avoid conflict with the

equal protection clause, a classification that denies a benefit, causes harm, or imposes a burden must not be based on race. In that sense, the Constitution is color blind. But the Constitution is color conscious to prevent discrimination being perpetuated and to undo the effects of past discrimination. The criterion is the relevancy of color to a legitimate governmental purpose.

John Minor Wisdom, *United States v. Jefferson County Bd. of Educ.*, 372 F.2d 836, 876 (5th Cir. 1966)

2 Our society cannot be completely colorblind in the short term if we are to have a colorblind society in the long term. After centuries of viewing through colored lenses, eyes do not quickly adjust when the lenses are removed. Discrimination has a way of perpetuating itself, albeit unintentionally, because the resulting inequalities make new opportunities less accessible. Preferential treatment is one partial prescription to remedy our society's most intransigent and deeply rooted inequalities.

Frank M. Coffin, *Associated Gen. Contractors v. Altshuler*, 490 F.2d 9, 16 (1st Cir. 1971)

3 The purpose of the University of Washington cannot be to produce black lawyers for blacks, Polish lawyers for Poles, Jewish lawyers for Jews, Irish lawyers for Irish. It should be to produce good lawyers for Americans and not to place First Amendment barriers against anyone.

William O. Douglas, *DeFunis v. Odegaard*, 416 U.S. 312, 342 (1974) (dissenting)

4 If discrimination based on race is constitutionally permissible when those who hold the reins can come up with "compelling" reasons to justify it, then constitutional guarantees acquire an accordionlike quality.

William O. Douglas, *DeFunis v. Odegaard*, 416 U.S. 312, 343 (1974) (dissenting)

5 The lesson of the great decisions of the Supreme Court and the lesson of contemporary history have been the same for at least a generation: discrimination on the basis of race is illegal, immoral, unconstitutional, inherently wrong, and destructive of democratic society. Now this is to be unlearned and we are told that this is not a

matter of fundamental principle but only a matter of whose ox is gored.

Alexander M. Bickel, *The Morality of Consent* 133 (1975)

6 The Fourteenth Amendment has expanded beyond its original 1868 concept and now is recognized to have reached a point where, ... it embraces a "broader principle." This enlargement does not mean ... that the Fourteenth Amendment has broken away from its moorings and its original intended purposes. Those original aims persist. And that, in a distinct sense, is what "affirmative action" in the face of proper facts, is all about. If this conflicts with idealistic equality, that tension is original Fourteenth Amendment tension, constitutionally conceived and constitutionally imposed, and it is part of the Amendment's very nature until complete equality is achieved in the area.

Harry A. Blackmun, *University of California Regents v. Bakke*, 438 U.S. 265, 405 (1978) (concurring in part and dissenting in part)

7 I suspect that it would be impossible to arrange an affirmative-action program in a racially neutral way and have it successful. ... In order to get beyond racism, we must first take account of race. There is no other way. And in order to treat some persons equally, we must treat them differently. We cannot—we dare not—let the Equal Protection Clause perpetuate racial supremacy.

Harry A. Blackmun, *University of California Regents v. Bakke*, 438 U.S. 265, 407 (1978) (concurring in part and dissenting in part)

8 Government may take race into account when it acts not to demean or insult any racial group, but to remedy disadvantages cast on minorities by past racial prejudice, at least when appropriate findings have been made by judicial, legislative, or administrative bodies with competence to act in this area.

William J. Brennan, Jr., *University of California Regents v. Bakke*, 438 U.S. 265, 325 (1978) (concurring in part and dissenting in part)

9 We cannot ... let color blindness become myopia which masks the reality that many "created equal" have been treated within

our lifetimes as inferior both by the law and by their fellow citizens.

> William J. Brennan, Jr., *University of California Regents v. Bakke*, 438 U.S. 265, 327 (1978) (concurring in part and dissenting in part)

10 It must be remembered that, during most of the past 200 years, the Constitution as interpreted by this Court did not prohibit the most ingenious and pervasive forms of discrimination against the Negro. Now, when a State acts to remedy the effects of that legacy of discrimination, I cannot believe that this same Constitution stands as a barrier.

> Thurgood Marshall, *University of California Regents v. Bakke*, 438 U.S. 265, 387 (1978) (concurring in part and dissenting in part)

11 At every point from birth to death the impact of the past is reflected in the still disfavored position of the Negro. In light of the sorry history of discrimination and its devastating impact on the lives of Negroes, bringing the Negro into the mainstream of American life should be a state interest of the highest order.

> Thurgood Marshall, *University of California Regents v. Bakke*, 438 U.S. 265, 396 (1978) (concurring in part and dissenting in part)

12 The guarantee of equal protection cannot mean one thing when applied to one individual and something else when applied to a person of another color. If both are not accorded the same protection, then it is not equal.

> Lewis F. Powell, Jr., *University of California Regents v. Bakke*, 438 U.S. 265, 289–90 (1978)

13 If petitioner's purpose is to assure within its student body some specified percentage of a particular group merely because of its race or ethnic origin, such a preferential purpose must be rejected not as insubstantial but as facially invalid. Preferring members of any one group for no reason other than race or ethnic origin is discrimination for its own sake. This the Constitution forbids.

> Lewis F. Powell, Jr., *University of California Regents v. Bakke*, 438 U.S. 265, 307 (1978)

14 The fourth goal asserted by petitioner is the attainment of a diverse student body. This clearly is a constitutionally permissible goal for an institution of higher education. Academic freedom, though not a specifically enumerated constitutional right, long has been viewed as a special concern of the First Amendment. The freedom of a university to make its own judgments as to education includes the selection of its student body.

> Lewis F. Powell, Jr., *University of California Regents v. Bakke*, 438 U.S. 265, 311–12 (1978)

15 The fatal flaw in petitioner's preferential program is its disregard of individual rights as guaranteed by the Fourteenth Amendment. . . . Such rights are not absolute. But when a State's distribution of benefits or imposition of burdens hinges on ancestry or the color of a person's skin, that individual is entitled to a demonstration that the challenged classification is necessary to promote a substantial state interest.

> Lewis F. Powell, Jr., *University of California Regents v. Bakke*, 438 U.S. 265, 320 (1978)

16 Racial classifications drawn for the purpose of remedying the effects of discrimination that itself was race based have a highly pertinent basis: the tragic and indelible fact that discrimination against blacks and other racial minorities in this Nation has pervaded our Nation's history and continues to scar our society.

> Thurgood Marshall, *City of Richmond v. J. A. Croson Co.*, 488 U.S. 469, 552 (1989) (dissenting)

17 So-called formal equal opportunity has done a lot but misses the heart of the problem. It put the vampire back in its coffin, but it was no silver stake. The rules may be color-blind but people are not. The question remains, therefore, whether the law can truly shed, or exist apart from the color-conscious society in which it exists, as a skeleton is devoid of flesh; or whether law is the embodiment of society, either the creation or the reflection of a particular citizenry's arranged complexity of relations.

> Patricia Williams, "The Obliging Shell: An Informal Essay on Formal Equal Opportunity," 87 *Michigan Law Review* 2128, 2142 (1989)

AGREEMENTS

See CONTRACTS

ALCOHOL

See INTOXICATION

AMENDMENT

See CONSTITUTIONAL AMENDMENT

AMERICAN INDIAN LAW

1 Religion, Morality and knowledge being necessary to good government and the happiness of mankind, Schools and the means of education shall forever be encouraged. The utmost good faith shall always be observed towards the Indians, their lands and property shall never be taken from them without their consent; and in their property, rights and liberty, they never shall be invaded or disturbed, unless in just and lawful wars authorized by Congress; but laws founded in justice and humanity shall from time to time be made, for preventing wrongs being done to them, and for preserving peace and friendship with them.

Northwest Ordinance, art. 3, 13 July 1787, in *Journals of the Continental Congress* 32:340–41 (Roscoe R. Hill ed. 1936)

2 The case is now entirely altered. The general Government only has the power, to treat with the Indian Nations, . . . No State nor person, can purchase your lands, unless at some public treaty, held under the authority of the United States.

George Washington, Letter to Cornplanter, HalfTown, and Great Tree, Chiefs and Counselors of the Seneca Nation, 29 Dec. 1790, in *Writings of George Washington* 31:180 (John C. Fitzpatrick ed. 1939)

3 On the discovery of this immense continent, the great nations of Europe were eager to appropriate to themselves so much of it as they could respectively acquire. Its vast extent offered an ample field to the ambition and enterprise of all; and the character and religion of its inhabitants afforded an apology for considering them as a people over whom the superior genius of Europe might claim an ascendency. . . .

But, as they were all in pursuit of nearly the same object, it was necessary, in order to avoid conflicting settlements, and consequent war with each other, to establish a principle, which all should acknowledge as the law by which the right of acquisition, which they all asserted, should be regulated as between themselves. This principle was, that discovery gave title to the government by whose subjects, or by whose authority, it was made, against all other European governments, which title might be consummated by possession.

John Marshall, *Johnson v. M'Intosh,* 21 U.S. (8 Wheat.) 543, 572–73 (1823)

4 [American Indian tribes'] rights to complete sovereignty, as independent nations, were necessarily diminished, and their power to dispose of the soil at their own will, to whomsoever they pleased, was denied by the original fundamental principle, that discovery gave exclusive title to those who made it.

John Marshall, *Johnson v. M'Intosh,* 21 U.S. (8 Wheat.) 543, 574 (1823)

5 [The tribes'] relation [to the United States] was that of a nation claiming and receiving the protection of one more powerful; not that of individuals abandoning their national character, and submitting as subjects to the laws of a master.

John Marshall, *Worcester v. Georgia,* 31 U.S. (6 Pet.) 515, 555 (1832)

6 Indian nations had always been considered as distinct, independent political communities, retaining their original natural rights, as the undisputed possessors of the soil. . . . The very term "nation," so generally applied to them, means "a people distinct from others."

John Marshall, *Worcester v. Georgia,* 31 U.S. (6 Pet.) 515, 559 (1832)

7 The Cherokee nation, then, is a distinct community occupying its own territory . . . in which the laws of Georgia can have no force.

John Marshall, *Worcester v. Georgia,* 31 U.S. (6 Pet.) 515, 561 (1832)

8 The right of the Indians to the occupancy of the lands pledged to them, may be one of occupancy only, but it is "as sacred as

that of the United States to the fee." . . . Spoliation is not management.

Benjamin N. Cardozo, *Shoshone Tribe of Indians v. United States,* 299 U.S. 476, 497– 98 (1937)

9 It is well for our younger men to know our law. It is well for our older men and our younger men to agree about our law. It is not good to wait until trouble comes up before our law becomes clear to all. This is our law.

Karl N. Llewellyn, "Draft Preamble for a Code for the Pueblo of Zia," 1947, in William Twining, *Karl Llewellyn and the Realist Movement* 547 (1973)

10 Like the miner's canary, the Indian marks the shifts from fresh air to poison gas in our political atmosphere; and our treatment of Indians, even more than our treatment of other minorities, reflects the rise and fall in our democratic faith.

Felix S. Cohen, "The Erosion of Indian Rights, 1950–1953: A Case Study in Bureaucracy," 62 *Yale Law Journal* 348, 390 (1953)

11 Great nations, like great men, should keep their word.

Hugo L. Black, *Federal Power Comm'n v. Tuscarora Indian Nation,* 362 U.S. 99, 142 (1960) (dissenting)

ANTITRUST

See also CORPORATIONS

1 That monopolies are odious, contrary to the spirit of a free government, and the principles of commerce; and ought not to be suffered.

Maryland Constitution of 1776, § 39, in *Federal and State Constitutions* 3:1686, 1690 (Francis N. Thorpe ed. 1909)

2 Every contract, combination in the form of trust or otherwise, or conspiracy, in restraint of trade or commerce among the several States, or with foreign nations, is hereby declared to be illegal. Every person who shall make any such contract or engage in any such combination or conspiracy, shall be deemed guilty of a misdemeanor, and, on conviction thereof, shall be punished by fine not exceeding five thousand dollars, or by imprisonment not exceeding one year, or by both said punishments, in the discretion of the court.

Sherman Antitrust Act, ch. 647, § 1, 26 Stat. 209, 209 (1890)

3 Every person who shall monopolize, or attempt to monopolize, or combine or conspire with any other person or persons, to monopolize any part of the trade or commerce among the several States, or with foreign nations, shall be deemed guilty of a misdemeanor, and, on conviction thereof, shall be punished by fine not exceeding five thousand dollars, or by imprisonment not exceeding one year, or by both said punishments, in the discretion of the court.

Sherman Antitrust Act, ch. 647, § 2, 26 Stat. 209, 209 (1890)

4 Any person who shall be injured in his business or property by any other person or corporation by reason of anything forbidden or declared to be unlawful by this act, may sue therefor . . . and shall recover three fold the damages by him sustained, and the costs of suit, including a reasonable attorney's fee.

Sherman Antitrust Act, ch. 647, § 7, 26 Stat. 209, 210 (1890)

5 Free competition is worth more to society than it costs.

Oliver Wendell Holmes, Jr., *Vegelahn v. Guntner,* 167 Mass. 92, 106, 44 N.E. 1077 (1896)

6 Where a trust becomes a monopoly the State has an immediate right to interfere.

Theodore Roosevelt, Annual Message to New York Legislature, 3 Jan. 1900, in *Works of Theodore Roosevelt* 17:34, 54 (Hermann Hagedorn ed. 1925)

7 [Describing the breakup by the Supreme Court of the Northern Securities Company trust:] Two certificates of stock are now issued instead of one; they are printed in different colors, and that is the main difference.

James J. Hill, quoted in Matthew Josephson, *The Robber Barons* 450 (1934)

8 Intent is . . . essential to . . . an attempt [to monopolize]. Where acts are not sufficient in themselves to produce a result which the law seeks to prevent—for instance, the mo-

nopoly—but require further acts in addition to the mere forces of nature to bring that result to pass, an intent to bring it to pass is necessary in order to produce a dangerous probability that it will happen. . . . But when that intent and the consequent dangerous probability exist, this statute [the Sherman Act], like many others and like the common law in some cases, directs itself against that dangerous probability as well as against the completed result.

Oliver Wendell Holmes, Jr., *Swift & Co. v. United States*, 196 U.S. 375, 396 (1905)

9 Is there not a causal connection between the development of these huge, indomitable trusts and the horrible crimes now under investigation? . . . Is it not irony to speak of the equality of opportunity in a country cursed with bigness?*

Louis D. Brandeis, Letter to the editor, 27 *Survey* 1428 (1911)

10 [The Sherman Act was designed to prohibit] all contracts or acts which were unreasonably restrictive of competitive conditions, either from the nature or character of the contract or act or where the surrounding circumstances were such as to justify the conclusion that they had not been entered into or performed with the legitimate purpose of reasonably forwarding personal interest and developing trade, but on the contrary were of such a character as to give rise to the inference or presumption that they had been entered into or done with the intent to do wrong to the general public and to limit the right of individuals.

Edward D. White, *Standard Oil Co. v. United States*, 221 U.S. 1, 58 (1911)

11 It shall be unlawful for any person engaged in commerce, in the course of such commerce, either directly or indirectly to discriminate in price between different purchasers of commodities, which commodities are sold for use, consumption, or resale within the United States . . . , where the effect of such discrimination may be to substantially lessen competition

or tend to create a monopoly in any line of commerce.

Clayton Act, ch. 323, § 2, 38 Stat. 730, 730 (1914)

12 The labor of a human being is not a commodity or article of commerce. Nothing contained in the antitrust laws shall be construed to forbid the existence and operation of labor, agricultural, or horticultural organizations, instituted for the purposes of mutual help, and not having capital stock or conducted for profit, or to forbid or restrain individual members of such organizations from lawfully carrying out the legitimate objects thereof; nor shall such organizations, or the members thereof, be held or construed to be illegal combinations or conspiracies in restraint of trade, under the antitrust laws.

Clayton Act, ch. 323, § 6, 38 Stat. 730, 731 (1914)

13 No restraining order or injunction shall be granted by any court of the United States, or a judge or the judges thereof, in any case between an employer and employees, or between employers and employees, or between employees, or between persons employed and persons seeking employment, involving, or growing out of, a dispute concerning terms or conditions of employment, unless necessary to prevent irreparable injury to property, or to a property right, of the party making application, for which injury there is no adequate remedy at law.

Clayton Act, ch. 323, § 20, 38 Stat. 730, 738 (1914)

14 The legality of an agreement or regulation cannot be determined by so simple a test, as whether it restrains competition. Every agreement concerning trade, every regulation of trade, restrains. To bind, to restrain, is of their very essence.

Louis D. Brandeis, *Chicago Bd. of Trade v. United States*, 246 U.S. 231, 238 (1918)

15 The true test of legality is whether the restraint imposed is such as merely regulates and perhaps thereby promotes competition or whether it is such as may suppress or even destroy competition. To determine that question the court must ordinarily consider the facts peculiar to the business to which the restraint is applied; its con-

---

* A Curse of Bigness.—Louis D. Brandeis, Title of article, *Harper's Weekly*, 10 Jan. 1914, at 18

dition before and after the restraint was imposed; the nature of the restraint and its effect, actual or probable. The history of the restraint, the evil believed to exist, the reason for adopting the particular remedy, the purpose or end sought to be attained, are all relevant facts. This is not because a good intention will save an otherwise objectionable regulation or the reverse; but because knowledge of intent may help the court to interpret facts and to predict consequences.

> **Louis D. Brandeis,** *Chicago Bd. of Trade v. United States,* 246 U.S. 231, 238 (1918)

16 The corporation is undoubtedly of impressive size and it takes an effort of resolution not to be affected by it or to exaggerate its influence. But we must adhere to the law and the law does not make mere size an offense or the existence of unexerted power an offense.

> **Joseph McKenna,** *United States v. U.S. Steel Corp.,* 251 U.S. 417, 451 (1920)

17 It certainly is not the purpose of our competitive system that it should produce a competition which destroys stability in an industry and reduces to poverty all those within it. Its purpose is rather to maintain that degree of competition which induces progress and protects the consumer. If our regulatory laws be at fault they should be revised.

> **Herbert C. Hoover,** Speech, Boston, 7 Oct. 1930, in *State Papers and Other Public Writings of Herbert Hoover* 1:390, 394 (William S. Myers ed. 1934)

18 As a charter of freedom, the [Sherman] Act has a generality and adaptability comparable to that found to be desirable in constitutional provisions.

> **Charles Evans Hughes,** *Appalachian Coals, Inc. v. United States,* 288 U.S. 344, 359–60 (1933)

19 There must be outright dismantling of our gigantic corporations, and persistent prosecution of producers who organize, by whatever methods, for price maintenance or output limitation. There must be explicit and unqualified repudiation of the so-called "rule of reason". . . . In short, restraint of trade must be treated as a major

crime, and prosecuted unremittingly by a vigilant administrative body.

> **Henry C. Simons,** *A Positive Program for Laissez Faire* 19 (1934)

20 Any combination which tampers with price structures is engaged in unlawful activity.

> **William O. Douglas,** *United States v. Socony-Vacuum Oil Co.,* 310 U.S. 150, 221 (1940)

21 Under the Sherman Act a combination formed for the purpose and with the effect of raising, depressing, fixing, pegging, or stabilizing the price of a commodity in interstate or foreign commerce is illegal *per se.*

> **William O. Douglas,** *United States v. Socony-Vacuum Oil Co.,* 310 U.S. 150, 223 (1940)

22 Price-fixing agreements may or may not be aimed at complete elimination of price competition. The group making those agreements may or may not have power to control the market. But the fact that the group cannot control the market prices does not necessarily mean that the agreement as to prices has no utility to the members of the combination. The effectiveness of price-fixing agreements is dependent on many factors, such as competitive tactics, position in the industry, the formula underlying price policies. Whatever economic justification particular price-fixing agreements may be thought to have, the law does not permit an inquiry into their reasonableness. They are all banned because of their actual or potential threat to the central nervous system of the economy.

> **William O. Douglas,** *United States v. Socony-Vacuum Oil Co.,* 310 U.S. 150, 225–26 n.59 (1940)

23 This court has never applied the Sherman Act in any case, whether or not involving labor organizations or activities, unless the Court was of opinion that there was some form of restraint upon commercial competition in the marketing of goods or services.

> **Harlan F. Stone,** *Apex Hosiery Co. v. Leader,* 310 U.S. 469, 495 (1940)

24 Beware of that profound enemy of the free enterprise system who pays lip-service to free competition—but also labels every anti-trust prosecution as a "persecution."

You know, it depends a good deal on whose baby has the measles.

Franklin D. Roosevelt, Campaign Address at Soldier's Field, Chicago, 28 Oct. 1944, in *Public Papers and Addresses of Franklin D. Roosevelt, 1944–45,* at 369, 377 (Samuel I. Rosenman ed. 1950)

25 [Ninety per cent] is enough to constitute a monopoly; it is doubtful whether sixty or sixty-four per cent would be enough; and certainly thirty-three per cent is not.

Learned Hand, *United States v. Aluminum Co. of Am.,* 148 F.2d 416, 424 (2d Cir. 1945)

26 Many people believe that possession of unchallenged economic power deadens initiative, discourages thrift and depresses energy; that immunity from competition is a narcotic, and rivalry is a stimulant, to industrial progress; that the spur of constant stress is necessary to counteract an inevitable disposition to let well enough alone.... [Congress] did not condone "good trusts" and condemn "bad" ones; it forbad all.

Learned Hand, *United States v. Aluminum Co. of Am.,* 148 F.2d 416, 427 (2d Cir. 1945)

27 It is possible, because of its indirect social or moral effect, to prefer a system of small producers, each dependent for his success upon his own skill and character, to one in which the great mass of those engaged must accept the direction of a few.

Learned Hand, *United States v. Aluminum Co. of Am.,* 148 F.2d 416, 427 (2d Cir. 1945)

28 It does not follow because "Alcoa" had such a monopoly, that it "monopolized" the ingot market: it may not have achieved monopoly; monopoly may have been thrust upon it.

Learned Hand, *United States v. Aluminum Co. of Am.,* 148 F.2d 416, 429 (2d Cir. 1945)

29 The only question is whether [Alcoa] falls within the exception established in favor of those who do not seek, but cannot avoid, the control of a market. It seems to us that that question scarcely survives its statement. It was not inevitable that it should always anticipate increase in the demand for ingot and be prepared to supply them. Nothing compelled it to keep doubling and redoubling its capacity before others entered the field.

Learned Hand, *United States v. Aluminum Co. of Am.,* 148 F.2d 416, 431 (2d Cir. 1945)

30 The use of monopoly power, however lawfully acquired, to foreclose competition, to gain a competitive advantage, or to destroy a competitor, is unlawful.

William O. Douglas, *United States v. Griffith,* 334 U.S. 100, 107 (1948)

31 Taken as a whole, the legislative history [of the Sherman Act] illuminates congressional concern with the protection of competition, not *competitors,* and its desire to restrain mergers only to the extent that such combinations may tend to lessen competition.

Earl Warren, *Brown Shoe Co. v. United States,* 370 U.S. 294, 320 (1962)

32 The fact that a restraint operates upon a profession as distinguished from a business is, of course, relevant in determining whether that particular restraint violates the Sherman Act. It would be unrealistic to view the practice of professions as interchangeable with other business activities, and automatically to apply to the professions antitrust concepts which originated in other areas. The public service aspect, and other features of the professions, may require that a particular practice, which could properly be viewed as a violation of the Sherman Act in another context, be treated differently.

Warren E. Burger, *Goldfarb v. Virginia State Bar,* 421 U.S. 773, 788–89 n.17 (1975)

APPEALS

1 I perceive at present no impediment to the establishment of an appeal from the State courts to the subordinate national tribunals; and many advantages attending the power of doing it may be imagined. It would diminish the motives to the multiplication of federal courts, and would admit of arrangements calculated to contract the appellate jurisdiction of the supreme court. The State tribunals may then be left with a more entire charge of federal causes; and appeals in most cases in which they may be deemed proper instead of being carried to the supreme court, may be

made to lie from the state courts to district courts of the union.

> **Alexander Hamilton,** *The Federalist* No. 82, at 2:326–27 (1788)

2 A final judgment or decree in any suit, in the highest court of law or equity of a State in which a decision in the suit could be had, where is drawn in question the validity of a treaty or statute of, or an authority exercised under the United States, and the decision is against their validity; or where is drawn in question the validity of a statute of, or an authority exercised under any State, on the ground of their being repugnant to the constitution, treaties or laws of the United States, and the decision is in favour of such their validity, or where is drawn in question the construction of any clause of the constitution, or of a treaty, or statute of, or commission held under the United States, and the decision is against the title, right, privilege or exemption specially set up or claimed by either party, under such clause of the said Constitution, treaty, statute or commission, may be re-examined and reversed or affirmed in the Supreme Court of the United States upon a writ of error.

> Judiciary Act of 1789, ch. 20, § 25, 1 Stat. 73, 85–86

3 There is nothing in the nature of the thing which makes it improper for a Judge to sit in review upon his own judgments. If he is what a judge ought to be—wise enough to know that he is fallible, and therefore ever ready to learn; great and honest enough to discard all mere pride of opinion, and follow truth wherever it may lead; and courageous enough to acknowledge his errors—he is then the very best man to sit in review upon his own judgments. He will have the benefit of a double discussion. If right at the first, he will be confirmed in his opinion; and if wrong, he will be quite as likely to find it out as any one else.*

> **Greene C. Bronson,** *Pierce v. Delamater,* 1 N.Y. 3, 18–19 (1847)

---

* In this, the first opinion of the New York Court of Appeals, that court decided the question of whether a judge, Greene Bronson, could review on appeal his own judgment on a court on which he had previously sat. The Court of Appeals opinion, answering that question affirmatively and upholding Bronson's lower court decision, was written by Greene Bronson.

4 It not infrequently happens that a judgment is affirmed upon a theory of the case which did not occur to the court that rendered it, or which did occur and was expressly repudiated. The human mind is so constituted that in many instances it *finds the truth* when wholly unable to *find the way* that leads to it. "The pupil of impulse, it forc'd him along, / His conduct still right, with his argument wrong; / Still aiming at honor, yet fearing to roam, / The coachman was tipsy, the chariot drove Home."

> **Logan E. Bleckley,** *Lee v. Porter,* 63 Ga. 345, 346 (1879)

5 An appeal, Hinnissy, is where ye ask wan coort to show its contempt f'r another coort.

> **Finley Peter Dunne,** "The Big Fine," *Mr. Dooley Says,* 1910, in *Mr. Dooley: Now and Forever* 281, 283 (Louis Filler ed. 1954)

6 APPEAL, *v.t.* In law, to put the dice into the box for another throw.

> **Ambrose Bierce,** *The Devil's Dictionary* 25 (1911)

7 Motions, objections, exceptions, demurrers and appeals, many of them wholly pointless and preposterous, waste half the time of our courts, and particularly of our courts of first instance. Their one practical use seems to be to confuse and browbeat the trial judge. They lead him into trackless morasses; they increase his chance of making mistakes; they take away from him his necessary and proper dignity; they put a premium upon mere sharpness and talent for trickery in lawyers. It is seldom, indeed, that a case of any importance closes without innumerable loopholes for appeal. The public would be vastly surprised if a verdict in such a case were received as final by both sides. No wonder the harassed trial judge, knowing that everything he does is thus subject to unrestrained criticism and review, falls into indifference and formalism. No wonder he plays the mere umpire.

> **H. L. Mencken,** "The Free Lance," Baltimore *Evening Sun,* 21 Apr. 1913, quoted in *The Gist of Mencken* 453 (Mayo DuBasky ed. 1990)

8 Th' lawyer f'r th' definse objicts to all th' questions an' whin th' coort overrules him he takes an exciption. That is as much as

to say to th' judge: "I'll make a jack iv ye in th' supreem coort."

Finley Peter Dunne, "On Criminal Trials," in *On Making a Will* 212, 217 (1919)

9 A business man, who had to leave on a journey before the end of a case begun against him by a neighbor, gave orders to his lawyer to let him know the result by telegraph. After several days he got the following telegram: "Right has triumphed." He at once telegraphed back, "Appeal immediately!"

The World's Best Jokes 242 (Lewis Copeland ed. 1936)

10 Finality as a condition of review is an historic characteristic of federal appellate procedure. It was written into the first Judiciary Act and has been departed from only when observance of it would practically defeat the right to any review at all. Since the right to a judgment from more than one court is a matter of grace and not a necessary ingredient of justice, Congress from the very beginning has, by forbidding piecemeal disposition on appeal of what for practical purposes is a single controversy, set itself against enfeebling judicial administration. Thereby is avoided the obstruction to just claims that would come from permitting the harassment and cost of a succession of separate appeals from the various rulings to which a litigation may give rise, from its initiation to entry of judgment. To be effective, judicial administration must not be leaden-footed.

Felix Frankfurter, *Cobbledick v. United States*, 309 U.S. 323, 324–25 (1940)

11 Ordinarily an application for habeas corpus by one detained under a state court judgment of conviction for crime will be entertained by a federal court only after all state remedies available, including all appellate remedies in the state courts and in this Court by appeal or writ of certiorari, have been exhausted.

Ex parte Hawk, 321 U.S. 114, 116–17 (1944) (per curiam)

12 A finding is "clearly erroneous" when although there is evidence to support it, the reviewing court on the entire evidence is left with the definite and firm conviction that a mistake has been committed.

Stanley F. Reed, *United States v. United States Gypsum Co.*, 333 U.S. 364, 395 (1948)

13 There is no doubt that if there were a super-Supreme Court, a substantial proportion of our reversals of state courts would also be reversed. We are not final because we are infallible, but we are infallible only because we are final.

Robert H. Jackson, *Brown v. Allen*, 344 U.S. 443, 540 (1953) (concurring)

APPOINTMENTS

See JUDICIAL APPOINTMENTS

ARGUMENT

See ADVOCACY

ARREST

See SEARCHES AND SEIZURES

ATTORNEY-CLIENT PRIVILEGE

See CLIENT

ATTORNEYS

See LAWYER JOKES; LAWYERS; LAWYERS (PRO); LAWYERS (CON); LAWYERS, INDIVIDUAL

ATTORNEYS' FEES

See FEES

AUTHORITY

See LAW; PRECEDENT

BANKRUPTCY

1 I hold, it [the bankruptcy power] extends to all cases where the law causes to be distributed, the property of the debtor among his creditors: this is its least limit. Its greatest, is a discharge of the debtor from his contracts. And all intermediate legislation, affecting substance and form, but tending to further the great end of the subject—distribution and discharge—are in the competency and discretion of Congress.

John Catron, *In re Klein [reported in a note to Nelson v. Carland]*, 42 U.S. (1 How.) 265, 281 (1843)

2 Such a construction of the statute is consonant with equity, and consistent with the object and intention of Congress in enacting a general law by which the honest citizen may be relieved from the burden of hopeless insolvency. A different construction would be inconsistent with the liberal spirit which pervades the entire bankrupt system.

> **John M. Harlan** (1833–1911), *Neal v. Clark*, 95 U.S. 704, 709 (1878)

3 Systems of bankruptcy are designed to relieve the honest debtor from the weight of indebtedness which has become oppressive and to permit him to have a fresh start in business or commercial life, freed from the obligation and responsibilities which may have resulted from business misfortunes.

> **William R. Day,** *Wetmore v. Markoe*, 196 U.S. 68, 77 (1904)

4 The situs of intangibles is in truth a legal fiction, but there are times when justice or convenience requires that a legal situs be ascribed to them. The locality selected is for some purposes, the domicile of the creditor; for others, the domicile or place of business of the debtor, the place, that is to say, where the obligation was created or was meant to be discharged; for others, any place where the debtor can be found. . . . At the root of the selection is generally a common sense appraisal of the requirements of justice and convenience in particular conditions.

> **Benjamin N. Cardozo,** *Severnoe Securities Corp. v. London & Lancashire Ins. Co.*, 255 N.Y. 120, 123–24, 174 N.E. 299 (1931)

5 One of the primary purposes of the bankruptcy act is to "relieve the honest debtor from the weight of oppressive indebtedness and permit him to start afresh free from the obligations and responsibilities consequent upon business misfortunes." *Williams v. U.S. Fidelity & G. Co.*, 236 U.S. 549, 554–555. This purpose of the act has been again and again emphasized by the courts as being of public as well as private interest, in that it gives to the honest but unfortunate debtor who surrenders for distribution the property which he owns *at the time of bankruptcy,* a new opportunity in life and a clear field for future effort, un-

hampered by the pressure and discouragement of preëxisting debt.

> **George Sutherland,** *Local Loan Co. v. Hunt,* 292 U.S. 234, 244 (1934)

6 One could always begin again in America, even again and again. Bankruptcy, which in the fixed society of Europe was the tragic end of a career, might be merely a step in personal education.

> **John A. Krout and Dixon Ryan Fox,** *The Completion of Independence* 3 (1944)

7 The Court today holds that Congress may say that some of the poor are too poor even to go bankrupt. I cannot agree.

> **Potter Stewart,** *United States v. Kras,* 409 U.S. 434, 457 (1973) (dissenting)

8 Bankruptcy serves a role in corporate life eerily similar to that of the doctrine of reincarnation in some eastern religions. Bankruptcy is the belief that the souls of a corporate entity, the equityholders, do not just vanish when their corporeal form dies. Rather, they learn from the mistakes of a previous incarnation and can once again live on the earth in corporate form. True, they may suffer for the sins of previous incarnations and have trouble raising venture capital, but such is the karmic burden. With luck, some day a corporation may achieve enlightenment and reach a plane of eternal bliss and nirvana—the Fortune 500.

> **Irving L. Goldberg,** *In re Gary Aircraft Corp.,* 698 F.2d 775, 779–80 (5th Cir. 1983)

BAR ASSOCIATIONS

1 All associations are dangerous to good Government . . . and associations of Lawyers the most dangerous of any next to the Military.

> **Cadwallader Colden,** Letter to Earl of Halifax, 22 Feb. 1765, quoted in Anton-Hermann Chroust, *The Rise of the Legal Profession in America* 1:186 (1965)

2 Bar organizations have generally taken only a perfunctory interest in the real problems of the profession. They have been chiefly organizations which, when not given over to petty politics, have been devoted to honoring the leaders of the profession and to describing in sonorous

phrases the noble traditions of the bar and the perfection of the common law.

> Harlan F. Stone, Letter to Frederick L. Allen, Oct. 1926, in Alpheus T. Mason, *Harlan Fiske Stone: Pillar of the Law* 377 n. (1956)

3 One can scarcely imagine a speaker at a meeting of a county medical society discussing the possible elimination of some disease by public health measures, and then qualifying his observations by the statement that many practitioners make a living out of treating the disease in question; and that unless the physicians are vigilant to prevent the adoption of such measures, this source of business will be taken from them. Yet speakers at bar association meetings are frequently heard to make similar observations about the effect of proposed reforms.

> Arthur E. Sutherland, Jr., "A New Society and an Old Calling," 23 *Cornell Law Quarterly* 545, 552 (1938)

BIGAMY

See MARRIAGE

BILL OF RIGHTS

See also FOURTEENTH AMENDMENT

1 I will now add what I do not like [about the Constitution]. First the omission of a bill of rights providing clearly and without the aid of sophisms for freedom of religion, freedom of the press, protection against standing armies, restriction against monopolies, the eternal and unremitting force of the habeas corpus laws, and trials by jury in all matters of fact triable by the laws of the land and not by the law of Nations.

> Thomas Jefferson, Letter to James Madison, 20 Dec. 1787, in *Papers of Thomas Jefferson* 12:440 (Julian P. Boyd ed. 1955)

2 A bill of rights is what the people are entitled to against every government on earth, general or particular, and what no just government should refuse, or rest on inference.

> Thomas Jefferson, Letter to James Madison, 20 Dec. 1787, in *Papers of Thomas Jefferson* 12:440 (Julian P. Boyd ed. 1955)

3 For instance, the liberty of the press, which has been a copious subject of declamation and opposition: what controul can proceed from the federal government, to shackle or destroy that sacred palladium of national freedom? . . . the proposed system possesses no influence whatever upon the press; and it would have been merely nugatory, to have introduced a formal declaration upon the subject; nay, that very declaration might have been construed to imply that some degree of power was given, since we undertook to define its extent.

> James Wilson, Address, Philadelphia, 1787, in *The Bill of Rights: A Documentary History* 1:528, 529 (Bernard Schwartz ed. 1971)

4 Bills of rights . . . are not only unnecessary in the proposed constitution, but would even be dangerous. They would contain various exceptions to powers which are not granted; and, on this very account, would afford a colourable pretext to claim more than were granted. For why declare that things shall not be done which there is no power to do? Why for instance, should it be said, that the liberty of the press shall not be restrained, when no power is given by which restrictions may be imposed?

> Alexander Hamilton, *The Federalist* No. 84, at 2:349 (1788)

5 Excisemen may come in multitudes; for the limitation of their numbers no man knows. They may, unless the general government be restrained by a bill of rights, or some similar restriction, go into your cellars and rooms, and search, ransack, and measure, every thing you eat, drink, and wear.

> Patrick Henry, Debates in the Virginia Convention on the adoption of the Federal Constitution, 14 June 1788, in *Debates on the Adoption of the Federal Constitution* 3:448–49 (Jonathan Elliot ed., 2d ed. 1888)

6 I am glad to hear that the new constitution is received with favor. I sincerely wish that the 9 first conventions may receive, and the 4. last reject it. The former will secure it finally while the latter will oblige them to offer a declaration of rights in order to complete the union.

> Thomas Jefferson, Letter to James Madison, 6 Feb. 1788, in *Papers of Thomas Jefferson* 12:569 (Julian P. Boyd ed. 1955)

7 If they [the amendments in the Bill of Rights] are incorporated into the Constitution, independent tribunals of justice will consider themselves in a peculiar manner the guardians of those rights; they will be an impenetrable bulwark against every assumption of power in the Legislative or Executive; they will be naturally led to resist every encroachment upon rights expressly stipulated for in the Constitution by the declaration of rights.

   James Madison, in 1 *Annals of Congress* 457 (Joseph Gales ed. 1789)

8 These amendments [the Bill of Rights] contain no expression indicating an intention to apply them to the state governments. This court cannot so apply them.

   John Marshall, *Barron v. Baltimore,* 32 U.S. (7 Pet.) 243, 250 (1833)

9 No judicial tribunal has authority to say that some of [the Bill of Rights] may be abridged by the States while others may not be abridged.

   John M. Harlan (1833–1911), *Maxwell v. Dow,* 176 U.S. 581, 616 (1900) (dissenting)

10 It is possible that some of the personal rights safeguarded by the first eight Amendments against National action may also be safeguarded against state action, because a denial of them would be a denial of due process of law. . . . If this is so, it is not because those rights are enumerated in the first eight Amendments, but because they are of such a nature that they are included in the conception of due process of law.

   William H. Moody, *Twining v. New Jersey,* 211 U.S. 78, 99 (1908)

11 The very purpose of a Bill of Rights was to withdraw certain subjects from the vicissitudes of political controversy, to place them beyond the reach of majorities and officials and to establish them as legal principles to be applied by the courts. One's right to life, liberty, and property, to free speech, a free press, freedom of worship and assembly, and other fundamental rights may not be submitted to vote; they depend on the outcome of no elections.

   Robert H. Jackson, *West Virginia State Bd. of Educ. v. Barnette,* 319 U.S. 624, 638 (1943)

12 I fear to see the consequences of the Court's practice of substituting its own concepts of decency and fundamental justice for the language of the Bill of Rights as its point of departure in interpreting and enforcing that Bill of Rights.

   Hugo L. Black, *Adamson v. California,* 332 U.S. 46, 89 (1947) (dissenting)

13 The choice is not between order and liberty. It is between liberty with order and anarchy without either. There is danger that, if the Court does not temper its doctrinaire logic with a little practical wisdom, it will convert the constitutional Bill of Rights into a suicide pact.

   Robert H. Jackson, *Terminiello v. Chicago,* 337 U.S. 1, 37 (1949) (dissenting)

14 When public excitement runs high as to alien ideologies, is the time when we must be particularly alert not to impair the ancient landmarks* set up in the Bill of Rights.

   Luther W. Youngdahl, *United States v. Lattimore,* 112 F. Supp. 507, 518 (D.D.C. 1953)

15 It is my belief that there *are* "absolutes" in our Bill of Rights, and that they were put there on purpose by men who knew what words meant, and meant their prohibitions to be "absolutes."

   Hugo L. Black, "The Bill of Rights," 35 *New York University Law Review* 865, 867 (1960)

16 The foregoing cases suggest that specific guarantees in the Bill of Rights have penumbras, formed by emanations from those guarantees that help give them life and substance. . . . Various guarantees create zones of privacy.

   William O. Douglas, *Griswold v. Connecticut,* 381 U.S. 479, 484 (1965)

BOOKS

See LAW BOOKS; LAW LIBRARIES; LEGAL RESEARCH

BRITISH LAW

See ENGLISH LAW

---

* Do not remove the ancient landmark.—*Proverbs* 22.28 (NRSV)

BUSINESS

See also CORPORATIONS; REGULATION

1 Commerce is entitled to a complete and efficient protection in all its legal rights, but the moment it presumes to control a country, or to substitute its fluctuating expedients for the high principles of natural justice that ought to lie at the root of every political system, it should be frowned on, and rebuked.

James Fenimore Cooper, *The American Democrat* 167 (1956) (1838)

2 As our industrial conditions have developed, we have found that men may be oppressed quite as effectively and disastrously through business methods and practices as by force and violence. The law, therefore, must be invoked for the protection of the individual against the abuse of power.

Louis D. Brandeis, 1911, quoted in Alfred Lief, *The Brandeis Guide to the Modern World* 85 (1941)

3 Our laws are still meant for business done by *individuals;* they have not been satisfactorily adjusted to business done by great *combinations,* and we have got to adjust them. . . . there is no choice.

Woodrow Wilson, Address, Richmond, Va., 1 Feb. 1912, in *Public Papers of Woodrow Wilson* 2:367, 376 (Ray Stannard Baker & William E. Dodd eds. 1925)

CAPITAL PUNISHMENT

See also PUNISHMENT

1 The reformation of offenders . . . is not effected at all by capital punishments, which exterminate instead of reforming, and should be the last melancholy resource against those whose existence is become inconsistent with the safety of their fellow citizens, which also weaken the state, by cutting off so many who, if reformed, might be restored sound members to society, who, even under a course of correction, might be rendered useful in various labors for the public, and would be living and long continued spectacles to deter others from committing the like offences.

Thomas Jefferson, "A Bill for Proportioning Crimes and Punishments in Cases Heretofore Capital," 1779, in *Papers of Thomas Jefferson* 2:492, 493 (Julian P. Boyd ed. 1950)

2 The gallows has long been the penalty of murder, and yet we scarcely open a newspaper, that does not relate a new case of that crime.

Abraham Lincoln, Speech on the Sub-Treasury, Springfield, Ill., 26 Dec. 1839, in *Collected Works of Abraham Lincoln* 1:169 (Roy P. Basler ed. 1953)

3 Thank God! that I have lived to see the time
When the great truth begins at last to find
An utterance from the deep heart of mankind,
Earnest and clear, that all Revenge is Crime!

John Greenleaf Whittier, "Lines," 1843, in *Poetical Works of Whittier* 352, 353 (Hyatt H. Waggoner ed. 1975)

4 The best of us being unfit to die, what an inexpressible absurdity to put the worst to death!

Nathaniel Hawthorne, Journal entry, 13 Oct. 1851, in *The Heart of Hawthorne's Journals* 149 (Newton Arvin ed. 1929)

5 In England there was a time when one hundred different offences were punishable with death, and it made no difference. The English people strangely found out that so fast as they repealed the severe penalties and so fast as they did away with punishing men by death, crime decreased instead of increased; that the smaller the penalty the fewer the crimes. Hanging men in our county jails does not prevent murder. It makes murderers.

Clarence S. Darrow, Address to prisoners in Cook County Jail, 1902, in *Attorney for the Damned* 3, 14 (Arthur Weinberg ed. 1957)

6 I don't believe in capital punishment, Hinnissy, but 'twill niver be abolished while th' people injye it so much.

Finley Peter Dunne, "The Law's Delays," in *Observations by Mr. Dooley* 15, 16 (1906) (1902)

7 So long as governments set the example of killing their enemies, private individuals will occasionally kill theirs.

Elbert Hubbard, *Contemplations* 56 (1902)

8 CAPITAL PUNISHMENT, a penalty regarding the justice and expediency of which many worthy persons—including all the assassins—entertain grave misgivings.

> Ambrose Bierce, *The Devil's Dictionary* 44 (1911)

9 So there is a killer to be killed and I am the killer of the killer for today.

. . .

I am the high honorable killer today.
There are five million people in the state, five million killers for whom I kill.
I am the killer who kills today for five million killers who wish a killing.

> Carl Sandburg, "Killers," 1920, in *Complete Poems of Carl Sandburg* 197 (1969)

10 But why not do a good job of it? . . . Why not boil them in oil, as they used to do? Why not burn them at the stake? Why not sew them into a bag with serpents and throw them out to sea? . . . Why not break every bone in their body on the wrack, as has been done for such serious offenses as heresy and witchcraft?

> Clarence S. Darrow, in League for Public Discussion, *Debate, Resolved: That Capital Punishment is a Wise Public Policy* 32–33 (1924)

11 This world has been one long slaughterhouse from the beginning until today, and killing goes on and on and on, and will forever. Why not read something, why not study something, why not think instead of blindly shouting for death?

> Clarence S. Darrow, Closing argument in Leopold-Loeb trial, Chicago, 1924, in *Attorney for the Damned* 35–36 (Arthur Weinberg ed. 1957)

12 What is my friend's idea of justice? He says to this court, whom he says he respects—and I believe he does—Your Honor, who sits here patiently, holding the lives of these two boys in your hands:

"Give them the same mercy that they gave to Bobby Franks."

Is that the law? Is that justice? Is this what a court should do? Is this what a state's attorney should do? If the state in which I live is not kinder, more humane, more considerate, more intelligent than the mad act of these two boys, I am sorry that I have lived so long.

> Clarence S. Darrow, Closing argument in Leopold-Loeb trial, Chicago, 1924, in *Attorney for the Damned* 38 (Arthur Weinberg ed. 1957)

13 And for what [should the defendants die]? Because the people are talking about it. Nothing else. It would not mean, Your Honor, that your reason was convinced. It would mean in this land of ours, where talk is cheap, where newspapers are plenty, where the most immature expresses his opinion, and the more immature the stronger, that a court couldn't help feeling the great pressure of the public opinion which they say exists in this case.

> Clarence S. Darrow, Closing argument in Leopold-Loeb trial, Chicago, 1924, in *Attorney for the Damned* 47 (Arthur Weinberg ed. 1957)

14 Do I need to argue to Your Honor that cruelty only breeds cruelty?—that hatred only causes hatred?—that if there is any way to soften this human heart, which is hard enough at its best, if there is any way to kill evil and hatred and all that goes with it, it is not through evil and hatred and cruelty; it is through charity, and love and understanding?

> Clarence S. Darrow, Closing argument in Leopold-Loeb trial, Chicago, 1924, in *Attorney for the Damned* 52 (Arthur Weinberg ed. 1957)

15 I am not pleading so much for these boys as I am for the infinite number of others to follow, those who perhaps cannot be as well defended as these have been, those who may go down in the storm and the tempest without aid. It is of them I am thinking, and for them I am begging of this court not to turn backward toward the barbarous and cruel past.

> Clarence S. Darrow, Closing argument in Leopold-Loeb trial, Chicago, 1924, in *Attorney for the Damned* 53 (Arthur Weinberg ed. 1957)

16 Your Honor stands between the past and the future. You may hang these boys; you may hang them by the neck until they are dead. But in doing it you will turn your face toward the past. In doing it you are making it harder for every other boy who, in ignorance and darkness, must grope his way through the mazes which only childhood knows. In doing it you will make it harder for unborn children. You may save them

and make it easier for every child that sometime may stand where these boys stand. You will make it easier for every human being with an aspiration and a vision and a hope and a fate.

Clarence S. Darrow, Closing argument in Leopold-Loeb trial, Chicago, 1924, in *Attorney for the Damned* 86 (Arthur Weinberg ed. 1957)

17 I am pleading for the future; I am pleading for a time when hatred and cruelty will not control the hearts of men, when we can learn by reason and judgment and understanding and faith that all life is worth saving, and that mercy is the highest attribute of man.

Clarence S. Darrow, Closing argument in Leopold-Loeb trial, Chicago, 1924, in *Attorney for the Damned* 86–87 (Arthur Weinberg ed. 1957)

18 If I should succeed in saving these boys' lives and do nothing for the progress of the law, I should feel sad, indeed. If I can succeed, my greatest reward and my greatest hope will be that I have done something for the tens of thousands of other boys, for the countless unfortunates who must tread the same road in blind childhood that these poor boys have trod; that I have done something to help human understanding, to temper justice with mercy, to overcome hate with love.

Clarence S. Darrow, Closing argument in Leopold-Loeb trial, Chicago, 1924, in *Attorney for the Damned* 87 (Arthur Weinberg ed. 1957)

19 Those who would seek to take away from the State the power to impose capital punishment seek to despoil the symbol of justice. They would leave in her hands the scales that typify that in this country at least all are equal before the law, and that these scales must never tip from one side to the other, loaded on either side with power or influence of the litigant that comes to the temple of justice. They would leave over her eyes the bandage that typifies that she must be no respecter of persons, but they would take from her hand the sword, without which the other symbols would be meaningless things. For if justice has not the right to enforce her

edicts and her mandates, then her laws may be lost upon a senseless people.

Alfred J. Talley, in League for Public Discussion, *Debate, Resolved: That Capital Punishment is a Wise Public Policy* 22 (1924)

20 If I were having a philosophical talk with a man I was going to have hanged (or electrocuted) I should say, I don't doubt that your act was inevitable for you but to make if more avoidable by others we propose to sacrifice you to the common good. You may regard yourself as a soldier dying for your country if you like. But the law must keep its promises.

Oliver Wendell Holmes, Jr., Letter to Harold J. Laski, 17 Dec. 1925, in *Holmes-Laski Letters* 1:806 (Mark DeWolfe Howe ed. 1953)

21 The state continues to kill its victims, not so much to defend society against them—for it could do that equally well by imprisonment—but to appease the mob's emotions of hatred and revenge.

Clarence S. Darrow, "The Futility of the Death Penalty," *Forum*, Sept. 1928, at 327, 327

22 Perhaps the whole business of the retention of the death penalty will seem to the next generation, as it seems to many even now, an anachronism too discordant to be suffered, mocking with grim reproach all our clamorous professions of the sanctity of life.

Benjamin N. Cardozo, *Law and Literature* 93–94 (1931)

23 This Court may not disregard the Constitution because an appeal in this case, as in others, has been made on the eve of execution. We must be deaf to all suggestions that a valid appeal to the Constitution, even by a guilty man, comes too late, because courts, including this Court, were not earlier able to enforce what the Constitution demands. The proponent before the Court is not the petitioner but the Constitution of the United States.

John M. Harlan (1899–1971), *Chessman v. Teets*, 354 U.S. 156, 165 (1957)

24 Unless a vinireman states unambiguously that he would automatically vote against the imposition of capital punishment no

matter what the trial might reveal, it simply cannot be assumed that that is his position.

Potter Stewart, *Witherspoon v. Illinois,* 391 U.S. 510, 516 n.9 (1968)

25 To identify before the fact those characteristics of criminal homicides and their perpetrators which call for the death penalty, and to express these characteristics in language which can be fairly understood and applied by the sentencing authority, appear to be tasks which are beyond present human ability. . . . In light of history, experience, and the present limitations of human knowledge, we find it quite impossible to say that committing to the untrammeled discretion of the jury the power to pronounce life or death in capital cases is offensive to anything in the Constitution. . . . The infinite variety of cases and facets to each case would make general standards either meaningless "boiler-plate" or a statement of the obvious that no jury would need.

John M. Harlan (1899–1971), *McGautha v. California,* 402 U.S. 183, 204, 207-08 (1971)

26 In sum, the punishment of death is inconsistent with . . . four principles: Death is an unusually severe and degrading punishment; there is a strong probability that it is inflicted arbitrarily; its rejection by contemporary society is virtually total; and there is no reason to believe that it serves any penal purpose more effectively than the less severe punishment of imprisonment. The function of these principles is to enable a court to determine whether a punishment comports with human dignity. Death, quite simply, does not.

William J. Brennan, Jr., *Furman v. Georgia,* 408 U.S. 238, 305 (1972) (concurring)

27 In striking down capital punishment, this Court does not malign our system of government. . . . Only in a free society could right triumph in difficult times, and could civilization record its magnificent advancement. In recognizing the humanity of our fellow beings, we pay ourselves the highest tribute. We achieve "a major milestone in the long road up from barbarism" and join the approximately seventy other jurisdictions in the world which celebrate their regard for civilization and humanity by shunning capital punishment.

Thurgood Marshall, *Furman v. Georgia,* 408 U.S. 238, 371 (1972) (concurring)

28 The penalty of death differs from all other forms of criminal punishment, not in degree but in kind. It is unique in its total irrevocability. It is unique in its rejection of rehabilitation of the convict as a basic purpose of criminal justice. And it is unique, finally, in its absolute renunciation of all that is embodied in our concept of humanity.

Potter Stewart, *Furman v. Georgia,* 408 U.S. 238, 306 (1972) (concurring)

29 These death sentences are cruel and unusual in the same way that being struck by lightning is cruel and unusual.

Potter Stewart, *Furman v. Georgia,* 408 U.S. 238, 309 (1972) (concurring)

30 This Court inescapably has the duty, as the ultimate arbiter of the meaning of our Constitution, to say whether, when individuals condemned to death stand before our Bar, "moral concepts" require us to hold that the law has progressed to the point where we should declare that the punishment of death, like punishments on the rack, the screw and the wheel, is no longer morally tolerable in our civilized society.

William J. Brennan, Jr., *Gregg v. Georgia,* 428 U.S. 153, 229 (1976) (dissenting)

31 The penalty of death is qualitatively different from a sentence of imprisonment, however long. Death, in its finality, differs more from life imprisonment than a 100-year term differs from one of only a year or two.

Potter Stewart, Lewis F. Powell, Jr., and John Paul Stevens, *Woodson v. North Carolina,* 428 U.S. 280, 305 (1976)

32 Because of the unique finality of the death penalty, its imposition must be the result of careful procedures and must survive close scrutiny on post-trial review.

Thurgood Marshall, *Coleman v. Balkcom,* 451 U.S. 949, 955 (1981) (dissenting)

33 The Court . . . has recognized that the qualitative difference of death from all other punishments requires a correspondingly greater degree of scrutiny of the capital sentencing determination.

Sandra Day O'Connor, *California v. Ramos,* 463 U.S. 992, 998–99 (1983)

34 The calculated killing of a human being by the state involves, by its very nature, an ab-

solute denial of the executed person's humanity. . . . The most vile murder does not, in my view, release the state from Constitutional restraints on the destruction of human dignity. . . . The fatal constitutional infirmity of capital punishment is that it treats members of the human race as nonhumans, as objects to be toyed with and discarded.

> William J. Brennan, Jr., Address at Hastings College of Law, San Francisco, 18 Nov. 1985, quoted in *Los Angeles Times*, 19 Nov. 1985, at 13

35 Mutilations and tortures are not unconstitutional merely because they are painful— they would not, I submit, be saved from unconstitutionality by having the convicted person sufficiently anesthetized such that no physical pain were felt; rather, they are unconstitutional because they are inconsistent with the fundamental premise of the eighth amendment that "even the vilest criminal remains a human being possessed of common human dignity." A punishment is "cruel and unusual" if it does not comport with human dignity. The calculated killing of a human being by the state involves, by its very nature, an absolute denial of the executed person's humanity and thus violates the command of the eighth amendment.

> William J. Brennan, Jr., "Constitutional Adjudication and the Death Penalty: A View from the Court," 100 *Harvard Law Review* 313, 330 (1986)

36 It is tempting to pretend that minorities on death row share a fate in no way connected to our own, that our treatment of them sounds no echoes beyond the chambers in which they die. Such an illusion is ultimately corrosive, for the reverberations of injustice are not so easily confined. . . . the way in which we choose those who will die reveals the depth of moral commitment among the living.

> William J. Brennan, Jr., *McCleskey v. Kemp*, 481 U.S. 279, 344 (1987) (dissenting)

CASE SYSTEM

See also CASES; LAW SCHOOL; LEGAL EDUCATION

1 Law, considered as a science, consists of certain principles or doctrines. To have such a mastery of these as to be able to apply them with constant facility and certainty to the ever-tangled skein of human affairs, is what constitutes a true lawyer; and hence to acquire that mastery should be the business of every earnest student of law. Each of these doctrines has arrived at its present state by slow degrees; in other words, it is a growth, extending in many cases through centuries. This growth is to be traced in the main through a series of cases; and much the shortest and best, if not the only way of mastering the doctrine effectually is by studying the cases in which it is embodied.

> Christopher C. Langdell, *A Selection of Cases on the Law of Contracts* vi (1871)

2 The number of fundamental legal doctrines is much less than is commonly supposed. . . . If these doctrines could be so classified and arranged that each should be found in its proper place, and nowhere else, they would cease to be formidable from their number.

> Christopher C. Langdell, *A Selection of Cases on the Law of Contracts* vi-vii (1871)

3 It seemed to me, therefore, to be possible to take such a branch of the law as Contracts, for example, and, without exceeding comparatively moderate limits, to select, classify, and arrange all the cases which had contributed in any important degree to the growth, development, or establishment of any of its essential doctrines; and that such a work could not fail to be of material service to all who desire to study that branch of law systematically and in its original sources.

> Christopher C. Langdell, *A Selection of Cases on the Law of Contracts* vii (1871)

4 There is just as much sense in endeavoring to instruct students in the principles of law by the exclusive reading of cases as there would be in endeavoring to instruct the students of the West Point Military Academy in the art of war by compelling them to read the official reports of all the leading battles which have been fought in the world's history.

> Book Review, 5 *Southern Law Review* 872 (1880) (reviewing Christopher C. Langdell, *Selected Cases on Contracts* (2d ed. 1879))

5 Reading law cases in a hap-hazard way, leads to mental dissipation. . . . Law deci-

sions are but a labyrinth. Woe to the man who busies himself with them without a clue (in the form of a legal principle) to guide him.

> **Theodore Dwight,** "What Shall We Do When We Leave the Law School?," 1 *Counsellor* 63, 64 (1891)

6 The day came for its first trial. The class gathered in the old amphitheatre of Dane Hall—the one lecture room of the School— and opened their strange new pamphlets, reports bereft of their only useful part, the head-notes! The lecturer opened his.

"Mr. Fox, will you state the facts in the case of *Payne v. Cave?*"

Mr. Fox did his best with the facts of the case.

"Mr. Rawle, will you give the plaintiff's argument?"

Mr. Rawle gave what he could of the plaintiff's argument.

"Mr. Adams, do you agree with that?"

And the case-system of teaching law had begun.

> **Samuel F. Batchelder,** "Christopher C. Langdell," 18 *Green Bag* 437, 440 (1906)

7 Discussion is . . . ended at a question-begging phrase about "competing social policies" at the very point where it should properly begin. . . . Those higher domains where the important truths are examined and revealed are outside the province of a mere legal technician. Thus law, which is the keystone of the arch of public policy, is robbed of vitality and significance . . . the consequence of pedagogic failure which for three years drowns imagination in technique.

> **David Riesman, Jr.,** "Law and Social Science: A Report on Michael and Wechsler's Casebook on Criminal Law and Administration," 50 *Yale Law Journal* 636, 651 (1941)

8 American legal education went badly wrong some seventy years ago when it was seduced by a brilliant neurotic. I refer to the well-known founder of the so-called case system, Christopher Columbus Langdell.

> **Jerome N. Frank,** "A Plea for Lawyer-Schools," 56 *Yale Law Journal* 1303, 1303 (1947)

9 It is obvious that man could hardly devise a more wasteful method of imparting *information about subject matter* than the case-class. Certainly man never has.

> **Karl N. Llewellyn,** "The Current Crisis in Legal Education," 1 *Journal of Legal Education* 211, 215 (1948)

10 Students trained by the Langdell method are like dog breeders who only see stuffed dogs.

> **Jerome N. Frank,** quoted in *Guide to American Law* 2:254 (1983)

11 David . . . showed me around [Harvard] law school. . . . "This is Langdell Hall," he said. . . . "The building is named for the late Christopher Columbus Langdell, who was the dean of Harvard Law School in the late nineteenth century. Dean Langdell is best known as the inventor of the Socratic method."

David lowered his hand and looked sincerely at the building.

"May he rot in hell," David said.

> **Scott Turow,** *One L* 40 (1977)

12 Harvard Law's most enduring contribution to legal education was the mixing of the case method of study with the Socratic method of teaching. . . . these techniques were tailor-made to transform intellectual arrogance into pedagogical systems that humbled the student into accepting its premises, levels of abstractions, and choice of subjects. Law professors take delight in crushing egos in order to acculturate the students to what they called "legal reasoning" or "thinking like a lawyer." The process is a highly sophisticated form of mind control that trades off breadth of vision and factual inquiry for freedom to roam in an intellectual cage.

> **Ralph Nader,** in Joel Seligman, *The High Citadel* xv (1978)

13 The Socratic method is a game at which only one (the professor) can play.

> **Ralph Nader,** in Joel Seligman, *The High Citadel* xv (1978)

14 The key to the Socratic method is that the professor never reveals what the answer is. He keeps insisting that THERE IS NO ANSWER. Consistent with this view, he spends the whole class period asking questions that no

one even begins to understand. To get the answers, you have to buy commercial outlines, which cost $16.95 apiece and are published by the same people who publish Cliffs Notes and Key Comics. The commercial outlines are written by the professors and provide them with a handsome income on the side. To insure that you will buy them, the professors tell you that, whatever you do, DO NOT buy any commercial outlines, because they will make it TOO EASY for you, and you will not develop the analytical skills and hard work ethic that law school is supposed to teach. Pretty cagey, these professors.

> **James D. Gordon III,** "How Not to Succeed in Law School," 100 *Yale Law Journal* 1679, 1685 (1991)

```
                    CASES
```

See also CASE SYSTEM; LITIGATION; PRECEDENT; TRIALS

1 I look into my book in which I keep a docket of the decisions of the full court which fall to me to write, and find about a thousand cases. A thousand cases, many of them upon trifling or transitory matters, to represent nearly half a lifetime! A thousand cases, when one would have liked to study to the bottom and to say his say on every question which the law ever has presented, and then to go on and invent new problems which should be the test of doctrine, and then to generalize it all and write it in continuous, logical, philosophic exposition, setting forth the whole corpus with its roots in history and its justifications of expedience real or supposed!

> **Oliver Wendell Holmes, Jr.,** Speech to Bar Association of Boston, 7 Mar. 1900, in *Collected Legal Papers* 244, 245 (1920)

2 My keenest interest is excited, not by what are called great questions and great cases, but by little decisions which the common run of selectors would pass by because they did not deal with the Constitution or a telephone company, yet which have in them the germ of some wider theory, and therefore of some profound interstitial change in the very tissue of the law. The men whom I should be tempted to commemo-

rate would be the originators of transforming thought.

> **Oliver Wendell Holmes, Jr.,** "John Marshall" (speech), Boston, 4 Feb. 1901, in *Collected Legal Papers* 266, 269 (1920)

3 The ordinary man of business cares little for a "beautiful" case. He wishes it settled somehow on the most favorable terms he can obtain.

> **W. G. Miller,** *The Data of Jurisprudence* 1 (1903)

4 Great cases like hard cases make bad law. For great cases are called great, not by reason of their real importance in shaping the law of the future, but because of some accident of immediate overwhelming interest which appeals to the feelings and distorts the judgment. These immediate interests exercise a kind of hydraulic pressure which makes what previously was clear seem doubtful, and before which even well settled principles of law will bend.

> **Oliver Wendell Holmes, Jr.,** *Northern Securities Co. v. United States,* 193 U.S. 197, 400–01 (1904) (dissenting)

5 General propositions do not decide concrete cases. The decision will depend on a judgment or intuition more subtle than any articulate major premise.

> **Oliver Wendell Holmes, Jr.,** *Lochner v. New York,* 198 U.S. 45, 76 (1905) (dissenting)

6 I do not suppose that civilization will come to an end whichever way this case is decided.

> **Oliver Wendell Holmes, Jr.,** *Haddock v. Haddock,* 201 U.S. 562, 628 (1906) (dissenting)

7 A "controversy" in this sense must be one that is appropriate for judicial determination. . . . A justiciable controversy is thus distinguished from a difference or dispute of a hypothetical or abstract character; from one that is academic or moot. . . . The controversy must be definite and concrete, touching the legal relations of parties having adverse legal interests. . . . It must be a real and substantial controversy admitting of specific relief through a decree of a conclusive character, as distinguished from an opinion advising what the law would be upon a hypothetical state of facts.

> **Charles Evans Hughes,** *Aetna Life Ins. Co. v. Haworth,* 300 U.S. 227, 240–41 (1937)

CENSORSHIP

See also FIRST AMENDMENT; FREEDOM OF SPEECH; OBSCENITY; SEX

1 If we advert to the nature of Republican Government, we shall find that the censorial power is in the people over the Government, and not in the Government over the people.

James Madison, 27 Nov. 1794, in 4 *Annals of Congress* 934 (1855)

2 I am ... mortified to be told that, *in the United States of America* ... a question about the sale of a book can be carried before the civil magistrate. ... are we to have a censor whose imprimatur shall say what books may be sold, and what we may buy? ... Whose foot is to be the measure to which ours are all to be cut or stretched? ... It is an insult to our citizens to question whether they are rational beings or not.

Thomas Jefferson, Letter to N. G. DuFief, 19 Apr. 1814, in *Writings of Thomas Jefferson* 14:127 (Andrew A. Lipscomb ed. 1904)

3 Time is a great legalizer, even in the field of morals.

H. L. Mencken, *A Book of Prefaces* 282 (1917)

4 The censor believes that he can hold back the mighty traffic of life with a tin whistle and a raised right hand. For, after all, it is life with which he quarrels.

Heywood Broun, quoted in Ezra Goodman, *The Fifty-Year Decline and Fall of Hollywood* 423 (1961)

5 The power of the licensor against which John Milton directed his assault by his "Appeal for the Liberty of Unlicensed Printing" is pernicious not merely by reason of the censure of particular comments but by reason of the threat to censure comments on matters of public concern. It is not merely the sporadic abuse of power by the censor but the pervasive threat inherent in its very existence that constitutes the danger to freedom of discussion.

Frank Murphy, *Thornhill v. Alabama,* 310 U.S. 88, 97 (1940)

6 We all know that books burn—yet we have the greater knowledge that books can not be killed by fire. People die, but books never die. No man and no force can abolish memory. No man and no force can put thought in a concentration camp forever. No man and no force can take from the world the books that embody man's eternal fight against tyranny of every kind. In this war, we know, books are weapons. And it is a part of your dedication always to make them weapons for man's freedom.

Franklin D. Roosevelt, "Message to the Booksellers of America," *Publishers' Weekly,* 9 May 1942, at 1741

7 Murder is a crime. Describing murder is not. Sex is not a crime. Describing sex *is.*

Gershon Legman, *Love & Death: A Study in Censorship* 94 (1949)

8 The priceless heritage of our society is the unrestricted constitutional right of each member to think as he will. Thought control is a copyright of totalitarianism, and we have no claim to it. It is not the function of our Government to keep the citizen from falling into error; it is the function of the citizen to keep the Government from falling into error. We could justify any censorship only when the censors are better shielded against error than the censored.

Robert H. Jackson, *American Communications Ass'n v. Douds,* 339 U.S. 382, 442–43 (1950)

9 The function of the censor is to censor. He has a professional interest in finding things to suppress.

Thomas I. Emerson, "The Doctrine of Prior Restraint," 20 *Law and Contemporary Problems* 648, 659 (1955)

10 Any test that turns on what is offensive to the community's standards is too loose, too capricious, too destructive of freedom of expression to be squared with the First Amendment. Under that test, juries can censor, suppress, and punish what they don't like, provided the matter relates to "sexual impurity" or has a tendency "to excite lustful thoughts." This is community censorship in one of its worst forms. It creates a regime where in the battle between the literati and the Philistines, the Philistines are certain to win.

William O. Douglas, *Roth v. United States,* 354 U.S. 476, 512 (1957) (dissenting)

11 I assume there is nothing in the Constitution which forbids Congress from using its

power over the mails to proscribe *conduct* on the grounds of good morals. No one would suggest that the First Amendment permits nudity in public places, adultery, and other phases of sexual misconduct.

> William O. Douglas, *Roth v. United States,* 354 U.S. 476, 512 (1957) (dissenting)

12 Thus, if the First Amendment guarantee of freedom of speech and press is to mean anything in this field, it must allow protests even against the moral code that the standard of the day sets for the community. In other words, literature should not be suppressed merely because it offends the moral code of the censor.

> William O. Douglas, *Roth v. United States,* 354 U.S. 476, 513 (1957) (dissenting)

13 I'm going to introduce a resolution to have the Postmaster General stop reading dirty books and deliver the mail.

> Gale McGee, quoted in *The Home Book of Humorous Quotations* 53 (A. K. Adams ed. 1969)

14 When there is official censorship it is a sign that speech is serious. When there is none, it is pretty certain that the official spokesmen have all the loud-speakers.

> Paul Goodman, *Growing Up Absurd* 40 (1960)

15 The censor's sword pierces deeply into the heart of free expression.

> Earl Warren, *Times Film Corp. v. City of Chicago,* 365 U.S. 43, 75 (1961) (dissenting)

16 Censorship reflects a society's lack of confidence in itself.... Long ago those who wrote our First Amendment charted a different course. They believed a society can be truly strong only when it is truly free. In the realm of expression they put their faith, for better or for worse, in the enlightened choice of the people, free from the interference of a policeman's intrusive thumb or a judge's heavy hand. So it is that the Constitution protects coarse expression as well as refined, and vulgarity no less than elegance.

> Potter Stewart, *Ginzburg v. United States,* 383 U.S. 463, 498 (1966)

17 I never read or see the materials coming to the Court under charges of "obscenity," because I have thought the First Amendment made it unconstitutional for me to act as a censor.... As a parent or a priest or as a teacher I would have no compunction in edging my children or wards away from the books and movies that did no more than excite man's base instincts. But I never supposed that government was permitted to sit in judgment on one's tastes or beliefs.

> William O. Douglas, *Paris Adult Theatre I v. Slaton,* 413 U.S. 49, 71–72 (1973) (dissenting)

18 The idea that the First Amendment permits government to ban publications that are "offensive" to some people puts an ominous gloss on freedom of the press. That test would make it possible to ban any paper or any journal or magazine in some benighted place.... The idea that the First Amendment permits punishment for ideas that are "offensive" to the particular judge or jury sitting in judgment is astounding. No greater leveler of speech or literature has ever been designed. To give the power to the censor, as we do today, is to make a sharp and radical break with the traditions of a free society.

> William O. Douglas, *Miller v. California,* 413 U.S. 15, 44 (1973) (dissenting)

19 Censorship of erotica is pretty ridiculous too. What kind of people make a career of checking to see whether the covering of a woman's nipples is fully opaque, as the law requires? ... Many of us do not admire busybodies who want to bring the force of law down on the heads of adults whose harmless private pleasures the busybodies find revolting.

> Richard A. Posner, *Miller v. Civil City of South Bend,* 904 F.2d 1081, 1099–1100 (7th Cir. 1990) (concurring)

CERTAINTY

1 Certainty generally is illusion, and repose is not the destiny of man.

> Oliver Wendell Holmes, Jr., "The Path of the Law," 10 *Harvard Law Review* 457, 465 (1897)

2 Certitude is not the test of certainty. We have been cock-sure of many things that were not so.

> Oliver Wendell Holmes, Jr., "Natural Law," 32 *Harvard Law Review* 40, 40–41 (1918)

3 In our worship of certainty, we must distinguish between the sound certainty and the sham, between what is gold and what is tinsel; and then, when certainty is attained, we must remember that it is not the only good; that we can buy it at too high a price; that there is danger in perpetual quiescence as well as in perpetual motion; and that a compromise must be found in a principle of growth.

Benjamin N. Cardozo, *The Growth of the Law* 16–17 (1924)

CHANGE

See LAW, GROWTH OF

CHILDREN

See also CUSTODY

1 The wants and weaknesses of children render it necessary that some person maintain them, and the voice of nature has pointed out the parent as the most fit and proper person. The laws and customs of all nations have enforced this plain precept of universal law. . . . The obligation on the part of the parent to maintain the child, continues until the latter is in a condition to provide for its own maintenance.

James Kent, *Commentaries on American Law* 2:159–60 (1827)

2 As the pressure of economic competition intensifies with social consolidation, the family regularly disintegrates, the children rejecting the parental authority at a steadily decreasing age; until, finally, the population fuses into a compact mass, in which all individuals are equal before the law, and all are forced to compete with each other for the means of subsistence.

Brooks Adams, *The Law of Civilization and Decay* 368–69 (1896)

3 The problem for determination by the judge is not, Has this boy or girl committed a specific wrong, but What is he, how has he become what he is, and what had best be done in his interest and in the interest of the state to save him from a downward career.

Julian W. Mack, "The Juvenile Court," 23 *Harvard Law Review* 104, 119–20 (1909)

4 In the light of these features of the act [Child Labor Law], a court must be blind not to see that the so-called tax is imposed to stop the employment of children within the age limits prescribed. Its prohibitory and regulatory effect and purpose are palpable. All others can see and understand this. How can we properly shut our minds to it?

William Howard Taft, *Child Labor Tax Case,* 259 U.S. 20, 37 (1922)

5 The powers of the Star Chamber were a trifle in comparison with those of our juvenile courts.

Roscoe Pound, Foreword, in Pauline Young, *Social Treatment in Probation and Delinquency* xxvii (1937)

6 It is cardinal with us that the custody, care and nurture of the child reside first in the parents, whose primary function and freedom include preparation for obligations the state can neither supply nor hinder.

Wiley B. Rutledge, *Prince v. Massachusetts,* 321 U.S. 158, 166 (1944)

7 As I read the cases, there has been a steady effort in law toward establishing a greater appreciation of human life and a higher responsibility on the part of people toward other people. This advance has not been continuous or regular, but important decisions have been rendered which hold the development on its course, and although from time to time a decision seems to retard this progress, in the main the responsibility toward increased care has gained considerably. Particularly is this true where children may be the potential victims of negligence and want of care. . . .

The spontaneity of children in responding to invitation to play, without calculating the risk, is as well known as the sequence of the seasons or the regularity with which night follows day. It is not an imponderable, or a matter of speculation. It is simply fact.

Michael A. Musmanno, *Jennings v. Glen Alden Coal Co.,* 369 Pa. 532, 543–44, 87 A.2d 206 (1952) (dissenting)

8 This [a surrogate-motherhood contract] is the sale of a child, or, at the very least, the sale of a mother's right to her child, the

only mitigating factor being that one of the purchasers is the father.

Robert N. Wilentz, *In re Baby M.,* 109 N.J. 396, 437–38, 537 A.2d 1227 (1988)

CHOICE OF LAW

See CONFLICT OF LAWS

CINEMA

See COURTROOM SCENES

CIVIL DISOBEDIENCE

See also CIVIL RIGHTS; OBEDIENCE TO LAW

1 When I refuse to obey an unjust law, I do not contest the right of the majority to command, but I simply appeal from the sovereignty of the people to the sovereignty of mankind. Some have not feared to assert that a people can never outstep the boundaries of justice and reason in those affairs which are peculiarly its own; and that consequently full power may be given to the majority by which they are represented. But this is the language of a slave.

Alexis de Tocqueville, *Democracy in America* 1:330 (Francis Bowen trans. 1862) (1835)

2 I think that we should be men first, and subjects afterwards. It is not desirable to cultivate a respect for the law, so much as for the right. The only obligation which I have a right to assume is to do at any time what I think right.

Henry David Thoreau, *Civil Disobedience,* 1849, in *Writings of Henry David Thoreau* 4:356, 358 (1906)

3 A common and natural result of an undue respect for law is, that you may see a file of soldiers, colonel, captain, corporal, privates, powder-monkeys, and all, marching in admirable order over hill and dale to the wars, against their wills, ay, against their common sense and consciences, which makes it very steep marching indeed, and produces a palpitation of the heart. They have no doubt that it is a damnable business in which they are concerned; they are all peaceably inclined. Now, what are they? Men at all? or small movable forts and

magazines, at the service of some unscrupulous man in power?

Henry David Thoreau, *Civil Disobedience,* 1849, in *Writings of Henry David Thoreau* 4:356, 358–59 (1906)

4 Most legislators, politicians, lawyers, ministers, and office-holders . . . serve the state chiefly with their heads; and, as they rarely make any moral distinctions, they are as likely to serve the devil, without *intending* it, as God.

Henry David Thoreau, *Civil Disobedience,* 1849, in *Writings of Henry David Thoreau* 4:356, 359 (1906)

5 Unjust laws exist: shall we be content to obey them, or shall we endeavor to amend them, and obey them until we have succeeded, or shall we transgress them at once? Men generally, under such a government as this, think that they ought to wait until they have persuaded the majority to alter them. They think that, if they should resist, the remedy would be worse than the evil. But it is the fault of the government itself that the remedy *is* worse than the evil.

Henry David Thoreau, *Civil Disobedience,* 1849, in *Writings of Henry David Thoreau* 4:356, 367 (1906)

6 Under a government which imprisons any unjustly, the true place for a just man is also a prison.

Henry David Thoreau, *Civil Disobedience,* 1849, in *Writings of Henry David Thoreau* 4:356, 370 (1906)

7 I have never declined paying the highway tax, because I am as desirous of being a good neighbor as I am of being a bad subject.

Henry David Thoreau, *Civil Disobedience,* 1849, in *Writings of Henry David Thoreau* 4:356, 380 (1906)

8 It is not to be forgotten, that while the law holds fast the thief and murderer, it lets itself go loose. When I have not paid the tax which the State demanded for that protection which I did not want, itself has robbed me; when I have asserted the liberty it presumed to declare, itself has imprisoned me. Poor creature! if it knows no better I will not blame it. If it cannot live but by these means, I can.

Henry David Thoreau, *A Week on the Concord and Merrimack Rivers,* 1849, in

Selected Works of Thoreau 52, 118 (Walter Harding ed. 1975)

9 Much has been made of the willingness of . . . devotees of nonviolent social action to break the law. Paradoxically, although they have embraced Thoreau's and Gandhi's civil disobedience on a scale dwarfing any past experience in American history, they do respect law. They feel a moral responsibility to obey just laws. But they recognize that there are also unjust laws.

> **Martin Luther King, Jr.,** "The Time for Freedom Has Come," 1961, in *A Testament of Hope: The Essential Writings of Martin Luther King, Jr.* 160, 164 (James M. Washington ed. 1986)

10 One has not only a legal but a moral responsibility to obey just laws. Conversely, one has a moral responsibility to disobey unjust laws.

> **Martin Luther King, Jr.,** "Letter from Birmingham Jail," 16 Apr. 1963, in *Why We Can't Wait* 84 (1964)

11 I submit that an individual who breaks a law that conscience tells him is unjust, and who willingly accepts the penalty of imprisonment in order to arouse the conscience of the community over its injustice, is in reality expressing the highest respect for law. . . . We should never forget that everything Adolf Hitler did in Germany was "legal" and everything the Hungarian freedom fighters did in Hungary was "illegal."

> **Martin Luther King, Jr.,** "Letter from Birmingham Jail," 16 Apr. 1963, in *Why We Can't Wait* 86–87 (1964)

CIVIL PROCEDURE

See also APPEALS; JURISDICTION; PLEADINGS; PROCEDURE; STANDING

1 The court here points out three classes of parties to a bill in equity. They are: 1. Formal parties. 2. Persons having an interest in the controversy, and who ought to be made parties, in order that the court may act on that rule which requires it to decide on, and finally determine the entire controversy, and do complete justice, by adjusting all the rights involved in it. These persons are commonly termed necessary parties; but if their interests are separable from those of the parties before the court, so that the court can proceed to a decree, and do complete and final justice, without affecting other persons not before the court, the latter are not indispensable parties. 3. Persons who not only have an interest in the controversy, but an interest of such a nature that a final decree cannot be made without either affecting that interest, or leaving the controversy in such a condition that its final termination may be wholly inconsistent with equity and good conscience.

> **Benjamin R. Curtis,** *Shields v. Barrow,* 58 U.S. (17 How.) 130, 139 (1855)

2 Where the second action between the same parties is upon a different claim or demand, the judgment in the prior action operates as an estoppel only as to those matters in issue or points controverted, upon the determination of which the finding or verdict was rendered. In all cases, therefore, where it is sought to apply the estoppel of a judgment rendered upon one cause of action to matters arising in a suit upon a different cause of action, the inquiry must always be as to the point or question actually litigated and determined in the original action, not what might have been thus litigated and determined. Only upon such matters is the judgment conclusive in another action.

> **Stephen J. Field,** *Cromwell v. County of Sac,* 94 U.S. (4 Otto) 351, 353 (1877)

3 A right, question or fact distinctly put in issue and directly determined by a court of competent jurisdiction, as a ground of recovery, cannot be disputed in a subsequent suit between the same parties or their privies; and even if the second suit is for a different cause of action, the right, question or fact once so determined must, as between the same parties or their privies, be taken as conclusively established, so long as the judgment in the first suit remains unmodified.

> **John M. Harlan** (1833–1911), *Southern Pac. R.R. v. United States,* 168 U.S. 1, 48–49 (1897)

4 A judgment may be a merger or bar, or it may be an estoppel. For the first, the cause of action must be the same; for the second, they may be as different as possible. On the other hand, the merger or bar extends, not only to all matters pleaded, but to all that

might have been, while the estoppel extends only to facts decided and necessary to the decision. All this is very old law.

Learned Hand, *Irving Nat'l Bank v. Law*, 10 F.2d 721, 724 (2d Cir. 1926)

5 A judgment in one action is conclusive in the later one not only as to any matters actually litigated therein, but also as to any that might have been so litigated, when the two causes of action have such a measure of identity that a different judgment in the second would destroy or impair rights or interests established by the first.

Benjamin N. Cardozo, *Schuylkill Fuel Corp. v. B. & C. Nieberg Realty Corp.*, 250 N.Y. 304, 306-07, 165 N.E. 456 (1929)

6 Verdict can be directed only where there is no substantial evidence to support recovery by the party against whom it is directed or where the evidence is all against him or so overwhelmingly so as to leave no room to doubt what the fact is. . . . Verdict may be set aside and new trial granted, when the verdict is contrary to the clear weight of the evidence, or whenever in the exercise of a sound discretion the trial judge thinks this action necessary to prevent a miscarriage of justice.

John J. Parker, *Garrison v. United States*, 62 F.2d 41, 42 (4th Cir. 1932)

7 The Supreme Court of the United States shall have the power to prescribe, by general rules, for the district courts of the United States and for the courts of the District of Columbia, the forms of process, writs, pleadings, and motions, and the practice and procedure in civil actions at law. Said rules shall neither abridge, enlarge, nor modify the substantive rights of any litigant.

Enabling Act, ch. 651, § 1, 48 Stat. 1064, 1064 (1934)

8 The court may at any time unite the general rules prescribed by it for cases in equity with those in actions at law so as to secure one form of civil action and procedure for both: *Provided, however,* That in such union of rules the right of trial by jury as at common law and declared by the seventh amendment to the Constitution shall be preserved to the parties inviolate.

Enabling Act, ch. 651, § 2, 48 Stat. 1064, 1064 (1934)

9 The power to stay proceedings is incidental to the power inherent in every court to control the disposition of the causes on its docket with economy of time and effort for itself, for counsel, and for litigants. How this can best be done calls for the exercise of judgment, which must weigh competing interests and maintain an even balance.

Benjamin N. Cardozo, *Landis v. North American Co.*, 299 U.S. 248, 254–55 (1936)

10 Rule 1. Scope of Rules. These rules govern the procedure in the district courts of the United States in all suits of a civil nature whether cognizable as cases at law or in equity, with the exceptions stated in Rule 81. They shall be construed to secure the just, speedy, and inexpensive determination of every action.

Rule 2. One Form of Action. There shall be one form of action to be known as "civil action."

Federal Rules of Civil Procedure (1938)

11 Were the law to be recast, it would . . . be a pertinent inquiry whether the conclusiveness . . . of facts decided in the first [suit], might not properly be limited to future controversies which could be thought reasonably in prospect when the first suit was tried. . . . Logical relevance is of infinite possibility; there is no conceivable limit which can be put to it. Defeat in one suit might entail results beyond all calculation by either party; a trivial controversy might bring utter disaster in its train.

Learned Hand, *The Evergreens v. Nunan*, 141 F.2d 927, 929 (2d Cir. 1944)

12 Statutes of limitations, like the equitable doctrine of laches, in their conclusive effects are designed to promote justice by preventing surprises through the revival of claims that have been allowed to slumber until evidence has been lost, memories have faded, and witnesses have disappeared.

Robert H. Jackson, *Order of Railroad Telegraphers v. Railway Express Agency*, 321 U.S. 342, 348–49 (1944)

13 Statutes of limitation find their justification in necessity and convenience rather than in logic. They represent expedients, rather than principles. They are practical and pragmatic devices to spare the courts from litigation of stale claims, and the cit-

izen from being put to his defense after memories have faded, witnesses have died or disappeared, and evidence has been lost. . . . They are by definition arbitrary, and their operation does not discriminate between the just and the unjust claim, or the avoidable and unavoidable delay. They have come into the law not through the judicial process but through legislation. They represent a public policy about the privilege to litigate. Their shelter has never been regarded as what now is called a "fundamental" right.

> Robert H. Jackson, *Chase Securities Corp. v. Donaldson*, 325 U.S. 304, 314 (1945)

14 A common law trial is and always should be an adversary proceeding. Discovery was hardly intended to enable a learned profession to perform its functions either without wits or on wits borrowed from the adversary.

> Robert H. Jackson, *Hickman v. Taylor*, 329 U.S. 495, 516 (1947)

15 An interest to be considered [in deciding a forum non conveniens issue], and the one likely to be most pressed, is the private interest of the litigant. Important considerations are the relative ease of access to sources of proof; availability of compulsory process for attendance of unwilling, and the cost of obtaining attendance of willing, witnesses; possibility of view of premises, if view would be appropriate to the action, and all other practical problems that make trial of a case easy, expeditious and inexpensive. There may also be questions as to the enforcibility of a judgment if one is obtained. The court will weigh relative advantages and obstacles to fair trial. It is often said that the plaintiff may not, by choice of an inconvenient forum, "vex," "harass," or "oppress" the defendant by inflicting upon him expense or trouble not necessary to his own right to pursue his remedy. But unless the balance is strongly in favor of the defendant, the plaintiff's choice of forum should rarely be disturbed.

> Robert H. Jackson, *Gulf Oil Corp. v. Gilbert*, 330 U.S. 501, 508 (1947)

16 Jury duty is a burden that ought not to be imposed upon the people of a community which has no relation to the litigation. In cases which touch the affairs of many persons, there is reason for holding the trial in their view and reach rather than in remote parts of the country where they can learn of it by report only. There is a local interest in having localized controversies decided at home.

> Robert H. Jackson, *Gulf Oil Corp. v. Gilbert*, 330 U.S. 501, 508-09 (1947)

17 The situation is so tangled and bewildering that I sometimes wonder whether the world would be any the worse off if the class-suit device had been left buried in the learned obscurity of Calvert on *Parties to Suits in Equity*.

> Zechariah Chafee, Jr., *Some Problems of Equity* 200 (1950)

18 We need not consider all the reasons advanced by defendant in support of its motion. One arrow, if fatal, is fatal enough.

> Earl R. Hoover, *Inland Properties Co. v. Union Properties, Inc.*, 60 O.L. Abs. 150, 151, 44 Ohio Op. 485, 98 N.E.2d 444 (1951)

19 The fundamental premise of the federal rules is that a trial is an orderly search for the truth in the interest of justice rather than a contest between two legal gladiators with surprise and technicalities as their chief weapons.

> Arthur T. Vanderbilt, *Cases and Other Materials on Modern Procedure and Judicial Administration* 10 (1952)

CIVIL RIGHTS

See also AFFIRMATIVE ACTION; CIVIL DISOBEDIENCE; EQUAL PROTECTION; FOURTEENTH AMENDMENT; HUMAN RIGHTS; SEGREGATION; SLAVERY; VOTING

1 In what I have done I cannot claim to have acted from any peculiar consideration of the colored people as a separate and distinct class in the community, but from the simple conviction that all the individuals of that class are members of the community, and, in virtue of their manhood, entitled to every original right enjoyed by any other member. We feel, therefore, that all legal distinction between individuals of the same community, founded in any such circumstances as color, origin, and the like, are hostile to the genius of our institutions,

and incompatible with the true history of American liberty.

Abraham Lincoln, Speech, Cincinnati, 6 May 1842, in Emanuel Hertz, *Abraham Lincoln: A New Portrait* 2:531 (1931)

2 All persons without distinction of age or sex, birth or color, origin or condition, are equal before the law. . . . the rights of all, as they are settled and regulated by law, are equally entitled to the paternal consideration and protection of the law. . . . What those rights are, to which individuals, in the infinite variety of circumstances by which they are surrounded in society, are entitled, must depend on laws adapted to their respective relations and conditions.

Lemuel Shaw, *Roberts v. City of Boston,* 59 Mass. (5 Cush.) 198, 206 (1849)

3 All persons born in the United States and not subject to any foreign power, excluding Indians not taxed, are hereby declared to be citizens of the United States; and such citizens, of every race and color, without regard to any previous condition of slavery or involuntary servitude, . . . shall have the same right, in every State and Territory . . . , to make and enforce contracts, to sue, be parties, and give evidence, to inherit, purchase, lease, sell, hold, and convey real and personal property, and to full and equal benefit of all laws and proceedings for the security of person and property, as is enjoyed by white citizens, and shall be subject to like punishment, pains, and penalties, and to none other.

Civil Rights Act of 1866, ch. 31, § 1, 14 Stat. 27, 27

4 If two or more persons shall band or conspire together, or go in disguise upon the public highway, or upon the premises of another, with intent to violate any provision of this act, or to injure, oppress, threaten, or intimidate any citizen with intent to prevent or hinder his free exercise and enjoyment of any right or privilege granted or secured to him by the Constitution or laws of the United States, or because of his having exercised the same, such persons shall be held guilty of felony, and, on conviction thereof, shall be fined or imprisoned, or both, at the discretion of the court, . . . and shall, moreover, be thereafter ineligible to, and disabled from holding, any office or place of honor, profit or trust created by the Constitution or laws of the United States.

Civil Rights Act of 1870, ch. 114, § 6, 16 Stat. 140, 141

5 Any person who, under color of any law, statute, ordinance, regulation, custom, or usage of any State, shall subject, or cause to be subjected, any person within the jurisdiction of the United States to the deprivation of any rights, privileges, or immunities secured by the Constitution of the United States, shall, any such law, statute, ordinance, regulation, custom, or usage of the State to the contrary notwithstanding, be liable to the party injured in any action at law, suit in equity, or other proper proceeding for redress.

Civil Rights Act of 1871 (Ku Klux Klan Act), ch. 22, § 1, 17 Stat. 13, 13

6 On the most casual examination of the language of these amendments [the Thirteenth, Fourteenth, and Fifteenth Amendments], no one can fail to be impressed with the one pervading purpose found in them all, lying at the foundation of each, and without which none of them would have been even suggested; we mean the freedom of the slave race, the security and firm establishment of that freedom, and the protection of the newly-made freeman and citizen from the oppressions of those who had formerly exercised unlimited dominion over him.

Samuel F. Miller, *Slaughter-House Cases,* 83 U.S. (16 Wall.) 36, 71 (1873)

7 We want a state of things . . . which allows every man the largest liberty compatible with the liberty of every other man. . . . The genius of the country has marked out our true policy,—opportunity. Opportunity of civil rights, of education, . . . doors wide open . . . to every nation, to every race and skin, white men, red men, yellow men, black men; hospitality of fair field and equal laws to all. Let them compete and success to the strongest, the wisest, and the best.

Ralph Waldo Emerson, *The Fortune of the Republic,* 1874, in *Complete Works of Ralph Waldo Emerson* 11:511, 541 (1904)

8 Whereas, it is essential to just government we recognize the equality of all men before the law, and hold that it is the duty of gov-

ernment in its dealings with the people to mete out equal and exact justice to all, of whatever nativity, race, color, or persuasion, religious or political; and it being the appropriate object of legislation to enact great fundamental principles into law: Therefore,

Be it enacted . . . , That all persons within the jurisdiction of the United States shall be entitled to the full and equal enjoyment of the accommodations, advantages, facilities, and privileges of inns, public conveyances on land or water, theaters, and other places of public amusement; subject only to the conditions and limitations established by law, and applicable alike to citizens of every race and color, regardless of any previous condition of servitude.

Civil Rights Act of 1875, ch. 114, § 1, 18 Stat. 335, 335–36

9 When a man has emerged from slavery, and by aid of beneficent legislation has shaken off the inseparable concomitants of that state, there must be some stage in the progress of his elevation when he takes the rank of a mere citizen, and ceases to be the special favorite of the laws, and when his rights as a citizen, or a man, are to be protected in the ordinary modes by which other men's rights are protected.

Joseph P. Bradley, *Civil Rights Cases,* 109 U.S. 3, 25 (1883)

10 To-day, it is the colored race which is denied, by corporations and individuals wielding public authority, rights fundamental in their freedom and citizenship. At some future time, it may be that some other race will fall under the ban of race discrimination. If the constitutional amendments be enforced, according to the intent with which, as I conceive, they were adopted, there cannot be, in this republic, any class of human beings in practical subjection to another class, with power in the latter to dole out to the former just such privileges as they may choose to grant. The supreme law of the land has decreed that no authority shall be exercised in this country upon the basis of discrimination, in respect of civil rights, against freemen and citizens because of their race, color, or previous condition of servitude.

John M. Harlan (1833–1911), *Civil Rights Cases,* 109 U.S. 3, 62 (1883) (dissenting)

11 That there exists a serious and difficult problem arising from a feeling of race hostility which the law is powerless to control, and to which it must give a measure of consideration, may be freely admitted. But its solution cannot be promoted by depriving citizens of their constitutional rights and privileges.

William R. Day, *Buchanan v. Warley,* 245 U.S. 60, 80–81 (1917)

12 I do not believe in the law of hate. I may not be true to my ideals always, but I believe in the law of love, and I believe you can do nothing with hatred. I would like to see a time when man loves his fellow-man, and forgets his color or his creed. We will never be civilized until that time comes. I know the Negro race has a long road to go. I believe the life of the Negro race has been a life of tragedy, of injustice, of oppression. The law has made him equal, but man has not. And, after all, the last analysis is, what has man done?—and not what has the law done?

Clarence S. Darrow, Summation in Sweet Case, Detroit, 1926, in *Attorney for the Damned* 229, 262 (Arthur Weinberg ed. 1957)

13 The Japanese race is an enemy race and while many second and third generation Japanese born on United States soil, possessed of United States citizenship, have become "Americanized," the racial strains are undiluted. . . . There are indications that these [Japanese-Americans] are organized and ready for concerted action at a favorable opportunity. The very fact that no sabotage has taken place to date is a disturbing and confirming indication that such action will be taken.

John DeWitt, Final Recommendation of the Commanding General, Western Defense Command and Fourth Army, Submitted to the Secretary of War, 14 Feb. 1942, in U.S. Dep't of War, *Final Report, Japanese Evacuation from West Coast* 34 (1943)

14 It should be noted, to begin with, that all legal restrictions which curtail the civil rights of a single racial group are immediately suspect. That is not to say that all such restrictions are unconstitutional. It is to say that courts must subject them to the most rigid scrutiny. Pressing public necessity may sometimes justify the existence of

such restrictions; racial antagonism never can.

    Hugo L. Black, *Korematsu v. United States,* 323 U.S. 214, 216 (1944)

15 Once a judicial opinion rationalizes such an order to show that it conforms to the Constitution, or rather rationalizes the Constitution to show that the Constitution sanctions such an order, the Court for all time has validated the principle of racial discrimination in criminal procedure and of transplanting American citizens. The principle then lies about like a loaded weapon ready for the hand of any authority that can bring forward a plausible claim of an urgent need.

    Robert H. Jackson, *Korematsu v. United States,* 323 U.S. 214, 246 (1944) (dissenting)

16 The Constitution voices its disapproval whenever economic discrimination is applied under authority of law against any race, creed or color. A sound democracy cannot allow such discrimination to go unchallenged. Racism is far too virulent today to permit the slightest refusal, in the light of a Constitution that abhors it, to expose and condemn it wherever it appears in the course of a statutory interpretation.

    Frank Murphy, *Steele v. Louisville & Nashville R.R.,* 323 U.S. 192, 209 (1944) (concurring)

17 The constitution does not provide for first and second class citizens.

    Wendell L. Willkie, *An American Program* 8 (1944)

18 It's detestable, but that's the way it is. It's even worse in New Canaan. There, nobody can sell or rent to a Jew. . . . There's sort of a gentlemen's agreement . . .

    Moss Hart, *Gentlemen's Agreement* (screenplay), 1947, quoted in Gerald Gardner, *I Coulda Been a Contender* 192 (1992)

19 Section 1979 [of 42 U.S.C.] should be read against the background of tort liability that makes a man responsible for the natural consequences of his actions.

    William O. Douglas, *Monroe v. Pape,* 365 U.S. 167, 187 (1961)

20 The statute becomes more than a jurisdictional provision only if one attributes to the enacting legislature the view that a deprivation of a constitutional right is significantly different from and more serious than a violation of a state right and therefore deserves a different remedy even though the same act may constitute both a state tort and the deprivation of a constitutional right.

    John M. Harlan (1899–1971), *Monroe v. Pape,* 365 U.S. 167, 196 (1961) (concurring)

21 There will be many cases in which the relief provided by the state to the victim of a use of state power which the state either did not or could not constitutionally authorize will be far less than what Congress may have thought would be fair reimbursement for deprivation of a constitutional right. I will venture only a few examples. There may be no damage remedy for the loss of voting rights or for the harm from psychological coercion leading to a confession. And what is the dollar value of the right to go to unsegregated schools? Even the remedy for such an unauthorized search and seizure as Monroe was allegedly subjected to may be only the nominal amount of damages to physical property allowable in an action for trespass to land. It would indeed be the purest coincidence if the state remedies for violations of common-law rights by private citizens were fully appropriate to redress those injuries which only a state official can cause and against which the Constitution provides protection.

    John M. Harlan (1899–1971), *Monroe v. Pape,* 365 U.S. 167, 196 n.5 (1961) (concurring)

22 The man said, "I believe they are short-handed, but I don't believe they're employing any colored boys in the reconversion jobs."

    I said, "What makes you think I'm colored? They done took such words off of jobs in New York State by law."

    I know he wanted to say, "But they ain't took the black off of your face."

    Langston Hughes, *The Best of Simple* 187 (1961)

23 We have talked long enough in this country about equal rights. We have talked for one hundred years or more. It is time now to

write the next chapter, and to write it in the books of law.

> **Lyndon B. Johnson,** Address before Joint Session of Congress, 27 Nov. 1963, in *Public Papers of the Presidents: Lyndon B. Johnson, 1963–64,* at 8, 9 (1965)

24 Every American ought to have the right to be treated as he would wish to be treated, as one would wish his children to be treated. But this is not the case.

> **John F. Kennedy,** Radio and Television Report on Civil Rights, 11 June 1963, in *Public Papers of the Presidents: John F. Kennedy, 1963,* at 468 (1964)

25 No one has been barred on account of his race from fighting or dying for America— there are no "white" or "colored" signs on the foxholes or graveyards of battle.

> **John F. Kennedy,** Special Message to Congress on Civil Rights, 19 June 1963, in *Public Papers of the Presidents: John F. Kennedy, 1963,* at 485 (1964)

26 When the architects of our republic wrote the magnificent words of the Constitution and the Declaration of Independence, they were signing a promissory note to which every American was to fall heir. This note was the promise that all men, yes, black men as well as white men, would be guaranteed the unalienable rights of life, liberty, and the pursuit of happiness. It is obvious today that America has defaulted on this promissory note in so far as her citizens of color are concerned.

> **Martin Luther King, Jr.,** Speech at Civil Rights March, Washington, D.C., 28 Aug. 1963, in *Martin Luther King, Jr.: A Documentary* 218 (Flip Schulke ed. 1976)

27 All persons shall be entitled to the full and equal enjoyment of the goods, services, facilities, privileges, advantages, and accommodations of any place of public accommodation, as defined in this section, without discrimination or segregation on the ground of race, color, religion, or national origin.

> Civil Rights Act of 1964, Pub. L. No. 88–352, § 201(a), 78 Stat. 241, 243

28 All persons shall be entitled to be free, at any establishment or place, from discrimination or segregation of any kind on the ground of race, color, religion, or national

origin, if such discrimination or segregation is or purports to be required by any law, statute, ordinance, regulation, rule, or order of a State or any agency or political subdivision thereof.

> Civil Rights Act of 1964, Pub. L. No. 88–352, § 202, 78 Stat. 241, 244

29 No person in the United States shall, on the ground of race, color, or national origin, be excluded from participation in, be denied the benefits of, or be subjected to discrimination under any program or activiity receiving Federal financial assistance.

> Civil Rights Act of 1964, Pub. L. No. 88–352, § 601, 78 Stat. 241, 252

30 It shall be an unlawful employment practice for an employer—

(1) to fail or refuse to hire or to discharge any individual, or otherwise to discriminate against any individual with respect to his compensation, terms, conditions, or privileges of employment, because of such individual's race, color, religion, sex, or national origin; or

(2) to limit, segregate, or classify his employees in any way which would deprive or tend to deprive any individual of employment opportunities or otherwise adversely affect his status as an employee, because of such individual's race, color, religion, sex, or national origin.

> Civil Rights Act of 1964, Pub. L. No. 88–352, § 703(a), 78 Stat. 241, 255

31 The age-old dream for recognition of the inherent dignity and of the equal and inalienable rights of all members of the human family, . . . in that recognition is indeed the foundation of freedom, justice and peace in the world. The dream, though always old, is never old, like the Poor Old Woman in Yeats' play. "Did you see an old woman going down the path?" asked Bridget. "I did not," replied Patrick, who had come into the house just after the old woman left it, "but I saw a young girl and she had the walk of a queen."

> **William J. Brennan, Jr.,** Address, New York, 15 Nov. 1964, quoted in Stephen J. Friedman, "Mr. Justice Brennan: The First Decade," 80 *Harvard Law Review* 7, 22 (1966)

32 The court has not merely the power but the duty to render a decree which will so far

as possible eliminate the discriminatory effects of the past as well as bar like discrimination in the future.

> Hugo L. Black, *Louisiana v. United States,* 380 U.S. 145, 154 (1965)

33 Once loosed, the idea of Equality is not easily cabined.

> Archibald Cox, "The Supreme Court, 1965 Term—Foreword: Constitutional Adjudication and the Promotion of Human Rights," 80 *Harvard Law Review* 91, 91 (1966)

34 It is the policy of the United States to provide, within constitutional limitations, for fair housing throughout the United States.

> Fair Housing Act of 1968, Pub. L. No. 90–284, § 801, 82 Stat. 73, 81

35 When racial discrimination herds men into ghettos and makes their ability to buy property turn on the color of their skin, then it too is a relic of slavery.

> Potter Stewart, *Jones v. Alfred H. Mayer Co.,* 392 U.S. 409, 442–43 (1968)

36 At the very least, the freedom that Congress is empowered to secure under the Thirteenth Amendment includes the freedom to buy whatever a white man can buy, the right to live wherever a white man can live. If Congress cannot say that being a free man means at least this much, then the Thirteenth Amendment made a promise the Nation cannot keep.

> Potter Stewart, *Jones v. Alfred H. Mayer Co.,* 392 U.S. 409, 443 (1968)

37 What is required by Congress is the removal of artificial, arbitrary, and unnecessary barriers to employment when the barriers operate invidiously to discriminate on the basis of racial or other impermissible classification.

> Warren E. Burger, *Griggs v. Duke Power Co.,* 401 U.S. 424, 430–31 (1971)

38 Earlier today, we heard the beginning of the Preamble to the Constitution of the United States. "We the people." It is a very eloquent beginning. But, when that document was completed on the 17th of September in 1787, I was not included in that "We, the people." I felt somehow for many years that George Washington and Alexander Hamilton just left me out by mistake.

But, through the process of amendment, interpretation and court decision, I have finally been included in "We, the people."

> Barbara C. Jordan, Testimony before House Judiciary Committee, 25 July 1974, in Ira B. Bryant, *Barbara Charline Jordan* 51 (1977)

39 I testified for a proposal which was not to intern in concentration camps *all* Japanese, but to require them to move from what was designated as the theater of operations, extending seven hundred and fifty miles inland from the Pacific Ocean. Those who did not move by a certain date were to be confined to concentration camps established by the United States Government.... I have since deeply regretted the removal order and my own testimony advocating it, because it was not in keeping with our American concept of freedom and the rights of citizens. Whenever I thought of the innocent little children who were torn from home, school friends, and congenial surroundings, I was conscience-striken. It was wrong to react so impulsively, without positive evidence of disloyalty, even though we felt we had a good motive in the security of our state.

> Earl Warren, *The Memoirs of Earl Warren* 148, 149 (1977)

40 It may be assumed that parents have a First Amendment right to send their children to educational institutions that promote the belief that racial segregation is desirable, and that the children have an equal right to attend such institutions. But it does not follow that the *practice* of excluding racial minorities from such institutions is also protected by the same principle.

> Potter Stewart, *Runyon v. McCrary,* 427 U.S. 160, 176 (1976)

41 Our cases have not embraced the proposition that a law or other official act, without regard to whether it reflects a racially discriminatory purpose, is unconstitutional *solely* because it has a racially disproportionate impact.

> Byron R. White, *Washington v. Davis,* 426 U.S. 229, 239 (1976)

42 Of course, a simple mechanism for deterring violations such as this [police brutality] would be to amend section 1983 to provide that violators will be drawn and quartered. This seems like a very powerful

deterrent and might substantially reduce violations of federal rights under color of state law.

> **Irving L. Goldberg,** *Dobson v. Camden,* 705 F.2d 759, 765 (5th Cir. 1983)

43 One wonders whether the majority still believes that race discrimination—or, more accurately, race discrimination against nonwhites—is a problem in our society, or even remembers that it ever was.

> **Harry A. Blackmun,** *Wards Cove Packing Co. v. Atonio,* 109 S. Ct. 2115, 2136 (1989) (dissenting)

CLIENT

See also FEES; LAWYER JOKES

1 He who is always his own counseller will often have a fool for his client.*

> *Port Folio* (Philadelphia), Aug. 1809, at 132

2 This principle we take to be this; that so numerous and complex are the laws by which the rights and duties of citizens are governed, so important is it that they should be permitted to avail themselves of the superior skill and learning of those who are sanctioned by the law as its ministers and expounders, both in ascertaining their rights in the country, and maintaining them most safely in courts, without publishing those facts, which they have a right to keep secret, but which must be disclosed to a legal advisor and advocate, to enable him successfully to perform the duties of his office, that the law has considered it the wisest policy to encourage and sanction this confidence, by requiring that on such facts the mouth of the attorney shall be for ever sealed.

> **Lemuel Shaw,** *Hatton v. Robinson,* 31 Mass. (14 Pick.) 416, 422 (1834)

3 A reputable lawyer will advise you to keep out of the law, make the best of a foolish bargain, and not get caught again.

> **Mark Twain,** Letter to Charles H. Webb, 8 Apr. 1875, in *Mark Twain's Letters to His Publishers* 86 (Hamlin Hill ed. 1967)

---

* The *Concise Oxford Dictionary of Proverbs* lists this as the earliest known example of the proverb "A man who is his own lawyer has a fool for his client."

4 I would rather have clients than be somebody's lawyer.

> **Louis D. Brandeis,** quoted in Ernest Poole, "Brandeis: A Remarkable Record of Unselfish Work Done in the Public Interest," 71 *American Magazine* 481, 492 (1911)

5 I don't know as I want a lawyer to tell me what I cannot do. I hire him to tell me how to do what I want to do.

> **J. P. Morgan,** quoted in Ida M. Tarbell, *The Life of Elbert H. Gary* 81 (1925)

6 CLIENT, *n.* A person who has made the customary choice between the two methods of being legally robbed.

> **Ambrose Bierce,** *The Enlarged Devil's Dictionary* 40 (Ernest J. Hopkins ed. 1967)

7 DEFENDANT, *n.* In law, an obliging person who devotes his time and character to preserving property for his lawyer.

> **Ambrose Bierce,** *The Enlarged Devil's Dictionary* 60 (Ernest J. Hopkins ed. 1967)

8 "Yes," I said, "but you advised him to make the assignment. For whom were you counsel when you advised him to do that, if not for the Lennoxes?" He said, "I should say that I was counsel for the situation."

> **Louis D. Brandeis,** reported in *Nomination of Louis D. Brandeis: Hearings before the Senate Judiciary Comm.* 64th Cong., 1st Sess. 287 (1916)

9 [The ideal client is] the very wealthy man in very great trouble.

> **John Sterling,** quoted in John C. Payne, "Lawyers and the Laws of Economics," 46 *American Bar Association Journal* 365, 366 (1960)

10 A smart-Aleck client is apt to engage a smart-Aleck lawyer, much as men are said, out of personal vanity, to marry women who in general resemble them.

> **Arthur Train,** "The Liberty of the Jail," in *Tut, Tut! Mr. Tutt* 83, 91 (1923)

11 No one in all this list of clients has ever controlled or even fancied that he could control my personal or my political conscience. I am vain enough to imagine that no one ever will. The only limitation upon a right-thinking lawyer's independence is the duty which he owes to his clients, once

selected, to serve them without the slightest thought of the effect such a service may have upon his personal popularity or his political fortunes. Any lawyer who surrenders this independence or shades this duty by trimming his professional course to fit the gusts of popular opinion in my judgment not only dishonors himself but disparages and degrades the great profession to which he should be proud to belong.

John W. Davis, Letter to Theodore Huntley, 4 Mar. 1924, quoted in William H. Harbaugh, *Lawyer's Lawyer: The Life of John W. Davis* 199–200 (1990)

12 Its [the work of any criminal law office] object is precisely the same as that of the best offices where civil law is practised—that is, to make money out of the client. But inasmuch as the client who seeks the aid of a criminal attorney is usually in dread of losing not merely money but liberty, reputation, and perhaps life as well, he is correspondingly ready to pay generously for any real or fancied service on the part of the lawyer. Thus the fees of a criminal practitioner—when the client has any money—are ridiculously high, and he usually gets sooner or later all that the client has.

Arthur Train, *The Confessions of Artemas Quibble* 76–77 (1924)

13 There are three golden rules in the profession [criminal law] ... the first ... thoroughly terrify your client. Second, find out how much money he has and where it is. Third, get it. The merest duffer can usually succeed in following out the first two of these precepts, but to accomplish the third requires often a master's art. The ability actually to get one's hands on the coin is what differentiates the really great criminal lawyer from his inconspicuous brethren.

Arthur Train, *The Confessions of Artemas Quibble* 77 (1924)

14 The object of the lawyer being to hang on to the client until he has got his money, it follows that if the latter is locked up in jail it is all for the better for the lawyer, unless it be expedient to let him out to raise funds. Thus criminal attorneys are not, as a rule, particularly anxious to secure the release of a client from jail. Solitary confinement

increases his apprehension and discomfort and renders him more complacent about paying well for liberty. The English king who locked up the money-lender and had one of his teeth drawn out each day until he made the desired loan knew his business. Once the fellow is out of jail—pfft! He is gone, and neither the place nor you know him more. Very likely also he will jump his bail and you will have to make good your bond. One client in jail is worth two at large.

Arthur Train, *The Confessions of Artemas Quibble* 78–79 (1924)

15 About half the practice of a decent lawyer consists in telling would-be clients that they are damned fools and should stop.

Elihu Root, quoted in Philip C. Jessup, *Elihu Root* 1:132–33 (1938)

16 The main qualifications which are necessary [to successfully assert the attorney-client privilege]: (1) The asserted holder of the privilege is or sought to become a client; (2) the person to whom the communication was made (a) is a member of the bar of a court, or his subordinate and (b) in connection with this communication is acting as a lawyer; (3) the communication relates to a fact of which the attorney was informed (a) by his client (b) without the presence of strangers (c) for the purpose of securing primarily either (i) an opinion on law or (ii) legal services or (iii) assistance in some legal proceeding, and not (d) for the purpose of committing a crime or tort; and (4) the privilege has been (a) claimed and (b) not waived by the client.

Charles E. Wyzanski, Jr., *United States v. United Shoe Machinery Corp.,* 89 F. Supp. 357, 358–59 (D. Mass. 1950)

17 Everybody loved Mickie Joe, everybody tried to throw business in his way, but nobody ever took him seriously. He had a tendency which was very obvious in the Lynam case to identify himself with his client, a thing no real lawyer will do. A client is a fact, and a true lawyer hates facts. A lawyer is like an actor who can never bother about what sort of play he appears in, but tells himself some little story to cover as many of the incidents as he can be bothered to remember. The only thing he hates is to be reminded—for instance

by the author—what the real story is about.

Frank O'Connor, "Counsel for Oedipus," in *More Stories* 225, 228–29 (1954)

18 The easiest thing in the world is for a layman to poke fun at the law. Lawyers and the law are sitting ducks for ridicule and always have been. The average layman may in all his lifetime collide with but one small branch of the law, which he understands but imperfectly. He usually knows whether he won or lost. He may also remember that Dickens, grumbling through Mr. Bumble, once called the law an ass. So for him all the law is henceforth an ass, and, overnight, he becomes its severest critic.

Robert Traver, *Anatomy of a Murder* 62 (1958)

19 [Perry Mason speaking:] I'd rather have my hand cut off than betray the interests of a client.

Erle Stanley Gardner, *The Case of the Singing Skirt* 128 (1959)

20 While it is the great purpose of law to ascertain the truth, there is the countervailing necessity of insuring the right of every person to freely and fully confer and confide in one having knowledge of the law, and skilled in its practice, in order that the former may have adequate advice and a proper defense.

Stanley N. Barnes, *Baird v. Koerner*, 279 F.2d 623, 629 (9th Cir. 1960)

21 Praise the adversary. He is the catalyst by which you bill your client. Damn the client. He is your true enemy.

Steven J. Kumble, quoted in Kim Eisler, *Shark Tank: Greed, Politics, and the Collapse of Finley Kumble* 32 (1990)

22 An investigation is underway, and for the first time in my life I may actually have to stoop to retaining a lawyer. This is the end of something pure and good. Once a fellow breaks down and hires his first attorney, he has gone and booked himself passage aboard the hand basket to Hades.

Tom Robbins, *Skinny Legs and All* 358 (1990)

1 The distinction between actions at law and suits in equity, and the forms of all such actions and suits heretofore existing, are abolished; and, there shall be in this state, hereafter, but one form of action, for the enforcement or protection of private rights and the redress or prevention of private wrongs, which shall be denominated a civil action.

Act of Apr. 12, 1848 (Field Code), ch. 379, § 62, 1848 N.Y. Laws 497, 510

2 The complaint shall contain:
1. The title of the cause, specifying the name of the court in which the action is brought, the name of the county in which the plaintiff desires the trial to be had, and the names of the parties to the action, plaintiff and defendant:
2. A statement of the facts constituting the cause of action, in ordinary and concise language, without repetition, and in such a manner as to enable a person of common understanding to know what is intended:
3. A demand of the relief, to which the plaintiff supposes himself entitled. If the recovery of money be demanded, the amount thereof shall be stated.

Act of Apr. 12, 1848 (Field Code), ch. 379, § 120, 1848 N.Y. Laws 497, 521

3 I respectfully recommend to the consideration of Congress the present condition of the statute laws, with the hope that Congress will be able to find an easy remedy for many of the inconveniences and evils which constantly embarrass those engaged in the practical administration of them. Since the organization of the government, Congress has enacted some five thousand acts and joint resolutions, which fill more than six thousand closely printed pages, and are scattered through many volumes. Many of these acts have been drawn in haste and without sufficient caution, so that their provisions are often obscure in themselves, or in conflict with each other, or at least so doubtful as to render it very difficult for even the best informed persons to ascertain precisely what the statute law really is.

Abraham Lincoln, Annual Message to Congress, 3 Dec. 1861, in *Collected Works of Abraham Lincoln* 5:42 (Roy P. Basler ed. 1953)

4 It seems to me very important that the statute laws should be made as plain and intelligible as possible, and be reduced to as small a compass as may consist with the fullness and precision of the will of the legislature and the perspicuity of its language. This, well done, would, I think, greatly facilitate the labors of those whose duty it is to assist in the administration of the laws, and would be a lasting benefit to the people, by placing before them, in a more accessible and intelligible form, the laws which so deeply concern their interests and their duties.

> **Abraham Lincoln,** Annual Message to Congress, 3 Dec. 1861, in *Collected Works of Abraham Lincoln* 5:42 (Roy P. Basler ed. 1953)

COLLECTIVE BARGAINING

See LABOR LAW

COMMERCE CLAUSE

1 Commerce, undoubtedly, is traffic, but it is something more: it is intercourse. It describes the commercial intercourse between nations, and parts of nations, in all its branches, and is regulated by prescribing rules for carrying on that intercourse.

> **John Marshall,** *Gibbons v. Ogden,* 22 U.S. (9 Wheat.) 1, 189–90 (1824)

2 The commerce of the United States with foreign nations, is that of the whole United States. Every district has a right to participate in it. The deep streams which penetrate our country in every direction, pass through the interior of almost every State in the Union, and furnish the means of exercising this right. If Congress has the power to regulate it, that power must be exercised whenever the subject exists. If it exists within the States . . . then the power of Congress may be exercised within a State.

> **John Marshall,** *Gibbons v. Ogden,* 22 U.S. (9 Wheat.) 1, 195 (1824)

3 It [the commerce power] is the power to regulate; that is, to prescribe the rule by which commerce is to be governed. This power, like all others vested in Congress, is complete in itself, may be exercised to its utmost extent, and acknowledges no limitations, other than are prescribed in the constitution.

> **John Marshall,** *Gibbons v. Ogden,* 22 U.S. (9 Wheat.) 1, 196 (1824)

4 If, as has always been understood, the sovereignty of Congress, though limited to specified objects, is plenary as to those objects, the power over commerce with foreign nations, and among the several States, is vested in Congress as absolutely as it would be in a single government, having in its constitution the same restrictions on the exercise of the power as are found in the constitution of the United States. The wisdom and the discretion of Congress, their identity with the people, and the influence which their constituents possess at elections, are, in this, as in many other instances, as that, for example, of declaring war, the sole restraints on which they have relied, to secure them from its abuse. They are the restraints on which the people must often rely solely, in all representative governments.

> **John Marshall,** *Gibbons v. Ogden,* 22 U.S. (9 Wheat.) 1, 197 (1824)

5 Whatever subjects of this [commerce] power are in their nature national, or admit only of one uniform system, or plan of regulation, may justly be said to be of such a nature as to require exclusive Legislation by Congress.

> **Benjamin R. Curtis,** *Cooley v. Board of Wardens of the Port of Philadelphia,* 53 U.S. (12 How.) 299, 319 (1852)

6 Commerce succeeds to manufacture, and is not a part of it.

> **Melville W. Fuller,** *United States v. E. C. Knight Co.,* 156 U.S. 1, 12 (1895)

7 The power to regulate interstate commerce is, as stated by Chief Justice Marshall, full and complete in Congress, and there is no limitation in the grant of the power which excludes private contracts of the nature in question from the jurisdiction of that body. Nor is any such limitation contained in that other clause of the Constitution which provides that no person shall be deprived of life, liberty or property without due process of law. . . . the power of Congress to regulate interstate commerce compromises the right to enact a law prohibiting

the citizen from entering into those private contracts which directly and substantially . . . regulate to a greater or lesser degree commerce among the States.

> **Rufus W. Peckham,** *Addyston Pipe & Steel Co. v. United States,* 175 U.S. 211, 228–29 (1899)

8 When cattle are sent for sale from a place in one State, with the expectation that they will end their transit, after purchase, in another, and when in effect they do so, with only the interruption necessary to find a purchaser at the stock yards, and when this is a typical, constantly recurring course, the current thus existing is a current of commerce among the States, and the purchase of the cattle is a part and incident of such commerce.

> **Oliver Wendell Holmes, Jr.,** *Swift & Co. v. United States,* 196 U.S. 375, 398–99 (1905)

9 It remains only to consider the contention which we have previously quoted, that the act [Employers' Liability Act] is constitutional, although it embraces subjects not within the power of Congress to regulate commerce, because one who engages in interstate commerce thereby submits all his business concerns to the regulating power of Congress. To state the proposition is to refute it.

> **Edward D. White,** *Employers' Liability Cases,* 207 U.S. 463, 502 (1908)

10 I see nothing in the commerce clause to prevent a State from giving a preference to its inhabitants in the enjoyment of its natural advantages.

> **Oliver Wendell Holmes, Jr.,** *Pennsylvania v. West Virginia,* 262 U.S. 553, 602 (1923) (dissenting)

11 In determining how far the federal government may go in controlling intrastate transactions upon the ground that they "affect" interstate commerce, there is a necessary and well-established distinction between direct and indirect effects. The precise line can be drawn only as individual cases arise, but the distinction is clear in principle.

> **Charles Evans Hughes,** *Schechter Poultry Corp. v. United States,* 295 U.S. 495, 546 (1935)

12 It is not the province of the Court to consider the economic advantages or disadvantages of such a centralized system. It is sufficient to say that the Federal Constitution does not provide for it. Our growth and development have called for wide use of the commerce power of the federal government in its control over the expanded activities of interstate commerce, and in protecting that commerce from burdens, interferences, and conspiracies to restrain and monopolize it. But the authority of the federal government may not be pushed to such an extreme as to destroy the distinction, which the commerce clause itself establishes, between commerce "among the several States" and the internal concerns of a State.

> **Charles Evans Hughes,** *Schechter Poultry Corp. v. United States,* 295 U.S. 495, 549–50 (1935)

13 We have been relegated to the horse-and-buggy definition of interstate commerce.

> **Franklin D. Roosevelt,** Press conference in response to Supreme Court decisions overturning New Deal legislation, 31 May 1935, in *Public Papers and Addresses of Franklin D. Roosevelt* 4:200, 221 (Samuel I. Rosenman ed. 1938)
> See also CONSTITUTIONAL LAW 23

14 The authority of the federal government may not be pushed to such an extreme as to destroy the distinction, which the commerce clause itself establishes, between commerce "among the several States" and the internal concerns of a State. That distinction between what is national and what is local in the activities of commerce is vital to the maintenance of our federal system.

> **Charles Evans Hughes,** *NLRB v. Jones & Laughlin Steel Corp.,* 301 U.S. 1, 30 (1937)

15 If it is interstate commerce that feels the pinch, it does not matter how local the operation which applies the squeeze.

> **Robert H. Jackson,** *United States v. Women's Sportswear Mfrs. Ass'n,* 336 U.S. 460, 464 (1949)

16 The Commerce Clause is one of the most prolific sources of national power and an equally prolific source of conflict with legislation of the state. While the Constitution vests in Congress the power to regulate commerce among the states, it does not say

what the states may or may not do in the absence of congressional action. . . . Perhaps even more than by interpretation of its written word, this Court has advanced the solidarity and prosperity of this Nation by the meaning it has given to these great silences of the Constitution.

Robert H. Jackson, *H.P. Hood & Sons v. Du Mond,* 336 U.S. 525, 534–35 (1949)

17 This principle that our economic unit is the Nation, which alone has the gamut of powers necessary to control of the economy . . . has as its corollary that the states are not separable economic units.

Robert H. Jackson, *H.P. Hood & Sons v. Du Mond,* 336 U.S. 525, 537–38 (1949)

18 The material success that has come to inhabitants of the states which make up this federal free trade unit has been the most impressive in the history of commerce, but the established interdependence of the states only emphasizes the necessity of protecting interstate movement of goods against local burdens and repressions.

Robert H. Jackson, *H.P. Hood & Sons v. Du Mond,* 336 U.S. 525, 538 (1949)

19 Our system, fostered by the Commerce Clause, is that every farmer and every craftsman shall be encouraged to produce by the certainty that he will have free access to every market in the Nation, that no home embargoes will withold his exports, and no foreign state will by customs duties or regulations exclude them. Likewise, every customer may look to the free competition from every producing area in the Nation to protect him from exploitation by any. Such was the vision of the Founders; such has been the doctrine of this Court which has given it reality.

Robert H. Jackson, *H.P. Hood & Sons v. Du Mond,* 336 U.S. 525, 539 (1949)

20 Where the statute regulates evenhandedly to effectuate a legitimate local public interest, and its effects on interstate commerce are only incidental, it will be upheld unless the burden imposed on such commerce is clearly excessive in relation to the putative local benefits. . . . If a legitimate local purpose is found, then the question becomes one of degree. And the extent of the burden that will be tolerated will of course depend

on the nature of the local interest involved, and on whether it could be promoted as well with a lesser impact on interstate activities.

Potter Stewart, *Pike v. Bruce Church, Inc.,* 397 U.S. 137, 142 (1970)

COMMERCIAL LAW

1 A negotiable bill or note is a courier without luggage.

John B. Gibson, *Overton v. Tyler,* 3 Pa. 346, 347 (1846)

2 Some of the teaching of the law books and of the classroom seemed to me to be against justice. The *caveat emptor* side of the law, like the *caveat emptor* side of business, seemed to me repellent; it did not make for social fair dealing. The "let the buyer beware" maxim, when translated into actual practice, whether in law or business, tends to translate itself further into the seller making his profit at the expense of the buyer, instead of a bargain which shall be to the profit of both. It did not seem to me that the law was framed to discourage as it should sharp practice, and all other kinds of bargains except those which are fair and of benefit to both sides.

Theodore Roosevelt, *An Autobiography* 61 (1913)

3 Wealth, in a commercial age, is made up largely of promises. An important part of everyone's substance consists of advantages which others have promised to provide for or to render to him; of demands to have the advantages promised which he may assert not against the world at large but against particular individuals.

Roscoe Pound, *An Introduction to the Philosophy of Law* 236 (1922)

4 Since they [judicial techniques for balancing bargains] purport to construe and do not really construe, nor are intended to, but are instead tools of intentional and creative misconstruction, they seriously embarrass later efforts at true construction, later efforts to get at the true meaning of those wholly legitimate contracts and clauses which call for their meaning to be got at instead of avoided. The net effect is unnecessary confusion and unpredictability, together with inadequate remedy, and evil

persisting that calls for remedy. Covert tools are never reliable tools.

Karl N. Llewellyn, Book Review, 52 *Harvard Law Review* 700, 703 (1939)

COMMON LAW

See also LAW, GROWTH OF; PRECEDENT

1 Our ancestors were entitled to the common law of England when they emigrated, that is, to just so much of it as they pleased to adopt, and no more. They were not bound or obliged to submit to it, unless they chose it.

John Adams, *Novanglus,* 1774, in *Works of John Adams* 4:122 (Charles Francis Adams ed. 1851)

2 Of all the doctrines which have ever been broached by the federal goverment, the novel one, of the common law being in force & cognizable as an existing law in their courts, is to me the most formidable. All their other assumptions of un-given powers have been in the detail. The bank law, the treaty doctrine, the sedition act, alien act, the undertaking to change the state laws of evidence in the state courts by certain parts of the stamp act, &c., &c., have been solitary, unconsequential, timid things, in comparison with the audacious, barefaced and sweeping pretension to a system of law for the U S, without the adoption of their legislature, and so infinitely beyond their power to adopt.

Thomas Jefferson, Letter to Edmund Randolph, 18 Aug. 1799, in *Writings of Thomas Jefferson* 7:383–84 (Paul L. Ford ed. 1896)

3 I consider all the encroachments made on that [the Constitution] heretofore as nothing, as mere retail stuff compared with the wholesale doctrine, that there is a common law in force in the U.S. of which & of all the cases within its provisions their courts have cognizance.

Thomas Jefferson, Letter to Charles Pinckney, 29 Oct. 1799, in *Writings of Thomas Jefferson* 7:398 (Paul L. Ford ed. 1896)

4 The *common law* . . . pervades everything, and everything is interwoven with it. Its extent is unlimited, its bounds are unknown; it varies with the successions of ages, and takes its colour from the spirit of the times, the learning of the age, and the temper and disposition of the Judges. It has experienced great changes at different periods, and is destined to experience more. It is from its very nature uncertain and fluctuating; while to vulgar eyes it appears fixed and stationary.

Peter S. Du Ponceau, *A Dissertation on the Nature and Extent of the Jurisdiction of the Courts* viii (1824)

5 We live in the midst of the common law, we inhale it at every breath, imbibe it at every pore; we meet it when we wake and when we lay down to sleep, when we travel and when we stay at home; it is interwoven with the very idiom that we speak, and we cannot learn another system of laws without learning at the same time another language.

Peter S. Du Ponceau, *A Dissertation on the Nature and Extent of the Jurisdiction of the Courts* 91 (1824)

6 The common law is destined to acquire in this country the highest degree of perfection of which it is susceptible, and which will raise it in all respects above every other system of laws, ancient or modern. But it will not have fully reached that towering height, until the maxim shall be completely established in practice as well as in theory, THAT PURE ETHICS AND SOUND LOGIC ARE ALSO PARTS OF THE COMMON LAW.

Peter S. Du Ponceau, *A Dissertation on the Nature and Extent of the Jurisdiction of the Courts* 132 (1824)

7 The common law is gradually changing its old channels and wearing new.

Joseph Story, "Growth of the Commercial Law," 1825, in *Miscellaneous Writings of Joseph Story* 262, 278 (William W. Story ed. 1852)

8 Though the judiciary of the United States cannot take cognizance of offences at common law unless they have jurisdiction over the person or subject matter, given them by the constitution or laws made in pursuance of it; yet when the jurisdiction is once granted, the common law, under the correction of the constitution and statute law of the United States, would seem to be a necessary and a safe guide, in all cases, civil and criminal, arising under the exer-

cise of that jurisdiction, and not specially provided for by statute. Without such a guide, the courts would be left to a dangerous discretion, and to roam at large in the trackless field of their own imaginations.

James Kent, *Commentaries on American Law* 1:320–21 (1826)

9 The common law of England is not to be taken in all respects to be that of America. Our ancestors brought with them its general principles, and claimed it as their birthright; but they brought with them and adopted only that portion which was applicable to their situation.

Joseph Story, *Van Ness v. Pacard*, 27 U.S. (2 Pet.) 137, 144 (1829)

10 Older, nobler, clearer, and more glorious, then, is everlasting justice, than ambiguous, baseborn, purblind, perishable Common Law. That which is older than the creation may indeed be extolled for its venerable age; but among created things, the argument from antiquity is a false criterion of worth. Sin and death are older than the Common Law; are they, therefore, to be preferred to it? The mortal transgression of Cain was anterior to the Common Law: does it therefore furnish a better precedent? Judge-made law is *ex post facto* law, and therefore unjust.

Robert Rantoul, Jr., Oration, Scituate, Mass., 4 July 1836, in *The Legal Mind in America* 222, 223 (Perry Miller ed. 1962)

11 The Common Law is the perfection of human reason,—just as alcohol is the perfection of sugar. The subtle spirit of the Common Law is reason double distilled, till what was wholesome and nutritive becomes rank poison. Reason is sweet and pleasant to the unsophisticated intellect; but this sublimated perversion of reason bewilders, and perplexes, and plunges its victims into mazes of error.

Robert Rantoul, Jr., Oration, Scituate, Mass., 4 July 1836, in *The Legal Mind in America* 222, 224 (Perry Miller ed. 1962)

12 It is one of the great merits and advantages of the common law, that, instead of a series of detailed practical rules, established by positive provisions, and adapted to the precise circumstances of particular cases, which would become obsolete and fail, when the practice and course of business, to which they apply, should cease or change, the common law consists of a few broad and comprehensive principles, founded on reason, natural justice, and enlightened public policy, modified and adapted to the circumstances of all the particular cases which fall within it.

Lemuel Shaw, *Norway Plains Co. v. Boston & Maine R.R.*, 67 Mass. 263, 267 (1854)

13 This flexibility and capacity for growth and adaptation is the peculiar boast and excellence of the common law.

Stanley Matthews, *Hurtado v. California*, 110 U.S. 516, 530 (1884)

14 The Constitution of the United States was ordained, it is true, by descendants of Englishmen, who inherited the traditions of English law and history; but it was made for an undefined and expanding future, and for a people gathered and to be gathered from many nations and of many tongues. . . . There is nothing in Magna Charta, rightly construed as a broad charter of public right and law, which ought to exclude the best ideas of all systems and of every age; and as it was the characteristic principle of the common law to draw its inspiration from every fountain of justice, we are not to assume that the sources of its supply have been exhausted. On the contrary, we should expect that the new and various experiences of our own situation and system will mould and shape it into new and not less useful forms.

Stanley Matthews, *Hurtado v. California*, 110 U.S. 516, 530–31 (1884)

15 The common law is not a brooding omnipresence in the sky but the articulate voice of some sovereign or quasi-sovereign that can be identified.

Oliver Wendell Holmes, Jr., *Southern Pacific Co. v. Jensen*, 244 U.S. 205, 222 (1917) (dissenting)

16 Now, if you can have the law systematically, scientifically stated, the principles stated by competent men, giving their discussions of the theories upon which their statements are based, giving a presentation and discussion of all the judicial decisions

upon which their statements are based, and if such a statement can be revised and criticized and tested by a competent group of lawyers of eminence, and where their work is done if their conclusions can be submitted to the bar that we have here, if that can be done when the work is completed, we will have a statement of the common law of America which will be the *prima facie* basis on which judicial action will rest; and any lawyer, whose interest in litigation requires him to say that a different view of the law shall be taken, will have upon his shoulders the burden to overturn the statement.

> **Elihu Root,** "An Account of the Proceedings at the Organization of the Institute," in *Proceedings of the American Law Institute* 48, 51 (1923)

COMMUNICATIONS LAW

1 If any licensee shall permit any person who is a legally qualified candidate for any public office to use a broadcasting station, he shall afford equal opportunities to all other such candidates for that office in the use of such broadcasting station.

> Communications Act of 1934, ch. 652, § 315, 48 Stat. 1064, 1088

2 It is idle to posit an unabridgeable First Amendment right to broadcast comparable to the right of every individual to speak, write or publish.

> **Byron R. White,** *Red Lion Broadcasting Co. v. FCC,* 395 U.S. 367, 388 (1969)

3 The people as a whole retain their interest in free speech by radio and their collective right to have the medium function consistently with the ends and purposes of the First Amendment. It is the right of the viewers and listeners, not the right of the broadcasters, which is paramount. . . . It is the purpose of the First Amendment to preserve an uninhibited marketplace of ideas in which truth will ultimately prevail, rather than to countenance monopolization of that market, whether it be by the Government itself or a private licensee.

> **Byron R. White,** *Red Lion Broadcasting Co. v. FCC,* 395 U.S. 367, 390 (1969)

COMPETITION

See ANTITRUST

COMPUTERS AND THE LAW

1 In short, members of the Bar will be well advised to stay very far away from computers if they want to remain—or become—lawyers rather than simply attorneys at law. Computers are fine for inertial guidance problems—but the law is neither a missile nor an atomic submarine.

> **Frederick B. Wiener,** "Decision Prediction by Computers: Nonsense Cubed—and Worse," 48 *American Bar Association Journal* 1023, 1028 (1962)

2 The costs [of overreliance on computer-assisted legal research] in the short-run may be more limited lawyers, stale arguments, and dependence on prior creativity. . . . The long-run offers a worse picture as the law itself begins to reflect this smaller outlook and a rigid definition of "relevance." The impact on law may be a "freeze effect" since in a common-law system the law is molded by the profession and its materials. Reform and evolution will be slow in a system of law challenged only by on-point cases.

> **Steven A. Childress,** "Warning Label for Lexis: The Hazards of Computer-Assisted Research to the Legal Profession," 13 *Lincoln Law Review* 91, 98–99 (1982)

3 The computer has clearly made research much more powerful for the lawyer who knows how to use it. Any time you give a good lawyer additional lines of inquiry, different lines, different research channels, you are saying, You can be better. You can use these materials more effectively. You can massage them in a way that they've never been massaged before. . . . In a real sense, the lawyer and the tools become interactive.

> **Arthur R. Miller,** quoted in Fred R. Shapiro, *LEXIS: The Complete User's Guide* 8 (1989)

CONFESSIONS

See also CRIMINAL PROCEDURE; FIFTH AMENDMENT

1 There is no refuge from confession but suicide, and suicide is confession.

> **Daniel Webster,** Summation in murder trial of John Francis Knapp, 3 Aug. 1830, in *Writings and Speeches of Daniel Webster* 11:54 (J. W. McIntyre ed. 1903)

2 It may be that the whole of the evidence would be inadmissible according to the true meaning and spirit of the rule, if it appeared that criminal violence, such as whipping, was used in coercing the act or extorting the speech which led to the discovery. The fruits of physical torture as distinguished from those of mere fear, it would seem, ought to be unavailing. The honor and decency of the law would seem to be involved in rejecting them. The law ought to hold out no encouragement to violent and lawless men to commit crime for the sake of detecting a previous crime and bringing the offender to punishment. The law should never suffer itself to become an enemy or antagonist to its own reign. . . .

It must be remembered that confessions as such are equally inadmissible when they are the fruits of hope as when they are the product of fear.

Logan E. Bleckley, *Rusher v. State,* 94 Ga. 363, 366, 368, 21 S.E. 593 (1894)

3 Of course, after an accused has once let the cat out of the bag by confessing, no matter what the inducement, he is never thereafter free of the psychological and practical disadvantages of having confessed. He can never get the cat back in the bag. The secret is out for good. In such a sense, a later confession always may be looked upon as fruit of the first. But this Court has never gone so far as to hold that making a confession under circumstances which preclude its use, perpetually disables the confessor from making a usable one after those conditions have been removed.

Robert H. Jackson, *United States v. Bayer,* 331 U.S. 532, 540–41 (1947)

4 One serious situation seems to me to stand out in these [confession] cases. The suspect neither had nor was advised of his right to get counsel. This presents a real dilemma in a free society. To subject one without counsel to questioning which may and is intended to convict him, is a real peril to individual freedom. To bring in a lawyer means a real peril to solution of the crime, because, under our adversary system, he deems that his sole duty is to protect his client—guilty or innocent—and that in such a capacity he owes no duty whatever to help society solve its crime problem. Under this conception of criminal procedure, any lawyer worth his salt will tell the suspect in no uncertain terms to make no statement to police under any circumstances.

Robert H. Jackson, *Watts v. Indiana,* 338 U.S. 49, 59 (1949) (concurring)

5 Of course, no confession that has been obtained by any form of physical violence to the person is reliable and hence no conviction should rest upon one obtained in that manner. Such treatment not only breaks the will to conceal or lie, but may even break the will to stand by the truth. Nor is it questioned that the same result can sometimes be achieved by threats, promises, or inducements, which torture the mind but put no scar on the body.

Robert H. Jackson, *Watts v. Indiana,* 338 U.S. 49, 59–60 (1949) (concurring)

6 The abhorrence of society to the use of involuntary confessions does not turn alone on their inherent untrustworthiness. It also turns on the deep-rooted feeling that the police must obey the law while enforcing the law; that in the end life and liberty can be as much endangered from illegal methods used to convict those thought to be criminals as from the actual criminals themselves.

Earl Warren, *Spano v. New York,* 360 U.S. 315, 320–21 (1959)

7 It is only a sterile syllogism—an unsound one, besides—to say that because Massiah had a right to counsel's aid before and during the trial, his out-of-court conversations and admissions must be excluded if obtained without counsel's consent or presence. The right to counsel has never meant as much before. . . . Since the new rule would exclude all admissions made to the police, no matter how voluntary and reliable, the requirement of counsel's presence or approval would seem to rest upon the probability that counsel would foreclose any admissions at all.

Byron R. White, *Massiah v. United States,* 377 U.S. 201, 209 (1964) (dissenting)

8 Our holding will be spelled out with some specificity in the pages which follow but briefly stated it is this: the prosecution may not use statements, whether exculpatory or inculpatory, stemming from custodial interrogation of the defendant unless it demonstrates the use of procedural safeguards

effective to secure the privilege against self-incrimination. By custodial interrogation, we mean questioning initiated by law enforcement officers after a person has been taken into custody or otherwise deprived of his freedom of action in any significant way.

Earl Warren, *Miranda v. Arizona*, 384 U.S. 436, 444 (1966)

9 Prior to any questioning, the person must be warned that he has a right to remain silent, that any statement he does make may be used as evidence against him, and that he has a right to the presence of an attorney, either retained or appointed. The defendant may waive effectuation of these rights, provided the waiver is made voluntarily, knowingly, and intelligently. If, however, he indicates in any manner and at any stage of the process that he wishes to consult with an attorney before speaking there can be no questioning. Likewise, if the individual is alone and indicates in any manner that he does not wish to be interrogated, the police may not question him. The mere fact that he may have answered some questions or volunteered some statements on his own does not deprive him of the right to refrain from answering any further inquiries until he has consulted with an attorney and thereafter consents to be questioned.

Earl Warren, *Miranda v. Arizona*, 384 U.S. 436, 444–45 (1966)

10 While a warning that the indigent may have counsel appointed need not be given to the person who is known to have an attorney or is known to have ample funds to secure one, the expedient of giving a warning is too simple and the rights involved too important to engage in *ex post facto* inquiries into financial ability when there is any doubt at all on that score.

Earl Warren, *Miranda v. Arizona*, 384 U.S. 436, 473 n.43 (1966)

11 The principles announced today deal with the protection which must be given to the privilege against self-incrimination when the individual is first subjected to police interrogation while in custody at the station or otherwise deprived of his freedom of action in any significant way. It is at this point that our adversary system of criminal proceedings commences, distinguishing itself at the outset from the inquisitorial system recognized in some countries.

Earl Warren, *Miranda v. Arizona*, 384 U.S. 436, 477 (1966)

12 To summarize, we hold that when an individual is taken into custody or otherwise deprived of his freedom by the authorities in any significant way and is subjected to questioning, the privilege against self-incrimination is jeopardized. Procedural safeguards must be employed to protect the privilege, and unless other fully effective means are adopted to notify the person of his right of silence and to assure that the exercise of the right will be scrupulously honored, the following measures are required. He must be warned prior to any questioning that he has the right to remain silent, that anything he says can be used against him in a court of law, that he has the right to the presence of an attorney, and that if he cannot afford an attorney one will be appointed for him prior to any questioning if he so desires.

Earl Warren, *Miranda v. Arizona*, 384 U.S. 436, 478–79 (1966)

13 It is wrong, and subtly corrosive of our criminal justice system, to regard an honest confession as a "mistake." While every person is entitled to stand silent, it is more virtuous for the wrongdoer to admit his offense and accept the punishment he deserves. . . . A confession is rightly regarded by the sentencing guidelines as warranting a reduction of sentence, because it "demonstrates a recognition and affirmative acceptance of personal responsibility for . . . criminal conduct," U.S. Sentencing Commission, Guidelines Manual § 3E1.1 (1988), which is the beginning of reform. We should, then, rejoice at an honest confession, rather than pity the "poor fool" who has made it; and we should regret the attempted retraction of that good act, rather than seek to facilitate and encourage it.

Antonin Scalia, *Minnick v. Mississippi*, 111 S. Ct. 486, 498 (1990) (dissenting)

14 The Constitution requires that I inform you of your rights:

You have a right to remain silent. If you talk to any police officer, anything you say can and will be used against you in court.

You have a right to consult with a lawyer before you are questioned, and may have him with you during questioning.

If you cannot afford a lawyer, one will be appointed for you, if you wish, before any questioning.

If you wish to answer questions, you have the right to stop answering at any time.

You may stop answering questions at any time if you wish to talk to a lawyer, and may have him with you during any further questioning.

"Miranda Warning Card," quoted in Jay M. Shafritz, *HarperCollins Dictionary of American Government and Politics* 367 (1992)

CONFLICT OF LAWS

1 The laws of the several states, except where the constitution, treaties or statutes of the United States shall otherwise require or provide, shall be regarded as rules of decision in trials at common law in the courts of the United States in cases where they apply.

Judiciary Act of 1789, ch. 20, § 34, 1 Stat. 73, 92

2 The injustice, as well as the absurdity of [federal courts] deciding by one rule, and [state courts] by another, would be too monstrous to find a place in any system of government.

Bushrod Washington, *Golden v. Prince,* 10 F. Cas. 542, 543–44 (C.C.D. Pa. 1814) (No. 5,509)

3 The Gordian Knot of the Constitution seems to lie in the problem of collision between the federal & State powers, especially as eventually exercised by their respective Tribunals. If the knot cannot be untied by the text of the Constitution it ought not, certainly, to be cut by any Political Alexander. I have always thought that a construction of the instrument ought to be favoured, as far as the text would warrent, which would obviate the dilemma of a Judicial rencounter or a material paralysis; and that on the abstract question Whether the federal or the State decisions ought to prevail, the sounder policy would yield to the claims of the former.

James Madison, Letter to Spencer Roane, 29 June 1821, in *Writings of James Madison* 9:65–66 (Gaillard Hunt ed. 1910)

4 It would be strange, if in the now well understood rights of nations to organize their judicial tribunals according to their notions of policy, it should be conceded to them in every other respect than that of prescribing the time within which suits shall be litigated in their courts. Prescription is a thing of policy, growing out of the experience of its necessity.

James M. Wayne, *M'Elmoyle v. Cohen,* 38 U.S. (13 Pet.) 312, 327 (1839)

5 In the ordinary use of language it will hardly be contended that the decisions of Courts constitute laws. They are, at most, only evidence of what the laws are; and are not of themselves laws.

Joseph Story, *Swift v. Tyson,* 41 U.S. (16 Pet.) 1, 18 (1842)

6 A party by going into a National court does not lose any right or appropriate remedy of which he might have availed himself in the State courts of the same locality. The wise policy of the Constitution gives him a choice of tribunals.

Noah H. Swayne, *Davis v. Gray,* 83 U.S. (16 Wall.) 203, 221 (1873)

7 If a foreign statute gives the right, the mere fact that we do not give a like right is no reason for refusing to help the plaintiff in getting what belongs to him. We are not so provincial as to say that every solution of a problem is wrong because we deal with it otherwise at home.

Benjamin N. Cardozo, *Loucks v. Standard Oil Co.,* 224 N.Y. 99, 110–11, 120 N.E. 198 (1918)

8 The question for decision is whether the oft-challenged doctrine of *Swift v. Tyson* [41 U.S. (16 Pet.) 1 (1842)] shall now be disapproved.

Louis D. Brandeis, *Erie R.R. v. Tompkins,* 304 U.S. 64, 69 (1938)

9 Except in matters governed by the Federal Constitution or by Acts of Congress, the law to be applied in any case is the law of the State. And whether the law of the State shall be declared by its Legislature in a statute or by its highest court in a decision is not a matter of federal concern. There is no federal general common law.

Louis D. Brandeis, *Erie R.R. v. Tompkins,* 304 U.S. 64, 78 (1938)

10 Congress has no power to declare substantive rules of common law applicable in a State. . . . And no clause in the Constitution purports to confer such a power upon the federal courts. . . . in applying the doctrine [of *Swift v. Tyson*, 41 U.S. (16 Pet.) 1 (1842)] this Court and the lower courts have invaded rights which in our opinion are reserved by the Constitution to the several States.

> **Louis D. Brandeis**, *Erie R.R. v. Tompkins*, 304 U.S. 64, 78, 80 (1938)

11 People repeatedly subjected, like Pavlov's dogs, to two or more inconsistent sets of directions, without means of resolving the inconsistencies, could not fail in the end to react as the dogs did. The society, collectively, would suffer a nervous breakdown.

> **Henry M. Hart, Jr.**, "The Relations Between State and Federal Law," 54 *Columbia Law Review* 489, 489 (1954)

12 The general rule, bottomed deeply in belief in the importance of state control of state judicial procedure, is that federal law takes the state courts as it finds them.

> **Henry M. Hart, Jr.**, "The Relations Between State and Federal Law," 54 *Columbia Law Review* 489, 508 (1954)

13 Our principle task, in this diversity of citizenship case, is to determine what the New York courts would think the California courts would think on an issue about which neither has thought.

> **Henry J. Friendly**, *Nolan v. Transocean Air Lines*, 276 F.2d 280, 281 (2d Cir. 1960)

CONGRESS

See also LEGISLATION; LEGISLATIVE HISTORY; LEGISLATIVE INTENT; SEPARATION OF POWERS; STATUTES; STATUTORY CONSTRUCTION

1 I have much doubted whether, in case of a war, Congress would find it practicable to do their part of the business. That a body containing 100 lawyers in it, should direct the measures of a war, is, I fear, impossible; and that thus that member of our Constitution, which is its bulwark, will prove to be an impracticable one from it's [*sic*] cacoethes loquendi.

> **Thomas Jefferson**, Letter to James Madison, 19 Feb. 1812, in *Writings of Thomas Jefferson* 9:337 (Paul L. Ford ed. 1898)

2 If the present Congress errs in too much talking, how can it be otherwise in a body to which the people send 150. lawyers, whose trade it is to question everything, yield nothing, and talk by the hour? That 150. lawyers should do business together ought not to be expected.

> **Thomas Jefferson**, *Autobiography*, 1821, in *Writings of Thomas Jefferson* 1:82 (Paul L. Ford ed. 1892)

3 The United States Senate may not be the most refined and deliberative body in existence but they got the most unique rules. Any member can call anybody in the world anything he can think of and they can't answer him, sue him, or fight him. Our Constitution protects aliens, drunks and United States Senators. There ought to be one day a year (just one) when there is an open season on Senators.

> **Will Rogers**, "Mr. Rogers Takes Notice of the Senatorial Storm," 7 Mar. 1935, in *Will Rogers' Daily Telegrams* 4:284 (James M. Smallwood ed. 1979)

4 Read some of the Bills that they have passed, if you think they ain't Joke makers. I could study all my life and not think up half the amount of funny things they can think of in one Session of Congress. Besides my jokes don't do anybody any harm. You don't have to pay any attention to them. But everyone of the jokes those Birds make is a LAW and hurts somebody (generally everybody).

> **Will Rogers**, *The Autobiography of Will Rogers* 111 (Donald Day ed. 1949)

CONSPIRACY

1 A conspiracy must be a combination of two or more persons, by some concerted action, to accomplish some criminal or unlawful purpose, or to accomplish some purpose, not in itself criminal or unlawful, by criminal or unlawful means. We use the terms criminal or unlawful, because it is manifest that many acts are unlawful, which are not punishable by indictment or other public prosecution; and yet there is no doubt, we think, that a combination by numbers to do them would be an unlawful conspiracy, and punishable by indictment.

> **Lemuel Shaw**, *Commonwealth v. Hunt*, 45 Mass. (4 Met.) 111, 123 (1842)

2 When to the idea of an offence plurality of agents is logically necessary, conspiracy, which assumes the voluntary accession of a person to a crime of such a character that it is aggravated by a plurality of agents, cannot be maintained.

Francis Wharton, *A Treatise on the Criminal Law of the United States* 2:634 (7th ed. 1874)

3 A conspiracy is a partnership in criminal purposes.

Oliver Wendell Holmes, Jr., *United States v. Kissel,* 218 U.S. 601, 608 (1910)

4 A doctrine so vague in its outlines and uncertain in its fundamental nature as criminal conspiracy lends no strength or glory to the law; it is a veritable quicksand of shifting opinion and ill-considered thought.

Francis B. Sayre, "Criminal Conspiracy," 35 *Harvard Law Review* 393, 393 (1922)

5 While one may, for instance, be guilty of running past a traffic light of whose existence one is ignorant, one cannot be guilty of conspiring to run past such a light, for one cannot agree to run past a light unless one supposes that there is a light to run past.

Learned Hand, *United States v. Crimmins,* 123 F.2d 271, 273 (2d Cir. 1941)

6 The modern crime of conspiracy is so vague that it almost defies definition. Despite certain elementary and essential elements, it also, chameleon-like, takes on a special coloration from each of the many independent offenses on which it may be overlaid. It is always "predominantly mental in composition" because it consists primarily of a meeting of minds and an intent.

Robert H. Jackson, *Krulewitch v. United States,* 336 U.S. 440, 446–48 (1949) (concurring)

7 There is, of course, strong temptation to relax rigid standards when it seems the only way to sustain convictions of evildoers. But statutes authorize prosecution for substantive crimes for most evil-doing without the dangers to the liberty of the individual and the integrity of the judicial process that are inherent in conspiracy charges. We should disapprove the doc-

trine of implied or constructive crime in its entirety and in every manifestation.

Robert H. Jackson, *Krulewitch v. United States,* 336 U.S. 440, 457 (1949) (concurring)

8 The Constitution does not make conspiracy a civil right.

Robert H. Jackson, *Dennis v. United States,* 341 U.S. 494, 572 (1951) (concurring)

9 There is no constitutional right to "gang up" on the Government.

Robert H. Jackson, *Dennis v. United States,* 341 U.S. 494, 577 (1951) (concurring)

CONSTITUTION

See also CONSTITUTIONAL AMENDMENT; CONSTITUTIONAL CONVENTION; CONSTITUTIONAL LAW; ORIGINAL INTENTION

1 But had this writ been in any book whatever it would have been illegal. ALL PRECEDENTS ARE UNDER THE CONTROUL OF THE PRINCIPLES OF THE LAW. . . . No Acts of Parliament can establish such a writ; Though it should be made in the very words of the petition, it would be void, "AN ACT AGAINST THE CONSTITUTION IS VOID."

James Otis, Argument against the writs of assistance, Boston, Feb. 1761, quoted in John Adams, "Abstract of the Argument for and against the Writts of Assistance," 1761, in *Legal Papers of John Adams* 2:134, 144 (L. Kinvin Wroth & Hiller B. Zobel eds. 1965)

2 In all free States the Constitution is fixd; & as the supreme Legislative derives its Power & Authority from the Constitution, it cannot overleap the Bounds of it without destroying its own foundation: That the Constitution ascertains & limits both Sovereignty & allegiance, & therefore, his Majestys American Subjects who acknowledge themselves bound by the Ties of Allegiance, have an equitable Claim to the full enjoymt of the fundamental Rules of the British Constitution. That it is an essential unalterable Right in nature, ingrafted into the British Constitution, as a fundamental Law & ever held sacred & irrevocable by the Subjects within the Realm, that what a man has honestly acquird is absolutely his own, which he may freely give, but cannot be taken from him without his consent: That the American Subjects may therefore

exclusive of any Consideration of Charter Rights, with a decent firmness adapted to the Character of free men & Subjects assert this natural and constitutional Right.

> Massachusetts Circular Letter, 11 Feb. 1768, in *Writings of Samuel Adams* 1:184, 185 (Harry A. Cushing ed. 1904)

3 I wish most sincerely . . . that a Constitution [were] formed and settled for America, that we might know what we are and what we have, what our Rights and what our Duties, in the Judgment of this Country as well as in our own. Till such a Constitution is settled, different Sentiments, will ever occasion Misunderstandings.

> **Benjamin Franklin,** Letter to Joseph Galloway, 18 Feb. 1774, in *Papers of Benjamin Franklin* 21:110–11 (William B. Willcox ed. 1978)

4 I trust the friends of the proposed constitution will never concur with its enemies in questioning that fundamental principle of republican government, which admits the right of the people to alter or abolish the established constitution whenever they find it inconsistent with their happiness.

> **Alexander Hamilton,** *The Federalist* No. 78, at 2:296 (1788)

5 Constitutions should consist only of general provisions: The reason is, that they must necessarily be permanent, and that they cannot calculate for the possible changes of things.

> **Alexander Hamilton,** Speech at New York Ratifying Convention, 28 June 1788, in *Papers of Alexander Hamilton* 1:118 (Harold C. Syrett ed. 1961)

6 It [the Constitution] is a good canvas, on which some strokes only want retouching.

> **Thomas Jefferson,** Letter to James Madison, 31 July 1788, in *Papers of Thomas Jefferson* 13:442 (Julian P. Boyd ed. 1956)

7 The danger of disturbing the public tranquillity by interesting too strongly the public passions, is a still more serious objection against a frequent reference of constitutional questions, to the decision of the whole society.

> **James Madison,** *The Federalist* No. 49, at 2:109 (1788)

8 No society can make a perpetual constitution, or even a perpetual law. The earth be-

longs always to the living generation. They may manage it then, and what proceeds from it, as they please, during their usufruct. They are masters too of their own persons, and consequently may govern them as they please. But persons and property make the sum of the objects of government. The constitution and the laws of their predecessors extinguished then in their natural course with those who gave them being. This could preserve that being till it ceased to be itself, and no longer. Every constitution, then, and every law, naturally expires at the end of 19 years.

> **Thomas Jefferson,** Letter to James Madison, 6 Sept. 1789, in *Papers of Thomas Jefferson* 15:395–96 (Julian P. Boyd ed. 1958)

9 The American Constitutions were to liberty, what a grammar is to language: they define its parts of speech, and practically construct them into syntax.

> **Thomas Paine,** *The Rights of Man,* 1791, in *Complete Writings of Thomas Paine* 1:243, 300 (Philip S. Foner ed. 1969)

10 The basis of our political systems is the right of the people to make and to alter their Constitutions of Government. But the Constitution which at any time exists, 'till changed by an explicit and authentic act of the whole People, is sacredly obligatory upon all. The very idea of the power and the right of the People to establish Government presupposes the duty of every Individual to obey the established Government.

> **George Washington,** Farewell Address, 19 Sept. 1796, in *Writings of George Washington* 35:214, 224 (John C. Fitzpatrick ed. 1940)

11 It would be a dangerous delusion were a confidence in the men of our choice to silence our fears for the safety of our rights; that confidence is every where the parent of despotism; free government is founded in jealousy, and not in confidence; it is jealousy, and not confidence, which prescribes limited constitutions to bind down those whom we are obliged to trust with power; that our Constitution has accordingly fixed the limits to which, and no farther, our confidence may go.

> Kentucky Resolutions of 1798, Resolution 9, in *Debates in the Several State Conventions* 4:540, 543 (Jonathan Elliot ed., 2d ed. 1888)

12 In questions of power, then, let no more be said of confidence in man, but bind him

down from mischief by the chains of the Constitution.

Kentucky Resolutions of 1798, Resolution 9, in *Debates in the Several State Conventions* 4:540, 543 (Jonathan Elliot ed., 2d ed. 1888)

13 It is still certain that tho' written constitutions may be violated in moments of passion or delusion, yet they furnish a text to which those who are watchful may again rally and recall the people; they fix too for the people the principles of their political creed.

Thomas Jefferson, Letter to Joseph Priestley, 19 June 1802, in *Writings of Thomas Jefferson* 8:159–60 (Paul L. Ford ed. 1897)

14 The powers of the legislature are defined, and limited; and that those limits may not be mistaken, or forgotten, the constitution is written. To what purpose are powers limited, and to what purpose is that limitation committed to writing, if these limits may, at any time, be passed by those intended to be restrained? The distinction, between a government with limited and unlimited powers, is abolished, if those limits do not confine the persons on whom they are imposed, and if acts prohibited and acts allowed, are of equal obligation.

John Marshall, *Marbury v. Madison*, 5 U.S. (1 Cranch) 137, 176–77 (1803)

15 Some men look at constitutions with sanctimonious reverence, and deem them like the ark of the covenant, too sacred to be touched. They ascribe to the men of the preceding age a wisdom more than human, and suppose what they did to be beyond amendment. . . . I am certainly not an advocate for frequent and untried changes in laws and constitutions. . . . But I know also, that laws and institutions must go hand in hand with the progress of the human mind. . . . We might as well require a man to wear still the coat which fitted him when a boy, as civilized society to remain ever under the regimen of their barbarous ancestors.

Thomas Jefferson, Letter to Samuel Kercheval, 12 July 1816, in *Writings of Thomas Jefferson* 10:42–43 (Paul L. Ford ed. 1899)

16 Let us [Virginia] provide in our constitution for its revision at stated periods. . . . of

the adults living at any one moment of time, a majority will be dead in about nineteen years. At the end of that period, then, a new majority is coming into place; or in other words, a new generation. Each generation . . . [has] a right to choose for itself the form of government it believes most promotive of its own happiness . . . a solemn opportunity of doing this every nineteen or twenty years, should be provided by the constitution; so that it may be handed on, with periodical repairs, from generation to generation, to the end of time, if anything human can so long endure.

Thomas Jefferson, Letter to Samuel Kercheval, 12 July 1816, in *Writings of Thomas Jefferson* 10:43 (Paul L. Ford ed. 1899)

17 A constitution, to contain an accurate detail of all the subdivisions of which its great powers will admit, and of all the means by which they may be carried into execution, would partake of the prolixity of a legal code, and could scarcely be embraced by the human mind. It would probably never be understood by the public. Its nature, therefore, requires, that only its great outlines should be marked, its important objects designated, and the minor ingredients which compose those objects be deduced from the nature of the objects themselves. That this idea was entertained by the framers of the American constitution, is not only to be inferred from the nature of the instrument, but from the language.

John Marshall, *McCulloch v. Maryland*, 17 U.S. (4 Wheat.) 316, 407 (1819)

18 We must never forget, that it is *a constitution* we are expounding.

John Marshall, *McCulloch v. Maryland*, 17 U.S. (4 Wheat.) 316, 407 (1819)

19 This provision is made in a constitution intended to endure for ages to come, and, consequently, to be adapted to the various *crises* of human affairs.

John Marshall, *McCulloch v. Maryland*, 17 U.S. (4 Wheat.) 316, 415 (1819)

20 I believe . . . that constitutions are the work of time and not the invention of ingenuity; and that to frame a complete system of government, depending on the habits of reverence and experience, was an attempt as

absurd as to build a tree or manufacture an opinion.

> **Martin Van Buren**, Remarks at New York State Constitutional Convention, 25 Sept. 1820, quoted in Denis T. Lynch, *An Epoch and a Man* 226 (1929)

21 But a constitution is framed for ages to come, and is designed to approach immortality as nearly as human institutions can approach it.

> **John Marshall**, *Cohens v. Virginia,* 19 U.S. (6 Wheat.) 264, 387 (1821)

22 The people made the constitution, and the people can unmake it. It is the creature of their will, and lives only by their will. But this supreme and irresistible power to make or unmake, resides only in the whole body of the people; not in any sub-division of them.

> **John Marshall**, *Cohens v. Virginia,* 19 U.S. (6 Wheat.) 264, 389 (1821)

23 I yield slowly and reluctantly to the conviction that our constitution cannot last.... The union has been prolonged thus far by miracles. I fear they cannot continue.

> **John Marshall**, Letter to Joseph Story, 22 Sept. 1832, in Albert J. Beveridge, *Life of John Marshall* 4:559 (1919)

24 Constitutions are not designed for metaphysical or logical subtleties, for niceties of expression, for critical propriety, for elaborate shades of meaning, or for the exercise of philosophical acuteness, or judicial research.... The people make them; the people adopt them; the people must be supposed to read them, with the help of common sense; and cannot be presumed to admit in them any recondite meaning, or any extraordinary gloss.

> **Joseph Story**, *Commentaries on the Constitution of the United States* 1:436 (1833)

25 In examining the Constitution of the United States, which is the most perfect federal constitution that ever existed, one is startled at the variety of information and the amount of discernment which it presupposes in the people whom it is meant to govern. The government of the Union depends almost entirely upon legal fictions; the Union is an ideal nation, which exists, so to speak, only in the mind, and whose limits and extent can only be discerned by the understanding.

> **Alexis de Tocqueville**, *Democracy in America* 1:210–11 (Francis Bowen trans. 1862) (1835)

26 Gentlemen, the citizens of this republic cannot sever their fortunes.... Let us then stand by the Constitution as it is, and by our country as it is, one, united, and entire: let it be a truth engraven on our hearts, let it be borne on the flag under which we rally, in every exigency, that we have ONE COUNTRY, ONE CONSTITUTION, ONE DESTINY.

> **Daniel Webster**, Speech at Niblo's Saloon, New York, 15 Mar. 1837, in *Papers of Daniel Webster: Speeches and Formal Writings* 2:118, 124 (Charles M. Wiltse ed. 1988)

27 We may be tossed upon an ocean where we can see no land—nor, perhaps, the sun or stars. But there is a chart and a compass for us to study, to consult, and to obey. That chart is the Constitution.

> **Daniel Webster**, Speech, Springfield, Mass., 29 Sept. 1847, in *Writings and Speeches of Daniel Webster* 13:365 (J. W. McIntyre ed. 1903)

28 I think that the Constitution of the thirteen States was made, not merely for the generation which then existed, but for posterity, undefined, unlimited, permanent and perpetual—for their posterity, and for every subsequent State which might come into the Union, binding themselves by that indissoluble bond.

> **Henry Clay**, Speech on the Compromise Resolutions, 6 Feb. 1850, in *Life and Speeches of Henry Clay* 2:663 (1860)

29 Much babble will always be heard in the land about the Federal Constitution, this, that, and the other concerning it. The Federal Constitution is a perfect and entire thing, an edifice put together not for the accommodation of a few persons, but for the whole human race; not for a day or a year, but for many years, perhaps a thousand, perhaps many thousands. Its architecture is not a single brick, a beam, an apartment, but only the whole. It is the grandest piece of moral building ever constructed; I believe its architects were some mighty prophets and gods. Few appreciate it, Americans just as few as any. Like all perfect works or persons, time only is great enough to give it area. Five or six centuries

hence, it will be better understood from results, growths.

Walt Whitman, "The Federal Constitution," 1856, in *Walt Whitman: Complete Poetry and Collected Prose* 1307, 1318 (Justin Kaplan ed. 1982)

30 Your constitution is all sail and no anchor. As I said before, when a society has entered on this downward progress, either civilization or liberty must perish. Either some Caesar or Napoleon will seize the reins of government with a strong hand; or your republic will be as fearfully plundered and laid waste by barbarians in the twentieth Century as the Roman Empire was in the fifth;—with this difference, that the Huns and Vandals who ravaged the Roman Empire came from without, and that your Huns and Vandals will have been engendered within your own country by your own institutions.

Thomas B. Macaulay, Letter to Henry S. Randall, 23 May 1857, in *Letters of Thomas Babington Macaulay* 6:96 (Thomas Pinney ed. 1981)

31 The public could not rest on its faith in the "fidelity of the legislature". . . . Limitations of power, established by written constitutions, have their origin in a distrust of the infirmity of man. That distrust is fully justified by the history of the rise and fall of nations.

Ellis Lewis, *Mott v. Pennsylvania R.R.,* 30 Pa. 9, 28 (1858)

32 I hold, that in contemplation of universal law, and of the Constitution, the Union of these states is perpetual. Perpetuity is implied, if not expressed, in the fundamental law of all national governments. It is safe to assert that no government proper, ever had a provision in its organic law for its own termination. Continue to execute all the express provisions of our national Constitution, and the Union will endure forever—it being impossible to destroy it, except by some action not provided for in the instrument itself.

Abraham Lincoln, First Inaugural Address, 4 Mar. 1861, in *Collected Works of Abraham Lincoln* 4:264–65 (Roy P. Basler ed. 1953)

33 All that is valuable in the United States Constitution is a thousand years old. What is good is not new and what is new is not good.

Wendell Phillips, Speech, Boston, 17 Feb. 1861, in *Speeches, Lectures, and Letters* 371, 377 (1863)

34 These rebels are violating the Constitution to destroy the Union; I will violate the Constitution, if necessary, to save the Union: and I suspect, Chase, that our Constitution is going to have a rough time of it before we get done with this row.

Abraham Lincoln, Conversation with Salmon P. Chase, 1863, quoted in Emanuel Hertz, *Abraham Lincoln: A New Portrait* 2:897 (1931)

35 Was it possible to lose the nation, and yet preserve the constitution? By general law life *and* limb must be protected; yet often a limb must be amputated to save a life; but a life is never wisely given to save a limb. I felt that measures, otherwise unconstitutional, might become lawful, by becoming indispensable to the preservation of the constitution, through the preservation of the nation.

Abraham Lincoln, Letter to Albert G. Hodges, 4 Apr. 1864, in *Collected Works of Abraham Lincoln* 7:281 (Roy P. Basler ed. 1953)

36 The Constitution of the United States is a law for rulers and people, equally in war and in peace, and covers with the shield of its protection all classes of men, at all times, and under all circumstances. No doctrine, involving more pernicious consequences, was ever invented by the wit of man than that any of its provisions can be suspended during any of the great exigencies of government.

David Davis, *Ex parte Milligan,* 71 U.S. (4 Wall.) 2, 120–21 (1867)

37 What cannot be done directly cannot be done indirectly. The Constitution deals with substance, not shadows.

Stephen J. Field, *Cummings v. Missouri,* 71 U.S. (4 Wall.) 277, 325 (1867)

38 The Constitution, in all its provisions, looks to an indestructible Union, composed of indestructible States.

Salmon P. Chase, *Texas v. White,* 74 U.S. (7 Wall.) 700, 725 (1869)

39 But, as the British Constitution is the most subtile organism which has proceeded from the womb and the long gestation of progressive history, so the American Constitution is, so far as I can see, the most wonderful work ever struck off at a given time by the brain and purpose of man.

> **William E. Gladstone,** "Kin Beyond Sea," 127 *North American Review* 179, 185 (1878)

40 The American Constitution is no exception to the rule that everything which has power to win the obedience and respect of men must have its roots deep in the past, and that the more slowly every institution has grown, so much the more enduring is it likely to prove. There is little in this Constitution that is absolutely new. There is much that is as old as Magna Charta.

> **James Bryce,** *The American Commonwealth* 1:25–26 (1888)

41 The Constitution follows the flag.

> Slogan used by Republican Party in 1900 after the conquest of the Philippines by the United States

42 An amusing story is told of a legislator who, endeavoring to persuade a friend and colleague to aid him in the passage of a certain measure in which he was personally interested, met the remark that his bill was unconstitutional with the exclamation, "What does the Constitution amount to between friends?"*

> **Grover Cleveland,** *Presidential Problems* 28–29 (1904)

43 Constitutions are intended to preserve practical and substantial rights, not to maintain theories.

> **Oliver Wendell Holmes, Jr.,** *Davis v. Mills,* 194 U.S. 451, 457 (1904)

44 What is a constitution for—does it exist to grant power or to organize it? The former of these views is undoubtedly the older one, not only of the national Constitution, but of the state constitutions as well. For the written constitution, wherever found, was at first regarded as a species of social compact, entered into by sovereign individuals in a state of nature. From this point of view . . . governmental authority, wherever centered, is a trust which, save for the grant of it effected by the written constitution, were non-existent, and private rights, since they precede the constitution, gain nothing of authoritativeness from being enumerated in it, though possibly something of security. These rights are not, in other words, fundamental because they find mention in the written instrument; they find mention there because they are fundamental.

> **Edward S. Corwin,** "The Basic Doctrine of American Constitutional Law," 12 *Michigan Law Review* 247, 247–48 (1914)

45 The United States Constitution has proved itself the most marvelously elastic compilation of rules of government ever written.

> **Franklin D. Roosevelt,** Radio Address on States' Rights, 2 Mar. 1930, in *Public Papers and Addresses of Franklin D. Roosevelt* 1:569, 570 (Samuel I. Rosenman ed. 1938)

46 Our Constitution is so simple and practical that it is possible always to meet extraordinary needs by changes in emphasis and arrangement without loss of essential form. That is why our constitutional system has proved itself the most superbly enduring political mechanism the modern world has produced. It has met every stress of vast expansion of territory, of foreign wars, of bitter internal strife, of world relations.

> **Franklin D. Roosevelt,** Inaugural Address, 4 Mar. 1933, in *Public Papers and Addresses of Franklin D. Roosevelt* 2:14–15 (Samuel I. Rosenman ed. 1938)

47 It well may be that guarantees which must be written are less secure than those so embedded in the hearts of men that they need not be written.

> **William O. Douglas,** *We the Judges* 259 (1956)

48 I hold the view that the Constitution is the most revolutionary document . . . ever written, and it should to the new countries serve as a source of stimulation and enterprise.

> **John F. Kennedy,** Campaign speech, Greensboro, N.C., 17 Sept. 1960, quoted in Maxwell Meyersohn, *Memorable Quotations of John F. Kennedy* 133 (1965)

---

* This is usually quoted as "What's the Constitution between friends?" and often attributed to Timothy J. Campbell.

49 It is, after all, a national Constitution we are expounding.

> **William J. Brennan, Jr.,** *Jacobellis v. Ohio,* 378 U.S. 184, 195 (1964)

50 It is of paramount importance to me that our country has a written constitution. This great document is the unique American contribution to man's continuing search for a society in which individual liberty is secure against governmental oppression.

> **Hugo L. Black,** *A Constitutional Faith* 3 (1968)

51 My fellow Americans, our long national nightmare is over. Our Constitution works; our great Republic is a government of laws and not of men. Here the people rule.

> **Gerald R. Ford,** Remarks upon taking oath of office, 9 Aug. 1974, in *Public Papers of the Presidents: Gerald R. Ford, 1974,* at 1, 2 (1975)
> See also OBEDIENCE TO LAW 2

52 We will see that the true miracle was not the birth of the Constitution, but its life, a life nurtured through two turbulent centuries of our own making, and a life embodying much good fortune that was not. Thus, in this bicentennial year, we may not all participate in the festivities with flag-waving fervor. Some may more quietly commemorate the suffering, struggle and sacrifice that has triumphed over much of what was wrong with the original document, and observe the anniversary with hopes not realized and promises not fulfilled.

> **Thurgood Marshall,** Speech, Maui, Hawaii, 6 May 1987, quoted in *New York Times,* 7 May 1987, at B18

CONSTITUTIONAL AMENDMENT

See also BILL OF RIGHTS; CONSTITUTION

1 We, the people, possessing all power, form a government, such as we think will secure happiness: and suppose, in adopting this plan, we should be mistaken in the end; where is the cause of alarm on that quarter? In the same plan we point out an easy and quiet method of reforming what may be found amiss. No, but, say gentlemen, we have put the introduction of that method in the hands of our servants, who will interrupt it from motives of self-interest. What then? . . . Who shall dare to resist the people? No, we will assemble in Convention; wholly recall our delegated powers, or reform them so as to prevent such abuse; and punish those servants who have perverted powers, designed for our happiness, to their own emolument.

> **Edmund Pendleton,** Remarks before the Virginia Convention on the Adoption of the Federal Constitution, 5 June 1788, in *Debates on the Adoption of the Federal Constitution* 3:37 (Jonathan Elliot ed., 2d ed. 1888)

2 Towards the preservation of your Government and the permanency of your present happy state, it is requisite, not only that you steadily discountenance irregular oppositions to its acknowledged authority, but also that you resist with care the spirit of innovation upon its principles however specious the pretexts. One method of assault may be to effect, in the forms of the Constitution, alterations which will impair the energy of the system, and thus to undermine what cannot be directly overthrown.

> **George Washington,** Farewell Address, 19 Sept. 1796, in *Writings of George Washington* 35:225 (John C. Fitzpatrick ed. 1940)

3 I wish now to submit a few remarks on the general proposition of amending the constitution. As a general rule, I think, we would [do] much better [to] let it alone. No slight occasion should tempt us to touch it. Better not take the first step, which may lead to a habit of altering it. Better, rather, habituate ourselves to think of it, as unalterable. It can scarcely be made better than it is. New provisions, would introduce new difficulties, and thus create, an increased appetite for still further change. No sir, let it stand as it is. New hands have never touched it. The men who made it, have done their work, and have passed away. Who shall improve, on what *they* did?

> **Abraham Lincoln,** Speech in United States House of Representatives on Internal Improvements, 20 June 1848, in *Collected Works of Abraham Lincoln* 1:488 (Roy P. Basler ed. 1953)

4 To me, the convention mode [of amending the Constitution] seems preferable, in that it allows amendments to originate with the people themselves, instead of only permit-

ting them to take, or reject, propositions, originated by others, not especially chosen for the purpose, and which might not be precisely such, as they would wish to either accept or refuse.

> Abraham Lincoln, First Inaugural Address, 4 Mar. 1861, in *Collected Works of Abraham Lincoln* 4:270 (Roy P. Basler ed. 1953)

5 Amendments to the Constitution ought to not be too frequently made; . . . [if] continually tinkered with it would lose all its prestige and dignity, and the old instrument would be lost sight of altogether in a short time.

> Andrew Johnson, Speech, Washington, D.C., 22 Feb. 1866, quoted in *Respectfully Quoted* 67 (Suzy Platt ed. 1989)

6 The present process of constitutional amendment is too long, too cumbrous, and too uncertain to afford an adequate remedy, and, moreover, after the amendment has been carried, the law must once more be submitted to the same court which was, perhaps, originally at fault, in order to decide whether the new law comes within the amendment.

> Theodore Roosevelt, "The Progressive Party," 1913, in *Works of Theodore Roosevelt* 19:551 (1925)

7 One generalization, at least, may be made about constitutional amendments: that they never work. But perhaps the word never is a shade too strong. It may be that the first half of the Third has worked. . . . All the other amendments seem to be complete failures. The Seventeenth was to purge the United States Senate of undesirables. . . . The Nineteenth was to introduce female virtue into politics: it has been followed by the worst series of scandals in American history. The Fifteenth was to give the Aframerican the franchise in the late Confederate States: he still pines for it. The Thirteenth was to abolish slavery: it still exists in every mill-town, with white slaves substituted for black. The Seventh was to safeguard the right to trial by jury: the Volstead Act has blown it full of holes. The Fourth was to put down lawless raids and seizures by the police: they go on every day. And so with all the rest.

> H. L. Mencken, "Note Upon a Fatal Curse," *American Mercury,* Feb. 1930, at 152, 154

8 Rejecting the old concept of government as a kind of primal entity, ordained of God and beyond human control, they [the Framers] tried to make it a mere creature of the people. So far it could go, but no further. Within its proper provinces it had all the prerogatives that were necessary to its existence, but beyond that province it had none at all. It could do what it was specifically authorized to do, but nothing else. The Constitution was simply a record specifying its bounds. The Fathers, taught by their own long debates, knew that efforts would be made, from time to time, to change the Constitution as they had framed it, so they made the process as difficult as possible, and hoped that they had prevented frequent resort to it. Unhappily, they did not foresee the possibility of making changes, not by formal act, but by mere political intimidation—not by recasting its terms, but by distorting its meaning.

> H. L. Mencken, "The Suicide of Democracy," Baltimore *Sun,* 12 May 1940, quoted in *The Gist of Mencken* 349–50 (Mayo DuBasky ed. 1990)

9 Recalling that it is a Constitution "intended to endure for ages to come" we also remember that the Founders wisely provided the means for that endurance: changes in the Constitution, when thought necessary, are to be proposed by Congress or conventions and ratified by the States. The Founders gave no such amending power to this Court.

> Hugo L. Black, *Bell v. Maryland,* 378 U.S. 226, 342 (1964) (dissenting)

CONSTITUTIONAL CONVENTION

See also CONSTITUTION; ORIGINAL INTENTION

1 Your Commissioners, with the most respectful deference, beg leave to suggest their unanimous conviction, that it may essentially tend to advance the interests of the union, if the States, by whom they have been respectively delegated, would themselves concur, and use their endeavors to procure the concurrence of the other States, in the appointment of Commissioners, to meet at Philadelphia on the second Monday in May next, to take into consideration the situation of the United States, to devise such further provisions as shall

appear to them necessary to render the constitution of the Federal Government adequate to the exigencies of the Union; and to report such an Act for that purpose to the United States in Congress assembled, as when agreed to, by them, and afterwards confirmed by the Legislatures of every State, will effectually provide for the same.

Proceedings of Commissioners to Remedy Defects of the Federal Government (Annapolis Convention), 14 Sept. 1786, in *Documents Illustrative of the Formation of the Union of the American States* 39, 42–43 (1927)

2 Whereas there is provision in the Articles of Confederation and perpetual Union for making alterations therein by the Assent of a Congress of the United States and of the legislatures of the several States; And whereas experience hath evinced that there are defects in the present Confederation, as a mean to remedy which several of the states and particularly the state of New York by express instructions to their delegates in Congress have suggested a Convention for the purposes expressed in the following resolution and such Convention appearing to be the most probable mean of establishing in these states a firm national government.

Resolved that in the opinion of Congress it is expedient that on the second Monday in May next a Convention of delegates who shall have been appointed by the several States be held at Philadelphia for the sole and express purpose of revising the Articles of Confederation and reporting to Congress and the several legislatures such alterations and provisions therein as shall when agreed to in Congress and confirmed by the States render the federal Constitution adequate to the exigencies of Government and the preservation of the Union.

Resolution, 21 Feb. 1787, in *Journals of the Continental Congress* 32:73–74 (Roscoe R. Hill ed. 1936)

3 The Father of the Constitution.

Epithet of James Madison

4 In all our deliberations on this subject we kept steadily in our view, that which appears to us the greatest interest of every true American, the consolidation of our Union, in which is involved our prosperity, felicity, safety, perhaps our national exis-

tence. This important consideration, seriously and deeply impressed on our minds, led each state in the Convention to be less rigid on points of inferior magnitude, than might have been otherwise expected; and thus the Constitution, which we now present, is the result of a spirit of amity, and of that mutual deference and concession which the peculiarity of our political situation rendered indispensable.

Letter of the President of the Federal Convention [George Washington] Transmitting the Constitution, 17 Sept. 1787, in *Documents Illustrative of the Formation of the Union of the American States* 1003, 1003-04 (1927)

5 Congress having received the report of the Convention lately assembled in Philadelphia

Resolved Unanimously that the said Report with the resolutions and letter accompanying the same be transmitted to the several legislatures in Order to be submitted to a convention of Delegates chosen in each state by the people thereof in conformity to the resolves of the Convention made and provided in that case.

Resolution of Congress Submitting the Constitution to the States, 28 Sept. 1787, in *Documents Illustrative of the Formation of the Union of the American States* 1007, 1007 (1927)

6 I confess, that I do not entirely approve of this Constitution at present; but, Sir, I am not sure I shall never approve it; for, having lived long, I have experienced many instances of being obliged, by better information or fuller consideration, to change my opinions even on important subjects, which I once thought right, but found to be otherwise.

Benjamin Franklin, Speech at Constitutional Convention, Philadelphia, 17 Sept. 1787, in *Writings of Benjamin Franklin* 9:607, 607 (Albert H. Smyth ed. 1906)

7 In these sentiments, Sir, I agree to this Constitution, with all its faults,—if they are such; because I think a general Government necessary for us, and there is no *form* of Government but what may be a blessing to the people, if well administered; and I believe further that this is likely to be well administered for a course of years, and can only end in despotism, as other forms have

done before it, when the People shall become so corrupted as to need despotic government, being incapable of any other.

> Benjamin Franklin, Speech at Constitutional Convention, Philadelphia, 17 Sept. 1787, in *Writings of Benjamin Franklin* 9:607, 607-08 (Albert H. Smyth ed. 1906)

8 I doubt, too, whether any other Convention we can obtain, may be able to make a better constitution; for, when you assemble a number of men, to have the advantage of their joint wisdom, you inevitably assemble with those men all their prejudices, their passions, their errors of opinion, their local interests, and their selfish views. From such an assembly can a *perfect* production be expected? It therefore astonishes me, Sir, to find this system approaching so near to perfection as it does.

> Benjamin Franklin, Speech at Constitutional Convention, Philadelphia, 17 Sept. 1787, in *Writings of Benjamin Franklin* 9:607, 608 (Albert H. Smyth ed. 1906)

9 On the whole, Sir, I cannot help expressing a wish, that every member of the Convention who may still have objections to it, would with me on this occasion doubt a little of his own infallibility, and, to make *manifest* our *unanimity*, put his name to this Instrument.

> Benjamin Franklin, Speech at Constitutional Convention, Philadelphia, 17 Sept. 1787, in *Writings of Benjamin Franklin* 9:607, 609 (Albert H. Smyth ed. 1906)

10 Painters had found it difficult to distinguish in their art a rising from a setting sun. I have often and often in the course of the Session [of the Constitutional Convention], and the vicissitudes of my hopes and fears as to its issue, looked at that [sun painted] behind the [chair of the] President without being able to tell whether it was rising or setting: but now at length I have the happiness to know that it is a rising and not a setting Sun.

> Benjamin Franklin, Remarks upon the signing of the Constitution, Philadelphia, 17 Sept. 1787, quoted in *Records of the Federal Convention of 1787*, at 2:648 (Max Farrand ed. 1966)

11 It [the Constitutional Convention at Philadelphia] is really an assembly of demigods.

> Thomas Jefferson, Letter to John Adams, 30 Aug. 1787, in *Writings of Thomas Jefferson* 2:260 (H. A. Washington ed. 1853)

12 It is too probable that no plan we propose will be adopted. Perhaps another dreadful conflict is to be sustained. If to please the people, we offer what we ourselves disapprove, how can we afterwards defend our work? Let us raise a standard to which the wise and the honest can repair. The event is in the hand of God.

> George Washington, Speech at the Constitutional Convention, Philadelphia, 1787, in Max Farrand, *The Framing of the Constitution of the United States* 66 (1913)

13 Should the States reject this excellent Constitution, the probability is that an opportunity will never again offer to cancel another in peace—the next will be drawn in blood.*

> George Washington, Attributed speech, quoted in *Pennsylvania Journal and Weekly Advertiser*, 14 Nov. 1787, at 3

14 After the lapse of six thousand years since the Creation of the world, America now presents the first instance of a people assembled to weigh deliberately and calmly, and to decide leisurely and peaceably, upon the form of government by which they will bind themselves and their posterity.

> James Wilson, Speech on Proposed Federal Constitution, 24 Nov. 1787, in *Documentary History of the Ratification of the Constitution* 2:340, 342 (Merrill Jensen ed. 1976)

15 After an unequivocal experience in the inefficacy of the subsisting federal government, you are called upon to deliberate on a new constitution for the United States of America. The subject speaks its own importance; comprehending in its consequences, nothing less than ... the fate of an empire, in many respects, the most interesting in the world. It has been frequently remarked, that it seems to have been reserved to the people of this country, by their conduct and example, to decide the important question, whether societies of men are really capable or not, of establishing good government from reflection and choice, or whether they are forever destined to depend, for their political constitutions, on accident and force. . . . a wrong

---

* The authenticity of this quotation is questioned by Charles Warren, *The Making of the Constitution* 717 (1928).

election of the part we shall act, may, in this view, deserve to be considered as the general misfortune of mankind.

Alexander Hamilton, *The Federalist* No. 1, at 1:1–2 (1788)

16 You will permit me to say, that a greater Drama is now acting on this Theatre than has heretofore been brought on the American Stage, or any other in the World. We exhibit at present the Novel and astonishing Spectacle of a whole People deliberating calmly on what form of government will be most conducive to their happiness; and deciding with an unexpected degree of unanimity in favour of a System which they conceive calculated to answer the purpose.

George Washington, Letter to Edward Newenham, 29 Aug. 1788, in *Writings of George Washington* 30:73 (John C. Fitzpatrick ed. 1939)

17 The American Constitution, one of the few modern political documents drawn up by men who were forced by the sternest circumstances to think out what they really had to face instead of chopping logic in a university classroom.

George Bernard Shaw, Preface to *Getting Married,* 1908, in *Works of George Bernard Shaw* 12:181, 237 (1930)

18 The movement for the Constitution of the United States was originated and carried through principally by four groups of personalty interests which had been adversely affected under the Articles of Confederation: money, public securities, manufactures, and trade and shipping.

Charles A. Beard, *An Economic Interpretation of the Constitution of the United States* 324 (1913)

CONSTITUTIONAL LAW

See also CONSTITUTION; CONSTITUTIONAL AMENDMENT; JUDICIAL LEGISLATION; MARSHALL, JOHN; ORIGINAL INTENTION; SUPREME COURT

1 Our peculiar security is in the possession of a written Constitution. Let us not make it a blank paper by construction.

Thomas Jefferson, Letter to Wilson C. Nicholas, 7 Sept. 1803, in *Life and Selected Writings of Thomas Jefferson* 572 (Adrienne Koch & William Peden eds. 1944)

2 It cannot be presumed that any clause in the constitution is intended to be without effect; and therefore such a construction is inadmissible, unless the words require it.

John Marshall, *Marbury v. Madison,* 5 U.S. (1 Cranch) 137, 174 (1803)

3 Strained constructions . . . loosen all the bands of the constitution.

Thomas Jefferson, Letter to George Ticknor, 7 May 1817, in *Writings of Thomas Jefferson* 10:81 (Paul L. Ford ed. 1899)

4 For intending to establish three departments, co-ordinate and independent, that they might check and balance one another, it [the Constitution] has given, . . . to one of them alone, the right to prescribe rules for the government of the others, and to that one too, which is unelected by, and independent of the nation. . . . The constitution, on this hypothesis, is a mere thing of wax in the hands of the judiciary, which they may twist and shape into any form they please. It should be remembered, as an axiom of eternal truth in politics, that whatever power in any government is independent, is absolute also.

Thomas Jefferson, Letter to Spencer Roane, 6 Sept. 1819, in *Writings of Thomas Jefferson* 10:141 (Paul L. Ford ed. 1899)

5 The judiciary of the United States is the subtle corps of sappers and miners constantly working under ground to undermine the foundations of our confederated fabric. They are construing our constitution from a co-ordination of a general and special government to a general and supreme one alone. This will lay all things at their feet, and they are too well versed in English law to forget the maxim, *"boni judicis est ampliare jurisdictionem."*

Thomas Jefferson, Letter to Thomas Ritchie, 25 Dec. 1820, in *Writings of Thomas Jefferson* 10:170 (Paul L. Ford ed. 1899)

6 If a State be a party, the jurisdiction of this Court is original; if the case arise under a constitution or a law, the jurisdiction is appellate. But a case to which a State is a party may arise under the constitution or a law of the United States. What rule is applicable to such a case? What, then, becomes the duty of the Court? Certainly, we think, so to construe the constitution as to give effect to both provisions, so far as it is

possible to reconcile them, and not to permit their seeming repugnancy to destroy each other. We must endeavor so to construe them as to preserve the true intent and meaning of the instrument.

John Marshall, *Cohens v. Virginia*, 19 U.S. (6 Wheat.) 264, 393 (1821)

7 The wise, and the learned, and the virtuous, have been nearly unanimous in supporting that doctrine, which courts of justice have uniformly asserted, that the constitution is not the law for the legislature only, but is the law, and the supreme law, which is to direct and control all judicial proceedings.

Joseph Story, Address before Suffolk Bar, Boston, 4 Sept. 1821, in *Miscellaneous Writings of Joseph Story* 198, 227 (William W. Story ed. 1852)

8 In attempts to construe the constitution, I have never found much benefit resulting from the inquiry, whether the whole, or any part of it, is to be construed strictly, or literally. The simple, classical, precise, yet comprehensive language, in which it is couched, leaves, at most, but very little latitude for construction; and when its intent and meaning is discovered, nothing remains but to execute the will of those who made it, in the best manner to effect the purposes intended. The great and paramount purpose, was, to unite this mass of wealth and power, for the protection of the humblest individual; his rights, civil and political, his interests and prosperity, are the sole *end;* the rest are nothing but the *means.*

William Johnson, *Gibbons v. Ogden*, 22 U.S. (9 Wheat.) 1, 223 (1824) (separate opinion)

9 It has been said, that these [enumerated] powers ought to be construed strictly. But why ought they to be so construed? Is there one sentence in the constitution which gives countenance to this rule?

John Marshall, *Gibbons v. Ogden*, 22 U.S. (9 Wheat.) 1, 187 (1824)

10 What do gentlemen mean, by a strict construction? . . . If they contend for that narrow construction which . . . would cripple the government, and render it unequal to the objects for which it is declared to be instituted, and to which the powers given, as fairly understood, render it competent;

then we cannot perceive the propriety of this strict construction, nor adopt it as the rule by which the constitution is to be expounded.

John Marshall, *Gibbons v. Ogden*, 22 U.S. (9 Wheat.) 1, 188 (1824)

11 Powerful and ingenious minds, taking, as postulates, that the powers expressly granted to the government of the Union, are to be contracted by construction, into the narrowest possible compass, . . . may, by a course of well-digested, but refined and metaphysical reasoning, founded on these premises, explain away the constitution of our country, and leave it, a magnificent structure, indeed, to look at, but totally unfit for use. They may so entangle and perplex the understanding, as to obscure principles, which were before thought quite plain, and induce doubts where, if the mind were to pursue its own course, none would be perceived.

John Marshall, *Gibbons v. Ogden*, 22 U.S. (9 Wheat.) 1, 222 (1824)

12 In construing the constitution of the United States, we are, in the first instance, to consider, what are its nature and objects, its scope and design, as apparent from the structure of the instrument, viewed as a whole, and also viewed in its component parts. Where its words are plain, clear, and determinate, they require no interpretation. . . . Where the words admit of two senses, each of which is conformable to common usage, that sense is to be adopted, which, without departing from the literal import of the words, best harmonizes with the nature and objects, the scope and design of the instrument.

Joseph Story, *Commentaries on the Constitution of the United States* 1:387 (1833)

13 It is obvious, that there can be no security to the people in any constitution of government, if they are not to judge of it by the fair meaning of the words of the text.

Joseph Story, *Commentaries on the Constitution of the United States* 1:391 n.1 (1833)

14 Nor should it ever be lost sight of, that the government of the United States is one of limited and enumerated powers; and that a departure from the true import and sense of its powers is, *pro tanto*, the establish-

ment of a new constitution. It is doing for the people, what they have not chosen to do for themselves. It is usurping the functions of a legislator.

Joseph Story, *Commentaries on the Constitution of the United States* 1:410 (1833)

15 Let us never forget, that our constitutions of government are solemn instruments, addressed to the common sense of the people and designed to fix, and perpetuate their rights and their liberties. They are not to be frittered away to please the demagogues of the day. They are not to be violated to gratify the ambition of political leaders. They are to speak in the same voice now, and for ever. They are of no man's private interpretation. They are ordained by the will of the people; and can be changed only by the sovereign command of the people.

Joseph Story, *Commentaries on the Constitution of the United States* 3:754 (1833)

16 It will, indeed, probably, be found, when we look to the character of the Constitution itself, the objects which it seeks to attain, the powers which it confers, the duties which it enjoins, and the rights which it secures, as well as the known historical fact that many of its provisions were matters of compromise of opposing interests and opinions; that no uniform rule of interpretation can be applied to it which may not allow, even if it does not positively demand, many modifications in its actual application to particular clauses. And, perhaps, the safest rule of interpretation after all will be found to be to look to the nature and objects of the particular powers, duties, and rights, with all the lights and aids of contemporary history; and to give to the words of each just such operation and force, consistent with their legitimate meaning, as may fairly secure and attain the ends proposed. . . . If by one mode of interpretation the right must become shadowy and unsubstantial, and without any remedial power adequate to the end; and by another mode it will attain its just end and secure its manifest purpose; it would seem, upon principles of reasoning, absolutely irresistible, that the latter ought to prevail.

Joseph Story, *Prigg v. Pennsylvania,* 41 U.S. (16 Pet.) 539, 610–12 (1842)

17 We have seen that the American Constitution has changed, is changing, and by the law of its existence must continue to change, in its substance and practical working even when its words remain the same.

James Bryce, *The American Commonwealth* 1:390 (1888)

18 Constitutional provisions do not change, but their operation extends to new matters as the modes of business and the habits of life of the people vary with each succeeding generation.

David J. Brewer, *In re Debs,* 158 U.S. 564, 591 (1895)

19 Great constitutional provisions must be administered with caution. Some play must be allowed for the joints of the machine, and it must be remembered that legislatures are ultimate guardians of the liberties and welfare of the people in quite as great a degree as the courts.

Oliver Wendell Holmes, Jr., *Missouri, Kansas & Texas Ry. v. May,* 194 U.S. 267, 270 (1904)

20 The Constitution was not made to fit us like a strait jacket. In its elasticity lies its chief greatness.

Woodrow Wilson, Speech, New York, 19 Nov. 1904, in *Papers of Woodrow Wilson* 15:537 (Arthur S. Link ed. 1973)

21 Under the guise of interpreting the Constitution we must take care that we do not import into the discussion our own personal views of what would be wise, just and fitting rules of government to be adopted by a free people and confound them with constitutional limitations.

William H. Moody, *Twining v. New Jersey,* 211 U.S. 78, 106-07 (1908)

22 But the Constitution of the United States is not a mere lawyers' document: it is a vehicle of life, and its spirit is always the spirit of the age.

Woodrow Wilson, *Constitutional Government in the United States* 69 (1908)

23 The Constitution was not meant to hold the government back to the time of horses and wagons.

Woodrow Wilson, *Constitutional Government in the United States* 169 (1908)
See also COMMERCE CLAUSE 13

24 Time works changes, brings into existence new conditions and purposes. Therefore a principle to be vital must be capable of wider application than the mischief which gave it birth. This is peculiarly true of constitutions. They are not ephemeral enactments, designed to meet passing occasions. They are, to use the words of Chief Justice John Marshall, "designed to appproach immortality as nearly as human institutions can approach it." The future is their care and provision for events of good and bad tendencies of which no prophecy can be made. In the application of a constitution, therefore, our contemplation cannot be only of what has been but of what may be.

Joseph McKenna, *Weems v. United States,* 217 U.S. 349, 373 (1910)

25 Now and then an extraordinary case may turn up, but constitutional law like other mortal contrivances has to take some chances, and in the great majority of instances no doubt justice will be done.

Oliver Wendell Holmes, Jr., *Blinn v. Nelson,* 222 U.S. 1, 7 (1911)

26 But the provisions of the Constitution are not mathematical formulas having their essence in their form; they are organic living institutions transplanted from English soil. Their significance is vital not formal; it is to be gathered not simply by taking the words and a dictionary, but by considering their origin and the line of their growth.

Oliver Wendell Holmes, Jr., *Gompers v. United States,* 233 U.S. 604, 610 (1914)

27 When we are dealing with words that also are a constituent act, like the Constitution of the United States, we must realize that they have called into life a being the development of which could not have been foreseen completely by the most gifted of its begetters. It was enough for them to realize or to hope that they had created an organism; it has taken a century and has cost their successors much sweat and blood to prove that they created a nation. The case before us must be considered in the light of our whole experience and not merely in that of what was said a hundred years ago.

Oliver Wendell Holmes, Jr., *Missouri v. Holland,* 252 U.S. 416, 433 (1920)

28 The great generalities of the constitution have a content and a significance that vary from age to age.

Benjamin N. Cardozo, *The Nature of the Judicial Process* 17 (1921)

29 A *constitution* states or ought to state not rules for the passing hour, but principles for an expanding future. In so far as it deviates from that standard, and descends into details and particulars, it loses its flexibility, the scope of interpretation contracts, the meaning hardens. While it is true to its function, it maintains its power of adaptation, its suppleness, its play.

Benjamin N. Cardozo, *The Nature of the Judicial Process* 83–84 (1921)

30 However the Court may interpret the provisions of the Constitution, it is still the Constitution which is the law and not the decision of the Court.

Charles Warren, *The Supreme Court in United States History* 3:470–71 (1922)

31 Chief Justice Taft once said that a constitutional lawyer was one who had abandoned the practice of the law and had gone into politics.

William Howard Taft, 1926, reported in Merlo J. Pusey, *Charles Evans Hughes* 2:625 (1951)

32 The meaning of "due process" and the content of terms like "liberty" are not revealed by the Constitution. It is the Justices who make the meaning. They read into the neutral language of the Constitution their own economic and social views. . . . Let us face the fact that five Justices of the Supreme Court *are* molders of policy, rather than impersonal vehicles of revealed truth.

Felix Frankfurter, "The Supreme Court and the Public," *Forum,* June 1930, at 329, 332–33, 334

33 I venture to believe that it is as important to a judge called upon to pass on a question of constitutional law, to have at least a bowing acquaintance with Acton and Maitland, with Thucydides, Gibbon and Carlyle, with Homer, Dante, Shakespeare and Milton, with Machiavelli, Montaigne and Rabelais, with Plato, Bacon, Hume and Kant, as with the books which have been specifically written on the subject. For in such

matters everything turns upon the spirit in which he approaches the questions before him. The words he must construe are empty vessels into which he can pour nearly anything he will.

Learned Hand, "Sources of Tolerance," 79 *University of Pennsylvania Law Review* 1, 12 (1930)

34 The theory that the Constitution is a written document is a legal fiction. The idea that it can be understood by a study of its language and the history of its past development is equally mythical. It is what the Government and the people who count in public affairs recognize and respect as such, what they think it is. More than this. It is not merely what it has been, or what it is today. It is always becoming something else, and those who criticize it and the acts done under it, as well as those who praise, help to make it what it will be tomorrow.

Charles A. Beard and William Beard, *The American Leviathan* 39 (1931)

35 The Court developed, for its own governance in the cases confessedly within its jurisdiction, a series of rules under which it has avoided passing upon a large part of all the constitutional questions pressed upon it for decision. They are:

1. The Court will not pass upon the constitutionality of legislation in a friendly, non-adversary, proceeding. . . .

2. The Court will not "anticipate a question of constitutional law in advance of the necessity of deciding it." . . .

3. The Court will not "formulate a rule of constitutional law broader than is required by the precise facts to which it is to be applied." . . .

4. The Court will not pass upon a constitutional question although properly presented by the record, if there is also present some other ground upon which the case may be disposed of. . . .

5. The Court will not pass upon the validity of a statute upon complaint of one who fails to show that he is injured by its operation. . . .

6. The Court will not pass upon the constitutionality of a statute at the instance of one who has availed himself of its benefits. . . .

7. "When the validity of an act of the Congress is drawn in question, and even if a serious doubt of constitutionality is raised, it is a cardinal principle that this Court will first ascertain whether a construction of the statute is fairly possible by which the question may be avoided."

Louis D. Brandeis, *Ashwander v. Tennessee Valley Authority*, 297 U.S. 288, 346–48 (1936) (concurring)

36 Sometimes it is said that the relation must be "direct" to bring that power into play. In many circumstances such a description will be sufficiently precise to meet the needs of the occasion. But a great principle of constitutional law is not susceptible of comprehensive statement in an adjective.

Benjamin N. Cardozo, *Carter v. Carter Coal Co.*, 298 U.S. 238, 327 (1936) (separate opinion)

37 The suggestion that the only check upon the exercise of the judicial power, when properly invoked, to declare a constitutional right superior to an unconstitutional statute is the judge's own faculty of self-restraint, is both ill considered and mischievous. Self-restraint belongs in the domain of will and not of judgment. The check upon the judge is that imposed by his oath of office, by the Constitution and by his own conscientious and informed convictions; and since he has the duty to make up his own mind and adjudge accordingly, it is hard to see how there could be any other restraint.

George Sutherland, *West Coast Hotel Co. v. Parrish*, 300 U.S. 379, 402 (1937) (dissenting)

38 It is urged that the question involved should now receive fresh consideration, among other reasons, because of "the economic conditions which have supervened"; but the meaning of the Constitution does not change with the ebb and flow of economic events. We frequently are told in more general words that the Constitution must be construed in the light of the present. . . . But to say, if that be intended, that the words of the Constitution mean today what they did not mean when written . . . is to rob that instrument of the essential element which continues it in force as the people have made it until they, and not

their official agents, have made it otherwise.

> George Sutherland, *West Coast Hotel Co. v. Parrish*, 300 U.S. 379, 402–03 (1937) (dissenting)

39 The judicial function is that of interpretation; it does not include the power of amendment under the guise of interpretation. To miss the point of difference between the two is to miss all that the phrase "supreme law of the land" stands for and to convert what was intended as inescapable and enduring mandates into mere moral reflections.

> George Sutherland, *West Coast Hotel Co. v. Parrish*, 300 U.S. 379, 404 (1937) (dissenting)

40 The ultimate touchstone of constitutionality is the Constitution itself and not what we have said about it.

> Felix Frankfurter, *Graves v. New York ex rel. O'Keefe*, 306 U.S. 466, 491–92 (1939) (concurring)

41 If it be the part of wisdom to avoid unnecessary decision of constitutional questions, it would seem to be equally so to avoid the unnecessary creation of novel constitutional doctrine, inadequately supported by the record, in order to attain an end easily and certainly reached by following the beaten paths of constitutional decision.

> Harlan F. Stone, *Hague v. Committee for Industrial Organization*, 307 U.S. 496, 525 (1939)

42 In determining whether a provision of the Constitution applies to a new subject matter, it is of little significance that it is one with which the framers were not familiar. For in setting up an enduring framework of government they undertook to carry out for the indefinite future and in all the vicissitudes of the changing affairs of men, those fundamental purposes which the instrument itself discloses. Hence we read its words, not as we read legislative codes which are subject to continuous revision with the changing course of events, but as the revelation of the great purposes which were intended to be achieved by the Constitution as a continuing instrument of government.

> Harlan F. Stone, *United States v. Classic*, 313 U.S. 299, 316 (1941)

43 As a member of this Court I am not justified in writing my private notions of policy into the Constitution, no matter how deeply I may cherish them or how mischievous I may deem their disregard. . . . It can never be emphasized too much that one's own opinion about the wisdom or evil of a law should be excluded altogether when one is doing one's duty on the bench.

> Felix Frankfurter, *West Virginia State Bd. of Educ. v. Barnette*, 319 U.S. 624, 647 (1943) (dissenting)

44 Our constant preoccupation with the constitutionality of legislation rather than with its wisdom tends to preoccupation of the American mind with a false value. The tendency of focussing attention on constitutionality is to make constitutionality synonymous with wisdom, to regard a law as all right if it is constitutional. Such an attitude is a great enemy of liberalism. Particularly in legislation affecting freedom of thought and freedom of speech, much which should offend a free-spirited society is constitutional. Reliance for the most precious interests of civilization, therefore, must be found outside of their vindication in courts of law. Only a persistent positive translation of the faith of a free society into the convictions and habits and actions of a community is the ultimate reliance against unabated temptations to fetter the human spirit.

> Felix Frankfurter, *West Virginia State Bd. of Educ. v. Barnette*, 319 U.S. 624, 670–71 (1943) (dissenting)

45 The constitutional fathers, fresh from a revolution, did not forge a political straitjacket for the generations to come.

> Frank Murphy, *Schneiderman v. United States*, 320 U.S. 118, 137 (1943)

46 Humility means an alert self-scrutiny so as to avoid infusing into the vagueness of a Constitutional command one's merely private notions.

> Felix Frankfurter, *Haley v. Ohio*, 332 U.S. 596, 602 (1948) (joining in reversal of judgment)

47 When only one new judge is appointed during a short period, the unsettling effect in Constitutional law may not be great. But when a majority of a Court is suddenly reconstituted, there is likely to be substantial

unsettlement. . . . During that time—which may extend a decade or more—Constitutional law will be in flux. That is the necessary consequence of our system and to my mind a healthy one. The alternative is to let the Constitution freeze in the pattern which one generation gave it. But the Constitution was designed for the vicissitudes of time. It must never become a code which carries the overtones of one period that may be hostile to another.

William O. Douglas, *Stare Decisis* 9 (1949)

48 It is an inadmissibly narrow conception of American constitutional law to confine it to the words of the Constitution and to disregard the gloss which life has written upon them.

Felix Frankfurter, *Youngstown Sheet & Tube Co. v. Sawyer*, 343 U.S. 579, 610 (1952) (concurring)

49 In nations like America and India that have written constitutions, the judiciary must do more than dispense justice in cases and controversies. It must also keep the charter of government current with the times and not allow it to become archaic or out of tune with the needs of the day.

William O. Douglas, *We the Judges* 428 (1956)

50 I put it to you that the main constituent of the judicial process is precisely that it must be genuinely principled, resting with respect to every step that is involved in reaching judgment on analysis and reasons quite transcending the immediate result that is achieved.

Herbert Wechsler, "Toward Neutral Principles of Constitutional Law," 73 *Harvard Law Review* 1, 15 (1959)

51 The Court should declare as law only such principles as will—in time, but in a rather immediate foreseeable future—gain general assent.

Alexander M. Bickel, *The Least Dangerous Branch* 239 (1962)

52 Judicial self-restraint . . . will be achieved . . . only by continual insistence upon respect for the teachings of history, solid recognition of the basic values that underlie our society, and wise appreciation of the great roles that the doctrines of federalism and separation of powers have played in

establishing and preserving American freedoms.

John M. Harlan (1899–1971), *Griswold v. Connecticut*, 381 U.S. 479, 501 (1965) (concurring)

53 That the Court's holding today is neither compelled nor even strongly suggested by the language of the Fifth Amendment, is at odds with American and English legal history, and involves a departure from a long line of precedent does not prove either that the Court has exceeded its powers or that the Court is wrong or unwise in its present reinterpretation of the Fifth Amendment. It does, however, underscore the obvious— that the Court has not discovered or found the law in making today's decision, nor has it derived it from some irrefutable sources; what it has done is to make new law and new public policy in much the same way that it has in the course of interpreting other great clauses of the Constitution. This is what the Court historically has done. Indeed, it is what it must do . . . until and unless there is some fundamental change in the constitutional distribution of governmental powers.

Byron R. White, *Miranda v. Arizona*, 384 U.S. 436, 531 (1966) (dissenting)

54 Our Constitution was not written in the sands to be washed away by each wave of new judges blown in by each successive political wind.

Hugo L. Black, *Turner v. United States*, 396 U.S. 398, 426 (1970) (dissenting)

55 Where constitutional materials do not clearly specify the value to be preferred, there is no principled way to prefer any claimed human value to any other. . . . There is no way of deciding [human rights questions] other than by reference to some system of moral or ethical values that has no objective or intrinsic validity of its own and about which men can and do differ.

Robert H. Bork, "Neutral Principles and Some First Amendment Problems," 47 *Indiana Law Journal* 1, 8, 10 (1971)

56 It is perfectly proper for judges to disagree about what the Constitution requires. But it is disgraceful for an interpretation of the Constitution to be premised upon un-

founded assumptions about how people live.

Thurgood Marshall, *United States v. Kras,* 409 U.S. 434, 460 (1973) (dissenting)

57 The authoritative status of the written constitution is a legitimate matter of debate for political theorists interested in the nature of political obligation. That status is, however, an incontestable first principle for theorizing about American constitutional law. . . . For the purpose of *legal* reasoning, the binding quality of the constitutional text is itself incapable of and not in need of further demonstration. It is our master rule of recognition, one initially so intended and understood, and one which our "tradition" in fact continues to perpetuate.

Henry P. Monaghan, "Our Perfect Constitution," 56 *New York University Law Review* 353, 383–84 (1981)

58 There is no constitutional right to be protected by the state against being murdered by criminals or madmen. It is monstrous if the state fails to protect its residents against such predators but it does not violate the due process clause of the Fourteenth Amendment or, we suppose, any other provision of the Constitution. The Constitution is a charter of negative liberties; it tells the state to let people alone; it does not require the federal government or the state to provide services, even so elementary a service as maintaining law and order.

Richard A. Posner, *Bowers v. DeVito,* 686 F.2d 616, 618 (7th Cir. 1982)

59 The fact that a given law or procedure is efficient, convenient, and useful in facilitating functions of government, standing alone, will not save it if it is contrary to the Constitution.

Warren E. Burger, *Immigration & Naturalization Serv. v. Chadha,* 462 U.S. 919, 944 (1983)

60 Charles Warren did not mean that a constitutional decision by the Supreme Court lacks the character of law. Obviously it does have binding quality: It binds the parties in a case and also the executive branch for whatever enforcement is necessary. But such a decision does not establish a supreme law of the land that is binding on all persons and parts of government henceforth and forevermore.

Edwin Meese III, "The Law of the Constitution" (speech at Tulane University), New Orleans, 21 Oct. 1986, in 61 *Tulane Law Review* 979, 983 (1987)

61 Once we understand the distinction between constitutional law and the Constitution, once we see that constitutional decisions need not be seen as the last words in constitutional construction, once we comprehend that these decisions do not necessarily determine future public policy, once we see all of this, we can grasp a correlative point: that constitutional interpretation is not the business of the Court only, but also properly the business of all branches of government. The Supreme Court, then, is not the only interpreter of the Constitution. Each of the three coordinate branches of government created and empowered by the Constitution—the executive and legislative no less than the judicial—has a duty to interpret the Constitution in the performance of its official functions. In fact, every official takes an oath precisely to that effect.

Edwin Meese III, "The Law of the Constitution" (speech at Tulane University), New Orleans, 21 Oct. 1986, in 61 *Tulane Law Review* 979, 985–86 (1987)

62 The Court is most vulnerable and comes nearest to illegitimacy when it deals with judge-made constitutional law having little or no cognizable roots in the language or design of the Constitution. . . . There should be, therefore, great resistance to expand the substantive reach of those Clauses, particularly if it requires redefining the category of rights deemed to be fundamental.

Byron R. White, *Bowers v. Hardwick,* 478 U.S. 186, 194–95 (1986)

63 Our Constitution is a covenant running from the first generation of Americans to us and then to future generations. It is a coherent succession. Each generation must learn anew that the Constitution's written terms embody ideas and aspirations that must survive more ages than one. We ac-

cept our responsibility not to retreat from interpreting the full meaning of the covenant in light of all of our precedents. We invoke it once again to define the freedom guaranteed by the Constitution's own promise, the promise of liberty.

Sandra Day O'Connor, Anthony M. Kennedy, and David H. Souter, *Planned Parenthood v. Casey*, 112 S. Ct. 2791, 2833 (1992) (joint opinion)

CONSTITUTIONALITY

See CONSTITUTIONAL LAW; DUE PROCESS; JUDICIAL LEGISLATION; JUDICIAL REVIEW; STATUTORY CONSTRUCTION

CONTEMPT

1 The law will not bargain with anybody to let its courts be defied for a specified term of imprisonment. There are many persons who would gladly purchase the honours of martyrdom in a popular cause at almost any given price, while others are deterred by a mere show of punishment. Each is detained until he finds himself willing to conform. This is merciful to the submissive, and not too severe upon the refractory. The petitioner, therefore, carries the key of his prison in his own pocket.

Jeremiah S. Black, *Passmore Williamson's Case*, 26 Pa. 9, 24 (1855)

2 *Judge:* Are you trying to show contempt for the court?
Flower Belle Lee [played by Mae West]: No, I'm doing my best to hide it.*

Mae West and W. C. Fields, *My Little Chickadee* (screenplay), 1940, quoted in *The Wit and Wisdom of Mae West* 51 (Joseph Weintraub ed. 1970)

3 There is an unedifying moral to be drawn from this case of *The Man in High Office*

---

* One day when old Thaddeus Stevens was practicing in the courts he didn't like the ruling of the presiding judge. A second time when the judge ruled against "old Thad," the old man got up with scarlet face and quivering lips and commenced tying up his papers as if to quit the court room.
"Do I understand, Mr. Stevens," asked the judge, eyeing "old Thad" indignantly, "that you wish to show your contempt for this court?"
"No, sir; no, sir," replied Stevens. "I don't want to show my contempt, sir. I'm trying to conceal it." —*The World's Best Jokes* 241 (Lewis Copeland ed. 1936)

Who Defied the Nation: The mills of the law grind slowly—but not inexorably. If they grind slowly enough, they may even come, unaccountably, to a gradual stop, short of the trial and judgment an ordinary citizen expects when accused of criminal contempt. There is just one compensating thought: Hubris is grist for other mills, which grind exceeding small and sure.

John Minor Wisdom, *United States v. Barnett*, 346 F.2d 99, 109 (5th Cir. 1965) (dissenting)

CONTRACTS

1 The principle asserted is, that one legislature is competent to repeal any act which a former legislature was competent to pass; and that one legislature cannot abridge the powers of a succeeding legislature. The correctness of this principle, so far as respects general legislation, can never be controverted. But, if an act be done under a law, a succeeding legislature cannot undo it. The past cannot be recalled by the most absolute power. Conveyances have been made, those conveyances have vested legal estates, and, if those estates may be seized by the sovereign authority, still, that they originally vested is a fact, and cannot cease to be a fact. When, then, a law is in its nature a contract, when absolute rights have vested under that contract, a repeal of the law cannot divest those rights.

John Marshall, *Fletcher v. Peck*, 10 U.S. (6 Cranch) 87, 135 (1810)

2 Any act of a legislature which takes away any powers or franchises vested by its charter in a private corporation or its corporate officers, or which restrains or controls the legitimate exercise of them, or transfers them to other persons, without its assent, is a violation of the obligations of that charter.

Joseph Story, *Trustees of Dartmouth College v. Woodward*, 17 U.S. (4 Wheat.) 518, 712 (1819) (separate opinion)

3 A cent or a pepper corn, in legal estimation, would constitute a valuable consideration.

Nicholas Emery, *Whitney v. Stearns*, 16 Me. 394, 397 (1839)

4 Public policy is in its nature so uncertain and fluctuating, varying with the habits

and fashions of the day, with the growth of commerce and the usages of trade, that it is difficult to determine its limits with any degree of exactness. It has never been defined by the courts, but has been left loose and free of definition, in the same manner as fraud. This rule may, however, be safely laid down, that whenever any contract conflicts with the morals of the time, and contravenes any established interest of society, it is void, as being against public policy.

> **William W. Story,** *A Treatise on the Law of Contracts* 480–81 (2d ed. 1847)

5 It is the essence of a consideration, that, by the terms of the agreement, it is given and accepted as the motive or inducement of the promise. Conversely, the promise must be made and accepted as the conventional motive or inducement for furnishing the consideration. The root of the whole matter is the relation of reciprocal conventional inducement, each for the other, between consideration and promise.

> **Oliver Wendell Holmes, Jr.,** *The Common Law* 293–94 (1881)

6 If there is a difference or misapprehension as to the substance of the thing bargained for . . . and intended to be sold, then there is no contract; but if it be only a difference in some quality or accident, even though the mistake may have been the actuating motive to the purchaser or seller, or both of them, yet the contract remains binding. . . . A barren cow is substantially a different creature than a breeding one. . . . She was not in fact the animal, or the kind of animal, the defendants intended to sell or the plaintiff to buy.

> **Allen B. Morse,** *Sherwood v. Walker,* 66 Mich. 568, 577, 33 N.W. 919 (1887)

7 You cannot prove a mere private convention between the two parties to give language a different meaning from its common one. . . . It would open too great risks if evidence were admissible to show that when they said five hundred feet they agreed it should mean one hundred inches, or that Bunker Hill Monument should signify the Old South Church. As an artificial construction cannot be given to plain words by express agreement, the same rule is applied when there is a mutual mistake not apparent on the face of the instrument.

> **Oliver Wendell Holmes, Jr.,** *Goode v. Riley,* 153 Mass. 585, 586, 28 N.E. 228 (1891)

8 Consideration is as much a form as a seal.*

> **Oliver Wendell Holmes, Jr.,** *Krell v. Codman,* 154 Mass. 454, 456, 28 N.E. 578 (1891)

9 Nowhere is the confusion between legal and moral ideas more manifest than in the law of contract. . . . The duty to keep a contract at common law means a prediction that you must pay damages if you do not keep it—and nothing else.

> **Oliver Wendell Holmes, Jr.,** "The Path of the Law," 10 *Harvard Law Review* 457, 462 (1897)

10 One whose rights, such as they are, are subject to state restriction, cannot remove them from the power of the State by making a contract about them.

> **Oliver Wendell Holmes, Jr.,** *Hudson County Water Co. v. McCarter,* 209 U.S. 349, 357 (1908)

11 A contract has, strictly speaking, nothing to do with the personal, or individual, intent of the parties. A contract is an obligation attached by the mere force of law to certain acts of the parties, usually words, which ordinarily accompany and represent a known intent. If, however, it were proved by twenty bishops that either party, when he used the words, intended something else than the usual meaning which the law imposes upon them, he would still be held, unless there were some mutual mistake, or something else of the sort.

> **Learned Hand,** *Hotchkiss v. National City Bank,* 200 F. 287, 293 (S.D.N.Y. 1911)

12 Freedom of contract is a qualified and not an absolute right. There is no absolute freedom to do as one wills or to contract as one chooses. . . . Liberty implies the absence of arbitrary restraint, not immunity from reasonable regulations and prohibitions imposed in the interests of the community.

> **Charles Evans Hughes,** *Chicago, Burlington & Quincy R.R. v. McGuire,* 219 U.S. 549, 567 (1911)

---

* Consideration is a form as much as a seal. —**Oliver Wendell Holmes, Jr.,** *The Common Law* 273 (1881)

13 The law has outgrown its primitive stage of formalism when the precise word was the sovereign talisman, and every slip was fatal. It takes a broader view to-day. A promise may be lacking, and yet the whole writing may be "instinct with an obligation," imperfectly expressed. . . . If that is so, there is a contract.*

Benjamin N. Cardozo, *Wood v. Lucy, Lady Duff-Gordon*, 222 N.Y. 88, 91, 118 N.E. 214 (1917)

14 Whenever two men contract, no limitation self-imposed can destroy their power to contract again.

Benjamin N. Cardozo, *Beatty v. Guggenheim Exploration Co.*, 225 N.Y. 380, 388, 122 N.E. 378 (1919)

15 The modern law rightly construes both acts and words as having the meaning which a reasonable person present would put upon them in view of the surrounding circumstances. Even where words are used "a contract includes not only what the parties said, but also what is necessarily to be implied from what they said." And it may be said broadly that any conduct of one party, from which the other may reasonably draw the inference of a promise, is effective in law as such.

Samuel Williston, *The Law of Contracts* 1:27 (1920)

16 In order to enter into most of the relations of life people have to give up some of their Constitutional rights. If a man makes a contract he gives up the Constitutional right that previously he had to be free from the hamper that he puts upon himself.

Oliver Wendell Holmes, Jr., *Power Mfg. Co. v. Saunders*, 274 U.S. 490, 497 (1927) (dissenting)

17 One turns from contemplation of the work of contract as from the experience of Greek tragedy. Life struggling against form, or through form to its will—"pity and terror." Law means so pitifully little to life.

_____
* It is true that plaintiff does not by precise words engage to employ defendant for the term specified, but the whole contract is instinct with such an obligation on its part. —Francis M. Scott, *McCall Co. v. Wright*, 133 A.D. 62, 68, 117 N.Y.S. 775 (Sup. Ct. 1909)

Life is so terrifyingly dependent on the law.

Karl N. Llewellyn, "What Price Contract?— An Essay in Perspective," 40 *Yale Law Journal* 704, 751 (1931)

18 If an offer for a unilateral contract is made, and part of the consideration requested in the offer is given or tendered by the offeree in response thereto, the offeror is bound by a contract, the duty of immediate performance of which is conditional on the full consideration being given or tendered within the time stated in the offer, or, if no time is stated therein, within a reasonable time.

Restatement of Contracts § 45 (1932)

19 A promise which the promisor should reasonably expect to induce action or forbearance of a definite and substantial character on the part of the promisee and which does induce such action or forbearance is binding if injustice can be avoided only by enforcement of the promise.

Restatement of Contracts § 90 (1932)

20 Liberty of contract is not an absolute concept. . . . It is relative to many conditions of time and place and circumstance. The constitution has not ordained that the forms of business shall be cast in imperishable moulds.

Benjamin N. Cardozo, *Hartford Accident & Indemnity Co. v. N.O. Nelson Mfg. Co.*, 291 U.S. 352, 360–61 (1934)

21 *Fiorello* [played by Chico Marx]: Hey, wait—wait! What does this say here? This thing here?
Otis B. Driftwood [played by Groucho Marx]: Oh, that? Oh, that's the usual clause. That's in every contract. That just says, uh, it says, uh, if any of the parties participating in this contract is shown not to be in their right mind, the entire agreement is automatically nullified.
Fiorello: Well, I don't know.
Driftwood: It's all right. That's—that's in every contract. That's—that's what they call a sanity clause.
Fiorello: You can't fool me. There ain't no Sanity Claus.

George S. Kaufman and Morrie Ryskind, *A Night at the Opera* (published screenplay) 121–22 (1972) (1935)

22 A verbal contract isn't worth the paper it's written on.*

> **Samuel Goldwyn,** Attributed remark, quoted in Alva Johnston, *The Great Goldwyn* 16 (1937)

23 Freedom of contract enables enterprisers to legislate by contract and, what is even more important, to legislate in a substantially authoritarian manner without using the appearance of authoritarian forms. Standard contracts in particular could thus become effective instruments in the hands of powerful industrial and commercial overlords enabling them to impose a new feudal order of their own making upon a vast host of vassals.

> **Friedrich Kessler,** "Contracts of Adhesion— Some Thoughts about Freedom of Contract," 43 *Columbia Law Review* 629, 640 (1943)

24 The purpose of a contract is to place the risks of performance upon the promisor, and the relation of the parties, terms of the contract, and circumstances surrounding its formation must be examined to determine whether it can be fairly inferred that the risk of the event that has supervened to cause the alleged frustration was not reasonably foreseeable. If it was foreseeable there should have been provision for it in the contract, and the absence of such a provision gives rise to the inference that the risk was assumed.

> **Roger J. Traynor,** *Lloyd v. Murphy,* 25 Cal. 2d 48, 54, 153 P.2d 47 (1944)

25 To separate labor from other activities of life and to subject it to the laws of the market was to annihilate all organic forms of existence and to replace them by a different type of organization, an atomistic and individualistic one. Such a scheme of destruction was best served by the application of the principle of freedom of contract. In practice this meant that the noncontractual organizations of kinship, neighborhood, profession, and creed were to be liquidated since they claimed the allegiance of the individual and thus restrained his freedom. To represent this principle as one of non-interference . . . was merely the expression of an ingrained prejudice in favor of a definite kind of interference, namely, such as would destroy noncontractual relations between individuals and prevent their spontaneous re-formation.

> **Karl Polanyi,** *The Great Transformation* 163 (1957)

26 The contract law system . . . serves massively and systematically as an *intensifier* of economic advantage and disadvantage. It does this because people and businesses who are in strong bargaining positions, or who can afford expensive legal advice, can and epidemically do exact of necessitous and ignorant people contractual engagements which the general law never would impose.

> **Charles L. Black, Jr.,** "Some Notes on Law Schools in the Present Day," 79 *Yale Law Journal* 505, 508 (1970)

27 We might say that what is happening is that "contract" is being reabsorbed into the mainstream of "tort." Until the general theory of contract was hurriedly run up late in the nineteenth century, tort had always been our residual category of civil liability. As the contract rules dissolve, it is becoming so again.

> **Grant Gilmore,** *The Death of Contract* 87 (1974)

28 We seem to be in the presence of the phenomenon which, in the history of comparative religion, is called syncretism—that is, according to Webster, "the reconciliation or union of conflicting beliefs." I have occasionally suggested to my students that a desirable reform in legal education would be to merge the first-year courses in Contracts and Torts into a single course which we could call Contorts.

> **Grant Gilmore,** *The Death of Contract* 89–90 (1974)

29 (1) Where an offer invites an offeree to accept by rendering a performance and does not invite a promissory acceptance, an option contract is created when the offeree tenders or begins the invited performance or tenders a beginning of it.

(2) The offeror's duty of performance under any option contract so created is

---

* According to Norman Zierold, *The Moguls* 128 (1969), Goldwyn actually said, in praise of the trustworthiness of motion picture executive Joseph M. Schenck, that "His verbal contract is worth more than the paper it's written on." The sentence was then "improved," like many other Goldwynisms, and became famous in the form above.

conditional on completion or tender of the invited performance in accordance with the terms of the offer.

Restatement (Second) of Contracts § 45 (1979)

30 act of God. . . . The late J.A. MacLachlan of Harvard used to define it, impiously but usefully, as "that which no reasonable God would do."

Arthur A. Leff, "The Leff Dictionary of Law: A Fragment," 94 *Yale Law Journal* 1855, 1915–16 (1985)

COPYRIGHT

1 No reporter has or can have any copyright in the written opinions delivered by this court; and . . . the judges . . . cannot confer on any reporter any such right.

John McLean, *Wheaton v. Peters,* 33 U.S. (8 Pet.) 591, 668 (1834)

2 Patents and copyrights approach, nearer than any other class of cases belonging to forensic discussions, to what may be called the metaphysics of the law, where the distinctions are, or at least may be, very subtile and refined, and, sometimes, almost evanescent.

Joseph Story, *Folsom v. Marsh,* 9 F. Cas. 342, 344 (C.C.D. Mass. 1841) (No. 4,901)

3 A reviewer may fairly cite largely from the original work, if his design be really and truly to use the passages for the purposes of fair and reasonable criticism. On the other hand, it is as clear, that if he thus cites the most important parts of the work, with a view, not to criticize, but to supersede the use of the original work, and substitute the review for it, such a use will be deemed in law a piracy.

Joseph Story, *Folsom v. Marsh,* 9 F. Cas. 342, 344–45 (C.C.D. Mass. 1841) (No. 4,901)

4 There must be real, substantial condensation of the materials, and intellectual labor and judgment bestowed thereon; and not merely the facile use of the scissors; or extracts of the essential parts, constituting the chief value of the original work.

Joseph Story, *Folsom v. Marsh,* 9 F. Cas. 342, 345 (C.C.D. Mass. 1841) (No. 4,901)

5 Neither does it necessarily depend upon the quantity taken, whether it is an in-

fringement of the copyright or not. . . . In short, we must often, in deciding questions of this sort, look to the nature and objects of the selections made, the quantity and value of the materials used, and the degree in which the use may prejudice the sale, or diminish the profits, or supersede the objects, of the original work.

Joseph Story, *Folsom v. Marsh,* 9 F. Cas. 342, 348 (C.C.D. Mass. 1841) (No. 4,901)

6 In truth, in literature, in science and in art, there are, and can be, few, if any, things, which, in an abstract sense, are strictly new and original throughout. Every book in literature, science and art, borrows, and must necessarily borrow, and use much which was well known and used before.

Joseph Story, *Emerson v. Davies,* 8 F. Cas. 615, 619 (C.C.D. Mass. 1845) (No. 4,436)

7 A day will come when, in the eye of the law, literary property will be as sacred as whiskey, or any other of the necessaries of life. In this age of ours, if you steal another man's label to advertise your own brand of whiskey with, you will be heavily fined and otherwise punished for violating that trade-mark; if you steal the whiskey without the trade-mark, you go to jail; but if you could prove that the whiskey was literature, you can steal them both, and the law wouldn't say a word. It grieves me to think how far more profound and reverent a respect the law would have for literature if a body could only get drunk on it.

Mark Twain, quoted in *New York Times,* 10 Dec. 1881, at 2

8 In vain we call old notions fudge, And bend our conscience to our dealing; The Ten Commandments will not budge, And stealing will continue stealing.*

James Russell Lowell, "International Copyright," 1885, in *Complete Poetical Works of James Russell Lowell* 433 (Horace E. Scudder ed. 1925)

9 Others are free to copy the original. They are not free to copy the copy. . . . The copy is the personal reaction of an individual upon nature. Personality always contains something unique. It expresses its singu-

---

* This was adopted as the motto of the American Copyright League.

79

larity even in handwriting, and a very modest grade of art has in it something irreducible, which is one man's alone. That something he may copyright unless there is a restriction in the words of the act.

Oliver Wendell Holmes, Jr., *Bleistein v. Donaldson Lithographing Co.,* 188 U.S. 239, 249–50 (1903)

10 It would be a dangerous undertaking for persons trained only to the law to constitute themselves final judges of the worth of pictorial illustrations, outside of the narrowest and most obvious limits. At the one extreme some works of genius would be sure to miss appreciation. Their very novelty would make them repulsive until the public had learned the new language in which their author spoke. It may be more than doubted, for instance, whether the etchings of Goya or the paintings of Manet would have been sure of protection when seen for the first time. At the other end, copyright would be denied to pictures which appealed to a public less educated than the judge. Yet if they command the interest of any public, they have a commercial value—it would be bold to say that they have not an aesthetic and educational value—and the taste of any public is not to be treated with contempt.

Oliver Wendell Holmes, Jr., *Bleistein v. Donaldson Lithographing Co.,* 188 U.S. 239, 251–52 (1903)

11 Only one thing, is impossible for God: to find any sense in any copyright law on the planet.

Mark Twain, Notebook, 23 May 1903, in *Mark Twain's Notebook* 381 (Albert B. Paine ed. 1935)

12 Whenever a copyright law is to be made or altered, then the idiots assemble.

Mark Twain, Notebook, 23 May 1903, in *Mark Twain's Notebook* 382 (Albert B. Paine ed. 1935)

13 The ground of this extraordinary right is that the person to whom it is given has invented some new collocation of visible or audible points,—of lines, colors, sounds, or words. The restraint is directed against reproducing this collocation, although but for the invention and the statute any one would be free to combine the contents of the dictionary, the elements of the spectrum, or the notes of the gamut in any way

that he had the wit to devise. The restriction is confined to the specific form, to the collocation devised, of course, but one would expect that, if it was to be protected at all, that collocation would be protected according to what was its essence. One would expect the protection to be coextensive not only with the invention, which, though free to all, only one had the ability to achieve, but with the possibility of reproducing the result which gives to the invention its meaning and worth.

Oliver Wendell Holmes, Jr., *White-Smith Music Publishing Co. v. Apollo Co.,* 209 U.S. 1, 19 (1908) (concurring)

14 While there must be originality in a work of art . . . this means little more than a prohibition of actual copying.

R. R. Bowker, *Copyright* 229 (1912)

15 The general rule of law is, that the noblest of human productions—knowledge, truths ascertained, conceptions and ideas—become, after voluntary communication to others, free as the air to common use.

Louis D. Brandeis, *International News Serv. v. Associated Press,* 248 U.S. 215, 250 (1918) (dissenting)

16 But we do not doubt that two plays may correspond in plot closely enough for infringement. How far that correspondence must go is another matter. Nor need we hold that the same may not be true as to the characters, quite independently of the "plot" proper, though, as far as we know, such a case has never arisen. If Twelfth Night were copyrighted, it is quite possible that a second comer might so closely imitate Sir Toby Belch or Malvolio as to infringe, but it would not be enough that for one of his characters he cast a riotous knight who kept wassail to the discomfort of the household, or a vain and foppish steward who became amorous of his mistress. These would be no more than Shakespeare's "ideas" in the play, as little capable of monopoly as Einstein's Doctrine of Relativity, or Darwin's theory of the Origin of Species. It follows that the less developed the characters, the less they can be copyrighted; that is the penalty an author must bear.

Learned Hand, *Nichols v. Universal Pictures Corp.,* 45 F.2d 119, 121 (2d Cir. 1930)

17 Upon any work, and especially upon a play, a great number of patterns of increasing

generality will fit equally well, as more and more of the incident is left out. The last may perhaps be no more than the most general statement of what the play is about, and at times might consist only of its title; but there is a point in this series of abstractions where they are no longer protected, since otherwise the playwright could prevent the use of his "ideas," to which, apart from their expression, his property is never extended.

> Learned Hand, *Nichols v. Universal Pictures Corp.*, 45 F.2d 119, 121 (2d Cir. 1930)

18 Anticipation as such cannot invalidate a copyright. Borrowed the work must indeed not be, for a plagiarist is not himself pro tanto an "author"; but if by some magic a man who had never known it were to compose anew Keats's Ode on a Grecian Urn, he would be an "author," and, if he copyrighted it, others might not copy that poem, though they might of course copy Keats's.

> Learned Hand, *Sheldon v. Metro-Goldwyn Pictures Corp.*, 81 F.2d 49, 54 (2d Cir. 1936)

19 A play may be pirated without using the dialogue. . . . Were it not so, there could be no piracy of a pantomime, where there cannot be any dialogue; yet nobody would deny to pantomime the name of drama. Speech is only a small part of a dramatist's means of expression; he draws on all the arts and compounds his play from words and gestures and scenery and costume and from the very looks of the actors themselves. Again and again a play may lapse into pantomime at its most poignant and significant moments; a nod, a movement of the hand, a pause, may tell the audience more than words could tell. . . . The play is the sequence of the confluents of all these means, bound together in an inseparable unity; it may often be most effectively pirated by leaving out the speech, for which a substitute can be found, which keeps the whole dramatic meaning.

> Learned Hand, *Sheldon v. Metro-Goldwyn Pictures Corp.*, 81 F.2d 49, 55–56 (2d Cir. 1936)

20 No plagiarist can excuse the wrong by showing how much of his work he did not pirate.

> Learned Hand, *Sheldon v. Metro-Goldwyn Pictures Corp.*, 81 F.2d 49, 56 (2d Cir. 1936)

21 Such simple, trite themes as these are likely to recur spontaneously; indeed the defendants have been able to discover substantial equivalents of that at bar in a number of pieces which appeared earlier than the plaintiff's. . . . It must be remembered that, while there are an enormous number of possible permutations of the musical notes of the scale, only a few are pleasing; and much fewer still suit the infantile demands of the popular ear. Recurrence is not therefore an inevitable badge of plagiarism.

> Learned Hand, *Darrell v. Joe Morris Music Co.*, 113 F.2d 80, 80 (2d Cir. 1940)

22 Fair use may be defined as a privilege in others than the owner of a copyright to use the copyrighted material in a reasonable manner without his consent, notwithstanding the monopoly granted to the owner by the copyright.

> Horace G. Ball, *The Law of Copyright and Literary Property* 260 (1944)

23 Copyright is the Cinderella of the law. Her rich older sisters, Franchises and Patents, long crowded her into the chimney-corner. Suddenly the fairy godmother, Invention, endowed her with mechanical and electrical devices as magical as the pumpkin coach and the mice footmen. Now she whirls through the mad mazes of a glamorous ball.

> Zechariah Chafee, Jr., "Reflections on the Law of Copyright," 45 *Columbia Law Review* 503, 503 (1945)

24 You claim you own Casablanca and that no one else can use that name without your permission. What about "Warner Brothers"? Do you own that, too? You probably have the right to use the name Warner, but what about Brothers? Professionally, we were brothers long before you were. We were touring the sticks as The Marx Brothers when Vitaphone was still a gleam in the inventor's eye, and even before us there had been other brothers—the Smith Brothers; the Brothers Karamazov; Dan Brothers, an outfielder with Detroit; and "Brother, Can You Spare a Dime?"

> Groucho Marx, Letter to Warner Brothers, in *The Groucho/phile* 207 (1976)

25 "Original" in reference to a copyrighted work means that the particular work "owes

its origin" to the "author." No large measure of novelty is necessary.

> **Jerome N. Frank**, *Alfred Bell & Co. v. Catalda Fine Arts, Inc.*, 191 F.2d 99, 102 (2d Cir. 1951)

26 The trial court found that the art work in plaintiff's greeting cards was copyrightable, but not infringed. . . . the wording or textual matter . . . consist[s] of common and ordinary English words and phrases which are not original with Roth and were in the public domain. . . . It appears to us that in total concept and feel the cards of United are the same as the copyrighted cards of Roth.

> **Frederick G. Hamley**, *Roth Greeting Cards v. United Card Co.*, 429 F.2d 1106, 1109–10 (9th Cir. 1970)

27 One may search the Copyright Act in vain for any sign that the elected representatives of the millions of people who watch television every day have made it unlawful to copy a program for later viewing at home, or have enacted a flat prohibition against the sale of machines that make such copying possible.

> **John Paul Stevens**, *Sony Corp. v. Universal City Studios, Inc.*, 464 U.S. 417, 456 (1983)

CORPORATIONS

See also ANTITRUST; BUSINESS

1 A corporation is an artificial being, invisible, intangible, and existing only in contemplation of law. . . . it possesses only those properties which the charter of its creation confers upon it. . . . Among the most important are immortality, and . . . individuality; properties, by which a perpetual succession of many persons are considered as the same, and may act as a single individual. They enable a corporation to manage its own affairs, and to hold property without the perplexing intricacies, the hazardous and endless necessity, of perpetual conveyances for the purpose of transmitting it from hand to hand. . . . By these means, a perpetual succession of individuals are capable of acting for the promotion of the particular object, like one immortal being.

> **John Marshall**, *Trustees of Dartmouth College v. Woodward*, 17 U.S. (4 Wheat.) 518, 636 (1819)

2 It is very true that a corporation can have no legal existence out of the boundaries of the sovereignty by which it is created. It exists only in contemplation of law, and by force of the law; and where that law ceases to operate, and is no longer obligatory, the corporation can have no existence.

> **Roger B. Taney**, *Bank of Augusta v. Earle*, 38 U.S. (13 Pet.) 519, 588–89 (1839)

3 A corporation . . . seems to us to be a person, though an artificial one, inhabiting and belonging to that state [of incorporation], and therefore entitled, for the purpose of suing and being sued, to be deemed a citizen of that state.

> **James M. Wayne**, *Louisville, Cincinnati & Charleston R.R. v. Letson*, 43 U.S. (2 How.) 497, 555 (1844)

4 A corporation is an imaginary being. It has no mind but the mind of its servants; it has no voice but the voice of its servants; and it has no hands with which to act but the hands of its servants. All its schemes of mischief, as well as its schemes of public enterprise, are conceived by . . . its servants' minds and hands. All attempts, therefore, to distinguish between the guilt of the servant and the guilt of the corporation; or the malice of the servant and the malice of the corporation; or the punishment of the servant and the punishment of the corporation, is sheer nonsense. . . . Neither guilt, malice, nor suffering is predicable of this ideal existence, called a corporation. And yet under cover of its name and authority, there is in fact as much wickedness, and as much that is deserving of punishment, as can be found anywhere else. And since these ideal existences can neither be hung, imprisoned, whipped, or put in the stocks,—since in fact no corrective influence can be brought to bear upon them except that of pecuniary loss,—it does seem to us that the doctrine of exemplary damages is more beneficial in its application to them, than in its application to natural persons.

> **Charles W. Walton**, *Goddard v. Grand Trunk Ry.*, 57 Me. 202, 223–24 (1869)

5 It would be a most singular result if a constitutional provision intended for the protection of every person against partial and discriminating legislation by the states, should cease to exert such protection the

moment the person becomes a member of a corporation. We cannot accept such a conclusion. On the contrary, we think that it is well established . . . that whenever a provision of the constitution . . . guaranties to persons the enjoyment of property, . . . or prohibits legislation . . . affecting it, . . . the courts will always look beyond the name of the artificial being to the individuals whom it represents.

> **Stephen J. Field,** *County of San Mateo v. Southern Pacific R.R.,* 13 F. 722, 744 (C.C.D. Cal. 1882)

6 Corporations, which should be the carefully restrained creatures of the law and the servants of the people, are fast becoming the people's masters.

> **Grover Cleveland,** Fourth Annual Message to Congress, 3 Dec. 1888, in *Messages and Papers of the Presidents* 8:773, 774 (James D. Richardson ed. 1898)

7 It is no limitation upon property rights or freedom of contract to require that when men receive from government the privilege of doing business under corporate form, which frees them from individual responsibility, and enables them to call into their enterprises the capital of the public, they shall do so upon absolutely truthful representations as to the value of the property in which the capital is to be invested. Corporations engaged in interstate commerce should be regulated if they are found to exercise a license working to the public injury.

> **Theodore Roosevelt,** First Annual Message to Congress, 3 Dec. 1901, in *Works of Theodore Roosevelt* 17:104-05 (Hermann Hagedorn ed. 1925)

8 The biggest corporation, like the humblest private citizen, must be held to strict compliance with the will of the people as expressed in the fundamental law.

> **Theodore Roosevelt,** Speech, Cincinnati, 20 Sept. 1902, in *Outlook,* 27 Sept. 1902, at 206, 206

9 Philosophy may have gained by the attempts in recent years to look through the fiction to the fact and to generalize corporations, partnerships and other groups into a single conception. But to generalize is to omit, and in this instance to omit one characteristic of the complete corporation, as called into being under modern statutes, that is most important in business and law. A leading purpose of such statutes and of those who act under them is to interpose a nonconductor, through which in matters of contract it is impossible to see the men behind.

> **Oliver Wendell Holmes, Jr.,** *Donnell v. Herring-Hall-Marvin Safe Co.,* 208 U.S. 267, 273 (1908)

10 That fiction of the United States Federal Courts that all the stockholders in a corporation are citizens of the State which incorporates it . . . is remarkable for the late date of its origin and for its absurd results.

> **John Chipman Gray,** *The Nature and Sources of the Law* 34 (1909)

11 Liberty is always personal, never aggregate. . . . the individual . . . cannot be merged . . . without being lost to liberty, because lost to independence. Make of him a fraction instead of an integer, and you have broken his spirit, cut off the sources of his life. That is why I plead so earnestly for the individualization of responsibility within the corporation, for the establishment of the principle by law that a man has no more right to do a wrong as a member of a corporation than as an individual. Establish that principle, cut away the undergrowth of law that has sprung up so rankly about the corporation and make of it an ambush and covert, and it will give every man the right to say No again, to refuse to do wrong, no matter who orders him to do it.

> **Woodrow Wilson,** Address to American Bar Association, Chattanooga, Tenn., 31 Aug. 1910, in *Public Papers of Woodrow Wilson* 2:266–67 (Ray Stannard Baker & William E. Dodd eds. 1925)

12 CORPORATION, *n.* An ingenious device for obtaining individual profit without individual responsibility.

> **Ambrose Bierce,** *The Devil's Dictionary* 57 (1911)

13 There is one thing that political parties dare not do now. They do not dare to put corporation lawyers up for office, particularly lawyers who have been the advisers of railway corporations. Now I used to be a lawyer myself before I repented, and I don't see anything dishonest in giving legal ad-

vice to a railway company. . . . [but] corporations are having a bigger voice in the government of this country than you are, and . . . you don't want to put their particular advisers in control of the government.

Woodrow Wilson, Speech, Elk Point, S.D., 17 Sept. 1912, in *Papers of Woodrow Wilson* 25:157 (Arthur S. Link ed. 1978)

14 INCORPORATION, *n.* The act of uniting several persons into one fiction called a corporation, in order that they may be no longer responsible for their actions. A, B, and C are a corporation. A robs, B steals and C (it is necessary that there be one gentleman in the concern) cheats. It is a plundering, thieving, swindling corporation. But A, B and C, who have jointly determined and severally executed every crime of the corporation, are blameless. It is wrong to mention them by name when censuring their acts as a corporation, but right when praising. Incorporation is somewhat like the ring of Gyges: it bestows the blessing of invisibility—comfortable to knaves. The scoundrel who invented incorporation is dead—he has disincorporated.

Ambrose Bierce, *The Enlarged Devil's Dictionary* 152 (Ernest J. Hopkins ed. 1967)

15 It leads nowhere to call a corporation a fiction. If it is a fiction it is a fiction created by law with intent that it should be acted on as if true.

Oliver Wendell Holmes, Jr., *Klein v. Board of Tax Supervisors*, 282 U.S. 19, 24 (1930)

16 All powers granted to a corporation or to the management of a corporation, . . . whether derived from statute or charter or both, are necessarily and at all times exercisable only for the ratable benefit of all the shareholders as their interest appears.

Adolf A. Berle, Jr., "Corporate Powers as Powers in Trust," 44 *Harvard Law Review* 1049, 1049 (1931)

17 Able, discerning scholars have pictured for us the economic and social results of . . . removing all limitations upon the size and activities of business corporations and of vesting in their managers vast powers once exercised by stockholders—results not designed by the States and long unsuspected. They show that size alone gives to giant corporations a social significance not attached ordinarily to smaller units of private

enterprise. Through size, corporations, once merely an efficient tool employed by individuals in the conduct of private business, have become an institution—an institution which has brought such concentration of economic power that so-called private corporations are sometimes able to dominate the State. . . . Such is the Frankenstein monster which States have created by their corporation laws.

Louis D. Brandeis, *Louis K. Liggett Co. v. Lee*, 288 U.S. 517, 564–65, 567 (1933) (dissenting in part)

18 A public policy, existing through the years, and derived from a profound knowledge of human characteristics and motives, has established a rule that demands of a corporate officer or director, peremptorily and inexorably, the most scrupulous observance of his duty, not only affirmatively to protect the interests of the corporation committed to his charge, but also to refrain from doing anything that would work injury to the corporation, or to deprive it of profit or advantage which his skill and ability might properly bring to it, or to enable it to make in the reasonable and lawful exercise of its powers. The rule that requires an undivided and unselfish loyalty to the corporation demands that there shall be no conflict between duty and self-interest.

Daniel J. Layton, *Guth v. Loft, Inc.*, 5 A.2d 503, 510 (Del. 1939)

19 It is . . . clearly established that mistakes or errors in the exercise of honest business judgment do not subject the officers and directors to liability for negligence in the discharge of their appointed duties.

Harry E. Kalodner, *Otis & Co. v. Pennsylvania R.R.*, 61 F. Supp. 905, 911 (D. Pa. 1945)

20 It may be most desirable to give corporations this protection from the operation of the legislative process. But that question is not for us. It is for the people. If they want corporations to be treated as humans are treated, if they want to grant corporations this large degree of emancipation from state regulation, they should say so. The Constitution provides a method by which they may do so.

William O. Douglas, *Wheeling Steel Corp. v. Glander*, 337 U.S. 562, 581 (1949) (dissenting)

21 The young graduate of a law school who went to one of the more prominent lawyers in town who had a fine corporate practice. He said, "Mr. Smith, how does one become a corporation lawyer?" Mr. Smith replied: "That is the easiest question to answer I have had today. Just get yourself a corporation for a client."

John Eckler, in 30 *Bar Examiner* 42 (1961)

22 In summary, as long as we operate within a capitalist society and as long as confidence in management is prerequisite to its continuance, there should be a federal interest in the proper conduct of the corporation itself as much as in the market for its securities. A civilizing jurisprudence should import lifting standards; certainly there is no justification for permitting them to deteriorate. The absurdity of this race for the bottom, with Delaware in the lead—tolerated and indeed fostered by corporate counsel—should arrest the conscience of the American bar when its current reputation is in low estate.

William L. Cary, "Federalism and Corporate Law: Reflections Upon Delaware," 83 *Yale Law Journal* 663, 705 (1974)

```
                    COSTS
```

See FEES; WEALTH AND POVERTY

```
                   COUNSEL
```

See CRIMINAL PROCEDURE

```
              COURTROOM SCENES
```

1 *Jane Faulkner* [played by Margaret Seddon, testifying at Longfellow Deeds's sanity hearing]: Why, *everybody* in Mandrake Falls is pixilated—except us.

Robert Riskin, *Mr. Deeds Goes to Town* (screenplay), 1936, quoted in Harry Haun, *The Movie Quote Book* 49 (1980)

2 *Longfellow Deeds* [played by Gary Cooper, at Deeds's sanity hearing]: Other people are doodlers. . . . That's a name we made up back home for people who make foolish designs on paper when they're thinking. It's called doodling.* Almost everybody's a

---

* This represents the coinage of the term *doodle*.

doodler. Did you ever see a scratch pad in a telephone booth? People draw the most idiotic pictures when they're thinking.

Robert Riskin, *Mr. Deeds Goes to Town* (screenplay) (1936)

3 *Babe Bennett* [played by Jean Arthur, addressing judge at Longfellow Deeds's sanity hearing]: Certainly I wrote those articles. I was going to get a raise—and a month's vacation! But I stopped writing them when I found out what he was all about! When I realized how real he was—when I found out he could never fit in with our distorted viewpoint—because *his* was honest and sincere and good. If that man is crazy, Your Honor, the rest of us belong in straitjackets.

Robert Riskin, *Mr. Deeds Goes to Town* (screenplay), 1936, quoted in *Actor's Book of Movie Monologues* 14 (Marisa Smith & Amy Schewel eds. 1986)

4 *Judge Walker* [played by H. B. Warner, ruling on Longfellow Deeds's sanity hearing]: Mr. Deeds, there has been a great deal of damaging testimony against you. Your behavior, to say the least, has been most strange. But, in the opinion of the court, you are not only sane but you're the sanest man that ever walked into this courtroom.

Robert Riskin, *Mr. Deeds Goes to Town* (screenplay), 1936, quoted in Harry Haun, *The Movie Quote Book* 47 (1980)

5 *Emile Zola* [played by Paul Muni, speaking at Zola's libel trial]: They warned me that my actions would be mercilessly crushed . . . that I would be destroyed! But what does it matter if an individual is shattered, if only Justice is resurrected? It has been said that the State summoned me to this Court. That is not true. I am here because *I* wished it! *I* alone have chosen you as my judges! *I* alone decided that this abominable affair should see the light so that France might at last know all and voice her opinion! My act has no other object—my person is of no account. I am satisfied!

Heinz Herald, Geza Herczeg, and Norman Reilly Raine, *The Life of Emile Zola* (screenplay), 1937, in *Twenty Best Film Plays* 2:654, 695 (John Gassner & Dudley Nichols eds. 1977)

6 *Emile Zola* [played by Paul Muni, speaking at Zola's libel trial]: At this solemn mo-

ment, in the presence of this tribunal which is the representative of human justice, before you, gentlemen of the jury, before France, before the whole world—I swear that Dreyfus is innocent! By my forty years of work, by all that I have won, by all that I have written to spread the spirit of France, I swear that Dreyfus is innocent! May all that melt away—may my name perish!—if Dreyfus be not innocent! *He is innocent!*

> **Heinz Herald, Geza Herczeg, and Norman Reilly Raine,** *The Life of Emile Zola* (screenplay), 1937, in *Twenty Best Film Plays* 2:654, 696 (John Gassner & Dudley Nichols eds. 1977)

7 *Michael Lightcap* [played by Ronald Colman, in courtroom speech to a mob]: This is your law and your finest possession. It makes you free men in a free country. Why have you come here to destroy it? . . . Think of this country and of the law that makes it what it is. Think of a world crying for this very law. Then maybe you'll understand why you ought to guard it, why the law has got to be the personal concern of every citizen, to uphold it for your neighbor as well as yourself.

Violence against it is one mistake. Another mistake is for any man to look upon the law as just a set of principles, just so much language printed on fine heavy paper, something he recites and then leans back and takes it for granted that justice is automatically being done. Both kinds of men are equally wrong. The law must be engraved in our hearts and practiced every minute to the letter and spirit. We can't even exist unless we are willing to go down into the dust and blood and fight a battle every day of our lives to preserve it, for our neighbor as well as ourself.

> **Irwin Shaw and Sidney Buchman,** *The Talk of the Town* (screenplay) (1942)

8 *Fred Gailey* [played by John Payne]: You believe yourself to be Judge Harper, and nobody questions your sanity, Your Honor, because you *are* Judge Harper.
Judge Harper [played by Gene Lockhart]: I know all about myself, young man. Mr. Kringle is the subject of this hearing.
Fred: Yes, Your Honor—and if he is the person he believes himself to be—just as you are—then he is just as sane.
Harper: Granted—but he isn't.

Fred: Oh, but he *is*, Your Honor!
Harper: Is what?
Fred: I intend to prove that Mr. Kringle *is* Santa Claus.

> **George Seaton,** *Miracle on 34th Street* (screenplay), 1947, in *Best American Screenplays* 169, 205 (Sam Thomas ed. 1986)

9 *Fred Gailey* [played by John Payne]: Your Honor—every one of these letters is addressed to Santa Claus. The Post Office has delivered them. The Post Office is a branch of the Federal Government. Therefore, the United States Government recognizes this man, Kris Kringle, as the one and only Santa Claus.
Judge Harper [played by Gene Lockhart]: Since the United States of America believes this man to be Santa Claus, this Court will not dispute it. Case dismissed!

> **George Seaton,** *Miracle on 34th Street* (screenplay), 1947, in *Best American Screenplays* 169, 212 (Sam Thomas ed. 1986)

10 *Amanda Bonner* [played by Katharine Hepburn, in defense attorney's summation to jury]: Law, like man, is composed of two parts. Just as a man is body and soul, so is the law letter and spirit. The law says, "Thou shalt not kill!" Yet men *have* killed and proved a reason and been set free. Self-defense—defense of others, of wife or children or home. If a thief breaks into your home and you shoot him, the law will not deal harshly with you. Nor, indeed, should it. Thus, you are asked here to judge not whether or not these acts were committed, but to what extent they were justified.

> **Ruth Gordon and Garson Kanin,** *Adam's Rib* (published screenplay) 87 (1972) (1949)

11 *Adam Bonner* [played by Spencer Tracy, in prosecutor's summation to jury]: Now as to the character of this Doris Attinger. I'm afraid we know little about it—or about Doris Attinger. We have not seen Doris Attinger here. What we have seen has been a performance complete with costume and make-up. Carefully coached by her artful counsel, she has presented a gentle facade. A sweet face, crowned by a tenderly trimmed little bonnet. I found it difficult to be taken in, ladies and gentlemen, since *I* am the one who paid for the bonnet!

> **Ruth Gordon and Garson Kanin,** *Adam's Rib* (published screenplay) 92 (1972) (1949)

12 *Captain Queeg* [played by Humphrey Bogart, testifying at Queeg's court martial]: Ah, but the strawberries! That's—that's where I had them. They laughed and made jokes, but I proved beyond a shadow of a doubt, and with geometric logic, that a duplicate key to the wardroom icebox did exist. And I'd have produced that key if they hadn't have pulled the Caine out of action. I know now they were out to protect some fellow officer.

> Stanley Roberts, *The Caine Mutiny* (screenplay), 1954, quoted in Harry Haun, *The Movie Quote Book* 206 (1980)

13 *Juror # 8* [played by Henry Fonda]: I have a proposition to make to all of you. I want to call for a vote. I'd like you eleven men to vote by secret written ballot. I'll abstain. If there are still eleven votes for guilty I won't stand alone. We'll take a guilty verdict in to the judge right now. But if anyone votes not guilty we'll stay and talk this thing out.

> Reginald Rose, *Twelve Angry Men* (screenplay), 1957, in *Film Scripts Two* 156, 212–13 (George P. Garrett, O. B. Hardison, Jr., & Jane R. Gelfman eds. 1971)

14 *Juror # 3* [played by Lee J. Cobb]: You're talking about a matter of seconds here. Nobody can be that accurate!
Juror # 8 [played by Henry Fonda]: Well, I kind of think that testimony which could put a human being into the electric chair should be reasonably accurate.

> Reginald Rose, *Twelve Angry Men* (screenplay), 1957, in *Film Scripts Two* 156, 239 (George P. Garrett, O. B. Hardison, Jr., & Jane R. Gelfman eds. 1971)

15 *Juror # 3* [played by Lee J. Cobb]: What's the matter with you people? Every one of you knows this kid is guilty! He's got to burn! We're letting him slip through our fingers here!
Juror # 8 [played by Henry Fonda]: Slip through our fingers? Are you his executioner?
 # 3: I'm one of 'em.
 # 8: Maybe you'd like to pull the switch. . . .
 # 3: For this kid? You bet I'd like to pull the switch!
 # 8: I'm sorry for you. . . .
 # 3: Don't start with me now!
 # 8: What it must feel like to want to pull the switch!

> Reginald Rose, *Twelve Angry Men* (screenplay), 1957, in *Film Scripts Two* 156,

272–73 (George P. Garrett, O. B. Hardison, Jr., & Jane R. Gelfman eds. 1971)

16 *Juror # 8* [played by Henry Fonda]: Ever since we walked into this room you've been behaving like a self-appointed public avenger!
Juror # 3 [played by Lee J. Cobb]: I'm telling you now! Shut up!
 # 8: You want to see this boy die because you personally want it, not because of the facts.
 # 3: Shut up!
 # 8: You're a sadist. . . .

> Reginald Rose, *Twelve Angry Men* (screenplay), 1957, in *Film Scripts Two* 156, 273 (George P. Garrett, O. B. Hardison, Jr., & Jane R. Gelfman eds. 1971)

17 *Henry Drummond* [played by Spencer Tracy]: I say that you cannot administer a wicked law impartially. You can only destroy. You can only punish. I warn you that a wicked law, like cholera, destroys everyone it touches—its upholders as well as its defiers.

> Nathan E. Douglas and Harold J. Smith, *Inherit the Wind* (screenplay), 1960, quoted in Harry Haun, *The Movie Quote Book* 178 (1980)

18 *Frank Galvin* [played by Paul Newman, in attorney's summation to jury]: You know, so much of the time we're lost. We say "Please, God, tell us what is right. Tell us what's true. There is no justice. The rich win, the poor are powerless . . . " We become tired of hearing people lie. After a time we become dead. A little dead. We start thinking of ourselves as victims. And we *become* victims. And we *become* weak . . . and *doubt* ourselves, and doubt our *institutions* . . . and doubt our *beliefs* . . . we say for example, "The law is a sham—there *is* no law. . . . I was a fool for having *believed* that there was." But today *you* are the law. *You* are the law. . . . And not some *book* and not the *lawyers*, or the marble *statues* and the trappings of the court . . . all that they are is *symbols*. Of our desire to be just. . . . All that they are, in effect, is a *prayer*. . . . A fervent, and a frightened prayer. In my religion we say, "Act as if you had faith, and faith will be given to you." If. If we would have faith in *justice*, we must only believe in *ourselves*. And *act* with

justice. And I believe that there is justice in our hearts. Thank you.

> **David Mamet,** *The Verdict* (screenplay),
> 1982, quoted in *Actor's Book of Movie
> Monologues* 191–92 (Marisa Smith & Amy
> Schewel eds. 1986)

19 *Jim Garrison* [played by Kevin Costner]: We have all become Hamlets in our country—children of a slain father-leader whose killers still possess the throne. The ghost of John F. Kennedy confronts us with the secret murder at the heart of the American dream.

> **Oliver Stone and Zachary Sklar,** *JFK*
> (screenplay), 1991, in *JFK: The Book of the
> Film* 176 (1992)

COURTS

See also JUDGES; JUDICIARY; JURISDICTION; SUPREME COURT

1 Laws are a dead letter without courts to expound and define their true meaning and operation.

> **Alexander Hamilton,** *The Federalist* No. 22,
> at 1:140 (1788)

2 However true the fact may be, that the tribunals of the states will administer justice as impartially as those of the nation, to parties of every description, it is not less true that the constitution itself either entertains apprehensions on this subject, or views with such indulgence the possible fears and apprehensions of suitors, that it has established national tribunals for the decision of controversies between aliens and a citizen, or between citizens of different states.

> **John Marshall,** *Bank of the United States v.
> Deveaux,* 9 U.S. (5 Cranch) 61, 87 (1809)

3 If the legislatures of the several states may, at will, annul the judgments of the courts of the United States, and destroy the rights acquired under those judgments, the constitution itself becomes a solemn mockery; and the nation is deprived of the means of enforcing its laws by the instrumentality of its own tribunals.

> **John Marshall,** *United States v. Peters,* 9 U.S.
> (5 Cranch) 115, 136 (1809)

4 The judgment of a state court should have the same credit, validity, and effect, in every other court in the United States,

which it had in the state where it was pronounced, and that whatever pleas would be good to a suit thereon in such state, and none others, could be pleaded in any other court in the United States.

> **John Marshall,** *Hampton v. M'Connel,* 16
> U.S. (3 Wheat.) 234, 235 (1818)

5 And it requires no uncommon spirit of prophecy to foresee, that, whenever the liberties of this country are to be destroyed, the first step in the conspiracy will be to bring courts of justice into odium; and, by overawing the timid and removing the incorruptible, to break down the last barrier between the people and universal anarchy or despotism.

> **Joseph Story,** Address before Suffolk Bar,
> Boston, 4 Sept. 1821, in *Miscellaneous
> Writings of Joseph Story* 198, 229–30
> (William W. Story ed. 1852)

6 Courts are the mere instruments of the law, and can will nothing. . . . Judicial power is never exercised for the purpose of giving effect to the will of the Judge; always for the purpose of giving effect to the will of the Legislature; or, in other words, to the will of the law.

> **John Marshall,** *Osborn v. Bank of the United
> States,* 22 U.S. (9 Wheat.) 738, 866 (1824)

7 When they [the courts] are said to exercise a discretion, it is a mere legal discretion, a discretion to be exercised in discerning the course prescribed by law; and, when that is discerned, it is the duty of the Court to follow it.

> **John Marshall,** *Osborn v. Bank of the United
> States,* 22 U.S. (9 Wheat.) 738, 866 (1824)

8 The gravest and learnedest courts in this country shudder to face a new question, and will wait months and years for a case to occur that can be tortured into a precedent, and thus throw on a bolder party the *onus* of an initiative.

> **Ralph Waldo Emerson,** "Success," *Society
> and Solitude,* 1870, in *Complete Works of
> Ralph Waldo Emerson* 7:283, 292 (1904)

9 Every citizen is entitled to resort to all the courts of the country, and to invoke the protection which all the laws or all those courts may afford him. A man may not bar-

88

ter away his life or his freedom, or his substantial rights.

> Ward Hunt, *Insurance Co. v. Morse*, 87 U.S. (20 Wall.) 445, 451 (1874)

10 Probability cannot be made the measure of progress in the dispatch of business. As we all know, sometimes there is a drag and sometimes a run; and those having business to attend to in court must bear in mind that a wide variation from the average rate of progress may occur. Indeed, it is always probable that something improbable will happen.

> Logan E. Bleckley, *Warren v. Purtell*, 63 Ga. 428, 430 (1878)

11 Be that as it may, the courts of the United States are not required to give effect to judgments of this character when any right is claimed under them. Whilst they are not foreign tribunals in their relations to the State courts, they are tribunals of a different sovereignty, exercising a distinct and independent jurisdiction, and are bound to give to the judgments of the State courts only the same faith and credit which the courts of another State are bound to give to them.

Since the adoption of the Fourteenth Amendment to the Federal Constitution, the validity of such judgments may be directly questioned, and their enforcement in the State resisted on the ground that proceedings in a court of justice to determine the personal rights and obligations of parties over whom that court has no jurisdiction do not constitute due process of law.

> Stephen J. Field, *Pennoyer v. Neff*, 95 U.S. 714, 732–33 (1878)

12 Even righteous indignation and holy horror are impertinent intruders in an affair of justice. Emotional justice has no standing in the forum of right reason, and ought to have none anywhere. . . . With less emotional justice inside the courthouse, there would be less, perhaps none at all, on the outside. No greater good could be done than by withdrawing emotion as a force from the administration of justice.

> Logan E. Bleckley, "Emotional Justice," 9 *Georgia Bar Association Annual Report* 54, 61 (1892)

13 I [the judge] am not acquainted with the customs of other courts, and am not concerned to know what they are. I am responsible for this court, and I cannot conscientiously allow my judgment to be warped and my judicial liberty hampered by trying to conform to the caprices of other courts.

> Mark Twain, *Those Extraordinary Twins*, 1893–94, in *Writings of Mark Twain* 16:207, 259 (1929)

14 Naturally enough, in a country of innumerable courts the supply of judicial decisions and pronunciamentos is practically unlimited. They pour down from the bench, in truth, in such an appalling stream that no single man, nor even any combination or syndicate of men, is ever able to grapple with and master them. They are not only without number, but also without order. The decisions of one court give the lie, perhaps, to the decisions of all other courts; the jurisprudence of one State, or one group of States, is violently antagonistic, upon small matters or great, to the jurisprudence of all other States. It is impossible, in a word, to collate and classify these endless judgments and theories. They come too fast, and too many of them are unearthly and unique. As well try to count the teeth of a revolving buzz-saw.

> H. L. Mencken, "On Jurisprudence," Baltimore *Evening Sun*, 6 June 1910, quoted in *The Gist of Mencken* 442 (Mayo DuBasky ed. 1990)

15 Jurisprudence is eternally at it, conditioning, modifying, mutilating, coloring and obfuscating the laws. When those laws come from the legislative rolling mills they are rough and unlovely, like casts from an iron foundry. Large globules of asininity stand out upon their surfaces; their corners are sharp; they are sprinkled with sand from the mold; they need a lot of filing and polishing. It is the business of the higher courts to do that filing and polishing—to translate all new laws out of the loose, barbarous quasi-English of the legislative donkeys and into the refined and unintelligible jargon of jurisprudence—to fit them, in brief, with a thousand little details and offshoots, a million little sub-meanings and nicities, that their exact purport and bearing, in all conceivable emergencies, may be plain to the legal mind and entirely incom-

prehensible to the human mind. Upon such labors the learned judges expend their energies.

H. L. Mencken, "On Jurisprudence," Baltimore *Evening Sun*, 6 June 1910, quoted in *The Gist of Mencken* 442 (Mayo DuBasky ed. 1990)

16 I love judges, and I love Courts. They are my ideals, that typify on earth what we shall meet hereafter in heaven under a just God.

William Howard Taft, Campaign speech, Pocatello, Idaho, 1912, quoted in Max Lerner, "Constitution and Court as Symbols," 46 *Yale Law Journal* 1290, 1311 n.58 (1937)

17 A court of law, in the United States, is not a thing above and apart from the stream of everyday life, but a bobbing craft upon that stream, subject to infinite suctions and hazards. The least citizen is competent to criticize the highest judge, and he exercises that divine right whenever he is sufficiently attracted by the judge's doings. Nine times out of ten, of course, he is not attracted by them, and could not understand them if he were, but the tenth time he lifts his voice in hideous objurgation, and brave indeed is the rare Taney who disregards him. The result is that a case of any public interest whatever commonly resolves itself into a mixture of circus and camp meeting, with the newspapers in the dual role of clown and exhorter. Whether the defendant be a corporation accused of making money or an individual accused of murder, the actual weighing of the evidence is conducted outside the courtroom, and the verdict reached within is merely a weak echo and ratification of the circumambient *vox populi*.

H. L. Mencken, "The American," *The Smart Set*, June 1913, at 92

18 Frequently new conditions arise which those who were responsible for the written law could not have had in view, and to which existing common law principles have never before been applied, and it becomes necessary for the Court to make new applications of both. . . . [This] is not the exercise of legislative power . . . [but] the exercise of a sound judicial discretion in supplementing the provisions of constitu-

tions and laws and custom, which are necessarily incomplete or lacking in detail essential to their proper application, especially to new facts and situations constantly arising. . . . Indeed, it is one of the highest and most useful functions that courts have to perform in making a government of law practical and uniformly just.

William Howard Taft, *Popular Government* 222–23 (1913)

19 Courtroom—A place where Jesus Christ and Judas Iscariot would be equals, with the betting odds in favor of Judas.

H. L. Mencken, "Sententiae," 1916, in *A Mencken Chrestomathy* 616, 623 (1949)

20 The courts are not helped as they could and ought to be in the adaptation of law to justice. The reason they are not helped is because there is no one whose business it is to give warning that help is needed. . . . We must have a courier who will carry the tidings of distress. . . . To-day courts and legislature work in separation and aloofness. The penalty is paid both in the wasted effort of production and in the lowered quality of the product. On the one side, the judges, left to fight against anachronism and injustice by the methods of judge-made law, are distracted by the conflicting promptings of justice and logic, of consistency and mercy, and the output of their labors bears the tokens of the strain. On the other side, the legislature, informed only casually and intermittently of the needs and problems of the courts, without expert or responsible or disinterested or systematic advice as to the workings of one rule or another, patches the fabric here and there, and mars often when it would mend. Legislature and courts move on in proud and silent isolation. Some agency must be found to mediate between them.

Benjamin N. Cardozo, "A Ministry of Justice," 35 *Harvard Law Review* 113, 113–14 (1921)

21 This Court has stated many times the deference due to the understanding of the local courts upon matters of purely local concern . . . This is especially true in dealing with the decisions of a Court inheriting and brought up in a different system from that which prevails here. When we contem-

plate such a system from the outside it seems like a wall of stone, every part even with all the others, except so far as our own local education may lead us to see subordinations to which we are accustomed. But to one brought up within it, varying emphasis, tacit assumptions, unwritten practices, a thousand influences gained only from life, may give to the different parts wholly new values that logic and grammar never could have got from the books.

Oliver Wendell Holmes, Jr., *Diaz v. Gonzalez*, 261 U.S. 102, 105-06 (1923)

22 Some of the errors of courts have their origin in imperfect knowledge of the economic and social consequences of a decision, or of the economic and social needs to which a decision will respond. In the complexities of modern life there is a constantly increasing need for resort by the judges to some fact-finding agency which will substitute exact knowledge of factual conditions for conjecture and impression.

Benjamin N. Cardozo, *The Growth of the Law* 116–17 (1924)

23 The prevailing doctrine has been accepted upon a subtle fallacy that never has been analyzed. If I am right the fallacy has resulted in an unconstitutional assumption of powers by Courts of the United States which no lapse of time or respectable array of opinion should make us hesitate to correct. Therefore, I think it proper to state what I think the fallacy is.—The often repeated proposition of this and the lower Courts is that the parties are entitled to an independent judgment on matters of general law.

Oliver Wendell Holmes, Jr., *Black & White Taxicab Co. v. Brown & Yellow Taxicab Co.*, 276 U.S. 518, 532–33 (1928) (dissenting)

24 The "judicial power" of Article III of the Constitution is the power of the federal government, and not of any inferior tribunal.

Louis D. Brandeis, *Crowell v. Benson*, 285 U.S. 22, 86 (1932) (dissenting)

25 Proceedings in court should be conducted with fitting dignity and decorum. The taking of photographs in the court room, during sessions of the court or recesses between sessions, and the broadcasting of court proceedings are calculated to detract from the essential dignity of the proceedings, degrade the court and create misconceptions with respect thereto in the mind of the public and should not be permitted.

Canons of Judicial Ethics Canon 35 (1937)

26 Freedom of speech and of the press are essential to the enlightenment of a free people and in restraining those who wield power. Particularly should this freedom be employed in comment upon the work of courts, who are without many influences ordinarily making for humor and humility, twin antidotes to the corrosion of power.

Felix Frankfurter, *Bridges v. California*, 314 U.S. 252, 284 (1941) (dissenting)

27 The Court, moreover, is almost never a really contemporary institution. The operation of life tenure in the judicial department, as against elections at short intervals of the Congress, usually keeps the average viewpoint of the two institutions a generation apart. The judiciary is thus the check of a preceding generation on the present one; a check of conservative legal philosophy upon a dynamic people, and nearly always the check of a rejected regime on the one in being.

Robert H. Jackson, *The Struggle for Judicial Supremacy* 315 (1941)

28 This much I think I do know—that a society so riven that the spirit of moderation is gone, no court *can* save; that a society where that spirit flourishes, no court *need* save; that in a society which evades its responsibility by thrusting upon the courts the nurture of that spirit, that spirit in the end will perish.

Learned Hand, "The Contribution of an Independent Judiciary to Civilization" (speech), Boston, 21 Nov. 1942, in *The Spirit of Liberty* 155, 164 (Irving Dilliard ed., 2d ed. 1953)
See also LIBERTY 6

29 Nor is it desirable for a lower court to embrace the exhilarating opportunity of anticipating a doctrine which may be in the womb of time, but whose birth is distant; on the contrary I conceive that the measure

of its duty is to divine, as best it can, what would be the event of an appeal in the case before it.

> **Learned Hand,** *Spector Motor Service v. Walsh,* 139 F.2d 809, 823 (2d Cir. 1944) (dissenting)

30 Above all, the courthouse: the center, the focus, the hub; sitting looming in the center of the county's circumference like a single cloud in its ring of horizon, laying its vast shadow to the uttermost rim of horizon; musing, brooding, symbolic and ponderable, tall as cloud, solid as rock, dominating all: protector of the weak, judiciate and curb of the passions and lusts, repository and guardian of the aspirations and the hopes.

> **William Faulkner,** *Requiem for a Nun* 40 (1951)

31 But how are competing interests to be assessed? Since they are not subject to quantitive ascertainment, the issue necessarily resolves itself into asking, who is to make the adjustment?—who is to balance the relevant factors and ascertain which interest is in the circumstances to prevail? Full responsibility for the choice cannot be given to the courts. Courts are not representative bodies. They are not designed to be a good reflex of a democratic society. Their judgment is best informed, and therefore most dependable, within narrow limits. Their essential quality is detachment, founded on independence.

> **Felix Frankfurter,** *Dennis v. United States,* 341 U.S. 494, 525 (1951) (concurring)

32 One utterance of [Oliver Cromwell] . . . has always hung in my mind. It was just before the Battle of Dunbar; he beat the Scots in the end . . . but he wrote them before the battle, trying to get them to accept a reasonable composition. These were his words: "I beseech ye in the bowels of Christ, think ye may be mistaken."* I should like to have that written over the portals of every church, every school, and every court house, and, may I say, of every legislative body in the United States. I

---

* I beseech you, in the bowels of Christ, think it possible you may be mistaken. —**Oliver Cromwell,** Letter to General Assembly of the Kirk of Scotland, 3 Aug. 1650, in *Writings and Speeches of Oliver Cromwell* 2:303 (Wilbur C. Abbott ed. 1939)

should like to have every court begin, "I beseech ye in the bowels of Christ, think that we may be mistaken."

> **Learned Hand,** Testimony before Senate committee, 28 June 1951, in *The Spirit of Liberty* 229–30 (Irving Dilliard ed., 2d ed. 1953)

33 The penalty for laughing in the courtroom is six months in jail: if it were not for this penalty, the jury would never hear the evidence.

> **H. L. Mencken,** quoted in Andrew and Jonathan Roth, *Devil's Advocates* 127 (1989)

34 There are so many questions one could put to the Court, to any Court. But would one get a response? Can the Court of the Land ever be put in question? I am afraid not. The judicial body is a sacrosanct body. This is unfortunate, as I see it, for when issues of grave import arise the last court of reference, in my opinion, should be the public. When justice is at stake responsibility cannot be shifted to an elect few without injustice resulting. No Court could function if it did not follow the steel rails of precedent, taboo, and prejudice.

> **Henry Miller,** Letter to Trygve Hirsch, 27 Feb. 1959, in *The Henry Miller Reader* 378 (Lawrence Durrell ed. 1959)

35 But there is one way in this country in which all men are created equal—there is one human institution that makes a pauper the equal of a Rockefeller, the stupid man the equal of an Einstein, and the ignorant man the equal of any college president. That institution, gentlemen, is a court. It can be the Supreme Court of the United States or the humblest J.P. court in the land, or this honorable court which you serve. Our courts have their faults, as does any human institution, but in this country our courts are the great levelers, and in our courts all men are created equal.

> **Harper Lee,** *To Kill a Mockingbird* 218 (1960)

36 There is not under our Constitution a judicial remedy for every political mischief, for every undesirable exercise of legislative power. The Framers carefully and with deliberate forethought refused so to enthrone the judiciary. In this situation, as in others of like nature, appeal for relief does not be-

long here. Appeal must be to an informed, civically militant electorate.

Felix Frankfurter, *Baker v. Carr,* 369 U.S. 186, 270 (1962) (dissenting)

37 Do not waste your time looking up the law in advance, because you can find some Federal district court that will sustain any proposition you make.

Sam J. Ervin, Jr., quoted in Alan F. Pater and Jason R. Pater, *What They Said in 1973,* at 225 (1974)

38 My view always has been that anyone whose life, liberty or property was threatened or impaired by any branch of government—whether the President or one of his agencies, or Congress, or the courts (or any counterpart in a state regime)—had a justiciable controversy and could properly repair to a judicial tribunal for vindication of his rights. . . . Courts sit to determine questions on stormy as well as on calm days. The Constitution is the measure of their duty.

William O. Douglas, *The Court Years, 1939– 1975,* at 55–56 (1980)

39 About three years ago I was walking under the open windows of the conference room of our Supreme Court of Appeals when suddenly out of those olympian heights above and beyond the possibility of human error there came hurtling this hard wood cube which bounced off my head. I picked it up and knew at once that I ought to take it back, and am subject to grave criticism for failing to do so. But the unique features of this hard wood cube intrigued and tempted me. On its six sides were inscriptions which explained to us many things hitherto inexplicable: On one side, "Affirmed," on the next side, "Modified and Affirmed," then, "Affirmed in Part, Reversed in Part." On the other three sides were first, "Appeal Dismissed," then "Reversed and Final Judgment," and finally "Reversed and Remanded."

Now we can understand how the "family purpose doctrine" appeared, reappeared, and disappeared. Now we can understand the most recent statement of the law of the "last clear chance." It also explains how identical shares of stock of the Pittston Co. had entirely different values at the same instant.

Thomas C. Fletcher, quoted in Jacob A. Stein, *Legal Spectator* 218–19 (1981)

40 But courts do not sit to compensate the luckless; this is not Sherwood Forest.

Alex Kozinski, *Kern v. Levolor Lorentzen, Inc.,* 899 F.2d 772, 798 (9th Cir. 1990) (dissenting)

CRIME

See also CRIMINAL; CRIMINAL LAW; CRIMINAL PROCEDURE; ILLEGALITY; INSANITY; LAW ENFORCEMENT; MURDER; PRISON

1 Our age and history, for these thousand years, has not been the history of kindness, but of selfishness. Our distrust is very expensive. The money we spend for courts and prisons is very ill laid out. We make by distrust the thief, and burglar, and incendiary, and by our court and jail we keep him so.

Ralph Waldo Emerson, "Man the Reformer," 1841, in *Collected Works of Ralph Waldo Emerson* 1:141, 158 (Alfred R. Ferguson ed. 1971)

2 No man who has followed my advice has ever committed a crime. Crime is a technical word. It is the law's name for certain acts which it is pleased to define and punish with a penalty. . . . What the law permits is right, else it would prohibit it. What the law prohibits is wrong, because it punishes it.*

Melville D. Post, "The Grazier," in *The Man of Last Resort* 223, 252–53 (1897)

3 EXONERATE, *v.t.* To show that from a series of vices and crimes some particular crime or vice was accidentally omitted.

Ambrose Bierce, *The Enlarged Devil's Dictionary* 89 (Ernest J. Hopkins ed. 1967)

4 FAULT, *n.* One of my offenses, as distinguished from one of yours, the latter being crimes.

Ambrose Bierce, *The Enlarged Devil's Dictionary* 92 (Ernest J. Hopkins ed. 1967)

5 For de little stealin' dey gits you in jail soon or late. For de big stealin' dey makes you Emperor and puts you in de Hall o' Fame when you croaks.

Eugene O'Neill, *The Emperor Jones,* 1920, in *Eugene O'Neill: Complete Plays 1913–1920,* at 1030, 1035 (1988)

---

* This is the credo of Post's fictional detective, the unscrupulous lawyer Randolph Mason.

6 Each act, criminal or otherwise, follows a cause; . . . given the same conditions the same result will follow forever and ever.

　　Clarence S. Darrow, *Crime: Its Cause and Treatment* 36 (1922)

7 The professional prosecutor is continually surprised at the insignificant amount of crime compared with the extraordinary scope of criminal opportunity, so that his conviction grows that the world is astonishingly honest when one considers the unlikelihood that any specific offense will be discovered.

　　Arthur Train, *My Day in Court* 81 (1939)

8 Violations of law by persons in the upper socio-economic class are, for convenience, called "white collar crimes." This concept is not intended to be definitive, but merely to call attention to crimes which are not ordinarily included within the scope of criminology. White collar crime may be defined approximately as a crime committed by a person of respectability and high social status in the course of his occupation. Consequently, it excludes many crimes of the upper class, such as most of their cases of murder, adultery, and intoxication, since these are not customarily a part of their occupational procedures. Also, it excludes the confidence games of wealthy members of the underworld, since they are not persons of respectability and high social status.

　　Edwin H. Sutherland, *White Collar Crime* 9 (1949)

9 Crime is a sociopolitical artifact, not a natural phenomenon. We can have as much or as little crime as we please, depending on what we choose to count as criminal.

　　Herbert L. Packer, *The Limits of the Criminal Sanction* 364 (1968)

10 Kramer had reached that low point in the life of an assistant district attorney in the Bronx when he is assailed by Doubts. Every year forty thousand people, forty thousand incompetents, dimwits, alcoholics, psychopaths, knockabouts, good souls driven to some terrible terminal anger, and people who could only be described as stone evil, were arrested in the Bronx. Seven thousand of them were indicted and arraigned, and then they entered the maw of the criminal justice system. . . . And to what end? The same stupid, dismal, pathetic, horrifying crimes were committed day in and day out, all the same. What was accomplished by assistant D.A.'s, by any of them, through all this relentless stirring of the muck? The Bronx crumbled and decayed a little more, and a little more blood dried in the cracks.

　　Tom Wolfe, *The Bonfire of the Vanities* 41 (1987)

11 When guns are outlawed, only outlaws will have guns.

　　Slogan of opponents of gun control

12 Guns don't kill people, people kill people.

　　Slogan of opponents of gun control

13 Guns don't die, people die.

　　Slogan of supporters of gun control

CRIMINAL

See also CRIME; CRIMINAL LAW

1 In the court of law the judge sits over the culprit, but in the court of life in the same hour the judge also stands as culprit before a true tribunal. Every judge is a culprit, every law an abuse.

　　Ralph Waldo Emerson, "The Sovereignty of Ethics," 1878, in *Collected Works of Ralph Waldo Emerson* 10:181, 187 (1904)

2 We enact many laws that manufacture criminals, and then a few that punish them.

　　Benjamin R. Tucker, *Instead of a Book* 27 (1897)

3 I really do not in the least believe in crime. There is no such thing as a crime as the word is generally understood. I do not believe there is any sort of distinction between the real moral conditions of the people in and out of jail. One is just as good as the other. . . . I do not believe that people are in jail because they deserve to be. They are in jail simply because they cannot avoid it on account of circumstances which are entirely beyond their control and for which they are in no way responsible.

　　Clarence S. Darrow, Address to prisoners in Cook County Jail, 1902, in *Attorney for the Damned* 3, 3–4 (Arthur Weinberg ed. 1957)

4 If every man and woman and child in the world had a chance to make a decent, fair, honest living, there would be no jails and no lawyers and no courts.

    Clarence S. Darrow, Address to prisoners in Cook County Jail, 1902, in *Attorney for the Damned* 3, 9 (Arthur Weinberg ed. 1957)

5 Crime is unsuccessful defiance of the existing order of things. Once rebellion rises to the dignity of revolution, murder becomes execution and the murderers become belligerents. Therefore, as all real progress involves a change in or defiance of existing law, those who advocate progress are essentially criminally minded, and if they attempt to secure progress by openly refusing to obey the law they are actual criminals. Then if they prevail, and from being in the minority come into power, they are taken out of jail, banquets are given in their honor, and they are called patriots and heroes. Hence the close connection between crime and progress.

    Arthur Train, "The Hepplewhite Tramp," in *Tutt and Mr. Tutt* 234, 243–44 (1920)

6 A rule protective of law-abiding citizens is not apt to flourish where its advocates are usually criminals.

    William O. Douglas, *Draper v. United States*, 358 U.S. 307, 314 (1959) (dissenting)

7 Yes, as through this world I've rambled
I've seen lots of funny men,
Some will rob you with a six gun,
And some with a fountain pen.
But as through your life you'll travel,
Wherever you may roam,
You won't never see no outlaw
Drive a family from their home.

    Woody Guthrie, "Pretty Boy Floyd" (song), in Alan Lomax, *The Folk Songs of North America* 437 (1960)

8 The trouble with Eichmann was precisely that so many were like him, and that the many were neither perverted nor sadistic, that they were, and still are, terribly and terrifyingly normal. From the viewpoint of our legal institutions and of our moral standards of judgment, this normality was much more terrifying than all the atrocities put together, for it implied—as had been said at Nuremberg over and over again by the defendants and their counsels—that this new type of criminal, who is in actual

fact *hostis generis humani*, commits his crimes under circumstances that make it well-nigh impossible for him to know or to feel that he is doing wrong.

    Hannah Arendt, *Eichmann in Jerusalem* 276 (rev. ed. 1964)

CRIMINAL JUSTICE

See also CRIMINAL LAW; LAW ENFORCEMENT

1 If every policeman, every prosecutor, every court, and every post-sentence agency performed his or its responsibility in strict accordance with rules of law, precisely and narrowly laid down, the criminal law would be ordered but intolerable. Living would be a sterile compliance with soul-killing rules and taboos. By comparison, a primitive tribal society would seem free, indeed.

    Charles D. Breitel, "Controls in Criminal Law Enforcement," 27 *University of Chicago Law Review* 427, 427 (1960)

2 It is commonly assumed that these three components—law enforcement (police, sheriffs, marshals), the judicial process (judges, prosecutors, defense lawyers) and corrections (prison officials, probation and parole officers)—add up to a "system" of criminal justice. A system implies some unity of purpose and organized interrelationship among component parts. In the typical American city and state, and under federal jurisdiction as well, no such relationship exists. There is, instead, a reasonably well-defined criminal *process*, a continuum through which each accused offender may pass: from the hands of the police, to the jurisdiction of the courts, behind the walls of a prison, then back onto the street. The inefficiency, fall-out and failure of purpose during this process is notorious.

    National Commission on the Causes and Prevention of Violence, *To Establish Justice, To Insure Domestic Tranquility* 149 (1969)

3 Killian looked out over the lobby of 100 Centre Street. Then he turned back to Sherman. "You ever hear of the Favor Bank?"
"The Favor Bank? No."
"Well, everything in this building, everything in the criminal justice system in New York ... operates on favors. Everybody

does favors for everybody else. Every chance they get, they make deposits in the Favor Bank. . . . A deposit in the Favor Bank is not *quid pro quo*. It's saving up for a rainy day. In criminal law there's a lotta gray areas, and you gotta operate in 'em, but if you make a mistake, you can be in a whole lotta trouble, and you're gonna need a whole lotta help in a hurry.

   Tom Wolfe, *The Bonfire of the Vanities* 400–01 (1987)

CRIMINAL LAW

See also CRIME; CRIMINAL; CRIMINAL JUSTICE; CRIMINAL PROCEDURE; GUILT; INNOCENCE; LAW ENFORCEMENT

1 No Person, House-holder or other, shall spend his time idly and unprofitably, under pain of such punishment as the Court or Assistants shall think meet to inflict: And the Select Men of the several Towns are hereby required to give in a List of the Names of such as mispend their time, whether House-holders or others; and of all single persons that live from under Family Government, or will not be Governed by their Parents or Masters where they live, that so the Court may proceed with them as the case may require.

   The Book of the General Laws of the Inhabitants of the Jurisdiction of New-Plimouth 27, 1672, in *The Laws of the Pilgrims* (1977)

2 There is a very wide difference, in reason and policy, between the mode of proceeding on the irregular conduct of scattered individuals, or even of bands of men, who disturb order within the state, and the civil dissensions which may, from time to time, on great questions, agitate the several communities which compose a great empire. It looks to me to be narrow and pedantic to apply the ordinary ideas of criminal justice to this great public contest. I do not know the method of drawing up an indictment against an whole people.

   Edmund Burke, "On Moving His Resolutions for Conciliation with the Colonies," 22 Mar. 1775, in *Works of the Right Honorable Edmund Burke* 2:101, 136 (1866)

3 If it be justifiable homicide to shoot down a burglar who forcibly invades your house, with intent to commit a felony, as it undoubtedly is, and yet if you fail to kill him, you subject yourself to the penalty of the Act of 1856,* the title of the statute should be amended. It should be "An Act to encourage good shooting."

   Joseph H. Lumpkin, *Biggs v. State,* 29 Ga. 723, 727 (1860)

4 The object of the indictment is, first, to furnish the accused with such a description of the charge against him as will enable him to make his defense, and avail himself of his conviction or acquittal for protection against a further prosecution for the same cause; and, second, to inform the court of the facts alleged, so that it may decide whether they are sufficient in law to support a conviction, if one should be had. For this, facts are to be stated, not conclusions of law alone. A crime is made up of acts and intent; and these must be set forth in the indictment, with reasonable particularity of time, place and circumstances.

   Morrison R. Waite, *United States v. Cruikshank,* 92 U.S. 542, 558 (1875)

5 Every man should be able to know with certainty when he is committing a crime. . . . It would certainly be dangerous if the legislature could set a net large enough to catch all possible offenders and leave it to the courts to step inside and say who could be rightfully detained, and who should be set at large.

   Morrison R. Waite, *United States v. Reese,* 92 U.S. 214, 220–21 (1876)

6 The true explanation of the rule is the same as that which accounts for the law's indifference to a man's particular temperament, faculties, and so forth. Public policy sacrifices the individual to the general good. It is desirable that the burden of all should be equal, but it is still more desirable to put an end to robbery and murder.

   Oliver Wendell Holmes, Jr., *The Common Law* 48 (1881)

---

* The act referred to provided that any person who shot another except in self-defense would be punished. A husband committed a shooting in defense of his wife and was indicted for assault with intent to murder. The trial judge charged that, although the shooting might be justifiable homicide if it resulted in death, it would be a crime if death did not ensue.

7 For the most part, the purpose of the criminal law is only to induce external conformity to rule.

    Oliver Wendell Holmes, Jr., *The Common Law* 49 (1881)

8 ARREST, *v.t.* Formally to detain one accused of unusualness.

    Ambrose Bierce, *The Devil's Dictionary* 26 (1911)

9 Detached reflection cannot be demanded in the presence of an uplifted knife. Therefore in this Court, at least, it is not a condition of immunity that one in that situation should pause to consider whether a reasonable man might not think it possible to fly with safety or to disable his assailant rather than to kill him.

    Oliver Wendell Holmes, Jr., *Brown v. United States,* 256 U.S. 335, 343 (1921)

10 The first duties of the officers of the law are to prevent, not to punish crime. It is not their duty to incite to and create crime for the sole purpose of prosecuting and punishing it. Here the evidence strongly tends to prove, if it does not conclusively do so, that their first and chief endeavor was to cause, to create, crime in order to punish it, and it is unconscionable, contrary to public policy, and to the established law of the land.

    Walter H. Sanborn, *Butts v. United States,* 273 F. 35, 38 (8th Cir. 1921)

11 Although it is not likely that a criminal will carefully consider the text of the law before he murders or steals, it is reasonable that a fair warning should be given to the world in lanaguage that the common world will understand, of what the law intends to do if a certain line is passed. To make the warning fair, so far as possible the line should be clear.

    Oliver Wendell Holmes, Jr., *McBoyle v. United States,* 283 U.S. 25, 27 (1931)

12 But justice, though due to the accused, is due to the accuser also. The concept of fairness must not be strained till it is narrowed to a filament. We are to keep the balance true. . . . There is danger that the criminal law will be brought into contempt—that discredit will even touch the great immunities assured by the Fourteenth Amendment—if gossamer possibilities of prejudice to a defendant are to nullify a sentence pronounced by a court of competent jurisdiction in obedience to local law, and set the guilty free.

    Benjamin N. Cardozo, *Snyder v. Massachusetts,* 291 U.S. 97, 122 (1934)

13 It will be observed that all these definitions [of aiding and abetting] have nothing whatever to do with the probability that the forbidden result would follow upon the accessory's conduct; and that they all demand that he in some sort associate himself with the venture, that he participate in it as in something that he wishes to bring about, that he seek by his action to make it succeed.

    Learned Hand, *United States v. Peoni,* 100 F.2d 401, 402 (2d Cir. 1938)

14 No one may be required at peril of life, liberty or property to speculate as to the meaning of penal statutes. All are entitled to be informed as to what the State commands or forbids.

    Pierce Butler, *Lanzetta v. New Jersey,* 306 U.S. 451, 453 (1939)

15 The criminal law represents the pathology of civilization.

    Morris R. Cohen, "Moral Aspects of the Criminal Law," 49 *Yale Law Journal* 987, 1025 (1940)

16 Law, including the criminal law, must in a free society be judged ultimately on the basis of its success in promoting human autonomy and the capacity for individual human growth and development. The prevention of crime is an essential aspect of the environmental protection required if autonomy is to flourish. It is, however, a negative aspect and one which, pursued with single-minded zeal, may end up creating an environment in which all are safe but none is free.

    Herbert L. Packer, *The Limits of the Criminal Sanction* 65 (1968)

17 The idea of free will in relation to conduct is not, in the legal system, a statement of fact, but rather a value preference having very little to do with the metaphysics of determinism or free will. . . . Very simply, the law treats man's conduct as autonomous

and willed, not because it is, but because it is desirable to proceed as if it were.

Herbert L. Packer, *The Limits of the Criminal Sanction* 74–75 (1968)

18 The use of deadly force to prevent the escape of all felony suspects, whatever the circumstances, is constitutionally unreasonable. It is not better that all felony suspects die than that they escape.

Byron R. White, *Tennessee v. Garner,* 471 U.S. 1, 11 (1985)

19 As many commentators have pointed out, the definition of a "pattern of racketeering activity" differs from the other provisions in § 1961 in that it states that a pattern *"requires* at least two acts of racketeering activity," § 1961(5) (emphasis added), not that it "means" two such acts. The implication is that while two acts are necessary, they may not be sufficient. Indeed, in common parlance two of anything do not generally form a "pattern." The legislative history supports the view that two isolated acts of racketeering activity do not constitute a pattern. As the Senate Report explained: "The target of [RICO] is thus not sporadic activity. The infiltration of legitimate business normally requires more than one 'racketeering activity' and the threat of continuing activity to be effective. It is this factor of *continuity plus relationship* which combines to produce a pattern." S. Rep. No. 91–617, p. 158 (1969) (emphasis added).

Byron R. White, *Sedima S.P.R.L. v. IMREX Co.,* 473 U.S. 479, 496 n.14 (1985)

20 The system of criminal justice contemplated by the Due Process Clause—indeed, by all of the criminal justice guarantees of the Bill of Rights—is a system of announcing in statutes of adequate clarity what conduct is prohibited and then invoking the penalties of the law against those who have committed crimes. The liberty protected under that system is premised on the accountability of free men and women for what they have done, not for what they may do. The Due Process Clause reflects the constitutional imperative that incarceration to protect society from criminals may be accomplished only as punishment of those convicted for past crimes and not as

regulation of those feared likely to commit future crimes.

Jon O. Newman, *United States v. Melandez-Carrion,* 790 F.2d 984, 1001 (2d Cir. 1986)

CRIMINAL PROCEDURE

See also CONFESSIONS; CRIMINAL LAW; DOUBLE JEOPARDY; DUE PROCESS; PROCEDURE; PROSECUTION; SEARCHES AND SEIZURES

1 That all Criminals shall have the same Privileges of Witnesses and Council as their Prosecutors.

Pennsylvania Charter of Privileges of 1701, § 5, in *Federal and State Constitutions* 5:3076, 3079 (Francis N. Thorpe ed. 1909)

2 The next great right is that of trial by jury. This provides that neither life, liberty nor property, can be taken from the possessor, until twelve of his unexceptionable countrymen and peers of his vicinage . . . shall pass their sentence upon oath against him. . . .

Another right relates merely to the liberty of the person. If a subject is seized and imprisoned, tho' by order of Government, he may, by virtue of this right, immediately obtain a writ, termed a Habeas Corpus, from a Judge . . . and thereupon procure any illegal restraint to be quickly enquired into and redressed.

Address from the Continental Congress to the inhabitants of Quebec, 26 Oct. 1774, in *Journals of the Continental Congress* 1:105, 107 (Worthington C. Ford ed. 1904)

3 That in all prosecutions for criminal offences, every man hath a right to be informed of the accusation against him, to be allowed counsel, to be confronted with the accusers or witnesses, to examine evidence on oath in his favour, and to a speedy trial by an impartial jury, without whose unanimous consent he ought not to be found guilty.

Delaware Declaration of Rights of 1776, § 14, in *Sources of Our Liberties* 338, 339 (Richard L. Perry & John C. Cooper eds. 1959)

4 That in all capital or criminal prosecutions a man hath a right to demand the cause and nature of his accusation, to be confronted with the accusers and witnesses, to call for evidence in his favor, and to a

speedy trial by an impartial jury of twelve men of his vicinage, without whose unanimous consent he cannot be found guilty; nor can he be compelled to give evidence against himself; that no man be deprived of his liberty, except by the law of the land or the judgment of his peers.

Virginia Declaration of Rights of 1776, § 8, in *Federal and State Constitutions* 7:3812, 3813 (Francis N. Thorpe ed. 1909)

5 The privilege and benefit of the writ of *habeas corpus* shall be enjoyed in this commonwealth, in the most free, easy, cheap, expeditious, and ample manner; and shall not be suspended by the legislature, except upon the most urgent and pressing occasions, and for a limited time, not exceeding twelve months.

Massachusetts Constitution of 1780, pt. 2, ch. 6, art. 7, in *Federal and State Constitutions* 3:1888, 1910 (Francis N. Thorpe ed. 1909)

6 [Describing a riot in New York over graverobbing:] The people of more reflection, thinking it more dangerous that even a guilty person should be punished without the forms of law than that he should escape, armed themselves and went to protect the physician.

Thomas Jefferson, Letter to William Carmichael, 3 June 1788, in *Papers of Thomas Jefferson* 13:233 (Julian P. Boyd ed. 1956)

7 A valid affidavit being wanting, the bottom is knocked out of the case. It is a tub with only staves and hoops, and will hold nothing.

Logan E. Bleckley, *Scroggins v. State*, 55 Ga. 380, 382 (1875)

8 The primary object of the [Confrontation Clause of the Sixth Amendment] . . . was to prevent depositions or *ex parte* affidavits, such as were sometimes admitted in civil cases, being used against the prisoner in lieu of a personal examination and crossexamination of the witness in which the accused has an opportunity, not only of testing the recollection and sifting the conscience of the witness, but of compelling him to stand face to face with the jury in order that they may look at him, and judge by his demeanor upon the stand and the

manner in which he gives his testimony whether he is worthy of belief.

Henry B. Brown, *Mattox v. United States*, 156 U.S. 237, 242–43 (1895)

9 Centuries ago it was especially needful to throw every safeguard round the accused. The danger then was lest he be wronged by the State. The danger is now exactly the reverse. Our laws and customs tell immensely in favor of the criminal and against the interests of the public he has wronged.

Theodore Roosevelt, Fifth Annual Message, 5 Dec. 1905, in *Works of Theodore Roosevelt* 17:365–66 (Hermann Hagedorn ed. 1925)

10 HABEAS CORPUS. A writ by which a man may be taken out of jail when confined for the wrong crime.

Ambrose Bierce, *The Devil's Dictionary* 126 (1911)

11 *Habeas corpus* cuts through all forms and goes to the very tissue of the structure. It comes in from the outside, not in subordination to the proceedings, and although every form may have been preserved opens the inquiry whether they have been more than an empty shell. . . . Whatever disagreement there may be as to the scope of the phrase "due process of law," there can be no doubt that it embraces the fundamental conception of a fair trial, with opportunity to be heard. Mob law does not become due process of law by securing the assent of a terrorized jury. . . . it is our duty . . . to declare lynch law as little valid when practiced by a regularly drawn jury as when administered by one elected by a mob intent on death.

Oliver Wendell Holmes, Jr., *Frank v. Mangum*, 237 U.S. 309, 346, 347, 350 (1915) (dissenting)

12 Our procedure has been always haunted by the ghost of the innocent man convicted. It is an unreal dream. What we need to fear is the archaic formalism and the watery sentiment that obstructs, delays, and defeats the prosecution of crime.

Learned Hand, *United States v. Garsson*, 291 F. 646, 649 (S.D.N.Y. 1923)

13 Under our criminal procedure the accused has every advantage. While the prosecution is held rigidly to the charge, he need not

disclose the barest outline of his defense. He is immune from question or comment on his silence; he cannot be convicted when there is the least fair doubt in the minds of any one of the twelve. Why in addition he should in advance have the whole evidence against him to pick over at his leisure, and make his defense, fairly or foully, I have never been able to see.

Learned Hand, *United States v. Garsson,* 291 F. 646, 649 (S.D.N.Y. 1923)

14 Every procedure which would offer a possible temptation to the average man as a judge to forget the burden of proof required to convict the defendant, or which might lead him not to hold the balance nice, clear and true between the State and the accused, denies the latter due process of law.

William Howard Taft, *Tumey v. Ohio,* 273 U.S. 510, 532 (1927)

15 During perhaps the most critical period of the proceedings against these defendants, that is to say, from the time of their arraignment until the beginning of their trial, when consultation, thoroughgoing investigation and preparation were vitally important, the defendants did not have the aid of counsel in any real sense, although they were as much entitled to such aid during that period as at the trial itself.

George Sutherland, *Powell v. Alabama,* 287 U.S. 45, 57 (1932)

16 The prompt disposition of criminal cases is to be commended and encouraged. But in reaching that result a defendant, charged with a serious crime, must not be stripped of his right to have sufficient time to advise with counsel and prepare his defense. To do that is not to proceed promptly in the calm spirit of regulated justice but to go forward with the haste of the mob.

George Sutherland, *Powell v. Alabama,* 287 U.S. 45, 59 (1932)

17 The right to be heard would be, in many cases, of little avail if it did not comprehend the right to be heard by counsel. Even the intelligent and educated layman has small and sometimes no skill in the science of law. If charged with crime, he is incapable, generally, of determining for himself whether the indictment is good or bad. He

is unfamiliar with the rules of evidence. Left without the aid of counsel he may be put on trial without a proper charge, and convicted upon incompetent evidence, or evidence irrelevant to the issue or otherwise inadmissible. He lacks both the skill and knowledge adequately to prepare his defense, even though he have a perfect one. He requires the guiding hand of counsel at every step in the proceedings against him. Without it, though he be not guilty, he faces the danger of conviction because he does not know how to establish his innocence. If that be true of men of intelligence, how much more true is it of the ignorant and illiterate, or those of feeble intellect.

George Sutherland, *Powell v. Alabama,* 287 U.S. 45, 68–69 (1932)

18 In a capital case, where the defendent is unable to employ counsel, and is incapable adequately of making his own defense because of ignorance, feeble mindedness, illiteracy, or the like, it is the duty of the court, whether requested or not, to assign counsel for him as a necessary requisite of due process of law.

George Sutherland, *Powell v. Alabama,* 287 U.S. 45, 71 (1932)

19 A waiver is ordinarily an intentional relinquishment or abandonment of a known right or privilege. The determination of whether there has been an intelligent waiver of the right to counsel must depend, in each case, upon the particular facts and circumstances surrounding that case, including the background, experience, and conduct of the accused.

Hugo L. Black, *Johnson v. Zerbst,* 304 U.S. 458, 464 (1938)

20 As applied to a criminal trial, denial of due process is the failure to observe that fundamental fairness essential to the very concept of justice. In order to declare a denial of it we must find that the absence of that fairness fatally infected the trial; the acts complained of must be of such quality as necessarily prevents a fair trial.

Owen J. Roberts, *Lisenba v. California,* 314 U.S. 219, 236 (1941)

21 But the Constitution does not force a lawyer upon a defendant. He may waive his

Constitutional right to assistance of counsel if he knows what he is doing and his choice is made with eyes open.

Felix Frankfurter, *Adams v. United States ex rel. McCann*, 317 U.S. 269, 279 (1942)

22 The right to have the assistance of counsel is too fundamental and absolute to allow the courts to indulge in nice calculations as to the amount of prejudice arising from its denial.

Frank Murphy, *Glasser v. United States*, 315 U.S. 60, 76 (1942)

23 The protection of the individual from oppression and abuse by the police and other enforcing officers is indeed a major interest in a free society; but so is the effective prosecution of crime, an interest which at times seems to be forgotten. Perfection is impossible; like other human institutions criminal proceedings must be a compromise.

Learned Hand, *In re Fried*, 161 F.2d 453, 465 (2d Cir. 1947) (concurring)

24 A person's right to reasonable notice of a charge against him, and an opportunity to be heard in his defense—a right to his day in court—are basic in our system of jurisprudence; and these rights include, as a minimum, a right to examine the witnesses against him, to offer testimony, and to be represented by counsel.

Hugo L. Black, *In re Oliver*, 333 U.S. 257, 273 (1948)

25 All governments, democracies as well as autocracies, believe that those they seek to punish are guilty; the impediment of constitutional barriers are galling to all governments when they prevent the consummation of that just purpose. But those barriers were devised and are precious because they prevent that purpose and its pursuit from passing unchallenged by the accused, and unpurged by the alembic of public scrutiny and public criticism. A society which has come to wince at such exposure of the methods by which it seeks to impose its will upon its members, has already lost the feel of freedom and is on the path towards absolutism.

Learned Hand, *United States v. Coplon*, 185 F.2d 629, 638 (2d Cir. 1950)

26 Security is like liberty in that many are the crimes committed in its name. The menace to the security of this country, be it great as it may, from this girl's admission is as nothing compared to the menace to free institutions inherent in procedures of this pattern. In the name of security the police state justifies its arbitrary oppressions on evidence that is secret, because security might be prejudiced if it were brought to light in hearings. The plea that evidence of guilt must be secret is abhorrent to free men, because it provides a cloak for the malevolent, the misinformed, the meddlesome, and the corrupt to play the role of informer undetected and uncorrected.

Robert H. Jackson, *United States v. Shaughnessy*, 338 U.S. 537, 551 (1950) (dissenting)

27 The prompt and vigorous administration of the criminal law is to be commended and encouraged. But swift justice demands more than just swiftness.

Potter Stewart, *Henderson v. Bannan*, 256 F.2d 363, 390 (6th Cir. 1958) (dissenting)

28 More than one student of society has expressed the view that not the least significant test of the quality of a civilization is its treatment of those charged with crime, particularly with offenses which arouse the passions of a community. One of the rightful boasts of Western civilization is that the State has the burden of establishing guilt solely on the basis of evidence produced in court and under circumstances assuring an accused all the safeguards of a fair procedure. These rudimentary conditions for determining guilt are inevitably wanting if the jury which is to sit in judgment on a fellow human being comes to its task with its mind ineradicably poisoned against him. How can fallible men and women reach a disinterested verdict based exclusively on what they heard in court, when, before they entered the jury box, their minds were saturated by press and radio for months preceding by matter designed to establish the guilt of the accused? A conviction so secured obviously constitutes a denial of due process of law in its most rudimentary conception.

Felix Frankfurter, *Irvin v. Dowd*, 366 U.S. 717, 729–30 (1961) (concurring)

29 The right of one charged with crime to counsel may not be deemed fundamental and essential to fair trials in some countries, but it is in ours.

Hugo L. Black, *Gideon v. Wainwright,* 372 U.S. 335, 344 (1963)

30 From the very beginning, our state and national constitutions and laws have laid great emphasis on procedural and substantive safeguards designed to assure fair trials before impartial tribunals in which every defendant stands equal before the law. This noble ideal cannot be realized if the poor man charged with crime has to face his accusers without a lawyer to assist him.

Hugo L. Black, *Gideon v. Wainwright,* 372 U.S. 335, 344 (1963)

31 We now hold that the suppression by the prosecution of evidence favorable to an accused upon request violates due process where the evidence is material either to guilt or to punishment, irrespective of the good faith or bad faith of the prosecution.

William O. Douglas, *Brady v. Maryland,* 373 U.S. 83, 87 (1963)

32 We have . . . learned the companion lesson of history that no system of criminal justice can, or should, survive if it comes to depend for its continued effectiveness on the citizens' abdication through unawareness of their constitutional rights. No system worth preserving should have to *fear* that if an accused is permitted to consult with a lawyer, he will become aware of, and exercise, these rights.

Arthur J. Goldberg, *Escobedo v. Illinois,* 378 U.S. 478, 490 (1964)

33 Lest there remain any doubt about the constitutional stature of the reasonable-doubt standard, we explicitly hold that the Due Process Clause protects the accused against conviction except upon proof beyond a reasonable doubt of every fact necessary to constitute the crime with which he is charged.

William J. Brennan, Jr., *In re Winship,* 397 U.S. 358, 364 (1970)

34 It is indeed an odd business that it has taken this Court nearly two centuries to "discover" a constitutional mandate to have counsel at a preliminary hearing.

Warren E. Burger, *Coleman v. Alabama,* 399 U.S. 1, 22 (1970) (dissenting)

35 It was Mr. Justice Frankfurter—no watery sentimentalist—who reminded us that "The history of liberty has largely been the history of observance of procedural safeguards." And the history of the destruction of liberty, one may add, has largely been the history of the relaxation of those safeguards in the face of plausible-sounding governmental claims of a need to deal with widely frightening and emotion-freighted threats to the good order of society.

Anthony G. Amsterdam, "Perspectives on the Fourth Amendment," 58 *Minnesota Law Review* 349, 354 (1974)

36 The assumption on which the Court's holding rests is that the only purpose of the constitutional guarantee of effective assistance of counsel is to reduce the chance that innocent persons will be convicted. In my view, the guarantee also functions to ensure that convictions are obtained only through fundamentally fair procedures. The majority contends that the Sixth Amendment is not violated when a manifestly guilty defendant is convicted after a trial in which he was represented by a manifestly ineffective attorney. I cannot agree. Every defendant is entitled to a trial in which his interests are vigorously and conscientiously advocated by an able lawyer. A proceeding in which the defendant does not receive meaningful assistance in meeting the forces of the State does not, in my opinion, constitute due process.

Thurgood Marshall, *Strickland v. Washington,* 466 U.S. 668, 711 (1984) (dissenting)

37 A convicted defendant's claim that counsel's assistance was so defective as to require reversal of a conviction or death sentence has two components. First, the defendant must show that counsel's performance was deficient. This requires showing that counsel made errors so serious that counsel was not functioning as the "counsel" guaranteed the defendant by the Sixth Amendment. Second, the defendant must show that the deficient performance prejudiced the defense. This requires showing that counsel's errors were so serious as

to deprive the defendant of a fair trial, a trial whose result is reliable.

Sandra Day O'Connor, *Strickland v. Washington,* 466 U.S. 668, 687 (1984)

CRITICAL LEGAL STUDIES

See also LEGAL REALISM

1 But the point is also to reconceive the internal issues of firm hierarchy as an important part of one's political life, fighting the oligarchy of senior partners, opposing the oppression of secretaries by arrogant young men who turn around and grovel before their mentors. It means engaging in indirect struggle to control the political tone of the office, say by refusing to laugh at jokes. Blank expressions where the oppressor expects a compliant smile can be the beginning of actual power.

Duncan Kennedy, "Rebels from Principle: Changing the Corporate Law Firm from Within," *Harvard Law School Bulletin,* Fall 1981, at 36, 39

2 The general thesis is that law schools are intensely *political* places, in spite of the fact that they seem intellectually unpretentious, barren of theoretical ambition or practical vision of what social life might be. The trade school mentality, the endless attention to trees at the expense of forests, the alternating grimness and chumminess of focus on the limited task at hand, all these are only a part of what is going on. The other part is ideological training for willing service in the hierarchies of the corporate welfare state.

Duncan Kennedy, *Legal Education and the Reproduction of Hierarchy* i (1983)

3 This whole body of implicit messages is nonsense. Legal reasoning is not distinct, *as a method for reaching correct results,* from ethical and political discourse in general (i.e., from policy analysis). It is true that there is a distinctive lawyers' body of knowledge of the rules in force. It is true that there are distinctive lawyers' argumentative techniques for spotting gaps, conflicts and ambiguities in the rules, for arguing broad and narrow holdings of cases, and for generating pro and con policy arguments. But these are *only* argumentative techniques. There is never a "correct legal solution" that is other than the correct ethical and political solution to that legal problem.

Duncan Kennedy, *Legal Education and the Reproduction of Hierarchy* 20 (1983)

4 Without such a guiding vision, legal reasoning seems condemned to a game of easy analogies. It will always be possible to find, retrospectively, more or less convincing ways to make a set of distinctions, or failures to distinguish, look credible. A common experience testifies to this possibility; every thoughtful law student or lawyer has had the disquieting sense of being able to argue too well or too easily for too many conflicting solutions.

Roberto Mangabeira Unger, "The Critical Legal Studies Movement," 96 *Harvard Law Review* 563, 570 (1983)

5 When we [the critical legal studies movement] came, they [legal scholars] were like a priesthood that had lost their faith and kept their jobs. They stood in tedious embarrassment before cold altars. But we turned away from those altars, and found the mind's opportunity in the heart's revenge.

Roberto Mangabeira Unger, "The Critical Legal Studies Movement," 96 *Harvard Law Review* 561, 675 (1983)

CROSS-EXAMINATION

See also WITNESSES

1 A lawyer should never ask a witness on cross-examination a question unless in the first place he knew what the answer would be, or in the second place he didn't care.

David Graham, quoted in Francis L. Wellman, *The Art of Cross-Examination* 44 (1903)

2 [Cross-examination] is beyond any doubt the greatest legal engine ever invented for the discovery of truth. . . . cross-examination, not trial by jury, is the great and permanent contribution of the Anglo-American system of law to improved methods of trial-procedure.

John H. Wigmore, *A Treatise on the System of Evidence in Trials at Common Law* 2:1697–98 (1904)

3 More cross-examinations are suicidal than homicidal.

> Emory R. Buckner, "Some Comments on the 'Uses and Abuses' of Cross-Examination," in Francis L. Wellman, *The Art of Cross-Examination* 204, 204 (4th ed. 1936)

4 At one point in the trial Darrow had started to cross-examine a particularly vitriolic witness but, after merely asking her name, excused her. In view of the fact that she had given damaging testimony on direct examination Toms asked Darrow, "Why didn't you cross-examine Mrs. Blank?" He answered, "Because I didn't know what she would say. I never ask a question unless I know beforehand what the answer will be."

> Clarence S. Darrow, quoted in Irving Stone, *Clarence Darrow for the Defense* 481 (1941)

5 A browbeating lawyer was demanding that a witness answer a certain question in the negative or affirmative.

"I cannot do it," said the witness. "There are some questions that cannot be answered by a 'yes' or a 'no,' as any one knows."

"I defy you to give an example to the court," thundered the lawyer.

The retort came like a flash: "Are you still beating your wife?"

> Lewis Copeland and Faye Copeland, *10,000 Jokes, Toasts & Stories* 479 (1939)

6 [Perry Mason speaking:] If you've followed my cases, you'll note that most of them have been cleared up in the courtroom. I can suspect the guilty, but about the only way I can really prove my point is by cross-examining witnesses.

> Erle Stanley Gardner, *The Case of the Perjured Parrot* 9 (1939)

7 Never, never, never, on cross-examination ask a witness a question you don't already know the answer to, was a tenet I absorbed with my baby-food. Do it, and you'll often get an answer you don't want, an answer that might wreck your case.

> Harper Lee, *To Kill A Mockingbird* 188 (1960)

8 The classic story about the extra question has to do with the man who was charged with mayhem. The allegation was that he was in a fight and the fight got rough and he bit the complainant's ear off. . . .

So the case went to trial. A witness was on the stand and the defense lawyer took him over on cross-examination. "Now, you saw this fight, did you?"

"Well," he said, "I didn't see all of it."

"As a matter of fact, you didn't see very much of it, did you?"

"I didn't see very much of it, no."

The lawyer said, "As a matter of fact, you never saw the defendant bite the complainant's ear, did you?"

And the witness said, "No, I didn't."

. . . But this lawyer could not stop. He had to go on and he said, "But you testified that he bit it off, didn't you?"

"Yes."

"Well, how did you know that the defendant bit the complainant's ear off?"

"Because I saw him spit it out."

> Edward Bennett Williams, "You in Trial Law," in *Listen to Leaders in Law* 97, 124–25 (Albert Love & James S. Childers eds. 1963)

9 "Razzle-dazzle is not good cross-examination," Mason said. "The purpose of cross-examination is to find out whether a witness is telling the truth."

Lovett laughed sarcastically. "That's the line they try to teach you in the lawbooks and in the colleges. Actually, when you come right down to it, you know and I know, Mason, that the object of cross-examination is first to find out to your own satisfaction if a witness is telling the truth. If you find out the witness *is* telling the truth, then you go on to the next step—which is to try and confuse the witness so that any testimony the witness has given is open to doubt."

> Erle Stanley Gardner, *The Case of the Queenly Contestant* 63 (1967)

10 My efforts to elicit information from Stans were not pleasing to Senator Gurney, who uttered this protest: "I for one have not appreciated the harassment of this witness by the Chairman in the questioning that has just finished. I think this Senate Committee ought to act in fairness."

As a practitioner of the Biblical admonition "A soft answer turneth away wrath," I said, "I have asked the witness questions to find out what the truth is. . . . I am sorry that my distinguished friend from Florida does not approve of my method of examining the witness. I am an old country lawyer and I don't know the finer ways to do it. I just have to do it my way."

Sam J. Ervin, Jr., *The Whole Truth: The Watergate Conspiracy* 148 (1980)

11 I've felt a little bit like that farmer that was driving his horse and wagon to town for some grain and had a head-on collision with a truck. And later was the litigation involving claims for his injuries, some of them permanent. And he was on the stand and a lawyer said to him, "Isn't it true that while you were lying there at the scene of the accident someone came over to you and asked you how you were feeling, and you said you never felt better in your life?" And he said, "Yes, I remember that." Well, later he's on the stand and the witnesses were there—the lawyer for the other side is questioning—and he said, "When you gave that answer about how you felt, what were the circumstances?" "Well," he said, "I was lying there and a car came up and a deputy sheriff got out." He said, "My horse was screaming with pain—had broken two legs." The deputy took out his gun, put it in the horse's ear, and finished him off. "And," he said, "my dog was whining with pain—had a broken back." "And," he said, "he went over to him and put the gun to his ear." "And then," he says, "he turned to me and says now, how are you feeling?"

Ronald W. Reagan, Remarks at the Conservative Political Action Conference, 20 Feb. 1987, in *Public Papers of the Presidents: Ronald Reagan, 1987*, at 1:165, 166 (1989)

CRUEL AND UNUSUAL PUNISHMENT

See CAPITAL PUNISHMENT; PUNISHMENT

CUSTODY

1 Even a court of common law will not go so far as to hold nature in contempt, and snatch helpless, pulling infancy from the bosom of an affectionate mother and place it in the coarse hands of the father. The mother is the softest and safest nurse of infancy, and with her it will be left in opposition to this general right of the father.

Theodorick Bland, *Helms v. Franciscus*, 2 Bl. Ch. 544, 563 (Md. 1830)

2 In such cases [when the parents are living separately or apart] a court may conclude that the best interests of the child and due regard for the interests of the parents require that one or the other be given complete custody of the child. It may conclude that such action would be unjust, and unable like Solomon to carve the child, it may carve out of the sum of custodial rights, certain rights to be exercised by each parent.

Roger J. Traynor, *Burge v. City and County of San Francisco*, 41 Cal. 2d 608, 618, 262 P.2d 6 (1953)

3 *Ted Kramer* [played by Dustin Hoffman, testifying at a trial for custody of Kramer's son]: Joanna says she loves Billy. I believe she does. So do I. But the way it was explained to me, that's not the issue. The only thing that's supposed to matter here is what's best for Billy. . . . When Joanna said why shouldn't a woman have the same ambitions as a man, I suppose she's right. But by the same token what law is it that says a woman is a better parent simply by virtue of her sex? I guess I've had to think a lot about whatever it is that makes somebody a good parent: constancy, patience, understanding . . . love. Where is it written that a man has any less of those qualities than a woman? Billy has a home with me, I've tried to make it the best I could. It's not perfect. I'm not a perfect parent. I don't have enough patience. Sometimes I forget he's just a little kid. . . . But I love him. . . . More than anything in this world I love him.

Robert Benton, *Kramer vs. Kramer* (screenplay), 1979, quoted in *Actor's Book of Movie Monologues* 155–56 (Marisa Smith & Amy Schewel eds. 1986)

4 The [surrogate parenting] contract's basic premise, that the natural parents can decide in advance of birth which one is to have custody of the child, bears no relationship to the settled law that the child's best interests shall determine custody.

Robert N. Wilentz, *In re Baby M.*, 109 N.J. 396, 434, 537 A.2d 1227 (1988)

CUSTOM

See LAW

DAMAGES

1 It is not enough to say, that in the opinion of the court, the damages are too high and that we would have given much less. It is the judgment of the jury, and not the judgment of the court, which is to assess the damages in actions for personal torts and injuries. . . . The damages, therefore, must be so excessive as to strike mankind, at first blush, as being beyond all measure, unreasonable and outrageous, and such as manifestly show the jury to have been actuated by passion, partiality, prejudice, or corruption. In short, the damages must be flagrantly outrageous and extravagant, or the court cannot undertake to draw the line; for they have no standard by which to ascertain the excess.

James Kent, *Coleman v. Southwick,* 9 Johns. 45, 51–52 (N.Y. 1812)

2 The only universal consequence of a legally binding promise is, that the law makes the promisor pay damages if the promised event does not come to pass.

Oliver Wendell Holmes, Jr., *The Common Law* 301 (1881)

3 Before the verdict will be set aside on the ground that it is excessive, where there is no direct proof of prejudice or bias, the amount thereof, when considered in connection with all the facts, must shock the moral sense, appear "exorbitant," "flagrantly outrageous," and "extravagant." "It must be monstrous indeed and such as all mankind must be ready to exclaim against at first blush." It must carry its death warrant upon its face.

Oliver H. Bloodworth, *Realty Bond & Mortgage Co. v. Harley,* 19 Ga. App. 186, 187–88, 91 S.E. 254 (1917)

4 The "restitution interest," involving a combination of unjust impoverishment with unjust gain, presents the strongest case for relief. If, following Aristotle, we regard the purpose of justice as the maintenance of an equilibrium of goods among members of society, the restitution interest presents twice as strong a claim to judicial intervention as the reliance interest, since if A not only causes B to lose one unit but appropriates that unit to himself, the resulting discrepancy between A and B is not one unit but two.

Lon L. Fuller and William R. Perdue, Jr., "The Reliance Interest in Contract Damages: 1," 46 *Yale Law Journal* 52, 56 (1936)

5 On the other hand, the promisee who has actually relied on the promise, even though he may not thereby have enriched the promisor, certainly presents a more pressing case for relief than the promisee who merely demands satisfaction for his disappointment in not getting what was promised him. In passing from compensation for change of position to compensation for loss of expectancy we pass, to use Aristotle's terms again, from the realm of corrective justice to that of distributive justice. The law no longer seeks to heal a disturbed status quo, but to bring into being a new situation. It ceases to act defensively or restoratively, but assumes a more active role. With the transition, the justification for legal relief loses its self-evident quality. It is as a matter of fact no easy thing to explain why the normal rule of contract recovery should be that which measures damages by the value of the promised performance.

Lon L. Fuller and William R. Perdue, Jr., "The Reliance Interest in Contract Damages: 1," 46 *Yale Law Journal* 52, 56–57 (1936)

6 We have a judge in Boston named Donahue, who is indeed brilliant, but a character. A couple of years ago, a jury case was being tried before him, a personal injury case, and the jury sent a note in to him with a question asking if, even though there was not any liability, could they still give the plaintiff some money. The judge sent for the jury. He said to them, "I have your written question, and I assume from the question that you have found there is no liability." The foreman said, "That is so, Your Honor." He said, "All right, sign this slip then."

After they had signed the slip, which directed a verdict for the defendant, he said, "I will now answer your question. You may retire to the jury room and pass the hat."

Samuel P. Sears, "In Defense of the Defense," 25 *Insurance Counsel Journal* 428, 429 (1958)

DARROW, CLARENCE

1 The Defender of the Damned [also "Attorney for the Damned"].

Epithet of Clarence S. Darrow

2 I have lived my life, and I have fought my battles, not against the weak and the poor—anybody can do that—but against power, against injustice, against oppression, and I have asked no odds from them, and I never shall.

Clarence S. Darrow, Defense against charge of jury bribing in McNamara Case, 1912, in *Attorney for the Damned* 491, 497 (Arthur Weinberg ed. 1957)

3 The law is work for some law clerks who ought not to be in it. It isn't work for me; just one fascinating moment after another.

Clarence S. Darrow, quoted in *Chicago Daily News*, 20 May 1925, in Arthur Weinberg and Lila Weinberg, *Clarence Darrow: A Sentimental Rebel* 22 (1980)

4 I do not consider it an insult, but rather a compliment to be called an agnostic. I do not pretend to know where many ignorant men are sure; that is all that agnosticism means.

Clarence S. Darrow, Speech at Scopes Trial, Dayton, Tenn., 15 July 1925, in *The World's Most Famous Court Trial* 99 (1925)

5 I don't believe in God because I don't believe in Mother Goose.

Clarence S. Darrow, Speech, Toronto, 1930, quoted in John Bartlett, *Familiar Quotations* 684 (Emily Morison Beck ed., 15th ed. 1980)

6 I may hate the sin but never the sinner.

Clarence S. Darrow, quoted in Irving Stone, *Clarence Darrow for the Defense* 410 (1941)

DEATH PENALTY

See CAPITAL PUNISHMENT

DEBT

See BANKRUPTCY

DEFAMATION

See LIBEL

DEFENSE

1 Whether a jury is a good one or a bad one depends on the point of view. I have always been an attorney for the defense. I can think of nothing, not even war, that has brought so much misery to the human race as prisons. And all of it so futile!

Clarence S. Darrow, "Attorney for the Defense," *Esquire*, May 1936, in *Verdicts Out of Court* 313, 321 (Arthur Weinberg & Lila Weinberg eds. 1963)

2 "You mean," [attorney Paul Biegler's client] said, "that my only possible defense in this case is to find some justification or excuse?"

My [Biegler's] lecture was proceeding nicely to schedule. "You're learning rapidly," I said, nodding approvingly. "Merely add *legal* justification or excuse and I'll mark you an A."

"And you say that a man is not justified in killing a man who has just raped and beat up his wife?"

"Morally, perhaps, but not legally."

Robert Traver, *Anatomy of a Murder* 37 (1958)

3 But defense counsel has no comparable obligation to ascertain or present the truth. Our system assigns him a different mission. . . . Defense counsel need present nothing, even if he knows what the truth is. He need not furnish any witnesses to the police, or reveal any confidences of his client, or furnish any other information to help the prosecution's case. If he can confuse a witness, even a truthful one, or make him appear at a disadvantage, unsure or indecisive, that will be his normal course. Our interest in not convicting the innocent permits counsel to put the State to its proof, to put the State's case in the worst possible light, regardless of what he thinks or knows to be the truth. . . . more often than not, defense counsel will cross-examine a prosecution witness, and impeach him if he can, even if he thinks the witness is telling the truth. . . . In this respect, as part of our modified adversary system and as part of the duty imposed on the most honorable defense counsel, we countenance or require conduct which in many instances has little, if any, relation to the search for truth.

Byron R. White, *United States v. Wade*, 388 U.S. 218, 256–58 (1967) (dissenting in part and concurring in part)

4 In their uniforms of charcoal gray, the prosecutors appeared dignified and orderly. We defense attorneys wore easier clothes day-to-day, slacks and jackets, and those donned grudgingly, scarcely concealing the denim souls within. We were individuals, we were free. We worked for freedom, not justice, not freedom when merited, not freedom for the innocent—for freedom itself, for being loose, for staying outside.

> **James S. Kunen,** *"How Can You Defend Those People?": The Making of a Criminal Lawyer* 182 (1983)

5 An Oklahoma man, charged with armed robbery, elected to defend himself. He handled his case well until the store manager identified him as the robber, at which point the defendant leaped to his feet, accused the woman of lying, and exclaimed, "I should have blown your f———head off." He then paused, sat down, and muttered, "If I'd been the one that was there."

> **Rodney R. Jones and Gerald F. Uelmen,** *Supreme Folly* 14 (1990)

DEGREE

See DISTINCTIONS

DEMOCRACY

See also VOTING

1 It is, Sir, the people's Constitution, the people's government, made for the people, made by the people, and answerable to the people.*

> **Daniel Webster,** Second Speech on Foot's Resolution in United States Senate, 26–27 Jan. 1830, in *Writings and Speeches of Daniel Webster* 6:3, 54 (1903)

2 It is a besetting vice of democracies to substitute publick opinion for law. This is the usual form in which masses of men exhibit their tyranny. When the majority of the entire community commits this fault it is a sore grievance, but when local bodies, influenced by local interests, pretend to style themselves the publick, they are assuming powers that properly belong to the whole body of the people, and to them only under constitutional limitations. No tyranny of one, nor any tyranny of the few, is worse than this.

> **James Fenimore Cooper,** *The American Democrat* 69 (1956) (1838)

3 Where every man in a State has a vote, brutal laws are impossible.

> **Mark Twain,** *A Connecticut Yankee in King Arthur's Court,* 1889, in *Works of Mark Twain* 9:288 (Bernard L. Stein ed. 1979)

4 The authority of law here is not something which is imposed upon the people; it is the will of the people themselves. The decision of the court here is not something which is apart from the people; it is the judgment of the people themselves. The right of the ownership of property here is not something withheld from the people; it is the privilege of the people themselves. Their sovereignty is absolute and complete. A definition of the relationship between the institutions of our government and the American people entirely justifies the assertion that: "All things were made by *them;* and without *them* was not anything made that was made." It is because the American Government is the sole creation and possession of the people that they have always cherished it and defended it, and always will.

> **Calvin Coolidge,** Memorial Day address, Northampton, Mass., 30 May 1923, in *The Price of Freedom* 331, 333 (1924)

5 I have many theoretical objections to democracy, and sometimes urge them with such heat that it probably goes beyond the bounds of sound taste, but I am thoroughly convinced, nevertheless, that the democratic nations are happier than any other. The United States today, indeed, is probably the happiest the world has ever seen. Taxes are high, but they are still well within the means of the taxpayer: he could pay twice as much and yet survive. The laws are innumerable and idiotic, but only prisoners in the penitentiaries and persons under religious vows ever obey them.

> **H. L. Mencken,** "The Master Illusion," *American Mercury,* Mar. 1925, at 319, 319

---

* We here highly resolve . . . that government of the people, by the people, for the people, shall not perish from the earth. —**Abraham Lincoln,** Address, Gettysburg, Pa., 19 Nov. 1863, in *Collected Works of Abraham Lincoln* 7:17, 23 (Roy P. Basler ed. 1953)
John Bartlett, *Familiar Quotations* 657 (Emily Morison Beck ed., 14th ed. 1968) suggests that an 1858 sermon by Theodore Parker inspired Lincoln's phrase.

6 At no time, at no place, in solemn convention assembled, through no chosen agents, had the American people officially proclaimed the United States to be a democracy. The Constitution did not contain the word or any word lending countenance to it, except possibly the mention of "we, the people," in the preamble. . . . when the Constitution was framed no respectable person called himself or herself a democrat.

Charles A. Beard and Mary R. Beard, *America in Midpassage* 2:922–23 (1939)

DEPARTMENT OF JUSTICE

See JUSTICE DEPARTMENT

DESEGREGATION

See EDUCATION; SEGREGATION

DIFFERENCES

See DISTINCTIONS

DISCRIMINATION

See AFFIRMATIVE ACTION; CIVIL RIGHTS; EQUAL PROTECTION; SEGREGATION; SEX DISCRIMINATION; WOMEN'S RIGHTS

DISHONESTY

See ETHICS; LAWYER JOKES; LAWYERS (CON)

DISSENT

1 I am of opinion, . . . that upon constitutional questions, the public have a right to know the opinion of every judge who dissents from the opinion of the Court, and the reasons of his dissent.

Joseph Story, *Briscoe v. Bank of Kentucky*, 36 U.S. (11 Pet.) 257, 350 (1837)

2 When I differ with the court, I hope I am wrong, for I would rather err in opinion than for the court to err in judgment. Still, I must abide by my convinctions [*sic*], and declare them. I do so in the present instance, with no zeal whatever to establish like convictions in the minds of others.

Logan E. Bleckley, *Queen v. City of Atlanta*, 59 Ga. 318, 324 (1877) (dissenting)

3 The only purpose which an elaborate dissent can accomplish, if any, is to weaken the effect of the opinion of the majority, and thus engender want of confidence in the conclusions of courts of last resort.

Edward D. White, *Pollock v. Farmers' Loan & Trust Co.*, 157 U.S. 429, 608 (1895) (dissenting)

4 I think it useless and undesirable, as a rule, to express dissent.

Oliver Wendell Holmes, Jr., *Northern Securities Co. v. United States*, 193 U.S. 197, 400 (1904) (dissenting)

5 A dissent in a court of last resort is an appeal to the brooding spirit of the law, to the intelligence of a future day, when a later decision may possibly correct the error into which the dissenting judge believes the court to have been betrayed.

Charles Evans Hughes, *The Supreme Court of the United States* 68 (1928)

6 Comparatively speaking at least, the dissenter is irresponsible. The spokesman of the court is cautious, timid, fearful of the vivid word, the heightened phrase. He dreams of an unworthy brood of scions, the spawn of careless *dicta*, disowned by the *ratio decidendi*, to which all legitimate offspring must be able to trace their lineage. The result is to cramp and paralyze. One fears to say anything when the peril of misunderstanding puts a warning finger to the lips. Not so, however, the dissenter. He has laid aside the role of the hierophant, which he will be only too glad to resume when the chances of war make him again the spokesman of the majority. For the moment, he is the gladiator making a last stand against the lions.

Benjamin N. Cardozo, *Law and Literature* 34 (1931)

7 More truly characteristic of dissent is a dignity, an elevation, of mood and thought and phrase. Deep conviction and warm feeling are saying their last say with knowledge that the cause is lost. The voice of the majority may be that of force triumphant, content with the plaudits of the hour, and recking little of the morrow. The dissenter speaks to the future, and his voice is pitched to a key that will carry through the years.

Benjamin N. Cardozo, *Law and Literature* 36 (1931)

8 Those who begin coercive elimination of dissent soon find themselves exterminating dissenters. Compulsory unification of opinion achieves only the unanimity of the graveyard.

> **Robert H. Jackson,** *West Virginia State Bd. of Educ. v. Barnette,* 319 U.S. 624, 641 (1943)

9 There has been much undiscriminating eulogy of dissenting opinions. It is said they clarify the issues. Often they do the exact opposite. The technique of the dissenter often is to exaggerate the holding of the Court beyond the meaning of the majority and then to blast away at the excess. So the poor lawyer with a similar case does not know whether the majority opinion meant what it seemed to say or what the minority said it meant. . . . Each dissenting opinion is a confession of failure to convince the writer's colleagues, and the true test of a judge is his influence in leading, not in opposing, his court.

> **Robert H. Jackson,** *The Supreme Court in the American System of Government* 18–19 (1955)

10 The right to dissent is the only thing that makes life tolerable for a judge of an appellate court.

> **William O. Douglas,** *America Challenged* 4 (1960)

DISTINCTIONS

1 The growth of law is very apt to take place in this way: Two widely different cases suggest a general distinction, which is a clear one when stated broadly. But as new cases cluster around the opposite poles, and begin to approach each other, the distinction becomes more difficult to trace . . . at last a mathematical line is arrived at by the contact of contrary decisions, which is so far arbitrary that it might equally well have been drawn a little further to the one side or to the other. . . . it is better to have a line drawn somewhere in the penumbra* between darkness and light, than to remain in uncertainty.

> **Oliver Wendell Holmes, Jr.,** "The Theory of Torts," 7 *American Law Review* 652, 654 (1873)

---

* This appears to be the first use of the "penumbra" metaphor in American law.

2 But it does not follow that the rule is the same for a boundary fence unnecessarily built more than six feet high. It may be said that the difference is only one of degree: most differences are, when nicely analyzed.

> **Oliver Wendell Holmes, Jr.,** *Rideout v. Knox,* 148 Mass. 368, 372, 19 N.E. 390 (1889)

3 I have heard it suggested that the difference is one of degree. I am the last man in the world to quarrel with a distinction simply because it is one of degree. Most distinctions, in my opinion, are of that sort, and are none the worse for it.

> **Oliver Wendell Holmes, Jr.,** *Haddock v. Haddock,* 201 U.S. 562, 631 (1906) (dissenting)

4 The law is full of instances where a man's fate depends on his estimating rightly, that is, as a jury subsequently estimates it, some matter of degree. If his judgment is wrong, not only may he incur a fine or a short imprisonment, as here; he may incur the penalty of death.

> **Oliver Wendell Holmes, Jr.,** *Nash v. United States,* 229 U.S. 373, 377 (1913)

5 I do not think we need trouble ourselves with the thought that my view depends upon differences of degree. The whole law does so as soon as it is civilized. . . . Negligence is all degree—that of the defendant here degree of the nicest sort; and between the variations according to distance that I suppose to exist and the simple universality of the rules in the Twelve Tables of the Leges Barbarorum, there lies the culture of two thousand years.

> **Oliver Wendell Holmes, Jr.,** *LeRoy Fibre Co. v. Chicago, Milwaukee & St. Paul Ry.,* 232 U.S. 340, 354 (1914) (concurring)

6 Life has relations not capable always of division into inflexible compartments. The moulds expand and shrink.

> **Benjamin N. Cardozo,** *Glanzer v. Shepard,* 233 N.Y. 236, 241, 135 N.E. 275 (1922)

7 Neither are we troubled by the question where to draw the line. That is the question in pretty much everything worth arguing in the law. . . . Day and night, youth and age are only types.

> **Oliver Wendell Holmes, Jr.,** *Irwin v. Gavit,* 268 U.S. 161, 168 (1925)

8 While I should not dream of asking where the line can be drawn, since the great body of the law consists in drawing such lines, yet when you realize that you are dealing with a matter of degree you must realize that reasonable men may differ widely as to the place where the line should fall. . . . The law allows a penumbra to be embraced that goes beyond the outline of its object in order that the object may be secured.

Oliver Wendell Holmes, Jr., *Schlesinger v. Wisconsin,* 270 U.S. 230, 241 (1926) (dissenting)

9 When a legal distinction is determined, as no one doubts that it may be, between night and day, childhood and maturity, or any other extremes, a point has to be fixed or a line has to be drawn, or gradually picked out by successive decisions, to mark where the change takes place. Looked at by itself without regard to the necessity behind it the line or point seems arbitrary. It might as well or nearly as well be a little more to one side or the other. But when it is seen that a line or point there must be, and that there is no mathematical or logical way of fixing it precisely, the decision of the Legislature must be accepted unless we can say that is very wide of any reasonable mark.

Oliver Wendell Holmes, Jr., *Louisville Gas & Electric Co. v. Coleman,* 277 U.S. 32, 41 (1928) (dissenting)

10 Whenever the law draws a line there will be cases very near each other on opposite sides. The precise course of the line may be uncertain, but no one can come near it without knowing that he does so, if he thinks, and if he does so it is familiar to the criminal law to make him take the risk.

Oliver Wendell Holmes, Jr., *United States v. Wurzbach,* 280 U.S. 396, 399 (1930)

11 Here, indeed, as so often in other branches of the law, the decisive distinctions are those of degree and not of kind. One struggles in vain for any verbal formula that will supply a ready touchstone. The standard set up by the statute is not a rule of law; it is rather a way of life. Life in all its fullness must supply the answer to the riddle.

Benjamin N. Cardozo, *Welch v. Helvering,* 290 U.S. 111, 114–15 (1933)

DIVORCE

See also CUSTODY

1 But not always was Lawyer Gooch the keen, armed, wily belligerent, ready with his two-edged sword to lop off the shackles of Hymen. He had been known to build up instead of demolishing, to reunite instead of severing, to lead erring and foolish ones back into the fold instead of scattering the flock. Often had he by his eloquent and moving appeals sent husband and wife, weeping, back into each other's arms. Frequently he had coached childhood so successfully that, at the psychological moment (and at a given signal) the plaintive pipe of "Papa, won't you tum home adain to me and muvver?" had won the day and upheld the pillars of a tottering home.

Unprejudiced persons admitted that Lawyer Gooch received as big fees from these re-yoked clients as would have been paid him had the cases been contested in court. Prejudiced ones intimated that his fees were doubled, because the penitent couples always came back later for the divorce, anyhow.

O. Henry, "The Hypotheses of Failure," in *Whirligigs* 37 (1910)

2 No course of bad treatment on one side more than on the other.
Blame balanced as six and half a dozen.
Mutually mean.
He mean enough to seek divorce.
She mean enough to resist.
Parties too much alike ever to have been joined in marriage.
Also too much alike to be separated by divorce.
Having made their own bed must lie down in it.
Lying out of it, no standing in court.
Decree refused.

Henry A. Fuller, *Kmicz v. Kmicz,* 50 Pa. C. 588, 588 (1921)

3 Watch him smile he thinks it's Christmas or his fifth birthday;
And he thinks c-u-s-t-o-d-y spells fun or play.
I spell out all the hurtin' words and turn my head when I speak,
Because I can't spell away this hurt that's drippin' down my cheeks.
Our d-i-v-o-r-c-e becomes final today;
Me and little Joe will be going away.

Bobby Braddock and Curly Putman, "D-I-V-O-R-C-E" (song), 1968, in *The Best Country Songs Ever* 41–43 (1991)

4 Neither a sexual revolution nor enlightened legislation can eliminate overnight more than a thousand years of divorce taboo. It lives on like a ghost, chilly and half-perceived, generating a kind of moral shudder even in those to whom religion no longer means much and society does not accuse. Pride, or the superego, takes over where the Church and community leave off, and no amount of acceptance or understanding or social indifference lessens the sense of personal failure.

    A. Alvarez, *Life After Marriage* 138 (1981)

| DOMESTIC RELATIONS |

See CHILDREN; DIVORCE; MARRIAGE

| DOUBLE JEOPARDY |

1 No man shall be twise sentenced by Civill Justice for one and the same Crime, offence, or Trespasse.

    Massachusetts Body of Liberties of 1641, § 42, in *Collections of the Massachusetts Historical Society (3d series)* 8:216, 223 (1843)

2 Everie Action betweene partie and partie, and proceedings against delinquents in Criminall causes shall be briefly and destinctly entered on the Rolles of every Court by the Recorder thereof. That such actions be not afterwards brought againe to the vexation of any man.

    Massachusetts Body of Liberties of 1641, § 64, in *Collections of the Massachusetts Historical Society (3d series)* 8:216, 226–27 (1843)

3 No subject shall be liable to be tried, after an acquittal, for the same crime or offence.

    New Hampshire Constitution of 1784, pt. 1, art. 1, § 16, in *Federal and State Constitutions* 4:2453, 2455 (Francis N. Thorpe ed. 1909)

4 If the trial had been infected with error adverse to the accused, there might have been [appellate] review at his instance, and as often as necessary to purge the vicious taint. A reciprocal privilege, subject at all times to the discretion of the presiding judge, . . . has now been granted to the state. There is here no seismic innovation.

The edifice of justice stands, its symmetry, to many, greater than before.

    Benjamin N. Cardozo, *Palko v. Connecticut,* 302 U.S. 319, 328 (1937)

5 The underlying idea, one that is deeply ingrained in at least the Anglo-American system of jurisprudence, is that the State with all its resources and power should not be allowed to make repeated attempts to convict an individual for an alleged offense, thereby subjecting him to embarrassment, expense and ordeal and compelling him to live in a continuing state of anxiety and insecurity, as well as enhancing the possibility that even though innocent he may be found guilty.

    Hugo L. Black, *Green v. United States,* 355 U.S. 184, 187–88 (1957)

| DRAMA |

See COURTROOM SCENES

| DRINKING |

See INTOXICATION

| DUE PROCESS |

See also CRIMINAL PROCEDURE; FOURTEENTH AMENDMENT

1 No mans life shall be taken away, no mans honour or good name shall be stayned, no mans person shall be arested, restrayned, banished, dismembred, nor any wayes punished, no man shall be deprived of his wife or children, no mans goods or estaite shall be taken away from him, nor any way indammaged under colour of law or Countenance of Authoritie, unlesse it be by vertue or equitie of some expresse law of the Country waranting the same, established by a generall Court and sufficiently published, or in case of the defect of a law in any parteculer case by the word of God. And in Capitall cases, or in cases concerning dismembring or banishment according to that word to be judged by the Generall Court.

    Massachusetts Body of Liberties of 1641, § 1, in *Collections of the Massachusetts Historical Society (3d series)* 8:216, 216–17 (1843)

2 Every person within this Jurisdiction, whether Inhabitant or forreiner shall enjoy

the same justice and law, that is generall for the plantation, which we constitute and execute one towards another without partialitie or delay.

> Massachusetts Body of Liberties of 1641, § 2, in *Collections of the Massachusetts Historical Society (3d series)* 8:216, 217 (1843)

3 That no Person or Persons shall or may, at any Time hereafter, be obliged to answer any Complaint, Matter or Thing whatsoever, relating to Property, before the Governor and Council, or in any other Place, but in ordinary Course of Justice, unless Appeals thereunto shall be hereafter by Law appointed.

> Pennsylvania Charter of Privileges of 1701, § 6, in *Federal and State Constitutions* 5:3076, 3079 (Francis N. Thorpe ed. 1909)

4 The words *"due process"* have a precise technical import, and are only applicable to the process and proceedings of the courts of justice; they can never be referred to an act of legislature.

> Alexander Hamilton, Remarks on an Act for Regulating Elections, New York Assembly, 6 Feb. 1787, in *Papers of Alexander Hamilton* 4:34, 35 (Harold C. Syrett ed. 1962)

5 What are the privileges and immunities of citizens in the several states? We feel no hesitation in confining these expressions to those privileges and immunities which are, in their nature, fundamental; which belong, of right, to the citizens of all free governments; and which have, at all times, been enjoyed by the citizens of the several states which compose this Union, from the time of their becoming free, independent, and sovereign.... They may [be] comprehended under the following general heads: Protection by the government; the enjoyment of life and liberty, with the right to acquire and possess property of every kind, and to pursue and obtain happiness and safety; subject nevertheless to such restraints as the government may justly prescribe for the general good of the whole. The right of a citizen of one state to pass through, or to reside in any other state, for purposes of trade, agriculture, professional pursuits, or otherwise; to claim the benefit of the writ of habeas corpus; to institute and maintain actions of any kind in the courts of the state; to take, hold and dispose of property, either real or personal;

and an exemption from higher taxes or impositions than are paid by the other citizens of the state.

> Bushrod Washington, *Corfield v. Coryell*, 6 F. Cas. 546, 551–52 (C.C.E.D. Pa. 1823) (No. 3,230)

6 The words, "due process of law," were undoubtedly intended to convey the same meaning as the words, "by the law of the land," in *Magna Charta*.

> Benjamin R. Curtis, *Murray's Lessee v. Hoboken Land & Improvement Co.*, 59 U.S. (18 How.) 272, 276 (1856)

7 To what principles, then, are we to resort to ascertain whether this process, enacted by congress, is due process? ... We must examine the constitution itself, to see whether this process be in conflict with any of its provisions. If not found to be so, we must look to those settled usages and modes of proceeding existing in the common and statute law of England, before the emigration of our ancestors, and which are shown not to have been unsuited to their civil and political condition by having been acted on by them after the settlement of this country.

> Benjamin R. Curtis, *Murray's Lessee v. Hoboken Land & Improvement Co.*, 59 U.S. (18 How.) 272, 276–77 (1856)

8 To hold that such a characteristic is essential to due process of law, would be to deny every quality of the law but its age, and to render it incapable of progress or improvement. It would be to stamp upon our jurisprudence the unchangeableness attributed to the laws of the Medes and Persians.... it is better not to go too far back into antiquity for the best securities for our "ancient liberties." It is more consonant to the true philosophy of our historical legal institutions to say that the spirit of personal liberty and individual right, which they embodied, was preserved and developed by a progressive growth and wise adaptation to new circumstances and situations of the forms and processes found fit to give, from time to time, new expression and greater effect to modern ideas of self-government.

> Stanley Matthews, *Hurtado v. California*, 110 U.S. 516, 529, 530 (1884)

9 The question of the reasonableness of a rate of charge for transportation by a rail-

road company . . . is eminently a question for judicial investigation, requiring due process of law for its determination. If the company is deprived of the power of charging reasonable rates for the use of its property, and such deprivation takes place in the absence of an investigation by judicial machinery, it is deprived of the lawful use of its property, and thus, in substance and effect, of the property itself.

Samuel Blatchford, *Chicago, Milwaukee & St. Paul Ry. v. Minnesota,* 134 U.S. 418, 458 (1890)

10 To justify the State in . . . interposing its authority in behalf of the public, it must appear, first, that the interests of the public . . . require such interference; and, second, that the means are reasonably necessary for the accomplishment of the purpose, and not unduly oppressive upon individuals.

Henry B. Brown, *Lawton v. Steele,* 152 U.S. 133, 137 (1894)

11 The liberty mentioned in that amendment [the Fourteenth] means not only the right of the citizen to be free from the mere physical restraint of his person . . . but the term is deemed to embrace the right of the citizen to be free in the enjoyment of all his faculties; to be free to use them in all lawful ways; to live and work where he will; to earn his livelihood by any lawful calling; to pursue any livelihood or avocation, and for that purpose to enter into all contracts which may be proper, necessary and essential to his carrying out to a successful conclusion the purposes above mentioned.

Rufus W. Peckham, *Allgeyer v. Louisiana,* 165 U.S. 578, 589 (1897)

12 While the courts must exercise a judgment of their own, it by no means is true that every law is void which may seem to the judges who pass upon it excessive, unsuited to its ostensible end, or based upon conceptions of morality with which they disagree. Considerable latitude must be allowed for differences of view as well as for possible peculiar conditions which this court can know but imperfectly, if at all. Otherwise a constitution, instead of embodying only relatively fundamental rules of right, as generally understood by all English-speaking communities, would become the partisan of a particular set of eth-

ical or economical opinions, which by no means are held *semper ubique et ab omnibus.*

Oliver Wendell Holmes, Jr., *Otis v. Parker,* 187 U.S. 606, 609 (1903)

13 This case is decided upon an economic theory which a large part of the country does not entertain. If it were a question whether I agreed with that theory, I should desire to study it further and long before making up my mind. But I do not conceive that to be my duty, because I strongly believe that my agreement or disagreement has nothing to do with the right of a majority to embody their opinions in law.

Oliver Wendell Holmes, Jr., *Lochner v. New York,* 198 U.S. 45, 75 (1905) (dissenting)

14 It is settled by various decisions of this court that state constitutions and state laws may regulate life in many ways which we as legislators might think as injudicious or if you like as tyrannical as this, and which equally with this interfere with the liberty to contract. Sunday laws and usury laws are ancient examples. A more modern one is the prohibition of lotteries. The liberty of the citizen to do as he likes so long as he does not interfere with the liberty of others to do the same, which has been a shibboleth for some well-known writers, is interfered with by school laws, by the Post Office, by every state or municipal institution which takes his money for purposes thought desirable, whether he likes it or not. The Fourteenth Amendment does not enact Mr. Herbert Spencer's Social Statics.

Oliver Wendell Holmes, Jr., *Lochner v. New York,* 198 U.S. 45, 75 (1905) (dissenting)

15 A constitution is not intended to embody a particular economic theory, whether of paternalism and the organic relation of the citizen to the State or of *laissez faire.* It is made for people of fundamentally differing views, and the accident of our finding certain opinions natural and familiar or novel and even shocking ought not to conclude our judgment upon the question whether statutes embodying them conflict with the Constitution of the United States.

Oliver Wendell Holmes, Jr., *Lochner v. New York,* 198 U.S. 45, 75–76 (1905) (dissenting)

16 I think that the word liberty in the Fourteenth Amendment is perverted when it is

held to prevent the natural outcome of a dominant opinion, unless it can be said that a rational and fair man necessarily would admit that the statute proposed would infringe fundamental principles as they have been understood by the traditions of our people and our law.

Oliver Wendell Holmes, Jr., *Lochner v. New York,* 198 U.S. 45, 76 (1905) (dissenting)

17 Statutes of the nature of that under review, limiting the hours in which grown and intelligent men may labor to earn their living, are mere meddlesome interferences with the rights of the individual, and they are not saved from condemnation by the claim that they are passed in the exercise of the police power and upon the subject of the health of the individual whose rights are interfered with, unless there be some fair ground, reasonable in and of itself, to say that there is material danger to the public health or to the health of the employés, if the hours of labor are not curtailed. If this be not clearly the case, the individuals, whose rights are thus made the subject of legislative interference, are under the protection of the Federal Constitution regarding their liberty of contract as well as of person; and the legislature of the State has no power to limit their right as proposed in this statute.

Rufus W. Peckham, *Lochner v. New York,* 198 U.S. 45, 61 (1905)

18 What is due process of law depends on circumstances. It varies with the subject-matter and the necessities of the situation.

Oliver Wendell Holmes, Jr., *Moyer v. Peabody,* 212 U.S. 78, 84 (1909)

19 There is nothing that I more deprecate than the use of the Fourteenth Amendment beyond the absolute compulsion of its words to prevent the making of social experiments that an important part of the community desires, in the insulated chambers afforded by the several States, even though the experiments may seem futile or even noxious to me and to those whose judgment I most respect.

Oliver Wendell Holmes, Jr., *Truax v. Corrigan,* 257 U.S. 312, 344 (1921) (dissenting)

20 The Fourteenth Amendment, itself a historical product, did not destroy history for the States and substitute mechanical compartments of law all exactly alike. If a thing has been practised for two hundred years by common consent, it will need a strong case for the Fourteenth Amendment to affect it.

Oliver Wendell Holmes, Jr., *Jackman v. Rosenbaum Co.,* 260 U.S. 22, 31 (1922)

21 [Liberty] denotes not merely freedom from bodily restraint but also the right of the individual to contract, to engage in any of the common occupations of life, to acquire useful knowledge, to marry, establish a home and bring up children, to worship God according to the dictates of his own conscience, and generally to enjoy those privileges long recognized at common law as essential to the orderly pursuit of happiness by free men.

James C. McReynolds, *Meyer v. Nebraska,* 262 U.S. 390, 399 (1923)

22 I tell them that if the rate-making power will only say I have considered A. B. & C., all the elements enumerated, we accept the judgment unless it makes us puke.

Oliver Wendell Holmes, Jr., Letter to Harold J. Laski, 23 Oct. 1926, in *Holmes-Laski Letters* 2:888 (Mark DeWolfe Howe ed. 1953)

23 I think the proper course is to recognize that a state legislature can do whatever it sees fit to do unless it is restrained by some express prohibition in the Constitution of the United States or of the State, and that Courts should be careful not to extend such prohibitions beyond their obvious meaning by reading into them conceptions of public policy that the particular Court may happen to entertain.

Oliver Wendell Holmes, Jr., *Tyson v. Banton,* 273 U.S. 418, 446 (1927) (dissenting)

24 In delimiting the field of liberty, courts have professed for the most part to go about their work empirically and have rather prided themselves on doing so. They have said, we will not define due process of law. We will leave it to be "pricked out" by a process of inclusion and exclusion in individual cases. That was to play safely, and very likely at the beginning to play wisely. The question is how long we are to be satisfied with a series of *ad hoc* conclusions. It is all very well to go on pricking the lines, but the time must come when we shall do

prudently to look them over, and see whether they make a pattern or a medley of scraps and patches.

Benjamin N. Cardozo, *The Paradoxes of Legal Science* 96 (1928)

25 I have not yet adequately expressed the more than anxiety that I feel at the ever increasing scope given to the Fourteenth Amendment in cutting down what I believe to be the constitutional rights of the States. As the decisions now stand, I see hardly any limit but the sky to the invalidating of those rights if they happen to strike a majority of this Court as for any reason undesirable. I cannot believe that the Amendment was intended to give us *carte blanche* to embody our economic or moral beliefs in its prohibitions.

Oliver Wendell Holmes, Jr., *Baldwin v. Missouri,* 281 U.S. 586, 595 (1930) (dissenting)

26 Under certain circumstances, the constitutional requirement of due process is a requirement of judicial process.

Louis D. Brandeis, *Crowell v. Benson,* 285 U.S. 22, 87 (1932) (dissenting)

27 A regulation valid for one kind of business may, of course, be invalid for another; since the reasonableness of every regulation is dependent upon the relevant facts. But so far as concerns the power to regulate, there is no difference in essence, between a business called private and one called a public utility. . . . In my opinion, the true principle is that the state's power extends to every regulation of any business reasonably required and appropriate for the public protection. I find in the due process clause no other limitation upon the character or the scope of regulation permissible.

Louis D. Brandeis, *New State Ice Co. v. Liebmann,* 285 U.S. 262, 301-03 (1932) (dissenting)

28 There must be power in the States . . . to remould, through experimentation, our economic practices and institutions to meet changing social and economic needs. . . . To stay experimentation in things social and economic is a grave responsibility. Denial of the right to experiment may be fraught with serious consequences to the Nation. . . . It is one of the

happy incidents of the federal system that a single courageous State may, if its citizens choose, serve as a laboratory; and try novel social and economic experiments without risk to the rest of the country. This Court has the power to prevent an experiment. . . . But in the exercise of this high power, we must be ever on our guard, lest we erect our prejudices into legal principles. If we would guide by the light of reason, we must let our minds be bold.*

Louis D. Brandeis, *New State Ice Co. v. Liebmann,* 285 U.S. 262, 311 (1932) (dissenting)

29 While emergency does not create power, emergency may furnish the occasion for the exercise of power.

Charles Evans Hughes, *Home Building & Loan Ass'n v. Blaisdell,* 290 U.S. 398, 426 (1934)

30 Neither property rights nor contract rights are absolute; for government cannot exist if the citizen may at will use his property to the detriment of his fellows, or exercise his freedom of contract to work them harm.

Owen J. Roberts, *Nebbia v. New York,* 291 U.S. 502, 523 (1934)

31 The guaranty of due process, as has often been held, demands only that the law shall not be unreasonable, arbitrary or capricious, and that the means selected shall have a real and substantial relation to the object sought to be attained. It results that a regulation valid for one sort of business, or in given circumstances, may be invalid for another sort, or for the same business under other circumatances.

Owen J. Roberts, *Nebbia v. New York,* 291 U.S. 502, 525 (1934)

32 So far as the requirement of due process is concerned, and in the absence of other constitutional restriction, a state is free to adopt whatever economic policy may reasonably be deemed to promote public welfare, and to enforce that policy by legislation adapted to its purpose. The courts are without authority either to declare such

---

* If we would guide by the light of reason, we must let our minds be bold. —**Louis D. Brandeis,** *Jay Burns Baking Co. v. Bryan,* 264 U.S. 504, 520 (1924) (dissenting)

policy, or, when it is declared by the legislature, to override it.

> Owen J. Roberts, *Nebbia v. New York*, 291 U.S. 502, 537–38 (1934)

33 It is difficult to imagine any grounds, other than our own personal economic predilections, for saying that the contract of employment is any the less an appropriate subject of legislation than are scores of others, in dealing with which this Court has held that legislatures may curtail individual freedom in the public interest.

> Harlan F. Stone, *Morehead v. New York*, 298 U.S. 587, 633 (1936) (dissenting)

34 The Constitution does not recognize an absolute and uncontrollable liberty.... The liberty safeguarded is liberty in a social organization which requires the protection of law against the evils which menace the health, safety, morals and welfare of the people. Liberty under the Constitution is thus necessarily subject to the restraints of due process, and regulation which is reasonable in relation to its subjects and is adopted in the interests of the community is due process.

> Charles Evans Hughes, *West Coast Hotel Co. v. Parrish*, 300 U.S. 379, 391 (1937)

35 There may be narrower scope for operation of the presumption of constitutionality when legislation appears on its face to be within a specific prohibition of the Constitution.... It is unnecessary to consider now whether legislation which restricts those political processes which can ordinarily be expected to bring about repeal of undesirable legislation, is to be subjected to more exacting judicial scrutiny under the general prohibitions of the Fourteenth Amendment than are most other types of legislation.... Nor need we enquire whether similar considerations enter into the review of statutes directed at particular religious ... or national ... or racial minorities ... whether prejudice against discrete and insular minorities may be a special condition, which tends seriously to curtail the operation of those political processes ordinarily to be relied upon to protect minorities, and which may call for a correspondingly more searching judicial inquiry.

> Harlan F. Stone, *United States v. Carolene Products Co.*, 304 U.S. 144, 152 n.4 (1938)

36 Under our constitutional system, courts stand against any winds that blow as havens of refuge for those who might otherwise suffer because they are helpless, weak, outnumbered, or because they are nonconforming victims of prejudice and public excitement. Due process of law, preserved for all by our Constitution, commands that no such practice as that disclosed by this record shall send any accused to his death. No higher duty, no more solemn responsibility, rests upon this Court, than that of translating into living law and maintaining this constitutional shield deliberately planned and inscribed for the benefit of every human being subject to our Constitution—of whatever race, creed or persuasion.

> Hugo L. Black, *Chambers v. Florida*, 309 U.S. 227, 240–41 (1940)

37 The use of the due process clause to disable the States in protection of society from crime is quite as dangerous and delicate a use of federal judicial power as to use it to disable them from social or economic experimentation.

> Robert H. Jackson, *Ashcraft v. Tennessee*, 322 U.S. 137, 174 (1944)

38 Therefore, in considering what interests are so fundamental as to be enshrined in the Due Process Clause, those liberties of the individual which history has attested as the indispensable conditions of an open as against a closed society come to this Court with a momentum for respect lacking when appeal is made to liberties which derive merely from shifting economic arrangements.

> Felix Frankfurter, *Kovacs v. Cooper*, 336 U.S. 77, 95 (1949) (concurring)

39 Many controversies have raged about the cryptic and abstract words of the Due Process Clause but there can be no doubt that at a minimum they require that deprivation of life, liberty or property by adjudication be preceded by notice and opportunity for hearing appropriate to the nature of the case.

> Robert H. Jackson, *Mullane v. Central Hanover Bank & Trust Co.*, 339 U.S. 306, 313 (1950)

40 An elementary and fundamental requirement of due process in any proceeding

which is to be accorded finality is notice reasonably calculated, under all the circumstances, to apprise interested parties of the pendency of the action and afford them an opportunity to present their objections.... The notice must be of such nature as reasonably to convey the required information.

> **Robert H. Jackson,** *Mullane v. Central Hanover Bank & Trust Co.,* 339 U.S. 306, 314 (1950)

41 "Due process," unlike some legal rules, is not a technical conception with a fixed content unrelated to time, place and circumstances. Expressing as it does in its ultimate analysis respect enforced by law for that feeling of just treatment which has been evolved through centuries of Anglo-American constitutional history and civilization, "due process" cannot be imprisoned within the treacherous limits of any formula. Representing a profound attitude of fairness between man and man, and more particularly between the individual and government, "due process" is compounded of history, reason, the past course of decisions, and stout confidence in the strength of the democratic faith which we profess.

> **Felix Frankfurter,** *Joint Anti-Fascist Refugee Comm. v. McGrath,* 341 U.S. 123, 162–63 (1951) (concurring)

42 That a conclusion satisfies one's private conscience does not attest its reliability. The validity and moral authority of a conclusion largely depend on the mode by which it was reached. Secrecy is not congenial to truth-seeking and self-righteousness gives too slender an assurance of rightness. No better instrument has been devised for arriving at truth than to give a person in jeopardy of serious loss notice of the case against him and opportunity to meet it. Nor has a better way been found for generating the feeling, so important to a popular government, that justice has been done.

> **Felix Frankfurter,** *Joint Anti-Fascist Refugee Comm. v. McGrath,* 341 U.S. 123, 171–72 (1951) (concurring)

43 The vague contours of the Due Process Clause do not leave judges at large. We may not draw on our merely personal and private notions and disregard the limits that bind judges in their judicial function.

> **Felix Frankfurter,** *Rochin v. California,* 342 U.S. 165, 170 (1952)

44 At this time when many are worried about dismissal from public service, when only because of the overriding need to protect the public safety is the identity of informers kept secret, when we proudly contrast the full hearings before our courts with those in the benighted countries which have no due process protection, when many of our courts are so careful in the protection of those charged with crimes that they will not permit the use of evidence illegally obtained, our sense of justice should be outraged by denial to students of the normal safeguards. It is shocking that the officials of a state educational institution, which can function properly only if our freedoms are preserved, should not understand the elementary principles of fair play. It is equally shocking to find that a court supports them in denying to a student the protection given to a pickpocket.

> **Warren A. Seavey,** "Dismissal of Students: 'Due Process,'" 70 *Harvard Law Review* 1406, 1406-07 (1957)

45 As a generalization, it can be said that due process embodies the differing rules of fair play, which through the years, have become associated with differing types of proceedings. Whether the Constitution requires that a particular right obtain in a specific proceeding depends upon a complexity of factors. The nature of the alleged right involved, the nature of the proceeding, and the possible burden on that proceeding, are all considerations which must be taken into account.

> **Earl Warren,** *Hannah v. Larche,* 363 U.S. 420, 442 (1960)

46 Due process has not been reduced to any formula; its content cannot be determined by reference to any code. The best that can be said is that through the course of this Court's decisions it has represented the balance which our Nation, built upon postulates of respect for the liberty of the individual, has struck between that liberty and the demands of organized society.... The balance of which I speak is the balance struck by this country, having regard to

what history teaches are the traditions from which it developed as well as the traditions from which it broke. That tradition is a living thing. A decision of this Court which radically departs from it could not long survive, while a decision which builds on what has survived is likely to be sound.

John M. Harlan (1899–1971), *Poe v. Ullman*, 367 U.S. 497, 542 (1961) (dissenting)

47 The full scope of the liberty guaranteed by the Due Process Clause cannot be found in or limited by the precise terms of the specific guarantees elsewhere provided in the Constitution. This "liberty" is not a series of isolated points pricked out in terms of the taking of property; the freedom of speech, press, and religion; the right to keep and bear arms; the freedom from unreasonable searches and seizures; and so on. It is a rational continuum which, broadly speaking, includes a freedom from all substantial arbitrary impositions and purposeless restraints, . . . and which also recognizes, what a reasonable and sensitive judgment must, that certain interests require particularly careful scrutiny of the state needs asserted to justify their abridgement.

John M. Harlan (1899–1971), *Poe v. Ullman*, 367 U.S. 497, 543 (1961) (dissenting)

48 The suppression by the prosecution of evidence favorable to an accused upon request violates due process where the evidence is material either to guilt or to punishment, irrespective of the good faith or bad faith of the prosecution.

William J. Brennan, Jr., *Brady v. Maryland*, 373 U.S. 83, 87 (1963)

49 A fundamental requirement of due process is "the opportunity to be heard." . . . It is an opportunity which must be granted at a meaningful time and in a meaningful manner.

Potter Stewart, *Armstrong v. Manzo*, 380 U.S. 545, 552 (1965)

50 Where a person's good name, reputation, honor, or integrity is at stake because of what the government is doing to him, notice and an opportunity to be heard are essential.

William O. Douglas, *Wisconsin v. Constantineau*, 400 U.S. 433, 437 (1971)

51 Due process requires, at a minimum, that absent a countervailing state interest of overriding significance, persons forced to settle their claims of right and duty through the judicial process must be given a meaningful opportunity to be heard.

John M. Harlan (1899–1971), *Boddie v. Connecticut*, 401 U.S. 371, 377 (1971)

52 Not every push or shove, even if it may later seem unnecessary in the peace of a judge's chambers, violates a person's constitutional rights.

Henry J. Friendly, *Johnson v. Glick*, 481 F.2d 1028, 1033 (2d Cir. 1973)

53 I have always thought that one of this Court's most important roles is to . . . [protect] the legitimate expectations of every person to innate human dignity and sense of worth.

William J. Brennan, Jr., *Paul v. Davis*, 424 U.S. 693, 734–35 (1976) (dissenting)

DUTY

See NEGLIGENCE; TORTS

ECONOMICS

See LAW AND ECONOMICS

EDUCATION

See also SEGREGATION

1 It is, Sir, as I have said, a small college. And yet *there are those who love it!*

Daniel Webster, Argument in *Trustees of Dartmouth College v. Woodward*, 17 U.S. (4 Wheat.) 518, 10 Mar. 1818, in *Papers of Daniel Webster: Legal Papers* 3:153, 154 (Andrew J. King ed. 1989)

2 While this court would not interfere with any action of the board in so far as a pure question of "valid" academic freedom is concerned, it will not tolerate academic freedom being used as a cloak to promote the popularization in the minds of adolescents of acts forbidden by the Penal Law. This appointment [of Bertrand Russell to a chair of philosophy at the City College of New York] affects the health, safety and morals of the community and it is the duty of the court to act. Academic freedom does

119

not mean academic license. It is the freedom to do good and not to teach evil.

> **John E. McGeehan,** *Kay v. Board of Higher
> Educ.,* 173 Misc. 943, 950–51, 18 N.Y.S.2d
> 821 (Sup. Ct. 1940)

3 These [school boards] have, of course, important, delicate, and highly discretionary
functions, but none that they may not perform within the limits of the Bill of Rights.
That they are educating the young for citizenship is reason for scrupulous protection of Constitutional freedoms of the individual, if we are not to strangle the free
mind at its source and teach youth to discount important principles of our government as mere platitudes.

> **Robert H. Jackson,** *West Virginia State Bd.
> of Educ. v. Barnette,* 319 U.S. 624, 637 (1943)

4 That a child is offered an alternative may
reduce the constraint; it does not eliminate
the operation of influence by the school in
matters sacred to conscience and outside
the school's domain. The law of imitation
operates, and non-conformity is not an outstanding characteristic of children. The result is an obvious pressure upon children
to attend.

> **Felix Frankfurter,** *Illinois ex rel. McCollum
> v. Board of Educ.,* 333 U.S. 203, 227 (1948)
> (separate opinion)

5 If we are to eliminate everything that is objectionable to any of these warring sects or
inconsistent with any of their doctrines, we
will leave public education in shreds.

> **Robert H. Jackson,** *Illinois ex rel. McCollum
> v. Board of Educ.,* 333 U.S. 203, 235 (1948)
> (concurring)

6 To do so is to allow zeal for our own ideas
of what is good in public instruction to induce us to accept the role of a super board
of education for every school district in the
nation.

> **Robert H. Jackson,** *Illinois ex rel. McCollum
> v. Board of Educ.,* 333 U.S. 203, 237 (1948)
> (concurring)

7 Today, education is perhaps the most important function of state and local governments. Compulsory school attendance laws
and the great expenditures for education
both demonstrate our recognition of the
importance of education to our democratic
society. It is required in the performance

of our most basic public responsibilities,
even service in the armed forces. It is the
very foundation of good citizenship. Today
it is a principal instrument in awakening
the child to cultural values, in preparing
him for later professional training, and in
helping him to adjust normally to his environment. In these days, it is doubtful that
any child may reasonably be expected to
succeed in life if he is denied the opportunity of an education. Such an opportunity,
where the state has undertaken to provide
it, is a right which must be made available
to all on equal terms.

> **Earl Warren,** *Brown v. Board of Education,*
> 347 U.S. 483, 493 (1954)

8 It can hardly be argued that either students
or teachers shed their constitutional rights
to freedom of speech or expression at the
schoolhouse gate.

> **Abe Fortas,** *Tinker v. Des Moines Indep.
> Community School Dist.,* 393 U.S. 503, 506
> (1969)

ELECTIONS

See VOTING

EMINENT DOMAIN

1 It may well be doubted whether the nature
of society and of government does not prescribe some limits to the legislative power;
and, if any be prescribed, where are they
to be found, if the property of an individual, fairly and honestly acquired, may be
seized without compensation.

> **John Marshall,** *Fletcher v. Peck,* 10 U.S. (6
> Cranch) 87, 135 (1810)

2 [An eminent domain taking] is the purchase of a public easement, the consideration for which is settled by such appraise-
ment only because the parties are unable
to agree upon it. The true rule would be,
as in the case of other purchases, that the
price is due and ought to be paid, at the
moment the purchase is made, when credit
is not specially agreed on. And if a pie-pow-
der court could be called on the instant and
on the spot, the true rule of justice for the
public would be, to pay the compensation
with one hand, whilst they apply the axe
with the other; and this rule is departed
from only because some time is necessary,

by the forms of law, to conduct the inquiry; and this delay must be compensated by interest.

Lemuel Shaw, *Parks v. City of Boston,* 32 Mass. (15 Pick.) 198, 208 (1834)

3 The legislature may determine what private property is needed for public purposes—that is a question of a political and legislative character; but when the taking has been ordered, then the question of compensation is judicial. It does not rest with the public, taking the property, through Congress or the legislature, its representative, to say what compensation shall be paid, or even what shall be the rule of compensation. The Constitution has declared that just compensation shall be paid, and the ascertainment of that is a judicial inquiry.

David J. Brewer, *Monongahela Navigation Co. v. United States,* 148 U.S. 312, 327 (1893)

4 In the organic relations of modern society it may sometimes be hard to draw the line that is supposed to limit the authority of the legislature to exercise or delegate the power of eminent domain. But to gather the streams from waste and to draw from them energy, labor without brains, and so to save mankind from toil that it can be spared, is to supply what, next to intellect, is the very foundation of all our achievements and all our welfare. If that purpose is not public we should be at a loss to say what is.

Oliver Wendell Holmes, Jr., *Mt. Vernon-Woodberry Cotton Duck Co. v. Alabama Interstate Power Co.,* 240 U.S. 30, 32 (1916)

5 Government hardly could go on if to some extent values incident to property could not be diminished without paying for every such change in the general law. As long recognized, some values are enjoyed under an implied limitation and must yield to the police power. But obviously the implied limitation must have its limits, or the contract and due process clauses are gone. One fact for consideration in determining such limits is the extent of the diminution. When it reaches a certain magnitude, in most if not in all cases there must be an exercise of eminent domain and compensation to sustain the act.

Oliver Wendell Holmes, Jr., *Pennsylvania Coal Co. v. Mahon,* 260 U.S. 393, 413 (1922)

6 The general rule at least is, that while property may be regulated to a certain extent, if regulation goes too far it will be recognized as a taking. . . . In general it is not plain that a man's misfortunes or necessities will justify his shifting the damages to his neighbor's shoulders. . . . We are in danger of forgetting that a strong public desire to improve the public condition is not enough to warrant achieving the desire by a shorter cut than the constitutional way of paying for the change.

Oliver Wendell Holmes, Jr., *Pennsylvania Coal Co. v. Mahon,* 260 U.S. 393, 415–16 (1922)

7 The Fifth Amendment's guarantee that private property shall not be taken for a public use without just compensation was designed to bar Government from forcing some people alone to bear public burdens which, in all fairness and justice, should be borne by the public as a whole.

Hugo L. Black, *Armstrong v. United States,* 364 U.S. 40, 49 (1960)

EMPLOYMENT

See LABOR LAW

ENFORCEMENT

See LAW ENFORCEMENT

ENGLISH LAW

1 Our allegiance binds us not to the laws of England any longer than while we live in England, for the laws of the parliament of England reach no further, nor do the king's writs under the great seal go any further.

John Winthrop, 1646, in *The History of New England from 1630 to 1649,* at 289 (James Savage ed. 1826)

2 To say the Parliament is absolute and arbitrary is a contradiction. The Parliament cannot make 2 and 2, 5: omnipotency cannot do it. The supreme power in a state is *jus dicere* only: *jus dare,* strictly speaking, belongs alone to GOD. Parliaments are in all cases to *declare* what is for the good of the whole; but it is not the *declaration* of Parliament that makes it so. There must be in every instance a higher authority, viz., GOD. Should an act of Parliament be against any

of *his* natural laws, which are *immutably* true, *their* declaration would be contrary to eternal truth, equity, and justice, and consequently void: and so it would be adjudged by the Parliament itself when convinced of their mistake.

> James Otis, *The Rights of the British Colonies Asserted and Proved*, 1764, in *Pamphlets of the American Revolution* 1:419, 454 (Bernard Bailyn ed. 1965)

3 But in conquered or ceded countries, that have already laws of their own, the king may indeed alter and change those laws; but, till he does actually change them, the antient laws of the country remain, unless such as are against the law of God, as in the case of an infidel country. Our American plantations are principally of this latter sort, being obtained in the last century either by right of conquest and driving out the natives (with what natural justice I shall not at present enquire), or by treaties. And therefore the common law of England, as such, has no allowance or authority there; they being part of the mother country, but distinct (though dependent) dominions. They are subject however to the control of the parliament; though (like Ireland, Man, and the rest) not bound by any acts of parliament, unless particularly named.

> William Blackstone, *Commentaries on the Laws of England* 1:105 (1765)

4 The history of the present King of Great Britain is a history of repeated injuries and usurpations, all having in direct object the establishment of an absolute Tyranny over these States. To prove this, let Facts be submitted to a candid world.—He has refused his Assent to Laws, the most wholesome and necessary for the public good.—He has forbidden his Governors to pass Laws of immediate and pressing importance, unless suspended in their operation till his Assent should be obtained; and when so suspended, he has utterly neglected to attend to them.—He has refused to pass other Laws for the accommodation of large districts of people, unless those people would relinquish the right of Representation in the Legislature, a right inestimable to them and formidable to tyrants only.

> Declaration of Independence, 1776, in *Documents Illustrative of the Formation of the Union of the American States* 22, 22–23 (1927)

5 It is a proverb in England that it is safer to shoot a man than a hare. The severity of the game-laws certainly indicates an extravagant sympathy of the nation with horses and hunters.

> Ralph Waldo Emerson, "Race," *English Traits*, 1856, in *Complete Works of Ralph Waldo Emerson* 5:44, 73 (1903)

6 In the [English] courts the independence of the judges and the loyalty of the suitors are equally excellent. In parliament they have hit on that capital invention on freedom, a constitutional opposition. And when courts and parliament are both deaf, the plaintiff is not silenced. Calm, patient, his weapon of defence from year to year is the obstinate reproduction of the grievance, with calculations and estimates. . . . They are bound to see their measure carried, and stick to it through ages of defeat.

> Ralph Waldo Emerson, "Ability," *English Traits*, 1856, in *Complete Works of Ralph Waldo Emerson* 5:74, 81 (1903)

7 The Englishman is peaceably minding his business and earning his day's wages. But if you offer to lay hand on his day's wages, on his cow, or his right in common, or his shop, he will fight to the Judgment. Magnacharta, jury-trial, *habeas-corpus*, starchamber, ship-money, Popery, Plymouth colony, American Revolution, are all questions involving a yeoman's right to his dinner, and except as touching that, would not have lashed the British nation to rage and revolt.

> Ralph Waldo Emerson, "Ability," *English Traits*, 1856, in *Complete Works of Ralph Waldo Emerson* 5:74, 87–88 (1903)

8 A Western lawyer of eminence [Judge H. H. Emmons of Michigan] said to me he wished it were a penal offense to bring an English law-book into a court in this country, so pernicious had he found in his experience our deference to English precedent.

> Ralph Waldo Emerson, "Power," *The Conduct of Life*, 1860, in *Complete Works of Ralph Waldo Emerson* 6:53, 62 (1904)

9 BARRISTER, *n.* One of the ten thousand varieties of the genus Lawyer. In England the

functions of a barrister are distinct from those of a solicitor. The one advises, the other executes; but the thing advised and the thing executed is the client.

Ambrose Bierce, *The Enlarged Devil's Dictionary* 24 (Ernest J. Hopkins ed. 1967)

10 The United States pays heavy and inconvenient death duties upon its inheritance of English law. . . . the judges of the United States have added something a good deal worse, and that is the custom of widening the scope of specific laws by judicial interpretation. The English judges, whatever their barbarous delight in cruelty otherwise, at least observe the ancient rule that criminal statutes are to be construed strictly, and that no man is to be punished for a crime not clearly defined.

H. L. Mencken, "On Justice," *Smart Set,* July 1921, at 39, 40–41

ENVIRONMENTAL LAW

1 The State has an interest independent of and behind the titles of its citizens, in all the earth and air within its domain.

Oliver Wendell Holmes, Jr., *Georgia v. Tennessee Copper Co.,* 206 U.S. 230, 237 (1907)

2 The purposes of this Act are: To declare a national policy which will encourage productive and enjoyable harmony between man and his environment; to promote efforts which will prevent or eliminate damage to the environment and biosphere and stimulate the health and welfare of man; to enrich the understanding of the ecological systems and natural resources important to the Nation; and to establish a Council on Environmental Quality.

National Environmental Policy Act of 1969, Pub. L. No. 91–190, § 2, 83 Stat. 852, 852 (1970)

3 It is the continuing policy of the Federal Government, in cooperation with State and local governments, and other concerned public and private organizations, to use all practicable means and measures, including financial and technical assistance, in a manner calculated to foster and promote the general welfare, to create and maintain conditions under which man and nature can exist in productive harmony, and fulfill

the social, economic, and other requirements of present and future generations of Americans.

National Environmental Policy Act of 1969, Pub. L. No. 91–190, § 101(a), 83 Stat. 852, 852 (1970)

4 Each person should enjoy a healthful environment and . . . each person has a responsibility to contribute to the preservation and enhancement of the environment.

National Environmental Policy Act of 1969, Pub. L. No. 91–190, § 101(c), 83 Stat. 852, 853 (1970)

5 The critical question of "standing" would be simplified and also put neatly in focus if we fashioned a federal rule that allowed environmental issues to be litigated before federal agencies or federal courts in the name of the inanimate object about to be despoiled, defaced, or invaded by roads and bulldozers and where injury is the subject of public outrage. Contemporary public concern for protecting nature's ecological equilibrium should lead to the conferral of standing upon environmental objects to sue for their own preservation.

William O. Douglas, *Sierra Club v. Morton,* 405 U.S. 727, 741–42 (1972) (dissenting)

6 The river as plaintiff speaks for the ecological unit of life that is part of it.

William O. Douglas, *Sierra Club v. Morton,* 405 U.S. 727, 743 (1972) (dissenting)

7 I am quite seriously proposing that we give legal rights to forests, oceans, rivers and other so-called "natural objects" in the environment—indeed, to the natural environment as a whole.

Christopher D. Stone, "Should Trees Have Standing?—Toward Legal Rights for Natural Objects," 45 *Southern California Law Review* 450, 456 (1972)

8 It is not inevitable, nor is it wise, that natural objects should have no rights to seek redress in their own behalf. It is no answer to say that streams and forests cannot have standing because streams and forests cannot speak. Corporations cannot speak either; nor can states, estates, infants, incompetents, municipalities or universities. Lawyers speak for them, as they custom-

arily do for the ordinary citizen with legal problems.

> Christopher D. Stone, "Should Trees Have Standing?—Toward Legal Rights for Natural Objects," 45 *Southern California Law Review* 450, 464 (1972)

9 Approximately 80% of our air pollution stems from hydrocarbons released by vegetation, so let's not go overboard in setting and enforcing tough emission standards from man-made sources.*

> Ronald W. Reagan, 1980, quoted in *There He Goes Again: Ronald Reagan's Reign of Error* 99 (Mark Green & Gail MacColl eds. 1983)

EQUAL PROTECTION

See also CIVIL RIGHTS; FOURTEENTH AMENDMENT; SEX DISCRIMINATION; WOMEN'S RIGHTS

1 But the fundamental rights to life, liberty, and the pursuit of happiness, considered as individual possessions, are secured by those maxims of constitutional law which are the monuments showing the victorious progress of the race in securing to men the blessings of civilization under the reign of just and equal laws, so that, in the famous language of the Massachusetts Bill of Rights, the government of the commonwealth "may be a government of laws and not of men." For the very idea that one man may be compelled to hold his life, or the means of living, or any material right essential to the enjoyment of life, at the mere will of another, seems to be intolerable in any country where freedom prevails, as being the essence of slavery itself.

> Stanley Matthews, *Yick Wo v. Hopkins,* 118 U.S. 356, 370 (1886)
> See also OBEDIENCE TO LAW 3

2 The cases present the ordinances in actual operation, and the facts shown establish an administration directed so exclusively against a particular class of persons as to warrant and require the conclusion, that, whatever may have been the intent of the ordinances as adopted, they are applied by the public authorities charged with their

---

* This statement was widely disputed by scientists. Hecklers at a Reagan campaign rally at Claremont College hung a banner from a tree reading, "Chop Me Down Before I Kill Again."

administration, and thus representing the State itself, with a mind so unequal and oppressive as to amount to a practical denial by the State of that equal protection of the laws. . . . Though the law itself be fair on its face and impartial in appearance, yet, if it is applied and administered by public authority with an evil eye and an unequal hand, so as practically to make unjust and illegal discriminations between persons in similar circumstances, material to their rights, the denial of equal justice is still within the prohibition of the Constitution.

> Stanley Matthews, *Yick Wo v. Hopkins,* 118 U.S. 356, 373–74 (1886)

3 The provision in the Fourteenth Amendment, that no State shall deny to any person within its jurisdiction the equal protection of the laws, was not intended to prevent a State from adjusting its system of taxation in all proper and reasonable ways. . . . We think that we are safe in saying that the Fourteenth Amendment was not intended to compel the State to adopt an iron rule of equal taxation.

> Joseph P. Bradley, *Bell's Gap R.R. v. Pennsylvania,* 134 U.S. 232, 237 (1890)

4 The foregoing argument is one of the many attempts to construe the Fourteenth Amendment as introducing a factitious equality without regard to practical differences that are best met by corresponding differences of treatment.

> Oliver Wendell Holmes, Jr., *Standard Oil Co. of Kentucky v. Tennessee,* 217 U.S. 413, 420 (1910)

5 It requires no argument to show that the right to work for a living in the common occupations of the community is of the very essence of the personal freedom and opportunity that it was the purpose of the [Fourteenth] Amendment to secure. . . . If this could be refused solely upon the ground of race or nationality, the prohibition of the denial to any person of the equal protection of the laws would be a barren form of words.

> Charles Evans Hughes, *Traux v. Raich,* 239 U.S. 33, 41 (1915)

6 It is unnecessary to say that the "equal protection of the laws" required by the Fourteenth Amendment does not prevent the

States from resorting to classification for the purposes of legislation. . . . But the classification must be reasonable, not arbitrary, and must rest upon some ground of difference having a fair and substantial relation to the object of the legislation, so that all persons similarly circumstanced shall be treated alike.

Mahlon Pitney, *F.S. Royster Guano Co. v. Virginia,* 253 U.S. 412, 415 (1920)

7 It is the usual last resort of constitutional arguments to point out shortcomings of this sort [equal protection arguments]. But the answer is that the law does all that is needed when it does all that it can, indicates a policy, applies it to all within the lines, and seeks to bring within the lines all similarly situated so far and so fast as its means allow.

Oliver Wendell Holmes, Jr., *Buck v. Bell,* 274 U.S. 200, 208 (1927)

8 All legal restrictions which curtail the civil rights of a single racial group are immediately suspect . . . courts must subject them to the most rigid scrutiny.

Hugo L. Black, *Korematsu v. United States,* 323 U.S. 214, 216 (1944)

9 The unlawful administration by state officers of a state statute fair on its face, resulting in its unequal application to those who are entitled to be treated alike, is not a denial of equal protection unless there is shown to be present in it an element of intentional or purposeful discrimination. This may appear on the face of the action taken with respect to a particular class or person . . . , or it may only be shown by extrinsic evidence showing a discriminatory design to favor one individual or class over another not to be inferred from the action itself. . . . But a discriminatory purpose is not presumed . . . , there must be a showing of "clear and intentional discrimination."

Harlan F. Stone, *Snowden v. Hughes,* 321 U.S. 1, 8 (1944)

10 There is no more effective practical guaranty against arbitrary and unreasonable government than to require that the principles of law which officials would impose upon a minority must be imposed generally. Conversely, nothing opens the door to arbitrary action so effectively as to allow those officials to pick and choose only a few to whom they will apply legislation and thus to escape the political retribution that might be visited upon them if larger numbers were affected.

Robert H. Jackson, *Railway Express v. New York,* 336 U.S. 106, 112–13 (1949) (concurring)

11 We shall speak of the defining character or characteristics of the legislative classification as the trait. We can thus speak of the relation of the classification to the purpose of the law as the relation of the Trait to the Mischief. . . . There are five possible relationships between the class defined by the Trait and the class defined by the Mischief. . . . Classifications of the third type may be called "under-inclusive." All who are included in the class are tainted with the mischief, but there are others also tainted whom the classification does not include. . . . The fourth type of classification imposes a burden upon a wider range of individuals than are included in the class of those tainted with the mischief at which the law aims. It can thus be called "over-inclusive."

Joseph Tussman and Jacobus tenBroek, "The Equal Protection of the Laws," 37 *California Law Review* 341, 346–48, 351 (1949)

12 The problem of legislative classification is a perennial one, admitting of no doctrinaire definition. Evils in the same field may be of different dimensions and proportions, requiring different remedies. Or so the legislature may think. . . . Or the reform may take one step at a time, addressing itself to the phase of the problem which seems most acute to the legislative mind. . . . The legislature may select one phase of one field and apply a remedy there, neglecting the others. . . . The prohibition of the Equal Protection Clause goes no further than the invidious discrimination.

William O. Douglas, *Williamson v. Lee Optical Co.,* 348 U.S. 483, 489 (1955)

13 There can be no equal justice where the kind of trial a man gets depends on the amount of money he has.

Hugo L. Black, *Griffin v. Illinois,* 351 U.S. 12, 19 (1956)

14 Although no precise formula has been developed, the Court has held that the Fourteenth Amendment permits the States a wide scope of discretion in enacting laws which affect some groups of citizens differently than others. The constitutional safeguard is offended only if the classification rests on grounds wholly irrelevant to the achievement of the State's objective. State legislatures are presumed to have acted within their constitutional power despite the fact that, in practice, their laws result in some inequality. A statutory discrimination will not be set aside if any state of facts reasonably may be conceived to justify it.

Earl Warren, *McGowan v. Maryland,* 366 U.S. 420, 425 (1961)

15 Equal protection does not require that all persons be dealt with identically, but it does require that a distinction made have some relevance to the purpose for which the classification is made.

Earl Warren, *Baxstrom v. Herold,* 383 U.S. 107, 111 (1966)

16 The emergence of the "new" equal protection during the Warren Court's last decade brought a dramatic change. Strict scrutiny of selected types of legislation proliferated. The familiar signals of "suspect classification" and "fundamental interest" came to trigger the occasions for the new interventionist stance. The Warren Court embraced a rigid two-tiered attitude. Some situations evoked the aggressive "new" equal protection, with scrutiny that was "strict" in theory and fatal in fact; in other contexts, the deferential "old" equal protection reigned, with minimal scrutiny in theory and virtually none in fact.

Gerald Gunther, "The Supreme Court, 1971 Term—Foreword: In Search of Evolving Doctrine on a Changing Court: A Model for a Newer Equal Protection," 86 *Harvard Law Review* 1, 8 (1972)

17 As in all equal protection cases, . . . the crucial question is whether there is an appropriate governmental interest suitably furthered by the differential treatment.

Thurgood Marshall, *Police Department v. Mosley,* 408 U.S. 92, 95 (1972)

18 It is not the province of this Court to create substantive constitutional rights in the name of guaranteeing equal protection of the laws.

Lewis F. Powell, Jr., *San Antonio Indep. School Dist. v. Rodriguez,* 411 U.S. 1, 33 (1973)

19 In order to justify the use of a suspect classification, a State must show that its purpose or interest is both constitutionally permissible and substantial, and that its use of the classification is "necessary . . . to the accomplishment" of its purpose or the safeguarding of its interest.

Lewis F. Powell, Jr., *In re Griffiths,* 413 U.S. 717, 721–22 (1973)

20 Unless a classification trammels fundamental personal rights or is drawn upon inherently suspect distinctions such as race, religion, or alienage, our decisions presume the constitutionality of the statutory discriminations and require only that the classification challenged be rationally related to a legitimate state interest.

City of New Orleans v. Dukes, 427 U.S. 297, 303 (1976) (per curiam)

21 The Constitution requires that Congress treat similarly situated persons similarly, not that it engage in gestures of superficial equality.

William H. Rehnquist, *Rostker v. Goldberg,* 453 U.S. 57, 79 (1981)

22 Equality before the Law.

State Motto of Nebraska

EQUITY

1 Another maxim of no small extent is, that he, who seeks Equity, must do Equity.

Joseph Story, *Commentaries on Equity Jurisprudence* 1:77 (1836)

2 The powers of a court of equity are as vast, and its processes and procedure as elastic, as all the changing emergencies of increasingly complex business relations and the protection of rights can demand.

David J. Brewer, *Chicago, R.I. & P. Ry. v. Union Pac. R.R.,* 47 F. 15, 26 (C.C.D. Neb. 1891)

3 What equity exacts to-day as a condition of relief is the assurance that the decree, if rendered, will operate without injustice or

oppression either to plaintiff or to defendant. . . . Mutuality of remedy is important in so far only as its presence is essential to the attainment of that end. The formula had its origin in an attempt to fit the equitable remedy to the needs of equal justice. We may not suffer it to petrify at the cost of its animating principle.

Benjamin N. Cardozo, *Epstein v. Gluckin,* 233 N.Y. 490, 494, 135 N.E. 861 (1922)

4 If rich men thus suffer severe pains and penalties in the courts of law they get plenty of compensation in the courts of equity. The cause thereof is not occult. In the courts of law, and particularly the criminal courts, they have to face petit juries, which are composed, in the main, of poor men who envy and hate them. But in the courts of equity they are dealt with chiefly by judges, and most of those judges have either worked for them in the past or hope to work for them in the future. Equity's greatest remedy, the injunction, is thus theirs for the asking.

H. L. Mencken, "Equality Before the Law," *American Mercury,* July 1924, at 317

5 Equity does not demand that its suitors shall have led blameless lives.

Louis D. Brandeis, *Loughran v. Loughran,* 292 U.S. 216, 229 (1934)

6 We are dealing here with the requirements of equity practice with a background of several hundred years of history. . . . The essence of equity jurisdiction has been the power of the Chancellor to do equity and to mould each decree to the necessities of the particular case. Flexibility rather than rigidity has distinguished it. The qualities of mercy and practicality have made equity the instrument for nice adjustment and reconciliation between the public interest and private needs as well as between competing private claims.

William O. Douglas, *Hecht Co. v. Bowles,* 321 U.S. 321, 329–30 (1944)

ERROR

1 The court erred in some of the legal propositions announced to the jury; but all the errors were harmless. Wrong directions which do not put the traveler out of his way, furnish no reasons for repeating the journey.

Logan E. Bleckley, *Cherry v. Davis,* 59 Ga. 454, 456 (1877)

2 Delusive exactness is a source of fallacy throughout the law.

Oliver Wendell Holmes, Jr., *Truax v. Corrigan,* 257 U.S. 312, 342 (1921) (dissenting)

3 There is no reason to doubt that this Court may fall into error as may other branches of the Government. . . . The Court differs, however, from other branches of the Government in its ability to extricate itself from error. It can reconsider a matter only when it is again properly brought before it in a case or controversy; and if the case requires . . . a statutory basis for a case, the new case must have sufficient statutory support.

Robert H. Jackson, *Helvering v. Griffiths,* 318 U.S. 371, 400–01 (1943)

4 I concur in the judgment and opinion of the Court. But since it is contrary to an opinion which, as Attorney General, I rendered in 1940, I owe some word of explanation. . . . I am entitled to say of that opinion what any discriminating reader must think of it—that it was as foggy as the statute the Attorney General was asked to interpret. . . .

Precedent, however, is not lacking for ways by which a judge may recede from a prior opinion that has proven untenable and perhaps misled others. . . . Baron Bramwell extricated himself from a somewhat similar embarrassment by saying, "The matter does not appear to me now as it appears to have appeared to me then." . . . And Mr. Justice Story, accounting for his contradiction of his own former opinion, quite properly put the matter: "My own error, however, can furnish no ground for its being adopted by this Court. . . ." Perhaps Dr. Johnson really went to the heart of the matter when he explained a blunder in his dictionary—"Ignorance, sir, ignorance." But an escape less self-deprecating was taken by Lord Westbury, who, it is said, rebuffed a barrister's reliance upon an earlier opinion of his Lordship: "I can only say that I am amazed that a man of my intelligence should have been guilty of giving such an opinion." If there are other

ways of gracefully and good-naturedly surrendering former views to a better considered position, I invoke them all.

> **Robert H. Jackson,** *McGrath v. Kristensen*,
> 340 U.S. 162, 176–78 (1950) (concurring)

ESTATES

See WILLS

ETHICS

See also CLIENT; LAWYER JOKES; LAWYERS (PRO);
LAWYERS (CON); MORALITY

1 Sir, be prevailed withal, to keep constantly
a *court of chancery* in your breast; and
scorn and fear to do anything, but what
your *conscience* will pronounce, consistent
with, yea, conducing to, *glory to God in the
highest, on earth peace, good will towards
men.*

> **Cotton Mather,** *Bonifacius* 127 (David Levin
> ed. 1966) (1710)

2 You will abhor, Sir, to appear in a *dirty
cause.* If you discern, that your *client* has
an *unjust cause,* you will faithfully advise
him of it. . . . You will be sincerely desirous, *Truth* and *Right* may take place. You
will speak nothing that shall be to the prejudice of *either.* You will abominate the use
of all unfair arts, to confound *evidences,* to
browbeat *testimonies,* to suppress what
may give light in the case.

> **Cotton Mather,** *Bonifacius* 127 (David Levin
> ed. 1966) (1710)

3 There has been an old complaint, *that a
good lawyer seldom is a good neighbor.* You
know how to confute it, *gentlemen,* by making your *skill in the law,* a blessing to your
neighborhood. . . . You may, *gentlemen,* if
you please, be a vast accession to the *felicity*
of your countries. . . . Perhaps, you may
discover many things yet wanting in the
laws; mischiefs in the execution and application of the *laws,* which ought to be better
provided against; *mischiefs* annoying of
mankind, against which no *laws* are yet
provided. The *reformation of the law,* and
more *law* for the *reformation of the world,*
is what is mightily called for.

> **Cotton Mather,** *Bonifacius* 129–30 (David
> Levin ed. 1966) (1710)

4 My client's conscience, and my own, are
distinct entities . . . it would be dishonorable folly in me to endeavor to incorporate
[any unmeritorious claim] in the jurisprudence of the country.

> **David Hoffman,** *A Course of Legal Study*
> 2:755 (2d ed. 1836)

5 An eminent lawyer cannot be a dishonest
man. Tell me a man is dishonest, and I will
answer he is no lawyer. He cannot be, because he is careless and reckless of justice;
the law is not in his heart,—is not the standard and rule of his conduct.

> **Daniel Webster,** Speech, Charleston, S.C., 10
> May 1847, in *Writings and Speeches of Daniel
> Webster* 4:90 (J. W. McIntyre ed. 1903)

6 There is a vague popular belief that lawyers
are necessarily dishonest. I say vague, because when we consider to what extent
confidence and honors are reposed in and
conferred upon lawyers by the people, it
appears improbable that their impression
of dishonesty is very distinct and vivid. Yet
the impression is common, almost universal. Let no young man choosing the law for
a calling for a moment yield to the popular
belief—resolve to be honest at all events;
and if in your own judgment you cannot be
an honest lawyer, resolve to be honest
without being a lawyer. Choose some other
occupation, rather than one in the choosing of which you do, in advance, consent
to be a knave.

> **Abraham Lincoln,** "Notes for a Law
> Lecture," 1 July 1850?, in *Collected Works of
> Abraham Lincoln* 2:82 (Roy P. Basler ed.
> 1953)

7 There is, perhaps, no profession, after that
of the sacred ministry, in which a high-
toned morality is more imperatively necessary than that of the law. There is certainly, without any exception, no profession
in which so many temptations beset the
path to swerve from the line of strict duty
and propriety; in which so many delicate
and difficult questions of casuistry are continually arising. There are pitfalls and
man-traps at every step, and the youthful
adventurer needs often the prudence and
self-denial, as well as the moral courage,
which belong commonly to riper years.
High moral principle is his only safe guide;

the only torch to light his way amidst darkness and obstruction.

> **George Sharswood,** *A Compend of Lectures
> on the Aims and Duties of the Profession of
> the Law* 9 (1854)

8 The advocate . . . is not morally responsible
for the act of the party in maintaining an
unjust cause, nor for the error of the court,
if they fall into error, in deciding it in his
favor. . . . The lawyer, who refuses his professional assistance because in his judgment the case is unjust and indefensible,
usurps the function of both judge and jury.

> **George Sharswood,** *A Compend of Lectures
> on the Aims and Duties of the Profession of
> the Law* 26 (1854)

9 The advocate is bound in honor, as well as
duty, to disclose to the client at the time of
the retainer, every circumstance of his own
connection with the parties or prior relation to the controversy, which can or may
influence his determination in the selection
of him for the office. . . . No man can be
supposed to be indifferent to the knowledge of facts, which work directly on his
interests, or bear on the freedom of his
choice of counsel.

> **George Sharswood,** *A Compend of Lectures
> on the Aims and Duties of the Profession of
> the Law* 45–46 (1854)

10 It is the glory of our profession that its fidelity to its client can be depended on; that
a man may safely go to a lawyer and converse with him upon his rights or supposed
rights in any litigation with the absolute
assurance that that lawyer's tongue is tied
from ever disclosing it; and any lawyer who
proves false to such an obligation, and betrays or seeks to betray any information or
any facts that he has attained while employed on the one side, is guilty of the
grossest breach of trust. I can tolerate a
great many things that a lawyer may do,—
things that in and of themselves may perhaps be criticised or condemned when
done in obedience to the interest or supposed interest of his own client, and when
he is seeking simply to protect and uphold
those interests. If he goes beyond, perhaps,
the limits of propriety, I can tolerate and
pass that by; but I cannot tolerate for a moment, neither can the profession, neither
can the community, any disloyalty on the
part of a lawyer to his client. In all things

he must be true to that trust, or, failing it,
he must leave the profession.

> **David J. Brewer,** *United States v. Costen,* 38
> F. 24, 24 (C.C.D. Colo. 1889)

11 I noticed the burst of applause when Judge
O'Brien got up to speak, and I knew that
he was either an exceedingly able man or
else that a lot of you practice in his
court. . . . One speaker got up here and
urged you to be honest, and there was no
response.

> **Mark Twain,** Speech to Society of Medical
> Jurisprudence, 8 Mar. 1902, in *Mark Twain
> Speaking* 429 (Paul Fatout ed. 1972)

12 And here in America, where justice reigns
only by and through the people under
forms of law, the lawyer is and must ever
be the high priest at the shrine of justice.
Under our form of government, unless the
system for establishing and dispensing justice is so developed and maintained that
there shall be continued confidence on the
part of the public in the fairness, integrity
and impartiality of its administration,
there can be no lasting permanence to our
republican institutions. Our profession is
necessarily the keystone of the republican
arch of government. Weaken this keystone
by allowing it to be increasingly subject to
the corroding and demoralizing influence
of those who are controlled by graft, greed
and gain, or other unworthy motive, and
sooner or later the arch must fall. It follows
that the future of the republic depends
upon our maintenance of the shrine of justice pure and unsullied. We know it cannot
be so maintained unless the conduct and
motives of the members of our profession,
of those who are the high-priests of justice,
are what they ought to be.

> **American Bar Association,** Committee on
> Code of Professional Ethics, "Report," 29
> *American Bar Association Report* 600, 600–01
> (1906)

13 In America, where the stability of Courts
and of all departments of governments
rests upon the approval of the people, it is
peculiarly essential that the system for establishing and dispensing Justice be developed to a high point of efficiency and so
maintained that the public shall have absolute confidence in the integrity and impartiality of its administration. The future
of the Republic, to a great extent, depends

upon our maintenance of Justice pure and unsullied. It cannot be so maintained unless the conduct and the motives of the members of our profession are such as to merit the approval of all just men.

Canons of Professional Ethics Preamble (1908)

14 The office of attorney does not permit, much less does it demand of him for any client, violation of law or any manner of fraud or chicane. He must obey his own conscience and not that of his client.

Canons of Professional Ethics Canon 15 (1908)

15 The conduct of the lawyer before the Court and with other lawyers should be characterized by candor and fairness.

Canons of Professional Ethics Canon 22 (1908)

16 Solicitation of business by circulars or advertisements, or by personal communications or interviews, not warranted by personal relations, is unprofessional. It is equally unprofessional to procure business by indirection through touters of any kind. . . . Indirect advertisement for business by furnishing or inspiring newspaper comments concerning causes in which the lawyer has been or is engaged, or concerning the manner of their conduct, the magnitude of the interests involved, the importance of the lawyer's positions, and all other like self-laudation, defy the traditions and lower the tone of our high calling, and are intolerable.

Canons of Professional Ethics Canon 27 (1908)

17 I will not counsel or maintain any suit or proceeding which shall appear to me to be unjust, nor any defense except such as I believe to be honestly debatable under the law of the land.

American Bar Association, Model oath for candidates for admission to the bar, 33 *American Bar Association Report* 585 (1908)

18 Consequences cannot alter statutes, but may help to fix their meaning. Statutes must be so construed, if possible, that absurdity and mischief may be avoided. The claim of immunity from disbarment cannot survive the application of that test. If the exemption protects lawyers, it must

equally protect physicians, whose licenses have long been subject to revocation for misconduct. . . . Two great and honorable professions have in that view been denied the right to purify their membership and vindicate their honor. The charlatan and rogue may assume to heal the sick. The knave and criminal may pose as a minister of justice. Such things cannot have been intended, and will not be allowed.

Benjamin N. Cardozo, *In re Rouss*, 221 N.Y. 81, 91, 116 N.E. 782 (1917)

19 Just addressed the California State Legislature and helped them pass a bill to form a lawyers' association to regulate their conduct. Personally I don't think you can make a lawyer honest by an act of the Legislature. You've got to work on his conscience. And his lack of conscience is what makes him a lawyer.

Will Rogers, "Opinion of Will Rogers On the Legal Conscience," 15 Mar. 1927, in *Will Rogers' Daily Telegrams* 1:67 (James M. Smallwood ed. 1978)

20 The professional services of a lawyer should not be controlled or exploited by any lay agency, personal or corporate, which intervenes between client and lawyer.

Canons of Professional Ethics Canon 35 (1928)

21 When a lawyer discovers that some fraud or deception has been practiced, which has unjustly imposed upon the court or a party, he should endeavor to rectify it; at first by advising his client, and if his client refuses to forego the advantage thus unjustly gained, he should promptly inform the injured person or his counsel, so that they may take appropriate steps.

Canons of Professional Ethics Canon 41 (1928)

22 Two generations ahead of me there was a well known lawyer in Boston, Charles G. Loring, whom my mother-in-law pronounced a really good man because he never took a case that he didn't believe in — perhaps a more sardonic way of putting it would be that he believed in every case that he took.

Oliver Wendell Holmes, Jr., Letter to Harold J. Laski, 23 Jan. 1928, in *Holmes-Laski*

Letters 2:1019 (Mark DeWolfe Howe ed. 1953)

23 I will join with my adversary in waiving a jury trial wherever and whenever it can possibly be done without the sacrifice of a fundamental right.

I will join with my adversary in supporting a trial justice in fair comment upon the evidence and reasonable direction to a jury on the facts.

I will join with my adversary in fair concession of undisputed facts.

I will not put an adversary to his proof in respect to facts whose existence my client admits.

I will refrain from merely formal or technical objection to the admission of evidence.

I will co-operate with the trial justice and my adversary to secure a speedy, prompt and complete presentation of the facts of the case.

I will neither make nor oppose interlocutory motions unless they are of real and practical importance.

I will take no appeal unless I am satisfied that a substantial error has been committed and that a new trial should reasonably give a different result.

Joseph M. Proskauer, "Credo," 1928, in 13 *New York County Lawyers Association Bar Bulletin* 146 (1956)

24 Here is about the best crime prevention news I have seen: "The California Bar Association is to rid its ranks of any attorney found to have connection with the underworld." The first thing they do now if they are taking up crime as a profession (even before they buy the gun) is to engage their lawyer. He works on a percentage. He acts as their advance agent, too, he picks out the banks they are to rob. Bar associations invented the word "ethics," then forgot about it.

Will Rogers, "Mr. Rogers Sees Progress In the War on Crime," 30 Dec. 1934, in *Will Rogers' Daily Telegrams* 4:258 (James M. Smallwood ed. 1979)

25 California has been lucky, we escaped the winds, the floods, the drouths, and the heat, but pestilence has finally caught us, the boweevil descended on us in trainloads, 3500 lawyers of the American Bar Association are here eating us out of house and home. They are here, they say, "to save the Constitution, to preserve State rights." What they ought to be here for, that would make this convention immortal, is to kick the crooks out of their profession. They should recommend a law that every case that went on trial, the lawyer defending should be tried first, then if he come clear, he was eligible to defend. As it is now they are trying the wrong man.

Will Rogers, "Will Rogers' Remarks," 14 July 1935, in *Will Rogers' Daily Telegrams* 4:332–33 (James M. Smallwood ed. 1979)

26 Went down and spoke at some lawyers' meeting last night. They didn't think much of my little squib yesterday about driving the shysters out of their profession. They seemed to kinder doubt just who would have to leave.

Will Rogers, "Mr. Rogers is Hob Nobbing With Leaders of the Bar," 16 July 1935, in *Will Rogers' Daily Telegrams* 4:333 (James M. Smallwood ed. 1979)

27 Now here is a thing. I am in the movies. When there was so much talk of cleaning-up the movies, there wasent a lawyer, or any other profession but what said, "Why don't they clean those things up? My wife and children can't go to see 'em."

Now you offered an opinion in my business, but the minute a comedian offers an opinion in your business, I am out of place. Your business is sacred and no one should mention it only in the highest terms. The movies cleaned up and they dident write editorials against the lawyers for saying they should. If all lawyers are not honest how are clients to tell when they might go to a bad one any more than a movie fan might go to a bad movie? There is no reason of knowing till you go and see. Lawyers is everybody's business the same as the movies are.

Will Rogers, "Now About These Lawyers," 11 Aug. 1935, in *Will Rogers' Weekly Articles* 6:246, 247 (Steven K. Gragert ed. 1982)

28 [Perry Mason speaking:] I wish people would learn to differentiate between the reputable lawyer who represents persons accused of crime, and the criminal lawyer who becomes a silent partner in the profits of crime. . . . I never take a case unless I

am convinced my client was incapable of committing the crime charged.

Erle Stanley Gardner, *The Case of the Perjured Parrot* 3 (1939)

29 In the course of his remarks the Chief Justice stated as one reason for his decision a supposed fact which I knew to be unfounded. I had in front of me a letter that showed his error. Though I have no doubt of the propriety of my behavior in keeping silent, I was somewhat uncomfortable at the time.

Samuel Williston, *Life and Law: An Autobiography* 271 (1940)

30 Ours is a learned profession, not a mere money-getting trade.

ABA Comm. on Professional Ethics and Grievances, Formal Op. 250 (1943)

31 I don't see why we should not come out roundly and say that one of the functions of a lawyer is to lie for his client; and on rare occasions, as I think I have shown, I believe it is.

Charles P. Curtis, "The Ethics of Advocacy," 4 *Stanford Law Review* 3, 9 (1951)

32 I don't know of any other career that offers ampler opportunity for both the enjoyment of virtue and the exercise of vice, or, if you please, the exercise of virtue and the enjoyment of vice, except possibly the ancient rituals which were performed in some temples by vestal virgins, in others by sacred prostitutes.

Charles P. Curtis, "The Ethics of Advocacy," 4 *Stanford Law Review* 3, 18 (1951)

33 From a profession charged with such responsibilities there must be exacted those qualities of truth-speaking, of a high sense of honor, of granite discretion, of the strictest observance of fiduciary responsibility, that have, throughout the centuries, been compendiously described as "moral character."

Felix Frankfurter, *Schware v. Board of Bar Examiners*, 353 U.S. 232, 247 (1957) (concurring)

34 The Lecture is an ancient device that lawyers use to coach their clients so that the client won't quite know he has been coached and his lawyer can still preserve the face-saving illusion that he hasn't done

any coaching. . . . "Who, me? I didn't tell him what to say," the lawyer can later comfort himself. "I merely explained the law, see."

Robert Traver, *Anatomy of a Murder* 35 (1958)

35 In civilized life, law floats in a sea of ethics. Each is indispensable to civilization. Without law, we should be at the mercy of the least scrupulous; without ethics, law could not exist.

Earl Warren, quoted in Fred J. Cook, "The Corrupt Society," *The Nation*, 1–8 June 1963, at 453

36 When a client engages the services of a lawyer in a given piece of business he is entitled to feel that, until that business is finally disposed of in some manner, he has the undivided loyalty of the one upon whom he looks as his advocate and champion.

John N. Comley, *Grievance Committee v. Rottner*, 152 Conn. 59, 65, 203 A.2d 82 (1964)

37 Bar associations are notoriously reluctant to disbar or even suspend a member unless he has murdered a judge downtown at high noon, in the presence of the entire Committee on Ethical Practices.

Sydney J. Harris, quoted in Murray Teigh Bloom, *The Trouble with Lawyers* 157 (1968)

38 Each lawyer must find within his own conscience the touchstone against which to test the extent to which his actions should rise above minimum standards. But in the last analysis it is the desire for the respect and confidence of the members of his profession and of the society which he serves that should provide to a lawyer the incentive for the highest possible degree of ethical conduct. The possible loss of that respect and confidence is the ultimate sanction. So long as its practitioners are guided by these principles, the law will continue to be a noble profession. This is its greatness and its strength, which permit of no compromise.

Model Code of Professional Responsibility Preamble (1970)

39 Regardless of his personal feelings, a lawyer should not decline representation be-

cause a client or a cause is unpopular or community reaction is adverse.

Model Code of Professional Responsiblity EC 2–27 (1970)

40 A Lawyer Should Exercise Independent Professional Judgment on Behalf of a Client.

Model Code of Professional Responsibility Canon 5 (1970)

41 A Lawyer Should Represent a Client Zealously Within the Bounds of the Law.

Model Code of Professional Responsibility Canon 7 (1970)

42 The duty of a lawyer, both to his client and to the legal system, is to represent his client zealously within the bounds of the law, which includes Disciplinary Rules and enforceable professional regulations. The professional responsibility of a lawyer derives from his membership in a profession which has the duty of assisting members of the public to secure and protect available legal rights and benefits. In our government of laws and not of men, each member of our society is entitled to have his conduct judged and regulated in accordance with the law; to seek any lawful objective through legally permissible means; and to present for adjudication any lawful claim, issue, or defense.

Model Code of Professional Responsibility EC 7–1 (1970)

43 A Lawyer Should Avoid Even the Appearance of Professional Impropriety.

Model Code of Professional Responsibility Canon 9 (1970)

44 He believed in the justice of his using any legal methods he could improvise to force the other side into compromise or into dismissals of charges, or to lead a jury into the verdict he wanted. Why not? He was a defense lawyer, not a judge or a juror or a policeman or a legislator or a theoretician or an anarchist or a murderer.

Joyce Carol Oates, *Do With Me What You Will* 284 (1973)

EVIDENCE

See also PROOF

1 Circumstantial evidence is, in the *abstract*, nearly, though perhaps not altogether, as strong as positive evidence; in the *concrete*, it may be infinitely stronger. A fact positively sworn to by a single eye-witness of blemished character, is not so satisfactorily proved, as is a fact which is the necessary consequence of a chain of other facts sworn to by many witnesses of undoubted credibility.

John B. Gibson, *Commonwealth v. Harman,* 4 Pa. 269, 271–72 (1846)

2 I would sooner trust the smallest slip of paper for truth, than the strongest and most retentive memory, ever bestowed on mortal man.

Joseph H. Lumpkin, *Miller v. Cotten,* 5 Ga. 341, 349 (1848)

3 Some circumstantial evidence is very strong, as when you find a trout in the milk.

Henry David Thoreau, Journal, 11 Nov. 1850, in *Journal of Henry D. Thoreau* 2:94 (Bradford Torrey & Francis H. Allen eds. 1962)

4 Tell me not of technical rules of evidence! They have excluded the light of day from the jury box long enough. Not only open wide doors and windows, but unroof the temples of justice, that all the rays of truth may beam brilliantly upon those who are set for the administration of the law.

Joseph H. Lumpkin, *Ganahl v. Shore,* 24 Ga. 17, 26 (1858)

5 While courts, in the administration of the law of evidence, should be careful not to open the door to falsehood, they should be equally careful not to shut out truth. They should not encumber the law with rules which will involve labor and expense to the parties, and delay the progress of the remedy—itself a serious evil—without giving any additional safeguard to the interests of justice.

Noah H. Swayne, *In re Cliquot's Champagne,* 70 U.S. (3 Wall.) 114, 141 (1865)

6 This policy of the Anglo-American law is perhaps more or less due to the inborn sporting instinct of Anglo-Normandom— the instinct of giving the game fair play. . . . The deep tendency of human nature to punish, not because our victim is guilty this time, but because he is a bad man and may as well be condemned now that he is caught, is a tendency which cannot help

operating with any jury, in or out of court. . . . Our rule, then, firmly and universally established in policy and tradition, is that the prosecution may not initially attack the defendant's character.

> **John H. Wigmore,** *A Treatise on the System of Evidence in Trials at Common Law* 1:126–27 (1904)

7 "Presumptions," as happily stated by a scholarly counselor, *ore tenus*, in another case, "may be looked on as the bats of the law, flitting in the twilight but disappearing in the sunshine of actual facts."

> **Henry Lamm,** *Mockowik v. Kansas City, St. Joseph & Council Bluffs R.R.,* 196 Mo. 550, 571, 94 S.W. 256 (1906)

8 Heresay [sic] evidence is inadmissible because the person quoted was unsworn and is not before the court for examination; yet most momentous actions, military, political, commercial and of every other kind, are daily undertaken on hearsay evidence. There is no religion in the world that has any other basis than hearsay evidence. . . . It cannot be proved that the battle of Blenheim ever was fought, that there was such a person as Julius Caesar, such an empire as Assyria.

> **Ambrose Bierce,** *The Devil's Dictionary* 153–54 (1911)

9 PRODUCIBLE, *adj.* Evidence as to a murderer's good moral character.

> **Ambrose Bierce,** *The Enlarged Devil's Dictionary* 229 (Ernest J. Hopkins ed. 1967)

10 If we were to reframe the law of evidence and were still to preserve the hearsay rule, it might be better to keep out all such, for the practice, though well settled, is an evasion, and evasions are discreditable. There is no reason why the prosecution, if it chooses to indict several defendants together, should not be confined to evidence admissible against all, and if real injustice were done, the result would be undesirable. In effect, however, the rule probably furthers, rather than impedes, the search for truth, and this perhaps excuses the device which satisfies form while it violates substance; that is, the recommendation to the jury of a mental gymnastic which is beyond, not only their powers, but anybody's else.

> **Learned Hand,** *Nash v. United States,* 54 F.2d 1006, 1006-07 (2d Cir. 1932)

11 The reverberating clang of those accusatory words would drown all weaker sounds. It is for ordinary minds, and not for psychoanalysts, that our rules of evidence are framed. They have their source very often in considerations of administrative convenience, of practical expediency, and not in rules of logic. When the risk of confusion is so great as to upset the balance of advantage, the evidence goes out.

> **Benjamin N. Cardozo,** *Shepard v. United States,* 290 U.S. 96, 104 (1933)

12 To say that the rules of evidence may be relaxed in Juvenile Court is like saying that during a surgical operation on a child the surgeon may relax the rules of precise hygiene. Hygienic precautions in the operating room are taken to keep out microbes and germs of infection in the same way that rules of evidence in court erect barriers to bar the microbes of lies, the germs of prejudice, and the infection of rumor.

> **Michael A. Musmanno,** *In re Holmes,* 379 Pa. 599, 616, 109 A.2d 523 (1954) (dissenting)

13 Hearsay is merely a legal term for unconfirmed rumor. Pouring rumored scandal into the bent ear of blabbering busybodies in a pool room or gambling house is no more disreputable than pronouncing it with clipped accent in a courtroom. Hearsay is not dross in one proceeding and gold in another. It is a deceptive commodity which should not be accepted in any market of freedom except under the most unusual circumstances.

> **Michael A. Musmanno,** *In re Holmes,* 379 Pa. 599, 617–18, 109 A.2d 523 (1954) (dissenting)

14 Common sense, of course, is not the only thing a system of law relies on. It is not a substitute for knowledge. It cannot compete with "expertise." But it is common sense which determines the relevance and weight of knowledge in specific situations.

> **Sidney Hook,** *Common Sense and the Fifth Amendment* 17 (1957)

15 When I took courses on Evidence in law school, the explanation given for this giant collection of rules was simply that Juries were stupid. . . . this does appear to be the only explanation for the development of this branch of the law.

> **Gordon Tullock,** *The Logic of the Law* 93–94 (1971)

EXCLUSIONARY RULE

See SEARCHES AND SEIZURES

EXPERTS

1 Just when a scientific principle or discovery crosses the line between the experimental and demonstrable stages is difficult to define. Somewhere in this twilight zone the evidential force of the principle must be recognized, and while courts will go a long way in admitting expert testimony deduced from a well-recognized scientific principle or discovery, the thing from which the deduction is made must be sufficiently established to have gained general acceptance in the particular field in which it belongs.

> **Josiah A. Van Orsdel,** *Frye v. United States,* 293 F. 1013, 1014 (D.C. Cir. 1923)

2 In response to the question: "Is that your conclusion that this man is a malingerer?" Dr. Unsworth responded: "I wouldn't be testifying if I didn't think so, unless I was on the other side, then it would be a post traumatic condition."

> **Godfrey Z. Regan,** *Ladner v. Higgins,* 71 So. 2d 242, 244 (La. Ct. App. 1954)

3 Expert opinion ... is only an ordinary guess in evening clothes.

> **Curtis Bok,** *Earl M. Kerstetter, Inc. v. Commonwealth,* 404 Pa. 168, 173, 171 A.2d 163 (1961)

4 Why would you, the diligent lawyer, settle for a scientist who will say that PCBs may in some circumstances affect health, though how and at what concentrations is most unclear, if you can find one who will swear that they are one of the most lethal substances known to man, that they subvert the immune system, and they undoubtedly were to blame for this plaintiff's migraine headaches? Why settle for one who will say that 60-cycle electromagnetic fields probably don't injure human health, though one must concede certain small pieces of disquieting evidence to the contrary, if you can find one who will take the Federal Express pledge, and absolutely, positively promise that the fields do no harm, nohow? The middle of the road, in law even more so than in politics, belongs

to the yellow stripes and the dead armadillos. ... It is the strength of the expert's support for *your* position that comes first.

> **Peter W. Huber,** *Galileo's Revenge: Junk Science in the Courtroom* 17–18 (1991)

FACTS

1 If facts are changing, law cannot be static.

> **Felix Frankfurter,** "The Zeitgeist and the Judiciary" (address), 1912, in *Law and Politics: Occasional Papers of Felix Frankfurter* 3, 6 (Archibald MacLeish & E.F. Prichard, Jr. eds. 1939)

2 They [questions of law and questions of fact] are not two mutually exclusive *kinds* of questions, based upon a difference of subject-matter. Matters of law grow downward into roots of fact, and matters of fact reach upward, without a break, into matters of law. The knife of policy alone effects an artificial cleavage at the point where the court chooses to draw the line between public interest and private right.

> **John Dickinson,** *Administrative Justice and the Supremacy of Law* 55 (1927)

3 We stress this matter because of the grave importance of factfinding. ... The trial court is the most important agency of the judicial branch of the government precisely because on it rests the responsibility of ascertaining the facts. When a federal trial judge sits without a jury, that responsibility is his. And it is not a light responsibility since, unless his findings are "clearly erroneous," no upper court may disturb them. To ascertain the facts is not a mechanical act. It is a difficult art, not a science. It involves skill and judgment. As fact-finding is a human undertaking, it can, of course, never be perfect and infallible. For that very reason every effort should be made to render it as adequate as it humanly can be.

> **Jerome N. Frank,** *United States v. Forness,* 125 F.2d 928, 942–43 (2d Cir. 1942)

4 Perhaps the most fatuous of all notions solemnly voiced by learned men who ought to know better is that when legal rules are "clear and complete" litigation is unlikely to occur. ... Such writers surely cannot be unaware that thousands of decisions yearly turn on disputes concerning the facts, i.e., as to whether clear-cut legal rules were in

fact violated. It is the uncertainty about the "facts" that creates most of the unpredictability of decisions.

> **Jerome N. Frank,** *Ricketts v. Pennsylvania R.R.,* 153 F.2d 757, 761–62 n. (2d Cir. 1946) (concurring)

5 Any distinction posited between "law" and "fact" does not imply the existence of static, polar opposites. Rather, law and fact have a nodal quality; they are points of rest and relative stability on a continuum of experience. In our legal system, the categories have functioned as crucially important constructs that permit us to understand, organize, and regulate certain forms of social experience.

> **Henry P. Monaghan,** "Constitutional Fact Review," 85 *Columbia Law Review* 229, 233 (1985)

FAMILY LAW

See CHILDREN; DIVORCE; MARRIAGE

FEDERALISM

1 Each state retains its sovereignty, freedom, and independence, and every Power, Jurisdiction and right, which is not by this confederation expressly delegated to the United States, in Congress assembled.

> Articles of Confederation, art. II, 1781, in *Journals of the Continental Congress* 19:214 (Gaillard Hunt ed. 1912)

2 I confess, as I enter the Building, I stumble at the Threshold. I meet with a National Government, instead of a Federal Union of Sovereign States. I am not able to conceive why the Wisdom of the Convention led them to give the Preference to the former before the latter. If the several States in the Union are to become one entire Nation, under one Legislature, the Powers of which shall extend to every Subject of Legislation, and its Laws be supreme & controul the whole, the Idea of Sovereignty in these States must be lost.

> **Samuel Adams,** Letter to Richard Henry Lee, 3 Dec. 1787, in *Writings of Samuel Adams* 4:324 (Harry A. Cushing ed. 1968)

3 That two supreme powers cannot act together, is false. . . . the laws of the United States are supreme, as to all their proper,

constitutional objects: The laws of the states are supreme in the same way.

> **Alexander Hamilton,** Remarks at New York Ratifying Convention, 27 June 1788, in *Papers of Alexander Hamilton* 1:94, 103 (Harold C. Syrett ed. 1961)

4 The powers delegated by the proposed constitution to the federal government, are few and defined. Those which are to remain in the state governments are numerous and indefinite. The former will be exercised principally on external objects, as war, peace, negociation [*sic*], and foreign commerce; with which last the power of taxation will for the most part be connected. The powers reserved to the several states will extend to all the objects, which, in the ordinary course of affairs, concern the lives, liberties and properties of the people; and the internal order, improvement, and prosperity of the state.

> **James Madison,** *The Federalist* No. 45, at 2:82 (1788)

5 I consider the foundation of the Constitution as laid on this ground: That "all powers not delegated to the United States, by the Constitution, nor prohibited by it to the States, are reserved to the States or to the people." . . . To take a single step beyond the boundaries thus specially drawn around the powers of Congress, is to take possession of a boundless field of power, no longer susceptible of any definition. The incorporation of a bank, and the powers assumed by this bill, have not, in my opinion, been delegated to the United States, by the Constitution.*

> **Thomas Jefferson,** "Opinion against the Constitutionality of a National Bank," 15 Feb. 1791, in *Writings of Thomas Jefferson* 7:556 (H. A. Washington ed. 1854)

6 This Assembly doth explicitly and peremptorily declare, that it views the powers of the federal government as resulting from the compact to which the states are parties, . . . and that, in case of a deliberate, palpable, and dangerous exercise of other powers, not granted by the said compact,

---

* This opinion was Jefferson's response to President George Washington's request for advice on the constitutionality of the bill establishing a national bank. The sentence quoted by Jefferson is the Tenth Amendment to the Constitution.

the states, who are parties thereto, have the right, and are in duty bound, to interpose, for arresting the progress of the evil, and for maintaining, within their respective limits, the authorities, rights, and liberties, appertaining to them.

Virginia Resolutions of 1798, in *Debates in the Several State Conventions* 4:528, 528 (Jonathan Elliot ed., 2d ed. 1888)

7 The several states composing the United States of America are not united on the principle of unlimited submission to their general government; but that, by compact, under the style and title of a Constitution for the United States, and of amendments thereto, they constituted a general government for special purposes, delegated to that government certain definite powers, reserving, each state to itself, the residuary mass of right to their own self-government; and that whensoever the general government assumes undelegated powers, its acts are unauthoritative, void, and of no force; that to this compact each state acceded as a state, and is an integral party; that this government, created by this compact, was not made the exclusive or final judge of the extent of the powers delegated to itself, since that would have made its discretion, and not the Constitution, the measure of its powers; but that, as in all other cases of compact among parties having no common judge, *each party has an equal right to judge for itself, as well of infractions as of the mode and measure of redress.*

Kentucky Resolutions of 1798, Resolution 1, in *Debates in the Several State Conventions* 4:540, 540 (Jonathan Elliot ed., 2d ed. 1888)

8 All these [state governments] as well as their central government, like the planets revolving around their common sun ... will produce that beautiful equilibrium on which our Constitution is founded, and which I believe it will exhibit to the world in a degree of perfection, unexampled but in the planetary system itself. The enlightened statesmen, therefore, will endeavor to preserve the weight and influence of every part, as too much given to any member of it would destroy the general equilibrium.

Thomas Jefferson, Letter to Peregrine Fitzhugh, 23 Feb. 1798, in *Writings of Thomas Jefferson* 7:210 (Paul L. Ford ed. 1896)

9 Our country is too large to have all its affairs directed by a single government. Public servants at such a distance, & from under the eye of their constituents, must, from the circumstance of distance, be unable to administer & overlook all the details necessary for the good government of the citizens, and the same circumstance, by rendering detection impossible to their constituents, will invite the public agents to corruption, plunder & waste. And I do verily believe, that if the principle were to prevail, of a common law being in force in the U S, (which principle possesses the general government at once of all the powers of the state governments, and reduces us to a single consolidated government,) it would become the most corrupt government on the earth.

Thomas Jefferson, Letter to Gideon Granger, 13 Aug. 1800, in *Writings of Thomas Jefferson* 7:451 (Paul L. Ford ed. 1896)

10 What an augmentation of the field for jobbing, speculating, plundering, office-building and office-hunting would be produced by an assumption of all the state powers into the hands of the general government.

Thomas Jefferson, Letter to Gideon Granger, 13 Aug. 1800, in *Writings of Thomas Jefferson* 7:451 (Paul L. Ford ed. 1896)

11 In the case now to be determined, the defendant, a sovereign state, denies the obligation of a law enacted by the legislature of the Union, and the plaintiff, on his part, contests the validity of an act which has been passed by the legislature of that State. The constitution of our country, in its most interesting and vital parts, is to be considered; the conflicting powers of the government of the Union and of its members, as marked in that constitution, are to be discussed; and an opinion given, which may essentially influence the great operations of the government. No tribunal can approach such a question without a deep sense of its importance, and of the awful responsibility involved in its decision. But it must be decided peacefully, or remain a source of hostile legislation, perhaps of hostility of a still more serious nature; and if it is to be so decided, by this tribunal alone can the decision be made. On the Supreme Court of

the United States has the constitution of our country devolved this important duty.

John Marshall, *McCulloch v. Maryland*, 17 U.S. (4 Wheat.) 316, 400–01 (1819)

12 If any one proposition could command the universal assent of mankind, we might expect it would be this—that the government of the Union, though limited in its powers, is supreme within its sphere of action. This would seem to result necessarily from its nature. It is the government of all; its powers are delegated by all; it represents all; and acts for all. . . . The nation, on those subjects on which it can act, must necessarily bind its component parts.

John Marshall, *McCulloch v. Maryland*, 17 U.S. (4 Wheat.) 316, 405 (1819)

13 The States have no power, by taxation or otherwise, to retard, impede, burden, or in any manner control, the operations of the constitutional laws enacted by Congress to carry into execution the powers vested in the general government. This is, we think, the unavoidable consequence of that supremacy which the constitution has declared.

John Marshall, *McCulloch v. Maryland*, 17 U.S. (4 Wheat.) 316, 436 (1819)

14 The framers of the constitution were . . . able to provide against the operation of measures adopted in any one State, whose tendency might be to arrest the execution of the laws, and this it was the part of true wisdom to attempt.

John Marshall, *Cohens v. Virginia*, 19 U.S. (6 Wheat.) 264, 390 (1821)

15 In a government acknowledgedly supreme, with respect to objects of vital interest to the nation, there is nothing inconsistent with sound reason, nothing incompatible with the nature of government, in making all its departments supreme, so far as respects those objects, and so far as is necessary to their attainment. The exercise of the appellate power over those judgments of the State tribunals which may contravene the constitution or laws of the United States, is, we believe, essential to the attainment of those objects.

John Marshall, *Cohens v. Virginia*, 19 U.S. (6 Wheat.) 264, 414–15 (1821)

16 It is very clear that a great republic, in which there is room for talents; in which thoughts and actions are not restrained by religious or political despotism; in which education is encouraged, and moral character is esteemed; in which the law rules, and not the sword; in which each one asserts his rights by law, and not by force; and in which there is representation, jury-trial, and a free press, is the natural field of law and equity: but to produce these in perfection, there must be a *national* character. The rules of law and equity, in important matters, must be uniform, and pervade the whole nation.

Nathan Dane, *A General Abridgment and Digest of American Law* 1:xv (1823)

17 The genius and character of the whole government seems to be, that its action is to be applied to all the external concerns of the nation and to those internal concerns which affect the States generally; but not to those which are completely within a particular State, which do not affect other States, and with which it is not necessary to interfere, for the purpose of executing some of the general powers of the government.

John Marshall, *Gibbons v. Ogden*, 22 U.S. (9 Wheat.) 1, 195 (1824)

18 In our complex system, presenting the rare and difficult scheme of one general government, whose action extends over the whole, but which possesses only certain enumerated powers; and of numerous State governments, which retain and exercise all powers not delegated to the Union, contests respecting power must arise.

John Marshall, *Gibbons v. Ogden*, 22 U.S. (9 Wheat.) 1, 204–05 (1824)

19 The happy Union of these States is a wonder; their Constitution a miracle; their example the hope of Liberty throughout the world.*

James Madison, "Outline," Sept. 1829, in *Writings of James Madison* 9:351, 357 (Gaillard Hunt ed. 1910)

20 Who . . . are the friends of the Union? Those who would confine the Federal Gov-

---

* This quotation is inscribed in the Madison Memorial Hall of the James Madison Building of the Library of Congress.

ernment strictly within the limits prescribed by the constitution; who would
preserve to the States and the People all
powers not expressly delegated; who would
make this a Federal and not a National
Union.

> Robert Y. Hayne, Speech in United States
> Senate, 25 Jan. 1830, in *Register of Debates
> in Congress* 43, 56 (1830)

21 If the Federal Government, in all or any, of
its departments, are to prescribe the limits
of its own authority, and the States are
bound to submit to the decision, and are
not to be allowed to examine and decide
for themselves, when the barriers of the
constitution shall be overleaped, this is
practically "a government without limitation of powers." The States are at once reduced to mere petty corporations.

> Robert Y. Hayne, Speech in United States
> Senate, 25 Jan. 1830, in *Register of Debates
> of Congress* 43, 58 (1830)

22 But, Sir, the people have wisely provided,
in the Constitution itself, a proper, suitable
mode and tribunal for settling questions of
constitutional law. . . . By declaring, Sir,
that *"the Constitution, and the laws of the
United States made in pursuance thereof,
shall be the supreme law of the land, any
thing in the constitution or laws of any State
to the contrary notwithstanding. . . ."*

This, Sir, was the first great step. By this
the supremacy of the Constitution and laws
of the United States is declared. The people
so will it. No State law is to be valid which
comes in conflict with the Constitution, or
any law of the United States. . . . But who
shall decide this question of interference?
To whom lies the last appeal? This, sir, the
Constitution itself decided also, by declaring *"that the judicial power shall extend to
all cases arising under the Constitution and
laws of the United States."* These two provisions cover the whole ground. They are,
in truth, the keystone of the arch! With
these it is a government; without them it is
a confederation.

> Daniel Webster, Second Reply to Senator
> Robert Y. Hayne of South Carolina (speech
> in United States Senate), 26–27 Jan. 1830, in
> *Papers of Daniel Webster: Speeches and
> Formal Writings* 1:287, 341 (Charles M.
> Wiltse ed. 1986)

23 The people have preserved this, their own
chosen Constitution, for forty years, and

have seen their happiness, prosperity, and
renown grow with its growth, and
strengthen with its strength. They are now,
generally strongly attached to it. Overthrown by direct assault, it cannot be;
evaded, undermined, NULLIFIED, it will not
be, if we, and those who shall succeed us
here, as agents and representatives of the
people, shall conscientiously and vigilantly
discharge the two great branches of our
public trust, faithfully to preserve, and
wisely to administer it.

> Daniel Webster, Second Reply to Senator
> Robert Y. Hayne of South Carolina (speech
> in United States Senate), 27 Jan. 1830, in
> *Papers of Daniel Webster: Speeches and
> Formal Writings* 1:287, 346 (Charles M.
> Wiltse ed. 1988)

24 *We, therefore, the People of the State of
South Carolina, in Convention assembled,
do Declare and Ordain, . . .* That the several
acts and parts of acts of the Congress of
the United States, purporting to be laws for
the imposing of duties and imposts on the
importation of foreign commodities, . . .
and more especially [the tariff cuts of 1828
and 1832] are unauthorized by the Constitution of the United States, and violate the
true meaning and intent thereof, and are
null, void, and no law, nor binding upon
this State, its officers, or citizens; and all
promises, contracts and obligations, made
or entered into, or to be made or entered
into, with purpose to secure the duties imposed by said acts, and all judicial proceedings which shall be hereafter had in
affirmance thereof, are, and shall be held,
utterly null and void.

> South Carolina Ordinance of Nullification,
> 24 Nov. 1832, in *Statutes at Large of South
> Carolina* 1:329, 329–30 (Thomas Cooper ed.
> 1836)

25 I consider, then, the power to annul a law
of the United States, assumed by one State,
*incompatible with the existence of the
Union, contradicted expressly by the letter of
the Constitution, unauthorized by its spirit,
inconsistent with every principle on which
it was founded, and destructive to the great
object for which it was formed.*

> Andrew Jackson, Proclamation, 10 Dec.
> 1832, in *Messages and Papers of the
> Presidents* 2:640, 643 (James D. Richardson
> ed. 1898)

26 The Constitution of the United States, then, forms a *government*, not a league ... in which all the people are represented, which operates directly on the people individually.

> **Andrew Jackson**, Proclamation, 10 Dec. 1832, in *Messages and Papers of the Presidents* 2:640, 648 (James D. Richardson ed. 1898)

27 The fifth amendment must be understood as restraining the power of the general government, not as applicable to the states.

> **John Marshall**, *Barron v. Baltimore*, 32 U.S. (7 Pet.) 243, 247 (1833)

28 And we think it clear, that the Federal Government, under the Constitution, has no power to impose on a State officer, as such, any duty whatever, and compel him to perform it; for if it possessed this power, it might overload the officer with duties which would fill up all his time, and disable him from performing his obligations to the State, and might impose on him duties of a character incompatible with the rank and dignity to which he was elevated by the State.

> **Roger B. Taney**, *Kentucky v. Dennison*, 65 U.S. (24 How.) 66, 107-08 (1861)

29 The question of the relation of the States to the federal government is the cardinal question of our constitutional system. At every turn of our national development we have been brought face to face with it, and no definition either of statesmen or of judges has ever quieted or decided it. It cannot, indeed, be settled by the opinion of any one generation, because it is a question of growth, and every successive stage of our political and economic development gives it a new aspect, makes it a new question.

> **Woodrow Wilson**, *Constitutional Government in the United States* 173 (1908)

30 This theory [of the first Federal Judiciary Act] and practice is but an expression of the principles underlying the Constitution and which cause the governments and courts of both the Nation and the several States not to be strange or foreign to each other in the broad sense of that word, but to be all courts of a common country.

> **Edward D. White**, *Minneapolis & St. Paul R.R. v. Bombolis*, 241 U.S. 211, 222 (1916)

31 The subject is national. Local interests must yield to the common welfare. The Constitution is supreme.

> **James C. McReynolds**, *Washington v. W.C. Dawson & Co.*, 264 U.S. 219, 228 (1924)

32 The Constitution ... was framed upon the theory that the peoples of the several states must sink or swim together, and that in the long run prosperity and salvation are in union and not division.

> **Benjamin N. Cardozo**, *Baldwin v. Seelig*, 294 U.S. 511, 523 (1935)

33 Every journey to a forbidden end begins with the first step; and the danger of such a step by the federal government in the direction of taking over the powers of the states is that the end of the journey may find the states so despoiled of their powers, or—what may amount to the same thing—so relieved of the responsibilities which possession of the powers necessarily enjoins, as to reduce them to little more than geographical subdivisions of the national domain.

> **George Sutherland**, *Carter v. Carter Coal Co.*, 298 U.S. 238, 295 (1936)

34 The purge of nation-wide calamity that began in 1929 has taught us many lessons. Not the least is the solidarity of interests that may once have seemed to be divided. Unemployment spreads from State to State, the hinterland now settled that in pioneer days gave an avenue of escape.... Rescue becomes necessary irrespective of the cause. The hope behind this statute is to save men and women from the rigors of the poor house as well as from the haunting fear that such a lot awaits them when journey's end is near.

> **Benjamin N. Cardozo**, *Helvering v. Davis*, 301 U.S. 619, 641 (1937)

35 The notion of "comity," that is, a proper respect for state functions, a recognition of the fact that the entire country is made up of a Union of separate state governments, and a continuance of the belief that the National Government will fare best if the States and their institutions are left free to perform their separate functions in their separate ways. This, perhaps for lack of a better and clearer way to describe it, is referred to by many as "Our Federalism," and one familiar with the profound debates

that ushered our Federal Constitution into existence is bound to respect those who remain loyal to the ideals and dreams of "Our Federalism." The concept does not mean blind deference to "States' Rights" any more than it means centralization of control over every important issue in our National Government and its courts. . . . What the concept does represent is a system in which there is sensitivity to the legitimate interests of both State and National Governments, and in which the National Government, anxious though it may be to vindicate and protect federal rights and federal interests, always endeavors to do so in ways that will not unduly interfere with the legitimate activities of the States.

Hugo L. Black, *Younger v. Harris,* 401 U.S. 37, 44 (1971)

36 State courts cannot rest when they have afforded their citizens the full protections of the federal Constitution. State constitutions, too, are a font of individual liberties, their protections often extending beyond those required by the Supreme Court's interpretation of federal law. The legal revolution which has brought federal law to the fore must not be allowed to inhibit the independent protective force of state law—for without it, the full realization of our liberties cannot be guaranteed.

William J. Brennan, Jr., "State Constitutions and the Protection of Individual Rights," 90 *Harvard Law Review* 489, 491 (1977)

37 The fact that Congress generally does not transgress constitutional limits on its power to reach state activities does not make judicial review any less necessary to rectify the cases in which it does do so. The States' role in our system of government is a matter of constitutional law, not of legislative grace.

Lewis F. Powell, Jr., *Garcia v. San Antonio Metro. Transit Auth.,* 469 U.S. 528, 566–67 (1985) (dissenting)

38 In our federal system, the States have a major role that cannot be pre-empted by the National Government. As contemporaneous writings and the debates at the ratifying conventions make clear, the States' ratification of the Constitution was predicated on this understanding of federalism. Indeed, the Tenth Amendment was adopted specifically to ensure that the important role promised the States by the

proponents of the Constitution was realized. . . . The Framers believed that the separate sphere of sovereignty reserved to the States would ensure that the States would serve as an effective "counterpoise" to the power of the Federal Government. . . . by usurping functions traditionally performed by the States, federal overreaching under the Commerce Clause undermines the constitutionally mandated balance of power between the States and the Federal Government, a balance designed to protect our fundamental liberties.

Lewis F. Powell, Jr., *Garcia v. San Antonio Metro. Transit Auth.,* 469 U.S. 528, 568, 571–72 (1985) (dissenting)

FEES

See also WEALTH AND POVERTY

1 Every man that findeth himselfe unfit to plead his owne cause in any Court shall have Libertie to imploy any man against whom the Court doth not except, to helpe him, Provided he give him noe fee or reward for his paines.

Massachusetts Body of Liberties of 1641, § 26, in *Collections of the Massachusetts Historical Society (3d series)* 8:216, 220–21 (1843)

2 It shall be a base and vile thing to plead for money or reward; nor shall any one (except he be a near kinsman, not farther off than cousin-german to the party concerned) be permitted to plead another man's cause, till, before the judge in open court, he hath taken an oath that he doth not plead for money or reward, nor hath nor will receive, nor directly nor indirectly bargained with the party whose cause he is going to plead, for money or any other reward for pleading his cause.

Fundamental Constitutions of Carolina of 1669, § 70, in *Federal and State Constitutions* 5:2772, 2781 (Francis N. Thorpe ed. 1909)

3 *Blind Plaintiff, lame Defendant, share*
The Friendly Laws impartial care,
A Shell for him, a Shell for thee,
The Middle is the Lawyer's Fee.*

Benjamin Franklin, *Poor Richard's Almanack,* 1733, in *Papers of Benjamin*

---

* In Jean de La Fontaine's *Fables* (1668), one fable concerns a dispute over the ownership of an oyster. The suit is settled by the judge's eating the oyster and giving the litigants the shells.

Franklin 1:318 (Leonard W. Labaree ed. 1959)

4 Since I arrived here, I have had an application to be concerned, professionally, against the Bank, which I have declined, of course, although I believe my retainer has not been renewed, or *refreshed*, as usual.

Daniel Webster, Letter (enclosure) to Nicholas Biddle, 21 Dec. 1833, in *Papers of Daniel Webster: Correspondence* 3:288 (Charles M. Wiltse ed. 1977)

5 Whatever fees we [Judge Logan and I] earn at a distance, if not paid *before*, we have noticed we never hear of after the work is done. We therefore, are growing a little sensitive on that point.

Abraham Lincoln, Letter to James S. Irwin, 2 Nov. 1842, in *Collected Works of Abraham Lincoln* 1:304 (Roy P. Basler ed. 1953)

6 The matter of fees is important, far beyond the mere question of bread and butter involved. Properly attended to, fuller justice is done to both lawyer and client. An exorbitant fee should never be claimed. As a general rule never take your whole fee in advance, nor any more than a small retainer. When fully paid beforehand, you are more than a common mortal if you can feel the same interest in the case, as if something was still in prospect for you, as well as for your client. And when you lack interest in the case the job will very likely lack skill and diligence in the performance. Settle the amount of fee and take a note in advance. Then you will feel that you are working for something, and you are sure to do your work faithfully and well.

Abraham Lincoln, "Notes for a Law Lecture," 1 July 1850?, in *Collected Works of Abraham Lincoln* 2:82 (Roy P. Basler ed. 1953)

7 I have heard news from Ottawa, that we *win* our Galatin and Saline county cases. As the dutch Justice said, when he married folks, "Now, vere ish my hundred tollars."

Abraham Lincoln, Letter to Andrew McCallen, 4 July 1851, in *Collected Works of Abraham Lincoln* 2:106 (Roy P. Basler ed. 1953)

8 I have just received yours of 16th, with check on Flagg & Savage for twenty-five dollars. You must think I am a high-priced man. You are too liberal with your money. Fifteen dollars is enough for the job. I send you a receipt for fifteen dollars, and return to you a ten-dollar bill.

Abraham Lincoln, Letter to George P. Floyd, 21 Feb. 1856, in *Collected Works of Abraham Lincoln* 2:332 (Roy P. Basler ed. 1953)

9 The value of a lawyer's services is not measured by time or labor merely. The practice of law is an art in which success depends as much as in any other art on the application of imagination—and sometimes inspiration—to the subject-matter.

John M. Woolsey, *Woodbury v. Andrew Jergens Co.*, 37 F. Supp. 749, 750 (S.D.N.Y. 1930)

10 I get paid for seeing that my clients have every break the law allows. I have knowingly defended a number of guilty men. But the guilty never escape unscathed. My fees are sufficient punishment for anyone.

F. Lee Bailey, quoted in *Los Angeles Times*, 9 Jan. 1972, at 43

11 As a moth is drawn to the light, so is a litigant drawn to the United States. If he can only get his case into their courts, he stands to win a fortune. At no cost to himself; and at no risk of having to pay anything to the other side.

Alfred Denning, *Smith Kline & French Laboratories Ltd. v. Bloch*, [1983] 1 W.L.R. 730, 733 (C.A. 1982)

12 Lawyers charge a fortune to handle a bond offering. You know what it takes to handle a bond offering? The mental capabilities of a filing cabinet.

Jimmy Breslin, quoted in *Legal Times*, 17 Jan. 1983, at 6

13 Finally, a response arrived that left Ms. Klemt stunned. "Without sounding pretentious," wrote Stephen G. Corris, a solo practitioner in Irvine, Calif., "my current retainer for cases is a flat $100,000, with an additional charge of $1,000 per hour. Since I specialize in international trade and geopolitical relations between the Middle East and Europe, my clientel [*sic*] is very unique and limited, and I am afraid I am unable to accept other work at this time."

Ms. Klemt responded: "Steve, I've got news—you can't say you charge a $100,000 retainer fee and an additional $1,000 an hour without sounding pretentious. . . . Especially when you're writing to someone in Laramie, Wyoming, where you're considered pretentious if you wear socks to Court. . . . Hell, Steve, all the lawyers in Laramie, put together, don't charge $1,000 an hour." . . .

"P.S.: Incidentally, we have advised our client of your hourly rate. She is willing to pay you $1,000 per hour to collect this judgment provided it doesn't take you more than four seconds."

Becky Klemt, reported in *Wall Street Journal*, 6 Sept. 1990, at A1, A8

FEMINISM

See ABORTION; RAPE; SEX DISCRIMINATION; WOMEN; WOMEN'S RIGHTS

FICTIONS

See LEGAL FICTIONS

FIFTH AMENDMENT

See also DUE PROCESS

1 It [the privilege against self-incrimination] had a use once. Has it a use now? There was a demand for it three centuries ago, as a safeguard against an extraordinary kind of oppression, which, like witchcraft, has passed away forever. Is there a demand now? I think that the history of the privilege shows us that in deciding these questions we may discard any sanction which its age would naturally carry. As a bequest of the seventeenth century, it is but a relic of controversies and dangers which have disappeared. As a rule of canon law, it never was accepted as we accept it. . . . As to its intrinsic merits, then, may we not express the general opinion in this way, that the privilege is not needed by the innocent, and that the only question can be how far the guilty are entitled to it?

John H. Wigmore, "Nemo Tenetur Seipsum Prodere," 5 *Harvard Law Review* 71, 85–86 (1891)

2 The prohibition of compelling a man in a criminal court to be witness against himself is a prohibition of the use of physical or moral compulsion to extort communications from him, not an exclusion of his body as evidence when it may be material.

Oliver Wendell Holmes, Jr., *Holt v. United States*, 218 U.S. 245, 252–53 (1910)

3 Justice . . . would not perish if the accused were subject to a duty to respond to orderly inquiry.

Benjamin N. Cardozo, *Palko v. Connecticut*, 302 U.S. 319, 326 (1937)

4 Answers to the questions asked by the grand jury would have furnished a link in the chain of evidence needed in a prosecution of petitioner for violation of (or conspiracy to violate) the Smith Act. Prior decisions of this Court have clearly established that under such circumstances, the Constitution gives a witness the privilege of remaining silent. The attempt by the courts below to compel petitioner to testify runs counter to the Fifth Amendment as it has been interpreted from the beginning.

Hugo L. Black, *Blau v. United States*, 340 U.S. 159, 161 (1950)

5 I do not like subversion or disloyalty in any form and if I had ever seen any I would have considered it my duty to have reported it to the proper authorities. But to hurt innocent people whom I knew many years ago in order to save myself is, to me, inhuman and indecent and dishonorable. I cannot and will not cut my conscience to fit this year's fashions, even though I long ago came to the conclusion that I was not a political person and could have no comfortable place in any political group.*

Lillian Hellman, Letter to John S. Wood, 19 May 1952, in *Scoundrel Time* 93 (1976)

6 Every intellectual who is called before one of the [congressional internal security] committees ought to refuse to testify, i.e., he must be prepared . . . for the sacrifice of his personal welfare in the interest of the cultural welfare of his country. . . . this kind of inquisition violates the spirit of the Constitution. If enough people are ready to take this grave step they will be successful. If not, then the intellectuals of this country

---

* Hellman declared in this letter to the Chairman of the House Un-American Activities Committee that she would testify about her own leftist political associations but not about those of others.

deserve nothing better than the slavery which is intended for them.

Albert Einstein, Letter to William Frauenglass, 16 May 1953, in *New York Times,* 12 June 1953, at 1, 9

7 The Fifth Amendment is an old friend and a good friend. It is one of the great landmarks in man's struggle to be free of tyranny, to be decent and civilized. It is our way of escape from the use of torture.

William O. Douglas, *An Almanac of Liberty* 238 (1954)

8 I would like to venture the suggestion that the privilege against self-incrimination is one of the greatest landmarks in man's struggle to make himself civilized.

Erwin N. Griswold, *The 5th Amendment Today* 7 (1955)

9 The Fifth Amendment was designed to protect the accused against infamy as well as against prosecution.

William O. Douglas, *Ullmann v. United States,* 350 U.S. 422, 450 (1956) (dissenting)

10 It is no answer to say that a witness who exercises his Fifth Amendment right of silence and stands mute may bring himself into disrepute. If so, that is the price he pays for exercising the right of silence granted by the Fifth Amendment. The critical point is that the Constitution places the right of silence *beyond the reach of government.* The Fifth Amendment stands between the citizen and his government when public opinion casts a person into the outer darkness, as happens today when a person is exposed as a Communist, the government brings infamy on the head of the witness when it compels discosure. That is precisely what the Fifth Amendment prohibits.

William O. Douglas, *Ullmann v. United States,* 350 U.S. 422, 454 (1956) (dissenting)

11 If this is only a problem in the law of evidence, that is one thing. The great name of Wigmore will be invoked against some of the exclusionary principles laid down by the Supreme Court. The law of evidence is concerned primarily with workable rules for determining the truth. . . . [But the] Supreme Court does not sit to . . . enforce Wigmore on Evidence. . . . [In] asserting the voice of the Constitution the Court rises far above the mere law of evidence.

Charles Fairman, "Compulsory Self-Incrimination," in *Fundamental Law in Criminal Prosecutions* 59, 71 (Arthur L. Harding ed. 1959)

12 The American system of criminal prosecution is accusatorial, not inquisitorial, and . . . the Fifth Amendment privilege is its essential mainstay.

William J. Brennan, Jr., *Malloy v. Hogan,* 378 U.S. 1, 7 (1964)

13 It [the privilege against self-incrimination] reflects many of our fundamental values and most noble aspirations: our unwillingness to subject those suspected of crime to the cruel trilemma of self-accusation, perjury or contempt; our preference for an accusatorial rather than an inquisitorial system of criminal justice; our fear that self-incriminating statements will be elicited by inhumane treatment and abuses; our sense of fair play . . . our respect for the inviolability of the human personality and of the right of each individual "to a private enclave where he may lead a private life," . . . our distrust of self-deprecatory statements; and our realization that the privilege, while sometimes "a shelter to the guilty," is often "a protection to the innocent."

Arthur J. Goldberg, *Murphy v. Waterfront Commission,* 378 U.S. 52, 55 (1964)

14 There is no right to escape detection. There is no right to commit a perfect crime or to an equal opportunity to that end. The Constitution is not at all offended when a guilty man stubs his toe. On the contrary, it is decent to hope that he will. Nor is it dirty business to use evidence a defendant himself may furnish in the detectional stage. Voluntary confessions accord with high moral values, and as to the culprit who reveals his guilt unwittingly with no intent to shed his inner burden, it is no more unfair to use the evidence he thereby reveals than it is to turn against him clues at the scene of the crime which a brighter, better informed, or more gifted criminal would not have left. Thus the Fifth Amendment does not say that a man shall not be permitted to incriminate himself, or that he shall not be persuaded to do so. It says no more than

a man shall not be "compelled" to give evidence against himself.

Joseph Weintraub, *State v. McKnight,* 52 N.J. 35, 52, 243 A.2d 240 (1968)

FIRMS

See LAW FIRMS

FIRST AMENDMENT

See also CENSORSHIP; FREEDOM OF EXPRESSION; FREEDOM OF RELIGION; FREEDOM OF SPEECH; FREEDOM OF THE PRESS; LIBEL; OBSCENITY

1 That the people have a right to freedom of speech, and of writing, and publishing their sentiments; therefore the freedom of the press ought not to be restrained.

Pennsylvania Constitution of 1776, Declaration of Rights, § 12, in *Federal and State Constitutions* 5:3081, 3083 (Francis N. Thorpe ed. 1909)

2 That the people have a right to assemble together, to consult for their common good, to instruct their representatives, and to apply to the legislature for redress of grievances, by address, petition, or remonstrance.

Pennsylvania Constitution of 1776, Declaration of Rights, § 16, in *Federal and State Constitutions* 5:3081, 3084 (Francis N. Thorpe ed. 1909)

3 Driven from every other corner of the earth, freedom of thought and the right of private judgment in matters of conscience direct their course to this happy country as their last asylum.

Samuel Adams, Oration at the State-House, Philadelphia, 1 Aug. 1776, in *Life and Public Services of Samuel Adams* 3:413 (William V. Wells ed., 2d ed. 1888)

4 This state having, by its Convention, which ratified the Federal Constitution, expressly declared that, among other essential rights, "the liberty of conscience and the press cannot be cancelled, abridged, restrained, or modified, by any authority of the United States," and from its extreme anxiety to guard these rights from every possible attack of sophistry and ambition, having, with other states, recommended an amendment for that purpose, . . . it would mark a reproachful inconsistency, and criminal degeneracy, if an indifference were now shown to the most palpable violation of one of the rights thus declared and secured, and to the establishment of a precedent which may be fatal to the other.

Virginia Resolutions of 1798, in *Debates in the Several State Conventions* 4:528, 529 (Jonathan Elliot ed., 2d ed. 1888)

5 It is by the goodness of God that in our country we have those three unspeakably precious things: freedom of speech, freedom of conscience, and the prudence never to practise either of them.

Mark Twain, *Following the Equator,* 1897, in *Writings of Mark Twain* 20:175 (1929)

6 It shall be unlawful for any teacher in any of the Universitis [*sic*], Normals and all other public schools of the State which are supported in whole or in part by the public school funds of the State, to teach any theory that denies the story of the Divine Creation of man as taught in the Bible, and to teach instead that man has descended from a lower order of animals.

Act of Mar. 13, 1925, ch. 27, § 1, 1925 Tenn. Pub. Acts 50, 50–51

7 If today you can take a thing like evolution and make it a crime to teach it in the public school, tomorrow you can make it a crime to teach it in the private schools, and the next year you can make it a crime to teach it to the hustings or in the church. At the next session you may ban books and the newspapers. Soon you may set Catholic against Protestant and Protestant against Protestant, and try to foist your own religion upon the minds of men. If you can do one you can do the other. Ignorance and fanaticism is ever busy and needs feeding. Always it is feeding and gloating for more. Today it is the public school teachers, tomorrow the private. The next day the preachers and the lecturers, the magazines, the books, the newspapers. After while, your honor, it is the setting of man against man and creed against creed until with flying banners and beating drums we are marching backward to the glorious ages of the sixteenth century when bigots lighted fagots to burn the men who dared to bring any intelligence and enlightenment and culture to the human mind.

Clarence S. Darrow, Speech at Scopes Trial, Dayton, Tenn., 13 July 1925, in *The World's Most Famous Court Trial* 87 (1925)

8 The greater the importance of safeguarding the community from incitements to the overthrow of our institutions by force and violence, the more imperative is the need to preserve inviolate the constitutional rights of free speech, free press and free assembly in order to maintain the opportunity for free political discussion, to the end that government may be responsive to the will of the people and that changes, if desired, may be obtained by peaceful means. Therein lies the security of the Republic, the very foundation of constitutional government. . . . The holding of meetings for peaceable political action cannot be proscribed. . . . The question, if the rights of free speech and peaceable assembly are to be preserved, is not as to the auspices under which the meeting is held but as to its purpose; not as to the relations of the speakers, but whether their utterances transcend the bounds of the freedom of speech which the Constitution protects.

Charles Evans Hughes, *DeJonge v. Oregon*, 299 U.S. 353, 365–66 (1937)

9 Do the people of this land . . . desire to preserve those [liberties] so carefully protected by the First Amendment . . . ? If so, let them withstand all *beginnings* of encroachment. For the saddest epitaph which can be carved in memory of a vanished liberty is that it was lost because its possessors failed to stretch forth a saving hand while yet there was time.

George Sutherland, *Associated Press v. NLRB*, 301 U.S. 103, 141 (1937) (dissenting)

10 Wherever the title of streets and parks may rest, they have immemorially been held in trust for the use of the public and, time out of mind, have been used for purposes of assembly, communicating thoughts between citizens, and discussing public questions. Such use of the streets and public places has, from ancient times, been a part of the privileges, immunities, rights, and liberties of citizens.

Owen J. Roberts, *Hague v. CIO*, 307 U.S. 496, 515 (1939)

11 The streets are natural and proper places for the dissemination of information and opinion; and one is not to have the exercise of his liberty of expression in appropriate places abridged on the plea that it may be exercised in some other place.

Owen J. Roberts, *Schneider v. State*, 308 U.S. 147, 163 (1939)

12 The First Amendment does not speak equivocally. It prohibits any law "abridging the freedom of speech, or of the press." It must be taken as a command of the broadest scope that explicit language, read in the context of a liberty-loving society, will allow.

Hugo L. Black, *Bridges v. California*, 314 U.S. 252, 263 (1941)

13 In the future days, which we seek to make secure, we look forward to a world founded upon four essential human freedoms. The first is freedom of speech and expression— everywhere in the world. The second is freedom of every person to worship God in his own way—everywhere in the world.

Franklin D. Roosevelt, Annual Message to Congress, 6 Jan. 1941, in *Public Papers and Addresses of Franklin D. Roosevelt, 1940*, at 663, 672 (Samuel I. Rosenman ed. 1941)

14 I view the guarantees of the First Amendment as the foundation upon which our governmental structure rests and without which it could not continue to endure as conceived and planned. Freedom to speak and write about public questions is as important to the life of our government as is the heart to the human body. In fact, this privilege is the heart of our government. If that heart be weakened, the result is debilitation; if it be stilled, the result is death.

Hugo L. Black, *Drivers v. Meadowmore Dairies*, 312 U.S. 287, 301-02 (1942) (dissenting)

15 If this Court is to err in evaluating claims that freedom of speech, freedom of the press, and freedom of religion have been invaded, far better that it err in being overprotective of these precious rights.

Frank Murphy, *Jones v. Opelika*, 316 U.S. 584, 623 (1942) (dissenting)

16 The First Amendment is not confined to safeguarding freedom of speech and freedom of religion against discriminatory attempts to wipe them out. On the contrary, the Constitution, by virtue of the First and

Fourteenth Amendments, has put those freedoms in a preferred position.

> Harlan F. Stone, *Jones v. Opelika*, 316 U.S. 584, 608 (1942) (dissenting)

17 Words uttered under coercion are proof of loyalty to nothing but self-interest. Love of country must spring from willing hearts and free minds, inspired by a fair administration of wise laws enacted by the people's elected representatives within the bounds of express constitutional prohibitions. These laws must, to be consistent with the First Amendment, permit the widest toleration of conflicting viewpoints consistent with a society of free men.

> Hugo L. Black, *West Virginia State Bd. of Educ. v. Barnette*, 319 U.S. 624, 644 (1943) (dissenting)

18 The very purpose of the First Amendment is to foreclose public authority from assuming a guardianship of the public mind through regulating the press, speech, and religion. In this field every person must be his own watchman for truth, because the forefathers did not trust any government to separate the true from the false for us. . . . Nor would I.

> Robert H. Jackson, *Thomas v. Collins*, 323 U.S. 516, 545 (1945) (concurring)

19 The usual presumption supporting legislation is balanced by the preferred place given in our scheme to the great, the indispensable democratic freedoms secured by the First Amendment. . . . The rational connection between the remedy provided and the evil to be curbed, which in other contexts might support legislation against attack on due process grounds, will not suffice.

> Wiley B. Rutledge, *Thomas v. Collins*, 323 U.S. 516, 529–30 (1945)

20 It was not by accident or coincidence that the rights to freedom in speech and press were coupled in a single guaranty with the rights of the people peaceably to assemble and to petition for redress of grievances. All these, though not identical, are inseparable. They are cognate rights, . . . and therefore are united in the First Article's assurance.

> Wiley B. Rutledge, *Thomas v. Collins*, 323 U.S. 516, 530 (1945)

21 The First Amendment . . . does not require that, on every occasion, every citizen shall take part in public debate. . . . What is essential is not that everyone shall speak, but that everything worth saying shall be said.

> Alexander Meiklejohn, *Free Speech and its Relation to Self-Government* 25 (1948)

22 When men govern themselves, it is they—and no one else—who must pass judgment upon unwisdom and unfairness and danger. . . . Just so far as, at any point, the citizens who are to decide an issue are denied acquaintance with information or opinion or doubt or disbelief or criticism which is relevant to that issue, just so far the result must be ill-considered, ill-balanced planning for the general good. *It is that mutilation of the thinking process of the community against which the First Amendment to the Constitution is directed.*

> Alexander Meiklejohn, *Free Speech and Its Relation to Self-Government* 26 (1948)

23 Conflicting views may be expressed, must be expressed, not because they are valid, but because they are relevant. If they are responsibly entertained by anyone, we, the voters, need to hear them. . . . To be afraid of ideas, any idea, is to be unfit for self-government. Any such suppression of ideas about the common good, the First Amendment condemns with its absolute disapproval. The freedom of ideas shall not be abridged.

> Alexander Meiklejohn, *Free Speech and Its Relation to Self-Government* 27 (1948)

24 Public opinion being what it now is, few will protest the conviction of these Communist petitioners. There is hope, however, that in calmer times, when present pressures, passions, and fears subside, this or some later Court will restore the First Amendment liberties to the high preferred place where they belong in a free society.

> Hugo L. Black, *Dennis v. United States*, 341 U.S. 494, 581 (1951) (dissenting)

25 I do not agree that the Constitution leaves freedom of petition, assembly, speech, press or worship at the mercy of a case-by-case, day-by-day majority of this Court. I had supposed that our people could rely for their freedom on the Constitution's com-

mands, rather than on the grace of this Court on an individual case basis.

Hugo L. Black, *Beauharnais v. Illinois,* 343 U.S. 250, 274–75 (1952) (dissenting)

26 Those who want the Government to regulate matters of the mind and spirit are like men who are so afraid of being murdered that they commit suicide to avoid assassination.

Harry S. Truman, Address at the National Archives, Washington, D.C., 15 Dec. 1952, in *Public Papers of the Presidents: Harry S. Truman, 1952–53,* at 1077, 1079 (1966)

27 That [the First] Amendment provides, in simple words, that "Congress shall make no law . . . abridging the freedom of speech, or of the press." I read "no law . . . abridging" to mean *no law abridging.*

Hugo L. Black, *Smith v. California,* 361 U.S. 147, 157 (1959) (concurring)

28 [The First Amendment] is not confined to the expression of ideas that are conventional or shared by a majority. It protects advocacy of the opinion that adultery may sometimes be proper, no less than advocacy of socialism or the single tax. And in the realm of ideas it protects expression which is eloquent no less than that which is unconvincing.

Potter Stewart, *Kingsley Int'l Pictures Corp. v. Regents,* 360 U.S. 684, 689 (1959)

29 Since the earliest days philosophers have dreamed of a country where the mind and spirit of man would be free; where there would be no limits to inquiry; where men would be free to explore the unknown and to challenge the most deeply rooted beliefs and principles. Our First Amendment was a bold effort to adopt this principle—to establish a country with no legal restrictions of any kind upon the subjects people could investigate, discuss and deny. The Framers knew, better perhaps than we do today, the risks they were taking. They knew that free speech might be the friend of change and revolution. But they also knew that it is always the deadliest enemy of tyranny. With this knowledge they still believed that the ultimate happiness and security of a nation lies in its ability to explore, to change, to grow and ceaselessly to adapt itself to new knowledge born of inquiry free from any kind of governmental control over the

mind and spirit of man. Loyalty comes from love of good government, not fear of a bad one.

Hugo L. Black, "The Bill of Rights," 35 *New York University Law Review* 865, 880–81 (1960)

30 Even though the governmental purpose be legitimate and substantial, that purpose cannot be pursued by means that broadly stifle fundamental personal liberties when the end can be more narrowly achieved. The breadth of legislative abridgment must be viewed in the light of less drastic means for achieving the same basic purpose.

Potter Stewart, *Shelton v. Tucker,* 364 U.S. 479, 488 (1960)

31 I believe that the First Amendment's unequivocal command that there shall be no abridgment of the rights of free speech and assembly shows that the men who drafted our Bill of Rights did all the "balancing" that was to be done in this field. . . . the very object of adopting the First Amendment, as well as the other provisions of the Bill of Rights, was to put the freedoms protected there completely out of the area of any congressional control that may be attempted through the exercise of precisely those powers that are now being used to "balance" the Bill of Rights out of existence.

Hugo L. Black, *Konigsberg v. State Bar,* 366 U.S. 36, 61 (1961) (dissenting)

32 But that is the present trend, not only in the legal profession but in almost every walk of life. Too many men are being driven to become government-fearing and time-serving because the Government is being permitted to strike out at those who are fearless enough to think as they please and say what they think. This trend must be halted if we are to keep with the Founders of our Nation and pass on to future generations of Americans the great heritage of freedom which they sacrificed so much to leave to us. The choice is clear to me. If we are to pass on that great heritage of freedom, we must return to the original language of the Bill of Rights. We must not be afraid to be free.

Hugo L. Black, *In re Anastaplo,* 366 U.S. 82, 116 (1961) (dissenting)

33 In time of "clear and present danger," the courts have held that even the privileged

rights of the First Amendment must yield to the public's need for national security.

John F. Kennedy, Address before American Newspaper Publishers Association, New York, 27 Apr. 1961, in *Public Papers of the Presidents: John F. Kennedy, 1961*, at 336 (1962)

34 I do not believe that it can be too often repeated that the freedoms of speech, press, petition and assembly guaranteed by the First Amendment must be accorded to the ideas we hate or sooner or later they will be denied to the ideas we cherish.

Hugo L. Black, *Communist Party v. Subversive Activities Control Bd.*, 367 U.S. 1, 137 (1961) (dissenting)

35 I took an obligation to support and defend the Constitution as I understand it. And being a rather backward country fellow, I understand it to mean what the words say.

Hugo L. Black, quoted in Edmond Cahn, "Justice Black and the First Amendment 'Absolutes': A Public Interview," 37 *New York University Law Review* 549, 553–54 (1962)

36 Standards of permissible statutory vagueness are strict in the area of free expression.... Because First Amendment freedoms need breathing space to survive, government may regulate in the area only with narrow specificity.

William J. Brennan, Jr., *NAACP v. Button*, 371 U.S. 415, 432–33 (1963)

37 Freedom of expression embraces more than the right of an individual to speak his mind. It includes also his right to advocate and his right to join with his fellows in an effort to make that advocacy effective.... And just as it includes the right jointly to petition the legislature for redress of grievances ... so it must include the right to join together for purposes of obtaining judicial redress.

John M. Harlan (1899–1971), *NAACP v. Button*, 371 U.S. 415, 452–53 (1963) (dissenting)

38 An unconditional right to say what one pleases about public affairs is what I consider to be the minimum guarantee of the First Amendment.

Hugo L. Black, *New York Times Co. v. Sullivan*, 376 U.S. 254, 297 (1964) (concurring)

39 Because of the sensitive nature of constitutionally protected expression, we have not required that all of those subject to overbroad regulations risk prosecution to test their rights.... Moreover, we have not thought that the improbability of successful prosecution makes the case different. The chilling effect upon the exercise of First Amendment rights may derive from the fact of the prosecution, unaffected by the prospects of its success or failure.*

William J. Brennan, Jr., *Dombrowski v. Pfister*, 380 U.S. 479, 486–87 (1965)

40 It is true that the First Amendment contains no specific guarantee of access to publications. However, the protection of the Bill of Rights goes beyond the specific guarantees to protect from congressional abridgment those equally fundamental personal rights necessary to make the express guarantees meaningful.... I think the right to receive publications is such a fundamental right.

William J. Brennan, Jr., *Lamont v. Postmaster General*, 381 U.S. 301, 308 (1965) (concurring)

41 Our Nation is deeply committed to safeguarding academic freedom, which is of transcendent value to all of us and not merely to the teachers concerned. That freedom is therefore a special concern of the First Amendment, which does not tolerate laws that cast a pall of orthodoxy over the classroom.

William J. Brennan, Jr., *Keyishian v. Board of Regents*, 385 U.S. 589, 603 (1967)

42 To characterize the quality of the governmental interest which must appear, the Court has employed a variety of descriptive terms: compelling; substantial; subordinating; paramount; cogent; strong. Whatever imprecision inheres in these terms, we think it clear that a government regulation is sufficiently justified if it is within the constitutional power of the Government; if it furthers an important or substantial governmental interest; if the governmental interest is unrelated to the suppression of free expression; and if the incidental restriction on alleged First Amendment free-

---

* This passage popularized the use of the term "chilling effect" to describe inhibition of freedom of expression.

149

doms is no greater than is essential to the furtherance of that interest.

> **Earl Warren,** *United States v. O'Brien,* 391 U.S. 367, 376–77 (1968)

43 The framers seem to have had no coherent theory of free speech. . . . The First Amendment, like the rest of the Bill of Rights, appears to have been a hastily drafted document upon which little thought was expended.

> **Robert H. Bork,** "Neutral Principles and Some First Amendment Problems," 47 *Indiana Law Journal* 1, 22 (1971)

44 The associational rights which our system honors permit all white, all black, all brown, and all yellow clubs to be formed. They also permit all Catholic, all Jewish, or all agnostic clubs to be established. Government may not tell a man or woman who his or her associates must be.

> **William O. Douglas,** *Moose Lodge No. 107 v. Irvis,* 407 U.S. 163, 179–80 (1972) (dissenting)

45 Above all else, the First Amendment means that government has no power to restrict expression because of its message, its ideas, its subject matter, or its content.

> **Thurgood Marshall,** *Police Department v. Mosley,* 408 U.S. 92, 95 (1972)

46 In the oscillating movement of the planets man is a tiny speck—a microcosm. We seek truth, and in that search, a medley of voices is essential. That is why the First Amendment is our most precious inheritance. It gives equal time to my opponents, as it gives to me.

I hope it is always that way in this great land, which, in spite of its shortcomings, is still the hope of mankind across the globe.

> **William O. Douglas,** *Go East Young Man* 470 (1974)

47 But the concept that government may restrict the speech of some elements of our society in order to enhance the relative voice of others is wholly foreign to the First Amendment.

> *Buckley v. Valeo,* 424 U.S. 1, 48–49 (1976) (per curiam)

48 The First Amendment bars the state from imposing upon its citizens an authoritative vision of truth. It prohibits the state from interfering with the communicative processes through which its citizens exercise and prepare to exercise their rights of self-government. And the Amendment shields those who would censure the state or expose its abuses.

> **William J. Brennan, Jr.,** *Herbert v. Lando,* 441 U.S. 153, 184–85 (1979) (dissenting in part)

49 We hold that the right to attend criminal trials is implicit in the guarantees of the First Amendment.

> **Warren E. Burger,** *Richmond Newspapers, Inc. v. Virginia,* 448 U.S. 555, 580 (1980)

50 If there is a bedrock principle underlying the First Amendment, it is that the Government may not prohibit the expression of an idea simply because society finds the idea itself offensive and disagreeable. . . . We decline, therefore, to create for the flag an exception to the joust of principles protected by the First Amendment.

> **William J. Brennan, Jr.,** *Texas v. Johnson,* 109 S. Ct. 2533, 2544, 2546 (1989)

51 We can imagine . . . no better way to counter a flag-burner's message than by saluting the flag that burns. . . . We do not consecrate the flag by punishing its desecration, for in doing so we dilute the freedom that this cherished emblem represents.

> **William J. Brennan, Jr.,** *Texas v. Johnson,* 109 S. Ct. 2533, 2547–48 (1989)

52 The hard fact is that sometimes we must make decisions we do not like. We make them because they are right, right in the sense that the law and the Constitution, as we see them, compel the result. . . . Though symbols often are what we ourselves make of them, the flag is constant in expressing beliefs Americans share, beliefs in law and peace and that freedom which sustains the human spirit. The case here today forces recognition of the costs to which those beliefs commit us. It is poignant but fundamental that the flag protects those who hold it in contempt.

> **Anthony M. Kennedy,** *Texas v. Johnson,* 491 U.S. 397, 420–21 (1989) (concurring)

53 In order for the flag to endure as a symbol of freedom in this nation, we must protect

with equal vigor the right to wave it and the right to destroy it.

> **Barbara J. Rothstein,** *United States v. Haggerty,* 731 F. Supp. 415, 422 (W.D. Wash. 1990)

54 A formerly dramatic expression of protest is now rather commonplace. In today's marketplace of ideas, the public burning of a Vietnam draft card is probably less provocative than lighting a cigarette. Tomorrow flag burning may produce a similar reaction.

> **John Paul Stevens,** *United States v. Eichman,* 110 S. Ct. 2404, 2412 (1990) (dissenting)

FOURTEENTH AMENDMENT

See also BILL OF RIGHTS; CIVIL RIGHTS; DUE PROCESS; EQUAL PROTECTION

1 To these [Article IV] privileges and immunities, whatever they may be—for they are not and cannot be fully defined . . . to these should be added the personal rights guarantied and secured by the first eight amendments of the Constitution. . . . The great object of the first section of this [Fourteenth] amendment is, therefore, to restrain the power of the States and compel them at all times to respect these great fundamental guarantees.

> **Jacob M. Howard,** in *Congressional Globe,* 39th Cong., 1st Sess. 2765–66 (1866)

2 "The hand that rounded Peter's dome, / And groined the aisles of Christian Rome, / Wrought in a sad sincerity. / He builded better than he knew!"

Those who devised the Fourteenth Amendment wrought in grave sincerity. They may have builded better than they knew.

They vitalized and energized a principle, as old and as everlasting as human rights. To some of them, the sunset of life may have given mystical lore.

They builded, not for a day, but for all time; not for a few, or for a race; but for man. They planted in the Constitution a monumental truth . . . the golden rule.

> **Roscoe Conkling,** Oral argument in *County of San Mateo v. Southern Pacific R.R.,* 116 U.S. 138, in *Oral Argument on Behalf of Defendant by Roscoe Conkling* 34 (1883)

3 The court does not wish to hear argument on the question whether the provision in the Fourteenth Amendment to the Constitution, which forbids a State to deny to any person within its jurisdiction the equal protection of the laws, applies to these corporations. We are all of opinion that it does.

> **Morrison R. Waite,** *Santa Clara County v. Southern Pacific R.R.,* 118 U.S. 394, 396 (1886) (statement before argument)

4 If the Fourteenth Amendment is not to be a greater hamper upon the established practices of the States in common with other governments than I think was intended, they must be allowed a certain latitude in the minor adjustments of life, even though by their action the burdens of a part of the community are somewhat increased. The traditions and habits of centuries were not intended to be overthrown when that amendment was passed.

> **Oliver Wendell Holmes, Jr.,** *Interstate Consol. Street Ry. v. Massachusetts,* 207 U.S. 79, 87 (1907)

5 We must be cautious about pressing the broad words of the Fourteenth Amendment to a drily logical extreme.

> **Oliver Wendell Holmes, Jr.,** *Noble State Bank v. Haskell,* 219 U.S. 104, 110 (1911)

6 The Fourteenth Amendment is not a pedagogical requirement of the impracticable.

> **Oliver Wendell Holmes, Jr.,** *Dominion Hotel v. Arizona,* 249 U.S. 265, 268 (1919)

7 Freedom of speech and of the press . . . are among the fundamental personal rights and "liberties" protected by the due process clause of the Fourteenth Amendment from impairment by the States.

> **Edward T. Sanford,** *Gitlow v. New York,* 268 U.S. 652, 666 (1925)

8 We have said that in appellant's view the Fourteenth Amendment is to be taken as embodying the prohibitions of the Fifth. His thesis is even broader. Whatever would be a violation of the original bill of rights (Amendments I to VIII) if done by the federal government is now equally unlawful by force of the Fourteenth Amendment if done by a state. There is no such general rule.

> **Benjamin N. Cardozo,** *Palko v. Connecticut,* 302 U.S. 319, 323 (1937)

9 Immunities that are valid as against the federal government by force of the specific pledges of particular amendments have been found to be implicit in the concept of ordered liberty, and thus, through the Fourteenth Amendment, become valid as against the states.

> **Benjamin N. Cardozo,** *Palko v. Connecticut,* 302 U.S. 319, 324–25 (1937)

10 The right to trial by jury and the immunity from prosecution except as the result of an indictment may have value and importance. Even so, they are not of the very essence of a scheme of ordered liberty. . . . Few would be so narrow or provincial as to maintain that a fair and enlightened system of justice would be impossible without them.

> **Benjamin N. Cardozo,** *Palko v. Connecticut,* 302 U.S. 319, 325 (1937)

11 A contention that a citizen's duty to render military service is suspended by "indigence" would meet with little favor. Rich or penniless, Duncan's citizenship under the Constitution pledges his strength to the defense of California as a part of the United States, and his right to migrate to any part of the land he must defend is something she must respect under the same instrument. Unless this Court is willing to say that citizenship of the United States means at least this much to the citizen, then our heritage of constitutional privileges and immunities is only a promise to the ear to be broken to the hope, a teasing illusion like a munificent bequest in a pauper's will.

> **Robert H. Jackson,** *Edwards v. California,* 314 U.S. 160, 185–86 (1941) (concurring)

12 My study of the historical events that culminated in the Fourteenth Amendment, and the expressions of those who sponsored and favored, as well as those who opposed its submission and passage, persuades me that one of the chief objects that the provisions of the Amendment's first section, separately, and as a whole, were intended to accomplish was to make the Bill of Rights, applicable to the states.

> **Hugo L. Black,** *Adamson v. California,* 332 U.S. 46, 71–72 (1947) (dissenting)

13 Of all these judges, only one [the first Justice John M. Harlan], who may respectfully be called an eccentric exception, ever indicated the belief that the Fourteenth Amendment was a shorthand summary of the first eight Amendments theretofore limiting only the Federal Government, and that due process incorporated those eight Amendments as restrictions upon the powers of the States.

> **Felix Frankfurter,** *Adamson v. California,* 332 U.S. 46, 62 (1947) (concurring)

14 It is far too late in the day to contend that the Fourteenth Amendment prohibits only racial discrimination; and to me, singling out the poor to bear a burden not placed on any other class of citizens tramples the values that the Fourteenth Amendment was designed to protect.

> **Thurgood Marshall,** *James v. Valtierra,* 402 U.S. 137, 145 (1971) (dissenting)

15 No patent medicine was ever put to wider and more varied use than the Fourteenth Amendment.

> **William O. Douglas,** quoted in Hugo Black, Jr., *My Father: A Remembrance* 242 (1975)

FOURTH AMENDMENT

See SEARCHES AND SEIZURES

FRAUD

1 Fraud, or breach of trust, ought not lightly to be imputed to the living; for, the legal presumption is the other way; and as to the dead, who are not here to answer for themselves, it would be the height of injustice and cruelty to disturb their ashes, and violate the sanctity of the grave, unless the evidence of fraud be clear, beyond a reasonable doubt.

> **Joseph Story,** *Prevost v. Gratz,* 19 U.S. (6 Wheat.) 481, 498 (1821)

2 [Fraud] therefore has to be ferreted out by carefully following its marks and signs; for fraud will, in most instances, though never so artfully and secretly contrived, like the snail in its passage, leaves its slime by which it may be traced.

> *Floyd v. Goodwin,* 16 Tenn. 484, 490 (1835) (jury charge in court below)

3 The defendant insists that the false representations must have been such as to deceive a man of ordinary care and prudence;

i.e., if a man is not endowed with those faculties he is at the mercy of every swindler who makes him prey, excluding from the benefits of the law the very class around whom its arm should be thrown,—thus protecting the strong and robbing the weak. As well adopt Rob Roy's rule: "That they should take who have the power, / And they should keep who can." No rogue should enjoy his ill-gotten plunder for the simple reason that his victim is by chance a fool.

Russell S. Taft, *Chamberlin v. Fuller*, 59 Vt. 247, 256, 9 A. 832 (1886)

4 No one shall be permitted to profit by his own fraud, or to take advantage of his own wrong, or to found any claim upon his own iniquity, or to acquire property by his own crime.

Robert Earl, *Riggs v. Palmer*, 115 N.Y. 506, 511, 22 N.E. 188 (1889)

5 Fresh news is got only by enterprise and expense.... If the plaintiff produces the news at the same time that the defendant does, the defendant's presentation impliedly denies to the plaintiff the credit of collecting the facts and assumes that credit to the defendant.... The falsehood is a little more subtle, the injury a little more indirect, than in ordinary cases of unfair trade, but I think that the principle that condemns the one condemns the other. It is a question of how strong an infusion of fraud is necessary to turn a flavor into a poison. The dose seems to me strong enough here to need a remedy from the law.

Oliver Wendell Holmes, Jr., *International News Service v. Associated Press*, 248 U.S. 215, 247–48 (1918) (separate opinion)

6 Fraud is the homage that force pays to reason.

Charles P. Curtis, *A Commonplace Book* 15 (1957)

FREE SPEECH

See FIRST AMENDMENT; FREEDOM OF EXPRESSION; FREEDOM OF SPEECH

FREEDOM

See also LIBERTY; RIGHTS

1 Since the general civilization of mankind, I believe there are more instances of the abridgment of the freedom of the people, by gradual and silent encroachments of those in power, than by violent and sudden usurpations.

James Madison, Speech at Virginia Convention, 5 June 1788, in *Writings of James Madison* 5:123, 126 (Gaillard Hunt ed. 1904)

2 You can only protect your liberties in this world by protecting the other man's freedom. You can only be free if I am free.

Clarence S. Darrow, Address to jury, Communist Trial, 1920, in *Attorney for the Damned* 121, 140 (Arthur Weinberg ed. 1957)

3 The case is made difficult, not because the principles of its decision are obscure, but because the flag involved is our own. Nevertheless, we apply the limitations of the Constitution with no fear that freedom to be intellectually and spiritually diverse or even contrary will disintegrate the social organization. To believe that patriotism will not flourish if patriotic ceremonies are voluntary and spontaneous instead of a compulsory routine is to make an unflattering estimate of the appeal of our institutions to free minds.

Robert H. Jackson, *West Virginia State Bd. of Educ. v. Barnette*, 319 U.S. 624, 641 (1943)

4 We can have intellectual individualism and the rich cultural diversities that we owe to exceptional minds only at the price of occasional eccentricity and abnormal attitudes. When they are so harmless to others or to the State as those we deal with here, the price is not too great.

Robert H. Jackson, *West Virginia State Bd. of Educ. v. Barnette*, 319 U.S. 624, 641–42 (1943)

5 To abolish the fences of laws between men—as tyranny does—means to take away man's liberties and destroy freedom as a living political reality; for the space between men as it is hedged in by laws, is the living space of freedom.

Hannah Arendt, *The Origins of Totalitarianism* 466 (2d ed. 1958)

6 The American feels so rich in his opportunities for free expression that he often no

longer knows what it is he is free from. Neither does he know where he is not free; he does not recognize his native autocrats when he sees them.

> Erik H. Erikson, *Childhood and Society* 321 (2d ed. 1963)

FREEDOM OF CONTRACT

See CONTRACTS; DUE PROCESS

FREEDOM OF EXPRESSION

See also FIRST AMENDMENT; FREEDOM OF SPEECH; FREEDOM OF THE PRESS

1 The jaws of power are always opened to devour, and her arm is always stretched out, if possible, to destroy the freedom of thinking, speaking, and writing.

> John Adams, *Dissertation on the Canon and the Feudal Law,* 1765, in *Works of John Adams* 3:457 (Charles Francis Adams ed. 1851)

2 If any person shall write, print, utter or publish, or shall cause or procure to be written, printed, uttered or published, or shall knowingly and willingly assist or aid in writing, printing, uttering or publishing any false, scandalous and malicious writing or writings against the government of the United States, or either house of the Congress of the United States, or the President of the United States, with intent to defame the said government, or either house of the said Congress, or the said President, or to bring them, or either of them, into contempt or disrepute; or to excite against them, or either or any of them, the hatred of the good people of the United States, or to stir up sedition within the United States, or to excite any unlawful combinations therein, for opposing or resisting any law of the United States, or any act of the President of the United States, done in pursuance of any such law, or of the powers in him vested by the constitution of the United States, or to resist, oppose, or defeat any such law or act, or to aid, encourage or abet any hostile designs of any foreign nation against the United States, their people or government, then such person, . . . shall be punished by a fine

not exceeding two thousand dollars, and by imprisonment not exceeding two years.

> Sedition Act of 1798, ch. 74, § 2, 1 Stat. 596, 596–97

3 I cannot contemplate human Affairs, without laughing or crying. I choose to laugh. When People talk of the Freedom of Writing Speaking or thinking, I cannot choose but laugh. No such thing ever existed. No such thing now exists: but I hope it will exist. But it must be hundreds of years after you and I shall write and speak no more.

> John Adams, Letter to Thomas Jefferson, 15 July 1817, in *The Adams-Jefferson Letters* 2:519 (Lester J. Cappon ed. 1959)

4 In America, the majority raises formidable barriers around the liberty of opinion: within these barriers, an author may write what he pleases; but woe to him if he goes beyond them.

> Alexis de Tocqueville, *Democracy in America* 1:337–38 (Francis Bowen trans. 1862) (1835)

5 And I honor the man who is willing to sink
Half his present repute for the freedom to think,
And, when he has thought, be his cause strong or weak,
Will risk t' other half for the freedom to speak.

> James Russell Lowell, "A Fable for Critics," 1848, in *Complete Poetical Works of James Russell Lowell* 114, 136 (Horace E. Scudder ed. 1925)

6 The very aim and end of our institutions is just this: that we may think what we like and say what we think.

> Oliver Wendell Holmes, Sr., *The Professor at the Breakfast-Table,* 1859, in *Works of Oliver Wendell Holmes* 2:118 (1892)

7 I cannot assent to that view, if it be meant that the legislature may impair or abridge the rights of a free press and of free speech whenever it thinks that the public welfare required that to be done. The public welfare cannot override constitutional privileges, and if the rights of free speech and of a free press are, in their essence, attributes of national citizenship, as I think they are, then neither Congress nor any State since the adoption of the Fourteenth Amendment can, by legislative enactments

or by judicial action, impair or abridge them.

John M. Harlan (1833–1911), *Patterson v. Colorado*, 205 U.S. 454, 465 (1907) (dissenting)

8 Words are not only the keys of persuasion, but the triggers of action, and those which have no purport but to counsel the violation of law cannot by any latitude of interpretation be a part of that public opinion which is the final source of government in a democratic state.

Learned Hand, *Masses Publishing Co. v. Patten*, 244 F. 535, 540 (S.D.N.Y. 1917)

9 Like the course of the heavenly bodies, harmony in national life is a resultant of the struggle between contending forces. In frank expression of conflicting opinion lies the greatest promise of wisdom in governmental action; and in suppression lies ordinarily the greatest peril.

Louis D. Brandeis, *Gilbert v. Minnesota*, 254 U.S. 325, 338 (1920) (dissenting)

10 Freedom of speech and press . . . does not protect disturbances to the public peace or the attempt to subvert the government. It does not protect publications or teachings which tend to subvert or imperil the government or to impede or hinder it in the performance of its governmental duties. . . . It does not protect publications prompting the overthrow of the government by force.

Edward T. Sanford, *Gitlow v. New York*, 268 U.S. 652, 667–68 (1925)

11 The State cannot reasonably be required to measure the danger from every such utterance in the nice balance of a jeweler's scale. A single revolutionary spark may kindle a fire that, smouldering for a time, may burst into a sweeping and destructive conflagration.

Edward T. Sanford, *Gitlow v. New York*, 268 U.S. 652, 669 (1925)

12 If there is any principle of the Constitution that more imperatively calls for attachment than any other it is the principle of free thought—not free thought for those who agree with us but freedom for the thought that we hate.

Oliver Wendell Holmes, Jr., *United States v. Schwimmer*, 279 U.S. 644, 654–55 (1929) (dissenting)

13 We reach a different plane of social and moral values when we pass to the privileges and immunities that have been taken over from the earlier articles of the federal bill of rights and brought within the Fourteenth Amendment by a process of absorption. These in their origin were effective against the federal government alone. If the Fourteenth Amendment has absorbed them, the process of absorption has had its source in the belief that neither liberty nor justice would exist if they were sacrificed. . . . This is true, for illustration, of freedom of thought and speech. Of that freedom one may say that it is the matrix, the indispensable condition, of nearly every other form of freedom.

Benjamin N. Cardozo, *Palko v. Connecticut*, 302 U.S. 319, 326–27 (1937)

14 Nothing is more certain than the fact that the restriction of the right of freedom of expression to those holding certain beliefs, and its denial to those holding other beliefs, would sooner or later destroy the right for those holding any belief. The very essence of the right is that it should be effective against majorities and that it should protect the most unpopular opinions. To set up one political exception is to set up all political exceptions. And so even though the exception is phrased in terms of the right itself. It is as dangerous to deny the right of free speech to those who do not believe in free speech as to deny that right to those who do not believe in war or Herbert Hoover or fundamentalist Baptist biology. The one certain and fixed point in the entire discussion is this: that freedom of expression is guaranteed to the citizens of a liberal democracy not for the pleasure of the citizens but for the health of the state.

Archibald MacLeish, "Freedom to End Freedom," 1939, in *A Time to Speak* 131, 136 (1940)

15 Laws alone cannot secure freedom of expression; in order that every man may present his views without penalty there must be a spirit of tolerance in the entire population.

Albert Einstein, "On Freedom," 1940, in *Out of My Later Years* 12, 13 (1950)

16 One man, with views contrary to the rest of his compatriots, is entitled to the privi-

155

lege of expressing his ideas by speech or broadside to anyone willing to listen or to read. Too many settled beliefs have in time been rejected to justify this generation in refusing a hearing to its own dissentients.

> Stanley F. Reed, *Jones v. Opelika*, 316 U.S. 584, 594 (1942)

17 Right conclusions are more likely to be gathered out of a multitude of tongues, than through any kind of authoritative selection. To many this is, and always will be, folly; but we have staked upon it our all.

> Learned Hand, *United States v. Associated Press*, 52 F. Supp. 362, 372 (S.D.N.Y. 1943)

18 Progress generally begins in skepticism about accepted truths. Intellectual freedom means the right to re-examine much that has been long taken for granted. A free man must be a reasoning man, and he must dare to doubt what a legislative or electoral majority may most passionately assert. The danger that citizens will think wrongly is serious, but less dangerous than atrophy from not thinking at all. Our Constitution relies on our electorate's complete ideological freedom to nourish independent and responsible intelligence and preserve our democracy from that submissiveness, timidity and hard-mindedness of the masses which would foster a tyranny of mediocrity. The priceless heritage of our society is the unrestricted constitutional right of each member to think as he will. Thought control is a copyright of totalitarianism, and we have no claim to it.

> Robert H. Jackson, *American Communications Ass'n v. Douds*, 339 U.S. 382, 442–43 (1950)

19 I think that under our system, it is time enough for the law to lay hold of the citizen when he acts illegally, or in some rare circumstances when his thoughts are given illegal utterance. I think we must let his mind alone.

> Robert H. Jackson, *American Communications Ass'n v. Douds*, 339 U.S. 382, 444 (1950)

20 The Framers of the Constitution knew human nature as well as we do. They too had lived in dangerous days; they too knew the suffocating influence of orthodoxy and standardized thought. They weighed the compulsions for restrained speech and thought against the abuses of liberty. They chose liberty.

> William O. Douglas, *Beauharnais v. Illinois*, 342 U.S. 250, 287 (1952)

21 For myself I had rather take my chance that some traitors will escape detection than spread abroad a spirit of general suspicion and distrust, which accepts rumor and gossip in place of undismayed and unintimidated inquiry. I believe that that community is already in process of dissolution where each man begins to eye his neighbor as a possible enemy, where nonconformity with the accepted creed, political as well as religious, is a mark of disaffection; where denunciation, without specification or backing, takes the place of evidence; where orthodoxy chokes freedom of dissent; where faith in the eventual supremacy of reason has become so timid that we dare not enter our convictions in the open lists, to win or lose.

> Learned Hand, "A Plea for the Open Mind and Free Discussion" (speech), Albany, N.Y., 24 Oct. 1952, in *The Spirit of Liberty* 274, 284 (Irving Dilliard ed., 2d ed. 1953)

22 The mere summoning of a witness and compelling him to testify, against his will, about his beliefs, expressions or associations is a measure of governmental interference. And when those forced revelations concern matters that are unorthodox, unpopular, or even hateful to the general public, the reaction in the life of the witness may be disastrous.

> Earl Warren, *Watkins v. United States*, 354 U.S. 178, 197 (1957)

23 All political ideas cannot and should not be channeled into the programs of our two major parties. History has amply proved the virtue of political activity by minority, dissident groups, who innumerable times have been in the vanguard of democratic thought and whose programs were ultimately accepted. Mere unorthodoxy or dissent from the prevailing mores is not to be condemned. The absence of such voices would be a symptom of grave illness in our society.

> Earl Warren, *Sweezy v. New Hampshire*, 354 U.S. 234, 250–51 (1957)

24 The primary social fact which blocks and hinders the success of our experiment in self-government is that our citizens are not

educated for self-government. We are terrified by ideas, rather than challenged and stimulated by them. Our dominant mood is not the courage of people who dare to think. It is the timidity of those who fear and hate whenever conventions are questioned.

Alexander Meiklejohn, "The First Amendment is an Absolute," 1961 *Supreme Court Review* 245, 263

25 The constitutional guarantees of free speech and free press do not permit a State to forbid or proscribe advocacy of the use of force or of law violation except where such advocacy is directed to inciting or producing imminent lawless action and is likely to incite or produce such action.

Brandenburg v. Ohio, 395 U.S. 444, 447 (1969) (per curiam)

26 The constitutional right of free expression is powerful medicine in a society as diverse and populous as ours. It is designed and intended to remove governmental restraints from the arena of public discussion, putting the decision as to what views shall be voiced largely into the hands of each of us, in the hope that use of such freedom will ultimately produce a more capable citizenry and more perfect polity and in the belief that no other approach would comport with the premise of individual dignity and choice upon which our political system rests.

John M. Harlan (1899–1971), *Cohen v. California,* 403 U.S. 15, 24 (1971)

27 Prior restraints fall on speech with a brutality and a finality all their own. Even if they are ultimately lifted they cause irremediable loss—a loss in the immediacy, the impact, of speech. . . . The violator of a prior restraint may be assured of being held in contempt; the violator of a statute punishing speech criminally knows that he will go before a jury, and may be willing to take his chance, counting on a possible acquittal. A prior restraint, therefore, stops speech more effectively. A criminal statute chills, prior restraint freezes.

Alexander M. Bickel, *The Morality of Consent* 61 (1975)

FREEDOM OF RELIGION

See also FIRST AMENDMENT; RELIGION

1 Be it Therefore . . . enacted (except as in this psent Act is before Declared and sett forth) that noe person or psons whatsoever within this Province, or the Islands, Ports, Harbors, Creekes, or havens thereunto belonging professing to beleive [*sic*] in Jesus Christ, shall from henceforth bee any waies troubled, Molested or discountenanced for or in respect of his or her religion nor in the free exercise thereof within this Province or the Islands thereunto belonging nor any way compelled to the beleife [*sic*] or exercise of any other Religion against his or her consent.

Act Concerning Religion of 1649 (Toleration Act), in *Archives of Maryland* 1:246 (William H. Browne ed. 1883)

2 *Whereas,* . . . they [the colonists] have ffreely declared, . . . that a most flourishing civill state may stand and best bee maintained, . . . with a full libertie in religious concernements; and that true pietye rightly grounded upon gospell principles, will give the best and greatest security to sovereigne-tye, and will lay in the hearts of men the strongest obligations to true loyaltye: *Now know yee,* that wee beinge willing to . . . secure them in the free exercise and enjoyment of all theire civill and religious rights, . . . and to preserve unto them that libertye, in the true Christian ffaith and worshipp of God, which they have sought . . . to enjoye; . . . doe hereby publish, graunt, ordeyne and declare, . . . that noe person within the sayd colonye, at any tyme hereafter, shall bee any wise molested, punished, disquieted, or called in question, for any differences in opinione in matters of religion, . . . but that all and everye person and persons may, from tyme to tyme, and at all tymes hereafter, freelye and fullye have and enjoye his and theire owne judgments and consciences, in matters of religious concernments.

Rhode Island Charter of 1663, in *Federal and State Constitutions* 6:3211, 3212–13 (Francis N. Thorpe ed. 1909)

3 Because no People can be truly happy, though under the greatest Enjoyment of Civil Liberties, if abridged of the Freedom of their Consciences, . . . I do hereby grant and declare, That no Person or Persons, inhabiting in this Province or Territories, who shall confess and acknowledge *One* almighty God, the Creator, Upholder and Ruler of the World; and profess him or

themselves obliged to live quietly under the Civil Government, shall be in any Case molested or prejudiced, in his or their Person or Estate, because of his or their conscientious Persuasion or Practice, nor be compelled to frequent or maintain any religious Worship, Place or Ministry, contrary to his or their Mind, or to do or suffer any other Act or Thing, contrary to their religious Persuasion.

> Pennsylvania Charter of Privileges of 1701, § 1, in *Federal and State Constitutions* 5:3076, 3077 (Francis N. Thorpe ed. 1909)

4 Because the Happiness of Mankind depends so much upon the Enjoying of Liberty of their Consciences as aforesaid, I do hereby solemnly declare, promise and grant, for me, my Heirs and Assigns, That the *First* Article of this Charter relating to Liberty of Conscience, and every Part and Clause therein, according to the true Intent and Meaning thereof, shall be kept and remain, without any Alteration, inviolably for ever.

> Pennsylvania Charter of Privileges of 1701, § 8, in *Federal and State Constitutions* 5:3076, 3079–80 (Francis N. Thorpe ed. 1909)

5 That all men have a natural and unalienable right to worship Almighty God according to the dictates of their own consciences and understanding: And that no man ought or of right can be compelled to attend any religious worship, or erect or support any place of worship, or maintain any ministry, contrary to, or against, his own free will and consent: Nor can any man, who acknowledges the being of a God, be justly deprived or abridged of any civil right as a citizen, on account of his religious sentiments or peculiar mode of religious worship: And that no authority can or ought to be vested in, or assumed by any power whatever, that shall in any case interfere with, or in any manner controul, the right of conscience in the free exercise of religious worship.

> Pennsylvania Constitution of 1776, Declaration of Rights, § 2, in *Federal and State Constitutions* 5:3081, 3082 (Francis N. Thorpe ed. 1909)

6 That religion, or the duty which we owe to our Creator, and the manner of discharging it, can be directed only by reason and conviction, not by force or violence; and therefore all men are equally entitled to the free exercise of religion, according to the dictates of conscience; and that it is the mutual duty of all to practise Christian forbearance, love, and charity towards each other.

> Virginia Declaration of Rights of 1776, § 16, in *Federal and State Constitutions* 7:3812, 3814 (Francis N. Thorpe ed. 1909)

7 As to religion, I hold it to be the indispensable duty of all government, to protect all conscientious professors thereof, and I know of no other business which government hath to do therewith.

> **Thomas Paine,** *Common Sense* 108–109 (Isaac Kramnick ed. 1976) (1776)

8 That Almighty God hath created the mind free . . . that all attempts to influence it by temporal punishments, or burthens, or by civil incapacitations, tend only to beget habits of hypocrisy and meanness, . . . to compel a man to furnish contributions of money for the propagation of opinions which he disbelieves and abhors is sinful and tyrannical; . . . that our civil rights have no dependence on our religious opinions, any more than our opinions in physics or geometry.

> **Thomas Jefferson,** "A Bill for Establishing Religious Freedom," 1779, in *Papers of Thomas Jefferson* 2:545–46 (Julian P. Boyd ed. 1950)

9 No man shall be compelled to frequent or support any religious worship, place, or ministry . . . nor shall otherwise suffer on account of his religious opinions or belief; but . . . all men shall be free to profess, and by argument to maintain, their opinions in matters of religion.*

> **Thomas Jefferson,** "A Bill for Establishing Religious Freedom," 1779, in *Papers of Thomas Jefferson* 2:546 (Julian P. Boyd ed. 1950)

10 The opinions of men are not the object of civil government, nor under its jurisdiction.

> **Thomas Jefferson,** "A Bill for Establishing Religious Freedom," 1779, in *Papers of*

---

* This quotation is inscribed on the Jefferson Memorial, Washington, D.C.

Thomas Jefferson 2:546 (Julian P. Boyd ed. 1950)

11 Proscribing any citizen as unworthy the public confidence by laying upon him an incapacity of being called to offices of trust and emolument, unless he profess or renounce this or that religious opinion, is depriving him injuriously of those privileges and advantages to which, in common with his fellow-citizens, he has a natural right.

Thomas Jefferson, "A Bill for Establishing Religious Freedom," 1779, in *Papers of Thomas Jefferson* 2:546 (Julian P. Boyd ed. 1950)

12 To suffer the civil magistrate to intrude his powers into the field of opinion and to restrain the profession or propagation of principles on supposition of their ill tendency is a dangerous falacy [*sic*], which at once destroys all religious liberty, because he being of course judge of that tendency will make his opinions the rule of judgment, and approve or condemn the sentiments of others only as they shall square with or differ from his own. . . . it is time enough for the rightful purposes of civil government for its officers to interfere when principles break out into overt acts against peace and good order.

Thomas Jefferson, "A Bill for Establishing Religious Freedom," 1779, in *Papers of Thomas Jefferson* 2:546 (Julian P. Boyd ed. 1950)

13 The legitimate powers of government extend to such acts only as are injurious to others. But it does me no injury for my neighbour to say there are twenty gods, or no god. It neither picks my pocket nor breaks my leg.

Thomas Jefferson, *Notes on Virginia*, 1782, in *Works of Thomas Jefferson* 4:78 (Paul L. Ford ed. 1904)

14 The Religion . . . of every man must be left to the conviction and conscience of every man; and it is the right of every man to exercise it as these may dictate.

James Madison, "Memorial and Remonstrance Against Religious Assessments," 1785, in *Papers of James Madison* 8:295, 299 (Robert A. Rutland & William M. E. Rachal eds. 1973)

15 It is the duty of every man to render to the Creator such homage and such only as he

believes to be acceptable to him. This duty is precedent, both in order of time and in degree of obligation, to the claims of Civil Society. . . . in matters of Religion, no mans [*sic*] right is abridged by the institution of Civil Society.

James Madison, "Memorial and Remonstrance Against Religious Assessments," 1785, in *Papers of James Madison* 8:295, 299 (Robert A. Rutland & William M. E. Rachal eds. 1973)

16 It is proper to take alarm at the first experiment on our liberties. . . . Who does not see that the same authority which can establish Christianity, in exclusion of all other Religions, may establish with the same ease any particular sect of Christians, in exclusion of all other Sects? that the same authority which can force a citizen to contribute three pence only of his property for the support of any one establishment, may force him to conform to any other establishment in all cases whatsoever?

James Madison, "Memorial and Remonstrance Against Religious Assessments," 1785, in *Papers of James Madison* 8:295, 300 (Robert A. Rutland & William M. E. Rachal eds. 1973)

17 No person demeaning himself in a peaceable and orderly manner shall ever be molested on account of his mode of worship or religious sentiments in the said territory.

Northwest Ordinance, art. 1, 13 July 1787, in *Journals of the Continental Congress* 32:340 (Roscoe R. Hill ed. 1936)

18 Happily the government of the United States, which gives to bigotry no sanction, to persecution no assistance, requires only that they who live under its protection should demean themselves as good citizens.

George Washington, Letter to Hebrew congregation of Newport, R.I., 17 Aug. 1790, in *Writings of George Washington* 31:93 n.65 (John C. Fitzpatrick ed. 1939)

19 Believing with you that religion is a matter which lies solely between man and his God, that he owes account to none other for his faith or his worship, that the legislative powers of government reach actions only, and not opinions, I contemplate with sovereign reverence that act of the whole American people which declared that their

legislature should "make no law respecting an establishment of religion, or prohibiting the free exercise thereof," thus building a wall of separation between church and State.

> **Thomas Jefferson,** Reply to Nehemiah Dodge, Ephraim Robbins, and Stephen S. Nelson [committee of the Danbury, Conn., Baptist Association], 1 Jan. 1802, in *Writings of Thomas Jefferson* 8:113 (H. A. Washington ed. 1854)

20 It behoves every man who values liberty of conscience for himself, to resist invasions of it in the case of others; or their case may, by change of circumstances, become his own.

> **Thomas Jefferson,** Letter to Benjamin Rush, 21 Apr. 1803, in *Writings of Thomas Jefferson* 8:224 n. (Paul L. Ford ed. 1897)

21 It was under a solemn consciousness of the dangers from ecclesiastical ambition, the bigotry of spiritual pride, and the intolerance of sects . . . that it was deemed advisable to exclude from the national government all power to act upon the subject.

> **Joseph Story,** *Commentaries on the Constitution of the United States* 3:730 (1833)

22 In this country the full and free right to entertain any religious belief, to practice any religious principle, and to teach any religious doctrine which does not violate the laws of morality and property, and which does not infringe personal rights, is conceded to all. The law knows no heresy, and is committed to the support of no dogma, the establishment of no sect.

> **Samuel F. Miller,** *Watson v. Jones,* 80 U.S. (13 Wall.) 679, 728 (1872)

23 Encourage free schools, and resolve that not one dollar appropriated for their support shall be appropriated for the support of any sectarian schools. Resolve that neither the State nor nation, nor both combined, shall support institutions of learning other than those sufficient to afford every child growing up in the land the opportunity of a good common-school education, unmixed with sectarian, pagan, or atheistical dogmas. Leave the matter of religion to the family altar, the church, and the private school, supported entirely by private contributions. Keep the church and the state for ever separate.

> **Ulysses S. Grant,** Speech to Convention of the Army of the Tennessee, Des Moines, Ia.,

29 Sept. 1875, in 22 *Catholic World* 433, 434–35 (1876)

24 [In Germany] they recognize two sects, Catholic and Lutheran. . . . These receive State support; and their schools receive State support. Other sects are taxed to support these sects and schools, and have to run their own churches and schools at their own cost. It is infamous. Just as infamous as it is with us—where no church property is taxed and so the infidel and the atheist and the man without religion are taxed to make up the deficit in the public income thus caused.

> **Mark Twain,** Notebook, 14 Feb. 1892, in *Mark Twain's Notebook* 223 (Albert B. Paine ed. 1935)

25 God was left out of the Constitution but was furnished a front seat on the coins of the country.

> **Mark Twain,** 1906, in *Mark Twain in Eruption* 49 (Bernard De Voto ed. 1940)

26 All stand equal before the law,—the Protestant, the Catholic, the Mohammedan, the Jew, the Mormon, the free-thinker, the atheist. Whatever may be the view of the majority of the people, the court has no right, and the majority has no right, to force that view upon the minority, however small. It is precisely for the protection of the minority that the constitutional limitations exist. Majorities need no such protection,—they can take care of themselves.

> **Frank K. Dunn,** *People ex rel. Ring v. Board of Education,* 245 Ill. 334, 346, 92 N.E. 251 (1910)

27 The realm of religion . . . is where knowledge leaves off, and where faith begins, and it never has needed the arm of the State for support, and wherever it has received it, it has harmed both the public and the religion that it would pretend to serve.

> **Clarence S. Darrow,** quoted in John Paul Stevens, *Wolman v. Walter,* 433 U.S. 229, 264 (1977) (concurring in part and dissenting in part)

28 The purport, though not the letter, of its [the First Amendment's] first two strophes is that every free-born Americano shall stand clear of ecclesiastical domination, and be at liberty to serve, dodge or bam-

boozle Omnipotence by whatever devices appeal to his taste, or his lack of it. As the common phrase has it, church and state are separate in the Federal Union, with the province of each plainly marked out, and each forbidden to invade the province of the other. But in the common phrase, as usual, there is only wind. The fact is that the United States, save for a short while in its infancy, while the primal infidels survived, has always diluted democracy with theocracy. Practically all our political campaigns have resolved themselves into witch-hunts by the consecrated, and all our wars have been fought to hymn tunes.

H. L. Mencken, Editorial, *American Mercury*, Oct. 1928, at 156, 156

29 The essence of religion is belief in a relation to God involving duties superior to those arising from any human relation.

Charles Evans Hughes, *United States v. Macintosh*, 283 U.S. 605, 633–34 (1931) (dissenting)

30 When [Macintosh] speaks of putting his allegiance to the will of God above his allegiance to the government, it is evident . . . that he means to make *his own interpretation* of the will of God the decisive test which shall conclude the government and stay its hand. We are a Christian people . . . , according to one another the equal right of religious freedom, and acknowledging with reverence the duty of obedience to the will of God. But, also, we are a Nation with the duty to survive; a Nation whose Constitution contemplates war as well as peace; whose government must go forward upon the assumption . . . that unqualified allegiance to the Nation and submission and obedience to the laws of the land, as well those made for war as those made for peace, are not inconsistent with the will of God.

George Sutherland, *United States v. Macintosh*, 283 U.S. 605, 625 (1931)

31 Never in our history has the notion been accepted, or even, it is believed, advanced, that acts thus indirectly related to service in the camp or field are so tied to the practice of religion as to be exempt, in laws or in morals, from regulation by the state. . . . The right of private judgment has never yet been so exalted above the powers and the compulsion of the agencies of government.

One who is a martyr to a principle . . . does not prove by his martyrdom that he has kept within the law.

Benjamin N. Cardozo, *Hamilton v. Regents of the Univ. of California*, 293 U.S. 245, 267–68 (1934) (concurring)

32 The [First] Amendment embraces two concepts—freedom to believe and freedom to act. The first is absolute but, in the nature of things, the second cannot be. . . . In every case the power to regulate must be so exercised as not, in attaining a permissible end, unduly to infringe the protected freedom.

Owen J. Roberts, *Cantwell v. Connecticut*, 310 U.S. 296, 303-04 (1940)

33 One who belongs to the most vilified and persecuted minority in history is not likely to be insensible to the freedoms guaranteed by our Constitution. . . . But as judges we are neither Jew nor Gentile, neither Catholic nor agnostic.

Felix Frankfurter, *West Virginia State Bd. of Educ. v. Barnette*, 319 U.S. 624, 646–47 (1943) (dissenting)

34 The constitutional protection of religious freedom terminated disabilities, it did not create new privileges. It gave religious equality, not civil immunity. Its essence is freedom from conformity to religious dogma, not freedom from conformity to law because of religious dogma.

Felix Frankfurter, *West Virginia State Bd. of Educ. v. Barnette*, 319 U.S. 624, 653 (1943) (dissenting)

35 The First Amendment grew out of an experience which taught that society cannot trust the conscience of a majority to keep its religious zeal within the limits that a free society can tolerate. I do not think it any more intended to leave the conscience of a minority to fix its limits. Civil government can not let any group ride rough-shod over others simply because their "consciences" tell them to do so.

Robert H. Jackson, *Douglas v. Jeannette*, 319 U.S. 157, 179 (1943) (concurring)

36 But freedom to differ is not limited to things that do not matter much. That would be a mere shadow of freedom. The test of its substance is the right to differ as

to things that touch the heart of the existing order.

If there is any fixed star in our constitutional constellation, it is that no official, high or petty, can prescribe what shall be orthodox in politics, nationalism, religion, or other matters of opinion or force citizens to confess by word or act their faith therein.

Robert H. Jackson, *West Virginia State Bd. of Educ. v. Barnette,* 319 U.S. 624, 642 (1943)

37 Men may believe what they cannot prove. They may not be put to the proof of their religious doctrines or beliefs. Religious experiences which are as real as life to some may be incomprehensible to others.

William O. Douglas, *United States v. Ballard,* 322 U.S. 78, 86 (1944)

38 Some who profess belief in the Bible read literally what others read as allegory or metaphor, as they read Aesop's fables. Religious symbolism is even used by some with the same mental reservations one has in teaching of Santa Claus or Uncle Sam or Easter bunnies or dispassionate judges.

Robert H. Jackson, *United States v. Ballard,* 322 U.S. 78, 94 (1944)

39 The wrong of these things, as I see it, is not in the money the victims part with half so much as in the mental and spiritual poison they get. But that is precisely the thing the Constitution put beyond the reach of the prosecutor, for the price of freedom of religion or of speech or of the press is that we must put up with, and even pay for, a good deal of rubbish. . . . I would dismiss the indictment and have done with this business of judicially examining other people's faiths.

Robert H. Jackson, *United States v. Ballard,* 322 U.S. 78, 95 (1944)

40 The "establishment of religion" clause of the First Amendment means at least this: Neither a state nor the Federal Government can set up a church. Neither can pass laws which aid one religion, aid all religions, or prefer one religion over another. Neither can force nor influence a person to go to or to remain away from church against his will or force him to profess a belief or disbelief in any religion. No person can be punished for entertaining or professing any religious beliefs or disbe-

liefs, for church attendance or non-attendance. No tax in any amount, large or small, can be levied to support any religious activities or institutions, whatever they may be called, or whatever form they may adopt to teach or practice religion. Neither a state nor the Federal Government can, openly or secretly, participate in the affairs of any religious organizations or groups and *vice versa.*

Hugo L. Black, *Everson v. Board of Educ.,* 330 U.S. 1, 15–16 (1947)

41 The First Amendment has erected a wall between church and state. That wall must be kept high and impregnable. We could not approve the slightest breach.

Hugo L. Black, *Everson v. Board of Educ.,* 330 U.S. 1, 18 (1947)
See also FREEDOM OF RELIGION 19

42 The First Amendment . . . requires the state to be a neutral in its relations with groups of religious believers and non-believers; it does not require the state to be their adversary. State power is no more to be used so as to handicap religions than it is to favor them.

Hugo L. Black, *Everson v. Board of Educ.,* 330 U.S. 1, 18 (1947)

43 In fact, the undertones of the opinion, advocating complete and uncompromising separation of Church from State, seem utterly discordant with its conclusion yielding support to their commingling in educational matters. The case which irresistibly comes to mind as the most fitting precedent is that of Julia who, according to Byron's reports, "whispering 'I will ne'er consent,'—consented."

Robert H. Jackson, *Everson v. Board of Educ.,* 330 U.S. 1, 19 (1947) (dissenting)

44 This freedom [of religion] was first in the Bill of Rights because it was first in the forefathers' minds; it was set forth in absolute terms, and its strength is its rigidity.

Robert H. Jackson, *Everson v. Board of Educ.,* 330 U.S. 1, 26 (1947) (dissenting)

45 Two great drives are constantly in motion to abridge, in the name of education, the complete division of religion and civil authority which our forefathers made. One is to introduce religious education and observances into the public schools. The other,

to obtain public funds for the aid and support of various private religious schools. . . . In my opinion both avenues were closed by the Constitution. Neither should be opened by this Court.

Wiley B. Rutledge, *Everson v. Board of Educ.*, 330 U.S. 1, 63 (1947) (dissenting)

46 I think it remains to be demonstrated whether it is possible, even if desirable . . . to isolate and cast out of secular education all that some people may reasonably regard as religious instruction. Perhaps subjects such as mathematics, physics or chemistry are, or can be, completely secularized. But it would not seem practical to teach either practice or appreciation of the arts if we are to forbid exposure of youth to any religious influences. Music without sacred music, architecture minus the cathedral, or painting without the scriptural themes would be eccentric and incomplete, even from a secular point of view. Yet the inspirational appeal of religion in these guises is often stronger than in forthright sermon. Even such a "science" as biology raises the issue between evolution and creation as an explanation of our presence on this planet. Certainly a course in English literature that omitted the Bible and other powerful uses of our mother tongue for religious ends would be pretty barren. And I should suppose it is a proper, if not an indispensable, part of preparation for a worldly life to know the roles that religions have played in the tragic story of mankind.

Robert H. Jackson, *Illinois ex rel. McCollum v. Board of Educ.*, 333 U.S. 203, 235–36 (1948) (concurring)

47 It is idle to pretend that this task is one for which we can find in the Constitution one word to help us as judges to decide where the secular ends and the sectarian begins in education. Nor can we find guidance in any other legal source. It is a matter on which we can find no law but our own prepossessions.

Robert H. Jackson, *Illinois ex rel. McCollum v. Board of Educ.*, 333 U.S. 203, 237–38 (1948) (concurring)

48 The "wall of separation between church and State" that Mr. Jefferson built at the University which he founded did not exclude religious education from that school. The difference between the generality of his statements on the separation of church and state and the specificity of his conclusions on education are considerable. A rule of law should not be drawn from a figure of speech.

Stanley F. Reed, *Illinois ex rel. McCollum v. Board of Educ.*, 333 U.S. 203, 247 (1948) (dissenting)
See also FREEDOM OF RELIGION 19

49 The First Amendment has lost much if the religious follower and the atheist are no longer to be judicially regarded as entitled to equal justice under law.

Hugo L. Black, *Zorach v. Clauson*, 343 U.S. 306, 320 (1952) (dissenting)

50 State help to religion injects political and party prejudices into a holy field. It too often substitutes force for prayer, hate for love, and persecution for persuasion. Government should not be allowed, under cover of the soft euphemism of "co-operation," to steal into the sacred area of religious choice.

Hugo L. Black, *Zorach v. Clauson*, 343 U.S. 306, 320 (1952) (dissenting)

51 The First Amendment, however, does not say that in every and all respects there shall be a separation of church and State. Rather, it studiously defines the manner, the specific ways, in which there shall be no concert or union or dependency one on the other. That is the common sense of the matter. Otherwise the state and religion would be aliens to each other—hostile, suspicious, and even unfriendly. Churches could not be required to pay even property taxes. Municipalities would not be permitted to render police or fire protection to religious groups. Policemen who helped parishioners into their places of worship would violate the Constitution. Prayers in our legislative halls; the appeals to the Almighty in the messages of the Chief Executive; the proclamations making Thanksgiving Day a holiday; "so help me God" in our courtroom oaths—these and all other references to the Almighty that run through our laws, our public rituals, our ceremonies would be flouting the First Amendment. A fastidious atheist or agnostic could even object to the supplication with which the Court opens each session:

"God save the United States and this Honorable Court."

> **William O. Douglas,** *Zorach v. Clauson,* 343 U.S. 306, 312–13 (1952)

52 We are a religious people whose institutions presuppose a Supreme Being. We guarantee the freedom to worship as one chooses. We make room for as wide a variety of beliefs and creeds as the spiritual needs of man deem necessary. We sponsor an attitude on the part of government that shows no partiality to any one group and that lets each flourish according to the zeal of its adherents and the appeal of its dogma.

> **William O. Douglas,** *Zorach v. Clauson,* 343 U.S. 306, 313 (1952)

53 When the state encourages religious instruction or cooperates with religious authorities by adjusting the schedule of public events to sectarian needs, it follows the best of our traditions. For then it respects the religious nature of our people and accommodates the public service to their spiritual needs. To hold that it may not would be to find in the Constitution a requirement that the government show a callous indifference to religious groups. That would be preferring those who believe in no religion over those who do believe.

> **William O. Douglas,** *Zorach v. Clauson,* 343 U.S. 306, 313–14 (1952)

54 The day that this country ceases to be free for irreligion it will cease to be free for religion—except for the sect that can win political power.

> **Robert H. Jackson,** *Zorach v. Clauson,* 343 U.S. 306, 325 (1952) (dissenting)

55 The First Amendment protects one against action by the government, though even then, not in all circumstances; but it gives no one the right to insist that in the pursuit of their own interests others must conform their conduct to his own religious necessities.

> **Learned Hand,** *Otten v. Baltimore & Ohio R.R.,* 205 F.2d 58, 61 (2d Cir. 1953)

56 I believe in an America where the separation of church and state is absolute . . . where no church or church school is granted any public funds or political preference. . . . I believe in an America that is officially neither Catholic, Protestant nor Jewish . . . where no religious body seeks to impose its will directly or indirectly upon the general populace or the public acts of its officials—and where religious liberty is so indivisible that an act against one church is treated as an act against all.

> **John F. Kennedy,** Campaign speech to Greater Houston Ministerial Association, 12 Sept. 1960, quoted in Maxwell Meyersohn, *Memorable Quotations of John F. Kennedy* 142–43 (1965)

57 The constitutional prohibition against laws respecting an establishment of religion must at least mean that in this country it is no part of the business of government to compose official prayers for any group of the American people to recite as a part of a religious program carried on by government.

> **Hugo L. Black,** *Engel v. Vitale,* 370 U.S. 421, 425 (1962)

58 It has been argued that to apply the Constitution in such a way as to prohibit state laws respecting an establishment of religious services in public schools is to indicate a hostility toward religion or toward prayer. Nothing, of course, could be more wrong.

> **Hugo L. Black,** *Engel v. Vitale,* 370 U.S. 421, 433–34 (1962)

59 It is neither sacrilegious nor antireligious to say that each separate government in this country should stay out of the business of writing or sanctioning official prayers and leave that purely religious function to the people themselves and to those the people choose to look to for religious guidance.

> **Hugo L. Black,** *Engel v. Vitale,* 370 U.S. 421, 435 (1962)

60 I cannot see how an "official religion" is established by letting those who want to say a prayer say it. On the contrary, I think that to deny the wish of these school children to join in reciting this prayer is to deny them the opportunity of sharing in the spiritual heritage of our Nation.

> **Potter Stewart,** *Engel v. Vitale,* 370 U.S. 421, 445 (1962) (dissenting)

61 Awareness of history and an appreciation of the aims of the Founding Fathers do not always resolve concrete problems. . . . A

more fruitful inquiry, it seems to me, is whether the practices here challenged threaten those consequences which the Framers deeply feared; whether, in short, they tend to promote that type of interdependence between religion and state which the First Amendment was designed to prevent.

William J. Brennan, Jr., *Abington School Dist. v. Schempp*, 374 U.S. 203, 234, 236 (1963) (concurring)

62 What the Framers meant to foreclose, and what our decisions under the Establishment Clause have forbidden, are those involvements of religious with secular institutions which (a) serve the essentially religious activities of religious institutions; (b) employ the organs of government for essentially religious purposes; or (c) use essentially religious means to serve governmental ends, where secular means would suffice.

William J. Brennan, Jr., *Abington School Dist. v. Schempp*, 374 U.S. 203, 294–95 (1963) (concurring)

63 The door of the Free Exercise Clause [of the First Amendment] stands tightly closed against any governmental regulation of religious *beliefs* as such. . . . Government may neither compel affirmation of a repugnant belief, . . . nor penalize or discriminate against individuals or groups because they hold religious views abhorrent to the authorities.

William J. Brennan, Jr., *Sherbert v. Verner*, 374 U.S. 398, 402 (1963)

64 The test may be stated as follows: what are the purpose and the primary effect of the enactment? If either is the advancement or inhibition of religion then the enactment exceeds the scope of legislative power as circumscribed by the Constitution. That is to say that to withstand the strictures of the Establishment Clause there must be a secular legislative purpose and a primary effect that neither advances nor inhibits religion.

Tom C. Clark, *Abington School Dist. v. Schempp*, 374 U.S. 203, 222 (1963)

65 In the relationship between man and religion, the State is firmly committed to a position of neutrality.

Tom C. Clark, *Abington School Dist. v. Schempp*, 374 U.S. 203, 226 (1963)

66 There are neutral principles of law, developed for use in all property disputes, which can be applied without "establishing" churches to which property is awarded. . . . the [First] Amendment therefore commands civil courts to decide church property disputes without resolving underlying controversies over religious doctrine. Hence, States, religious organizations, and individuals must structure relationships involving church property so as not to require the civil courts to resolve ecclesiastical questions.

William J. Brennan, Jr., *Presbyterian Church v. Mary Elizabeth Blue Hull Memorial Presbyterian Church*, 393 U.S. 440, 449 (1969)

67 Every analysis in this area must begin with consideration of the cumulative criteria developed by the Court over many years. Three such tests may be gleaned from our cases. First, the statute must have a secular legislative purpose; second, its principal or primary effect must be one that neither advances nor inhibits religion . . . ; finally, the statute must not foster "an excessive government entanglement with religion."

Warren E. Burger, *Lemon v. Kurtzman*, 403 U.S. 602, 612–13 (1971)

68 Only those interests of the highest order and those not otherwise served can overbalance legitimate claims to the free exercise of religion.

Warren E. Burger, *Wisconsin v. Yoder*, 406 U.S. 205, 215 (1972)

69 There can be no assumption that today's majority is "right" and the Amish and others like them are "wrong." A way of life that is odd or even erratic but interferes with no right or interests of others is not to be condemned because it is different.

Warren E. Burger, *Wisconsin v. Yoder*, 406 U.S. 205, 223–24 (1972)

70 I have never believed that the oft-quoted amendment [the First Amendment] was supposed to protect us from religion: It was to protect religion from government tyranny.

Ronald W. Reagan, Remarks in Observance of National Day of Prayer, 6 May 1982, in *Public Papers of the Presidents: Ronald Reagan, 1982*, at 1:573, 574 (1983)

71 The concept of a "wall" of separation is . . . not a wholly accurate description of the

practical aspects of the relationship that in fact exists between church and state. No significant segment of our society and no institution within it can exist in a vacuum or in total or absolute isolation from all the other parts, much less from government.... Nor does the Constitution require complete separation of church and state; it affirmatively mandates accommodation, not merely tolerance, of all religions, and forbids hostility toward any.

> **Warren E. Burger,** *Lynch v. Donnelly,* 465 U.S. 668, 673 (1984)
> See also FREEDOM OF RELIGION 19

72 To forbid the use of this one passive symbol—the crèche—at the very time people are taking note of the season with Christmas hymns and carols in public schools and other public places, and while the Congress and legislatures open sessions with prayers by paid chaplains, would be a stilted overreaction contrary to our history and to our holdings. If the presence of the crèche in this display violates the Establishment Clause, a host of other forms of taking official note of Christmas, and of our religious heritage, are equally offensive to the Constitution.

> **Warren E. Burger,** *Lynch v. Donnelly,* 465 U.S. 668, 686 (1984)

73 The attitude that regards entanglement with religion as something akin to entanglement with an infectious disease must be confronted broadly and directly.

> **William J. Bennett,** quoted in *New York Times,* 8 Aug. 1985, at A18

74 The argument [that attendance at a graduation, featuring prayers, is voluntary] lacks all persuasion. Law reaches past formalism. And to say a teenage student has a real choice not to attend her high school graduation is formalistic in the extreme. True, Deborah could elect not to attend commencment without renouncing her diploma; but we shall not allow the case to turn on this point. Everyone knows that in our society and in our culture high school graduation is one of life's most significant occasions.

> **Anthony M. Kennedy,** *Lee v. Weisman,* 112 S. Ct. 2649, 2659 (1992)

FREEDOM OF SPEECH

See also CENSORSHIP; FIRST AMENDMENT; FREEDOM OF EXPRESSION; FREEDOM OF THE PRESS; LIBEL; OBSCENITY

1 Printers are educated in the Belief, that when Men differ in Opinion, both Sides ought equally to have the Advantage of being heard by the Publick; and that when Truth and Error have fair Play, the former is always an overmatch for the latter.

> **Benjamin Franklin,** "Apology for Printers," 1731, in *Papers of Benjamin Franklin* 1:195 (Leonard W. Labaree ed. 1959)

2 Truth is great and will prevail if left to herself; that she is the proper and sufficient antagonist to error, and has nothing to fear from the conflict unless by human interposition disarmed of her natural weapons, free argument and debate; errors ceasing to be dangerous when it is permitted freely to contradict them.

> **Thomas Jefferson,** "A Bill for Establishing Religious Freedom," 1779, in *Papers of Thomas Jefferson* 2:546 (Julian P. Boyd ed. 1950)

3 It is error alone which needs the support of government. Truth can stand by itself.

> **Thomas Jefferson,** *Notes on Virginia,* 1782, in *Writings of Thomas Jefferson* 3:264 (Paul L. Ford ed. 1894)

4 If there be any among us who would wish to dissolve this Union or to change its republican form, let them stand undisturbed as monuments of the safety with which error of opinion may be tolerated where reason is left free to combat it.

> **Thomas Jefferson,** First Inaugural Address, 4 Mar. 1801, in *Messages and Papers of the Presidents* 1:321, 322 (James D. Richardson ed. 1898)

5 The petitioner may have a constitutional right to talk politics, but he has no constitutional right to be a policeman. There are few employments for hire in which the servant does not agree to suspend his constitutional right of free speech, as well as of idleness, by the implied terms of his contract. The servant cannot complain, as he takes the employment on the terms which are offered him.

> **Oliver Wendell Holmes, Jr.,** *McAuliffe v. Mayor of New Bedford,* 155 Mass. 216, 220, 29 N.E. 517 (1892)

6 The wisest thing to do with a fool is to encourage him to hire a hall and discourse to his fellow-citizens. Nothing chills nonsense like exposure to the air.

Woodrow Wilson, *Constitutional Government in the United States* 38 (1908)

7 Make no laws whatever concerning speech, and speech will be free; so soon as you make a declaration on paper that speech shall be free, you will have a hundred lawyers proving that "freedom does not mean abuse, nor liberty license"; and they will define and define freedom out of existence.

Voltarine De Cleyre, quoted in *The Great Thoughts* 84–85 (George Seldes ed. 1985)

8 The character of every act depends upon the circumstances in which it is done. . . . The most stringent protection of free speech would not protect a man in falsely shouting fire in a theatre and causing a panic.* It does not even protect a man from an injunction against uttering words that may have all the effect of force. . . . The question in every case is whether the words used are used in such circumstances and are of such a nature as to create a clear and present danger that they will bring about the substantive evils that Congress has a right to prevent. It is a question of proximity and degree.

Oliver Wendell Holmes, Jr., *Schenck v. United States*, 249 U.S. 47, 52 (1919)

9 The First Amendment while prohibiting legislation against free speech as such cannot have been, and obviously was not, intended to give immunity for every possible use of language.

Oliver Wendell Holmes, Jr., *Frohwerk v. United States*, 249 U.S. 204, 206 (1919)

10 Every year if not every day we have to wager our salvation upon some prophecy based upon imperfect knowledge. While that experiment is part of our system I think that we should be eternally vigilant against attempts to check the expression of opinions that we loathe and believe to be fraught with death, unless they so imminently threaten immediate interference with the lawful and pressing purposes of the law that an immediate check is required to save the country.

Oliver Wendell Holmes, Jr., *Abrams v. United States*, 250 U.S. 616, 624 (1919) (dissenting)

11 I do not doubt for a moment that by the same reasoning that would justify punishing persuasion to murder, the United States constitutionally may punish speech that produces or is intended to produce a clear and imminent danger that it will bring about forthwith certain substantive evils that the United States constitutionally may seek to prevent.

Oliver Wendell Holmes, Jr., *Abrams v. United States*, 250 U.S. 616, 627 (1919) (dissenting)

12 Persecution for the expression of opinions seems to me perfectly logical. If you have no doubt of your premises or your power and want a certain result with all your heart you naturally express your wishes in law and sweep away all opposition. To allow opposition by speech seems to indicate that you think the speech impotent, as when a man says that he has squared the circle, or that you do not care whole-heartedly for the result, or that you doubt either your power or your premises.

Oliver Wendell Holmes, Jr., *Abrams v. United States*, 250 U.S. 616, 630 (1919) (dissenting)

13 But when men have realized that time has upset many fighting faiths, they may come to believe even more than they believe the very foundations of their own conduct that the ultimate good desired is better reached by free trade in ideas—that the best test of truth is the power of the thought to get itself accepted in the competition of the market, and that truth is the only ground upon which their wishes safely can be carried out. That at any rate is the theory of our Constitution. It is an experiment, as all life is an experiment.*

Oliver Wendell Holmes, Jr., *Abrams v. United States*, 250 U.S. 616, 630 (1919) (dissenting)

---

* The sentence about "falsely shouting fire" is often misquoted by omitting the word "falsely."

---

* And though all the windes of doctrin were let loose to play upon the earth, so Truth be in the field, we do injuriously by licencing and prohibiting to misdoubt her strength. Let her and Falshood grapple; who ever knew Truth put to the wors, in a free and open encounter.
—**John Milton**, *Areopagitica*, 1644, in *Works* 4:293, 347 (1931)

14 I . . . probably take the extremest view in favor of free speech, (in which, in the abstract, I have no very enthusiastic belief, though I hope I would die for it).

> Oliver Wendell Holmes, Jr., Letter to Frederick Pollock, 26 Oct. 1919, in *Holmes-Pollock Letters* 2:28–29 (Mark DeWolfe Howe ed. 1941)

15 I have always been among those who believed that the greatest freedom of speech was the greatest safety, because if a man is a fool, the best thing to do is to encourage him to advertise the fact by speaking. . . . So it is by the exposure of folly that it is defeated; not by the seclusion of folly, and in this free air of free speech men get into that sort of communication with one another which constitutes the basis of all common achievement.

> Woodrow Wilson, Speech, Paris, 10 May 1919, in *Public Papers of Woodrow Wilson* 3:482, 484 (Ray Stannard Baker & William E. Dodd eds. 1927)

16 The constitutional right of free speech has been declared to be the same in peace and in war. In peace, too, men may differ widely as to what loyalty to our country demands; and an intolerant majority, swayed by passion or by fear, may be prone in the future, as it has often been in the past, to stamp as disloyal opinions with which it disagrees.

> Louis D. Brandeis, *Schaefer v. United States*, 251 U.S. 466, 495 (1920) (dissenting)

17 I have difficulty in believing that the liberty guaranteed by the Constitution, which has been held to protect against state denial the right of an employer to discriminate against a workman because he is a member of a trade union, . . . the right of a business man to conduct a private employment agency, . . . or to contract outside the State for insurance of his property, . . . although the legislature deems it inimical to the public welfare, does not include liberty to teach, either in the privacy of the home or publicly, the doctrine of pacifism; so long, at least, as Congress has not declared that the public safety demands its suppression. I cannot believe that the liberty guaranteed by the Fourteenth Amendment includes only liberty to acquire and to enjoy property.

> Louis D. Brandeis, *Gilbert v. Minnesota*, 254 U.S. 325, 343 (1920) (dissenting)

18 The United States may give up the Post Office when it sees fit, but while it carries it on the use of the mails is almost as much a part of free speech as the right to use our tongues.

> Oliver Wendell Holmes, Jr., *Milwaukee Social Democratic Publishing Co. v. Burleson*, 255 U.S. 407, 437 (1921) (dissenting)

19 It is said that this manifesto was more than a theory, that it was an incitement. Every idea is an incitement. It offers itself for belief and if believed it is acted on unless some other belief outweighs it or some failure of energy stifles the movement at its birth. The only difference between the expression of an opinion and an incitement in the narrower sense is the speaker's enthusiasm for the result. Eloquence may set fire to reason. But whatever may be thought of the redundant discourse before us it had no chance of starting a present conflagration. If in the long run the beliefs expressed in proletarian dictatorship are destined to be accepted by the dominant forces of the community, the only meaning of free speech is that they should be given their chance and have their way.

> Oliver Wendell Holmes, Jr., *Gitlow v. New York*, 268 U.S. 652, 673 (1925) (dissenting)

20 Those who won our independence believed that the final end of the State was to make men free to develop their faculties; and that in its government the deliberative forces should prevail over the arbitrary. They valued liberty both as an end and as a means. They believed liberty to be the secret of happiness and courage to be the secret of liberty. They believed that freedom to think as you will and to speak as you think are means indispensable to the discovery and spread of political truth; that without free speech and assembly discussion would be futile; that with them, discussion affords ordinarily adequate protection against the dissemination of noxious doctrine; that the greatest menace to freedom is an inert people; that public discussion is a political duty; and that this should be a fundamental principle of the American government.

> Louis D. Brandeis, *Whitney v. California*, 274 U.S. 357, 375 (1927) (concurring)

21 [Those who won our independence knew] that fear breeds repression; that repression breeds hate; that hate menaces stable gov-

ernment; that the path of safety lies in the opportunity to discuss freely supposed grievances and proposed remedies; and that the fitting remedy for evil counsels is good ones.

Louis D. Brandeis, *Whitney v. California,*
274 U.S. 357, 375 (1927) (concurring)

22 Fear of serious injury cannot alone justify suppression of free speech and assembly. Men feared witches and burnt women. It is the function of speech to free men from the bondage of irrational fears. To justify suppression of free speech there must be reasonable ground to fear that serious evil will result if free speech is practiced. There must be reasonable ground to believe that the danger apprehended is imminent. There must be reasonable ground to believe that the evil to be prevented is a serious one. Every denunciation of existing law tends in some measure to increase the probability that there will be violation of it. Condonation of a breach enhances the probability.

Louis D. Brandeis, *Whitney v. California,*
274 U.S. 357, 376 (1927) (concurring)

23 Those who won our independence by revolution were not cowards. They did not fear political change. They did not exalt order at the cost of liberty. To courageous, self-reliant men, with confidence in the power of free and fearless reasoning applied through the processes of popular government, no danger flowing from speech can be deemed clear and present, unless the incidence of the evil apprehended is so imminent that it may befall before there is opportunity for full discussion. If there be time to expose through discussion the falsehood and fallacies, to avert the evil by the processes of education, the remedy to be applied is more speech, not enforced silence. Only an emergency can justify repression. Such must be the rule if authority is to be reconciled with freedom.

Louis D. Brandeis, *Whitney v. California,*
274 U.S. 357, 377 (1927) (concurring)

24 The real issue in every free speech controversy is this: whether the state can punish all words which have some tendency, however remote, to bring about acts in violation of law, or only words which directly incite to acts in violation of law.

Zechariah Chafee, Jr., *Free Speech in the United States* 23 (1941)

25 Picketing by an organized group is more than free speech, since it involves patrol of a particular locality and since the very presence of a picket line may induce action of one kind or another, quite irrespective of the nature of the ideas which are being disseminated. Hence those aspects of picketing make it the subject of restrictive regulation.

William O. Douglas, *Bakery & Pastry Drivers Local 802 v. Wohl,* 315 U.S. 769, 776–77 (1942) (concurring)

26 There are certain well-defined and narrowly limited classes of speech, the prevention and punishment of which have never been thought to raise any Constitutional problem. These include the lewd and obscene, the profane, the libelous, and the insulting or "fighting" words—those which by their very utterance inflict injury or tend to incite an immediate breach of the peace. It has been well observed that such utterances are no essential part of any exposition of ideas, and are of such slight social value as a step to truth that any benefit that may be derived from them is clearly outweighed by the social interest in order and morality.

Frank Murphy, *Chaplinsky v. New Hampshire,* 315 U.S. 568, 571–72 (1942)

27 This court has unequivocally held that the streets are proper places for the exercise of the freedom of communicating information and disseminating opinion and that, though the states and municipalities may appropriately regulate the privilege in the public interest, they may not unduly burden or proscribe its employment in these public thoroughfares. We are equally clear that the Constitution imposes no such restraint on government as respects purely commercial advertising.

Owen J. Roberts, *Valentine v. Chrestensen,* 316 U.S. 52, 54 (1942)

28 A function of free speech under our system of government is to invite dispute, It may indeed best serve its high purpose when it induces a condition of unrest, creates dissatisfaction with conditions as they are, or even stirs people to anger. Speech is often provocative and challenging. It may strike at prejudices and preconceptions and have profound unsettling effects as it presses for acceptance of an idea. That is why freedom

of speech, though not absolute, . . . is nevertheless protected against censorship or punishment, unless shown likely to produce a clear and present danger of a serious substantive evil that rises far above public inconvenience, annoyance, or unrest.

> **William O. Douglas,** *Terminiello v. Chicago,*
> 337 U.S. 1, 4 (1949)

29 [The preferred position of freedom of speech] is a phrase that has uncritically crept into some recent opinions of this Court. I deem it a mischievous phrase, if it carries the thought, which it may subtly imply, that any law touching communication is infected with presumptive invalidity.

> **Felix Frankfurter,** *Kovacs v. Cooper,* 336
> U.S. 77, 90 (1949) (concurring)

30 It is argued that the Constitution protects freedom of speech: freedom of speech means the right to communicate, whatever the physical means for so doing; sound trucks are one form of communication; *ergo* that form is entitled to the same protection as any other means of communication, whether by tongue or pen. Such sterile argumentation treats society as though it consisted of bloodless categories.

> **Felix Frankfurter,** *Kovacs v. Cooper,* 336
> U.S. 77, 96 (1949) (concurring)

31 In each case [the courts] must ask whether the gravity of the "evil," discounted by its improbability, justifies such invasion of free speech as is necessary to avoid the danger.

> **Learned Hand,** *United States v. Dennis,* 183
> F.2d 201, 212 (2d Cir. 1950)

32 But the command of the First Amendment is so clear that we should not allow Congress to call a halt to free speech except in the extreme case of peril from the speech itself. The First Amendment makes confidence in the common sense of our people and in their maturity of judgment the great postulate of our democracy. Its philosophy is that violence is rarely, if ever, stopped by denying civil liberties to those advocating resort to force.

> **William O. Douglas,** *Dennis v. United States,*
> 341 U.S. 494, 590 (1951) (dissenting)

33 Overthrow of the Government by force and violence is certainly a substantial enough interest for the Government to limit speech. Indeed, this is the ultimate value of any society, for if a society cannot protect its very structure from armed internal attack, it must follow that no subordinate value can be protected.

> **Fred M. Vinson,** *Dennis v. United States,* 341
> U.S. 494, 509 (1951)

34 The First Amendment and other parts of the law erect a fence inside which men can talk. The law-makers, legislators and officials stay on the outside of that fence. But what the men inside the fence say when they are let alone is no concern of the law.

> **Zechariah Chafee, Jr.,** *The Blessings of*
> *Liberty* 108 (1956)

35 Free speech is not to be regulated like diseased cattle and impure butter. The audience . . . that hissed yesterday may applaud today, even for the same performance.

> **William O. Douglas,** *Kingsley Books, Inc. v.*
> *Brown,* 354 U.S. 436, 447 (1957) (dissenting)

36 Government should be concerned with antisocial conduct, not with utterances.

> **William O. Douglas,** *Roth v. United States,*
> 354 U.S. 476, 512–13 (1957) (dissenting)

37 General regulatory statutes, not intended to control the content of speech but incidentally limiting its unfettered exercise, have not been regarded as the type of law the First or Fourteenth Amendment forbade Congress or the States to pass, when they have been found justified by subordinating valid governmental interests, a prerequisite to constitutionality which has necessarily involved a weighing of the governmental interest involved.

> **John M. Harlan** (1899–1971), *Konigsberg v.*
> *State Bar,* 366 U.S. 36, 50–51 (1961)

38 Speech is often provocative and challenging. It may strike at prejudices and preconceptions and have profound unsettling effects as it presses for acceptance of an idea. That is why freedom of speech . . . is . . . protected against censorship or punishment, unless shown likely to produce a clear and present danger of a serious substantive evil that rises far above public inconvenience, annoyance, or unrest. . . .

There is no room under our Constitution for a more restrictive view.

> Potter Stewart, *Edwards v. South Carolina,* 372 U.S. 229, 237–38 (1963)

39 Speech concerning public affairs is more than self-expression; it is the essence of self-government.

> William J. Brennan, Jr., *Garrison v. Louisiana,* 379 U.S. 64, 74–75 (1964)

40 The sound of tireless voices is the price we pay for the right to hear the music of our own opinions.

> Adlai E. Stevenson, quoted in *The Guide to American Law* 9:340 (1984)

41 A constitutional distinction between speech and conduct is specious. Speech *is* conduct, and actions speak.

> Louis Henkin, "Foreword: On Drawing Lines," 82 *Harvard Law Review* 63, 79 (1968)

42 Constitutional protection should be accorded only to speech that is explicitly political.

> Robert H. Bork, "Neutral Principles and Some First Amendment Problems," 47 *Indiana Law Journal* 1, 20 (1971)

43 One man's vulgarity is another's lyric.

> John M. Harlan (1899–1971), *Cohen v. California,* 403 U.S. 15, 25 (1971)

44 Leaving aside for the moment the question whether there are greater dangers in trying to define and control the sort of speech I have been reciting than in risking that it will achieve the results it advocates, one may allow such speech on one of two premises: either the cynical premise that words don't matter, that they make nothing happen and are too trivial to bother with; or else the premise taken by Justice Brandeis in *Whitney v. California* that "discussion affords ordinarily adequate protection against the dissemination of noxious doctrine."

The first premise is inconsistent with the idea of a First Amendment; if speech doesn't matter we might as well suppress it, because it is sometimes a nuisance. As to the second, we have lived through too much to believe it.

> Alexander M. Bickel, *The Morality of Consent* 71 (1975)

45 The theory of the truth of the marketplace, determined ultimately by a count of noses—this total relativism—cannot be the theory of our Constitution.

> Alexander M. Bickel, *The Morality of Consent* 77 (1975)

46 The concept that government may restrict the speech of some elements of our society in order to enhance the relative voice of others is wholly foreign to the First Amendment.

> *Buckley v. Valeo,* 424 U.S. 1, 48–49 (1976) (per curiam)

47 There is no claim . . . that the prohibition on prescription drug price advertising is a mere time, place, and manner restriction. We have often approved restrictions of that kind provided that they are justified without reference to the content of the regulated speech, that they serve a significant governmental interest, and that in so doing they leave open ample alternative channels for communication of the information.

> Harry A. Blackmun, *Virginia State Bd. of Pharmacy v. Virginia Citizens Consumer Council, Inc.,* 425 U.S. 748, 771 (1976)

48 Free speech carries with it some freedom to listen.

> Warren E. Burger, *Richmond Newspapers, Inc. v. Virginia,* 448 U.S. 555, 576 (1980)

49 In commercial speech cases, then, a four-part analysis has developed. At the outset, we must determine whether the expression is protected by the First Amendment. For commercial speech to come within that provision, it at least must concern lawful activity and not be misleading. Next we ask whether the asserted governmental interest is substantial. If both inquiries yield positive answers, we must determine whether the regulation directly advances the governmental interest asserted, and whether it is not more extensive than is necessary to serve that interest.

> Lewis F. Powell, Jr., *Central Hudson Gas & Elec. Corp. v. Public Serv. Comm'n,* 447 U.S. 557, 566 (1980)

50 But for purposes of presenting political views in connection with a nationwide Presidential election, allowing the presentation of views while forbidding the expenditure of more that $1,000 to present them

is much like allowing a speaker in a public hall to express his views while denying him the use of an amplifying system.

William H. Rehnquist, *Federal Election Comm'n v. National Conservative Political Action Comm.,* 470 U.S. 480, 493 (1985)

51 It is a paradox of modern life that speech, although highly prized, enjoys its great protection in part because it is so often of no concern to anyone. To an almost alarming degree, tolerance depends not on principle but on indifference.

Harry Kalven, Jr., *A Worthy Tradition* 6 (1988)

FREEDOM OF THE PRESS

See also CENSORSHIP; FIRST AMENDMENT; FREEDOM OF EXPRESSION; FREEDOM OF SPEECH; LIBEL

1 The loss of liberty in general would soon follow the suppression of the liberty of the press; for as it is an essential branch of liberty, so perhaps it is the best preservation of the whole.

New York Weekly Journal, 19 Nov. 1733, in *A Brief Narrative of the Case and Trial of John Peter Zenger* 115 (Stanley N. Katz ed. 1963)

2 The last right . . . regards the freedom of the press. The importance of this consists, besides the advancement of truth, science, morality, and arts in general, in its diffusion of liberal sentiments on the administration of Government, . . . whereby oppressive officers are shamed or intimidated, into more honourable and just modes of conducting affairs.

Address from the Continental Congress to the inhabitants of Quebec, 26 Oct. 1774, in *Journals of the Continental Congress* 1:105, 108 (Worthington C. Ford ed. 1904)

3 That the freedom of the press is one of the great bulwarks of liberty, and can never be restrained but by despotic governments.

Virginia Declaration of Rights of 1776, § 12, in *Federal and State Constitutions* 7:3812, 3814 (Francis N. Thorpe ed. 1909)

4 Our liberty depends on the freedom of the press, and that cannot be limited without being lost.

Thomas Jefferson, Letter to James Currie, 28 Jan. 1786, in *Papers of Thomas Jefferson* 9:239 (Julian P. Boyd ed. 1954)

5 The basis of our governments being the opinion of the people, the very first object should be to keep that right; and were it left to me to decide whether we should have a government without newspapers, or newspapers without a government, I should not hesitate a moment to prefer the latter.

Thomas Jefferson, Letter to Edward Carrington, 16 Jan. 1787, in *Papers of Thomas Jefferson* 11:49 (Julian P. Boyd ed. 1955)

6 *The Liberty of the Press;* a Liberty which every Pennsylvanian would fight and die for; tho' few of us, I believe, have distinct Ideas of its Nature and Extent. It seems indeed somewhat like the *Liberty of the Press* that Felons have, by the Common Law of England, before Conviction, that is, to be *press'd* to death or hanged. If by the *Liberty of the Press* were understood merely the Liberty of discussing the Propriety of Public Measures and political opinions, let us have as much of it as you please: But if it means the Liberty of affronting, calumniating, and defaming one another, I, for my part, own myself willing to part with my Share of it when our Legislators shall please so to alter the Law, and shall cheerfully consent to exchange my *Liberty* of Abusing others for the *Privilege* of not being abus'd myself.

Benjamin Franklin, "An Account of the Supremest Court of Judicature in Pennsylvania," 1789, in *Writings of Benjamin Franklin* 10:36, 37–38 (Albert H. Smyth ed. 1907)

7 My proposal then is, to leave the liberty of the press untouched, to be exercised in its full extent, force, and vigor; but to permit the *liberty of the cudgel* to go with it *pari passu.* Thus, my fellow-citizens, if an impudent writer attacks your reputation, dearer to you perhaps than your life, and puts his name to the charge, you may go to him as openly and break his head. If he conceals himself behind the printer, and you can nevertheless discover who he is, you may in like manner way-lay him in the night, attack him behind, and give him a good drubbing. Thus far goes my project as to *private* resentment and retribution. But if the public should ever happen to be affronted, *as it ought to be,* with the conduct of such writers, I would not advise

proceeding immediately to these extremities; but that we should in moderation content ourselves with tarring and feathering, and tossing them in a blanket.

> **Benjamin Franklin,** "An Account of the Supremest Court of Judicature in Pennsylvania," 1789, in *Writings of Benjamin Franklin* 10:36, 40 (Albert H. Smyth ed. 1907)

8 If, however, it should be thought that this proposal of mine may disturb the public peace, I would then humbly recommend to our legislators to take up the consideration of both liberties, that of the *press,* and that of the *cudgel,* and by an explicit law mark their extent and limits; and, at the same time that they secure the person of a citizen from *assaults,* they would likewise provide for the security of his *reputation.*

> **Benjamin Franklin,** "An Account of the Supremest Court of Judicature in Pennsylvania," 1789, in *Writings of Benjamin Franklin* 10:36, 40 (Albert H. Smyth ed. 1907)

9 The press shall be free to every citizen who undertakes to examine the official conduct of men acting in a public capacity; and any citizen may print on any subject, being responsible for the abuse of that liberty.

> Delaware Constitution of 1792, art. I, § 5, in *Federal and State Constitutions* 1:568, 569 (Francis N. Thorpe ed. 1909)

10 No government ought to be without censors: and where the press is free, no one ever will.

> **Thomas Jefferson,** Letter to George Washington, 9 Sept. 1792, in *Writings of Thomas Jefferson* 6:108 (Paul L. Ford ed. 1895)

11 It is true, as a general principle, and is also expressly declared by one of the amendments to the Constitution, that "the powers not delegated to the United States by the Constitution, nor prohibited by it to the states, are reserved to the states respectively, or to the people;" and that, no power over the freedom of religion, freedom of speech, or freedom of the press, being delegated to the United States by the Constitution, not prohibited by it to the states, all lawful powers respecting the same did of right remain, and were reserved to the states, or to the people; . . . therefore [the

Sedition Act] . . . which does abridge the freedom of the press, is not law, but is altogether void, and of no force.

> Kentucky Resolutions of 1798, Resolution 3, in *Debates in the Several State Conventions* 4:540, 540–41 (Jonathan Elliot ed., 2d ed. 1888)

12 Some degree of abuse is inseparable from the proper use of every thing; and in no instance is this more true than in that of the press. It has accordingly been decided, by the practice of the states, that it is better to leave a few of its noxious branches to their luxuriant growth, than, by pruning them away, to injure the vigor of those yielding the proper fruits.

> **James Madison,** "Report on the Virginia Resolutions," 1799–1800, in *Debates on the Adoption of the Federal Constitution* 4:571 (Jonathan Elliot ed., 2d ed. 1888)

13 The abuses of the freedom of the press here have been carried to a length never before known or borne by any civilized nation.

> **Thomas Jefferson,** Letter to M. Pictet, 5 Feb. 1803, in *Writings of Thomas Jefferson* 4:463 (H. A. Washington ed. 1854)

14 It is so difficult to draw a clear line of separation between the abuse and the wholesome use of the press, that as yet we have found it better to trust the public judgment, rather than the magistrate, with the discrimination between truth and falsehood.

> **Thomas Jefferson,** Letter to M. Pictet, 5 Feb. 1803, in *Writings of Thomas Jefferson* 4:463 (H. A. Washington ed. 1854)

15 The Liberty of the Press consists, in my idea, in publishing the truth, from good motives and for justifiable ends, though it reflect on government, on magistrates, or individuals. If it be not allowed, it excludes the privilege of canvassing men, and our rulers. It is in vain to say, you may canvass measures. This is impossible without the right of looking to men.

> **Alexander Hamilton,** Speech before the court in *People v. Croswell,* 13 Feb. 1804, in *The Law Practice of Alexander Hamilton* 1:808, 809 (Julius Goebel, Jr. ed. 1964)

16 No experiment can be more interesting than that we are now trying, and which we trust will end in establishing the fact, that men may be governed by reason and truth.

Our first object should therefore be, to leave open to him all the avenues to truth. The most effectual hitherto found, is the freedom of the press. It is, therefore, the first shut up by those who fear the investigation of their actions.

> **Thomas Jefferson,** Letter to Judge Tyler, 28 June 1804, in *Life and Selected Writings of Thomas Jefferson* 576 (Adrienne Koch & William Peden eds. 1944)

17 The press, confined to truth, needs no other legal restraint; the public judgment will correct false reasonings and opinions, on a full hearing of all parties; and no other definite line can be drawn between the inestimable liberty of the press and its demoralizing licentiousness. If there be still improprieties which this rule would not restrain, its supplement must be sought in the censorship of public opinion.

> **Thomas Jefferson,** Second Inaugural Address, 4 Mar. 1805, in *Writings of Thomas Jefferson* 8:346–47 (Paul L. Ford ed. 1897)

18 The functionaries of every government have propensities to command at will the liberty and property of their constituents. There is no safe deposit for these but with the people themselves; nor can they be safe with them without information. Where the press is free, and every man able to read, all is safe.

> **Thomas Jefferson,** Letter to Charles Yancey, 6 Jan. 1816, in *Writings of Thomas Jefferson* 10:4 (Paul L. Ford ed. 1899)

19 A popular Government, without popular information, or the means of acquiring it, is but a Prologue to a Farce or a Tragedy; or perhaps both. Knowledge will forever govern ignorance: And a people who mean to be their own Governors, must arm themselves with the power which knowledge gives.

> **James Madison,** Letter to W. T. Barry, 4 Aug. 1822, in *Writings of James Madison* 9:103 (Gaillard Hunt ed. 1910)

20 In countries where the doctrine of the sovereignty of the people ostensibly prevails, the censorship of the press is not only dangerous, but absurd. When the right of every citizen to a share in the government of society is acknowledged, every one must be presumed to be able to choose between the various opinions of his contemporaries, and to appreciate the different facts from which inferences may be drawn.

> **Alexis de Tocqueville,** *Democracy in America* 1:232 (Francis Bowen trans. 1862) (1835)

21 In order to enjoy the inestimable benefits which the liberty of the press insures, it is necessary to submit to the inevitable evils which it creates.

> **Alexis de Tocqueville,** *Democracy in America* 1:234 (Francis Bowen trans. 1862) (1835)

22 The more I consider the independence of the press in its principal consequences, the more am I convinced that, in the modern world, it is the chief, and, so to speak, the constitutive element of liberty. A nation which is determined to remain free is therefore right in demanding, at any price, the exercise of this independence.

> **Alexis de Tocqueville,** *Democracy in America* 1:245 (Francis Bowen trans. 1862) (1835)

23 There are laws to protect the freedom of the press's speech, but none that are worth anything to protect the people from the press.

> **Mark Twain,** "License of the Press" (speech), Hartford, 1873, in *Writings of Mark Twain* 28:46, 46–47 (Albert B. Paine ed. 1929)

24 Nor can any regulations be enforced against the transportation of printed matter in the mail, which is open to examination, so as to interfere in any manner with the freedom of the press. Liberty of circulating is as essential to that freedom as liberty of publishing; indeed, without the circulation, the publication would be of little value. If, therefore, printed matter be excluded from the mails, its transportation in any other way cannot be forbidden by Congress.

> **Stephen J. Field,** *Ex parte Jackson,* 96 U.S. 727, 733 (1878)

25 The liberty of the press is most generally approved when it takes liberties with the other fellow, and leaves us alone.

> **Edgar W. Howe,** *Country Town Sayings* 198 (1911)

26 No one would question but that a government might prevent actual obstruction to its recruiting service or the publication of sailing dates of transports or the number and location of troops. On similar grounds,

the primary requirements of decency may be enforced against obscene publications. The security of the community life may be protected against incitements to acts of violence and the overthrow by force of orderly government.

Charles Evans Hughes, *Near v. Minnesota,* 283 U.S. 697, 716 (1931)

27 The exceptional nature of its limitations places in a strong light the general conception that liberty of the press, historically considered and taken up by the Federal Constitution, has meant, principally although not exclusively, immunity from previous restraints or censorship.

Charles Evans Hughes, *Near v. Minnesota,* 283 U.S. 697, 716 (1931)

28 The fact that for approximately one hundred and fifty years there has been almost an entire absence of attempts to impose previous restraints upon publications relating to the malfeasance of public officers is significant of the deep-seated conviction that such restraints would violate constitutional right. Public officers, whose character and conduct remain open to debate and free discussion in the press, find their remedies for false accusations in actions under libel laws providing for redress and punishment, and not in proceedings to restrain the publication of newspapers and periodicals. The general principle that the constitutional guaranty of the liberty of the press gives immunity from previous restraints has been approved in many decisions under the provisions of state constitutions.

Charles Evans Hughes, *Near v. Minnesota,* 283 U.S. 697, 718–19 (1931)

29 The fact that the liberty of the press may be abused by miscreant purveyors of scandal does not make any the less necessary the immunity of the press from previous restraint in dealing with official misconduct. Subsequent punishment for such abuses as may exist is the appropriate remedy, consistent with constitutional privilege.

Charles Evans Hughes, *Near v. Minnesota,* 283 U.S. 697, 720 (1931)

30 A free press stands as one of the great interpreters between the government and the people. To allow it to be fettered is to fetter ourselves.

George Sutherland, *Grosjean v. American Press Co.,* 297 U.S. 233, 250 (1936)

31 Freedom to publish means freedom for all and not for some. Freedom to publish is guaranteed by the Constitution, but freedom to combine to keep others from publishing is not. Freedom of the press from governmental interference under the First Amendment does not sanction repression of that freedom by private interests.

Hugo L. Black, *Associated Press v. United States,* 326 U.S. 1, 20 (1945)

32 Freedom of the press . . . is not an end in itself but a means to the end of a free society.

Felix Frankfurter, *Pennekamp v. Florida,* 328 U.S. 331, 354–55 (1946) (concurring)

33 Freedom of the press is guaranteed only to those who own one.

A. J. Liebling, "The Wayward Press: Do you belong in Journalism?" *New Yorker,* 14 May 1960, at 105, 109

34 The Government's position in this court, Your Honor, was that grave danger to the national security would occur if another installment of a story that The Times had were published. Another installment of that story has been published. The republic stands and it stood the first three days.

Alexander M. Bickel, Argument in Pentagon Papers Case, quoted in *New York Times,* 19 June 1971, at 10

35 In the First Amendment the Founding Fathers gave the free press the protection it must have to fulfill its essential role in our democracy. The press was to serve the governed, not the governors. The Government's power to censor the press was abolished so that the press would remain forever free to censure the Government. The press was protected so that it could bare the secrets of government and inform the people.

Hugo L. Black, *New York Times Co. v. United States,* 403 U.S. 713, 717 (1971) (concurring)

36 Paramount among the responsibilities of a free press is the duty to prevent any part of the government from deceiving the people

175

and sending them off to distant lands to die of foreign fevers and foreign shot and shell.

> **Hugo L. Black,** *New York Times Co. v. United States,* 403 U.S. 713, 717 (1971) (concurring)

37 In revealing the workings of government that led to the Vietnam war, the newspapers nobly did precisely that which the Founders hoped and trusted they would do.

> **Hugo L. Black,** *New York Times Co. v. United States,* 403 U.S. 713, 717 (1971) (concurring)

38 In my view, far from deserving condemnation for their courageous reporting, the New York Times, the Washington Post, and other newspapers should be commended for serving the purpose that the Founding Fathers saw so clearly.

> **Hugo L. Black,** *New York Times Co. v. United States,* 403 U.S. 713, 717 (1971) (concurring)

39 The security of the Nation is not at the ramparts alone. Security also lies in the value of our free institutions. A cantankerous press, an obstinate press, an ubiquitous press must be suffered by those in authority in order to preserve the even greater values of freedom of expression and the right of the people to know. . . . it is not merely the opinion of the editorial writer or of the columnist which is protected by the First Amendment. It is the free flow of information so that the public will be informed about the Government and its actions.

> **Murray I. Gurfein,** *United States v. New York Times Co.,* 328 F. Supp. 324, 331 (S.D.N.Y. 1971)

40 Without an informed and free press there cannot be an enlightened people. Yet it is elementary that the successful conduct of international diplomacy and the maintenance of an effective national defense require both confidentiality and secrecy. . . . It is an awesome responsibility, requiring judgment and wisdom of a high order. I should suppose that moral, political, and practical considerations would dictate that a very first principle of that wisdom would be an insistence upon avoiding secrecy for its own sake. For when everything is classified, then nothing is classified, and the system becomes one to be disregarded by the cynical or the careless, and to be manipulated by those intent on self-protection or self-promotion.

> **Potter Stewart,** *New York Times Co. v. United States,* 403 U.S. 713, 728–29 (1971) (concurring)

41 The First Amendment is not so construed, however, to award merit badges for intrepid but mistaken or careless reporting. Misinformation has no merit in itself; standing alone it is as antithetical to the purposes of the First Amendment as the calculated lie. . . . The sole basis for protecting publishers who spread false information is that otherwise the truth would too often be suppressed.

> **Byron R. White,** *Ocala Star-Banner Co. v. Damron,* 401 U.S. 295, 301 (1971) (concurring)

42 What kind of First Amendment would best serve our needs as we approach the 21st century may be an open question. But the old-fashioned First Amendment that we have is the Court's only guideline; and one hard and fast principle which it announces is that Government shall keep its hands off the press. That principle has served us through days of calm and eras of strife and I would abide by it until a new First Amendment is adopted. That means, as I view it, that TV and radio, as well as the more conventional methods for disseminating news, are all included in the concept of "press" as used in the First Amendment and therefore are entitled to live under the laissez-faire regime which the First Amendment sanctions.

> **William O. Douglas,** *CBS v. Democratic Nat'l Comm.,* 412 U.S. 94, 160–61 (1973) (concurring)

43 There is no constitutional right to have access to particular government information, or to require openness from the bureaucracy. . . . The public's interest in knowing about its government is protected by the guarantee of a Free Press, but the protection is indirect. The Constitution itself is neither a Freedom of Information Act nor an Official Secrets Act.

> **Potter Stewart,** "Or of the Press," 26 *Hastings Law Journal* 631, 636 (1975)

44 We reaffirm that the guarantees of freedom of expression are not an absolute prohibi-

tion under all circumstances, but the barriers to prior restraint remain high and the presumption against its use continues intact.

Warren E. Burger, *Nebraska Press Ass'n v. Stuart,* 427 U.S. 539, 570 (1976)

GOVERNMENT

See also DEMOCRACY; FEDERALISM; SOVEREIGN IMMUNITY; VOTING

1 Government implies the power of making laws. It is essential to the idea of a law, that it be attended with a sanction; or, in other words, a penalty or punishment for disobedience.

Alexander Hamilton, *The Federalist* No. 15, at 1:92 (1788)

2 No axiom is more clearly established in law, or in reason, than that wherever the end is required, the means are authorized; wherever a general power to do a thing is given, every particular power necessary for doing it, is included.

James Madison, *The Federalist* No. 44, at 2:74 (1788)

3 The aim of every political constitution is, or ought to be, first to obtain for rulers men who possess most wisdom to discern, and most virtue to pursue, the common good of the society; and in the next place, to take the most effectual precautions for keeping them virtuous, whilst they continue to hold their public trust.

James Madison, *The Federalist* No. 57, at 2:153 (1788)

4 Every power vested in a Government is in its nature *sovereign,* and includes by *force* of the *term,* a right to employ all the *means* requisite . . . to the attainment of the *ends* of such power.

Alexander Hamilton, Opinion on the Constitutionality of an Act to Establish a Bank, 1791, in *Papers of Alexander Hamilton* 8:98 (Harold C. Syrett ed. 1965)

5 If the end be clearly comprehended with any of the specified powers, and if the measure have an obvious relation to that end, and is not forbidden by any particular provision of the constitution—it may safely be

deemed to come within the compass of the national authority.

Alexander Hamilton, Opinion on the Constitutionality of an Act to Establish a Bank, 1791, in *Papers of Alexander Hamilton* 8:107 (Harold C. Syrett ed. 1965)

6 The very essence of civil liberty certainly consists in the right of every individual to claim the protection of the laws, whenever he receives an injury. One of the first duties of government is to afford that protection.

John Marshall, *Marbury v. Madison,* 5 U.S. (1 Cranch) 137, 163 (1803)

7 The government, then, of the United States, can claim no powers which are not granted to it by the constitution, and the powers actually granted, must be such as are expressly given, or given by necessary implication.

Joseph Story, *Martin v. Hunter's Lessee,* 14 U.S. (1 Wheat.) 304, 326 (1818)

8 The government of the Union . . . is emphatically, and truly, a government of the people. In form and in substance it emanates from them. Its powers are granted by them, and are to be exercised directly on them, and for their benefit.

John Marshall, *McCulloch v. Maryland,* 17 U.S. (4 Wheat.) 316, 404-05 (1819)

9 This government is acknowledged by all to be one of enumerated powers. . . . But the question respecting the extent of the powers actually granted, is perpetually arising, and will probably continue to arise, so long as our system shall exist.

John Marshall, *McCulloch v. Maryland,* 17 U.S. (4 Wheat.) 316, 405 (1819)

10 The sword and the purse, all the external relations, and no inconsiderable portion of the industry of the nation, are entrusted to its government. . . . a government entrusted with such ample powers, on the due execution of which the happiness and prosperity of the nation so vitally depends, must also be entrusted with ample means for their execution. The power being given, it is the interest of the nation to facilitate its execution. It can never be their interest, and cannot be presumed to have been their intention, to clog and embarrass its execution.

John Marshall, *McCulloch v. Maryland,* 17 U.S. (4 Wheat.) 316, 407-08 (1819)

11 The government which has a right to do an act, and has imposed on it the duty of performing that act, must, according to the dictates of reason, be allowed to select the means; and those who contend that it may not select any appropriate means, that one particular mode of effecting the object is excepted, take upon themselves the burden of establishing that exception.

John Marshall, *McCulloch v. Maryland*, 17 U.S. (4 Wheat.) 316, 409–10 (1819)

12 But we think the sound construction of the constitution must allow to the national legislature that discretion, with respect to the means by which the powers it confers are to be carried into execution, which will enable that body to perform the high duties assigned to it, in the manner most beneficial to the people. Let the end be legitimate, let it be within the scope of the constitution, and all means which are appropriate, which are plainly adapted to that end, which are not prohibited, but consist with the letter and spirit of the constitution, are constitutional.

John Marshall, *McCulloch v. Maryland*, 17 U.S. (4 Wheat.) 316, 421 (1819)

13 No government ought to be so defective in its organization, as not to contain within itself the means of securing the execution of its own laws against other dangers than those which occur every day.

John Marshall, *Cohens v. Virginia*, 19 U.S. (6 Wheat.) 264, 387 (1821)

14 That the United States form, for many, and for most important purposes, a single nation, has not yet been denied. In war, we are one people. In making peace, we are one people. In all commercial regulations, we are one and the same people. In many other respects, the American people are one; and the government which is alone capable of controling and managing their interests in all these respects, is the government of the Union. It is their government, and in that character they have no other. America has chosen to be, in many respects, and to many purposes, a nation; and for all these purposes, her government is complete; to all these objects, it is competent.

John Marshall, *Cohens v. Virginia*, 19 U.S. (6 Wheat.) 264, 413–14 (1821)

15 The less government we have the better,—the fewer laws, and the less confided power.

Ralph Waldo Emerson, "Politics," *Essays: Second Series*, 1844, in *Complete Works of Ralph Waldo Emerson* 3:199, 215 (1903)

16 It rests with Congress to decide what government is the established one in a State. . . . And its decision is binding on every other department of the government, and could not be questioned in a judicial tribunal.

Roger B. Taney, *Luther v. Borden*, 48 U.S. (7 How.) 1, 42 (1849)

17 The world is made wrong; kings should go to school to their own laws, at times, and so learn mercy.

Mark Twain, *The Prince and the Pauper*, 1881, in *Works of Mark Twain* 6:284 (Victor Fischer & Lin Salamo eds. 1979)

18 No man in this country is so high that he is above the law. No officer of the law may set that law at defiance with impunity. All the officers of the government, from the highest to the lowest, are creatures of the law, and are bound to obey it.

Samuel F. Miller, *United States v. Lee*, 106 U.S. 196, 220 (1882)

19 The paternal theory of government is to me odious. The utmost possible liberty to the individual, and the fullest possible protection to him and his property, is both the limitation and the duty of government.

David J. Brewer, *Budd v. New York*, 143 U.S. 517, 551 (1892) (dissenting)

20 Men must turn square corners when they deal with the Government.

Oliver Wendell Holmes, Jr., *Rock Island, Arkansas & Louisiana Ry. v. United States*, 254 U.S. 141, 143 (1920)

21 We fear to grant power and are unwilling to recognize it when it exists. The States very generally have stripped jury trials of one of their most important characteristics by forbidding the judges to advise the jury upon the facts . . . and when legislatures are held to be authorized to do anything considerably affecting public welfare it is covered by apologetic phrases like the police power, or the statement that the busi-

ness concerned has been dedicated to a public use.

Oliver Wendell Holmes, Jr., *Tyson v. Banton,* 273 U.S. 418, 445 (1927) (dissenting)

22 Experience should teach us to be most on our guard to protect liberty when the Government's purposes are beneficent. Men born to freedom are naturally alert to repel invasion of their liberty by evil-minded rulers. The greatest dangers to liberty lurk in insidious encroachment by men of zeal, well-meaning but without understanding.

Louis D. Brandeis, *Olmstead v. United States,* 277 U.S. 438, 479 (1928) (dissenting)

23 Decency, security and liberty alike demand that government officials shall be subjected to the same rules of conduct that are commands to the citizen. In a government of laws, existence of the government will be imperilled if it fails to observe the law scrupulously. Our Government is the potent, the omnipresent teacher. For good or for ill, it teaches the whole people by its example. Crime is contagious. If the Government becomes a lawbreaker, it breeds contempt for law; it invites every man to become a law unto himself; it invites anarchy. To declare that in the administration of the criminal law the end justifies the means—to declare that the Government may commit crimes in order to secure the conviction of a private criminal—would bring terrible retribution. Against that pernicious doctrine this Court should resolutely set its face.

Louis D. Brandeis, *Olmstead v. United States,* 277 U.S. 438, 485 (1928) (dissenting)

24 A city acts for city purposes when it builds a dock or a bridge or a street or a subway. . . . Its purpose is not different when it builds an airport. . . . Aviation is today an established method of transportation. The future, even the near future, will make it still more general. The city that is without the foresight to build the ports for the new traffic may soon be left behind in the race of competition. Chalcedon was called the city of the blind, because its founder rejected the nobler site of Byzantium lying at their feet. The need for vision of the future in the governance of cities has not lessened with the years. The dweller within the gates, even more than the stranger from afar, will pay the price of blindness.

Benjamin N. Cardozo, *Hesse v. Rath,* 249 N.Y. 436, 438, 164 N.E. 342 (1928)

25 The philosophy that constitutional limitations and legal restraints upon official action may be brushed aside upon the plea that good, perchance, may follow, finds no countenance in the American system of government.

George Sutherland, *Jones v. SEC,* 298 U.S. 1, 27 (1936)

26 "We live by symbols." The flag is the symbol of our national unity, transcending all internal differences, however large, within the framework of the Constitution.

Felix Frankfurter, *Minersville School Dist. v. Gobitis,* 310 U.S. 586, 596 (1940)

27 There is no mysticism in the American concept of the State or of the nature or origin of its authority. We set up government by consent of the governed, and the Bill of Rights denies those in power any legal opportunity to coerce that consent. Authority here is to be controlled by public opinion, not public opinion by authority.

Robert H. Jackson, *West Virginia State Bd. of Educ. v. Barnette,* 319 U.S. 624, 641 (1943)

28 Men are more often bribed by their loyalties and ambitions than by money.

Robert H. Jackson, *United States v. Wunderlich,* 342 U.S. 98, 103 (1951) (dissenting)

29 Each one of us must in the end choose for himself how far he would like to leave our collective fate to the wayward vagaries of popular assemblies. No one can fail to recognize the perils to which the last forty years have exposed such governments. We are not indeed forced to choose between absolutism and the kind of democracy that so often prevailed in Greek cities during the sixth to fourth centuries before our era. The Founding Fathers were acutely, perhaps overacutely, aware of the dangers that had followed that sort of rule, though, as you all know, they differed widely as to what curbs to impose. For myself it would be most irksome to be ruled by a bevy of Platonic Guardians, even if I knew how to choose them, which I assuredly do not.

Learned Hand, *The Bill of Rights* 73 (1958)

30 I think the Government in moving against the citizen should also turn square corners.

> William O. Douglas, *Commissioner of Internal Revenue v. Lester*, 366 U.S. 299, 306 (1961) (concurring)

31 No society, certainly not a large and heterogeneous one, can fail in time to explode if it is deprived of the arts of compromise, if it knows no ways of muddling through. No good society can be unprincipled; and no viable society can be principle-ridden.

> Alexander M. Bickel, *The Least Dangerous Branch* 64 (1962)

32 Yet as I read the Constitution, one of its essential purposes was to take government off the backs of people and keep it off.

> William O. Douglas, *W.E.B. Du Bois Clubs v. Clark*, 389 U.S. 309, 318 (1967) (dissenting)

GRAND JURY

1 The natural and obvious inference is, that in the sense of the Constitution, "due process of law" was not meant or intended to include . . . the institution and procedure of a grand jury in any case.

> Stanley Matthews, *Hurtado v. California*, 110 U.S. 516, 534 (1884)

2 Save for torture, it would be hard to find a more effective tool of tyranny than the power of unlimited and unchecked *ex parte* examination.

> Learned Hand, *United States v. Remington*, 208 F.2d 567, 573 (2d Cir. 1953) (dissenting)

3 The concept, which had originated in England in 1681, was that the grand jury would protect the citizenry against unscrupulous prosecutors. That was the concept, and the concept had become a joke. If a defendant wanted to testify before the grand jury, he could bring his lawyer into the grand-jury room. If he was (a) perplexed or (b) petrified or (c) grievously abused by the prosecutor's questions, he could leave the room and confer with a lawyer outside in the hall—and thereby look like someone who was (b) petrified, a defendant with something to hide. Not many defendants took the chance. Grand-jury hearings had become a show run by the prosecutor. With rare exceptions, a grand jury did whatever a prosecutor indicated he wanted them to do. Ninety-nine percent of the time he wanted them to indict the defendant, and they obliged without a blink.

> Tom Wolfe, *The Bonfire of the Vanities* 628–29 (1987)

GROWTH OF LAW

See LAW, GROWTH OF

GUILT

See also INNOCENCE

1 The sword of the law could never fall but on those whose guilt is so apparent as to be pronounced by their friends as well as foes.

> Thomas Jefferson, Letter to Sarah Mease, 26 Mar. 1801, in *Writings of Thomas Jefferson* 8:35 (Paul L. Ford ed. 1897)

2 GUILT, *n*. The condition of one who is known to have committed an indiscretion, as distinguished from the state of him who has covered his tracks.

> Ambrose Bierce, *The Enlarged Devil's Dictionary* 122 (Ernest J. Hopkins ed. 1967)

3 In the absence of eye-witnesses there's always a doubt, sometimes only the shadow of a doubt. The law says "reasonable doubt," but I think a defendant's entitled to the shadow of a doubt. There's always the possibility, no matter how improbable, that he's innocent.

> Harper Lee, *To Kill a Mockingbird* 232 (1960)

4 *Foreman* [returning jury's verdict on Max Bialystock and Leo Bloom, played by Zero Mostel and Gene Wilder]: We find the defendants incredibly guilty.

> Mel Brooks, *The Producers* (screenplay), 1967, quoted in Harry Haun, *The Movie Quote Book* 128 (1980)

5 In former days, everyone found the assumption of innocence so easy; today we find fatally easy the assumption of guilt.

> Amanda Cross, *Poetic Justice* 38 (1970)

6 Again Ottinger spoke carefully, and tactfully. "You must understand, Ian, that the law is incapable of calibrating anything so subtle as metaphysical distinctions. It tries

to measure intent, but it cannot measure what one might call the swerve, or the inclination of the soul. . . . If you retain me as your defense attorney you will have to allow me to defend you as if I were defending—which indeed I am—an action, and not, in the most abstract terms, a man. Do you understand?"

Joyce Carol Oates, *American Appetites* 193 (1989)

HARVARD LAW SCHOOL

See also CASE SYSTEM; LAW SCHOOL; LEGAL EDUCATION

1 I give devise and bequeath to the Overseers and Corporation of Harvard College in Cambridge in the County of Middlesex aforesaid to be appropriated towards the Endowing a Professor of Laws in said College or a Professor of Physick and Anatomy which ever the said Overseers and Corporation shall judge to be best for the benefit of said College and they hereby shall have full power to sell said Lands and to put the money out to Interest the income whereof shall be for the aforesaid purpose.

Isaac Royall, Will, 1778, quoted in Arthur E. Sutherland, *The Law at Harvard* 37–38 (1967)

2 A science like this, is worthy to be taught, for it cannot be understood without instruction; it should be admitted into fellowship with its sister sciences, for like theirs, its ends are noble. Its fundamental and general principles should be a branch of liberal education, in every country, but especially in those where freedom prevails, and where every citizen has an equal interest in its preservation and improvement. Justice ought therefore to be done to the memory of *Royall*, whose prospective wisdom, and judicious liberality, provided the means of introducing to the University the study of the law. . . . At some future time, perhaps, a school for the instruction of resident graduates in jurisprudence may be usefully ingrafted on this professorship.

Isaac Parker, Inaugural Address as Royall Professor of Law at Harvard, in 3 *North-American Review* 11, 19, 25 (1816)

3 I will tell you honestly that I am sick at heart of this place [Harvard Law School] and almost everything connected with it. I know not what the temple of the law may be to those who have entered it, but to me it seems very cold and cheerless about the threshold.

Oliver Wendell Holmes, Sr., Letter to Phineas Barnes, 13 Jan. 1830, in *Life and Letters of Oliver Wendell Holmes* 1:65 (John T. Morse, Jr. ed. 1896)

4 [At Harvard Law School] were instilled into me without difficulty the dictums that the law was the most important of all professions, that those who entered it were a priestly class set aside to guard from profanation that Ark of the Covenant, the Constitution of the United States. In short, I was taught law precisely as I had been taught religion,—scriptural infallibility over again,—a static law and a static theology,—a set of concepts that were supposed to be equal to any problems civilization would have to meet until the millennium.

Winston Churchill, *A Far Country* 113–14 (1915)

5 I know of no title that I deem more honorable than that of Professor of the Harvard Law School.

Felix Frankfurter, "Dean James Barr Ames and the Harvard Law School," 1956, in *Of Law and Life and Other Things That Matter* 26, 28 (1965)

6 For some years now I have been concerned about the effect of our legal education on the idealism of our students. . . . They bring to this School [Harvard Law School] a large measure of idealism. Do they leave with less? And if they do, is that something we can view with indifference? If they do, what is the cause? What do we do to them that makes them turn another way?

Erwin N. Griswold, Speech at Harvard Law School sesquicentennial celebration, Cambridge, Mass., 22 Sept. 1967, in *The Path of the Law from 1967*, at 142, 150–51 (Arthur E. Sutherland ed. 1968)

7 You are ready to aid in the shaping and application of those wise restraints that make men free.

Declaration used for conferring law degrees at Harvard, composed by John M. Maguire

HEARSAY

See EVIDENCE

HISTORY

1 The law, as far as it depends on learning, is indeed . . . the government of the living by the dead. To a very considerable extent no doubt it is inevitable that the living should be so governed. The past gives us our vocabulary and fixes the limits of our imagination; we cannot get away from it. . . . But the present has a right to govern itself so far as it can; and it ought always to be remembered that historic continuity with the past is not a duty, it is only a necessity.

> **Oliver Wendell Holmes, Jr.**, "Learning and Science" (speech to Harvard Law School Association), Cambridge, Mass., 25 June 1895, in *Collected Legal Papers* 138, 138–39 (1920)

2 History . . . is a part of the rational study [of law], because it is the first step toward an enlightened scepticism, that is, toward a deliberate reconsideration of the worth of those rules. When you get the dragon out of his cave on to the plain and in the daylight, you can count his teeth and claws, and see just what is his strength. But to get him out is only the first step. The next is either to kill him, or tame him and make him a useful animal.

> **Oliver Wendell Holmes, Jr.**, "The Path of the Law," 10 *Harvard Law Review* 457, 469 (1897)

3 It is revolting to have no better reason for a rule of law than that so it was laid down in the time of Henry IV. It is still more revolting if the grounds upon which it was laid down have vanished long since, and the rule simply persists from blind imitation of the past.

> **Oliver Wendell Holmes, Jr.**, "The Path of the Law," 10 *Harvard Law Review* 457, 469 (1897)

4 The tendency of a principle to expand itself to the limit of its logic may be counteracted by the tendency to confine itself within the limits of its history.

> **Benjamin N. Cardozo**, *The Nature of the Judicial Process* 51 (1921)

5 Upon this point a page of history is worth a volume of logic.

> **Oliver Wendell Holmes, Jr.**, *New York Trust Co. v. Eisner*, 256 U.S. 345, 349 (1921)

6 Not lightly vacated is the verdict of quiescent years.

> **Benjamin N. Cardozo**, *Coler v. Corn Exch. Bank*, 250 N.Y. 136, 141, 164 N.E. 882 (1928)

HOLMES, OLIVER WENDELL

1 The Great Dissenter.

> Epithet of Oliver Wendell Holmes, Jr.

2 No society has ever admitted that it could not sacrifice individual welfare to its own existence. If conscripts are necessary for its army, it seizes them, and marches them, with bayonets in their rear, to death. It runs highways and railroads through old family places in spite of the owner's protest, paying in this instance the market value, to be sure, because no civilized government sacrifices the citizen more than it can help, but still sacrificing his will and his welfare to that of the rest.

> **Oliver Wendell Holmes, Jr.**, *The Common Law* 43 (1881)

3 We pause to become conscious of our national life and to rejoice in it, to recall what our country has done for each of us, and to ask ourselves what we can do for our country in return.*

> **Oliver Wendell Holmes, Jr.**, Memorial Day Address, 30 May 1884, in *Speeches* 1, 2–3 (1913)

4 I think that, as life is action and passion, it is required of a man that he should share the passion and action of his time at peril of being judged not to have lived.

> **Oliver Wendell Holmes, Jr.**, Memorial Day Address, 30 May 1884, in *Speeches* 1, 3 (1913)

5 Through our great good fortune, in our youth our hearts were touched with fire.

> **Oliver Wendell Holmes, Jr.**, Memorial Day Address, 30 May 1884, in *Speeches* 1, 11 (1913)

6 No man has earned the right to intellectual ambition until he has learned to lay his

---

* And so, my fellow Americans: ask not what your country can do for you—ask what you can do for your country. —**John F. Kennedy**, Inaugural Address, 20 Jan. 1961, in *Public Papers of the Presidents: John F. Kennedy, 1961*, at 1, 2 (1962)

course by a star which he has never seen,— to dig by the divining rod for springs which he may never reach.

> **Oliver Wendell Holmes, Jr.,** "The Profession of the Law" (lecture to Harvard undergraduates), Cambridge, Mass., 17 Feb. 1886, in *Speeches* 22, 24 (1913)

7 Only when you have worked alone, . . . then only will you have achieved. Thus only can you gain the secret isolated joy of the thinker, who knows that, a hundred years after he is dead and forgotten, men who never heard of him will be moving to the measure of his thought,—the subtile rapture of a postponed power, which the world knows not because it has no external trappings, but which to his prophetic vision is more real than that which commands an army.

> **Oliver Wendell Holmes, Jr.,** "The Profession of the Law" (lecture to Harvard undergraduates), Cambridge, Mass., 17 Feb. 1886, in *Speeches* 22, 24–25 (1913)

8 In the midst of doubt, in the collapse of creeds, there is one thing I do not doubt . . . and that is that the faith is true and adorable which leads a soldier to throw away his life in obedience to a blindly accepted duty, in a cause which he little understands, in a plan of campaign of which he has no notion, under tactics of which he does not see the use.

> **Oliver Wendell Holmes, Jr.,** "The Soldier's Faith" (address to graduating class of Harvard University), Cambridge, Mass., 30 May 1895, in *Speeches* 56, 59 (1913)

9 The rule of joy and the law of duty seem to me all one. I confess that altruistic and cynically selfish talk seem to me about equally unreal. With all humility, I think "Whatsoever thy hand findeth to do, do it with thy might," infinitely more important than the vain attempt to love one's neighbor as one's self. If you want to hit a bird on the wing, you must have all your will in a focus, you must not be thinking about yourself, and equally, you must not be thinking about your neighbor; you must be living in your eye on that bird. Every achievement is a bird on the wing.

> **Oliver Wendell Holmes, Jr.,** Speech to Bar Association of Boston, 7 Mar. 1900, in *Collected Legal Papers* 244, 247 (1920)

10 Life is an end in itself, and the only question as to whether it is worth living is whether you have enough of it.

> **Oliver Wendell Holmes, Jr.,** Speech to Bar Association of Boston, 7 Mar. 1900, in *Collected Legal Papers* 244, 248 (1920)

11 A great man represents a great ganglion in the nerves of society, or, to vary the figure, a strategic point in the campaign of history, and part of his greatness consists in his being *there*.

> **Oliver Wendell Holmes, Jr.,** "John Marshall" (speech), Boston, 4 Feb. 1901, in *Collected Legal Papers* 266, 267–68 (1920)

12 It is said that as Justice Holmes was leaving the banquet hall after the farewell dinner tendered him by the Boston Bar, before he left for Washington to take his seat on the Bench of the Supreme Court of the United States, someone called out:

"Now justice will be administered in Washington."

To this the new justice is reported to have replied:

"Don't be too sure. I am going there to administer *the law*. "

> **Charles Henry Butler,** *A Century at the Bar of the Supreme Court of the United States* 50–51 (1942)

13 My intellectual furniture consists of an assortment of general propositions which grow fewer and more general as I grow older. I always say that the chief end of man is to frame them and that no general proposition is worth a damn.

> **Oliver Wendell Holmes, Jr.,** Letter to Frederick Pollock, 24 Sept. 1904, in *Holmes-Pollock Letters* 1:118 (Mark DeWolfe Howe ed. 1941)

14 I could carve out of a banana a Justice with more backbone than that.*

> **Theodore Roosevelt,** quoted in Silas Bent, *Justice Oliver Wendell Holmes* 251 (1932)

15 The great act of faith is when a man decides that he is not God.

> **Oliver Wendell Holmes, Jr.,** Letter to William James, 24 Mar. 1907, in Ralph

---

* [William] McKinley has no more backbone than a chocolate éclair! —**Theodore Roosevelt,** quoted in Harry T. Peck, *Twenty Years of the Republic* 642 (1906)

Barton Perry, *The Thought and Character of William James* 459 (1935)

16 Life is painting a picture, not doing a sum.

Oliver Wendell Holmes, Jr., "The Class of '61" (speech), Cambridge, Mass., 28 June 1911, in *Speeches* 95, 96 (1913)

17 The only prize much cared for by the powerful is power. The prize of the general is not a bigger tent, but command.

Oliver Wendell Holmes, Jr., "Law and the Court" (speech to Harvard Law School Association of New York), 15 Feb. 1913, in *Collected Legal Papers* 291, 293 (1920)

18 When twenty years ago a vague terror went over the earth and the word socialism began to be heard, I thought and still think that fear was translated into doctrines that had no proper place in the Constitution or the common law.

Oliver Wendell Holmes, Jr., "Law and the Court" (speech to Harvard Law School Association of New York), 15 Feb. 1913, in *Collected Legal Papers* 291, 295 (1920)

19 I do not pin my dreams for the future to my country or even to my race. I think it probable that civilization somehow will last as long as I care to look ahead—perhaps with smaller numbers, but perhaps also bred to greatness and splendor by science. I think it not improbable that man, like the grub that prepares a chamber for the winged thing it never has seen but is to be—that man may have cosmic destinies that he does not understand.

Oliver Wendell Holmes, Jr., "Law and the Court" (speech to Harvard Law School Association of New York), 15 Feb. 1913, in *Collected Legal Papers* 291, 296 (1920)

20 To rest upon a formula is a slumber that, prolonged, means death.

Oliver Wendell Holmes, Jr., "Ideals and Doubts," 10 *Illinois Law Review* 1, 3 (1915)

21 To have doubted one's own first principles is the mark of a civilized man.

Oliver Wendell Holmes, Jr., "Ideals and Doubts," 10 *Illinois Law Review* 1, 3 (1915)

22 The notion that with socialized property we should have women free and a piano for everybody seems to me an empty humbug.

Oliver Wendell Holmes, Jr., "Ideals and Doubts," 10 *Illinois Law Review* 1, 3 (1915)

23 The chief end of man is to frame general ideas—and . . . no general idea is worth a straw.

Oliver Wendell Holmes, Jr., Letter to Morris R. Cohen, 12 Apr. 1915, in Felix S. Cohen, "The Holmes-Cohen Correspondence," 9 *Journal of the History of Ideas* 7, 8 (1948)

24 I used to say, when I was young, that truth was the majority vote of that nation that could lick all others.

Oliver Wendell Holmes, Jr., "Natural Law," 32 *Harvard Law Review* 40, 40 (1918)

25 I always say, as you know, that if my fellow citizens want to go to Hell I will help them. It's my job.

Oliver Wendell Holmes, Jr., Letter to Harold J. Laski, 4 Mar. 1920, in *Holmes-Laski Letters* 1:249 (Mark DeWolfe Howe ed. 1953)

26 Your general line of thought I agree with, but your first proposition (as to this being the best possible world) strikes me as speculation *in vacuo*—what I call churning the void to make cheese. The only cosmic possibilities I know anything about are the actualities.

Oliver Wendell Holmes, Jr., Letter to John C. H. Wu, 26 July 1923, in *Justice Holmes to Doctor Wu* 14 (1947)

27 We have seen more than once that the public welfare may call upon the best citizens for their lives. It would be strange if it could not call upon those who already sap the strength of the State for these lesser sacrifices, often not felt to be such by those concerned, in order to prevent our being swamped with incompetence. It is better for all the world, if instead of waiting to execute degenerate offspring for crime, or to let them starve for their imbecility, society can prevent those who are manifestly unfit from continuing their kind. The principle that sustains compulsory vaccination is broad enough to cover cutting the Fallopian tubes. . . . Three generations of imbeciles are enough.

Oliver Wendell Holmes, Jr., *Buck v. Bell,* 274 U.S. 200, 207 (1927)

28 But if we are to yield to fashionable conventions, it seems to me that theatres are as much devoted to public use as anything well can be. We have not that respect for art that is one of the glories of France. But

to many people the superfluous is the necessary, and it seems to me that Government does not go beyond its sphere in attempting to make life livable for them.

Oliver Wendell Holmes, Jr., *Tyson v. Banton,* 273 U.S. 418, 447 (1927) (dissenting)

29 I have always thought that not place, or power or popularity makes the success that one desires, but a trembling hope that one has come near to an ideal.

Oliver Wendell Holmes, Jr., Letter to Benjamin N. Cardozo, 15 Dec. 1928, quoted in Benjamin N. Cardozo, "Mr. Justice Holmes," 44 *Harvard Law Review* 682, 691 (1931)

30 [At the age of eighty-seven, viewing a beautiful woman:] Oh, to be sixty again!*

Oliver Wendell Holmes, Jr., quoted in *The American Treasury* 783 (Clifton Fadiman ed. 1955)

31 Style is thus a form of honor and courage, just as, Santayana tells us, is the pursuit of truth always. One can not read these opinions without seeing honor and courage written down on every page.

Benjamin N. Cardozo, "Mr. Justice Holmes," 44 *Harvard Law Review* 682, 690 (1931)

32 To quote from Mr. Justice Holmes' opinions is to string pearls.

Felix Frankfurter, "Mr. Justice Holmes and the Constitution: A Review of His Twenty-five Years on the Supreme Court," in *Mr. Justice Holmes* 46, 85 (Felix Frankfurter ed. 1931)

33 Serenely dwelling above the sound of passing shibboleths, Mr. Justice Holmes has steadfastly refused to hearken to the murmur of the moment. . . . He has built himself into the structure of our national life. He has written himself into the slender volume of the literature of all time.

Felix Frankfurter, "Mr. Justice Holmes and the Costitution: A Review of His Twenty-five Years on the Supreme Court," in *Mr. Justice Holmes* 46, 118 (Felix Frankfurter ed. 1931)

34 The riders in a race do not stop short when they reach the goal. There is a little finishing canter before coming to a standstill. There is time to hear the kind voice of friends and to say to one's self: "The work is done."

But just as one says that, the answer comes: "The race is over, but the work never is done while the power to work remains."

The canter that brings you to a standstill need not be only coming to rest. It cannot be, while you still live. For to live is to function. That is all there is in living.

And so I end with a line from a Latin poet who uttered the message more than fifteen hundred years ago:

"Death plucks my ears and says, Live—I am coming."

Oliver Wendell Holmes, Jr., Radio address on his 90th birthday, 8 Mar. 1931, in *New York Times,* 9 Mar. 1931, at 1

35 [Explaining why he wrote opinions while standing:] Nothing conduces to brevity like a caving in of the knees.

Oliver Wendell Holmes, Jr., attributed in Catherine Drinker Bowen, *Yankee from Olympus* 324 (1944)

36 The former secretaries, who adore the Justice, delight in such stories. One of them objected to the phrasing of a certain opinion, maintaining that the shading given to one word meant that "there isn't more than one man in a thousand who will understand it."

"I write for that man," the Justice retorted.

Oliver Wendell Holmes, Jr., reported in Silas Bent, *Justice Oliver Wendell Holmes* 306 (1932)

37 Remember what Justice Holmes said about "justice." I don't know what you think about him, but on the whole he was to me the master craftsman certainly of our time; and he said: "I hate justice," which he didn't quite mean. What he did mean was this. I remember once I was with him; it was a Saturday when the Court was to confer. It was before we had a motorcar, and we jogged along in an old coupé. When we got down to the Capitol, I wanted to provoke a response, so as he walked off, I said to him: "Well, sir, goodbye. Do justice!" He

* Fontenelle . . . said, you remember, to the damsel of eighteen, "Ah, Madam, would that I were eighty once more." —Harold J. Laski, Letter to Oliver Wendell Holmes, Jr., 1 Apr. 1921, in *Holmes-Laski Letters* 1:324 (Mark DeWolfe Howe ed. 1953)

turned quite sharply and he said: "Come here. Come here." I answered: "Oh, I know, I know." He replied: "That is not my job. My job is to play the game according to the rules."

> **Oliver Wendell Holmes, Jr.,** reported in Learned Hand, *The Spirit of Liberty* 306-07 (Irving Dilliard ed., 3d ed. 1960)

38 Life seems to me like a Japanese picture which our imagination does not allow to end with the margin. We aim at the infinite and when our arrow falls to earth it is in flames.

> **Oliver Wendell Holmes, Jr.,** Letter to Federal Bar Association, 29 Feb. 1932, in 1 *Federal Bar Association Journal* 35 (1932)

39 All the rest . . . I give, devise and bequeath to the United States of America.

> **Oliver Wendell Holmes, Jr.,** Will, quoted in *Literary Digest*, 16 Mar. 1935, at 6

40 This is in no sense a memorial volume. It is rather an attempt to select and gather the best of Holmes's writings in every form . . . to give a rounded portrait of the mind and faith of one who was perhaps the most complete personality in the history of American thought.

> **Max Lerner,** *The Mind and Faith of Justice Holmes* vii (1943)

41 There have been, and still are, those who believe that words will be privileged, even though they satisfy the definition, if the unlawful conduct they seek to induce is to be after a substantial interval. That is the doctrine of "clear and present danger." The only ground for this exception that I have ever heard is that during the interval between the provocation and its realization correctives may arise, and that it is better to accept the risk that they may not be sufficient than to suppress what, however guilty in itself, may prove innocuous. I confess that I cannot understand why it should not be adequate protection of the speaker's privilege if he were allowed to show that the interval made it reasonably certain that the provocation would not be realized. It is always a difficult matter to forecast what will be the effect of such a pause, and by hypothesis the words proceed from an un-

lawful purpose and do not therefore fall within any interest that the amendment is designed to protect. I doubt that the doctrine will persist, and I cannot help thinking that for once Homer nodded.

> **Learned Hand,** *The Bill of Rights* 58–59 (1958)

HOMICIDE

See MURDER

HONESTY

See ETHICS; LAWYER JOKES; LAWYERS (PRO); LAWYERS (CON); WITNESSES

HUMAN RIGHTS

See also CIVIL RIGHTS

1 We yet like to believe that wherever the Federal courts sit, human rights under the Federal Constitution are always a proper subject for adjudication.

> **Alfred P. Murrah,** *Stapleton v. Mitchell*, 60 F. Supp. 51, 55 (D. Kan. 1945)

2 Human rights is the soul of our foreign policy . . . because human rights is the soul of our sense of nationhood.

> **Jimmy Carter,** "Universal Declaration of Human Rights" (speech), Washington, D.C., 6 Dec. 1978, in *Public Papers of the Presidents: Jimmy Carter, 1978*, at 2161, 2164 (1979)

3 America did not invent human rights. In a very real sense it's the other way around. Human rights invented America.

> **Jimmy Carter,** Farewell Address, 14 Jan. 1981, in *Public Papers of the Presidents: Jimmy Carter, 1980–81*, at 2889, 2892

HUMOR

See LAWYER JOKES

HUSBAND

See MARRIAGE

ILLEGALITY

See also CRIME; LAWLESSNESS

1 Oh, Mr. President, do not let so great an achievement suffer from any taint of legality.*

Philander C. Knox, 1903, quoted in Tyler Dennett, *John Hay: From Poetry to Politics* 381 (1933)

2 [W. C. Fields:] According to you, everything I like to do is either illegal, immoral or fattening.

Walter DeLeon and Harry Ruskin, *Six of a Kind* (screenplay), 1934, quoted in *The Quotations of W. C. Fields* 154 (Martin Lewis ed. 1976)

3 All the things I really like to do are either immoral, illegal, or fattening.

Alexander Woollcott, quoted in *The Algonquin Wits* 145 (Robert E. Drennan ed. 1968)

4 The illegal we do immediately. The unconstitutional takes a little longer.†

Henry Kissinger, quoted in Morris K. Udall, *Too Funny to Be President* 173 (1988)

5 I never threw an illegal pitch. The trouble is, once in a while I toss one that ain't never been seen by this generation.

Leroy Robert (Satchel) Paige, quoted in *Washington Post,* 10 June 1982, at A16

6 Nothing is illegal if one hundred well-placed businessmen decide to do it.

Andrew Young, quoted in Morris K. Udall, *Too Funny to be President* 223 (1988)

IMMIGRATION

1 *Hannah Bainbridge* [played by Almira Sessions]: My ancestors came on the Mayflower. *Fay Lawrence* [played by Mae West]: You're lucky. Now they have immigration laws.

Fitzroy Davis, George S. George, and Fred Schiller, *The Heat's On* (screenplay), 1943, quoted in Harry Haun, *Movie Quote Book* 202-03 (1980)

2 American citizenship is not a right granted on a condition subsequent that the naturalized citizen refrain in the future from uttering any remark or adopting an attitude favorable to his original homeland or those there in power, no matter how distasteful such conduct may be to most of us. He is not required to imprison himself in an intellectual or spiritual strait-jacket; nor is he obliged to retain a static mental attitude. Moreover, he does not lose the precious right of citizenship because he subsequently dares to criticize his adopted government in vituperative or defamatory terms.

Frank Murphy, *Baumgartner v. United States,* 322 U.S. 665, 679 (1944) (separate opinion)

3 I have never discovered that disregard of the Nation's liquor taxes excluded a citizen from our best society and I see no reason why it should banish an alien from our worst.

Robert H. Jackson, *Jordan v. DeGeorge,* 341 U.S. 223, 241 (1951) (dissenting)

4 It is inconceivable to me that this measure of simple justice and fair dealing [hearing and notice before exclusion of an alien] would menace the security of this country. No one can make me believe that we are that far gone.

Robert H. Jackson, *Shaughnessy v. United States,* 345 U.S. 206, 228 (1953) (dissenting)

5 Citizenship *is* man's basic right for it is nothing less than the right to have rights. Remove this priceless possession and there remains a stateless person, disgraced and degraded in the eyes of his countrymen. He has no lawful claim to protection from any nation, and no nation may assert rights on his behalf. His very existence is at the sufferance of the state within whose borders he happens to be. In this country the expatriate would presumably enjoy, at most, only the limited rights and privileges of aliens, and like the alien he might even be subject to deportation and thereby deprived of the right to assert any rights. This government was not established with power to decree this fate.

Earl Warren, *Perez v. Brownell,* 356 U.S. 44, 64–65 (1958) (dissenting)

6 It was prior to this New York trip that Harding originated a quip which at least two well known television entertainers have

---

* This was Knox's reply, as Attorney General, to Theodore Roosevelt's request for a legal justification of his acquisition of the Panama Canal Zone.
† Kissinger was National Security Advisor and Secretary of State in the corrupt Nixon Administration.

since regaled as their own. Before he could go to New York he had to get a U.S. visa at the American consulate in Toronto. He was called upon to fill in a long form with many questions, including "Is it your intention to overthrow the Government of the United States by force?" By the time Harding got to that one he was so irritated that he answered: "Sole purpose of visit."

> **Gilbert Harding,** reported in Wallace Reyburn, *Gilbert Harding* 4 (1978)

7 The classification at issue deprives a group of children of the opportunity for education afforded all other children simply because they have been assigned a legal status due to a violation of law by their parents. These children thus have been singled out for a lifelong penalty and stigma. A legislative classification that threatens the creation of an underclass of future citizens and residents cannot be reconciled with one of the fundamental purposes of the Fourteenth Amendment.

> **Lewis F. Powell, Jr.,** *Plyler v. Doe,* 457 U.S. 202, 238–39 (1982)

IMPEACHMENT

See also PRESIDENT

1 Experience has already shown that the impeachment the Constitution has provided is not even a scarecrow.

> **Thomas Jefferson,** Letter to Spencer Roane, 6 Sept. 1819, in *Writings of Thomas Jefferson* 10:141 (Paul L. Ford ed. 1899)

2 Having found, from experience, that impeachment is an impracticable thing, a mere scare-crow, they [the judiciary] consider themselves secure for life.

> **Thomas Jefferson,** Letter to Thomas Ritchie, 25 Dec. 1820, in *Writings of Thomas Jefferson* 10:170–71 (Paul L. Ford ed. 1899)

3 In the general government in this instance, we have gone even beyond the English caution, by requiring a vote of two thirds in one of the Houses for removing a judge; a vote so impossible where any defence is made, before men of ordinary prejudices and passions, that our judges are effectually independent of the nation. But this ought not to be.

> **Thomas Jefferson,** *Autobiography,* 1821, in *Writings of Thomas Jefferson* 1:112 (Paul L. Ford ed. 1892)

4 An impeachable offense is whatever a majority of the House of Representatives considers [it] to be at a given moment in history.

> **Gerald R. Ford,** Remarks in House of Representatives on proposed impeachment of Justice William O. Douglas, 15 Apr. 1970, in 116 *Congressional Record* 11913 (1970)

5 Whether ours shall continue to be a Government of laws and not of men is now for Congress and ultimately the American people [to decide].*

> **Archibald Cox,** Statement, 20 Oct. 1973, quoted in *New York Times,* 21 Oct. 1973, at 60
> See also OBEDIENCE TO LAW 2

6 In his conduct of the office of President of the United States, Richard M. Nixon, in violation of his constitutional oath faithfully to execute the office of President of the United States and, to the best of his ability, preserve, protect, and defend the Constitution of the United States, and in violation of his constitutional duty to take care that the laws be faithfully executed, has prevented, obstructed, and impeded the administration of justice, in that: . . . [lists elements of Watergate "coverup"] . . .

In all of this, Richard M. Nixon has acted in a manner contrary to his trust as President and subversive of constitutional government, to the great prejudice of the cause of law and justice and to the manifest injury of the people of the United States.

Wherefore Richard M. Nixon, by such conduct, warrants impeachment and trial, and removal from office.

> Article I of Impeachment against President Nixon, 1974, in H.R. Rep. No. 1305, 93d Cong., 2d Sess. 1–3 (1974)

7 Using the powers of the office of President of the United States, Richard M. Nixon, in violation of his constitutional oath faithfully to execute the office of President of the United States and, to the best of his ability, preserve, protect, and defend the Constitution of the United States, and in disregard of his constitutional duty to take care that the laws be faithfully executed, has repeatedly engaged in conduct violat-

---

* Cox had just been dismissed by President Richard M. Nixon because he refused to drop his lawsuit to obtain Watergate-related White House tapes.

ing the constitutional rights of citizens, impairing the due and proper administration of justice and the conduct of lawful inquiries, or contravening the laws governing agencies of the executive branch and the purposes of these agencies.

Article II of Impeachment against President Nixon, 1974, in H.R. Rep. No. 1305, 93d Cong., 2d Sess. 3 (1974)

8 In his conduct of the office of President of the United States, Richard M. Nixon, contrary to his oath faithfully to execute the office of President of the United States and, to the best of his ability, preserve, protect, and defend the Constitution of the United States, and in violation of his constitutional duty to take care that the laws be faithfully executed, has failed without lawful cause or excuse to produce papers and things as directed by duly authorized subpoenas issued by the Committee on the Judiciary of the House of Representatives on April 11, 1974, May 15, 1974, May 30, 1974, and June 24, 1974, and willfully disobeyed such subpoenas.

Article III of Impeachment against President Nixon, 1974, in H.R. Rep. No. 1305, 93d Cong., 2d Sess. 4 (1974)

9 In his conduct of the office of President of the United States, Richard M. Nixon, in violation of his constitutional oath faithfully to execute the office of President of the United States and, to the best of his ability, preserve, protect, and defend the Constitution of the United States, and in disregard of his constitutional duty to take care that the laws be faithfully executed, on and subsequent to March 17, 1969, authorized, ordered, and ratified the concealment from the Congress of the facts and the submission to the Congress of false and misleading statements concerning the existence, scope and nature of American bombing operations in Cambodia in derogation of the power of the Congress to declare war, to make appropriations and to raise and support armies, and by such conduct warrants impeachment and trial and removal from office.

Proposed Article of Impeachment against President Nixon, 1974, in H.R. Rep. No. 1305, 93d Cong., 2d Sess. 217 (1974)

10 In his conduct of the office of President of the United States, Richard M. Nixon, in vi-

olation of his constitutional oath faithfully to execute the office of the President of the United States, and, to the best of his ability, preserve, protect, and defend the Constitution of the United States, and in violation of his constitutional duty to take care that the laws be faithfully executed, did receive emoluments from the United States in excess of the compensation provided by law pursuant to Article II, Section 1, of the Constitution, and did willfully attempt to evade the payment of a portion of Federal income taxes due and owing by him for the years 1969, 1970, 1971, and 1972.

Proposed Article of Impeachment against President Nixon, 1974, in H.R. Rep. No. 1305, 93d Cong., 2d Sess. 220 (1974)

IMPRISONMENT

See PRISON

INCOME TAX

See TAXATION

INDIANS

See AMERICAN INDIAN LAW

INFANTS

See CHILDREN

INFRINGEMENT

See COPYRIGHT; PATENTS; TRADEMARKS

INJUNCTIONS

1 I care not who makes th' laws iv a nation iv I can get out an injunction.

Finley Peter Dunne, "Casual Observations," in *Mr. Dooley's Philosophy* 251, 253 (1906)

2 There is need to keep in mind steadily the limits of inquiry proper to the case before us. We are not framing a decree. We are asking ourselves whether anything has happened that will justify us now in changing a decree. The injunction, whether right or wrong, is not subject to impeachment in its application to the conditions that existed at its making. We are not at liberty to reverse under the guise of readjusting. . . .

189

The inquiry for us is whether the changes are so important that dangers, once substantial, have become attenuated to a shadow.... Nothing less than a clear showing of grievous wrong evoked by new and unforeseen conditions should lead us to change what was decreed after years of litigation with the consent of all concerned.

> **Benjamin N. Cardozo,** *United States v. Swift & Co.,* 286 U.S. 106, 119 (1932)

3 To disarm the court [of power to enjoin] it must appear that there is no reasonable expectation that the wrong will be repeated.

> **Learned Hand,** *United States v. Aluminum Co. of Am.,* 148 F.2d 416, 448 (2d Cir. 1945)

4 To justify a temporary injunction it is not necessary that the plaintiff's right to a final decision, after a trial, be absolutely certain, wholly without doubt; if the other elements are present (i.e., the balance of hardships tips decidedly toward plaintiff), it will ordinarily be enough that the plaintiff has raised questions going to the merits so serious, substantial, difficult and doubtful, as to make them a fair ground for deliberative investigation.

> **Jerome N. Frank,** *Hamilton Watch Co. v. Benrus Watch Co.,* 206 F.2d 738, 740 (2d Cir. 1953)

INJUSTICE

See also JUSTICE

1 Law never made men a whit more just; and, by means of their respect for it, even the well-disposed are daily made the agents of injustice.

> **Henry David Thoreau,** *Civil Disobedience,* 1849, in *Writings of Henry David Thoreau* 4:356, 358 (1906)

2 If the injustice is part of the necessary friction of the machine of government, let it go, let it go: perchance it will wear smooth,— certainly the machine will wear out. If the injustice has a spring, or a pulley, or a rope, or a crank, exclusively for itself, then perhaps you may consider whether the remedy will not be worse than the evil; but if it is of such a nature that it requires you to be the agent of injustice to another, then, I

say, break the law. Let your life be a counter-friction to stop the machine.

> **Henry David Thoreau,** *Civil Disobedience,* 1849, in *Writings of Henry David Thoreau* 4:356, 368 (1906)

3 The sense of injustice revolts against whatever is unequal by caprice.

> **Edmond N. Cahn,** *The Sense of Injustice* 14 (1949)

4 Injustice anywhere is a threat to justice everywhere. We are caught in an inescapable network of mutuality, tied in a single garment of destiny. Whatever affects one directly, affects all indirectly.

> **Martin Luther King, Jr.,** "Letter from Birmingham Jail," 16 Apr. 1963, in *Why We Can't Wait* 77, 79 (1964)

INNOCENCE

See also GUILT

1 How can we adjudge to summary and shameful death a fellow creature innocent before God, and whom we feel to be so?— Does that state it aright? You sign sad assent. Well, I too feel that, the full force of that. It is Nature. But do these buttons that we wear attest that our allegiance is to Nature? No, to the King.

> **Herman Melville,** *Billy Budd, Sailor* 110 (Harrison Hayford & Merton M. Sealts, Jr. eds. 1962) (1924)

2 INNOCENCE, *n.* The state or condition of a criminal whose counsel has fixed the jury.
"My client, gentlemen," the lawyer cried,
"Is innocent as any babe unborn—
As spotless as the snows upon the side
Of giant Blanc or skyward Matterhorn.

"What! *he* steal hogs—this honorable youth?
A thought so monstrous makes the angels weep!
When that vile felony was wrought, in truth,
My client was in jail for stealing sheep."

> **Ambrose Bierce,** *The Enlarged Devil's Dictionary* 158–59 (Ernest J. Hopkins ed. 1967)

3 In England a man is presoomed to be innocent till he's proved guilty an' they take

it f'r granted he's guilty. In this counthry a man is presoomed to be guilty ontil he's proved guilty an' afther that he's presoomed to be innocent.

Finley Peter Dunne, "On Criminal Trials," in *On Making a Will* 212, 212 (1919)

4 Honoring the presumption of innocence is often difficult; sometimes we must pay substantial social costs as a result of our commitment to the values we espouse. But at the end of the day the presumption of innocence protects the innocent; the shortcuts we take with those whom we believe to be guilty injure only those wrongfully accused and, ultimately, ourselves.

Thurgood Marshall, *United States v. Salerno*, 481 U.S. 739, 767 (1987) (dissenting)

INSANITY

1 If then it is proved, to the satisfaction of the jury, that the mind of the accused was in a diseased and unsound state, the question will be, whether the disease existed to so high a degree, that for the time being it overwhelmed the reason, conscience, and judgment, and whether the prisoner, in committing the homicide, acted from an irresistible and uncontrollable impulse: If so, then the act was not the act of a voluntary agent, but the involuntary act of the body, without the concurrence of a mind directing it.

Lemuel Shaw, *Commonwealth v. Rogers*, 49 Mass. (8 Met.) 500, 502 (1845)

2 Charles O'Neil was, it seems, temporarily insane when he threw his wife off the balcony, and broke her precious neck. Charles O'Neil, would that we had but had the sentencing of thee—there would have been another neck broken. We yearn for a law making temporary insanity a capital offense.

Ambrose Bierce, "Make It a Capital Offense," *News Letter*, 26 Dec. 1868, in *The Ambrose Bierce Satanic Reader* 59 (Ernest J. Hopkins ed. 1968)

3 Heaven knows insanity was disreputable enough, long ago; but now that the lawyers have got to cutting every gallows rope and picking every prison lock with it, it is become a sneaking villainy that ought to hang and keep on hanging its sudden possessors until evil-doers should conclude that the

safest plan was to never claim to have it until they came by it legitimately. The very calibre of the people the lawyers most frequently try to save by the insanity subterfuge, ought to laugh the plea out of the courts, one would think.

Mark Twain, "Unburlesquable Things," *Galaxy Magazine*, July 1870, at 137

4 In view of these considerations, we are led to the conclusion that the instruction given to the jury in this case, that "If the defendant killed his wife in a manner that would be criminal and unlawful if the defendant were sane, the verdict should be 'not guilty by reason of insanity,' if the killing was the offspring or product of mental disease in the defendant," was right.

William S. Ladd, *State v. Jones*, 50 N.H. 369, 398 (1871)

5 To the Late Cain, This Book is Dedicated, Not on account of respect for his memory, for it merits little respect; not on account of sympathy with him, for his bloody deed placed him without the pale of sympathy, strictly speaking; but out of a mere human commiseration for him in that it was his misfortune to live in a dark age that knew not the beneficent Insanity Plea.

Mark Twain, Deleted dedication of *Roughing It*, in Letter to Elisha Bliss, 15 May 1871, in *Selected Letters of Mark Twain* 73 (Charles Neider ed. 1982)

6 We have an insanity plea that would have saved Cain.

Mark Twain, "Americans and the English" (speech), London, 4 July 1872, in *Writings of Mark Twain* 28:34, 35 (Albert B. Paine ed. 1929)

7 By the argument of counsel it was shown that at half-past ten in the morning on the day of the murder, . . . [the defendant] became insane, and remained so for eleven hours and a half exactly.

Mark Twain, "A New Crime," *Sketches New and Old*, 1875, in *Writings of Mark Twain* 7:220, 220–21 (1929)

8 One of these men [Baldwin murdered] he had notoriously been threatening to kill for twelve years. The poor creature happened, by the merest piece of ill fortune, to come along a dark alley at the very moment . . .

[the defendant's] insanity came upon him, and so he was shot in the back.

> Mark Twain, "A New Crime," *Sketches New and Old*, 1875, in *Writings of Mark Twain* 7:220, 221 (1929)

9 Insanity certainly is on the increase in the world, and crime is dying out. There are no longer any murders—Formerly, if you killed a man, it was possible that you were insane—but now, if you, having friends and money, kill a man, it is *evidence* that you are a lunatic. . . . what we want now, is not laws against crime, but a law against *insanity*.

> Mark Twain, "A New Crime," *Sketches New and Old*, 1875, in *Writings of Mark Twain* 7:220, 225–26 (1929)

10 There must exist either one of two conditions: (1) Such mental defect as to render the defendant unable to distinguish between right [and] wrong in relation to the particular act; or (2), the overmastering of defendant's will in consequence of the insane delusion under the influence of which he acts, produced by disease of the mind or brain.

> H. M. Somerville, *Parsons v. State*, 81 Ala. 577, 596 (1886)

11 I have scant sympathy with the plea of insanity advanced to save a man from the consequences of crime, when unless that crime had been committed it would have been impossible to persuade any responsible authority to commit him to an asylum as insane.

> Theodore Roosevelt, Letter replying to petition for pardon, 8 Aug. 1904, in *Works of Theodore Roosevelt* 22:425 (Hermann Hagedorn ed. 1925)

12 SANITY, *n*. A state of mind which immediately precedes and follows murder.

> Ambrose Bierce, *The Enlarged Devil's Dictionary* 257 (Ernest J. Hopkins ed. 1967)

13 An accused is not criminally responsible if his unlawful act was the product of mental disease or mental defect.

> David L. Bazelon, *Durham v. United States*, 214 F.2d 862, 874–75 (D.C. Cir. 1954)

14 The legal and moral traditions of the western world require that those who, of their own free will and with evil intent . . . commit acts which violate the law, shall be criminally responsible for those acts. Our traditions also require that where such acts stem from and are the product of a mental disease or defect . . . moral blame shall not attach, and hence there will not be criminal responsibility.

> David L. Bazelon, *Durham v. United States*, 214 F.2d 862, 876 (D.C. Cir. 1954)

15 Upon consideration of the entire record we agree with the Solicitor General that "the record in this case does not sufficiently support the findings of competency to stand trial," for to support those findings under 18 U.S.C. section 4244 the district judge "would need more information than this record presents." We also agree with the suggestion of the Solicitor General that it is not enough for the district judge to find that "the defendant [is] oriented to time and place and [has] some recollection of events," but that the "test must be whether he has sufficient present ability to consult with his lawyer with a reasonable degree of rational understanding—and whether he has a rational as well as factual understanding of the proceedings against him.

> *Dusky v. United States*, 362 U.S. 402, 402 (1960) (per curiam)

INTENT

See also LEGISLATIVE INTENT; ORIGINAL INTENTION

1 The intention of the law-giver is the law.

> Abraham Lincoln, First Inaugural Address, 4 Mar. 1861, in *Collected Works of Abraham Lincoln* 4:263 (Roy P. Basler ed. 1953)

2 Vengeance imports a feeling of blame, and an opinion, however distorted by passion, that a wrong has been done. It can hardly go very far beyond the case of a harm intentionally inflicted: even a dog distinguishes between being stumbled over and being kicked.

> Oliver Wendell Holmes, Jr., *The Common Law* 3 (1881)

3 If a man intentionally adopts certain conduct in certain circumstances known to him; and that conduct is forbidden by the law under those circumstances, he intentionally breaks the law in the only sense in which the law ever considers intent.

> Oliver Wendell Holmes, Jr., *Ellis v. United States*, 206 U.S. 246, 257 (1907)

4 The attempted distinction between accidental results and accidental means will plunge this branch of the law into a Serbonian Bog.

    Benjamin N. Cardozo, *Landress v. Phoenix Mut. Life Ins. Co.*, 291 U.S. 491, 499 (1934) (dissenting)

5 The contention that an injury can amount to a crime only when inflicted by intention is no provincial or transient notion. It is as universal and persistent in mature systems of law as belief in freedom of the human will and a consequent ability and duty of the normal individual to choose between good and evil. A relation between some mental element and punishment for a harmful act is almost as instinctive as the child's familiar exculpatory "But I didn't mean to," and has afforded the rational basis for a tardy and unfinished substitution of deterrence and reformation in place of retaliation and vengeance as the motivation for public prosecution. Unqualified acceptance of this doctrine by English common law in the Eighteenth Century was indicated by Blackstone's sweeping statement that to constitute any crime there must first be a "vicious will."

    Robert H. Jackson, *Morissette v. United States*, 342 U.S. 246, 250–51 (1952)

INTERNATIONAL LAW

See also HUMAN RIGHTS; TREATIES; WAR; WAR CRIMES

1 The jurisdiction of the nation within its own territory is necessarily exclusive and absolute. It is susceptible of no limitation not imposed by itself. Any restriction upon it, deriving validity from an external source, would imply a diminution of its sovereignty to the extent of the restriction, and an investment of that sovereignty to the same extent in that power which could impose such restriction.

    John Marshall, *The Schooner Exchange v. M'Faddon*, 11 U.S. (7 Cranch) 116, 136 (1812)

2 No principle of general law is more universally acknowledged, than the perfect equality of nations. Russia and Geneva have equal rights. It results from this equality, that no one can rightfully impose a rule on another. . . . As no nation can prescribe

a rule for others, none can make a law of nations.

    John Marshall, *The Antelope*, 23 U.S. (10 Wheat.) 66, 122 (1825)

3 The settled doctrine of the law of nations is, that a weaker power does not surrender its independence—its right to self government, by associating with a stronger, and taking its protection.

    John Marshall, *Worcester v. Georgia*, 31 U.S. (6 Pet.) 515, 560–61 (1832)

4 I am desirous that our two countries should trade with each other for the benefit both of Japan and the United States. We know that the ancient laws of Your Imperial Majesty's government do not allow of foreign trade except with the Dutch. But as the state of the world changes, and new governments are formed, it seems to be wise from time to time to make new laws. There was a time when the ancient laws of Your Imperial Majesty's government were first made. . . . If Your Imperial Majesty is not satisfied that it would be safe, altogether, to abrogate the ancient laws which forbid foreign trade, they might be suspended for five or ten years, so as to try the experiment. If it does not prove as beneficial as was hoped, the ancient laws can be restored.

    Millard Fillmore, Letter to Emperor of Japan, 13 Nov. 1852, in *The Japan Expedition 1852–1854*, at 220 (Roger Pineau ed. 1968)

5 We think that, by the universal comity of nations and the established rules of international law, the courts of one country are bound to abstain from sitting in judgment on the acts of another government done within its own territory.

    Jasper W. Gilbert, *Hatch v. Baez*, 14 N.Y. Sup. Ct. 596, 599 (1876)

6 "Comity," in the legal sense, is neither a matter of absolute obligation, on the one hand, nor of mere courtesy and goodwill, upon the other. But it is the recognition which one nation allows within its territory to the legislative, executive or judicial acts of another nation, having due regard both to international duty and convenience, and to the rights of its own citizens or of other

persons who are under the protection of its laws.

Horace Gray, *Hilton v. Guyot*, 159 U.S. 113, 163–64 (1895)

7 Where there has been opportunity for a full and fair trial abroad before a court of competent jurisdiction, conducting the trial upon regular proceedings, after due citation or voluntary appearance of the defendant, and under a system of jurisprudence likely to secure an impartial administration of justice between the citizens of its own country and those of other countries, and there is nothing to show either prejudice in the court, or in the system of laws under which it was sitting, or fraud in procuring the judgment, or any other special reason why the comity of this nation should not allow it full effect, the merits of the case should not, in an action brought in this country upon the judgment, be tried afresh, as on a new trial or an appeal, upon the mere assertion of the party that the judgment was erroneous in law or in fact.

Horace Gray, *Hilton v. Guyot*, 159 U.S. 113, 202–03 (1895)

8 Every sovereign State is bound to respect the independence of every other sovereign State, and the courts of one country will not sit in judgment on the acts of the government of another done within its own territory. Redress of grievances by reason of such acts must be obtained through the means open to be availed of by sovereign powers as between themselves.

Melville W. Fuller, *Underhill v. Hernandez*, 168 U.S. 250, 252 (1897)

9 Neither the sanctions of international law nor the justice of a cause can be depended upon for a fair settlement of differences, when they come into conflict with a strong political necessity on the one side opposed to comparative weakness on the other.

Alfred Thayer Mahan, *The Interest of America in Sea Power* 9 (1897)

10 International law is part of our law, and must be ascertained and administered by the courts of justice of appropriate jurisdiction, as often as questions of right depending upon it are duly presented for their determination. For this purpose, where there is no treaty, and no controlling executive or legislative act or judicial de-

cision, resort must be had to the customs and usages of civilized nations.

Horace Gray, *The Paquete Habana*, 175 U.S. 677, 700 (1900)

11 There is an indefinite and almost mysterious influence exercised by the general opinion of the world regarding the nation's character and conduct. The greatest and strongest governments recognize this influence and act with reference to it. They dread the moral isolation created by general adverse opinion and the unfriendly feeling that accompanies it, and they desire general approval and the kindly feeling that goes with it.

Elihu Root, Address, Washington, D.C., 24 Apr. 1908, in 2 *Proceedings of the American Society of International Law* 14, 19 (1908)

12 The whole fabric of municipal law, of law within each nation, rests ultimately upon the judge and the policeman; and the complete absence of the policeman, and the almost complete absence of the judge, in international affairs, prevents there being as yet any real homology between municipal and international law.

Theodore Roosevelt, *Autobiography*, 1913, in *Works of Theodore Roosevelt* 22:605 (Hermann Hagedorn ed. 1925)

13 ARBITRATION, *n*. A patent medicine for allaying international heat, designed to supersede the old-school treatment of bloodletting. It makes the unsuccessful party to the dispute hate two or more nations instead of one—to the unspeakable advantage of peace.

Ambrose Bierce, *The Enlarged Devil's Dictionary* 16 (Ernest J. Hopkins ed. 1967)

14 What we seek [in creating the League of Nations] is the reign of law, based upon the consent of the governed, and sustained by the organized opinion of mankind.

Woodrow Wilson, Speech, Mount Vernon, 4 July 1918, in *Wilson's Ideals* 96 (Saul K. Padover ed. 1942)

15 The current argument in favor of this or that scheme for the abolition of war is largely based upon the fact that men have long since abandoned the appeal to arms in their private disputes and submitted themselves to the jurisdiction of courts. Starting from this fact, it is contended that

disputes between nations should be settled in the same manner, and that the adoption of the reform would greatly promote the happiness of the world. Unluckily, the proponents of the argument overlook . . . the circumstance that the courts of justice now in existence do not actually dispense justice at all, but only law, . . . If they could ladle out actual justice it might be different, for justice sometimes contents even the loser; his finer feelings conquer his selfishness. But never law. The mildest man, when the law bites him, yells for its repeal; the average man denounces all its agents and catchpolls as scoundrels.

> **H. L. Mencken,** "The Dream of Peace," *The Smart Set,* Oct. 1919, at 82, 82–83

16 The Government of the United States merely adverts to a self-evident fact when it notes that the applicable precedents and recognized authorities on international law support its declaration that, under every rule of law and equity, no government is entitled to expropriate private property, for whatever purpose, without provision for prompt, adequate, and effective payment therefor.

> **Cordell Hull,** Note to Mexican Ambassador, 22 Aug. 1938, in 19 *Department of State Press Releases,* No. 465, 27 Aug. 1938, at 135, 140

17 By "genocide" we mean the destruction of a nation or of an ethnic group.*

> **Raphael Lemkin,** *Axis Rule in Occupied Europe* 79 (1944)

18 Both agreements would clearly have been unlawful, had they been made within the United States; and it follows from what we have just said that both were unlawful, though made abroad, if they were intended to affect imports and did affect them.

> **Learned Hand,** *United States v. Aluminum Co. of Am.,* 148 F.2d 416, 444 (2d Cir. 1945)

19 I am standing here with the degree of Doctor of Laws. That means that we live, in this country at least, in an age of law and an age of reason, an age in which we can get along with our neighbors.

Now we must do that internationally. It will be just as easy for nations to get along in a republic of the world as it is for us to get along in the republic of the United States.

Now, if Kansas and Colorado have a quarrel over a watershed they don't call out the National Guard of each State and go to war over it. They bring suit in the Supreme Court and abide by its decision. There isn't a reason in the world why we can't do that internationally.

> **Harry S. Truman,** Remarks upon receiving honorary degree, University of Kansas City, 28 June 1945, in *Public Papers of the Presidents: Harry S. Truman,* at 151 (1961)

20 Peace requires positive American leadership in a more effective United Nations, working toward the establishment of a worldwide system of law, enforced by worldwide sanctions of justice. In this age of jets and atoms, we can no longer put our faith in war as a method of settling international disputes. We can no longer tolerate a world which is like a frontier town, without a sheriff or a magistrate.

> **John F. Kennedy,** Campaign speech to Democratic Women's luncheon, New York, 14 Sept. 1960, quoted in Maxwell Meyersohn, *Memorable Quotations of John F. Kennedy* 126–27 (1965)

21 If a beach-head of cooperation may push back the jungle of suspicion, let both sides join in creating a new endeavor, not a new balance of power, but a new world of law, where the strong are just and the weak secure and the peace preserved. All this will not be finished in the first one hundred days. Nor will it be finished in the first one thousand days, nor in the life of this Administration, nor even perhaps in our lifetime on this planet. But let us begin.

> **John F. Kennedy,** Inaugural address, 20 Jan. 1961, in *Public Papers of the Presidents: John F. Kennedy, 1961,* at 1, 1 (1962)

22 Rather than laying down or reaffirming an inflexible and all-encompassing rule in this case, we decide only that the Judicial Branch will not examine the validity of a taking of property within its own territory by a foreign sovereign government, extant and recognized by this country at the time of suit, in the absence of a treaty or other unambiguous agreement regarding controlling legal principles, even if the com-

---

* Lemkin coined the word *genocide* in this book.

plaint alleges that the taking violates customary international law.

> **John M. Harlan** (1899–1971), *Banco Nacional de Cuba v. Sabbatino*, 376 U.S. 398, 428 (1964)

23 Almost all nations observe almost all principles of international law and almost all of their obligations almost all of the time.

> **Louis Henkin,** *How Nations Behave* 42 (1968)

24 We have before us the opportunity to forge for ourselves and for future generations a new world order—a world where the rule of law, not the law of the jungle, governs the conduct of nations.

> **George Bush,** Address to the Nation Announcing Allied Military Action in the Persian Gulf, 27 *Weekly Compilation of Presidential Documents* 50, 51 (Jan. 16, 1991)

25 What is at stake is more than one small country; it is a big idea: a new world order, where diverse nations are drawn together in common cause to achieve the universal aspirations of mankind—peace and security, freedom and the rule of law.

> **George Bush,** State of the Union Address, 27 *Weekly Compilation of Presidential Documents* 90, 90 (Jan. 29, 1991)

INTERPRETATION

See also CONSTITUTIONAL LAW; ORIGINAL INTENTION; STATUTORY CONSTRUCTION

1 As courts become increasingly sure of themselves, interpretation more and more involves an imaginative projection of the expressed purpose upon situations arising later, for which the parties did not provide and which they did not have in mind. Out of the rivers of ink that have been spilled upon that subject I know nothing that has emerged which enlightens us beyond the caution that departure from the text—necessary as it is—must always be made with circumspection.

> **Learned Hand,** *Jackson & Co. v. Royal Norwegian Gov't,* 177 F.2d 694, 702 (2d Cir. 1949) (dissenting)

2 There are as many plausible readings of the United States Constitution as there are versions of *Hamlet,* even though each interpreter, like each director, might genuinely believe that he or she has stumbled onto the one best answer to the conundrums of the texts.

> **Sanford Levinson,** "Law as Literature," 60 *Texas Law Review* 373, 391 (1982)

3 Legal interpretation takes place in a field of pain and death. This is true in several senses. Legal interpretive acts signal and occasion the imposition of violence upon others: A judge articulates her understanding of a text, and as a result, somebody loses his freedom, his property, his children, even his life. Interpretations in law also constitute justifications for violence which has already occurred or which is about to occur. When interpreters have finished their work, they frequently leave behind victims whose lives have been torn apart by these organized, social practices of violence. Neither legal interpretation nor the violence it occasions may be properly understood apart from one another.

> **Robert M. Cover,** "Violence and the Word," 95 *Yale Law Journal* 1601, 1601 (1986)

4 Like veteran police officers who cannot find innocence in their crime-filled world, lawyers almost never see meaning as simple or clear. It is something to be argued about and, ultimately, may seem to be no more than the momentary outcome of argumentation. In short, legal thinking builds upon and accentuates contemporary tendencies toward relativism and solipsism. Oddly, then, those most entrusted with the meaning of our fundamental document are by training, role, and instinct inclined to think that it is difficult to discover meaning.

> **Robert F. Nagel,** *Constitutional Cultures* 8 (1989)

INTERSTATE COMMERCE

See COMMERCE CLAUSE

INTOXICATION

1 Prohibition only drives drunkenness behind doors.

> **Mark Twain,** Letter for *Alta California,* 28 May 1867, in *Mark Twain's Travels with Mr. Brown* 238, 248 (Franklin Walker & G. Ezra Dane eds. 1940)

2 It is extremely difficult to draw the line on a "drunk." There are various stages such as "quarter dunk [*sic*], half drunk, and dead drunk;" there are the stages of being vivacious, foxy, tipsy, and on a "high lonesome," and it is about as difficult to determine when a young lady gets to be an old maid as it is to tell when a man has taken enough alcoholic stimulant to pass the line between a "jolly sober" and a "gentlemanly drunk."

> **A. J. Harper,** *Ex parte Townsend*, 64 Tex. Crim. 350, 356–57, 144 S.W. 628 (1911)

3 There is in all men a demand for the superlative, so much so that the poor devil who has no other way of reaching it attains it by getting drunk.

> **Oliver Wendell Holmes, Jr.,** "Natural Law," 32 *Harvard Law Review* 40, 40 (1918)

4 I cannot for a moment believe that apart from the Eighteenth Amendment special constitutional principles exist against strong drink. The fathers of the Constitution so far as I know approved it.

> **Oliver Wendell Holmes, Jr.,** *Knickerbocker Ice Co. v. Stewart*, 253 U.S. 149, 169 (1920) (dissenting)

5 Our country has deliberately undertaken a great social and economic experiment, noble in motive and far-reaching in purpose.*

> **Herbert C. Hoover,** Letter to William E. Borah, 23 Feb. 1928, in Claudius O. Johnson, *Borah of Idaho* 420 (1936)

6 The appellant's theory seems to have been that [a] stranger had in some way found a mysteriously hidden receptacle in the upholstering of his car and played him the mean trick of filling it with whiskey. Like a cuckoo bird, this unfeathered follower of Bacchus surreptitiously slipped a whole settin' of eggs into appellant's nest, after which he was apparently swallowed up by space, leaving his troublesome brood to be hatched by another. We believe in Santa Claus all right, but we confess the increasingly frequent appearance of this same stranger in whiskey cases inclines us to relegate him to the mythical realm of Dido and Aeneas. This ubiquitous disciple of John Barleycorn seems to have a peculiar habit of hovering around places just prior to their raid and search by officers, and then as mysteriously evaporating as the mists of an April morning.

> **Albert B. Martin,** *Epple v. State*, 112 Tex. Crim. 612, 613–14, 18 S.W.2d 625 (1929)

7 Although I was brought up to believe that Scotch whisky would need a tax preference to survive in competition with Kentucky bourbon, I never understood the Constitution to require a State to give such preference. (My dissenting Brother asks me to say that this statement does not necessarily represent his views on the respective merits of Scotch and bourbon.)

> **Hugo L. Black,** *Department of Revenue v. James B. Beam Distilling Co.*, 377 U.S. 341, 348–49 (1964) (dissenting)

INVENTION

See PATENTS

JAIL

See PRISON

JOKES

See LAWYER JOKES

JUDGES

See also COURTS; HOLMES, OLIVER WENDELL; JUDGES, INDIVIDUAL; JUDICIARY; MARSHALL, JOHN; SUPREME COURT

1 It is essential to the preservation of the rights of every individual, his life, liberty, property, and character, that there be an impartial interpretation of the laws, and administration of justice. It is the right of every citizen to be tried by judges as free, impartial, and independent as the lot of humanity will admit.

> Massachusetts Constitution of 1780, pt. 1, art. 29, in *Federal and State Constitutions* 3:1888, 1893 (Francis N. Thorpe ed. 1909)

2 In truth, it is better to toss up cross and pile in a cause, than to refer it to a judge whose mind is warped by any motive whatever, in that particular case. But the com-

---

* Hoover referred to the prohibition of liquor, thereafter known as "the noble experiment."

mon sense of twelve honest men gives still a better chance of just decision, than the hazard of cross and pile.

> **Thomas Jefferson,** *Notes on Virginia,* 1782, in *Writings of Thomas Jefferson* 3:236 (Paul L. Ford ed. 1894)

3 We all know that permanent judges acquire an Esprit de corps, that being known they are liable to be tempted by bribery, that they are misled by favor, by relationship, by a spirit of party, by a devotion to the Executive or Legislative; that it is better to leave a cause to the decision of cross and pile, than to that of a judge biassed to one side.

> **Thomas Jefferson,** Letter to L'Abbé Arnoux, 19 July 1789, in *Papers of Thomas Jefferson* 15:283 (Julian P. Boyd ed. 1958)

4 Yet knowing that religion does not furnish grosser bigots than law, I expect little from old judges. Those now at the bar may be bold enough to follow reason rather than precedent, and may bring that principle on the bench when promoted to it; but I fear this effort is not for my day.

> **Thomas Jefferson,** Letter to Thomas Cooper, 6 Aug. 1810, in *Writings of Thomas Jefferson* 5:532 (H. A. Washington ed. 1853)

5 "Talk not to me of law, Marmaduke Temple," [said] the hunter. "Did the beast of the forest mind your laws, when it was thirsty and hungering for the blood of your own child! . . .
"My private feelings must not enter into—"

> **James Fenimore Cooper,** *The Pioneers,* 1823, in *Writings of James Fenimore Cooper* 370 (James F. Beard ed. 1980)

6 My practice was first to make myself perfectly & accurately (mathematically accurately) master of the facts. . . . I saw where justice lay and the moral sense decided the cause half the time, & I then sed [*sic*] down to search the authorities until I had exhausted my books, & I might once & a while be embarrassed by a technical rule, but I *most always found principles suited to my views of the case.*

> **James Kent,** Letter to Thomas Washington, 6 Oct. 1828, in 9 *Green Bag* 206, 210 (1897)

7 There is no happiness, there is no liberty, there is no enjoyment of life, unless a man can say when he rises in the morning, I shall be subject to the decision of no unjust judge to-day.

> **Daniel Webster,** Speech, New York, 24 Mar. 1831, in *Papers of Daniel Webster: Speeches and Formal Writings* 1:459–60 (Charles M. Wiltse ed. 1986)

8 The world, my fellow citizens, has produced fewer instances of truly great judges, than it has of great men in almost every other department of civil life. A large portion of the ages that are past, have been altogether incapable of producing this excellence. It is the growth only of a government of laws, and of a political Constitution so free as to invite to the acquisition of the highest attainments, and to permit the exercise of the purest virtues, without exposure to degradation and contempt, under the frown of power.

> **Horace Binney,** *An Eulogy on the Life and Character of John Marshall* 70 (1835)

9 As unerring justice dwells in a unity, and as one judge will at last judge the world beyond all appeal; so—though often here below justice be hard to attain—does man come nearest the mark, when he imitates that model divine. Hence, one judge is better than twelve.

> **Herman Melville,** *Mardi,* 1849, in *Writings of Herman Melville* 3:185 (Harrison Hayford ed. 1970)

10 A law should be "universal," and include in its possible penal operations the very judge himself who gives decisions upon it; nay, the very judge who expounds it.

> **Herman Melville,** *White Jacket,* 1850, in *Writings of Herman Melville* 5:145 (Harrison Hayford ed. 1970)

11 The judge weighs the arguments and puts a brave face on the matter, and, since there must be a decision, decides as he can, and hopes he has done justice.

> **Ralph Waldo Emerson,** "Considerations by the Way," *The Conduct of Life,* 1860, in *Complete Works of Ralph Waldo Emerson* 6:243, 245–46 (1904)

12 The perfect judge fears nothing—he could go front to front before God,
Before the perfect judge all shall stand back—life and death shall stand back—heaven and hell shall stand back.

> **Walt Whitman,** "Great Are the Myths," in *Leaves of Grass* 585, 587 (Harold W. Blodgett & Sculley Bradley eds. 1965) (1860)

13 The strongest example of "rigid government" and "close construction" I ever knew, was that of Judge——. It was once said of him that he would *hang* a man for blowing his nose in the street, but that he would *quash* the indictment if it failed to specify which *hand* he blew it with!*

> **Abraham Lincoln,** quoted in Francis B. Carpenter, *Six Months at the White House with Abraham Lincoln* 254 (1866)

14 It is not the will of the sovereign that makes lawyers' law, even when that is its source, but what . . . the judges, by whom it is enforced, *say* is his will. The judges have other motives for decision, outside their own arbitrary will, beside the commands of their sovereign. And whether those other motives are, or are not, equally compulsory, is immaterial, if they are sufficiently likely to prevail to afford a ground for prediction. The only question for the lawyer is, how will the judges act?

> **Oliver Wendell Holmes, Jr.,** "Book Notices," 6 *American Law Review* 723, 724 (1872)

15 If the appellant, who was personally present in the court, was unable to determine whether the judge was really asleep or only had his eyes closed, how are we to determine? It is said to have occurred while the appellant was reading his written evidence. If he had reason to suppose that the judge was indulging in a gentle doze after dinner, he should have suspended his reading, or awakened the judge. Nor does it appear what portion of the written evidence was being read. There was much of it wholly immaterial and irrelevant. We might reasonably conclude that the judge but imitated the example of many of the profoundest thinkers and most distinguished judges, and closed his eyes that he might hear the more accurately and more fully comprehend what he heard.

> **Samuel H. Buskirk,** *Musselman v. Musselman,* 44 Ind. 106, 118 (1873)

16 Judges commonly are elderly men, and are more likely to hate at sight any analysis to which they are not accustomed, and which disturbs repose of mind, than to fall in love with novelties.

> **Oliver Wendell Holmes, Jr.,** "Law in Science and Science in Law," 12 *Harvard Law Review* 443, 455 (1899)

17 "If I had me job to pick out," said Mr. Dooley, "I'd be a judge. I've looked over all th' others an' that's th' on'y wan that suits. I have th' judicyal timperamint. I hate wurruk."

> **Finley Peter Dunne,** "The Law's Delays," in *Observations by Mr. Dooley* 15, 15 (1906) (1902)

18 An Associate Justice of the Supreme Court was sitting by a river when a Traveler approached and said:

"I wish to cross. Will it be lawful to use this boat?"

"It will," was the reply; "it is my boat."

The Traveler thanked him, and pushing the boat into the water embarked and rowed away. But the boat sank and he was drowned.

"Heartless man!" said an Indignant Spectator. "Why did you not tell him that your boat had a hole in it?"

"The matter of the boat's condition," said the great jurist, "was not brought before me."

> **Ambrose Bierce,** *Fantastic Fables,* in *Collected Works of Ambrose Bierce* 6:294 (1911)

19 I believe that our judges are as honest as you can make men. But like all the rest of us they are subject to their environment. And law has always been a narrowing, conservatizing profession. In England it was always easy for a Tory government to find great lawyers for judicial office, but for a Liberal government it was hard. And so it has been throughout history. Nearly all of England's great lawyers were Tories.

> **Louis D. Brandeis,** quoted in Ernest Poole, "Brandeis: A Remarkable Record of Unselfish Work Done in the Public Interest," 71 *American Magazine* 481, 493 (1911)

20 Judges are apt to be naif, simple-minded men, and they need something of Mephistopheles. We too need education in the obvious—to learn to transcend our own convictions and to leave room for much that

---

* He [the lawyer Sar Kasm] might approve of a law making it death for a man to blow his nose in the street, but would be for rebelling if it allowed the indictment to dispense with stating in which hand he held it. —**Joseph G. Baldwin,** *Flush Times of Alabama and Mississippi* 24 (1853)

we hold dear to be done away with short of revolution by the orderly change of law.

> **Oliver Wendell Holmes, Jr.,** "Law and the Court" (speech to Harvard Law School Association of New York), 15 Feb. 1913, in *Collected Legal Papers* 291, 295 (1920)

21 It is a misfortune if a judge reads his conscious or unconscious sympathy with one side or the other prematurely into the law, and forgets that what seem to him to be first principles are believed by half his fellow men to be wrong.

> **Oliver Wendell Holmes, Jr.,** "Law and the Court" (speech to Harvard Law School Association of New York), 15 Feb. 1913, in *Collected Legal Papers* 291, 295 (1920)

22 JUDGE, *n.* A person who is always interfering in disputes in which he has no personal interest.

> **Ambrose Bierce,** *The Enlarged Devil's Dictionary* 168 (Ernest J. Hopkins ed. 1967)

23 Conservative political opinion in America cleaves to the tradition of the judge as passive interpreter.... His is the role of a faithful administrator whose success depends upon his interpretation of the written word, not of the full heart. In its passionate adherence to this tradition such opinion is not disinterested; it would as eagerly encourage judicial initiative, if the laws were framed by labor unions, as it insists upon rigid obedience in a system framed for the most part for the protection of property and for the prevention of thoroughgoing social regulation.

> **Learned Hand,** "The Speech of Justice," 29 *Harvard Law Review* 617, 617 (1916)

24 It is not as the priests of a completed revelation that the living successors of past lawmakers can most truly show their reverence or continue the traditions which they affect to regard.... Only as an articulate organ of the half-understood aspirations of living men, constantly recasting and adapting existing forms, bringing to the high light of expression the dumb impulses of the present, can they continue in the course of the ancestors whom they revere.

> **Learned Hand,** "The Speech of Justice," 29 *Harvard Law Review* 617, 618–19 (1916)

25 Judge—A law student who marks his own examination papers.

> **H. L. Mencken,** "Sententiae," 1916, in *A Mencken Chrestomathy* 616, 623 (1949)

26 How well this figure represents the Law—
This pose of neuter Justice, sterile Cant;
This Roman Emperor with the iron jaw,
Wrapped in the black silk of a maiden-aunt.

> **Louis Untermeyer,** "Portrait of a Supreme Court Judge," in *These Times* 77 (1917)

27 Adams [Henry Adams speaking of himself in the third person] felt no moral obligation to defend Judges, who, as far as he knew, were the only class of society specially adapted to defend themselves.

> **Henry Adams,** *The Education of Henry Adams* 191 (1918)

28 We are not to close our eyes as judges to what we must perceive as men.

> **Benjamin N. Cardozo,** *People v. Knapp,* 230 N.Y. 48, 63, 129 N.E. 202 (1920)
> See also JUDGES 48

29 There is in each of us a stream of tendency, whether you choose to call it philosophy or not, which gives coherence and direction to thoughts and action. Judges cannot escape that current any more than other mortals. All their lives, forces which they do not recognize and cannot name, have been tugging at them—inherited instincts, traditional beliefs, acquired convictions.... In this mental background every problem finds its setting. We may try to see things as objectively as we please. None the less, we can never see them with any eyes except our own.

> **Benjamin N. Cardozo,** *The Nature of the Judicial Process* 12–13 (1921)

30 Therefore in the main there shall be adherence to precedent. There shall be symmetrical development, consistently with history or custom ..., logic or philosophy.... But symmetrical development may be bought at too high a price. Uniformity ceases to be a good when it becomes uniformity of oppression. The social interest served by symmetry or certainty must then be balanced against the social interest served by equity and fairness or other elements of social welfare. These may enjoin

upon the judge the duty of drawing the line at another angle, of staking the path along new courses, of marking a new point of departure from which others who come after him will set out upon their journey. If you ask how he is to know when one interest outweighs another, I can only answer that he must get his knowledge just as the legislator gets it, from experience and study and reflection; in brief, from life itself.

Benjamin N. Cardozo, *The Nature of the Judicial Process* 112–13 (1921)

31 The judge, even when he is free, is still not wholly free. He is not to innovate at pleasure. He is not a knight-errant, roaming at will in pursuit of his own ideal of beauty or of goodness. He is to draw his inspiration from consecrated principles. He is not to yield to spasmodic sentiment, to vague and unregulated benevolence. He is to exercise a discretion informed by tradition, methodized by analogy, disciplined by system, and subordinated to "the primordial necessity of order in the social life." Wide enough in all conscience is the field of discretion that remains.

Benjamin N. Cardozo, *The Nature of the Judicial Process* 141 (1921)

32 I was much troubled in spirit, in my first years upon the bench, to find how trackless was the ocean on which I had embarked. I sought for certainty. I was oppressed and disheartened when I found that the quest for it was futile. . . . As the years have gone by, and as I have reflected more and more upon the nature of the judicial process, I have become reconciled to the uncertainty, because I have grown to see it as inevitable. I have grown to see that the process in its highest reaches is not discovery, but creation; and that the doubts and misgivings, the hopes and fears, are part of the travail of mind, the pangs of death and the pangs of birth, in which principles that have served their day expire, and new principles are born.

Benjamin N. Cardozo, *The Nature of the Judicial Process* 166–67 (1921)

33 I do not doubt the grandeur of the conception which lifts them [judges] into the realm of pure reason, above and beyond the sweep of perturbing and deflecting forces. None the less, if there is anything of reality in my analysis of the judicial process, they do not stand aloof on these chill and distant heights; and we shall not help the cause of truth by acting and speaking as if they do. The great tides and currents which engulf the rest of men, do not turn aside in their course, and pass the judges by.

Benjamin N. Cardozo, *The Nature of the Judicial Process* 168 (1921)

34 My duty as judge may be to objectify in law, not my own aspirations and convictions and philosophies, but the aspirations and convictions and philosophies of the men and women of my time. Hardly shall I do this well if my own sympathies and beliefs and passionate devotions are with a time that is past.

Benjamin N. Cardozo, *The Nature of the Judicial Process* 173 (1921)

35 Judges march at times to pitiless conclusions under the prod of a remorseless logic which is supposed to leave them no alternative. They deplore the sacrificial rite. They perform it, none the less, with averted gaze, convinced as they plunge the knife that they obey the bidding of their office. The victim is offered up to the gods of jurisprudence on the altar of regularity.

Benjamin N. Cardozo, *The Growth of the Law* 66 (1924)

36 Judges tend to show . . . decay of the faculties in an exaggerated form; they become mere automata, bound by arbitrary rules, precedents, the accumulated imbecilities of generations; to their primary lack of sense as lawyers they add the awful manner of bureaucrats. It is thus too much to hope for a judge showing any originality or courage; one Holmes is an era of Hardings and Coolidges is probably more than a fair allotment.

H. L. Mencken, Editorial, *American Mercury*, Feb. 1924, at 161, 164

37 Technically, he was learned in the law; actually, so far as life was concerned, absolutely unconscious of that subtle chemistry of things that transcends all written law and makes for the spirit and, beyond that, the inutility of all law, as all wise judges know.

Theodore Dreiser, *The Financier* 323 (rev. ed. 1927)

38 When did a judge ever think? He's paid not
to.

Maxwell Anderson and Harold Hickerson,
Gods of the Lightning 42 (1928)

39 Judge Ulman . . . is one of the few judges
in American history who have ever ven-
tured to write (or even, perhaps, to think)
about the nature of the judicial art and
mystery. . . . His book ought to be read by
judges, but it is not likely that many of
them will look into it. They are, as a class,
very backward men. Only too often they
reach the bench without having given the
slightest thought to its problems, and so it
is no wonder that many of them perform
their duties in the manner of checkers at a
race-track or pump-men at a filling-station.
Under our system of government there is
no training for them. If they are intelligent
they learn gradually at the public expense;
if not, they help to keep their trade at its
present low level. If they were required, like
the schoolma'ams, to give over their long
vacations to professional studies they
might be appreciably improved.

H. L. Mencken, Book Review, *American
Mercury*, July 1933, at 381, 381–83

40 There is no certain harm in turning a politician into a judge. He may be or become
a good judge. The curse of the elective system is the converse, that it turns almost
every judge into a politician.

Henry T. Lummus, *The Trial Judge* 138
(1937)

41 It has been said that a judge is a member
of the Bar who once knew a Governor.

Curtis Bok, *The Backbone of the Herring* 3
(1941)

42 The position of a judge has been likened to
that of an oyster—anchored in one place,
unable to take the initiative, unable to go
out after things, restricted to working on
and digesting what the fortuitous eddies
and currents of litigation may wash his
way.

Calvert Magruder, "Mr. Justice Brandeis," 55
Harvard Law Review 193, 194 (1941)

43 A certain judge in the mining territory of
Nevada had a reputation for probity. In
keeping with this opinion, he opened a
mining claim case one morning with the
following words to the court: "Gentlemen,

this court has received from the plaintiff in
this case a check for $10,000. He has re-
ceived from the defendant a check for
$15,000. The court has returned $5,000 to
the defendant and will now try the case on
its merits."

Thesaurus of Anecdotes 444 (Edmund Fuller
ed. 1942)

44 The movies are the only court where the
judge goes to the lawyer for advice.

F. Scott Fitzgerald, *The Crack-up* 122 (1945)

45 But the law of contempt is not made for
the protection of judges who may be sensitive to the winds of public opinion.
Judges are supposed to be men of fortitude,
able to thrive in a hardy climate.

William O. Douglas, *Craig v. Harney*, 331
U.S. 367, 376 (1947)

46 I do not know whether it is the view of the
Court that a judge must be thick-skinned
or just thickheaded, but nothing in my experience or observation confirms the idea
that he is insensitive to publicity. Who does
not prefer good to ill report of his work?
And if fame—a good public name—is, as
Milton said, the "last infirmity of noble
mind," it is frequently the first infirmity of
a mediocre one.

Robert H. Jackson, *Craig v. Harney*, 331 U.S.
367, 396 (1947) (dissenting)

47 We need a new kind of courage—the courage to face unconquerable imperfections in
the solution of human problems.

Jerome N. Frank, *Courts on Trial* 425 (1949)

48 And there comes a point where this Court
should not be ignorant as judges of what
we know as men.

Felix Frankfurter, *Watts v. Indiana*, 338 U.S.
49, 52 (1949)
See also JUDGES 28

49 Judicial humor is a dreadful thing. In the
first place, the jokes are usually bad; I have
seldom heard a judge utter a good one. . . .
In the second place, the bench is not an
appropriate place for unseemly levity. The
litigant has vital interests at stake. His entire future, or even his life, may be trembling in the balance, and the robed buffoon
who makes merry at his expense should be
choked with his own wig.

William L. Prosser, *The Judicial Humorist*
vii (1952)

50 What is essential for the discharge of functions that are almost too much, I think, for any nine mortal men, but have to be discharged by nine fallible creatures, what is essential is that you get men who bring to their task, first and foremost, humility and an understanding of the range of the problems and of their own inadequacy in dealing with them; disinterestedness, allegiance to nothing except the search, amid tangled words, amid limited insights, loyalty and allegiance to nothing except the effort to find their path through precedent, through policy, through history, through their own gifts of insight to the best judgment that poor fallible creatures can arrive at in that most difficult of all tasks, the adjudication between man and man, between man and state, through reason called law.

Felix Frankfurter, "Chief Justices I Have Known," 39 *Virginia Law Review* 883, 905 (1953)

51 Of course personal attacks or innuendoes by a lawyer against a judge, with a view to provoking him, only aggravate what may be an obstruction to the trial. The vital point is that in sitting in judgment on such a misbehaving lawyer the judge should not himself give vent to personal spleen or respond to a personal grievance. These are subtle matters, for they concern the ingredients of what constitutes justice. Therefore, justice must satisfy the appearance of justice.

Felix Frankfurter, *Offutt v. United States,* 348 U.S. 11, 14 (1954)

52 After the young man had gotten his client's name, age, and address on the record, the court interrupted and started to ask questions. The young lawyer stood first on one foot and then on the other as the court's questioning continued. He finally sat down, and in due course the court came to the end of his questioning and said, "Counselor, you may now continue with the witness. Proceed." The young man arose and said, "If your Honor please, I have no more questions to ask because I think the court has covered my case very thoroughly. But," he added, "I would like to make a statement. If your Honor please, this is my first case, my first client. I have prepared my case thoroughly. I have gone back to the Year Books on the law; I have questioned all eye witnesses to the accident with the

greatest care; but if your Honor wants to try this case, it is all right with me, except, for goodness' sake, don't lose it!"

John M. Harlan (1899–1971), "What Part Does the Oral Argument Play in the Conduct of an Appeal," 41 *Cornell Law Quarterly* 6, 10 (1955)

53 Judges, like people, may be divided roughly into four classes: judges with neither head nor heart—they are to be avoided at all costs; judges with head but no heart—they are almost as bad; then judges with heart but no head—risky but better than the first two; and finally, those rare judges who possess both head and a heart—thanks to blind luck, that's our judge.

Robert Traver, *Anatomy of a Murder* 313–14 (1958)

54 After all, why isn't it in the nature of an art? It is a bit of craftsmanship, isn't it? It is what a poet does, it is what a sculptor does. He has some vague purposes and he has an indefinite number of what you might call frames of preference among which he must choose; for choose he has to, and he does. So, I like to think that the work of a judge is an art.

Learned Hand, Remarks at special session of United States Court of Appeals for the Second Circuit commemorating his fifty years of federal judicial service, 10 Apr. 1959, 264 F.2d (separately paginated section) 28–29 (1959)

55 When I read the decision of the Oslo Town Court, which you sent me some months ago, I did so with mingled feelings. If occasionally I was obliged to roll with laughter—partly because of the inept translation, partly because of the nature and the number of infractions listed—I trust no one will take offense. Taking the world for what it is, and the men who made and execute the laws for what they are, I thought the decision as fair and honest as any theorem of Euclid's. Nor was I unaware of, or indifferent to, the efforts made by the Court to render an interpretation beyond the strict letter of the law. (An impossible task, I would say, for if laws are made for men and not men for laws, it is also true that certain individuals are made for the law and can only see things through the eyes of the law.)

Henry Miller, Letter to Trygve Hirsch, 27 Feb. 1959, in *The Henry Miller Reader* 372 (Lawrence Durrell ed. 1959)

56 "Mr. Kinney: May the record also show that I object to the comments of the trial judge as being unfair to counsel for defendant and prejudicial to my client.

"The Court: Take this, lady. Whenever I see a lawyer interrupt another lawyer for the purpose of disrupting another lawyer's line of thought, I think it's unfair and I say so, and that's exactly what happened here. As a general rule I don't let lawyers interrupt other lawyers, and I ain't a going to start it. I'm too old to start doing that sort of thing. Now, anything else you want to put in there?

    Campbell Thornal, *Giglio v. Valdez*, 114 So. 2d 305, 306 (Fla. Dist. Ct. App. 1959)

57 After many years of effort to attain at once that degree of detachment in the discharge of what is inevitably a duty to fabricate, I have not yet lost a sense of joy when, for the moment anyway, I hope that in a given controversy I may have found a solution that will seem at least tolerable to those who are not committed in advance.

    Learned Hand, in *Proceedings in Honor of Mr. Justice Frankfurter and Distinguished Alumni* (Occasional Pamphlet Number 3, Harvard Law School) 62 (1960)

58 [On the sentencing of criminal defendants:] Here I am an old man in a long nightgown making muffled noises at people who may be no worse then I am.

    Learned Hand, quoted in Marvin E. Frankel, *Criminal Sentences: Law Without Order* 16 (1973)

59 Haywood looked at Janning, sympathy welling up in him. He felt impotent, wanting to say something to this man but unable to. Understand, said Haywood to himself. I understand the pressures you were under. From my own experience here I understand that. But how can I understand the death of millions of men, women, and children in gas ovens, Herr Janning? How can I understand that? How can I tell you I understand it?

Janning looked at Haywood, sensitive to what he must be feeling. He spoke finally. It seemed almost as though he were reading Haywood's mind.

"I did not know it would come to that. You must believe it. You must believe it."

Haywood stood staring at the man before him. Then, almost without thinking, he said the words, as though he were speaking to a child.

"Herr Janning. It came to that the first time you sentenced to death a man you knew to be innocent."

    Abby Mann, *Judgment at Nuremberg* 136 (1961)

60 Indeed, I was so gouged myself just recently when I purchased some ordinary eye-wash drops and later learned that I paid 10 times the price the drops should have cost. Likewise, a year or so ago I purchased a brand name drug for the treatment of labyrinthitis at a cost of some $12, which I later learned to buy by its established name for about $1.

    Tom C. Clark, *Abbott Laboratories v. Gardner*, 387 U.S. 136, 201 (1967) (dissenting)

61 Here comes the judge.*

    Dewey Markham et al., Title of song (1968)

62 Some of my lawyer friends say I ought to be cool and dignified and not talk about the judges that have just about ruined this country. . . . Why not? They talk about me, don't they? They don't hang their britches on the wall and go jump in 'em—, they pull 'em on one leg at a time just like regular folks. And the people didn't elect them, either, like they did me.

    George C. Wallace, quoted in *National Observer*, 19 Feb. 1972, at 4

63 A judge is not free, like a loose cannon, to inflict indiscriminate damage whenever he announces that he is acting in his judicial capacity.

    Potter Stewart, *Stump v. Sparkman*, 435 U.S. 349, 367 (1978) (dissenting)

64 The *function* of the judge—a statement of social purpose and a definition of role—is not to resolve disputes, but to give the proper meaning to our public values.

    Owen M. Fiss, "The Supreme Court, 1978 Term—Foreword: The Forms of Justice," 93 *Harvard Law Review* 1, 30 (1979)

---

* In the form "Here come de judge," this was popularized as a catch-phrase by the television series *Rowan and Martin's Laugh-In* (1967–73).

65 JUDGE, *n.* Ringmaster. *v.* To toss a coin.

Robert J. Morris, "The New (Legal) Devil's Dictionary," 6 *Journal of Contemporary Law* 231, 234 (1979)

66 When I ran for Mayor in 1973 . . . I went to a Senior Citizen center in the Bronx. I was immediately asked about crime and what we were going to do about it. And I said to these elderly people, "You know, ladies and gentlemen, crime is terrible. A judge that I know was mugged this week and do you know what he did? He called a press conference and said that mugging would in no way affect his judicial decisions in matters of that kind." And an elderly lady stood up in the back of the room and said, "Then mug him again!"

Edward I. Koch, quoted in Jay M. Shafritz, *The HarperCollins Dictionary of American Government and Politics* 312 (1992)

67 I well know I resemble the man at the fair who needs all three baseballs to knock over the milk bottles. The good coming of all this is the knowledge that, having taken all conceivable sides on the issue, I must certainly at some point have been right. Unfortunately, it too obviously follows that at some point I must also have been wrong.

Richard M. Sims III, *People v. Webb,* 186 Cal. App. 3d 401, 413, 230 Cal. Rptr. 755 (1986) (concurring)

68 I don't want to know what the law is, I want to know who the judge is.

Roy M. Cohn, quoted in *New York Times Book Review,* 3 Apr. 1988, at 24

JUDGES, INDIVIDUAL

See also HOLMES, OLIVER WENDELL; JUDGES; MARSHALL, JOHN

1 The American Blackstone.

Epithet of James Kent

2 The Law West of the Pecos.

Epithet of Roy Bean

3 The People's Attorney [also "The People's Lawyer"].

Epithet of Louis D. Brandeis

4 The Tenth Justice of the Supreme Court.*

Epithet of Learned Hand

5 I always approach Judge [Lemuel] Shaw as a savage approaches his fetish, knowing that he is ugly, but feeling that he is great.

Rufus Choate, quoted in Van Wyck Brooks, *The Flowering of New England* 325 (1936)

6 When I suggested to him [William Howard Taft, who weighed over 300 pounds] . . . that he occupy a Chair of Law at the University, he said that he was afraid that a Chair would not be adequate, but that if we would provide a Sofa of Law, it might be all right.

William Howard Taft, reported in Anson Phelps Stokes, Letter to Frederick C. Hicks, 10 May 1940, in Frederick C. Hicks, *William Howard Taft: Yale Professor of Law and New Haven Citizen* 112 (1945)

7 Some judges have stayed too long on the bench. An unfortunate illustration was that of Justice Grier.... A committee of the Court waited upon Justice Grier to advise him of the desirability of his retirement.... Justice Field tarried too long on the bench.... It occurred to the other members of the Court that Justice Field had served on a committee which waited upon Justice Grier to suggest his retirement, and it was thought that recalling that to his memory might aid him to decide to retire. Justice Harlan was deputed to make the suggestion.... Justice Harlan asked if Justice Field did not remember what had been said to Justice Grier on that occasion. The old man listened, gradually becoming alert and finally, with his eyes blazing with the old fire of youth, he burst out: "Yes! And a dirtier day's work I never did in my life!"

Charles Evans Hughes, *The Supreme Court of the United States* 75–76 (1928)

8 [Responding in 1932 to President Herbert Hoover showing him a list of ten leading prospects for a Supreme Court appointment, with Benjamin N. Cardozo in tenth place:] Your list is all right, but you handed it to me upside down.

William E. Borah, quoted in Henry J. Abraham, *Justices and Presidents* 202-03 (2d ed. 1985)

---

* "The tenth justice" has also been used as a description of the position of the Solicitor General.

9 On the bench ... [Chief Justice Hughes] held each speaker to exactly his allotted time. It is said, with some exaggeration, that once he called time on a leader of the New York Bar in the middle of the word "if." When John W. Davis asked how much time remained and Hughes snapped, "exactly one minute and a half," counsel suavely replied, "I present the court with one minute and a half."

Merlo J. Pusey, *Charles Evans Hughes* 2:664–65 (1951)

10 Quote Learned, and follow "Gus" [referring to Judges Learned and Augustus Hand].

Robert H. Jackson, quoted in Hershel Shanks, *The Art and Craft of Judging* 4 (1968)

JUDGMENT

See also JUDGES

1 The rest, finding themselves left sole judges [of the cripple] in the case, could not resist the opportunity of acting the part: not because it is a human weakness to take pleasure in sitting in judgment upon one in a box, as surely this unfortunate negro now was, but that it strangely sharpens human perceptions, when, instead of standing by and having their fellow-feelings touched by the sight of an alleged culprit severely handled by some one justiciary, a crowd suddenly come to be all justiciaries in the same case themselves.

Herman Melville, *The Confidence-Man,* 1857, in *Writings of Herman Melville* 10:12–13 (Harrison Hayford ed. 1984)

2 The two parties being confronted before him [Governor Wouter Van Twiller of New York], each produced a book of accounts, written in a language and character that would have puzzled any but a High-Dutch commentator, or a learned decipherer of Egyptian obelisks. The sage Wouter took them one after the other, and having poised them in his hands, and attentively counted over the number of leaves, fell straightway into a very great doubt, and smoked for half an hour without saying a word; at length, laying his finger beside his nose, and shutting his eyes for a moment, with the air of a man who has just caught a subtle idea by the tail, he slowly took his pipe from his mouth, puffed forth a column of tobacco-smoke, and with a marvellous gravity and solemnity pronounced, that, having carefully counted over the leaves and weighed the books, it was found, that one was just as thick and as heavy as the other: therefore, it was the final opinion of the court that the accounts were equally balanced: therefore, Wandle should give Barent a receipt, and Barent should give Wandle a receipt, and the constable should pay the costs. . . .

I am the more particular in dwelling on this transaction, . . . because I deem it one of the most sage and righteous judgments on record, and well worthy the attention of modern magistrates.

Washington Irving, *A History of New York* 177–179 (1868)

3 ACQUIT, *v.t.* To render judgment in a murder case in San Francisco.

Ambrose Bierce, *The Enlarged Devil's Dictionary* 9 (Ernest J. Hopkins ed. 1967)

4 Summary Judgment. A dispositive judicial ruling. The term "summary" is ironic, in that it suggests that *other* rulings by a judge are the product of deliberation and care.

Daniel R. White, *Trials and Tribulations* 181 (1989)

JUDICIAL APPOINTMENTS

See also HOLMES, OLIVER WENDELL; MARSHALL, JOHN

1 [On the nomination of Salmon P. Chase to be Chief Justice of the Supreme Court:] We cannot ask a man what he will do, and if we should, and he should answer us, we should despise him for it. Therefore we must take a man whose opinions are known.

Abraham Lincoln, quoted in George S. Boutwell, *Reminiscences of Sixty Years in Public Affairs* 2:29 (1902)

2 Nothing has been so strongly borne in on me concerning lawyers on the bench as that the *nominal* politics of the man has nothing to do with his actions on the bench. His *real* politics are all important. From his antecedents, Holmes should have been an ideal man on the bench. As a mat-

ter of fact he has been a bitter disappointment.

> **Theodore Roosevelt,** Letter to Henry Cabot Lodge, 1906, in *New England Quarterly,* Sept. 1949, at 301

3 [Looking back on his appointment of Herbert O'Brien as a judge:] When I make a mistake, it's a beaut.

> **Fiorello H. La Guardia,** quoted in William Manners, *Patience and Fortitude* 219 (1976)

4 If by that phrase "packing the Court" it is charged that I wish to place on the bench spineless puppets who would disregard the law and would decide specific cases as I wished them to be decided, I make this answer: that no President fit for his office would appoint, and no Senate of honorable men fit for their office would confirm, that kind of appointees to the Supreme Court.

But if by that phrase the charge is made that I would appoint and the Senate would confirm Justices worthy to sit beside present members of the Court who understand those modern conditions, that I will appoint Justices who will not undertake to override the judgment of the Congress on legislative policy, that I will appoint Justices who will act as Justices and not as legislators—if the appointment of such Justices can be called "packing the Courts," then I say that I and with me the vast majority of the American people favor doing just that thing—now.

> **Franklin D. Roosevelt,** "Fireside Chat on Reorganization of Judiciary," Washington, D.C., 9 Mar. 1937, in *Public Papers and Addresses of Franklin D. Roosevelt* 6:122, 129 (1941)

5 [Turning down an appointment to the Supreme Court:] I would rather talk to the damned fools than listen to them.

> **John G. Johnson,** quoted in Dean Acheson, Letter to Harry S. Truman, 8 Oct. 1957, in *Among Friends: Personal Letters of Dean Acheson* 131 (David S. McLellan & David C. Acheson eds. 1980)

6 [Packing the Supreme Court] can't be done. . . . I've tried it and it doesn't work. Whenever you put a man on the Supreme Court, he ceases to be your friend.

> **Harry S. Truman,** Lecture at Columbia University, New York, 28 Apr. 1959, quoted in *New York Herald Tribune,* 29 Apr. 1959, at 4

7 I believe it is the right thing to do, the right time to do it, the right man and the right place.

> **Lyndon B. Johnson,** Remarks to the Press Announcing the Nomination of Thurgood Marshall as Associate Justice of the Supreme Court, 13 June 1967, in *Public Papers of the Presidents: Lyndon B. Johnson, 1967,* at 1:611, 611 (1968)

8 There are a lot of mediocre judges and people and lawyers, and they are entitled to a little representation [on the Supreme Court], aren't they? We can't have all Brandeises, Frankfurters, and Cardozos.

> **Roman L. Hruska,** Interview after speech in United States Senate, quoted in *New York Times,* 17 Mar. 1970, at 21

9 It may be some comfort to describe to the fearful realtors what lawyers . . . believe is the shortest interval of time known to man: that fleeting moment when a lawyer takes his oath as a judge and immediately forgets that he was ever a lawyer.

> **Joseph H. Stamler,** *New Jersey State Bar Ass'n v. New Jersey Ass'n of Realtor Boards,* 118 N.J. Super. 203, 210, 287 A.2d 14 (1972)

10 [When asked if he had made any mistakes while he had been President:] Yes, two, and they are both sitting on the Supreme Court.*

> **Dwight D. Eisenhower,** Attributed remark, quoted in Henry J. Abraham, *Justices and Presidents* 246 (1974)

11 Earlier today, I was asked whether I had ever used drugs. To the best of my recollection, once as a college student in the '60s, and then on a few occasions in the '70s, I used marijuana. That was the only drug I ever used. I have not used it since. It was a mistake, and I regret it.

> **Douglas H. Ginsburg,** Statement issued while nominee for Supreme Court Associate Justice, quoted in *New York Times,* 6 Nov. 1987, at 1

---

* This attributed comment is probably apocryphal. Elmo Richardson, in his book *The Presidency of Dwight D. Eisenhower* 108 (1979), states that the remark, "Yes, and both of them are sitting on the Supreme Court," has been "ascribed to several other presidents." The generic joke may have combined with actual statements by Eisenhower about his disappointment with appointee Earl Warren to inspire an apocryphal story about Eisenhower's disappointment with *two* justices (usually said to be Warren and William J. Brennan, Jr.).

12 Robert Bork's America is a land in which women would be forced into back-alley abortions, blacks would sit at segregated lunch counters, rogue police could break down citizens' doors in midnight raids, schoolchildren could not be taught about evolution, writers and artists would be censored at the whim of government, and the doors of the Federal courts would be shut on the fingers of millions of citizens for whom the judiciary is often the only protector of the individual rights that are the heart of our democracy.

> **Edward M. Kennedy,** Statement on nomination of Robert H. Bork to Supreme Court, 133 *Congressional Record* S9188 (daily ed. July 1, 1987)

13 [Criticizing the Senate Judiciary Committee's treatment of Supreme Court nominee Robert H. Bork:] What's at issue is that we make sure the process of appointing and confirming judges never again is turned into such a political joke. And if I have to appoint another one [if Bork is not confirmed], I'll try to find one that they'll object to just as much as they did for this one.

> **Ronald W. Reagan,** Remarks to New Jersey Republican State Committee, Whippany, N.J., 13 Oct. 1987, in *Public Papers of the Presidents: Ronald Reagan, 1987,* at 2:1172, 1175 (1989)

14 One of the oddest episodes I remember was an occasion in which [Supreme Court nominee Clarence] Thomas was drinking a Coke in his office. He got up from the table at which we were working, went over to his desk to get the Coke, looked at the can and asked, "Who has put pubic hair on my Coke?"

> **Anita Hill,** quoted in *New York Times,* 12 Oct. 1991, at 11

15 This is a circus. It's a national disgrace. From my standpoint as a black American, it is a high-tech lynching for uppity blacks who in any way deign to think for themselves, to do for themselves.

> **Clarence Thomas,** quoted in *New York Times,* 12 Oct. 1991, at 1, 9

JUDICIAL LEGISLATION

See also CONSTITUTIONAL LAW; JUDICIAL REVIEW

1 There is one general Observation I would make; that the End of Government is the Happiness of every Individual, so far as is consistent with the Good of *the Whole.* To attain this End is impossible without Laws, and their due Execution. 'Tis necessary that Laws should be established, else Judges and Juries must go according to their Reason, that is, their Will; and this is in the strictest Sense arbitrary. On this Reason, I take to be grounded that well-known Maxim, that *the Judge* should never be *the Legislator:* Because, then, the Will of the Judge would be the Law; and this tends directly to a State of Slavery. The Rules and Orders of a State must be known, and must be certain, that People may know how to act; or else they are equally uncertain, as if the Law depended upon the arbitrary Opinion of Another.

> **Thomas Hutchinson,** *Charge to the Grand Jury,* Quincy's Reports 232, 234 (1767)

2 I recognize without hesitation that judges do and must legislate, but they can do so only interstitially; they are confined from molar to molecular motions. A common-law judge could not say I think the doctrine of consideration a bit of historical nonsense and shall not enforce it in my court.

> **Oliver Wendell Holmes, Jr.,** *Southern Pacific Co. v. Jensen,* 244 U.S. 205, 221 (1917) (dissenting)

3 It is the function of our courts to keep the doctrines up to date with the *mores* by continual restatement and by giving them a continually new content. This is judicial legislation, and the judge legislates at his peril. Nevertheless, it is the necessity and duty of such legislation that gives to judicial office its highest honor; and no brave and honest judge shirks the duty or fears the peril.

> **Arthur L. Corbin,** "The Offer of an Act for a Promise," 29 *Yale Law Journal* 767, 771–72 (1920)

4 All rights are derived from the purposes of the society in which they exist; above all rights rises duty to the community. The conditions developed in industry may be such that those engaged in it cannot continue their struggle without danger to the community. But it is not for judges to determine whether such conditions exist, nor is it their function to set the limits of per-

missible contest and to declare the duties which the new situation demands. This is the function of the legislature which, while limiting individual and group rights of aggression and defense, may substitute processes of justice for the more primitive method of trial by combat.

Louis D. Brandeis, *Duplex Printing Press Co. v. Deering*, 254 U.S. 443, 488 (1921) (dissenting)

5 We must keep within those interstitial limits which precedent and custom and the long and silent and almost indefinable practice of other judges through the centuries of the common law have set to judge-made innovations. But within the limits thus set, within the range over which choice moves, the final principle of selection for judges, as for legislators, is one of fitness to an end. . . . We do not pick our rules of law full-blossomed from the trees.

Benjamin N. Cardozo, *The Nature of the Judicial Process* 103 (1921)

6 Each [common-law judge] indeed is legislating within the limits of his competence. No doubt the limits for the judge are narrower. He legislates only between gaps. He fills the open spaces in the law. . . . within the confines of these open spaces and those of precedent and tradition, choice moves with a freedom which stamps its action as creative. The law which is the resulting product is not found, but made.

Benjamin N. Cardozo, *The Nature of the Judicial Process* 113, 115 (1921)

JUDICIAL REVIEW

See also CONSTITUTIONAL LAW; DUE PROCESS; JUDICIAL LEGISLATION; STATUTORY CONSTRUCTION

1 There is no position which depends on clearer principles, than that every act of a delegated authority, contrary to the tenor of the commission under which it is exercised, is void. No legislative act therefore contrary to the constitution, can be valid. To deny this would be to affirm that the deputy is greater than his principal; that the servant is above his master; that the representatives of the people are superior to the people themselves; that men acting by virtue of powers may do not only what

their powers do not authorise, but what they forbid.

Alexander Hamilton, *The Federalist* No. 78, at 2:293 (1788)

2 The interpretation of the laws is the proper and peculiar province of the courts. A constitution is in fact, and must be, regarded by the judges as a fundamental law. It therefore belongs to them to ascertain its meaning as well as the meaning of any particular act proceeding from the legislative body. If there should happen to be an irreconcilable variance between the two, that which has the superior obligation and validity ought of course to be prefered [*sic*]; or in other words, the constitution ought to be prefered [*sic*] to the statute, the intention of the people to the intention of their agents.

Alexander Hamilton, *The Federalist* No. 78, at 2:294 (1788)

3 Nor does this conclusion by any means suppose a superiority of the judicial to the legislative power. It only supposes that the power of the people is superior to both; and that where the will of the legislature declared in its statutes, stands in opposition to that of the people declared in the constitution, the judges ought to be governed by the latter, rather than the former.

Alexander Hamilton, *The Federalist* No. 78, at 2:294 (1788)

4 The Constitution ought to be the standard of construction for the laws, and . . . wherever there is an evident opposition, the laws ought to give place to the constitution.

Alexander Hamilton, *The Federalist* No. 81, at 2:312 (1788)

5 The legislative authority of any country, can only be restrained by its own municipal constitution. This is a principle that springs from the very nature of society; and the judicial authority can have no right to question the validity of a law, unless such a jurisdiction is expressly given by the constitution.*

John Marshall, Argument as counsel in *Ware v. Hilton*, 3 U.S. (3 Dall.) 199, 211 (1796)

---

* Here Marshall contradicts the position in support of judicial review which he took seven years later in *Marbury v. Madison.*

6 Where the heads of departments are the political or confidential agents of the executive, merely to execute the will of the President, or rather to act in cases in which the executive possesses a constitutional or legal discretion, nothing can be more perfectly clear than that their acts are only politically examinable. But where a specific duty is assigned by law, and individual rights depend upon the performance of that duty, it seems equally clear that the individual who considers himself injured, has a right to resort to the laws of his country for a remedy.

John Marshall, *Marbury v. Madison*, 5 U.S. (1 Cranch) 137, 166 (1803)

7 The distinction, between a government with limited and unlimited powers, is abolished, if those limits do not confine the persons on whom they are imposed, and if acts prohibited and acts allowed, are of equal obligation. It is a proposition too plain to be contested, that the constitution controls any legislative act repugnant to it; or, that the legislature may alter the constitution by an ordinary act.

John Marshall, *Marbury v. Madison*, 5 U.S. (1 Cranch) 137, 176–77 (1803)

8 Certainly all those who have framed written constitutions contemplate them as forming the fundamental and paramount law of the nation, and consequently the theory of every such government must be, that an act of the legislature, repugnant to the constitution, is void.

John Marshall, *Marbury v. Madison*, 5 U.S. (1 Cranch) 137, 177 (1803)

9 It is emphatically the province and duty of the judicial department to say what the law is. Those who apply the rule to particular cases, must of necessity expound and interpret that rule. If two laws conflict with each other, the courts must decide on the operation of each. So if a law be in opposition to the constitution; if both the law and the constitution apply to a particular case, so that the court must either decide that case conformably to the law, disregarding the constitution; or conformably to the constitution, disregarding the law; the court must determine which of these conflicting rules governs the case. This is of the very essence of judicial duty. If then the courts are to regard the constitution; and

the constitution is superior to any ordinary act of the legislature; the constitution, and not such ordinary act, must govern the case to which they both apply.

John Marshall, *Marbury v. Madison*, 5 U.S. (1 Cranch) 137, 177–78 (1803)

10 It is also not entirely unworthy of observation, that in declaring what shall be the *supreme* law of the land, the *constitution* itself is first mentioned; and not the laws of the United States generally, but those only which shall be made in *pursuance* of the constitution, have that rank. Thus, the particular phraseology of the constitution of the United States confirms and strengthens the principle, supposed to be essential to all written constitutions, that a law repugnant to the constitution is void; and that *courts*, as well as other departments, are bound by that instrument.

John Marshall, *Marbury v. Madison*, 5 U.S. (1 Cranch) 137, 180 (1803)

11 Whether a law be void for its repugnancy to the Constitution, is, at all times, a question of much delicacy, which ought seldom, if ever, to be decided in the affirmative, in a doubtful case. . . . But it is not on slight implication and vague conjecture that the legislature is to be pronounced to have transcended its powers, and its acts to be considered as void. The opposition between the constitution and the law should be such that the judge feels a clear and strong conviction of their incompatibility with each other.

John Marshall, *Fletcher v. Peck*, 10 U.S. (6 Cranch) 87, 128 (1810)

12 There is not a word in the constitution which has given that power [to review the acts of Congress or the President] to them [the courts] more than to the executive or legislative branches.

Thomas Jefferson, Letter to W. H. Torrance, 11 June 1815, in *Works of Thomas Jefferson* 11:473 (Paul L. Ford ed. 1905)

13 My construction of the Constitution . . . is that each department is truly independent of the others, and has an equal right to decide for itself what is the meaning of the constitution in the cases submitted to its action; and especially, where it is to act ultimately and without appeal.

Thomas Jefferson, Letter to Spencer Roane, 6 Sept. 1819, in *Writings of Thomas Jefferson* 10:141 (Paul L. Ford ed. 1899)

14 Should Congress, in the execution of its powers, adopt measures which are prohibited by the constitution; or should Congress, under the pretext of executing its powers, pass laws for the accomplishment of objects not entrusted to the government; it would become the painful duty of this tribunal, should a case requiring such a decision come before it, to say that such an act was not the law of the land.

John Marshall, *McCulloch v. Maryland,* 17 U.S. (4 Wheat.) 316, 423 (1819)

15 But where the law is not prohibited, and is really calculated to effect any of the objects entrusted to the government, to undertake here to inquire into the degree of its necessity, would be to pass the line which circumscribes the judicial department, and to tread on legislative ground. This court disclaims all pretensions to such a power.

John Marshall, *McCulloch v. Maryland,* 17 U.S. (4 Wheat.) 316, 423 (1819)

16 You seem . . . to consider the judges as the ultimate arbiters of all constitutional questions; a very dangerous doctrine indeed, and one which would place us under the despotism of an oligarchy. Our judges are as honest as other men, and not more so. They have, with others, the same passions for party, for power, and the privilege of their corps. Their maxim is *"boni judicis est ampliare jurisdictionem,"* and their power the more dangerous as they are in office for life, and not responsible, as the other functionaries are, to the elective control. The constitution has erected no such single tribunal, knowing that to whatever hands confided, with the corruptions of time and party, its members would become despots. It has more wisely made all the departments co-equal and co-sovereign within themselves.

Thomas Jefferson, Letter to William C. Jarvis, 28 Sept. 1820, in *Writings of Thomas Jefferson* 10:160 (Paul L. Ford ed. 1899)

17 The most delicate and at the same time, the proudest attribute of American jurisprudence, is the right of its judicial tribunals to decide questions of constitutional law. In other governments these questions cannot be entertained or decided by courts of justice; and, therefore, whatever may be the theory of the constitution, the legislative authority is practically omnipotent, and there is no means of contesting the legality or justice of a law but by an appeal to arms. This can be done only when oppression weighs heavily and grievously on the whole people, and is then resisted by all because it is felt by all. But the oppression that strikes at a humble individual, though it robs him of character, or fortune, or life, is remediless; and, if it becomes the subject of judicial inquiry, judges may lament, but cannot resist, the mandates of the legislature.

Joseph Story, Address before Suffolk Bar, Boston, 4 Sept. 1821, in *Miscellaneous Writings of Joseph Story* 198, 226–27 (William W. Story ed. 1852)

18 Now, in questions of this sort, precedents ought to go for absolutely nothing. The constitution is a collection of fundamental laws, not to be departed from in practice nor altered by judicial decision, and in the construction of it, nothing would be so alarming as the doctrine of *communis error,* which offers a ready justification for every usurpation that has not been resisted *in limine* . . . the judge who asserts [the right of judicial review] ought to be prepared to maintain it on the principles of the constitution.

John B. Gibson, *Eakin v. Raub,* 12 S.& R. 330, 346 (Pa. 1825) (dissenting)

19 It is but a decent respect due to the wisdom, the integrity, and the patriotism of the legislative body, by which any law is passed, to presume in favor of its validity, until its violation of the constitution is proved beyond all reasonable doubt.

Bushrod Washington, *Ogden v. Saunders,* 25 U.S. (12 Wheat.) 213, 270 (1827)

20 No questions can be brought before a judicial tribunal of greater delicacy than those which involve the constitutionality of a legislative act. If they become indispensably necessary to the case, the court must meet and decide them; but if the case may be determined on other points, a just respect for the legislature requires, that the obligation of its laws should not be unnecessarily and wantonly assailed.

John Marshall, *Ex parte Randolph,* 20 F. Cas. 242, 254 (C.C.D. Va. 1833) (No. 11,558)

21 The power vested in the American courts of justice, of pronouncing a statute to be

unconstitutional, forms one of the most powerful barriers which has ever been devised against the tyranny of political assemblies.

> Alexis de Tocqueville, *Democracy in America* 1:129–30 (Francis Bowen trans. 1862) (1835)

22 If the policy of the government, upon vital questions, affecting the whole people, is to be irrevocably fixed by decisions of the Supreme Court, the instant they are made, in ordinary litigation between parties, in personal actions, the people will have ceased, to be their own rulers, having, to that extent, practically resigned their government, into the hands of that eminent tribunal.

> Abraham Lincoln, First Inaugural Address, 4 Mar. 1861, in *Collected Works of Abraham Lincoln* 4:268 (Roy P. Basler ed. 1953)

23 For protection against abuses by legislatures the people must resort to the polls, not to the courts.

> Morrison R. Waite, *Munn v. Illinois*, 94 U.S. 113, 134 (1877)

24 Having regard to the great, complex, ever-unfolding exigencies of government, much which will seem unconstitutional to one man, or body of men, may reasonably not seem so to another; that the constitution often admits of different interpretations; that there is often a range of choice and judgment; that in such cases the constitution does not impose upon the legislature any one specific opinion, but leaves open this range of choice; and that whatever choice is rational is constitutional.

> James Bradley Thayer, "The Origin and Scope of the American Doctrine of Constitutional Law," 7 *Harvard Law Review* 129, 144 (1893)

25 The legislature in determining what shall be done, what it is reasonable to do, does not divide its duty with the judges, nor must it conform to their conception of what is prudent or reasonable legislation. The judicial function is merely that of fixing the outside border of reasonable legislative action.

> James Bradley Thayer, "The Origin and Scope of the American Doctrine of Constitutional Law," 7 *Harvard Law Review* 129, 148 (1893)

26 Is the judiciary to supervise the action of the legislative branch of the government

upon questions of public policy? ... The vast powers committed to the present government may be abused. ... But the remedy for such abuses is to be found at the ballot-box, and in a wholesome public opinion which the representatives of the people will not long, if at all, disregard.

> John M. Harlan (1833–1911), *Pollock v. Farmers' Loan & Trust Co.*, 158 U.S. 601, 679–80 (1895) (dissenting)

27 Great and, indeed, inestimable as are the advantages in a popular government of this conservative influence,—the power of the judiciary to disregard unconstitutional legislation,—it should be remembered that the exercise of it, even when unavoidable, is always attended with a serious evil, namely, that the correction of legislative mistakes comes from the outside, and the people thus lose the political experience, and the moral education and stimulus that come from fighting the question out in the ordinary way, and correcting their own errors.

> James Bradley Thayer, *John Marshall* 106 (1901)

28 The tendency of a common and easy resort to this great function [judicial review], now lamentably too common, is to dwarf the political capacity of the people, and to deaden its sense of moral possibility.

> James Bradley Thayer, *John Marshall* 107 (1901)

29 I do not think the United States would come to an end if we lost our power to declare an Act of Congress void. I do think the Union would be imperiled if we could not make that declaration as to the laws of the several States.

> Oliver Wendell Holmes, Jr., "Law and the Court" (speech to Harvard Law School Association of New York), 15 Feb. 1913, in *Collected Legal Papers* 291, 295–96 (1920)

30 The utility of an external power restraining the legislative judgment is not to be measured by counting the occasions of its exercise. The great ideals of liberty and equality are preserved against the assaults of opportunism, the expediency of the passing hour, the erosion of small encroachments, the scorn and derision of those who have no patience with general principles, by enshrining them in constitutions, and

consecrating to the task of their protection a body of defenders. By conscious or subconscious influence, the presence of this restraining power, aloof in the background, but none the less always in reserve, tends to stabilize and rationalize the legislative judgment, to infuse it with the glow of principle, to hold the standard aloft and visible for those who must run the race and keep the faith.

Benjamin N. Cardozo, *The Nature of the Judicial Process* 92–93 (1921)

31 There should be no misunderstanding as to the function of this court. . . . It is sometimes said that the court assumes a power to overrule or control the action of the people's representatives. This is a misconception. The Constitution is the supreme law of the land ordained and established by the people. All legislation must conform to the principles it lays down. When an act . . . is appropriately challenged in the courts as not conforming to the constitutional mandate the judicial branch of the Government has only one duty,—to lay the article of the Constitution which is involved beside the statute which is challenged and to decide whether the latter squares with the former. All the Court does, or can do, is to announce its considered judgment upon the question. The only power it has, if such it may be called, is the power of judgment. This court neither approves nor condemns any legislative policy. Its delicate and difficult office is to ascertain and declare whether the legislation is in accordance with, or in contravention of, the provisions of the Constitution; and, having done that, its duty ends.

Owen J. Roberts, *United States v. Butler,* 297 U.S. 1, 62–63 (1936)

32 The power of courts to declare a statute unconstitutional is subject to two guiding principles of decision which ought never to be absent from judicial consciousness. One is that courts are concerned only with the power to enact statutes, not with their wisdom. The other is that while unconstitutional exercise of power by the executive and legislative branches of the government is subject to judicial restraint, the only check upon our own exercise of power is our own sense of self-restraint. For the removal of unwise laws from the statute books appeal lies not to the courts but to

the ballot and to the processes of democratic government.

Harlan F. Stone, *United States v. Butler,* 297 U.S. 1, 78 (1936) (dissenting)

33 Our only power over state judgments is to correct them to the extent that they incorrectly adjudge federal rights. And our power is to correct wrong judgments, not to revise opinions. We are not permitted to render an advisory opinion, and if the same judgment would be rendered by the state court after we corrected its views of federal laws, our review could amount to nothing more than an advisory opinion.

Robert H. Jackson, *Herb v. Pitcairn,* 324 U.S. 117, 125–26 (1945)

34 What is always basic when the power of Congress to enact legislation is challenged is the appropriate approach to judicial review of congressional legislation. . . . When the power of Congress to pass a statute is challenged, the function of this Court is to determine whether legislative action lies clearly outside the constitutional grant of power to which it has been, or may fairly be, referred. In making this determination, the Court sits in judgment on the action of a co-ordinate branch of the Government while keeping into itself—as it must under our constitutional system—the final determination of its own power to act.

Felix Frankfurter, *Trop v. Dulles,* 356 U.S. 86, 119–20 (1958) (dissenting)

35 Judicial review is a counter-majoritarian force in our system.

Alexander M. Bickel, *The Least Dangerous Branch* 16 (1962)

36 The reality [is] that when the Supreme Court declares unconstitutional a legislative act or the action of an elected executive, it thwarts the will of representatives of the actual people of the here and now; it exercises control, not in behalf of the prevailing majority, but against it. That, without mystic overtones, is what actually happens.

Alexander M. Bickel, *The Least Dangerous Branch* 16–17 (1962)

37 We [the Supreme Court] do not sit as a super-legislature to determine the wisdom, need, and propriety of laws that touch eco-

nomic problems, business affairs, or social conditions.

William O. Douglas, *Griswold v. Connecticut,* 381 U.S. 479, 482 (1965)

38 The Constitution presumes that, absent some reason to infer antipathy, even improvident decisions will eventually be rectified by the democratic process and that judicial intervention is generally unwarranted no matter how unwisely we may think a political branch has acted.

Byron R. White, *Vance v. Bradley,* 440 U.S. 93, 97 (1979)

JUDICIARY

See also COURTS; JUDGES; JUDGES, INDIVIDUAL; SEPARATION OF POWERS; SUPREME COURT

1 He has obstructed the Administration of Justice, by refusing his Assent to Laws for establishing Judiciary powers.—He has made Judges dependent on his Will alone, for the tenure of their offices, and the amount and payment of their salaries.

Declaration of Independence, 1776, in *Documents Illustrative of the Formation of the Union of the American States* 22, 23 (1927)

2 The dignity and stability of government in all its branches, the morals of the people, and every blessing of society, depend so much upon an upright and skillful administration of justice, that the judicial power ought to be distinct from both the legislature and executive, and *independent* upon both, that so it may be a *check* upon both, as both should be checks upon that. The judges, therefore, should always be men of learning and experience in the laws, of exemplary morals, great patience, calmness and attention; their minds should not be *distracted with jarring interests;* they should not be *dependent upon any man, or body of men.* To these ends they should hold *estates for life* in their offices, or, in other words, their commissions should be *during good behavior,* and their salaries ascertained and established by law.

Thomas Jefferson, Letter to George Wythe, June 1776, in *Papers of Thomas Jefferson* 1:410 (Julian P. Boyd ed. 1950)

3 The judiciary, from the nature of its functions, will always be the least dangerous to the political rights of the constitution; because it will be least in a capacity to annoy or injure them. . . . The judiciary . . . has no influence over either the sword or the purse, no direction either of the strength or of the wealth of the society, and can take no active resolution whatever. It may truly be said to have neither FORCE nor WILL, but merely judgment; and must ultimately depend upon the aid of the executive arm even for the efficacy of its judgments.

Alexander Hamilton, *The Federalist* No. 78, at 2:291 (1788)

4 The judiciary is beyond comparison the weakest of the three departments. . . . it is in continual jeopardy of being overpowered, awed or influenced by its coordinate branches.

Alexander Hamilton, *The Federalist* No. 78, at 2:292 (1788)

5 Though individual oppression may now and then proceed from the courts of justice, the general liberty of the people can never be endangered from that quarter: I mean, so long as the judiciary remains truly distinct from both the legislature and executive.

Alexander Hamilton, *The Federalist* No. 78, at 2:292 (1788)

6 The complete independence of the courts of justice is peculiarly essential in a limited constitution.

Alexander Hamilton, *The Federalist* No. 78, at 2:292 (1788)

7 Impressed with a conviction that the due administration of justice is the firmest pillar of good Government,* I have considered the first arrangement of the Judicial department as essential to the happiness of our Country, and to the stability of its political system; hence the selection of the fittest characters to expound the laws, and dispense justice, has been an invariable object of my anxious concern.

George Washington, Letter to Edmund Randolph, 27 Sept. 1789, in *Writings of George Washington* 30:418–19 (John C. Fitzpatrick ed. 1939)

---

* "The administration of justice is the firmest pillar of government" is inscribed on the New York County courthouse.

8 A judiciary independent of a king or executive alone, is a good thing; but independence of the will of the nation is a solecism, at least in a republican government.

Thomas Jefferson, Letter to Thomas Ritchie, 25 Dec. 1820, in *Writings of Thomas Jefferson* 10:171 (Paul L. Ford ed. 1899)

9 The legislative and executive branches may sometimes err, but elections and dependence will bring them to rights. The judiciary branch is the instrument which, working like gravity, without intermission, is to press us at last into one consolidated mass.

Thomas Jefferson, Letter to Archibald Thweat, 19 Jan. 1821, in *Writings of Thomas Jefferson* 10:184 (Paul L. Ford ed. 1899)

10 They [the judges] are then in fact the corps of sappers and miners, steadily working to undermine the independent rights of the States, and to consolidate all power in the hands of that government in which they have so important a freehold estate.

Thomas Jefferson, *Autobiography*, 1821, in *Writings of Thomas Jefferson* 1:113 (Paul L. Ford ed. 1892)

11 The great object of my fear is the federal judiciary. That body, like gravity, ever acting, with noiseless foot, and unalarming advance, gaining ground step by step, and holding what it gains, is ingulphing insidiously the special governments into the jaws of that which feeds them.

Thomas Jefferson, Letter to Spencer Roane, 9 Mar. 1821, in *Writings of Thomas Jefferson* 10:189 (Paul L. Ford ed. 1899)

12 The germ of dissolution of our federal government is in the constitution of the federal judiciary; an irresponsible body, (for impeachment is scarcely a scare-crow,) working like gravity by night and by day, gaining a little to-day and a little to-morrow, and advancing its noiseless step like a thief, over the field of jurisdiction, until all shall be usurped from the States, and the government of all be consolidated into one.

Thomas Jefferson, Letter to Charles Hammond, 18 Aug. 1821, in *Writings of Thomas Jefferson* 15:331–32 (Andrew A. Lipscomb ed. 1904)

13 Frame constitutions of government with what wisdom and foresight we may, they must be imperfect, and leave something to discretion, and much to public virtue. It is in vain, that we insert bills of rights in our constitutions, as checks upon legislative power, unless there be firmness in courts, in the hour of trial, to resist the fashionable opinions of the day.

Joseph Story, Address before Suffolk Bar, Boston, 4 Sept. 1821, in *Miscellaneous Writings of Joseph Story* 198, 229 (William W. Story ed. 1852)

14 At the establishment of our constitutions, the judiciary bodies were supposed to be the most helpless and harmless members of our government. Experience, however, soon showed in what way they were to become the most dangerous; that the insufficiency of the means provided for their removal gave them a freehold and irresponsibility in office; that their decisions, seeming to concern individual suitors only, pass silent and unheeded by the public at large; that these decisions, nevertheless, become law by precedent, sapping, by little and little, the foundations of the constitution, and working its change by construction, before any one has perceived that that invisible and helpless worm has been busily employed in consuming its substance. In truth, man is not made to be trusted for life, if secured against all liability to account.

Thomas Jefferson, Letter to A. Coray, 31 Oct. 1823, in *Writings of Thomas Jefferson* 15:486–87 (Andrew A. Lipscomb ed. 1904)

15 This member of the government [the judiciary] was at first considered as the most harmless and helpless of all its organs. But it has proved that the power of declaring what the law is, *ad libitum*, by sapping and mining, slily, and without alarm, the foundations of the constitution, can do what open force would not dare to attempt.

Thomas Jefferson, Letter to Edward Livingston, 25 Mar. 1825, in *Writings of Thomas Jefferson* 7:404 (H.A. Washington ed. 1854)

16 The Judicial Department comes home in its effects to every man's fireside: it passes on his property, his reputation, his life, his all. Is it not, to the last degree important, that he [the judge] should be rendered perfectly and completely independent, with nothing

to influence or controul him but God and his conscience?

John Marshall, in Debates of the Virginia State Convention, 11 Dec. 1829, in *Proceedings and Debates of the Virginia State Convention of 1829–30,* at 616 (1830)

17 The greatest scourge an angry Heaven ever inflicted upon an ungrateful and a sinning people, was an ignorant, a corrupt, or a dependent Judiciary.

John Marshall, in Debates of the Virginia State Convention, 11 Dec. 1829, in *Proceedings and Debates of the Virginia State Convention of 1829–30,* at 619 (1830)

18 I have the highest regard for the courts. My whole life has been spent in work conditioned upon respect for the courts. I reckon him one of the worst enemies of the community who will talk lightly of the dignity of the bench. We are under a Constitution, but the Constitution is what the judges say it is,* and the judiciary is the safeguard of our liberty and of our property under the Constitution.

Charles Evans Hughes, Speech, Elmira, N.Y., 3 May 1907, in *Addresses and Papers of Charles Evans Hughes* 133, 139 (1908)

19 I have gr-reat respect f'r th' joodicyary, as fine a lot iv cross an' indignant men as ye'll find annywhere.

Finley Peter Dunne, "The Big Fine," *Mr. Dooley Says,* 1910, in *Mr. Dooley: Now and Forever* 281, 283 (Louis Filler ed. 1954)

20 It [the Constitution] gave the courts of the United States a power possessed by the judicial tribunals of no other country. It brought within the scope of the lawyer's

---

* This remark ["the Constitution is what the judges say it is"] has been used, regardless of its context, as if permitting the inference that I was picturing constitutional interpretation by the courts as a matter of judicial caprice. This was farthest from my thought.... I was speaking of the essential function of the courts under our system in interpreting and applying constitutional safeguards, and I was emphasizing the importance of maintaining the courts in the highest public esteem as our final judicial arbiters and the inadvisability of needlessly exposing them to criticism and disrespect by throwing upon them the burden of dealing with purely administrative questions. —**Charles Evans Hughes,** *The Autobiographical Notes of Charles Evans Hughes* 143–44 (1973)

business cases of a kind that could arise nowhere else—it married law and politics.

Frederick W. Lehmann, quoted in Champ Clark, *My Quarter Century of American Politics* 2:133 (1920)

21 Judicial restraint is but another form of judicial activism.

Laurence H. Tribe, *American Constitutional Law* iv (1978)

JURISDICTION

See also COURTS

1 The honorable gentleman says that no law of Congress can make any exception to the federal appellate jurisdiction of facts as well as law. He has frequently spoken of technical terms, and the meaning of them. What is the meaning of the term *exception*? Does it not mean an alteration and diminution? Congress is empowered to make exceptions to the appellate jurisdiction, as to law and fact, of the Supreme Court. These exceptions certainly go as far as the legislature may think proper for the interest and liberty of the people.

John Marshall, Speech to Virginia ratifying convention, 1788, in *Debates on the Adoption of the Federal Constitution* 3:559–60 (Jonathan Elliot ed., 2d ed. 1888)

2 What do we mean by the words *arising under the Constitution?* What do they relate to? I conceive this to be very ambiguous. If my interpretation be right, the word *arising* will be carried so far that it will be made use of to aid and extend the federal jurisdiction.

Edmund Randolph, Speech before the Virginia Convention on the Adoption of the Federal Constitution, 21 June 1788, in *Debates on the Adoption of the Federal Constitution,* 3:572 (Jonathan Elliot ed., 2d ed. 1888)

3 The circuit courts shall have original cognizance, concurrent with the courts of the several States, of all suits of a civil nature at common law or in equity, where the matter in dispute exceeds, exclusive of costs, the sum or value of five hundred dollars, and the United States are plaintiffs, or petitioners; or an alien is a party, or the suit is between a citizen of the State where the suit is brought, and a citizen of another State. And shall have exclusive cognizance

of all crimes and offences cognizable under the authority of the United States, except where this act otherwise provides, or the laws of the United States shall otherwise direct, and concurrent jurisdiction with the district courts of the crimes and offences cognizable therein.

Judiciary Act of 1789, ch. 20, § 11, 1 Stat. 73, 78–79

4 The political truth is, that the disposal of the judicial power, (except in a few specified instances) belongs to congress. If congress has given the power to this Court, we possess it, not otherwise.

Samuel Chase, *Turner v. Bank of North America,* 4 U.S. (4 Dall.) 8, 10 n.1 (1799)

5 It is most true that this Court will not take jurisdiction if it should not: but it is equally true, that it must take jurisdiction if it should. The judiciary cannot, as the legislature may, avoid a measure because it approaches the confines of the constitution. We cannot pass it by because it is doubtful. With whatever doubts, with whatever difficulties, a case may be attended, we must decide it, if it be brought before us. We have no more right to decline the exercise of jurisdiction which is given, than to usurp that which is not given. The one or the other would be treason to the constitution.

John Marshall, *Cohens v. Virginia,* 19 U.S. (6 Wheat.) 264, 404 (1821)

6 The universally received opinion is, that no suit can be commenced or prosecuted against the United States; that the judiciary act does not authorize such suits.

John Marshall, *Cohens v. Virginia,* 19 U.S. (6 Wheat.) 264, 411–12 (1821)

7 The jurisdiction claimed for the Federal Judiciary is truly the *only* defensive armour of the Federal Government, or, rather, for the Constitution and laws of the United States. Strip it of that armour, and the door is wide open for nullification, anarchy, and convulsion.

James Madison, Letter to Joseph C. Cabell, 1 Apr. 1833, in *Letters and Other Writings of James Madison* 4:294, 296–97 (William C. Rives ed. 1865)

8 We do not consider congress can either withdraw from judicial cognizance any matter which, from its nature, is the subject of a suit at the common law, or in equity, or admiralty; nor, on the other hand, can it bring under the judicial power a matter which, from its nature, is not a subject for judicial determination. At the same time there are matters, involving public rights, which may be presented in such form that the judicial power is capable of acting on them, and which are susceptible of judicial determination, but which congress may or may not bring within the cognizance of the courts of the United States, as it may deem proper.

Benjamin R. Curtis, *Murray's Lessee v. Hoboken Land & Improvement Co.,* 59 U.S. (18 How.) 272, 284 (1856)

9 We disclaim altogether any jurisdiction in the courts of the United States upon the subject of divorce, or for the allowance of alimony.

James M. Wayne, *Barber v. Barber,* 62 U.S. (21 How.) 582, 584 (1858)

10 We are not at liberty to inquire into the motives of the legislature. We can only examine into its power under the Constitution; and the power to make exceptions to the appellate jurisdiction of this court is given by express words. . . . Without jurisdiction the court cannot proceed at all in any cause. Jurisdiction is power to declare the law, and when it ceases to exist, the only function remaining to the court is that of announcing the fact and dismissing the cause.

Salmon P. Chase, *Ex parte McCardle,* 74 U.S. (7 Wall.) 506, 514 (1869)

11 The State courts are the appropriate tribunals, as this court has repeatedly held, for the decision of questions arising under their local laws, whether statutory or otherwise. And it is not lightly to be presumed that Congress acted upon a principle which implies a distrust of their integrity or of their ability to construe those laws correctly.

Samuel F. Miller, *Murdock v. City of Memphis,* 87 U.S. (20 Wall.) 590, 626 (1875)

12 Every State possesses exclusive jurisdiction and sovereignty over persons and property within its territory. . . . no State can exer-

217

cise direct jurisdiction and authority over persons or property without its territory.

Stephen J. Field, *Pennoyer v. Neff,* 95 U.S. 714, 722 (1878)

13 If the act which the state [official] seeks to enforce be a violation of the Federal Constitution, the officer in proceeding under such enactment comes into conflict with the superior authority of that Constitution, and he is in that case stripped of his official or representative character and is subjected in his person to the consequences of his individual conduct. The State has no power to impart to him any immunity from responsibility to the supreme authority of the United States.

Rufus W. Peckham, *Ex parte Young,* 209 U.S. 123, 159–60 (1908)

14 Of course the party who brings a suit is master to decide what law he will rely upon and therefore does determine whether he will bring a "suit arising under" . . . [any] law of the United States by his declaration or bill. That question cannot depend upon the answer, and accordingly jurisdiction cannot be conferred by the defense even when anticipated and replied to in the bill.

Oliver Wendell Holmes, Jr., *The Fair v. Kohler Die & Specialty Co.,* 228 U.S. 22, 25 (1913)

15 Ordinarily jurisdiction over a person is based on the power of the sovereign asserting it to seize that person and imprison him to await the sovereign's pleasure. But when that power exists and is asserted by service at the beginning of a cause, or if the party submits to the jurisdiction in whatever form may be required, we dispense with the necessity of maintaining the physical power and attribute the same force to the judgment or decree whether the party remain within the jurisdiction or not. This is one of the decencies of civilization that no one would dispute.

Oliver Wendell Holmes, Jr., *Michigan Trust Co. v. Ferry,* 228 U.S. 346, 353 (1913)

16 A suit arises under the law that creates the cause of action.

Oliver Wendell Holmes, Jr., *American Well Works Co. v. Layne & Bowler Co.,* 241 U.S. 257, 260 (1916)

17 A foreign corporation is amenable to process to enforce a personal liability, in the absence of consent, only if it is doing business within the State in such manner and to such extent as to warrant the inference that it is present there.

Louis D. Brandeis, *Philadelphia & Reading Ry. v. McKibbin,* 243 U.S. 264, 265 (1917)

18 The foundation of jurisdiction is physical power.

Oliver Wendell Holmes, Jr., *McDonald v. Mabee,* 243 U.S. 90, 91 (1917)

19 Jurisdiction exists that rights may be maintained. Rights are not maintained that jurisdiction may exist.

Benjamin N. Cardozo, *Berkovitz v. Arbib,* 230 N.Y. 261, 274, 130 N.E. 288 (1921)

20 We are to inquire whether the extent and continuity of what it [the corporation] has done in the state in question makes it reasonable to bring it before one of its courts. . . . It is quite impossible to establish any rule from the decided cases; we must step from tuft to tuft across the morass.

Learned Hand, *Hutchinson v. Chase & Gilbert,* 45 F.2d 139, 141–42 (2d Cir. 1930)

21 How and when a case arises "under the Constitution or laws of the United States" has been much considered in the books. . . . To bring a case within the statute, a right or immunity created by the Constitution or laws of the United States must be an element, and an essential one, of the plaintiff's cause of action. . . . The right or immunity must be such that it will be supported if the Constitution or laws of the United States are given one construction or effect, and defeated if they receive another. . . . the controversy must be disclosed upon the face of the complaint, unaided by the answer or by the petition for removal. . . . Indeed, the complaint itself will not avail as a basis of jurisdiction in so far as it goes beyond a statement of the plaintiff's cause of action and anticipates or replies to a probable defense.

Benjamin N. Cardozo, *Gully v. First Nat'l Bank,* 299 U.S. 109, 112–13 (1936)

22 What is needed is something of that common-sense accommodation of judgment to kaleidoscopic situations which characterizes the law in its treatment of problems of causation. One could carry the search for

causes backward, almost without end. . . . Instead, there has been a selective process which picks the substantial causes out of the web and lays the other ones aside. As in problems of causation, so here in the search for the underlying law. If we follow the ascent far enough, countless claims of right can be discovered to have their source or their operative limits in the provisions of a federal statute or in the Constitution itself with its circumambient restrictions upon legislative power. To set bounds to the pursuit, the courts have formulated the distinction between controversies that are basic and those that are collateral, between disputes that are necessary and those that are merely possible. We shall be lost in a maze if we put that compass by.

    Benjamin N. Cardozo, *Gully v. First Nat'l Bank,* 299 U.S. 109, 117–18 (1936)

23 The rule governing dismissal for want of jurisdiction in cases brought in the federal court is that, unless the law gives a different rule, the sum claimed by the plaintiff controls if the claim is apparently made in good faith. It must appear to a legal certainty that the claim is really for less than the jurisdictional amount to justify dismissal. . . . But if, from the face of the pleadings, it is apparent, to a legal certainty, that the plaintiff cannot recover the amount claimed, or if, from the proofs, the court is satisfied to a like certainty that the plaintiff never was entitled to recover that amount, and that his claim was therefore colorable for the purpose of conferring jurisdiction, the suit will be dismissed.

    Owen J. Roberts, *Saint Paul Mercury Indemnity Co. v. Red Cab Co.,* 303 U.S. 283, 288–89 (1938)

24 It is settled law . . . that any state may impose liabilities, even upon persons not within its allegiance, for conduct outside its borders that has consequences within its borders which the state reprehends; and these liabilities other states will ordinarily recognize.

    Learned Hand, *United States v. Aluminum Co. of Am.,* 148 F.2d 416, 443 (2d Cir. 1945)

25 Due process requires only that in order to subject a defendant to a judgment *in personam,* if he be not present within the territory of the forum, he have certain minimum contacts with it such that the

maintenance of the suit does not offend "traditional notions of fair play and substantial justice." Milliken v. Meyer, 311 U.S. 457, 463.

    Harlan F. Stone, *International Shoe Co. v. Washington,* 326 U.S. 310, 316 (1945)

26 This is a horse soon curried. Congress, in conferring jurisdiction on the district courts in cases based solely on diversity of citizenship, has been explicit to confine such suits to "the judicial district where all plaintiffs or all defendants reside."

    Felix Frankfurter, *Olberding v. Illinois Cent. R.R.,* 346 U.S. 338, 340 (1953)

27 It is essential in each case that there be some act by which the defendant purposefully avails itself of the privilege of conducting activities within the forum State, thus invoking the benefits and protections of its laws.

    Earl Warren, *Hanson v. Denckla,* 357 U.S. 235, 253 (1958)

28 He alleges that Satan has on numerous occasions caused plaintiff misery and unwarranted threats, against the will of plaintiff, that Satan has placed deliberate obstacles in his path and has caused plaintiff's downfall. Plaintiff alleges that by reason of these acts Satan has deprived him of his constitutional rights. . . . We question whether plaintiff may obtain personal jurisdiction over the defendant in this judicial district.

    Gerald J. Weber, *United States ex rel. Mayo v. Satan & His Staff,* 54 F.R.D. 282, 283 (W.D. Pa. 1971)

29 The district courts shall have original jurisdiction of all civil actions arising under the Constitution, laws, or treaties of the United States.

    Federal Question Jurisdictional Amendments Act of 1980, Pub. L. No. 96–486, § 2(a), 94 Stat. 2369, 2369

JURISPRUDENCE

See also CRITICAL LEGAL STUDIES; LAW

1 There is another study which sometimes is undervalued by the practical minded, for which I wish to say a good word, although I think a good deal of pretty poor stuff goes under that name. I mean the study of what

is called jurisprudence. Jurisprudence, as I look at it, is simply law in its most generalized part. Every effort to reduce a case to a rule is an effort of jurisprudence, although the name as used in English is confined to the broadest rules and most fundamental conceptions. One mark of a great lawyer is that he sees the application of the broadest rules.

> **Oliver Wendell Holmes, Jr.,** "The Path of the Law," 10 *Harvard Law Review* 457, 474 (1897)

2 Legal systems have their periods in which science degenerates, in which system decays into technicality, in which a scientific jurisprudence becomes a mechanical jurisprudence.

> **Roscoe Pound,** "Mechanical Jurisprudence," 8 *Columbia Law Review* 605, 607 (1908)

3 Our written Constitution, by cutting off legal speculation and experiment in the precise fields wherein such adventuring is most tempting and useful, has reduced the science of jurisprudence to purely historical interest, and made all lawyers the slaves of words. . . . [The lawyer] is bound by a text, and every year that text grows more rigid and inconvenient. Justice has no place in it, nor reason: it is simply a series of unyielding mandates. Some of those mandates, at an early stage, were found to be unworkable, and so the courts had to find ways to get around them. But it was not possible to get around them by setting the principles of justice and reason against them: The business had to be achieved by the arts of casuistry and obfuscation, of what on other planes would be called hypocrisy and trickery.

> **H. L. Mencken,** Editorial, *American Mercury,* Jan. 1928, at 35, 37

JURY

See also GRAND JURY

1 That in controversies respecting property, and in suits between man and man, the ancient trial by jury is preferable to any other, and ought to be held sacred.

> Virginia Declaration of Rights of 1776, § 11, in *Federal and State Constitutions* 7:3812, 3814 (Francis N. Thorpe ed. 1909)

2 I consider that [trial by jury] as the only anchor, ever yet imagined by man, by which a government can be held to the principles of it's [sic] constitution.

> **Thomas Jefferson,** Letter to Thomas Paine, 11 July 1789, in *Papers of Thomas Jefferson* 15:269 (Julian P. Boyd ed. 1958)

3 It is left therefore to the juries, if they think permanent judges are under any biass [sic] whatever in any cause, to take upon themselves to judge the law as well as the fact. They never exercise this power but when they suspect partiality in the judges, and by the exercise of this power they have been the firmest bulwarks of English liberty.

> **Thomas Jefferson,** Letter to Abbé Arnoux, 19 July 1789, in *Papers of Thomas Jefferson* 15:283 (Julian P. Boyd ed. 1958)

4 Were I called upon to decide whether the people had best be omitted in the Legislative or Judiciary department, I would say it is better to leave them out of the Legislature. The execution of the laws is more important than the making of them.

> **Thomas Jefferson,** Letter to Abbé Arnoux, 19 July 1789, in *Papers of Thomas Jefferson* 15:283 (Julian P. Boyd ed. 1958)

5 But it must be observed that by the same law, which recognizes this reasonable distribution of jurisdiction, you have nevertheless a right to take upon yourselves to judge of both, and to determine the law as well as the fact in controversy. On this, and on every other occasion, however, we have no doubt, you will pay that respect which is due to the opinion of the court: For, as on the one hand, it is presumed, that juries are the best judges of facts; it is, on the other hand, presumable, that the court are the best judges of law. But still both objects are lawfully, within your power of decision.

> **John Jay,** *Georgia v. Brailsford,* 3 U.S. (3 Dall.) 1, 4 (1794) (charge to jury)

6 Light impressions which may fairly be supposed to yield to the testimony that may be offered, which may leave the mind open to a fair consideration of the testimony, constitute no sufficient objection to a juror; but . . . those strong and deep impressions which will close the mind against the testimony that may be offered in opposition to them, which will combat that testimony,

and resist its force, do constitute a sufficient objection to him.

John Marshall, *United States v. Burr,* 25 F. Cas. 49, 51 (C.C.D. Va. 1807) (No. 14,692g)

7 We think, that in all cases of this nature, the law has invested Courts of justice with the authority to discharge a jury from giving any verdict, whenever, in their opinion, taking all the circumstances into consideration, there is a manifest necessity for the act, or the ends of public justice would otherwise be defeated. They are to exercise a sound discretion on the subject; and it is impossible to define all the circumstances, which would render it proper to interfere. To be sure, the power ought to be used with the greatest caution, under urgent circumstances, and for very plain and obvious causes; and, in capital cases especially, Courts should be extremely careful how they interfere with any of the changes of life, in favour of the prisoner. But, after all, they have the right to order the discharge; and the security which the public have for the faithful, sound, and conscientious exercise of this discretion, rests, in this, as in other cases, upon the responsibility of the Judges, under their oaths of office.

Joseph Story, *United States v. Perez,* 22 U.S. (9 Wheat.) 579, 580 (1824)

8 The jury is, above all, a political institution, and it must be regarded in this light in order to be duly appreciated.

Alexis de Tocqueville, *Democracy in America* 1:361 (Francis Bowen trans. 1862) (1835)

9 He who punishes the criminal is therefore the real master of society. Now, the institution of the jury raises the people itself, or at least a class of citizens, to the bench of judges. The institution of the jury consequently invests the people, or that class of citizens, with the direction of society.

Alexis de Tocqueville, *Democracy in America* 1:361 (Francis Bowen trans. 1862) (1835)

10 The jury . . . may be regarded as a gratuitous public school, ever open, in which every juror learns his rights.

Alexis de Tocqueville, *Democracy in America* 1:364 (Francis Bowen trans. 1862) (1835)

11 The jury, which is the most energetic means of making the people rule, is also the most efficacious means of teaching it how to rule well.

Alexis de Tocqueville, *Democracy in America* 1:367 (Francis Bowen trans. 1862) (1835)

12 Juries . . . have the effect . . . of placing the control of the law in the hands of those who would be most apt to abuse it.

James Fenimore Cooper, *The Redskins,* 1846, in *Complete Works of J. Fenimore Cooper* 146 (1893)

13 The law was dead against us they say, and the facts were against us; but the verdict was in our favor. That's what I call practising the law! . . . I can beat any railroad in the State, with a jury of a neighborhood, let the question or facts be what they may; but in this instance I beat the neighborhood, and all through the faith the jury had in me.

James Fenimore Cooper, *The Ways of the Hour,* 1850, in *Complete Works of J. Fenimore Cooper* 194 (1893)

14 As for the jurors, they were just what that ancient institution might be supposed to be, in a country where so many of the body of the people are liable to be summoned. An unusually large proportion of these men, when all the circumstances are considered, were perhaps as fit to be thus employed as could be obtained from the body of the community of any country of earth; but a very serious number were altogether unsuited to perform the delicate duties of their station. Fortunately, the ignorant are very apt to be influenced by the more intelligent . . . and by this exercise of a very natural power less injustice is committed than might otherwise occur.

James Fenimore Cooper, *The Ways of the Hour,* 1850, in *Complete Works of J. Fenimore Cooper* 250–51 (1893)

15 Reasonable doubt . . . is a term often used, probably pretty well understood, but not easily defined. It is not a mere possible doubt; because every thing relating to human affairs, and depending on moral evidence, is open to some possible or imaginary doubt. It is that state of the case, which, after the entire comparison and consideration of all the evidence, leaves the minds of jurors in that condition that they cannot say they feel an abiding conviction,

to a moral certainty, of the truth of the charge.

Lemuel Shaw, *Commonwealth v. Webster*, 59 Mass. (5 Cush.) 295, 320 (1850)

16 It has been truly said, that more instructive lessons are taught in Courts of Justice, than the Church is able to inculcate. Morals come in the cold abstract from the pulpit; but men smart under them practically when Juries are the preachers.

Joseph H. Lumpkin, *Kendrick v. McCrary*, 11 Ga. 603, 606 (1852)

17 For more than six hundred years—that is, since Magna Carta, in 1215—there has been no clearer principle of English or American constitutional law, than that, in criminal cases, it is not only the right and duty of juries to judge what are the facts, what is the law, and what was the moral intent of the accused; *but that it is also their right, and their primary and paramount duty, to judge of the justice of the law, and to hold all laws invalid, that are, in their opinion, unjust or oppressive, and all persons guiltless in violating, or resisting the execution of, such laws. . . .*

Any people, that judge of, and determine authoritatively for the government, what are their own liberties against the government, of course retain all the liberties they wish to enjoy. *And this is freedom.* At least, it is freedom *to them;* because, although it may be theoretically imperfect, it, nevertheless, corresponds to *their* highest notions of freedom.

Lysander Spooner, *An Essay on the Trial by Jury* 5–6 (1852)

18 A jury too frequently have at least one member, more ready to hang the panel than to hang the traitor.

Abraham Lincoln, Letter to Erastus Corning and others, 12 June 1863, in *Collected Works of Abraham Lincoln* 6:264 (Roy P. Basler ed. 1953)

19 In the McFarland case the defendant set up the plea of insanity, and succeeded in proving himself a fool. And he was acquitted by a jury of his peers.

Ambrose Bierce, "Jury of His Peers," *News Letter*, 14 May 1870, in *The Ambrose Bierce Satanic Reader* 59 (Ernest J. Hopkins ed. 1968)

20 We have a criminal jury system which is superior to any in the world; and its efficiency is only marred by the difficulty of finding twelve men every day who don't know anything and can't read.

Mark Twain, "Americans and the English" (speech), London, 4 July 1872, in *Writings of Mark Twain* 28:34, 35 (Albert B. Paine ed. 1929)

21 Alfred the Great, when he invented trial by jury, and knew that he had admirably framed it to secure justice in his age of the world, was not aware that in the nineteenth century the condition of things would be so entirely changed that unless he rose from the grave and altered the jury plan to meet the emergency, it would prove the most ingenious and infallible agency for *defeating* justice that human wisdom could contrive.

Mark Twain, *Roughing It*, 1872, in *Works of Mark Twain* 2:307 (Franklin R. Rogers ed. 1972)

22 When the peremptory challenges were all exhausted, a jury of twelve men were impaneled—a jury who swore that they had neither heard, read, talked about nor expressed an opinion concerning a murder which the very cattle in the corrals, the Indians in the sage-brush and the stones in the street were cognizant of!

Mark Twain, *Roughing It*, 1872, in *Works of Mark Twain* 2:308 (Franklin R. Rogers ed. 1972)

23 The jury system puts a ban upon intelligence and honesty, and a premium upon ignorance, stupidity, and perjury. It is a shame that we must continue to use a worthless system because it *was* good a thousand years ago. In this age, when a gentleman of high social standing, intelligence, and probity, swears that testimony given under solemn oath will outweigh, with him, street talk and newspaper reports based upon mere hearsay, he is worth a hundred jurymen who will swear to their own ignorance and stupidity, and justice would be far safer in his hands than in theirs. Why could not the jury law be so altered as to give men of brains and honesty an *equal chance* with fools and miscreants? Is it right to show the present favoritism to one class of men and inflict a

disability on another, in a land whose boast is that all its citizens are free and equal?

Mark Twain, *Roughing It*, 1872, in *Works of Mark Twain* 2:309 (Franklin R. Rogers ed. 1972)

24 I desire to tamper with the jury law. I wish to so alter it as to put a premium on intelligence and character, and close the jury box against idiots, blacklegs, and people who do not read newspapers. But no doubt I shall be defeated—every effort I make to save the country "misses fire."

Mark Twain, *Roughing It*, 1872, in *Works of Mark Twain* 2:309 (Franklin R. Rogers ed. 1972)

25 Trial by jury is the palladium of our liberties. I do not know what a palladium is, having never seen a palladium, but it is a good thing no doubt at any rate. Not less than a hundred men have been murdered in Nevada—perhaps I would be within bounds if I said three hundred—and as far as I can learn, only two persons have suffered the death penalty there. However, four or five who had no money and no political influence have been punished by imprisonment.

Mark Twain, *Roughing It*, 1872, in *Works of Mark Twain* 2:316–17 (Franklin R. Rogers ed. 1972)

26 The humorist who invented trial by jury played a colossal, practical joke upon the world, but since we have the system we ought to try to respect it. A thing which is not thoroughly easy to do, when we reflect that by command of the law a criminal juror must be an intellectual vacuum, attached to a melting heart and perfectly macaronian bowels of compassion.

Mark Twain, Letter to the Editor, *New York Tribune*, 10 Mar. 1873, at 5

27 Twelve men of the average of the community, comprising men of education and men of little education, men of learning and men whose learning consists only in what they have themselves seen and heard, the merchant, the mechanic, the farmer, the laborer; these sit together, consult, apply their separate experience of the affairs of life to the facts proven, and draw a unanimous conclusion. This average judgment thus given it is the great effort of the law to obtain. It is assumed that twelve

men know more of the common affairs of life than does one man, that they can draw wiser and safer conclusions from admitted facts thus occurring than can a single judge.

Ward Hunt, *Sioux City & P. Ry. v. Stout*, 84 U.S. (17 Wall.) 657, 664 (1874)

28 In trying a case depending upon circumstantial evidence, very few abstract principles should be given to the jury. Left to exercise their common-sense in their own way, the jury will generally determine correctly what is well proved, and what lacks further support. Furnished with a superfluity of rules, their attention is distracted, and the proffered help only obstructs. The better practice is, to decline charging refined speculations, and give only coarse, sharp-cut law. What shall come to the jury as evidence, is for the court. What it is worth when it arrives, is for the jury.

Logan E. Bleckley, *Moughon v. State*, 57 Ga. 102, 106 (1876)

29 The evidence is not conclusive. It pushes the mind into that great pit-fall called doubt, and there leaves it. The jury are the best doctors of doubt that we know of, especially when their treatment has been revised with approval by the presiding judge.

Logan E. Bleckley, *Central R.R. v. Ferguson*, 63 Ga. 83, 85 (1879)

30 A charge, torn to pieces and scattered in disjointed fragments, may seem objectionable, although when put together and considered as a whole, it may be perfectly sound. The full charge being in the record, what it lacks when divided is supplied when the parts are all united. United they stand, divided they fall.

Logan E. Bleckley, *Brown v. Matthews*, 79 Ga. 1, 7, 4 S.E. 13 (1887)

31 Marriage will relate the husband by affinity to the wife's blood relations, but will not relate the husband's brother to any of her relations. The husband of the juror's stepdaughter was not related to the juror, but only to the juror's wife. The husband's brother, the plaintiff, was further off still; he was not related even to the juror's wife. "The groom and bride each comes within / The circle of the other's kin; / But kin and

kin are still no more / Related than they were before."

Logan E. Bleckley, *Central R.R. & Banking Co. v. Roberts,* 91 Ga. 513, 516–17, 18 S.E. 315 (1893)

32 Whin th' case is all over, the jury'll pitch th' tistimony out iv th' window, an' consider three questions: "Did Lootgert look as though he'd kill his wife? Did his wife look as though she ought to be kilt? Isn't it time we wint to supper?"

Finley Peter Dunne, "On Expert Testimony," in *Mr. Dooley in Peace and in War* 141, 145 (1898)

33 I confess that in my experience I have not found juries specially inspired for the discovery of truth. I have not noticed that they could see further into things or form a saner judgment than a sensible and well trained judge. I have not found them freer from prejudice than an ordinary judge would be. Indeed one reason why I believe in our practice of leaving questions of negligence to them is what is precisely one of their gravest defects from the point of view of their theoretical function: that they will introduce into their verdict a certain amount—a very large amount, so far as I have observed—of popular prejudice, and thus keep the administration of the law in accord with the wishes and feelings of the community.

Oliver Wendell Holmes, Jr., "Law in Science and Science in Law," 12 *Harvard Law Review* 443, 459–60 (1899)

34 Th' lawyers make th' law; th' judges make th' errors, but th' iditors make th' juries.

Finley Peter Dunne, "Mr. Dooley on the Power of the Press," 62 *American Magazine* 607, 608 (1906)

35 JURY, *n.* A number of persons appointed by a court to assist the attorneys in preventing law from degenerating into justice.
Against all law and evidence,
    The prisoner was acquitted.
The judge exclaimed: "Is common sense
    To jurors not permitted?"
The prisoner's counsel rose and bowed:
    "Your Honor, why this fury?
By law the judge is not allowed
    To sit upon the jury."

Ambrose Bierce, *The Enlarged Devil's Dictionary* 168 (Ernest J. Hopkins ed. 1967)

36 Jury—A group of twelve men who, having lied to the judge about their hearing, health and business engagements, have failed to fool him.

H. L. Mencken, "Sententiae," 1916, in *A Mencken Chrestomathy* 616, 623 (1949)

37 In due time twelve men iv intilligence who have r-read th' pa-apers an' can't remimber what they've r-read, or who can't r-read, or ar-re out iv wurruk, ar-re injooced to sarve, an' th' awful wheels iv justice begins to go round.

Finley Peter Dunne, "On Criminal Trials," in *On Making a Will* 212, 216 (1919)

38 "And look at the jury," cried Tutt. "Just look at them! Ignorant, stupid, prejudiced—"
. . .
    I recall an accident case I tried once for a whole week before the Supreme Court, where, after the judge had finished charging with regard to the respective rights of the plaintiff and defendant, the foreman held up his hand and asked innocently, "Well, Your Honor, which is the plaintiff and which is the defendant?" . . .
    . . . "You wouldn't believe such people existed. But even if they had brains how on earth can they get at the real facts simply by listening to witnesses?"

Arthur Train, "The Hand is Quicker Than the Eye," in *Tutt and Mr. Tutt* 308, 322–23 (1920)

39 Juries are not leaves swayed by every breath.

Learned Hand, *United States v. Garsson,* 291 F. 646, 649 (S.D.N.Y. 1923)

40 Nothing is more conducive to the absurd formalism, which even yet at times invades a criminal trial, than to suppose that there is a ritual which must be repeated [by a judge instructing a jury] if the charm is to work. . . . It is enough if it appears that the jury has been told that the prosecution must establish all the facts to the required degree of satisfaction of the jury, and there is no fixed way in which this need be communicated, so long as that idea is evident.

Learned Hand, *Becher v. United States,* 5 F.2d 45, 51 (2d Cir. 1924)

41 And such men—odd and grizzled, or tan and wrinkled, farmers and country storekeepers, with here and there a Ford agent,

a keeper of an inn at Tom Dixon's Lake, a salesman in Hamburger's dry goods store at Bridgeburg, and a peripatetic insurance agent residing in Purday just north of Grass Lake. . . . And with but one exception, all religious, if not moral, and all convinced of Clyde's guilt before ever they sat down, but still because of their almost unanimous conception of themselves as fair and open-minded men, and because they were so interested to sit as jurors in this exciting case, convinced that they could pass fairly and impartially on the facts presented to them.

Theodore Dreiser, *An American Tragedy* 231 (1925)

42 I never saw twelve men in my life, that, if you could get them to understand a human case, were not true and right.

Clarence S. Darrow, Summation in Sweet Case, Detroit, 1926, in *Attorney for the Damned* 229, 261 (Arthur Weinberg ed. 1957)

43 The snap judgments of juries are inadequate in those knife-edge cases . . . where there is a subtler distinction to be made than the one between black and white. . . . There are decisions which casually chosen juries of men, unused to judge human motives and actions, are ludicrously unfit to render.

Theodore Dreiser, 1926, quoted in Robert H. Elias, *Theodore Dreiser: Apostle of Nature* 222–23 (1970)

44 Twelve men of limited information and intelligence, chosen precisely because of their lack of intellectual resilience.

H. L. Mencken, *Notes on Democracy* 172 (1926)

45 There is something so inherently constructive in the human mind that to leave a problem unsolved is plain misery. It haunts the average individual like any other important task left unfinished. Men in a juryroom, like those scientifically demonstrated atoms of a crystal which scientists and philosophers love to speculate upon, like finally to arrange themselves into an orderly and artistic whole, to present a compact, intellectual front, to be whatever they have set out to be, properly and rightly—a compact, sensible jury. One sees this same instinct magnificently displayed in every other phase of nature. . . . It would seem as though the physical substance of life—this apparition of form which the eye detects and calls real—were shot through with some vast subtlety that loves order, that is order. The atoms of our so-called *being*, in spite of our so-called *reason*—the dreams of a mood—know where to go and what to do. They represent an order, a wisdom, a willing that is not of us. They build orderly in spite of us. So the subconscious spirit of a jury.

Theodore Dreiser, *The Financier* 363–64 (rev. ed. 1927)

46 Up here, just loads of fun, of the most dismal sort. I'm just in the middle of serving on the jury. That is, I'm supposed to be; but every time I get into the jury box some lawyer throws me out. Sometimes it's the plaintiff and sometimes it's the defendant; they just can't stand me; they challenge away like madmen. I was getting rather sensitive about it; I was beginning to avoid my friends and talk to myself; but today I got elected into the nicest jury you ever saw, and now I'm going to have one twelfth of the responsibility of deciding whether Mr. Julius Singer really was at fault when his car collided with a taxi containing Mr. Harry Sperber at 2 o'clock in the morning of a Sunday in March 1928. Thus automatically I become a good citizen. At the same time that sour musty feeling I've had about the law has been confirmed.

Ogden Nash, Letter to Frances Leonard, 25 Jan. 1929, in *Loving Letters from Ogden Nash* 30–31 (Linell Nash Smith ed. 1990)

47 In a trial by jury in a federal court, the judge is not a mere moderator, but is the governor of the trial for the purpose of assuring its proper conduct and of determining questions of law. . . . It is within his province, whenever he thinks it necessary, to assist the jury in arriving at a just conclusion by explaining and commenting upon the evidence, by drawing their attention to the parts of it which he thinks important; and he may express his opinion upon the facts, provided he makes it clear to the jury that all matters of fact are submitted to their determination.

Charles Evans Hughes, *Quercia v. United States,* 289 U.S. 466, 469 (1933)

48 When the very merits of the case are clear; when only one result can honestly emerge; and when the jury has in fact been satisfied, we no longer look upon criminal procedure as a sacred ritual, no part of which can be omitted without breaking the charm. Trial by jury is a rough scales at best; the beam ought not to tip for motes and straws.

> **Learned Hand,** *United States v. Brown,* 79 F.2d 321, 326 (2d Cir. 1935)

49 Choosing jurors is always a delicate task. The more a lawyer knows of life, human nature, psychology, and the reactions of the human emotions, the better he is equipped for the subtle selection of his so-called "twelve men, good and true." In this undertaking, everything pertaining to the prospective juror needs to be questioned and weighed: his nationality, his business, religion, politics, social standing, family ties, friends, habits of life and thought; the books and newspapers he likes and reads, and many more matters that combine to make a man; all of these qualities and experiences have left their effect on ideas, beliefs and fancies that inhabit his mind.

> **Clarence S. Darrow,** "Attorney for the Defense," *Esquire,* May 1936, in *Verdicts Out of Court* 313, 315 (Arthur Weinberg & Lila Weinberg eds. 1963)

50 So far as possible, the lawyer should know both sides of the case. If the client is a landlord, a banker, or a manufacturer, or one of that type, then jurors sympathetic to that class will be wanted in the box; a man who looks neat and trim and smug.... Every knowing lawyer seeks for a jury of the same sort of men as his client; men who will be able to imagine themselves in the same situation and realize what verdict the client wants.

> **Clarence S. Darrow,** "Attorney for the Defense," *Esquire,* May 1936, in *Verdicts Out of Court* 313, 315 (Arthur Weinberg & Lila Weinberg eds. 1963)

51 Never take a wealthy man on a jury. He will convict, unless the defendant is accused of violating the anti-trust law, selling worthless stocks or bonds, or something of that kind. Next to the Board of Trade, for him, the penitentiary is the most important of all public buildings.

> **Clarence S. Darrow,** "Attorney for the Defense," *Esquire,* May 1936, in *Verdicts Out*

of Court 313, 319 (Arthur Weinberg & Lila Weinberg eds. 1963)

52 A jury consists of twelve persons chosen to decide who has the better lawyer.

> **Robert Frost,** Attributed remark, quoted in Lewis and Faye Copeland, *10,000 Jokes, Toasts & Stories* 655 (1939)

53 In a word I learned that juries, so far from doing what they were supposed to do, really treated crimes as sins, and temporarily acted as vicarious representatives of the Almighty in deciding what ought to be done about the transgressors; that on the whole, although it wasn't the Law, this was a good thing; and that, by and large, the Good Samaritan was better than the Man-who-passed-by-on-the-other-side, even if the chap in the gutter had got only what he legally deserved; that even the worst had something admirable about them and should be judged, not according to legislative standards, but by their own, for which usually they were not responsible—held good or bad "according to their lights"; that the really important thing was, not what their standards were, but that people should have standards at all; in fine that only sympathy and understanding could make life or law bearable; and that kindness, loyalty and courage were better tests of a man's rectitude than his respect for the letter of the statutes.

> **Arthur Train,** *My Day in Court* 114 (1939)

54 It is part of the established tradition in the case of juries as instruments of public justice that the jury be a body truly representative of the community. For racial discrimination to result in the exclusion from jury service of otherwise qualified groups not only violates our Constitution and the laws enacted under it but is at war with our basic concepts of a democratic society and a representative government.

> **Hugo L. Black,** *Smith v. Texas,* 311 U.S. 128, 130 (1940)

55 A jury has its uses.... It's like a cylinder head gasket. Between two things that don't give any, you have to have something that does give a little, something to seal the law to the facts. There isn't any known way to legislate with an allowance for right feeling.

> **James Gould Cozzens,** *The Just and the Unjust* 427 (1942)

56 The jury protects the Court. It's a question how long any system of courts could last in a free country if judges found the verdicts. It doesn't matter how wise and experienced the judges may be. Resentment would build up every time the findings didn't go with current notions or prejudices. Pretty soon half the community would want to lynch the judge. There's no focal point with a jury; the jury is the public itself. That's why a jury can say when a judge couldn't, "I don't care what the law is, that isn't right and I won't do it." It's the greatest prerogative of free men. They have to have a way of saying that and making it stand. They may be wrong, they may refuse to do the things they ought to do; but freedom just to be wise and good isn't any freedom. We pay a price for lay participation in the law; but it's a necessary expense.

James Gould Cozzens, *The Just and the Unjust* 427–28 (1942)

57 The institution of trial by jury—especially in criminal cases—has its hold upon public favor chiefly for two reasons. The individual can forfeit his liberty—to say nothing of his life—only at the hands of those who, unlike any official, are in no wise accountable, directly or indirectly, for what they do, and who at once separate and melt anonymously in the community from which they came. Moreover, since if they acquit their verdict is final, no one is likely to suffer of whose conduct they do not morally disapprove; and this introduces a slack into the enforcement of law, tempering its rigor by the mollifying influence of current ethical conventions. A trial by any jury, however small, preserves both these fundamental elements and a trial by a judge preserves neither, at least to anything like the same degree.

Learned Hand, *United States ex rel. McCann v. Adams*, 126 F.2d 774, 775–76 (2d Cir. 1942)

58 A keen observer has said that "next to perjury, prejudice is the main cause of miscarriages of justice." If government counsel in a criminal suit is allowed to inflame the jurors by irrelevantly arousing their deepest prejudices, the jury may become in his hands a lethal weapon directed against defendants who may be innocent. He should not be permitted to summon that thirteenth juror, prejudice.

Jerome N. Frank, *United States v. Antonelli Fireworks Co.*, 155 F.2d 631, 659 (2d Cir. 1946) (dissenting)

59 The American tradition of trial by jury, considered in connection with either criminal or civil proceedings, necessarily contemplates an impartial jury drawn from a cross-section of the community.... This does not mean, of course, that every jury must contain representatives of all economic, social, religious, racial, political, and geographical groups of the community; frequently such complete representation would be impossible. But it does mean that prospective jurors shall be selected by court officials without systematic and intentional exclusion of any of these groups. Recognition must be given to the fact that those eligible for jury service are to be found in every stratum of society. Jury competence is an individual rather than a group or class matter.

Frank Murphy, *Thiel v. Southern Pacific Co.*, 328 U.S. 217, 220 (1946)

60 There is no constitutional right to a jury drawn from a group of uneducated and unintelligent persons. Nor is there any right to a jury chosen solely from those at the lower end of the economic and social scale. But there is a constitutional right to a jury drawn from a group which represents a cross-section of the community. And a cross-section of the community includes persons with varying degrees of training and intelligence and with varying economic and social positions. Under our Constitution, the jury is not to be made the representative of the most intelligent, the most wealthy or the most successful, nor of the least intelligent, the least wealthy or the least successful. It is a democratic institution, representative of all qualified classes of people.

Frank Murphy, *Fay v. New York*, 332 U.S. 261, 299–300 (1947) (dissenting)

61 On one proposition I should expect trial lawyers to be nearly unanimous: that a jury, every member of which is in the hire of one of the litigants, lacks something of being an impartial jury. A system which has produced such an objectionable result and always tends to repeat it, should, in my opinion, be disapproved by this Court in exercise of its supervisory power over federal courts.

Robert H. Jackson, *Frazier v. United States,* 335 U.S. 497, 514 (1948) (dissenting)

62 In other words, a conspiracy often is proved by evidence that is admissible only upon assumption that conspiracy existed. The naive assumption that prejudicial effects can be overcome by instructions to the jury . . . all practicing lawyers know to be unmitigated fiction.

Robert H. Jackson, *Krulewitch v. United States,* 336 U.S. 440, 453 (1949) (concurring)

63 So long as accused persons who are Republicans, Dixiecrats, Socialists, or Democrats must put up with such a jury, it will have to do for Communists.

Robert H. Jackson, *Dennis v. United States,* 339 U.S. 162, 175 (1950)

64 *Juror # 11* [played by George Voskovec]: Pardon. This fighting. This is not why we are here, to fight. We have a responsibility. This, I have always thought, is a remarkable thing about democracy. That we are, uh, what is the word? . . . notified. That we are notified by mail to come down to this place and decide on the guilt or innocence of a man we have never heard of before. We have nothing to gain or lose by our verdict. This is one of the reasons why we are strong. We should not make it a personal thing.

Reginald Rose, *Twelve Angry Men* (screenplay), 1957, in *Film Scripts Two* 156, 276 (George P. Garrett, O. B. Hardison, Jr., & Jane R. Gelfman eds. 1971)

65 I'm no idealist to believe firmly in the integrity of our courts and in the jury system—that is no ideal to me, it is a living, working reality. Gentlemen, a court is no better than each man of you sitting before me on this jury. A court is only as sound as its jury, and a jury is only as sound as the men who make it up. I am confident that you gentlemen will review without passion the evidence you have heard, come to a decision, and restore this defendant to his family. In the name of God, do your duty.

Harper Lee, *To Kill a Mockingbird* 218 (1960)

66 This was not good enough for Jem. "No sir, they oughta do away with juries. He wasn't guilty in the first place and they said he was."

"If you had been on that jury, son, and eleven other boys like you, Tom would be a free man," said Atticus. "So far nothing in your life has interfered with your reasoning process. Those are twelve reasonable men in everyday life, Tom's jury, but you saw something come between them and reason. You saw the same thing that night in front of the jail. When that crew went away, they didn't go as reasonable men, they went because we were there. There's something in our world that makes men lose their heads—they couldn't be fair if they tried. In our courts, when it's a white man's word against a black man's, the white man always wins. They're ugly, but those are the facts of life."

Harper Lee, *To Kill a Mockingbird* 233 (1960)

67 The one place where a man ought to get a square deal is in a courtroom, be he any color of the rainbow, but people have a way of carrying their resentments right into a jury box. As you grow older, you'll see white men cheat black men every day of your life, but let me tell you something and don't you forget it—whenever a white man does that to a black man, no matter who he is, how rich he is, or how fine a family he comes from, that white man is trash.

Harper Lee, *To Kill a Mockingbird* 233 (1960)

68 Because we believe that trial by jury in criminal cases is fundamental to the American scheme of justice, we hold that the Fourteenth Amendment guarantees a right of jury trial in all criminal cases which—were they to be tried in a federal court—would come within the Sixth Amendment's guarantee.

Byron R. White, *Duncan v. Louisiana,* 391 U.S. 145, 149 (1968)

69 [The jury system is a] startling weakness in our legal machinery. You never get a jury of your peers. In most states you get a jury of elderly and retired, telephone company employees, civil servants, and so forth. The rest either duck jury duty or are eliminated in pretrial selection. When you see a lawyer trying to pick a smart jury, you know he's

got a strong case. Percy Foreman and I once had an argument as to which of us had picked the most stupid jury. I think I won with one that returned a verdict which amounted to "Not guilty with a recommendation of clemency because of reasonable doubt."

F. Lee Bailey, quoted in *Los Angeles Times*, 9 Jan. 1972, at 43

70 A juror is not some kind of a dithering nincompoop, brought in from never-never land and exposed to the harsh realities of life for the first time in the jury box.

Robert Gardner, *People v. Long*, 38 Cal. 3d 680, 689, 113 Cal. Rptr. 530 (1974)

JUSTICE

See also INJUSTICE; MORALITY; NATURAL LAW

1 Justice in the life and conduct of the State is possible only as first it resides in the hearts and souls of the citizens.*

Inscription at entrance to Department of Justice Building, Washington, D.C.

2 Justice is founded in the rights bestowed by nature upon man. Liberty is maintained in the security of justice.

Inscription on Department of Justice Building, Washington, D.C.

3 *393*. Our Law says well, 'To delay justice, is injustice.'

William Penn, *Fruits of Solitude* 69 (11th ed. 1906) (1693)

4 *407*. Justice is justly represented blind, because she sees no difference in the parties concerned.

408. She has but one scale and weight, for rich and poor, great and small.

409. Her sentence is not guided by the person, but the cause. . . .

411. Impartiality is the life of justice, as that is of government.

William Penn, *Fruits of Solitude* 71 (11th ed. 1906) (1693)

5 What pains our Justice takes his faults to hide,

---

* According to *Respectfully Quoted* 184 (Suzy Platt ed. 1989), "This has been attributed to Plato, but is unverified."

With half that pains sure he might cure 'em quite.

Benjamin Franklin, *Poor Richard's Almanack*, 1734, in *Papers of Benjamin Franklin* 1:353 (Leonard W. Labaree ed. 1959)

6 In some Countries the Course of the Courts is so tedious, and the Expence so high, that the Remedy, Justice, is worse than, Injustice, the Disease.

Benjamin Franklin, *Poor Richard's Almanack*, 1742, in *Papers of Benjamin Franklin* 2:339 (Leonard W. Labaree ed. 1960)

7 From Earth to Heav'n, when *Justice* fled, The Laws decided in her Stead; For Heav'n to Earth should she return, Lawyers might beg, and Lawbooks burn.

Benjamin Franklin, *Poor Richard's Almanack*, 1746, in *Papers of Benjamin Franklin* 3:67 (Leonard W. Labaree ed. 1961)

8 Justice is the end of government. It is the end of civil society. It ever has been, and ever will be pursued, until it be obtained, or until liberty be lost in the pursuit.

Alexander Hamilton, *The Federalist* No. 51, at 2:121 (1788)

9 I told him that I thought it was law logic—an artificial system of reasoning, exclusively used in Courts of justice, but good for nothing anywhere else. . . . Hence it is my firm belief that if, instead of the long robes of judges and the long speeches of lawyers, the suitors of every question debated in the Courts between individuals were led blindfolded up to a lottery wheel and there bidden to draw, each of them one of two tickets, one marked Right and the other Wrong, and execution should issue according to the sentence of the wheel, more substantial justice would be done than is now dispensed by Courts of law.

John Quincy Adams, Diary, May 1819, in *Memoirs of John Quincy Adams* 4:372–73 (Charles Francis Adams ed. 1875)

10 A general law, which bears the name of justice, has been made and sanctioned, not only by a majority of this or that people, but by a majority of mankind. The rights of every people are therefore confined within the limits of what is just. A nation may be considered as a jury which is em-

powered to represent society at large, and to apply justice, which is its law. Ought such a jury, which represents society, to have more power than the society itself, whose laws it executes?

Alexis de Tocqueville, *Democracy in America* 1:330 (Francis Bowen trans. 1862) (1835)

11 Justice, Sir, is the great interest of man on earth. It is the ligament which holds civilized beings and civilized nations together. Wherever her temple stands, and so long as it is duly honored, there is a foundation for social security, general happiness, and the improvement and progress of our race. And whoever labors on this edifice with usefulness and distinction, whoever clears its foundations, strengthens its pillars, adorns its entablatures, or contributes to raise its august dome still higher in the skies, connects himself, in name, and fame, and character, with that which is and must be as durable as the frame of human society.

Daniel Webster, Oration on day of Justice Story's funeral, Boston, 12 Sept. 1845, in *Writings and Speeches of Daniel Webster* 3:300 (J. W. McIntyre ed. 1903)

12 What men call justice lies chiefly in outward formalities.

Nathaniel Hawthorne, *The Marble Faun,* 1860, in *Works of Nathaniel Hawthorne* 4:211 (William Charvat et al. eds. 1968)

13 Great is Justice!
Justice is not settled by legislators and laws—it is in the Soul,
It cannot be varied by statutes, any more than love, pride, the attraction of gravity, can,
It is immutable—it does not depend on majorities—majorities or what not come at last before the same passionless and exact tribunal.

For justice are the grand natural lawyers and perfect judges—it is in their Souls,
It is well assorted—they have not studied for nothing—the great includes the less,
They rule on the highest grounds—they oversee all eras, states, administrations.

Walt Whitman, "Great Are the Myths," in *Leaves of Grass* 585, 587 (Harold W. Blodgett & Sculley Bradley eds. 1965) (1860)

14 *Justice,* plain and simple, is a thing which right-feeling men stand ready at all times

to accord to brothers and strangers alike.... If a thing is right *it ought to be done*—the thing called "expediency" or "policy" has no concern with such a matter.

Mark Twain, "Petition Concerning Copyright," 1875, in Albert B. Paine, *Mark Twain: A Biography* 1637, 1637 (1929)

15 No court can mould its decisions by a higher standard of morality than the morality of the law. Law is the measure of forensic justice. So far as I know, the courthouse is the only place on earth where the vicious and the virtuous may contend upon perfectly equal terms, receive the same patient and impartial hearing, and have their respective dues, whatever they may be, meted out in the decision. It is this characteristic, more than any other, which entitles the court-house to be called a temple of justice.

Logan E. Bleckley, *Gilham & Brown v. Wells,* 64 Ga. 192, 194 (1879)

16 Of relative justice law may know something; of expediency it knows much; with absolute justice it does not concern itself.

Oliver Wendell Holmes, Sr., *Pages from an Old Volume of Life,* 1883, in *Works of Oliver Wendell Holmes* 8:324 (1892)

17 Friend, your white beard sweeps the ground.
Why do you stand, expectant?
Do you hope to see it
In one of your withered days?
With your old eyes
Do you hope to see
The triumphal march of justice?
Do not wait, friend.
Take your white beard
And your old eyes
To more tender lands.

Stephen Crane, *The Black Riders,* 1895, in *Stephen Crane: Poems and Literary Remains* 10:3, 40 (Fredson Bowers ed. 1975)

18 I tell ye Hogan's r-right when he says: "Justice is blind." Blind she is, an' deef an' dumb an' has a wooden leg!

Finley Peter Dunne, "Cross Examinations," in *Mr. Dooley's Opinions* 117, 118 (1906) (1901)

19 They [lawyers] talk about law—why, gentlemen, it's not law we want, but justice. They want to govern us by the common law

of England; trust me for it, common sense is a much safer guide for us. . . . It's our business to do justice between the parties; not by any quirks o' the law out of Coke or Blackstone—books that I never read and never will—but by common sense and common honesty between man and man.

John Dudley, quoted in "Law Versus Common Sense," 40 *American Law Review* 436, 437 (1906)

20 Justice, which is the end of law, is the ideal compromise between the activities of each and the activities of all in a crowded world.

Roscoe Pound, "The Causes of Popular Dissatisfaction with the Administration of Justice," 29 *American Bar Association Report* 395, 399 (1906)

21 His wife might be dying, his baby might be starving, his whole family might be perishing in the cold—and all the while they were ringing their Christmas chimes! And the bitter mockery of it—all this was punishment for him! They put him in a place where the snow could not beat in, where the cold could not eat through his bones; they brought him food and drink—why, in the name of heaven, if they must punish him, did they not put his family in jail and leave him outside—why could they find no better way to punish him than to leave three weak women and six helpless children to starve and freeze?

That was their law, that was their justice! Jurgis stood upright, trembling with passion, his hands clenched and his arms upraised, his whole soul ablaze with hatred and defiance. Ten thousand curses upon them and their law! Their justice—it was a lie, it was a lie, a hideous, brutal lie, a thing too black and hateful for any world but a world of nightmares. It was a sham and a loathsome mockery. There was no justice, there was no right, anywhere in it—it was only force, it was tyranny, the will and the power, reckless and unrestrained!

Upton Sinclair, *The Jungle* 191 (1906)

22 JUSTICE, *n*. A commodity which is a more or less adulterated condition the State sells to the citizen as a reward for his allegiance, taxes and personal service.

Ambrose Bierce, *The Devil's Dictionary* 176–77 (1911)

23 Administration of justice according to law means administration according to stan-dards, more or less fixed, which individuals may ascertain in advance of controversy and by which all are reasonably assured of receiving like treatment.

Roscoe Pound, "Justice According to Law," 13 *Columbia Law Review* 696, 705 (1913)

24 The profession of the law of which he [the judge] is a part is charged with the articulation and final incidence of the successive efforts towards justice; it must feel the circulation of the communal blood or it will wither and drop off, a useless member. . . . the form of justice will be without content till we fill it with the ardor of life.

Learned Hand, "The Speech of Justice," 29 *Harvard Law Review* 617, 618 (1916)

25 The sense of justice, like the sense of honor, is the exclusive possession of a small and usually miserable minority of men.

H. L. Mencken, "Campaign Notes," Baltimore *Evening Sun*, 13 Sept. 1920, quoted in *The Gist of Mencken* 449–50 (Mayo DuBasky ed. 1990)

26 The law has "its epochs of ebb and flow." One of the flood seasons is upon us. Men are insisting, as perhaps never before, that law shall be made true to its ideals of justice. Let us gather up the driftwood, and leave the waters pure.

Benjamin N. Cardozo, "A Ministry of Justice," 35 *Harvard Law Review* 113, 126 (1921)

27 Not for us the barren logomachy that dwells upon the contrasts between law and justice, and forgets their deeper harmonies.

Benjamin N. Cardozo, *The Nature of the Judicial Process* 134 (1921)

28 Injustice is relatively easy to bear; what stings is justice.

H. L. Mencken, *Prejudices, Third Series* 101 (1922)

29 Perhaps we shall even find at times that when talking about justice, the quality we have in mind is charity.

Benjamin N. Cardozo, *The Growth of the Law* 87 (1924)

30 As new problems arise, equity and justice will direct the mind to solutions which will be found, when they are scrutinized, to be

consistent with symmetry and order, or even to be the starting points of a symmetry and order theretofore unknown. Logic and history, the countless analogies suggested by the recorded wisdom of the past, will in turn inspire new expedients for the attainment of equity and justice. We find a kindred phenomenon in literature, alike in poetry and in prose. The search is for the just word, the happy phrase, that will give expression to the thought, but somehow the thought itself is transfigured by the phrase when found. There is emancipation in our very bonds. The restraints of rhyme or metre, the exigencies of period or balance, liberate at times the thought which they confine, and in imprisoning release.

> **Benjamin N. Cardozo,** *The Growth of the Law* 88–89 (1924)

31 Justice is not to be taken by storm. She is to be wooed by slow advances. Substitute statute for decision, and you shift the center of authority, but add no quota of inspired wisdom.

> **Benjamin N. Cardozo,** *The Growth of the Law* 133 (1924)

32 If there is such a thing as justice it could only be administered by one who knew the inmost thoughts of the man to whom he was meting it out. Aye, who knew the father and mother and the grandparents and the infinite number of people back of him. Who knew the origin of every cell that went into the body, who could understand the structure and how it acted. Who could tell how the emotions that sway the human being affected that particular frail piece of clay. It means more than that. It means that you must appraise every influence that moves men, the civilization where they live, and all society which enters into the making of the child or the man! If Your Honor can do it—if you can do it you are wise, and with wisdom goes mercy.

> **Clarence S. Darrow,** Closing argument in Leopold-Leob trial, Chicago, 1924, in *Attorney for the Damned* 43 (Arthur Weinberg ed. 1957)

33 Justice is not blind, nor is she evenhanded. The scales do not balance and they cannot be made to balance. Not, that is, until we are freed of our humanity and turned to demigods. And then justice will no longer be needed.

> **H. L. Mencken,** "Note on Justice," Baltimore *Evening Sun,* 19 Nov. 1925, quoted in *The Gist of Mencken* 443 (Mayo DuBasky ed. 1990)

34 I have said to my brethren many times that I hate justice, which means that I know if a man begins to talk about that, for one reason or another he is shirking thinking in legal terms.

> **Oliver Wendell Holmes, Jr.,** Letter to John C. H. Wu, 1 July 1929, in *Justice Holmes to Doctor Wu* 53 (1947)

35 There is no such thing as justice—in or out of court.

> **Clarence S. Darrow,** Interview, Chicago, 18 Apr. 1936, quoted in *New York Times,* 19 Apr. 1936, at 24

36 Justice, I think, is the tolerable accommodation of the conflicting interests of society, and I don't believe there is any royal road to attain such accommodations concretely.

> **Learned Hand,** quoted in Philip Hamburger, "The Great Judge," *Life,* 4 Nov. 1946, at 117, 122

37 Lawyers know, if others do not, that what may seem technical may embody a great tradition of justice.

> **Wiley B. Rutledge,** *Kotteakos v. United States,* 328 U.S. 750, 761 (1946)

38 To take appropriate measures in order to avert injustice even towards a member of a despised group is to enforce justice. . . . This is not to coddle Communists but to respect our professions of equal justice to all. It was a wise man who said that there is no greater inequality than the equal treatment of unequals.

> **Felix Frankfurter,** *Dennis v. United States,* 339 U.S. 162, 184 (1950) (dissenting)

39 If we are to keep our democracy, there must be one commandment: Thou shalt not ration justice.

> **Learned Hand,** "Thou Shalt Not Ration Justice," 9 *Brief Case,* No 4, at 3, 5 (1951)

40 "You had to play the big scene," he said coldly. "Stand on your rights, talk about the law. How ingenuous can a man get,

Marlowe? A man like you who is supposed to know his way around. The law isn't justice. It's a very imperfect mechanism. If you press exactly the right buttons and are also lucky, justice may show up in the answer. A mechanism is all the law was ever intended to be. I guess you're not in any mood to be helped. So I'll take myself off. You can reach me if you change your mind."

Raymond Chandler, *The Long Goodbye*, 1953, in *The Midnight Raymond Chandler* 464–65 (1971)

41 'Oh, Elizabeth, your justice would freeze beer!

Arthur Miller, *The Crucible* 55 (Gerald Weales ed. 1971) (1953)

42 In its wisdom, the law only aimed at certainty, could not, did not, really hope to get there. This science, as inexact as medicine, must do its justice with the imprecision of wisdom, the pragmatism of a long, a mighty experience. Those balances were to weigh, not what was just in general, but what might be just between these actual adversaries.

James Gould Cozzens, *By Love Possessed* 566 (1957)

43 The halls of justice. That's the only place you see the justice, is in the halls.

Lenny Bruce, in *The Essential Lenny Bruce* 271 (John Cohen ed. 1967)

44 One receives only imperfect justice in this world; only fools, children, left-wing Democrats, social scientists, and a few demented judges expect anything better.

Walter F. Murphy, *The Vicar of Christ* 93 (1979)

JUSTICE DEPARTMENT

1 The Place of Justice Is a Hallowed Place.

Inscription over Pennsylvania Avenue entrance to Department of Justice Building, Washington, D.C.

2 [To President Theodore Roosevelt on the antitrust prosecution of the Northern Securities Corporation:] If we have done anything wrong, send your man [the Attorney-

General] to my man [naming one of his lawyers] and they can fix it up.

J. P. Morgan, quoted in Matthew Josephson, *The Robber Barons* 449 (1934)

3 Of all the officers of the Government, those of the Department of Justice should be kept most free from any suspicion of improper action on partisan or factional grounds . . . so that there shall be gradually a growth, even though a slow growth, in the knowledge that the Federal courts and the representatives of the Federal Department of Justice insist on meting out evenhanded justice to all.

Theodore Roosevelt, Letter to William H. Moody, 9 Aug. 1904, in *Letters of Theodore Roosevelt* 4:885 (Elting E. Morison ed. 1951)

4 I marvel that no candidate for the doctorate has ever written a realistic history of the American Department of Justice, ironically so called. It has been engaged in sharp practices since the earliest days, and remains a fecund source of oppression and corruption to-day. It is hard to recall an administration in which it was not the center of grave scandal. . . . it has actually resorted to perjury in its efforts to undo men guilty of flouting it, and at all times it has laboured valiantly to nullify the guarantes of the Bill of Rights. The doings of its corps of spies and *agents provocateurs* are worthy the pen of some confectioner of dime novels.

H. L. Mencken, *Notes on Democracy* 183 (1926)

5 [On the appointment of his brother Robert F. Kennedy:] I see nothing wrong with giving Robert some legal experience as Attorney General before he goes out to practice law.

John F. Kennedy, 1961, quoted in Bill Adler, *The Complete Kennedy Wit* 179 (1967)

JUVENILE JUSTICE

See CHILDREN

LABOR LAW

1 With us the rule is inflexible, that a general or indefinite hiring is *prima facie* a hiring at will, and if the servant seeks to make it out a yearly hiring, the burden is upon him

to establish it by proof. A hiring at so much a day, week, month or year, no time being specified, is an indefinite hiring . . . and is determinable at the will of either party.

Horace G. Wood, *A Treatise on the Law of Master and Servant* 272 (1877)

2 Men must be left, without interference to buy and sell where they please, and to discharge or retain employees at will for good cause or for no cause, or even for bad cause without thereby being guilty of an unlawful act *per se*. It is a right which an employe [*sic*] may exercise in the same way, to the same extent, for the same cause or want of cause as the employer.

Henry H. Ingersoll, *Payne v. Western & Atlantic R.R.*, 81 Tenn. 507, 518–19 (1884)

3 Loss alone gives no right of action. Great corporations, strong associations, and wealthy individuals may thus do great mischief and wrong . . . but power is inherent in size and strength and wealth; and the law cannot set bound to it, unless it is exercised illegally. . . . The great and rich and powerful are guaranteed the same liberty and privilege as the poor and weak. All may buy and sell when they choose; they may refuse to employ or dismiss whom they choose, without being thereby guilty of a legal wrong, though it may seriously injure and even ruin others.

Henry H. Ingersoll, *Payne v. Western & Atlantic R.R.*, 81 Tenn. 507, 519 (1884)

4 It is not within the functions of government . . . to compel any person in the course of his business and against his will to accept or retain the personal services of another, to compel any person, against his will, to perform personal services for another. . . . Congress could not, consistently with the Fifth Amendment, make it a crime against the United States to discharge the employé because of his being a member of a labor organization.

John M. Harlan (1833–1911), *Adair v. United States*, 208 U.S. 161, 174, 176 (1908)

5 In present conditions a workman not unnaturally may believe that only by belonging to a union can he secure a contract that shall be fair to him. . . . If that belief, whether right or wrong, may be held by a reasonable man, it seems to me that it may be enforced by law in order to establish the equality of position between the parties in which liberty of contract begins.

Oliver Wendell Holmes, Jr., *Coppage v. Kansas*, 236 U.S. 1, 26–27 (1915) (dissenting)

6 There is no right to strike against the public safety by anybody, anywhere, any time.

Calvin Coolidge, Telegram to Samuel Gompers, 14 Sept. 1919, in *Have Faith in Massachusetts* 222, 223 (1919)

7 It is said that the pain cannot be shifted to another. Neither can the loss of a leg. But one can be paid for as well as the other. It is said that these elements do not constitute an economic loss, in the sense of diminished power to produce. They may. . . . But whether they do or not they are as much part of the workman's loss as the loss of a limb. The legislature may have reasoned thus. If a business is unsuccessful it means that the public does not care enough for it to make it pay. If it is successful the public pays its expenses and something more. It is reasonable that the public should pay the whole cost of producing what it wants and a part of that cost is the pain and mutilation incident to production. By throwing that loss upon the employer in the first instance we throw it upon the public in the long run and that is just. If a legislature should reason in this way and act accordingly it seems to me that it is within constitutional bounds.

Oliver Wendell Holmes, Jr., *Arizona Employers' Liability Cases*, 250 U.S. 400, 433 (1919) (concurring)

8 Gentlemen, there is one reason why this legislation is before Congress, and that one reason is disobedience of the law on the part of whom? On the part of organized labor? No. Disobedience of the law on the part of a few Federal judges. If the courts had been satisfied to construe the law as enacted by Congress, there would not be any need of legislation of this kind. If the courts had administered even justice to both employers and employees, there would be no need of considering a bill of this kind now. If the courts had not emasculated and purposely misconstrued the Clayton Act, we would not today be discussing the anti-injunction bill.

Fiorello H. La Guardia, in 75 *Congressional Record* 5478 (1932)

9 Every code of fair competition, agreement, and license approved, prescribed, or issued under this title shall contain the following conditions: (1) That employees shall have the right to organize and bargain collectively through representatives of their own choosing, and shall be free from the interference, restraint, or coercion of employers of labor, or their agents, in the designation of such representatives or in self-organization or in other concerted activities for the purpose of collective bargaining or other mutual aid or protection; (2) that no employee and no one seeking employment shall be required as a condition of employment to join any company union or to refrain from joining, organizing, or assisting a labor organization of his own choosing; and (3) that employers shall comply with the maximum hours of labor, minimum rates of pay, and other conditions of employment, approved or prescribed by the President.

National Industrial Recovery Act, ch. 90, § 7(a), 48 Stat. 195, 198–99 (1933)

10 The inequality of bargaining power between employees who do not possess full freedom of association or actual liberty of contract, and employers who are organized in the corporate or other forms of ownership association substantially burdens and affects the flow of commerce, and tends to aggravate recurrent business depressions, by depressing wage rates and the purchasing power of wage earners in industry and by preventing the stabilization of competitive wage rates and working conditions within and between industries.

National Labor Relations Act (Wagner Act), ch. 372, § 1, 49 Stat. 449, 449 (1935)

11 Experience has proved that protection by law of the right of employees to organize and bargain collectively safeguards commerce from injury, impairment, or interruption, and promotes the flow of commerce by removing certain recognized sources of industrial strife and unrest, by encouraging practices fundamental to the friendly adjustment of industrial disputes arising out of differences as to wages, hours, or other working conditions, and by restoring equality of bargaining power between employers and employees.

National Labor Relations Act (Wagner Act), ch. 372, § 1, 49 Stat. 449, 449 (1935)

12 It is hereby declared to be the policy of the United States to eliminate the causes of certain substantial obstructions to the free flow of commerce and to mitigate and eliminate these obstructions when they have occurred by encouraging the practice and procedure of collective bargaining and by protecting the exercise by workers of full freedom of association, self-organization, and designation of representatives of their own choosing, for the purpose of negotiating the terms and conditions of their employment or other mutual aid or protection.

National Labor Relations Act (Wagner Act), ch. 372, § 1, 49 Stat. 449, 449–50 (1935)

13 Employees shall have the right to self-organization, to form, join, or assist labor organizations, to bargain collectively through representatives of their own choosing, and to engage in concerted activities, for the purpose of collective bargaining or other mutual aid or protection.

National Labor Relations Act (Wagner Act), ch. 372, § 7, 49 Stat. 449, 452 (1935)

14 It shall be an unfair labor practice for an employer—

(1) To interfere with, restrain, or coerce employees in the exercise of the rights guaranteed in section 7.

(2) To dominate or interfere with the formation or administration of any labor organization or contribute financial or other support to it: *Provided*, That subject to rules and regulations made and published by the Board . . . , an employer shall not be prohibited from permitting employees to confer with him during working hours without loss of time or pay.

(3) By discrimination in regard to hire or tenure of employment or any term or condition of employment to encourage or discourage membership in any labor organization: *Provided*, That nothing in this Act, or in the National Industrial Recovery Act . . . or in any other statute of the United States, shall preclude an employer from making an agreement with a labor organization . . . to require as a condition of employment membership therein, if such labor organization is the representative of the employees as provided in section 9 (a), in the appropriate collective bargaining unit covered by such agreement when made.

(4) To discharge or otherwise discriminate against an employee because he has filed charges or given testimony under this Act.

(5) To refuse to bargain collectively with the representatives of his employees.

National Labor Relations Act (Wagner Act), ch. 372, § 8, 49 Stat. 449, 452–53 (1935)

15 Nothing in this Act shall be construed so as to interfere with or impede or diminish in any way the right to strike.

National Labor Relations Act (Wagner Act), ch. 372, § 13, 49 Stat. 449, 457 (1935)

16 Experience has abundantly demonstrated that the recognition of the right of employees to self-organization and to have representatives of their own choosing for the purpose of collective bargaining is often an essential condition of industrial peace. Refusal to confer and negotiate has been one of the most prolific causes of strife. This is such an outstanding fact in the history of labor disturbances that it is a proper subject of judicial notice.

Charles Evans Hughes, *NLRB v. Jones & Laughlin Steel Corp.,* 301 U.S. 1, 42 (1937)

17 Particularly, I want to emphasize my conviction that militant tactics have no place in the functions of any organization of Government employees. . . . A strike of public employees manifests nothing less than an intent on their part to prevent or obstruct the operations of Government until their demands are satisfied. Such action, looking toward the paralysis of Government by those who have sworn to support it, is unthinkable and intolerable.

Franklin D. Roosevelt, Letter to President of National Federation of Federal Employees, 16 Aug. 1937, in *Public Papers and Addresses of Franklin D. Roosevelt, 1937,* at 324, 325 (Samuel I. Rosenman ed. 1941)

18 Known hostility to one union and clear discrimination against it may indeed make seemingly trivial intimations of preference for another union powerful assistance for it. Slight suggestions as to the employer's choice between unions may have telling effect among men who know the consequences of incurring that employer's strong displeasure.

William O. Douglas, *International Ass'n of Machinists v. National Labor Relations Board,* 311 U.S. 72, 78 (1940)

19 Industrial strife which interferes with the normal flow of commerce and with the full production of articles and commodities for commerce, can be avoided or substantially minimized if employers, employees, and labor organizations each recognize under law one another's legitimate rights in their relations with each other, and above all recognize under law that neither party has any right in its relations with any other to engage in acts or practices which jeopardize the public health, safety, or interest.

Labor Management Relations Act of 1947 (Taft-Hartley Act), ch. 120, § 1(b), 61 Stat. 136, 136

20 It is the policy of the United States that—

(a) sound and stable industrial peace and the advancement of the general welfare, health, and safety of the Nation and of the best interests of employers and employees can most satisfactorily be secured by the settlement of issues between employers and employees through the processes of conference and collective bargaining between employers and the representatives of their employees.

Labor Management Relations Act of 1947 (Taft-Hartley Act), ch. 120, § 201, 61 Stat. 136, 152

21 Because a State may require payment of a minimum wage for hours that are worked it does not follow that it may compel payment for time that is not worked. To overlook a distinction so fundamental is to confuse the point in issue.

Robert H. Jackson, *Day-Brite Lighting v. Missouri,* 342 U.S. 421, 426 (1952) (dissenting)

22 An arbitrator is confined to interpretation and application of the collective bargaining agreement; he does not sit to dispense his own brand of industrial justice. He may of course look for guidance from many sources, yet his award is legitimate only so long as it draws its essence from the collective bargaining agreement. When the arbitrator's words manifest an infidelity to this obligation, courts have no choice but to refuse enforcement of the award.

William O. Douglas, *United Steelworkers v. Enterprise Wheel & Car Corp.,* 363 U.S. 593, 597 (1960)

23 So far as the arbitrator's decision concerns construction of the contract, the courts

have no business overruling him because their interpretation of the contract is different from his.

William O. Douglas, *United Steelworkers v. Enterprise Wheel & Car Corp.*, 363 U.S. 593, 599 (1960)

24 The statutory ban in this case affects only that aspect of the union's efforts to communicate its views that calls for an automatic response to a signal, rather than a reasoned response to an idea.

John Paul Stevens, *NLRB v. Retail Store Employees Union, Local 1001*, 447 U.S. 607, 619 (1980) (concurring in part and concurring in the result)

LAND

See PROPERTY

LANGUAGE

See also LEGAL WRITING; WORDS

1 No language is so copious as to supply words and phrases for every complex idea, or so correct as not to include many equivocally denoting different ideas. Hence it must happen, that however accurately objects may be discriminated in themselves, and however accurately the discrimination may be considered, the definition of them may be rendered inaccurate by the inaccuracy of the terms in which it is delivered. And this unavoidable inaccuracy must be greater or less, according to the complexity and novelty of the objects defined. When the Almighty himself condescends to address mankind in their own language, his meaning, luminous as it must be, is rendered dim and doubtful, by the cloudy medium through which it is communicated.

James Madison, *The Federalist* No. 37, at 2:7 (1788)

2 One-half the doubts in life arise from the defects of language.

William Johnson, *Gibbons v. Ogden*, 22 U.S. (9 Wheat.) 1, 232 (1824) (separate opinion)

3 We have heard Judge Story make the following statement to show the extreme difficulty of framing a statute so as to avoid all ambiguity in its language. Being once employed by Congress to draft an impor-

tant law, he spent six months in trying to perfect its phraseology, so that its sense would be clear beyond a shadow of a doubt, leaving not the smallest loophole for a lawyer to creep through. Yet, in less than a year, after having heard the arguments of two able attorneys, in a suit which came before him as a Judge of the United States Supreme Court, he was utterly at a loss to decide upon the statute's meaning!

William Mathews, *Words; Their Use and Abuse* 252 (1876)

4 The Chief Justice [Holt] here retires into that lawyer's Paradise where all words have a fixed, precisely ascertained meaning; where men may express their purposes, not only with accuracy, but with fulness; and where, if the writer has been careful, a lawyer, having a document referred to him, may sit in his chair, inspect the text, and answer all questions without raising his eyes. Men have dreamed of attaining for their solemn muniments of title such an absolute security; and some degree of security they have compassed by giving strict definitions and technical meanings to words and phrases, and by rigid rules of construction. But the fatal necessity of looking outside the text in order to identify persons and things, tends steadily to destroy such illusions and to reveal the essential imperfection of language, whether spoken or written.

James Bradley Thayer, *A Preliminary Treatise on Evidence* 428–29 (1898)

5 Metaphors in law are to be narrowly watched, for starting as devices to liberate thought, they end often by enslaving it.

Benjamin N. Cardozo, *Berkey v. Third Avenue Railway*, 244 N.Y. 84, 94, 155 N.E. 58 (1926)

6 There is something monstrous in commands couched in invented and unfamiliar language; an alien master is the worst of all. The language of the law must not be foreign to the ears of those who are to obey it.

Learned Hand, "Is There a Common Will," 28 *Michigan Law Review* 46, 52 (1929)

7 The Law is carried on in a foreign language.... law deals almost exclusively with the ordinary facts and occurrences of everyday business and government and liv-

ing. But it deals with them in a jargon which completely baffles and befoozles the ordinary literate man.

Fred Rodell, *Woe Unto You, Lawyers!* 7 (1939)

8 The whole abracadabra of The Law swings around a sort of circular paradox. Legal language—in statutes, documents, court opinions—makes use of strange unfamiliar words because those words tie up to the abstract principles of which The Law is composed. Except in reference to those principles the words, as used, mean even less than nothing. But the principles themselves are utterly unintelligible except in terms of the legal words in which *they* are phrased. Neither words nor principles have any direct relation to tangible, earthly things. Like Alphonse and Gaston, they can do no more than keep bowing back and forth to each other.

Fred Rodell, *Woe Unto You, Lawyers!* 191 (1939)

9 The principles of The Law are made of those outlandish words and phrases because they are not really reasons for decisions but obscure and thoroughly unconvincing rationalizations of decisions—and if they were written in ordinary English, everybody could see how silly, how irrelevant and inconclusive, they are. If everybody could see how silly legal principles are, The Law would lose its dignity and then its power—and so would the lawyers.

Fred Rodell, *Woe Unto You, Lawyers!* 193 (1939)

10 There is no more likely way to misapprehend the meaning of language—be it in a constitution, a statute, a will or a contract—than to read the words literally, forgetting the object which the document as a whole is meant to secure. Nor is a court ever less likely to do its duty than when, with an obsequious show of submission, it disregards the overriding purpose because the particular occasion which has arisen, was not foreseen. That there are hazards in this is quite true; there are hazards in all interpretation, at best a perilous course between dangers on either hand; but it scarcely helps to give so wide a berth to Charybdis's maw that one is in danger of being impaled upon Scylla's rocks.

Learned Hand, *Central Hanover Bank & Trust Co. v. Commissioner,* 159 F.2d 167, 169 (2d Cir. 1947)

11 I cannot believe that any of us would say that the "meaning" of an utterance is exhausted by the specific content of the utterer's mind at the moment.

Learned Hand, *The Bill of Rights* 18–19 (1958)

12 To be of any use, the language of the law (as any other language) must not only express but convey thought. With communication the object, the principle of simplicity would dictate that the language used by lawyers agree with the common speech, unless there are reasons for a difference.

David Mellinkoff, *The Language of the Law* vii (1963)

13 And *is* the difference between the law as the School teaches it and poetry as a man pursues it as deep and wide as all that? That there are differences, noticeable differences between the means of poetry and the means of the law is obvious. Both use words—more or less the same words now that poetry has shuffled off the "poetic" vocabulary which disfigured it in the last century and lawyers have stopped writing as though they were translating themselves out of Latin. But though the words are the same, the tunes are distinguishable. In more senses than one. Lawyers use words as signs standing for meanings whereas poets use them not only as signs but as sounds and as visible objects, as images, as metaphors.

Archibald MacLeish, "Art and Law," in *Riders on the Earth* 82, 83 (1978)

14 To conceive of the law as a rhetorical and social system, a way in which we use an inherited language to talk to each other and to maintain a community, suggests in a new way that the heart of the law is what we always knew it was: the open hearing in which one point of view, one construction of language and reality, is tested against another.

James B. White, *When Words Lose Their Meaning* 273 (1984)

LAW

See also LAW, DEFINITIONS OF; LAW, GROWTH OF; NATURAL LAW; OBEDIENCE TO LAW

1 Since multiplicity of comments, as well as of laws, have great inconveniencies, and

serve only to obscure and perplex, all manner of comments and expositions on any part of these fundamental constitutions, or on any part of the common or statute laws of Carolina, are absolutely prohibited.

Fundamental Constitutions of Carolina of 1669, § 80, in *Federal and State Constitutions* 5:2772, 2782 (Francis N. Thorpe ed. 1909)

2 I know what is said by the several admirers of *monarchy, aristocracy* and *democracy,* which are the rule of one, a few, and many, and are the three common ideas of government, when men discourse on the subject. But I chuse to solve the controversy with this small distinction, and it belongs to all three: *Any government is free to the people under it* (whatever be the frame) *where the laws rule, and the people are a party to those laws,* and more than this is tyranny, oligarchy, or confusion.

William Penn, Pennsylvania Frame of Government of 1682, Preface, in *Federal and State Constitutions* 5:3052, 3053–54 (Francis N. Thorpe ed. 1909)

3 Where carcasses are, eagles will gather, And where good laws are, much people flock thither.*

Benjamin Franklin, *Poor Richard's Almanack* 1734, in *Papers of Benjamin Franklin* 1:352 (Leonard W. Labaree ed. 1959)

4 Where there's no Law, there's no Bread.

Benjamin Franklin, *Poor Richard's Almanack,* 1744, in *Papers of Benjamin Franklin* 2:398 (Leonard W. Labaree ed. 1960)

5 Where there is Hunger, Law is not regarded; and where Law is not regarded, there will be Hunger.

Benjamin Franklin, *Poor Richard's Almanack,* 1755, in *Papers of Benjamin Franklin* 5:472 (Leonard W. Labaree ed. 1962)

6 The law, in all vicissitudes of government, fluctuations of the passions, or flights of enthusiasm, will preserve a steady undeviating course; it will not bend to the uncertain wishes, imaginations, and wanton

tempers of men. . . .* On the one hand it is inexorable to the cries and lamentations of the prisoners; on the other it is deaf, deaf as an adder† to the clamours of the populace.

John Adams, Argument in Defense of the British Soldiers in the Boston Massacre Trials, 4 Dec. 1770, in *Legal Papers of John Adams* 3:269–70 (L. Kinvin Wroth & Hiller B. Zobel eds. 1968)

7 But where, say some, is the king of America? I'll tell you, friend, he reigns above, and doth not make havoc of mankind like the royal brute of Great Britain. Yet that we may not appear to be defective even in earthly honors, let a day be solemnly set apart for proclaiming the charter; let it be brought forth placed on the divine law, the Word of God; let a crown be placed thereon, by which the world may know, that so far as we approve of monarchy, that in America the law is king. For as in absolute governments the king is law, so in free countries the law ought to be king; and there ought to be no other. But lest any ill should afterwards arise, let the crown at the conclusion of the ceremony be demolished, and scattered among the people whose right it is.

Thomas Paine, *Common Sense,* 1776, in *Complete Writings of Thomas Paine* 1:3, 29 (Philip S. Foner ed. 1969)

8 Law . . . is a field which is uninteresting and boundless. . . . so encumbered with voluminous rubbish and the baggage of folios that it requires uncommon assiduity and patience to manage so unwieldy a work.

James Kent, Letter to Simeon Baldwin, 10 Oct. 1782, quoted in William Kent, *Memoirs and Letters of James Kent, L.L.D.* 16 (1898)

9 Ignorance of the law is no excuse in any country. If it were, the laws would lose their effect, because it can always be pretended.

Thomas Jefferson, Letter to André Limozin, 22 Dec. 1787, in *Papers of Thomas Jefferson* 12:451 (Julian P. Boyd ed. 1955)

10 Were it made a question, whether no law, as among the savage Americans, or too

---

* Wherever the corpse is, there the vultures will gather. —*Matthew* 24.28 (NRSV)

* Adams here quotes Algernon Sidney's description of the law as "deaf, inexorable, inflexible," from Sidney's *Discourses Concerning Government* (2d ed. 1704)
† They have venom like the venom of a serpent, like the deaf adder that stops its ear. —*Psalms* 58.4 (NRSV)

much law, as among the civilized Europeans, submits man to the greatest evil, one who has seen both conditions of existence would pronounce it to be the last; and that the sheep are happier of themselves, than under the care of the wolves.

> Thomas Jefferson, *Notes on Virginia*, 1787, in *Works of Thomas Jefferson* 3:495 n.1 (Paul L. Ford ed. 1904)

11 The law,—a profession whose general principles enlighten and enlarge, but whose minutiae contract and distract the mind.

> Joseph Story, Letter to Samuel P. P. Fay, 6 Sept. 1798, in *Life and Letters of Joseph Story* 1:71 (William W. Story ed. 1851)

12 No man has a natural right to commit aggression on the equal rights of another; and this is all from which the laws ought to restrain him; every man is under the natural duty of contributing to the necessities of the society; and this is all the laws should enforce on him: and, no man having a natural right to be the judge between himself and another, it is his natural duty to submit to the umpirage of an impartial third. When the laws have declared and enforced all this, they have fulfilled their functions.

> Thomas Jefferson, Letter to Francis W. Gilmer, 7 June 1816, in *Writings of Thomas Jefferson* 10:32 (Paul L. Ford ed. 1899)

13 By the law of the land is most clearly intended the general law[;] a law which hears, before it condemns; which proceeds upon inquiry, & renders judgme[nt] only after trial. The meaning is, that every citizen shall hold his life, liberty, property, & immunities, under the protection of the general rules which govern society.

> Daniel Webster, Argument in *Trustees of Dartmouth College v. Woodward*, 17 U.S. (4 Wheat.) 518, 10 Mar. 1818, in *Papers of Daniel Webster: Legal Papers* 3:119, 140 (Andrew J. King ed. 1989)

14 Society cannot exist without wholesome restraints. Those restraints cannot be inflicted, without security and respect to the persons who administer them. . . . try to remember, Elizabeth, that the laws alone remove us from the condition of the savages.

> James Fenimore Cooper, *The Pioneers*, 1823, in *Writings of James Fenimore Cooper* 382–83 (James F. Beard ed. 1980)

15 The law—'Tis bad to have it, but, I sometimes think, it is worse to be entirely without it. . . . Yes—yes, the law is needed, when such as have not the gifts of strength and wisdom are to be taken care of.

> James Fenimore Cooper, *The Prairie: A Tale* 27 (James P. Elliot ed. 1985) (1827)

16 I will not say, with Lord Hale, that "The Law will admit of no rival" . . . but I will say, that it is a jealous mistress,* and requires a long and constant courtship. It is not to be won by trifling favors, but by lavish homage.

> Joseph Story, "The Value and Importance of Legal Studies," 1829, in *Miscellaneous Writings of Joseph Story* 503, 523 (William W. Story ed. 1852)

17 The law, unfortunately, has always been retained on the side of power: laws have uniformly been enacted for the protection and perpetuation of power.†

> Thomas Cooper, *A Treatise on the Law of Libel and the Liberty of the Press* ix (1830)

18 *Law*, in all its divisions, is the strong action of *Reason* upon wants, necessities, and imperfections. No matter whether its ministration is by a legislative or through a judicial faculty, or by the consentaneous acts of individuals under no manifest compulsion; it is still the act of those on whom it has pleased divine Providence to bestow the attribute of reason, as distinguished from those who are guided only by instinct, and can make no rules for themselves.

> William Rawle, *A Discourse on the Nature and Study of Law* 4 (1832)

19 In the United States, then, that numerous and turbulent multitude does not exist, who, regarding the law as their natural enemy, look upon it with fear and distrust.

---

* As the law is a jealous science, and will not have any partnership with the Eastern Muses, I must absolutely renounce their acquaintance for ten or twelve years to come. —**William Jones**, Letter to Mr. Howard, 4 Oct. 1774, in *Works of Sir William Jones* 1:225 (1807)

Mr. North's observations are correct and sensible; the law is not so jealous a mistress as to exclude every other object from the mind of her devotee, although she will vindicate the first place in his affections. —**Roger North**, *A Discourse on the Study of the Laws* 55 n.5 (1824) (note by "A Member of the Inner Temple")

† The quotation is from a "Preface by an unknown friend of the author."

It is impossible, on the contrary, not to perceive that all classes display the utmost reliance upon the legislation of their country, and are attached to it by a kind of parental affection.

> Alexis de Tocqueville, *Democracy in America* 1:316 (Francis Bowen trans. 1862) (1835)

20 Scarcely any political question arises in the United States which is not resolved, sooner or later, into a judicial question. Hence all parties are obliged to borrow, in their daily controversies, the ideas, and even the language, peculiar to judicial proceedings. As most public men are, or have been, legal practitioners, they introduce the customs and technicalities of their profession into the management of public affairs. The jury extends this habitude to all classes. The language of the law thus becomes, in some measure, a vulgar tongue; the spirit of the law, which is produced in the schools and courts of justice, gradually penetrates beyond their walls into the bosom of society, where it descends to the lowest classes, so that at last the whole people contract the habits and the tastes of the judicial magistrate.

> Alexis de Tocqueville, *Democracy in America* 1:357–58 (Francis Bowen trans. 1862) (1835)

21 Let reverence for the laws, be breathed by every American mother, to the lisping babe, that prattles on her lap—let it be taught in schools, in seminaries, and in colleges;—let it be written in Primmers [*sic*], spelling books, and in Almanacs;—let it be preached from the pulpit, proclaimed in legislative halls, and enforced in courts of justice. And, in short, let it become the *political religion* of the nation; and let the old and the young, the rich and the poor, the grave and the gay, of all sexes and tongues, and colors and conditions, sacrifice unceasingly upon its altars.

> Abraham Lincoln, Address before Young Men's Lyceum, Springfield, Ill., 27 Jan. 1838, in *Collected Works of Abraham Lincoln* 1:112 (Roy P. Basler ed. 1953)

22 It is in vain you pretend that you are not responsible for the evil law because you are not a magistrate, or a party to a civil process, or do not vote. You eat the law in a crust of bread, you wear it in your hat and shoes. The Man—it is his attitude: the attitude makes the man.

> Ralph Waldo Emerson, Journal, 1842, in *Journals of Ralph Waldo Emerson* 6:168 (Edward W. Emerson ed. 1911)

23 There are two laws discrete,
Not reconciled,—
Law for man, and law for thing;*
The last builds town and fleet,
But it runs wild,
And doth the man unking.
. . .
Let man serve law for man;
Live for friendship, live for love,
For truth's and harmony's behoof;
The state may follow how it can,
As Olympus follows Jove.

> Ralph Waldo Emerson, "Ode Inscribed to W. H. Channing," 1847, in *Complete Works of Ralph Waldo Emerson* 9:76, 78 (1904)

24 The man for whom law exists—the man of forms, the conservative—is a tame man.

> Henry David Thoreau, Journal, 30 Mar. 1851, in *Journal of Henry D. Thoreau* 2:187 (Bradford Torrey & Francis H. Allen eds. 1962)

25 The law will never make men free; it is men who have got to make the law free.

> Henry David Thoreau, "Slavery in Massachusetts" (address), Framingham, Mass., 4 July 1854, in *Writings of Henry David Thoreau* 4:388, 396 (1906)

26 I would remind my countrymen that they are to be men first, and Americans only at a late and convenient hour. No matter how valuable law may be to protect your property, even to keep soul and body together, if it do not keep you and humanity together.

> Henry David Thoreau, "Slavery in Massachusetts" (address), Framingham, Mass., 4 July 1854, in *Writings of Henry David Thoreau* 4:388, 401 (1906)

27 I think there never was a people so choked and stultified by forms. We adore the forms of law, instead of making them vehicles of wisdom and justice.

> Ralph Waldo Emerson, Speech, Cambridge, Mass., 10 Sept. 1856, in *Complete Works of Ralph Waldo Emerson* 11:255, 258 (1904)

---

* Emerson's "law for man" refers to justice founded on human values; "law for thing" refers to the conventional law of the commercial world.

28 When laws, customs, or institutions cease to be beneficial to man, they cease to be obligatory.

> **Henry Ward Beecher,** *Life Thoughts* 54 (1858)

29 Laws and institutions are constantly tending to gravitate. Like clocks, they must be occasionally cleansed, and wound up, and set to true time.

> **Henry Ward Beecher,** *Life Thoughts* 129 (1858)

30 Great is Law—great are the old few landmarks of the law,
They are the same in all times, and shall not be disturbed.

> **Walt Whitman,** "Great Are the Myths," in *Leaves of Grass* 585, 587 (Harold W. Blodgett & Sculley Bradley eds. 1965) (1860)

31 Why, law an' order, honor, civil right,
Ef they *ain't* wuth it, wut *is* wuth a fight?

> **James Russell Lowell,** *Bigelow Papers,* 1862, in *Complete Poetical Works of James Russell Lowell* 228, 237 (Horace E. Scudder ed. 1925)

32   . . . the plough, the axe, the mill,
All kin's o' labor an' all kin's o' skill,
Would be a rabbit in a wile-cat's claw,
Ef 't warn't for thet slow critter,
'stablished law.

> **James Russell Lowell,** *Bigelow Papers,* 1862, in *Complete Poetical Works of James Russell Lowell* 228, 237 (Horace E. Scudder ed. 1925)

33 The hardship of the particular case is no reason for melting down the law. For the sake of fixedness and uniformity, law must be treated as a solid, not as a fluid. It must have, and always retain, a certain degree of hardness, to keep its outlines firm and constant. Water changes shape with every vessel into which it is poured; and a liquid law would vary with the mental conformation of judges, and become a synonym for vagueness and instability.

> **Logan E. Bleckley,** *Southern Star Lightning Rod Co. v. Duvall,* 64 Ga. 262, 268 (1879)

34 The life of the law has not been logic: it has been experience. The felt necessities of the time, the prevalent moral and political theories, intuitions of public policy, avowed or unconscious, even the prejudices which judges share with their fellow-men, have had a good deal more to do than the syllogism in determining the rules by which men should be governed.*

> **Oliver Wendell Holmes, Jr.,** *The Common Law* 1 (1881)

35 The law embodies the story of a nation's development through many centuries, and it cannot be dealt with as if it contained only the axioms and corollaries of a book of mathematics.

> **Oliver Wendell Holmes, Jr.,** *The Common Law* 1 (1881)

36 In order to know what it [the law] is, we must know what it has been, and what it tends to become.

> **Oliver Wendell Holmes, Jr.,** *The Common Law* 1 (1881)

37 The substance of the law at any given time pretty nearly corresponds, so far as it goes, with what is then understood to be convenient; but its forms and machinery, and the degree to which it is able to work out desired results, depend very much upon its past.

> **Oliver Wendell Holmes, Jr.,** *The Common Law* 1–2 (1881)

38 The first requirement of a sound body of law is, that it should correspond with the actual feelings and demands of the community, whether right or wrong.

> **Oliver Wendell Holmes, Jr.,** *The Common Law* 41 (1881)

39 *Law* is an implement of society which is intended for every-day work. It is a coarse tool and not a mathematical instrument.

> **Oliver Wendell Holmes, Sr.,** *Pages from an Old Volume of Life,* 1883, in *Works of Oliver Wendell Holmes* 8:323 (1892)

---

* For reason is the life of the Law. —**Edward Coke,** *The First Part of the Institutes of the Lawes of England* 1:97 (1979) (1628)

The life of the law has not been logic: it has been experience. The seed of every new growth within its sphere has been a felt necessity. —**Oliver Wendell Holmes, Jr.,** Book Review, 14 *American Law Review* 233, 234 (1880) (reviewing Christopher C. Langdell, *A Selection of Cases on the Law of Contracts*)

40 The law, wherein, as in a magic mirror,* we see reflected, not only our own lives, but the lives of all men that have been! When I think on this majestic theme, my eyes dazzle.†

> Oliver Wendell Holmes, Jr., "The Law" (address to Suffolk Bar Association Dinner), Boston, 5 Feb. 1885, in *Speeches* 16, 17 (1913)

41 If we are to speak of the law as our mistress, we who are here know that she is a mistress only to be wooed with sustained and lonely passion,—only to be won by straining all the faculties by which man is likest to a god. Those who, having begun the pursuit, turn away uncharmed, do so either because they have not been vouchsafed the sight of her divine figure, or because they have not the heart for so great a struggle.

> Oliver Wendell Holmes, Jr., "The Law" (address to Suffolk Bar Association Dinner), Boston, 5 Feb. 1885, in *Speeches* 16, 17 (1913)
> See also LAW 16

42 When I think thus of the law, I see a princess mightier than she who once wrought at Bayeux, eternally weaving into her web dim figures of the ever-lengthening past—figures too dim to be noticed by the idle, too symbolic to be interpreted except by her pupils, but to the discerning eye disclosing every painful step and every world-shaking contest by which mankind has worked and fought its way from savage isolation to organic social life.‡

> Oliver Wendell Holmes, Jr., "The Law" (address to Suffolk Bar Association Dinner), Boston, 5 Feb. 1885, in *Speeches* 16, 17–18 (1913)

43 When I think of the Law as we know her in the courthouse and the market, she seems to me a woman sitting by the wayside, beneath whose overshadowing hood every man shall see the countenance of his

---

* The "magic mirror" is probably an allusion to Alfred Tennyson's poem, *The Lady of Shalott*, in which the Lady's only view of the world is through reflections in a mirror.
† Cover her face: Mine eyes dazell: she di'd yong. —John Webster, *The Duchess of Malfi* 109 (F. L. Lucas ed. 1959) (1623)
‡ This passage is inscribed on the exterior of Boalt Hall, University of California School of Law, Berkeley.

deserts or needs. The timid and overborne gain heart from her protecting smile. Fair combatants, manfully standing to their rights, see her keeping the lists with the stern and discriminating eye of even justice. The wretch who has defied her most sacred commands, and has thought to creep through ways where she was not, finds that his path ends with her, and beholds beneath her hood the inexorable face of death.

> Oliver Wendell Holmes, Jr., "The Law" (address to Suffolk Bar Association Dinner), Boston, 5 Feb. 1885, in *Speeches* 16, 18 (1913)

44 The law constantly is tending towards consistency of theory.

> Oliver Wendell Holmes, Jr., *Hanson v. Globe Newspaper Co.*, 159 Mass. 293, 302, 34 N.E. 462 (1893)

45 An ideal system of law should draw its postulates and its legislative justification from science. As it is now, we rely upon tradition, or vague sentiment, or the fact that we never thought of any other way of doing things, as our only warrant for rules. . . . Who here can give reasons of any different kind for believing that half the criminal law does not do more harm than good? Our forms of contract . . . are accidental relics of early notions. . . . And so I might go on through the whole law.

> Oliver Wendell Holmes, Jr., "Learning and Science" (speech to Harvard Law School Association), Cambridge, Mass., 25 June 1895, in *Collected Legal Papers* 138, 139 (1920)

46 A system of law at any time is the resultant of present needs and present notions of what is wise and right on the one hand, and, on the other, of rules handed down from earlier states of society and embodying needs and notions which more or less have passed away.

> Oliver Wendell Holmes, Jr., "The Bar as a Profession," 1896, in *Collected Legal Papers* 153, 156 (1920)

47 The aim of the law is not to punish sins, but is to prevent certain external results.

> Oliver Wendell Holmes, Jr., *Commonwealth v. Kennedy*, 170 Mass. 18, 20, 48 N.E. 770 (1897)

48 The way to gain a liberal view of your subject is . . . to get to the bottom of the subject itself. The means of doing that are, in the first place, to follow the existing body of dogma into its highest generalizations by the help of jurisprudence; next, to discover from history how it has come to be what it is; and, finally, so far as you can, to consider the ends which the several rules seek to accomplish, the reasons why those ends are desired, what is given up to gain them, and whether they are worth the price.

    Oliver Wendell Holmes, Jr., "The Path of the Law," 10 *Harvard Law Review* 457, 476 (1897)

49 It is perfectly proper to regard and study the law simply as a great anthropological document.

    Oliver Wendell Holmes, Jr., "Law in Science and Science in Law," 12 *Harvard Law Review* 443, 444 (1899)

50 This home iv opporchunity where ivry man is th' equal iv ivry other man befure th' law if he isn't careful.

    Finley Peter Dunne, "The Food We Eat," *Dissertations by Mr. Dooley,* 1906, in *Mr. Dooley: Now and Forever* 235, 236 (Louis Filler ed. 1954)

51 The Law! It is the arch-crime of the centuries. The path of Man is soaked with the blood it has shed. Can this great criminal determine Right? Is a revolutionist to respect such a travesty? It would mean the perpetuation of human slavery.

    Alexander Berkman, *Prison Memoirs of an Anarchist* 71 (1912)

52 If we desire respect for the law we must first make the law respectable.

    Louis D. Brandeis, 1912, quoted in Alfred Lief, *The Brandeis Guide to the Modern World* 166 (1941)

53 Men do not make laws. They do but discover them. Laws must be justified by something more than the will of the majority. They must rest on the eternal foundation of righteousness. That state is most fortunate in its form of government which has the aptest instruments for the discovery of laws.

    Calvin Coolidge, Speech to the Massachusetts State Senate, 7 Jan. 1914, in *Have Faith in Massachusetts* 3, 4 (1919)

54 It is the business of the law and the courts to discourage any change of insight or opinion.

    Thorstein Veblen, *The Vested Interests and the State of the Industrial Arts* 170–71 (1919)

55 The observance of the law is the greatest solvent of public ills. Men speak of natural rights, but I challenge any one to show where in nature any rights ever existed or were recognized until there was established for their declaration and protection a duly promulgated body of corresponding laws. The march of civilization has been ever under the protecting aegis of the law. It is the strong defence of the weak, the ever present refuge of innocence, a mighty fortress of the righteous. One with the law is a majority.

    Calvin Coolidge, Speech accepting Republican vice-presidential nomination, Northampton, Mass., 27 July 1920, in *New York Times,* 28 July 1920, at 6

56 Law never *is,* but is always about to be. It is realized only when embodied in a judgment, and in being realized, expires.

    Benjamin N. Cardozo, *The Nature of the Judicial Process* 126 (1921)

57 Life may be lived, conduct may be ordered, it *is* lived and ordered, for unnumbered human beings without bringing them within the field where the law can be misread, unless indeed the misreading be accompanied by conscious abuse of power. Their conduct never touches the border land, the penumbra, where controversy begins. They go from birth to death, their action restrained at every turn by the power of the state, and not once do they appeal to judges to mark the boundaries between right and wrong. I am unable to withhold the name of law from rules which exercise this compulsion over the fortunes of mankind.

    Benjamin N. Cardozo, *The Nature of the Judicial Process* 130 (1921)

58 But pretty much all law consists in forbidding men to do some things that they want to do.

    Oliver Wendell Holmes, Jr., *Adkins v. Children's Hospital,* 261 U.S. 525, 568 (1923) (dissenting)

59 Law, like other branches of social science, must be satisfied to test the validity of its

conclusions by the logic of probabilities rather than the logic of certainty.

Benjamin N. Cardozo, *The Growth of the Law* 33 (1924)

60 Law, if you had asked him, and he had accurately expressed himself, was a mist formed out of the moods and the mistakes of men, which befogged the sea of life and prevented plain sailing for the little commercial and social barques of men; it was a miasma of misinterpretation where the ills of life festered, and also a place where the accidentally wounded were ground between the upper and the nether millstones of force or chance; it was a strange, weird, interesting, and yet futile battle of wits where the ignorant and the incompetent and the shrewd and the angry and the weak were made pawns and shuttlecocks for men—lawyers, who were playing upon their moods, their vanities, their desires, and their necessities. It was an unholy and unsatisfactory disrupting and delaying spectacle, a painful commentary on the frailties of life, and men, a trick, a snare, a pit and gin.

Theodore Dreiser, *The Financier* 327–28 (rev. ed. 1927)

61 Law in the sense in which courts speak of it today does not exist without some definite authority behind it.

Oliver Wendell Holmes, Jr., *Black & White Taxicab Co. v. Brown & Yellow Taxicab Co.,* 276 U.S. 518, 533 (1928) (dissenting)

62 The theory that there is something sacred about law is always propagated very diligently by gentleman thirsty for power, and it has never been propagated so diligently as it is by such persons in the United States today. They erect upon it a cult that takes on a passionate and even mystical character. The thing that we must grovel to, so they teach, is not this or that law, not the good law as opposed to the bad law, but law in general, *all* law. But it takes no great acuity to see that what they are really arguing for, whatever their pretensions otherwise, is some law that they are especially interested in. They care nothing, in truth, for law in general.

H. L. Mencken, Editorial, *American Mercury,* Dec. 1929, at 409, 409

63 Ninety-nine per cent of the laws by which we are governed are unwritten laws, just as binding as the printed ones upon our statute books, which after all are only the crystallization of the sentiments and opinions of the community based upon its traditions, manners, customs and religious beliefs. For every statute in print there are a hundred that have no tangible existence, based on our sense of decency, of duty and of honor, which are equally controlling and which it has never been found necessary to reduce to writing, since their infraction usually brings its own penalty or infringes the more delicate domain of private conscience where the crude processes of the criminal law cannot follow. The laws of etiquette and fair play are just as obligatory as legislative enactments—the Ten Commandments as efficacious as the Penal Code.

Arthur Train, "Contempt of Court," in *By Advice of Counsel* 96, 108 (1929)

64 Rules of logic can no more produce legal or moral doctrines than they can produce kittens. On the whole, it is safe to assume that those legal doctrines that claim to be the offspring of logic are either not proud or not aware of their real parents.

Felix S. Cohen, "Modern Ethics and the Law: Ethics for Lawyers and Judges," 4 *Brooklyn Law Review* 33, 43 (1934)

65 Men insist upon believing that there are fundamental principles of law which exist apart from any particular case, or any particular human activity; that these principles must be sought with a reverent attitude; that they are being improved constantly; and that our sacrifices of efficiency and humanitarianism in their honor are leading us to a better government. The truth of such a philosophy cannot be demonstrated or proved. It exists only because we seem unable to find comfort without it.

Thurman W. Arnold, *The Symbols of Government* 32–33 (1935)

66 The Law's alleged certainty and consistency lie entirely in the never-never land of abstract principles and precepts. The Law has been forced to retreat from the world of facts into its own world of fancy in order to maintain the pose that it is a precise and solid science.

Fred Rodell, *Woe Unto You, Lawyers!* 251 (1939)

67 Law is through and through a social phenomenon; social in origin, in purpose or end, and in application.

> John Dewey, "My Philosophy of Law," in *My Philosophy of Law: Credos of Sixteen American Scholars* 73, 76 (1941)

68 We can judge what the law *is* as matter of fact only by telling how it operates, and what are its effects in and upon the human activities that are going on.

> John Dewey, "My Philosophy of Law," in *My Philosophy of Law: Credos of Sixteen American Scholars* 73, 77 (1941)

69 I have never seen any reason why law should make any more sense than the rest of life; and I think that the attitude of those of us who have anything to do with it should be that of the familiar sign in the western dance hall, "Don't shoot the piano player, he's doing the best he can."

> William L. Prosser, Book Review, 27 *Cornell Law Quarterly* 292, 294 (1942)

70 The law knows no finer hour than when it cuts through formal concepts and transitory emotions to protect unpopular citizens against discrimination and persecution.

> Frank Murphy, *Falbo v. United States*, 320 U.S. 549, 561 (1944) (dissenting)

71 "You're a lawyer," Hugh Miller said.

"No," the Boss corrected, "I'm not a lawyer. I know some law. In fact, I know a lot of law. And I made me some money out of law. But I'm not a lawyer. That's why I can see what the law is like. It's like a single-bed blanket on a double bed and three folks in the bed and a cold night. There ain't ever enough blanket to cover the case, no matter how much pulling and hauling, and somebody is always going to nigh catch pneumonia. Hell, the law is like the pants you bought last year for a growing boy, but it is always this year and the seams are popped and the shankbones to the breeze. The law is always too short and too tight for growing humankind. The best you can do is do something and then make up some law to fit and by the time that law gets on the books you would have done something different.

> Robert Penn Warren, *All the King's Men* 145 (1946)

72 There can be no free society without law administered through an independent judiciary. If one man can be allowed to determine for himself what is law, every man can. That means first chaos, then tyranny. Legal process is an essential part of the democratic process.

> Felix Frankfurter, *United States v. United Mine Workers*, 330 U.S. 258, 312 (1947) (concurring)

73 In the community develops the law behind law, the multi-sanctioned law that existed before governments began and that the law of government can never supersede. Without the prior laws of the community all the laws of the state would be empty formulas. Custom, the first "king of men," still rules. The *mores* still prescribe. Manners and modes still flourish. The laws made by governments cannot rescind them, cannot long defy them or deeply invade them.

> Robert M. MacIver, *The Web of Government* 193 (1947)

74 The fundamental social relationships regulated by official law change but slowly, providing the society with a necessary stability and order. An incessant change of such fundamental social relationships as property, the family, and forms of government would mean a continuous revolution — economic, social, and political — which would make stable order in the society impossible. These facts explain why the norms of official law tend to "harden" and in this "hardened" form tend to stay unchanged for decades, even centuries, until a profound change in the law-convictions of the members occurs. . . . *Official law, then, always lags somewhat behind unofficial law.*

> Pitirim A. Sorokin, *Society, Culture, and Personality* 82 (1947)

75 The law is not a series of calculating machines where definitions and answers come tumbling out when the right levers are pushed.

> William O. Douglas, "The Dissent, a Safeguard of Democracy," 32 *Journal of the American Judicature Society* 105 (1948)

76 As an admiring lay observer, I have always considered that W. S. Gilbert's Lord Chancellor, when he declared that the law is the true embodiment of everything that's excellent, stated no more than the truth. If it has a single fault or flaw, I lay that to the

unfortunate intrusion of the human element—a fallibility and unreasonableness of mankind that enters to disturb the law's own august order of right and reason. This, I think, the law itself feels. In its accumulated wisdom, work of the best minds of many centuries, the law moves—and not without resource and dexterity—to minimize the damage men can do its processes by being men.

James Gould Cozzens, "Notes on a Difficulty of Law by One Unlearned in It," 1951, in *Just Representations* 310 (Matthew J. Bruccoli ed. 1978)

77 Law cannot restrain evil; for the freedom of man is such that he can make the keeping of the law the instrument of evil.

Reinhold Niebuhr, *The Nature and Destiny of Man* 38 (1951)

78 I know of no way that we can have equal justice under law except we have some law.

Robert H. Jackson, *Brown v. Allen*, 344 U.S. 443, 546 (1953) (concurring)

79 The central idea of law . . . [is] *the principle of institutional settlement*. . . . when the principle . . . is plainly applicable, we say that the law "is" thus and so, and brush aside further discussion of what it "ought" to be. Yet the "is" is not really an "is" but a special kind of decision of "ought"—a statement that . . . a decision which is the duly arrived at result of a duly established procedure for making decisions of that kind "ought" to be accepted as binding upon the whole society unless and until it has been duly changed.

Henry M. Hart, Jr. and Albert M. Sacks, *The Legal Process* 4–5 (tent. ed. 1958)

80 For all its lurching and shambling imbecilities, the law—and only the law—is what keeps our society from bursting apart at the seams, from becoming a snarling jungle. While the law is not perfect, God knows, no other system has yet been found for governing men except violence. The law is society's safety valve, its most painless way to achieve social catharsis; any other way lies anarchy.

Robert Traver, *Anatomy of a Murder* 63 (1958)

81 All our fine Magna Chartas and constitutions and bills of right and all the rest would be nothing but a lot of archaic and high-flown rhetoric if we could not and did not at all times have the *law* to buttress them, to interpret them, to breathe meaning and force and life into them. Lofty abstractions about individual liberty and justice do not enforce themselves. These things must be reforged in men's hearts every day. And they are reforged by the law, for every jury trial in the land is a small daily miracle of democracy in action.

Robert Traver, *Anatomy of a Murder* 63 (1958)

82 The law is the busy fireman that puts out society's brush fires; that gives people a *nonphysical* method to discharge hostile feelings and settle violent differences; that substitutes orderly ritual for the rule of tooth and claw. The very slowness of the law, its massive impersonality, its insistence upon proceeding according to settled and ancient rules—all this tends to cool and bank the fires of passion and violence and replace them with order and reason.

Robert Traver, *Anatomy of a Murder* 63 (1958)

83 I fought the law, and the law won.

Sonny Curtis, *I Fought the Law* (song) (1961)

84 Law in latter days has gained much in realism, in hard-headedness, in disdain for orotundity and rhetorical glitter. This gain, like all gains, comes with its built-in peril—in this case the deadly peril of loss of the poetry of law. The poetry of law solves no legal problems; it was, in fact, brought into disrepute precisely by misbegotten attempts to make it solve legal problems—and herein all known schools of "natural law" have offended. The poetry of law is the motive for solving problems, the sacred stir toward justice, our priceless discontent at the remoteness of perfect law.

Charles L. Black, Jr., *The Occasions of Justice* 31 (1963)

85 I consider advocacy, jurisprudence, even justice, to have no more intrinsic importance than, say, oyster-shucking.

John Barth, *The Floating Opera* 73 (1967)

86 Respect for judicial process is a small price to pay for the civilizing hand of law, which

alone can give abiding meaning to constitutional freedom.

Potter Stewart, *Walker v. City of Birmingham*, 388 U.S. 307, 321 (1967)

87 Far more than money, law is capable of intervening between man and his humanity.... law gets into the individual's mind and substitutes its external standards, whatever they may be, for the individual's own standards. We are taught that it is our moral and civic duty to substitute the law's standards for our own. It is a virtue to obey the law, a sin to ignore it in favor of one's own personal desires. That doctrine serves a community well as long as law is formed in a human image.

Charles A. Reich, *The Greening of America* 126–27 (1970)

88 But what if the law becomes the betrayer of the people? ... The people's best instincts are then used to disable them from fighting an enemy; they are told it is morally right to surrender. Thus the people are led to deny their own inner values in favor of law which has become, unknown to them, corrupt, unjust, and antihuman.

Charles A. Reich, *The Greening of America* 127 (1970)

89 "It didn't satisfy me at all."
"It satisfied the law," the old woman said sharply.
"The law," Mr Shiftlet said and spit. "It's the law that don't satisfy me."

Flannery O'Connor, "The Life You Save May Be Your Own," in *Complete Stories* 145, 153 (1971)

90 There's no question of justice, or right and wrong. The law seeks order ... Order!

William Gaddis, *JR* 8 (1975)

91 As lawyers we will do well to be on our guard against any suggestion that, through law, our society can be reformed, purified, or saved. The function of law, in a society like our own, is altogether more modest and less apocalyptic. It is to provide a mechanism for the settlement of disputes in the light of broadly conceived principles on whose soundness, it must be assumed, there is general consensus among us. If the assumption is wrong, if there is no consensus, then we are headed for war, civil strife and revolution.

Grant Gilmore, *The Ages of American Law* 109 (1977)

92 Law reflects but in no sense determines the moral worth of a society. The values of a reasonably just society will reflect themselves in a reasonably just law. The better the society, the less law there will be. In Heaven there will be no law, and the lion will lie down with the lamb. The values of an unjust society will reflect themselves in an unjust law. The worse the society, the more law there will be. In Hell there will be nothing but law, and due process will be meticulously observed.

Grant Gilmore, *The Ages of American Law* 110–11 (1977)

93 The business of the law is to make sense of the confusion of what we call human life—to reduce it to order but at the same time to give it possibility, scope, even dignity.

Archibald MacLeish, "Art and Law," in *Riders on the Earth* 82, 85 (1978)

94 I have spent all my life under a Communist regime and I will tell you that a society without any objective legal scale is a terrible one indeed. But a society with no other scale but the legal one is also less than worthy of man.

Aleksandr I. Solzhenitsyn, Commencement address at Harvard University, 8 June 1978, in *A World Split Apart* 17 (1978)

95 A society based on the letter of the law and never reaching any higher fails to take advantage of the full range of human possibilities. The letter of the law is too cold and formal to have a beneficial influence on society. Whenever the tissue of life is woven of legalistic relationships, this creates an atmosphere of spiritual mediocrity that paralyzes man's noblest impulses.

Aleksandr I. Solzhenitsyn, Commencement address at Harvard University, 8 June 1978, in *A World Split Apart* 17–19 (1978)

96 After a certain level of the problem has been reached, legalistic thinking induces paralysis; it prevents one from seeing the scale and the meaning of events.

Aleksandr I. Solzhenitsyn, Commencement address at Harvard University, 8 June 1978, in *A World Split Apart* 39 (1978)

97 Law is the thing, the most sensible of all, because it works like a boa constrictor, the best of all snakes. My favorite. A boa doesn't actually squeeze anything. The snake just wraps itself around a man or a lamb or some unfortunate creature and waits for whatever it's wrapped around to exhale: the boa then takes up the slack. It's a procedure, and the law is nothing else if it's not a procedure.

  Craig Nova, *The Good Son* 63 (1982)

98 There is far too much law for those who can afford it and far too little for those who cannot.

  Derek C. Bok, "A Flawed System," *Harvard Magazine,* May-June 1983, at 38, 38

99 The elaborateness of our laws and the complexity of our procedures absorb the energies of this giant bar, raise the cost of legal services, and help produce the other great problem of our legal system—the lack of access for the poor and middle class. The results are embarrassing to behold. . . . The blunt, inexcusable fact is that this nation, which prides itself on efficiency and justice, has developed a legal system that is the most expensive in the world, yet cannot manage to protect the rights of most of its citizens.

  Derek C. Bok, "A Flawed System," *Harvard Magazine,* May-June 1983, at 38, 41

100 No set of legal institutions or prescriptions exists apart from the narratives that locate it and give it meaning. For every constitution there is an epic, for each decalogue a scripture. Once understood in the context of the narratives that give it meaning, law becomes not merely a system of rules to be observed, but a world in which we live.

  Robert M. Cover, "The Supreme Court, 1982 Term—Foreword: Nomos and Narrative," 97 *Harvard Law Review* 4, 4–5 (1983)

101 I myself do not think law is a humanity. It is a technique of government.

  Richard A. Posner, "Law and Literature: A Relation Reargued," 72 *Virginia Law Review* 1351, 1392 (1986)

102 Raphael Lemkin was once asked, "What good will it do to write mass murder down as a crime; will a piece of paper stop a new Hitler or Stalin?" He replied: "Only man

has law. Law must be built, do you understand me? You must build the law!"

  Raphael Lemkin, reported in *New York Times,* 18 Oct. 1988, at A31

103 Some spoke of the nobility of the law. Stern did not believe in that. Too much of the grubby boneshop, the odor of the abattoir, emanated from every courtroom he had entered. It was often a nasty business. But the law, at least, sought to govern misfortune, the slights and injuries of our social existence that were otherwise wholly random. The law's object was to let the seas engulf only those who had been selected for drowning on an orderly basis. In human affairs, reason would never fully triumph; but there was no better cause to champion.

  Scott Turow, *The Burden of Proof* 202 (1990)

LAW, DEFINITIONS OF

See also LAW

1 Law is merely the expression of the will of the strongest for the time being, and therefore laws have no fixity, but shift from generation to generation.

  Brooks Adams, *The Law of Civilization and Decay* 165 (1896)

2 The prophecies of what the courts will do in fact, and nothing more pretentious, are what I mean by the law.

  Oliver Wendell Holmes, Jr., "The Path of the Law," 10 *Harvard Law Review* 457, 460–61 (1897)

3 The true view, as I submit, is that the Law is what the judges declare; that statutes, precedents, the opinions of learned experts, customs and morality are the sources of the Law.

  John Chipman Gray, *The Nature and Sources of the Law* 267 (1909)

4 We shall unite in viewing as law that body of principle and dogma which with a reasonable measure of probability may be predicted as the basis for judgment in pending or in future controversies.

  Benjamin N. Cardozo, *The Growth of the Law* 44 (1924)

5 The real law in the modern state is the multitude of little decisions made daily by millions of men.

> **Walter Lippmann,** *A Preface to Morals* 275 (1929)

6 I am the law!*

> **Frank Hague,** quoted in *New York Times,* 11 Nov. 1937, at 1

7 Law is more than the words that put it on the books; law is more than any decisions that may be made from it; law is more than the particular code of it stated at any one time or in any one place or nation; more than any man, lawyer or judge, sheriff or jailer, who may represent it. True law, the code of justice, the essence of our sensations of right and wrong, is the conscience of society. It has taken thousands of years to develop, and it is the greatest, the most distinguishing quality which has evolved with mankind. None of man's temples, none of his religions, none of his weapons, his tools, his arts, his sciences, nothing else he has grown to, is so great a thing as his justice, his sense of justice. The true law is something in itself; it is the spirit of the moral nature of man; it is an existence apart, like God, and as worthy of worship as God. If we can touch God at all, where do we touch him save in the conscience? And what is the conscience of any man save his little fragment of the conscience of all men in all time?

> **Walter Van Tilburg Clark,** *The Ox-Bow Incident* 66–67 (1940)

8 That will-o'-the-wisp, the law: where shall I begin to speak of it? Is the law the legal rules, or their interpretations by judges, or

---

* William Safire explains in *Safire's Political Dictionary* 319 (1978) that "Mayor Frank Hague of Jersey City . . . received a bum rap from history on this quotation. The episode involved two youths who wanted to change from day school to night school so that they could go to work, but who were denied working papers by the Board of Education's Special Services Director because the law required them to stay in day school. Mayor Hague cut through the red tape and ordered the official to give the boys working papers. As he proudly recounted the matter before the Men's Club of Emory Church in Jersey City on November 10, 1937: when the school official told him, 'That's the law,' he replied, 'Listen, here is the law. I am the law! Those boys go to work!' Today such an action would be lauded . . . but Hague had a well-deserved reputation for high-handedness, and the phrase soon lost its context and was used against him."

by juries? Is it the precedent or the present fact? The norm or the practice?

> **John Barth,** *The Floating Opera* 84 (1967)

9 What's law? Control? Law filters chaos and what drips through? Serenity? Law—our highest ideal and our basest nature. Don't look too closely at the law. Do, and you'll find the rationalized interpretations, the legal casuistry, the precedents of convenience. You'll find the serenity, which is just another word for death.

> **Frank Herbert,** *Dune Messiah* 193 (1969)

10 What is law? Now I offer a different kind of answer. Law is not exhausted by any catalogue of rules or principles, each with its own dominion over some discrete theater of behavior. Nor by any roster of officials and their powers each over part of our lives. Law's empire is defined by attitude, not territory or power or process.

> **Ronald M. Dworkin,** *Law's Empire* 413 (1986)

LAW, GROWTH OF

See also LAW

1 The law is a living growth, not a changeless code.*

> Inscription carved over the entrance to the Yale Law School

2 New times demand new measures and
>   new men;
> The world advances, and in time
>   outgrows
> The laws which in our father's day were
>   best;
> And, doubtless, after us, some purer
>   scheme
> Will be shaped out by wiser men than we,
> Made wiser by the steady growth of truth.

> **James Russell Lowell,** "A Glance Behind the Curtain," 1843, in *Complete Poetical Works of James Russell Lowell* 49, 51 (Horace E. Scudder ed. 1925)

3 *Legislation* and *adjudication* must follow, and conform to, the progress of society.

> **Abraham Lincoln,** Notes of argument in law case, 15 June 1858?, in *Collected Works of*

---

* The inscription was suggested by Arthur L. Corbin.

Abraham Lincoln 2:459 (Roy P. Basler ed. 1953)

4 The truth is, that law hitherto has been, and it would seem by the necessity of its being is always approaching and never reaching consistency. It is for ever adopting new principles from life at one end, and it always retains old ones from history at the other which have not yet been absorbed or sloughed off. It will become entirely consistent only when it ceases to grow.

Oliver Wendell Holmes, Jr., "Common Carriers and the Common Law," 13 *American Law Review* 609, 631 (1879)

5 The truth is, that the law is always approaching, and never reaching, consistency. It is forever adopting new principles from life at one end, and it always retains old ones from history at the other, which have not yet been absorbed or sloughed off. It will become entirely consistent only when it ceases to grow.

Oliver Wendell Holmes, Jr., *The Common Law* 36 (1881)

6 Law is the business to which my life is devoted, and I should show less than devotion if I did not do what in me lies to improve it, and, when I perceive what seems to me the ideal of its future, if I hesitated to point it out and to press toward it with all my heart.

Oliver Wendell Holmes, Jr., "The Path of the Law," 10 *Harvard Law Review* 457, 473–74 (1897)

7 My analysis of the judicial process comes then to this, and little more: logic, and history, and custom, and utility, and the accepted standards of right conduct, are the forces which singly or in combination shape the progress of the law.

Benjamin N. Cardozo, *The Nature of the Judicial Process* 112 (1921)

8 Law must be stable and yet it cannot stand still.

Roscoe Pound, *Interpretations of Legal History* 1 (1923)

9 Existing rules and principles can give us our present location, our bearings, our latitude and longitude. The inn that shelters for the night is not the journey's end. The law, like the traveler, must be ready for the morrow. It must have a principle of growth.

Benjamin N. Cardozo, *The Growth of the Law* 19–20 (1924)

10 The legal structure still changes only in response to crisis: lawyers and judges, like laymen, are forever crying that there ought to be a law.

Martin Mayer, *The Lawyers* 137 (1967)

11 I am convinced that law can be a vital engine not merely of change but of other civilizing change. That is because law, when it merits the synonym justice, is based on reason and insight. Decisional law evolves as litigants and judges develop a better understanding of the world in which we live. Sometimes, these insights appear pedestrian, such as when we recognize, for example, that a suitcase is more like a home than it is like a car. On occasion, these insights are momentous, such as when we finally understand that separate can never be equal. I believe that these steps, which are the building blocks of progress, are fashioned from a great deal more than the changing views of judges over time. I believe that problems are susceptible to rational solution if we work hard at making and understanding arguments that are based on reason and experience.

William J. Brennan, Jr., "Constitutional Adjudication and the Death Penalty: A View from the Court," 100 *Harvard Law Review* 313, 331 (1986)

LAW AND ECONOMICS

1 For the rational study of the law the black-letter man may be the man of the present, but the man of the future is the man of statistics and the master of economics.

Oliver Wendell Holmes, Jr., "The Path of the Law," 10 *Harvard Law Review* 457, 469 (1897)

2 Under perfect competition private and social costs will be equal.*

George J. Stigler, *The Theory of Price* 113 (3d ed. 1966)

---

* This is a formulation of the "Coase Theorem" derived from the work of economist Ronald Coase.

3 The strict liability test we suggest does not require that a governmental institution make such a cost-benefit analysis. It requires of such an institution only a decision as to which of the parties to the accident *is in the best position to make the cost-benefit analysis between accident costs and accident avoidance costs and to act on that decision once it is made.* The question for the court reduces to a search for the cheapest cost avoider.

> **Guido Calabresi and Jon T. Hirschoff,** "Toward a Test for Strict Liability in Torts," 81 *Yale Law Journal* 1055, 1060 (1972)

4 An economic theory of law will not capture the full complexity, richness, and confusion of the phenomena.... But its lack of realism, far from invalidating the theory, is the essential precondition of theory.... The true test of a theory is its utility in predicting or explaining reality. Judged by this criterion, economic theory, despite (because of?) the unrealism of its assumptions, may be judged a success.

> **Richard A. Posner,** *Economic Analysis of Law* 13 (2d ed. 1977)

LAW BOOKS

See also LAW LIBRARIES; LEGAL RESEARCH

1 A lawyer without books would be like a workman without tools.

> **Thomas Jefferson,** Letter to Thomas Turpin, 5 Feb. 1769, in *Papers of Thomas Jefferson* 1:24 (Julian P. Boyd ed. 1950)

2 Indeed a Lawyer through his whole Life ought to have some Book on Ethicks or the Law of Nations always on his Table. They are all Treatises of individual or national Morality and ought to be the Study of our whole Lives.

> **John Adams,** Autobiography, 1802, in *Diary and Autobiography of John Adams* 3:272 (L. H. Butterfield ed. 1961)

3 At this Time October 1758 the Study of the Law was a dreary Ramble, in comparison to what it is at this day. The Name of Blackstone had not been heard.... I was desirous of seeking the Law as well as I could in its foundations and I obtained as much Knowledge as I could of Bracton, Britton, Fleta and Glanville, but I suffered very much for Want of Books, which deter-

mined me to furnish myself, at any Sacrifice, with a proper Library: and Accordingly by degrees I procured the best Library of Law in the State.

> **John Adams,** Autobiography, 1802, in *Diary and Autobiography of John Adams* 3:273–74 (L.H. Butterfield ed. 1961)

4 Blackstone, whose book, although the most elegant and best digested of our law catalogue, has been perverted more than all others, to the degeneracy of legal science. A student finds there a smattering of everything, and his indolence easily persuades him that if he understands that book, he is master of the whole body of the law. The distinction between these, and those who have drawn their stores from the deep and rich mines of Coke Littleton, seems well understood even by the unlettered common people, who apply the appellation of Blackstone lawyers to these ephemeral insects of the law.

> **Thomas Jefferson,** Letter to John Tyler, 17 June 1812, in *Writings of Thomas Jefferson* 6:66 (H. A. Washington ed. 1854)

5 The mass of the law is, to be sure, accumulating with an almost incredible rapidity.... It is impossible not to look without some discouragement upon the ponderous volumes, which the next half century will add to the groaning shelves of our jurists.

> **Joseph Story,** Address before Suffolk Bar, Boston, 4 Sept. 1821, in *Miscellaneous Writings of Joseph Story* 198, 237 (William W. Story ed. 1852)

6 It is strange to think of that monotonous series as a record of human lives. I have seen upon the section of an ancient tree the annual rings marked off which grew while the Black Prince was fighting the French, while Shakespeare wrote his plays, while England was a Commonwealth, while a later republic arose over the western waters, and grew so great as to shake the world. And so, I often think, may all our histories be marked off upon the backs of the unbroken series of our reports.

> **Oliver Wendell Holmes, Jr.,** "Daniel S. Richardson" (eulogy), 15 Apr. 1890, in *Speeches* 46, 47 (1913)

7 We must look away from the piecemeal law books, the miscellaneous and disconnected

statutes and legal maxims, the court decisions, to the life of men.

> Woodrow Wilson, "The Law and the Facts,"
> 5 *American Political Science Review* 1, 6
> (1911)

8 Of course there are books which a man or woman uses as instruments of a profession—law books, medical books, cookery books, and the like. I am not speaking of these, for they are not properly "books" at all; they come in the category of time-tables, telephone directories, and other useful agencies of civilized life.

> Theodore Roosevelt, *An Autobiography* 360
> (1913)

9 When the [Supreme] Court moved to Washington in 1800, it was provided with no books, which probably accounts for the high quality of early opinions.

> Robert H. Jackson, *The Supreme Court in
> the American System of Government* 30
> (1955)

LAW ENFORCEMENT

See also CRIME; CRIMINAL JUSTICE; CRIMINAL LAW;
SEARCHES AND SEIZURES

1 We preserve the so-called peace of a community by deeds of petty violence everyday. Look at the policeman's billy and handcuffs! Look at the jail! Look at the gallows!

> Henry David Thoreau, "A Plea for Captain
> John Brown," 1859, in *Writings of Henry
> David Thoreau* 4:407, 434 (1906)

2 I know no method to secure the repeal of bad or obnoxious laws so effective as their stringent execution.

> Ulysses S. Grant, First Inaugural Address, 4
> Mar. 1869, in *Messages and Papers of the
> Presidents* 7:6, 6 (James D. Richardson ed.
> 1898)

3 They [women] live in the midst of a country [the United States] where there is no end to the laws and no beginning to the execution of them.

> Mark Twain, "The Temperance Crusade and
> Woman's Rights," 1873, in *Complete Essays
> of Mark Twain* 664, 666 (Charles Neider ed.
> 1963)

4 The administration of law can never go lax where every individual sees to it that it grows not lax in his own case, or in cases which fall under his eyes.

> Mark Twain, "Notes for a New Book," 10
> June 1878, in *Mark Twain's Notebook* 140
> (Albert B. Paine ed. 1935)

5 I shall enforce the laws; I shall enforce them against men of vast wealth just exactly as I enforce them against ordinary criminals; and I shall not flinch from this course, come weal or come woe.

> Theodore Roosevelt, Letter to David Scull,
> 16 Aug. 1907, in *Letters of Theodore
> Roosevelt* 5:755 (Elting E. Morison ed. 1952)

6 The Government—I heard about the
Government and I went out to find it. I
said I would look closely at it when I
saw it.
Then I saw a policeman dragging a
drunken man to the calaboose. It was
the Government in action.
I saw a ward alderman slip into an office
one morning and talk with a judge.
Later in the day the judge dismissed a
case against a pickpocket who was a
live ward worker for the alderman.
Again I saw this was the Government,
doing things.

> Carl Sandburg, "Government," 1916, in
> *Complete Poems: Carl Sandburg* 71, 71–72
> (1950)

7 The truth is, and everybody knows it, that there are wise laws and there are laws which are far from wise. Every policeman on the beat recognizes the difference and acts accordingly. Every citizen knows that there are laws which are simply idiotic and he disobeys with impunity. When and if some stupid person calls him to account he expects and believes that the courts will take into consideration the fact that the law is idiotic. In nine times out of ten his expectation is realized. Honest policemen, honest district attorneys, honest judges and practically all juries are in a sort of tacit agreement not to enforce idiotic laws.

> H. L. Mencken, "Note on Law
> Enforcement," Baltimore *Evening Sun,* 3
> Nov. 1925, quoted in *The Gist of Mencken*
> 444 (Mayo DuBasky ed. 1990)

8 The Government may set decoys to entrap criminals. But it may not provoke or create

a crime and then punish the criminal, its creature.

Louis D. Brandeis, *Casey v. United States,* 276 U.S. 413, 423 (1928) (dissenting)

9 There's a lot of law at the end of a nightstick.*

Grover A. Whalen, quoted in Quentin Reynolds, *Courtroom* 33 (1950)

10 When the law fails of execution, when the conduct of the government is hampered by dishonesty and corruption, when crime is prevalent, the value of property is reduced, the area of the slums is widened, ignorance becomes more dense and the poverty of the people is increased. We are a rich nation, but our citizens cannot afford to be complacent about violations of the law or laxity in their government. Our whole credit structure rests on the general power to enforce the law.

Calvin Coolidge, 1931, in *Calvin Coolidge Says* (Edward C. Lathem ed. 1972)

11 It is well settled that the fact that officers or employees of the Government merely afford opportunities or facilities for the commission of the offense does not defeat the prosecution. Artifice and stratagem may be employed to catch those engaged in criminal enterprises. . . . The appropriate object of this permitted activity, frequently essential to the enforcement of the law, is to reveal the criminal design; to expose the illicit traffic, the prohibited publication, the fraudulent use of the mails, the illegal conspiracy, or other offenses, and thus to disclose the would-be violators of the law. A different question is presented when the criminal design originates with the officials of the Government, and they implant in the mind of an innocent person the disposition to commit the alleged offense and induce its commission in order that they may prosecute.

Charles Evans Hughes, *Sorrells v. United States,* 287 U.S. 435, 441–42 (1932)

12 "You're not exactly proud of the way you have handled things, are you, Marlowe?"

"I got off on the wrong foot. After that I just had to take my lumps."

"Don't you think you owe a certain obligation to the law?"

"I would—if the law was like you."

He ran his long pale fingers through his tousled black hair.

"I could make a lot of answers to that," he said. "They'd all sound about the same. The citizen is the law. In this country we haven't got around to understanding that. We think of the law as an enemy. We're a nation of cop-haters."

Raymond Chandler, *The Little Sister* 225 (1949)

13 There are not enough jails, not enough policemen, not enough courts to enforce a law not supported by the people.

Hubert H. Humphrey, Speech, Williamsburg, Va., 1 May 1965, quoted in *New York Times,* 2 May 1965, at 1:34

14 Entrapment is merely a facet of a much broader problem. Together with illegal searches and seizures, coerced confessions, wiretapping, and bugging, it represents lawless invasion of privacy. It is indicative of a philosophy that the ends justify the means.

William O. Douglas, *Osborn v. United States,* 385 U.S. 323, 343–44 (1966) (dissenting)

15 A policeman's lot is not so unhappy that he must choose between being charged with dereliction of duty if he does not arrest when he has probable cause, and being mulcted in damages if he does. Although the matter is not entirely free from doubt, the same consideration would seem to require excusing him from liability for acting under a statute that he reasonably believed to be valid but that was later held unconstitutional, on its face or as applied.

Earl Warren, *Pierson v. Ray,* 386 U.S. 547, 555 (1967)

16 [Addressing black civil rights workers protesting Nixon Administration actions regarding the Voting Rights Act:] You'd be better informed if instead of listening to what we say, you watch what we do.*

John N. Mitchell, quoted in *Washington Post,* 7 July 1969, at A22

---

* Whalen was New York City's Police Commissioner from 1928 to 1930. Reynolds also states, "Much earlier, in the 1870's, Inspector Alexander S. Williams . . . had observed, 'There is more law in the end of a policeman's nightstick than in a decision of the Supreme Court.'"

---

* Attorney General Mitchell's statement is usually misquoted as "Watch what we do, not what we say."

17 Law is not self-executing. Unfortunately, at times its execution rests in the hands of those who are faithless to it. And even when its enforcement is committed to those who revere it, law merely deters some human beings from offending, and punishes other human beings for offending. It does not make men good. This task can be performed only by ethics or religion or morality.

Sam J. Ervin, Jr., in Select Comm. on Presidential Campaign Activities, Final Report, S. Rep. No. 981, 93d Cong., 2d Sess. 1103 (1974)

LAW FIRMS

See also LAW PRACTICE

1 The story, doubtless apocryphal, has long been told that when some of his partners urged that the office was under such pressure as to make additions to the staff imperative, Moore [Hoyt A. Moore of Cravath, Swaine and Moore] replied: "That's silly. No one is under pressure. There wasn't a light on when I left at two o'clock this morning."

Robert T. Swaine, *The Cravath Firm and Its Predecessors, 1819–1948,* at 2:143 (1948)

2 Henry Fellows Everett was . . . one of the last of that great generation of lawyers, the generation of Paul D. Cravath and Francis Lynde Stetson, which had forged the modern corporate law firm, that bright and gleaming sword, out of the rusty materials lying about the old-fashioned city lawyer's office of seventy years ago. The members of these firms today, and indeed for the past thirty years, have unlike their predecessors conformed to a certain pattern: they have become genial, available, democratic with their clerks and sympathetic with their clients, ready with a generality for every emergency and a funny story for every banquet. Eccentricity, the prerogative of the older generation, has gone out of fashion, though the middle-aged lawyer still remembers it lovingly and tells nostalgic tales of his early clerkship when he was shouted at and abused by a ferocious but magnificent taskmaster. This nostalgia, of course, is not so much a nostalgia for the days of his own subordination as for the era of the lawyer's greater glory, that hal-cyon time when clients as well as clerks could be shouted at, even shown the door, when fees were paid in the stock of expanding companies, when a Joseph H. Choate could persuade the Supreme Court that an income tax was unconstitutional and a William Nelson Cromwell could negotiate the Panama Canal.

Louis Auchincloss, "The Legends of Henry Everett," in *The Romantic Egoists* 85, 85–86 (1954)

3 I regret that I have but one law firm to give to my country [referring to President John Kennedy's repeated selection of members of Stevenson's law firm to serve in his Administration].

Adlai E. Stevenson, quoted in Peter Hay, *Book of Legal Anecdotes* xii (1989)

4 Mr. Byrne [James Byrne, with whom Tweed apprenticed in a New York law office] demanded to know why [a memorandum] was not ready and I humbly pleaded that I had not had time to finish it. He glared at me and asked, "What time did you go home on Friday night?" I replied, "Three o'clock in the morning." "What time did you go home Saturday night?" I told him that I had quit at two o'clock in the morning. Then came the final "What time did you go home Sunday night?" And I had to confess that I had done so at eleven o'clock; whereupon he pounded the desk and said: "Don't tell me that you didn't have time to finish that memorandum. Tell me the truth—that you wanted to go home early Sunday night."

Harrison Tweed, "One Lawyer's Life," in *Listen to Leaders in Law* 303, 312–13 (Albert Love & James S. Childers eds. 1963)

5 Third though I was [in the narrator's class at Harvard Law School], I enjoyed one inestimable advantage in competing for the best legal spots. I was the only guy in the top ten who wasn't Jewish. (And anyone who says it doesn't matter is full of it.) Christ, there are dozens of firms who will kiss the ass of a WASP who can merely pass the bar.
. . . Jonas and Marsh paid [me] . . . the absolute highest salary received by any member of our graduating class.
So you see I was only third *academically.*

Erich Segal, *Love Story* 97–99 (1970)

6 Associates at Cravath [New York law firm Cravath, Swaine and Moore] are considered for partnerships in groups based on their year of graduation from law school. . . . During the period of frenzied discovery in 1974, the group of senior IBM team associates were entering the last crucial year or two before the fateful decision, and competition among them reached a fever pitch. . . . When Sahid scored another triumph by billing 24 hours in a single day, Rolfe—in a move that became the subject of legend in the firm—flew to California, worked on the plane and, by virtue of the change in time zones, managed to bill 27 hours in one day.

    James B. Stewart, *The Partners* 70 (1983)

7 A law student was hit by a truck and lapsed into a coma. The student found herself prematurely transported into hell, where the devil introduced her to her new surroundings—rivers of milk and honey, plentiful fruit and champagne, bedrooms with gold brocaded draperies and satin sheets, and beautiful music. When the student recovered from her coma and returned to earth, she committed herself to a life of sin, believing that ecstasy awaited her in hell. When she finally died and returned to hell, the student found a raging inferno, the stench of sulphur, and the screams of the dead being tortured. The student asked the devil why everything was so different from her earlier visit, and the devil replied, "Oh, that was our summer program."

    Harry T. Edwards, "Remarks: A Lawyer's Duty to Serve the Public Good," 65 *New York University Law Review* 1148, 1162 (1990)

LAW LIBRARIES

See also LAW BOOKS; LEGAL RESEARCH

1 It is a general practice to study law in the office of some lawyer. This indeed gives to the student the advantage of his instruction. But I have ever seen that the services expected in return have been more than the instructions have been worth. All that is necessary for a student is access to a library, and directions in what order the books are to be read.

    Thomas Jefferson, Letter to John Garland Jefferson, 11 June 1790, in *Papers of Thomas Jefferson* 16:480 (Julian P. Boyd ed. 1961)

2 Law is a science, and . . . all the available materials of that science are contained in printed books. . . . the library is the proper workshop of professors and students alike; . . . it is to us all that the laboratories of the university are to the chemists and physicists, the museum of natural history to the zoologists, the botanical garden to the botanists.

    Christopher C. Langdell, Speech at Harvard University, Cambridge, Mass., in 3 *Law Quarterly Review* 123, 124 (1887)

3 Headnotes arranged vertically make a digest. Headnotes arranged horizontally make a textbook. Textbooks arranged alphabetically make an encyclopedia. Every few years some investigator has to disintegrate one of these works into its constituent atoms, add some more headnotes from recent decisions, stir well, and give us the latest book on the subject. And so law libraries grow.

    Zechariah Chafee, Jr., Book Review, 30 *Harvard Law Review* 300, 300 (1917)

4 Adjudicated quarrels of mankind,
  Brown row on row!—how well these lawyers bind
Their records of dead sin,—as if they feared
The hate might spill and their long shelves be smeared
With slime of human souls,—brown row on row
Span on Philistine span, a greasy show
Of lust and lies and cruelty, dried grime
Streaked from the finger of the beggar, Time.

    Archibald MacLeish, "A Library of Law," in *Tower of Ivory* 46 (1917)

LAW PRACTICE

See also ETHICS; FEES; LAW FIRMS; LAWYERS

1 Never fear the want of business. A man who qualifies himself well for his calling never fails of employment in it.

    Thomas Jefferson, Letter to Peter Carr, 22 June 1792, in *Writings of Thomas Jefferson* 6:92 (Paul L. Ford ed. 1895)

2 Our profession is good, if practised in the spirit of it; it is damnable fraud and iniquity when its true spirit is supplied by a

spirit of mischief-making and money catching.

> **Daniel Webster,** Letter to James Hervey Bingham, 19 Jan. 1806, in *Papers of Daniel Webster: Legal Papers* 1:69 (Alfred S. Konefsky & Andrew J. King eds. 1982)

3 Law is quite overdone. It is fallen to the ground, and a man must have great powers to raise himself in it to either honor or profit. The mob of the profession gets as little money and less respect, than they would by digging the earth.

> **Thomas Jefferson,** Letter to David Campbell, 28 Jan. 1810, in *Writings of Thomas Jefferson* 5:499–500 (H. A. Washington ed. 1853)

4 The leading rule for the lawyer, as for the man of every other calling, is diligence. Leave nothing for to-morrow which can be done to-day. Never let your correspondence fall behind.

> **Abraham Lincoln,** "Notes for a Law Lecture," 1 July 1850?, in *Collected Works of Abraham Lincoln* 2:81 (Roy P. Basler ed. 1953)

5 Whatever piece of business you have in hand, before stopping, do all the labor pertaining to it which can then be done. When you bring a common-law suit, if you have the facts for doing so, write the declaration at once. If a law point be involved, examine the books, and note the authority you rely on upon the declaration itself, where you are sure to find it when wanted. The same of defenses and pleas. In business not likely to be litigated, —ordinary collection cases, foreclosures, partitions, and the like,— make all examinations of titles, and note them, and even draft orders and decrees in advance. This course has a triple advantage; it avoids omissions and neglect, saves your labor when once done, performs the labor out of court when you have leisure, rather than in court when you have not.

> **Abraham Lincoln,** "Notes for a Law Lecture," 1 July 1850?, in *Collected Works of Abraham Lincoln* 2:81 (Roy P. Basler ed. 1953)

6 A lawyer's time and advice are his stock in trade.*

> **Abraham Lincoln,** Attributed remark

---

* A study of Lincoln's accredited writings fails to pro-

7 Every person of good moral character, being a voter, shall be entitled to admission to practice law in all courts of justice.

> Indiana Constitution of 1851, art. VII, § 21

8 [When advised not to become a lawyer because the profession was overcrowded:] There is always room at the top.

> **Daniel Webster,** quoted in Edward Latham, *Famous Sayings and Their Authors* 65 (1904)

9 The law is the calling of thinkers. But to those who believe with me that not the least godlike of man's activities is the large survey of causes, that to know is not less than to feel, I say . . . that a man may live greatly in the law as well as elsewhere.

> **Oliver Wendell Holmes, Jr.,** "The Profession of the Law" (lecture to Harvard undergraduates), Cambridge, Mass., 17 Feb. 1886, in *Collected Legal Papers* 29, 29–30 (1920)

10 And happiness, I am sure from having known many successful men, cannot be won simply by being counsel for great corporations and having an income of fifty thousand dollars. An intellect great enough to win the prize needs other food beside success.

> **Oliver Wendell Holmes, Jr.,** "The Path of the Law," 10 *Harvard Law Review* 457, 478 (1897)

11 The remoter and more general aspects of the law are those which give it universal interest. It is through them that you not only become a great master in your calling, but connect your subject with the universe and catch an echo of the infinite, a glimpse of its unfathomable process, a hint of the universal law.

> **Oliver Wendell Holmes, Jr.,** "The Path of the Law," 10 *Harvard Law Review* 457, 478 (1897)

12 There is a little law business . . . now and then, but law is mostly thinking without

---

duce this aphorism. . . . The Lincoln National Life Foundation, which makes an effort to trace the origin of supposed Lincoln sayings, reports that this one . . . apparently came to life in a plaque produced by the Allen Smith Company in Indianapolis. . . . (Bulletin, Lincoln National Life Foundation No. 1057, July 11, 1949.) —**Michael J. Musmanno,** *Sterling v. Philadelphia,* 378 Pa. 538, 562–63, 106 A.2d 793 (1954) (dissenting)

much result. It consists of passing one question to take up another.

Wallace Stevens, Letter to Elsie Moll, 7 Dec. 1908, in *Letters of Wallace Stevens* 110 (Holly Stevens ed. 1981)

13 I still grapple with all the law business that comes my way, but it is surely the quaintest way of making a living in the world. Practicing law is only lending people the use of your bald-head.

Wallace Stevens, Letter to Elsie Moll, 19 Jan. 1909, in *Letters of Wallace Stevens* 124 (Holly Stevens ed. 1981)

14 "What wud I be doin' in a smelly coort room talkin' up to a man that was me chief clerk last year?" says he. "No, sir, th' law is a diff'rent profissyon fr'm what it was whin Dan'l Webster an' Rufus Choate an' thim gas bags used to make a mighty poor livin' be shoutin' at judges that made less. Th' law to-day is not only a profissyon. It's a business. I made a bigger honoraryum last year consolidatin' th' glue inthrests that afterwards wint into th' hands iv a receiver, which is me, thin Dan'l Webster iver thought was in th' goold mines iv th' wurruld. I can't promise to take a case f'r ye an' hoot me reasons f'r thinkin' ye'er right into th' ears iv a larned judge. I'm a poor speaker. But if iver ye want to do something that ye think ye oughtn't to do, come around to me an' I'll show ye how to do it," says he.

Finley Peter Dunne, "The Art of Advocacy," in *Mr. Dooley on the Choice of Law* 33, 35–36 (Edward J. Bander ed. 1963)

15 Whatever their failings as a class may be, and however likely to lose their immortal souls, lawyers do not generally lose papers.

Arthur Train, "Hocus-Pocus," in *Tut, Tut! Mr. Tutt* 119, 120 (1923)

16 The changed character of the lawyer's work has made it difficult for him to contemplate his function in its new setting, to see himself and his occupation in proper perspective. No longer does his list of clients represent a cross section of society; no longer do his contacts make him the typical representative and interpreter of his community. The demands of practice are more continuous and exacting. He has less time for reflection upon other than immediate professional undertakings. He is more the

man of action, less the philosopher and less the student of history, economics and government.

Harlan F. Stone, "The Public Influence of the Bar," 48 *Harvard Law Review* 1, 6 (1934)

17 The successful lawyer of our day more often than not is the proprietor or general manager of a new type of factory, whose legal product is increasingly the result of mass production methods. More and more the amount of his income is the measure of professional success. More and more he must look for his rewards to the material satisfactions derived from profits as from a successfully conducted business, rather than to the intangible and indubitably more durable satisfactions which are to be found in a professional service more consciously directed toward the advancement of the public interest.

Harlan F. Stone, "The Public Influence of the Bar," 48 *Harvard Law Review* 1, 6–7 (1934)

18 Steadily the best skill and capacity of the [legal] profession has been drawn into the exacting and highly specialized service of business and finance. At its best the changed system has brought to the command of the business world loyalty and a superb proficiency and technical skill. At its worst it has made the learned profession of an earlier day the obsequious servant of business, and tainted it with the morals and manners of the market place in its most anti-social manifestations.

Harlan F. Stone, "The Public Influence of the Bar," 48 *Harvard Law Review* 1, 7 (1934)

19 A man in the home office tends to conduct his business on the basis of the papers that come before him. After twenty-five years or more of that sort of thing, he finds it difficult sometimes to distinguish himself from the papers he handles and comes almost to believe that he and his papers constitute a single creature, consisting principally of hands and eyes: lots of hands and lots of eyes.

Wallace Stevens, "Surety and Fidelity Claims," 1938, in *Opus Posthumous* 237 (Milton J. Bates ed., 2d ed. 1989)

20 *Doris Walker* [played by Maureen O'Hara]: Look, darling, he's a nice old man and I admire you for wanting to help him, but

you've got to face facts and be realistic. You can't throw your career away because of a sentimental whim.

Fred Gailey [played by John Payne]: I'm *not* throwing my career away.

Doris: If Haislip feels that way so will every other law firm in town.

Fred: I'm sure they will. Then I'll open my own office.

Doris: And what kind of cases will you get?

Fred: Probably a lot of people like Kris who are being pushed around. That's the only fun in law anyway. And if you believe in me, have faith in me, I promise you everything will—

> George Seaton, *Miracle on 34th Street* (screenplay), 1947, in *Best American Screenplays* 169, 205 (Sam Thomas ed. 1986)

21 Law is one of the last citadels of wavering conservatism in an untidy world and the offices of most lawyers reflect it.

> Robert Traver, *Anatomy of a Murder* 5 (1958)

22 When I was about 14, I decided against seeking the Presidency. Fourteen being an impressionable age, I was accustomed to making such major decisions on the basis of a picture in a magazine or a line in a film. Around the same time, I had decided against a career in the law when I saw someone in a movie—someone like Clark Gable—snap shut his briefcase, jam on his hat, and say, as he walked out of the room, "I'll have my lawyers draw up the papers." I had no intention of being the person who, instead of saying that, said, "Christ! Now I'll have to go back to the office and draw up the wretched papers."

> Calvin Trillin, *Uncivil Liberties* 94 (1982)

LAW REFORM

See CODIFICATION; LAW, GROWTH OF

LAW REVIEWS

See also LEGAL WRITING

1 I shall continue to be worried by attacks from all the academic lawyers who write college law journals, but I suppose it is not a basis for impeachment.

> William Howard Taft, Letter to Horace Taft, 12 June 1928, quoted in Sheldon M. Novick, *Honorable Justice* 360 (1989)

2 There is not, as far as I know, in the world an academic faculty which pins its reputation before the public upon the work of undergraduate students—there is none, that is, except in the American law reviews.

> Karl N. Llewellyn, *The Bramble Bush* 107 (1930)

3 I don't mind when the lads on the Law Review say I'm wrong, what I object to is when they say I'm right.

> Oliver Wendell Holmes, Jr., attributed in Frederick B. Wiener, *Effective Appellate Advocacy* 130 (1950)

4 Though it is in the law reviews that the most highly regarded legal literature . . . is regularly embalmed, it is in the law reviews that a pennyworth of content is most frequently concealed beneath a pound of so-called style. The average law review writer is peculiarly able to say nothing with an air of great importance. When I used to read law reviews, I used constantly to be reminded of an elephant trying to swat a fly.

> Fred Rodell, "Goodbye to Law Reviews," 23 *Virginia Law Review* 38, 38 (1936)

5 Long sentences, awkward constructions, and fuzzy-wuzzy words that seem to apologize for daring to venture an opinion are part of the price the law reviews pay for their precious dignity. And circumlocution does not make for strong writing. I grant that a rapier in capable hands can be just as effective as a bludgeon. But the average law review writer, scorning the common bludgeon and reaching into his style for a rapier, finds himself trying to wield a barn door.

> Fred Rodell, "Goodbye to Law Reviews," 23 *Virginia Law Review* 38, 39 (1936)

6 One of the style quirks that inevitably detracts from the forcefulness and clarity of law review writing is the taboo on pronouns of the first person. An "I" or a "me" is regarded as a rather shocking form of disrobing in print. To avoid nudity, the back-handed passive is almost obligatory:—"It is suggested—," "It is proposed—," "It would seem—." Whether the writers really suppose that such constructions clothe them in anonymity so that people can not guess who is suggesting and who is proposing, I do not know. I do know that such forms frequently lead to the kind

of sentence that looks as though it had been translated from the German by someone with a rather meager knowledge of English.

> Fred Rodell, "Goodbye to Law Reviews," 23 *Virginia Law Review* 38, 39 (1936)

7 Moreover, the explosive touch of humor is considered just as bad taste as the hard sock of condemnation. I know no field of learning so vulnerable to burlesque, satire, or occasional pokes in the ribs as the bombastic pomposity of legal dialectic. Perhaps that is the very reason why there are no jesters or gag men in legal literature and why law review editors knit their brows overtime to purge their publications of every crack that might produce a real laugh. The law is a fat man walking down the street in a high hat. And far be it from the law reviews to be any party to the chucking of a snowball or the judicious placing of a banana-peel.

> Fred Rodell, "Goodbye to Law Reviews," 23 *Virginia Law Review* 38, 40 (1936)

8 I suspect that the law reviews will keep right on turning out stuff that is not fit to read, on subjects that are not worth the bother of writing about them.

> Fred Rodell, "Goodbye to Law Reviews," 23 *Virginia Law Review* 38, 45 (1936)

9 Any morning's mail may bring a law review from Harvard or Yale or Columbia or Pennsylvania or Michigan or a score of other places to disturb our self conceit and show with pitiless and relentless certainty how we have wandered from the path.

> Benjamin N. Cardozo, quoted in Stanley H. Fuld, "A Judge Looks at the Law Review," 28 *New York University Law Review* 915, 915 (1953)

10 Law reviews are unique among publications in that they do not exist because of any large demand on the part of a reading public. Whereas most periodicals are published primarily in order that they may be read, the law reviews are published primarily in order that they may be written.

> Harold C. Havighurst, "Law Reviews and Legal Education," 51 *Northwestern University Law Review* 22, 24 (1956)

11 Cititis was a disease abroad in the land. Victims of this mental disorder hold the de-

lusion that nothing *is*, except in print; and that even what is in print is tabu to use unless some print is cited. I have been fighting Cititis, especially in law reviews, now for many years. (The cure is to ask: Where did Aristotle get his stuff from?)

> Karl N. Llewellyn, *The Bramble Bush* 8 (2d ed. 1960)

12 Who else beside a law review deigns to "reverse" the Supreme Court of the United States?

> Frank R. Strong, "The Iowa Law Review at Age Fifty," 50 *Iowa Law Review* 12, 13 (1964)

13 The fact remains that the intensive two-year training of law review members in research and writing may be the most effective training presently offered in American law schools. All students deserve a comparable education. For law schools to accord frequent faculty contact and intensive research and training only to a chosen few is a fundamental failing of American legal education. Law schools provide the most attention to students who presumably need the least extra help.

> Joel Seligman, *The High Citadel* 185 (1978)

14 By subsidizing the reviews, law schools support a pedagogical strategy whereby a minority of their students are given an intensive training in some practical skills while the vast majority are inadequately trained.

> Joel Seligman, *The High Citadel* 185 (1978)

15 [Law review editing] does to the written word what the Cuisinart does to broccoli.

> David Margolick, "Law Journal is Caught in Corporate Crossfire," *New York Times*, 24 Sept. 1984, at D2

16 One of my favorite persons in the profession (a famous scholar whom I will not identify for fear of betraying his realist tendencies) described to me how to become a successful professor with a national reputation when I was a fledgling professor. He said: "Take an obscure little problem that no one has thought much about, blow it out of all proportion, and solve it, preferably several times, in prestigious law reviews."

> John E. Nowak, "Woe Unto You, Law Reviews!," 27 *Arizona Law Review* 317, 320 (1985)

LAW SCHOOL

See also CASE SYSTEM; HARVARD LAW SCHOOL; LEGAL EDUCATION; YALE LAW SCHOOL

1 Law schools are splendid institutions. Aside from the instruction there received, being able continually to associate with young-men who have the same interest and ambition, who are determined to make as great progress as possible in their studies and devote all their time to the same — must alone be of inestimable advantages. Add to this the instruction of consummate lawyers, who devote their whole time to *you*, and a complete law-library of over fifteen thousand volumes and then compare the opportunities for learning which a student of the law has at Harvard Law School and in a law-office. After one has grasped the principles which underlie the structure of the Common Law, I doubt not, that one can learn very much in an office — That first year at law is, however, surely ill-spent in an office.

Louis D. Brandeis, Letter to Otto A. Wehle, 12 Mar. 1876, in *Letters of Louis D. Brandeis* 1:6 (Melvin I. Urofsky & David W. Levy eds. 1971)

2 I say the business of a law school is not sufficiently described when you merely say that it is to teach law, or to make lawyers. It is to teach law in the grand manner, and to make great lawyers.

Oliver Wendell Holmes, Jr., "The Use of Law Schools" (oration before Harvard Law School Association), Cambridge, Mass., 5 Nov. 1886, in *Collected Legal Papers* 35, 37 (1920)

3 The law school belongs in the modern university no more than a school of fencing or dancing.

Thorstein Veblen, *The Higher Learning in America* 211 (1918)

4 The failure of the modern American law school to make any adequate provision in its curriculum for practical training constitutes a remarkable educational anomaly.

Alfred Z. Reed, *Training for the Public Profession of the Law* 281 (1921)

5 Look well to the right of you, look well to the left of you, for one of you three won't be here next year.

Edward H. Warren, quoted in W. Barton Leach, "Look Well to the Right . . . ," 58 *Harvard Law Review* 1137, 1138 (1945)

6 On one occasion a student made a curiously inept response to a question from Professor Warren. "The Bull" roared at him, "You will never make a lawyer. You might just as well pack up your books now and leave the school." The student rose, gathered his notebooks, and started to leave, pausing only to say in full voice, "I accept your suggestion, Sir, but I do not propose to leave without giving myself the pleasure of telling you to go plumb straight to Hell." "Sit down, Sir, sit down," said "The Bull." "Your response makes it clear that my judgment was too hasty."

Joseph N. Welch, "Edward Henry Warren," 58 *Harvard Law Review* 1134, 1136 (1945) See also LAW SCHOOL 9

7 If the weakness of the apprentice system was to produce advocates without scholarship, the weakness of the law school system is to turn out scholars with no skill at advocacy.

Robert H. Jackson, "Training the Trial Lawyer: A Neglected Area of Legal Education," 3 *Stanford Law Review* 48, 57 (1950)

8 [One type of law student] builds a "private self" as a counter-model to the "public self." . . . As this type's public life becomes more and more controlled and aggressive, often more and more dishonest and in any case less and less emotionally satisfying, his private life is invested with vast quantities of intense feeling, sentimentality, idealism and exaggerated protectiveness. There is something truly pathetic about his terror of talking about these "private matters" in any context which, no matter how appropriate in other ways, has even a whiff of the "legal" about it. . . . [This] division of life into hermetically sealed "private" (emotional) and "public" (effectiveness) compartments must lead to deformations in both. . . . [It also creates] a model of private life in direct opposition to public life as a lawyer [that] may make it possible to accept conduct in the public area which would otherwise be intolerable.

Duncan Kennedy, "How the Law School Fails: A Polemic," 1 *Yale Review of Law and Social Action* 77–78 (1970)

9 In the few days between arrival at Harvard Law School and the first classes, there are rumors. And stories. . . . One concerns a

boy who did a particularly bad job. His professor called him down to the front of the class, up to the podium, gave the student a dime and said, loudly:

"Go call your mother, and tell her you'll never be a lawyer."

Sometimes the story ends here, but the way I heard it, the crushed student bowed his head and limped slowly back through the one hundred and fifty students in the class. When he got to the door, his anger exploded. He screamed:

"You're a son of a bitch, Kingsfield."

"That's the first intelligent thing you've said," Kingsfield replied. "Come back. Perhaps I've been too hasty."

John Jay Osborn, Jr., *The Paper Chase* 3 (1971)

See also LAW SCHOOL 6

10 Law school has been described as a place for the accumulation of learning. First-year students bring some in; third-year students take none away. Hence it accumulates.

Daniel R. White, *The Official Lawyer's Handbook* 23 (1983)

11 People often ask whether it's important that they attend a law school in the state where they intend to practice. The answer, of course, is NO. A good law school's curriculum is not tied to the law of any particular state. This is also true of the "elite" law schools, except that their curriculum is not tied to the law of any particular planet. You should attend one of those schools if you intend to practice law somewhere in the Andromeda Galaxy.

James D. Gordon III, "How Not to Succeed in Law School," 100 *Yale Law Journal* 1679, 1683–84 (1991)

LAWLESSNESS

See also CRIME; ILLEGALITY

1 Whereas, many of the inhabitants of the county of Pittsylvania . . . have sustained great and intolerable losses by a set of lawless men . . . that . . . we, the subscribers, being determined to put a stop to the iniquitous practices of those unlawful and abandoned wretches, do enter into the following association . . . and if they will not desist from their evil practices, we will inflict such corporeal punishment on him or them, as to us shall seem adequate to the crime committed or the damage sustained.*

William Lynch et al., Agreement, 1780, in 2 *Southern Literary Messenger* 389, 389 (1836)

2 Men know that the publick, or the community, rules, and becoming impatient of any evil that presses on them, or which they fancy presses on them, they overstep all the forms of law, overlook deliberation and consultation, and set up their own local interests, and not infrequently their passions, in the place of positive enactments and the institutions.

James Fenimore Cooper, *The American Democrat* 148 (1956) (1838)

3 There were none of those thousand sources of irritation that the ingenuity of civilized man has created to mar his own felicity. There were no foreclosures of mortgages, no protested notes, no bills payable, no debts of honor in Typee; no unreasonable tailors and shoemakers, perversely bent on being paid; no duns of any description; no assault and battery attorneys, to foment discord, backing their clients up to a quarrel, and then knocking their heads together.

Herman Melville, *Typee,* 1846, in *Writings of Herman Melville* 1:123, 126 (Harrison Hayford ed. 1968)

4 How were these people [the Typees] governed? . . . It must have been by an inherent principle of honesty and charity towards each other. They seemed to be governed by that sort of tacit common-sense law which, say what they will of the inborn lawlessness of the human race, has its precepts graven on every breast.

Herman Melville, *Typee,* 1846, in *Writings of Herman Melville* 1:200, 200–01 (Harrison Hayford ed. 1968)

---

* This agreement was drawn up by Captain William Lynch and his Pittsylvania County, Virginia, neighbors. They agreed to "take the law into their own hands to protect their community from horse-stealing, counterfeiting, and 'other species of villainy'" (*Dictionary of Americanisms*). The term *lynch law* and the verb *lynch,* referring to punishment without due process of law, derived from William Lynch's name.

5 Standing alone in the world . . . she cast away the fragments of a broken chain. The world's law was no law for her mind.

Nathaniel Hawthorne, *The Scarlet Letter*, 1850, in *Works of Nathaniel Hawthorne* 1:164 (William Charvat, Roy H. Pearce, & Claude M. Simpson eds. 1962)

6 We certainly think that even the looseness of law, legislation, and justice, that is so widely spreading itself over the land, is not exactly unsuited to sustain the rapid settlement of a country. No doubt men accomplish more in the earlier stages of society when perfectly unfettered, than when brought under the control of those principles and regulations which alone can render society permanently secure or happy.

James Fenimore Cooper, *The Towns of Manhattan* 48 (1930)

7 I have a room all to myself; it is nature. It is a place beyond the jurisdiction of human governments. Pile up your books, the records of sadness, your saws and your laws. Nature is glad outside, and her merry worms will ere long topple them down. There is a prairie beyond your laws. Nature is a prairie for outlaws. There are two worlds, the post-office and nature. I know them both. I continually forget mankind and their institutions, as I do a bank.

Henry David Thoreau, Journal, 3 Jan. 1853, in *Selected Works of Thoreau* 12 (Walter Harding ed. 1975)

8 Are you going to hang him *anyhow*—and try him afterward?

Mark Twain, *Innocents at Home*, 1872, in *Works of Mark Twain* 2:321 (Franklin R. Rogers ed. 1972)

9 What do I care about the law? Hain't I got the power?

Cornelius Vanderbilt, quoted in Matthew Josephson, *The Robber Barons* 15 (1934)

10 These are the hands into which ordinary citizens have put the law. So you see, at best, when they lynch they only take back what they once gave. . . . in the South they take a negro from jail where he was waiting to be duly hung. The South has never claimed that the law would let him go. But in Wyoming the law has been letting our cattle-thieves go for two years. We are in a very bad way, and we are trying to make that way a little better until civilization can reach us. At present we lie beyond its pale. The courts, or rather the juries, into whose hands we have put the law, are not dealing the law. They are withered hands, or rather they are imitation hands made for show, with no life in them, no grip. They cannot hold a cattle-thief. And so when your ordinary citizen sees this, and sees that he has placed justice in a dead hand, he must take justice back into his own hands where it was once at the beginning of all things. Call this primitive, if you will. But so far from being a *defiance* of the law, it is an *assertion* of it—the fundamental assertion of self-governing men, upon whom our whole social fabric is based.

Owen Wister, *The Virginian* 435–36 (1902)

11 *Joe Wilson* [played by Spencer Tracy, on the lynch mob that almost killed Wilson]: They're murderers. I know the law says they're not because I'm still alive, but that's not their fault.

Bartlett Cormack and Fritz Lang, *Fury* (screenplay), 1936, quoted in Harry Haun, *Movie Quote Book* 187 (1980)

12 *Gil Carter* [played by Henry Fonda, reading letter home written by Martin, played by Dana Andrews, before Martin was lynched]: Mr. Davies will tell you what's happening here tonight. He's a good man, and he's done everything he can for me. I suppose there's some other good men here, too, only they don't seem to realize what they're doing. They're the ones I feel sorry for 'cause it'll be over for me in a little while, but they'll have to go on remembering for the rest of their lives. A man just naturally can't take the law into his own hands and hang people without hurting everybody in the world, 'cause then he's not just breaking one law but all laws.

Lamar Trotti, *The Ox-Bow Incident* (screenplay), 1943, quoted in Harry Haun, *The Movie Quote Book* 181 (1980)

13 The first essential step on the road to total domination is to kill the juridical person in man . . . by putting certain categories of people outside the protection of the law and forcing at the same time, through the instrument of denationalization, the non-

totalitarian world into recognition of lawlessness.

Hannah Arendt, *The Origins of Totalitarianism* 419 (1951)

14 But to live outside the law, you must be honest.

Bob Dylan, "Absolutely Sweet Marie" (song), 1966, in *Lyrics, 1962–1985,* at 233 (1985)

LAWSUITS

See CASES; COURTS; LITIGATION; TRIALS

LAWYER JOKES

See also LAWYERS; LAWYERS (CON)

1 "I am looking for a criminal lawyer. . . . Have you one here?"

"Well, . . . we think we have, but we can't prove it on him."

The World's Best Humorous Anecdotes 160–161 (J. Gilchrist Lawson ed. 1923)

2 An Irishman stopped before a grave in a cemetery, containing the tombstone declaring: "Here lies a lawyer and an honest man."

"An' who'd ever think," he murmured, "there'd be room for two men in that one little grave!"

The World's Best Jokes 242 (Lewis Copeland ed. 1936)

3 A lawyer and his wife were taking an ocean cruise. The ship hit a storm and the lawyer fell overboard. Almost immediately eight sharks formed a two-lane escort for the guy and helped him all the way back to the ship.

"It was a miracle," the lawyer told his wife. "No," said his wife, "JUST PROFESSIONAL COURTESY."

James C. Humes, *Podium Humor* 82–83 (1975)

4 An immediately deceased lawyer arrived at the Pearly Gates to seek admittance from St. Peter. The Keeper of the Keys was surprisingly warm in his welcome: "We are so glad to see you, Mr. — —. We are particularly happy to have you here, not only because we get so few lawyers up here, but because you lived to the wonderful age of 165." Mr. — —was a bit doubtful and hesi-

tant. "Now, St. Peter, if there's one place I don't want to get into under false pretenses, it's Heaven. I really died at age 78." St. Peter looked perplexed, frowned, and consulted the scroll in his hand. "Ah, I see where we made our mistake as to your age. We just added up your time sheets!"

Malcolm R. Wilkey, *Copeland v. Marshall,* 641 F.2d 880, 929–30 n.53 (D.C. Cir. 1980) (dissenting)

5 The best description of "utter waste" would be a busload of lawyers to go over a cliff with three empty seats.

Lamar Hunt, *San Francisco Examiner,* 1982, quoted in Bob Chieger and Pat Sullivan, *Football's Greatest Quotes* 114 (1990)

6 A psychological test was prepared to see how members of different professions would answer the same question. An engineer and a lawyer were called in. The examiner asked the engineer, "How much is two times two?"

The engineer replied, "Three point nine, nine, nine, nine . . . "

Then he asked the lawyer, "How much is two times two?"

The lawyer said, "How much do you want it to be?"

Larry Wilde, *The Official Lawyers Joke Book* 77 (1982)

7 There was a young lawyer named Rex
Who was sadly deficient in sex.
    Arraigned for exposure,
    He said with composure,
"De minimis non curat lex."*

Larry Wilde, *The Official Lawyers Joke Book* 20 (1982)

8 "Before I take your case," said the counselor, "you'll have to give me a $50 retainer."

"All right, here's the $50," agreed Nyman, handing over the money.

"Thank you," the lawyer retorted. "This entitles you to two questions!"

"What! Fifty dollars for just two questions? Isn't that awfully high?"

"Yes, I suppose it is," said the lawyer. "Now what's your second question?"

Larry Wilde, *The Official Lawyers Joke Book* 82 (1982)

---

* The last line is Latin for "the law does not concern itself with trifles."

9 How can you tell if a lawyer is lying?
His lips are moving.

Los Angeles Times, 9 July 1986, at 3

10 The deans of Florida's medical schools
have announced they will use lawyers instead of rats for experiments. They cited
three reasons: Lawyers are more numerous; students don't become attached to
them; and there are some things even rats
won't do.

Stephen M. Masterson, quoted in *National
Law Journal,* 7 July 1986, at 6

11 What's the difference between a dead lawyer and a dead snake lying in the road?
There are skid marks leading up to the
snake.

Larry Wilde, *The Ultimate Lawyers Joke Book*
135 (1987)

12 What is the difference between a dead
skunk and a dead lawyer in the middle of
the road?
There are skid marks in front of the
skunk.

Michael Rafferty, *Skid Marks* 8–9 (1988)

13 Upon seeing an elderly lady for the drafting
of her will, the attorney charged her $100.
She gave him a $100 bill, not noticing that
stuck to it was a second $100 bill. Imme-
diately the ethical question arose in the attorney's mind: "Do I tell my partner?"

Michael Rafferty, *Skid Marks* 23 (1988)

14 What do you call 2,000 attorneys chained
together at the bottom of the sea?
A good beginning.

Michael Rafferty, *Skid Marks* 14–15 (1988)

15 At a revival meeting, a young lawyer was
called upon to deliver a prayer. Totally unprepared, he got to his feet, and these
words tumbled out: "Oh, Lord, stir up
much strife amongst Thy people lest Thy
humble servant perish . . ."

Harry T. Shafer and Angie Papadakis, *The
Howls of Justice* 142 (1988)

16 Whatever their other contributions to our
society, lawyers could be an important
source of protein.

Richard G. Guindon, Cartoon caption,
quoted in *The Quotable Quote Book* 155
(Merrit Maloy & Shauna Sorensen eds.
1990)

17 A lawyer, an avid golfer, was pursuing a
solo round at his country club. He played
well until shanking his approach toward
the seventh green. As he flailed away in a
bunker, he grumbled, "Damn, I'd give anything to have a million dollars in the bank
and shoot scratch golf." With that, the devil
appeared, and said, "You will never have
less than $1 million in your checking ac-
count, and you will shoot lower than par.
All I want in exchange is your soul." The
lawyer thought about that, and demanded,
"What's the catch?"

Sam Steiger, *Kill the Lawyers!* 1 (1990)

LAWYERS

See also LAWYER JOKES; LAWYERS (PRO); LAWYERS
(CON); LAWYERS, INDIVIDUAL

1 *Necessity* has no Law; I know some Attorneys of the name.*

Benjamin Franklin, *Poor Richard's
Almanack,* 1734, in *Papers of Benjamin
Franklin* 1:357 (Leonard W. Labaree ed.
1959)

2 In no country, perhaps, in the world is the
law so general a study. The profession itself
is numerous and powerful, and in most
provinces it takes the lead. The greater
number of the deputies sent to the Congress were lawyers. . . . I hear that they
have sold nearly as many of Blackstone's
"Commentaries" in America as in England.

Edmund Burke, "On Moving His Resolution
for Conciliation with the Colonies," 22 Mar.
1775, in *Works of the Right Honorable
Edmund Burke* 2:101, 124–25 (1866)

3 They have a proverb here [in London],
which I do not know how to account for;—
in speaking of a difficult point, they say, *it
would puzzle a Philadelphia lawyer.*†

"A Humorous Description of the Manners
and Fashions of London; in a Letter from a
Citizen of America to his Correspondent in
Philadelphia," 2 *Columbian Magazine* 181,
182 (1788)

---

* The last word is usually misquoted as "same."
† This is the earliest known usage of the phrase *Philadelphia lawyer* to mean "a shrewd lawyer expert in legal
technicalities." This term may have been inspired by
Philadelphia attorney Andrew Hamilton's successful defense of John Peter Zenger in a New York court in 1735.

4 Accuracy and diligence are much more necessary to a lawyer, than great comprehension of mind, or brilliancy of talent. His business is to refine, define, and split hairs, to look into authorities, and compare cases. A man can never gallop over the fields of law on Pegasus, nor fly across them on the wing of oratory. If he would stand on *terra firma* he must descend; if he would be a great lawyer, he must first consent to be only a great drudge.

Daniel Webster, Letter to Thomas Merrill, 11 Nov. 1803, in *Writings and Speeches of Daniel Webster* 1:150–51 (Fletcher Webster ed. 1903)

5 No profession is open to stronger antipathies than that of the law.

Thomas Jefferson, Letter to William Wirt, 10 Jan. 1808, in *Writings of Thomas Jefferson* 5:233 (H. A. Washington ed. 1853)

6 It is well known that on every question the lawyers are about equally divided, . . . and were we to act but in cases where no contrary opinion of a lawyer can be had, we should never act.

Thomas Jefferson, Letter to Albert Gallatin, 20 Sept. 1808, in *Writings of Thomas Jefferson* 5:369 (H. A. Washington ed. 1853)

7 Let me not be thought as intending anything derogatory to the profession of the law, or to the distinguished members of that illustrious order. Well am I aware that we have in this ancient city innumerable worthy gentlemen, the knights-errant of modern days, who go about redressing wrongs and defending the defenceless, not for the love of filthy lucre, nor the selfish cravings of renown, but merely for the pleasure of doing good. Sooner would I throw this trusty pen into the flames and cork up my ink bottle forever, than infringe even for a nail's breadth upon the dignity of these truly benevolent champions of the distressed. On the contrary, I allude merely to those caitiff scouts who, in these latter days of evil, infest the skirts of the profession, as did the recreant Cornish knights of yore the honorable order of chivalry,—who under its auspices, commit flagrant wrongs,—who thrive by quibbles, by quirks and chicanery, and like vermin increase the corruption in which they are engendered.

Washington Irving, *The History of New York* 261–62 (1868) (1809)

8 The New England folks have a saying, that *three Philadelphia lawyers* are a match for the very devil himself.

Salem Observer, 13 Mar. 1824, quoted in Richard H. Thornton, *An American Glossary* 2:659 (1962)

9 The special information which lawyers derive from their studies insures them a separate rank in society, and they constitute a sort of privileged body in the scale of intellect. This notion of their superiority perpetually recurs to them in the practice of their profession: they are the masters of a science which is necessary, but which is not very generally known: they serve as arbiters between the citizens; and the habit of directing to their purpose the blind passions of parties in litigation, inspires them with a certain contempt for the judgment of the multitude.

Alexis de Tocqueville, *Democracy in America* 1:349 (Francis Bowen trans. 1862) (1835)

10 I cannot believe that a republic could hope to exist at the present time, if the influence of lawyers in public business did not increase in proportion to the power of the people.

Alexis de Tocqueville, *Democracy in America* 1:352–53 (Francis Bowen trans. 1862) (1835)

11 A French observer is surprised to hear how often an English or an American lawyer quotes the opinions of others, and how little he alludes to his own; . . . This abnegation of his own opinion, and this implicit deference to the opinion of his forefathers, which are common to the English and American lawyer, this servitude of thought which he is obliged to profess, necessarily give him more timid habits and more conservative inclinations in England and America than in France.

Alexis de Tocqueville, *Democracy in America* 1:353 (Francis Bowen trans. 1862) (1835)

12 In America, there are no nobles or literary men, and the people are apt to mistrust the wealthy; lawyers consequently form the highest political class, and the most cultivated portion of society. They have therefore nothing to gain by innovation, which adds a conservative interest to their natural taste for public order. If I were asked where I place the American aristocracy, I should reply, without hesitation, that it is not

among the rich, who are united by no common tie, but that it occupies the judicial bench and the bar.

Alexis de Tocqueville, *Democracy in America* 1:355 (Francis Bowen trans. 1862) (1835)

13 The more we reflect upon all that occurs in the United States, the more shall we be persuaded that the lawyers, as a body, form the most powerful, if not the only, counterpoise to the democratic element. In that country, we easily perceive how the legal profession is qualified by its attributes, and even by its faults, to neutralize the vices inherent in popular government.

Alexis de Tocqueville, *Democracy in America* 1:355–56 (Francis Bowen trans. 1862) (1835)

14 When the American people are intoxicated by passion, or carried away by the impetuosity of their ideas, they are checked and stopped by the almost invisible influence of their legal counsellors. These secretly oppose their aristocratic propensities to the nation's democratic instincts, their superstitious attachment to what is old to its love of novelty, their narrow views to its immense designs, and their habitual procrastination to its ardent impatience.

Alexis de Tocqueville, *Democracy in America* 1:356 (Francis Bowen trans. 1862) (1835)

15 The lawyers of the United States form a party which is but little feared and scarcely perceived, which has no badge peculiar to itself, which adapts itself with great flexibility to the exigencies of the time, and accommodates itself without resistance to all the movements of the social body. But this party extends over the whole community, and penetrates into all the classes which compose it; it acts upon the country inperceptibly, but finally fashions it to suit its own purposes.

Alexis de Tocqueville, *Democracy in America* 1:358 (Francis Bowen trans. 1862) (1835)

16 To fit up a village with tackle for tillage
    Jack Carter he took to the saw.
To pluck and to pillage, the same little village
    Tim Gordon he took to the law.

Marcus Smith, *The Boston Speaker*, 1844, quoted in Ruth Miller Elson, *Guardians of Tradition: American Schoolbooks of the Nineteenth Century* 26 (1964)

17 I can give it as the condensed history of most, if not all, good lawyers, that they lived well and died poor.

Daniel Webster, Speech, Charleston, S.C., 10 May 1847, in *Writings and Speeches of Daniel Webster* 4:88 (J. W. McIntyre ed. 1903)

18 I am a man who, from his youth upwards, has been filled with a profound conviction that the easiest way of life is the best. Hence, though I belong to a profession proverbially energetic and nervous, even to turbulence, at times, yet nothing of that sort have I ever suffered to invade my peace. I am one of the unambitious lawyers who never addresses a jury, or in any way draws down public applause; but in the cool tranquility of a snug retreat, do a snug business among rich men's bonds and mortgages and title-deeds.

Herman Melville, "Bartleby, the Scrivener," *The Piazza Tales*, 1853, in *Writings of Herman Melville* 9:13, 14 (Harrison Hayford ed. 1987)

19 When legislators keep the law, / When banks dispense with bolts and locks, / . . . / When lawyers take what they would give, / And doctors give what they would take.

Oliver Wendell Holmes, Sr., "Latter Day Warnings," 1858, in *Works of Oliver Wendell Holmes* 1:24–25 (1892)

20 The lawyer's vacation is the space between the question put to a witness and his answer!

Rufus Choate, quoted in *Works of Rufus Choate* 1:137 (Samuel G. Brown ed. 1862)

21 I do not believe in lawyers, in that mode of attacking or defending a man . . . you descend to meet the judge on his own ground, and, in cases of the highest importance, it is of no consequence whether a man breaks a human law or not. . . . Let lawyers decide trivial cases. Business men may arrange that among themselves. If they were the interpreters of the everlasting laws which rightfully bind man, that would be another thing.

Henry David Thoreau, "A Plea for Captain John Brown," 1859, in *Writings of Henry David Thoreau* 4:407, 438 (1906)

22 The good judge is not he who does hairsplitting justice to every allegation, but who, aiming at substantial justice, rules

something intelligible for the guidance of suitors. The good lawyer is not the man who has an eye to every side and angle of contingency, and qualifies all his qualifications, but who throws himself on your part so heartily that he can get you out of a scrape.

> Ralph Waldo Emerson, "Power," *The Conduct of Life*, 1860, in *Complete Works of Ralph Waldo Emerson* 6:53, 76 (1904)

23 How many times I have laughed at you telling me plainly that I was too lazy to be anything but a lawyer.

> Abraham Lincoln, Letter to E. D. Taylor, Dec. 1864, in Emanuel Hertz, *Abraham Lincoln: A New Portrait* 2:957 (1931)

24 Novelists and lawyers understand the art of "cramming" better than any other persons in the world.

> Oliver Wendell Holmes, Sr., *A Mortal Antipathy*, 1885, in *Works of Oliver Wendell Holmes* 7:80 (1892)

25 The law is not the place for the artist or the poet. The law is the calling of thinkers.

> Oliver Wendell Holmes, Jr., "The Profession of the Law" (lecture to Harvard undergraduates), Cambridge, Mass., 17 Feb. 1886, in *Speeches* 22, 22 (1913)

26 Your education begins when what is called your education is over,—when you no longer are stringing together the pregnant thoughts, the "jewels five words long," which great men have given their lives to cut from the raw material, but have begun yourselves to work upon the raw material for results which you do not see, cannot predict, and which may be long in coming,—when you take the fact which life offers you for your appointed task.

> Oliver Wendell Holmes, Jr., "The Profession of the Law" (lecture to Harvard undergraduates), Cambridge, Mass., 17 Feb. 1886, in *Speeches* 22, 24 (1913)

27 The growth of enormously rich and powerful corporations, willing to pay vast sums for questionable services, has seduced the virtue of some counsel whose eminence makes their example important.

> James Bryce, *The American Commonwealth* 2:492 (1888)

28 The glory of lawyers, like that of men of science, is more corporate than individual.

Our labor is an endless organic process. The organism whose being is recorded and protected by the law is the undying body of society.

> Oliver Wendell Holmes, Jr., "Daniel S. Richardson" (eulogy), 15 Apr. 1890, in *Speeches* 46, 47 (1913)

29 I am not certain whether to know the world and to know human nature be not two distinct branches of knowledge. . . . I have seen a girl wind an old lawyer about her little finger. Nor was it the dotage of senile love. Nothing of the sort. But he knew law better than he knew the girl's heart. Coke and Blackstone hardly shed so much light into obscure spiritual places as the Hebrew prophets. And who were they? Mostly recluses.

> Herman Melville, *Billy Budd, Sailor* 75 (Harrison Hayford & Merton M. Sealts, Jr. eds. 1962) (1924)

30 How large was Alexander, father,
    That parties designate
The historic gentleman as rather
    Inordinately great?

Why, son, to speak with conscientious
    Regard for history,
Waiving all claims, of course, to heights
  pretentious,—
    About the size of me.

> James Whitcomb Riley, "Lawyer and Child," in *Rhymes of Childhood* 111 (1891)

31 Your law may be perfect, your knowledge of human affairs may be such as to enable you to apply it with wisdom and skill, and yet without individual acquaintance with men, their haunts and habits, the pursuit of the profession becomes difficult, slow, and expensive. A lawyer who does not know men is handicapped.

> Louis D. Brandeis, Letter to William H. Dunbar, 2 Feb. 1893, in *Letters of Louis D. Brandeis* 1:108 (Melvin I. Urofsky & David W. Levy eds. 1971)

32 A certain amount of education a man must have who constantly is using books. It will save him trouble if he understands an occasional scrap of Latin when he comes across it. But a man may sweep juries before him, command the attention of judges, counsel sagely in great affairs, or be a

leader in any senate of the country with nothing of the scholarly about him.

> Oliver Wendell Holmes, Jr., "The Bar as a Profession," 1896, in *Collected Legal Papers* 153, 154 (1920)

33 A law, Hinnissy, that might look like a wall to you or me wud look like a triumphal arch to th' expeeryenced eye iv a lawyer.

> Finley Peter Dunne, "Mr. Dooley on the Power of the Press," 62 *American Magazine* 607, 607 (1906)

34 What the lawyer needs to redeem himself is not more ability or physical courage but the moral courage in the face of financial loss and personal ill-will to stand for right and justice. Law has ceased to be a profession and has become a business. The lawyer no longer has clients but rather we speak of him as the lawyer of this or that great capitalist or corporation. We feel today that the lawyer belongs to another and is no longer a free man.

> Louis D. Brandeis, Speech before Harvard Law Review Association, 22 June 1907, quoted in Alfred Lief, *The Brandeis Guide to the Modern World* 171 (1941)

35 America is the paradise of lawyers.

> David J. Brewer, Attributed remark, quoted in Champ Clark, *My Quarter Century of American Politics* 2:130 (1920)

36 There is not a greater delusion than the belief that a lawyer is, *per se*, also a statesman. On the contrary, the mere lawyer is rather more unfit than, say, the mere dentist, or mere bricklayer, or mere banker, to be a public man. . . . I could go still further and say that to be a great lawyer is, while a good thing in a judge, very far from being the most important thing.

> Theodore Roosevelt, Letter to Henry Cabot Lodge, 11 Apr. 1910, in *Letters of Theodore Roosevelt* 7:74 (Elting E. Morison ed. 1954)

37 PETTIFOGGER, *n.* A competing or opposing lawyer.

> Ambrose Bierce, *The Enlarged Devil's Dictionary* 217 (Ernest J. Hopkins ed. 1967)

38 The artist sees the line of growth in a tree, the business man an opportunity in a muddle, the lawyer a principle in a lot of dramatic detail.

> Oliver Wendell Holmes, Jr., Letter to John C. H. Wu, 16 June 1923, in *Justice Holmes to Dr. Wu* 13 (1947)

39 I have always noticed that any time a man can't come and settle with you without bringing his lawyer, why, look out for him.

> Will Rogers, "Slipping the Lariat Over," 14 Jan. 1923, in *Will Rogers' Weekly Articles* 1:10, 12 (James M. Smallwood ed. 1980)

40 Of course, people are getting smarter nowadays; they are letting lawyers instead of their conscience be their guides.

> Will Rogers, "How to Stop the Bootleggin'," 8 Apr. 1923, in *Will Rogers' Weekly Articles* 1:48, 50 (James M. Smallwood ed. 1980)

41 There are two qualities that make for the highest success in the law—honesty and dishonesty. To get ahead you must have one or the other. You must either be so irreproachable in your conduct and elevated in your ideals that your reputation for virtue becomes your chief asset, or, on the other hand, so crooked that your very dishonesty makes you invaluable to your clients. . . . the crooked lawyer has got to be so crooked that everybody is afraid of him, even the judge.

> Arthur Train, *The Confessions of Artemas Quibble* 45 (1924)

42 This is no life of cloistered ease to which you dedicate your powers. This is a life that touches your fellow men at every angle of their being, a life that you must live in the crowd, and yet apart from it, man of the world and philosopher by turns.

> Benjamin N. Cardozo, "The Game of the Law and Its Prizes" (speech at Albany Law School commencement), 10 June 1925, in *Law and Literature* 160, 175 (1931)

43 You will study the wisdom of the past, for in a wilderness of conflicting counsels, a trail has there been blazed.
>
> You will study the life of mankind, for this is the life you must order, and, to order with wisdom, must know.
>
> You will study the precepts of justice, for these are the truths that through you shall come to their hour of triumph.

> Benjamin N. Cardozo, "The Game of the Law and Its Prizes" (speech at Albany Law School commencement), 10 June 1925, in *Law and Literature* 160, 175 (1931)

44 Reputation in such a calling [practicing law] is a plant of tender growth, and its bloom, once lost, is not easily restored.

> Benjamin N. Cardozo, *Karlin v. Culkin*, 248 N.Y. 465, 478, 162 N.E. 487 (1928)

45 The sad thing about lawyers is not that so many of them are stupid, but that so many of them are intelligent. The craft is a great devourer of good men; it sucks in and wastes almost as many as the monastic life consumed in the Middle Ages.... Nevertheless, it must be plain that the law, *as the law*, has few rewards for a man of genuine ambition, with a yearning to leave his mark upon his time. How many American lawyers are remembered, as lawyers?

> **H. L. Mencken**, Editorial, *American Mercury*, Jan. 1928, at 35, 35

46 Why ... are lawyers, in essence, such obscure men? Why do their undoubted talents yield so poor a harvest of immortality? The answer, it seems to me ... is their professional aim and function [is] not to get at the truth, but simply to carry on combats between ancient rules.

> **H. L. Mencken**, Editorial, *American Mercury*, Jan. 1928, at 35, 36

47 "Horace is a poet," the other woman said.... "Poets must be excused for what they do. You should remember that, Belle."

Horace bowed toward her. "Your race never fails in tact, Belle," he said. "Mrs. Marders is one of the few people I know who give the law profession its true evaluation."

"It's like any other business, I suppose," Belle said....

"I mean, dubbing me a poet," Horace explained. "The law, like poetry, is the final resort of the lame, the halt, the imbecile, and the blind. I dare say Caesar invented the law business to protect himself against poets."

> **William Faulkner**, *Sartoris* 184 (1929)

48 If you think that you can think about a thing inextricably attached to something else without thinking of the thing which it is attached to, then you have a legal mind.

> **Thomas Reed Powell**, quoted in Thurman W. Arnold, *The Symbols of Government* 101 (1935)

49 His name was Fentry. I remembered all their names, because Uncle Gavin said that to be a successful lawyer and politician in our country you did not need a silver tongue nor even an intelligence; you needed only an infallible memory for names.

> **William Faulkner**, "Tomorrow," 1940, in *Tomorrow and Tomorrow and Tomorrow* 38 (David G. Yellin & Marie Connors eds. 1985)

50 A philosopher is a blind man in a dark cellar at midnight looking for a black cat that isn't there. He is distinguished from a theologian, in that the theologian finds the cat. He is also distinguished from a lawyer, who smuggles in a cat in his overcoat pocket, and emerges to produce it in triumph.

> **William L. Prosser**, Book Review, 27 *Cornell Law Quarterly* 292, 294 (1942)

51 What do you got in place of a conscience? Don't answer. I know—a lawyer.

> **Philip Yordan and Robert Wyler**, *Detective Story* (screenplay), 1951, quoted in Gerald Gardner, *I Coulda Been a Contender* 184 (1992)

52 It is as craftsmen that we get our satisfactions and our pay.

> **Learned Hand**, *The Bill of Rights* 77 (1958)

53 Lawyers who practise alone—at least a sample of them taken in Chicago—are utter captives and choreboys of their clients. They have no freedom to choose a branch of law and make themselves expert or learned in it. Most of them, in time, do find their practice narrowed to a special line of chores: they have become specialists by default.

> **Everett C. Hughes**, "The Professions in Society," 26 *Canadian Journal of Economics and Political Science* 54, 60–61 (1960)

54 Courage is the most important attribute of a lawyer. It is more important than competence or vision. It can never be an elective in any law school. It can never be delimited, dated or outworn, and it should pervade the heart, the halls of justice and the chambers of the mind.

> **Robert F. Kennedy**, Speech at University of San Francisco Law School, San Francisco, 29 Sept. 1962, quoted in Sue G. Hall, *The Quotable Robert F. Kennedy* 111 (1967)

55 "Old Bull" Warren at Harvard was right when he said that one didn't need brains to be a lawyer, only a cast-iron bottom.

> **Edward H. Warren**, reported in Edward Lamb, *No Lamb for Slaughter* 25 (1963)

56 One hires lawyers as one hires plumbers, because one wants to keep one's hands off the beastly drains.

Amanda Cross, *The Question of Max* 61 (1976)

57 The function of the lawyer is to preserve a skeptical relativism in a society hell-bent for absolutes.

Grant Gilmore, *The Ages of American Law* 110 (1977)

58 Send lawyers, guns and money, the shit has hit the fan.

Warren Zevon, "Lawyers, Guns and Money" (song) (1978)

59 "A lawyer's relationship to justice and wisdom," Greenfield observed, "is on a par with a piano tuner's relationship to a concert. He neither composes the music, nor interprets it—he merely keeps the machinery running."

Lucille Kallen, *Introducing C. B. Greenfield* 140 (1979)

60 Not only does the law absorb many more young people in America than in any other industrialized nation; it attracts an unusually large proportion of the exceptionally gifted. The average College Board scores of the top 2,000 or 3,000 law students easily exceed those of their counterparts entering other graduate schools and occupations, with the possible exception of medicine. The share of all Rhodes scholars who go on to law school has approximated 40 percent in recent years, dwarfing the figures for any other occupational group. Some readers may dismiss these statistics on the ground that lawyers often move to careers in business or public life. But the facts fail to support this rationalization, for roughly three quarters of all law school graduates are currently practicing their profession.

Derek C. Bok, "A Flawed System," *Harvard Magazine,* May-June 1983, at 38, 41

61 People think lawyers become sexual dullards in part because of the deadening influence of the legal texts they work with. Of course, we insiders know that precisely the opposite is true, and that legal literature is far more titillating than the uninitiated could possibly imagine. . . . I find that I am gripped by an urgent passion at the *bare mention* of certain sections of the Internal

Revenue Code. . . . For many of my friends, the thinly-veiled eroticism of Blackstone's *Commentaries* has the same effect. I happen to know that among our kinkier classmates the Model Penal Code and the Uniform Simultaneous Death Act are perennial favorites.

Lee Christie, "The Sexiest Profession," *Harvard Law Record,* 16 Sept. 1983, at 5

62 [Upon being told to allow his client, Lieutenant Colonel Oliver North, to object for himself if he wished, at the Senate hearings on the Iran-Contra scandal:] I'm not a potted plant. . . . I'm here as the lawyer. That's my job.

Brendan V. Sullivan, Jr., Remarks at Senate hearing, 9 July 1987, quoted in *New York Times,* 10 July 1987, at A7

63 I'm not an ambulance chaser. I'm usually there before the ambulance.

Melvin Belli, quoted in Robert Byrne, *1,911 Best Things Anybody Ever Said* 345 (1988)

64 [Dutch Schultz speaking:] The law is not majestic. The law is what public opinion says it is. I could tell you a lot about the law. . . . We got a man to argue for me tomorrow who wouldn't have me to dinner in his house. He talks on the phone with the president. But I have paid his price and he will be at my side for as long as it takes.

E. L. Doctorow, *Billy Bathgate* 209 (1989)

LAWYERS (PRO)

See also ETHICS; LAWYERS; LAWYERS (CON)

1 All who read, and most do read, endeavor to obtain some smattering of that science [law]. I have been told by an eminent bookseller, that in no branch of his business, after tracts of popular devotion, were so many books as those on the law exported to the plantations. . . . This study renders men acute, inquisitive, dexterous, prompt in attack, ready in defense, full of resources. In other countries, the people, more simple, and of a less mercurial cast, judge of an ill principle in government only by an actual grievance; here they anticipate the evil, and judge of the pressure of the grievance by the badness of the principle. They augur misgovernment at a distance,

and snuff the approach of tyranny in every tainted breeze.

Edmund Burke, "On Moving His Resolutions for Conciliation with the Colonies," 22 Mar. 1775, in *Works of the Right Honorable Edmund Burke* 2:101, 124–25 (1866)

2 As well as any other, better than any other profession or business or sphere, more directly, more palpably, it enables and commands [a lawyer] to perform certain grand and difficult and indispensable duties of patriotism. . . . In the language of our system, the law is not the transient and arbitrary creation of the major will, nor of any will. It is not the offspring of will at all. It is the absolute justice of the State, enlightened by the perfect reason of the State. That is law. Enlightened justice assisting the social nature to perfect itself by the social life.

Rufus Choate, "The Position and Functions of the American Bar, as an Element of Conservatism in the State" (address to Harvard Law School), Cambridge, Mass., 3 July 1845, in *Addresses and Orations of Rufus Choate* 133, 135, 156 (3d ed. 1879)

3 The world has its fling at lawyers sometimes, but its very denial is an admission. It feels, what I believe to be the truth, that of all secular professions this has the highest standards.

Oliver Wendell Holmes, Jr., "The Law" (address to Suffolk Bar Association Dinner), Boston, 5 Feb. 1885, in *Speeches* 16, 16 (1913)

4 And what a profession it [the law] is! . . . Every calling is great when greatly pursued. But what other gives such scope to realize the spontaneous energy of one's soul? In what other does one plunge so deep in the stream of life,—so share its passions, its battles, its despair, its triumphs, both as witness and actor?

Oliver Wendell Holmes, Jr., "The Law" (address to Suffolk Bar Association Dinner), Boston, 5 Feb. 1885, in *Speeches* 16, 16–17 (1913)

5 A man may live greatly in the law as well as elsewhere; that there as well as elsewhere his thought may find its unity in an infinite perspective; that there as well as elsewhere he may wreak himself upon life,

may drink the bitter cup of heroism, may wear his heart out after the unattainable.

Oliver Wendell Holmes, Jr., "The Profession of the Law" (lecture to Harvard undergraduates), Cambridge, Mass., 17 Feb. 1886, in *Speeches* 22, 23 (1913)

6 The external and immediate result of an advocate's work is but to win or lose a case. But remotely what the lawyer does is to establish, develop, or illuminate rules which are to govern the conduct of men for centuries; to set in motion principles and influences which shape the thought and action of generations which know not by whose command they move.

Oliver Wendell Holmes, Jr., "Sidney Bartlett" (eulogy), Boston, 23 Mar. 1889, in *Speeches* 41, 43 (1913)

7 I started in life with a belief that our profession in its highest walks afforded the most noble employment in which any man could engage, and I am of the same opinion still. . . . To be a priest, and possibly a high priest, in the temple of justice, to serve at her altar and aid in her administration, to maintain and defend those inalienable rights of life, liberty, and property upon which the safety of society depends, to succor the oppressed and to defend the innocent, to maintain constitutional rights against all violations, . . . to rescue the scapegoat and restore him to his proper place in the world—all this seemed to me to furnish a field worthy of any man's ambition.

Joseph H. Choate, "Farewell to the English Bar" (speech), London, 14 April 1905, in *Arguments and Addresses of Joseph Hodges Choate* 1107, 1109 (Frederick C. Hicks ed. 1926)

8 More than once, serving as a reporter for the press, I have lolled humbly in the bullring of jurisprudence, marvelling at the amazing dexterity and resilience of the embattled jurisconsults. What goes on there every day, year in and year out, far surpasses anything ever heard in any other arena. Compared to the jousting of lawyers, even of middling bad lawyers, the best that such theologians as the nation tolerates ever emit from their pulpits is as a crossword puzzle to a problem in the differential calculus. Even in the halls of legislation nothing so apt, ingenious and per-

suasive is on tap, for though most legislators are lawyers they are all well aware that, as legislators, it would be fatal to them to talk sense. But in their strictly legal character, performing on the stage assigned to them, they let themselves go, and the result is often a series of intellectual exercises of the first chop.

H. L. Mencken, Editorial, *American Mercury*, Jan. 1928, at 35, 36

9 This vanishing country lawyer left his mark on his times, and he was worth knowing. . . . He did not specialize, nor did he pick and choose clients. He rarely declined service to worthy ones because of inability to pay. Once enlisted for a client, he took his obligation seriously. . . . He identified himself with the client's cause fully, sometimes too fully. He would fight the adverse party and fight his counsel, fight every hostile witness, and fight the court, fight public sentiment, fight any obstacle to his client's success. He never quit. . . . He moved for new trials, he appealed; and if he lost out in the end, he joined the client at the tavern in damning the judge—which is the last rite in closing an unsuccessful case, and I have officiated at many.

Robert H. Jackson, "Tribute to Country Lawyers: A Review," 30 *American Bar Association Journal* 136, 139 (1944) (book review)

10 The law to [the country lawyer] was like a religion, and its practice was more than a means of support; it was a mission. He was not always popular in his community, but he was respected. Unpopular minorities and individuals often found in him their only mediator and advocate. He was too independent to court the populace—he thought of himself as a leader and lawgiver, not as a mouthpiece. . . . Often his name was, in a generation or two, forgotten. It was from this brotherhood that America has drawn its statesmen and its judges. A free and self-governing Republic stands as a monument for the little known and unremembered as well as for the famous men of our profession.

Robert H. Jackson, "Tribute to Country Lawyers: A Review," 30 *American Bar Association Journal* 136, 139 (1944) (book review)

11 True, we build no bridges. We raise no towers. We construct no engines. We paint no pictures—unless as amateurs for our own principal amusement. There is little of all that we do which the eye of man can see. But we smooth out difficulties; we relieve stress; we correct mistakes; we take up other men's burdens and by our efforts we make possible the peaceful life of men in a peaceful state.

John W. Davis, Address, New York, 16 Mar. 1946, in 1 *Record of the Association of the Bar of the City of New York* 101, 102 (1946)

12 Every would-be despot has found it necessary to silence the tongues of his country's lawyers. For this, brethren of the Bar, is our supreme function—to be sleepless sentinels on the ramparts of human liberty and there to sound the alarm whenever an enemy appears. What duty could be more transcendent and sublime? What cause more holy?

John W. Davis, Address, New York, 16 Mar. 1946, in 1 *Record of the Association of the Bar of the City of New York* 101, 103 (1946)

13 But it too often is overlooked that the lawyer and the law office are indispensable parts of our administration of justice. Law-abiding people can go nowhere else to learn the ever changing and constantly multiplying rules by which they must behave and to obtain redress for their wrongs.

Robert H. Jackson, *Hickman v. Taylor*, 329 U.S. 495, 514–15 (1947) (concurring)

14 I have a high opinion of lawyers. With all their faults, they stack up well against those in every other occupation or profession. They are better to work with or play with or fight with or drink with than most other varieties of mankind.

Harrison Tweed, quoted in Bernard Botein, *Trial Judge* 149 (1952)

15 The lawyers' contribution to the civilizing of humanity is evidenced in the capacity of lawyers to argue furiously in the courtroom, then sit down as friends over a drink or dinner. This habit is often interpreted by the layman as a mark of their ultimate corruption. In my opinion, it is their greatest moral achievement: It is a characteristic of humane tolerance that is most desperately needed at the present time.

John R. Silber, quoted in *Wall Street Journal*, 16 Mar. 1972, at 14

16 Anyone who believes a better day dawns when lawyers are eliminated bears the burden of explaining who will take their place. Who will protect the poor, the injured, the victims of negligence, the victims of racial discrimination and the victims of racial violence?

John J. Curtin, Jr., Remarks to American Bar Association, Atlanta, 13 Aug. 1991, quoted in *Time*, 26 Aug. 1991, at 54

LAWYERS (CON)

See also ETHICS; LAWYER JOKES; LAWYERS; LAWYERS (PRO)

1 Of Lawyers and Physicians I shall say nothing, because this Countrey is very Peaceable and Healthy; long may it so continue and never have occasion for the Tongue of the one, nor the Pen of the other, both equally destructive of Men's Estates and Lives.

Gabriel Thomas, *Pennsylvania and West Jersey*, 1698, quoted in Anton-Hermann Chroust, *The Rise of the Legal Profession in America* 211 (1965)

2 God works wonders now and then; Behold! a Lawyer, an honest Man!

Benjamin Franklin, *Poor Richard's Almanack*, 1733, in *Papers of Benjamin Franklin* 1:317 (Leonard W. Labaree ed. 1959)

3 Lawyers, Preachers, and Tomtits Eggs, there are more of them hatch'd than come to perfection.

Benjamin Franklin, *Poor Richard's Almanack*, 1734, in *Papers of Benjamin Franklin* 1:354 (Leonard W. Labaree ed. 1959)

4 A Lawyer being sick and extream ill
Was moved by his Friends to make his Will,
Which soon he did, gave all the Wealth he had
To frantic Persons, lunatick and mad;
And to his Friends this Reason did reveal
(That they might see with Equity he'd deal).
From Madmen's Hands I did my Wealth receive,

Therefore that Wealth to Madmen's Hands I'll leave.

Benjamin Franklin, *Poor Richard's Almanack*, 1734, in *Papers of Benjamin Franklin* 1:355 (Leonard W. Labaree ed. 1959)

5 Certainlie these things agree,
The Priest, the Lawyer, & Death all three:
Death takes both the weak and the strong.
The lawyer takes from both right and wrong,
And the priest from living and dead has his Fee.

Benjamin Franklin, *Poor Richard's Almanack*, 1737, in *Papers of Benjamin Franklin* 2:169 (Leonard W. Labaree ed. 1960)

6 [Lawyers] are plants that will grow in any soil that is cultivated by the hands of others; and when once they have taken root they will extinguish every other vegetable that grows around them. . . . The most ignorant, the most bungling member of that profession, will, if placed in the most obscure part of the country, promote litigiousness, and amass more wealth without labour, than the most opulent farmer, with all his toils.

J. Hector St. John Crèvecoeur, *Letters from an American Farmer* 146 (1968) (1782)

7 The order [of lawyers] is becoming continually more and more powerful. . . . There is danger of lawyers becoming powerful as a combined body. The people should be guarded against it as it might subvert every principle of law and establish a perfect aristocracy. . . . This order of men should be annihilated.

Benjamin Austin, *Observations on the Pernicious Practice of the Law*, 1786, quoted in Roscoe Pound, *The Lawyer from Antiquity to Modern Times* 234 (1953)

8 The practice of the law, it is said, tends to brutalize the feelings, to subvert the judgment, and to annihilate every virtuous principle of the human heart. . . . A lawyer, from the first moment he enters into business, becomes habituated to scenes of injustice and oppression; from which, if he possess the smallest particle of sensibility, he turns at first with disgust and abhorrence; but custom soon renders them fa-

miliar, and in process of time, he can view them with the utmost coolness and indifference. This lamentable consequence is the frequent result of the practice of the law. For, it is evident, that a perpetual fellowship with dishonesty, and a constant intercourse with villainy, will in time, destroy every tender emotion and sap by degrees the foundation of the most rigid virtue.

George Watterson, *The Lawyer, or Man as he ought not to be* 55–56 (1808)

9 The physician is happy in the attachment of the families in which he practices. All think he has saved some one of them, and he finds himself everywhere a welcome guest, a home in every house. . . . he will enjoy, in age, the happy reflection of not having lived in vain; while the lawyer has only to recollect how many, by his dexterity, have been cheated of their right and reduced to beggary.

Thomas Jefferson, Letter to David Campbell, 28 Jan. 1810, in *Writings of Thomas Jefferson* 5:500 (H. A. Washington ed. 1853)

10 The Counsellor expressed the utmost surprise at our ignorance of the true meaning of that expressive appellation, "shiseter,"* after which, by special request, he gave us the definition, which we would now give our readers, were it not that it would certainly subject us to a prosecution for libel and obscenity.

Mike Walsh, "The Pettifogger," *The Subterranean,* 29 July 1843, at 22, quoted in Gerald L. Cohen, *Origin of the Term "Shyster"* 65 (1982)

11 The lawyer's truth is not Truth, but consistency or a consistent expediency. Truth is always in harmony with herself, and is not concerned chiefly to reveal the justice that may consist with wrong-doing.

Henry David Thoreau, *Civil Disobedience,* 1849, in *Writings of Henry David Thoreau* 4:356, 384 (1906)

---

* This is the earliest recorded usage of the word *shyster,* which came to signify an unethical lawyer. The passage makes it clear that the word's etymology derives from the German *Scheisser* ("incompetent person," literally "shitter"). Other theories, such as a derivation from the name of an actual attorney, are without foundation. See Cohen's book for detailed discussion.

12 I do not believe in lawyers,—in that mode of defending or attacking a man,—because you descend to meet the judge on his own ground, and, in cases of the highest importance, it is of no consequence whether a man breaks a human law or not. Let lawyers decide trivial cases. If they were interpreters of the everlasting laws which rightfully bind men, that would be another thing.

Henry David Thoreau, Journal, 22 Oct. 1859, in *Journal of Henry D. Thoreau* 12:431 (Bradford Torrey & Francis H. Allen eds. 1962)

13 The more I see of lawyers, the more I despise them. They seem to be natural, born *cowards,* and on top of that they are God damned idiots.

Mark Twain, Letter to James R. Osgood, 26 Jan. 1876, in *Mark Twain's Letters to His Publishers* 95 (Hamlin Hill ed. 1967)

14 [After "Twain had just finished addressing a New England society banquet when the attorney William M. Evarts stood up with his hands in his pockets, as was his custom, and remarked: 'Does it not seem unusual to this gathering that a professional humorist should really appear funny?'":] Does it not also appear strange to this assembly that a lawyer should have his hands in his own pockets?

Mark Twain, "Plymouth Rock and the Pilgrims," 1881, quoted in Alex Ayres, *The Wit and Wisdom of Mark Twain* 135–36 (1987)

15 In Salem, the lawyers, and the judges, and the great counselors of the day were of the first, after the clergy, to incite, and the last to repent of the shedding of blood; here, as always and everywhere, law being behind all other branches, and filling up the rear in the slow evolution of the race.

George M. Beard, *The Psychology of the Salem Witchcraft Excitement* 5 (1882)

16 What chance has the ignorant, uncultivated liar against the educated expert? What chance have I . . . against a lawyer?

Mark Twain, "On the Decay of the Art of Lying," 1882, in *The Mark Twain Reader* 823, 824 (1981)

17 To succeed in other trades, capacity must be shown; in the law, concealment of it will do.

Mark Twain, *Following the Equator,* 1897, in *Writings of Mark Twain* 21:1 (1929)

18 The profession of the law does not imply large ownership; but since no taint of usefulness, for other than the competitive purpose, attaches to the lawyer's trade, it grades high in the conventional scheme.

Thorstein Veblen, *The Theory of the Leisure Class* 231 (1899)

19 The lawyer is exclusively occupied with the details of predatory fraud, either in achieving or in checkmating chicane, and success in the profession is therefore accepted as marking a large endowment of that barbarian astuteness which has always commanded men's respect and fear.

Thorstein Veblen, *The Theory of the Leisure Class* 231 (1899)

20 In mousing over Mary Cowden Clarke's Concordance of Shakespeare, I find that the man who so successfully ran the Globe Theatre had small use for lawyers. He refers to attorneys just eleven times, & seems to hold that to take a tainted plea and season it with gracious speech so as to obscure the show of evil, to set decrees at naught, pluck down justice, trip the course of law and blunt the sword that guards the peace and person,—these things are the work and occupation of lawyers.

Elbert Hubbard, *Contemplations* 25 (1902)

21 Every lawyer is an officer of the court, & yet fully one half of all the lawyers in the land are thorough rogues. And the curious fact is, all lawyers admit it. A lawyer is a moral strabismic, who revels in sharked up reasons. Lawyers are the jackals of commerce, and get their living by preying on the people.

Lawyers are men whom we hire to protect us from lawyers. . . .

The average attorney has but two objects in life, grand and petit larceny. . . .

Then there are succubi lawyers whose sole business is to drink the blood of corporations and railroad companies. Their grip is that of the horse-leech—their hunger is insatiable.

Elbert Hubbard, *Contemplations* 26 (1902)

22 Instead of holding a position of independence, between the wealthy and the people, prepared to curb the excesses of either, able lawyers have, to a large extent, allowed themselves to become adjuncts of great corporations and have neglected their obligation to use their powers for the protection of the people. We hear much of the "corporation lawyer," and far too little of the "people's lawyer."

Louis D. Brandeis, "The Opportunity in the Law," 39 *American Law Review* 555, 559 (1905)

23 I deceived myself for a long time by believing that I earned my living as the attorney for the Northeastern Railroads. I've drawn up some pretty good papers for them, and I've won some pretty difficult suits. I'm not proud of 'em all, but let that go. Do you know what I am? . . .

I'm merely their paid political tool. . . . I've sold them my brain, and my right of opinion as a citizen.

Winston Churchill, *Mr. Crewe's Career* 443 (1908)

24 Lawyer: The only man in whom ignorance of the law is not punished.

Elbert Hubbard, quoted in *Home Book of Proverbs, Maxims and Familiar Phrases* 1371 (Burton Stevenson ed. 1948)

25 ACCOMPLICE, *n.* One associated with another in a crime, having guilty knowledge and complicity, as an attorney who defends a criminal, knowing him guilty. This view of the attorney's position in the matter has not hitherto commanded the assent of attorneys, no one having offered them a fee for assenting.

Ambrose Bierce, *The Devil's Dictionary* 17 (1911)

26 LAWYER, *n.* One skilled in circumvention of the law.

Ambrose Bierce, *The Devil's Dictionary* 187 (1911)

27 LIAR, *n.* A lawyer with a roving commission.

Ambrose Bierce, *The Devil's Dictionary* 191 (1911)

28 ATTORNEY, *n.* A person legally appointed to mismanage one's affairs which one has not himself the skill to rightly mismanage.

Ambrose Bierce, *The Enlarged Devil's Dictionary* 18 (Ernest J. Hopkins ed. 1967)

29 DICE, *n.* Small polka-dotted cubes of ivory, constructed like a lawyer to lie on any side, but commonly on the wrong one.

Ambrose Bierce, *The Enlarged Devil's Dictionary* 66 (Ernest J. Hopkins ed. 1967)

30 Happy the lawyer!—at his favored hands
Nor truth nor decency the world
    demands.
Secure in his immunity from shame,
His cheek ne'er kindles with the tell-tale
    flame.
His brains for sale, morality for hire,
In every land and century a licensed liar!

Ambrose Bierce, "To an Insolent Attorney,"
in *Collected Works of Ambrose Bierce* 5:241
(1911)

31 The laws are mostly made by lawyers, and
so made as to encourage and compel litigation. By lawyers they are interpreted and
by lawyers enforced for their own profit
and advantage. The over-intricate and in-
terminable machinery of precedent, over-
rulings, writs of error, motions for new trials, appeals, reversals, affirmations and the
rest of it, is mostly a transparent and iniquitous system of exaction. What remedy
would I propose? None. There is none to
propose. The lawyers have us and mean to
keep us.

Ambrose Bierce, "Some Features of the
Law," in *Collected Works of Ambrose Bierce*
11:99, 101 (1912)

32 A lawyer is not like a doctor. No real good
for the community comes from the development of legalism, from the development
of that kind of ability shown by the great
corporation lawyers who lead our bar,
whereas good does come from medical development. The high-priced lawyer means,
when reduced to his simplest expression,
that justice tends to go to the man with the
longest purse.

Theodore Roosevelt, Letter to William R.
Nelson, 30 July 1912, in *Letters of Theodore
Roosevelt* 7:583 (Elting E. Morison ed. 1954)

33 FLINT, *n.* A substance much in use as a material for hearts. Its composition is silica,
98.00; oxide of iron, 0.25; alumina, 0.25;
water, 1.50. When an editor's heart is
made, the water is commonly left out; in a
lawyer's more water is added—and frozen.

Ambrose Bierce, *The Enlarged Devil's
Dictionary* 96–97 (Ernest J. Hopkins ed.
1967)

34 I was attorney for the "Q"
And the Indemnity Company which
    insured
The owners of the mine.

I pulled the wires with judge and jury,
And the upper courts, to beat the claims
Of the crippled, the widow and orphan,
And made a fortune thereat.
The bar association sang my praises
In a high-flown resolution.
And the floral tributes were many—
But the rats devoured my heart
And a snake made a nest in my skull!

Edgar Lee Masters, "John M. Church," in
Spoon River Anthology 75 (1915)

35 Lawyer—one who protects us against rob-
bers by taking away the temptation.

H. L. Mencken, "Sententiae," 1916, in *A
Mencken Chrestomathy* 616, 623 (1949)

36   Why is there always a secret singing
    When a lawyer cashes in?
    Why does a hearse horse snicker
    Hauling a lawyer away?

The work of a bricklayer goes to the blue.
The knack of a mason outlasts a moon.
The hands of a plasterer hold a room
    together,
The land of a farmer wishes him back
    again.
        Singers of songs and dreamers of
plays
        Build a house no wind blows over.
The lawyers—tell me why a hearse horse
snickers hauling a lawyer's bones.

Carl Sandburg, "The Lawyers Know Too
Much," 1920, in *Complete Poems of Carl
Sandburg* 189 (1969)

37 In the heels of the higgling lawyers, Bob
Too many slippery ifs and buts and
    howevers,
Too much hereinbefore provided whereas,
Too many doors to go in and out of.

    When the lawyers are through
    What is there left, Bob?
    Can a mouse nibble at it
    And find enough to fasten a tooth in?

Carl Sandburg, "The Lawyers Know Too
Much," 1920, in *Complete Poems of Carl
Sandburg* 189 (1969)

38 Is there any reason to believe that, among
lawyers, the best are much better than the
worst? I can find none. All the extravagance
and incompetence of our present government is due, in the main, to lawyers, and,
in part at least, to good ones. They are re-

sponsible for nine-tenths of the useless and vicious laws tht now clutter the statute-books, and for all the evils that go with the vain attempt to enforce them. Every Federal judge is a lawyer. So are most Congressmen. Every invasion of the plain rights of the citizen has a lawyer behind it. If all lawyers were hanged tomorrow, and their bones sold to a mah jong factory, we'd all be freer and safer, and our taxes would be reduced by almost a half.

> **H. L. Mencken,** "Breathing Space," Baltimore *Evening Sun,* 4 Aug. 1924, quoted in *The Gist of Mencken* 449 (Mayo DuBasky ed. 1990)

39 Ever' once in a while I meet some buddy in some honorable walk in life that wuz once admitted t' th' bar.

> **Kin Hubbard,** *Abe Martin: Hoss Sense and Nonsense* 60 (1926)

40 There is a limited number of the entire membership of the bar . . . who are counted as its leaders. They are men of high character, distinct intellectual power, great skill, and devoted to the practice of their profession. Their success is measured by the profession and the public very largely in terms of their professional income. . . . You rarely find their services enlisted in any case which does not involve substantial professional remuneration, and almost never on the unpopular side of a case involving human rights and personal liberty.

> **Harlan F. Stone,** Letter to Frederick L. Allen, Oct. 1926, in Alpheus T. Mason, *Harlan Fiske Stone: Pillar of the Law* 376 n. (1956)

41 There may be a pleasant paunch upon your client. His wallet may look fat. Suppose now that his case does not at first blush seem appealing. Then what to do? Courage, my friend, there is another ethic! There is that admirable ethic of the profession which makes it clear that the lawyer is neither judge nor jury; that the lawyer has neither duty nor right to usurp the constitutional function of the judicial tribunal. . . .

For your totem, for your ideal, you can then take the squid, the cuttlefish. Spine he has not, but O, a beak he has. The spine is absent, but the beak is strong. There are ten counted legs, each leg alive with suckers, all waving through the water after prey. The world, the whole world, offers hope for prey. When pressed some time too hard by enemies, most lawyer-like he hides himself behind a cloud of ink. *Why does a hearse horse snicker?*

> **Karl N. Llewellyn,** *The Bramble Bush* 155–57 (1930)
> See also LAWYERS (CON) 36

42 One level headed smart man could interpret every law there is. If you commit a crime you either did or you dident, without habus corpus, change of venue, or any other legal shindig. But Lord if we go into the things that are useless why two thirds of the world would have to turn to manual labor. That's really the only essential thing there is.

> **Will Rogers,** "The Lawyers Talking," 28 July 1935, in *Will Rogers' Weekly Articles* 6:243, 244 (Steven K. Gragert ed. 1982)

43 I'm not sayin' all lawyers deserved to be hanged, but they'd be no gr-reat har-rm done if they was all hanged. . . . String thim all up, says I, an' if anny iv thim can prove an allibyi give him a Christian burial with th' rites iv th' church.

> **Finley Peter Dunne,** "Law and Lawyers," in *Mr. Dooley on the Choice of Law* 27 (Edward J. Bander ed. 1963)

44 It is pretty hard to find a group less concerned with serving society and more concerned with serving themselves than the lawyers.

> **Fred Rodell,** "Goodbye to Law Reviews," 23 *Virginia Law Review* 38, 42 (1936)

45 Daniel Webster: You seem to have an excellent acquaintance with the law, sir.
The Devil: Sir, that is no fault of mine. Where I come from, we have always gotten the pick of the Bar.

> **Stephen Vincent Benét,** *The Devil and Daniel Webster* 52 (1939)

46 In tribal times, there were the medicine-men. In the Middle Ages, there were the priests. Today there are the lawyers. For every age, a group of bright boys, learned in their trade and jealous of their learning, who blend technical competence with plain and fancy hocus-pocus to make themselves masters of their fellow men. For every age, a pseudo-intellectual autocracy, guarding

the tricks of its trade from the uninitiated, and running, after its own pattern, the civilization of its day.

Fred Rodell, *Woe Unto You, Lawyers!* 3 (1939)

47 If you want to take dough from a murderer for helping him beat the rap you must be admitted to the bar.

Rex Stout, *In the Best Families* 199 (1950)

48 [Philip Marlowe speaking:] Let the law enforcement people do their own dirty work. Let the lawyers work it out. They write the law for other lawyers to dissect in front of other lawyers called judges so that other judges can say the first judges were wrong and the Supreme Court can say the second lot were wrong. Sure there's such a thing as law. We're up to our necks in it. About all it does is make business for lawyers. How long do you think the big-shot mobsters would last if the lawyers didn't show them how to operate?

Raymond Chandler, *The Long Goodbye,* 1953, in *The Midnight Raymond Chandler* 419, 681–82 (1971)

49 He was wrong. He's a lawyer, and to a lawyer, if it aint complicated it dont matter whether it works or not because if it aint complicated up enough it aint right and so even if it works, you dont believe it.

William Faulkner, *The Town* 296 (1957)

50 Next to the confrontation between two highly trained, finely honed batteries of lawyers, jungle warfare is a stately minuet.

Bill Veeck, *The Hustler's Handbook* 335 (1965)

51 He recalled what his favorite professor, Leonard Leech, once told him about getting ahead in law. Leech said that, just as a good airplane pilot should always be looking for places to land, so should a lawyer be looking for situations where large amounts of money were about to change hands.

"In every big transaction," said Leech, "There is a magic moment during which a man has surrendered a treasure, and during which the man who is due to receive it has not yet done so. An alert lawyer will make that moment his own, possessing the treasure for a magic microsecond, taking a little of it, passing it on. If the man who is to receive the treasure is unused to wealth, has an inferiority complex and shapeless feelings of guilt, as most people do, the lawyer can often take as much as half the bundle, and still receive the recipient's blubbering thanks."

Kurt Vonnegut, Jr., *God Bless You, Mr. Rosewater* 17–18 (1965)

52 A lawyer with his briefcase can steal more than a hundred men with guns.

Mario Puzo, *The Godfather* 51 (1969)

53 The public regards lawyers with great distrust. They think lawyers are smarter than the average guy but use their intelligence deviously. Well, they're wrong: Usually they're not smarter.

F. Lee Bailey, quoted in *Los Angeles Times,* 9 Jan. 1972, at 43

54 *Boris Grushenko* [played by Woody Allen]: Some men are heterosexual and some men are bisexual and some men don't think about sex at all, you know, they become lawyers.

Woody Allen, *Love and Death* (screenplay) (1975)

55 [In working as a corporate lawyer] even worse than the violation of spirit was the destruction of consciousness. Few people respected my right to have my own thoughts and feelings for very long. Usually the whole day was one series of things that jangled the mind until it could no longer function. . . . destruction of thought and feeling plus the repressed anger that went with it made it impossible for me to regain any sense of self when the working day was over. You cannot strike your head all day with a hammer and then expect that the person within will want to come out when you get home.

Charles A. Reich, *The Sorcerer of Bolinas Reef* 30–31 (1976)

56 Reason, arguments, theories could only be of lesser importance in such a process [a dam license proceeding], the sort of thing that would help to rationalize what was otherwise decided. The person who con-

tributed intellect to such a process was helping to create and perpetuate a lie about how things really happened; he was an unintentional conspirator in the cover-up of social truth.

Charles A. Reich, *The Sorcerer of Bolinas Reef* 35 (1976)

57 Who ran the country then? I learned that there was an elite group, a class that shared certain assumptions and values, and made basic decisions without offering them to anyone as a choice. It was sometimes called The Club. Its members held controlling positions in government, in [law] firms like mine, in the courts, and in the law schools. They were mostly male lawyers from Ivy League schools—all top-notch achievers. Although they were fiercely competitive, and gave the appearance of representing many different sides of the issues of the day, it gradually dawned on me that the values they shared, rather than those they debated, represented the true decisions which governed the country.

Charles A. Reich, *The Sorcerer of Bolinas Reef* 39 (1976)

58 The line between a bank robber and a lawyer is a very thin one, anyway.... The criminal attacks society head on; the lawyer is trying to set you free after you have been caught so that you can go out and steal some more. Whether he succeeds or not, he profits from your crime. The only way you can pay him is out of the money you have got away with at one time or another, everybody knows that. It isn't called his share of the loot, of course. It's called "the fee." But that's only because he has a license that entitles him to do what he's doing, and you haven't.

Willie Sutton, *Where the Money Was* 28 (1976)

59 We have the heaviest concentration of lawyers on Earth—1 for every 500 Americans; three times as many as are in England, four times as many as are in West Germany, twenty-one times as many as there are in Japan. We have more litigation, but I am not sure that we have more justice. No resources of talent and training in our own society, even including the medical care, is more wastefully or unfairly distributed than legal skills. Ninety percent of our law-

yers serve 10 percent of our people. We are over-lawyered and under-represented.

Jimmy Carter, Remarks at 100th Anniversary Banquet of the Los Angeles County Bar Association, 4 May 1978, in *Public Papers of the Presidents: Jimmy Carter, 1978,* at 1:834, 836 (1979)

60 The net result of these trends is a massive diversion of exceptional talent into pursuits that often add little to the growth of the economy, the pursuit of culture, or the enhancement of the human spirit. I cannot press this point too strongly. As I travel around the country looking at different professions and institutions, I am constantly struck by how complicated many jobs have become, how difficult many institutions are to administer, how pressing are the demands for more creativity and intelligence. However aggressive our schools and colleges are in searching out able youths and giving them a good education, the supply of exceptional people is limited. Yet far too many of these rare individuals are becoming lawyers at a time when the country cries out for more talented business executives, more enlightened public servants, more inventive engineers, more able high-school principals and teachers.

Derek C. Bok, "A Flawed System," *Harvard Magazine,* May-June 1983, at 38, 41

61 A nation's values and problems are mirrored in the ways in which it uses its ablest people. In Japan, a country only half our size, 30 percent more engineers graduate each year than in all the United States. But Japan boasts a total of less than 15,000 lawyers, while American universities graduate 35,000 *every year.* It would be hard to claim that these differences have no practical consequences. As the Japanese put it, "Engineers make the pie grow larger; lawyers only decide how to carve it up."

Derek C. Bok, "A Flawed System," *Harvard Magazine,* May-June 1983, at 38, 41

62 *Kate Sullivan:* For someone who has nothing nice to say about lawyers you certainly have enough of them around.
Lawrence Garfinkle: You have to. They're like nuclear warheads. They have theirs so you need yours—but once you use them

they fuck everything up. They're only good in their silos.

> **Jerry Sterner,** *Other People's Money* 58 (1991) (1989)

63 Our system of civil justice is, at times, a self-inflicted competitive disadvantage. . . . Let's ask ourselves: Does America really need 70 percent of the world's lawyers? . . . Is it healthy for our economy to have 18 million new lawsuits coursing through the system annually? Is it right that people with disputes come up against staggering expense and delay?

> **Dan Quayle,** Speech to American Bar Association, Atlanta, 13 Aug. 1991, quoted in *New York Times,* 14 Aug. 1991, at A14

LAWYERS, INDIVIDUAL

See also DARROW, CLARENCE

1 The Lawyer's Lawyer.

> Epithet of John W. Davis

2 This is [Rufus] Choate, who made it safe to murder; and of whose health thieves asked before they began to steal.

> **Wendell Phillips,** "Idols" (lecture), Boston, 4 Oct. 1859, in *Speeches, Lectures, and Letters* 242, 254 (1863)

3 A bronzed, lank man! His suit of ancient black,
A famous high top-hat and plain worn shawl
Make him the quaint great figure that men love,
The prairie-lawyer, master of us all.

> **Vachel Lindsay,** "Abraham Lincoln Walks at Midnight," 1913, in *Collected Poems* 53 (1925)

LEGAL EDUCATION

See also CASE SYSTEM; HARVARD LAW SCHOOL; LAW SCHOOL; YALE LAW SCHOOL

1 In reading the Reporters, enter in a common-place book every case of value, condensed into the narrowest compass possible. . . . This operation is doubly useful, insomuch as it obliges the student to seek out the pith of the case, and habituates him to a condensation of thought, and to an acquisition of the most valuable of all talents,

that of never using two words where one will do. It fixes the case, too, more indelibly in the mind.

> **Thomas Jefferson,** Letter to Bernard Moore, 1765, in Henry S. Randall, *The Life of Thomas Jefferson* 1:55 (1857)

2 I always was of opinion that the placing a youth to study with an attorney was rather a prejudice than a help. We are all too apt by shifting on them our business, to incroach on that time which should be devoted to their studies. The only help a youth wants is to be directed what books to read, and in what order to read them.

> **Thomas Jefferson,** Letter to Thomas Turpin, 5 Feb. 1769, in *Papers of Thomas Jefferson* 1:24 (Julian P. Boyd ed. 1950)

3 Your resolution to apply to the study of the law is wise in my opinion, and at the same time to mix with it a good degree of attention to the farm. The one will relieve the other. The study of the law is useful in a variety of points of view. It qualifies a man to be useful to himself, to his neighbors, and to the public. It is the most certain stepping stone to preferment in the political line.

> **Thomas Jefferson,** Letter to Thomas Mann Randolph, Jr., 30 May 1790, in *Papers of Thomas Jefferson* 16:449 (Julian P. Boyd ed. 1961)

4 Other branches of science, and especially history, are necessary to form a lawyer.

> **Thomas Jefferson,** Letter to John Garland Jefferson, 11 June 1790, in *Papers of Thomas Jefferson* 16:480 (Julian P. Boyd ed. 1961)

5 Study is *truly* the grand requisite for a lawyer. Men may be born poets, and leap from their cradle painters; nature may have made them musicians, and called on them only to exercise, and not to acquire, ability. But law is artificial. It is a human science to be learnt, not inspired.

> **Daniel Webster,** Letter to James Hervey Bingham, 19 Jan. 1806, in *Papers of Daniel Webster: Legal Papers* 1:69 (Alfred S. Konefsky & Andrew J. King eds. 1982)

6 I have long lamented with you the depreciation of law science. The opinion seems to be that Blackstone is to us what the Alcoran is to the Mahometans, that everything which is necessary is in him, and

what is not in him is not necessary. . . .
Now, men are born scholars, lawyers, doctors; in our day this was confined to poets.

Thomas Jefferson, Letter to John Tyler, 26
May 1810, in *Writings of Thomas Jefferson*
9:276 n. (Paul L. Ford ed. 1898)

7 But the student should not imagine, that
enough is done, if he has so far mastered
the general doctrines of the common law,
that he may enter with some confidence
into practice. There are other studies,
which demand his attention. He should addict
himself to the study of philosophy, of
rhetoric, of history, and of human nature.
It is from the want of this enlarged view of
duty, that the profession has sometimes
been reproached with a sordid narrowness,
with a low chicane, with a cunning avarice,
and with a deficiency in liberal and enlightened
policy.

Joseph Story, "The Value and Importance of
Legal Studies," 1829, in *Miscellaneous
Writings of Joseph Story* 503, 527 (William
W. Story ed. 1852)

8 The perfect lawyer, like the perfect orator,
must accomplish himself for his duties by
familiarity with every study. . . . He should
search the human heart, and explore to
their sources the passions, and appetites,
and feelings of mankind. . . . He should unlock
all the treasures of history for illustration,
and instruction, and admonition. . . .
He will thus see man, as he has been, and
thereby best know what he is. He will thus
be taught to distrust theory, and cling to
practical good; to rely more upon experience
than reasoning; more upon institutions
than laws. . . . If the melancholy infirmities
of his race shall make him trust men
less, he may yet learn to love man more.

Joseph Story, "The Value and Importance of
Legal Studies," 1829, in *Miscellaneous
Writings of Joseph Story* 503, 527–28
(William W. Story ed. 1852)

9 Eminence in [the law] can never be attained
without the most laborious study,
united with talents of a superior order.
There is no royal road to guide us through
its labyrinths. They are to be penetrated by
skill, and mastered by a frequent survey of
landmarks. It has almost passed into a
proverb, that the lucubrations of twenty
years will do little more than conduct us to
the vestibule of the temple; and an equal

period may well be devoted to exploring the
recesses.

Joseph Story, Discourse on John H.
Ashmun, Apr. 1833, in *Life and Letters of
Joseph Story* 2:143, 145 (William W. Story
ed. 1851)

10 They tell me I must study law.
They say that I have dreamed, and
    dreamed too long;
    That I must rouse and seek for fame
    and gold;
That I must scorn this idle gift of song,
    And mingle with the vain and proud
    and cold.
        Is, then, this petty strife
        The end and aim of life,
All that is worth the living for below?
*O God! then call me hence, for I would
gladly go!*

James Russell Lowell, Letter to G. B.
Loring, 25 Aug. 1840, in *Letters of James
Russell Lowell* 1:60 (Charles Eliot Norton ed.
1893)

11 A mind confined exclusively to law is narrow,
and not of a high order. Other and
various learning is indispensable, as we
gather clearness from seeing things in various
relations. Coke and Bacon were universally
learned.

Rufus Choate, Conversation, 24 Sept. 1850,
quoted in Edward G. Parker, *Reminiscences
of Rufus Choate* 241 (1860)

12 I am from home too much of my time, for
a young man to read law with me advantageously.
If you are resolutely determined
to make a lawyer of yourself, the thing is
more than half done already. It is but a
small matter whether you read *with* any
body or not. I did not read with any one.
Get the books, and read and study them till,
you understand them in their principal features;
and that is the main thing. It is of no
consequence to be in a large town while
you are reading. I read at New-Salem,
which never had three hundred people living
in it. The *books,* and your *capacity* for
understanding them, are just the same in
all places.

Abraham Lincoln, Letter to Isham Reavis, 5
Nov. 1855, in *Collected Works of Abraham
Lincoln* 2:327 (Roy P. Basler ed. 1953)

13 If you wish to be a lawyer, attach no consequence
to the *place* you are in, or the *per-*

son you are with; but get books, sit down anywhere, and go to reading for yourself. That will make a lawyer of you quicker than any other way.

> Abraham Lincoln, Letter to William H. Grigsby, 3 Aug. 1858, in *Collected Works of Abraham Lincoln* 2:535 (Roy P. Basler ed. 1953)

14 I am absent altogether too much to be a suitable instructor for a law-student. When a man has reached the age that Mr. [John H.] Widmer has, and has already been doing for himself, my judgment is that he reads the books for himself without an instructer [*sic*]. That is precisely the way I came to the law. . . . That is my judgment of the cheapest, quickest, and best way.

> Abraham Lincoln, Letter to James T. Thornton, 2 Dec. 1858, in *Collected Works of Abraham Lincoln* 3:344 (Roy P. Basler ed. 1953)

15 [You ask] "the best mode of obtaining a thorough knowledge of the law." . . . The mode is very simple, though laborious, and tedious. It is only to get the books, and read, and study them carefully. . . . Work, work, work, is the main thing.

> Abraham Lincoln, Letter to John M. Brockman, 25 Sept. 1860, in *Collected Works of Abraham Lincoln* 4:121 (Roy P. Basler ed. 1953)

16 I had studied law an entire week, and then given it up because it was so prosy and tiresome.

> Mark Twain, *Roughing It*, 1872, in *Works of Mark Twain* 2:265 (Franklin R. Rogers ed. 1972)

17 If your subject is law, the roads are plain to anthropology, the science of man, to political economy, the theory of legislation, ethics, and thus by several paths to your final view of life. It would be equally true of any subject. The only difference is in the ease of seeing the way. To be master of any branch of knowledge, you must master those which lie next to it; and thus to know anything you must know all.

> Oliver Wendell Holmes, Jr., "The Profession of the Law" (lecture to Harvard undergraduates), Cambridge, Mass., 17 Feb. 1886, in *Speeches* 22, 23 (1913)

18 It seems to me that nearly all the education which men can get from others is moral, not intellectual. The main part of intellectual education is not the acquisition of facts, but learning how to make facts live. Culture, in the sense of fruitless knowledge, I for one abhor. The mark of a master is, that facts which before lay scattered in an inorganic mass, when he shoots through them the magnetic current of his thought, leap into an organic order, and live and bear fruit.

> Oliver Wendell Holmes, Jr., "The Use of Law Schools" (oration before Harvard Law School Association), Cambridge, Mass., 5 Nov. 1886, in *Collected Legal Papers* 35, 36–37 (1920)

19 The Professors of this School have said to themselves more definitely than ever before, We will not be contented to send forth students with nothing but a rag-bag full of general principles—a throng of glittering generalities, like a swarm of little bodiless cherubs fluttering at the top of one of Correggio's pictures.

> Oliver Wendell Holmes, Jr., "The Use of Law Schools" (oration before Harvard Law School Association), Cambridge, Mass., 5 Nov. 1886, in *Collected Legal Papers* 35, 42 (1920)

20 I cannot but believe that if the training of lawyers led them habitually to consider more definitely and explicitly the social advantage on which the rule they lay down must be justified, they sometimes would hesitate where now they are confident, and see that really they were taking sides upon debatable and often burning questions.

> Oliver Wendell Holmes, Jr., "The Path of the Law," 10 *Harvard Law Review* 457, 468 (1897)

21 Don't imagine that the time that you spend in "a commercial house" is wasted. What a lawyer needs is knowledge, not only of law, but of affairs; and above all, of men and of human nature. The time that you spend in business may ultimately prove to be the most profitable preparation for an honorable and useful pursuit of your profession. Learn, above all things, to understand thoroughly business, business habit of mind, business practices, and business men; and treat every activity in life with which you come in contact as simply educating you to a better performance later of the specific duties of the profession which you are

choosing for yourself. Remember every person you meet.

In the next place, proper preparation for law involves good general education; and the education not only of books, but of life outside of business as well as in it.

In the third place, the best part of that education is the struggle,—the determination to overcome difficulties; and those difficulties with which you are now wrestling will probably do more to strengthen your will and your mind than conditions which might seem more favorable.

> **Louis D. Brandeis**, Letter to Jacob Meyer Rudy, 14 Apr. 1913, in *Letters of Louis D. Brandeis* 3:62–63 (Melvin I. Urofsky & David Levy eds. 1973)

22 High ability, resourcefulness, imagination, the essentially legal mind, come, like kissing, by the favor of the gods (although there is much in the way of development that training may do in them).

> **Louis D. Brandeis**, Letter to Felix Frankfurter, 3 Feb. 1922, in *Letters of Louis D. Brandeis* 5:44 (Melvin I. Urofsky & David W. Levy eds. 1978)

23 The first year [of law school] . . . aims, in the old phrase, to get you to "thinking like a lawyer." The hardest job of the first year is to lop off your commonsense, to knock your ethics into temporary anesthesia. Your view of social policy, your sense of justice—to knock these out of you along with woozy thinking, along with ideas all fuzzed along their edges. You are to acquire ability to think precisely, to analyze coldly, to work within a body of materials that is given, to see, and see only, and manipulate, the machinery of the law.

> **Karl N. Llewellyn**, *The Bramble Bush* 102 (1930)

24 It is not easy thus to turn human beings into lawyers. Neither is it safe. . . . None the less, it is an almost impossible process to achieve the technique without sacrificing some humanity first.

> **Karl N. Llewellyn**, *The Bramble Bush* 102-03 (1930)

25 Your commonsense has gone [in the second year of law school]. It is time now to seek to regain it; to reshape it. It is time, too, to bring your ethics out from under ether. This time, however, in a better guise,

a commonsense, a body of ethics, no longer at war with law, preventing you from seeing the legal question, but informing law, helping you solve and criticize; no longer impeding your techniques, but furthering them.

> **Karl N. Llewellyn**, *The Bramble Bush* 105 (1930)

26 Logic across your path, and history, and the social bearings of the rules, Hohfeld's analysis, and clashing schools of jurisprudence. Details, unnumbered, shifting, sharp, disordered, unchartable, jagged. And all of this that goes on in class but an excuse to start you on a wilderness of other matters you need. The thicket presses in, the great hooked spikes rip clothes and hide and eyes. High sun, no path, no light, thirst and the thorns.—I fear there is no cure. No cure for law but more law. No vision save at the cost of plunging deeper. But men do say that if you stand these thousand vicious gaffs, if you fight through to the next bush, the gashing there brings sight.

> **Karl N. Llewellyn**, *The Bramble Bush* 108 (1930)

27 The English teacher [of law] emphasizes what the judge has said: the American professor explains what the judge should have said.

> **Arthur L. Goodhart**, *Essays in Jurisprudence and the Common Law* 70 (1931)

28 If legal education in the contemporary world is adequately to serve the needs of a free and productive commonwealth, it must be conscious, efficient, and systematic *training for policy-making*. The proper function of our law schools is, in short, to contribute to the training of policy-makers for the ever more complete achievement of the democratic values that constitute the professed end of American polity.

> **Harold D. Lasswell and Myres S. McDougal**, "Legal Education and Public Policy: Professional Training in the Public Interest," 52 *Yale Law Journal* 203, 206 (1943)

29 No one can be a truly competent lawyer unless he is a cultivated man. If I were you, I would forget all about any technical preparation for the law. The best way to prepare for the law is to come to the study of the

law as a well-read person. Thus alone can one acquire the capacity to use the English language on paper and in speech and with the habits of clear thinking which only a truly liberal education can give. No less important for a lawyer is the cultivation of the imaginative faculties by reading poetry, seeing great paintings, in the original or in easily available reproductions, and listening to great music. Stock your mind with the deposit of much good reading, and widen and deepen your feelings by experiencing vicariously as much as possible the wonderful mysteries of the universe, and forget all about your future career.

  Felix Frankfurter, Letter to M. Paul Claussen, Jr., May 1954, in *Of Law and Men: Papers and Addresses of Felix Frankfurter* 103–104 (Philip Elman ed. 1956)

30 The truth, the truth which cries out, is that the good work, the most effective work, of the lawyer in practice roots in and depends on vision, range, depth, balance, and rich humanity—those things which it is the function, frequently the fortune, of the liberal arts to introduce and indeed to induce. The truth is therefore that the best *practical* training a University can give to any lawyer who is not by choice or by unendowment doomed to be hack or shyster—the best *practical* training, along with the best human training, is the study of law, within the professional school itself, as a liberal art.

  Karl N. Llewellyn, *Jurisprudence: Realism in Theory and Practice* 376 (1962)

31 The body of "knowledge" pounded into the heads of law students does not survive long after Bar examinations are passed. Law, like engineering, changes fast. The so-called "practical" facts soon become obsolete. The only knowledge of permanent value—in law as elsewhere—is theoretical knowledge. Theoretical knowledge, critical judgment, and the discipline of learning are the only enduring aspects of legal education which make the individual readily adaptable to changing situations and problems.

  William O. Douglas, *Go East, Young Man* 169 (1974)

LEGAL FEES

See FEES

LEGAL FICTIONS

1 It overworks legal fiction to say that one is free in law when by the commonest of common sense he is bound.

  Robert H. Jackson, *Shaughnessy v. United States*, 345 U.S. 206, 220 (1953) (dissenting)

2 The users of any system—scientific, theological, legal—encounter points where their premises and their practices are inconsistent. These gaps in the system must be bridged or the system changed. To bridge the gaps, those who accept the system employ fictions. . . . fictions are a necessity of law.

  John T. Noonan, Jr., *Persons and Masks of the Law* 25 (1976)

3 Thinking like a lawyer involved being suspicious and distrustful. You reevaluated statements, inferred from silences, looked for loopholes and ambiguities. You did everything but take a statement at face value. So on one hand you believed nothing. And on the other, for the sake of logical consistency, and to preserve long-established rules, you would accept the most ridiculous fictions—that a corporation was a person, that an apartment tenant was renting land and not a dwelling.

  Scott Turow, *One L* 93 (1977)

LEGAL HUMOR

See LAWYER JOKES

LEGAL PROFESSION

See also BAR ASSOCIATIONS; ETHICS; LAW PRACTICE; LAWYERS

1 The discussion of constitutional questions throws a lustre round the bar, and gives a dignity to its functions, which can rarely belong to the profession in any other country. Lawyers are here emphatically placed as sentinels upon the outposts of the constitution; and no nobler end can be proposed for their ambition or patriotism, than to stand as faithful guardians of the constitution, ready to defend its legitimate powers, and to stay the arm of legislative, executive, or popular oppression.

  Joseph Story, Address before Suffolk Bar, Boston, 4 Sept. 1821, in *Miscellaneous Writings of Joseph Story* 198, 227–28 (William W. Story ed. 1852)

2 I think the legal profession, as a whole, presents a very sad spectacle. I fear that it has become so legalized and commercialized in its higher strata and has so little professional and public spirit throughout that it is lagging behind the other professions.

> **Harlan F. Stone,** Letter to Nicholas Murray Butler, 3 Dec. 1926, in Alpheus T. Mason, *Harlan Fiske Stone: Pillar of the Law* 210 (1956)

3 The office of the lawyer . . . is too delicate, personal and confidential to be occupied by a corporation.

> **Robert H. Jackson,** "The Trust Company in the Field of Law," 1 *New York State Bar Association Bulletin* 192, 194 (1929)

4 The legal profession, like many another, tends to become over-professionalized. We forget that law is the rule for simple and untaught people to live by. We complicate and over-refine it as a weapon in legal combat until we take it off the ground where people live and into the thin atmosphere of sheer fiction.

> **Robert H. Jackson,** *The Struggle for Judicial Supremacy* 292 (1941)

LEGAL REALISM

See also CRITICAL LEGAL STUDIES

1 LAWFUL, *adj.* Compatible with the will of a judge having jurisdiction.

> **Ambrose Bierce,** *The Devil's Dictionary* 186 (1911)

2 COMMON-LAW, *n.* The will and pleasure of the judge.

> **Ambrose Bierce,** *The Enlarged Devil's Dictionary* 43 (Ernest J. Hopkins ed. 1967)

3 I have spoken of the forces of which judges avowedly avail to shape the form and content of their judgments. . . . Deep below consciousness are other forces, the likes and the dislikes, the predilections and the prejudices, the complex of instincts and emotions and habits and convictions, which make the man, whether he be litigant or judge.

> **Benjamin N. Cardozo,** *The Nature of the Judicial Process* 167 (1921)

4 The constant development of unprecedented problems requires a legal system capable of fluidity and pliancy. Our society would be strait-jacketed were not the courts, with the able assistance of the lawyers, constantly overhauling the law and adapting it to the realities of ever-changing social, industrial and political conditions; although changes cannot be made lightly, yet law must be more or less impermanent, experimental and therefore not nicely calculable. *Much of the uncertainty of law is not an unfortunate accident: it is of immense social value.*

> **Jerome N. Frank,** *Law and the Modern Mind* 6–7 (1930)

5 The law is not a machine and the judges not machine-tenders. There never was and there never will be a body of fixed and predetermined rules alike for all.

> **Jerome N. Frank,** *Law and the Modern Mind* 120 (1930)

6 Lawyers and judges purport to make large use of precedents; that is, they purport to rely on the conduct of judges in past cases as a means of procuring analogies for action in new cases. But since what was actually decided in the earlier cases is seldom revealed, it is impossible, in a real sense, to rely on these precedents. What the courts in fact do is to manipulate the language of former decisions. They could approximate a system of real precedents only if the judges, in rendering those former decisions, had reported with fidelity the precise steps by which they arrived at their decisions. The paradox of the situation is that, granting there is value in a system of precedents, our present use of illusory precedents makes the employment of real precedents impossible.

> **Jerome N. Frank,** *Law and the Modern Mind* 148–49 (1930)

7 What, then, is this law business about? It is about the fact that our society is honeycombed with disputes. . . . This doing of something about disputes, this doing of it reasonably, is the business of law. And the people who have the doing in charge, whether they be judges or sheriffs or clerks or jailers or lawyers, are officials of the law. *What these officials do about disputes is, to my mind, the law itself.*

> **Karl N. Llewellyn,** *The Bramble Bush* 2–3 (1930)

8 Within the law, I say, therefore, rules *guide*, but they do not *control* decision. There is no precedent the judge may not at his need either file down to razor thinness or expand into a bludgeon. Why should you expect the ethics of the game to be different from the game itself?

Karl N. Llewellyn, *The Bramble Bush* 180 (1930)

9 Ferment is abroad in the law. The sphere of interest widens; men become interested again in the life that swirls around things legal. Before rules, were facts; in the beginning was not a Word, but a Doing. Behind decisions stand judges; judges are men; as men they have human backgrounds. Beyond rules, again, lie effects: beyond decisions stand people whom rules and decisions directly or indirectly touch. The field of Law reaches both forward and back from the Substantive Law of school and doctrine. The sphere of interest is widening: so, too, is the scope of doubt. *Beyond rules lie effects*—but do they? Are some rules mere paper? And if effects, what effects? Hearsay, unbuttressed guess, assumption or assertion unchecked by test—can such be trusted on this matter of what law is *doing*?

Karl N. Llewellyn, "Some Realism about Realism—Responding to Dean Pound," 44 *Harvard Law Review* 1222, 1222 (1931)

10 The object of a realistic legal criticism will be not the divine vision which follows the words "Be it enacted:" but the probable reaction between the words of the legislature and the professional prejudices and distorting apparatus of the bench, between the ideas that emerge from this often bloody encounter and the social pressures that play upon enforcing officials. Words are frail packages for legislative hopes. The voyage to the realm of law-observance is long and dangerous. Seldom do meanings arrive at their destination intact. Whether or not we approve of storms and pirates, let us be aware of them when we appraise the cargo.

Felix S. Cohen, *Ethical Systems and Legal Ideals* 240 (1933)

11 By another route this general program led us toward another absurdity. The law is what the courts will do. Courts are people. What people do largely depends on their visceral reactions. The law may thus depend on what the judge has had for breakfast. The conclusion is that legal scholars, adopting the slogan of Shredded Wheat, "Tell me what you eat and I'll tell you what you are," should devote themselves to studying the domestic larder of judicial wives.

Robert M. Hutchins, "The Autobiography of an Ex-Law Student," 7 *American Law School Review* 1051, 1054 (1934)

12 The theory that rules decide cases seems for a century to have fooled not only library-ridden recluses, but judges. . . . the theory flew in the face of common sense and professional experience. If rules decided cases, one judge would be as good as another, provided only the rules had been adduced before him.

Karl N. Llewellyn, "The Constitution as an Institution," 34 *Columbia Law Review* 1, 7 (1934)

13 Although judges and lawyers need not be legal scientists, it is of some practical importance that they should recognize that the traditional language of argument and opinion neither explains nor justifies court decisions. When the vivid fictions and metaphors of traditional jurisprudence are thought of as reasons for decisions, rather than poetical or mnemonic devices for formulating decisions reached on other grounds, then the author, as well as the reader, of the opinion or argument, is apt to forget the social forces which mold the law and the social ideals by which the law is to be judged.

Felix S. Cohen, "Transcendental Nonsense and the Functional Approach," 35 *Columbia Law Review* 809, 812 (1935)

14 We may summarize the basic assumptions of traditional legal theory in the following terms: *Legal concepts* (for example, *corporations* or *property rights*) are supernatural entities which do not have a verifiable existence except to the eyes of faith.

Felix S. Cohen, "Transcendental Nonsense and the Functional Approach," 35 *Columbia Law Review* 809, 820–21 (1935)

15 Legal criticism is empty without objective description of the causes and consequences of legal decisions. Legal description is blind without the guiding light of a theory

of values. It is through the union of objective legal science and a critical theory of social values that our understanding of the human significance of law will be enriched.

> Felix S. Cohen, "Transcendental Nonsense and the Functional Approach," 35 *Columbia Law Review* 809, 849 (1935)

16 Interests, points of view, preferences, are the essence of living. Only death yields complete dispassionateness, for such dispassionateness signifies utter indifference. . . . The judge in our society owes a duty to act in accordance with those basic predilections inhering in our legal system (although, of course, he has the right, at times, to urge that some of them be modified or abandoned). The standard of dispassionateness obviously does not require the judge to rid himself of the unconscious influence of such social attitudes.

> Jerome N. Frank, *Courts on Trial* 413 (1949)

LEGAL RESEARCH

See also LAW BOOKS; LAW LIBRARIES

1 It is also to be borne in mind, that digests and elementary treatises are only the abstracts of adjudicated cases, and not always sure therefore of stating accurately the points decided. In fact, experienced counsel will never, in a case of importance, trust to a short sentence, which, the laborious compiler says, contains in an abbreviated form the principles of a question settled, when they have the original case itself within their reach; for they have learned by observation the errors and the imperfections of digests.

> James Madison Porter, Book Review, 27 *North American Review* 167, 182 (1828)

2 It is a great mistake to be frightened by the ever increasing number of reports. The reports of a given jurisdiction in the course of a generation take up pretty much the whole body of the law, and restate it from the present point of view. We could reconstruct the corpus from them if all that went before were burned.

> Oliver Wendell Holmes, Jr., "The Path of the Law," 10 *Harvard Law Review* 457, 458 (1897)

3 There is another case bearing upon this proposition which neither counsel nor we

have been able to find; but it holds that there was no such defect in the ballot used as to defeat the election. The departure from the statute in that case was much greater than in this one.

> Horace E. Deemer, *Kinney v. Howard,* 133 Iowa 94, 103, 110 N.W. 282 (1907)

4 I do not feel that any one ever really masters the law, but it is not difficult to master the approaches to the law, so that given a certain state of facts it is possible to know how to marshal practically all the legal decisions which apply to them.

> Calvin Coolidge, *The Autobiography of Calvin Coolidge* 76 (1929)

5 I made no preparations for the trial. It is not my policy to look up law in advance of the trial of a lawsuit. I have learned from experience that no matter how strange and fantastic is my own notion of the law, it is safe to assume that somewhere in the reports there will be decision that will support it. And maybe I won't have to look it up at all. I really have, I must confess, a singular aversion to looking up law. At one time I seriously considered specializing exclusively in a certain class of cases dealing with what is commonly referred to as "the unwritten law," but I didn't seem able to work up that type of practice.

> Robert T. Sloan, "Daisy Whiffle v. The Twitter Bird Seed Company," in *The Judicial Humorist* 20, 22–23 (William L. Prosser ed. 1952)

6 Justice Robert H. Jackson liked to tell of the time when, as a young lawyer before an upstate New York judge, he cited in his support a case newly decided by the Supreme Court, and handed up the advance sheets to prove his point. The judge handed them back, glaring, and said, "I don't take no law from no magazines."

> Martin Mayer, *The Lawyers* 497 (1967)

LEGAL WRITING

See also LANGUAGE; LAW REVIEWS; QUOTATIONS; WORDS

1 I should apologize, perhaps, for the style of this bill. I dislike the verbose and intricate style of the English statutes, and in our revised code I endeavored to restore it to the

simple one of the ancient statutes, in such original bills as I drew in that work. I suppose the reformation has not been acceptable, as it has been little followed. You, however, can easily correct this bill to the taste of my brother lawyers, by making every other word a "said" or "aforesaid," and saying everything over two or three times, so that nobody but we of the craft can untwist the diction, and find out what it means; and that, too, not so plainly but that we may conscientiously divide one half on each side. Mend it, therefore, in form and substance to the orthodox taste, and make it what it should be; or, if you think it radically wrong, try something else, and let us make a beginning in some way. No matter how wrong, experience will amend it as we go along, and make it effectual in the end.

> **Thomas Jefferson,** Letter to Joseph C. Cabell, 9 Sept. 1817, in *Writings of Thomas Jefferson* 17:417–18 (Andrew A. Lipscomb ed. 1904)

2 [Jefferson disliked statutes] which from their verbosity, their endless tautologies, their involutions of case within case, and parenthesis within parenthesis, and their multiplied efforts at certainty by *saids* and *aforesaids,* by *ors* and by *ands,* to make them more plain, do really render them more perplexed and incomprehensible, not only to common readers, but to the lawyers themselves.

> **Thomas Jefferson,** *Autobiography,* 1821, in *Writings of Thomas Jefferson* 1:61 (Paul L. Ford ed. 1892)

3 Legislatures are not grammar schools, and in this country, at least, it is hardly reasonable to expect legislative acts to be drawn with strict grammatical or logical accuracy.

> **Isaac P. Christiancy,** *Whipple v. Judge of Saginaw Circuit,* 26 Mich. 342, 344–45 (1873)

4 There is a useless lawsuit in every useless word of a statute and every loose, sloppy phrase plays the part of the typhoid carrier.

> **Elihu Root,** "The Layman's Criticism of the Lawyer," 39 *American Bar Association Report* 386, 395 (1914)

5 I abhor, loathe and despise these long discourses, and agree with Carducci the Italian poet who died some years ago that a man who takes half a page to say what can be said in a sentence will be damned.

> **Oliver Wendell Holmes, Jr.,** Letter to Frederick Pollock, 1 June 1917, in *Holmes-Pollock Letters* 1:245 (Mark DeWolfe Howe ed. 1941)

6 The pen of an indictment clerk is oft mightier than the sword of a Lion heart, the brain behind the subtle quill far defter than said swordsman's skill. Moreover, the ingenuity necessary to draft one of these documents is not confined to its mere successful composition, for having achieved the miraculous feat of alleging in fourteen ways without punctuation that the defendant did something, and with a final fanfare of "saids" and "to wits" inserted his verb where no one will ever find it, the indicter must then be able to unwind himself, rolling in and out among the "dids" and "thens" and "theres" until he is once more safely upon the terra firma of foolscap at the head of the first page. . . .

Therefore was Caput Magnus held in high honor among the pack of human hounds who bayed at the call of Huntsman Peckhan's horn. Others might lose the scent of what it was all about in the tropical jungle of an indictment eleven pages long, but not he. Like the old dog in Masefield's "Reynard the Fox," Mr. Magnus would work through ditches full of legal slime, nose through thorn thickets of confusion, dash through copses and spinneys of words and phrases, until he snapped close at the heels of intelligibility.

> **Arthur Train,** "By Advice of Counsel," in *By Advice of Counsel* 149–50 (1929)

7 Write an opinion, and read it a few years later when it is dissected in the briefs of counsel. You will learn for the first time the limitations of the power of speech, or, if not those of speech in general, at all events your own.

> **Benjamin N. Cardozo,** *Law and Literature* 8 (1931)

8 Clearness, though the sovereign quality, is not the only one to be pursued, and even if it were, may be gained through many avenues of approach. The opinion will need persuasive force, or the impressive virtue of sincerity and fire, or the mnemonic power of alliteration and antithesis, or the

terseness and tang of the proverb and the maxim. Neglect the help of these allies, and it may never win its way.

> **Benjamin N. Cardozo,** *Law and Literature* 9 (1931)

9 I seem to discern six types or methods [of judicial opinion-writing] which divide themselves from one another with measurable distinctness. There is the type magisterial or imperative; the type laconic or sententious; the type conversational or homely; the type refined or artificial, smelling of the lamp, verging at times upon preciosity or euphuism; the type demonstrative or persuasive; and finally the type tonsorial or agglutinative, so called from the shears and the pastepot which are its implements and emblem.

> **Benjamin N. Cardozo,** *Law and Literature* 10 (1931)

10 [There is] something more important than mere felicities of turn or phrase. Above and beyond all these are what we may term the architectonics of opinions. The groupings of fact and argument and illustration so as to produce a cumulative and mass effect; these, after all, are the things that count above all others.

> **Benjamin N. Cardozo,** *Law and Literature* 32–33 (1931)

11 Everytime a lawyer writes something, he is not writing for posterity, he is writing so that endless others of his craft can make a living out of trying to figure out what he said, course perhaps he hadent really said anything, that's what makes it hard to explain.

> **Will Rogers,** "The Lawyers Talking," 28 July 1935, in *Will Rogers' Weekly Articles* 6:243, 244 (Steven K. Gragert ed. 1982)

12 The minute you read something and you can't understand it you can almost be sure that it was drawn up by a lawyer. Then if you give it to another lawyer to read and he don't know just what it means, why then you can be sure it was drawn up by a lawyer. If it's in a few words and is plain and understandable only one way, it was written by a non-lawyer.

> **Will Rogers,** "The Lawyers Talking," 28 July 1935, in *Will Rogers' Weekly Articles* 6:243, 244 (Steven K. Gragert ed. 1982)

13 There are two things wrong with almost all legal writing. One is its style. The other is its content.

> **Fred Rodell,** "Goodbye to Law Reviews," 23 *Virginia Law Review* 38, 38 (1936)

14 Then there is this business of footnotes, the flaunted Phi Beta Kappa keys of legal writing, and the pet peeve of everyone who has ever read a law review piece for any other reason than that he was too lazy to look up his own cases. So far as I can make out, there are two distinct types of footnote. There is the explanatory or you-didn't-understand-what-I-said-in-the-text-this-may-help-you type. And there is the probative or if-you're-from-Missouri-just-take-a-look-at-all-this type.

> **Fred Rodell,** "Goodbye to Law Reviews," 23 *Virginia Law Review* 38, 40 (1936)

15 The footnote foible breeds nothing but sloppy thinking, clumsy writing, and bad eyes. Any article that has to be explained or proved by being cluttered up with little numbers until it looks like the Acrosses and Downs of a cross-word puzzle has no business being written.

> **Fred Rodell,** "Goodbye to Law Reviews," 23 *Virginia Law Review* 38, 41 (1936)

16 The words of such an act as the Income Tax . . . merely dance before my eyes in a meaningless procession: cross-reference to cross-reference, exception upon exception. . . . at times I cannot help recalling a saying of William James about certain passages of Hegel: that they were no doubt written with a passion of rationality; but that one cannot help wondering whether to the reader they have any significance save that the words are strung together with syntactical correctness.

> **Learned Hand,** "Thomas Walter Swan," 57 *Yale Law Journal* 167, 169 (1947)

17 To one digging into the bowels of the law, a fat footnote is a mother lode, a vein of purest gold.

> **Stanley H. Fuld,** "A Judge Looks at the Law Review," 28 *New York University Law Review* 915, 919 (1953)

18 Style, as you all know, is a matter for which the law has been taken severely to task. Recalling the frequent jibes of exasperated laymen, some of you may remember one

that floated around during the days of federal price control. A business man was charged with violating a complicated regulation setting ceiling prices on the articles he sold. When he betrayed some unfamiliarity with the regulation, the judge asked him whether he had ever read it. The defendant replied indignantly, "Read it, Judge? I can't even *lift* it!"

Reed Dickerson, "How to Write a Law," 31 *Notre Dame Lawyer* 14, 22–23 (1955)

19 From the exactness, brevity, and simplicity of the Twelve Tables to the wordiness of the *Novels* of Justinian, from the 1321 words of the Declaration of Independence to the 12,962 words of the order of the Office of Price Stabilization establishing the ceiling price of manually operated foghorns and other manufactured items, legal prose seems in the grip of an iron law. Literary prose changes from the ornate to the plain, and back again, as men become tired of one or the other; more often the two streams run parallel. Official legal prose, however, seems an illustration of Herbert Spencer's evolutionary law of a development from homogeneity to heterogeneity; it appears to be an instance of unilinear evolution, perhaps the only known example.

Huntington Cairns, in *Language: An Enquiry into its Meaning and Function* 237 (Ruth N. Anshen ed. 1957)

20 One of Judge Jerome Frank's law clerks objected to the length of one of his opinions. He spent all of a week and finally cut it down from sixty-five pages to one-half page. He left both on Judge Frank's desk without comment. The following morning Judge Frank rushed into his clerk's office and shouted, "Bully for you," displaying the clerk's work, "we'll add it to the end."

Jerome N. Frank, reported in Ed Bander, "Doing Justice," 72 *Law Library Journal* 150, 150 (1979)

21 There are only two cures for the long sentence:
(1) Say less;
(2) Put a period in the middle.
Neither expedient has taken hold in the law.

David Mellinkoff, *The Language of the Law* 366 (1963)

22 Defendants say in their brief: "The duty owing from defendants to plaintiffs in the abstract will vary, under *White,* relative to the juxtaposition of the real world environmental encasement of the two sides. The concept of causation would seem less plastic." Briefs should be written in the English language!

Ben C. Duniway, *Gottreich v. San Francisco Investment Corp.,* 552 F.2d 866, 867 n.2 (9th Cir. 1977)

23 The *Blue Book* [*A Uniform System of Citation*] . . . champions *technical due process.* According to this doctrine, it does not matter who wrote the article; it does not matter how he wrote it. It does not matter what the article says; it does not matter that it says nothing at all. The doctrine of technical due process maintains that *if the footnotes are wrong, the article is worthless.*

Alan Strasser, Book Review, 12 *Harvard Civil Rights-Civil Liberties Law Review* 507, 509 (1977)

24 For a public figure to recover in a defamation suit, actual malice must be proved with clear and convincing clarity.*

William C. Hill, *Burns v. Times Argus Ass'n,* 139 Vt. 381, 388, 430 A.2d 773 (1981)

25 When reading a footnoted opinion one's eyes are constantly moving from text to footnotes and back again. . . . If footnotes were a rational form of communication, Darwinian selection would have resulted in the eyes being set vertically rather than on an inefficient horizontal plane.†

Abner J. Mikva, "Goodbye to Footnotes," 56 *University of Colorado Law Review* 647, 648 (1985)

26 Legal writing is one of those rare creatures, like the rat and the cockroach, that would attract little sympathy even as an endangered species.

Richard Hyland, "A Defense of Legal Writing," 134 *University of Pennsylvania Law Review* 599, 600 (1986)

---

* The Vermont Supreme Court here created a remarkably redundant standard. The Hawaii Supreme Court also came up with "clear and convincing clarity" in *Fong v. Merena,* 66 Haw. 72, 74, 655 P.2d 875 (1982) (per curiam).

† Judge Mikva, who sits on the United States Court of Appeals for the District of Columbia Circuit, uses no footnotes in his opinions.

27 Anthropologists use the word "hypertrophy" to describe the tendency of human beings to mindless elaboration of social practices. The pyramids in Egypt are the hypertrophy of burial. The hypertrophy of law is *A Uniform System of Citation*.

> **Richard A. Posner,** "Goodbye to the Bluebook," 53 *University of Chicago Law Review* 1343, 1343 (1986)

28 The vacuity and tendentiousness of so much legal reasoning are concealed by the awesome scrupulousness with which a set of intricate rules governing the form of citations is observed.

> **Richard A. Posner,** "Goodbye to the Bluebook," 53 *University of Chicago Law Review* 1343, 1344 (1986)

29 The rightful objects of our condemnation are the bombastic, vestigial Latinisms that serve no purpose but to give the writer a false sense of erudition. These terms convey no special legal meanings, no delicate nuances apprehended only by lawyers. They are pompous, turgid deadwood. Just as a mathematician would seem ludicrous to write 386/1544 rather than 1/4 for purposes of thereby seeming more scholarly, so the lawyer who writes *sub suo periculo* instead of *at his own risk*, strikes his reader as a laughable, if vexatious, figure.

> **Bryan A. Garner,** *A Dictionary of Modern Legal Usage* 329 (1987)

30 If there is a malady endemic in legal writing, it is the practice or habit of mechanically repeating previously received ideas or images that reflect neither true reasoning nor feeling, the parrot-like repetition of words.

> **Bryan A. Garner,** *A Dictionary of Modern Legal Usage* 447 (1987)

31 In the third year of law school, they ought to teach English as a Second Language.

> **Stephen Wermiel,** quoted in Tom Goldstein and Jethro K. Lieberman, *The Lawyer's Guide to Writing Well* 80 (1989)

32 Law is not just a bunch of dusty old precepts to be applied with humdrum objectivity. It is alive; blood courses through its veins. As often as not, to apply legal rules you must weigh, judge, and argue about human folkways and human foibles. And to do that well, you must have a heart. . . .

in the end, the law has something to do with justice.

> **Bryan A. Garner,** *The Elements of Legal Style* 174 (1991)

LEGISLATION

See also CONGRESS; JUDICIAL LEGISLATION; LEGISLATIVE HISTORY; LEGISLATIVE INTENT; STATUTES; STATUTORY CONSTRUCTION

1 In ye name of God, Amen. We whose names are underwriten, the loyall subjects of our dread soveraigne Lord, King James, by ye grace of God, of Great Britaine, Franc, & Ireland king, defender of ye faith, &c., haveing undertaken, for ye glorie of God, and advancemente of ye Christian faith, and honour of our king & countrie, a voyage to plant ye first colonie in ye Northerne parts of Virginia, doe by these presents solemnly & mutualy in ye presence of God, and one of another, covenant & combine our selves togeather into a civill body politick, for our better ordering & preservation & furtherance of ye ends aforesaid; and by vertue hearof to enacte, constitute, and frame such just & equall lawes, ordinances, acts, constitutions, & offices, from time to time, as shall be thought most meete & convenient for ye generall good of ye Colonie, unto which we promise all due submission and obedience.

> Mayflower Compact of 1620, in William Bradford, *Of Plimouth Plantation* 110 (1898) (1646)

2 The Governor, or in his absence, the Deputie Governor of the saide Company for the tyme being, and such of the Assistants and Freeman of the saide Company as shalbe present, or the greater nomber of them so assembled, . . . shall have full Power and authoritie . . . to make Lawes and Ordinnces for the Good and Welfare of the saide Company, and for the Government and ordering of the saide Landes and Plantacõn, and the People inhabiting and to inhabite the same, as to them from tyme to tyme shalbe thought meete, soe as such Lawes and Ordinances be not contrarie or repugnant to the Lawes and Statuts of this our Realme of England.

> Massachusetts Bay Charter of 1629, in *Federal and State Constitutions* 3:1846, 1853 (Francis N. Thorpe ed. 1909)

3 We, for Us, our Heirs and Successors, do grant unto the said now Baron, (in whose Fidelity, Prudence, Justice, and provident Circumspection of Mind, We repose the greatest Confidence) and to his Heirs, for the good and happy Government of the said Province, free, full, and absolute Power, by the Tenor of these Presents, to Ordain, Make, and Enact Laws, of what Kind soever, according to their sound Discretions, whether relating to the Public State of the said Province, or the private Utility of Individuals, of and with the Advice, Assent, and Approbation of the Free-Men of the same Province, or the greater Part of them, or of their Delegates or Deputies, whom We shall be called together for the framing of Laws, when, and as often as Need shall require, by the aforesaid now Baron of Baltimore, and his Heirs.

Maryland Charter of 1632, § 7, in *Federal and State Constitutions* 3:1677, 1679 (Francis N. Thorpe ed. 1909)

4 Laws *too gentle* are seldom *obeyed; too severe,* seldom *executed.*

Benjamin Franklin, *Poor Richard's Almanack,* 1756, in *Papers of Benjamin Franklin* 6:324 (Leonard W. Labaree ed. 1963)

5 That retrospective laws, punishing offences committed before the existence of such laws, are oppressive and unjust, and ought not to be made.

Delaware Declaration of Rights of 1776, § 11, in *Sources of Our Liberties* 338, 339 (Richard L. Perry & John C. Cooper eds. 1959)

6 It will be of little avail to the people that the laws are made by men of their own choice, if the laws be so voluminous that they cannot be read, or so incoherent that they cannot be understood; if they be repealed or revised before they are promulgated, or undergo such incessant changes that no man who knows what the law is to day can guess what it will be to morrow.

Alexander Hamilton or James Madison, *The Federalist* No. 62, at 2:190 (1788)

7 It may perhaps be said, that the power of preventing bad laws includes that of preventing good ones; and may be used to the one purpose as well as to the other. But this objection will have little weight with those who can properly estimate the mischiefs of that inconstancy and mutability in the laws which form the greatest blemish in the character and genius of our governments. They will consider every institution calculated to restrain the excess of law-making, and to keep things in the same state in which they may happen to be at any given period, as much more likely to do good than harm.

Alexander Hamilton, *The Federalist* No. 73, at 2:265 (1788)

8 I will state *what laws* I consider *ex post facto laws,* within the *words* and the *intent* of the prohibition. 1st. Every law that makes an action done before the passing of the law, and which was *innocent* when done, criminal; and punishes such action. 2d. Every law that *aggravates* a *crime,* or makes it *greater* than it was, when committed. 3d. Every law that *changes the punishment,* and inflicts a *greater punishment,* than the law annexed to the crime, when committed. 4th. Every law that alters the *legal* rules of *evidence,* and receives less, or different, testimony, than the law required at the time of the commission of the offence, *in order to convict the offender.* All these, and similar laws, are manifestly *unjust and oppressive.*

Samuel Chase, *Calder v. Bull,* 3 U.S. (3 Dall.) 386, 390–91 (1798)

9 For my own part, until the learned have come to an agreement among themselves, I shall content myself with the account [of creation] handed down to us by Moses; in which I do but follow the example of our ingenious neighbors of Connecticut; who at their first settlement proclaimed, that the colony should be governed by the laws of God—until they had time to make better.

Washington Irving, *A History of New York* 60 (1868) (1809)

10 He [William the Testy] ordained that, whoever proposed a new law should do it with a halter about his neck; whereby, in case his proposition were rejected, they just hung him up—and there the matter ended. The effect was, that for more than two hundred years there was but one trifling alteration in the judicial code; and legal matters

were so clear and simple that the whole race of lawyers starved to death for want of employment.

Washington Irving, *A History of New York* 260 (1868) (1809)

11 Republics abound in young civilians who believe that the laws make the city, that grave modifications of the policy and modes of living and employments of the population, that commerce, education and religion may be voted in or out; and that any measure, though it were absurd, may be imposed on a people if only you can get sufficient voices to make it a law. But the wise know that foolish legislation is a rope of sand which perishes in the twisting; that the State must follow and not lead the character and progress of the citizen; . . . that the form of government which prevails is the expression of what cultivation exists in the population which permits it. The law is only a memorandum.

Ralph Waldo Emerson, "Politics," *Essays: Second Series,* 1844, in *Complete Works of Ralph Waldo Emerson* 3:199, 199–200 (1903)

12 We must trust infinitely to the beneficent necessity which shines through all laws. Human nature expresses itself in them as characteristically as in statues, or songs, or railroads; and an abstract of the codes of nations would be a transcript of the common conscience.

Ralph Waldo Emerson, "Politics," *Essays: Second Series,* 1844, in *Complete Works of Ralph Waldo Emerson* 3:199, 212 (1903)

13 When people pass wise and needful laws, but leave them without public sentiment, it is as if a child were born into an exhausted receiver instead of a cradle.

Henry Ward Beecher, *Life Thoughts* 141 (1858)

14 A law is valuable, not because it is law, but because there is right in it; and because of this rightness it is like a vessel carrying perfume—like the alabaster enclosure of a lamp.

Henry Ward Beecher, *Life Thoughts* 206 (1858)

15 We bury men when they are dead, but we try to embalm the dead body of laws. . . . It

usually takes a hundred years to make a law; and then, after it has done its work, it usually takes a hundred years to get rid of it.

Henry Ward Beecher, *Life Thoughts* 239 (1858)

16 The error arose from want of diligent watchfulness in respect to legislative changes. He did not remember that it might be necessary to look at the statutes of the year before. Perhaps he had forgotten the saying, that "no man's life, liberty or property are safe while the Legislature is in session."

Gideon J. Tucker, *Final Accounting in the Estate of A.B.,* 1 Tucker (N.Y. Surr.) 247, 249 (1866)

17 The struggle for life . . . does not stop in the ascending scale with the monkeys, but is equally the law of human existence. Outside of legislation this is undeniable. It is mitigated by sympathy, prudence, and all the social and moral qualities. But in the last resort a man rightly prefers his own interest to that of his neighbors. And this is as true in legislation as in any other form of corporate action.

Oliver Wendell Holmes, Jr., "Summary of Events: The Gas-Stokers' Strike," 7 *American Law Review* 582, 583 (1873)

18 All that can be expected from modern improvements is that legislation should easily and quickly, yet not too quickly, modify itself in accordance with the will of the *de facto* supreme power in the community, and . . . the spread of an educated sympathy should reduce the sacrifice of minorities to a minimum. But whatever body may possess the supreme power for the moment is certain to have interests inconsistent with others which have competed unsuccessfully. The more powerful interests must be more or less reflected in legislation; which, like every other device of man or beast, must tend in the long run to aid the survival of the fittest. The objection to class legislation is not that it favors a class, but either that it fails to benefit the legislators, or that it is dangerous to them because a competing class has gained in power, or that it transcends the limits of

self-preference which are imposed by sympathy.

> Oliver Wendell Holmes, Jr., "Summary of Events: The Gas-Stokers' Strike," 7 *American Law Review* 582, 583–84 (1873)

19 Our [railroad] tracks ought to be fenced on the principle that the majority of human beings, being fools, the laws ought to be made in the interest of the majority.

> Mark Twain, "Mississippi River, 1882," in *Mark Twain's Notebook* 164 (Albert B. Paine ed. 1935)

20 It is not every act, legislative in form, that is law. Law is something more than mere will exerted as an act of power. . . . The enforcement of these limitations by judicial process . . . protect[s] the rights of individuals and minorities . . . against the violence of public agents transcending the limits of lawful authority, even when acting in the name and wielding the force of the government.

> Stanley Matthews, *Hurtado v. California,* 110 U.S. 516, 535–36 (1884)

21 No law can be effective which does not take into consideration the conditions of the community for which it is designed; no law can be a good law—every law must be a bad law—that remains unenforced. That is a fundamental truth in legislation.

> Louis D. Brandeis, Statement before Massachusetts Joint Legislative Committee on Liquor Law, 27 Feb. 1891, quoted in Alfred Lief, *The Brandeis Guide to the Modern World* 165–66 (1941)

22 It is said that the power here asserted is inherent in sovereignty. This doctrine of powers inherent in sovereignty is one both indefinite and dangerous. Where are the limits to such powers to be found, and by whom are they to be pronounced? Is it within the legislative capacity to declare the limits? If so, then the mere assertion of an inherent power creates it, and despotism exists.

> David J. Brewer, *Fong Yue Ting v. United States,* 149 U.S. 698, 737 (1893) (dissenting)

23 If a legislature undertakes to exert the taxing power, that of eminent domain, or any part of that vast, unclassified residue of legislative authority which is called, not al-

ways intelligently, the police power, this action must not degenerate into an irrational excess, so as to become, in reality, something different and forbidden,—e.g., the depriving people of their property without due process of law; and whether it does so or not, must be determined by the judges.

> James Bradley Thayer, "The Origin and Scope of the American Doctrine of Constitutional Law," 7 *Harvard Law Review* 129, 148 (1893)

24 It is difficult to make our material condition better by the best laws, but it is easy enough to ruin it by bad laws.

> Theodore Roosevelt, Address, Providence, R.I., 23 Aug. 1902, in *Works of Theodore Roosevelt* 18:73, 74 (1925)

25 Laws are sand, customs are rock. Laws can be evaded and punishment escaped, but an openly transgressed custom brings sure punishment.

> Mark Twain, "The Gorky Incident," 1906, in *Mark Twain: Letters From the Earth* 155, 156 (Bernard De Voto ed. 1939)

26 A judicial inquiry investigates, declares and enforces liabilities as they stand on present or past facts and under laws supposed already to exist. That is its purpose and end. Legislation on the other hand looks to the future and changes existing conditions by making a new rule to be applied thereafter to all or some part of those subject to its power.

> Oliver Wendell Holmes, Jr., *Prentis v. Atlantic Coast Line Co.,* 211 U.S. 210, 226 (1908)

27 Establishment of a rate is the making of a rule for the future, and therefore is an act legislative not judicial.

> Oliver Wendell Holmes, Jr., *Prentis v. Atlantic Coast Line Co.,* 211 U.S. 210, 226 (1908)

28 The question relates to matters of public policy . . . and Congress alone can deal with the subject; [a] court would encroach upon the authority of Congress if, under the guise of construction, it should assume to determine a matter of public policy. . . . [The opponents of a statute] must go to Congress and obtain an amendment of the [statute] if they think [it wrong]. . . . [The Supreme Court] cannot and will not *judi-*

cially legislate, since its function is to declare the law, while it belongs to the legislative department to make the law.

> **John M. Harlan** (1833–1911), *Standard Oil Co. of New Jersey v. United States,* 221 U.S. 1, 102 (1911) (concurring in part and dissenting in part)

29 By tyranny, as we now fight it, we mean control of the law, of legislation and adjudication, by organizations which do not represent the people, by means which are private and selfish. We mean, specifically, the conduct of our affairs and the shaping of our legislation in the interest of special bodies of capital and those who organize their use. We mean the alliance, for this purpose, of political machines with selfish business. We mean the exploitation of the people by legal and political means. We have seen many of our governments under these influences cease to be representative governments, cease to be governments representative of the people, and become governments representative of special interests, controlled by machines, which in their turn are not controlled by the people.

> **Woodrow Wilson,** *The New Freedom* 49–50 (1913)

30 Publicity is justly commended as a remedy for social and industrial diseases. Sunlight is said to be the best of disinfectants; electric light the most efficient policeman.

> **Louis D. Brandeis,** *Other People's Money* 92 (1914)

31 Legislation cannot save society. Legislation cannot even rectify society. The law that will work is merely the summing up in legislative form of the moral judgment that the community has already reached.

> **Woodrow Wilson,** Address to the Federal Council of Churches, Columbus, Ohio, 10 Dec. 1915, in *Papers of Woodrow Wilson* 35:329, 334 (Arthur S. Link ed. 1980)

32 The American method, from the beginning of things, has been to ignore the obnoxious law, not to repeal it. Our statute books are cluttered with enactments which prove the truth of this assertion. . . . repeals require action by legislatures, and legislatures are notoriously timid, particularly when they are beset by fanatics. There are many men in legislatures and elsewhere who will see

a law ignored with a wholly clear conscience but wouldn't have the courage to vote for its repeal.

> **H. L. Mencken,** "'Law' Enforcement," Baltimore *Evening Sun,* 10 Nov. 1925, quoted in *The Gist of Mencken* 426 (Mayo DuBasky ed. 1990)

33 What we need to do is to stop passing laws. We have enough laws now to govern the world for the next 10,000 years. Every crank who has a foolish notion that he would like to impose upon everybody else hastens to some legislative body and demands that it be graven upon the statutes. Every fanatic who wants to control his neighbor's conduct is here or at some other legislative body demanding that a law be passed to regulate that neighbor's conduct.

> **James A. Reed,** in 67 *Congressional Record* 10,708 (1926)

34 But here are men and women coming constantly to the legislative halls wanting to tie around the liberties of the American people first this thread and then that thread, until finally, as the Lilliputians bound the full-sized and athletic Gulliver with threads until he was inert and helpless on the ground, we ourselves will be bound.

Sir, what we need is less law, less interference, less legislative guidance. What boots it to be called a free man if when you are born you fall into a legislative cradle, your swaddling clothes are regulated by statute, your steps through life are all in accordance with the law, and a policeman is there to see that you take them, your course in life is marked out for you from the cradle to the grave, all the time you have moved in gyves and all the time you have been a slave to the laws of a Republic? And one might as well be a slave to the decrees of a tyrant as to the decrees of a Senate or of a House of Representatives.

> **James A. Reed,** in 67 *Congressional Record* 10,708 (1926)

35 When a people lose respect for one bad law, it is but a short step before they include the good laws with the bad and are shortly in rebellion against all law.

> **Oscar W. Underwood,** *Drifting Sands of Party Politics* 42 (1928)

36 If the moral and physical fibre of its manhood and its womanhood is not a State concern, the question is, what is?

> Benjamin N. Cardozo, *Adler v. Deegan*, 251 N.Y. 467, 484, 167 N.E. 705 (1929) (concurring)

37 I hope your committee will not permit doubts as to constitutionality, however reasonable, to block the suggested legislation [the Bituminous Coal Conservation Act of 1935].*

> Franklin D. Roosevelt, Letter to Samuel B. Hill [chairman of House Ways and Means Committee], 6 July 1935, in *Public Papers and Addresses of Franklin D. Roosevelt* 4:297, 298 (Samuel I. Rosenman ed. 1938)

38 The line must still be drawn between one welfare and another. . . . The discretion belongs to Congress. . . . Nor is the concept of the general welfare static. Needs that were narrow or parochial a century ago may be interwoven in our day with the well-being of the Nation. What is critical or urgent changes with the times.

> Benjamin N. Cardozo, *Helvering v. Davis*, 301 U.S. 619, 640–41 (1937)

39 That cats destroy some birds, I well know, but I believe this legislation [a bill protecting birds by restraining cats] would further but little the worthy cause to which its proponents give such unselfish effort. The problem of cat versus bird is as old as time. If we attempt to resolve it by legislation who knows but what we may be called upon to take sides as well in the age old problems of dog versus cat, bird versus bird, or even bird versus worm. In my opinion, the State of Illinois and its local governing bodies already have enough to do without trying to control feline delinquency.

> Adlai E. Stevenson, Veto message, 23 Apr. 1949, in *Papers of Adlai E. Stevenson* 3:73–74 (Walter Johnson ed. 1973)

---

* The last paragraph of the foregoing letter to Congressman Hill should, of course, be read as a whole. When it is, it will be seen that the paragraph merely sets forth the traditional rule which the Courts are supposed to follow in determining whether or not a statute is unconstitutional. . . . During the past two years certain newspaper publishers and columnists have quoted only the last sentence of the letter [quoted above], taken completely from its text, so as to give a wholly false impression of the letter. —Franklin D. Roosevelt, Note, *Id.* at 298

40 Legislators are immune from deterrents to the uninhibited discharge of their legislative duty, not for their private indulgence but for the public good. One must not expect uncommon courage even in legislators. The privilege would be of little value if they could be subjected to the cost and inconvenience and distractions of a trial upon a conclusion of the pleader, or to the hazard of a judgment against them based on a jury's speculation as to motives.

> Felix Frankfurter, *Tenney v. Brandhove*, 341 U.S. 367, 377 (1951)

LEGISLATIVE HISTORY

See also LEGISLATIVE INTENT; STATUTES; STATUTORY CONSTRUCTION

1 Great weight has always been attached, and very rightly attached, to contemporaneous exposition.

> John Marshall, *Cohens v. Virginia*, 19 U.S. (6 Wheat.) 264, 418 (1821)

2 It is said that when the meaning of language is plain we are not to resort to evidence in order to raise doubts. That is rather an axiom of experience than a rule of law, and does not preclude consideration of persuasive evidence if it exists.

> Oliver Wendell Holmes, Jr., *Boston Sand & Gravel Co. v. United States*, 278 U.S. 41, 48 (1928)

3 Moreover, it is only the words of the bill that have presidential approval, where that approval is given. It is not to be supposed that, in signing a bill, the President endorses the whole Congressional Record.

> Robert H. Jackson, *Schwegmann Bros. v. Calvert Distillers Corp.*, 341 U.S. 384, 396 (1951) (concurring)

4 There are practical reasons why we should accept whenever possible the meaning which an enactment reveals on its face. Laws are intended for all of our people to live by; and the people go to law offices to learn what their rights under those laws are. Here is a controversy which affects every little merchant in many States. Aside from a few offices in the larger cities, the materials of legislative history are not available to the lawyer who can afford neither the cost of acquisition, the cost of

housing, or the cost of repeatedly examining the whole congressional history. Moreover, if he could, he would not know any way of anticipating what would impress enough members of the Court to be controlling. To accept legislative debates to modify statutory provisions is to make the law inaccessible to a large part of the country.

> **Robert H. Jackson,** *Schwegmann Bros. v. Calvert Distillers Corp.,* 341 U.S. 384, 396–97 (1951) (concurring)

5 I should concur in this result more readily if the Court could reach it by analysis of the statute instead of by psychoanalysis of Congress. When we decide from legislative history, including statements of witnesses at hearings, what Congress probably had in mind, we must put ourselves in the place of a majority of Congressmen and act according to the impression we think this history should have made on them. Never having been a Congressman, I am handicapped in that weird endeavor. That process seems to me not interpretation of a statute but creation of a statute.

> **Robert H. Jackson,** *United States v. Public Utilities Comm'n,* 345 U.S. 295, 319 (1953) (concurring)

6 But this is a case for applying the canon of construction of the wag who said, when the legislative history is doubtful, go to the statute.

> **Felix Frankfurter,** *Greenwood v. United States,* 350 U.S. 366, 374 (1956)

7 Neither due process nor the First Amendment requires legislation to be supported by committee reports, floor debates, or even consideration, but only by a vote.

> **Antonin Scalia,** *Sable Communications v. FCC,* 492 U.S. 115, 133 (1989) (concurring)

LEGISLATIVE INTENT

See also LEGISLATIVE HISTORY; STATUTES;
STATUTORY CONSTRUCTION

1 Where the mind labours to discover the design of the legislature, it seizes everything from which aid can be derived.

> **John Marshall,** *United States v. Fisher,* 6 U.S. (2 Cranch) 358, 386 (1805)

2 The intent of the Legislature is sometimes little more than a useful legal fiction, save as it describes in a general way certain outstanding purposes which no one disputes, but which are frequently of little aid in dealing with the precise points presented in litigation. Moreover, legislative ambiguity may at times not be wholly unintentional. It is not to be forgotten that important legislation sometimes shows the effect of compromises which have been induced by exigencies in its progress, and phrases with a convenient vagueness are referred to the courts for appropriate delimitation, each group interested in the measure claiming that the language adopted embodies its views.

> **Charles Evans Hughes,** Address before the New York State Bar Association, 1 *Massachusetts Law Quarterly,* No. 2, at 13, 15 (1916)

3 The intention of the legislature is undiscoverable in any real sense.... The chances that of several hundred men each will have exactly the same determinate situations in mind as possible reductions of a given determinable, are infinitesimally small.

> **Max Radin,** "Statutory Interpretation," 43 *Harvard Law Review* 863, 870 (1930)

4 The courts in England and America have generally qualified the "golden rule" that intent governs the meaning of a statute, by saying that it must be the intent "as expressed in the statute." In that case, it would obviously be better to use the expression alone, without reference to the intent at all, since if the intent is not in the expression, it is nowhere. If the doctrine means anything, it means that, once the expression is before the court, the intent becomes irrelevant.

> **Max Radin,** "Statutory Interpretation," 43 *Harvard Law Review* 863, 872 (1930)

5 The judgment of the court, if I interpret the reasoning aright, does not rest upon a ruling that Congress would have gone beyond its power if the purpose that it professed was the purpose truly cherished. The judgment of the court rests upon the ruling that another purpose, not professed, may be read beneath the surface, and by the purpose so imputed the statute is destroyed.

Thus the process of psychoanalysis has spread to unaccustomed fields.

Benjamin N. Cardozo, *United States v. Constantine,* 296 U.S. 287, 298–99 (1935) (dissenting)

LIABILITY

See NEGLIGENCE; PRODUCTS LIABILITY; TORTS

LIBEL

1 If any person shall be prosecuted under this act, for the writing or publishing any libel aforesaid, it shall be lawful for the defendant, upon the trial of the cause, to give in evidence in his defence, the truth of the matter contained in the publication charged as a libel. And the jury who shall try the cause, shall have a right to determine the law and the fact, under the direction of the court, as in other cases.

Sedition Act of 1798, ch. 74, § 3, 1 Stat. 596, 597

2 Human reputation is complex in its nature. Because a man has a single vice or even more than a single vice, it does not necessarily follow from that circumstance that he is totally depraved. . . . The man may have vices, and yet his virtues may so predominate over them, that it may truthfully be said that his general reputation is good. He may be an incorrigible liar, and yet strictly honest in all his dealings. He may be a great scoundrel in pecuniary matters, and yet perfectly chaste. . . . Where a person's character for truth and veracity is falsely assailed, and he brings his action against the assailant to recover damages therefor, if his reputation for truth and veracity is good, on what sound principle can it be said that if such plaintiff is unchaste, or dishonest in business matters, or covetous, profane or a sabbath-breaker, the damages to which he would otherwise be entitled shall be reduced perhaps to a sum which is merely nominal?

William P. Lyon, *Wilson v. Noonan,* 27 Wis. 598, 614–15 (1871)

3 Over and over again did the Attorney-General cry out loud, in the agony of his cause, "What is to become of painting if the critics withhold their lash?" As well might he ask what is to become of mathematics under similar circumstances, were they possible. I maintain that two and two the mathematician would continue to make four, in spite of the whine of the amateur for three, or the cry of the critic for five. We are told that Mr. Ruskin has devoted his long life to art, and as a result—is "Slade Professor" at Oxford. In the same sentence, we have thus his position and its worth. It suffices not, Messieurs! a life passed among pictures makes not a painter—else the policeman in the National Gallery might assert himself.

James McNeill Whistler, "Whistler v. Ruskin: Art and Art Critics," 1878, in *The Gentle Art of Making Enemies* 25, 26 (2d ed. 1892)

4 A man cannot justify a libel by proving that he had contracted to libel.

Oliver Wendell Holmes, Jr., *Weston v. Barnicoat,* 175 Mass. 454, 458, 56 N.E. 619 (1900)

5 Where an article is published and circulated among voters for the sole purpose of giving what the defendant believes to be truthful information concerning a candidate for public office and for the purpose of enabling such voters to cast their ballot more intelligently, and the whole thing is done in good faith, and without malice, the article is privileged, although the principal matters contained in the article may be untrue in fact and derogatory to the character of the plaintiff; and in such a case the burden is on the plaintiff to show actual malice in the publication of the article.

Rousseau A. Burch, *Coleman v. MacLennan,* 78 Kan. 711, 712–13, 98 P. 281 (1908) See also LIBEL 11

6 It may be that the action for libel is of little use, but while it is maintained it should be governed by the general principles of tort. If the advertisement obviously would hurt the plaintiff in the estimation of an important and respectable part of the community, liability is not a question of a majority vote.

Oliver Wendell Holmes, Jr., *Peck v. Tribune Co.,* 214 U.S. 185, 189–90 (1909)

7 TECHNICALITY, *n.* In an English court a man named Home was tried for slander in having accused a neighbor of murder. His exact words were: "Sir Thomas Holt hath taken a cleaver and stricken his cook upon

the head, so that one side of the head fell upon one shoulder and the other side upon the other shoulder." The defendant was acquitted by instruction of the court, the learned judges holding that the words did not charge murder, for they did not affirm the death of the cook, that being only an inference.

Ambrose Bierce, *The Devil's Dictionary* 340–41 (1911)

8 Many things that are defamatory may be said with impunity through the medium of speech. Not so, however, when speech is caught upon the wing and transmuted into print. What gives the sting to the writing is its permanence of form. The spoken word dissolves, but the written one abides and "perpetuates the scandal."

Benjamin N. Cardozo, *Ostrowe v. Lee,* 256 N.Y. 36, 39, 175 N.E. 505 (1931)

9 We consider this case against the background of a profound national commitment to the principle that debate on public issues should be uninhibited, robust, and wide-open, and that it may well include vehement, caustic, and sometimes unpleasantly sharp attacks on government and public officials.

William J. Brennan, Jr., *New York Times Co. v. Sullivan,* 376 U.S. 254, 270 (1964)

10 A rule compelling the critic of official conduct to guarantee the truth of all his factual assertions—and to do so on pain of libel judgments virtually unlimited in amount—leads to a comparable "self-censorship." . . . Under such a rule, would-be critics of official conduct may be deterred from voicing their criticism, even though it is believed to be true and even though it is in fact true, because of doubt whether it can be proved in court or fear of the expense of having to do so. . . . The rule thus dampens the vigor and limits the variety of public debate.

William J. Brennan, Jr., *New York Times Co. v. Sullivan,* 376 U.S. 254, 279 (1964)

11 The constitutional guarantees require, we think, a federal rule that prohibits a public official from recovering damages for a defamatory falsehood relating to his official conduct unless he proves that the statement was made with "actual malice"—that is, with knowledge that it was false or with reckless disregard of whether it was false or not.

William J. Brennan, Jr., *New York Times Co. v. Sullivan,* 376 U.S. 254, 279–80 (1964)
See also LIBEL 5

12 Under the First Amendment there is no such thing as a false idea. However pernicious an opinion may seem, we depend for its correction not on the conscience of judges and juries but on the competition of other ideas.

Lewis F. Powell, Jr., *Gertz v. Robert Welch, Inc.,* 418 U.S. 323, 339–40 (1974)

13 The First Amendment requires that we protect some falsehood in order to protect speech that matters.

Lewis F. Powell, Jr., *Gertz v. Robert Welch, Inc.,* 418 U.S. 323, 341 (1974)

14 Truth is a journalist's stock in trade. To invoke the right to deliberately distort what someone else has said is to assert the right to lie in print. To have that assertion made by *The New Yorker,* widely acknowledged as the flagship publication when it comes to truth and accuracy, debases the journalistic profession as a whole. Whatever it might have taken to refute Masson's allegations on the merits is not, in my view, worth the unsettling implications left by defeating him on these grounds. Masson has lost his case, but the defendants, and the profession to which they belong, have lost far more.

Alex Kozinski, *Masson v. The New Yorker Magazine, Inc.,* 881 F.2d 1452, 1486 (9th Cir. 1989) (dissenting)

LIBERTY

See also FREEDOM; RIGHTS

1 I do hereby promise, grant and declare, That the Inhabitants of both Province and Territories, shall separately enjoy all other Liberties, Privileges and Benefits, granted jointly to them in this Charter, any Law, Usage or Custom of this Government heretofore made and practised, or any Law made and passed by this General Assembly, to the Contrary hereof, notwithstanding.

Pennsylvania Charter of Privileges of 1701, in *Federal and State Constitutions* 5:3076, 3080 (Francis N. Thorpe ed. 1909)

2 Liberty is the soul's right to breathe, and, when it cannot take a long breath, laws are girdled too tight.

> Henry Ward Beecher, *Life Thoughts* 70 (1858)

3 "Liberty to all" ... the assertion of that *principle* ... has proved an "apple of gold" to us. The *Union*, and the *Constitution* are the *picture* of *silver*, subsequently framed around it. The picture was made, not to *conceal*, or *destroy* the apple; but to *adorn* and *preserve* it. The *picture* was made *for* the apple—*not* the apple for the picture.

> Abraham Lincoln, "Fragment on the Constitution and the Union," ca. Jan. 1861, in *Collected Works of Abraham Lincoln* 4:169 (Roy P. Basler ed. 1953)

4 We only attain to freedom by a knowledge of, and implicit obedience to, Law. Great— unspeakably great—is the Will! the free Soul of man! At its greatest, understanding and obeying the laws, it can then, and then only, maintain true liberty.... The shallow, as intimated, consider liberty a release from all law, from every constraint. The wise see in it, on the contrary, the potent Law of Laws.

> Walt Whitman, "Freedom," *Notes Left Over*, 1892, in *Walt Whitman: Complete Poetry and Collected Prose* 1050, 1073 (Justin Kaplan ed. 1982)

5 Civil liberties had their origin and must find their ultimate guaranty in the faith of the people. If that faith should be lost, five or nine men in Washington could not long supply its want.

> Robert H. Jackson, *Douglas v. Jeannette*, 319 U.S. 157, 182 (1943) (concurring)

6 I often wonder whether we do not rest our hopes too much upon constitutions, upon laws and upon courts. These are false hopes; believe me, these are false hopes. Liberty lies in the hearts of men and women; when it dies there, no constitution, no law, no court can save it; no constitution, no law, no court can even do much to help it. While it lies there it needs no constitution, no law, no court to save it.

> Learned Hand, "The Spirit of Liberty" (speech), New York, 21 May 1944, in *The Spirit of Liberty* 189, 189–90 (Irving Dilliard ed., 2d ed. 1953)
> See also COURTS 28

7 What then is the spirit of liberty? I cannot define it; I can only tell you my own faith. The spirit of liberty is the spirit which is not too sure that it is right; the spirit of liberty is the spirit which seeks to understand the minds of other men and women; the spirit of liberty is the spirit which weighs their interests alongside its own without bias.

> Learned Hand, "The Spirit of Liberty" (speech), New York, 21 May 1944, in *The Spirit of Liberty* 189, 190 (Irving Dilliard ed., 2d ed. 1953)

8 Liberty is too priceless to be forfeited through the zeal of an administrative agent.

> Frank Murphy, *Oklahoma Press Pub. Co. v. Walling*, 327 U.S. 186, 219 (1946) (dissenting)

9 It is a fair summary of history to say that the safeguards of liberty have frequently been forged in controversies involving not very nice people.

> Felix Frankfurter, *United States v. Rabinowitz*, 339 U.S. 56, 69 (1950) (dissenting)

10 The task of this Court to maintain a balance between liberty and authority is never done, because new conditions today upset the equilibriums of yesterday. The seesaw between freedom and power makes up most of the history of governments, which, as Bryce points out, on a long view consists of repeating a painful cycle from anarchy to tyranny and back again. The Court's day-to-day task is to reject as false, claims in the name of civil liberty which, if granted, would paralyze or impair authority to defend existence of our society, and to reject as false, claims in the name of security which would undermine our freedoms and open the way to oppression. These are the competing considerations involved in judging any measures which government may take to suppress or disadvantage its opponents and critics.

> Robert H. Jackson, *American Communications Ass'n v. Douds*, 339 U.S. 382, 445 (1950)

11 World conditions seem to frustrate the policy of deportation of subversives.... While we would not join in a strained construction of the Constitution to create captious

or trivial obstacles or delays to solution of this problem, we cannot sanction sending aliens to prison except upon compliance with constitutional procedures. We can afford no liberties with liberty itself.

Robert H. Jackson, *United States v. Spector,* 343 U.S. 169, 180 (1952) (dissenting)

12 Liberty is not the mere absence of restraint, it is not a spontaneous product of majority rule, it is not achieved merely by lifting underprivileged classes to power, nor is it the inevitable by-product of technological expansion. It is achieved only by a rule of law.

Robert H. Jackson, *The Supreme Court in the American System of Government* 76 (1955)

13 Liberty is always unfinished business.

Title of 36th Annual Report of the American Civil Liberties Union (1956)

LIBRARIES

See LAW BOOKS; LAW LIBRARIES; LEGAL RESEARCH

LIQUOR

See INTOXICATION

LITIGATION

See also CASES; COURTS; TRIALS

1 In my Travels I once saw a Sign call'd *The Two Men at Law;* One of them was painted on one Side, in a melancholy Posture, all in Rags, with this Scroll, *I have lost my Cause.* The other was drawn capering for Joy, on the other Side, with these Words, *I have gain'd my Suit;* but he was stark naked.

Benjamin Franklin, *Poor Richard's Almanack,* 1742, in *Papers of Benjamin Franklin* 2:339 (Leonard W. Labaree ed. 1960)

2 Then rather let two Neighbors end your Cause,
And split the Difference; tho' you lose one Half;
Than spend the Whole, entangled in the Laws,

While merry Lawyers sly, at both sides laugh.

Benjamin Franklin, *Poor Richard's Almanack,* 1750, in *Papers of Benjamin Franklin* 3:455–56 (Leonard W. Labaree ed. 1961)

3 It will be a pleasure to me to find it so, that I may have no occasion to have recourse to the law, which is so disagreeable a thing to me, that through the whole course of my life I have never entered an action against any man.

Benjamin Franklin, Letter to Rev. M., 30 Mar. 1762, in *Papers of Benjamin Franklin* 10:72 (Leonard W. Labaree ed. 1966)

4 It is for the public interest and policy to make an end to litigation . . . [so] that suits may not be immortal, while men are mortal.

Joseph Story, *Ocean Ins. Co. v. Fields,* 18 F. Cas. 532, 539 (C.C.D. Mass. 1841) (No. 10,406)

5 Discourage litigation. Persuade your neighbors to compromise whenever you can. Point out to them how the nominal winner is often a real loser—in fees, expenses, and waste of time. As a peacemaker the lawyer has a superior opportunity of being a good man. There will still be business enough.

Abraham Lincoln, "Notes for a Law Lecture," 1 July 1850?, in *Collected Works of Abraham Lincoln* 2:81 (Roy P. Basler ed. 1953)

6 Never stir up litigation. A worse man can scarcely be found than one who does this. Who can be more nearly a fiend than he who habitually overhauls the register of deeds in search of defects in titles, whereon to stir up strife, and put money in his pocket? A moral tone ought to be infused into the profession which should drive such men out of it.

Abraham Lincoln, "Notes for a Law Lecture," 1 July 1850?, in *Collected Works of Abraham Lincoln* 2:81–82 (Roy P. Basler ed. 1953)

7 Gentlemen: You have undertaken to cheat me. I will not sue you, for law takes too long. I will ruin you.

Cornelius Vanderbilt, Letter, quoted in Matthew Josephson, *The Robber Barons* 15 (1934)

8 Gentlemen of the Jury: I want to thank you in the first place for your inexhaustible patience. When we started in here the sunny days of October were still with us, and now it is the dead of winter. If we had stayed here a little longer we should have all become antiquities. I know that I have felt, as I sat here, the corroding surface of antiquity stealing over me and I have thought at times that the incrustations we have heard discussed were slowly covering His Honor and yourselves, so that in a short time we would have been worthy of gathering into the Museum.

Joseph H. Choate, Closing argument in *Cesnola* case, 1882, quoted in Edward S. Martin, *Life of Joseph Hodges Choate* 1:349–50 (1927)

9 In the ornithology of litigation this case is a tomtit, furnished with a garb of feathers ample enough for a turkey. Measured by the verdict, its tiny body has only the bulk of twenty-five dollars, but it struts with a display of record expanded into eighty-three pages of manuscript. It seems to us that a more contracted plumage might serve for so small a bird, but perhaps we are mistaken. In every forensic season, we have a considerable flock of such cases, to be stripped and dissected for the cabinets of jurisprudence. We endeavor to pick our overfledged poultry with judicial assiduity and patience.

Logan E. Bleckley, *Lukens v. Ford*, 87 Ga. 541, 542, 13 S.E. 949 (1891)

10 The sporting theory of justice, the "instinct of giving the game fair play," as Professor Wigmore has put it, is so rooted in the profession in America that most of us take it for a fundamental legal tenet. But it is probably only a survival of the days when a lawsuit was a fight between two clans . . . it is peculiar to Anglo-American law. . . . in America we take it as a matter of course that a judge should be a mere umpire. . . . The idea that procedure must of necessity be wholly contentious disfigures our judicial administration at every point. It leads the most conscientious judge to feel that he is merely to decide the contest, as counsel present it, according to the rules of the game, not to search independently for truth and justice. . . . It creates vested rights in errors of procedure, of the benefit whereof parties are not to be deprived. The inquiry is not, What do substantive law and justice require? Instead, the inquiry is, Have the rules of the game been carried out strictly? . . . put back the offending team five or ten or fifteen yards.

Roscoe Pound, "The Causes of Popular Dissatisfaction with the Administration of Justice," 29 *American Bar Association Report* 395, 404-06 (1906)
See also EVIDENCE 6

11 COURT FOOL, *n.* The plaintiff.

Ambrose Bierce, *The Devil's Dictionary* 57 (1911)

12 FORMA PAUPERIS (Latin). In the character of a poor person—a method by which a litigant without money for lawyers is considerately permitted to lose his case.

Ambrose Bierce, *The Devil's Dictionary* 106 (1911)

13 LITIGANT, *n.* A person about to give up his skin for the hope of retaining his bones.

Ambrose Bierce, *The Devil's Dictionary* 194 (1911)

14 LITIGATION, *n.* A machine which you go into as a pig and come out of as a sausage.

Ambrose Bierce, *The Devil's Dictionary* 194 (1911)

15 Most of us live our lives in conscious submission to rules of law, yet without necessity of resort to the courts to ascertain our rights and duties. Lawsuits are rare and catastrophic experiences for the vast majority of men, and even when the catastrophe ensues, the controversy relates most often not to the law, but to the facts. In countless litigations, the law is so clear that judges have no discretion. They have the right to legislate within gaps, but often there are no gaps. We shall have a false view of the landscape if we look at the waste spaces only, and refuse to see the acres already sown and fruitful.

Benjamin N. Cardozo, *The Nature of the Judicial Process* 128–29 (1921)

16 No rules in the end will help us. We shall succeed in making our results conform with our professions only by a change of heart in ourselves. It is hard to expect lawyers who are half litigants to forego the advantages which come from obscuring the case and supporting contentions which

they know to be false.... It is important nevertheless that we should realize the price we pay for it, the atmosphere of contention over trifles, the unwillingness to concede what ought to be conceded, and to proceed to the things which matter. Courts have fallen out of repute; many of you avoid them whenever you can, and rightly. About trials hang a suspicion of trickery and a sense of a result depending upon cajolery or worse. I wish I could say that it was all unmerited.

> Learned Hand, "The Deficiencies of Trials to Reach the Heart of the Matter," 1921, in *Lectures on Legal Topics* 3:89, 104-05 (1926)

17 I must say that as a litigant I should dread a lawsuit beyond almost anything else short of sickness and death.

> Learned Hand, "The Deficiencies of Trials to Reach the Heart of the Matter," 1921, in *Lectures on Legal Topics* 3:89, 105 (1926)

18 American law and procedure have taken shape under the hand of legislatures and courts which have habitually and as a matter of course been made up of investors and lawyers, with no control from outside these classes; and the upshot of it has been an arrangement such as to serve the convenience and profit of these two classes of persons,—such as to increase the cost, volume, uncertainty and intricacy of litigation.

> Thorstein Veblen, *Absentee Ownership and Business Enterprise in Recent Times* 12 (1923)

19 To seek the redress of grievances by going to law, is like sheep running for shelter to a bramble bush.

> Lewis W. Dilwyn, quoted in Tryon Edwards, *Useful Quotations* 325 (1936)

20 Litigation is the pursuit of practical ends, not a game of chess.

> Felix Frankfurter, *Indianapolis v. Chase Nat'l Bank*, 314 U.S. 63, 69 (1941)

21 *This is government by lawsuit.* These constitutional lawsuits are the stuff of power politics in America.

> Robert H. Jackson, *The Struggle for Judicial Supremacy* 287 (1941)

22 The vice of the litigation process in broad constitutional questions is that since we cannot expand the lawsuit process to include an era, a people, and a continent, we simply cut down the problem to the scope of a lawsuit.

> Robert H. Jackson, *The Struggle for Judicial Supremacy* 299 (1941)

23 It could not be said to have taken many minutes; but when you heard them waste time and waste more time complaining about whether they were wasting time or not, what could you say, except that the law was an ass? They acted as though all eternity were at their disposal. If it did not get through this afternoon, there was always tomorrow, and the next day; and next week, and for that matter, next month, and even next year.

> James Gould Cozzens, *The Just and the Unjust* 323 (1942)

24 I want, therefore, to stress the fact that litigation in our courts is still a fight. The fighting, to be sure, occurs in a court-room, and is supervised by a government officer known as a judge. Yet, for the most part, a law-suit remains a sort of sublimated, regulated brawl, a private battle conducted in a court-house.

> Jerome N. Frank, *Courts on Trial* 7 (1949)

25 Sue me!*

> Catch-phrase

26 It is not to be overlooked that the ends of human dignity are often served by encouraging litigation. In cultures where non-elite elements have long been intimidated from asserting their just claims, a new era of public order is signalized by an upsurge of formal complaint and adjudication.

> Myres S. McDougal, Harold D. Lasswell, and Ivan A. Vlasic, *Law and Public Order in Space* 1071 (1963)

27 Sue the Bastards!

> Victor J. Yannacone, Jr. Speech, East Lansing, Mich., 22 Apr. 1970, quoted in *A Dictionary of Environmental Quotations* 27 (Barbara K. Rodes & Rice Odell eds. 1992)

---

* According to Eric Partridge, *A Dictionary of Catch Phrases* 286 (Paul Beale ed., rev. ed. 1986), this was originally "(c. 1930) chiefly New York City, but from 1950s some general U.S. use, propelled by the song of that title sung by 'Nathan Detroit' in the musical comedy, later film, *Guys and Dolls*, one of Frank Loesser's masterpieces."

28 This is often how you meet your first lawyers, a section of the population who charge only what they hope the traffic can bear. Which is a lot. They are employed by people who desperately don't want to roll up their sleeves and have a fair fight. So get ready for plenty of turpitude and plan for the long haul. It takes time and money to sue you. Before final judgments are handed down your opponent may be crazy, bankrupt, or dead. If you spot a lawyer's letter without opening it and can return it marked deceased, this is a trump card.

J. P. Donleavy, *The Unexpurgated Code* 222 (1975)

29 For no good cause shown each side will be entitled to three (3) time outs between now and the date of trial. A time out is defined as a one week period in which no discovery can be served, all deadlines are postponed and counsel can generally goof off.

1. The procedure for calling a time out will be as follows: Both plaintiffs and defendants will designate one individual as the official time out persons (hereinafter referred to as the "Designated Whistler"). The designated whistler will be issued a whistle from the case liaison logistics committee which will be strung around his, her, or its neck. When a time out is desired, the designated whistler will go to the offices of opposing lead counsel . . . and blow the whistle three (3) times. Thereafter there will be a one (1) week time out.

Edward R. Becker, *Zenith Radio Corp. v. Matsushita Electric Industrial Co.,* 478 F. Supp. 889, 959–60 (E.D. Pa. 1979)

30 Until the day when our institutions can be trusted to serve us as fiduciaries and when we can be educated to understand the limitations of the world we have constructed, litigation will remain the hallmark of a free and just society.

Jethro K. Lieberman, *The Litigious Society* 190 (1981)

31 Contrary to popular belief, it is not clear that we are a madly litigious society. It is true that we have experienced a rapid growth in the number of complaints filed in our courts. But filings are often only a prelude to some kind of voluntary settlement. The number of disputes *actually litigated* in the United States does not appear to be rising much faster than the population as a whole. Our courts may *seem* crowded, since we have relatively few judges compared with many industrial nations. Nevertheless, our volume of litigated cases is not demonstrably larger in relation to our total population than that of other Western nations.

Derek C. Bok, "A Flawed System," *Harvard Magazine,* May-June 1983, at 38, 40

32 It strikes me that litigation has survived in a world of computers like a Toonerville trolley on the track of a Metroliner. Yet its very survival has made it curiously revered. The tricks and winks and chuckles of the courtroom technique, the voice of thunder, the sly insinuations, the throat clearings, the whispered conferences, the whole hammy vaudeville adored by judge and jury—and by television audiences—has become too sacred to be touched, has even in some crazy way taken the place of our empty churches as the shrine of the oldest American virtue.

Louis Auchincloss, *Diary of a Yuppie* 8 (1986)

LYING

See LAWYER JOKES; LAWYERS (CON)

LYNCHING

See LAWLESSNESS

MARRIAGE

See also DIVORCE

1 Of the unjust rights which, in virtue of this ceremony, an iniquitous law tacitly gives me over the person and property of another, I cannot legally, but I can morally divest myself. And I hereby distinctly and emphatically declare, that I consider myself, and earnestly desire to be considered by others, as utterly divested, now and during the rest of my life, of any such rights; the barbarous relics of a feudal and despotic system, soon destined . . . to be wholly swept away.

Robert Dale Owen, Contract of marriage to Mary Jane Robinson, 1832, in Richard W. Leopold, *Robert Dale Owen: A Biography* 111 (1940)

2 The barbarous custom of wresting from a woman whatever she possesses, whether by inheritance, donation, or her own industry, and conferring it all upon the man she marries, to be used at his discretion and will, perhaps wasted on his wicked indulgences, without allowing her any control or redress, is such a monstrous perversion of *justice* by *law*, that we might well marvel how it could obtain in a Christian community.

Sarah Josepha Hale, "Rights of Married Women," *Godey's Lady's Book*, May 1837, at 212, 212

3 § 1. The real and personal property of any female who may hereafter marry, and which she shall own at the time of marriage, and the rents issues and profits thereof shall not be subject to the disposal of her husband, nor be liable for his debts, and shall continue her sole and separate property, as if she were a single female.

§ 2. The real and personal property, and the rents issues and profits thereof of any female now married shall not be subject to the disposal of her husband; but shall be her sole and separate property as if she were a single female except so far as the same may be liable for the debts of her husband heretofore contracted.

§ 3. It shall be lawful for any married female to receive, by gift, grant devise or bequest, from any person other than her husband and hold to her sole and separate use, as if she were a single female, real and personal property, and the rents, issues and profits thereof, and the same shall not be subject to the disposal of her husband, nor be liable for his debts.

Act of Apr. 7, 1848, ch. 200, 1848 N.Y. Laws 307, 307-08

4 While acknowledging our mutual affection by publicly assuming the relationship of husband and wife, . . . we deem it a duty to declare that this act on our part implies no sanction of, nor promise of voluntary obedience to such of the present laws of marriage, as refuse to recognize the wife as an independent, rational being, while they confer upon the husband an injurious and unnatural superiority.

Lucy Stone and Henry B. Blackwell, Statement read at marriage, 1855, in *Loving Warriors* 135 (Leslie Wheeler ed. 1981)

5 We believe that personal independence and equal human rights can never be forfeited, except for crime; that marriage should be equal and permanent partnership, and so recognized by law; that until it is so recognized, married partners should provide against the radical injustice of present laws, by every means in their power.

Lucy Stone and Henry B. Blackwell, Statement read at marriage, 1855, in *Loving Warriors* 136 (Leslie Wheeler ed. 1981)

6 The presumption of marriage, from a cohabitation, apparently matrimonial, is one of the strongest presumptions known to the law. This is especially true in a case involving legitimacy. The law presumes morality, and not immorality; marriage, and not concubinage; legitimacy, and not bastardy. Where there is enough to create a foundation for the presumption of marriage, it can be repelled only by the most cogent and satisfactory evidence.

Charles Andrews, *Hynes v. McDermott*, 91 N.Y. 451, 459 (1883)

7 *Captain Jeffrey Spaulding* [played by Groucho Marx]: Are we all going to get married?
Mrs. Rittenhouse [played by Margaret Irving]: All of us?
Spaulding : All of us!
Rittenhouse : But that's bigamy!
Spaulding : Yes, and it's bigamy, too.*

Morrie Ryskind and Pierre Collings, *Animal Crackers* (screenplay), 1930, quoted in Groucho Marx, *The Groucho/phile* 81 (1976)

8 If there is one thing that the people are entitled to expect from their lawmakers, it is rules of law that will enable individuals to tell whether they are married and, if so to whom.

Robert H. Jackson, *Estin v. Estin*, 334 U.S. 541, 553 (1948) (dissenting)

9 Adultery, homosexuality and the like are sexual intimacies which the State forbids . . . but the intimacy of husband and wife is necessarily an essential and accepted feature of the institution of marriage, an institution which the State not only must allow, but which always and in every age

---

* These lines first appeared in the Marx Brothers' play, *I'll Say She Is!* (1923).

it has fostered and protected. It is one thing when the State exerts its power either to forbid extra-marital sexuality . . . , or to say who may marry, but it is quite another when, having acknowledged a marriage and the intimacies inherent in it, it undertakes to regulate by means of the criminal law the details of that intimacy.

> **John M. Harlan** (1899–1971), *Poe v. Ullman*, 367 U.S. 497, 553 (1961) (dissenting)

10 We deal with a right of privacy older than the Bill of Rights—older than our political parties, older than our school system. Marriage is a coming together for better or for worse, hopefully enduring, and intimate to the degree of being sacred. It is an association that promotes a way of life, not causes; a harmony in living, not political faiths; a bilateral loyalty, not commercial or social projects. Yet it is an association for as noble a purpose as any involved in our prior decisions.

> **William O. Douglas**, *Griswold v. Connecticut*, 381 U.S. 479, 486 (1965)

11 The freedom to marry has long been recognized as one of the vital personal rights essential to the orderly pursuit of happiness by free men.

> **Earl Warren**, *Loving v. Virginia*, 388 U.S. 1, 12 (1967)

MARSHALL, JOHN

1 His [John Marshall's] twistifications in the case of Marbury, in that of Burr, and the late Yazoo case shew how dexterously he can reconcile law to his personal biasses.

> **Thomas Jefferson**, Letter to James Madison, 25 May 1810, in *Writings of Thomas Jefferson* 9:276 (Paul L. Ford ed. 1898)

2 They [the judiciary] skulk from responsibility to public opinion, the only remaining hold on them, under a practice first introduced in England by Lord Mansfield. An opinion is huddled up in conclave, perhaps by a majority of one, delivered as if unanimous, and with the silent acquiescence of lazy or timid associates, by a crafty chief judge, who sophisticates the law to his mind, by the turn of his own reasoning.

> **Thomas Jefferson**, Letter to Thomas Ritchie, 25 Dec. 1820, in *Writings of Thomas Jefferson* 10:171 (Paul L. Ford ed. 1899)

3 My gift of John Marshall to the people of the United States was the proudest act of my life.

> **John Adams**, quoted in Charles Warren, *The Supreme Court in United States History* 1:178 (1922)

4 [My greatest satisfaction is that the Supreme Court has] never sought to enlarge the judicial power beyond its proper bounds, nor feared to carry it to the fullest extent that duty required.

> **John Marshall**, Letter to the Philadelphia Bar, 1831, quoted in Albert J. Beveridge, *Life of John Marshall* 4:522 (1919)

5 Now Story, that is the law; you find the precedents for it.

> **John Marshall**, attributed in Edward S. Corwin, *John Marshall and the Constitution* 116 (1919)

6 The acme of judicial distinction means the ability to look a lawyer straight in the eyes for two hours and not hear a damned word he says.

> **John Marshall**, quoted in Albert J. Beveridge, *Life of John Marshall* 4:83 (1919)

7 He boasted of the fact that he never took wine except in wet weather; but as he was as liberal in his definition of the weather as he was in his interpretation of the Constitution, if the sun shone in Washington, he used to say that the country was so large that the chances were all the greater that it must be raining somewhere within the jurisdiction of his court. The consequence was that the Chief Justice always lived in a moist climate.

> **John Marshall**, reported in Henry B. Brown, Oration on John Marshall, 4 Feb. 1901, in *John Marshall: Life, Character and Judicial Services* 2:58 (John F. Dillon ed. 1903)

8 When I examine a question, I go from headland to headland, from case to case; Marshall has a compass, puts out to sea, and goes directly to his result.

> **Joseph Story**, quoted in "John Marshall," 1 *American Law Review* 432, 436 (1867)

9 There fell to Marshall perhaps the greatest place that ever was filled by a judge; but when I consider his might, his justice, and his wisdom, I do fully believe that if American law were to be represented by a single

figure, sceptic and worshipper alike would agree without dispute that the figure could be one alone, and that one, John Marshall.

> **Oliver Wendell Holmes, Jr.**, "John Marshall" (speech), Boston, 4 Feb. 1901, in *Collected Legal Papers* 266, 270 (1920)

10 The flag is but a bunting to one who insists on prose. Yet, thanks to Marshall and to the men of his generation—and for this above all we celebrate him and them—its red is our lifeblood, its stars our world, its blue our heaven. It owns our land. At will it throws away our lives.

> **Oliver Wendell Holmes, Jr.**, "John Marshall" (speech), Boston, 4 Feb. 1901, in *Collected Legal Papers* 266, 271 (1920)

11 Lacking, perforce, any solid basis in precedent, vulnerable in theory and in logic, its central core of reasoning reversed within a week by another Court decision, Marbury v. Madison may seem scarcely worthy of the plaudits that have been heaped on it or the deference that has been paid it in the intervening century and a half. But both the plaudits and the deference, like the decision itself, and like every significant Supreme Court decision since, were and are rooted in politics, not in law. This only the ignorant would deny and only the naive deplore.

> **Fred Rodell**, *Nine Men* 90 (1955)

MEDICAL JURISPRUDENCE

1 Every human being of adult years and sound mind has a right to determine what shall be done with his own body.

> **Benjamin N. Cardozo**, *Schloendorff v. Society of New York Hosp.*, 211 N.Y. 125, 129, 105 N.E. 92 (1914)

2 The final, and compelling, reason for granting the emergency writ was that a life hung in the balance. There was no time for research and reflection. Death could have mooted the cause in a matter of minutes, if action were not taken to preserve the *status quo*. To refuse to act, only to find later that the law required action, was a risk I was unwilling to accept. I determined to act on the side of life.

> **J. Skelly Wright**, *In re President & Directors of Georgetown College*, 331 F.2d 1000, 1009–10 (D.C. Cir. 1964)

3 The State's interest *contra* weakens and the individual's [patient's] right to privacy grows as the degree of bodily invasion increases and the prognosis dims. Ultimately there comes a point at which the individual's rights overcome the State interest.

> **Richard J. Hughes**, *In re Quinlan*, 70 N.J. 10, 41, 355 A.2d 647 (1976)

MENTAL ILLNESS

See INSANITY

MERCY

See CAPITAL PUNISHMENT; SENTENCING

MILITARY JUSTICE

See also WAR; WAR CRIMES

1 Every Officer, be his rank what it may, who shall betray his Country, dishonour the Army and his General, by basely keeping back and shrinking from his duty in any engagement; shall be held up as an infamous Coward and punished as such, with the utmost martial severity; and no Connections, Interest, or Intercessions in his behalf will avail to prevent the strict execution of justice.

> **George Washington**, General Orders, 7 July 1775, in *Papers of George Washington, Revolutionary War Series* 1:72 (W. W. Abbot ed. 1985)

2 Another guarantee of freedom was broken when Milligan was denied a trial by jury. The great minds of the country have differed on the correct interpretation to be given to various provisions of the Federal Constitution; and judicial decision has been often invoked to settle their true meaning; but until recently no one ever doubted that the right of trial by jury was fortified in the organic law against the power of attack. It is now assailed; but if ideas can be expressed in words, and language has any meaning, this right—one of the most valuable in a free country—is preserved to every one accused of crime who is not attached to the army, or navy, or militia in actual service.

> **David Davis**, *Ex parte Milligan*, 71 U.S. (4 Wall.) 2, 123 (1867)

3 For suppose condemnation to follow these present proceedings. Would it be so much we ourselves that would condemn as it would be martial law operating through us? For that law and the rigor of it, we are not responsible. Our vowed responsibility is in this: That however pitilessly that law may operate in any instances, we nevertheless adhere to it and administer it.

Herman Melville, *Billy Budd, Sailor* 110–11 (Harrison Hayford & Merton M. Sealts, Jr. eds. 1962) (1924)

4 "... But surely Budd proposed neither mutiny nor homicide."

"Surely not, my good man. And before a court less arbitrary and more merciful than a martial one, that plea would largely extenuate. At the Last Assizes it shall acquit. But how here? We proceed under the law of the Mutiny Act. ... War looks but to the frontage, the appearance. And the Mutiny Act, War's child, takes after the father. Budd's intent or non-intent is nothing to the purpose."

Herman Melville, *Billy Budd, Sailor* 111–12 (Harrison Hayford & Merton M. Sealts, Jr. eds. 1962) (1924)

5 *Roger Byam* [played by Franchot Tone, speaking at court-martial of mutineer]: I don't speak here for myself alone, nor for these men you've condemned. I speak in their names, in Fletcher Christian's name, for all men at sea. These men don't ask for comfort, they don't ask for safety! If they could speak to you they'd say: Let us choose to do our duty willingly, not the choice of a slave, but the choice of free English men. They ask only freedom that England expects for every man. Oh, if one man among you believed that. One man! He could command the fleets of England, he could sweep the seas for England. If he called his men to duty, not by flaying their backs, but by lifting their hearts!

Talbot Jennings, Jules Furthman, and Carey Wilson, *Mutiny on the Bounty* (screenplay), 1935, quoted in *Actor's Book of Movie Monologues* 12 (Marisa Smith & Amy Schewel eds. 1986)

6 One of the great defects in our military establishment is the giving of weak sentences for military offenses. The purpose of military law is administrative rather than legal. ... in justice to other men, soldiers who go to sleep on post, who go absent for an unreasonable time during combat, who shirk in battle, should be executed; and ... Army Commanders or Corps Commanders should have the authority to approve the death sentence. It is utterly stupid to say that General Officers, as a result of whose orders thousands of gallant and brave men have been killed, are not capable of knowing how to remove the life of one miserable poltroon.

George S. Patton, Jr., *War As I Knew It* 362 (1947)

7 I better tell you one more thing. I'd rather be prosecuting you than defending you. I don't know yet just how guilty you are. But you're either a mutineer or one of the dumbest goofs in the whole Navy. There's no third possibility.

Herman Wouk, *The Caine Mutiny* 356 (1951)

8 The contrast between Challee's manner and Greenwald's could not have been sharper. The pilot was soft, apologetic, hesitant after the judge advocate's passionate shouting. He kept looking from Blakely to Challee. He started by mentioning that he had undertaken Maryk's defense reluctantly at the judge advocate's request. "I was reluctant," he said, "because I knew that the only possible defense of the accused was to show in court the mental incompetence of an officer of the Navy. It has been the most unpleasant duty I've ever had to perform. Let me make one thing clear. It is not and never has been the contention of the defense that Commander Queeg is a coward. The entire case of the defense rests on the opposite assumption: that no man who rises to command of a United States naval ship can possibly be a coward. And that therefore if he commits questionable acts under fire the explanation must lie elsewhere.

Herman Wouk, *The Caine Mutiny* 437 (1951)

9 I [Navy defense attorney Barney Greenwald] defended [accused mutineer Steve Maryk] because I found out the wrong guy was on trial. Only way I could defend him was to sink Queeg for you. I'm sore that I was pushed into that spot, and ashamed of what I did.

Herman Wouk, *The Caine Mutiny* 448 (1951)

10 Judges are not given the task of running the Army. The responsibility for setting up the channels through which such grievances can be considered and fairly settled rests upon the Congress and upon the President of the United States and his subordinates. The military constitutes a specialized community governed by a separate discipline from that of the civilian. Orderly government requires that the judiciary be as scrupulous not to interfere with legitimate Army matters as the Army must be scrupulous not to interfere in judicial matters.

Robert H. Jackson, *Orloff v. Willoughby,* 345 U.S. 83, 93–94 (1953)

11 *Billy Mitchell* [played by Gary Cooper]: I've been wearing the uniform of the United States Army most of my adult life. And I've worn it with pride. But, if being a good soldier is your kind of good soldier, of being unable to think for himself and say what he thinks, of being narrow and blind and insensible to a higher duty, you can have the uniform and all that goes with it.

Milton Sperling and Emmet Lavery, *The Court Martial of Billy Mitchell* (screenplay) (1955)

12 I fired him [General Douglas MacArthur] because he wouldn't respect the authority of the President. That's the answer to that. I didn't fire him because he was a dumb son of a bitch, although he was, but that's not against the law for generals. If it was, half to three-quarters of them would be in jail.

Harry S. Truman, quoted in Merle Miller, *Plain Speaking: An Oral Biography of Harry S. Truman* 287 (1974)

13 The First Amendment does not evaporate with the mere intonation of interests such as national defense, military necessity, or domestic security. . . . In all cases where such interests have been advanced, the inquiry has been whether the exercise of First Amendment rights necessarily must be circumscribed in order to secure those interests.

William J. Brennan, Jr., *Greer v. Spock,* 424 U.S. 828, 852–53 (1976) (dissenting)

MONEY

See FEES; WEALTH AND POVERTY

MORALITY

See also ETHICS; JUSTICE; LAW

1 Tastes cannot be controuled by law.

Thomas Jefferson, "Notes on Coinage," 1784, in *Papers of Thomas Jefferson* 7:180 (Julian P. Boyd ed. 1953)

2 While the law does . . . measure legal liability by moral standards, it nevertheless, by the very necessity of its nature, is continually transmuting those moral standards into external or objective ones, from which the actual guilt of the party concerned is wholly eliminated.

Oliver Wendell Holmes, Jr., *The Common Law* 38 (1881)

3 A man may have as bad a heart as he chooses, if his conduct is within the rules.

Oliver Wendell Holmes, Jr., *The Common Law* 110 (1881)

4 Ethical considerations can no more be excluded from the administration of justice, which is the end and purpose of all civil laws, than one can exclude the vital air from his room and live.

John F. Dillon, *The Laws and Jurisprudence of England and America* 17 (1895)

5 You can see very plainly that a bad man has as much reason as a good one for wishing to avoid an encounter with the public force, and therefore you can see the practical importance of the distinction between morality and law. A man who cares nothing for an ethical rule which is believed and practised by his neighbors is likely nevertheless to care a good deal to avoid being made to pay money, and will want to keep out of jail if he can.

Oliver Wendell Holmes, Jr., "The Path of the Law," 10 *Harvard Law Review* 457, 459 (1897)

6 The law is the witness and external deposit of our moral life. Its history is the history of the moral development of the race.

Oliver Wendell Holmes, Jr., "The Path of the Law," 10 *Harvard Law Review* 457, 459 (1897)

7 If you want to know the law and nothing else, you must look at it as a bad man, who cares only for the material consequences

which such knowledge enables him to predict, not as a good one, who finds his reasons for conduct, whether inside the law or outside of it, in the vaguer sanctions of conscience.

Oliver Wendell Holmes, Jr., "The Path of the Law," 10 *Harvard Law Review* 457, 459 (1897)

8 Nothing but confusion of thought can result from assuming that the rights of man in a moral sense are equally rights in the sense of the Constitution and the law.

Oliver Wendell Holmes, Jr., "The Path of the Law," 10 *Harvard Law Review* 457, 460 (1897)

9 For my own part, I often doubt whether it would not be a gain if every word of moral significance could be banished from the law altogether, and other words adopted which should convey legal ideas uncolored by anything outside the law.

Oliver Wendell Holmes, Jr., "The Path of the Law," 10 *Harvard Law Review* 457, 464 (1897)

10 You cannot legislate virtue into any people. There is no man ever any better than he wants to be.

Elbert Hubbard, *Contemplations* 65 (1902)

11 The worst of tyrannies is moral tyranny. Smoking may be bad, but it is not so bad as prohibiting smoking by law. Commendable as it may be for people to go to church, eat with a fork, and shave off their whiskers, we don't want laws to compel these things.

Frank Crane, "The Smoker," in *Four Minute Essays* 8:125, 127 (1919)

12 The shelves of our law libraries are packed to suffocation and moldering to decay with laws ethically intended to govern things which man has never yet been able to govern entirely and probably never will be, although the instinct so to legislate probably conforms to the mechanistic instinct for balance and proportion in all things.

Theodore Dreiser, *Hey Rub-a-Dub-Dub* 162–63 (1920)

13 Man, or at least a part of him, a fragment of the chemical whole of which he is a part or an expression, wishes and writes laws to confirm these, but in spite of all so-called

spiritual instruction, an ordered scheme of spiritual rewards and punishments, he is still not chemically able to accommodate himself to these things—not all of him, at least. Nature, his sheer, rank human nature, which sinks deep below into mechanistic, chemical and physical laws and substances, will not let him.

Theodore Dreiser, *Hey Rub-A-Dub-Dub* 163 (1920)

14 Puritan legislation, especially in the field of public law, is a thing of many grandiose pretensions and a few simple and ignoble realities. The Puritan, discussing it voluptuously, always tries to convince himself (and the rest of us) that it is grounded upon altruistic and evangelical motives—that its aim is to work the other fellow's benefit against the other fellow's will. Such is the theory behind Prohibition, comstockery, vice crusading and all its other familiar devices of oppression. That theory, of course, is false. The Puritan's actual motives are (a) to punish the other fellow for having a better time in the world, and (b) to bring the other fellow down to his own unhappy level.

H. L. Mencken, *Notes on Democracy* 155 (1926)

15 Law accepts as the pattern of its justice the morality of the community whose conduct it assumes to regulate.

Benjamin N. Cardozo, *The Paradoxes of Legal Science* 37 (1928)

16 There are certain things that we can accomplish by law and there are certain things that we cannot accomplish by law or by any process of government. We cannot legislate intelligence. We cannot legislate morality. No, and we cannot legislate loyalty, for loyalty is a kind of morality. We cannot produce these things by decrees or commissions or public inquisitions.

A. Whitney Griswold, *Essays on Education* 139 (1954)

17 It may be true that morality cannot be legislated, but behavior can be regulated. It may be true that the law cannot make a man love me, but it can keep him from lynching me, and I think that's pretty important.

Martin Luther King, Jr., Address at Cornell College, Mount Vernon, Iowa, quoted in *Wall Street Journal*, 13 Nov. 1962, at 18

18 Morality cannot be legislated, but behavior can be regulated. Judicial decrees may not change the heart, but they can restrain the heartless.

> **Martin Luther King, Jr.,** *Strength to Love* 22 (1963)

19 The highest morality almost always is the morality of process.

> **Alexander M. Bickel,** *The Morality of Consent* 123 (1975)

20 All I can say is this: it looks as if we are all we have. . . . Only if ethics were something unspeakable by us, could law be unnatural, and therefore unchallengeable. As things now stand, everything is up for grabs.
> Nevertheless:
> Napalming babies is bad.
> Starving the poor is wicked.
> Buying and selling each other is depraved.
> Those who stood up to and died resisting Hitler, Stalin, Amin, and Pol Pot—and General Custer too—have earned salvation.
> Those who acquiesced deserve to be damned.
> There is in the world such a thing as evil. [All together now:] Sez who? God help us.

> **Arthur A. Leff,** "Unspeakable Ethics, Unnatural Law," 1979 *Duke Law Journal* 1229, 1249

21 The law . . . is constantly based on notions of morality, and if all laws representing essentially moral choices are to be invalidated under the Due Process Clause, the courts will be very busy indeed.

> **Byron R. White,** *Bowers v. Hardwick,* 478 U.S. 186, 196 (1986)

22 *Alan Dershowitz* [played by Ron Silver, speaking as attorney to his client Claus von Bülow, played by Jeremy Irons, after von Bülow's appeal has succeeded]: One thing, Claus. Legally, this was an important victory. Morally, you're on your own.

> **Nicholas Kazan,** *Reversal of Fortune* (screenplay) (1991)

MOVIES

See COURTROOM SCENES

MURDER

---

1 Every unpunished murder takes away something from the security of every man's life.

> **Daniel Webster,** Summation in murder trial of John Francis Knapp, 3 Aug. 1830, in *Writings and Speeches of Daniel Webster* 11:59 (J. W. McIntyre ed. 1903)

2 If, then, the persons in and about Brown Street were the plotters and executers of the murder of Captain White, we know who they were, and you know that *there* is one of them. This fearful concatenation of circumstances puts him to an account.

> **Daniel Webster,** Summation in murder trial of John Francis Knapp, 3 Aug. 1830, in *Writings and Speeches of Daniel Webster* 11:88 (J. W. McIntyre ed. 1903)

3 The clerk then read the indictment, which was in the usual form. It charged Laura Hawkins, in effect, with the premeditated murder of George Selby, by shooting him with a pistol, with a revolver, shotgun, rifle, repeater, breech-loader, cannon, six-shooter, with a gun, or some other weapon; with killing him with a slung-shot, a bludgeon, carving-knife, bowie-knife, penknife, rolling-pin, carhook, dagger, hairpin, with a hammer, with a screwdriver, with a nail, and with all other weapons and utensils whatsoever, at the Southern Hotel and in all other hotels and places wheresoever, on the thirteenth day of March and all other days of the Christian era whensoever.

> **Mark Twain and Charles Dudley Warner,** *The Gilded Age,* 1873, in *Writings of Mark Twain* 6:227 (1929)

4 HOMICIDE, *n.* The slaying of one human being by another. There are four kinds of homicide: felonious, excusable, justifiable and praiseworthy, but it makes no great difference to the person slain whether he fell by one kind or another—the classification is for advantage of the lawyers.

> **Ambrose Bierce,** *The Devil's Dictionary* 139–40 (1911)

5 Everybody is a potential murderer. I've never killed any one, but I frequently get satisfaction reading the obituary notices.

> **Clarence S. Darrow,** Interview, Chicago, quoted in *New York Times Magazine,* 18 Apr. 1937, at 31

6 Just as murder itself is one of the most elemental and primitive of crimes, so also the law of murder is, for all the torrent of words written about it, still pretty elemental and primitive in its basic concepts. The human tribe learned early that indiscriminate killing was not only poor for tribal decorum and well-being but threatened its very survival and was therefore bad in itself. So murder became taboo.

Robert Traver, *Anatomy of a Murder* 38 (1958)

NATURAL LAW

See also JUSTICE; LAW; RELIGION

1 Now all acts of legislature apparently contrary to natural right and justice, are, in our laws, and must be in the nature of things, considered as void. The laws of nature are the laws of God; whose authority can be superseded by no power on earth. A legislature must not obstruct our obedience to him from whose punishments they cannot protect us. All human constitutions which contradict his laws, we are in conscience bound to disobey.

George Mason, Argument for plaintiffs, *Robin v. Hardaway,* Jefferson's Virginia Reports 109, 114 (1772)

2 Good and wise men ... have supposed, that the deity, from the relations, we stand in, to himself and to each other, has constituted an eternal and immutable law, which is, indispensibly, obligatory upon all mankind, prior to any human institution whatever.

Alexander Hamilton, "The Farmer Refuted," 1775, in *Papers of Alexander Hamilton* 1:81, 87 (Harold C. Syrett ed. 1961)

3 When the first principles of civil society are violated, and the rights of a whole people are invaded, the common forms of municipal law are not to be regarded. Men may then betake themselves to the law of nature; and, if they but conform their actions, to that standard, all cavils against them, betray either ignorance or dishonesty. There are some events in society, to which human laws cannot extend; but when applied to them lose all their force and efficacy. In short, when human laws contradict or dis-

countenance the means, which are necessary to preserve the essential rights of any society, they defeat the proper end of all laws, and so become null and void.

Alexander Hamilton, "The Farmer Refuted," 1775, in *Papers of Alexander Hamilton* 1:81, 136 (Harold C. Syrett ed. 1961)

4 There are certain *vital* principles in our *free Republican governments,* which will determine and over-rule an *apparent and flagrant* abuse of *legislative* power.

Samuel Chase, *Calder v. Bull,* 3 U.S. (3 Dall.) 386, 388 (1798)

5 An Act of the Legislature (for I cannot call it a *law,*) contrary to the *great first principles* of the *social compact,* cannot be considered a *rightful exercise* of *legislative* authority.

Samuel Chase, *Calder v. Bull,* 3 U.S. (3 Dall.) 386, 388 (1798)

6 Game is game, and he who finds may kill; that has been the law in these mountains for forty years, to my sartain knowledge; and I think one old law is worth two new ones.

James Fenimore Cooper, *The Pioneers,* 1823, in *Writings of James Fenimore Cooper* 160 (James F. Beard ed. 1980)

7 No law can be sacred to me but that of my nature. Good and bad are but names very readily transferable to that or this; the only right is what is after my constitution; the only wrong what is against it.

Ralph Waldo Emerson, "Self-Reliance," *Essays: First Series,* 1841, in *Complete Works of Ralph Waldo Emerson* 2:45, 50 (1903)

8 The Constitution regulates our stewardship; the Constitution devotes the domain to union, to justice, to defense, to welfare, and to liberty. But there is a higher law than the Constitution, which regulates our authority over the domain, and devotes it to the same noble purposes. The territory is a part—no inconsiderable part—of the common heritage of mankind, bestowed upon them by the Creator of the universe. We are his stewards, and must so discharge our trust as to secure, in the highest attainable degree, their happiness.

William H. Seward, Speech in United States Senate during debate on Compromise of 1850, 11 Mar. 1850, in *Congressional Globe,* 31st Cong., 1st Sess. 260, 265 (1850)

9 Laws are merely declaratory of the natural sentiments of mankind, and the language of all permanent laws will be in contradiction to any immoral enactment.

> **Ralph Waldo Emerson,** Speech, Concord, Mass., 3 May 1851, in *Complete Works of Ralph Waldo Emerson* 11:179, 195 (1904)

10 He who lives according to the highest law is in one sense lawless. That is an unfortunate discovery, certainly, that of a law which binds us where we did not know we were bound. Live free, child of the mist! He for whom the law is made, who does not obey the law but whom the law obeys, reclines on pillows of down and is wafted at will whither he pleases, for man is superior to all laws, both of heaven and earth, when he takes his liberty.

> **Henry David Thoreau,** Journal, 27 Feb. 1851, in *Journal of Henry D. Thoreau* 2:187 (Bradford Torrey & Francis H. Allen eds. 1962)

11 In the matter of the sexual relation man's statutory regulations of it [were] a distinct interference with a higher law, the law of Nature. . . . I [can not] call to mind a written law of any kind that had been promulgated in any age of the world in any statute book or any Bible for the regulation of man's conduct in *any* particular, from assassination all the way up to Sabbath-breaking, that [was not] a violation of the law of Nature, which I regard as the highest of laws.

> **Mark Twain,** 1908, in *Mark Twain in Eruption* 315 (Bernard De Voto ed. 1940)

12 While the laws of Nature, that is to say the laws of God, plainly made every human being a law unto himself, we must steadfastly refuse to obey those laws, and we must as steadfastly stand by the conventions which ignore them, since the statutes furnish us peace, fairly good government, and stability, and therefore are better for us then the laws of God, which would soon plunge us into confusion and disorder and anarchy, if we should adopt them.

> **Mark Twain,** 1908, in *Mark Twain in Eruption* 316 (Bernard De Voto ed. 1940)

13 The jurists who believe in natural law seem to me to be in that naïve state of mind that accepts what has been familiar and accepted by them and their neighbors as something that must be accepted by all men everywhere.

> **Oliver Wendell Holmes, Jr.,** "Natural Law," 32 *Harvard Law Review* 40, 41 (1918)

14 Deep-seated preferences can not be argued about—you can not argue a man into liking a glass of beer—and therefore, when differences are sufficiently far reaching, we try to kill the other man rather than let him have his way. But that is perfectly consistent with admitting that, so far as appears, his grounds are just as good as ours. . . . It is true that beliefs and wishes have a transcendental basis in the sense that their foundation is arbitrary. You can not help entertaining and feeling them, and there is an end of it.

> **Oliver Wendell Holmes, Jr.,** "Natural Law," 32 *Harvard Law Review* 40, 41 (1918)

15 If "natural rights" means anything it means that the individual rights are to be determined by the conduct of Nature. But Nature knows nothing about rights in the sense of human conception. Nothing is so cruel, so wanton, so unfeeling as Nature; she moves with the weight of a glacier carrying everything before her.

> **Clarence S. Darrow,** *The Story of My Life* 53 (1932)

16 The rule of law in America means nothing outside constitutional government and constitutionalism, and these are simply unintelligible without a higher law. Men cannot rule others by their consent unless their common humanity is understood in light of transcendent standards provided by the Declaration's "Laws of Nature and of Nature's God." Natural law provides a basis in human dignity by which we can judge whether human beings are just or unjust, noble or ignoble.

> **Clarence Thomas,** "Affirmative Action: Cure or Contradiction?," *The Center Magazine,* Nov./Dec. 1987, at 20, 21

17 Natural rights and higher law arguments are the best defense of liberty and of limited government. Moreover, without recourse to higher law, we abandon our best defense of judicial review—a judiciary active in defending the Constitution, but judicious in its restraint and moderation. Rather than being a justification of the worst type of judicial activism, higher law

is the only alternative to the willfulness of both run-amok majorities and run-amok judges.

> **Clarence Thomas,** "The Higher Law Background of the Privileges or Immunities Clause of the Fourteenth Amendment," 12 *Harvard Journal of Law & Public Policy* 63, 63–64 (1989)

NATURAL RESOURCES

See also ENVIRONMENTAL LAW

1 A river is more than an amenity, it is a treasure. It offers a necessity of life that must be rationed among those who have power over it.

> **Oliver Wendell Holmes, Jr.,** *New Jersey v. New York,* 283 U.S. 336, 342 (1931)

2 The meek shall inherit the earth, but not the mineral rights.

> **J. Paul Getty,** Attributed remark, quoted in Robert Lenzner, *The Great Getty* 93 (1985)

NEGLIGENCE

See also TORTS

1 If the defendants were at fault in leaving an uncovered hole in the sidewalk of a public street, the intoxication of the plaintiff cannot excuse such gross negligence. A drunken man is as much entitled to a safe street, as a sober one, and much more in need of it.

> **Solomon Heydenfeldt,** *Robinson v. Pioche, Bayerque & Co.,* 5 Cal. 460, 461 (1855)

2 The standards of the law are standards of general application. The law takes no account of the infinite varieties of temperament, intellect, and education which make the internal character of a given act so different in different men. It does not attempt to see men as God sees them, for more than one sufficient reason. In the first place, the impossibility of nicely measuring a man's powers and limitations is far clearer than that of ascertaining his knowledge of law, which has been thought to account for what is called the presumption that every man knows the law. But a more satisfactory explanation is, that, when men live in society, a certain average of conduct, a sacrifice of individual peculiarites going be-

yond a certain point, is necessary to the general welfare. If, for instance, a man is born hasty and awkward, is always having accidents and hurting himself or his neighbors, no doubt his congenital defects will be allowed for in the courts of Heaven, but his slips are no less troublesome to his neighbors than if they sprang from guilty neglect. His neighbors accordingly require him, at his proper peril, to come up to their standard, and the courts which they establish decline to take his personal equation into account.

> **Oliver Wendell Holmes, Jr.,** *The Common Law* 108 (1881)

3 It is perfectly consistent with the views maintained in this Lecture that the courts have been very slow to withdraw questions of negligence from the jury, without distinguishing nicely whether the doubt concerned the facts or the standard to be applied. Legal, like natural divisions, however clear in their general outline, will be found on exact scrutiny to end in a penumbra or debatable land. This is the region of the jury, and only cases falling on this doubtful border are likely to be carried far in court. Still, the tendency of the law must always be to narrow the field of uncertainty.

> **Oliver Wendell Holmes, Jr.,** *The Common Law* 126–27 (1881)

4 With purely moral obligations the law does not deal. For example, the priest and Levite who passed by on the other side were not . . . liable at law for the continued suffering of the man who fell among thieves, which they might and morally ought to have prevented or relieved. Suppose A., standing close by a railroad, sees a two-year-old babe on the track and a car approaching. He can easily rescue the child with entire safety to himself, and the instincts of humanity require him to do so. If he does not, he may, perhaps, justly be styled a ruthless savage and a moral monster; but he is not liable in damages for the child's injury, or indictable under the statute for its death.

> **Alonzo P. Carpenter,** *Buch v. Amory Mfg. Co.,* 69 N.H. 257, 260, 44 A. 809 (1898)

5 What usually is done may be evidence of what ought to be done, but what ought to be done is fixed by a standard of reasonable

prudence, whether it usually is complied with or not.

Oliver Wendell Holmes, Jr., *Texas & Pac. Ry. v. Behymer*, 189 U.S. 468, 470 (1903)

6 The friend whom I invite to ride with me in my car, and who occupies the rear seat beside me, while the car is in the care of my chauffeur, is charged with active vigilance to watch for tracks and trains, and is without a remedy if in the exuberance of jest or anecdote or reminiscence, he relies upon the vigilance of the driver to carry him in safety. I find it hard to imagine a rule more completely unrelated to the realities of life.

Benjamin N. Cardozo, "A Ministry of Justice," 35 *Harvard Law Review* 113, 121 (1921)

7 The rights of bathers do not depend upon these nice tinctions. . . . Jumping from a boat or a barrel, the boy would have been a bather in the river. Jumping from the end of a springboard, he was no longer, it is said, a bather, but a trespasser on a right of way. Rights and duties in systems of living law are not built upon such quicksands.

Benjamin N. Cardozo, *Hynes v. New York Cent. R.R.*, 231 N.Y. 229, 233, 131 N.E. 898 (1921)

8 Landowners are not bound to regulate their conduct in contemplation of the presence of trespassers intruding upon private structures. Landowners *are* bound to regulate their conduct in contemplation of the presence of travelers upon the adjacent public ways. . . . Rules appropriate to spheres which are conceived of as separate and distinct cannot, both, be enforced when the spheres become concentric. There must then be readjustment or collision. In one sense, and that a highly technical and artificial one, the diver at the end of the springboard is an intruder on the adjoining lands. In another sense, and one that realists will accept more readily, he is still on public waters in the exercise of public rights. The law must say whether it will subject him to the rule of the one field or of the other, of this sphere or of that. We think that considerations of analogy, of convenience, of policy, and of justice, exclude him from the field of the defendant's

immunity and exemption, and place him in the field of liability and duty.

Benjamin N. Cardozo, *Hynes v. New York Cent. R.R.*, 231 N.Y. 229, 235–36, 131 N.E. 898 (1921)

9 Danger invites rescue. The cry of distress is the summons to relief. The law does not ignore these reactions of the mind in tracing conduct to its consequences. It recognizes them as normal. It places their effects within the range of the natural and probable. The wrong that imperils life is a wrong to the imperilled victim; it is a wrong also to his rescuer. . . . The risk of rescue, if only it be not wanton, is born of the occasion. The emergency begets the man. The wrongdoer may not have foreseen the coming of a deliverer. He is accountable as if he had.

Benjamin N. Cardozo, *Wagner v. International Railway Co.*, 232 N.Y. 176, 180, 133 N.E. 437 (1921)

10 It is ancient learning that one who assumes to act, even though gratuitously, may thereby become subject to the duty of acting carefully, if he acts at all.

Benjamin N. Cardozo, *Glanzer v. Shepard*, 233 N.Y. 236, 239, 135 N.E. 275 (1922)

11 When a man goes upon a railroad track he knows that he goes to a place where he will be killed if a train comes upon him before he is clear of the track. He knows that he must stop for the train, not the train stop for him. In such circumstances it seems to us that if a driver cannot be sure otherwise whether a train is dangerously near he must stop and get out of his vehicle, although obviously he will not often be required to do more than to stop and look. It seems to us that if he relies upon not hearing the train or any signal and takes no further precaution he does so at his own risk.

Oliver Wendell Holmes, Jr., *Baltimore & Ohio R.R. v. Goodman*, 275 U.S. 66, 69–70 (1927)

12 Due care is a duty imposed on each one of us to protect society from unnecessary danger, not to protect A, B, or C alone.

William S. Andrews, *Palsgraf v. Long Island R.R.*, 248 N.Y. 339, 349, 162 N.E. 99 (1928) (dissenting)

13 What we do mean by the word "proximate" is, that because of convenience, of public policy, of a rough sense of justice, the law arbitrarily declines to trace a series of events beyond a certain point. This is not logic. It is practical politics.

> William S. Andrews, *Palsgraf v. Long Island R.R.*, 248 N.Y. 339, 352, 162 N.E. 99 (1928) (dissenting)

14 One who jostles one's neighbor in a crowd does not invade the rights of others standing at the outer fringe when the unintended contact casts a bomb upon the ground. The wrongdoer as to them is the man who carries the bomb, not the one who explodes it without suspicion of the danger. Life will have to be made over, and human nature transformed, before prevision so extravagant can be accepted as the norm of conduct, the customary standard to which behavior must conform.

> Benjamin N. Cardozo, *Palsgraf v. Long Island R.R.*, 248 N.Y. 339, 343, 162 N.E. 99 (1928)

15 The orbit of the danger as disclosed to the eye of reasonable vigilance would be the orbit of the duty.

> Benjamin N. Cardozo, *Palsgraf v. Long Island R.R.*, 248 N.Y. 339, 343, 162 N.E. 99 (1928)

16 The risk reasonably to be perceived defines the duty to be obeyed, and risk imports relation; it is risk to another or to others within the range of apprehension.

> Benjamin N. Cardozo, *Palsgraf v. Long Island R.R.*, 248 N.Y. 339, 344, 162 N.E. 99 (1928)

17 One who takes part in such a sport accepts the dangers that inhere in it so far as they are obvious and necessary, just as a fencer accepts the risk of a thrust by his antagonist or a spectator at a ball game the chance of contact with the ball. . . . The antics of the clown are not the paces of the cloistered cleric. The rough and boisterous joke, the horse-play of the crowd, evokes its own guffaws, but they are not the pleasures of tranquillity. The plaintiff was not seeking a retreat for meditation. Visitors were tumbling about the belt to the merriment of onlookers when he made his choice to join them. He took the chance of a like fate, with whatever damage to his body might ensue from such a fall. The timorous may stay at home.

> Benjamin N. Cardozo, *Murphy v. Steeplechase Amusement Co.*, 250 N.Y. 479, 482–83, 166 N.E. 173 (1929)

18 If liability for negligence exists, a thoughtless slip or blunder, the failure to detect a theft or forgery beneath the cover of deceptive entries, may expose accountants to a liability in an indeterminate amount for an indeterminate time to an indeterminate class. The hazards of a business conducted on these terms are so extreme as to enkindle doubt whether a flaw may not exist in the implication of a duty that exposes to these consequences.

> Benjamin N. Cardozo, *Ultramares Corp. v. Touche*, 255 N.Y. 170, 179–80, 174 N.E. 441 (1931)

19 In most cases reasonable prudence is in fact common prudence; but strictly it is never its measure; a whole calling may have unduly lagged in the adoption of new and available devices. It never may set its own tests, however persuasive be its usages. Courts must in the end say what is required; there are precautions so imperative that even their universal disregard will not excuse their omission.

> Learned Hand, *The T. J. Hooper*, 60 F.2d 737, 740 (2d Cir. 1932)

20 Standards of prudent conduct are declared at times by courts, but they are taken over from the facts of life.

> Benjamin N. Cardozo, *Pokora v. Wabash Ry.*, 292 U.S. 98, 104 (1934)

21 The degree of care demanded of a person by an occasion is the resultant of three factors: the likelihood that his conduct will injure others, taken with the seriousness of the injury if it happens, and balanced against the interest which he must sacrifice to avoid the risk. All these are practically not susceptible of any quantitative estimate, and the second two are generally not so, even theoretically. For this reason a solution always involves some preference, or choice between incommensurables, and it is consigned to a jury because their decision is thought most likely to accord with commonly accepted standards, real or fancied.

> Learned Hand, *Conway v. O'Brien*, 111 F. 2d 611, 612 (2d Cir. 1940)

22 There are those who stem the turbulent current for bubble fame, or who bridge the yawning chasm with a leap for the leap's sake or who "outstare the sternest eyes that look, outbrave the heart most daring on the earth, pluck the young sucking cubs from the she-bear, yea, mock the lion when he roars for prey" to win a fair lady and these are the admiration of the generality of men; but they are made of sterner stuff than the ordinary man upon whom the law places no duty of emulation. The law would indeed be fond if it imposed upon the ordinary man the obligation to so demean himself when suddenly confronted with a danger, not of his creation, disregarding the likelihood that such a contingency may darken the intellect and palsy the will of the common legion of the earth, the fraternity of ordinary men,—whose acts or omissions under certain conditions or circumstances make the yardstick by which the law measures culpability or innocense [sic], negligence or care.

> **Frank A. Carlin,** *Cordas v. Peerless Transp. Co.,* 27 N.Y.S.2d 198, 201 (N.Y. City Ct. 1941)

23 *Willie Gingrich* [played by Walter Matthau, speaking as lawyer to injured client]: I mean, too bad it didn't happen further down the street—in front of the May Company. From *them* you can collect! Couldn't you have dragged yourself another twenty feet?

> **Billy Wilder and I. A. L. Diamond,** *The Fortune Cookie* (screenplay), 1966, in *The Apartment and The Fortune Cookie* 137 (1971)

24 [The plaintiff in a lawsuit] had brought suit against a large store, claiming he had fallen on its slippery floor and was totally paralyzed from the waist down. The insurance lawyer defending the suit was sure the injury was a fake and tried his best to prove it. But the jury brought in an award of $200,000.

After the trial, the lawyer walked over to the plaintiff and said, "You got your money. But you're never going to be able to enjoy it. I'm going to dog your steps until I prove you are a fake. Wherever you go, I'll be watching you. You'll never be able to get out of that wheelchair. You're not going to be any better off than if you really were paralyzed."

"Listen, Counsellor" said the plaintiff, "now that we're being frank, I'll tell you something. Tomorrow the sleekest ambulance in town calls for me at my home and takes me to the airport. I get on a plane for Paris. In Paris, another ambulance meets me with a pretty French nurse. That ambulance drives me, oh so carefully, down to the shrine at Lourdes, in the south of France.

"AND THEN YOU'RE GOING TO SEE THE GREATEST MIRACLE TAKE PLACE THAT THEY HAVE EVER HAD."

> **James C. Humes,** *Podium Humor* 74–75 (1975)

25 *Frank Galvin* [played by Paul Newman]: It just struck me how neatly three goes into this amount. That means I'd keep seventy.... So that's it—I take the money—and no one will ever know the truth: that that girl was turned into a vegetable because of two doctors' negligence and that rather than face what they did they'd rather buy me off to keep my mouth shut about it.... If I take the money, I'm lost—I'll just be a rich ambulance chaser.

> **David Mamet,** *The Verdict* (screenplay), 1982, quoted in Thomas J. Harris, *Courtroom's Finest Hour in American Cinema* 156 (1987)

26 Dr. Gavin and Allison, an attorney, were driving in separate autos along the California Coast Highway one foggy night. The cars collided, but the fault was questionable. Both men were shaken up, and the lawyer offered the doctor some whiskey from a pocket flask.

Gavin took the flask with a shaking hand and took several long swallows. When Allison started to cap the flask, the doctor said, "A stiff drink could help the nerves. Why don't you have one, also?"

"Oh, I will," replied the lawyer, "right after the highway patrol gets here."

> **Larry Wilde,** *The Official Lawyers Joke Book* 160 (1982)

27 We therefore hold that a host who serves liquor to an adult social guest, knowing both that the guest is intoxicated and [that he] will thereafter be operating a motor vehicle, is liable for injuries inflicted on a third party as a result of the negligent operation of a motor vehicle by the adult

guest when such negligence is caused by the intoxication.

Robert N. Wilentz, *Kelly v. Gwinnell,* 96 N.J. 538, 548, 476 A.2d 1219 (1984)

NUISANCE

See TORTS

OBEDIENCE TO LAW

See also CIVIL DISOBEDIENCE; ILLEGALITY; LAW; LAW ENFORCEMENT; LAWLESSNESS

1 The magistrate should obey the Laws, the People should obey the magistrate.

Benjamin Franklin, *Poor Richard's Almanack,* 1734, in *Papers of Benjamin Franklin* 1:357 (Leonard W. Labaree ed. 1959)

2 A government of laws, and not of men.*

John Adams, "Novanglus Papers," No. 7, 1774, in *Works of John Adams* 4:106 (Charles Francis Adams ed. 1851)
See also OBEDIENCE TO LAW 3; OBEDIENCE TO LAW 5

3 In the government of this commonwealth, the legislative department shall never exercise the executive and judicial powers, or either of them: the executive shall never exercise the legislative and judicial powers, or either of them: the judicial shall never exercise the legislative and executive powers, or either of them: to the end it may be a government of laws and not of men.

Massachusetts Constitution of 1780, pt. 1, art. 30, in *Federal and State Constitutions* 3:1888, 1893 (Francis N. Thorpe ed. 1909)
See also OBEDIENCE TO LAW 2; OBEDIENCE TO LAW 5

4 It is not true . . . that any people ever existed who loved the public better than

---

* These I conceive to be the principles upon which Aristotle and Livy . . . have grounded their assertion that a commonwealth is an empire of laws and not of men.
—**James Harrington,** *The Commonwealth of Oceana,* 1656, in *Political Works of James Harrington* 170 (J. G. A. Pocock ed. 1977)

Adams almost certainly derived his formulation from Harrington, but it was Adams's use of the phrase which gave it wide circulation in America. He also employed "government of laws, and not of men" in the Declaration of Rights which he drafted for the Massachusetts Constitution in 1780.

themselves, their private friends, neighbors, etc., and therefore this kind of virtue, this sort of love, is as precarious a foundation for liberty as honor or fear; it is the laws alone that really love the country, the public, the whole better than any part; and that form of government which unites all the virtue, honor, and fear of the citizens, in a reverence and obedience to the laws, is the only one in which liberty can be secure, and all orders, and ranks, and parties, compelled to prefer the public good before their own; that is the government for which we plead.

John Adams, "A Defence of the Constitutions of Government of the United States of America," 1787–88, in *Works of John Adams* 6:208 (Charles Francis Adams ed. 1851)

5 The government of the United States has been emphatically termed a government of laws, and not of men. It will certainly cease to deserve this high appellation, if the laws furnish no remedy for the violation of a vested legal right.

John Marshall, *Marbury v. Madison,* 5 U.S. (1 Cranch) 137, 163 (1803)
See also OBEDIENCE TO LAW 2; OBEDIENCE TO LAW 3

6 The question you propose, whether circumstances do not sometimes occur, which make it a duty in officers of high trust, to assume authorities beyond the law, is easy of solution in principle, but sometimes embarrassing in practice. A strict observance of the written laws is doubtless *one* of the high duties of a good citizen, but it is not *the highest.* The laws of necessity, of self-preservation, of saving our country when in danger, are of higher obligation. To lose our country by a scrupulous adherence to written law, would be to lose the law itself, with life, liberty, property and all those who are enjoying them with us; thus absurdly sacrificing the end to the means.

Thomas Jefferson, Letter to John B. Colvin, 20 Sept. 1810, in *Writings of Thomas Jefferson* 9:279 (Paul L. Ford ed. 1898)

7 In the United States, every one is personally interested in enforcing the obedience of the whole community to the law; for as the minority may shortly rally the majority to its principles, it is interested in profess-

ing that respect for the decrees of the legislator which it may soon have occasion to claim for its own. However irksome an enactment may be, the citizen of the United States complies with it, not only because it is the work of the majority, but because it is his own, and he regards it as a contract to which he is himself a party.

> **Alexis de Tocqueville,** *Democracy in America* 1:316 (Francis Bowen trans. 1862) (1835)

8 The people in America obey the law, not only because it is their work, but because it may be changed if it be harmful; a law is observed because, first, it is a self-imposed evil, and, secondly, it is an evil of transient duration.

> **Alexis de Tocqueville,** *Democracy in America* 1:317 (Francis Bowen trans. 1862) (1835)

9 As [a citizen] is a "law-maker," he should not be a "law-breaker," for he ought to be conscious that every departure from the established ordinances of society is an infraction of his rights. His power can only be maintained by the supremacy of the laws, as in monarchies, the authority of the king is asserted by obedience to his orders. The citizen in lending a cheerful assistance to the ministers of the law, on all occasions, is merely helping to maintain his own power. This feature in particular, distinguishes the citizen from the subject.

> **James Fenimore Cooper,** *The American Democrat* 83 (1956) (1838)

10 Let every man remember that to violate the law, is to trample on the blood of his father, and to tear the character [*this word may be a mistake for "charter"*] of his own, and his children's liberty.

> **Abraham Lincoln,** Address before Young Men's Lyceum, Springfield, Ill., 27 Jan. 1838, in *Collected Works of Abraham Lincoln* 1:112 (Roy P. Basler ed. 1953)

11 Let every American, every lover of liberty, every well wisher to his posterity, swear by the blood of the Revolution, never to violate in the least particular, the laws of the country; and never to tolerate their violation by others.

> **Abraham Lincoln,** Address before Young Men's Lyceum, Springfield, Ill., 27 Jan. 1838, in *Collected Works of Abraham Lincoln* 1:112 (Roy P. Basler ed. 1953)

12 Let me not be understood as saying there are no bad laws, nor that grievances may not arise, for the redress of which, no legal provisions have been made. I mean to say no such thing. But I do mean to say, that, although bad laws, if they exist, should be repealed as soon as possible, still while they continue in force, for the sake of example, they should be religiously observed.

> **Abraham Lincoln,** Address before Young Men's Lyceum, Springfield, Ill., 27 Jan. 1838, in *Collected Works of Abraham Lincoln* 1:112 (Roy P. Basler ed. 1953)

13 Good men must not obey the laws too well.

> **Ralph Waldo Emerson,** "Politics," *Essays: Second Series,* 1844, in *Complete Works of Ralph Waldo Emerson* 3:199, 208 (1903)

14 We live in a very low state of the world, and pay unwilling tribute to governments founded on force. There is not, among the most religious and instructed men of the most religious and civil nations, a reliance on the moral sentiment and a sufficient belief in the unity of things, to persuade them that society can be maintained without artificial restraints. . . . I do not call to mind a single human being who has steadily denied the authority of the laws, on the simple ground of his own moral nature.

> **Ralph Waldo Emerson,** "Politics," *Essays: Second Series,* 1844, in *Complete Works of Ralph Waldo Emerson* 3:197, 220–21 (1903)

15 A very wise father once remarked, that in the government of his children, he forbade as few things as possible; a wise legislation would do the same. It is folly to make laws on subjects beyond human prerogative, knowing that in the very nature of things they must be set aside. To make laws that man can not and will not obey, serves to bring all law into contempt. It is very important in a republic, that the people should respect the laws, for if we throw them to the winds, what becomes of civil government?

> **Elizabeth Cady Stanton,** Address before 10th National Woman's Rights Convention, New York, May 1860, in *History of Woman Suffrage* 1:716, 721 (Elizabeth Cady Stanton, Susan B. Anthony, & Matilda J. Gage eds. 1881)

16 He [the King] knew his own laws just as other people so often know the laws: by

words, not by effects. They take a *meaning*, and get to be very vivid, when you come to apply them to yourself.

> Mark Twain, *A Connecticut Yankee in King Arthur's Court*, 1889, in *Works of Mark Twain* 9:392 (Bernard L. Stein ed. 1979)

17 Ours is a government of liberty by, through, and under the law. No man is above it, and no man is below it.

> Theodore Roosevelt, Speech, Spokane, Wash., 26 May 1903, in *Works of Theodore Roosevelt* 18:20 (Hermann Hagedorn ed. 1925)

18 We ask no man's permission when we require him to obey the law; neither the permission of the poor man nor yet of the rich man.

> Theodore Roosevelt, Speech, Syracuse, N.Y., 7 Sept. 1903, in *Works of Theodore Roosevelt* 18:64 (Hermann Hagedorn ed. 1925)

19 No man is above the law and no man is below it; nor do we ask any man's permission when we require him to obey it. Obedience to the law is demanded as a right; not asked as a favor.

> Theodore Roosevelt, Third Annual Message, 7 Dec. 1903, in *Works of Theodore Roosevelt* 17:200 (Hermann Hagedorn ed. 1925)

20 I niver bow to a decision iv a judge onless, first, it's pleasant to me, an', second, other judges bow to it. Ye can't be too careful about what decisions ye bow to. A decision that seems agreeable may turn out like an acquaintance ye scrape up at a picnic. Ye may be ashamed iv it to-morrah. Manny's th' time I've bowed to a decree iv a coort on'y to see it go up gayly to th' Supreme Coort, knock at th' dure, an' be kicked downstairs be an angry old gintleman in a black silk petticoat. A decree iv th' coort has got to be pretty vinrable befure I do more thin greet it with a pleasant smile.

> Finley Peter Dunne, "The Big Fine," *Mr. Dooley Says*, 1910, in *Mr. Dooley: Now and Forever* 281, 283–84 (Louis Filler ed. 1954)

21 Of the contrivances which mankind has devised to lift itself from savagery there are few to compare with the habit of assent, not to a facitious common-will, but to the law as it is.

> Learned Hand, "Is There a Common Will," 28 *Michigan Law Review* 46, 52 (1929)

22 The power does not lie in the guns, or the ships, or the walls of stone, or the lines of steel. Important as these are, the real political power lies in a definite common pattern of impulse. If the soldiers choose to disobey or even shoot their officers, if the guns are turned against the government, if the citizenry connives at disobedience of the law, and makes of it even a virtue, then authority is impotent and may drag its bearer down to doom.

> Charles E. Merriam, *Political Power*, 1934, in *A Study of Power* 3, 7–8 (1950)

23 *Peaches O'Day* [played by Mae West]: It ain't no sin if you crack a few laws now and then, just so long as you don't break any.

> Mae West, *Every Day's a Holiday* (screenplay), 1938, quoted in *The Wit and Wisdom of Mae West* 47 (Joseph Weintraub ed. 1970)

OBSCENITY

See also CENSORSHIP; SEX

1 I question whether in the end men will regard that as obscene which is honestly relevant to the adequate expression of innocent ideas, and whether they will not believe that truth and beauty are too precious to society at large to be mutilated in the interests of those most likely to pervert them to base *uses*.

> Learned Hand, *United States v. Kennerley*, 209 F. 119, 120–21 (S.D.N.Y. 1913)

2 If there be no abstract definition, . . . should not the word "obscene" be allowed to indicate the present critical point in the compromise between candor and shame at which the community may have arrived here and now?

> Learned Hand, *United States v. Kennerley*, 209 F. 119, 121 (S.D.N.Y. 1913)

3 The words which are criticized as dirty [in James Joyce's *Ulysses*] are old Saxon words known to almost all men and, I venture, to many women, and are such words as would be naturally and habitually used, I believe, by the types of folk whose life, physical, and mental, Joyce is seeking to describe. In respect of the recurrent emergence of the theme of sex in the minds of

his characters, it must always be remembered that his locale was Celtic and his season spring.

> **John M. Woolsey,** *United States v. One Book Called "Ulysses",* 5 F. Supp. 182, 183–84 (S.D.N.Y. 1933)

4 The meaning of the word "obscene" as legally defined by the courts is: Tending to stir the sex impulses or to lead to sexually impure and lustful thoughts. . . . Whether a particular book would tend to excite such impulses and thoughts must be tested by the court's opinion as to its effect on a person with average sex instincts—what the French would call *l'homme moyen sensuel*—who plays, in this branch of legal inquiry, the same role of hypothetical reagent as does the "reasonable man" in the law of torts and "the man learned in the art" on questions of invention in patent law.

> **John M. Woolsey,** *United States v. One Book Called "Ulysses",* 5 F. Supp. 182, 184 (S.D.N.Y. 1933)

5 I am quite aware that owing to some of its scenes *Ulysses* is a rather strong draught to ask some sensitive, though normal, persons to take. But my considered opinion, after long reflection, is that, whilst in many places the effect of *Ulysses* on the reader undoubtedly is somewhat emetic, nowhere does it tend to be an aphrodisiac.*

Ulysses may, therefore, be admitted into the United States.

> **John M. Woolsey,** *United States v. One Book Called "Ulysses",* 5 F. Supp. 182, 185 (S.D.N.Y. 1933)

6 We believe that the proper test of whether a given book is obscene is in its dominant effect. I applying this test, relevancy of the objectionable parts to the theme, the established reputation of the work in the estimation of approved critics, if the book is modern, and the verdict of the past, if it is ancient, are persuasive pieces of evidence.

> **Augustus N. Hand,** *United States v. One Book Entitled "Ulysses",* 72 F.2d 705, 708 (2d Cir. 1934)

---

* [Deciding that the book *Forever Amber* could be sold in Massachusetts:] The book . . . acts like a soporific rather than an aphrodisiac. While conducive to sleep it is not conducive to a desire to sleep with a member of the opposite sex. —Frank J. Donahue, 1947, quoted in Clifton Fadiman, *The American Treasury, 1455–1955,* at 785 (1955)

7 This then? This is not a book. This is libel, slander, defamation of character. This is not a book, in the ordinary sense of the word. No, this is a prolonged insult, a gob of spit in the face of Art, a kick in the pants to God, Man, Destiny, Time, Love, Beauty . . . what you will. I am going to sing for you, a little off key, perhaps, but I will sing. I will sing while you croak, I will dance over your dirty corpse.

> **Henry Miller,** *Tropic of Cancer* 11–12 (1934)

8 As so often happens, the problem is to find a passable compromise between opposing interests, whose relative importance, like that of all social or personal values, is incommensurable. We impose such a duty upon a jury, because the standard they fix is likely to be an acceptable mesne, and because in such matters a mesne most nearly satisfies the moral demands of the community. There can never be constitutive principles for such judgments, or indeed more than cautions to avoid the personal aberrations of the jurors. We mentioned some of these in United States v. One Book Entitled Ulysses; the work must be taken as a whole, its merits weighed against its defects; if it is old, its accepted place in the arts must be regarded; if new, the opinions of competent critics in published reviews or the like may be considered; what counts is its effect, not upon any particular class, but upon all those whom it is likely to reach. Thus "obscenity" is a function of many variables, and the verdict of the jury is not the conclusion of a syllogism of which they are to find only the minor premiss, but really a small bit of legislation ad hoc, like the standard of care.

> **Learned Hand,** *United States v. Levine,* 83 F.2d 156, 157 (2d Cir. 1936)

9 All ideas having even the slightest redeeming social importance—unorthodox ideas, controversial ideas, even ideas hateful to the prevailing climate of opinion—have the full protection of the guaranties. . . . But implicit in the history of the First Amendment is the rejection of obscenity as utterly without redeeming social importance. . . . We hold that obscenity is not within the area of constitutionally protected speech or press.

> **William J. Brennan, Jr.,** *Roth v. United States,* 354 U.S. 476, 484–85 (1957)

10 Sex and obscenity are not synonymous.

    William J. Brennan, Jr., *Roth v. United States,* 354 U.S. 476, 487 (1957)

11 [Standard for obscenity:] Whether to the average person, applying contemporary community standards, the dominant theme of the material taken as a whole appeals to prurient interest.

    William J. Brennan, Jr., *Roth v. United States,* 354 U.S. 476, 489 (1957)

12 Should a mature and sophisticated reading public be kept in blinders because a government official thinks reading certain works of power and literary value is not good for it? We agree with the court below in believing and holding that definitions of obscenity consistent with modern intellectual standards and morals neither require nor permit such a restriction.

    Charles E. Clark, *Grove Press, Inc. v. Christenberry,* 276 F.2d 433, 439 (2d Cir. 1960)

13 Indeed, a legal proscription cannot in any event constrict artistic creation. Man's drive for self-expression, which over the centuries has built his monuments, does not stay within set bounds; the creations which yesterday were the detested and the obscene become the classics of today. The quicksilver of creativity will not be solidified by legal pronouncement; it will necessarily flow into new and sometimes frightening fields. If, indeed, courts try to forbid new and exotic expression they will surely and fortunately fail. The new forms of expression, even though formally banned, will, as they always have, remain alive in man's consciousness. The court-made excommunication, if it is too wide or if it interferes with true creativity, will be rejected like incantations of forgotten witch-doctors. Courts must therefore move here with utmost caution; they tread in a field where a lack of restraint can only invite defeat and only impair man's most precious potentiality: his capacity for self-expression.

    Mathew O. Tobriner, *Zeitlin v. Arnebergh,* 59 Cal. 2d 901, 922–23, 383 P.2d 152, 31 Cal. Rptr. 800 (1963)

14 I have reached the conclusion ... that under the First and Fourteenth Amendments criminal laws in this area [obscen-ity] are constitutionally limited to hard-core pornography. I shall not today attempt further to define the kinds of material I understand to be embraced within that shorthand description; and perhaps I could never succeed in intelligibly doing so. But I know it when I see it; and the motion picture involved in this case is not that.

    Potter Stewart, *Jacobellis v. Ohio,* 378 U.S. 184, 197 (1964) (concurring)

15 Three elements must coalesce [before a work can be deemed obscene]: it must be established that (a) the dominant theme of the material taken as a whole appeals to a prurient interest in sex; (b) the material is patently offensive because it affronts contemporary community standards relating to the description or representation of sexual matters; and (c) the material is utterly without redeeming social value.

    William J. Brennan, Jr., *A Book Named "John Cleland's Memoirs of a Woman of Pleasure" v. Attorney General,* 383 U.S. 413, 418 (1966)

16 The decision of the Majority of the Court in this case has dealt a staggering blow to the forces of morality, decency and human dignity in the Commonwealth of Pennsylvania. If, by this decision, a thousand rattlesnakes had been let loose, they could not do as much damage to the well-being of the people of this state as the unleashing of all the scorpions and vermin of immorality swarming out of that volume of degeneracy called the "Tropic of Cancer." Policemen, hunters, constables and foresters could easily and quickly kill a thousand rattlesnakes but the lice, lizards, maggots and gangrenous roaches scurrying out from beneath the covers of the "Tropic of Cancer" will enter into the playground, the study desks, the cloistered confines of children and immature minds to eat away moral resistance and wreak damage and harm which may blight countless lives for years and decades to come.

    Michael A. Musmanno, *Commonwealth v. Robin,* 421 Pa. 70, 73–74, 218 A.2d 546 (1966) (dissenting)

17 Then the defendants say that "Cancer" is entitled to immunity under the First Amendment because court decisions have declared that only worthless trash may be

proscribed as obscene. To say that "Cancer" is worthless trash is to pay it a compliment. "Cancer" is the sweepings of the Augean stables, the stagnant bilge of the slimiest mudscow, the putrescent corruption of the most noisome dump pile, the dreggiest filth in the deepest morass of putrefaction.

> Michael A. Musmanno, *Commonwealth v. Robin*, 421 Pa. 70, 83, 218 A.2d 546 (1966) (dissenting)

18 "Cancer" is not a book. It is a cesspool, an open sewer, a pit of putrefaction, a slimy gathering of all that is rotten in the debris of human depravity. And in the center of all this waste and stench, besmearing himself with its foulest defilement, splashes, leaps, cavorts and wallows a bifurcated specimen that responds to the name of Henry Miller. One wonders how the human species could have produced so lecherous, blasphemous, disgusting and amoral a human being as Henry Miller. One wonders why he is received in polite society.

> Michael A. Musmanno, *Commonwealth v. Robin*, 421 Pa. 70, 91, 218 A.2d 546 (1966) (dissenting)

19 I would prefer to have as a visitor in my home the most impecunious tramp that ever walked railroad ties, a tramp whose raggedy clothes are held together by faith and a safety pin, a tramp, who, throughout his entire life, always moved at a lazy pace, ... a tramp who rides the rods of freight cars with the aplomb of a railroad president in his private train, a tramp who knows as much about Emily Post's etiquette as a chattering chimpanzee, and who couldn't care less; I would prefer to invite that lazy, bewhiskered cavalier of the road to my residence for a short visit, than even to see on the highway that hobo of the mind, that licentious nomad called Henry Miller, whose literary clothes are plastered with filth, whose language is dirtier than any broken sewer that pollutes and contaminates a whole community;—Henry Miller who shuns a bath of clean words, as the devil avoids holy water, who reduces human beings to animals, home standards to the pigsty, and dwells in a land of his own fit only for lice, bedbugs, cockroaches and tapeworms.

> Michael A. Musmanno, *Commonwealth v. Robin*, 421 Pa. 70, 91, 218 A.2d 546 (1966) (dissenting)

20 "Cancer" is not a book. It is malignancy itself. It is a cancer on the literary body of America. I wonder that it can remain stationary on the bookshelf. One would expect it to generate self-locomotion just as one sees a moldy, maggoty rock move because of the creepy, crawling creatures underneath it.

> Michael A. Musmanno, *Commonwealth v. Robin*, 421 Pa. 70, 92, 218 A.2d 546 (1966) (dissenting)

21 The First Amendment guarantees liberty of human expression in order to preserve in our Nation what Mr. Justice Holmes called a "free trade in ideas." To that end, the Constitution protects more than just a man's freedom to say or write or publish what he wants. It secures as well the liberty of each man to decide for himself what he will read and to what he will listen. The Constitution guarantees, in short, a society of free choice.

> Potter Stewart, *Ginsberg v. New York*, 390 U.S. 629, 649 (1968) (concurring)

22 Whatever may be the justifications for other statutes regulating obscenity, we do not think they reach into the privacy of one's own home. If the First Amendment means anything, it means that a State has no business telling a man, sitting alone in his own house, what books he may read or what films he may watch. Our whole constitutional heritage rebels at the thought of giving government the power to control men's minds.

> Thurgood Marshall, *Stanley v. Georgia*, 394 U.S. 557, 565 (1969)

23 The worst that can be said of pornography is that it leads not to "antisocial" sexual acts but to the reading of more pornography.

> Gore Vidal, *Reflections upon a Sinking Ship* 85, 90 (1969)

24 The term "f-----g pigs" in the context in which it was used referred not to copulation of porcine animals but was rather a highly insulting epithet directed to the police officers. . . . Appellant's use of the vulgarism describing the filial partner in an oedipal relationship is fairly to be viewed as an epithet rather than as a phrase appealing to a shameful or morbid interest in intra-family sex. . . . There is, after all, a strong possibility that an expert witness

called in the matter before us might have testified to the occasional use of the offending profane adjective in bar association quarters or in trial judges' lounges—alas, all too often in reference to a decision of the Court of Appeal.

> Robert S. Thompson, *People v. Price*, 4 Cal. App. 3d 941, 948–49, 84 Cal. Rptr. 585 (1970) (dissenting)

25 It is neither realistic nor constitutionally sound to read the First Amendment as requiring that the people of Maine or Mississippi accept public depiction of conduct found tolerable in Las Vegas, or New York City.

> Warren E. Burger, *Miller v. California*, 413 U.S. 15, 32 (1973)

26 One can concede that the "sexual revolution" of recent years may have had useful byproducts in striking layers of prudery from a subject long irrationally kept from needed ventilation. But it does not follow that no regulation of patently offensive "hard core" materials is needed or permissible; civilized people do not allow unregulated access to heroin because it is a derivative of medicinal morphine.

> Warren E. Burger, *Miller v. California*, 413 U.S. 15, 36 (1973)

27 It would appear that such an argument ought only to be advanced by depraved, mentally deficient, mind-warped queers. Judges who seek to find technical excuses to permit such pictures to be shown under the pretense of finding some intrinsic value to it are reminiscent of a dog that returns to his vomit in search of some morsel in that filth which may have some redeeming value to his own taste.

> Albert H. Ellett, *Salt Lake City v. Piepenburg*, 571 P.2d 1299, 1299–300 (Utah 1977)

28 Pornography is the theory, and rape the practice.

> Robin Morgan, *Going Too Far* 169 (1978)

29 I put sixteen years into that damn obscenity thing. I tried and I tried, and I waffled back and forth, and I finally gave up. If you can't define it, you can't prosecute people for it. And that's why, in the Paris Adult Theatre decision, I finally abandoned the whole effort. I reached the conclusion that every criminal-obscenity statute—and most obscenity laws are criminal—was

necessarily unconstitutional, because it was impossible, from the statute, to define obscenity. Accordingly, anybody charged with violating the statute would not have known that his conduct was a violation of the law. He wouldn't know whether the material was obscene until the court told him.

> William J. Brennan, Jr., quoted in Nat Hentoff, "Profiles: The Constitutionalist," *New Yorker*, 12 Mar. 1990, at 45, 56

30 The purpose of Indiana's nudity law would be violated, I think, if 60,000 fully consenting adults crowded into the Hoosierdome to display their genitals to one another, even if there were not an offended innocent in the crowd.

> Antonin Scalia, *Barnes v. Glen Theatre, Inc.*, 111 S. Ct. 2456, 2465 (1991) (concurring)

31 Pasties and a G-string moderate the expression [of nude dancing] to some degree, to be sure, but only to a degree. Dropping the final stitch is prohibited, but the limitation is minor when measured against the dancer's remaining capacity and opportunity to express the erotic message.

> David H. Souter, *Barnes v. Glen Theatre, Inc.*, 111 S. Ct. 2456, 2471 (1991) (concurring)

OPINIONS, CURIOUS

1 From which mortal wound he, the said Hurva Garnett, then and there died, contrary to the form of the statute.

> James H. Jordan, *Potter v. State*, 162 Ind. 213, 214, 70 N.E. 129 (1904)

2 For some time after his death, plaintiff in error, *John G. Holmes*, worked in a brewery as an employee of Mrs. Walter, who had charge of the business for herself and children.

> Roujet D. Marshall, *Holmes v. State*, 124 Wis. 133, 134–35, 102 N.W. 321 (1905)

3 The appellant has attempted to distinguish the factual situation in this case from that in *Renfroe v. Higgins Rack Coating and Manufacturing Co., Inc.* (1969), 17 Mich App 259. He didn't. We couldn't.
Affirmed. Costs to appellee.
All concurred.*

> John H. Gillis, *Denny v. Radar Industries*, 28 Mich. App. 294, 294 (1970)

---

* This is the opinion in its entirety.

4 Literary license allows an avid alliteration-ist authority to postulate parenthetically that the predominating principles presented here may be summarized thusly: Preventing public pollution permits promiscuous perusal of personalty but persistent perspicacious patron persuasively provided pertinent perdurable preponderating presumption precedent preventing prison.

H. Sol Clark, *Banks v. State*, 132 Ga. App. 809, 810, 209 S.E.2d 252 (1974)

5 We feel compelled by the nature of the attack in the dissenting opinion to spell out a response:
1. Some answer is required to dissent's charge.
2. Certainly we do not endorse "victimless crime."
3. How that question is involved escapes us.
4. Moreover, the constitutional issue is significant.
5. Ultimately it must be addressed in light of precedent.
6. Certainly the course of precedent is clear.
7. Knowing that, our result is compelled.*

Robert S. Thompson, *People v. Arno*, 90 Cal. App. 3d 505, 514 n.2, 153 Cal. Rptr. 624 (1979)

ORAL ARGUMENT

See ADVOCACY

ORIGINAL INTENTION

See also CONSTITUTION; CONSTITUTIONAL CONVENTION; CONSTITUTIONAL LAW

1 The legitimate meaning of the Instrument must be derived from the text itself; or if a key is to be sought elsewhere, it must be not in the opinions or intentions of the Body which planned & proposed the Constitution, but in the sense attached to it by the people in their respective State Conventions where it recd. all the Authority which it possesses.

James Madison, Letter to Thomas Ritchie, 15 Sept. 1821, in *Writings of James Madison* 9:71, 72 n.1 (Gaillard Hunt ed. 1910)

---

* The first letters of the numbered sentences spell out a common Yiddish insult.

2 On every question of construction, carry ourselves back to the time when the constitution was adopted, recollect the spirit manifested in the debates, and instead of trying what meaning may be squeezed out of the text, or invented against it, conform to the probable one in which it was passed.

Thomas Jefferson, Letter to William Johnson, 12 June 1823, in *Writings of Thomas Jefferson* 10:231 n. (Paul L. Ford ed. 1899)

3 I entirely concur in the propriety of resorting to the sense in which the Constitution was accepted and ratified by the nation. In that sense alone it is the legitimate Constitution. And if that be not the guide in expounding it, there can be no security for a consistent and stable, more than for a faithful exercise of its powers. If the meaning of the text be sought in the changeable meaning of the words composing it, it is evident that the shape and attributes of the Government must partake of the changes to which the words and phrases of all living languages are constantly subject. What a metamorphosis would be produced in the code of law if all its ancient phraseology were to be taken in its modern sense.

James Madison, Letter to Henry Lee, 25 June 1824, in *Writings of James Madison* 9:191 (Gaillard Hunt ed. 1910)

4 No one, we presume, supposes that any change in public opinion or feeling, in relation to this unfortunate race, in the civilized nations of Europe or in this country, should induce the court to give to the words of the Constitution a more liberal construction in their favor than they were intended to bear when the instrument was framed and adopted. Such an argument would be altogether inadmissible in any tribunal called on to interpret it. If any of its provisions are deemed unjust, there is a mode prescribed in the instrument itself by which it may be amended; but while it remains unaltered, it must be construed now as it was understood at the time of its adoption.

Roger B. Taney, *Dred Scott v. Sandford*, 60 U.S. (19 How.) 393, 426 (1857)

5 As long as [the Constitution] continues to exist in its present form, it speaks not only in the same words, but with the same meaning and intent with which it spoke

when it came from the hands of its framers.

> Roger B. Taney, *Dred Scott v. Sandford,* 60 U.S. (19 How.) 393, 426 (1857)

6 It is never to be forgotten that, in the construction of the language of the Constitution ... as indeed in all other instances where construction becomes necessary, we are to place ourselves as nearly as possible in the condition of the men who framed that instrument.

> Samuel F. Miller, *Ex parte Bain,* 121 U.S. 1, 12 (1887)

7 So it is that words, separately considered and in the strictly technical sense in which used in a Constitution, and as defined at the day of their original use therein, do not of themselves immovably fetter the sense or intention, for, if that were held to be the case, the Constitution intended to stand for all time, or at least for a long time, would by such restriction make of itself only a temporary document; it would so enchain itself as to be incapable, in a healthful and uniform manner, of any expansion or development or movement with the living current of the times, and would thereby hold within its embrace the certain means of its own ultimate destruction.

> V. A. Griffith, *Moore v. General Motors Acceptance Corp.,* 155 Miss. 818, 823–24, 125 So. 411 (1930)

8 If by the statement that what the Constitution meant at the time of its adoption it means to-day, it is intended to say that the great clauses of the Constitution must be confined to the interpretation which the framers, with the conditions and outlook of their time, would have placed upon them, the statement carries its own refutation.

> Charles Evans Hughes, *Home Building & Loan Ass'n v. Blaisdell,* 290 U.S. 398, 442–43 (1934)

9 Just what our forefathers did envision, or would have envisioned had they foreseen modern conditions, must be divined from materials almost as enigmatic as the dreams Joseph was called upon to interpret for Pharaoh. A century and a half of partisan debate and scholarly speculation yields no net result but only supplies more

or less apt quotations from respected sources on each side of any question.

> Robert H. Jackson, *Youngstown Sheet & Tube Co. v. Sawyer,* 343 U.S. 579, 634–35 (1952) (concurring)

10 It is ... impossible to fabricate how the "Framers" would have answered the problems that arise in a modern society had they been reared in the civilization that has produced those problems. We should indeed have to be sorcerers to conjure up how they would have responded.

> Learned Hand, *The Bill of Rights* 34–35 (1958)

11 It is not true that the Framers intended the First Amendment to guarantee all speech against all possible infringement by government regulation; but they did not foreclose such a policy and may indeed have invited something like it. It is not true that the Framers intended the Fourteenth Amendment to outlaw segregation or to make applicable to the states all restrictions on government that may be evolved under the Bill of Rights; but they did not foreclose such policies and may indeed have invited them.

> Alexander M. Bickel, *The Least Dangerous Branch* 103 (1962)

12 One perpetrates no violence upon logic or known historical facts by assuming that the Founding Fathers *intended* ... to empower the Court to serve as the Founders' surrogate for the indefinite future—interpreting the Constitution not as they themselves would have directed if they had been consulted in 1787, but as is thought right *by men who accept the Founders' political philosophy—their commitment to self-government and the open society—and consider themselves obligated to effectuate that philosophy in the America of their own day.*

> Louis Lusky, *By What Right?* 21 (1975)

13 It is necessary to establish the proposition that the framers' intentions ... are the sole legitimate premise from which constitutional analysis may proceed.

> Robert H. Bork, *Tradition and Morality in Constitutional Law* 10 (1984)

14 Our amended Constitution is the lodestar for our aspirations. Like every text worth reading, it is not crystalline. The phrasing

is broad and the limitations of its provisions are not clearly marked. Its majestic generalities and ennobling pronouncements are both luminous and obscure. This ambiguity of course calls forth interpretation, the interaction of reader and text. The encounter with the Constitutional text has been, in many senses, my life's work.

> William J. Brennan, Jr., "The Constitution of the United States: Contemporary Ratification" (speech), Washington, D.C., 12 Oct. 1985, in *Original Meaning Jurisprudence: A Sourcebook* 151, 152 (1987).

15 There are those who find legitimacy in fidelity to what they call "the intentions of the Framers." In its most doctrinaire incarnation, this view demands that Justices discern exactly what the Framers thought about the question under consideration and simply follow that intention in resolving the case before them. It is a view that feigns self-effacing deference to the specific judgments of those who forged our original social compact. But in truth it is little more than arrogance cloaked as humility. It is arrogant to pretend that from our vantage we can gauge accurately the intent of the Framers on application of principle to specific, contemporary questions. All too often, sources of potential enlightenment such as records of the ratification debates provide sparse or ambiguous evidence of the original intention.

> William J. Brennan, Jr., "The Constitution of the United States: Contemporary Ratification" (speech), Washington, D.C., 12 Oct. 1985, in *Original Meaning Jurisprudence: A Sourcebook* 151, 155 (1987).

16 We current Justices read the Constitution in the only way that we can: as Twentieth Century Americans. We look to the history of the time of framing and to the intervening history of interpretation. But the ultimate question must be, what do the words of the text mean in our time. For the genius of the Constitution rests not in any static meaning it might have had in a world that is dead and gone, but in the adaptability of its great principles to cope with current problems and current needs.

> William J. Brennan, Jr., "The Constitution of the United States: Contemporary Ratification" (speech), Washington, D.C., 12 Oct. 1985, in *Original Meaning Jurisprudence: A Sourcebook* 151, 158 (1987).

17 No one, including a judge, can be above the law. Only in that way will justice be done and the freedom of Americans assured. How should a judge go about finding the law? The only legitimate way, in my opinion, is by attempting to discern what those who made the law intended. . . . If a judge abandons intention as his guide, there is no law available to him and he begins to legislate a social agenda for the American people. That goes well beyond his legitimate power. He or she then diminishes liberty instead of enhancing it.

> Robert H. Bork, Testimony before Senate Judiciary Committee hearing on his nomination to the Supreme Court, 15 Sept. 1987, quoted in *New York Times*, 16 Sept. 1987, at A28

OWNERSHIP

See PROPERTY

PARDONS

1 I, ANDREW JOHNSON, . . . hereby proclaim and declare unconditionally, and without reservation, to all and to every person who directly or indirectly participated in the late insurrection or rebellion, a full pardon and amnesty for the offence of treason against the United States, or of adhering to their enemies during the late civil war, with restoration of all rights, privileges, and immunities under the Constitution and the laws which have been made in pursuance thereof.

> Proclamation, 25 Dec. 1868, 15 Stat. 711, 712

2 I have had no experience in making laws or amending them, but still I cannot understand why, when it takes twelve men to inflict the death penalty upon a person, it should take any less than 12 more to undo their work. If I were a legislature, and had just been elected and had not time to sell out, I would put the pardoning and commuting power into the hands of twelve able men instead of dumping so huge a burden upon the shoulders of one poor petition-persecuted individual.

> Mark Twain, Letter to the Editor, *New York Tribune*, 10 Mar. 1873, at 5

3 Now, THEREFORE, I, Gerald R. Ford, President of the United States, pursuant to the

pardon power conferred upon me by Article II, Section 2, of the Constitution, have granted and by these presents do grant a full, free, and absolute pardon unto Richard Nixon for all offenses against the United States which he, Richard Nixon, has committed or may have committed or taken part in during the period from January 20, 1969 through August 9, 1974.

> **Gerald R. Ford,** Proclamation 4311, 8 Sept. 1974, in *Public Papers of the Presidents: Gerald R. Ford, 1974,* at 103, 104 (1975)

PATENTS

1 If nature has made any one thing less susceptible than all others of exclusive property, it is the action of the thinking power called an idea, which an individual may exclusively possess as long as he keeps it to himself; but the moment it is divulged, it forces itself into the possession of every one, and the receiver cannot dispossess himself of it. Its peculiar character, too, is that no one possesses the less, because every other possesses the whole of it. He who receives an idea from me, receives instruction himself without lessening mine; as he who lights his taper at mine, receives light without darkening me.

> **Thomas Jefferson,** Letter to Isaac McPherson, 13 Aug. 1813, in *Writings of Thomas Jefferson* 13:333–34 (Andrew A. Lipscomb ed. 1904)

2 All that the law requires is, that the invention should not be frivolous or injurious to the well-being, good policy, or sound morals of society. The word "useful," therefore, is incorporated into the act in contradistinction to mischievous or immoral. For instance, a new invention to poison people, or to promote debauchery, or to facilitate private assassination, is not a patentable invention. But if the invention steers wide of these objections, whether it be more or less useful is a circumstance very material to the interests of the patentee, but of no importance to the public. If it be not extensively useful, it will silently sink into contempt and disregard.

> **Joseph Story,** *Lowell v. Lewis,* 15 F. Cas. 1018, 1019 (C.C.D. Mass. 1817) (No. 8,568)

3 It [the patent] is the reward stipulated for the advantages derived by the public for the exertions of the individual, and is intended as a stimulus to those exertions. . . . The public yields nothing which it has not agreed to yield; it receives all which it has contracted to receive. The full benefit of the discovery, after its enjoyment by the discoverer for fourteen years, is preserved; and for his exclusive enjoyment of it during that time the public faith is pledged.

> **John Marshall,** *Grant v. Raymond,* 31 U.S. (6 Pet.) 218, 241–42 (1832)

4 Unless more ingenuity and skill . . . were required . . . than were possessed by an ordinary mechanic acquainted with the business, there was an absence of that degree of skill and ingenuity which constitute essential elements of every invention. In other words, the improvement is the work of the skilful mechanic, not of the inventor.

> **Samuel Nelson,** *Hotchkiss v. Greenwood,* 52 U.S. (11 How.) 248, 267 (1851)

5 The right of an inventor to his invention is no monopoly . . . in any other sense than as a man's own house is a monopoly.

> **Daniel Webster,** Argument in Goodyear Rubber case, Mar. 1852, in *Writings and Speeches of Daniel Webster* 15:438–39 (J. W. McIntyre ed. 1903)

6 The patentee, having described his invention, and shown its principles, and claimed it in that form which most perfectly embodies it, is, in contemplation of law, deemed to claim every form in which his invention may be copied, unless he manifests an intention to disclaim some of those forms.

> **Benjamin R. Curtis,** *Winans v. Denmead,* 56 U.S. (15 How.) 330, 343 (1854)

7 The patent system . . . added the fuel of *interest* to the *fire* of genius.

> **Abraham Lincoln,** Second Lecture on Discoveries and Inventions, Jacksonville, Ill., 11 Feb. 1859, in *Collected Works of Abraham Lincoln* 3:363 (Roy P. Basler ed. 1953)

8 If, in the eye of an ordinary observer, giving such attention as a purchaser usually gives, two designs are substantially the same, if the resemblance is such as to deceive such an observer, inducing him to purchase one supposing it to be the other, the first one patented is infringed by the other.

> **William Strong,** *Gorham Mfg. Co. v. White,* 81 U.S. (14 Wall.) 511, 528 (1871)

9 Irrespective of this testimony, and of any testimony, upon looking this reissue in the face, and examining its several claims by their own light, we find nothing that brings any of them within the sphere of what is properly patentable. There is no novelty and no utility. It does not appear (to use the language of appellants' brief) that there was "a flash of thought" by which such a result as to either was reached, or that there was any exercise of the inventive faculty, more or less thoughtful, whereby anything entitled to the protection of a patent was produced.

Noah H. Swayne, *Densmore v. Scofield,* 102 U.S. 375, 378 (1880)

10 Letters-patent [are] invalid if the invention which they cover was in public use, with the consent and allowance of the inventor, for more than two years prior to his application. . . . to constitute the public use of an invention it is not necessary that more than one of the patented articles should be publicly used. . . .

The evidence of the complainant herself shows that for more than two years before the application for the original letters there was . . . a public use of the invention [the invention, a type of corset, had been used by the inventor's wife]. . . . The inventor slept on his rights for eleven years.

William B. Woods, *Egbert v. Lippmann,* 104 U.S. 333, 334, 336, 337 (1881)

11 The process of development in manufactures creates a constant demand for new appliances, which the skill of ordinary head-workmen and engineers is generally adequate to devise, and which, indeed, are the natural and proper outgrowth of such development. Each step forward prepares the way for the next, and each is usually taken by spontaneous trials and attempts in a hundred different places. To grant to a single party a monopoly of every slight advance made, except where the exercise of invention, somewhat above ordinary mechanical or engineering skill, is distinctly shown, is unjust in principle and injurious in its consequences. . . . It was never the object of those laws to grant a monopoly for every trifling device, every shadow of a shade of an idea, which would naturally and spontaneously occur to any skilled mechanic or operator in the ordinary progress of manufactures.

Joseph P. Bradley, *Atlantic Works v. Brady,* 107 U.S. 192, 199–200 (1882)

12 Had the complainant's invention been first in time and patented, the Binghamton sheath would have been an infringement; and, conversely, had the Binghamton sheath been patented, the complainant's would have been an infringement. That which infringes, if later, would anticipate, if earlier.

Samuel Blatchford, *Peters v. Active Manufacturing Co.,* 129 U.S. 530, 537 (1889)

13 It should be borne in mind that this process was one not accidentally discovered, but was the result of a long search for the very purpose. The surprise is that the manufacturers of steel, having felt the want for so many years, should never have discovered from the multiplicity of patents and of processes introduced into this suit, and well known to the manufacturers of steel, that it was but a step from what they already knew to that which they had spent years in endeavoring to find out. It only remains now for the wisdom which comes after the fact to teach us that Jones discovered nothing, invented nothing, accomplished nothing.

Henry B. Brown, *Carnegie Steel Co. v. Cambria Iron Co.,* 185 U.S. 403, 445–46 (1902)

14 It is hardly necessary to say that unless the present record discloses new facts which materially change the issues involved we cannot alter our former decision; every question there determined is stare decisis. Even patent litigation must end somewhere.

Alfred C. Coxe, *American Graphophone Co. v. Leeds & Catlin Co.,* 170 F. 327, 329 (2d Cir. 1909)

15 Knowledge after the event is always easy, and problems once solved present no difficulties, indeed, may be represented as never having had any, and expert witnesses may be brought forward to show that the new thing which seemed to have eluded the search of the world was always ready at hand and easy to be seen by a merely skillful attention. But the law has other tests of the invention than subtle conjectures of

what might have been seen and yet was not. It regards a change as evidence of novelty, the acceptance and utility of change as a further evidence, even as demonstration.

Joseph McKenna, *Diamond Rubber Co. v. Consolidated Tire Co.*, 220 U.S. 428, 435 (1911)

16 The imitation of a thing patented by a defendant, who denies invention, has often been regarded, perhaps especially in this circuit, as conclusive evidence of what the defendant thinks of the patent, and persuasive of what the rest of the world ought to think.

Charles M. Hough, *Kurtz v. Belle Hat Lining Co.*, 280 F. 277, 281 (2d Cir. 1922)

17 The new device, however useful it may be, must reveal the flash of creative genius, not merely the skill of the calling.

William O. Douglas, *Cuno Engineering Corp. v. Automatic Devices Corp.*, 314 U.S. 84, 91 (1941)

18 We have disposed of the patent as a whole because it has seemed to us proper that it should not remain in the art as a scarecrow.

Learned Hand, *Bresnick v. United States Vitamin Corp.*, 139 F.2d 239, 242 (2d Cir. 1943)

19 As to ethics, the parties seem to me as much on a parity as the pot and the kettle. But want of knowledge or innocent intent is not ordinarily available to diminish patent protection. I do not see how intent can make infringement of what otherwise is not. The less legal rights depend on someone's state of mind, the better.

Robert H. Jackson, *Mercoid Corp. v. Mid-Continent Investment Co.*, 320 U.S. 661, 679–80 (1944) (dissenting)

20 A patent may have lain for years unheeded, as little a contribution to the sum of knowledge as though it had never existed, an idle gesture long since drifted into oblivion. Nevertheless, it will be as effective to invalidate a new patent, as though it had entered into the very life blood of the industry. . . . Perhaps this should not be so; perhaps there should be some equivalent of a "lost art," which would put even prior patents in Limbo, when they have really

gone to the place of departed spirits. That is another question: it is not for courts.

Learned Hand, *Western States Mach. Co. v. S.S. Hepworth Co.*, 147 F.2d 345, 350 (2d Cir. 1945)

21 In determining whether an accused device or composition infringes a valid patent, resort must be had in the first instance to the words of the claim. If accused matter falls clearly within the claim, infringement is made out and that is the end of it.

Robert H. Jackson, *Graver Tank & Mfg. Co. v. Linde Air Products Co.*, 339 U.S. 605, 607 (1950)

22 One who seeks to pirate an invention, like one who seeks to pirate a copy-righted book or play, may be expected to introduce minor variations to conceal and shelter the piracy. Outright and forthright duplication is a dull and very rare type of infringement.

Robert H. Jackson, *Graver Tank & Mfg. Co. v. Linde Air Products Co.*, 339 U.S. 605, 607 (1950)

23 Courts should scrutinize combination patent claims with a care proportioned to the difficulty and improbability of finding invention in an assembly of old elements. The function of a patent is to add to the sum of useful knowledge. Patents cannot be sustained when, on the contrary, their effect is to subtract from former resources freely available to skilled artisans. A patent for a combination which only unites old elements with no change in their respective functions, such as is presented here, obviously withdraws what already is known into the field of its monopoly and diminishes the resources available to skillful men. This patentee has added nothing to the total stock of knowledge, but has merely brought together segments of prior art and claims them in congregation as a monopoly.

Robert H. Jackson, *Great Atlantic & Pacific Tea Co. v. Supermarket Equipment Corp.*, 340 U.S. 147, 152–53 (1950)

24 The economic philosophy behind the clause empowering Congress to grant patents and copyrights is the conviction that encouragement of individual effort by personal gain is the best way to advance public welfare through the talents of authors and inventors in "Science and useful Arts." Sac-

rificial days devoted to such creative activities deserve rewards commensurate with the services rendered.

> **Stanley F. Reed,** *Mazer v. Stein,* 347 U.S. 201, 219 (1954)

25 While the ultimate question of patent validity is one of law, . . . the § 103 condition, which is but one of three conditions, each of which must be satisfied, lends itself to several basic factual inquiries. Under § 103, the scope and content of the prior art are to be determined; differences between the prior art and the claims at issue are to be ascertained; and the level of ordinary skill in the pertinent art resolved. Against this background, the obviousness or nonobviousness of the subject matter is determined. Such secondary considerations as commercial success, long felt but unsolved needs, failure of others, etc., might be utilized to give light to the circumstances surrounding the origin of the subject matter sought to be patented. As indicia of obviousness or nonobviousness, these inquiries may have relevancy.

> **Tom C. Clark,** *Graham v. John Deere Co.,* 383 U.S. 1, 17–18 (1966)

PERPETUITIES

See WILLS

PLEADINGS

1 In law it is good policy never to *plead* what you *need* not, lest you oblige yourself to *prove* what you *can* not.

> **Abraham Lincoln,** Letter to Usher F. Linder, 20 Feb. 1848, in *Collected Works of Abraham Lincoln* 1:453 (Roy P. Basler ed. 1953)

2 Amendment is a resource against waste. In pleading, as in every other art, the philosophy of amendment . . . is comprehended in the frank recognition of two things, both of which are made manifest by actual experience: the first is, that in the practice of any art, it is generally better to preserve what has been done . . . than to throw it away and begin over. . . . The law has all the wisdom and prudence of all the trades. When practicable, it will conserve its own work, the work of its magistrates and ministers, and that of suitors in its courts, and their counsel.

> **Logan E. Bleckley,** *Ellison v. Georgia R.R.,* 87 Ga. 691, 697, 13 S.E. 809 (1891)

3 Demurrers were no doubt an invention of the Bar to prevent justice, . . . a cursed cheat. . . . Let me advise you, young man, not to come here with your new-fangled law — you must try your cases as others do, by the court and jury.

> **John Dudley,** quoted in Charles Warren, *A History of the American Bar* 136 (1911)

4 And yet I dare say that an ingenious actuary might find upon irrefragable computation that in general loss of time, misprision of judges, consequent appeals, discouragement of suitors and the like, the annual loss to our country through bad pleadings equalled the cost of four new battleships, or a complete refashioning of primary education.

> **Learned Hand,** "The Deficiencies of Trials to Reach the Heart of the Matter," 1921, in *Lectures on Legal Topics* 3:89, 94–95 (1926)

POLICE

See CRIMINAL JUSTICE; LAW ENFORCEMENT; SEARCHES AND SEIZURES

PORNOGRAPHY

See CENSORSHIP; OBSCENITY; SEX

POVERTY

See WEALTH AND POVERTY

POWER

See GOVERNMENT

PRACTICE

See LAW FIRMS; LAW PRACTICE; LAWYERS

PRECEDENT

See also CASES

1 It is a maxim not to be disregarded, that general expressions, in every opinion, are to be taken in connection with the case in

which those expressions are used. If they go beyond the case, they may be respected, but ought not to control the judgment in a subsequent suit when the very point is presented for decision. The reason of this maxim is obvious. The question actually before the Court is investigated with care, and considered in its full extent. Other principles which may serve to illustrate it, are considered in their relation to the case decided, but their possible bearing on all other cases is seldom completely investigated.

John Marshall, *Cohens v. Virginia*, 19 U.S. (6 Wheat.) 264, 399–400 (1821)

2 The law is progressive and expansive, adapting itself to the new relations and interests which are constantly springing up in the progress of society. But this progress must be by analogy to what is already settled.

Richard W. Greene, *Hodges v. New England Screw Co.*, 1 R.I. 312, 356 (1850)

3 *Stare decisis* 's itself a principle of great magnitude and importance. It is absolutely necessary to the formation and permanence of any system of jurisprudence. Without it we may fairly be said to have no law; for law is a fixed and established *rule*, not depending in the slightest degree on the caprice of those who may happen to administer it. I take it that the adjudications of this Court, when they are free from absurdity, not mischievous in practice, and consistent with one another, are the law of the land. It is this law which we are bound to execute, and not any "higher law," manufactured for each special occasion out of our own private feelings and opinions. . . . The uncertainty of the law—an uncertainty inseparable from the nature of the science—is a great evil at best, and we would aggravate it terribly if we could be blown about by every wind of doctrine, holding for true to-day what we repudiate as false to-morrow.

Jeremiah S. Black, *McDowell v. Oyer*, 21 Pa. 417, 423 (1853)

4 Of course I am not saying that we must consecrate the mere blunders of those who went before us, and stumble every time we come to the place where they have stumbled. A palpable mistake, violating justice, reason, and law, must be corrected, no matter by whom it may have been made. There are cases in our books which bear such marks of haste and inattention, that they demand reconsideration. There are some which must be disregarded, because they cannot be reconciled with others. There are old decisions of which the authority has become obsolete, by a total alteration in the circumstances of the country and the progress of opinion. *Tempora mutantur.* We change with the change of the times, as necessarily as we move with the motion of the earth. But in ordinary cases, to set up our mere notions above the principles which the country has been acting upon as settled and established, is to make ourselves not the ministers and agents of the law, but the masters of the law and the tyrants of the people.

Jeremiah S. Black, *McDowell v. Oyer*, 21 Pa. 417, 423 (1853)

5 If it [the point or matter commented upon] might have been decided either way without affecting any right brought into question, then, according to the principles of the common law, an opinion on such a question is not a decision.

Benjamin R. Curtis, *Carroll v. Lessee of Carroll*, 57 U.S. (16 How.) 275, 286–87 (1854)

6 [To the Court requesting a precedent for his position during the Crafts trial:] I will look, your Honor, and endeavor to find a precedent, if you require it; though it would seem to be a pity that the Court should lose the honor of being the first to establish so just a rule.

Rufus Choate, quoted in *Works of Rufus Choate* 1:292 (Samuel G. Brown ed. 1862)

7 Once git a smell o' musk into a draw,
An' it clings hold like precerdents in law.

James Russell Lowell, *Bigelow Papers*, 1862, in *Complete Poetical Works of James Russell Lowell* 228, 260 (Horace E. Scudder ed. 1925)

8 The maxim which, taken literally, requires courts to follow decided cases, is shown by the thousands of overruled decisions, to be a figurative expression requiring only a reasonable respect for decided cases.

Charles Doe, *Lisbon v. Lyman*, 49 N.H. 553, 602 (1870)

9 We sincerely hope that the editors [of the *American Civil Law Journal*] will fail in their expressed desire to diminish the weight of precedents with our courts. We believe the weight attached to them is about the best thing in our whole system of law.

> **Oliver Wendell Holmes, Jr.,** "Summary of Events," 7 *American Law Review* 579 (1873)

10 The official theory [of the development of law] is that each new decision follows syllogistically from existing precedents. But just as the clavicle in the cat only tells of the existence of some earlier creature to which a collar-bone was useful, precedents survive in the law long after the use they once served is at an end and the reason for them has been forgotten. . . . as the law is administered by able and experienced men, who know too much to sacrifice good sense to a syllogism, it will be found that, when ancient rules maintain themselves . . . new reasons more fitted to the time have been found for them, and that they gradually receive a new content, and at last a new form, from the grounds to which they have been transplanted.

> **Oliver Wendell Holmes, Jr.,** *The Common Law* 35–36 (1881)

11 A precedent, my little ruffians, is the most respectable thing in the world, for it has no binding force, but sways by the stress of professional etiquette; precisely as the first monkey that leaps into the stream determines the point at which all shall leave it on the other side. It is revered for its priority and observed for its badness. A decision, for illustration, that is obviously just and legal cannot become a true precedent. There may be a parallel decision, but there is the law for that. It is only when a decision is to be rendered for which there is no law that your true precedent rears its venerated head and gives the Jovian, irrevocable nod. American law, which is based upon English law, which is based upon French law, which is based upon Roman law, has the advantage of hoarier precedents than English law, which has the advantage of hoarier precedents than French law, which has the advantage of hoarier precedents than Roman law, under which Pontius Pilate had himself to establish a precedent by convicting a prisoner in whom he found no sin.

> **Ambrose Bierce,** "Prohibiting of Weapons Prohibited," *Wasp,* 24 Mar. 1883, in *The Ambrose Bierce Satanic Reader* 66–67 (Ernest J. Hopkins ed. 1968)

12 Some courts live by correcting the errors of others and adhering to their own. On these terms courts of final review hold their existence, or those of them which are strictly and exclusively courts of review, without any original jurisdiction, and with no direct function but to find fault or see that none can be found. With these exalted tribunals, who live only to judge the judges, the rule of *stare decisis* is not only a canon of the public good, but a law of self-preservation. At the peril of their lives they must discover error abroad and be discreetly blind to its commission at home. Were they as ready to correct themselves as others, they could no longer speak as absolute oracles of legal truth; the reason for their existence would disappear, and their destruction would speedily supervene.

> **Logan E. Bleckley,** *Ellison v. Georgia R.R.,* 87 Ga. 691, 695–96, 13 S.E. 809 (1891)

13 Every direct authority known to us is against us; nevertheless, we are right and these authorities are all wrong, as time and further judicial study of the subject will manifest.

> **Logan E. Bleckley,** *Green v. Coast Line R.R.,* 97 Ga. 15, 36–37, 24 S.E. 814 (1895)

14 A recent President of the American Bar Association has criticised the present conditions in radical language: "A judge may decide almost any question any way, and still be supported by an array of cases."

> **John H. Wigmore,** *A Treatise on the System of Evidence in Trials at Common Law* 1:ix (1904)

15 It may not be amiss . . . to notice the course of legislation as well as expressions of opinion from other than judicial sources. In the brief filed by Mr. Louis D. Brandeis, for the defendant in error, is a very copious collection of all these matters. . . . The legislation and opinions referred to in the margin may not be, technically speaking, authorities, . . . yet they are significant of a widespread belief that woman's physical

structure, and the functions she performs in consequence thereof, justify special legislation. . . . when a question of fact is debated and debatable, . . . a widespread and long continued belief concerning it is worthy of consideration. We take judicial cognizance of all matters of general knowledge.*

David J. Brewer, *Muller v. Oregon,* 208 U.S. 412, 419–21 (1908)

16 The rules and principles of case-law have never been treated as final truths but as working hypotheses, continually retested in those great laboratories of the law, the courts of justice. Every new case is an experiment; and if the accepted rule which seems applicable yields a result which is felt to be unjust, the rule is reconsidered. It may not be modified at once, for the attempt to do absolute justice in every single case would make the development and maintenance of general rules impossible; but if a rule continues to work injustice, it will eventually be reformulated.

Munroe Smith, *Jurisprudence* 21 (1909)

17 PRECEDENT, *n.* In Law, a previous decision, rule or practice which, in the absence of a definite statute, has whatever force and authority a Judge may choose to give it, thereby greatly simplifying his task of doing as he pleases. As there are precedents for everything, he has only to ignore those that make against his interest and accentuate those in the line of his desire. Invention of the precedent elevates the trial-at-law from the low estate of a fortuitous ordeal to the noble attitude of a dirigible arbitrament.

Ambrose Bierce, *The Devil's Dictionary* 262 (1911)

18 That court best serves the law which recognizes that the rules of law which grew up in a remote generation may, in the fullness of experience, be found to serve another generation badly, and which discards the old rule when it finds that another rule of law represents what should be according to the established and settled judgment of society. . . . [The common law] is not and it should not be stationary. Change of this character should not be left to the legislature.

George W. Wheeler, *Dwy v. Connecticut Co.,* 89 Conn. 74, 99, 92 A. 112 (1915) (concurring)

19 Courts of law follow precedent, on the general theory that experience is more just than individual decision.

Precedent, however, tends to carry forward the ignorance and injustice of the past.

Mankind is constantly learning, getting new views of truth, seeing new values in social justice. Precedent clogs this advance.

Frank Crane, "Precedent," in *Four Minute Essays* 10:18, 19 (1919)

20 A decided case is worth as much as it weighs in reason and righteousness, and no more.

R. M. Wanamaker, *Adams Express Co. v. Beckwith,* 100 Ohio St. 348, 352, 126 N.E. 300 (1919)

21 [Some judges'] notion of their duty is to match the colors of the case at hand against the colors of many sample cases spread out upon their desk. The sample nearest in shade supplies the applicable rule. . . . If that were all there was to our calling, there would be little of intellectual interest about it. The man who had the best card index of the cases would also be the wisest judge. It is when the colors do not match, when the references in the index fail, when there is no decisive precedent, that the serious business of the judge begins. He must then fashion law for the litigants before him.

Benjamin N. Cardozo, *The Nature of the Judicial Process* 20–21 (1921)

22 Not all the progeny of principles begotten of a judgment survive . . . to maturity. Those that cannot prove their worth and strength by the test of experience, are sacrificed mercilessly and thrown into the void.

Benjamin N. Cardozo, *The Nature of the Judicial Process* 22–23 (1921)

23 It will not do to decide the same question one way between one set of litigants and the opposite way between another.

Benjamin N. Cardozo, *The Nature of the Judicial Process* 33 (1921)

---

* The type of brief filed by Brandeis in the *Muller* case, relying heavily on extralegal data, became known as a "Brandeis brief."

24 The sordid controversies of litigants are the stuff out of which great and shining truths will ultimately be shaped.

> **Benjamin N. Cardozo,** *The Nature of the Judicial Process* 35 (1921)

25 The labor of judges would be increased almost to the breaking point if every past decision could be reopened in every case, and one could not lay one's own course of bricks on the secure foundation of the courses laid by others who had gone before him.

> **Benjamin N. Cardozo,** *The Nature of the Judicial Process* 149 (1921)

26 But I am ready to concede that the rule of adherence to precedent, though it ought not to be abandoned, ought to be in some degree relaxed. I think that when a rule, after it has been duly tested by experience, has been found to be inconsistent with the sense of justice or with the social welfare, there should be less hesitation in frank avowal and full abandonment.

> **Benjamin N. Cardozo,** *The Nature of the Judicial Process* 150 (1921)

27 If judges have wofully [*sic*] misinterpreted the *mores* of their day, or if the *mores* of their day are no longer those of ours, they ought not to tie, in helpless submission, the hands of their successors.

> **Benjamin N. Cardozo,** *The Nature of the Judicial Process* 152 (1921)

28 Such limitation of principles previously announced, and such express disapproval of *dicta*, are often necessary. It is an unavoidable incident of the search by courts of last resort for the true rule. The process of inclusion and exclusion, so often applied in developing a rule, cannot end with its first enunciation. The rule as announced must be deemed tentative. For the many and varying facts to which it will be applied cannot be foreseen. Modification implies growth. It is the life of the law.

> **Louis D. Brandeis,** *Washington v. W.C. Dawson & Co.,* 264 U.S. 219, 236 (1924) (dissenting)

29 *Stare decisis* is ordinarily a wise rule of action. But it is not a universal, inexorable command. The instances in which the court has disregarded its admonition are many.

> **Louis D. Brandeis,** *Washington v. W.C. Dawson & Co.,* 264 U.S. 219, 238 (1924) (dissenting)

30 The fecundity of our case law would make Malthus stand aghast. Adherence to precedent was once a steadying force, the guarantee, as it seemed, of stability and certainty. We would not sacrifice any of the brood, and now the spawning progeny, forgetful of our mercy, are rending those who spared them. Increase of numbers has not made for increase of respect. The output of a multitude of minds must be expected to contain its proportion of vagaries. So vast a brood includes the defective and the helpless. An avalanche of decisions by tribunals great and small is producing a situation where citation of precedent is tending to count for less, and appeal to an informing principle is tending to count for more.

> **Benjamin N. Cardozo,** *The Growth of the Law* 4–5 (1924)

31 So far as we have been able to determine the diligence of counsel has spread before us all "the law and the Gospels" touching the question at issue. Four chapters of the Bible, department bulletin No. 1151 of the United States Department of Agriculture, Belden on Fur Farming for Profit, Harding on Fox Raising, Darwin's Origin of Species, Shakespeare's Henry IV, St. John Lucas, Suetonius, Aesop's Fables, the Tale of the Spartan Youth, the Harvard Law Review, the Albany Law Journal, the Central Law Journal, the London Law Times, the Criminal Law Magazine, and certain anonymous writers, not to mention numerous statutes and court decisions, adorn and illuminate their briefs.

> **Haslett P. Burke,** *E.A. Stephens & Co. v. Albers,* 81 Colo. 488, 491, 256 P. 15 (1927)

32 What has once been settled by a precedent will not be unsettled overnight, for certainty and uniformity are gains not lightly to be sacrificed. Above all is this true when honest men have shaped their conduct upon the faith of the pronouncement.

> **Benjamin N. Cardozo,** *The Paradoxes of Legal Science* 29–30 (1928)

33 Every lawyer knows that a prior case may, at the will of the court, "stand" either for

the narrowest point to which its holding may be reduced, or for the widest formulation that its *ratio decidendi* will allow.

Karl N. Llewellyn, *Cases and Materials on the Law of Sales* x (1930)

34 Toward its [precedent's] operation drive all those phases of human make up which build habit in the individual and institutions in the group: laziness as to the reworking of a problem once solved; the time and energy saved by routine, especially under any pressure of business; the values of routine as a curb on arbitrariness and as a prop of weakness, inexperience, and instability; the social values of predictability; the power of whatever exists to produce expectations and the power of expectations to become normative. The force of precedent in the law is heightened by an additional factor: that curious, almost universal sense of justice which urges that all men are properly to be treated alike in like circumstances. As the social system varies we meet infinite variations as to what men or treatments or circumstances are to be classed as "like"; but the pressure to accept the views of the time and place remains.

Karl N. Llewellyn, "Case Law," in *Encyclopedia of the Social Sciences* 3:249, 249 (1930)

35 *Stare decisis* is usually the wise policy, because in most matters it is more important that the applicable rule of law be settled than that it be settled right.... But in cases involving the Federal Constitution, where correction through legislative action is practically impossible, this Court has often overruled its earlier decisions. The Court bows to the lessons of experience and the force of better reasoning, recognizing that the process of trial and error, so fruitful in the physical sciences, is appropriate also in the judicial function.*

Louis D. Brandeis, *Burnet v. Colorado Oil & Gas Co.,* 285 U.S. 393, 406–408 (1932) (dissenting)

* It is almost as important that the law should be settled permanently, as that it should be settled correctly. —**Noah H. Swayne,** *Gilman v. Philadelphia,* 70 U.S. (3 Wall.) 713, 724 (1865)
No question is ever settled / Until it is settled right. —**Ella Wheeler Wilcox,** "Settle the Question Right," 1900, quoted in *Home Book of Quotations* 1727 (Burton Stevenson ed., 9th ed. 1958)
The fact that we are here today is due to the inexo-

36 At least it is a considered dictum, and not comment merely *obiter*. It has capacity, though it be less than a decision, to tilt the balanced mind toward submission and agreement.... In controversies so purely local, little gain is to be derived from drawing nice distinctions between dicta and decisions. Disagreement with either, even though permissible, is at best a last resort, to be embraced with caution and reluctance. The stranger from afar, unacquainted with the local ways, permits himself to be guided by the best evidence available, the directions or the counsel of those who dwell upon the spot.

Benjamin N. Cardozo, *Hawks v. Hamill,* 288 U.S. 52, 59–60 (1933)

37 No two cases are exactly alike. A young attorney found two opinions in the New York Reports where the facts seemed identical although the law was in conflict, but an older and more experienced attorney pointed out to him that the names of the parties were different.

Cuthbert W. Pound, "American Law Institute Speech of Judge Pound," 5 *New York State Bar Journal* 267 (1933)

38 The Law is the killy-loo bird of the sciences. The killy-loo, of course, was the bird that insisted on flying backward because it didn't care where it was going but was mightily interested in where it had been. And certainly The Law, when it moves at all, does so by flapping clumsily and uncertainly along, with its eye unswervingly glued on what lies behind.... Only The Law, inexorably devoted to all its most ancient principles and precedents, makes a vice of innovation and a virtue of hoariness. Only The Law resists and resents the notion that it should ever change its anti-

rable law that nothing is settled until it is settled right. —**Louis D. Brandeis,** Speech, Boston, 6 Mar. 1913, quoted in Alpheus T. Mason, *Brandeis: A Free Man's Life* 204 (1946)
It is important, of course, that controversies be settled right, but there are many civil questions which arise between individuals in which it is not so important that the controversy be settled one way or another as that it be settled. —**William Howard Taft,** "Adequate Machinery for Judicial Business," 7 *American Bar Association Journal* 453, 453 (1921)
It is usually more important that a rule of law be settled than that it be settled right. —**Louis D. Brandeis,** *DiSanto v. Pennsylvania,* 273 U.S. 34, 42 (1927) (dissenting)

quated ways to meet the challenge of a changing world.

Fred Rodell, *Woe Unto You, Lawyers!* 23 (1939)

39 We recognize that *stare decisis* embodies an important social policy. It represents an element of continuity in law, and is rooted in the psychologic need to satisfy reasonable expectations. But *stare decisis* is a principle of policy and not a mechanical formula of adherence to the latest decision, however recent and questionable, when such adherence involves collision with a prior doctrine more embracing in its scope, intrinsically sounder, and verified by experience. . . . This Court, unlike the House of Lords, has from the beginning rejected a doctrine of disability at self-correction.

Felix Frankfurter, *Helvering v. Hallock,* 309 U.S. 106, 119, 121 (1940)

40 Cases get distinguished and distinguished till they provoke the aphorism that a distinguished case is a case that is no longer distinguished.

Thomas Reed Powell, "Some Aspects of American Constitutional Law," 53 *Harvard Law Review* 529, 537 (1940)

41 In actual practice, two cases are rarely, if ever, exactly alike. . . . Thus a judge may have a wide discretion in deciding in a given case to follow either precedent A, or precedent B, both of which seem to have considerable bearing on this case but which, unfortunately, are completely contradictory to one another.

Robert K. Carr, *The Supreme Court and Judicial Review* 19 (1942)

42 However, when convinced of former error, this Court has never felt constrained to follow precedent. In constitutional questions, where correction depends upon amendment and not upon legislative action this Court throughout its history has freely exercised its power to reexamine the basis of its constitutional decisions.

Stanley F. Reed, *Smith v. Allwright,* 321 U.S. 649, 665 (1944)

43 The evil resulting from overruling earlier considered decisions must be evident. . . . the law becomes not a chart to govern conduct but a game of chance; the administration of justice will fall into disrepute. Re-

spect for tribunals must fall when the bar and the public come to understand that nothing that has been said in prior adjudications has force in a current controversy.

Owen J. Roberts, *Mahnich v. Southern Steamship Co.,* 321 U.S. 96, 112–13 (1944)

44 The reason for my concern is that the instant decision, overruling that announced about nine years ago, tends to bring adjudications of this tribunal into the same class as a restricted railroad ticket, good for this day and train only. I have no assurance, in view of current decisions, that the opinion announced today may not shortly be repudiated and overruled by justices who deem they have new light on the subject.

Owen J. Roberts, *Smith v. Allwright,* 321 U.S. 649, 665 (1944) (dissenting)

45 While Judge Cardozo pointed out with great accuracy that the power of the precedent is only "the power of the beaten track," still the mere fact that a path is a beaten one is a persuasive reason for following it.

Robert H. Jackson, "Full Faith and Credit— The Lawyer's Clause of the Constitution," 45 *Columbia Law Review* 1, 26 (1945)

46 But throughout the history of the Court *stare decisis* has had only a limited application in the field of constitutional law. And it is a wise policy which largely restricts it to those areas of the law where correction can be had by legislation. Otherwise the Constitution loses the flexibility necessary if it is to serve the needs of successive generations.

William O. Douglas, *New York v. United States,* 326 U.S. 572, 590 (1946) (dissenting)

47 Precedent is not all-controlling in law. There must be room for growth, since every precedent has an origin. But it is the essence of our tradition for judges, when they stand at the end of the marked way, to go forward with caution keeping sight, so far as they are able, upon the great landmarks left behind and the direction they point ahead.

Wiley B. Rutledge, *In re Yamashita,* 327 U.S. 1, 43 (1946) (dissenting)

48 But if I have agreed to any prior decision which forecloses what now seems to be a sensible construction of this Act, I must frankly admit that I was unaware of it. . . . Under these circumstances, except for any personal humiliation involved in admitting that I do not always understand the opinions of this Court, I see no reason why I should be consciously wrong today because I was unconsciously wrong yesterday.

> **Robert H. Jackson,** *Massachusetts v. United States,* 333 U.S. 611, 639–40 (1948) (dissenting)

49 The search for a static security—in the law or elsewhere—is misguided. The fact is that security can only be achieved through constant change, through the wise discarding of old ideas that have outlived their usefulness, and through the adapting of others to current facts.

> **William O. Douglas,** *Stare Decisis* 7 (1949)

50 *Stare decisis* provides some moorings so that men may trade and arrange their affairs with confidence. *Stare decisis* serves to take the capricious element out of law and to give stability to a society. It is a strong tie which the future has to the past.

> **William O. Douglas,** *Stare Decisis* 8 (1949)

51 A judge looking at a constitutional decision may have compulsions to revere past history and accept what was once written. But he remembers above all else that it is the Constitution which he swore to support and defend, not the gloss which his predecessors may have put on it. So he comes to formulate his own views, rejecting some earlier ones as false and embracing others. He cannot do otherwise unless he lets men long dead and unaware of the problems of the age in which he lives do his thinking for him.

> **William O. Douglas,** *Stare Decisis* 9 (1949)

52 "Equality before the law" is a properly cherished principle. Yet it ought not to be pushed to ridiculous limits. Merely because a court was outrageously unfair to Mr. Simple in 1900 is a poor reason for being equally unfair to Mr. Timid in 1947. Thus to perpetuate a markedly unjust rule seems a queer way of doing justice.

> **Jerome N. Frank,** *Courts on Trial* 268 (1949)

53 Wisdom too often never comes, and so one ought not to reject it merely because it comes late.

> **Felix Frankfurter,** *Henslee v. Union Planters Bank,* 335 U.S. 595, 600 (1949) (dissenting)

54 These decisions do not justify today's decision. They merely prove how a hint becomes a suggestion, is loosely turned into dictum and finally elevated to a decision. This progressive distortion is due to . . . uncritical confusion.

> **Felix Frankfurter,** *United States v. Rabinowitz,* 339 U.S. 56, 75 (1950) (dissenting)

55 Somewhere, sometime to every principle comes a moment of repose when it has been so often announced, so confidently relied upon, so long continued, that it passes the limits of judicial discretion and disturbance.

> **John W. Davis,** Argument before the Supreme Court, *Brown v. Board of Education,* Dec. 1953, in *Argument* 215 (Leon Friedman ed. 1969)

56 The law is the only profession which records its mistakes carefully, exactly as they occurred, and yet does not identify them as mistakes.

> **Elliott Dunlap Smith,** quoted in Louis M. Brown, "Legal Autopsy," *Journal of the American Judicature Society,* June 1955, at 47

57 If I were to attempt to generalize, as indeed I should not, I should say that most depends upon the judge's unspoken notion as to the function of his court. If he views the role of the courts as a passive one, he will be willing to delegate the responsibility for change, and he will not greatly care whether the delegated authority is exercised or not. If he views the court as an instrument of society designed to reflect in its decisions the morality of the community, he will be more likely to look precedent in the teeth and to measure it against the ideals and the aspirations of his time.

> **Walter V. Schaefer,** "Precedent and Policy," 34 *University of Chicago Law Review* 3, 23 (1966)

58 DISTINGUISH, *v.* . . . To explain crucial differences between apparently similar cases—such as differences in typeface, the

names of judges and their spellings, uses of commas, and paragraphing.

> Robert J. Morris, "The New (Legal) Devil's Dictionary," 6 *Journal of Contemporary Law* 231, 232–33 (1979)

59 I would rather create a precedent than find one.

> William O. Douglas, *The Court Years: 1939–1975*, at 179 (1980)

60 Power, not reason, is the new currency of this Court's decisionmaking. . . . Neither the law nor the facts supporting [previous opinions barring victim-impact statements] underwent any change in the last four years. Only the personnel of this Court did. . . . This truncation of the Court's duty to stand by its own precedents is astonishing. . . . the majority sends a clear signal that essentially *all* decisions implementing the personal liberties protected by the Bill of Rights and the Fourteenth Amendment are open to reexamination.

> Thurgood Marshall, *Payne v. Tennessee*, 111 S. Ct. 2597, 2619, 2623 (1991) (dissenting)

PRESIDENT

See also IMPEACHMENT; PARDONS; SEPARATION OF POWERS

1 [Explaining the rationale for Presidential appointment of judges:] I proceed to lay it down as a rule, that one man of discernment is better fitted to analise and estimate the peculiar qualities adapted to particular offices, than a body of men of equal, or perhaps even of superior discernment. The sole and undivided responsibility of one man will naturally beget a livelier sense of duty and a more exact regard to reputation. He will on this account feel himself under stronger obligations, and more interested to investigate with care the qualities requisite to the stations to be filled, and to prefer with impartiality the persons who may have the fairest pretensions to them.

> Alexander Hamilton, *The Federalist* No. 76, at 2:279 (1788)

2 The President is the sole organ of the nation in its external relations, and its sole representative with foreign nations.

> John Marshall, in 10 *Annals of Congress* 613 (1800)

3 The intimate political relation, subsisting between the president of the United States and the heads of departments, necessarily renders any legal investigation of the acts of one of those high officers peculiarly irksome, as well as delicate; and excites some hesitation with respect to the propriety of entering into such investigation.

> John Marshall, *Marbury v. Madison*, 5 U.S. (1 Cranch) 137, 169 (1803)

4 The province of the court is, solely, to decide on the rights of individuals, not to enquire how the executive, or executive officers, perform duties in which they have a discretion. Questions, in their nature political, or which are, by the constitution and laws, submitted to the executive, can never be made in this court.

> John Marshall, *Marbury v. Madison*, 5 U.S. (1 Cranch) 137, 170 (1803)

5 Every person holding any civil office to which he has been appointed by and with the advice and consent of the Senate, and every person who shall hereafter be appointed to any such office, and shall become duly qualified to act therein, is, and shall be entitled to hold such office until a successor shall have been in like manner appointed and duly qualified.

> Tenure of Office Act, ch. 154, § 1, 14 Stat. 430, 430 (1867)

6 After an existence of nearly twenty years of almost innocuous desuetude these laws [the Tenure of Office Acts] are brought forth.

> Grover Cleveland, Message to Senate, 1 Mar. 1886, in *Messages and Papers of the Presidents* 8:375, 381 (James D. Richardson ed. 1898)

7 The President is at liberty, both in law and conscience, to be as big a man as he can. His capacity will set the limit; and if Congress be overborne by him, it will be no fault of the makers of the Constitution.

> Woodrow Wilson, *Constitutional Government in the United States* 70 (1908)

8 It is important to bear in mind that we are here dealing not alone with an authority vested in the President by an exertion of legislative power, but with such an authority plus the very delicate, plenary and exclusive power of the President as the sole

organ of the federal government in the field of international relations—a power which does not require as a basis for its exercise an act of Congress, but which, of course, like every other governmental power, must be exercised in subordination to the applicable provisions of the Constitution.

George Sutherland, *United States v. Curtiss-Wright Export Corp.*, 299 U.S. 304, 319–20 (1936)

9 It would be intolerable that courts, without the relevant information, should review and perhaps nullify actions of the Executive taken on information properly held secret. . . . the very nature of executive decisions as to foreign policy is political, not judicial. Such decisions are wholly confided by our Constitution to the political departments of the government, Executive and Legislative. They are delicate, complex, and involve large elements of prophecy. They are and should be undertaken only by those directly responsible to the people whose welfare they advance or imperil. They are decisions of a kind for which the Judiciary has neither aptitude, facilities nor responsibility and which has long been held to belong in the domain of political power not subject to judicial intrusion or inquiry.

Robert H. Jackson, *Chicago & Southern Air Lines v. Waterman Steamship Corp.*, 333 U.S. 103, 111 (1948)

10 Presidential powers are not fixed but fluctuate, depending upon their disjunction or conjunction of those of Congress. 1. When the President acts pursuant to an express or implied authorization of Congress, his authority is at its maximum, for it includes all that he possesses in his own right plus all that Congress can delegate. In these circumstances . . . may he be said . . . to personify the federal sovereignty.

Robert H. Jackson, *Youngstown Sheet & Tube Co. v. Sawyer*, 343 U.S. 579, 635–36 (1952) (concurring)

11 When the President acts in absence of either a congressional grant or denial of authority, he can only rely upon his own independent powers, but there is a zone of twilight in which he and Congress may have concurrent authority, or in which its distribution is uncertain. Therefore, congressional inertia, indifference or quies-

cence may sometimes, at least as a practical matter, enable, if not invite, measures on independent presidential responsibility. In this area, any actual test of power is likely to depend on the imperatives of events and contemporary imponderables rather than on abstract theories of law.

Robert H. Jackson, *Youngstown Sheet & Tube Co. v. Sawyer*, 343 U.S. 579, 637 (1952) (concurring)

12 When the President takes measures incompatible with the expressed or implied will of Congress, his power is at its lowest ebb, for then he can rely only upon his own constitutional powers minus any constitutional powers of Congress over the matter.

Robert H. Jackson, *Youngstown Sheet & Tube Co. v. Sawyer*, 343 U.S. 579, 637 (1952) (concurring)

13 What did the President know, and when did he know it?

Howard H. Baker, Jr., quoted in Sam J. Ervin, Jr., *The Whole Truth: The Watergate Conspiracy* 174 (1980)

14 Under the doctrine of separation of powers, the manner in which the President personally exercises his assigned executive powers is not subject to questioning by another branch of Government.

Richard M. Nixon, Statement about Executive Privilege, 12 Mar. 1973, in *Public Papers of the Presidents: Richard Nixon, 1973*, at 184, 185 (1975)

15 I made mistakes, but in all my years of public life, I have never profited, never profited from public service—I have earned every cent. And in all of my years of public life, I have never obstructed justice. And I think, too, that I could say that in my years of public life, that I welcome this kind of examination, because people have got to know whether or not their President is a crook. Well, I am not a crook. I have earned everything I have got.

Richard M. Nixon, Speech, Orlando, Fla., 17 Nov. 1973, in *Public Papers of the Presidents: Richard Nixon, 1973*, at 946, 956 (1975)

16 In all candor, the Court fails to perceive any reason for suspending the power of courts to get evidence and rule on questions of privilege in criminal matters sim-

ply because it is the President of the United States who holds the evidence.

John J. Sirica, *In re Grand Jury Subpoena Duces Tecum Issued to Richard M. Nixon,* 360 F. Supp. 1, 10 (D.D.C. 1973)

17 Neither the doctrine of separation of powers, nor the need for confidentiality of high-level communications, without more, can sustain an absolute, unqualified Presidential privilege of immunity from judicial process under all circumstances. The President's need for complete candor and objectivity from advisers calls for great deference from the courts. However, when the privilege depends solely on the broad, undifferentiated claim of public interest in the confidentiality of such conversations, a confrontation with other values arises.

Warren E. Burger, *United States v. Nixon,* 418 U.S. 683, 706 (1974)

18 Nowhere in the Constitution ... is there any explicit reference to a privilege of confidentiality, yet to the extent this interest relates to the effective discharge of a President's powers, it is constitutionally based.

Warren E. Burger, *United States v. Nixon,* 418 U.S. 683, 711 (1974)

19 We conclude that when the ground for asserting [executive] privilege as to subpoenaed materials sought for use in a criminal trial is based only on the generalized interest in confidentiality, it cannot prevail over the fundamental demands of due process of law in the fair administration of criminal justice. The generalized assertion of privilege must yield to the demonstrated, specific need for evidence in a pending criminal trial.

Warren E. Burger, *United States v. Nixon,* 418 U.S. 683, 713 (1974)

20 In all the decisions I have made in my public life, I have always tried to do what was best for the Nation. Throughout the long and difficult period of Watergate, I have felt it was my duty to persevere, to make every possible effort to complete the term of office to which you elected me.

In the past few days, however, it has become evident to me that I no longer have a strong enough political base in the Congress to justify continuing that effort. As long as there was such a base, I felt strongly that it was necessary to see the

constitutional process through to its conclusion, that to do otherwise would be unfaithful to the spirit of that deliberately difficult process and a dangerously destabilizing precedent for the future.

But with the disappearance of that base, I now believe that the constitutional purpose has been served, and there is no longer a need for the process to be prolonged.

Richard M. Nixon, Address to the Nation Announcing Decision to Resign the Office of President of the United States, 8 Aug. 1974, in *Public Papers of the Presidents: Richard Nixon, 1974,* at 626, 627 (1975)

21 When the President does it, that means that it is not illegal.

Richard M. Nixon, Interview by David Frost, quoted in *New York Times,* 20 May 1977, at A16

PRESS

See CENSORSHIP; FREEDOM OF THE PRESS; LIBEL

PRISON

1 Imprisonment to protect society from predicted but unconsummated offenses is so unprecedented in this country and so fraught with danger of excesses and injustice that I am loath to resort to it, even as a discretionary judicial technique to supplement conviction of such offenses as those of which defendants stand convicted.

Robert H. Jackson, *Williamson v. United States,* 184 F.2d 280, 282–83 (2d Cir. 1950)

2 If the position implies that the prisoners in state institutions are wholly without the protections of the Constitution and the Due Process Clause, it is plainly untenable. Lawful imprisonment necessarily makes unavailable many rights and privileges of the ordinary citizen, a "retraction justified by the considerations underlying our penal system." But though his rights may be diminished by the needs and exigencies of the institutional environment, a prisoner is not wholly stripped of constitutional protections when he is imprisoned for crime. There is no iron curtain drawn between the Constitution and the prisons of this country.

Byron R. White, *Wolff v. McDonnell,* 418 U.S. 539, 555–56 (1974)

3 Prisoners are persons whom most of us would rather not think about. . . . It is thus easy to think of prisoners as members of a separate netherworld. . . . Nothing can change the fact, however, that the society that these prisoners inhabit is our own. . . . When prisoners emerge from the shadows to press a constitutional claim . . . they speak the language of a charter upon which all of us rely to hold official power accountable.

William J. Brennan, Jr., *O'Lone v. Estate of Shabazz,* 482 U.S. 342, 354–55 (1987) (dissenting)

PRIVACY

See also ABORTION; SEARCHES AND SEIZURES

1 Political, social, and economic changes entail the recognition of new rights, and the common law, in its eternal youth, grows to meet the demands of society. . . . now the right to life has come to mean the right to enjoy life,—the right to be let alone; the right to liberty secures the exercise of extensive civil privileges; and the term "property" has grown to comprise every form of possession—intangible, as well as tangible.

Samuel D. Warren and Louis D. Brandeis, "The Right to Privacy," 4 *Harvard Law Review* 193, 193 (1890)
See also PRIVACY 3

2 The so-called right of privacy is, as the phrase suggests, founded upon the claim that a man has the right to pass through this world, if he wills, without having his picture published, his business enterprises discussed, his successful experiments written up for the benefit of others, or his eccentricities commented upon either in handbills, circulars, catalogues, periodicals or newspapers.

Alton B. Parker, *Roberson v. Rochester Folding Box Co.,* 171 N.Y. 538, 544 (1902)

3 The makers of our Constitution undertook to secure conditions favorable to the pursuit of happiness. They recognized the significance of man's spiritual nature, of his feelings and of his intellect. They knew that only a part of the pain, pleasure and satisfactions of life are to be found in material things. They sought to protect Americans in their beliefs, their thoughts, their emotions and their sensations. They conferred,

as against the Government, the right to be let alone*—the most comprehensive of rights and the right most valued by civilized men.

Louis D. Brandeis, *Olmstead v. United States,* 277 U.S. 438, 478 (1928) (dissenting)
See also PRIVACY 1

4 A man can still control a small part of his environment, his house; he can retreat thence from outsiders, secure in the knowledge that they cannot get at him without disobeying the Constitution. That is still a sizable hunk of liberty—worth protecting from encroachment. A sane, decent, civilized society must provide some such oasis, some shelter from public scrutiny, some insulated enclosure, some enclave, some inviolate place which is a man's castle.

Jerome N. Frank, *United States v. On Lee,* 193 F.2d 306, 315–16 (2d Cir. 1951) (dissenting)

5 There is . . . unanimity that opportunists, for private gain, cannot be permitted to arm themselves with an acceptable principle, such as that of a right to work, a privilege to engage in interstate commerce, or a free press, and proceed to use it as an iron standard to smooth their path by crushing the living rights of others to privacy and repose.

Stanley F. Reed, *Breard v. Alexandria,* 341 U.S. 622, 625–26 (1951)

6 The right to be let alone is indeed the beginning of all freedom.

William O. Douglas, *Public Utilities Comm'n v. Pollak,* 343 U.S. 451, 467 (1952) (dissenting)

7 I like my privacy as well as the next one, but I am nevertheless compelled to admit that government has a right to invade it unless prohibited by some specific constitutional provision.

Hugo L. Black, *Griswold v. Connecticut,* 381 U.S. 479, 510 (1965) (dissenting)

8 In other words, the First Amendment has a penumbra where privacy is protected from governmental intrusion.

William O. Douglas, *Griswold v. Connecticut,* 381 U.S. 479, 483 (1965)

---

* The right to one's person may be said to be a right of complete immunity: to be let alone. —**Thomas M. Cooley,** *A Treatise on the Law of Torts* 29 (1880)

9 Would we allow the police to search the sacred precincts of marital bedrooms for telltale signs of the use of contraceptives?

> William O. Douglas, *Griswold v. Connecticut*, 381 U.S. 479, 485 (1965)

10 To hold that a right so basic and fundamental and so deep-rooted in our society as the right of privacy in marriage may be infringed because that right is not guaranteed in so many words by the first eight amendments to the Constitution is to ignore the Ninth Amendment and to give it no effect whatsoever.

> Arthur J. Goldberg, *Griswold v. Connecticut*, 381 U.S. 479, 491 (1965) (concurring)

11 Since 1879 Connecticut has had on its books a law which forbids the use of contraceptives by anyone. I think this is an uncommonly silly law.... But we are not asked in this case to say whether we think this law is unwise, or even asinine. We are asked to hold that it violates the United States Constitution. And that I cannot do.

> Potter Stewart, *Griswold v. Connecticut*, 381 U.S. 479, 527 (1965) (dissenting)

12 We are rapidly entering the age of no privacy, where everyone is open to surveillance at all times; where there are no secrets from government.

> William O. Douglas, *Osborn v. United States*, 385 U.S. 323, 341 (1966) (dissenting)

13 The good society must have its hiding places—its protected crannies for the soul. Under the pitiless eye of safety the soul will wither. If I choose to get in my car and drive somewhere, it seems to me that where I am coming from, and where I am going, are nobody's business; I know of no law that requires me to have either a purpose or a destination. If I choose to take an evening walk to see if Andromeda has come up on schedule, I think I am entitled to look for the distant light of Almach and Mirach without finding myself staring into the blinding beam of a police flashlight.

> Charles A. Reich, "Police Questioning of Law Abiding Citizens," 75 *Yale Law Journal* 1161, 1172 (1966)

14 My understanding of the rule that has emerged from prior decisions is that there is a twofold requirement, first that a person have exhibited an actual (subjective) ex-pectation of privacy and, second, that the expectation be one that society is prepared to recognize as "reasonable." Thus a man's home is, for most purposes, a place where he expects privacy, but objects, activities, or statements that he exposes to the "plain view" of outsiders are not "protected" because no intention to keep them to himself has been exhibited. On the other hand, conversations in the open would not be protected against being overheard, for the expectation of privacy under the circumstances would be unreasonable.

> John M. Harlan (1899–1971), *Katz v. United States*, 389 U.S. 347, 361 (1967) (concurring)

15 The marital couple is not an independent entity with a mind and heart of its own, but an association of two individuals each with separate intellectual and emotional makeup. If the right of privacy means anything, it is the right of the *individual*, married or single, to be free from unwarranted governmental intrusion into matters so fundamentally affecting a person as the decision whether to bear or beget a child.

> William J. Brennan, Jr., *Eisenstadt v. Baird*, 405 U.S. 438, 453 (1972)

16 The Constitution does not explicitly mention any right of privacy. In a line of decisions, however ... the Court has recognized that a right of personal privacy, or a guarantee of certain areas or zones of privacy, does exist under the Constitution.

> Harry A. Blackmun, *Roe v. Wade*, 410 U.S. 113, 152 (1973)
> See also BILL OF RIGHTS 16

17 The Fourth Amendment protects the individual's privacy in a variety of settings. In none is the zone of privacy more clearly defined than when bounded by the unambiguous physical dimensions of an individual's home—a zone that finds its roots in clear and specific constitutional terms: "the right of the people to be secure in their ... houses ... shall not be violated."

> John Paul Stevens, *Payton v. New York*, 445 U.S. 573, 589 (1980)

18 Our cases long have recognized that the Constitution embodies a promise that a certain private sphere of individual liberty will be kept largely beyond the reach of government.

> Harry A. Blackmun, *Thornburgh v. American College of Obstetricians & Gynecologists*, 476 U.S. 747, 772 (1986)

19 The right of an individual to conduct intimate relationships in the intimacy of his or her own home seems to me to be the heart of the Constitution's protection of privacy.

Harry A. Blackmun, *Bowers v. Hardwick,* 478 U.S. 186, 208 (1986) (dissenting)

```
┌─────────────────────────────────────┐
│              PRIVILEGE               │
└─────────────────────────────────────┘
```

See CLIENT; FIFTH AMENDMENT

```
┌─────────────────────────────────────┐
│              PROCEDURE               │
└─────────────────────────────────────┘
```

See also CIVIL PROCEDURE; CRIMINAL PROCEDURE

1 Those who are impatient with the forms of law ought to reflect that it is through form that all organization is reached. Matter without form is chaos; power without form is anarchy. The state, were it to disregard forms, would not be a government, but a mob. Its action would not be administration, but violence.

Logan E. Bleckley, *Cochran v. State,* 62 Ga. 731, 732 (1879)

2 A system of procedure is perverted from its proper function when it multiplies impediments to justice without the warrant of clear necessity.

Benjamin N. Cardozo, *Reed v. Allen,* 286 U.S. 191, 209 (1932) (dissenting)

3 It is characteristic of the prevailing rationalistic systems of legal philosophy that they minimize the importance of procedure by calling it adjective law, etc. But the tendency of all modern scientific and philosophic thought is to weaken the distinction between substance and attribute . . . and to emphasize the importance of method, process, or procedure.

Morris R. Cohen, *Law and the Social Order* 128 (1933)

4 The history of liberty has largely been the history of observance of procedural safeguards.

Felix Frankfurter, *McNabb v. United States,* 318 U.S. 332, 347 (1943)

5 The history of American freedom is, in no small measure, the history of procedure.

Felix Frankfurter, *Malinski v. New York,* 324 U.S. 401, 414 (1945) (concurring)

6 Matters of "substance" and matters of "procedure" are much talked about in the books as though they defined a great divide cutting across the whole domain of law. But . . . [they] are the same keywords to very different problems. Neither . . . represents the same invariants. Each implies different variables depending upon the particular problem for which it is used. . . . And the different problems are only distantly related at best, for the terms are in common use in connection with situations turning on such different considerations as those that are relevant to questions pertaining to *ex post facto* legislation, the impairment of the obligations of contract, the enforcement of federal rights in the State courts and the multitudinous phases of the conflict of laws.

Felix Frankfurter, *Guaranty Trust Co. v. York,* 326 U.S. 99, 108 (1945)

7 At times in our system the way in which courts perform their function becomes as important as what they do in the result. In some respects matters of procedure constitute the very essence of ordered liberty under the Constitution.

Wiley B. Rutledge, *United States v. United Mine Workers,* 330 U.S. 258, 363 (1947)

8 Unfortunately by a kind of Gresham's Law, the bad, or harsh, procedural decisions drive out the good, so that in time a rule becomes entirely obscured by its interpretive barnacles.

Charles E. Clark, "Special Problems in Drafting and Interpreting Procedural Codes and Rules," 3 *Vanderbilt Law Review* 493, 498 (1950)

9 It is procedure that spells much of the difference between rule by law and rule by whim or caprice. Steadfast adherence to strict procedural safeguards is our main assurance that there will be equal justice under law.

William O. Douglas, *Joint Anti-Fascist Refugee Committee v. McGrath,* 341 U.S. 123, 179 (1951) (concurring)

10 Procedural fairness and regularity are of the indispensable essence of liberty. Severe substantive laws can be endured if they are fairly and impartially applied. Indeed, if put to the choice, one might well prefer to live under Soviet substantive law applied in

good faith by our common-law procedures than under our substantive law enforced by Soviet procedural practices.

> Robert H. Jackson, *Shaughnessy v. United States*, 345 U.S. 206, 224 (1953) (dissenting)

11 Our system of government is one in which procedure is greatly important: because procedure takes into account the ways of a people, their customs, their tradition, their way of looking at things—their way of life.

> William F. Buckley, Jr., Newspaper column, 17 Sept. 1964, quoted in *Quotations from Chairman Bill* 6 (1970)

12 Procedure is the blindfold of Justice.

> Robert M. Cover, Owen M. Fiss, and Judith Resnik, *Procedure* 1232 (1988)

PRODUCTS LIABILITY

1 The remedies of injured consumers ought not to be made to depend upon the intricacies of the law of sales. The obligation of the manufacturer should not be based alone upon privity of contract. It should rest, as was once said, upon "the demands of social justice."

> Walter C. Noyes, *Ketterer v. Armour & Co.*, 200 F. 322, 323 (S.D.N.Y. 1912)

2 If the nature of a thing is such that it is reasonably certain to place life and limb in peril when negligently made, it is then a thing of danger. Its nature gives warning of the consequences to be expected. If to the element of danger there is added knowledge that the thing will be used by persons other than the purchaser, and used without new tests, then, irrespective of contract, the manufacturer of this thing of danger is under a duty to make it carefully.

> Benjamin N. Cardozo, *MacPherson v. Buick Motor Co.*, 217 N.Y. 382, 389, 111 N.E. 1050 (1916)

3 We have put aside the notion that the duty to safeguard life and limb, when the consequences of negligence may be foreseen, grows out of contract and nothing else. We have put the source of the obligation where it ought to be. We have put its source in the law.

> Benjamin N. Cardozo, *MacPherson v. Buick Motor Co.*, 217 N.Y. 382, 390, 111 N.E. 1050 (1916)

4 The maker of this car supplied it for the use of purchasers from the dealer just as plainly as the contractor in *Devlin v. Smith* supplied the scaffold for use by the servants of the owner. The dealer was indeed the one person of whom it might be said with some approach to certainty that by him the car would not be used. Yet the defendant would have us say that he was the one person whom it was under a legal duty to protect. The law does not lead us to so inconsequent a conclusion. Precedents drawn from the days of travel by stage coach do not fit the conditions of travel today. The principle that the danger must be imminent does not change, but the things subject to the principle do change. They are whatever the needs of life in a developing civilization require them to be.

> Benjamin N. Cardozo, *MacPherson v. Buick Motor Co.*, 217 N.Y. 382, 391, 111 N.E. 1050 (1916)

5 I believe the manufacturer's negligence should no longer be singled out as the basis of a plaintiff's right to recover in cases like the present one. In my opinion it should now be recognized that a manufacturer incurs an absolute liability when an article that he has placed on the market, knowing that it is to be used without inspection, proves to have a defect that causes injury to human beings. . . . Even if there is no negligence . . . public policy demands that responsibility be fixed wherever it will most effectively reduce the hazards to life and health inherent in defective products that reach the market. It is evident that the manufacturer can anticipate some hazards and guard against the recurrence of others, as the public cannot. Those who suffer injury from defective products are unprepared to meet its consequences. The cost of an injury and the loss of time or health may be an overwhelming misfortune to the person injured, and a needless one, for the risk of injury can be insured by the manufacturer and distributed among the public as a cost of doing business. It is to the public interest to discourage the marketing of products having defects that are a menace to the public. If such products nevertheless find their way into the market it is to the public interest to place the responsibility for whatever injury they may cause upon the manufacturer, who, even if he is not negligent in the manufacture of the prod-

uct, is responsible for its reaching the market. However intermittently such injuries may occur and however haphazardly they may strike, the risk of their occurrence is a constant risk and a general one. Against such a risk there should be general and constant protection and the manufacturer is best situated to afford such protection.

> Roger J. Traynor, *Escola v. Coca Cola Bottling Co. of Fresno*, 24 Cal. 2d. 453, 462, 150 P.2d 436 (1944) (concurring)

6 One who sells any product in a defective condition unreasonably dangerous to the user or consumer or to his property is subject to liability for physical harm thereby caused to the ultimate user or consumer, or to his property, if (a) the seller is engaged in the business of selling such a product, and (b) it is expected to and does reach the user or consumer without substantial change in the condition in which it is sold.

> Restatement (Second) of Torts § 402A(1) (1964)

7 The fall of a citadel is a dramatic moment. . . . In the field of products liability, the date of the fall of the citadel of privity can be fixed with some certainty. It was May 9, 1960, when the Supreme Court of New Jersey announced the decision in *Henningsen v. Bloomfield Motors, Inc.*

> William L. Prosser, "The Fall of the Citadel (Strict Liability to the Consumer)," 50 *Minnesota Law Review* 791, 791 (1966)

PROFESSION

See LEGAL PROFESSION

PROFESSIONAL CONDUCT

See CLIENT; LAWYER JOKES; LAWYERS (PRO); LAWYERS (CON)

PROHIBITION

See INTOXICATION

PROOF

See also EVIDENCE

1 In a word, justice was like to be in what is by no means an unusual dilemma for that upright functionary, namely, unable to show a fact that no one doubted.

> James Fenimore Cooper, *The Wing-and-Wing*, 1842, in *Complete Works of James Fenimore Cooper* 273 (1893)

2 It is not sufficient to establish a probability, though a strong one arising from the doctrine of chances, that the fact charged is more likely to be true than the contrary; but the evidence must establish the truth of the fact to a reasonable and moral certainty.

> Lemuel Shaw, *Commonwealth v. Webster*, 59 Mass. (5 Cush.) 295, 320 (1850)

3 We better know there is fire whence we see much smoke rising than [we] could know it by one or two witnesses swearing to it. The witnesses may commit perjury, but the smoke can not.

> Abraham Lincoln, Unfinished draft of letter to John R. Underwood and Henry Grider, 26 Oct. 1864, in *Collected Works of Abraham Lincoln* 7:77–78 (Roy P. Basler ed. 1953)

4 PROOF, *n.* Evidence having a shade more of plausibility than of unlikelihood. The testimony of two credible witnesses as opposed to that of only one.

> Ambrose Bierce, *The Devil's Dictionary* 268–69 (1911)

5 As long as th' courts kin hardly ever prove what ever'buddy knows we needn' expect too much o' them.

> Kin Hubbard, *Abe Martin: Hoss Sense and Nonsense* 37 (1926)

6 The burden of proof that is on the plaintiff in this case does not require him to establish beyond all doubt, or beyond a reasonable doubt, that the insured died from accidental injury within the policy. He must prove that by a preponderance of the evidence. It has been held not enough that mathematically the chances somewhat favor a proposition to be proved; for example, the fact that colored automobiles made in the current year outnumber black ones would not warrant a finding that an undescribed automobile of the current year is colored and not black, nor would the fact that only a minority of men die of cancer warrant a finding that a particular man did not die of cancer. . . . The weight or ponderance of evidence is its power to con-

vince the tribunal which has the determination of the fact, of the actual truth of the proposition to be proved. After the evidence has been weighed, that proposition is proved by a preponderance of the evidence if it is made to appear more likely or probable in the sense that actual belief in its truth, derived from the evidence, exists in the mind or minds of the tribunal notwithstanding any doubts that may still linger there.

> **Henry T. Lummus,** *Sargent v. Massachusetts Accident Co.,* 307 Mass. 246, 250, 29 N.E.2d 825 (1940)

PROPERTY

See also EMINENT DOMAIN

1 Whenever there is in any country, uncultivated lands and unemployed poor, it is clear that the laws of property have been so far extended as to violate natural right. The earth is given as a common stock for man to labour and live on.

> **Thomas Jefferson,** Letter to James Madison, 28 Oct. 1785, in *Papers of Thomas Jefferson* 8:682 (Julian P. Boyd ed. 1953)

2 Property is surely a right of mankind as really as liberty.

> **John Adams,** "A Defence of the Constitutions of Government of the United States of America," 1787, in *Works of John Adams* 6:8–9 (Charles Francis Adams ed. 1851)

3 The most common and durable source of factions, has been the various and unequal distribution of property. Those who hold, and those who are without property, have ever formed distinct interests in society. Those who are creditors, and those who are debtors, fall under a like discrimination. A landed interest, a manufacturing interest, a mercantile interest, a moneyed interest, with many lesser interests, grow up of necessity in civilized nations, and divide them into different classes, actuated by different sentiments and views. The regulation of these various and interfering interests forms the principal task of modern legislation, and involves the spirit of party and faction in the necessary and ordinary operations of government.

> **James Madison,** *The Federalist* No. 10, at 1:55 (1788)

4 Private Property therefore is a Creature of Society, and is subject to the Calls of that Society, whenever its Necessities shall require it, even to its last Farthing.

> **Benjamin Franklin,** "On the Legislative Branch," 1789, in *Writings of Benjamin Franklin* 10:54, 59 (Albert H. Smyth ed. 1907)

5 As a man is said to have a right to his property, he may be equally said to have a property in his rights.*

> **James Madison,** "Property," 1792, in *Papers of James Madison* 14:266, 266 (Robert A. Rutland et al. eds. 1983)

6 If there be a government then which prides itself in maintaining the inviolability of property; which provides that none shall be taken *directly* even for public use without indemnification to the owner; and yet *directly* violates the property which individuals have in their opinions, their religion, their persons, and their faculties; nay more, which *indirectly* violates their property, in their actual possessions, in the labor that acquires their daily subsistence, and in the hallowed remnant of time which ought to relieve their fatigues and soothe their cares, the influence will have been anticipated, that such a government is not a pattern for the United States.

> **James Madison,** "Property," 1792, in *Papers of James Madison* 14:266, 267–68 (Robert A. Rutland et al. eds. 1983)

7 "Owners!" echoed the squatter, "I am as rightful an owner of the land I stand on, as any governor in the States! Can you tell me, stranger, where the law or the reason, is to be found, which says that one man shall have . . . perhaps a county, to his use, and another have to beg for 'arth to make his grave in. This is not natur [sic] and I deny that it is law. That is, your legal law."

> **James Fenimore Cooper,** *The Prairie: A Tale* 61 (James P. Elliot ed. 1985) (1827)

8 The personal right to acquire property, which is a natural right, gives to property,

---

* This quotation is inscribed in the Madison Memorial Hall of the James Madison Building of the Library of Congress.

when acquired, a right to protection, as a social right.

James Madison, Speech in Virginia Constitutional Convention, 2 Dec. 1829, in *Writings of James Madison* 9:358, 361 (Gaillard Hunt ed. 1910)

9 The sacred rights of property are to be guarded at every point. I call them sacred, because, if they are unprotected, all other rights become worthless or visionary. What is personal liberty, if it does not draw after it the right to enjoy the fruits of our own industry? What is political liberty, if it imparts only perpetual poverty to us and all our posterity? What is the privilege of a vote, if the majority of the hour may sweep away the earnings of our whole lives, to gratify the rapacity of the indolent, the cunning, or the profligate, who are borne into power upon the tide of a temporary popularity?

Joseph Story, "The Value and Importance of Legal Studies," 1829, in *Miscellaneous Writings of Joseph Story* 503, 519 (William W. Story ed. 1852)

10 In no country in the world is the love of property more active and more anxious than in the United States; nowhere does the majority display less inclination for those principles which threaten to alter, in whatever manner, the laws of property.

Alexis de Tocqueville, *Democracy in America* 2:314 (Francis Bowen trans. 1862) (1835)

11 Property always carries with it a portion of indirect political influence, and it is unwise, and even dangerous, to strengthen this influence by adding to it constitutional privileges; the result always being to make the strong stronger, and the weak weaker.

James Fenimore Cooper, *The American Democrat* 136 (1956) (1838)

12 We think it is a settled principle, growing out of the nature of well ordered civil society, that every holder of property, however absolute and unqualified may be his title, holds it under the implied liability that his use of it may be so regulated, that it shall not be injurious to the equal enjoyment of others having an equal right to the enjoyment of their property, nor injurious

to the rights of the community. All property in the commonwealth, as well that in the interior as that bordering on tide waters, is derived directly or indirectly from the government, and held subject to those general regulations, which are necessary to the common good and general welfare. Rights of property, like all other social and conventional rights, are subject to such reasonable limitations in their enjoyment, as shall prevent them from being injurious, and to such reasonable restraints and regulations established by law, as the legislature, under the governing and controlling power vested in them by the constitution, may think necessary and expedient.

Lemuel Shaw, *Commonwealth v. Alger*, 61 Mass. (7 Cush.) 53, 84–85 (1851)

13 Any person who is the head of a family, or who has arrived at the age of twenty-one years, and is a citizen of the United States, or who shall have filed his declaration of intention to become such, as required by the naturalization laws of the United States, and who has never borne arms against the United States Government or given aid and comfort to its enemies, shall, from and after the first January, eighteen hundred and sixty-three, be entitled to enter one quarter section or a less quantity of unappropriated public lands, upon which said person may have filed a preemption claim, or which may, at the time the application is made, be subject to preemption at one dollar and twenty-five cents, or less, per acre; or eighty acres or less of such unappropriated lands, at two dollars and fifty cents per acre, to be located in a body, in conformity to the legal subdivisions of the public lands, and after the same shall have been surveyed.

Homestead Act of 1862, ch. 75, § 1, 12 Stat. 392, 392

14 With the rise of property, considered as an institution, with the settlement of its rights, and, above all, with the established certainty of its transmission to lineal descendants, came the first possibility among mankind of the true family in its modern acceptation. . . . It is impossible to separate property, considered in the concrete, from civilization, or for civilization to exist without its presence, protection, and regulated inheritance. Of property in this sense, all

barbarous nations are necessarily ignorant.

>Lewis Henry Morgan, *Systems of Consanguinity and Affinity* 492 (1870)

15 Property does become clothed with a public interest when used in a manner to make it of public consequence, and affect the community at large. When therefore, one devotes his property to a use in which the public has an interest, he, in effect, grants to the public an interest in that use, and must submit to be controlled by the public for the common good, to the extent of the interest he has thus created.

>Morrison R. Waite, *Munn v. Illinois*, 94 U.S. 113, 126 (1877)

16 A vested right of action is property in the same sense in which tangible things are property, and is equally protected against arbitrary interference. Whether it springs from contract or from the principles of the common law, it is not competent for the legislature to take it away.

>Stanley Matthews, *Pritchard v. Norton*, 106 U.S. 124, 132 (1882)

17 All property in this country is held under the implied obligation that the owner's use of it shall not be injurious to the community.

>John M. Harlan (1833–1911), *Mugler v. Kansas*, 123 U.S. 623, 665 (1887)

18 I look upon this case with very different eyes from those of either the Attorney General or his associate who has just closed. I believe there are private rights of property here to be protected; that we have a right to come to this court and ask for their protection, and that this court has a right, without asking leave of the Attorney General or of any counsel, to hear our plea. The act of Congress which we are impugning before you is communistic in its purposes and tendencies, and is defended here upon principles as communistic, socialistic—what shall I call them—populistic as ever have been addressed to any political assembly in the world.

>Joseph H. Choate, Argument for appellant, in *Pollock v. Farmers' Loan & Trust Co.*, 157 U.S. 429, 532 (1895)

19 The rule in Shelley's Case, the Don Quixote of the law, which, like the last knight errant of chivalry, has long survived every cause that gave it birth and now wanders aimlessly through the reports, still vigorous, but equally useless and dangerous.

>Robert M. Douglas, *Stamper v. Stamper*, 121 N.C. 251, 254, 28 S.E. 20 (1897)

20 BONDSMAN, *n.* A fool who, having property of his own, undertakes to become responsible for that entrusted by another to a third.

>Ambrose Bierce, *The Devil's Dictionary* 39 (1911)

21 What I am interested in is having the government of the United States more concerned about human rights than about property rights. Property is an instrument of humanity. Humanity isn't an instrument of property.

>Woodrow Wilson, Speech, Minneapolis, 18 Sept. 1912, in John W. Davidson, *A Crossroads of Freedom* 190 (1956)

22 Next to the right of liberty, the right of property is the most important individual right guaranteed by the Constitution and the one which, united with that of personal liberty, has contributed more to the growth of civilization than any other institution established by the human race.

>William Howard Taft, *Popular Government* 90 (1913)

23 By calling a business "property" you make it seem like land, and lead up to the conclusion that a statute cannot substantially cut down the advantages of ownership existing before the statute was passed. An established business no doubt may have pecuniary value and commonly is protected by law against various unjustified injuries. But you cannot give it definiteness of contour by calling it a thing. It is a course of conduct and like other conduct is subject to substantial modification according to time and circumstances both in itself and in regard to what shall justify doing it a harm.

>Oliver Wendell Holmes, Jr., *Truax v. Corrigan*, 257 U.S. 312, 342 (1921) (dissenting)

24 The bundle of power and privileges to which we give the name of ownership is not constant through the ages. The faggots

must be put together and rebound from time to time.

Benjamin N. Cardozo, *The Paradoxes of Legal Science* 129 (1928)

25 Ownership does not always mean absolute dominion. The more an owner, for his advantage, opens up his property for use by the public in general, the more do his rights become circumscribed by the statutory and constitutional rights of those who use it. . . . Thus, the owners of privately held bridges, ferries, turnpikes and railroads may not operate them as freely as a farmer does his farm. Since these facilities are built and operated primarily to benefit the public and since their operation is essentially a public function, it is subject to state regulation.

Hugo L. Black, *Marsh v. Alabama,* 326 U.S. 501, 506 (1946)

26 The concept of the public welfare is broad and inclusive. . . . The values it represents are spiritual as well as physical, aesthetic as well as monetary. It is within the power of the legislature to determine that the community should be beautiful as well as healthy, spacious as well as clean, well-balanced as well as carefully patrolled.

William O. Douglas, *Berman v. Parker,* 348 U.S. 26, 33 (1954)

27 The institution called property guards the troubled boundary between individual man and the state. . . . in a society that chiefly values material well-being, the power to control a particular portion of that well-being is the very foundation of individuality.

Charles A. Reich, "The New Property," 73 *Yale Law Journal* 733, 733 (1964)

28 If an individual is to survive in a collective society, he must have protection against its ruthless pressures. There must be sanctuaries or enclaves where no majority can reach. . . . Just as the Homestead Act was a deliberate effort to foster individual values at an earlier time, so we must try to build an economic basis for liberty today—a Homestead Act for rootless twentieth century man. We must create a new property.

Charles A. Reich, "The New Property," 73 *Yale Law Journal* 733, 787 (1964)

29 It may be realistic today to regard welfare entitlements as more like "property" than a "gratuity." Much of the existing wealth in this country takes the form of rights that do not fall within traditional common-law concepts of property.

William J. Brennan, Jr., *Goldberg v. Kelly,* 397 U.S. 254, 262 (1970)

30 When American city dwellers, both rich and poor, seek "shelter" today, they seek a well known package of goods and services—a package which includes not merely walls and ceilings, but also adequate heat, light and ventilation, serviceable plumbing facilities, secure windows and doors, proper sanitation, and proper maintenance.

J. Skelly Wright, *Javins v. First Nat'l Realty Corp.,* 428 F.2d 1071, 1074 (D.C. Cir. 1970)

31 The dichotomy between personal liberties and property rights is a false one. Property does not have rights. People have rights. The right to enjoy property without unlawful deprivation, no less than the right to speak or the right to travel, is in truth, a "personal" right, whether the "property" in question be a welfare check, a home, or a savings account. In fact, a fundamental interdependence exists between the personal right to liberty and the personal right in property. Neither could have meaning without the other.

Potter Stewart, *Lynch v. Household Finance Corp.,* 405 U.S. 538, 552 (1972)

32 To have a property interest in a benefit, a person clearly must have more than an abstract need or desire for it. He must have more than a unilateral expectation of it. He must, instead, have a legitimate claim of entitlement to it. . . . Property interests, of course, are not created by the Constitution. Rather, they are created and their dimensions are defined by existing rules or understandings that stem from an independent source such as state law.

Potter Stewart, *Board of Regents v. Roth,* 408 U.S. 564, 577 (1972)

33 A quiet place where yards are wide, people few, and motor vehicles restricted are legitimate guidelines in a land-use project addressed to family needs. This goal is a permissible one within *Berman v. Parker.* . . . The police power is not confined to

elimination of filth, stench, and unhealthy places. It is ample to lay out zones where family values, youth values, and the blessings of quiet seclusion and clean air make the area a sanctuary for people.

William O. Douglas, *Village of Belle Terre v. Boraas*, 416 U.S. 1, 9 (1974)

34 That property interest is not a monolithic, abstract concept hovering in the legal stratosphere. It is a bundle of rights in personalty, the metes and bounds of which are determined by the decisional and statutory law of the State of New York. The validity of the property interest in these possessions which respondents previously acquired from some other private person depends on New York law, and the manner in which that same property interest in these same possessions may be lost or transferred to still another private person likewise depends on New York law.

William H. Rehnquist, *Flagg Bros., Inc. v. Brooks*, 436 U.S. 149, 160 n.10 (1978)

PROSECUTION

See also JUSTICE DEPARTMENT; SEARCHES AND SEIZURES

1 The primary duty of a lawyer engaged in public prosecution is not to convict, but to see that justice is done.

Canons of Professional Ethics Canon 5 (1908)

2 I, the scourge-wielder, balance-wrecker, Smiter with whips and swords; I, hater of the breakers of the law; I, legalist, inexorable and bitter.

Edgar Lee Masters, "State's Attorney Fallas," in *Spoon River Anthology* 80 (1915)

3 There is to be no traffic in the privilege of invoking the public justice of the state. One may press a charge or withhold it as one will. One may not make action or inaction dependent on a price. The state has, indeed, no interest to be promoted by the prosecution of the innocent. . . . The state has an interest, however, in preserving to complainants the freedom of choice, the incentives to sincerity, which are the safeguards and the assurance of the prosecution of the guilty. . . . Innocence will strangely multiply when the accuser is the paid defender. In such matters, the law looks beyond the specific instance where

the evil may be small or nothing. It throttles a corrupting tendency.

Benjamin N. Cardozo, *Union Exchange Nat'l Bank v. Joseph*, 231 N.Y. 250, 253–54, 131 N.E. 905 (1921)

4 There is always a district attorney at hand to launch the prosecution, for district attorneys are invariably men who aspire to higher office, and no more facile way to it is to be found than by assaulting and destroying a man above the general. . . . many an American Congressman comes to Washington from a district attorney's office: you may be sure that he is seldom promoted because he has been jealous of the liberties of the citizen.

H. L. Mencken, *Notes on Democracy* 160–61 (1926)

5 A prosecuting attorney's success depends very largely upon his ferocity. American practice permits him an extravagance of attack that would land him in jail, and perhaps even in a lunatic asylum, in any other country, and the more passionately he indulges in it the more certain becomes his promotion to higher office, including the judiciary.

H. L. Mencken, *Notes on Democracy* 169 (1926)

6 The United States Attorney is the representative not of an ordinary party to a controversy, but of a sovereignty whose obligation to govern impartially is as compelling as its obligation to govern at all; and whose interest, therefore, in a criminal prosecution is not that it shall win a case, but that justice shall be done. As such, he is in a peculiar and very definite sense the servant of the law, the twofold aim of which is that guilt shall not escape or innocence suffer.

George Sutherland, *Berger v. United States*, 295 U.S. 78, 88 (1935)

7 He [the prosecutor] may prosecute with earnestness and vigor—indeed, he should do so. But, while he may strike hard blows, he is not at liberty to strike foul ones. It is as much his duty to refrain from improper methods calculated to produce a wrongful conviction as it is to use every legitimate means to bring about a just one.

George Sutherland, *Berger v. United States*, 295 U.S. 78, 88 (1935)

8 No prosecution is tried with flawless perfection; if every slip is to result in reversal, we shall never succeed in enforcing the criminal law at all.

> Learned Hand, *United States v. Sherman,* 171 F.2d 619, 625 (2d Cir. 1948)

9 It does indeed go without saying that an official, who is in fact guilty of using his powers to vent his spleen upon others, or for any other personal motive not connected with the public good, should not escape liability for the injuries he may so cause; and, if it were possible in practice to confine such complaints to the guilty, it would be monstrous to deny recovery. The justification for doing so is that it is impossible to know whether the claim is well founded until the case has been tried, and that to submit all officials, the innocent as well as the guilty, to the burden of a trial and to the inevitable danger of its outcome, would dampen the ardor of all but the most resolute, or the most irresponsible, in the unflinching discharge of their duties. . . . As is so often the case, the answer must be found in a balance between the evils inevitable in either alternative. In this instance it has been thought in the end better to leave unredressed the wrongs done by dishonest officers than to subject those who try to do their duty to the constant dread of retaliation.

> Learned Hand, *Gregoire v. Biddle,* 177 F.2d 579, 581 (2d Cir. 1949)

10 To approve legally what we disapprove morally, on the ground of practical convenience, is to yield to a short-sighted view of practicality. . . . Nor are the needs of an effective penal code seen in the truest perspective by talk about a criminal prosecution's not being a game in which the Government loses because its officers have not played according to rule. Of course criminal prosecution is more than a game. But in any event it should not be deemed to be a dirty game in which "the dirty business" of criminals is out-witted by "the dirty business" of law officers. The contrast between morality professed by society and immorality practiced on its behalf makes for contempt of law. Respect for law cannot be turned off and on as though it were a hot-water faucet.

> Felix Frankfurter, *On Lee v. United States,* 343 U.S. 747, 758–59 (1952) (dissenting)

11 The Government wins its point when justice is done in its courts.*

> Frederick W. Lehmann, quoted in Simon E. Sobeloff, "Attorney for the Government: The Work of the Solicitor General's Office," 41 *American Bar Association Journal* 229, 229 (1955)

PUNISHMENT

See also CAPITAL PUNISHMENT; SENTENCING

1 No man shall be forced by Torture to confesse any Crime against himselfe nor any other unlesse it be in some Capitall case, where he is first fullie convicted by cleare and suffitient evidence to be guilty, After which if the cause be of that nature, That it is very apparent there be other conspiratours, or confederates with him, Then he may be tortured, yet not with such Tortures as be Barbarous and inhumane.

> Massachusetts Body of Liberties of 1641, § 45, in *Collections of the Massachusetts Historical Society (3d series)* 8:216, 224 (1843)

2 That excessive bail ought not to be required, nor excessive fines imposed, nor cruel and unusual punishments inflicted.

> Virginia Declaration of Rights of 1776, § 9, in *Federal and State Constitutions* 7:3812, 3813 (Francis N. Thorpe ed. 1909)

3 Punishments I know are necessary, and I would provide them, strict and inflexible, but proportioned to the crime. Death might be inflicted for murther and perhaps for treason if you would take out of the description of treason all crimes which are not such in their nature. Rape, buggery &c. punish by castration. All other crimes by working on high roads, rivers, gallies &c. a certain time proportioned to the offence. But as this would be no punishment or change of condition to slaves (me miserum!) let them be sent to other countries. By these means we should be freed from the wickedness of the latter, and the former would be living monuments of public ven-

---

* "The United States wins its point whenever justice is done its citizens in the courts" is inscribed on the wall of the Attorney General's rotunda in the Department of Justice Building in Washington.

geance. Laws thus proportionate and mild should never be dispensed with.

> **Thomas Jefferson**, Letter to Edmund Pendleton, 26 Aug. 1776, in *Papers of Thomas Jefferson* 1:505 (Julian P. Boyd ed. 1950)

4 Let mercy be the character of the law-giver, but let the judge be a mere machine. The mercies of the law will be dispensed equally and impartially to every description of men; those of the judge, or of the executive power, will be the eccentric impulses of whimsical, capricious designing man.

> **Thomas Jefferson**, Letter to Edmund Pendleton, 26 Aug. 1776, in *Papers of Thomas Jefferson* 1:505 (Julian P. Boyd ed. 1950)

5 And forasmuch the experience of all ages and countries hath shewn that cruel and sanguinary laws defeat their own purpose by engaging the benevolence of mankind to withold prosecutions, to smother testimony, or to listen to it with bias, when, if the punishment were only proportioned to the injury, men would feel it their inclination as well as their duty to see the laws observed.

> **Thomas Jefferson**, "A Bill for Proportioning Crimes and Punishments in Cases Heretofore Capital," 1779, in *Papers of Thomas Jefferson* 2:492, 493 (Julian P. Boyd ed. 1950)

6 The [cruel and unusual punishment] clause seems to express a great deal of humanity, on which account I have no objection to it; but as it seems to have no meaning in it, I do not think it necessary.... Who are to be the judges? ... No cruel and unusual punishment is to be inflicted; it is sometimes necessary to hang a man, villains often deserve whipping, and perhaps having their ears cut off; but are we in future to be prevented from inflicting these punishments because they are cruel?

> **Samuel Livermore**, in 1 *Annals of Congress* 754 (Joseph Gales ed. 1789)

7 Will the punishment of the thief bring back the stolen money? No more so than the hanging of a murderer restores his victim to life.

> **Abraham Lincoln**, Speech on the Sub-Treasury, Springfield, Ill., 26 Dec. 1839, in *Collected Works of Abraham Lincoln* 1:169 (Roy P. Basler ed. 1953)

8 Is not punishment out of place, irregular, anomalous, exceptional, unjust, unscientific, not to say absurd and ridiculous, when classed among civil remedies? What kind of a civil remedy for the plaintiff is the punishment of the defendant? The idea is wrong. It is a monstrous heresy. It is an unsightly and an unhealthy excrescence, deforming the symmetry of the body of the law.

> **William L. Foster**, *Fay v. Parker*, 53 N.H. 342, 382 (1873)

9 There is no such thing as moral responsibility for past acts, no such thing as real justice in punishing them, for the reason that human beings are not stationary existences, but changing, growing, incessantly progressive organisms, which in no two moments are the same. Therefore justice, whose only possible mode of proceeding is to punish in present time for what is done in past time, must always punish a person more or less similar to, but never identical with, the one who committed the offense, and therein must be no justice.

> **Edward Bellamy**, *Dr. Heidenhoff's Process* 121 (1880)

10 But when our neighbors do wrong, we sometimes feel the fitness of making them smart for it, whether they have repented or not.

> **Oliver Wendell Holmes, Jr.**, *The Common Law* 45 (1881)

11 A law which punished conduct which would not be blameworthy in the average member of the community would be too severe for that community to bear.

> **Oliver Wendell Holmes, Jr.**, *The Common Law* 50 (1881)

12 If the government is cruel, the governor's life is not safe. If you tax too high, the revenue will yield nothing. If you make the criminal code sanguinary, juries will not convict. If the law is too mild, private vengeance comes in.

> **Ralph Waldo Emerson**, "Compensation," *Essays: First Series*, in *Complete Works of Ralph Waldo Emerson* 2:93, 100 (1903)

13 All crimes should be punished with humiliations—life-long public exposure in ridiculous and grotesque situations—and never in any other way. Death Gallows makes a hero of the villain, and he is envied by some spectators and by and by imitated.

> **Mark Twain,** Notebook, 1887–88, in *Mark Twain's Notebooks and Journals* 3:346 (Robert P. Browning, Michael B. Frank, & Lin Salamo eds. 1979)

14 A man has never yet been hung for breaking the spirit of a law.

> **Grover Cleveland,** quoted in Paxton Hibben, *The Peerless Leader* 155 (1929)

15 AMNESTY, *n.* The state's magnanimity to those offenders whom it would be too expensive to punish.

> **Ambrose Bierce,** *The Devil's Dictionary* 23 (1911)

16 We have put away the blood feud, the vendetta, the other forms of private war, but in the framing of our penal codes we have not forgotten the passions that had their outlet and release in pursuit and retribution. I do not say that it is wise to forget them altogether. The thirst for vengeance is a very real, even if it be a hideous, thing; and states may not ignore it till humanity has been raised to greater heights than any that have yet been scaled in all the long ages of struggle and ascent.

> **Benjamin N. Cardozo,** *Law and Literature* 87–88 (1931)

17 Probation is thus conferred as a privilege and cannot be demanded as a right. It is a matter of favor, not of contract. There is no requirement that it must be granted on a specified showing. The defendant stands convicted; he faces punishment and cannot insist on terms or strike a bargain. To accomplish the purpose of the statute, an exceptional degree of flexibility in administration is essential. It is necessary to individualize each case, to give that careful, humane and comprehensive consideration to the particular situation of each offender which would be possible only in the exercise of a broad discretion.

> **Charles Evans Hughes,** *Burns v. United States,* 287 U.S. 216, 220 (1932)

18 If the state officials deliberately and intentionally had placed the relator in the electric chair five times and ... had applied electric current to his body in a manner not sufficient, until the final time, to kill him, such a form of torture would rival that of burning at the stake.... How many deliberate and intentional reapplications of electric current does it take to produce a cruel, unusual and unconstitutional punishment?

> **Harold H. Burton,** *Francis v. Resweber,* 329 U.S. 459, 476 (1947) (dissenting)

19 The exact scope of the constitutional phrase "cruel and unusual" has not been detailed by this Court.... The basic concept underlying the Eighth Amendment is nothing less than the dignity of man. While the State has the power to punish, the Amendment stands to assure that this power be exercised within the limits of civilized standards.... The Court [has] recognized ... that the words of the Amendment are not precise, and that their scope is not static. The Amendment must draw its meaning from the evolving standards of decency that mark the progress of a maturing society.

> **Earl Warren,** *Trop v. Dulles,* 356 U.S. 86, 99–101 (1958)

20 Even one day in prison would be a cruel and unusual punishment for the "crime" of having a common cold.

> **Potter Stewart,** *Robinson v. California,* 370 U.S. 660, 667 (1962)

21 Nothing can be right and balanced again until justice is won—the injured party has to have justice. Do you understand that? Nothing can be right, for years, for lifetimes, until that first crime is punished. Or else we'd all be animals.

> **Joyce Carol Oates,** "Norman and the Killer," in *Upon the Sweeping Flood and Other Stories* 144–45 (1965)

QUOTATIONS

1 Spare me quotations, which, though learn'd, are long,
On points remote at best, and rarely strong;
How sad to find our time consumed by speech,
Feeble in logic, feebler still in reach,

Yet urged in words of high and bold
pretense,
As if the sound made up the lack of
sense.

> **Joseph Story,** "Lines Written on Hearing an
> Argument in Court," 1842, in *Life and Letters
> of Joseph Story* 2:413 (William W. Story ed.
> 1851)

2 But I have long thought that if you knew a
column of advertisements by heart, you
could achieve unexpected felicities with
them. You can get a happy quotation anywhere if you have the eye.

> **Oliver Wendell Holmes, Jr.,** Letter to Harold
> J. Laski, 31 May 1923, in *Holmes-Laski
> Letters* 1:504 (Mark DeWolfe Howe ed. 1953)

3 For quotable good things, for pregnant
aphorisms, for touchstones of ready application, the opinions of the English judges
are a mine of instruction and a treasury of
joy.

> **Benjamin N. Cardozo,** *Law and Literature*
> 20–21 (1931)

4 The power of a sonorous phrase to command uncritical acceptance has often been
encountered in the law.

> **Calvert Magruder,** "Mental and Emotional
> Disturbance in the Law of Torts," 49 *Harvard
> Law Review* 1033, 1033 (1936)

RACE

See AFFIRMATIVE ACTION; CIVIL RIGHTS; EQUAL
PROTECTION; FOURTEENTH AMENDMENT;
SEGREGATION; SLAVERY

RAPE

1 Woman was and is condemned to a system
under which the lawful rapes exceed the
unlawful ones a million to one.

> **Margaret Sanger,** *Woman and the New Race*
> 178 (1920)

2 Man's discovery that his genitalia could
serve as a weapon to generate fear must
rank as one of the most important discoveries of prehistoric times, along with the
use of fire and the first crude stone axe.
From prehistoric times to the present, I believe, rape has played a critical function. It
is nothing more or less than a conscious

process of intimidation by which *all men*
keep *all women* in a state of fear.

> **Susan Brownmiller,** *Against Our Will* 14–15
> (1975)

3 My purpose in this book has been to give
rape its history. Now we must deny it a
future.

> **Susan Brownmiller,** *Against Our Will* 404
> (1975)

4 Whatever they may be in public life, whatever their relations with men, in their relations with women, all men are rapists,
and that's all they are. They rape us with
their eyes, their laws, and their codes.

> **Marilyn French,** *The Women's Room* 433
> (1977)

5 Certainly, then, a marriage license should
not be viewed as a license for a husband to
forcibly rape his wife with impunity. A
married woman has the same right to control her own body as does an unmarried
woman.

> **Sol Wachtler,** *People v. Liberta*, 64 N.Y.2d
> 152, 164, 474 N.E.2d 567, 485 N.Y.S.2d 207
> (1984)

REALISM

See LEGAL REALISM

REGULATION

See also ADMINISTRATIVE LAW

1 Trade and commerce, if they were not
made of india-rubber, would never manage
to bounce over the obstacles which legislators are continually putting in their way.

> **Henry David Thoreau,** *Civil Disobedience*,
> 1849, in *Writings of Henry David Thoreau*
> 4:356, 357 (1906)

2 This power to regulate is not a power to
destroy, and limitation is not the equivalent of confiscation. Under pretence of regulating fares and freights, the State cannot
. . . do that which in law amounts to a taking of private property for public use without just compensation, or without due process of law.

> **Morrison R. Waite,** *Railroad Commission
> Cases*, 116 U.S. 307, 331 (1886)

3 The provisions of this act shall apply to any common carrier or carriers engaged in the transportation of passengers or property wholly by railroad, or partly by railroad and partly by water when both are used, under a common control, management, or arrangement, for a continuous carriage or shipment, from one State or Territory of the United States, or the District of Columbia, to any other State or Territory of the United States, or the District of Columbia, ... All charges made for any service rendered or to be rendered in the transportation of passengers or property as aforesaid, or in connection therewith, or for the receiving, delivering, storage, or handling of such property, shall be reasonable and just; and every unjust and unreasonable charge for such service is prohibited and declared to be unlawful.

Interstate Commerce Act, ch. 104, § 1, 24 Stat. 379, 379 (1887)

4 If any common carrier subject to the provisions of this act shall, directly or indirectly, by any special rate, rebate, drawback, or other device, charge, demand, collect, or receive from any person or persons a greater or less compensation for any service rendered, or to be rendered, in the transportation of passengers or property, subject to the provisions of this act, than it charges, demands, collects, or receives from any other person or persons for doing for him or them a like and contemporaneous service in the transportation of a like kind of traffic under substantially similar circumstances and conditions, such common carrier shall be deemed guilty of unjust discrimination, which is hereby prohibited and declared to be unlawful.

Interstate Commerce Act, ch. 104, § 2, 24 Stat. 379, 379–80 (1887)

5 It shall be unlawful for any common carrier subject to the provisions of this act to make or give any undue or unreasonable preference or advantage to any particular person, company, firm, corporation, or locality, or any particular description of traffic, in any respect whatsoever, or to subject any particular person, company, firm, corporation, or locality, or any particular description of traffic, to any undue or unreasonable prejudice or disadvantage in any respect whatsoever.

Interstate Commerce Act, ch. 104, § 3, 24 Stat. 379, 380 (1887)

6 My impression would be that, looking at the matter from a railroad point of view exclusively, it would not be a wise thing to undertake to abolish the [Interstate Commerce] Commission.... The Commission, as its functions have now been limited by the Courts, is, or can be made of great use to the railroads. It satisfies the popular clamor for a government supervision of railroads, at the same time that the supervision is almost entirely nominal. Further, the older such a commission gets to be, the more inclined it will be found to be to take the business and railroad view of things. It thus becomes a sort of barrier between the railroad corporations and the people and a sort of protection against hasty and crude legislation hostile to railroad interests. The Commission costs something, of course. But so long as its powers are advisory merely, for the reasons just stated, it strikes me it is well worth the money. The part of wisdom is not to destroy the Commission, but to utilize it.

Richard Olney, Letter to Charles C. Perkins, 28 Dec. 1892, in *Liberty and Justice* 292–93 (James M. Smith & Paul L. Murphy eds. 1958)

7 The man who wrongly holds that every human right is secondary to his profit must now give way to the advocate of human welfare, who rightly maintains that every man holds his property subject to the general right of the community to regulate its use to whatever degree the public welfare may require it.

Theodore Roosevelt, Speech, Osawatomie, Kan., 31 Aug. 1910, in *Writings of Theodore Roosevelt* 315, 328 (William H. Harbaugh ed. 1967)

8 The first duty of law is to keep sound the society it serves. Sanitary laws, pure food laws, and laws determining conditions of labor which individuals are powerless to determine for themselves are intimate parts of the very business of justice and legal efficiency.

Woodrow Wilson, Inaugural Address, 4 Mar. 1913, in *Papers of Woodrow Wilson* 27:148, 151 (Arthur S. Link ed. 1978)

9 Property, like liberty, though immune under the Constitution from destruction, is not immune from regulation essential for the common good. What that regulation

shall be, every generation must work out for itself.

> **Benjamin N. Cardozo**, *The Nature of the Judicial Process* 87 (1921)

10 I think . . . that the notion that a business is clothed with a public interest and has been devoted to the public use is little more than a fiction intended to beautify what is disagreeable to the sufferers. The truth seems to me to be that, subject to compensation when compensation is due, the legislature may forbid or restrict any business when it has a sufficient force of public opinion behind it.

> **Oliver Wendell Holmes, Jr.**, *Tyson v. Banton*, 273 U.S. 418, 446 (1927) (dissenting)

11 It is of the essence of regulation that it lays a restraining hand on the self-interest of the regulated and that advantages from the regulation commonly fall to others. The conflicts of economic interest between the regulated and those who advantage by it are wisely left under our system to resolution by the Congress under its more flexible and responsible legislative process. Such conflicts rarely lend themselves to judicial determination. And with the wisdom, workability, or fairness, of the plan of regulation we have nothing to do.

> **Robert H. Jackson**, *Wickard v. Filburn*, 317 U.S. 111, 129 (1942)

12 It is hardly lack of due process for the Government to regulate that which it subsidizes.

> **Robert H. Jackson**, *Wickard v. Filburn*, 317 U.S. 111, 131 (1942)

13 It is a paradox of the acquisitive society in which we now live that although private morals are regulated by law, the entrepreneur is allowed considerable freedom to use—and abuse—the public in order to make money. The American pursuit of happiness might be less desperate if the situation were reversed.

> **Gore Vidal**, *Homage to Daniel Shays* 321 (1972)

14 Federal bureaucracy is legally permitted to execute congressional mandate with high degree of befuddlement as long as it acts no more befuddled than Congress must reasonably have anticipated.

> *American Petroleum Inst. v. Knecht*, 456 F. Supp. 889, 892 (C.D. Cal. 1978) (headnote prepared by West Publishing Co.)

15 Regulation is the substitution of error for chance.

> **Fred J. Emery**, quoted in Paul Dickson, *The Official Explanations* 56 (1980)

16 This case, involving legal requirements for the content and labeling of meat products such as frankfurters, affords a rare opportunity to explore simultaneously both parts of Bismarck's aphorism that "No man should see how laws or sausages are made."

> **Antonin Scalia**, *Community Nutrition Inst. v. Block*, 749 F.2d 50, 51 (D.C. Cir. 1984)

RELIGION

See also FREEDOM OF RELIGION; NATURAL LAW

1 A people [the Puritans] amongst whom religion and law were almost identical, and in whose character both were so thoroughly interfused, that the mildest and the severest acts of public discipline were alike made venerable and awful.

> **Nathaniel Hawthorne**, *The Scarlet Letter*, 1850, in *Nathaniel Hawthorne: Novels* 160 (Millicent Bell ed. 1983)

2 If we only had some God in the country's laws, instead of being in such a sweat to get Him into the Constitution, it would be better all around.

> **Mark Twain**, Letter to William Dean Howells, 18 Sept. 1875, in *Writings of Mark Twain* 34:262 (Albert B. Paine ed. 1929)

3 The term "religion" has reference to one's views of his relations to his Creator, and to the obligations they impose of reverence for his being and character, and of obedience to his will.

> **Stephen J. Field**, *Davis v. Beason*, 133 U.S. 333, 342 (1890)

4 We are a Christian people, and the morality of the country is deeply ingrafted upon Christianity. . . . If we pass beyond these matters to a view of American life as expressed by its laws, its business, its customs and its society, we find everywhere a clear recognition of the same truth. Among other matters note the following: The form of oath universally prevailing, concluding with an appeal to the Almighty; . . . the laws respecting the observance of the Sabbath. . . . These, and many other matters

... add a volume of unofficial declarations to the mass of organic utterances that this is a Christian nation.

David J. Brewer, *Church of the Holy Trinity v. United States,* 143 U.S. 457, 471 (1892)

5 Man is without any doubt the most interesting fool there is. Also the most eccentric. He hasn't a single written law, in his Bible or out of it, which has any but one purpose and intention—to *limit or defeat a law of God.*

Mark Twain, *Letters from the Earth* 37 (Bernard De Voto ed. 1939) (1905-09)

6 [William Jennings Bryan:] Your Honor, I think I can shorten this testimony. The only purpose Mr. Darrow has is to slur at the Bible, but I will answer his question. I will answer it all at once, and I have no objection in the world, I want the world to know that this man, who does not believe in a God, is trying to use a court in Tennessee—
[Clarence S. Darrow:] I object to that.
[Bryan:] to slur at it, and while it will require time, I am willing to take it.
[Darrow:] I object to your statement. I am exempting you on your fool ideas that no intelligent Christian on earth believes.

Clarence S. Darrow, Scopes Trial, Dayton, Tenn., 20 July 1925, in *The World's Most Famous Court Trial* 304 (1925)

7 Men may believe what they cannot prove. They may not be put to the proof of their religious doctrines or beliefs. Religious experiences which are as real as life to some may be incomprehensible to others.

William O. Douglas, *United States v. Ballard,* 322 U.S. 78, 86 (1944)

8 Among religions in this country which do not teach what would generally be considered a belief in the existence of God are Buddhism, Taoism, Ethical Culture, Secular Humanism and others.

Hugo L. Black, *Torcaso v. Watkins,* 367 U.S. 488, 495 n.11 (1961)

REMEDIES

See DAMAGES; INJUNCTIONS

RESEARCH

See LEGAL RESEARCH

REVENGE

See CAPITAL PUNISHMENT; PUNISHMENT

REVOLUTION

1 If, by the mere force of numbers, a majority should deprive a minority of any clearly written constitutional right, it might, in a moral point of view, justify revolution—certainly would, if such right were a vital one.

Abraham Lincoln, First Inaugural Address, 4 Mar. 1861, in *Collected Works of Abraham Lincoln* 4:267 (Roy P. Basler ed. 1953)

2 This country, with its institutions, belongs to the people who inhabit it. Whenever they shall grow weary of the existing government, they can exercise their *constitutional* right of amending it, or their *revolutionary* right to dismember, or overthrow it.

Abraham Lincoln, First Inaugural Address, 4 Mar. 1861, in *Collected Works of Abraham Lincoln* 4:269 (Roy P. Basler ed. 1953)

3 The advocacy of violence may, or may not, fail; but in neither case can there be any "right" to use it. Revolutions are often "right," but a "right of revolution" is a contradiction in terms, for a society which acknowledged it, could not stop at tolerating conspiracies to overthrow it, but must include their execution. The question before us, and the only one, is how long a government, having discovered such a conspiracy, must wait. When does the conspiracy become a "present danger"?

Learned Hand, *United States v. Dennis,* 183 F.2d 201, 213 (2d Cir. 1950)

4 The word "revolution" has of course acquired a subversive connotation in modern times. But it has roots that are eminently respectable in American history. This country is the product of revolution. Our very being emphasizes that when grievances pile high and there are no political remedies, the exercise of sovereign powers reverts to the people. Teaching and espousing revolution—as distinguished from indulging in overt acts—are therefore obviously within the range of the First Amendment.

William O. Douglas, *W.E.B. Du Bois Clubs v. Clark,* 389 U.S. 309, 315–16 (1967)

RIGHT TO COUNSEL

See CRIMINAL PROCEDURE

1 Noe ffreeman shall be compelled to receive any Marriners or Souldiers into his house and there suffer them to Sojourne, against their willes provided Always it be not in time of Actuall Warr within this province.

New York Charter of Libertyes of 1683, in *The Colonial Laws of New York* 1:111, 114 (1894)

2 5. That the respective colonies are entitled to the common law of England, and more especially to the great and inestimable privilege of being tried by their peers of the vicinage, according to the course of that law. . . .

6. That they are entitled to the benefit of such of the English statutes as existed at the time of their colonization; and which they have, by experience, respectively found to be applicable to their several local and other circumstances. . . .

7. That these, his majesty's colonies, are likewise entitled to all the immunities and privileges granted & confirmed to them by royal charters, or secured by their several codes of provincial laws. . . .

8. That they have a right peaceably to assemble, consider of their grievances, and petition the King; and that all prosecutions, prohibitory proclamations, and commitments for the same, are illegal.

Declarations and Resolves, 14 Oct. 1774, in *Journals of the Continental Congress* 1:63, 69–70 (Worthington C. Ford ed. 1904)

3 That the people have a right to bear arms for the defence of themselves and the state; and as standing armies in the time of peace are dangerous to liberty, they ought not to be kept up; And that the military should be kept under strict subordination to, and governed by, the civil power.

Pennsylvania Constitution of 1776, Declaration of Rights, § 13, in *Federal and State Constitutions* 5:3081, 3083 (Francis N. Thorpe ed. 1909)

4 The Inhabitants of the said territory shall always be entitled to the benefits of the writ of habeas corpus, and of the trial by Jury; of a proportionate representation of the people in the legislature, and of judicial proceedings according to the course of the common law; all persons shall be bailable unless for capital offences, where the proof shall be evident, or the presumption great; all fines shall be moderate, and no cruel or unusual punishments shall be inflicted; no man shall be deprived of his liberty or property but by the judgment of his peers, or the law of the land; and should the public exigencies make it necessary for the common preservation to take any persons property, or to demand his particular services, full compensation shall be made for the same; and in the just preservation of rights and property it is understood and declared; that no law ought ever to be made, or have force in the said territory, that shall in any manner whatever interfere with, or affect private contracts or engagements, bona fide and without fraud previously formed.

Northwest Ordinance, art. 2, 13 July 1787, in *Journals of the Continental Congress* 32:340 (Roscoe R. Hill ed. 1936)

5 If we cannot secure all our rights, let us secure what we can.

Thomas Jefferson, Letter to James Madison, 15 Mar. 1789, in *Papers of Thomas Jefferson* 14:660 (Julian P. Boyd ed. 1958)

6 All, too, will bear in mind this sacred principle, that though the will of the majority is in all cases to prevail, that will to be rightful must be reasonable; that the minority possess their equal rights, which equal law must protect, and to violate would be oppression.

Thomas Jefferson, First Inaugural Address, 4 Mar. 1801, in *Messages and Papers of the Presidents* 1:321, 322 (James D. Richardson ed. 1898)

7 Equal and exact justice to all men, of whatever state or persuasion, religious or political; . . . freedom of religion; freedom of the press, and freedom of person under the protection of the habeas corpus, and trial by juries impartially selected. These principles form the bright constellation which has gone before us and guided our steps through an age of revolution and reformation. The wisdom of our sages and blood of our heroes have been devoted to their attainment. They should be the creed of our political faith, the text of civic instruction, the touchstone by which to try the services of those we trust; and should

we wander from them in moments of error or of alarm, let us hasten to retrace our steps and to regain the road which alone leads to peace, liberty, and safety.

Thomas Jefferson, First Inaugural Address, 4 Mar. 1801, in *Messages and Papers of the Presidents* 1:321, 323–24 (James D. Richardson ed. 1898)

8 Equal laws protecting equal rights . . . the best guarantee of loyalty & love of country.*

James Madison, Letter to Jacob De La Motta, Aug. 1820, in *Writings of James Madison* 9:29, 30 (Gaillard Hunt ed. 1910)

9 The greatest praise government can win is, that its citizens know their rights, and dare to maintain them. The best use of good laws is to teach men to trample bad laws under their feet.

Wendell Phillips, Speech, Boston, 12 April 1852, in *Speeches, Lectures, and Letters* 71, 91 (1863)

10 The right to follow any of the common occupations of life is an inalienable right.

Joseph P. Bradley, *Butchers' Union Co. v. Crescent City Co.*, 111 U.S. 746, 762 (1884) (concurring)

11 Fiction always is a poor ground for changing substantial rights.

Oliver Wendell Holmes, Jr., *Haddock v. Haddock*, 201 U.S. 562, 630 (1906) (dissenting)

12 All rights tend to declare themselves absolute to their logical extreme. Yet all in fact are limited by the neighborhood of principles of policy which are other than those on which the particular right is founded, and which become strong enough to hold their own when a certain point is reached. . . . The boundary at which the conflicting interests balance cannot be determined by any general formula in advance, but points in the line, or helping to establish it, are fixed by decisions that this or that concrete case falls on the nearer or farther side.

Oliver Wendell Holmes, Jr., *Hudson County Water Co. v. McCarter*, 209 U.S. 349, 355 (1908)

13 An immortal right to bring an eternally prohibited action is a metaphysical subtlety that the present writer cannot pretend to understand.

James Barr Ames, *Lectures on Legal History* 199 (1913)

14 But for legal purposes a right is only the hypostasis of a prophecy—the imagination of a substance supporting the fact that the public force will be brought to bear upon those who do things said to contravene it. . . . No doubt behind these legal rights is the fighting will of the subject to maintain them, and the spread of his emotions to the general rules by which they are maintained; but that does not seem to me the same thing as the supposed *a priori* discernment of a duty or the assertion of a preëxisting right. A dog will fight for his bone.

Oliver Wendell Holmes, Jr., "Natural Law," 32 *Harvard Law Review* 40, 42 (1918)

15 But the word "right" is one of the most deceptive of pitfalls; it is so easy to slip from a qualified meaning in the premise to an unqualified one in the conclusion. Most rights are qualified.

Oliver Wendell Holmes, Jr., *American Bank & Trust Co. v. Federal Reserve Bank of Atlanta*, 256 U.S. 350, 358 (1921)

16 When houses are scarce and landlords are grasping, Blackstone's proposition that the public good is in nothing more essentially interested than in the protection of every individual's private rights is not the popular view. A crowded, urban, industrial community looks to society for protection against predatory individuals, natural or artificial, and resents doctrines that protect these individuals against society for fear society will oppress them.

Roscoe Pound, *The Spirit of the Common Law* 102-03 (1921)

17 "I understand it."

"No you don't. Every man's supposed to have certain rights."

"Certain inalienable rights," Starke said, "to liberty, equality and the pursuit of happiness. I learnt it in school, as a kid."

"Not that," Prew said. "That's The Constitution. Nobody believes that any more."

---

* This quotation is inscribed in the Madison Memorial Hall of the James Madison Building of the Library of Congress.

"Sure they do," Starke said. "They all believe it. They just dont do it. But they believe it."

"Sure," Prew said. "Thats what I mean."

"But at least in this country they believe it," Starke said, "even if they dont do it."

James Jones, *From Here to Eternity* 209 (1951)

18 Life is breathed into a judicial decision by the persistent exercise of legal rights until they become usual and ordinary in human experience.

Martin Luther King, Jr., "The Case against 'Tokenism,'" 1962, in *A Testament of Hope: The Essential Writings of Martin Luther King, Jr.* 106, 109 (James M. Washington ed. 1986)

19 This freedom of movement is the very essence of our free society, setting us apart. Like the right of assembly and the right of association, it often makes all other rights meaningful—knowing, studying, arguing, exploring, conversing, observing and even thinking. Once the right to travel is curtailed, all other rights suffer, just as when curfew or home detention is placed on a person.

William O. Douglas, *Aptheker v. Secretary of State,* 378 U.S. 500, 520 (1964) (concurring)

20 America is of course sovereign; but her sovereignty is woven in an international web that makes her one of the family of nations. The ties with all the continents are close—commercially as well as culturally. Our concerns are planetary, beyond sunrises and sunsets. Citizenship implicates us in those problems and perplexities, as well as in domestic ones. We cannot exercise and enjoy citizenship in world perspective without the right to travel abroad; and I see no constitutional way to curb it unless, as I said, there is the power to detain.

William O. Douglas, *Aptheker v. Secretary of State,* 378 U.S. 500, 520–21 (1964) (concurring)

21 Of course, I believe that every child has a right to decent education and shelter, food and medical care; of course, I believe that refugees from political oppression have a right to a haven in a free land; of course I believe that every person has a right to work in dignity and for a decent wage. I do believe and affirm the social contract that grounds these rights. But more to the point

I also believe that I am commanded—that we are obligated—to realize those rights.

Robert M. Cover, "Obligation: A Jewish Jurisprudence of the Social Order," 5 *Journal of Law and Religion* 65, 73–74 (1988)

RULE OF LAW

See LAW; OBEDIENCE TO LAW

RULES

See also DISTINCTIONS

1 Right law must be intelligible, intellectually accessible, to the people whom that law is to serve, whose law it is, the law-consumers and the citizen "makers" of the law. . . . Only the rule which shows its reason on its face has ground to claim maximum chance of *continuing* effectiveness; so that to satisfy, in this, the lay need of relative accessibility, of friendliness and meaningfulness of the reason, is at the same time to do a functionally more effective job on the side of pure technique. There is thus no need, in widening one's view of what the function of rules of law is, to risk confusion on the marks of beauty. Quite the contrary. For to see the wider function, is to find the road back to that rightest and most beautiful type of legal rule, the singing rule with purpose and with reason clear.

Karl N. Llewellyn, "On the Good, the True, the Beautiful in Law," 9 *University of Chicago Law Review* 224, 249–50 (1941)

2 If we are to communicate with each other at all, and if, as in the most elementary form of law, we are to express our intentions that a certain type of behavior be regulated by rules, then the general words we use . . . must have some standard instance in which no doubts are felt about its application. There must be a core of settled meaning, but there will be, as well, a penumbra of debatable cases in which words are neither obviously applicable nor obviously ruled out.

H. L. A. Hart, "Positivism and the Separation of Law and Morals," 71 *Harvard Law Review* 593, 607 (1958)

3 The history of the cases does not show the development of a logical rule but rather a

series of changes and abandonments. Upon the argument in each situation that the courts draw a Maginot Line to withstand an onslaught of false claims, the cases have assumed a variety of postures. . . . Legal history shows that artificial islands of exceptions, created from the fear that the legal process will not work, usually do not withstand the waves of reality and, in time, descend into oblivion.

> **Mathew O. Tobriner,** *Dillon v. Legg,* 68 Cal. 2d 728, 746–47, 441 P.2d 912, 69 Cal. Rptr. 72 (1968)

SCHOOLS

See EDUCATION; SEGREGATION

SEARCHES AND SEIZURES

See also CRIMINAL PROCEDURE; PRIVACY

1 And I take this opportunity to declare, that . . . I will to my dying day oppose, with all the powers and faculties God has given me, all such instruments of slavery on the one hand, and villainy on the other, as this writ of assistance is. It appears to me . . . the worst instrument of arbitrary power, the most destructive of English liberty, and the fundamental principles of the constitution, that ever was found in an English law-book.

> **James Otis,** Argument against the writs of assistance, Boston, Feb. 1761, quoted in John Adams, "Abstract of the Argument for and against the Writts of Assistance," 1761, in *Legal Papers of John Adams* 2:134, 139–40 (L. Kinvin Wroth & Hiller B. Zobel eds. 1965)

2 Your Honours will find in the old book, concerning the office of a justice of peace, precedents of general warrants to search suspected houses. But in more modern books you will find only special warrants to search such and such houses specially named, in which the complainant has before sworn he suspects his goods are concealed; and you will find it adjudged *that special warrants only are legal.* In the same manner I rely on it, that the writ prayed for in this petition being general is illegal. It is a power that places the liberty of every man in the hands of every petty officer.

> **James Otis,** Argument against the writs of assistance, Boston, Feb. 1761, quoted in

John Adams, "Abstract of the Argument for and against the Writts of Assistance," 1761, in *Legal Papers of John Adams* 2:134, 141–42 (L. Kinvin Wroth & Hiller B. Zobel eds. 1965)

3 Now one of the most essential branches of English liberty, is the freedom of one's house. A man's house is his castle;* and while he is quiet, he is as well guarded as a prince in his castle. This writ [of assistance], if it should be declared legal, would totally annihilate this privilege.

> **James Otis,** Argument against the writs of assistance, Boston, Feb. 1761, quoted in John Adams, "Abstract of the Argument for and against the Writts of Assistance," 1761, in *Legal Papers of John Adams* 2:134, 142 (L. Kinvin Wroth & Hiller B. Zobel eds. 1965)

4 That general warrants, whereby an officer or messenger may be commanded to search suspected places without evidence of a fact committed, or to seize any person or persons not named, or whose offence is not particularly described and supported by evidence, are grievous and oppressive, and ought not to be granted.

> Virginia Declaration of Rights of 1776, § 10, in *Federal and State Constitutions* 7:3812, 3814 (Francis N. Thorpe ed. 1909)

5 Every subject has a right to be secure from all unreasonable searches, and seizures, of his person, his houses, his papers, and all his possessions. All warrants, therefore, are contrary to this right, if the cause or foundation of them be not previously supported by oath or affirmation, and if the order in the warrant to a civil officer, to make search in suspected places, or to arrest one or more suspected persons, or to seize their property, be not accompanied with a special designation of the persons or objects of search, arrest, or seizure; and no warrant ought to be issued but in cases, and with the formalities prescribed by the laws.

> Massachusetts Constitution of 1780, pt. 1, art. 14, in *Federal and State Constitutions* 3:1888, 1891 (Francis N. Thorpe ed. 1909)

6 It may be added, that the term "probable cause," according to its usual acceptation,

---

* Burton Stevenson, *Home Book of Proverbs, Maxims and Familiar Phrases* 1192 (1948), traces the proverb, "A man's house is his castle," back to 1567 and notes legal usages of it by Sir Edward Coke in the 17th century.

means less than evidence which would justify condemnation. . . . It imports a seizure made under circumstances which warrant suspicion.

> **John Marshall**, *Locke v. United States*, 11
> U.S. (7 Cranch) 339, 348 (1813)

7 But Otis was a flame of fire!—with a promptitude of classical allusions, a depth of research, a rapid summary of historical events and dates, a profusion of legal authorities, a prophetic glance of his eye into futurity, and a torrent of impetuous eloquence, he hurried away every thing before him. American independence was then and there born; the seeds of patriots and heroes were then and there sown, to defend the vigorous youth, the *non sine Diis animosus infans*. Every man of a crowded audience appeared to me to go away, as I did, ready to take arms against writs of assistance. Then and there was the first scene of the first act of opposition to the arbitrary claims of Great Britain. Then and there the child Independence was born. In fifteen years, namely in 1776, he grew up to manhood, and declared himself free.

> **John Adams**, Letter to William Tudor, 29
> Mar. 1817, in *Works of John Adams* 10:247–
> 48 (Charles Francis Adams ed. 1856)

8 I shall only say, and I do say in the most solemn manner, that Mr. Otis's oration against *writs of assistance* breathed into this nation the breath of life.

> **John Adams**, Letter to H. Niles, 14 Jan.
> 1818, in *Works of John Adams* 10:276
> (Charles Francis Adams ed. 1856)

9 The principles laid down in this opinion [Lord Camden's opinion in *Entick v. Carrington*, 19 How. St. Tr. 1029 (1765)] affect the very essence of constitutional liberty and security. They reach farther than the concrete form of the case then before the court, with its adventitious circumstances; they apply to all invasions on the part of the government and its employés of the sanctity of a man's home and the privacies of life. It is not the breaking of his doors, and the rummaging of his drawers, that constitutes the essence of the offence; but it is the invasion of his indefeasible right of personal security, personal liberty and private property, where that right has never been forfeited by his conviction of some public offence,—it is the invasion of this

sacred right which underlies and constitutes the essence of Lord Camden's judgment. Breaking into a house and opening boxes and drawers are circumstances of aggravation; but any forcible and compulsory extortion of a man's own testimony or of his private papers to be used as evidence to convict him of crime or to forfeit his goods, is within the condemnation of that judgment. In this regard the Fourth and Fifth Amendments run almost into each other.

> **Joseph P. Bradley**, *Boyd v. United States*,
> 116 U.S. 616, 630 (1886)

10 It may be that it is the obnoxious thing in its mildest and least repulsive form; but illegitimate and unconstitutional practices get their first footing in that way, namely, by silent approaches and slight deviations from legal modes of procedure. This can only be obviated by adhering to the rule that constitutional provisions for the security of person and property should be liberally construed. A close and literal construction deprives them of half their efficacy, and leads to gradual depreciation of the right, as if it consisted more in sound than in substance. It is the duty of courts to be watchful for the constitutional rights of the citizen, and against any stealthy encroachments thereon.

> **Joseph P. Bradley**, *Boyd v. United States*,
> 116 U.S. 616, 635 (1886)

11 If letters and private documents can . . . be seized and held and used in evidence against a citizen accused of an offense, the protection of the Fourth Amendment declaring [a person's] right to be secure against such searches and seizures is of no value, and . . . might as well be stricken from the Constitution.

> **William R. Day**, *Weeks v. United States*, 232
> U.S. 383, 393 (1914)

12 The proposition could not be presented more nakedly. It is that although of course its seizure was an outrage which the Government now regrets, it may study the papers before it returns them, copy them, and then may use the knowledge that it has gained. . . . In our opinion such is not the law. It reduces the Fourth Amendment to a form of words.

> **Oliver Wendell Holmes, Jr.**, *Silverthorne
> Lumber Co. v. United States*, 251 U.S. 385,
> 391–92 (1920)

13 The essence of a provision forbidding the acquisition of evidence in a certain way is that not merely evidence so acquired shall not be used before the Court but that it shall not be used at all. Of course this does not mean that the facts thus obtained become sacred and inaccessible. If the knowledge of them is gained from an independent source they may be proved like any others, but the knowledge gained by the Government's own wrong cannot be used by it in the way proposed.

Oliver Wendell Holmes, Jr., *Silverthorne Lumber Co. v. United States*, 251 U.S. 385, 392 (1920)

14 We are not to strain an immunity to the point at which human nature rebels against honoring it in conduct. The peace officer empowered to arrest must be empowered to disarm. If he may disarm, he may search, lest a weapon be concealed. The search being lawful, he retains what he finds if connected with the crime. We may be sure that the law would be flouted and derided if, defeating its own ends, it drew too fine a point, after sanctioning the search, between the things to be retained and the things to be returned.

Benjamin N. Cardozo, *People v. Chiagles*, 237 N.Y. 193, 197, 142 N.E. 583 (1923)

15 The special protection accorded by the Fourth Amendment to the people in their "persons, houses, papers and effects," is not extended to the open fields. The distinction between the latter and the house is as old as the common law.

Oliver Wendell Holmes, Jr., *Hester v. United States*, 265 U.S. 57, 59 (1924)

16 The right without a search warrant contemporaneously to search persons lawfully arrested while committing crime and to search the place where the arrest is made in order to find and seize things connected with the crime as its fruits or as the means by which it was committed, as well as weapons and other things to effect an escape from custody, is not to be doubted.

Pierce Butler, *Agnello v. United States*, 269 U.S. 20, 30 (1925)

17 In determining what is probable cause, we are not called upon to determine whether the offense charged has in fact been committed. We are concerned only with the question whether the affiant had reasonable grounds at the time of his affidavit and the issuance of the warrant for the belief that the law was being violated on the premises to be searched; and if the apparent facts set out in the affidavit are such that a reasonably discreet and prudent man would be led to believe that there was a commission of the offense charged, there is probable cause justifying the issuance of a warrant.

Harlan F. Stone, *Dumbra v. United States*, 268 U.S. 435, 441 (1925)

18 We have made a somewhat extended reference to these statutes to show that the guaranty of freedom from unreasonable searches and seizures by the Fourth Amendment has been construed, practically since the beginning of the Government, as recognizing a necessary difference between a search of a store, dwelling house or other structure in respect of which a proper official warrant readily may be obtained, and a search of a ship, motor boat, wagon or automobile, for contraband goods, where it is not practicable to secure a warrant because the vehicle can be quickly moved out of the locality or jurisdiction in which the warrant must be sought.

William Howard Taft, *Carroll v. United States*, 267 U.S. 132, 153 (1925)

19 It is clear that the officers here had justification for the search and seizure. That is to say that the facts and circumstances within their knowledge and of which they had reasonably trustworthy information were sufficient in themselves to warrant a man of reasonable caution in the belief that intoxicating liquor was being transported in the automobile which they stopped and searched.

William Howard Taft, *Carroll v. United States*, 267 U.S. 132, 162 (1925)

20 It is enough if the description is such that the officer with a search warrant can with reasonable effort ascertain and identify the place intended.

William Howard Taft, *Steele v. United States*, 267 U.S. 498, 503 (1925)

21 The criminal is to go free because the constable has blundered.

Benjamin N. Cardozo, *People v. Defore*, 242 N.Y. 13, 21, 150 N.E. 585 (1926)

22 We are confirmed in this conclusion when we reflect how far-reaching in its effect upon society the new consequences would be. The pettiest peace officer would have it in his power through overzeal or indiscretion to confer immunity upon an offender for crimes the most flagitious. A room is searched against the law, and the body of a murdered man is found. If the place of discovery may not be proved, the other circumstances may be insufficient to connect the defendant with the crime. . . . Like instances can be multiplied. We may not subject society to these dangers until the Legislature has spoken with a clearer voice. . . . The question is whether protection for the individual would not be gained at a disproportionate loss of protection for society. On the one side is the social need that crime shall be repressed. On the other, the social need that law shall not be flouted by the insolence of office. There are dangers in any choice.

Benjamin N. Cardozo, *People v. Defore,* 242 N.Y. 13, 23–25, 150 N.E. 585 (1926)

23 After arresting a man in his house, to rummage at will among his papers in search of whatever will convict him, appears to us to be indistinguishable from what might be done under a general warrant; . . . True, by hypothesis the power would not exist, if the supposed offender were not found on the premises; but it is small consolation to know that one's papers are safe only so long as one is not at home. . . . Nor should we forget that what seems fair enough against a squalid huckster of bad liquor may take on a very different face, if used by a government determined to suppress political opposition under the guise of sedition.

Learned Hand, *United States v. Kirschenblatt,* 16 F.2d 202, 203 (2d Cir. 1926)

24 The requirement that warrants shall particularly describe the things to be seized makes general searches under them impossible and prevents the seizure of one thing under a warrant describing another. As to what is to be taken, nothing is left to the discretion of the officer executing the warrant.

Pierce Butler, *Marron v. United States,* 275 U.S. 192, 196 (1927)

25 As a means of espionage, writs of assistance and general warrants are but puny instruments of tyranny and oppression when compared with wire-tapping.

Louis D. Brandeis, *Olmstead v. United States,* 277 U.S. 438, 476 (1928) (dissenting)

26 The government ought not to use evidence obtained and only obtainable, by a criminal act. . . . for my part I think it a less evil that some criminals should escape than that the Government should play an ignoble part. . . . If the existing code does not permit district attorneys to have a hand in such dirty business [wiretapping], it does not permit the judge to allow such iniquities to succeed.

Oliver Wendell Holmes, Jr., *Olmstead v. United States,* 277 U.S. 438, 469–70 (1928) (dissenting)

27 It is desirable that criminals should be detected, and to that end that all available evidence should be used. It also is desirable that the Government should not itself foster and pay for other crimes, when they are the means by which the evidence is to be obtained.

Oliver Wendell Holmes, Jr., *Olmstead v. United States,* 277 U.S. 438, 470 (1928) (dissenting)

28 The burden is, of course, on the accused in the first instance to prove to the trial court's satisfaction that wire-tapping was unlawfully employed. Once that is established— as was plainly done here—the trial judge must give opportunity, however closely confined, to the accused to prove that a substantial portion of the case against him was a fruit of the poisonous tree.

Felix Frankfurter, *Nardone v. United States,* 308 U.S. 338, 341 (1939)

29 Titus, you have been found guilty of conducting a lottery; Flavius, you have confessedly violated the Constitution. Titus ought to suffer imprisonment for crime, and Flavius for contempt. But no! We shall let you *both* go free. We shall not punish Flavius directly, but shall do so by reversing Titus' conviction. This is our way of teaching people like Flavius to behave, and of teaching people like Titus to behave, and incidentally of securing respect for the Constitution. Our way of upholding the Constitution is not to strike at the man who

breaks it, but to let off somebody else who broke something else.

John H. Wigmore, *A Treatise on the Anglo-American System of Evidence in Trials at Common Law* 8:40 (3d ed. 1940)

30 The forefathers, after consulting the lessons of history, designed our Constitution to place obstacles in the way of a too permeating police surveillance, which they seemed to think was a greater danger to a free people than the escape of some criminals from punishment.

Robert H. Jackson, *United States v. Di Re,* 332 U.S. 581, 595 (1948)

31 A search is not to be made legal by what it turns up. In law it is good or bad when it starts and does not change character from its success.

Robert H. Jackson, *United States v. Di Re,* 332 U.S. 581, 595 (1948)

32 The point of the Fourth Amendment . . . is not that it denies law enforcement the support of the usual inferences which reasonable men draw from evidence. Its protection consists in requiring that those inferences be drawn by a neutral and detached magistrate instead of being judged by the officer engaged in the often competitive enterprise of ferreting out crime.

Robert H. Jackson, *Johnson v. United States,* 333 U.S. 10, 13–14 (1948)

33 The right of officers to thrust themselves into a home is . . . a grave concern, not only to the individual but to a society which chooses to dwell in reasonable security and freedom from surveillance. When the right of privacy must reasonably yield to the right of search is, as a rule, to be decided by a judicial officer, not by a policeman or government enforcement agent.

Robert H. Jackson, *Johnson v. United States,* 333 U.S. 10, 14 (1948)

34 Any assumption that evidence sufficient to support a magistrate's disinterested determination to issue a search warrant will justify the officers in making a search without a warrant would reduce the Amendment to a nullity and leave the people's homes secure only in the discretion of police officers.

Robert H. Jackson, *Johnson v. United States,* 333 U.S. 10, 14 (1948)

35 The knock at the door, whether by day or by night, as a prelude to a search, without authority of law but solely on the authority of the police, did not need the commentary of recent history to be condemned as inconsistent with the conception of human rights enshrined in the history and the basic constitutional documents of English-speaking peoples.

Felix Frankfurter, *Wolf v. Colorado,* 338 U.S. 25, 28 (1949)

36 The crux of that doctrine is that a search is a search by a federal official if he had a hand in it; it is not a search by a federal official if evidence secured by state authorities is turned over to the federal authorities on a silver platter.

Felix Frankfurter, *Lustig v. United States,* 338 U.S. 74, 78–79 (1949)

37 Indications are not wanting that Fourth Amendment freedoms are tacitly marked as secondary rights, to be relegated to a deferred position. . . . These, I protest, are not mere second-class rights but belong in the catalog of indispensable freedoms. Among deprivations of rights, none is so effective in cowing a population, crushing the spirit of the individual and putting terror in every heart. Uncontrolled search and seizure is one of the first and most effective weapons in the arsenal of every arbitrary government. And one need only briefly to have dwelt and worked among a people possessed of many admirable qualities but deprived of these rights to know that the human personality deteriorates and dignity and self-reliance disappear where homes, persons and possessions are subject at any hour to unheralded search and seizure by the police.

Robert H. Jackson, *Brinegar v. United States,* 338 U.S. 160, 180–81 (1949) (dissenting)

38 If we assume, for example, that a child is kidnaped [*sic*] and the officers throw a roadblock about the neighborhood and search every outgoing car, it would be a drastic and undiscriminating use of the search. The officers might be unable to show probable cause for searching any particular car. However, I should candidly strive hard to sustain such an action, executed fairly and in good faith, because it might be reasonable to subject travelers to that indignity if it was the only way to save

a threatened life and detect a vicious crime. But I should not strain to sustain such a roadblock and universal search to salvage a few bottles of bourbon and catch a bootlegger.

Robert H. Jackson, *Brinegar v. United States,* 338 U.S. 160, 183 (1949) (dissenting)

39 The conclusion is inescapable that but one remedy exists to deter violations of the search and seizure clause. That is the rule which excludes illegally obtained evidence. Only by exclusion can we impress upon the zealous prosecutor that violation of the Constitution will do him no good. And only when that point is driven home can the prosecutor be expected to emphasize the importance of observing constitutional demands in his instructions to the police.

Frank Murphy, *Wolf v. Colorado,* 338 U.S. 25, 44 (1949) (dissenting)

40 In dealing with probable cause, however, as the very name implies, we deal with probabilities. These are not technical; they are the factual and practical considerations of everyday life on which reasonable and prudent men, not legal technicians, act. The standard of proof is accordingly correlative to what must be proved.

Wiley B. Rutledge, *Brinegar v. United States,* 338 U.S. 160, 175 (1949)

41 The proceedings by which this conviction was obtained do more than offend some fastidious squeamishness or private sentimentalism about combatting crime too energetically. This is conduct that shocks the conscience. Illegally breaking into the privacy of the petitioner, the struggle to open his mouth and remove what was there, the forcible extraction of his stomach's contents—this course of proceeding by agents of government to obtain evidence is bound to offend even hardened sensibilities. They are methods too close to the rack and the screw to permit of constitutional differentiation.

Felix Frankfurter, *Rochin v. California,* 342 U.S. 165, 172 (1952)

42 It would be a stultification of the responsibility which the course of constitutional history has cast upon this Court to hold that in order to convict a man the police cannot extract by force what is in his mind but can extract what is in his stomach.

Felix Frankfurter, *Rochin v. California,* 342 U.S. 165, 173 (1952)

43 That the rule of exclusion and reversal results in the escape of guilty persons is more capable of demonstration than that it deters invasions of right by the police. The case is made, so far as the police are concerned, when they announce that they have arrested their man. Rejection of the evidence does nothing to punish the wrongdoing official, while it may, and likely will, release the wrong-doing defendant. It deprives society of its remedy against one lawbreaker because he has been pursued by another. It protects one against whom incriminating evidence is discovered, but does nothing to protect innocent persons who are the victims of illegal but fruitless searches. The disciplinary or educational effect of the court's releasing the defendant for police misbehavior is so indirect as to be no more than a mild deterrent at best.

Robert H. Jackson, *Irvine v. California,* 347 U.S. 128, 136–37 (1954)

44 Wherever a culprit is caught red-handed . . . it is difficult to adopt and enforce a rule that would turn him loose. A rule protective of law-abiding citizens is not apt to flourish where its advocates are usually criminals.

William O. Douglas, *Draper v. United States,* 358 U.S. 307, 314 (1959) (dissenting)

45 It must be remembered that what the Constitution forbids is not all searches and seizures, but unreasonable searches and seizures.

Potter Stewart, *Elkins v. United States,* 364 U.S. 206, 222 (1960)

46 Our holding that the exclusionary rule is an essential part of both the Fourth and Fourteenth Amendments is not only the logical dictate of prior cases, but it also makes very good sense. There is no war between the Constitution and common sense.

Tom C. Clark, *Mapp v. Ohio,* 367 U.S. 643, 657 (1961)

47 The criminal goes free, if he must, but it is the law that sets him free.

Tom C. Clark, *Mapp v. Ohio,* 367 U.S. 643, 659 (1961)

48 Having once recognized that the right to privacy embodied in the Fourth Amendment is enforceable against the States, and that the right to be secure against rude invasions of privacy by state officers is, therefore, constitutional in origin, we can no longer permit that right to remain an empty promise. Because it is enforceable in the same manner and to *like* effect as other basic rights secured by the Due Process Clause, we can no longer permit it to be revocable at the whim of any police officer who, in the name of law enforcement itself, chooses to suspend its enjoyment. Our decision, founded on reason and truth, gives no more than that which the Constitution guarantees him, to the police officer no less than that to which honest law enforcement is entitled, and, to the courts, that judicial integrity so necessary in the true administration of justice.

Tom C. Clark, *Mapp v. Ohio*, 367 U.S. 643, 660 (1961)

49 The Fourth Amendment and the personal rights which it secures have a long history. At the very core stands the right of a man to retreat into his own home and there be free from unreasonable governmental intrusion.

Potter Stewart, *Silverman v. United States*, 365 U.S. 505, 511 (1961)

50 Although an affidavit may be based on hearsay information and need not reflect the direct personal observations of the affiant, . . . the magistrate must be informed of some of the underlying circumstances from which the informant concluded that the narcotics were where he claimed they were, and some of the underlying circumstances from which the officer concluded that the informant, whose identity need not be disclosed, . . . was "credible" or his information "reliable."

Arthur J. Goldberg, *Aguilar v. Texas*, 378 U.S. 108, 114 (1964)

51 If the teachings of the Court's cases are to be followed and the constitutional policy served, affidavits for search warrants, such as the one involved here, must be tested and interpreted by magistrates and courts in a commonsense and realistic fashion. They are normally drafted by nonlawyers in the midst and haste of a criminal investigation. Technical requirements of elabo-

rate specificity once exacted under common law pleadings have no proper place in this area. A grudging or negative attitude by reviewing courts toward warrants will tend to discourage police officers from submitting their evidence to a judicial officer before acting.

Arthur J. Goldberg, *United States v. Ventresca*, 380 U.S. 102, 108 (1965)

52 Recital of some of the underlying circumstances in the affidavit is essential if the magistrate is to perform his detached function and not serve merely as a rubber stamp for the police. However, where these circumstances are detailed, where reason for crediting the source of the information is given, and when a magistrate has found probable cause, the courts should not invalidate the warrant by interpreting the affidavit in a hypertechnical, rather than a commonsense, manner.

Arthur J. Goldberg, *United States v. Ventresca*, 380 U.S. 102, 109 (1965)

53 If detectives and private intermeddlers may, without legal responsibility, peer through keyholes, eavesdrop at the table, listen at the transom and over the telephone, and crawl under the bed, then all constitutional guarantees become meaningless aggregation of words, as disconnected as a broken necklace whose beads have scattered on the floor.

Michael A. Musmanno, *Commonwealth v. Murray*, 423 Pa. 37, 51–52, 223 A.2d 102 (1966)

54 The Fourth Amendment protects people, not places. What a person knowingly exposes to the public, even in his own home or office, is not a subject of Fourth Amendment protection. . . . But what he seeks to preserve as private, even in an area accessible to the public, may be constitutionally protected.

Potter Stewart, *Katz v. United States*, 389 U.S. 347, 351–52 (1967)

55 Searches conducted outside the judicial process, without prior approval by judge or magistrate, are *per se* unreasonable under the Fourth Amendment—subject only to a few specifically established and well-delineated exceptions.

Potter Stewart, *Katz v. United States*, 389 U.S. 347, 357 (1967)

56 There have been powerful hydraulic pressures throughout our history that bear heavily on the Court to water down constitutional guarantees and give the police the upper hand. That hydraulic pressure has probably never been greater than it is today. Yet if the individual is no longer to be sovereign, if the police can pick him up whenever they do not like the cut of his jib, if they can "seize" and "search" him in their discretion, we enter a new regime. The decision to enter it should be made only after a full debate by the people of this country.

William O. Douglas, *Terry v. Ohio*, 392 U.S. 1, 39 (1968) (dissenting)

57 It must be recognized that whenever a police officer accosts an individual and restrains his freedom to walk away, he has "seized" that person. And it is nothing less than sheer torture of the English language to suggest that a careful exploration of the outer surfaces of a person's clothing all over his or her body in an attempt to find weapons is not a "search."

Earl Warren, *Terry v. Ohio*, 392 U.S. 1, 16 (1968)

58 In determining whether the seizure and search were "unreasonable" our inquiry is a dual one—whether the officer's action was justified at its inception, and whether it was reasonably related in scope to the circumstances which justified the interference in the first place.

Earl Warren, *Terry v. Ohio*, 392 U.S. 1, 19– 20 (1968)

59 In justifying the particular intrusion the police officer must be able to point to specific and articulable facts which, taken together with rational inferences from those facts, reasonably warrant that intrusion.

Earl Warren, *Terry v. Ohio*, 392 U.S. 1, 21 (1968)

60 We merely hold today that where a police officer observes unusual conduct which leads him reasonably to conclude in the light of his experience that criminal activity may be afoot and that the persons with whom he is dealing may be armed and presently dangerous, . . . he is entitled for the protection of himself and others in the area to conduct a carefully limited search of the outer clothing of such persons in an attempt to discover weapons which might be used to assault him.

Earl Warren, *Terry v. Ohio*, 392 U.S. 1, 30 (1968)

61 The history of the suppression doctrine demonstrates that it is both conceptually sterile and practically ineffective in accomplishing its stated objective. . . . Some clear demonstration of the benefits and effectiveness of the exclusionary rule is required to justify it in view of the high price it extracts from society—the release of countless guilty criminals.

Warren E. Burger, *Bivens v. Six Unknown Named Agents*, 403 U.S. 388, 415 (1971) (dissenting)

62 The ultimate question . . . is whether, if the particular form of surveillance practiced by the police is permitted to go unregulated by constitutional restraints, the amount of privacy and freedom remaining to citizens would be diminished to a compass inconsistent with the aims of a free and open society.

Anthony G. Amsterdam, "Perspectives on the Fourth Amendment," 58 *Minnesota Law Review* 349, 403 (1974)

63 A person who is aggrieved by an illegal search and seizure only through the introduction of damaging evidence secured by a search of a third person's premises or property has not had any of his Fourth Amendment rights infringed.

William H. Rehnquist, *Rakas v. Illinois*, 439 U.S. 128, 134 (1978)

64 Jones had a legitimate expectation of privacy in the premises he was using and therefore could claim the protection of the Fourth Amendment with respect to a government invasion of those premises, even though his "interest" in those premises might not have been a recognized property interest at common law.

William H. Rehnquist, *Rakas v. Illinois*, 439 U.S. 128, 143 (1978)

65 The test of reasonableness under the Fourth Amendment is not capable of precise definition or mechanical application. In each case it requires a balancing of the need for the particular search against the invasion of personal rights that the search entails. Courts must consider the scope of

the particular intrusion, the manner in which it is conducted, the justification for initiating it, and the place in which it is conducted.

William H. Rehnquist, *Bell v. Wolfish*, 441 U.S. 520, 559 (1979)

66 I suspect, therefore, that members of our society will be shocked to learn that the Court, the ultimate guarantor of liberty, deems unreasonable our expectation that the aspects of our private lives that are concealed safely in a trash bag will not become public.

William J. Brennan, Jr., *California v. Greenwood*, 486 U.S. 35, 45–46 (1988) (dissenting)

67 The issue in this case is not whether declaring a war on illegal drugs is good public policy. The importance of ridding our society of such drugs is, by now, apparent to all. Rather, the issue here is whether the Government's deployment in that war of a particularly draconian weapon—the compulsory collection and chemical testing of railroad workers' blood and urine—comports with the Fourth Amendment. Precisely because the need for action against the drug scourge is manifest, the need for vigilance against unconstitutional excess is great. History teaches that grave threats to liberty often come in times of urgency, when constitutional rights seem too extravagant to endure. The World War II relocation-camp cases, . . . and the Red scare and McCarthy-Era internal subversion cases, are only the most extreme reminders that when we allow fundamental freedoms to be sacrificed in the name of real or perceived exigency, we invariably come to regret it.

Thurgood Marshall, *Skinner v. Railway Labor Executives' Ass'n*, 489 U.S. 602, 635 (1989) (dissenting)

SECURITIES LAW

1 No member bank shall be affiliated . . . with any corporation, association, business trust, or other similar organization engaged principally in the issue, flotation, underwriting, public sale, or distribution . . . of stocks, bonds, debentures, notes, or other securities.

Banking Act of 1933 (Glass-Steagall Act), ch. 89, § 20, 48 Stat. 162, 188

2 An investment contract for purposes of the Securities Act means a contract, transaction or scheme whereby a person invests his money in a common enterprise and is led to expect profits solely from the efforts of the promoter or a third party. . . . It embodies a flexible rather than a static principle, one that is capable of adaptation to meet the countless and variable schemes devised by those who seek the use of the money of others on the promise of profits.

Frank Murphy, *SEC v. Howey Co.*, 328 U.S. 293, 298–99 (1946)

3 The Court's reasoning adds up to this: The Commission must be sustained because of its accumulated experience in solving a problem with which it had never before been confronted. . . . I give up. Now I realize fully what Mark Twain meant when he said, "The more you explain it, the more I don't understand it."

Robert H. Jackson, *SEC v. Chenery Corp.*, 332 U.S. 194, 213–14 (1947) (dissenting)

4 It shall be unlawful for any person, directly or indirectly, by the use of any means or instrumentality of interstate commerce, or of the mails . . .

(a) To employ any device, scheme, or artifice to defraud,

(b) To make any untrue statement of a material fact or to omit to state a material fact necessary in order to make the statements made, in the light of the circumstances under which they were made, not misleading, or

(c) To engage in any act, practice, or course of business which operates or would operate as a fraud or deceit upon any person, in connection with the purchase or sale of any security.

Rule 10b-5, 13 Fed. Reg. 8183–84 (1948) (codified at 17 C.F.R. § 240.10b-5)

5 [Definition of insider trading:] Stealing too fast.

Calvin Trillin, "The Inside on Insider Trading," in *If You Can't Say Something Nice* 141, 143 (1987)

SEGREGATION

See also CIVIL RIGHTS; EDUCATION

1 All railway companies carrying passengers in their coaches in this State, shall provide

equal but separate accommodations for the white, and colored races.

> Act of July 10, 1890, no. 111, 1890 La. Acts 152, 153

2 If railroad companies care to furnish separate but equal accommodations on equal terms to each race, no objection need be made.

> **Frank W. Gage,** *The Negro Problem in the United States* 92 (1892)

3 The object of the amendment was undoubtedly to enforce the absolute equality of the two races before the law, but in the nature of things it could not have been intended to abolish distinctions based upon color, or to enforce social, as distinguished from political equality, or a commingling of the two races upon terms unsatisfactory to either. Laws permitting, and even requiring, their separation in places where they are liable to be brought into contact do not necessarily imply the inferiority of either race to the other, and have been generally, if not universally, recognized as within the competency of the state legislatures in the exercise of their police power. The most common instance of this is connected with the establishment of separate schools for white and colored children, which has been held to be a valid exercise of the legislative power even by courts of States where the political rights of the colored race have been longest and most earnestly enforced.

> **Henry B. Brown,** *Plessy v. Ferguson,* 163 U.S. 537, 544 (1896)

4 We consider the underlying fallacy of the plaintiff's argument to consist in the assumption that the enforced separation of the two races stamps the colored race with a badge of inferiority. . . . The argument also assumes that social prejudices may be overcome by legislation, and that equal rights cannot be secured to the negro except by an enforced commingling of the two races. We cannot accept this proposition. If the two races are to meet upon terms of social equality, it must be the result of natural affinities, a mutual appreciation of each other's merits and a voluntary consent of individuals.

> **Henry B. Brown,** *Plessy v. Ferguson,* 163 U.S. 537, 551 (1896)

5 Legislation is powerless to eradicate racial instincts or to abolish distinctions based upon physical differences, and the attempt to do so can only result in accentuating the difficulties of the present situation. If the civil and political rights of both races be equal one cannot be inferior to the other civilly or politically. If one race be inferior to the other socially, the Constitution of the United States cannot put them upon the same plane.

> **Henry B. Brown,** *Plessy v. Ferguson,* 163 U.S. 537, 551–52 (1896)

6 By the Louisiana statute, the validity of which is here involved, all railway companies (other than street railroad companies) carrying passengers in that State are required to have separate but equal* accommodations for white and colored persons.

> **John M. Harlan** (1833–1911), *Plessy v. Ferguson,* 163 U.S. 537, 552 (1896) (dissenting)

7 The Constitution of the United States does not, I think, permit any public authority to know the race of those entitled to be protected in the enjoyment of such rights. Every true man has pride of race, and under appropriate circumstances when the rights of others, his equals before the law, are not to be affected, it is his privilege to express such pride and to take such action based upon it as to him seems proper. But I deny that any legislative body or judicial tribunal may have regard to the race of citizens when the civil rights of those citizens are involved.

> **John M. Harlan** (1833–1911), *Plessy v. Ferguson,* 163 U.S. 537, 554–55 (1896) (dissenting)

8 But in view of the Constitution, in the eye of the law, there is in this country no superior, dominant, ruling class of citizens. There is no caste here. Our Constitution is

---

* The statute used the phrase "equal but separate" (see quotation 1 above), but Harlan's opinion popularized "separate but equal." An earlier usage of the latter formulation was by F. W. Gage in 1892 (see quotation 2 above). The Declaration of Independence referred to "the separate and equal station to which the laws of Nature and of Nature's God entitle" a people. See also quotation 12 below.

color-blind,* and neither knows nor tolerates classes among citizens. In respect of civil rights, all citizens are equal before the law. The humblest is the peer of the most powerful.

> **John M. Harlan** (1833–1911), *Plessy v. Ferguson*, 163 U.S. 537, 559 (1896) (dissenting)

9 The sure guarantee of the peace and security of each race is the clear, distinct, unconditional recognition by our governments, National and State, of every right that inheres in civil freedom, and of the equality before the law of all citizens of the United States, without regard to race.

> **John M. Harlan** (1833–1911), *Plessy v. Ferguson*, 163 U.S. 537, 560 (1896) (dissenting)

10 The arbitrary separation of citizens, on the basis of race, while they are on a public highway, is a badge of servitude wholly inconsistent with the civil freedom and the equality before the law established by the Constitution. It cannot be justified upon any legal grounds. . . . We boast of the freedom enjoyed by our people above all other peoples. But it is difficult to reconcile that boast with a state of the law which, practically, puts the brand of servitude and degradation upon a large class of our fellow-citizens, our equals before the law. The thin disguise of "equal" accommodations for passengers in railroad coaches will not mislead any one, nor atone for the wrong this day done.

> **John M. Harlan** (1833–1911), *Plessy v. Ferguson*, 163 U.S. 537, 562 (1896) (dissenting)

11 Whatever may have been the extent of psychological knowledge at the time of *Plessy v. Ferguson*, this finding [that segregated schooling has a detrimental effect on black children] is amply supported by modern authority.†

> **Earl Warren**, *Brown v. Board of Education*, 347 U.S. 483, 494 (1954)

---

* Justice is pictured blind and her daughter, the Law, ought at least to be color-blind. —**Albion W. Tourgee**, Brief for Plaintiff in Error, *Plessy v. Ferguson*, 163 U.S. 537 (1896), in *Landmark Briefs and Arguments of the Supreme Court* 13:19, 46 (Philip B. Kurland & Gerhard Casper eds. 1975)

† This statement was accompanied by footnote 11 of the decision, which listed seven studies by social scientists concerning the effects of racial segregation.

12 To separate them [black children] from others of similar age and qualifications solely because of their race generates a feeling of inferiority as to their status in the community that may affect their hearts and minds in a way unlikely ever to be undone. . . . We conclude that in the field of public education the doctrine of "separate but equal" has no place. Separate educational facilities are inherently unequal.

> **Earl Warren**, *Brown v. Board of Education*, 347 U.S. 483, 494–95 (1954)
> See also SEGREGATION 1; SEGREGATION 2; SEGREGATION 6

13 The Constitution, in other words, does not require integration. It merely forbids discrimination.

> *Briggs v. Elliott*, 132 F. Supp. 776, 777 (E.D.S.C. 1955) (per curiam)

14 On May 17, [1954,] the Constitution of the United States was destroyed because the Supreme Court disregarded the law and decided integration was right. . . . You are not required to obey any court which passes out such a ruling. In fact, you are obligated to defy it.

> **James O. Eastland**, Speech, Senatobia, Miss., 12 Aug. 1955, quoted in *Look*, 3 Apr. 1956, at 24

15 Racial discrimination in public education is unconstitutional. . . . All provisions of federal, state or local law requiring or permitting such discrimination must yield to this principle.

> **Earl Warren**, *Brown v. Board of Education*, 349 U.S. 294, 298 (1955)

16 While giving weight to these public and private considerations, the courts will require that the defendants make a prompt and reasonable start toward full compliance with our May 17, 1954, ruling. Once such a start has been made, the courts may find that additional time is necessary to carry out the ruling in an effective manner. The burden rests upon the defendents to establish that such time is necessary in the public interest and is consistent with good faith compliance at the earliest practicable date.

> **Earl Warren**, *Brown v. Board of Education*, 349 U.S. 294, 300 (1955)

17 The judgments below . . . are accordingly reversed and the cases are remanded to the

District Courts to take such proceedings and enter such orders and decrees consistent with this opinion as are necessary and proper to admit to public schools on a racially nondiscriminatory basis with all deliberate speed* the parties to these cases.

Earl Warren, *Brown v. Board of Education,* 349 U.S. 294, 301 (1955)

18 We reaffirm our reliance on the Constitution as the fundamental law of the land.

We decry the Supreme Court's encroachments on rights reserved to the states and

---

* For that portion which he had converted into cash and expended in his own or on political intrigues, there was no mode of recovering it but by a suit at law, which was forthwith commenced, and proceeded, as our law-agents assured us, with all deliberate speed. —**Walter Scott,** *Rob Roy* 352 (Everyman's Library 1973) (1817)

I was obliged to reform my "way of life" which was conducting me from the "yellow leaf" to the Ground with all deliberate speed. —**George Gordon, Lord Byron,** Letter to John Murray, 6 Apr. 1819, in *Byron's Letters and Journals* 6:106 (Leslie A. Marchand ed. 1976)

But with unhurrying chase, / And with unperturbèd pace, / Deliberate speed, majestic instancy, / They beat— and a Voice beat / More instant than the Feet—/ 'All things betray thee, who betrayest Me.' —**Francis Thompson,** "The Hound of Heaven," 1893, in *Works of Francis Thompson* 1:107, 107 (1913)

We had to take steps to deal with the contempt of our authority—which we have done in your Chancery's delightful phrase, with all deliberate speed. —**Oliver Wendell Holmes, Jr.,** Letter to Frederick Pollock, 7 Mar. 1909, in *Holmes-Pollock Letters* 1:152 (Mark DeWolfe Howe ed. 1941)

A State cannot be expected to move with the celerity of a private business man; it is enough if it proceeds, in the language of the English Chancery, with all deliberate speed. —**Oliver Wendell Holmes, Jr.,** *Virginia v. West Virginia,* 222 U.S. 17, 19–20 (1911)

In order to justify a modification having such drastic business consequences, it was surely incumbent upon the Government to show that it had proceeded with all deliberate speed against General Motors. —**Felix Frankfurter,** *Chrysler Corp. v. United States,* 316 U.S. 556, 568 (1942) (dissenting)

This decree may lay out. . . . a plan for handling these cases in returning them to the lower courts for final disposition. We suggest a year for the presentation and consideration of a plan, not because that is an exact standard, but with the idea that it might involve the principle of handling the matter with deliberate speed. —**J. Lee Rankin,** Argument on behalf of United States as amicus curiae, *Briggs v. Elliott,* 8 Dec. 1953, in *Landmark Briefs and Arguments of the Supreme Court* 49A:537, 538 (Philip B. Kurland & Gerhard Casper eds. 1975)

It appears that Justice Felix Frankfurter contributed the crucial phrase "deliberate speed" to Chief Justice Earl Warren's opinion in the implementation stage of *Brown v. Board of Education* and, earlier, to the government's oral argument in a connected case. Frankfurter's source was Justice Oliver Wendell Holmes, Jr. Although Holmes attributed the phrase to "the language of the English chancery," assiduous investigations by scholars have uncovered only literary usages of it in England.

---

to the people, contrary to established law and to the Constitution.

We commend the motives of those states which have declared the intention to resist forced integration by any lawful means.

We appeal to the states and people who are not directly affected by these decisions to consider the constitutional principles involved against the time when they too, on issues vital to them, may be the victims of judicial encroachment.

Even though we constitute a minority in the present Congress, we have full faith that a majority of the American people believe in the dual system of government which has enabled us to achieve our greatness and will in time demand that the reserved rights of the states and of the people be made secure against judicial usurpation.

We pledge ourselves to use all lawful means to bring about a reversal of this decision which is contrary to the Constitution and to prevent the use of force in its implementation.

Southern Declaration on Integration, quoted in *New York Times,* 12 Mar. 1956, at 19

19 The problem of changing a people's mores, particularly those with an emotional overlay, is not to be taken lightly. It is a problem which will require the utmost patience, understanding, generosity and forbearance from all of us, of whatever race. But the magnitude of the problem may not nullify the principle. And that principle is that we are, all of us, freeborn Americans, with a right to make our way, unfettered by sanctions imposed by man because of the work of God.

J. Skelly Wright, *Bush v. Orleans Parish Sch. Bd.,* 138 F. Supp. 337, 342 (E.D. La. 1956)

20 State support of segregated schools through any arrangement . . . cannot be squared with the [Fourteenth] Amendment's command that no State shall deny to any person within its jurisdiction the equal protection of the laws. The right of a student not to be segregated on racial grounds . . . is indeed so fundamental and pervasive that it is embraced in the concept of due process of law. . . . The principles announced in [the Brown] decision and the obedience of the States to them, according to the command of the Constitution, are indispensable for the protection of the free-

doms guaranteed by our fundamental charter for all of us. Our constitutional ideal of equal justice under law is thus made a living truth.

> Cooper v. Aaron, 358 U.S. 1, 19–20 (1958) (joint opinion)

21 But if the freedom of association is denied by segregation, integration forces an association upon those for whom it is unpleasant or repugnant.... Given a situation where the state must practically choose between denying the association to those individuals who wish it or imposing it on those who would avoid it, is there a basis in neutral principles for holding that the Constitution demands that the claims for association should prevail? I should like to think there is, but I confess that I have not yet written the opinion.

> Herbert Wechsler, "Toward Neutral Principles of Constitutional Law," 73 Harvard Law Review 1, 34 (1959)

22 Then does segregation offend against equality? Equality, like all general concepts, has marginal areas where philosophic difficulties are encountered. But if a whole race of people finds itself confined within a system which is set up and continued for the very purpose of keeping it in an inferior station, and if the question is then solemnly propounded whether such a race is being treated "equally," I think we ought to exercise one of the sovereign prerogatives of philosophers—that of laughter. The only question remaining (after we get our laughter under control) is whether the segregation system answers to this description. Here I must confess to a tendency to start laughing all over again.

> Charles L. Black, Jr., "The Lawfulness of the Segregation Decisions," 69 Yale Law Journal 421, 424 (1960)

23 The time for mere "deliberate speed" has run out, and that phrase can no longer justify denying these Prince Edward County school children their constitutional rights to an education equal to that afforded by the public schools in the other parts of Virginia.

> Hugo L. Black, Griffin v. County School Bd., 377 U.S. 218, 234 (1964)

24 This is not to say, however, that the prima facie case may not be met by evidence sup-

porting a finding that a lesser degree of segregated schooling in the core city area would not have resulted even if the Board had not acted as it did.*

> William J. Brennan, Jr., Keyes v. School District No. 1, 413 U.S. 189, 211 (1973)

25 Desegregation is not and was never expected to be an easy task. Racial attitudes ingrained in our Nation's childhood and adolescence are not quickly thrown aside in its middle years. But just as the inconvenience of some cannot be allowed to stand in the way of the rights of others, so public opposition, no matter how strident, cannot be permitted to divert this Court from the enforcement of the constitutional principles at issue in this case. Today's holding, I fear, is more a reflection of a perceived public mood that we have gone far enough in enforcing the Constitution's guarantee of equal justice than it is the product of neutral principles of law. In the short run, it may seem to be the easier course to allow our great metropolitan areas to be divided up each into two cities—one white, the other black—but it is a course, I predict, our people will ultimately regret. I dissent.

> Thurgood Marshall, Milliken v. Bradley, 418 U.S. 717, 814–15 (1974) (dissenting)

26 [The Supreme Court's] opinion in Brown v. Board of Education ... represented nothing short of a reconsecration of American ideals. At a moment when the country had just begun to sense the magnitude of its global ideological contest with Communist authoritarianism and was quick to measure its own worth in terms of megaton power, the opinion of the Court said that the United States still stood for something more than material abundance, still moved to an inner spirit, however deeply it had been submerged by fear and envy and mindless hate.... The Court had restored to the American people a measure of the humanity that had been drained away in their climb to worldwide supremacy. The Court said, without using the words, that that ascent had been made over the backs of black America—and that when you

---

* This passage has been hailed as "the world's first and only quadruple negative."

stepped on a black man, he hurt. The time had come to stop.

Richard Kluger, *Simple Justice* 710 (1976)

SELF-INCRIMINATION

See FIFTH AMENDMENT

SENTENCING

See also CAPITAL PUNISHMENT; PUNISHMENT

1 The hardest case we ever heard of lived in Arkansas. He was only fourteen years old. One night he deliberately murdered his father and mother in cold blood, with a meat-axe. He was tried and found guilty. The Judge drew on his black cap, and in a voice choked with emotion asked the young prisoner if he had anything to say before the sentence of the Court was passed on him. . . . "Why, no," replied the prisoner, "I think I haven't, though I hope yer Honor will show some consideration FOR THE FEELINGS OF A POOR ORPHAN!"

Artemus Ward, "A Hard Case," in *Artemus Ward in London* 183, 183–84 (1867)
See also SENTENCING 3; SENTENCING 6

2 The newest "fad" of the penologists is "indeterminate sentences"—that is to say, criminals are to be simply sent to prison, to be, like patients in a hospital, "discharged when cured." This plan—which has the merit of Prison Director Hendrick's approval—will work first rate if God will agree to act as the discharging officer. It is hardly likely, though, that he would accept the position: he has long been out of politics.

Ambrose Bierce, "Determining the Indeterminate," *Wasp*, 6 Mar. 1886, in *The Ambrose Bierce Satanic Reader* 56 (Ernest J. Hopkins ed. 1968)

3 [After a lady had come from Alexandria demanding that a church that had been converted to a hospital be reconverted:] In speaking of this incident Mr. Lincoln said that the lady as a representative of her class in Alexandria reminded him of the story of the young man who had an aged father and mother owning considerable property. The young man being an only son and believing that the old people had lived out their usefullness assassinated them both. He was

accused, tried and convicted of the murder. When the judge came to pass sentence upon him and called upon him to give any reason he might have why the sentence of death should not be passed upon him, he with great promptness replied he hoped the court would be lenient upon him because he was a poor orphan.

Abraham Lincoln, reported in Ward Hill Lamon, *Administration of Lincoln*, 1886, in *Abe Lincoln Laughing* 91 (P. M. Zall ed. 1982)
See also SENTENCING 1; SENTENCING 6

4 There is two types of Larceny, Petty and Grand, and the courts will really give you a longer sentence for Petty than they do for Grand. They are supposed to be the same in the eyes of the law, but the Judges always put a little extra on you for Petty, which is a kind of a fine for stupidity. "If that's all you got you ought to go to jail longer."

Will Rogers, "Big or Little Corruption—Take Your Pick," 22 Apr. 1928, in *Will Rogers' Weekly Articles* 3:154, 156 (James M. Smallwood ed. 1981)

5 *Rufus T. Firefly* [played by Groucho Marx, addressing the bench]: Gentlemen, Chicolini here may talk like an idiot, and look like an idiot, but don't let that fool you. He really is an idiot. I implore you, send him back to his father and brothers who are waiting for him with open arms in the penitentiary. I suggest that we give him ten years in Leavenworth, or eleven years in Twelveworth.
Chicolini [played by Chico Marx]: I tell you what I'll do. I'll take five and ten in Woolworth.

Bert Kalmar and Harry Ruby, *Duck Soup* (screenplay), 1933, in *The Four Marx Brothers in Monkey Business and Duck Soup* 159 (1972)

6 *Chutzpa* is that quality enshrined in a man who, having killed his mother and father, throws himself on the mercy of the court because he is an orphan.

Leo Rosten, *The Joys of Yiddish* 93 (1968)
See also SENTENCING 1; SENTENCING 3

7 I'm often asked why there is such a great variation among sentences imposed by Texas judges. I can only quote the Texas judge who was asked why a killer some-

times doesn't even get indicted and a cattle thief can get ten years. The judge answered: "A lot of fellows ought to be shot, but we don't have any cows that need stealin'."

Percy Foreman, quoted in Michael Dorman, *King of the Courtroom* 104 (1969)

SEPARATION OF POWERS

See also CONGRESS; JUDICIARY; PRESIDENT

1 A legislative, an executive, and a judicial power comprehend the whole of what is meant and understood by government. It is by balancing each of these powers against the other two, that the efforts in human nature towards tyranny can alone be checked and restrained, and any degree of freedom preserved in the constitution.

John Adams, Letter to Richard Henry Lee, 15 Nov. 1775, in *Works of John Adams* 4:186 (Charles Francis Adams ed. 1851)

2 The judicial power ought to be distinct from both the legislative and executive, and independent upon both, that so it may be a check upon both, as both should be checks upon that.

John Adams, *Thoughts on Government,* 1776, in *Works of John Adams* 4:198 (Charles Francis Adams ed. 1851)

3 All the powers of government, legislative, executive, and judiciary, result to the legislative body. The concentrating these in the same hands is precisely the definition of despotic government. It will be no alleviation that these powers will be exercised by a plurality of hands, and not by a single one. 173 despots would surely be as oppressive as one. Let those who doubt it turn their eyes on the republic of Venice.

Thomas Jefferson, *Notes on Virginia,* 1782, in *Works of Thomas Jefferson* 4:20 (Paul L. Ford ed. 1904)

4 The accumulation of all powers legislative, executive and judiciary in the same hands, whether of one, a few or many, and whether hereditary, self appointed, or elective, may justly be pronounced the very definition of tyranny.

James Madison, *The Federalist* No. 47, at 2:92–93 (1788)

5 It was shewn in the last paper, that the political apothegm there examined, does not require that the legislative, executive and judiciary departments should be wholly unconnected with each other. I shall undertake in the next place, to shew that unless these departments be so far connected and blended, as to give to each a constitutional controul over the others, the degree of separation which the maxim requires as essential to a free government, can never in practice be duly maintained.

James Madison, *The Federalist* No. 48, at 2:101 (1788)

6 But the great security against a gradual concentration of the several powers in the same department, consists in giving to those who administer each department, the necessary constitutional means, and personal motives, to resist encroachments of the others. The provision for defence must in this, as in all other cases, be made commensurate to the danger of attack. Ambition must be made to counteract ambition. The interest of the man must be connected with the constitutional rights of the place. It may be a reflection on human nature, that such devices should be necessary to control the abuses of government. But what is government itself but the greatest of all reflections on human nature? If men were angels, no government would be necessary. If angels were to govern men, neither external nor internal controls on government would be necessary. In framing a government which is to be administered by men over men, the great difficulty lies in this: you must first enable the government to control the governed; and in the next place, oblige it to control itself.

James Madison, *The Federalist* No. 51, at 2:117–18 (1788)

7 In the compound republic of America, the power surrendered by the people, is first divided between two distinct governments, and then the portion allotted to each subdivided among distinct and separate departments. Hence a double security arises to the rights of the people. The different governments will control each other; at the same time that each will be controled [*sic*] by itself. . . . It is of great importance in a republic, not only to guard the society against the oppression of its rulers; but to

guard one part of the society against the injustice of the other part.

> James Madison, *The Federalist* No. 51, at 2:119–20 (1788)

8 It is important, likewise, that the habits of thinking in a free Country should inspire caution in those entrusted with its administration, to confine themselves within their respective Constitutional spheres; avoiding in the exercise of the Powers of one department to encroach upon another. . . . If in the opinion of the People, the distribution or modification of the Constitutional powers be in any particular wrong, let it be corrected by an amendment in the way which the Constitution designates. But let there be no change by usurpation; for though this, in one instance, may be the instrument of good, it is the customary weapon by which free governments are destroyed.

> George Washington, Farewell Address, 19 Sept. 1796, in *Writings of George Washington* 35:228–29 (John C. Fitzpatrick ed. 1940)

9 The difference between the departments undoubtedly is, that the legislature makes, the executive executes, and the judiciary construes the law; but the maker of the law may commit something to the discretion of the other departments, and the precise boundary of this power is a subject of delicate and difficult inquiry, into which a Court will not enter unnecessarily.

> John Marshall, *Wayman v. Southard*, 23 U.S. (10 Wheat.) 1, 46 (1825)

10 The interference of the Courts with the performance of the ordinary duties of the executive departments of the government, would be productive of nothing but mischief; and we are quite satisfied that such a power was never intended to be given to them.

> Roger B. Taney, *Decatur v. Paulding*, 39 U.S. (14 Pet.) 497, 516 (1840)

11 It is also essential to the successful working of this system that the persons intrusted with power in any one of these branches shall not be permitted to encroach upon the powers confided to the others, but that each shall by the law of its creation be limited to the exercise of the powers appropriate to its own department and no other.

> Samuel F. Miller, *Kilbourn v. Thompson*, 103 U.S. 168, 191 (1880)

12 The separation of powers of government did not make each branch completely autonomous. It left each, in some measure, dependent upon the others, as it left to each power to exercise, in some respects, functions in their nature executive, legislative, and judicial. Obviously the President cannot secure full execution of the laws, if Congress denies to him adequate means of doing so. Full execution may be defeated because Congress declines to create offices indispensable for that purpose. Or, because Congress, having created the office, declines to make the indispensable appropriation. Or, because Congress, having both created the office and made the appropriation, prevents, by restrictions which it imposes, the appointment of officials who in quality and character are indispensable to the efficient execution of the law. If, in any such way, adequate means are denied to the President, the fault will lie with Congress. The President performs his full constitutional duty, if, with the means and instruments provided by Congress and within the limitations prescribed by it, he uses his best endeavors to secure the faithful execution of the laws enacted.

> Louis D. Brandeis, *Myers v. United States*, 272 U.S. 52, 291–92 (1926) (dissenting)

13 The doctrine of the separation of powers was adopted by the Convention of 1787, not to promote efficiency but to preclude the exercise of arbitrary power. The purpose was, not to avoid friction, but, by means of the inevitable friction incident to the distribution of the governmental powers among three departments, to save the people from autocracy.

> Louis D. Brandeis, *Myers v. United States*, 272 U.S. 52, 293 (1926) (dissenting)

14 It does not seem to need argument to show that however we may disguise it by veiling words we do not and cannot carry out the distinction between legislative and executive action with mathematical precision and divide the branches into watertight compartments, were it ever so desirable to do so, which I am far from believing that it is, or that the Constitution requires.

> Oliver Wendell Holmes, Jr., *Springer v. Government of Philippine Islands*, 277 U.S. 189, 211 (1928) (dissenting)

15 This is not to say that the three branches are not co-ordinate parts of one government and that each in the field of its duties may not invoke the action of the two other branches in so far as the action invoked shall not be an assumption of the constitutional field of action of another branch. In determining what it may do in seeking assistance from another branch, the extent and character of that assistance must be fixed according to common sense and the inherent necessities of the governmental co-ordination. . . . The same principle that permits Congress to exercise its rate making power in interstate commerce, by declaring the rule which shall prevail in the legislative fixing of rates, and enables it to remit to a rate-making body created in accordance with its provisions the fixing of such rates, justifies a similar provision for the fixing of customs duties on imported merchandise. If Congress shall lay down by legislative act an intelligible principle to which the person or body authorized to fix such rates is directed to conform, such legislative action is not a forbidden delegation of legislative power.

   William Howard Taft, *J.W. Hampton, Jr. & Co. v. United States,* 276 U.S. 394, 406, 409 (1928)

16 Discretion is not unconfined and vagrant. It is canalized within banks that keep it from overflowing. . . . the separation of powers between the Executive and Congress is not a doctrinaire concept to be made use of with pedantic rigor. There must be sensible approximation, there must be elasticity of adjustment, in response to the practical necessities of government, which cannot foresee today the developments of tomorrow in their nearly infinite variety.

   Benjamin N. Cardozo, *Panama Refining Co. v. Ryan,* 293 U.S. 388, 440 (1935) (dissenting)

17 The delegated power of legislation which has found expression in this code [a code of fair competition for selling live kosher poultry] is not canalized within banks that keep it from overflowing. It is unconfined and vagrant. . . . Here in effect is a roving commission to inquire into evils and upon discovery correct them. . . . [If this delegation of power is upheld] anything that Congress may do within the limits of the commerce clause for the betterment of business may be done by the President upon the recommendation of a trade association by calling it a code. This is delegation running riot.

   Benjamin N. Cardozo, *Schechter Poultry Corp. v. United States,* 295 U.S. 495, 551–53 (1935) (concurring)

18 The Federal Trade Commission is an administrative body created by Congress to carry into effect legislative policies embodied in the statute in accordance with the legislative standard therein prescribed, and to perform other specified duties as a legislative or as a judicial aid. Such a body cannot in any proper sense be characterized as an arm or an eye of the executive. Its duties are performed without executive leave and, in the contemplation of the statute, must be free from executive control. . . . the commission acts in part quasi-legislatively and in part quasi-judicially.

   George Sutherland, *Humphrey's Executor v. United States,* 295 U.S. 602, 628 (1935)

19 The fundamental necessity of maintaining each of the three general departments of government entirely free from the control or coercive influence, direct or indirect, of either of the others, has often been stressed and is hardly open to serious question. So much is implied in the very fact of the separation of the powers of these departments by the Constitution; and in the rule which recognizes their essential co-equality.

   George Sutherland, *Humphrey's Executor v. United States,* 295 U.S. 602, 629–30 (1935)

20 While the Constitution diffuses power the better to secure liberty, it also contemplates that practice will integrate the dispersed powers into a workable government. It enjoins upon its branches separateness but interdependence, autonomy but reciprocity.

   Robert H. Jackson, *Youngstown Sheet & Tube Co. v. Sawyer,* 343 U.S. 579, 635 (1952) (concurring)

21 Such is the foundation, in both intellect and instinct, of the political-question doctrine: the Court's sense of lack of capacity, compounded in unequal parts of (a) the strangeness of the issue and its intractability to principled resolution; (b) the sheer momentousness of it, which tends to un-

balance judicial judgment; (c) the anxiety, not so much that the judicial judgment will be ignored, as that perhaps it should but will not be; (d) finally ("in a mature democracy"), the inner vulnerability, the self-doubt of an institution which is electorally irresponsible and has no earth to draw strength from.

> Alexander M. Bickel, *The Least Dangerous Branch* 184 (1962)

22 Prominent on the surface of any case held to involve a political question is found a textually demonstrable constitutional commitment of the issue to a coordinate political department; or a lack of judicially discoverable and manageable standards for resolving it; or the impossibility of deciding without an initial policy determination of a kind clearly for nonjudicial discretion; or the impossibility of a court's undertaking independent resolution without expressing lack of respect due coordinate branches of government; or an unusual need for unquestioning adherence to a political decision already made; or the potentiality of embarrassment from multifarious pronouncements by various departments on one question.

> William J. Brennan, Jr., *Baker v. Carr*, 369 U.S. 186, 217 (1962)

SEX

See also CENSORSHIP; OBSCENITY; RAPE

1 I regret to say that we of the FBI are powerless to act in cases of oral-genital intimacy, unless it has in some way obstructed interstate commerce.

> J. Edgar Hoover, quoted in Irving Wallace et al., *Intimate Sex Lives of Famous People* 536 (1981)

2 A contract between nonmarital partners is unenforceable only *to the extent* that it *explicitly* rests upon the immoral and illicit consideration of meretricious sexual services.

> Mathew O. Tobriner, *Marvin v. Marvin*, 18 Cal. 3d 660, 669, 557 P.2d 106, 134 Cal. Rptr. 815 (1976)

3 We protect those rights not because they contribute, in some direct and material way, to the general public welfare, but be-cause they form so central a part of an individual's life. . . . The fact that individuals define themselves in a significant way through their intimate sexual relationships with others suggests, in a Nation as diverse as ours, that there may be many "right" ways of conducting those relationships, and that much of the richness of a relationship will come from the freedom an individual has to *choose* the form and nature of these intensely personal bonds.

> Harry A. Blackmun, *Bowers v. Hardwick*, 478 U.S. 186, 204-05 (1986) (dissenting)

4 What the Court really has refused to recognize is the fundamental interest all individuals have in controlling the nature of their intimate associations with others.

> Harry A. Blackmun, *Bowers v. Hardwick*, 478 U.S. 186, 206 (1986) (dissenting)

5 It is precisely because the issue raised by this case touches the heart of what makes individuals what they are that we should be especially sensitive to the rights of those whose choices upset the majority.

> Harry A. Blackmun, *Bowers v. Hardwick*, 478 U.S. 186, 211 (1986) (dissenting)

6 This case involves no real interference with the rights of others, for the mere knowledge that other individuals do not adhere to one's value system cannot be a legally cognizable interest . . . let alone an interest that can justify invading the houses, hearts, and minds of citizens who choose to live their lives differently.

> Harry A. Blackmun, *Bowers v. Hardwick*, 478 U.S. 186, 213 (1986) (dissenting)

7 It took but three years for the Court to see the error in its analysis in *Minersville School District v. Gobitis*, 310 U.S. 586 (1940), and to recognize that the threat to national cohesion posed by a refusal to salute the flag was vastly outweighed by the threat to those same values posed by compelling such a salute. . . . I can only hope that here, too, the Court soon will reconsider its analysis and conclude that depriving individuals of the right to choose for themselves how to conduct their intimate relationships poses a far greater threat to the values most deeply rooted in our Nation's history than tolerance of noncon-

formity could ever do. Because I think the Court today betrays those values, I dissent.

Harry A. Blackmun, *Bowers v. Hardwick,* 478 U.S. 186, 213–14 (1986) (dissenting)

8 Sodomy was a criminal offense at common law and was forbidden by the laws of the original 13 States when they ratified the Bill of Rights. In 1868, when the Fourteenth Amendment was ratified, all but 5 of the 37 States in the Union had criminal sodomy laws. In fact, until 1961, all 50 States outlawed sodomy, and today, 24 States and the District of Columbia continue to provide criminal penalties for sodomy performed in private and between consenting adults. . . . Against this background, to claim that a right to engage in such conduct is "deeply rooted in this Nation's history and tradition" or "implicit in the concept of ordered liberty" is, at best, facetious.

Byron R. White, *Bowers v. Hardwick,* 478 U.S. 186, 192–94 (1986)

SEX DISCRIMINATION

See also CIVIL RIGHTS; WOMEN; WOMEN'S RIGHTS

1 Nature has tempered woman as little for the juridical conflicts of the court room, as for the physical conflicts of the battle field. Womanhood is moulded for gentler and better things. And it is not the saints of the world who chiefly give employment to our profession. It has essentially and habitually to do with all that is selfish and malicious, knavish and criminal, coarse and brutal, repulsive and obscene, in human life. It would be revolting to all female sense of the innocence and sanctity of their sex, shocking to man's reverence for womanhood and faith in woman, on which hinge all the better affections and humanities of life, that woman should be permitted to mix professionally in all the nastiness of the world which finds its way into courts of justice; . . . Discussions are habitually necessary in courts of justice, which are unfit for female ears. The habitual presence of women at these would tend to relax the public sense of decency and propriety. If, as counsel threatened, these things are to come, we will take no voluntary part in bringing them about.

Edward G. Ryan, *In re Goodell,* 39 Wis. 232, 245–46 (1875)

2 That woman's physical structure and the performance of maternal functions place her at a disadvantage in the struggle for subsistence is obvious. This is especially true when the burdens of motherhood are upon her . . . and as healthy mothers are essential to vigorous offspring, the physical well being of woman becomes an object of public interest and care in order to preserve the strength and vigor of the race. . . . Differentiated by these matters from the other sex, she is properly placed in a class by herself, and legislation designed for her protection may be sustained, even when like legislation is not necessary for men and could not be sustained.

David J. Brewer, *Muller v. Oregon,* 208 U.S. 412, 421–22 (1908)

3 It will need more than the Nineteenth Amendment to convince me that there are no differences between men and women, or that legislation cannot take those differences into account.

Oliver Wendell Holmes, Jr., *Adkins v. Children's Hospital,* 261 U.S. 525, 569–70 (1922) (dissenting)

4 The fact that women may now have achieved the virtues that men have long claimed as their prerogatives and now indulge in vices that men have long practiced, does not preclude the States from drawing a sharp line between the sexes, certainly in such matters as the regulation of the liquor traffic.

Felix Frankfurter, *Goesaert v. Cleary,* 335 U.S. 464, 466 (1948)

5 *Amanda Bonner* [played by Katharine Hepburn, speaking as defense attorney]: All I've been trying to say is this. Lots of things a man can do and in society's eyes it's all hunky-dory. A woman does the same things—the same, mind you, and she's an outcast. . . . All I say is why let this deplorable system seep into our courts of law, where women are supposed to be equal?

Ruth Gordon and Garson Kanin, *Adam's Rib* (published screenplay) 11–12 (1972) (1949)

6 *Amanda Bonner* [played by Katharine Hepburn, speaking as defense attorney]: May it please the Court, I submit that my entire line of defense is based upon the proposition that persons of the female sex should be dealt with, before the law, as the equals of

persons of the male sex. I submit that I cannot hope to argue this line before minds hostile to and prejudiced against the female sex.

Ruth Gordon and Garson Kanin, *Adam's Rib* (published screenplay) 47 (1972) (1949)

7 *Amanda Bonner* [played by Katharine Hepburn, speaking as defense attorney in summation to jury]: Now imagine her a man. Go on, now. Use your imaginations. Think of her as a man sitting there. Think of her as a man sitting there, accused of a like crime. All right, that's enough. Now, continuing. I ask you to hold that impression. And look at *Mr.* Attinger. And suppose him a woman. Try. Try hard. All right, thank you. And now, Miss Caighn. She's the third party. She's that slick homewrecker. Picture her so. A wolf. You know the type. All right. Now you have it. Judge it so. An unwritten law stands back of a man who fights to defend his home. Apply the same to this maltreated wife and neglected mother. We ask you no more. Equality!

Ruth Gordon and Garson Kanin, *Adam's Rib* (published screenplay) 87–89 (1972) (1949)

8 Law is a reflection and a source of prejudice. It both enforces and suggests forms of bias.

Diane B. Schulder, "Does the Law Oppress Women?," in *Sisterhood Is Powerful* 139 (Robin Morgan ed. 1970)

9 There can be no doubt that our Nation has had a long and unfortunate history of sex discrimination. Traditionally, such discrimination was rationalized by an attitude of "romantic paternalism" which, in practical effect, put women, not on a pedestal, but in a cage.

William J. Brennan, Jr., *Frontiero v. Richardson,* 411 U.S. 677, 684 (1973)

10 We can only conclude that classifications based upon sex, like classifications based upon race, alienage, or national origin, are inherently suspect, and must therefore be subjected to strict judicial scrutiny.

William J. Brennan, Jr., *Frontiero v. Richardson,* 411 U.S. 677, 688 (1973)

11 The program divides potential recipients into two groups—pregnant women and nonpregnant persons. While the first group is exclusively female, the second includes members of both sexes. The fiscal and actuarial benefits of the program thus accrue to members of both sexes.

Potter Stewart, *Geduldig v. Aiello,* 417 U.S. 484, 497 n.20 (1974)

12 To withstand constitutional challenge . . . classifications by gender must serve important governmental objectives and must be substantially related to achievement of those objectives.

William J. Brennan, Jr., *Craig v. Boren,* 429 U.S. 190, 197 (1976)

13 Because virtually all of the significant harmful and inescapably identifiable consequences of teenage pregnancy fall on the young female, a legislature acts well within its authority when it elects to punish only the participant who, by nature, suffers few of the consequences of his conduct.

William H. Rehnquist, *Michael M. v. Superior Court of Sonoma County,* 450 U.S. 464, 473 (1981)

14 The Constitution surely does not require a State to pretend that demonstrable differences between men and women do not really exist.

Potter Stewart, *Michael M. v. Superior Court of Sonoma County,* 450 U.S. 464, 481 (1981) (concurring)

15 The law sees and treats women the way men see and treat women.

Catharine MacKinnon, "Viewpoint: Feminism, Marxism, Method, and the State: Toward Feminist Jurisprudence," 8 *Signs* 635, 644 (1983)

16 A sign that says "men only" looks very different on a bathroom door than a courthouse door.

Thurgood Marshall, *City of Cleburne v. Cleburne Living Center, Inc.,* 473 U.S. 432, 468–69 (1985) (concurring in part and dissenting in part)

SLANDER

See LIBEL

SLAVERY

See also CIVIL RIGHTS

1 There shall be neither Slavery nor involuntary Servitude in the said territory oth-

erwise than in the punishment of crimes, whereof the party shall have been duly convicted; provided always that any person escaping into the same, from whom labor or service is lawfully claimed in any one of the original States, such fugitive may be lawfully reclaimed and conveyed to the person claiming his or her labor or service as aforesaid.

Northwest Ordinance, art. 6, 13 July 1787, in *Journals of the Continental Congress* 32:343 (Roscoe R. Hill ed. 1936)

2 There stands the bloody [fugitive slave] clause—you cannot fret the seal off the bond. The fault is in allowing such a constitution to live an hour. When I look upon these crowded thousands and see them trample on their consciences and the rights of their fellow-men, at the bidding of a piece of parchment, I say, my CURSE be on the Constitution of these United States.

Wendell Phillips, Speech at Faneuil Hall, Boston, 30 Oct. 1842, quoted in Irving H. Bartlett, *Wendell Phillips: Brahmin Radical* 117–18 (1961)

3 And herein consists the fallacy with which the holders of slaves often delude themselves, by assuming that the test of property is human law. The soul of one man cannot by human law be made the property of another. The owner of a slave is the owner of a living corpse; but he is not the owner of a man.

John Quincy Adams, Undelivered speech, 4 July 1843, in *Selected Writings of John and John Quincy Adams* 408 (Adrienne Koch & William Peden eds. 1946)

4 The traitor to Humanity is the traitor
    most accursed;
Man is more than Constitutions; better
    rot beneath the sod,
Than be true to Church and State while
    we are doubly false to God!

James Russell Lowell, "On the Capture of Fugitive Slaves Near Washington," 1845, in *Complete Poetical Works of James Russell Lowell* 82, 82 (Horace E. Scudder ed. 1925)

5 By the law of Congress, March 2, 1807, it is piracy and murder, punishable with death, to enslave a man on the coast of Africa. By law of Congress September, 1850,

it is a high crime and misdemeanor, punishable with fine and imprisonment, to resist the reënslaving a man on the coast of America. Off soundings, it is piracy and murder to enslave him. On soundings, it is fine and prison not to reënslave. What kind of legislation is this? What kind of constitution which covers it?

Ralph Waldo Emerson, Speech, Concord, Mass., 3 May 1851, in *Complete Works of Ralph Waldo Emerson* 11:179, 195 (1904)

6 A wicked law cannot be executed by good men, and must be by bad. . . . To serve it, low and mean people are found by the groping of the government. No government ever found it hard to pick up tools for base actions.

Ralph Waldo Emerson, Speech, Concord, Mass., 3 May 1851, in *Complete Works of Ralph Waldo Emerson* 11:179, 195–96 (1904)

7 When the pulpit preached slave-hunting, and the law bound the victim, and society said, "Amen! this will make money," we were "fanatics,"—"enthusiasts,"—"seditious,"—"disorganizers,"—"scorners of the pulpit,"—"traitors." Genius of the Past! drop not from thy tablets one of the honorable names. We claim them all as our surest title-deeds to the memory and gratitude of mankind. We indeed thought man more than constitutions, humanity and justice of more worth than law.

Wendell Phillips, Speech, Boston, 12 Apr. 1852, in *Speeches, Lectures, and Letters* 71, 75–76 (1863)

8 Whoever visits some estates there, and witnesses the good-humored indulgence of some masters and mistresses, and the affectionate loyalty of some slaves, might be tempted to dream the oft-fabled poetic legend of a patriarchal institution, and all that; but over and above the scene there broods a portentous shadow—the shadow of *law.* So long as the law considers all these human beings, with beating hearts and living affections, only as so many *things* belonging to a master,—so long as the failure, or misfortune, or imprudence, or death of the kindest owner, may cause them any day to exchange a life of kind protection and indulgence for one of hopeless misery and toil,—so long it is impossible to make anything beautiful or desir-

able in the best regulated administration of slavery.

Harriet Beecher Stowe, *Uncle Tom's Cabin* 19 (Kathryn Kish Sklar ed. 1982) (1852)

9 I defy anybody on earth to read our slave-code, as it stands in our lawbooks, and make anything else of it. Talk of the *abuses* of slavery! Humbug! The *thing itself* is the essence of all abuse! And the only reason why the land don't sink under it, like Sodom and Gomorrah, is because it is *used* in a way infinitely better than it is. For pity's sake, for shame's sake, because we are men born of women, and not savage beasts, many of us do not, and dare not,— we would *scorn* to use the full power which our savage laws put into our hands. And he who goes the furthest, and does the worst, only uses within limits the power that the law gives him.

Harriet Beecher Stowe, *Uncle Tom's Cabin* 261–62 (Kathryn Kish Sklar ed. 1982) (1852)

10 Who can speak the blessedness of that first day of freedom? Is not the *sense* of liberty a higher and finer one than any of the five? To move, speak, and breathe,—go out and come in unwatched, and free from danger! Who can speak the blessings of that rest which comes down on the free man's pillow, under laws which insure to him the rights that God has given to man?

Harriet Beecher Stowe, *Uncle Tom's Cabin* 452 (Kathryn Kish Sklar ed. 1982) (1852)

11 Slavery, as defined in American law, is no more capable of being regulated in its administration by principles of humanity than the torture system of the Inquisition. Every act of humanity of every individual owner is an illogical result from the legal definition; and the reason why the slave-code of America is more atrocious than any ever before exhibited under the sun, is that the Anglo-Saxon race are a more coldly and strictly logical race, and have an unflinching courage to meet the consequences of every premise which they lay down, and to work out an accursed principle, with mathematical accuracy, to its most accursed results. The decisions in American law-books show nothing so much as this severe, unflinching accuracy of logic. It is often and evidently, not because judges are inhuman or partial, but because they are logical and truthful, that they announce from the

bench, in the calmest manner, decisions which one would think might make the earth shudder, and the sun turn pale.

Harriet Beecher Stowe, *The Key to Uncle Tom's Cabin* 155 (1854)

12 The judges and lawyers . . . try this case by a very low and incompetent standard. They consider, not whether the Fugitive Slave Law is right, but whether it is what they call *constitutional.* Is virtue constitutional, or vice? Is equity constitutional, or iniquity? In important moral and vital questions . . . it is just as impertinent to ask whether a law is constitutional or not, as to ask whether it is profitable or not.

Henry David Thoreau, "Slavery in Massachusetts" (address), Framingham, Mass., 4 July 1854, in *Writings of Henry David Thoreau* 4:388, 401 (1906)

13 The Constitution is declared to be established for the people. And who are the people? The men and women of the country. We are a part of the people; and it is the most unkind—I was going to say it was the most wicked—concession ever made to the slave power from any quarter, to admit that the Constitution does not apply at all to colored people.

Frederick Douglass, "The Danger of the Republican Movement" (speech), Syracuse, N.Y., 28 May 1856, in *Life and Writings of Frederick Douglass* 5:385, 390 (Philip S. Foner ed. 1975)

14 They [slaves and their descendents] are not included, and were not intended to be included, under the word "citizens" in the Constitution, and can therefore, claim none of the rights and privileges which that instrument provides for and secures to citizens of the United States.

Roger B. Taney, *Dred Scott v. Sandford,* 60 U.S. (19 How.) 393, 404 (1857)

15 They had for more than a century before been regarded as beings of an inferior order, and altogether unfit to associate with the white race, either in social or political relations; and so far inferior, that they had no rights which the white man was bound to respect; and that the negro might justly and lawfully be reduced to slavery for his benefit. He was bought and sold, and treated as an ordinary article of merchandise and traffic, whenever a profit

could be made by it. This opinion was at that time fixed and universal in the civilized portion of the white race.

Roger B. Taney, *Dred Scott v. Sandford,* 60 U.S. (19 How.) 393, 407 (1857)

16 Now . . . the right of property in a slave is distinctly and expressly affirmed in the Constitution. The right to traffic in it, like an ordinary article of merchandise and property, was guarantied to the citizens of the United States, in every State that might desire it, for twenty years. And the Government in express terms is pledged to protect it in all future time, if the slave escapes from his owner. . . . And no word can be found in the Constitution which gives Congress a greater power over slave property, or which entitles property of that kind to less protection than property of any other description. The only power conferred is the power coupled with the duty of guarding and protecting the owner in his rights.

Roger B. Taney, *Dred Scott v. Sandford,* 60 U.S. (19 How.) 393, 451–52 (1857)

17 Upon these considerations, it is the opinion of the court that the act of Congress which prohibited a citizen from holding and owning property of this kind in the territory of the United States north of the line therein mentioned, is not warranted by the Constitution, and is therefore void; and that neither Dred Scott himself, nor any of his family, were made free by being carried into this territory; even if they had been carried there by the owner, with the intention of becoming a permanent resident.

Roger B. Taney, *Dred Scott v. Sandford,* 60 U.S. (19 How.) 393, 452 (1857)

18 I do not resist it [the *Dred Scott* decision]. If I wanted to take Dred Scott from his master, I would be interfering with property. . . . But I am doing no such thing as that, but all that I am doing is refusing to obey it as a political rule. If I were in Congress, and a vote should come up on a question whether slavery should be prohibited in a new territory, in spite of that Dred Scott decision, I would vote that it should.

Abraham Lincoln, Speech, Chicago, 10 July 1858, in *Collected Works of Abraham Lincoln* 2:495 (Roy P. Basler ed. 1953)

19 Judge Douglas has sung paeans to his "Popular Sovereignty" doctrine until his Supreme Court co-operating with him, has *squatted* his Squatter Sovereignty out. But he will keep up this species of humbuggery about Squatter Sovereignty. He has at last invented this sort of *do-nothing Sovereignty*—that the people may exclude slavery by a sort of "Sovereignty" that is exercised by doing nothing at all. Is not that running his Popular Sovereignty down awfully? Has it not got down as thin as the homeopathic soup that was made by boiling the shadow of a pigeon* that had starved to death? But at last, when it is brought to the test of close reasoning, there is not even that thin decoction of it left. It is a presumption impossible in the domain of thought. It is precisely no other than the putting of that most unphilosophical proposition, that two bodies may occupy the same space at the same time. The Dred Scott decision covers the whole ground, and while it occupies it, there is no room even for the shadow of a starved pigeon to occupy the same ground.

Abraham Lincoln, Sixth Debate with Stephen A. Douglas, Quincy, Ill., 13 Oct. 1858, in *Collected Works of Abraham Lincoln* 3:279 (Roy P. Basler ed. 1953)

20 The institution of slavery is only mentioned in the Constitution of the United States two or three times, and in neither of these cases does the word "slavery" or even "Negro race" occur: . . . Language is used not suggesting that slavery existed or that the black race were among us. . . . covert language was used with a purpose, and that purpose was that in our Constitution, which it was hoped and is still hoped will endure forever—when it should be read by intelligent and patriotic men, after the institution of slavery had passed from among us—there should be nothing on the face of the great charter of liberty suggesting that such a thing as Negro slavery had ever existed among us.

Abraham Lincoln, Seventh Debate with Stephen A. Douglas, Alton, Ill., 15 Oct. 1858,

---

* The learned Dr. FRANCIS once made himself "memorable" by a remark which he made in a Homeopathic discussion; namely, the boiling of the *shadow* of a pigeon in a bottle of water, and dividing the fluid into infinitesimal quantities, and administering this powerful "concentrated medicine to the patient once every six months," at night, before going to bed. —"Editor's Drawer," 6 *Harper's New Monthly Magazine* 565 (1853)

in *Collected Works of Abraham Lincoln* 3:307 (Roy P. Basler ed. 1953)

21 Now, therefore I, Abraham Lincoln, President of the United States, ... order and designate as the States and parts of States wherein the people thereof respectively, are this day in rebellion against the United States, the following, towit: ...

And by virtue of the power, and for the purpose aforesaid, I do order and declare that all persons held as slaves within said designated States, and parts of States, are, and henceforward shall be free; and that the Executive government of the United States, including the military and naval authorities thereof, will recognize and maintain the freedom of said persons.

... And upon this act, sincerely believed to be an act of justice, warranted by the Constitution, upon military necessity, I invoke the considerate judgment of mankind, and the gracious favor of Almighty God.

Abraham Lincoln, Emancipation Proclamation, 1 Jan. 1863, in *Collected Works of Abraham Lincoln* 6:28, 29–30 (Roy P. Basler ed. 1953)

SOVEREIGN IMMUNITY

1 A sovereign is exempt from suit, not because of any formal conception or obsolete theory, but on the logical and practical ground that there can be no legal right as against the authority that makes the law on which the right depends.

Oliver Wendell Holmes, Jr., *Kawananakoa v. Polyblank*, 205 U.S. 349, 353 (1907)

2 When you sue the government ... you must falsely pretend ... that the suit is not against the government but that it is against an officer. You may get relief against the sovereign if, but only if, you falsely pretend that you are not asking for relief against the sovereign. The judges often will falsely pretend that they are not giving you relief against the sovereign, even though you know and they know, and they know that you know, the relief is against the sovereign.

Kenneth C. Davis, "Suing the Government by Falsely Pretending to Sue an Officer," 29 *University of Chicago Law Review* 435, 435 (1962)

SPEECH

See FIRST AMENDMENT; FREEDOM OF EXPRESSION; FREEDOM OF SPEECH

SPORTS

1 How's it played, says ye? I don't exactly know. I niver studied law. ... If ye have a dispute over th' rules, th' quickest way to get a decision is to hire a lawyer, make a test case, an' carry it to th' supreem coort.

Finley Peter Dunne, "On Golf," in *On Making a Will* 144, 147 (1919)

2 We're doing this whole thing backward. Attorneys should wear numbers on their backs, and box scores should have entries for writs, dispositions and appeals.

Bill Veeck, 1976, quoted in *Baseball Quotations* 135 (David H. Nathan ed. 1991)

3 After twelve years of being in the major leagues, I do not feel I am a piece of property to be bought and sold irrespective of my wishes.

Curt Flood, quoted in *Guide to American Law* 2:49 (1983)

4 [On sentencing Pete Rose to a five-month prison term for income tax fraud:] Foremost, we must recognize that there are two people here: Pete Rose, the living legend, the all-time hit leader, and the idol of millions; and Pete Rose, the individual, who appears today convicted of two counts of cheating on his taxes. Today, we are not dealing with the legend. History and the tincture of time will decide his place among the all-time greats of baseball. With regard to Pete Rose, the individual, he has broken the law, admitted his guilt, and stands ready to pay the penalty.

S. Arthur Spiegel, Judge's statement, quoted in *New York Times*, 20 July 1990, at B10

5 Tony La Russa is the fifth major league manager to possess a law degree. The four other lawyer-managers (Branch Rickey, Miller Huggins, Hughie Jennings, Monte Ward) are in the Hall of Fame.

George F. Will, *Men at Work* 28 (1990)

STANDING

1 Congress can constitutionally enact a statute conferring on any non-official person, or on a designated group of non-official

persons, authority to bring a suit to prevent action by an officer in violation of his statutory powers; for then, in like manner, there is an actual controversy, and there is nothing constitutionally prohibiting Congress from empowering any person, official or not, to institute a proceeding involving such a controversy, even if the sole purpose is to vindicate the public interest. Such persons, so authorized, are, so to speak, private Attorney Generals.

Jerome N. Frank, *Associated Industries v. Ickes,* 134 F.2d 694, 704 (2d Cir. 1943)

2 Have the appellants alleged such a personal stake in the outcome of the controversy as to assure that concrete adverseness which sharpens the presentation of issues upon which the court so largely depends for illumination of difficult constitutional questions? This is the gist of the question of standing.

William J. Brennan, Jr., *Baker v. Carr,* 369 U.S. 186, 204 (1962)

3 The nexus demanded of federal taxpayers [in order to have standing to challenge the constitutionality of federal spending] has two aspects to it. First, the taxpayer must establish a logical link between that status and the type of legislative enactment attacked. . . . Secondly, the taxpayer must establish a nexus between that status and the precise nature of the constitutional infringement alleged. . . . When both nexuses are established, the litigant will have shown a taxpayer's stake in the outcome of the controversy and will be a proper and appropriate party to invoke a federal court's jurisdiction.

Earl Warren, *Flast v. Cohen,* 392 U.S. 83, 102-03 (1968)

STARE DECISIS

See PRECEDENT

STATES

See FEDERALISM

STATUTES

See also CONGRESS; LEGISLATION; LEGISLATIVE HISTORY; LEGISLATIVE INTENT; STATUTORY CONSTRUCTION

1 We are superstitious, and esteem the statute somewhat: so much life as it has in the character of living men is its force. The statute stands there to say, Yesterday we agreed so and so, but how feel ye this article to-day? Our statute is a currency which we stamp with our own portrait: it soon becomes unrecognizable, and in process of time will return to the mint.

Ralph Waldo Emerson, "Politics," *Essays: Second Series,* 1844, in *Complete Works of Ralph Waldo Emerson* 3:199–200 (1903)

2 I have not read far in the statutes of this Commonwealth. It is not profitable reading. They do not always say what is true; and they do not always mean what they say.

Henry David Thoreau, "Slavery in Massachusetts" (address), Framingham, Mass., 4 July 1854, in *Writings of Henry David Thoreau* 4:388, 391 (1906)

3 In thus considering the act, we cannot forbear remarking it as a most singular instance of the sparing hand of legislation in this state, that there should still be found upon our books a statute so old as this. . . . It stands, we believe, without rival or peer, as the only statute of the state of Wisconsin which has been permitted to attain the venerable age of nearly twenty-three years. This leads to the serious reflections as to the untimely fate of most of our legislative enactments, not only the companions of this, which have long since "faded and gone," but also those which have come after, a numerous progeny, nearly all of which seem to have been infected with some fatal disease, which was very soon to work their destruction. They have perished mostly in infancy, the average period of life being about one year; but those which have survived that period have seldom attained the age of ten or twelve. There must be something irregular and wrong in the birth and parentage, where such mortality prevails among the offspring—some malady and restlessness in the body politic, which demand the most careful attention and cure.

Luther S. Dixon, *Owens v. State,* 27 Wis. 456, 458–59 (1871)

4 Some rather weak cases must fall within any law which is couched in general words.

Oliver Wendell Holmes, Jr., *The Mangrove Prize Money,* 188 U.S. 720, 725 (1903)

5 A statute may indicate or require as its justification a change in the policy of the law, although it expresses that change only in the specific cases most likely to occur to the mind. The Legislature has the power to decide what the policy of the law shall be, and if it has intimated its will, however indirectly, that will should be recognized and obeyed.

Oliver Wendell Holmes, Jr., *Johnson v. United States,* 163 F. 30, 32 (1st Cir. 1908)

6 The tradition of English-speaking freedom has depended in no small part upon the merely procedural requirement that the state point with exactness to just that conduct which violates the law.

Learned Hand, *Masses Publishing Co. v. Patten,* 244 F. 535, 543 (S.D.N.Y. 1917)

7 Statutes are designed to meet the fugitive exigencies of the hour.

Benjamin N. Cardozo, *The Nature of the Judicial Process* 83 (1921)

8 That the terms of a penal statute creating a new offense must be sufficiently explicit to inform those who are subject to it what conduct on their part will render them liable to its penalties, is a well-recognized requirement, consonant alike with ordinary notions of fair play and the settled rules of law. And a statute which either forbids or requires the doing of an act in terms so vague that men of common intelligence must necessarily guess at its meaning and differ as to its application, violates the first essential of due process of law.

George Sutherland, *Connally v. General Construction Co.,* 269 U.S. 385, 391 (1926)

9 We do not pause to consider whether a statute differently conceived and framed would yield results more consonant with fairness and reason. We take the statute as we find it.

Benjamin N. Cardozo, *Anderson v. Wilson,* 289 U.S. 20, 27 (1933)

10 It would be a narrow conception of jurisprudence to confine the notion of "laws" to what is found written on the statute books, and to disregard the gloss which life has written upon it.

Felix Frankfurter, *Nashville, Chattanooga & St. Louis Ry. v. Browning,* 310 U.S. 362, 369 (1940)

11 Under our decisions, a statutory presumption cannot be sustained if there be no rational connection between the fact proved and the ultimate fact presumed, if the inference of the one from proof of the other is arbitrary because of lack of connection between the two in common experience. . . . where the inference is so strained as not to have a reasonable relation to the circumstances of life as we know them, it is not competent for the legislature to create it as a rule governing the procedure of courts.

Owen J. Roberts, *Tot v. United States,* 319 U.S. 463, 467–68 (1943)

12 The requirement that government articulate its aims with a reasonable degree of clarity ensures that state power will be exercised only on behalf of policies reflecting an authoritative choice among competing social values, reduces the danger of caprice and discrimination in the administration of the laws, enables individuals to conform their conduct to the requirements of law, and permits meaningful judicial review.

William J. Brennan, Jr., *Roberts v. United States JayCees,* 468 U.S. 609, 629 (1984)

STATUTORY CONSTRUCTION

See also INTERPRETATION; LEGISLATION; LEGISLATIVE HISTORY; LEGISLATIVE INTENT; STATUTES

1 Laws are made for men of ordinary understanding, and should, therefore, be construed by the ordinary rules of common sense. Their meaning is not to be sought for in metaphysical subtleties, which may make anything mean everything or nothing, at pleasure.

Thomas Jefferson, Letter to William Johnson, 12 June 1823, in *Works of Thomas Jefferson* 7:297 (H. A. Washington ed. 1854)

2 The departmental *interpreters* of the laws, in Washington, . . . can always be depended on to take any reasonably good law and interpret the common sense all out of it. They can be depended on, every time, to defeat a good law, and make it inoperative—yes, and utterly grotesque, too, mere matter for laughter and derision.

Mark Twain, Letter to H. C. Christiancy, 18 Dec. 1887, in *Writings of Mark Twain* 35:481 (Albert B. Paine ed. 1929)

3 We do not inquire what the legislature meant; we ask only what the statute means.

Oliver Wendell Holmes, Jr., "The Theory of Legal Interpretation," 12 *Harvard Law Review* 417, 419 (1898)

4 The major premise of the conclusion expressed in a statute, the change of policy that induces the enactment, may not be set out in terms, but it is not an adequate discharge of duty for courts to say: We see what you are driving at, but you have not said it, and therefore we shall go on as before.

Oliver Wendell Holmes, Jr., *Johnson v. United States*, 163 F. 30, 32 (1st Cir. 1908)

5 It has been sometimes said that the Law is composed of two parts,—legislative law and judge-made law, but, in truth, all the Law is judge-made law. The shape in which a statute is imposed on the community as a guide for conduct is that statute as interpreted by the courts. The courts put life into the dead words of the statute. To quote ... from Bishop Hoadly ...: "Nay, whoever hath an *absolute authority* to *interpret* any written or spoken laws, it is *He* who is truly the Law Giver to all intents and purposes, and not the Person who first wrote and spoke them."*

John Chipman Gray, *The Nature and Sources of the Law* 119–20 (1909)

6 Statutes do not interpret themselves; their meaning is declared by the courts, and *it is with the meaning declared by the courts, and with no other meaning, that they are imposed upon the community as Law.*

John Chipman Gray, *The Nature and Sources of the Law* 162 (1909)

7 The difficulties of so-called interpretation arise when the Legislature has had no meaning at all; when the question which is raised on the statute never occurred to it; when what the judges have to do is, not to determine what the Legislature did mean on a point which was present to its mind, but to guess what it would have intended on a point not present to its mind, if the point had been present.

John Chipman Gray, *The Nature and Sources of the Law* 165 (1909)

* The quotation is taken from Bishop Benjamin Hoadly's sermon preached before the King of England, 31 Mar. 1717.

8 It is not as speedy or as simple a process to interpret a statute out of existence as to repeal it, but with time and patient skill it can often be done.

John Chipman Gray, *The Nature and Sources of the Law* 180 (1909)

9 Some one has said, "Let me make the ballads of the country, and I care not who makes the laws." One might also say, paraphrasing this, "Let any one make the laws of the country, if I can construe them."

William Howard Taft, *Our Chief Magistrate and His Powers* 78 (1916)

10 The meaning of the statute must, in the first instance, be sought in the language in which the act is framed, and if that is plain, ... the sole function of the courts is to enforce it according to its terms.

William R. Day, *Caminetti v. United States*, 242 U.S. 470, 485 (1917)

11 The labors of the Supreme Court in applying general clauses of an undefined content are not limited to the duty of giving effect to the Constitution. The Court is the final interpreter of the acts of Congress. Statutes come to the judicial test not simply of constitutional validity but with respect to their true import, and a federal statute finally means what the Court says it means.

Charles Evans Hughes, *The Supreme Court of the United States* 229–30 (1928)

12 When the validity of an act of the Congress is drawn in question, and even if a serious doubt of constitutionality is raised, it is a cardinal principle that this Court will first ascertain whether a construction of the statute is fairly possible by which the question may be avoided.

Charles Evans Hughes, *Crowell v. Benson*, 285 U.S. 22, 62 (1932)

13 An example both of the defects of statutes and of the embarrassment courts may have in interpreting them was furnished a few years ago when a Chinese woman who had a permit to come to this country landed at San Francisco with a child born on the voyage. The immigration officer asked the authorities in Washington whether the child, having no permit to land, must be sent back to China. In view of the statute refusing immigration without a permit the legal question might have presented difficulties,

and the answer was appropriate: "Don't be a damned fool." Now suppose the question had come before a court. Obviously Congress had no such case in mind, and yet the statute was in terms explicit. If the court, relying on the language of the act, had decided that the child must be sent back, who would have been the "damned fool"?

A. Lawrence Lowell, *Conflicts of Principle* 82–83 (1932)

14 One school says that the judge must follow the letter of the law absolutely. I call this the dictionary school. No matter what the result is, he must read the words in their usual meaning and stop where they stop. No judges have ever carried on literally in that spirit, and they would not be long tolerated if they did. Nobody would in fact condemn the surgeon who bled a man in the street to cure him, because there was a law against drawing blood in the streets.

Learned Hand, "How Far Is a Judge Free in Rendering a Decision?" (radio broadcast), 14 May 1933, in *The Spirit of Liberty* 103, 107 (Irving Dilliard ed., 2d ed. 1953)

15 It is quite true . . . that as the articulation of a statute increases, the room for interpretation must contract; but the meaning of a sentence may be more than that of the separate words, as a melody is more than the notes, and no degree of particularity can ever obviate recourse to the setting in which all appear, and which all collectively create.

Learned Hand, *Helvering v. Gregory*, 69 F.2d 809, 810–11 (2d Cir. 1934)

16 Indeed, nothing is so likely to lead us astray as an abject reliance upon canons of any sort; so much the whole history of verbal interpretation teaches, if it teaches anything. At times one is more likely to reach the truth by an unanalyzed and intuitive conclusion from the text as a whole, than by following, step by step, the accredited guides.

Learned Hand, *Van Vranken v. Helvering*, 115 F.2d 709, 711 (2d Cir. 1940)

17 It is not enough for us to find in the vague penumbra of a statute some offense about which Congress could have legislated, and then to particularize it as a crime because it is highly offensive.

William O. Douglas, *United States v. Classic*, 313 U.S. 299, 331–32 (1941) (dissenting)

18 There is no surer way to misread any document than to read it literally.

Learned Hand, *Guiseppi v. Walling*, 144 F.2d 608, 624 (2d Cir. 1944) (dissenting)

19 The legislature is like a composer. It cannot help itself: It must leave interpretation to others, principally to the courts.

Jerome N. Frank, "Words and Music: Some Remarks on Statutory Interpretation," 47 *Columbia Law Review* 1259, 1264 (1947)

20 The troublesome phase of [statutory] construction is the determination of the extent to which extraneous documentation and external circumstances may be allowed to infiltrate the text on the theory that they were part of it, written in ink discernable to the judicial eye.

Felix Frankfurter, "Some Reflections on the Reading of Statutes," 47 *Columbia Law Review* 527, 529 (1947)

21 If the purpose of construction is the ascertainment of meaning, nothing that is logically relevant should be excluded.

Felix Frankfurter, "Some Reflections on the Reading of Statutes," 47 *Columbia Law Review* 527, 541 (1947)

22 It is always a dangerous business to fill in the text of a statute from its purposes, and, although it is a duty often unavoidable, it is utterly unwarranted unless the omission from, or corruption of, the text is plain.

Learned Hand, *Harris v. Commissioner*, 178 F.2d 861, 864 (2d Cir. 1949)

23 Legislation should not be read in such a decimating spirit unless the letter of Congress is inexorable. We are reminded from time to time that in enacting legislation Congress is not engaged in a scientific process which takes account of every contingency. Its laws are not to be read as though every *i* has to be dotted and every *t* crossed.

Felix Frankfurter, *United States ex rel. Knauff v. Shaughnessy*, 338 U.S. 537, 548–49 (1950) (dissenting)

24 The principle is old and deeply imbedded in our jurisprudence that this Court will construe a statute in a manner that requires decision of serious constitutional

questions only if the statutory language leaves no reasonable alternative.

Robert H. Jackson, *United States v. Five Gambling Devices,* 346 U.S. 441, 448 (1953)

STRICT LIABILITY

See PRODUCTS LIABILITY; TORTS

SUITS

See CASES; COURTS; LITIGATION; TRIALS

SUPREME COURT

See also CONSTITUTIONAL LAW; HOLMES, OLIVER WENDELL; JUDGES; JUDGES, INDIVIDUAL; JUDICIAL REVIEW; JUDICIARY; MARSHALL, JOHN; ORIGINAL INTENTION

1 To produce uniformity in these determinations, they ought to be submitted in the last resort, to one SUPREME TRIBUNAL. . . . If there is in each state a court of final jurisdiction, there may be as many different final determinations on the same point, as there are courts. There are endless diversities in the opinions of men. We often see not only different courts, but the judges of the same court differing from each other. To avoid the confusion which would unavoidably result from the contradictory decisions of a number of independent judicatories, all nations have found it necessary to establish one court paramount to the rest, possessing a general superintendance, and authorised to settle and declare in the last resort an uniform rule of civil justice.

Alexander Hamilton, *The Federalist* No. 22, at 1:140 (1788)

2 No nation can answer for perfect exactitude of proceedings in all their inferior courts. It suffices to provide a supreme judicature where all error and partiality will be ultimately corrected.

Thomas Jefferson, Letter to George Hammond, 29 May 1792, in *Writings of Thomas Jefferson* 6:55 (Paul L. Ford ed. 1895)

3 We have considered the previous question stated in a letter written by your direction to us by the Secretary of State on the 18th of last month, [regarding] the lines of separation drawn by the Constitution between the three departments of the government. These being in certain respects checks upon each other, and our being judges of a court in the last resort, are considerations which afford strong arguments against the propriety of our extra-judicially deciding the questions alluded to, especially as the power given by the Constitution to the President, of calling on the heads of departments for opinions, seems to have been *purposely* as well as expressly united to the *executive* departments.

John Jay, Letter to George Washington, 8 Aug. 1793, in *Correspondence and Public Papers of John Jay* 3:488–89 (Henry P. Johnston ed. 1891)

4 Another most condemnable practice of the supreme court to be corrected is that of cooking up a decision in Caucus and delivering it by one of their members as the opinion of the court, without the possibility of our knowing how many, who, and for what reasons each member concurred. . . . They would, were they to give their opinions seriatim and publicly, endeavor to justify themselves to the world by explaining the reasons which led to their opinion.

Thomas Jefferson, Letter to James Pleasants, 26 Dec. 1821, in *Writings of Thomas Jefferson* 10:199 (Paul L. Ford ed. 1899)

5 There is no danger I apprehend so much as the consolidation of our government by the noiseless, and therefore unalarming, instrumentality of the supreme court.

Thomas Jefferson, Letter to William Johnson, 4 Mar. 1823, in *Writings of Thomas Jefferson* 10:248 (Paul L. Ford ed. 1899)

6 I am no votary of the infallibility of any human tribunal; but it is no more than a just tribute to truth and candour to acknowledge, that the Supreme Court of the *United States* has hitherto discharged its high duties with such ability, firmness, and moderation, as to command the respect, and retain the confidence of the nation. I have always been much impressed with the immensity of the weight and value of its trust, and with the severe and majestic simplicity of its character. It may be said of that Court, and certainly with as much propriety as it has been said in reference to the *Roman sages,* that justice has there un-

veiled her mysteries and erected her temple.

> **James Kent,** Lecture at Columbia College, 2 Feb. 1824, in *The Legal Mind in America* 92, 104 (Perry Miller ed. 1962)

7 John Marshall has made his decision: *now let him enforce it!**

> **Andrew Jackson,** Attributed remark, 1832, quoted in Horace Greeley, *The American Conflict* 1:106 (1864)

8 When we have examined in detail the organization of the Supreme Court, and the entire prerogatives which it exercises, we shall readily admit that a more imposing judicial power was never constituted by any people.

> **Alexis de Tocqueville,** *Democracy in America* 1:190 (Francis Bowen trans. 1862) (1835)

9 The President, who exercises a limited power, may err without causing great mischief in the state. Congress may decide amiss without destroying the Union, because the electoral body in which the Congress originates may cause it to retract its decision by changing its members. But if the Supreme Court is ever composed of imprudent or bad men, the Union may be plunged into anarchy or civil war.

> **Alexis de Tocqueville,** *Democracy in America* 1:192 (Francis Bowen trans. 1862) (1835)

10 It is disgraceful, in Congress, or anybody at all, to question the honor and virtue of the highest tribunal in our country. If we cannot believe in the utter and spotless purity of the Judges of so sacred a tribunal, we ought at least to have the pride to keep such a belief unexpressed. I cannot conceive it possible that a man could occupy so royal a position as a Supreme Judge, and be base enough to let his decisions be tainted by any stain of his political predilections. I hate to hear people say this Judge will vote so and so, because he is a Democrat—and this one so and so, because he is a Republican. It is shameful. The Judges have the Constitution for their guidance; they have no right to any politics save the politics of rigid right and justice when

they are sitting in judgment upon the great matters that come before them. . . . When we become capable of believing our Supreme Judges can so belittle themselves and their great office as to read the Constitution of the United States through blurring and distorting political spectacles, it will be time for us to put on sackcloth and ashes.

> **Mark Twain,** Correspondence from Washington, *Alta California,* 19 Feb. 1868, quoted in *Mark Twain and the Government* 121–22 (Svend Peterson ed. 1960)

11 No matter whether th' constitution follows th' flag or not, th' supreme coort follows th' iliction returns.

> **Finley Peter Dunne,** "The Supreme Court's Decisions," in *Mr. Dooley's Opinions* 21, 26 (1906) (1901)
> See also CONSTITUTION 41

12 The Law of a great nation means the opinions of half-a-dozen old gentlemen. . . . If those half-a-dozen old gentlemen form the highest judicial tribunal of a country, then no rule or principle which they refuse to follow is Law in that country.

> **John Chipman Gray,** *The Nature and Sources of the Law* 82 (1909)

13 We are very quiet there [at the Supreme Court], but it is the quiet of a storm centre, as we all know.

> **Oliver Wendell Holmes, Jr.,** "Law and the Court" (speech to Harvard Law School Association of New York), 15 Feb. 1913, in *Collected Legal Papers* 291, 292 (1920)

14 The attacks upon the Court are merely an expression of the unrest that seems to wonder vaguely whether law and order pay. When the ignorant are taught to doubt they do not know what they safely may believe.

> **Oliver Wendell Holmes, Jr.,** "Law and the Court" (speech to Harvard Law School Association of New York), 15 Feb. 1913, in *Collected Legal Papers* 291, 292 (1920)

15 No one familiar with the history of the Supreme Court . . . need be told that its vast and singular power to curb legislation has always been exercised with one eye on the election returns. Practically all of its most celebrated decisions . . . have reflected popular outrages of the hour, and many of them have been modified, or even completely reversed afterward, as the second thought of the plain people has differed

---

* This response to the Supreme Court decision in *Worcester v. Georgia,* 31 U.S. (6 Pet.) 515 (1832), was first attributed to Jackson in the 1864 book indicated above. While the remark does represent Jackson's views, the actual words were probably never spoken by him.

from their first thought. This responsiveness to the shifts of popular opinion and passion is not alone due to the fact that the personnel of the court, owing to the high incidence of senile deterioration among its members, is constantly changing. . . . It is also due, and in no small measure, to the fact that the learned and puissant justices are, in the main, practical politicians themselves, and hence used to keeping their ears close to the grass-roots.

H. L. Mencken, *Notes on Democracy* 92–93 (1926)

16 How I dislike writing opinions! I prefer arguments—and let some one else have the responsibility of decision.

Charles Evans Hughes, Letter to Antoinette Carter Hughes, Mar. 1930, in Merlo J. Pusey, *Charles Evans Hughes* 2:643 (1951)

17 The issue may well simmer down to whether the judgment of the courts of the United States, the executive arm of the United States and, in fact though not in form, the apparent opinion of the great majority of the United States, considers essential this economic readjustment; or whether the nine old men of the Supreme Court are entitled to form their own opinion about it and to upset a movement of national scope solely on that opinion.

Adolf A. Berle, Jr., "The Law and the Social Revolution," *Survey Graphic,* Dec. 1933, at 592, 594
See also SUPREME COURT 19

18 It's not necessary to prove that the Supreme Court never made a mistake. But if the power is to be taken from them, it *is* necessary to prove that those who are to exercise it would be likely to make fewer mistakes.

Calvin Coolidge, quoted in Charles E. Whittaker, "Some Reminiscences," 43 *Nebraska Law Review* 352, 362 (1964)

19 The Nine Old Men [referring to the United States Supreme Court].

Drew Pearson and Robert S. Allen, Book title (1936)
See also SUPREME COURT 17

20 When any judge of a court of the United States, appointed to hold his office during good behavior, has heretofore or hereafter attained the age of seventy years and has held a commission or commissions as

judge of any such court or courts at least ten years, continuously or otherwise, and within six months thereafter has neither resigned nor retired, the President, for each such judge who has not so resigned or retired, shall nominate, and by and with the advice and consent of the Senate, shall appoint one additional judge to the court to which the former is commissioned.

Proposed bill, in S. Rep. No. 711, 75th Cong., 1st Sess. 31 (1937)

21 Modern complexities call also for a constant infusion of new blood in the courts, just as it is needed in executive functions of the Government and in private business. A lowered mental or physical vigor leads men to avoid an examination of complicated and changed conditions. Little by little, new facts become blurred through old glasses fitted, as it were, for the needs of another generation; older men, assuming that the scene is the same as it was in the past, cease to explore or inquire into the present or the future.

Franklin D. Roosevelt, Message to Congress recommending reorganization of judicial branch, 5 Feb. 1937, in *Public Papers and Addresses of Franklin D. Roosevelt, 1937,* at 55 (Samuel I. Rosenman ed. 1941)

22 This plan [the "court-packing plan" increasing the number of Supreme Court justices] will save our national Constitution from hardening of the judicial arteries.

Franklin D. Roosevelt, Radio broadcast, 9 Mar. 1937, in *Public Papers and Addresses of Franklin D. Roosevelt, 1937,* at 122, 128 (Samuel I. Rosenman ed. 1941)

23 We will no longer be permitted to sacrifice each generation in turn while the law catches up with life.

Franklin D. Roosevelt, Address on Constitution Day, Washington, D.C., 17 Sept. 1937, in *Public Papers and Addresses of Franklin D. Roosevelt, 1937,* at 359, 366 (Samuel I. Rosenman ed. 1941)

24 The switch in time that saved the Nine.*

Popular description of Justice Owen J. Roberts's changed position in *West Coast Hotel Co. v. Parrish,* 300 U.S. 379 (1937)

---

* *West Coast Hotel* was a decision which overruled previous Supreme Court decisions invalidating minimum wage laws and coincided with President Franklin D. Roosevelt's "court-packing" plan. In fact, however, Roberts had voted before Roosevelt proposed his plan.

25 The reason the public thinks so much of the Justices of the Supreme Court is that they are almost the only people in Washington who do their own work.

    Louis D. Brandeis, quoted in Charles E. Wyzanski, Jr., *Whereas—A Judge's Premises* 61 (1965)

26 [The] most important thing we do is not doing.

    Louis D. Brandeis, quoted in Henry J. Abraham, *The Judicial Process* 371 (3d ed. 1975)

27 Hughes made a statement to me which at the time was shattering but which over the years turned out to be true: "Justice Douglas, you must remember one thing. At the constitutional level where we work, ninety percent of any decision is emotional. The rational part of us supplies the reasons for supporting our predilections."

    Charles Evans Hughes, reported in William O. Douglas, *The Court Years, 1939–1975,* at 8 (1980)

28 As created, the Supreme Court seemed too anemic to endure a long contest for power. . . . Yet in spite of its apparently vulnerable position, this Court has repeatedly overruled and thwarted both the Congress and the Executive. It has been in angry collision with the most dynamic and popular Presidents in our history. . . . It is surprising that it should not only survive but, with no might except the moral force of its judgments, should attain actual supremacy as a source of constitutional dogma.

    Robert H. Jackson, *The Struggle for Judicial Supremacy* ix-x (1941)

29 The uncontrollable power wielded by this Court brings it very close to the most sensitive areas of public affairs. As appeal from legislation to adjudication becomes more frequent, and its consequences more far-reaching, judicial self-restraint becomes more and not less important, lest we unwarrantably enter social and political domains wholly outside our concern.

    Felix Frankfurter, *West Virginia State Bd. of Educ. v. Barnette,* 319 U.S. 624, 666 (1943) (dissenting)

30 We doubt if one can find in the long line of criticized cases one in which the Court has made a more extreme exertion of power or one so little supported or explained by either the statute or the record in the case. Power should answer to reason none the less because its fiat is beyond appeal.

    Robert H. Jackson, *Jewell Ridge Coal Corp. v. Local No. 6167, United Mine Workers of America,* 325 U.S. 161, 196 (1945) (dissenting)

31 After all, this is the Nation's ultimate judicial tribunal, not a super-legal-aid bureau.

    Felix Frankfurter, *Uveges v. Pennsylvania,* 335 U.S. 437, 449–50 (1948) (dissenting)

32 Rightly or wrongly, the belief is widely held by the practising profession that this Court no longer respects impersonal rules of law but is guided in these matters by personal impressions which from time to time may be shared by a majority of Justices. Whatever has been intended, this Court also has generated an impression . . . that regard for precedents and authorities is obsolete, that words no longer mean what they have always meant to the profession, that the law knows no fixed principles.

    Robert H. Jackson, *Brown v. Allen,* 344 U.S. 443, 535 (1953) (concurring)

33 It is often suggested that the Court could create a staff of assistants like those of administrative tribunals to take much of the drudgery of judicial work from the Justices. In fact, a suspicion has grown at the bar that the law clerks already constitute a kind of junior court which decides the fate of certiorari petitions. This idea of the law clerks' influence gave rise to a lawyer's waggish statement that the Senate no longer need bother about confirmation of Justices but ought to confirm the appointment of law clerks.

    Robert H. Jackson, *The Supreme Court in the American System of Government* 20 (1955)

34 The people have seemed to feel that the Supreme Court, whatever its defects, is still the most detached, dispassionate, and trustworthy custodian that one system affords for the translation of abstract into concrete constitutional commands.

    Robert H. Jackson, *The Supreme Court in the American System of Government* 23 (1955)

35 From the time of Chief Justice Marshall, the opinions of the Supreme Court have been a text unto the people. Read in the daily press, studied in the common school, knotted into the rope of enduring history, they may well be the largest single contribution to the philosophy of the American way of life.

> Charles E. Wyzanski, Jr., "Atlantic Portrait: Brandeis," *Atlantic Monthly,* Nov. 1956, at 66, 67

36 Marble Palace.

> John P. Frank, Title of book about United States Supreme Court (1961)

37 The least dangerous branch of the American government is the most extraordinarily powerful court of law the world has ever known.

> Alexander M. Bickel, *The Least Dangerous Branch* 1 (1962)
> See also JUDICIARY 3

38 The function of the Justices—and there is no question but what this accords with the great authoritative body of opinion on the subject—is to immerse themselves in the tradition of our society and of kindred societies that have gone before, in history and in the sediment of history which is law, and, as Judge Hand once suggested, in the thought and vision of the philosophers and the poets.

> Alexander M. Bickel, *The Least Dangerous Branch* 236 (1962)

39 Finally, these decisions give support to a current mistaken view of the Constitution and the constitutional function of this Court. This view, in a nutshell, is that every major social ill in this country can find its cure in some constitutional "principle," and that this Court should "take the lead" in promoting reform when other branches of government fail to act. The Constitution is not a panacea for every blot upon the public welfare, nor should this Court, ordained as a judicial body, be thought of as a general haven for reform movements. The Constitution is an instrument of government, fundamental to which is the premise that in a diffusion of governmental authority lies the greatest promise that this Nation will realize liberty for all its citizens. This Court, limited in function in accordance with that premise, does not serve its high purpose when it exceeds its authority, even to satisfy justified impatience with the slow workings of the political process. For when, in the name of constitutional interpretation, the Court *adds* something to the Constitution that was deliberately excluded from it, the Court in reality substitutes its view of what should be so for the amending process.

> John M. Harlan (1899–1971), *Reynolds v. Sims,* 377 U.S. 533, 624–25 (1964) (dissenting)

40 Virtually all important decisions of the Supreme Court are the beginnings of conversations between the Court and the people and their representatives. They are never, at the start, conversations between equals. The Court has an edge, because it initiates things with some immediate action, even if limited. But conversations they are, and to say that the Supreme Court lays down the law of the land is to state the ultimate result, following upon a complex series of events, in some cases, and in others it is a form of speech only.

> Alexander M. Bickel, *The Supreme Court and the Idea of Progress* 91 (1970)

41 [On being a Supreme Court Justice:] It's about a four-day-a-week job. . . . But that's a matter of working habits, a matter of energy. . . . Those three days with nothing to do much except take a walk, go out West on a trek, go to Europe, fly down to Knoxville for three days in the Smokies—these times of being away from the desk are a time when you are digesting a lot of things that have come in during those four days. It's one of the best decision-making processes: at the end of a 25-mile hike, your work is pretty well done.

> William O. Douglas, Interview, 28 Oct. 1973, in *New York Times,* 29 Oct. 1973, at 29

42 If this country wanted its Supreme Court to reflect the immediate social or political wishes of the nation's people, it would provide for the election of the Court. And if the Founding Fathers had wanted it that way, they could have said so—or at least hinted at it. They did just the opposite: they designed a system that tried to immunize the Court from the changing moods and passions of the people.

> Mario Cuomo, Speech to American Bar Association, New York, 11 Aug. 1986, quoted in *New York Times,* 12 Aug. 1986, at A20

43 Oyez, oyez, oyez! All persons having business before the honorable, the Supreme Court of the United States, are admonished to draw near and give their attention, for the court is now sitting. God save the United States and this honorable Court.

> Marshal's cry at the opening of public sessions of the United States Supreme Court

44 Equal Justice Under Law.

> Inscription on West Portico of Supreme Court Building, Washington. D.C.

45 Justice the Guardian of Liberty.

> Inscription on East Portico of Supreme Court Building, Washington, D.C.

TAKINGS

See EMINENT DOMAIN

TAXATION

1 Taxation without representation is tyranny.*

> **James Otis,** Attributed remark, 1761, quoted in William Tudor, *Life of James Otis* 77 (1823)

2 3d. That it is inseparably essential to the freedom of a people, and the undoubted rights of Englishmen, that no taxes should be imposed on them, but with their own consent, given personally, or by their representatives.

4th. That the people of these colonies are not, and from their local circumstances, cannot be represented in the house of commons in Great Britain.

---

* This maxim, which is often quoted as the rallying cry for the American Revolution, has been attributed to Otis's argument against the writs of assistance before the Superior Court of Massachusetts in February 1761. However, there is no contemporary record of these words being used by Otis. John Adams, in describing the event fifty-seven years later, wrote to William Tudor on 9 June 1818 that Otis "gave the reins to his genius, in declamation, invective, philippic, call it which you will, against *the tyranny of taxation without representation*" (*Works of John Adams* 10:319 (Charles Francis Adams ed. 1856)). Tudor then stated, in his *Life of James Otis* 76–77 (1823), "From the energy with which he urged this position, that taxation without representation is tyranny, it came to be a common maxim in the mouth of every one." Adams's recollections, based on rough notes at the argument, are the earliest source for the attribution to Otis, but Adams may have been summarizing Otis rather than quoting him.

5th. That the only representatives of the people of these colonies, are persons chosen therein by themselves; and that no taxes ever have been, or can be constitutionally imposed on them, but by their respective legislatures.

> Resolutions of the Stamp Act Congress, 19 Oct. 1765, in *Sources of Our Liberties* 270, 270 (Richard L. Perry & John C. Cooper eds., rev. ed. 1978)

3 Here this extraordinary man [Charles Townsend], then Chancellor of the Exchequer, found himself in great straits. To please universally was the object of his life; but to tax and to please, no more than to love and to be wise, is not given to men. However he attempted it.

> **Edmund Burke,** Speech on American Taxation, 19 April 1774, in *Writings and Speeches of Edmund Burke* 2:409, 454 (Paul Langford ed. 1981)

4 The genius of liberty reprobates every thing arbitrary or discretionary in taxation.

> **Alexander Hamilton,** "The Continentalist," No. 6, 1782, in *Papers of Alexander Hamilton* 3:104 (Harold C. Syrett ed. 1962)

5 Another means of silently lessening the inequality of property is to exempt all from taxation below a certain point, and to tax the higher portions of property in geometric progression as they rise.

> **Thomas Jefferson,** Letter to James Madison, 28 Oct. 1785, in *Papers of Thomas Jefferson* 8:682 (Julian P. Boyd ed. 1953)

6 Our new Constitution is now established, and has an appearance that promises permanency; but in this world nothing can be said to be certain, except death and taxes.*

> **Benjamin Franklin,** Letter to Jean Baptiste Le Roy, 13 Nov. 1789, in *Writings of Benjamin Franklin* 10:69 (Albert H. Smyth ed. 1907)

7 That the power to tax involves the power to destroy; that the power to destroy may defeat and render useless the power to create; that there is a plain repugnance, in

---

* Not the man in the moon, not the groaning-board, not the speaking of friar Bacon's brazen-head, not the inspiration of mother Shipton, or the miracles of Dr. Faustus, things as certain as death and taxes, can be more firmly believed. —Daniel Defoe, *The History of the Devil,* 1726, in *Defoe's Works* 3:283, 481 (1912)

conferring on one government a power to control the constitutional measures of another, which other, with respect to those very measures, is declared to be supreme over that which exerts the control, are propositions not to be denied.

John Marshall, *McCulloch v. Maryland*, 17 U.S. (4 Wheat.) 316, 431 (1819)
See also TAXATION 8; TAXATION 29

8 An *unlimited* right to tax, implies a right to destroy.

Daniel Webster, Argument in *McCulloch v. Maryland*, 17 U.S. (4 Wheat.) 316, 22 Feb. 1819, in *Papers of Daniel Webster: Legal Papers* 3:233, 235 (Andrew J. King ed. 1989)
See also TAXATION 7; TAXATION 29

9 The wisdom of man never yet contrived a system of taxation that would operate with perfect equality.

Andrew Jackson, Proclamation, 10 Dec. 1832, in *Messages and Papers of the Presidents* 2:640, 644 (James D. Richardson ed. 1898)

10 Of all debts men are least willing to pay the taxes. What a satire is this on government!

Ralph Waldo Emerson, "Politics," *Essays: Second Series*, 1844, in *Complete Works of Ralph Waldo Emerson* 3:199, 215 (1903)

11 The common people there . . . even have the effrontery to complain if they are not properly governed, and to take hold and help conduct the government themselves; if they had laws like ours, which give one dollar of every three a crop produces to the government for taxes, they would have that law altered; instead of paying thirty-three dollars in taxes, out of every one hundred they receive, they complain if they have to pay seven.

Mark Twain, *The Innocents Abroad* 212 (Guy Cardwell ed. 1984) (1869)

12 The thing generally raised on city land is taxes.

Charles Dudley Warner, *My Summer in a Garden* 143 (1870)

13 To lay, with one hand the power of the government on the property of the citizen, and with the other to bestow it upon favored individuals to aid private enterprises and build up private fortunes, is none the less

a robbery because it is done under the forms of law and is called taxation.

Samuel F. Miller, *Loan Association v. Topeka*, 87 U.S. (20 Wall.) 655, 664 (1875)

14 What I, therefore, propose, as the simple yet sovereign remedy, which will raise wages, increase the earnings of capital, extirpate pauperism, abolish poverty, give remunerative employment to whoever wishes it, afford free scope to human powers, lessen crime, elevate morals, and taste, and intelligence, purify government and carry civilization to yet nobler heights, is— *to appropriate rent by taxation.*

Henry George, *Progress and Poverty* 405-06 (1929) (1879)

15 The tax upon land values is therefore the most just and equal of all taxes. It falls only upon those who receive from society a peculiar and valuable benefit, and upon them in proportion to the benefit they receive. It is the taking by the community, for the use of the community, of that value which is the creation of the community.

Henry George, *Progress and Poverty* 421 (1929) (1879)

16 It is a matter of history that unequal and discriminating taxation, leveled against special classes, has been the fruitful means of oppressions, and the cause of more commotions and disturbance in society, of insurrections and revolutions, than any other cause in the world.

Stephen J. Field, *County of Santa Clara v. Southern Pac. R.R.*, 18 F. 385, 399 (C.C.D. Cal. 1883)

17 [A] tax is uniform when it operates with the same force and effect in every place where the subject of it is found.

Samuel F. Miller, *Head Money Cases*, 112 U.S. 580, 594 (1884)

18 Here I close my opinion. I could not say less in view of questions of such gravity that go down to the very foundation of the government. If the provisions of the Constitution can be set aside by an act of Congress, where is the course of usurpation to end? The present assault upon capital is but the beginning. It will be but the stepping-stone to others, larger and more sweeping, till our political contests will become a war of the poor against the rich; a

war constantly growing in intensity and bitterness.

> **Stephen J. Field,** *Pollock v. Farmers' Loan & Trust Co.,* 157 U.S. 429, 607 (1895) (separate opinion)

19 The income tax is just. It simply intends to put the burdens of government justly upon the backs of the people. I am in favor of an income tax. When I find a man who is not willing to bear his share of the burdens of the government which protects him, I find a man who is unworthy to enjoy the blessings of a government like ours.

> **William Jennings Bryan,** "The Cross of Gold" (speech at Democratic National Convention), Chicago, 8 July 1896, in *History of American Presidential Elections* 2:1845, 1847 (Arthur M. Schlesinger, Jr. & Fred L. Israel eds. 1971)

20 What is the difference between a taxidermist and a tax collector? The taxidermist takes only your skin.

> **Mark Twain,** Notebook, 30 Dec. 1902, in *Mark Twain's Notebook* 378 (Albert B. Paine ed. 1935)

21 There are two kinds of Christian morals, one private and the other public. These two are so distinct, so unrelated, that they are no more akin to each other than are archangels and politicians. During three hundred and sixty-three days in the year the American citizen is true to his Christian private morals, and keeps undefiled the nation's character at its best and highest; then in the other two days of the year he leaves his Christian private morals at home and carries his Christian public morals to the tax office and the polls, and does the best he can to damage and undo his whole year's faithful and righteous work. . . . Once a year he lays aside his Christian private morals . . . and gets out his Christian public morals and goes to the tax office and holds up his hands and swears he wishes he may never-never if he's got a cent in the world, so help him.

> **Mark Twain,** Speech at Carnegie Hall, New York, 22 Jan. 1906, in *Writings of Mark Twain* 28:276, 276–77 (Albert B. Paine ed. 1929)

22 Now that word—taxes, taxes, taxes! . . . that is a very sore subject to me. I was so relieved when Judge Leventritt did find something that was not taxable—when he said that the commissioner could not tax your patience. . . . We've got so much taxation. I don't know of a single foreign product that enters this country untaxed except the answer to prayer.

> **Mark Twain,** Speech to Freundschaft Society, 9 Mar. 1906, in *Writings of Mark Twain* 28:292, 292–93 (Albert B. Paine ed. 1929)

23 ALLEGIANCE, *n.* The traditional bond of duty between the taxer and the taxee. It is not reversible.

> **Ambrose Bierce,** *The Enlarged Devil's Dictionary* 12 (Ernest J. Hopkins ed. 1967)

24 In passing it might not be out of place to remark that should tax returns of many of our "good men and true" be conclusive as to the value of their property, numbers of fortunes in the State would shrink and shrivel even as a ripe plucked fig when exposed to a summer sun.

> **Oliver H. Bloodworth,** *City of Atlanta v. Sciple,* 19 Ga. App. 694, 697–98, 92 S.E. 28 (1917)

25 Logic and taxation are not always the best of friends.

> **James C. McReynolds,** *Sonneborn Bros. v. Cureton,* 262 U.S. 506, 522 (1923) (concurring)

26 The Income Tax has made more Liars out of the American people than Golf has. Even when you make one out on the level, you don't know when it's through if you are a Crook or a Martyr.

> **Will Rogers,** *The Illiterate Digest* 71–72 (1924)

27 I dont see why a man shouldn't pay an inheritance tax. If a Country is good enough to pay taxes to while you are living, it's good enough to pay in after you die. By the time you die you should be so used to paying taxes that it would just be almost second nature to you.

> **Will Rogers,** "They've Got a New Dictionary at Ellis Island," 28 Feb. 1926, in *Will Rogers' Weekly Articles* 2:157, 158 (James M. Smallwood ed. 1980)

28 Taxes are what we pay for civilized society.

> **Oliver Wendell Holmes, Jr.,** *Compañia General de Tabacos de Filipinas v. Collector of*

Internal Revenue 275 U.S. 87, 100 (1927)
(dissenting)
See also TAXATION 32; TAXATION 41

29 The power to tax is not the power to destroy while this Court sits.

> Oliver Wendell Holmes, Jr., *Panhandle Oil Co. v. Mississippi ex rel. Knox*, 277 U.S. 218, 223 (1928) (dissenting)
> See also TAXATION 7; TAXATION 8

30 But this case is not to be decided by attenuated subtleties. It turns on the import and reasonable construction of the taxing act. There is no doubt that the statute could tax salaries to those who earned them and provide that the tax could not be escaped by anticipatory arrangements and contracts however skilfully devised to prevent the salary when paid from vesting even for a second in the man who earned it. That seems to us the import of the statute before us and we think that no distinction can be taken according to the motives leading to the arrangement by which the fruits are attributed to a different tree from that on which they grew.

> Oliver Wendell Holmes, Jr., *Lucas v. Earl*, 281 U.S. 111, 114–15 (1930)

31 Taxation is not so much concerned with the refinements of title as it is with actual command over the property taxed—the actual benefit for which the tax is paid.

> Oliver Wendell Holmes, Jr., *Corliss v. Bowers*, 281 U.S. 376, 378 (1930)

32 I pay my tax bills more readily than any others—for whether the money is well or ill spent I get civilized society for it.

> Oliver Wendell Holmes, Jr., Letter to Harold J. Laski, 12 May 1930, in *Holmes-Laski Letters* 2:1247 (Mark DeWolfe Howe ed. 1953)
> See also TAXATION 28; TAXATION 41

33 If a taxpayer receives earnings under a claim of right and without restriction as to its disposition, he has received income which he is required to return, even though it may still be claimed that he is not entitled to retain the money, and even though he may still be adjudged liable to restore its equivalent.

> Louis D. Brandeis, *North American Oil Consol. v. Burnet*, 286 U.S. 417, 424 (1932)

34 Every time Congress starts to tax some particular industry, it rushes down with its main men and they scare 'em out of it. About the only way I see for 'em to do, so it would be fair to everybody, would be for Congress to go into secret session, allow no telephones, no telegrams, no visitors, so no outside lobbyist can get at 'em, then tax everything they want to, and should tax, then announce, "Boys, it's all over; there is no use shooting at us now." As it is now, we are taxing everybody without a lobby.

> Will Rogers, "Will Rogers Suggests A Way To Get New Taxes Fair To All," 29 Feb. 1932, in *Will Rogers' Daily Telegrams* 3:136 (James M. Smallwood ed. 1979)

35 Congress knocked the rich in the creek with a [72 per cent raise in the] income tax, then somebody must have told 'em "Yes, Congress you got 'em while they are living. But what if they die on you to keep from paying it?" Congress says, "Well, never thought of that, so we will frame one that will get 'em, alive or living, dead or deceased." Now they got such a high inheritance tax on 'em that you won't catch these old rich boys dying promiscuously like they did. This bill makes patriots out of everybody. You sure do die for your country if you die from now on.

> Will Rogers, "Mr. Rogers Airs Some Views on Congress and Taxpayers," 23 Mar. 1932, in *Will Rogers' Daily Telegrams* 3:146 (James M. Smallwood ed. 1979)

36 The respondent invokes the rule that in the construction of a taxing act doubt is to be resolved in favour of the taxpayer. . . . There are many facets to such a maxim. One must view them all, if one would apply it wisely. The construction that is liberal to one taxpayer may be illiberal to others. One must strike a balance of advantage.

> Benjamin N. Cardozo, *Burnet v. Guggenheim*, 288 U.S. 280, 286 (1933)

37 Now, what is ordinary, though there must always be a strain of constancy within it, is none the less a variable affected by time and place and circumstance. Ordinary in this context does not mean that the payments must be habitual or normal in the sense that the same taxpayer will have to make them often. A lawsuit affecting the safety of a business may happen once in a lifetime. The counsel fees may be so heavy

that repetition is unlikely. None the less, the expense is an ordinary one because we know from experience that payments for such a purpose, whether the amount is large or small, are the common and accepted means of defense against attack. . . . At such times there are norms of conduct that help to stabilize our judgment, and make it certain and objective. The instance is not erratic, but is brought within a known type.

Benjamin N. Cardozo, *Welch v. Helvering,* 290 U.S. 111, 113–14 (1933)

38 Collecting more taxes than is absolutely necessary is legalized robbery.

Calvin Coolidge, quoted in *New York Times Magazine,* 6 Mar. 1955, at 58

39 A transaction, otherwise within an exception of the tax law, does not lose its immunity, because it is actuated by a desire to avoid, or, if one choose, to evade, taxation. Any one may so arrange his affairs that his taxes shall be as low as possible; he is not bound to choose the pattern which will best pay the Treasury; there is not even a patriotic duty to increase one's taxes.

Learned Hand, *Helvering v. Gregory,* 69 F.2d 809, 810 (2d Cir. 1934)

40 Death and taxes and childbirth! There's never any convenient time for any of them!

Margaret Mitchell, *Gone With the Wind* 668 (1936)

41 In 1776 the fight was for democracy in taxation. In 1936 that is still the fight. Mr. Justice Oliver Wendell Holmes once said: "Taxes are the price we pay for civilized society." One sure way to determine the social conscience of a Government is to examine the way taxes are collected and how they are spent. And one sure way to determine the social conscience of an individual is to get his tax-reaction. Taxes, after all, are the dues that we pay for the privileges of membership in an organized society.

Franklin D. Roosevelt, Campaign address, Worcester, Mass., 21 Oct. 1936, in *Public Papers and Addresses of Franklin D. Roosevelt* 5:522, 523 (Samuel I. Rosenman ed. 1938)

See also TAXATION 28; TAXATION 32

42 Why shouldn't the American people take half my money from me? I took all of it from them.

Edward A. Filene, quoted in Arthur M. Schlesinger, Jr., *The Coming of the New Deal* 494 (1959)

43 The new tax we have authorized undermines the principle of graduation of tax burdens in proportion to ability to pay. No tax laid on anything less than the total net worth of the estate can be graduated even roughly according to the principle which progressive modern taxation strives to heed. The imposition of unpredictable assessments from many sources makes it impossible for the State of domicile to make intelligent use of its own taxing power as an instrument of enlightened social policy. Chaos serves no social end.

Robert H. Jackson, *State Tax Comm'n of Utah v. Aldrich,* 316 U.S. 174, 196 (1942)

44 The physical power to get the money does not seem to me a test of the right to tax. Might does not make right even in taxation.

Robert H. Jackson, *International Harvester Co. v. Wisconsin Dep't of Taxation,* 322 U.S. 435, 450 (1944) (dissenting)

45 It is not a tax bill but a tax relief bill providing relief not for the needy but for the greedy.

Franklin D. Roosevelt, Tax bill veto message, 22 Feb. 1944, in *Public Papers and Addresses of Franklin D. Roosevelt* 13:80 (Samuel I. Rosenman ed. 1950)

46 There is nothing sinister in so arranging one's affairs as to keep taxes as low as possible. Everybody does so, rich and poor; and all do right, for nobody owes any public duty to pay more than the law demands: taxes are enforced exactions, not voluntary contributions. To demand more in the name of morals is mere cant.

Learned Hand, *Commissioner v. Newman,* 159 F.2d 848, 850–51 (2d Cir. 1947) (dissenting)

47 Obviously, if the value of the property is less than the amount of the mortgage, a mortgagor who is not personally liable cannot realize a benefit equal to the mortgage. Consequently, a different problem might be encountered where a mortgagor abandoned the property or transferred it subject

to the mortgage without receiving boot. That is not this case.

Fred M. Vinson, *Crane v. Commissioner of Internal Revenue*, 331 U.S. 1, 14 n.37 (1947)

48 Except as otherwise provided in this subtitle, gross income means all income from whatever source derived.

Internal Revenue Code of 1954, Pub. L. No. 591, § 61(a), 68A Stat. 3, 17

49 Dear Mr. President, Internal Revenue regulations will turn us into a nation of bookkeepers. The life of every citizen is becoming a business. This, it seems to me, is one of the worst interpretations of the meaning of human life history has ever seen. Man's life is not a business.

Saul Bellow, *Herzog* 11 (1964)

50 [Describing tax reform:] Don't tax you, don't tax me, tax that fellow behind the tree.

Russell B. Long, quoted in *Forbes*, 15 Dec. 1976, at 46

51 [The Nation should] have a tax system which looks like someone designed it on purpose.

William E. Simon, quoted in United States Department of the Treasury, *Blueprints for Basic Tax Reform* 1 (1977)

52 The American taxing structure, the purpose of which was to serve the people, began instead to serve the insatiable appetite of government. If you will forgive me, you know someone has once likened government to a baby. It is an alimentary canal with an appetite at one end and no sense of responsibility at the other.

Ronald W. Reagan, Remarks before a joint session of Parliament, Ottawa, Canada, 11 Mar. 1981, in *Public Papers of the Presidents: Ronald Reagan, 1981*, at 229, 232 (1982)

53 Kemp-Roth [the Republican supply-side tax proposal] was always a Trojan horse to bring down the top rate [the tax rate for the wealthiest Americans].

David Stockman, quoted in William Greider, "The Education of David Stockman," *Atlantic Monthly*, Dec. 1981, at 27, 46

54 There is something wrong with any law that causes that many people to have to take a whole day off their jobs to find out how to comply.

T. Coleman Andrews, quoted in Michael Jackman, *Crown's Book of Political Quotations* 228 (1982)

55 There are some in government who have a very simple tax proposal in mind. There will only be two lines on the tax form: How much did you make last year? Send it.

Ronald W. Reagan, Remarks at a meeting with Puerto Rican leaders, 15 Mar. 1984, in *Public Papers of the Presidents: Ronald Reagan, 1984*, at 1:349, 350 (1986)

56 I have my veto pen drawn and ready for any tax increase that Congress might even think of sending up. And I have only one thing to say to the tax increasers: Go ahead, make my day.*

Ronald W. Reagan, Remarks to the American Business Conference, Washington, D.C., 13 Mar. 1985, in *Public Papers of the Presidents: Ronald Reagan, 1985*, at 1:278, 279 (1988)

57 Like the story of the man from Jefferson Parish—he sent a letter to the IRS saying: Enclosed is a check for $1,000. I cheated on my taxes last year, and I can't sleep at night. P.S. If I still can't sleep, I'll send you the rest I owe you.

Ronald W. Reagan, Remarks at Senate Campaign Rally, Metairie, La., 18 Sept. 1986, in *Public Papers of the Presidents: Ronald Reagan, 1986*, at 2:1204, 1204 (1989)

58 My opponent won't rule out raising taxes. But I will and the Congress will push me to raise taxes, and I'll say no, and they'll push, and I'll say no, and they'll push again. And I'll say to them, read my lips,† no new taxes.

George Bush, Speech accepting Republican nomination for President, New Orleans, 18 Aug. 1988, in *New York Times*, 19 Aug. 1988, at A14

59 The Rich aren't like us—they pay less taxes.

Peter De Vries, quoted in *Washington Post*, 30 July 1989, at C7

---

* *Harry Callahan* [played by Clint Eastwood]: Go ahead, make my day. —**Harry Julian Fink, Rita M. Fink, and Dean Riesner,** *Dirty Harry* (screenplay), 1971, quoted in Gerald Gardner, *I Coulda Been a Contender* 6 (1992)
† Read my lips. —**John Milius and Michael Cimino,** *Magnum Force* (screenplay), 1973, in Gerald Gardner, *I Coulda Been a Contender* 6 (1992)

60 We don't pay taxes. Only the little people pay taxes.

> **Leona Helmsley,** quoted in *New York Times*, 12 July 1989, at B2

61 [Response, while jogging, to questions on proposed tax increases:] Read my hips!

> **George Bush,** quoted in *Newsweek*, 22 Oct. 1990, at 21

62 Maybe I misread what some of their leaders said when they talked about now going back and trying to raise income tax rates. And they're going to do it over my dead veto or live veto or something like that, because it ain't going to happen, I'll guarantee you.

> **George Bush,** Remarks, in 26 *Weekly Compilation of Presidential Documents* 1781, 1785 (Nov. 8, 1990)

63 People hate taxes the way children hate brushing their teeth—and in the same shortsighted way.

> **Paul A. Samuelson,** quoted in Louis E. Boone, *Quotable Business* 224 (1992)

TESTIMONY

See CROSS-EXAMINATION; EXPERTS; WITNESSES

TORTS

See also INTENT; LIBEL; NEGLIGENCE; PRODUCTS LIABILITY

1 The general principle of our law is that loss from accident must lie where it falls, and this principle is not affected by the fact that a human being is the instrument of misfortune.

> **Oliver Wendell Holmes, Jr.,** *The Common Law* 94 (1881)

2 He who is intelligent and prudent does not act at his peril, in theory of law. On the contrary, it is only when he fails to exercise the foresight of which he is capable, or exercises it with evil intent, that he is answerable for the consequences.

> **Oliver Wendell Holmes, Jr.,** *The Common Law* 108-09 (1881)

3 A legal duty so called is nothing but a prediction that if a man does or omits certain things he will be made to suffer in this or

that way by judgment of the court;—and so of a legal right.

> **Oliver Wendell Holmes, Jr.,** "The Path of the Law," 10 *Harvard Law Review* 457, 458 (1897)

4 The torts with which our courts are kept busy to-day are mainly the incidents of certain well known businesses. . . . The liability for them is estimated, and sooner or later goes into the price paid by the public. The public really pays the damages, and the question of liability, if pressed far enough, is really the question how far it is desirable that the public should insure the safety of those whose work it uses. It might be said that in such cases the chance of a jury finding for the defendant is merely a chance, once in a while rather arbitrarily interrupting the regular course of recovery, most likely in the case of an unusually conscientious plaintiff, and therefore better done away with.

> **Oliver Wendell Holmes, Jr.,** "The Path of the Law," 10 *Harvard Law Review* 457, 467 (1897)

5 It has been considered that, *prima facie*, the intentional infliction of temporal damage is a cause of action, which, as a matter of substantive law, whatever may be the form of pleading, requires a justification if the defendant is to escape.

> **Oliver Wendell Holmes, Jr.,** *Aikens v. Wisconsin*, 195 U.S. 194, 204 (1904)

6 A nuisance may be merely a right thing in the wrong place,—like a pig in the parlor instead of the barnyard.

> **George Sutherland,** *Euclid v. Ambler Realty Co.*, 272 U.S. 365, 388 (1926)

7 The assault upon the citadel of privity [of contract] is proceeding in these days apace.

> **Benjamin N. Cardozo,** *Ultramares Corp. v. Touche*, 255 N.Y. 170, 180, 174 N.E. 441 (1931)

8 Quite apart from the question how far peace of mind is a good thing in itself, it would be quixotic indeed for the law to attempt a general securing of it. Against a large part of the frictions and irritations and clashing of temperaments incident to participation in a community life, a certain

toughening of the mental hide is a better protection than the law could ever be.

> Calvert Magruder, "Mental and Emotional Disturbance in the Law of Torts," 49 *Harvard Law Review* 1033, 1035 (1936)

9 There is danger of getting into the realm of the trivial in this matter of insulting language. No pressing social need requires that every abusive outburst be converted into a tort; upon the contrary, it would be unfortunate if the law closed all the safety valves through which irascible tempers might legally blow off steam.

> Calvert Magruder, "Mental and Emotional Disturbance in the Law of Torts," 49 *Harvard Law Review* 1033, 1053 (1936)

10 The chief reason relied upon by all these courts, however, is that personal tort actions between husband and wife would disrupt and destroy the peace and harmony of the home, which is against the policy of the law. This is on the bald theory that after a husband has beaten his wife, there is a state of peace and harmony left to be disturbed; and that if she is sufficiently injured or angry to sue him for it, she will be soothed and deterred from reprisals by denying her the legal remedy—and this even though she has left him or divorced him for that very ground, and though the same courts refuse to find any disruption of domestic tranquillity if she sues him for a tort to her property, or brings a criminal prosecution against him.

> William L. Prosser, *Handbook of the Law of Torts* 903-04 (1941)

11 It is not a tort for government to govern.

> Robert H. Jackson, *Dalehite v. United States,* 346 U.S. 15, 57 (1953) (dissenting)

12 There is a duty if the court says there is a duty; the law, like the Constitution, is what we make it. Duty is only a word with which we state our conclusion that there is or is not to be liability; it necessarily begs the essential question. . . . many factors interplay: the hand of history, our ideas of morals and justice, the convenience of administration of the rule, and our social ideas as to where the loss should fall.

> William L. Prosser, "Palsgraf Revisited," 52 *Michigan Law Review* 1, 15 (1953)

13 Ultimately, the infant's complaint is that he would be better off not to have been born.

Man, who knows nothing of death or nothingness, cannot possibly know whether that is so.

We must remember that the choice is not between being born with health or being born without it; it is not claimed the defendants failed to do something to prevent or reduce the ravages of rubella. Rather the choice is between a worldly existence and none at all. Implicit, beyond this claim against a physician for faulty advice, is the proposition that a pregnant woman who, duly informed, does not seek an abortion, and all who urge her to see the pregnancy through, are guilty of wrongful injury to the fetus, and indeed that every day in which the infant is sustained after birth is a day of wrong. To recognize a right not to be born is to enter an area in which no one could find his way.

> Joseph Weintraub, *Gleitman v. Cosgrove,* 49 N.J. 22, 63, 227 A.2d 689 (1967) (dissenting in part)

14 "Torts" more or less means "wrongs" and the subject is the study of the kinds of injuries done by private citizens to one another for which the law offers relief. . . . The cases concern virtually the entire range of misfortune and hurts which human beings can blame on one another— auto wrecks, beatings, medical malpractice, injuries from defective products—and the narratives of fact in the cases often offer accounts of bizarre calamities. One of my friends said during the year that Torts is the course which proves that your mother was right.

> Scott Turow, *One L* 60–61 (1977)

15 We thought that we would never see
A suit to compensate a tree.
A suit whose claim in tort is prest
Upon a mangled tree's behest;
A tree whose battered trunk was prest
Against a Chevy's crumpled crest;
A tree that faces each new day
With bark and limb in disarray;
A tree that may forever bear
A lasting need for tender care.
Flora lovers though we three,
We must uphold the court's decree.
Affirmed.

> John H. Gillis, *Fisher v. Lowe,* 122 Mich. App. 418, 419, 333 N.W.2d 67 (1983)

TRADE REGULATION

See ANTITRUST

1 The law is not made for the protection of experts, but for the public—that vast multitude which includes the ignorant, the unthinking and the credulous, who, in making purchases, do not stop to analyze, but are governed by appearances and general impressions.

Alfred C. Coxe, *Florence Mfg. Co. v. J.C. Dowd & Co.,* 178 F. 73, 75 (2d Cir. 1910)

2 It is so easy for the honest business man, who wishes to sell his goods upon their merits, to select from the entire material universe, which is before him, symbols, marks and coverings which by no possibility can cause confusion between his goods and those of competitors, that the courts look with suspicion upon one who, in dressing his goods for the market, approaches so near to his successful rival that the public may fail to distinguish between them.

Alfred C. Coxe, *Florence Mfg. Co. v. J.C. Dowd & Co.,* 178 F. 73, 75 (2d Cir. 1910)

3 Of course, the burden of proof always rests upon the moving party, but having shown the adoption of a similar trade name, arbitrary in character, I cannot see why speculation as to the chance that it will cause confusion should be at the expense of the man first in the field.

Learned Hand, *Lambert Pharmacal Co. v. Bolton Chemical Corp.,* 219 F. 325, 326 (S.D.N.Y. 1915)

4 The word property as applied to trademarks and trade secrets is an unanalyzed expression of certain secondary consequences of the primary fact that the law makes some rudimentary requirements of good faith. Whether the plaintiffs have any valuable secret or not the defendent knows the facts, whatever they are, through a special confidence that he accepted. The property may be denied but the confidence cannot be.

Oliver Wendell Holmes, Jr., *E.I. Du Pont De Nemours Powder Co. v. Masland,* 244 U.S. 100, 102 (1917)

5 The law of unfair trade comes down very nearly to this—as judges have repeated again and again—that one merchant shall not divert customers from another by representing what he sells as emanating from the second. This has been, and perhaps even more now is, the whole Law and the Prophets on the subject, though it assumes many guises. Therefore it was at first a debatable point whether a merchant's good will, indicated by his mark, could extend beyond such goods as he sold. How could he lose bargains which he had no means to fill? What harm did it do a chewing gum maker to have an ironmonger use his trade-mark? The law often ignores the nicer sensibilities.

Learned Hand, *Yale Electric Corp. v. Robertson,* 26 F.2d 972, 973–74 (2d Cir. 1928)

6 However, it has of recent years been recognized that a merchant may have a sufficient economic interest in the use of his mark outside the field of his own exploitation to justify interposition by a court. His mark is his authentic seal; by it he vouches for the goods which bear it; it carries his name for good or ill. If another uses it, he borrows the owner's reputation, whose quality no longer lies within his own control. This is an injury, even though the borrower does not tarnish it, or divert any sales by its use; for a reputation, like a face, is the symbol of its possessor and creator, and another can use it only as a mask. And so it has come to be recognized that, unless the borrower's use is so foreign to the owner's as to insure against any identification of the two, it is unlawful.

Learned Hand, *Yale Electric Corp. v. Robertson,* 26 F.2d 972, 974 (2d Cir. 1928)

7 The protection of trade-marks is the law's recognition of the psychological function of symbols. If it is true that we live by symbols, it is no less true that we purchase goods by them. A trade-mark is a merchandising short-cut which induces a purchaser to select what he wants, or what he has been led to believe he wants. The owner of a mark exploits this human propensity by making every effort to impregnate the atmosphere of the market with the drawing power of a congenial symbol. Whatever the means employed, the aim is the same—to convey through the mark, in the minds of potential customers, the desirability of the commodity upon which it appears. Once this is attained, the trade-mark owner has something of value. If another poaches

upon the commercial magnetism of the symbol he has created, the owner can obtain legal redress.

>   Felix Frankfurter, *Mishawaka Rubber & Woolen Mfg. Co. v. S.S. Kresge Co.,* 316 U.S. 203, 205 (1942)

TREASON

1 That no law, to attaint particular persons of treason or felony, ought to be made in any case, or at any time hereafter.

>   Maryland Constitution of 1776, § 16, in *Federal and State Constitutions* 3:1686, 1688 (Francis N. Thorpe ed. 1909)

2 Nolan was proved guilty enough, as I say; yet you and I would never have heard of him, reader, but that, when the president of the court asked him at the close whether he wished to say anything to show that he had always been faithful to the United States, he cried out, in a fit of frenzy,—

"Damn the United States! I wish I may never hear of the United States again!"

. . . "Prisoner, hear the sentence of the Court! The Court decides, subject to the approval of the President, that you never hear the name of the United States again."

>   Edward Everett Hale, *The Man Without a Country* 5, 7 (1906) (1865)

3 Your crime is worse than murder. . . . who knows but that millions more of innocent people may pay the price of your treason. Indeed, by your betrayal you undoubtedly have altered the course of history to the disadvantage of our country.

>   Irving R. Kaufman, Remarks sentencing Julius and Ethel Rosenberg to death for espionage of atomic secrets, quoted in *New York Times,* 6 Apr. 1951, at 10

TREATIES

See also INTERNATIONAL LAW

1 The treaties of the United States, to have force at all, must be considered as part of the law of the land. Their true import, as far as respects individuals, must, like all other laws, be ascertained by judicial determinations.

>   Alexander Hamilton, *The Federalist* No. 22, at 1:140 (1788)

2 The history of human conduct does not warrant that exalted opinion of human virtue which would make it wise in a nation to commit interests of so delicate and momentous a kind as those which concern its intercourse with the rest of the world to the sole disposal of a magistrate, created and circumstanced, as would be a president of the United States.

>   Alexander Hamilton, *The Federalist* No. 75, at 2:274 (1788)

3 All constitutional acts of power, whether in the executive or in the judicial department, have as much legal validity and obligation as if they proceeded from the legislature; and therefore, whatever name be given to the power of making treaties, or however obligatory they may be when made, certain it is that the people may with much propriety commit the power to a distinct body from the legislature, the executive, or the judicial.

>   John Jay, *The Federalist* No. 64, at 2:205 (1788)

4 We believe, that with nations as with individuals, dealings may be carried on as advantageously, perhaps more so, while their continuance depends on a voluntary good treatment, as if fixed by contract, which, when it becomes injurious to either, is made, by forced constructions, to mean what suits them, and becomes a cause of war instead of a bond of peace.

>   Thomas Jefferson, Letter to Philip Mazzei, 18 July 1804, in *Writings of Thomas Jefferson* 4:552–53 (H. A. Washington ed. 1854)

5 Treaties at best are but complied with so long as interest requires their fulfilment; consequently they are virtually binding on the weaker party only, or, in plain truth, they are not binding at all.

>   Washington Irving, *History of New York* 327–28 (1868) (1809)

6 No one can study the vague and wavering statements of treatise and decision in this field of international law with any feeling of assurance at the end that he has chosen the right path. One looks in vain either for uniformity of doctrine or for scientific accuracy of exposition. There are wise cautions for the statesman. There are few precepts for the judge. All the more, in this uncertainty, I am impelled to the belief that

until the political departments have acted, the courts, in refusing to give effect to treaties, should limit their refusal to the needs of the occasion; that they are not bound by any rigid formula to nullify the whole or nothing; and that in determining whether this treaty survived the coming of war, they are free to make choice of the conclusion which shall seem the most in keeping with the traditions of the law, the policy of the statutes, the dictates of fair dealing, and the honor of the nation.

> **Benjamin N. Cardozo,** *Techt v. Hughes,* 229 N.Y. 222, 247, 128 N.E. 185 (1920)

TRIALS

See also ADVOCACY; CASES; LITIGATION; TRIALS, FAMOUS

1 That in all publick courts of justice for tryals of causes, civil or criminal, any person or persons, inhabitants of the said Province may freely come into, and attend the said courts, and hear and be present, at all or any such tryals as shall be there had or passed, that justice may not be done in a corner nor in any covert manner, being intended and resolved, by the help of the Lord, and by these our Concessions and Fundamentals, that all and every person and persons inhabiting the said Province, shall, as far as in us lies, be free from oppression and slavery.

> West New Jersey Charter of 1676, ch. 23, in *Federal and State Constitutions* 5:2548, 2551 (Francis N. Thorpe ed. 1909)

2 Great causes are never tried on their merits.

> **Ralph Waldo Emerson,** "Nature," *Essays: Second Series,* 1844, in *Complete Works of Ralph Waldo Emerson* 3:169, 187 (1903)

3 Someone suggested that in case of a mistrial that the Judge should go ahead and hear the evidence and render the decision. Oh but what a howl the law profession put up at that suggestion. That was cutting right into their graft. What a justice seeking bunch of babies they turned out to be.

> **Will Rogers,** "How El Duce Put Sunday to Work," 20 Nov. 1927, in *Will Rogers' Weekly Articles* 3:97, 98–99 (James M. Smallwood ed. 1981)

4 How simply, Russia gets rid of such harpy bands of lawyers, sharpers, technical experts, et cetera, et cetera, as invariably infests and befogs every important trial here.

> **Theodore Dreiser,** *Dreiser Looks at Russia* 118 (1928)

5 It's the greatest murder trial of the century—about every two years another one of 'em comes along.

> **Frances Noyes Hart,** *The Bellamy Trial* 4 (1928)

6 I am appalled and ashamed that things should have come to such a pass in this country that I am skeptical of the ability of black revolutionaries to achieve a fair trial anywhere in the United States.

> **Kingman Brewster, Jr.,** Statement at Yale University faculty meeting, New Haven, Conn., quoted in *Washington Post,* 5 May 1970, at A16

TRIALS, FAMOUS

See also COURTROOM SCENES; DARROW, CLARENCE

1 I thank Your Honour. Then Gentlemen of the Jury, it is to you we must now appeal, for Witnesses to the Truth of the Facts we have offered, and are denied the Liberty to prove; and let it not seem strange, that I apply myself to you in this Manner, I am warranted so to do both by Law and Reason.

> **Andrew Hamilton,** Argument in Zenger Trial, 1735, in Livingston Rutherfurd, *John Peter Zenger: His Press, His Trial* 213 (1904)

2 Power may justly be compar'd to a great River, while kept within it's due Bounds, is both Beautiful and Useful; but when it overflows, it's Banks, it is then too impetuous to be stemm'd, it bears down all before it, and brings Destruction and Desolation wherever it comes. If then this is the Nature of Power, let us at least do our Duty, and like wise Men (who value Freedom) use our utmost Care to support Liberty, the only Bulwark against lawless Power, which in all Ages has sacrificed to it's wild Lust and boundless Ambition, the Blood of the best Men that ever liv'd.

> **Andrew Hamilton,** Argument in Zenger Trial, 1735, in Livingston Rutherfurd, *John Peter Zenger: His Press, His Trial* 238 (1904)

3 The Question before the Court and you Gentlemen of the Jury, is not of small nor private Concern, it is not the Cause of the poor Printer, nor of *New-York* alone, which you are now trying: No! It may in it's Consequence, affect every Freeman that lives under a British Government on the main of *America*. It is the best Cause. It is the Cause of Liberty; and I make no Doubt but your upright Conduct, this Day, will not only entitle you to the Love and Esteem of your Fellow-Citizens; but every Man who prefers Freedom to a Life of slavery will bless and honour You, as Men who have baffled the Attempt of Tyranny; and by an impartial and uncorrupt Verdict, have laid a noble Foundation for securing to ourselves, our Posterity, and our Neighbours, That, to which Nature and the Laws of our Country have given us a Right,—the Liberty—both of exposing and opposing arbitrary Power (in these Parts of the World, at least) by speaking and writing Truth.

> **Andrew Hamilton,** Argument in Zenger Trial, 1735, in Livingston Rutherfurd, *John Peter Zenger: His Press, His Trial* 239–40 (1904)

4 Much has been said in the course of the argument on points on which the court feels no inclination to comment particularly; but which may, perhaps not improperly, receive some notice. That this court dares not usurp power is most true. That this court dares not shrink from its duty is not less true. . . . No man is desirous of becoming the peculiar subject of calumny. No man might he let the bitter cup pass from him without self-reproach, would drain it to the bottom. But if he have no choice in the case, if there be no alternative presented to him but a dereliction of duty or the opprobrium of those who are denominated the world, he merits the contempt as well as the indignation of his country who can hesitate which to embrace.

> **John Marshall,** *United States v. Burr,* 25 F. Cas. 55, 179 (C.C.D. Va. 1807) (No. 14,693)

5 A sense of duty pursues us ever. It is omnipresent, like the Deity. If we take to ourselves the wings of the morning, and dwell in the uttermost parts of the sea, duty performed, or duty violated, is still with us, for our happiness or our misery. If we say the darkness shall cover us, in the darkness as

in the light our obligations are yet with us. We cannot escape their power, nor fly from their presence. They are with us in this life, will be with us at its close; and, in that scene of inconceivable solemnity, which lies yet farther onward, we shall still find ourselves surrounded by the consciousness of duty, to pain us whenever it has been violated, and to console us so far as God may have given us grace to perform it.

> **Daniel Webster,** Summation in murder trial of John Francis Knapp, 3 Aug. 1830, in *Writings and Speeches of Daniel Webster* 11:105 (J. W. McIntyre ed. 1903)

6 Had I interfered in the manner, which I admit, and which I admit has been fairly proved . . . had I so interfered in behalf of any of the rich, the powerful, the intelligent, the so-called great . . . and suffered and sacrificed what I have in this interference, it would have been all right, and every man in this court would have deemed it an act worthy of reward rather than punishment.

> **John Brown,** Speech at trial for treason and insurrection, Charlestown, Va., 1859, in *American State Trials* 6:801 (John D. Lawson ed. 1916)

7 I see a book kissed, which I suppose to be the Bible, or at least the New Testament, which teaches me that all things whatsoever I would that men should do to me, I should do even so to them. It teaches me further to remember them that are in bonds, as bound with them. I endeavored to act up to that instruction. I say I am yet too young to understand that God is any respecter of persons. I believe that to have interfered as I have done, as I have always freely admitted I have done in behalf of His despised poor, is no wrong, but right. Now, if it is deemed necessary that I should forfeit my life for the furtherance of the ends of justice, and mingle my blood further with the blood of my children and with the blood of millions in this slave country whose rights are disregarded by wicked, cruel, and unjust enactments, I say let it be done.

> **John Brown,** Speech at trial for treason and insurrection, Charlestown, Va., 1859, in *American State Trials* 6:801 (John D. Lawson ed. 1916)

8 [Responding to the question, in cross-examination, "The labor of two days is that

for which you ask two hundred guineas?":]
No. I ask it for the knowledge I have
gained in the work of a lifetime.

> **James McNeill Whistler,** Testimony in
> *Whistler v. Ruskin* libel trial, 1878, quoted in
> Linda Merrill, *A Pot of Paint* 148 (1992)

9 I have been accused of having obstructed
the war. I admit it. Gentlemen, I abhor war.
I would oppose the war if I stood alone.

> **Eugene V. Debs,** Speech before the jury at
> Federal Court, Cleveland, Sept. 1918, in
> *Speeches of Eugene V. Debs* 58, 59 (1928)

10 When great changes occur in history, when
great principles are involved, as a rule the
majority are wrong. The minority are right.

> **Eugene V. Debs,** Speech before jury at
> Federal Court, Cleveland, 12 Sept. 1918, in
> *Speeches of Eugene V. Debs* 65, 66 (1928)

11 Your Honor, years ago I recognized my
kinship with all living beings, and I made
up my mind that I was not one bit better
than the meanest of earth. I said then, I say
now, that while there is a lower class, I am
in it; while there is a criminal element, I
am of it; while there is a soul in prison, I
am not free.

> **Eugene V. Debs,** Speech at trial, Cleveland,
> 14 Sept. 1918, in *Liberator,* Nov. 1918, at 12

12 [Rejecting appeal for order delaying the execution of Sacco and Vanzetti:] The relation of the United States and the Courts of
the United States to the States and the
Courts of the States is a very delicate matter that has occupied the thoughts of
statesmen and judges for a hundred years
and can not be disposed of by a summary
statement that justice requires me to cut
red tape and to intervene.

> **Oliver Wendell Holmes, Jr.,** Memorandum,
> 20 Aug. 1927, in *The Sacco-Vanzetti Case,*
> *Transcript of the Record* 5:5516, 5516 (1927)

13 Sacco is a heart, a faith, a character, a man;
a man lover of nature and of mankind. A
man who gave all, who sacrifice all to the
cause of Liberty and to his love for mankind; money, rest, mundain ambitions, his
own wife, his children, himself and his own
life. . . .

Oh, yes, I may be more witfull, as some
have put it, I am a better babbler than he
is, but many, many times in hearing his
heartful voice ringing a faith sublime, in

considering his supreme sacrifice, remembering his heroism I felt small small at the
presence of his greatness and found myself
compelled to fight back from my eyes the
tears, and quanch my heart trobling to my
throat to not weep before him—this man
called thief and assasin and doomed. But
Sacco's name will live in the hearts of the
people and in their gratitude when Katz-
mann's and yours bones will be dispersed
by time, when your name, his [Katz-
mann's] name, your laws, institutions, and
your false god are but a *deem rememoring
of a cursed past in which man was wolf to
the man.*

> **Bartolomeo Vanzetti,** Speech to the court, 9
> Apr. 1927, in *The Letters of Sacco and
> Vanzetti* 379–80 (Marion Denman
> Frankfurter & Gardner Jackson eds. 1928)

14 If it had not been for these thing, I might
have live out my life talking at street corners to scorning men. I might have die, un-
marked, unknown, a failure. Now we are
not a failure. This is our career and our
triumph. Never in our full life could we
hope to do such work for tolerance, for
joostice, for man's onderstanding of man
as now we do by accident.

Our words—our lives—our pains—nothing! The taking of our lives—lives of a good
shoemaker and a poor fish-peddler—all!
That last moment belongs to us—that
agony is our triumph.

> **Bartolomeo Vanzetti,** Statement after being
> sentenced, 9 Apr. 1927, in *Letters of Sacco
> and Vanzetti* Preface (Marion Denman
> Frankfurter & Gardner Jackson eds. 1928)

15   No one can say
That the trial was not fair. The trial was
    fair,
Painfully fair by every rule of law,
And that it was made not the slightest
    difference.
The law's our yardstick, and it measures
    well
Or well enough when there are yards to
    measure.
Measure a wave with it, measure a fire,
Cut sorrow up in inches, weigh content.
You can weigh John Brown's body well
    enough,
But how and in what balance weigh John
    Brown?

> **Stephen Vincent Benét,** *John Brown's Body*
> 55 (1931)

16 The voice ceased. There was a deep, brief
　　pause.
　The judge pronounced the formal words
　　of death.
　One man, a stranger, tried to clap his
　　hands.
　The foolish sound was stopped.
　There was nothing but silence then.
　　　　　　　No cries in the court,
　No roar, no slightest murmur from the
　　thronged street,
　As Brown went back to jail between his
　　guards.
　The heavy door shut behind them.
　There was a noise of chairs scraped back
　　in the court-room,
　And that huge sigh of a crowd turning
　　back into men.

　　Stephen Vincent Benét, *John Brown's Body*
　　58 (1931)

17 . . . Justice once rendered
　in a clear burst of anger, righteously,
　upon a very common laborer,
　confessed an anarchist, the verdict found
　and the precise machinery of law
　invoked to know him guilty—think what
　　furor
　would rock the state if the court then
　　flatly said;
　all this was lies—must be reversed? It's
　　better,
　as any judge can tell you, in such cases,
　holding the common good to be worth
　　more
　than small injustice, to let the record
　　stand,
　let one man die.

　　Maxwell Anderson, *Winterset* 98–99 (1935)

18 We are innocent, as we have proclaimed
　and maintained from the time of our ar-
　rest. This is the whole truth. To forsake this
　truth is to pay too high a price even for the
　priceless gift of life—for life thus pur-
　chased we could not live out in dignity and
　self-respect.

　　Ethel Rosenberg and Julius Rosenberg,
　　Petition for executive clemency, 9 Jan. 1953,
　　in *Death House Letters of Ethel and Julius
　　Rosenberg* 149 (1953)

19 Suffice it to say that my husband and I
　shall die innocent before we lower our-
　selves to live guilty! And nobody, not even
　you, whom we continue to love as our own
　true brother, can dictate terms to the Ro-

senbergs, who follow only the dictates of
heart and soul, truth and conscience, and
the God-blessed love we bear our fellows!

　　Ethel Rosenberg, Letter to Emanuel H.
　　Bloch, 30 Jan. 1953, in *Death House Letters
　　of Ethel and Julius Rosenberg* 128, 129 (1953)

20 Ethel wants it made known that we are the
　first victims of American Fascism.

　　Ethel Rosenberg and Julius Rosenberg,
　　Letter to Emanuel Bloch, 19 June 1953, in
　　The Testament of Ethel and Julius Rosenberg
　　187 (2d ed. 1954)

21 Their [Sacco and Vanzetti's] fervor and
　human feelings gave the glow of life to the
　weary stock phrases of those writing about
　them, and we do know now, all of us, that
　the most appalling cruelties are committed
　by apparently virtuous governments in ex-
　pectation of a great good to come, never
　learning that the evil done now is the sure
　destroyer of the expected good. Yet, no
　matter what, it was a terrible miscarriage
　of justice; it was a most reprehensible
　abuse of legal power, in their attempt to
　prove that the law is something to be in-
　flicted—not enforced—and that it is above
　the judgment of the people.

　　Katherine Anne Porter, *The Never-Ending
　　Wrong* 57 (1977)

TRUSTS

See also ANTITRUST

1 And besides, what right has the State, or
　those called upon to administer a charity,
　to dictate conditions to its founder? Those
　conditions may seem to us foolish fancies;
　we may deem ourselves far more compe-
　tent to establish such as will secure the
　general object, but it is not ours to say.
　When we see fit to create such a foundation
　out of our own fortunes, we shall be at per-
　fect liberty to show our wisdom, but it is
　out of place in administering the fortunes
　of others. . . . One may do what he will with
　his own.

　　Philemon Bliss, *State v. Adams,* 44 Mo. 570,
　　581–82 (1869)

2 There is a strong and increasing feeling . . .
　that a main object of law is not to secure
　liberty of contract, but to restrain it, in the
　interest, or supposed interest, of the
　weaker, or supposed weaker, against the

stronger, or supposed stronger, portion of the community. Hence, for instance, laws enacted or contemplated for eight hours' labor, for weekly payments of wages by corporations, for "compulsory arbitration," &c., that is, laws intended to take away from certain classes of the community, for their supposed good, their liberty of action and their power of contract; in other words, attempts to bring society back to an organization founded on status and not upon contract. To a frame of mind and a state of public sentiment like this, spendthrift trusts are most congenial. If we are all to be cared for, and have our wants supplied, without regard to our mental and moral failings, in the socialistic Utopia, there is little reason why in the mean time, while waiting for that day, a father should not do for his son what the State is then to do for us all.

John Chipman Gray, *Restraints on the Alienation of Property* ix (2d ed. 1895)

3 A deposit by one person of his own money, in his own name as trustee for another, standing alone, does not establish an irrevocable trust during the lifetime of the depositor. It is a tentative trust merely, revocable at will, until the depositor dies or completes the gift in his lifetime by some unequivocal act or declaration, such as delivery of the pass book or notice to the beneficiary. In case the depositor dies before the beneficiary without revocation, or some decisive act or declaration of disaffirmance, the presumption arises that an absolute trust was created as to the balance on hand at the death of the depositor.

Irving G. Vann, *In re Totten*, 179 N.Y. 112, 125–26, 71 N.E. 748 (1904)

4 A constructive trust is the formula through which the conscience of equity finds expression. When property has been acquired in such circumstances that the holder of the legal title may not in good conscience retain the beneficial interest, equity converts him into a trustee.

Benjamin N. Cardozo, *Beatty v. Guggenheim Exploration Co.*, 225 N.Y. 380, 386, 122 N.E. 378 (1919)

5 Joint adventurers, like copartners, owe to one another, while the enterprise continues, the duty of the finest loyalty. Many forms of conduct permissible in a worka-

day world for those acting at arm's length, are forbidden to those bound by fiduciary ties. A trustee is held to something stricter than the morals of the market place. Not honesty alone, but the punctilio of an honor the most sensitive, is then the standard of behavior. As to this there has developed a tradition that is unbending and inveterate. Uncompromising rigidity has been the attitude of courts of equity when petitioned to undermine the rule of undivided loyalty by the "disintegrating erosion" of particular exceptions. . . . Only thus has the level of conduct for fiduciaries been kept at a level higher than that trodden by the crowd. It will not consciously be lowered by any judgment of this court.

Benjamin N. Cardozo, *Meinhard v. Salmon*, 249 N.Y. 458, 463–64, 164 N.E. 545 (1928)

6 To say that a man is a fiduciary only begins analysis; it gives direction to further inquiry. To whom is he a fiduciary? What obligations does he owe as a fiduciary?

Felix Frankfurter, *SEC v. Chenery Corp.*, 318 U.S. 80, 85–86 (1943)

TRUTH

See CROSS-EXAMINATION; EVIDENCE; PROOF; WITNESSES

UNCONSTITUTIONALITY

See CONSTITUTIONAL LAW; DUE PROCESS; JUDICIAL LEGISLATION; JUDICIAL REVIEW; STATUTORY CONSTRUCTION

UNIONS

See LABOR LAW

VOTING

1 I would not have the first wish, the momentary impulse of the public mind, become law. For it is not always the sense of the people, with whom, I admit, that all power resides. On great questions, we first hear the loud clamors of passion, artifice, and faction. I consider biennial elections as a security that the sober, second thought of the people shall be law.

Fisher Ames, Speech in Massachusetts Convention, Jan. 1788, in *Works of Fisher Ames* 2:1, 7 (Seth Ames ed. 1854)

2 Many state elections have been determined by a majority or plurality of fewer votes than that of the canvassed majority in the several precincts here involved. . . . It is sufficient to cause every liberty-loving American citizen to shudder in contemplation of the possibility that the private "industrial necessity" of some industrial company or corporation, employing large numbers of men, may thus determine the policies, or the fate of the republic. The result of the present contest is but infinitesimal as compared with that to which it might lead. . . . The links in the chains of tyranny are usually forged, singly and silently, and sometimes unconsciously, by those who are destined to wear them.

Tully Scott, *Neeley v. Farr*, 61 Colo. 485, 519, 158 P. 458 (1916)

3 New York, the state that is always telling the others about progress, this is written two weeks after election and their returns havent come in yet. All the primitive States were in by nine o'clock election night. They sent one hundred lawyers up state to see about the counting of the votes. Can you imagine 100 lawyers? Why two lawyers can make a scandal out of anything they have anything to do with. 100 will bring a revolution.

Will Rogers, "Shades of Jeff Davis," 18 Nov. 1928, in *Will Rogers' Weekly Articles* 3:221, 223 (James M. Smallwood ed. 1981)

4 Equality of representation in the legislative bodies of the state is a right preservative of all other rights. The source of the laws that govern the daily lives of the people, the control of the public purse from which the money of the taxpayer is distributed, and the power to make and measure the levy of taxes, are so essential, all-inclusive, and vital that the consent of the governed ought to be obtained through representatives chosen at equal, free and fair elections. If the principle of equality is denied, the spirit, purpose, and the very terms of the Constitution are emasculated. The failure to give a county or a district equal representation is not merely a matter of partisan strategy. It rises above any question of party, and reaches the very vitals of democracy itself.

Simeon S. Willis, *Stiglitz v. Schardien*, 239 Ky. 799, 811–12, 40 S.W.2d 315 (1931)

5 [The Fifteenth Amendment] nullifies sophisticated as well as simple-minded modes of discrimination. It hits onerous procedural requirements which effectively handicap exercise of the franchise by the colored race although the abstract right to vote may remain unrestricted as to race.

Felix Frankfurter, *Lane v. Wilson*, 307 U.S. 268, 275 (1939)

6 It may now be taken as a postulate that the right to vote in such a primary for the nomination of candidates without discrimination by the State, like the right to vote in a general election, is a right secured by the Constitution. . . . By the terms of the Fifteenth Amendment that right may not be abridged by any State on account of race. Under our Constitution the great privilege of the ballot may not be denied a man by the State because of his color.

Stanley F. Reed, *Smith v. Allwright*, 321 U.S. 649, 661 (1944)

7 Courts ought not to enter this political thicket.

Felix Frankfurter, *Colegrove v. Green*, 328 U.S. 549, 556 (1946)

8 While in form this is merely an act redefining metes and bounds . . . the inescapable human effect of this essay in geometry and geography is to despoil colored citizens, and only colored citizens, of their theretofore enjoyed voting rights.

Felix Frankfurter, *Gomillion v. Lightfoot*, 364 U.S. 339, 347 (1960)

9 The mere fact that the suit seeks protection of a political right does not mean it presents a political question. . . . The right asserted is within the reach of judicial protection under the Fourteenth Amendment.

William J. Brennan, Jr., *Baker v. Carr*, 369 U.S. 186, 209, 237 (1962)

10 In a democratic society like ours, relief must come through an aroused popular conscience that sears the conscience of the people's representatives.

Felix Frankfurter, *Baker v. Carr*, 369 U.S. 186, 270 (1962) (dissenting)

11 The conception of political equality from the Declaration of Independence, to Lincoln's Gettysburg Address, to the Fifteenth, Seventeenth, and Nineteenth Amendments

can mean only one thing—one person, one vote.*

> William O. Douglas, *Gray v. Sanders*, 372 U.S. 368, 381 (1963)

12 No right is more precious in a free country than that of having a voice in the election of those who make the laws under which, as good citizens, we must live. Other rights, even the most basic, are illusory if the right to vote is undermined.

> Hugo L. Black, *Wesberry v. Sanders*, 376 U.S. 1, 17 (1964)

13 The fact that Negro political leaders find advantage in this nearly solid Negro and Puerto Rican district is irrelevant. . . . Rotten boroughs were long a curse of democratic processes. Racial boroughs are also at war with democratic standards. . . . government has no business designing electoral districts along racial or religious lines.

> William O. Douglas, *Wright v. Rockefeller*, 376 U.S. 52, 62, 66 (1964)

14 The right to vote freely for the candidate of one's choice is of the essence of a democratic society, and any restrictions on that right strike at the heart of representative government. And the right of suffrage can be denied by a debasement or dilution of the weight of a citizen's vote just as effectively as by wholly prohibiting the free exercise of the franchise.

> Earl Warren, *Reynolds v. Sims*, 377 U.S. 533, 555 (1964)

15 Legislators represent people, not trees or acres. Legislators are elected by voters, not farms or cities or economic interests.

> Earl Warren, *Reynolds v. Sims*, 377 U.S. 533, 562 (1964)

16 As long as ours is a representative form of government, and our legislatures are those instruments of government elected directly by and directly representative of the people, the right to elect legislators in a free and unimpaired fashion is a bedrock of our political system.

> Earl Warren, *Reynolds v. Sims*, 377 U.S. 533, 562 (1964)

---

* One man shall have one vote. —**John Cartwright**, *People's Barrier Against Undue Influence and Corruption* 5 (1780)

WAR

See also MILITARY JUSTICE; WAR CRIMES

1 In war, in some sense, lies the very genius of law. . . . What is human warfare but just this,—an effort to make the laws of God and nature take sides with one party. Men make an arbitrary code, and, because it is not right, they try to make it prevail by might. The moral law does not want any champion. Its asserters do not go to war. It was never infringed with impunity. It is inconsistent to decry war and maintain law, for if there were no need of war there would be no need of law.

> Henry David Thoreau, Journal, 16 Mar. 1842, in *Journal of Henry D. Thoreau* 1:102 (Bradford Torrey & Francis H. Allen eds. 1962)

2 If I be wrong on this question of constitutional power, my error lies in believing that certain proceedings are constitutional when, in cases of rebellion or Invasion, the public Safety requires them, which would not be constitutional when, in the absence of rebellion or invasion, the public Safety does not require them—in other words, that the constitution is not in it's [*sic*] application in all respects the same, in cases of Rebellion or invasion, involving the public Safety, as it is in times of profound peace and public security. The constitution itself makes the distinction.

> Abraham Lincoln, Letter to Erastus Corning and others, 12 June 1863, in *Collected Works of Abraham Lincoln* 6:267 (Roy P. Basler ed. 1953)

3 The constitution is different, *in its application* in cases of Rebellion or Invasion, involving the Public Safety, from what it is in times of profound peace and public security; and this opinion I adhere to, simply because, by the constitution itself, things may be done in the one case which may not be done in the other.

> Abraham Lincoln, Letter to Matthew Birchard and others, 29 June 1863, in *Collected Works of Abraham Lincoln* 6:302 (Roy P. Basler ed. 1953)

4 I have found that men who have not even been suspected of disloyalty, are very averse to taking an oath of any sort as a

condition, to exercising an ordinary right of citizenship.

Abraham Lincoln, Letter to William S. Rosecrans, 4 Apr. 1864, in *Collected Works of Abraham Lincoln* 7:284 (Roy P. Basler ed. 1953)

5 Scarcely a day passes in a modern campaign that does not give the lie to the rules laid down in the ponderous tomes of the international law-writers. It is said that Gustavus Adolphus always had with him in camp a copy of "Grotius," as Alexander is said to have slept over Homer. The improbability of finding a copy of "Grotius" in a modern camp may be taken as an illustration of the neglect that has long since fallen on the restraints with which our publicists have sought to fetter our generals, and of the futility of all such endeavors.

James A. Farrer, *Military Manners and Customs* 22–23 (1885)

6 Absolute good faith with the enemy must be observed as a rule of conduct. Without it war will degenerate into excesses and violences, ending only in the total destruction of one or both of the belligerents.

United States War Department, *Rules of Land Warfare* 60 (1914)

7 There is an old saying that the laws are silent in the presence of war. Alas, yes; not only the civil laws of individual nations but also apparently the law that governs the relation of nations with one another must at times fall silent and look on in dumb impotency.

Woodrow Wilson, Speech, Chicago, 31 Jan. 1916, in *President Wilson's State Papers and Addresses* 181, 182 (Albert Shaw ed. 1917)

8 The Constitution was built for rough as well as smooth roads. In time of war the nation simply changes gears and takes the harder going under the same power.

Harold H. Burton, *Duncan v. Kahanamoku,* 327 U.S. 304, 342 (1946) (dissenting)

9 No one will question that this power [the war power] is the most dangerous one to free government in the whole catalogue of powers. It usually is involved in haste and excitement when calm legislative consideration of constitutional limitation is difficult. It is executed in a time of patriotic fervor that makes moderation unpopular.

And, worst of all, it is interpreted by judges under the influence of the same passions and pressures.

Robert H. Jackson, *Woods v. Miller Co.,* 333 U.S. 138, 146 (1948) (concurring)

WAR CRIMES

See also MILITARY JUSTICE; WAR

1 The privilege of opening the first trial in history for crimes against the peace of the world imposes a grave responsibility. The wrongs which we seek to condemn and punish have been so calculated, so malignant and so devastating, that civilisation cannot tolerate their being ignored, because it cannot survive their being repeated. That four great nations, flushed with victory and stung with injury, stay the hands of vengeance and voluntarily submit their captive enemies to the judgment of the law, is one of the most significant tributes that Power ever has paid to Reason.

Robert H. Jackson, Opening statement for the prosecution before International Military Tribunal, Nuremberg, Germany, 21 Nov. 1945, in *Trial of German Major War Criminals,* Part I, at 49, 49 (1946)

2 The common sense of mankind demands that law shall not stop with the punishment of petty crimes by little people. It must also reach men who possess themselves of great power and make deliberate and concerted use of it to set in motion evils which leave no home in the world untouched.

Robert H. Jackson, Opening statement for the prosecution before International Military Tribunal, Nuremberg, Germany, 21 Nov. 1945, in *Trial of German Major War Criminals,* Part I, at 49, 49 (1946)

3 We must never forget that the record on which we judge these defendants to-day is the record on which history will judge us to-morrow. To pass these defendants a poisoned chalice is to put it to our lips as well. We must summon such detachment and intellectual integrity to our task that this trial will commend itself to posterity as fulfilling humanity's aspirations to do justice.

Robert H. Jackson, Opening statement for the prosecution before International Military Tribunal, Nuremberg, Germany, 21 Nov. 1945, in *Trial of German Major War Criminals,* Part I, at 49, 51 (1946)

4 The idea that a State, any more than a corporation, commits crimes, is a fiction. Crimes always are committed only by persons.

> Robert H. Jackson, Opening statement for the prosecution before International Military Tribunal, Nuremberg, Germany, 21 Nov. 1945, in *Trial of German Major War Criminals*, Part I, at 49, 83 (1946)

5 But the ultimate step in avoiding periodic wars, which are inevitable in a system of international lawlessness, is to make statesmen responsible to law. And let me make clear that while this law is first applied against German aggressors, the law includes, and if it is to serve a useful purpose it must condemn, aggression by any other nations, including those which sit here now in judgment. We are able to do away with domestic tyranny and violence and aggression by those in power against the rights of their own people only when we make all men answerable to the law. This trial represents mankind's desperate effort to apply the discipline of the law to statesmen who have used their powers of state to attack the foundations of the world's peace, and to commit aggressions against the rights of their neighbors.

> Robert H. Jackson, Opening statement for the prosecution before International Military Tribunal, Nuremberg, Germany, 21 Nov. 1945, in *Trial of German Major War Criminals*, Part I, at 49, 85 (1946)

6 The real complaining party at your bar is Civilisation. In all our countries it is still a struggling and imperfect thing. It does not plead that the United States, or any other country, has been blameless of the conditions which made the German people easy victims to the blandishments and intimidations of the Nazi conspirators.

But it points to the dreadful sequence of aggressions and crimes I have recited, it points to the weariness of flesh, the exhaustion of resources, and the destruction of all that was beautiful or useful in so much of the world, and to greater potentialities for destruction in the days to come. It is not necessary among the ruins of this ancient and beautiful city with untold members of its civilian inhabitants still buried in its rubble, to argue the proposition that to start or wage an aggressive war has the moral qualities of the worst of crimes. The refuge of the defendants can be only their hope that International Law will lag so far behind the moral sense of mankind that conduct which is crime in the moral sense must be regarded as innocent in law.

> Robert H. Jackson, Opening statement for the prosecution before International Military Tribunal, Nuremberg, Germany, 21 Nov. 1945, in *Trial of German Major War Criminals*, Part I, at 49, 86 (1946)

7 Civilisation asks whether law is so laggard as to be utterly helpless to deal with crimes of this magnitude by criminals of this order of importance. It does not expect that you can make war impossible. It does expect that your juridical action will put the forces of International Law, its prospects, its prohibitions and most of all, its sanctions, on the side of peace, so that men and women of good will, in all countries, may have "leave to live by no man's leave, underneath the law."*

> Robert H. Jackson, Opening statement for the prosecution before International Military Tribunal, Nuremberg, Germany, 21 Nov. 1945, in *Trial of German Major War Criminals*, Part I, at 49, 86 (1946)

8 If you were to say of these men that they are not guilty, it would be as true to say there has been no war, there are no slain, there has been no crime.

> Robert H. Jackson, Concluding speech for the prosecution before International Military Tribunal, Nuremberg, Germany, 26 July 1946, in *Trial of German Major War Criminals*, Part 19, at 382, 406 (1948)

9 By the Agreement and this trial we have put International Law squarely on the side of peace as against aggressive warfare, and on the side of humanity as against persecution. In the present depressing world outlook it is possible that the Nurnberg trial may constitute the most important moral advance to grow out of this war.

> Robert H. Jackson, Report to the President, 7 Oct. 1946, in *International Conference on Military Trials* 432, 439 (1949)

---

* Ancient Right unnoticed as the breath we draw—/ Leave to live by no man's leave, underneath the Law. —Rudyard Kipling, "The Old Issue," 1899, in *The Five Nations* 104, 105 (1903)

10 The fact that the law of war has been violated pursuant to an order of a superior authority, whether military or civil, does not deprive the act in question of its character of a war crime, nor does it constitute a defense in the trial of an accused individual, unless he did not know and could not reasonably have been expected to know that the act ordered was unlawful.

United States Army, *The Law of Land Warfare* 182 (1956)

11 "Herr Rolfe further asserts that the defendant Janning was an extraordinary jurist who was acting in what he thought to be the best interests of his country."

Haywood paused.

"There is truth in this, also. Janning, to be sure, is a tragic character. We believe he loathed the evil he did."

. . . "But compassion for the present torture of his soul must not beget forgetfulness of the torture and death of millions by the government of which he was a part."

He looked over at Janning and spoke quietly.

"They can never be forgotten. Because to forget them would be to say there has been no war; there are no slain; there has been no crime."

. . . "Janning's record and his fate," continued Haywood, "illuminate the most shattering truth that has emerged from this trial. If he and the other defendants were all degraded perverts—if all the leaders of the Third Reich were sadistic monsters and maniacs—these events would have no more moral significance than an earthquake or other natural catastrophes. But this trial has shown that under the stress of a national crisis, ordinary men—even able and extraordinary men—can delude themselves into the commission of crimes and atrocities so vast and heinous that they beggar the imagination."

Abby Mann, *Judgment at Nuremberg* 129–30 (1961)

WEALTH AND POVERTY

See also FEES

1 To such a height th' Expence of COURTS is gone,

That poor Men are redress'd—*till they're undone.*

Benjamin Franklin, *Poor Richard's Almanack,* 1734, in *Papers of Benjamin Franklin* 1:359 (Leonard W. Labaree ed. 1959)

2 The son of Natty, or the son of nobody, I hope the young man is not going to let the matter drop. This is a country of laws; and I should like to see it fairly tried, whether a man who owns, or says he owns, a hundred thousand acres of land, has any more right to shoot a body, than another. What do you think of it, Dr. Todd?

James Fenimore Cooper, *The Pioneers,* 1823, in *Writings of James Fenimore Cooper* 151 (James F. Beard ed. 1980)

3 In the full enjoyment of the gifts of Heaven and the fruits of superior industry, economy, and virtue, every man is equally entitled to protection by law; but when the laws undertake to add to these natural and just advantages artificial distinctions, to grant titles, gratuities, and exclusive privileges, to make the rich richer and the potent more powerful, the humble members of society—the farmers, mechanics, and laborers—who have neither the time nor the means of securing like favors to themselves, have a right to complain of the injustice of their Government.

Andrew Jackson, Veto of Bank Bill, 10 July 1832, in *Messages and Papers of the Presidents* 2:576, 590 (James D. Richardson ed. 1898)

4 People say law, but they mean wealth.

Ralph Waldo Emerson, Journal, 9 Oct. 1841, in *Journals of Ralph Waldo Emerson* 6:86 (Edward W. Emerson ed. 1911)

5 [Responding to a statement that "laws should be considerate of the poor":] Not more so than of the rich. The laws should be equal and just; and the poor are the last people who ought to wish them otherwise, since they are certain to be the losers when any other principle governs. . . . No class suffers so much by a departure from the rule, as the rich have a thousand other means of attaining their ends, when the way is left clear to them, by setting up any other master than the right.

James Fenimore Cooper, *The Chainbearer,* 1845, in *Complete Works of J. Fenimore Cooper* 27:94–95 (1893)

6 Nine tenths of you are in jail because you did not have a good lawyer and, of course, you did not have a good lawyer because you did not have enough money to pay a good lawyer.

Clarence S. Darrow, Address to prisoners in Cook County Jail, 1902, in *Attorney for the Damned* 3, 7 (Arthur Weinberg ed. 1957)

7 Fine—A bribe paid by a rich man to escape the lawful penalty of his crime. In China such bribes are paid to the judge personally; in America they are paid to him as agent for the public. But it makes no difference to the men who pay them—nor to the men who can't pay them.

H. L. Mencken, "Sententiae," 1916, in *A Mencken Chrestomathy* 616, 623 (1949)

8 Don't I think a poor man has a chanst in coort? Iv coorse he has. He has th' same chanst there that he has outside. He has a splendid, poor man's chanst.

Finley Peter Dunne, "On the Recall of Judges," in *Mr. Dooley on the Choice of Law* 168, 173 (Edward J. Bander ed. 1963)

9 The Law not only can be bought . . . but most of the time it *has* to be bought. And since it has to be bought, its results tend to favor those who can afford to buy it.

Fred Rodell, *Woe Unto You, Lawyers!* 226 (1939)

10 The Law is bought . . . by hiring the services and the advice of the smartest lawyers, of the professional soothsayers who are most adept at manipulating the principles of which The Law is made. It is bought by paying a premium, in court and out of court, to the twentieth century medicine men who can best cast spells of legal language to protect and defend personal and financial interests of those who would be hard put to protect and defend such interests in terms of justice, undiluted by Law.

Fred Rodell, *Woe Unto You, Lawyers!* 228 (1939)

11 Poverty or wealth will make all the differences in securing the substance or only the shadow of constitutional protections.

Wiley B. Rutledge, *Foster v. Illinois,* 332 U.S. 134, 142 (1947) (dissenting)

12 The best lawyer in the world cannot competently defend an accused person if the lawyer cannot obtain existing evidence crucial to the defense, e.g., if the defendant cannot pay the fee of an investigator to find a pivotal missing witness or a necessary document, or that of an expert accountant or mining engineer or chemist. . . . In such circumstances, if the government does not supply the funds, justice is denied the poor—and represents but an upper-bracket privilege.

Jerome N. Frank, *United States v. Johnson,* 238 F.2d 565, 572 (2d Cir. 1956) (dissenting)

13 The indigent, where the record is unclear or the errors are hidden, has only the right to a meaningless ritual, while the rich man has a meaningful appeal.

William O. Douglas, *Douglas v. California,* 372 U.S. 353, 358 (1963)

14 A man's respect for law and order exists in precise relationship to the size of his paycheck.

Adam Clayton Powell, Jr., *Keep the Faith, Baby!* 17 (1967)

15 Where money determines not merely "the kind of trial a man gets," . . . but whether he gets into court at all, the great principle of equal protection becomes a mockery.

William J. Brennan, Jr., *Boddie v. Connecticut,* 401 U.S. 371, 389 (1971) (concurring in part)
See also EQUAL PROTECTION 13

16 [Lawyer to potential client:] You have a pretty good case, Mr. Pitkin. How much justice can you afford?

J. B. Handelsman, Cartoon caption, *New Yorker,* 24 Dec. 1973, at 52

17 At least where wealth is involved, the Equal Protection Clause does not require absolute equality or precisely equal advantages.

Lewis F. Powell, Jr., *San Antonio Indep. School Dist. v. Rodriguez,* 411 U.S. 1, 24 (1973)

18 Of course there's a different law for the rich and the poor; otherwise, who would go into business?

E. Ralph Stewart, quoted in Laurence J. Peter, *Peter's Quotations* 287 (1977)

19 Poor people have access to American courts in the same sense that the Christians

had access to the lions when they were dragged into a Roman arena.

> **Earl Johnson, Jr.**, quoted in Benjamin M. Becker and David L. Gibberman, *On Trial!* 17 (1987)

20 Lawyer, your briefcase is snappy with papers.
Whose justice do you argue? Money's? Is that it?
Money, money, money—
I hear the lawyer and his clients praying.

> **Donald Hall**, "The Grown-Ups," in *Old and New Poems* 55, 55 (1990)

WIFE

See MARRIAGE

WILLS

See also WILLS, FAMOUS

1 Man with all his wisdom, *toils for heirs he knows not who.*

> **Andrew Kirkpatrick**, *Nevison v. Taylor*, 8 N.J.L. 43, 46 (1824)

2 God bless you, Gentlemen! Learn to give Money to colleges while you live.
Don't be silly and think you'll try
To bother the colleges, when you die,
With codicil this, and codicil that,
That Knowledge may starve while Law grows fat?
For there never was pitcher that wouldn't spill,
And there's always a flaw in a donkey's will!

> **Oliver Wendell Holmes, Sr.**, "Parson Turell's Legacy," 1858, in *Works of Oliver Wendell Holmes* 1:297, 301 (1892)

3 You cannot live without the lawyers, and certainly you cannot die without them.

> **Joseph H. Choate**, "The Bench and the Bar" (speech), New York, 13 May 1879, in *Arguments and Addresses of Joseph Hodges Choate* 1060, 1061 (Frederick C. Hicks ed. 1926)

4 Whether a remainder is vested or contingent depends upon the language employed. If the conditional element is incorporated into the description of, or the gift to, the remainder-man, then the remainder is contingent; but if, after words giving a vested interest, a clause is added divesting it, the remainder is vested. Thus, on a devise to A. for life, remainder to his children, but if any child dies in the lifetime of A. his share to go to those who survive, the share of each child is vested, subject to be divested by his death. But on a devise to A. for life, remainder to such of his children as survive him, the remainder is contingent.

> **John Chipman Gray**, *The Rule Against Perpetuities* 66 (1886)

5 The true form of the Rule against Perpetuities is believed to be this:—NO INTEREST SUBJECT TO A CONDITION PRECEDENT IS GOOD, UNLESS THE CONDITION MUST BE FULFILLED, IF AT ALL, WITHIN TWENTY-ONE YEARS AFTER SOME LIFE IN BEING AT THE CREATION OF THE INTEREST.

> **John Chipman Gray**, *The Rule Against Perpetuities* 144 (1886)

6 If you wait till you are dead . . . you get credit for the *intention*, and the lawyers get the money. The stomachs of the lawyers of this land are distended to utter discomfort with the eleemosynary architecture that they have swallowed. In all this world there is no joy like to the joy a lawyer feels when he sees a good-hearted inconsiderate person erecting a free library or a town hall or a hospital in his will. He smiles the smile that only he knows how to smile, and goes into training for the anaconda act.

> **Mark Twain**, Speech, Fairhaven, Mass., 22 Feb. 1894, in *Mark Twain Speaking* 271–72 (Paul Fatout ed. 1976)

7 A Man died leaving a large estate and many sorrowful relations who claimed it. After some years, when all but one had had judgment given against them, that one was awarded the estate, which he asked his Attorney to have appraised.
"There is nothing to appraise," said the Attorney, pocketing his last fee.
"Then," said the Successful Claimant, "what good has all this litigation done me?"
"You have been a good client to me," the Attorney replied, gathering up his books and papers, "but I must say you betray a surprising ignorance of the purpose of litigation."

> **Ambrose Bierce**, *Fantastic Fables*, in *Collected Works of Ambrose Bierce* 6:234 (1911)

8 Doubtless the contesting of wills is a nuisance, generally speaking, the contestant devoid of moral worth and the verdict unrighteous; but as long as some testators really *are* daft, or subject to interested suasion, or wantonly sinful, all should be denied the power to stifle dissent by fining the luckless dissenter. The dead have too much to say in this world, at the best, and it is tyranny for them to stand at the door of the temple of justice to drive away the suitors that themselves have made.

> Ambrose Bierce, "Some Features of the Law," in *Collected Works of Ambrose Bierce* 11:99, 122 (1912)

9 BEQUEATH, *v.t.* To generously give to another that which can no longer be denied to *somebody.*

> Ambrose Bierce, *The Enlarged Devil's Dictionary* 27 (Ernest J. Hopkins ed. 1967)

10 NO INTEREST IS GOOD UNLESS IT MUST VEST, IF AT ALL, NOT LATER THAN TWENTY-ONE YEARS AFTER SOME LIFE IN BEING AT THE CREATION OF THE INTEREST.

> John Chipman Gray, *The Rule Against Perpetuities* 174 (3d ed. 1915)

11 To be injyeable a will must be at wan an' th' same time a practical joke on th' heirs an' an advertisemint iv th' man that made it.

> Finley Peter Dunne, "On Making a Will," in *On Making a Will* 3, 4 (1919)

12 If it wasn't for Wills, lawyers would have to go to work at an essential employment. There is only one way you can beat a Lawyer in a death case. That is to die with nothing. Then you can't get a Lawyer within 10 miles of your house.

> Will Rogers, "Well, All I Know Is What I Read in the Papers," 3 May 1925, in *Will Rogers' Weekly Articles* 2:34, 36 (James M. Smallwood ed. 1980)

13 The only authentic evidence which we have of the survival of life after death is the ability of the judges to read the intention of the testator long after he has been buried.

> Frederick E. Crane, "Quickening Imagination," 3 *New York State Bar Bulletin* 168 (1931)

14 Before I die, I shall leave a will, because if you want something done, sentimentality is effective.

> John Cage, "45' for a Speaker," in *Silence* 146, 188 (1939)

15 I think that I shall never see
A simple perpetuity;
A comprehensible bequest;
Devises where remainders vest;
A clause whose words are plain as day
And mean precisely what they say;
A state where Shelly doesn't care
To rise and shout, "Is 'B' an heir?"
A case where dying men refrain
From making lawyers share their pain.
If wills are made by fools like me,
Not even God can take a fee!

> "Kill Joycemer," "Forests," *Harvard Law Record*, 3 Mar. 1960, at 12

WILLS, FAMOUS

1 The King of France's Picture set with Four hundred and Eight Diamonds, I give to my Daughter Sarah Bache requesting however that she would not form any of those Diamonds into Ornaments either for herself or Daughters and thereby introduce or countenance the expensive vain and useless Fashion of wearing Jewels in this Country.

> Benjamin Franklin, Last Will and Testament, 17 July 1788, in *The Will of Benjamin Franklin* 5 (1904)

2 What is a charitable or pious gift . . . ? It is whatever is given for the love of God, or for the love of your neighbor, in the catholic and universal sense, — given from these motives, and to these ends, — free from the stain or taint of every consideration that is personal, private or selfish.

> Horace Binney, Argument, in *Arguments of Defendants' Counsel, in the Case of Vidal v. Mayor of Philadelphia* 41 (1844)

3 I enjoin and require that *no ecclesiastic, missionary, or minister of any sect whatsoever, shall ever hold or exercise any station or duty whatever in the said college; nor shall any such person ever be admitted for any purpose, or as a visiter, within the premises appropriated to the purposes of the said college.*

> Stephen Girard, Will, in *Arguments of the Defendant's Counsel, in the Case of Vidal v. Girard's Executors* 281, 298–99 (1844)

4 My will is that my sons should receive solid and useful education, and that no portion of their time be devoted to the study of abstract science. I greatly desire that they may possess a thorough knowledge of the English language, with a good knowledge of the Latin language. I request that they be instructed in the Holy Scriptures, and next to these that they be rendered thoroughly in a knowledge of geography and history. I wish my sons to be taught an entire contempt for novels and light reading, as well as for the morals and manners of those with whom they may be associated or instructed.

Sam Houston, Will, 1863, quoted in Alfred M. Williams, *Sam Houston* 376 (1893)

5 During my life, and now by my will and codicils, I have given considerable sums of money to promote public or humanitarian causes which have had my deliberate and sympathetic interest. If any of my children think excessive such gifts of mine outside of my family, I ask them to remember not only the merit of the causes and the corresponding usefulness of the gifts but also the dominating ideals of my life.

They should never forget the dangers which unfortunately attend the inheritance of large fortunes, even though the money come from the painstaking affections of a father. I beg of them to remember that such danger lies not only in the obvious temptation to enervating luxury, but in the inducement . . . to withdraw from the wholesome duty of vigorous, serious, useful work. In my opinion a life not largely dedicated to such work cannot be happy and honorable. And to such it is my earnest hope—and will be to my death—that my children shall, so far as their strength permits, be steadfastly devoted.

Joseph Pulitzer, Will, in James Wyman Barrett, *Joseph Pulitzer and His World* 295–96 (1941)

6 *Sonny* [played by Al Pacino]: Being of sound mind and body, and all that shit . . . To my darling wife Leon whom I love as no other man has loved another man in all eternity, I leave $2,700 from my $10,000 life insurance policy, to be used for your sex change operation. If there is money left over it is to go to you on the first anniversary of my death, at my grave. I expect you to be a real woman then, and your life full of happiness and joy. To my sweet wife, Heidi, five thousand from the same policy. You are the only woman I have ever loved, and I re-pledge my love to you in this sad moment, and to little Kimmy and Jimmy. I hope you remember me, Jimmy. You are the little man of the family now, and will have to look after them for me.

Frank Pierson, *Dog Day Afternoon* (screenplay), 1975, quoted in *Actor's Book of Movie Monologues* 133 (Marise Smith & Amy Schewel eds. 1986)

WIRETAPPING

See SEARCHES AND SEIZURES

WITNESSES

See also CROSS-EXAMINATION; EXPERTS

1 The trial chancellor . . . sees and hears much we cannot see and hear. We well know there are things of pith that cannot be preserved in or shown by the written page of a bill of exceptions. Truth does not always stalk boldly forth naked, but with modest withal, in a printed abstract in a court of last resort. She oft hides in nooks and crannies visible only to the mind's eye of the judge who tries the case. To him appears the furtive glance, the blush of conscious shame, the hesitation, the sincere or the flippant or sneering tone, the heat, the calmness, the yawn, the sigh, the candor or lack of it, the scant or full realization of the solemnity of an oath, the carriage and mien. The brazen face of the liar, the glibness of the schooled witness in reciting a lesson or the itching over-eagerness of the swift witness, as well as honest face of the truthful one, are alone seen by him. In short, one witness may give testimony that reads in print, here, as if falling from the lips of an angel of light and may testify so that it reads brokenly and obscurely in print and yet there was that about the witness that carried conviction of truth to every soul who heard him testify.

Henry Lamm, *Creamer v. Bivert*, 214 Mo. 473, 479–80, 113 S.W. 1118 (1908)

2 There are two great things that are essential to be a good witness—one is the desire to tell the truth, and the other is the ability to tell the truth. I mean the desire to tell

the full absolute truth under all circumstances, regardless of temptation and regardless of pressure. There are fortunately very many people who have that desire; but there are far less who have the ability. The ability to tell the exact truth involves four great qualities which are rarely found in combination with the desire to tell the truth, namely: perfection of observation . . . a perfect memory, power of expression, and ability to envisage the whole situation.

> **Louis D. Brandeis,** Investigation of Department of the Interior, 27 May 1910, quoted in Alfred Lief, *The Brandeis Guide to the Modern World* 314–15 (1941)

3 OATH, *n.* In law, a solemn appeal to the Deity, made binding upon the conscience by a penalty for perjury.

> **Ambrose Bierce,** *The Devil's Dictionary* 232 (1911)

4 The presiding justice then went on to say [to the jury]: "And now I am going to tell you what I think of the defendant's testimony. You may have noticed, Mr. Foreman and gentlemen, that he wiped his hands during his testimony. It is rather a curious thing, but that is almost always an indication of lying. Why it should be so we don't know, but that is the fact. I think that every single word that man said, except when he agreed with the Government's testimony, was a lie.

> **Scott Wilson,** *Quercia v. United States,* 62 F.2d 746, 747–48 (1st Cir. 1933)

5 Getting to the bottom of things like that was impossible. You just had to take the practical view that a man always lied on his own behalf, and paid his lawyer, who was an expert, a professional liar, to show him new and better ways of lying.

> **James Gould Cozzens,** *The Just and the Unjust* 330 (1942)

6 Every lawyer dislikes to take the witness stand and will do so only for grave reasons. This is partly because it is not his role; he is almost invariably a poor witness. But he steps out of professional character to do it. He regrets it; the profession discourages it.

> **Robert H. Jackson,** *Hickman v. Taylor,* 392 U.S. 495, 517 (1947) (concurring)

7 From considerable experience in observing witnesses on the stand, I had learned that those who are lying or trying to cover up something generally make a common mistake—they tend to overact, to overstate their case.

> **Richard M. Nixon,** *Six Crises* 7–8 (1962)

8 A witness who saw an automobile accident was out on the stand to testify when counsel said, "Did you see the accident?"

He said, "Yes, sir!"

Counsel added, "How far away were you when the accident happened?"

Witness said, "Twenty-two feet, nine and three-quarter inches."

Counsel looked at the court and looked at the jury and said, "Well, will you tell the court and jury how do you know it was twenty-two feet, nine and three-quarter inches?"

Witness replied, "When it happened, I took out a tape measure and measured from where I stood to the point of impact, BECAUSE I KNEW SOME DOGGONE LAWYER WAS GOING TO ASK ME THAT QUESTION."

> **James C. Humes,** *Podium Humor* 81 (1975)

WOMEN

See also ABORTION; RAPE; SEX DISCRIMINATION; WOMEN'S RIGHTS

1 I know you do not make the laws but I also know that *you are the wives and mothers, the sisters and daughters of those who do.*

> **Angelina Grimké,** "Appeal to the Christian Women of the South," *The Anti-Slavery Examiner,* Sept. 1836, at 1, 16

2 Let us have the true woman, the adorner, the hospitable, the religious heart, and no lawyer need be called in to write stipulations, the cunning clauses of provision, the strong investitures;—for woman moulds the lawgiver and writes the law.

> **Ralph Waldo Emerson,** "Woman" (lecture), Boston, 20 Sept. 1855, in *Complete Works of Ralph Waldo Emerson* 11:405, 425 (1904)

3 Man is, or should be, woman's protector and defender. The natural and proper timidity and delicacy which belongs to the female sex evidently unfits it for many of the occupations of civil life. The constitution of the family organization, which is founded in the divine ordinance, as well as in the nature of things, indicates the do-

mestic sphere as that which properly belongs to the domain and functions of womanhood. The harmony, not to say identity, of interests and views which belong, or should belong, to the family institution is repugnant to the idea of a woman adopting a distinct and independent career from that of her husband. . . . [The] paramount destiny and mission of woman are to fulfil the noble and benign offices of wife and mother. This is the law of the Creator.

Joseph P. Bradley, *Bradwell v. State,* 83 U.S. (16 Wall.) 130, 141 (1873) (concurring)

4 In some rare instances sympathetic juries act as if they were champions of the fair sex, and felt commissioned to protect ladies against their own weakness and folly. This is an amiable but mistaken chivalry. In the court-house, the standard of justice for both sexes is the same. Like the sun, the law shines on all who are in the same place with equal warmth and splendor. The most charming and attractive woman in the universe, loaded down with misfortune, is not to prevail as a suitor where she is in the wrong, be her adversary whom she may.

Logan E. Bleckley, *Boland v. Klink,* 63 Ga. 447, 453 (1879)

5 That woman's physical structure and the performance of maternal functions place her at a disadvantage in the struggle for subsistence is obvious. This is especially true when the burdens of motherhood are upon her. . . . as healthy mothers are essential to vigorous offspring, the physical well-being of woman becomes an object of public interest and care in order to preserve the strength and vigor of the race.

David J. Brewer, *Muller v. Oregon,* 208 U.S. 412, 421 (1908)

6 The pedestal upon which women have been placed has, . . . upon closer inspection, been revealed as a cage.

Raymond E. Peters, *Sail'er Inn, Inc. v. Kirby,* 5 Cal. 3d 1, 20, 485 P.2d 529, 95 Cal. Rptr. 329 (1971)

7 The controversy between rule of law and rule of men was never relevant to women—because, along with juveniles, imbeciles, and other classes of legal nonpersons, they had no access to law except through men.

Freda Adler, *Sisters in Crime* 203 (1975)

8 Men are generally more law-abiding than women. . . . Women have a feeling that since they didn't make the rules, the rules have nothing to do with them.

Diane Johnson, *Lying Low* 113 (1978)

9 It is a matter of some interest that, of the twelve federal judges to have considered this case to date, none has been female. This may be quite significant because this case, like other controversies of great potential consequence, demands, in addition to command of the disembodied rules, some insight into social reality. What is the situation of the pregnant woman, unemployed or working for the minimum wage and unprotected by health insurance in relation to her pregnant sister, exposed to an indeterminate lead risk but well-fed, housed and doctored? Whose fetus is at greater risk? Whose decision is this to make?

Richard D. Cudahy, *UAW v. Johnson Controls, Inc.,* 886 F.2d 871, 902 (7th Cir. 1989) (dissenting)

WOMEN'S RIGHTS

See also SEX DISCRIMINATION; WOMEN

1 In the new Code of Laws which I suppose it will be necessary for you to make I desire you would Remember the Ladies, and be more generous and favorable to them than your ancestors. Do not put such unlimited power into the hands of the Husbands. Remember all Men would be tyrants if they could. If perticular [*sic*] care and attention is not paid to the Ladies we are determined to foment a Rebelion [*sic*], and will not hold ourselves bound by any Laws in which we have no voice, or Representation.

Abigail Adams, Letter to John Adams, 31 Mar. 1776, in *Adams Family Correspondence* 1:370 (L. H. Butterfield ed. 1963)

2 As to your extraordinary Code of Laws, I cannot but laugh. We have been told that our Struggle has loosened the bands of Government every where. That Children and Apprentices were disobedient—that schools and Colledges were grown turbulent—that Indians slighted their Guardians and Negroes grew insolent to their Masters. But your Letter was the first Intimation that another Tribe more numerous

and powerfull than all the rest were grown discontented.

> **John Adams,** Letter to Abigail Adams, 14 Apr. 1776, in *Adams Family Correspondence* 1:381–82 (L. H. Butterfield ed. 1963)

3 As all Men of Delicacy and Sentiment are averse to Exercising the power they possess, yet as there is a natural propensity in Humane Nature to domination, I thought the most generous plan was to put it out of the power of the Arbitrary and tyranick to injure us with impunity by Establishing some Laws in our favour upon just and Liberal principals [*sic*].

> **Abigail Adams,** Letter to Mercy Otis Warren, 27 Apr. 1776, in *Adams Family Correspondence* 1:397 (L. H. Butterfield ed. 1963)

4 I can not say that I think you are very generous to the Ladies, for whilst you are proclaiming peace and good will to Men, Emancipating all Nations, you insist upon retaining an absolute power over Wives. But you must remember that Arbitrary power is like most other things which are very hard, very liable to be broken—and notwithstanding all your wise Laws and Maxims we have it in our power not only to free ourselves but to subdue our Masters, and without violence throw both your natural and legal authority at our feet— "Charm by accepting, by submitting sway Yet have our Humour most when we obey."

> **Abigail Adams,** Letter to John Adams, 7 May 1776, in *Adams Family Correspondence* 1:402-03 (L. H. Butterfield ed. 1963)

5 The history of mankind is a history of repeated injuries and usurpations on the part of man toward woman, having in direct object the establishment of an absolute tyranny over her. To prove this, let facts be submitted to a candid world.

He has never permitted her to exercise her inalienable right to the elective franchise.

He has compelled her to submit to laws, in the formation of which she had no voice.

He has withheld from her rights which are given to the most ignorant and degraded men—both natives and foreigners.

Having deprived her of this first right of a citizen, the elective franchise, thereby leaving her without representation in the halls of legislation, he has oppressed her on all sides.

He has made her, if married, in the eye of the law, civilly dead.

He has taken from her all right in property, even to the wages she earns.

He has made her, morally, an irresponsible being, as she can commit many crimes with impunity, provided they be done in the presence of her husband. In the covenant of marriage, she is compelled to promise obedience to her husband, he becoming, to all intents and purposes, her master—the law giving him power to deprive her of her liberty, and to administer chastisement.

He has so framed the laws of divorce, as to what shall be the proper causes, and in case of separation, to whom the guardianship of the children shall be given, as to be wholly regardless of the happiness of women—the law, in all cases, going upon a false supposition of the supremacy of man, and giving all power into his hands.

After depriving her of all rights as a married woman, if single, and the owner of property, he has taxed her to support a government which recognizes her only when her property can be made profitable to it.

> Declaration of Sentiments, Woman's Rights Convention, Seneca Falls, N.Y., 19 July 1848, in *History of Woman Suffrage* 1:70 (Elizabeth Cady Stanton, Susan B. Anthony, & Matilda J. Gage eds. 1881)

6 WHEREAS, The great precept of nature is conceded to be, that "man shall pursue his own true and substantial happiness." Blackstone in his Commentaries remarks, that this law of Nature being coeval with mankind, and dictated by God himself, is of course superior in obligation to any other. It is binding over all the globe, in all countries and at all times; no human laws are of any validity if contrary to this, and such of them as are valid, derive all their force, and all their validity, and all their authority, mediately and immediately, from this original; therefore,

Resolved, That such laws as conflict, in any way, with the true and substantial happiness of woman, are contrary to the great precept of nature and of no validity, for this is "superior in obligation to any other."

Resolved, That all laws which prevent woman from occupying such a station in society as her conscience shall dictate, or which place her in a position inferior to that of man, are contrary to the great precept of nature, and therefore of no force or authority.

Resolved, That woman is man's equal— was intended to be so by the Creator, and the highest good of the race demands that she should be recognized as such.

Resolved, That the women of this country ought to be enlightened in regard to the laws under which they live, that they may no longer publish their degradation by declaring themselves satisfied with their present position, nor their ignorance, by asserting that they have all the rights they want.

Declaration of Sentiments, Woman's Rights Convention, Seneca Falls, N.Y., 19 July 1848, in *History of Woman Suffrage* 1:71–72 (Elizabeth Cady Stanton, Susan B. Anthony, & Matilda J. Gage eds. 1881)

7 But the law never loses sight of the purse, no matter how low in the scale of being its owner may be. It sends its officers round every year to gather in the harvest for the public crib, and no widow who owns a piece of land two feet square ever escapes this reckoning. Our widow . . . has her annual tax to pay . . .—a tribute of gratitude that she is permitted to breathe the free air of this republic, where "taxation without representation," . . . has been declared "intolerable tyranny." Having glanced at the magnanimity of the law in its dealing with the widow, let us see how the individual man, under the influence of such laws, doles out justice to his helpmate. The husband has the absolute right to will away his property as he may see fit.

Elizabeth Cady Stanton, Address before New York State Legislature, Feb. 1854, in *History of Woman Suffrage* 1:595, 601-02 (Elizabeth Cady Stanton, Susan B. Anthony, & Matilda J. Gage eds. 1881)

8 Would to God you could know the burning indignation that fills woman's soul when she turns over the pages of your statute books, and sees there how like feudal barons you freemen hold your women. Would that you could know the humiliation she feels for [her] sex, when she thinks these ideas of one-sided justice—taking their first lessons in contempt for all womankind— being indoctrinated into the incapacities of their mothers, and the lordly, absolute

rights of man over all women, children, and property, and to know that these are to be our future presidents, judges, husbands, and fathers.

Elizabeth Cady Stanton, Address before New York State Legislature, Feb. 1854, in *History of Woman Suffrage* 1:595, 604 (Elizabeth Cady Stanton, Susan B. Anthony, & Matilda J. Gage eds. 1881)

9 Who of you appreciate the galling humiliation, the refinements of degradation, to which women (the mothers, wives, sisters, and daughters of freemen) are subject, in this the last half of the nineteenth century? How many of you have ever read even the laws concerning them that now disgrace your statute-books? In cruelty and tyranny, they are not surpassed by any slaveholding code in the Southern States.

Elizabeth Cady Stanton, Address to New York State Legislature, 18 Feb. 1860, in *History of Woman Suffrage* 1:679, 680 (Elizabeth Cady Stanton, Susan B. Anthony, & Matilda J. Gage eds. 1881)

10 Your laws degrade, rather than exalt woman; your customs cripple, rather than free; your system of taxation is alike ungenerous and unjust.

Elizabeth Cady Stanton, Address to New York State Constitutional Convention, 23 Jan. 1867, in *History of Woman Suffrage* 2:271, 273 (Elizabeth Cady Stanton, Susan B. Anthony, & Matilda J. Gage eds. 1882)

11 It was we, the people, not we, the white male citizens, nor yet we, the male citizens, but we, the whole people, who formed this Union. And we formed it, not to give the blessings of liberty, but to secure them; not to the half of ourselves and the half of our posterity, but to the whole people—women as well as men.

Susan B. Anthony, Speech, New York State, 1873, in *History of Woman Suffrage* 2:630, 632 (Elizabeth Cady Stanton, Susan B. Anthony, & Matilda J. Gage eds. 1882)

12 The rights of citizens of the state of Wyoming to vote and hold office shall not be denied or abridged on account of sex. Both male and female citizens of this state shall equally enjoy all civil, political and religious rights and privileges.

Wyoming Constitution of 1889, art. VI, § 1

13 The Nineteenth Amendment—I think that's the one that made Women humans by Act of Congress.

> **Will Rogers,** "Mr. Toastmaster and Democrats," 30 Mar. 1929, in *"How To Be Funny" & Other Writings of Will Rogers* 85, 89–90 (Steven K. Gragert ed. 1983)

WORDS

See also LANGUAGE; LEGAL WRITING; QUOTATIONS

1 Such is the character of human language, that no word conveys to the mind, in all situations, one single definite idea; and nothing is more common than to use words in a figurative sense. Almost all compositions contain words, which, taken in their rigorous sense, would convey a meaning different from that which is obviously intended. It is essential to just construction, that many words which import something excessive, should be understood in a more mitigated sense—in that sense which common usage justifies. The word "necessary" is of this description. It has not a fixed character peculiar to itself. It admits of all degrees of comparison; and it is often connected with other words, which increase or diminish the impression the mind receives of the urgency it imports.

> **John Marshall,** *McCulloch v. Maryland,* 17 U.S. (4 Wheat.) 316, 414 (1819)

2 As men, whose intentions require no concealment, generally employ the words which most directly and aptly express the ideas they intend to convey, the enlightened patriots who framed our constitution, and the people who adopted it, must be understood to have employed words in their natural sense, and to have intended what they have said.

> **John Marshall,** *Gibbons v. Ogden,* 22 U.S. (9 Wheat.) 1, 188 (1824)

3 The dictionary definition of a term is frequently the mere air of the music which the accused has attempted to execute with variations. Frequently, too, the variations are so luxuriant and ingenious that the air is much disguised, and to hum it over from the bench is but little assistance to the jury in following the real performance. It is

something easier for an offender to baffle the dictionary than the penal code.

> **Logan E. Bleckley,** *Minor v. State,* 63 Ga. 318, 321 (1879)

4 A word generally has several meanings, even in the dictionary. You have to consider the sentence in which it stands to decide which of those meanings it bears in the particular case, and very likely will see that it there has a shade of significance more refined than any given in the word-book.

> **Oliver Wendell Holmes, Jr.,** "The Theory of Legal Interpretation," 12 *Harvard Law Review* 417, 417 (1899)

5 We ask, not what this man meant, but what those words would mean in the mouth of a normal speaker of English, using them in the circumstances in which they were used.

> **Oliver Wendell Holmes, Jr.,** "The Theory of Legal Interpretation," 12 *Harvard Law Review* 417, 417–18 (1899)

6 It is not the first use but the tiresome repetition of inadequate catch words upon which I am observing,—phrases which originally were contributions, but which, by their very felicity, delay further analysis for fifty years. That comes from the same source as dislike of novelty,—intellectual intolerance or weakness,—a slackening in the eternal pursuit of the more exact.

> **Oliver Wendell Holmes, Jr.,** "Law in Science and Science in Law," 12 *Harvard Law Review* 443, 455 (1899)

7 My object is not so much to point out what seem to me to be fallacies in particular cases as to enforce . . . the need of scrutinizing the reasons for the rules which we follow, and of not being contented with hollow forms of words merely because they have been used very often and have been repeated from one end of the union to the other. We must think things not words, or at least we must constantly translate our words into the facts for which they stand, if we are to keep to the real and the true.

> **Oliver Wendell Holmes, Jr.,** "Law in Science and Science in Law," 12 *Harvard Law Review* 443, 460 (1899)

8 Whatever the consequences we must accept the plain meaning of plain words.

> **Oliver Wendell Holmes, Jr.,** *United States v. Brown,* 206 U.S. 240, 244 (1907)

9 It is one of the misfortunes of the law that ideas become encysted in phrases and thereafter for a long time cease to provoke further analysis.

Oliver Wendell Holmes, Jr., *Hyde v. United States,* 225 U.S. 347, 391 (1912) (dissenting)

10 We need to think of things instead of words—to drop ownership, money, etc., and to think of the stream of products; of wheat and cloth and railway travel. When we do, it is obvious that the many consume them; that they now as truly have substantially all there is, as if the title were in the United States; that the great body of property is socially administered now.

Oliver Wendell Holmes, Jr., "Law and the Court" (speech to Harvard Law School Association of New York), 15 Feb. 1913, in *Collected Legal Papers* 291, 293–94 (1920)

11 A word is not a crystal, transparent and unchanged, it is the skin of a living thought and may vary greatly in color and content according to the circumstances and the time in which it is used.

Oliver Wendell Holmes, Jr., *Towne v. Eisner,* 245 U.S. 418, 425 (1918)

12 I still have difficulty with philosophic as with economic language. As I have told you before that seems to me the chief trouble. Ideas are not often hard but words are the devil.

Oliver Wendell Holmes, Jr., Letter to Harold J. Laski, 21 Sept. 1923, in *Holmes-Laski Letters* 1:542 (Mark DeWolfe Howe ed. 1953)

13 We seek to find peace of mind in the word, the formula, the ritual. The hope is an illusion.

Benjamin N. Cardozo, *The Growth of the Law* 66–67 (1924)

14 The logic of words should yield to the logic of realities.

Louis D. Brandeis, *DiSanto v. Pennsylvania,* 273 U.S. 34, 43 (1927)

15 Weasel words will not avail to defeat the triumph of intention when once the words are read in the setting of the whole transaction.

Benjamin N. Cardozo, *Holyoke Water Power Co. v. American Writing Paper Co.,* 300 U.S. 324, 336 (1937)

16 Dealing in words is a dangerous business. . . . Dealing in long, vague, fuzzy-meaning words is even more dangerous business, and most of the words The Law deals in are long and vague and fuzzy. Making a habit of applying long, vague, fuzzy, general words to specific things and facts is perhaps the most dangerous of all, and The Law does that, too.

Fred Rodell, *Woe Unto You, Lawyers!* 59 (1939)

17 Words are not pebbles in alien juxtaposition; they have only a communal existence; and not only does the meaning of each interpenetrate the other, but all in their aggregate take their purport from the setting in which they are used, of which the relation between the speaker and the hearer is perhaps the most important part.

Learned Hand, *National Labor Relations Bd. v. Federbush Co.,* 121 F.2d 954, 957 (2d Cir. 1941)

18 Words are such temperamental beings that the surest way to lose their essence is to take them at their face.

Learned Hand, "The Contribution of an Independent Judiciary to Civilization," 1942, in *The Spirit of Liberty* 155, 157 (Irving Dilliard ed., 2d ed. 1953)

19 The phrase "assumption of risk" is an excellent illustration of the extent to which uncritical use of words bedevils the law. A phrase begins life as a literary expression; its felicity leads to its lazy repetition; and repetition soon establishes it as a legal formula, undiscriminatingly used to express different and sometimes contradictory ideas.

Felix Frankfurter, *Tiller v. Atlantic Coast Line R.R.,* 318 U.S. 54, 68 (1943) (concurring)

20 Of course it is true that the words used, even in their literal sense, are the primary, and ordinarily the most reliable, source of interpreting the meaning of any writing: be it a statute, a contract, or anything else. But it is one of the surest indexes of a mature and developed jurisprudence not to make a fortress out of the dictionary; but to remember that statutes always have some purpose or object to accomplish, whose

sympathetic and imaginative discovery is the surest guide to their meaning.

> Learned Hand, *Cabell v. Markham*, 148 F.2d 737, 739 (2d Cir. 1945)

21 Words are chameleons, which reflect the color of their environment.

> Learned Hand, *Commissioner v. National Carbide Corp.*, 167 F.2d 304, 306 (2d Cir. 1948)

22 It is added, though as something of an afterthought, that Dorsey in his brief to the Patent Office characterized Clarke as a "reluctant witness." I had supposed that such adjectives were in the nature of argument or, at most, of conclusion rather than representation or warranty. The arsenal of every advocate holds two bundles of adjectives for witnesses—such ones as "reluctant," "unbiased," "disinterested," and "honest" are reserved for his own; others, such as "partisan," "eager," "interested," "hostile," and even "perjured," for those of his adversary. I have the greatest difficulty believing that a mischoice among these adjectives has deceived anyone fit to decide facts, or that in any case other than this it would subject the advocate to disbarment.

> Robert H. Jackson, *Kingsland v. Dorsey*, 338 U.S. 318, 324 (1949) (dissenting)

23 Law has always been unintelligible, and I might say that perhaps it ought to be. And I will tell you why, because I don't want to deal in paradoxes. It ought to be unintelligible because it ought to be in words—and words are utterly inadequate to deal with the fantastically multiform occasions which come up in human life.

> Learned Hand, "Thou Shalt Not Ration Justice," 9 *Brief Case*, No. 4, at 3, 4 (1951)

24 It is certain that, although figures of speech have a literary charm, they may have unfortunate results in law suits if taken literally. . . . And a long experience in the use of words, by himself as well as by other men, had demonstrated that the thoughts that they express or convey are variables, depending on verbal context and surrounding circumstances and purposes in view of the linguistic education and experience of their users and their hearers or readers (not excluding judges). . . . A word has no meaning apart from these factors; much

less does it have an objective meaning, one true meaning.

> Arthur L. Corbin, "The Interpretation of Words and the Parol Evidence Rule," 50 *Cornell Law Quarterly* 161, 187 (1965)

25 The only tool of the lawyer is words. We have no marvelous pills to prescribe for our patients. We have no Superconducting Supercollider to help us find the Higgs boson. Whether we are trying a case, writing a brief, drafting a contract, or negotiating with an adversary, words are the only things we have to work with.

> Charles Alan Wright, Book Review, *Townes Hall Notes*, Spring 1988, at 5

WRITING

See LANGUAGE; LAW REVIEWS; LEGAL WRITING; QUOTATIONS; WORDS

YALE LAW SCHOOL

1 Let the school, then, be regarded no longer as simply the place for training men to plead causes, to give advice to clients, to defend criminals; but let it be regarded as the place of instruction in all sound learning relating to the foundations of justice, the history of law, the doctrine of government, to all those branches of knowledge to which the most finished statesman and legislator ought to know. . . . Let the plan of the library be expanded, so that it shall furnish the best books on all branches and topics connected with law, legislation, and government. Can it be doubted that such an institution, of which I have sketched a faint outline, would be of vast service; that its influence would reach into the halls of Congress, into the departments of government, that it might become a fountain of light through the whole land.

> Theodore D. Woolsey, *Historical Discourse* 1, 23–24 (1874)

2 When he was a dean of the Yale Law School, Hutchins had been invited to attend a reception for the justices of the Supreme Court. On that occasion, one of the stuffier old men on the court, either Mr. Justice [McReynolds] or Mr. Justice Butler, said to him: "I understand, Mr. Dean, that you are teaching your young men at New Haven what is wrong with our decisions."

To which Hutchins instantaneously replied: "Oh no, we let them find that out for themselves."

Robert M. Hutchins, reported in Mortimer J. Adler, *Philosopher at Large* 138 (1977)

3 [As Dean of Yale Law School, Sturges wired this response to a request from the Harvard Law School newspaper for comment on Harvard Law's decision to admit women students:] YALE LAW FACULTY AND STUDENT BODY DEEPLY MOVED. FEEL IT QUITE POSSIBLE HARVARD MAY MAKE CONTRIBUTION TO WOMANHOOD. DOUBT MANY ADVERSE CONSEQUENCES HARVARD FACULTY OR STUDENT BODY. WE HAVE ALWAYS FOLLOWED WITH GENUINE INTEREST LONG STRUGGLE HARVARD LIBERALS IN THIS MATTER. OUR MANY GENERATIONS OF WOMEN GRADUATES ARE OF COURSE A PRIDE AND JOY. BEST WISHES.

Wesley Sturges, quoted in *Yale Alumni Magazine*, Jan. 1950, at 2

4 Criminal lawyers help people who aren't criminals, too. We've used this fellow before ... He's very bright ... He went to Yale ... or at least he went to the law school. He's the only Irishman who ever graduated from the Yale Law School, and he's the only graduate of the Yale Law School who ever practiced criminal law. I'm exaggerating, of course.

Tom Wolfe, *The Bonfire of the Vanities* 295 (1987)

5 "Freddy tells me you went to the Yale Law School. When were you there?"

"The late seventies," said Killian.

"What did you think of it?"

"It was okay. . . . I liked it. It's a nice place. It's easy, as law schools go. They don't try to bury you in details. They give you the scholarly view, the overview. You get the grand design. They're very good at giving you that. Yale is terrific for anything you wanna do, so long as it don't involve people with sneakers, guns, dope, lust, or sloth."

Tom Wolfe, *The Bonfire of the Vanities* 389 (1987)

427

The Constitution of the United States

We the People of the United States, in Order to form a more perfect Union, establish Justice, insure domestic Tranquility, provide for the common defence, promote the general Welfare, and secure the Blessings of Liberty to ourselves and our Posterity, do ordain and establish this Constitution for the United States of America.

ARTICLE. I.

SECTION. 1. All legislative Powers herein granted shall be vested in a Congress of the United States, which shall consist of a Senate and House of Representatives.

SECTION. 2. The House of Representatives shall be composed of Members chosen every second Year by the People of the several States, and the Electors in each State shall have the Qualifications requisite for Electors of the most numerous Branch of the State Legislature.

No Person shall be a Representative who shall not have attained to the Age of twenty five Years, and been seven Years a Citizen of the United States, and who shall not, when elected, be an Inhabitant of that State in which he shall be chosen.

Representatives and direct Taxes shall be apportioned among the several States which may be included within this Union, according to their respective Numbers, which shall be determined by adding to the whole Number of free Persons, including those bound to Service for a Term of Years, and excluding Indians not taxed, three fifths of all other Persons. The actual Enumeration shall be made within three Years after the first Meeting of the Congress of the United States, and within every subsequent Term of ten Years, in such Manner as they shall by Law direct. The Number of Representatives shall not exceed one for every thirty Thousand, but each State shall have at Least one Representative; and until such enumeration shall be made, the State of New Hampshire shall be entitled to chuse three, Massachusetts eight, Rhode-Island and Providence Plantations one, Con-necticut five, New-York six, New Jersey four, Pennsylvania eight, Delaware one, Maryland six, Virginia ten, North Carolina five, South Carolina five, and Georgia three.

When vacancies happen in the Representation from any State, the Executive Authority thereof shall issue Writs of Election to fill such Vacancies.

The House of Representatives shall chuse their Speaker and other Officers; and shall have the sole Power of Impeachment.

SECTION. 3. The Senate of the United States shall be composed of two Senators from each State, chosen by the Legislature thereof, for six Years; and each Senator shall have one Vote.

Immediately after they shall be assembled in Consequence of the first Election, they shall be divided as equally as may be into three Classes. The Seats of the Senators of the first Class shall be vacated at the Expiration of the second Year, of the second Class at the Expiration of the fourth Year, and of the third Class at the Expiration of the sixth Year, so that one third may be chosen every second Year; and if Vacancies happen by Resignation, or otherwise, during the Recess of the Legislature of any State, the Executive thereof may make temporary Appointments until the next Meeting of the Legislature, which shall then fill such Vacancies.

No Person shall be a Senator who shall not have attained to the Age of thirty Years, and been nine Years a Citizen of the United States, and who shall not, when elected, be an Inhabitant of that State for which he shall be chosen.

The Vice President of the United States shall be President of the Senate, but shall have no Vote, unless they be equally divided.

The Senate shall chuse their other Officers, and also a President pro tempore, in the Absence of the Vice President, or when he shall exercise the Office of President of the United States.

The Senate shall have the sole Power to

try all Impeachments. When sitting for that Purpose, they shall be on Oath or Affirmation. When the President of the United States is tried, the Chief Justice shall preside: And no Person shall be convicted without the Concurrence of two thirds of the Members present.

Judgement in Cases of Impeachment shall not extend further than to removal from Office, and disqualification to hold and enjoy any Office of honor, Trust or Profit under the United States: but the Party convicted shall nevertheless be liable and subject to Indictment, Trial, Judgment and Punishment, according to Law.

SECTION. 4. The Times, Places and Manner of holding Elections for Senators and Representatives, shall be prescribed in each State by the Legislature thereof, but the Congress may at any time by Law make or alter such Regulations, except as to the Places of chusing Senators.

The Congress shall assemble at least once in every Year, and such Meeting shall be on the first Monday in December, unless they shall by Law appoint a different Day.

SECTION. 5. Each House shall be the Judge of the Elections, Returns and Qualifications of its own Members, and a Majority of each shall constitute a Quorum to do Business; but a smaller Number may adjourn from day to day, and may be authorized to compel the Attendance of absent Members, in such Manner, and under such Penalties as each House may provide.

Each House may determine the Rule of its Proceedings, punish its Members for disorderly Behaviour, and, with the Concurrence of two thirds, expel a Member.

Each House shall keep a Journal of its Proceedings, and from time to time publish the same, excepting such Parts as may in their Judgement require Secrecy; and the Yeas and Nays of the Members of either House on any question shall, at the Desire of one fifth of those Present, be entered on the Journal.

Neither House, during the Session of Congress, shall, without the Consent of the other, adjourn for more than three days, nor to any other Place than that in which the two Houses shall be sitting.

SECTION. 6. The Senators and Representatives shall receive a Compensation for their Services, to be ascertained by Law, and paid out of the Treasury of the United States. They shall in all Cases, except Treason, Felony and Breach of the Peace, be privileged from Arrest during their Attendance at the Session of their respective Houses, and in going to and returning from the same; and for any Speech or Debate in either House, they shall not be questioned in any other Place.

No Senator or Representative shall, during the Time for which he was elected, be appointed to any civil Office under the Authority of the United States, which shall have been created, or the Emoluments whereof shall have been encreased during such time; and no Person holding any Office under the United States, shall be a Member of either House during his Continuance in Office.

SECTION. 7. All Bills for raising Revenue shall originate in the House of Representatives; but the Senate may propose or concur with Amendments as on other Bills.

Every Bill which shall have passed the House of Representatives and the Senate, shall, before it become a Law, be presented to the President of the United States; If he approve he shall sign it, but if not he shall return it, with his Objections to that House in which it shall have originated, who shall enter the Objections at large on their Journal, and proceed to reconsider it. If after such Reconsideration two thirds of that House shall agree to pass the Bill, it shall be sent, together with the Objections, to the other House, by which it shall likewise be reconsidered, and if approved by two thirds of that House, it shall become a Law. But in all such Cases the Votes of both Houses shall be determined by yeas and Nays, and the Names of the Persons voting for and against the Bill shall be entered on the Journal of each House respectively. If any Bill shall not be returned by the President within ten days (Sundays excepted) after it shall have been presented to him, the Same shall be a Law, in like Manner as if he had signed it, unless the Congress by their Adjournment prevent its Return, in which case it shall not be a Law.

Every Order, Resolution, or Vote to which the Concurrence of the Senate and House of Representatives may be necessary (except on a question of Adjournment) shall be presented to the President of the United States; and before the Same shall take Effect, shall be approved by him, or being disapproved by him, shall be repassed by two thirds of the Senate and House of Representatives, according to the Rules and Limitations prescribed in the Case of a Bill.

SECTION. 8. The Congress shall have Power To lay and collect Taxes, Duties, Imposts and Excises, to pay the Debts and provide for the common Defence and general Welfare of the United States; but all Duties, Imposts and Excises shall be uniform throughout the United States;

To borrow Money on the credit of the United States;

To regulate Commerce with foreign Nations, and among the several States, and with the Indian Tribes;

To establish an uniform Rule of Naturalization, and uniform Laws on the subject of Bankruptcies throughout the United States;

To coin Money, regulate the Value thereof, and of foreign Coin, and fix the Standard of Weights and Measures;

To provide for the Punishment of counterfeiting the Securities and current Coin of the United States;

To establish Post Offices and post Roads;

To promote the Progress of Science and useful Arts, by securing for limited Times to Authors and Inventors the exclusive Right to their respective Writings and Discoveries;

To constitute Tribunals inferior to the supreme Court;

To define and punish Piracies and Felonies committed on the high Seas, and Offences against the Law of Nations;

To declare War, grant Letters of Marque and Reprisal, and make Rules concerning Captures on Land and Water;

To raise and support Armies, but no Appropriation of Money to that Use shall be for a longer Term than two years;

To provide and maintain a Navy;

To make Rules for the Government and Regulation of the land and naval Forces;

To provide for calling forth the Militia to execute the Laws of the Union, suppress Insurrections and repel Invasions;

To provide for organizing, arming, and disciplining, the Militia, and for governing such Part of them as may be employed in the Service of the United States, reserving to the States respectively, the Appointment of the Officers, and the Authority of training the Militia according to the discipline prescribed by Congress;

To exercise exclusive Legislation in all Cases whatsoever, over such District (not exceeding ten Miles square) as may, by Cession of particular States, and the Acceptance of Congress, become the Seat of Government of the United States, and to exercise like Authority over all Places purchased by the Consent of the Legislature of the State in which the Same shall be, for the Erection of Forts, Magazines, Arsenals, dock-Yards,and other needful Buildings;—And

To make all Laws which shall be necessary and proper for carrying into Execution the foregoing Powers, and all other Powers vested by this Constitution in the Government of the United States, or in any Department or Officer thereof.

SECTION. 9. The Migration or Importation of such Persons as any of the States now existing shall think proper to admit, shall not be prohibited by the Congress prior to the Year one thousand eight hundred and eight, but a Tax or duty may be imposed on such Importation, not exceeding ten dollars for each Person.

The Privilege of the Writ of Habeas Corpus shall not be suspended, unless when in Cases of Rebellion or Invasion the public Safety may require it.

No Bill of Attainder or ex post facto Law shall be passed.

No Capitation, or other direct, Tax, shall be laid, unless in Proportion to the Census or Enumeration herein before directed to be taken.

No Tax or Duty shall be laid on Articles exported from any State.

No Preference shall be given by any Regulation of Commerce or Revenue to the Ports of one State over those of another: nor shall Vessels bound to, or from, one State, be obliged to enter, clear, or pay Duties in another.

No Money shall be drawn from the Treasury, but in Consequence of Appropriations made by Law; and a regular Statement and Account of the Receipts and Expenditures of all public Money shall be published from time to time.

No Title of Nobility shall be granted by the United States: And no Person holding any Office of Profit or Trust under them, shall, without the Consent of the Congress, accept of any present, Emolument, Office, or Title, of any kind whatever, from any King, Prince, or foreign State.

SECTION. 10. No State shall enter into any Treaty, Alliance, or Confederation; grant Letters of Marque and Reprisal; coin Money; emit Bills of Credit; make any Thing but gold and silver Coin a Tender in Payment of Debts; pass any Bill of Attainder, ex post facto Law, or Law impairing the Obligation of Contracts, or grant any Title of Nobility.

No State shall, without the Consent of the Congress, lay any Imposts or Duties on Imports or Exports, except what may be absolutely necessary for executing it's inspection Laws: and the net Produce of all Duties and Imposts, laid by any State on Imports or Exports, shall be for the Use of the Treasury of the United States; and all such Laws shall be subject to the Revision and Controul of the Congress.

No State shall, without the Consent of Congress, lay any Duty of Tonnage, keep Troops, or Ships of War in time of Peace, enter into any Agreement or Compact with another State, or with a foreign Power, or engage in War, unless actually invaded, or in such imminent Danger as will not admit of delay.

ARTICLE. II.

SECTION. 1. The executive Power shall be vested in a President of the United States of America. He shall hold his Office during the Term of four Years, and, together with the Vice President, chosen for the same Term, be elected as follows

Each State shall appoint, in such Manner as the Legislature thereof may direct, a Number of Electors, equal to the whole Number of Senators and Representatives to which the State may be entitled in the Congress: but no Senator or Representative, or Person holding an Office of Trust or Profit under the United States, shall be appointed an Elector.

The Electors shall meet in their respective States, and vote by Ballot for two Persons, of whom one at least shall not be an Inhabitant of the same State with themselves. And they shall make a List of all the Persons voted for, and of the Number of Votes for each; which List they shall sign and certify, and transmit sealed to the Seat of the Government of the United States, directed to the President of the Senate. The President of the Senate shall, in the Presence of the Senate and House of Representatives, open all the Certificates, and the Votes shall then be counted. The Person having the greatest Number of Votes shall be the President, if such Number be a Majority of the whole Number of Electors appointed; and if there be more than one who have such Majority, and have an equal Number of Votes, then the House of Representatives shall immediately chuse by Ballot one of them for President; and if no Person have a Majority, then from the five highest on the List the said House shall in like Manner chuse the President. But in chusing the President, the Votes shall be taken by States, the Representation from each State having one Vote; A quorum for this Purpose shall consist of a Member or Members from two thirds of the States, and a Majority of all the States shall be necessary to a Choice. In every Case, after the Choice of President, the Person having the greatest Number of Votes of the Electors shall be the Vice President. But if there should remain two or more who have equal Votes, the Senate shall chuse from them by Ballot the Vice President.

The Congress may determine the Time of chusing the Electors, and the Day on which they shall give their Votes; which Day shall be the same throughout the United States.

No Person except a natural born Citizen, or a Citizen of the United States, at the time of the Adoption of this Constitution, shall be eligible to the Office of President; neither shall any Person be eligible to that Office who shall not have attained to the Age of thirty five Years, and been fourteen Years a Resident within the United States.

In Case of the Removal of the President from Office, or of his Death, Resignation, or Inability to discharge the Powers and Duties of the said Office, the Same shall devolve on the Vice President, and the Congress may by Law provide for the Case of Removal, Death, Resignation or Inability, both of the President and Vice President, declaring what Officer shall then act as President, and such Officer shall act accordingly, until the Disability be removed, or a President shall be elected.

The President shall, at stated Times, receive for his Services, a Compensation, which shall neither be increased nor diminished during the Period for which he shall have been elected, and he shall not receive within that Period any other Emolument from the United States, or any of them.

Before he enter on the Execution of his Office, he shall take the following Oath of

Affirmation:—"I do solemnly swear (or affirm) that I will faithfully execute the Office of President of the United States, and will to the best of my Ability, preserve, protect and defend the Constitution of the United States."

SECTION. 2. The President shall be Commander in Chief of the Army and Navy of the United States, and of the Militia of the several States, when called into the actual Service of the United States; he may require the Opinion, in writing, of the principal Officer in each of the executive Departments, upon any Subject relating to the Duties of their respective Offices, and he shall have Power to grant Reprieves and Pardons for Offences against the United States, except in Cases of Impeachment.

He shall have Power, by and with the Advice and Consent of the Senate, to make Treaties, provided two thirds of the Senators present concur; and he shall nominate, and by and with the Advice and Consent of the Senate, shall appoint Ambassadors, other public Ministers and Consuls, Judges of the supreme Court, and all other Officers of the United States, whose Appointments are not herein otherwise provided for, and which shall be established by Law: but the Congress may by Law vest the Appointment of such inferior Officers, as they think proper, in the President alone, in the Courts of Law, or in the Heads of Departments.

The President shall have Power to fill up all Vacancies that may happen during thc Recess of the Senate, by granting Commissions which shall expire at the End of their next Session.

SECTION. 3. He shall from time to time give to the Congress Information of the State of the Union, and recommend to their Consideration such Measures as he shall judge necessary and expedient; he may, on extraordinary Occasions, convene both Houses, or either of them, and in Case of Disagreement between them, with Respect to the Time of Adjournment, he may adjourn them to such Time as he shall think proper; he shall receive Ambassadors and other public Ministers; he shall take Care that the Laws be faithfully executed, and shall Commission all Officers of the United States.

SECTION. 4. The President, Vice President and all civil Officers of the United States, shall be removed from Office on Impeachment for, and Conviction of, Treason, Bribery, or other high Crimes and Misdemeanors.

ARTICLE. III.

SECTION. 1. The judicial Power of the United States, shall be vested in one supreme Court, and in such inferior Courts as the Congress may from time to time ordain and establish. The Judges, both of the supreme and inferior Courts, shall hold their Offices during good Behaviour, and shall, at stated Times, receive for their Services, a Compensation, which shall not be diminished during their Continuance in Office.

SECTION. 2. The judicial Power shall extend to all Cases, in Law and Equity, arising under this Constitution, the Laws of the United States, and Treaties made, or which shall be made, under their Authority;—to all Cases affecting Ambassadors, other public Ministers and Consuls;—to all Cases of admiralty and maritime Jurisdiction;—to Controversies to which the United States shall be a Party;—to Controversies between two or more States;—between a State and Citizens of another State;—between Citizens of different States;—between Citizens of the same State claiming Lands under Grants of different States, and between a State, or the Citizens thereof, and foreign States, Citizens or Subjects.

In all cases affecting Ambassadors, other public Ministers and Consuls, and those in which a State shall be Party, the supreme Court shall have original Jurisdiction. In all the other Cases before mentioned, the supreme Court shall have appellate Jurisdiction, both as to Law and Fact, with such Exceptions, and under such Regulations as the Congress shall make.

The Trial of all Crimes, except in Cases of Impeachment, shall be by Jury; and such Trial shall be held in the State where the said Crimes shall have been committed; but when not committed within any State, the Trial shall be at such Place or Places as the Congress may by Law have directed.

SECTION. 3. Treason against the United States, shall consist only in levying War against them, or in adhering to their Enemies, giving them Aid and Comfort. No Person shall be convicted of Treason unless on the Testimony of two Witnesses to the same overt Act, or on Confession in open Court.

The Congress shall have Power to declare the Punishment of Treason, but no Attainder of Treason shall work Corruption of Blood, or Forfeiture except during the Life of the Person attainted.

ARTICLE. IV.

SECTION. 1. Full Faith and Credit shall be given in each State to the public Acts, Records, and judicial Proceedings of every other State. And the Congress may by general Laws prescribe the Manner in which such Acts, Records and Proceedings shall be proved, and the Effect thereof.

SECTION. 2. The citizens of each State shall be entitled to all Privileges and Immunities of Citizens in the several States.

A person charged in any State with Treason, Felony, or other Crime, who shall flee from Justice, and be found in another State, shall on Demand of the executive Authority of the State from which he fled, be delivered up, to be removed to the State having Jurisdiction of the Crime.

No Person held to Service or Labour in one State, under the Laws thereof, escaping into another, shall, in Consequence of any Law or Regulation therein, be discharged from such Service or Labour, but shall be delivered up on Claim o the Party to whom such Service or Labour may be due.

SECTION. 3. New States may be admitted by the Congress into this Union; but no new State shall be formed or erected within the Jurisdiction of any other State; nor any State be formed by the Junction of two or more States, or Parts of States, without the Consent of the Legislatures of the States concerned as well as of the Congress.

The Congress shall have Power to dispose of and make all needful Rules and Regulations respecting the Territory or other Property belonging to the United States; and nothing in this Constitution shall be so construed as to Prejudice any Claims of the United States, or of any particular State.

SECTION. 4. The United States shall guarantee to every State in this Union a Republican Form of Government, and shall protect each of them against Invasion; and on Application of the Legislature, or of the Executive (when the Legislature cannot be convened) against domestic Violence.

ARTICLE. V.

The Congress, whenever two thirds of both Houses shall deem it necessary, shall propose Amendments to this Constitution, or, on the Application of the Legislatures of two thirds of the several States, shall call a Convention for proposing Amendments, which, in either Case, shall be valid to all Intents and Purposes, as Part of this Constitution, when ratified by the Legislatures of three fourths of the several States, or by Conventions in three fourths thereof, as the one or the other Mode of Ratification may be proposed by the Congress; Provided that no Amendment which may be made prior to the Year One thousand eight hundred and eight shall in any Manner affect the first and fourth Clauses in the Ninth Section of the first Article; and that no State, without its Consent, shall be deprived of it's equal Suffrage in the Senate.

ARTICLE. VI.

All Debts contracted and Engagements entered into, before the Adoption of this Constitution, shall be as valid against the United States under this Constitution, as under the Confederation.

This Constitution, and the Laws of the United States which shall be made in Pursuance thereof; and all Treaties made, or which shall be made, under the Authority of the United States, shall be the supreme Law of the Land; and the Judges in every State shall be bound thereby, any Thing in the Constitution or Laws of any State to the Contrary notwithstanding.

The Senators and Representatives before mentioned, and the Members of the several State Legislatures, and all executive and judicial Officers, both of the United States and of the several States, shall be bound by Oath or Affirmation, to support this Constitution; but no religious Test shall ever be required as a Qualification to any Office or public Trust under the United States.

ARTICLE. VII.

The Ratification of the Conventions of nine States, shall be sufficient for the Establishment of this Constitution between the States so ratifying the Same.

done in Convention by the Unanimous Consent of the States present the Seventeenth Day of September in the Year of our Lord one thousand seven hundred and Eighty seven and of the Independance of the United States of America the Twelfth In witness thereof We have hereunto subscribed our Names,

G°: Washington
Presid' and deputy from Virginia

New Hampshire	John Langdon
	Nicholas Gilman
Massachusetts	Nathaniel Gorham
	Rufus King
Connecticut	Wm Saml Johnson
	Roger Sherman
New York	Alexander Hamilton
New Jersey	Wil: Livingston
	David A. Brearley
	Wm Paterson
	Jona: Dayton
Pennsylvania	B. Franklin
	Thomas Mifflin
	Robt Morris
	Geo. Clymer
	Thos. FitzSimons
	Jared Ingersoll
	James Wilson
	Gouv Morris
Delaware	Geo: Read
	Gunning Bedford jun
	John Dickinson
	Richard Basset
	Jaco: Broom
Maryland	James McHenry
	Dan of St Thos Jenifer
	Danl Carroll
Virginia	John Blair-
	James Madison Jr.
North Carolina	Wm. Blount
	Richd Dobbs Spaight
	Hu Williamson
South Carolina	J. Rutledge
	Charles Cotesworth Pinckney
	Charles Pinckney
	Pierce Butler
Georgia	William Few
	Abr Baldwin

AMENDMENTS

ARTICLE I

Congress shall make no law respecting an establishment of religion, or prohibiting the free exercise thereof; or abriding the freedom of speech, or of the press; or of the right of the people peaceably to assemble, and to petition the Government for a redress of grievances.

ARTICLE II

A well regulated Militia, being necessary to the security of a free State, the right of the people to keep and bear Arms, shall not be infringed.

ARTICLE III

No Soldier shall, in time of peace be quartered in any house, without the consent of the Owner, nor in time of war, but in a manner to be prescribed by law.

ARTICLE IV

The right of the people to be secure in their persons, houses, papers, and effects, against unreasonable searches and seizures, shall not be violated, and no Warrants shall issue, but upon probable cause, supported by Oath or affirmation, and particularly describing the place to be searched, and the persons or things to be seized.

ARTICLE V

No person shall be held to answer for a capital, or otherwise infamous crime, unless on a presentment or indictment of a Grand Jury, except in cases arising in the land or naval forces, or in the Militia, when in actual service in time of War or public danger; nor shall any person be subject for the same offence to be twice put in jeopardy of life or limb; nor shall be compelled in any criminal case to be a witness against himself, nor be deprived of life, liberty, or property, without due process of law; nor shall private property be taken for public use, without just compensation.

ARTICLE VI

In all criminal prosecutions, the accused shall enjoy the right to a speedy and public trial, by an impartial jury of the State and district wherein the crime shall have been committed, which district shall have been previously ascertained by law, and to be informed of the nature and cause of the accusation; to be confronted with the witnesses against him; to have compulsory process for obtaining Witnesses in his favor, and to have the Assistance of Counsel for his defence.

ARTICLE VII

In Suits at common law, where the value in controversy shall exceed twenty dollars, the right of trial by jury shall be preserved, and no fact tried by a jury, shall be otherwise re-examined in any Court of the United States, than according to the rules of the common law.

ARTICLE VIII

Excessive bail shall not be required, nor excessive fines imposed, nor cruel and unusual punishments inflicted.

ARTICLE IX

The enumeration in the Constitution, of certain rights, shall not be construed to deny or disparage others retained by the people.

ARTICLE X

The powers not delegated to the United States by the Constitution, nor prohibited by it to the States, are reserved to the States respectively, or to the people.

ARTICLE XI

The Judicial power of the United States shall not be construed to extend to any suit in law or equity, commenced or prosecuted against one of the United States by Citizens of another State, or by Citizens or Subjects of any Foreign State.

ARTICLE XII

The Electors shall meet in their respective states, and vote by ballot for President and Vice-President, one of whom, at least, shall not be an inhabitant of the same state with themselves; they shall name in their ballots the person voted for as President, and in distinct ballots the person voted for as Vice-President, and they shall make distinct lists of all persons voted for as President and of all persons voted for as Vice-President, and of the number of votes for each, which lists they shall sign and certify, and transmit sealed to the seat of government of the United States, directed to the President of the Senate;—The President of the Senate shall, in the presence of the Senate and House of Representatives, open all the certificates and the votes shall then be counted;—The person having the greatest number of votes for President, shall be the President, if such number be a majority of the whole number of Electors appointed; and if no person have such majority, then from the persons having the highest numbers not exceeding three on the list of those voted for as President, the House of Representatives shall choose immediately, by ballot, the President. But, in choosing the President, the votes shall be taken by states, the representation from each state having one vote; a quorum for this purpose shall consist of a member or members from two-thirds of the states, and a majority of all the states shall be necessary to a choice. And if the House of Representatives shall not choose a President whenever the right of choice shall devolve upon them, before the fourth day of March next following, then the Vice-President shall act as President, as in the case of the death or other constitutional disability of the President.—The person having the greatest number of votes as Vice-President, shall be the Vice-President, if such number be a majority of the whole number of Electors appointed, and if no person have a majority, then from the two highest numbers on the list, the Senate shall choose the Vice-President; a quorum for the purpose shall consist of two-thirds of the whole number of Senators, and a majority of the whole number shall be necessary to a choice. But no person constitutionally ineligible to the office of President shall be eligible to that of Vice-President of the United States.

ARTICLE XIII

SECTION. 1. Neither slavery nor involuntary servitude, except as a punishment for crime whereof the party shall have been duly convicted, shall exist within the United States, or any place subject to their jurisdiction.

SECTION. 2. Congress shall have power to enforce this article by appropriate legislation.

ARTICLE XIV

SECTION. 1. All persons born or naturalized in the United States, and subject to the jurisdiction thereof, are citizens of the United States and of the State wherein they reside. No State shall make or enforce any law which shall abridge the privileges or immunities of citizens of the United States; nor shall any State deprive any person of life, liberty, or property, without due process of law; nor deny to any person within its jurisdiction the equal protection of the laws.

SECTION. 2. Representatives shall be apportioned among the several States according to their respective numbers, counting the whole number of persons in each State, excluding Indians not taxed. But when the right to vote at any election for the choice of electors for President and Vice President of the United States, Representatives in Congress, the Executive and Judicial officers of a State, or the members of the Legislature thereof, is denied to any of the male inhabitants of such State, being twenty-one years of age, and citizens of the United States, or in any way abridged, except for participation in rebellion, or other crime, the basis of representation therein shall be reduced in the proportion which the number of such male citizens shall bear to the whole number of male citizens twenty-one years of age in such State.

SECTION. 3. No person shall be a Senator or a Representative in Congress, or elector of President and Vice President, or hold any office, civil or military, under the United States, or under any State, who, having previously taken an oath, as a member of Congress, or as an officer of the United States, or as a member of any State legislature, or as an executive or judicial officer of any State, to support the Constitution of the United States, shall have engaged in insurrection or rebellion against the same, or given aid or comfort to the enemies thereof. But Congress may by a vote of two-thirds of each House, remove such disability.

SECTION. 4. The validity of the public debt of the United States, authorized by law, including debts incurred for payment of pensions and bounties for services in suppressing insurrection or rebellion, shall not be questioned. But neither the United States nor any State shall assume or pay any debt or obligation incurred in aid of insurrection or rebellion against the United States, or any claim for the loss or emancipation of any slave; but all such debts, obligations and claims shall be held illegal and void.

SECTION. 5. The Congress shall have power to enforce, by appropriate legislation, the provisions of this article.

ARTICLE XV

SECTION. 1. The right of citizens of the United States to vote shall not be denied or abridged by the United States or by any State on account of race, color, or previous condition of servitude.

SECTION. 2. The Congress shall have power to enforce this article by appropriate legislation.

ARTICLE XVI

The Congress shall have power to lay and collect taxes on incomes, from whatever source derived, without apportionment among the several States, and without regard to any census or enumeration.

ARTICLE XVII

(1) The Senate of the United States shall be composed of two Senators from each State, elected by the people thereof, for six years; and each Senator shall have one vote. The electors in each State shall have the qualifications requisite for electors of the most numerous branch of the State legislatures.
(2) When vacancies happen in the representation of any State in the Senate, the executive authority of such State shall issue writs of election to fill such vacancies: **Provided,** That the legislature of any State may empower the executive thereof to make temporary appointments until the people fill the vacancies by election as the legislature may direct.
(3) This amendment shall not be so construed as to affect the election or term of any Senator chosen before it becomes valid as part of the Constitution.

ARTICLE XVIII

SECTION. 1. After one year from the ratification of this article, the manufacture, sale, or transportation of intoxicating liquors within, the importation thereof into, or the exportation thereof from the United States and all territory subject to the jurisdiction thereof for beverage purposes is hereby prohibited.

SECTION. 2. The Congress and the several States shall have concurrent power to enforce this article by appropriate legislation.

SECTION. 3. This article shall be inoperative unless it shall have been ratified as an amendment to the Constitution by the legislatures of the several States, as provided in the Constitution, within seven years from the date of the submission hereof to the States by Congress.

ARTICLE XIX

The right of citizens of the United States to vote shall not be denied or abridged by the United States or by any State on account of sex.

Congress shall have power to enforce this article by appropriate legislation.

ARTICLE XX

SECTION. 1. The terms of the President and Vice President shall end at noon on the 20th day of January, and the terms of Senators and Representatives at noon on the 3d day of January, of the years in which such terms would have ended if this article had not been ratified; and the terms of their successors shall then begin.

SECTION. 2. The Congress shall assemble at least once in every year, and such meeting shall begin at noon on the 3d day of January, unless they shall by law appoint a different day.

SECTION. 3. If, at the time fixed for the beginning of the term of the President, the President elect shall have died, the Vice President elect shall become President. If a President shall not have been chosen before the time fixed for the beginning of his term, or if the President elect shall have failed to qualify, then the Vice President elect shall act as President until a President shall have qualified; and the Congress may by law provide for the case wherein neither a President elect or Vice President elect shall have qualified, declaring who shall then act as President, or the manner in which one is to act shall be selected, and such a person shall act accordingly until a President or Vice President shall have qualified.

SECTION. 4. The Congress may by law provide for the case of the death of any of the persons from whom the House of Representatives may choose a President whenever the right of choice shall have devolved upon them, and for the case of the death of any of the persons from whom the Senate may choose a Vice President whenever the right of choice shall have devolved upon them.

SECTION. 5. Sections 1 and 2 shall take place on the 15th day of October following the ratification of this article.

SECTION. 6. This article shall be inoperative unless it shall have been ratified as an amendment to the Constitution by the legislatures of three-fourths of the several States within seven years from the date of its submission.

ARTICLE XXI

SECTION. 1. The eighteenth article of amendment to the Constitution of the United States is hereby repealed.

SECTION. 2. The transportation or importation into any State, Territory, or possession of the United States for delivery or use therein of intoxicating liquors, in violation of the laws thereof, is hereby prohibited.

SECTION. 3. This article shall be inoperative unless it shall have been ratified as an amendment to the Constitution by conventions in the several States, as provided in the Constitution, within seven years from the date of the submission hereof to the States by the Congress.

ARTICLE XXII

SECTION. 1. No person shall be elected to the office of the President more than twice, and no person who has held the office of President, or acted as President, for more than two years of a term to which some other person was elected President shall be elected to the office of President more than once. But this Article shall not apply to any person holding the office of President when this Article was proposed by the Congress, and shall not prevent any person who may be holding the office of President, or acting as President, during the term within which this Article becomes operative from holding the office of President or acting as President during the remainder of such term.

SECTION. 2. This article shall be inoperative unless it shall have been ratified as an amendment to the Constitution by the legislatures of three-fourths of the several States within seven years from the date of its submission to the States by the Congress.

ARTICLE XXIII

SECTION. 1. The District constituting the seat of Government of the United States shall appoint in such manner as the Congress may direct:

A number of electors of President and Vice President equal to the whole number of

Senators and Representatives in Congress to which the District would be entitled if it were a State, but in no event more than the least populous state; they shall be in addition to those appointed by the States, but they shall be considered, for the purposes of the election of the President and Vice President, to be electors appointed by a State; and they shall meet in the District and perform such duties as provided by the twelfth article of amendment.

SECTION. 2. The Congress shall have the power to enforce this article by appropriate legislation.

ARTICLE XXIV

SECTION. 1. The right of citizens of the United States to vote in any primary or other election for President or Vice President, for electors for President or Vice President, or for Senator or Representative in Congress, shall not be denied or abridged by the United States or any State by reason of failure to pay any poll tax or other tax.

SECTION. 2. The Congress shall have power to enforce this article by appropriate legislation.

ARTICLE XXV

SECTION. 1. In case of the removal of the President from office or of his death or resignation, the Vice President shall become President.

SECTION. 2. Whenever there is a vacancy in the office of the Vice President, the President shall nominate a Vice President who shall take office upon confirmation by a majority vote of both Houses of Congress.

SECTION. 3. Whenever the President transmits to the President pro tempore of the Senate and the Speaker of the House of Representatives his written declaration that he is unable to discharge the powers and duties of his office, and until he transmits to them a written declaration to the contrary, such powers and duties shall be discharged by the Vice President as Acting President.

SECTION. 4. Whenever the Vice President and a majority of either the principal officers of the executive departments or of such other body as Congress may by law provide, transmit to the President pro tempore of the Senate and the Speaker of the House of Representatives their written declaration that the President is unable to discharge the powers and duties of his office, the Vice President shall immediately assume the powers and duties of the office as Acting President.

Thereafter, when the President transmits to the President pro tempore of the Senate and the Speaker of the House of Representatives his written declaration that no inability exists, he shall resume the powers and duties of his office unless the Vice President and a majority of either the principal officers of the executive departments or of such other body as Congress may by law provide, transmit within four days to the President pro tempore of the Senate and the Speaker of the House of Representatives their written declaration that the President is unable to discharge the powers and duties of his office. Thereupon Congress shall decide the issue, assembling within forty-eight hours for that purpose if not in session. If the Congress, within twenty-one days after receipt of the latter written declaration, or, if Congress is not in session, within twenty-one days after Congress is required to assemble, determines by two-thirds vote of both Houses that the President is unable to discharge the powers and duties of his office, the Vice President shall continue to discharge the same as Acting President; otherwise, the President shall resume the powers and duties of his office.

ARTICLE XXVI

SECTION. 1. The right of citizens of the United States, who are eighteen years of age or older, to vote shall not be denied or abridged by the United States or by any State on account of age.

SECTION. 2. The Congress shall have power to enforce this article by appropriate legislation.

ARTICLE XXVII

No law varying the compensation for the services of the Senators and Representatives shall take effect, until an election of Representatives shall have intervened.

SELECTED PROPOSED AMENDMENTS NOT RATIFIED BY THE STATES

CHILD LABOR AMENDMENT (1924)

SECTION 1. The Congress shall have power to limit, regulate, and prohibit the labor of persons under 18 years of age.

SECTION 2. The power of the several States is unimpaired by this article except that the operation of State laws shall be suspended to the extent necessary to give effect to legislation enacted by the Congress.

EQUAL RIGHTS AMENDMENT (1972)

SECTION 1. Equality of rights under the law shall not be denied or abridged by the United States or by any State on account of sex.

SECTION 2. The Congress shall have the power to enforce, by appropriate legislation, the provisions of this article.

SECTION 3. This amendment shall take effect two years after the date of ratification.

Index by Key Word

abandoned the practice of the law and had gone
CONST LAW 31
abhor Gentlemen, I a. war   TRIALS, FAMOUS 9
ability the a. to look a lawyer straight in the
MARSHALL 6
abject reliance upon canons of any sort
STATUTORY CONSTRUC 16
abolish the right of the people to alter or a.
CONSTITUTION 4
To a. the fences of laws between men   FREEDOM 5
abortion everybody that is for a. has already
ABORTION 13
factors that govern the a. decision   ABORTION 2
If men could get pregnant, a. would be a   ABORTION 8
personal privacy includes the a.   ABORTION 3
above No man is a. it, and no man is below it
OBEDIENCE TO LAW 17
No man is a. the law and no man is below
OBEDIENCE TO LAW 19
abracadabra The whole a. of The Law swings around a
LANGUAGE 8
absolute cannot be recalled by the most a. power
CONTRACTS 1
discretion is a ruthless master
ADMINISTRATIVE LAW 17
does not require a. equality or
WEALTH AND POVERTY 17
It is the a. justice of the State   LAWYERS (PRO) 2
retaining an a. power over Wives   WOMEN'S RIGHTS 4
The first is a. but, in the nature of
FREEDOM OF RELIGION 32
the separation of church and state is a.
FREEDOM OF RELIGION 56
There is no a. freedom to do as one   CONTRACTS 12
with a. justice it does not concern   JUSTICE 16
absolutely little in this Constitution that is a.
CONSTITUTION 40
more taxes than is a. necessary is   TAXATION 38
absolutes a society hell-bent for a.   LAWYERS 57
meant their prohibitions to be "a." BILL OF RIGHTS 15
there are "a." in our Bill of Rights BILL OF RIGHTS 15
absolutism is on the path towards a.
CRIMINAL PROCEDURE 25
absorbed not yet been a. or sloughed off
LAW, GROWTH 5
abstract in the a., I have no very enthusiastic
FREEDOM OF SPEECH 14
abstractions Lofty a. about individual liberty and
LAW 81
there is a point in this series of a.   COPYRIGHT 17
absurd as a. as to build a tree or manufacture
CONSTITUTION 20
formalism, which even yet at times   JURY 40
not only dangerous, but a. FREEDOM OF THE PRESS 20
absurdity inexpressible a. to put the worst to
CAPITAL PUNISHMENT 4

abuse every law an a.   CRIMINAL 1
separation between the a. and the
FREEDOM OF THE PRESS 14
Some degree of a. is inseparable from
FREEDOM OF THE PRESS 12
those who would be most apt to a. it   JURY 12
abuses The a. of the freedom of the press here
FREEDOM OF THE PRESS 13
academic an a. faculty which pins its reputation
LAW REVIEWS 2
committed to safeguarding a. freedom
FIRST AMEND 41
freedom does not mean academic license
EDUCATION 2
freedom, though not a specifically
AFFIRMATIVE ACTION 14
academically So you see I was only third a.
LAW FIRMS 5
accepted something that must be a. by all men
NATURAL LAW 13
access lack of a. for the poor and middle class   LAW 99
the Christians had a. to the lions when
WEALTH AND POVERTY 19
they had no a. to law except through men   WOMEN 7
to a library, and directions in what   LAW LIBRARIES 1
accident loss from a. must lie where it falls   TORTS 1
some a. of immediate overwhelming   CASES 4
accidentally particular crime or vice was a. omitted
CRIME 3
accommodation Justice, I think, is the tolerable a. of
JUSTICE 36
accommodations separate but equal a. for white and
SEGREGATION 6
accomplice n. One associated with another in a
LAWYERS (CON) 25
account Government may take race into ac. when
AFFIRMATIVE ACTION 8
accountants may expose a. to a liability in an
NEGLIGENCE 18
accounts the a. were equally balanced   JUDGMENT 2
accredited following, step by step, the a. guides
STATUTORY CONSTRUC 16
accumulating with an almost incredible rapidity
LAW BOOKS 5
accumulation The a. of all powers legislative
SEPARATION OF POWERS 4
accuracy and diligence are much more necessary to
LAWYERS 4
accurate electric chair should be reasonably a.
COURTROOM SCENES 14
accusatorial not inquisitorial   FIFTH AMEND 12
accused An a. is not criminally responsible if
INSANITY 13
Formally to detain one a. of   CRIMINAL LAW 8
justice, though due to the a., is due to
CRIMINAL LAW 12

441

Under our criminal procedure the a. has
CRIMINAL PROCEDURE 13

were subject to a duty to respond to   FIFTH AMEND 3

accuser due to the accused, is due to the a.
CRIMINAL LAW 12

achieved the immediate result that is a.   CONST LAW 50

achievement do not let so great an a. suffer from
ILLEGALITY 1

acme The a. of judicial distinction means the
MARSHALL 6

acquire includes only liberty to a. and enjoy
FREEDOM OF SPEECH 17

acquit At the Last Assizes it shall a.
MILITARY JUSTICE 4

v.t. To render judgment in a murder   JUDGMENT 3

acres represent people, not trees or a.   VOTING 15

act An a. against the constitution is void
CONSTITUTION 1

An A. to encourage good shooting   CRIMINAL LAW 3

an a. worthy of reward rather than   TRIALS, FAMOUS 6

believed to be an a. of justice   SLAVERY 21

constitution controls any legislative a.
JUDICIAL REVIEW 7

freedom to believe and freedom to a.
FREEDOM OF RELIGION 32

how will the judges a.   JUDGES 14

It is not every a., legislative in form   LEGISLATION 20

made Women humans by A. of Congress
WOMEN'S RIGHTS 13

make a lawyer honest by an a. of the   ETHICS 19

of the legislature, repugnant to the
JUDICIAL REVIEW 8

one who assumes to a., even though   NEGLIGENCE 10

the mad a. of these two boys, I am sorry
CAPITAL PUNISHMENT 12

The great a. of faith is when a man   HOLMES 15

was not the act of a voluntary agent   INSANITY 1

we should never a.   LAWYERS 6

words that are also a constituent a.   CONST LAW 27

acting subject to the duty of a. carefully, if
NEGLIGENCE 10

action A vested right of a. is property in the
PROPERTY 16

as life is a. and passion, it is   HOLMES 4

border of reasonable legislative a.   JUDICIAL REVIEW 25

form of action to be known as "civil a."
CIVIL PROCEDURE 10

one form of a., for the enforcement or
CODIFICATION 1

one form of a. to be known as "civil
CIVIL PROCEDURE 10

producing imminent lawless a. and is
FREEDOM OF EXPRESS 25

triggers of a.   FREEDOM OF EXPRESS 8

which shall be denominated a civil a.   CODIFICATION 1

actions nothing to do with his a. on the bench
JUDICIAL APPOINT 2

Speech is conduct, and a. speak
FREEDOM OF SPEECH 41

acts prohibited and acts allowed, are of
CONSTITUTION 14

sit in judgment on the a. of the
INTERNATIONAL LAW 8

actual show a. malice in the publication of the   LIBEL 5

the statement was made with "a. malice"   LIBEL 11

acute This study renders men a., inquisitive
LAWYERS (PRO) 1

adaptation capacity for growth and a. is the
COMMON LAW 13

add we'll a. it to the end   LEGAL WRITING 20

added We just a. up your time sheets   LAWYER JOKES 4

adder it is deaf, deaf as an a. to the   LAW 6

adjective comprehensive statement in an a.
CONST LAW 36

adjudge How can we a. to summary and shameful
INNOCENCE 1

adjudicated quarrels of mankind   LAW LIBRARIES 4

adjudication always a proper subject for a.
HUMAN RIGHTS 1

Legislation and a. must follow, and   LAW, GROWTH 3

the a. between man and man, between man
JUDGES 50

adjudications has been said in prior a. has force in a
PRECEDENT 43

adjuncts become a. of great corporations and have
LAWYERS (CON) 22

administer I am going there to a. the law   HOLMES 12

you cannot a. a wicked law impartially
COURTROOM SCENES 17

administration of justice is the firmest pillar of good
JUDICIARY 7

The a. of law can never go lax where
LAW ENFORCEMENT 4

administrative considerations of a. convenience
EVIDENCE 11

Our A. Law has largely "growed" like
ADMINISTRATIVE LAW 13

through the zeal of an a. agent   LIBERTY 8

admit to public schools on a racially   SEGREGATION 17

we shall readily a. that a more imposing
SUPREME COURT 8

admitted beat the rap you must be a. to the bar
LAWYERS (CON) 47

that wuz once a. t' th' bar   LAWYERS (CON) 39

adopted only that portion which was applicable
COMMON LAW 9

adore We a. the forms of law, instead of   LAW 27

adulterated A commodity which in a more or less a.
JUSTICE 22

advance never take your whole fee in a., nor any
FEES 6

waste your time looking up the law in a.   COURTS 37

advancement the a. or inhibition of religion then
FREEDOM OF RELIGION 64

advances effect that neither a. nor inhibits
FREEDOM OF RELIGION 64

neither a. nor inhibits religion
FREEDOM OF RELIGION 67

She is to be wooed by slow a.   JUSTICE 31

advantage One must strike a balance of a.   TAXATION 36

the accused has every a.   CRIMINAL PROCEDURE 13

advantages absolute equality or precisely equal a.
WEALTH AND POVERTY 17

adversary always should be an a. proceeding
CIVIL PROCEDURE 14

It is at this point that our a. system   CONFESSIONS 11

advertising as respects purely commercial a.
FREEDOM OF SPEECH 27

advice A lawyer's time and a. are his stock in
LAW PRACTICE 6

the judge goes to the lawyer for a.   JUDGES 44

advisory nothing more than an a. opinion
JUDICIAL REVIEW 33

advocacy is directed to inciting or producing

The present a. upon capital is but the   TAXATION 18
assembly been used for purposes of a.   FIRST AMEND 10
From such an a. can a perfect production
    CONST CONVENTION 8
It is really an a. of demigods   CONST CONVENTION 11
assent foreseeable future—gain general a.
    CONST LAW 51
has not hitherto commanded the a. of
    LAWYERS (CON) 25
the habit of a., not to a factitious
    OBEDIENCE TO LAW 21
assenting no one having offered them a fee for a.
    LAWYERS (CON) 25
asserted whatever is boldly a. and plausibly
    ADVOCACY 10
assizes At the Last A. it shall acquit
    MILITARY JUSTICE 4
associate he in some sort a. himself with the
    CRIMINAL LAW 13
associates tell a man or woman who his or her a.
    FIRST AMEND 44
association for as noble a purpose as any involved
    MARRIAGE 10
that promotes a way of life, not causes   MARRIAGE 10
associational The a. rights which our system honors
    FIRST AMEND 44
assumption admissible only upon a. that conspiracy
    JURY 62
everyone found the a. of innocence so   GUILT 5
unconstitutional a. of powers by Courts   COURTS 23
we find fatally easy the a. of guilt   GUILT 5
assumptions premised upon unfounded a. about how
    CONST LAW 56
astuteness that barbarian a. which has always
    LAWYERS (CON) 19
asylum perhaps even in a lunatic a., in any
    PROSECUTION 5
to this happy country as their last a.   FIRST AMEND 3
atone for the wrong this day done   SEGREGATION 10
attached a thing inextricably a. to something
    LAWYERS 48
students don't become a. to them   LAWYER JOKES 10
thinking of the thing which it is a. to   LAWYERS 48
to it by a kind of parental affection   LAW 19
attaches to the lawyer's trade, it grades high in
    LAWYERS (CON) 18
attacking that mode of a. or defending a man
    LAWYERS 21
attacks The a. upon the Court are merely an
    SUPREME COURT 14
attains reaching it a. it by getting drunk
    INTOXICATION 3
attend the right to a. criminal trials is   FIRST AMEND 49
attended that it be a. with a sanction; or, in
    GOVERNMENT 1
attitude Law's empire is defined by a., not
    LAW, DEFINITIONS 10
attorney an a. who defends a criminal, knowing
    LAWYERS (CON) 25
n. A person legally appointed to   LAWYERS (CON) 28
so to speak, private A. Generals   STANDING 1
some legal experience as A. General
    JUSTICE DEPARTMENT 5
the average a. has two objects in life
    LAWYERS (CON) 21
The People's A.   JUDGES, INDIVIDUAL 3
The United States A. is the   PROSECUTION 6

attribute mercy is the highest a. of man
    CAPITAL PUNISHMENT 17
augur They a. misgovernment at a distance, and
    LAWYERS (PRO) 1
authentic His mark is his a. seal; by it he
    TRADEMARKS 6
authoritative through any kind of a. selection
    FREEDOM OF EXPRESS 17
authorities these a. are all wrong, as time and
    PRECEDENT 13
authority does not exist without some definite a.
    LAW 61
every direct a. known to us is against   PRECEDENT 13
finding is amply supported by modern a.
    SEGREGATION 11
his a. is at its maximum, for it   PRESIDENT 10
if a. is to be reconciled with freedom
    FREEDOM OF SPEECH 23
justify the State in interposing its a.   DUE PROCESS 10
The courts are without a. either to   DUE PROCESS 32
the same a. which can establish
    FREEDOM OF RELIGION 16
within the compass of the national a.   GOVERNMENT 5
autocracy to save the people from a.
    SEPARATION OF POWERS 13
automatic calls for an a. response to a signal
    LABOR LAW 24
autonomy but reciprocity   SEPARATION OF POWERS 20
available a right which must be made a. to all on
    EDUCATION 7
avenger like a self-appointed public a.
    COURTROOM SCENES 16
avenue It is the lawyer's a. to the public   ADVOCACY 9
average a certain a. of conduct, a sacrifice of
    NEGLIGENCE 2
not be blameworthy in the a. member of
    PUNISHMENT 11
person, applying contemporary community
    OBSCENITY 11
the a. attorney has two objects in life
    LAWYERS (CON) 21
avoid A lawyer should a. even the appearance
    ETHICS 43
axiom rather an a. of experience than a rule
    LEGISLATIVE HISTORY 2
axioms contained only the a. and corollaries of   LAW 35

babe to the lisping b., that prattles on her   LAW 21
babies What a justice seeking bunch of b. they
    TRIALS 3
baby once likened government to a b.   TAXATION 52
which b. has the measles   ANTITRUST 24
back-alley women would be forced into b. abortions
    JUDICIAL APPOINT 12
backbone out of a banana a Justice with more b.
    HOLMES 14
background against the b. of a profound national
    LIBEL 9
backs take government off the b. of people and
    GOVERNMENT 32
backward flying b. because it didn't care where
    PRECEDENT 38
not to turn b. toward the barbarous and
    CAPITAL PUNISHMENT 15
bad a b. man has as much reason as a good
    MORALITY 5
A man may have as b. a heart as he   MORALITY 3

ever composed of imprudent or b. men
                                    SUPREME COURT 9
good government, not fear of a b. one
                                    FIRST AMEND 29
Great cases like hard cases make b. law   CASES 4
it is easy enough to ruin it by b. laws   LEGISLATION 24
neighbor as I am of being a b. subject
                                    CIVIL DISOBEDIENCE 7
people lose respect for one b. law   LEGISLATION 35
pleadings equalled the cost of four new   PLEADINGS 4
saying there are no b. laws, nor that
                                    OBEDIENCE TO LAW 12
secure the repeal of b. or obnoxious
                                    LAW ENFORCEMENT 2
teach men to trample b. laws under their   RIGHTS 9
The law—'Tis b. to have it, but, I   LAW 15
you must look at it as a b. man, who   MORALITY 7
balance hold the b. nice, clear and true between
                                    CRIMINAL PROCEDURE 14
how and in what b. weigh John Brown
                                    TRIALS, FAMOUS 15
in the nice b. of a jeweler's scale
                                    FREEDOM OF EXPRESS 11
One must strike a b. of advantage   TAXATION 36
the b. of hardships tips decidedly   INJUNCTIONS 4
the Bill of Rights out of existence   FIRST AMEND 31
We are to keep the b. true   CRIMINAL LAW 12
balanced the accounts were equally b.   JUDGMENT 2
balancing did all the "b." that was to be done in
                                    FIRST AMEND 31
ballot the b. and to the processes of
                                    JUDICIAL REVIEW 32
ban jury system puts a b. upon intelligence   JURY 23
banana I could carve out of a b. a Justice with
                                    HOLMES 14
banana-peel the judicious placing of a b.
                                    LAW REVIEWS 7
band or conspire together, or go in disguise
                                    CIVIL RIGHTS 4
bands loosen all the b. of the constitution   CONST LAW 3
banish why it should b. an alien from our worst
                                    IMMIGRATION 3
banished word of moral significance could be b.
                                    MORALITY 9
bank line between a b. robber and a lawyer is
                                    LAWYERS (CON) 58
    You ever hear of the Favor B.?   CRIMINAL JUSTICE 3
bankrupt too poor even to go b., I cannot agree
                                    BANKRUPTCY 7
banners with flying b. and beating drums we are
                                    FIRST AMEND 7
bar a judge is a member of the B. who once   JUDGES 41
    occupies the judicial bench and the b.   LAWYERS 12
    the great power at the b.   ADVOCACY 8
    The real complaining party at your b. is
                                    WAR CRIMES 6
    we have always gotten the pick of the B.
                                    LAWYERS (CON) 45
    you must be admitted to the b.   LAWYERS (CON) 47
barbarian that b. astuteness which has always
                                    LAWYERS (CON) 19
barbarous turn backward toward the b. and cruel
                                    CAPITAL PUNISHMENT 15
Barleycorn This ubiquitous disciple of John B.
                                    INTOXICATION 6
barn finds himself trying to wield a b. door
                                    LAW REVIEWS 5

barnacles entirely obscured by its interpretive b.
                                    PROCEDURE 8
barnyard pig in the parlor instead of the b.   TORTS 6
barred No one has been b. on account of his
                                    CIVIL RIGHTS 25
barren A b. cow is substantially a different
                                    CONTRACTS 6
    Not for us the b. logomachy that dwells   JUSTICE 27
barrier this same Constitution stands as a b.
                                    AFFIRMATIVE ACTION 10
barriers operate invidiously to discriminate on
                                    CIVIL RIGHTS 37
    the b. to prior restraint remain high
                                    FREEDOM OF THE PRESS 44
    the majority raises formidable b. around
                                    FREEDOM OF EXPRESS 4
barter A man may not b. away his life or his   COURTS 9
base a b. and vile thing to plead for money   FEES 2
basic Citizenship is man's b. right for it is
                                    IMMIGRATION 5
basis I suppose it is not a b. for impeachment
                                    LAW REVIEWS 1
    The b. of our political systems is the
                                    CONSTITUTION 10
bastards Sue the B.   LITIGATION 27
bath Henry Miller who shuns a b. of clean
                                    OBSCENITY 19
bathroom looks very different on a b. door than
                                    SEX DISCRIMINATION 16
bats of the law, flitting in the twilight   EVIDENCE 7
battle the foxholes or graveyards of b.   CIVIL RIGHTS 25
battleships equalled the cost of four new b., or a
                                    PLEADINGS 4
beach-head If a b. of cooperation may push back the
                                    INTERNATIONAL LAW 21
beam the b. ought not to tip for motes and   JURY 48
bear decision whether to b. or beget a child PRIVACY 15
    Injustice is relatively easy to b.; what   JUSTICE 28
beat a murderer for helping him b. the rap
                                    LAWYERS (CON) 47
beaten fact that a path is a b. one is a   PRECEDENT 45
beating Are you still b. your wife
                                    CROSS-EXAMINATION 5
beaut When I make a mistake, it's a b.
                                    JUDICIAL APPOINT 3
beautiful the community should be b. as well as
                                    PROPERTY 26
become they b. lawyers   LAWYERS (CON) 54
becomes Our d-i-v-o-r-c-e b. final today   DIVORCE 3
becoming It is always b. something else   CONST LAW 34
bed I thought of after going to b. that   ADVOCACY 20
bedevils uncritical use of words b. the law   WORDS 19
bedrock If there is a b. principle underlying
                                    FIRST AMEND 50
bedrooms sacred precincts of marital b. for   PRIVACY 9
beer your justice would freeze b.   JUSTICE 41
before I'm usually there b. the ambulance   LAWYERS 63
    was not brought b. me   JUDGES 18
begetters by the most gifted of its b.   CONST LAW 27
beggar Streaked from the finger of the b., Time
                                    LAW LIBRARIES 4
beggary cheated of their right and reduced to b.
                                    LAWYERS (CON) 9
begin But let us b.   INTERNATIONAL LAW 21
beginning A good b.   LAWYER JOKES 14
behalf had I so interfered in b. of any of the
                                    TRIALS, FAMOUS 6

behind Never let your correspondence fall b.
LAW PRACTICE 4

behold a Lawyer, an honest Man!   LAWYERS (CON) 2

belief I have no very enthusiastic b., though I
FREEDOM OF SPEECH 14

in a relation to God involving duties
FREEDOM OF RELIGION 29

It is my b. that there are "absolutes"
BILL OF RIGHTS 15

believe a lawyer who does not b. in his heart
ADVOCACY 5

I b. in an America where the separation
FREEDOM OF RELIGION 56

I b. in the law of love, and I believe   CIVIL RIGHTS 12

I do not b. in lawyers, in that mode of   LAWYERS 21

I do not b. in the law of hate   CIVIL RIGHTS 12

I don't b. in God because I don't   DARROW 5

I don't b. in Mother Goose   DARROW 5

Men may b. what they cannot prove
FREEDOM OF RELIGION 37

Men may b. what they cannot prove   RELIGION 7

two concepts—freedom to b. and freedom
FREEDOM OF RELIGION 32

we have lived through too much to b. it
FREEDOM OF SPEECH 44

believed by half his fellow men to be wrong   JUDGES 21

he b. in every case that he took   ETHICS 22

believes the majority still b. that race   CIVIL RIGHTS 43

this man to be Santa Claus, this Court
COURTROOM SCENES 9

belong the rest of us b. in straitjackets
COURTROOM SCENES 3

belongs One who b. to the most vilified and
FREEDOM OF RELIGION 33

The earth b. always to the living   CONSTITUTION 8

The law school b. in the modern   LAW SCHOOL 3

below No man is above it, and no man is b. it
OBEDIENCE TO LAW 17

the mistake I made in the Court b.   ADVOCACY 16

bench it occupies the judicial b. and the bar
LAWYERS 12

nothing to do with his actions on the b.
JUDICIAL APPOINT 2

beneficial cease to be b. to man, they cease to be
LAW 28

benefit actual benefit for which the t. is paid
TAXATION 31

will have the b. of a double discussion   APPEALS 3

benefits in order to enjoy the inestimable b.
FREEDOM OF THE PRESS 21

bequeath v. t. To generously give to another   WILLS 9

bequest like a munificent b. in a pauper's will
FOURTEENTH AMEND 11

beseech I b. ye in the bowels of Christ, think
COURTS 32

best excluded a citizen from our b. society
IMMIGRATION 3

he uses his b. endeavors to secure the
SEPARATION OF POWERS 12

he's doing the b. he can   LAW 69

Logic and taxation are not always the b.   TAXATION 25

No, I'm doing my b. to hide it   CONTEMPT 2

The b. of us being unfit to die, what an
CAPITAL PUNISHMENT 4

The b. use of good laws is to teach men   RIGHTS 9

betray my hand cut off than b. the interests of
CLIENT 19

better builded b. than they knew
FOURTEENTH AMEND 2

chosen to decide who has the b. lawyer   JURY 52

It can scarcely be made b. than it is
CONST AMENDMENT 3

It is not b. that all felony suspects   CRIMINAL LAW 18

may be able to make a b. constitution
CONST CONVENTION 8

The less government we have the b.   GOVERNMENT 15

They are b. to work with or play with or
LAWYERS (PRO) 14

betting with the b. odds in favor of Judas   COURTS 19

between the Constitution amount to b. friends
CONSTITUTION 42

bevy irksome to be ruled by a b. of Platonic
GOVERNMENT 29

Bible kissed, which I suppose to be the B.
TRIALS, FAMOUS 7

biennial I consider b. elections as a security   VOTING 1

big as b. a man as he can   PRESIDENT 7

For de b. stealin' dey makes you Emperor   CRIME 5

bigamy Yes, and it's b., too   MARRIAGE 7

bigness a country cursed with b.   ANTITRUST 9

bigotry which gives to b. no sanction, to
FREEDOM OF RELIGION 18

bigots religion does not furnish grosser b.   JUDGES 4

bill A b. of rights is what the people are
BILL OF RIGHTS 2

"balance" the B. of Rights out of   FIRST AMEND 31

First the omission of a b. of rights   BILL OF RIGHTS 1

make the B. of Rights, applicable to the
FOURTEENTH AMEND 12

managed to b. 27 hours in one day   LAW FIRMS 6

of Rights into a suicide pact   BILL OF RIGHTS 13

original language of the B. of Rights   FIRST AMEND 32

privacy older than the B. of Rights   MARRIAGE 10

specific guarantees in the B. of Rights
BILL OF RIGHTS 16

the protection of the B. of Rights goes
FIRST AMEND 40

The very purpose of a B. of Rights was
BILL OF RIGHTS 11

there are "absolutes" in our B. of   BILL OF RIGHTS 15

within the limits of the B. of Rights   EDUCATION 3

bills in vain, that we insert b. of rights in   JUDICIARY 13

of rights . . . are not only unnecessary in
BILL OF RIGHTS 4

bind him down from mischief by the chains of
CONSTITUTION 12

must necessarily b. its component parts
FEDERALISM 12

To b., to restrain, is of their very   ANTITRUST 14

binding law of the land that is b. on all   CONST LAW 60

made b. upon the conscience by a penalty
WITNESSES 3

they are not b. at all   TREATIES 5

virtually b. on the weaker party only   TREATIES 5

bird Every achievement is a b. on the wing   HOLMES 9

If you want to hit a b. on the wing, you   HOLMES 9

The problem of cat versus b. is as old   LEGISLATION 39

birds everyone of the jokes those B. make is a
CONGRESS 4

birth At every point from b. to death the
AFFIRMATIVE ACTION 11

than the mischief which gave it b.   CONST LAW 24

bishops proved by twenty b. that either party
CONTRACTS 11

SEPARATION OF POWERS 17
within banks that keep it from
SEPARATION OF POWERS 16
canary Like the miner's c., the Indian marks
AMERICAN INDIAN LAW 10
cancer is not a book OBSCENITY 18
is not a book OBSCENITY 20
is the sweepings of the Augean stables OBSCENITY 17
is worthless trash is to pay it a OBSCENITY 17
on the literary body of America OBSCENITY 20
candid let Facts be submitted to a c. world
ENGLISH LAW 4
candor the compromise between c. and shame at
OBSCENITY 2
The President's need for complete c. and
PRESIDENT 17
cannon A judge is not free, like a loose c., to JUDGES 63
cannot I want a lawyer to tell me what I c. do CLIENT 5
canons abject reliance upon c. of any sort
STATUTORY CONSTRUC 16
cant more in the name of morals is mere c.
TAXATION 46
canter There is a little finishing c. before HOLMES 34
canvas It is a good c., on which some strokes
CONSTITUTION 6
canvassing the privilege of c. men, and our rulers
FREEDOM OF THE PRESS 15
capacity and opportunity to express the erotic
OBSCENITY 31
must be shown; in the law concealment of
LAWYERS (CON) 17
This flexibility and c. for growth and COMMON LAW 13
capital I don't believe in c. punishment
CAPITAL PUNISHMENT 6
In a c. case, where the defendant is
CRIMINAL PROCEDURE 18
making temporary insanity a c. offense INSANITY 2
Punishment, a penalty regarding the
CAPITAL PUNISHMENT 8
The present assault upon c. is but the TAXATION 18
caprice against whatever is unequal by c. INJUSTICE 3
capricious arbitrary, c., an abuse of discretion
ADMINISTRATIVE LAW 22
not be unreasonable, arbitrary or c. DUE PROCESS 31
captain The law was not made for the C. ADMIRALTY 4
captives utter c. and choreboys of their clients
LAWYERS 53
carcasses Where c. are, eagles will gather LAW 3
care I c. little who lays down the general
ADMINISTRATIVE LAW 5
I c. not who makes th' laws iv a nation INJUNCTIONS 1
I don't c. what the law is, that isn't JURY 56
If perticular c. and attention is not WOMEN'S RIGHTS 1
The degree of c. demanded of a person by
NEGLIGENCE 21
they can take c. of themselves
FREEDOM OF RELIGION 26
What do I c. about the law LAWLESSNESS 9
careful befure th' law if he isn't c. LAW 50
carefully subject to the duty of acting c., if he
NEGLIGENCE 10
carrier plays the part of the typhoid c.
LEGAL WRITING 4
carries the key of his prison in his own pocket
CONTEMPT 1
the statement c. its own refutation
ORIGINAL INTENTION 8

carry It must c. its death warrant upon its DAMAGES 3
carrying their resentments right into a jury box
JURY 67
carte blanche to embody our economic or moral
DUE PROCESS 25
carve I could c. out of a banana a Justice HOLMES 14
lawyers only decide how to c. it up LAWYERS (CON) 61
unable like Solomon to c. the child CUSTODY 2
carved For the saddest epitaph which can be c.
FIRST AMEND 9
case A decided c. is worth as much as it PRECEDENT 20
a distinguished c. is a case that is no PRECEDENT 40
concrete c. falls on the nearer or RIGHTS 12
he believed in every c. that he took ETHICS 22
I never take a c. unless I am convinced ETHICS 28
is decided upon an economic theory which
DUE PROCESS 13
It is that state of the c., which, after JURY 15
match the colors of the c. at hand PRECEDENT 21
principles suited to my views of the c. JUDGES 6
The c. is made difficult, not because FREEDOM 3
The fecundity of our c. law would make
PRECEDENT 30
we will try the c. strictly on its JUDGES 43
cases A thousand c., many of them upon CASES 1
and still be supported by an array of c. PRECEDENT 14
Great c. like hard cases make bad law CASES 4
in the main through a series of c. CASE SYSTEM 1
select, classify, and arrange all the c. CASE SYSTEM 3
Some rather weak c. must fall within any STATUTES 4
studying the c. in which it is embodied
CASE SYSTEM 1
cashes When a lawyer c. in LAWYERS (CON) 36
cast the forms of business shall be c. in CONTRACTS 20
caste There is no c. here SEGREGATION 8
cast-iron brains to be a lawyer, only a c. bottom
LAWYERS 55
castle A man's house is his c.; and while he
SEARCHES AND SEIZ 3
some inviolate place which is a man's c. PRIVACY 4
casts into darkness the hopes and visions of
ABORTION 18
cat just as the clavicle in the c. only PRECEDENT 10
The problem of c. versus bird is as old
LEGISLATION 39
catalogue in the whole c. of powers WAR 9
catch an echo of the infinite, a glimpse of
LAW PRACTICE 11
demanded, "What's the c.?" LAWYER JOKES 17
repetition of inadequate c. words WORDS 6
categories as though it consisted of bloodless c.
FREEDOM OF SPEECH 30
Catholic Soon you may set C. against Protestant
FIRST AMEND 7
caucus cooking up a decision in C. and
SUPREME COURT 4
caught not get c. again CLIENT 3
cause It is the C. of Liberty; and I make no
TRIALS, FAMOUS 3
there was no better c. to champion LAW 103
causes Great c. are never tried on their merits TRIALS 2
caution to warrant a man of reasonable c. in the
SEARCHES AND SEIZ 19
cautious The spokesman of the court is c., timid
DISSENT 6
cave When you get the dragon out of his c. on
HISTORY 2

caving brevity like a c. in of the knees HOLMES 35
cease to provoke further analysis WORDS 9
ceased the people will have c., to be their own
JUDICIAL REVIEW 22
ceases consistent only when it c. to grow
LAW, GROWTH 4
consistent only when it c. to grow LAW, GROWTH 5
Supreme Court, he c. to be your friend
JUDICIAL APPOINT 6
Celtic locale was C. and his season spring OBSCENITY 3
censor Are we to have a c. whose imprimatur
CENSORSHIP 2
The c.'s sword pierces deeply into the CENSORSHIP 15
unconstitutional for me to act as a c. CENSORSHIP 17
censorial the c. power is in the people over the
CENSORSHIP 1
censors No government ought to be without c.
FREEDOM OF THE PRESS 10
censorship reflects a society's lack of confidence
CENSORSHIP 16
the c. of the press is not only
FREEDOM OF THE PRESS 20
This is community c. in one of its worst
CENSORSHIP 10
When there is official c. it is a sign CENSORSHIP 14
cent A c. or a pepper corn, in legal CONTRACTS 3
central The c. idea of law . . . [is] the principle LAW 79
centre it is the quiet of a storm c., as we all
SUPREME COURT 13
centuries govern the conduct of men for c.
LAWYERS (PRO) 6
it has taken this Court nearly two c. to
CRIMINAL PROCEDURE 34
traditions and habits of c. were not
FOURTEENTH AMEND 4
century It's the greatest murder trial of the c. TRIALS 5
certain It is the most c. stepping stone to
LEGAL EDUCATION 3
nothing can be said to be c., except TAXATION 6
certainty an abiding conviction, to a moral c. JURY 15
Certitude is not the test of c. CERTAINTY 2
generally is illusion, and repose is not CERTAINTY 1
I sought for c. JUDGES 32
the law only aimed at c., could not, did JUSTICE 42
to a reasonable and moral c. PROOF 2
certificates Two c. of stock are now issued instead
ANTITRUST 7
certitude is not the test of certainty CERTAINTY 2
chained together at the bottom of the sea
LAWYER JOKES 14
chains bind him down from mischief by the c. of
CONSTITUTION 12
The links in the c. of tyranny are VOTING 2
chair a C. would not be adequate, but that if
JUDGES, INDIVIDUAL 6
should be reasonably accurate
COURTROOM SCENES 14
Chalcedon was called the city of the blind
GOVERNMENT 24
chalice To pass these defendants a poisoned c.
WAR CRIMES 3
chameleons Words are c., which reflect the color of
WORDS 21
champion there was no better cause to c. LAW 103
chance chart to govern conduct but a game of c.
PRECEDENT 43
He has a splendid, poor man's c.

WEALTH AND POVERTY 8
the substitution of error for c. REGULATION 15
chancery keep constantly a court of c. in your ETHICS 1
chances contrivances has to take some c., and in
CONST LAW 25
when the c. of war make him again the DISSENT 6
change constitutional way of paying for the c.
EMINENT DOMAIN 6
Judicial decrees may not c. the heart MORALITY 18
changed the American Constitution has c., is
CONST LAW 17
changeless law is a living growth, not a c. code
LAW, GROWTH 1
changes cannot calculate for the possible c. of
CONSTITUTION 5
the nation simply c. gears and takes the WAR 8
Time works c., brings into existence new
CONST LAW 24
changing growing, incessantly progressive
PUNISHMENT 9
channels gradually changing its old c. and
COMMON LAW 7
leave open ample alternative c. for
FREEDOM OF SPEECH 47
chanst He has a splendid, poor man's c.
WEALTH AND POVERTY 8
chaos serves no social end TAXATION 43
chapter time now to write the next c., and to
CIVIL RIGHTS 23
character compendiously described as "moral c."
ETHICS 33
Every person of good moral c., being a
LAW PRACTICE 7
of every act depends upon the FREEDOM OF SPEECH 8
put a premium on intelligence and c. JURY 24
Such is the c. of human language, that WORDS 1
characteristic More truly c. of dissent is a dignity
DISSENT 7
non-conformity is not an outstanding c. EDUCATION 4
characters quite independently of the "plot" proper
COPYRIGHT 16
chariot The coachman was tipsy, the c. drove
APPEALS 4
charity the quality we have in mind is c. JUSTICE 29
charm can be omitted without breaking the c. JURY 48
chart That c. is the Constitution of the
CONSTITUTION 27
the law becomes not a c. to govern PRECEDENT 43
there is a c. and a compass for us to CONSTITUTION 27
charted those who wrote our First Amendment c. a
CENSORSHIP 16
charter As a c. of freedom, the Act has a ANTITRUST 18
nothing on the face of the great c. of SLAVERY 20
The Constitution is a c. of negative CONST LAW 58
Charybdis so wide a berth to C.'s maw that one is
LANGUAGE 10
cheapest the c., quickest, and best way
LEGAL EDUCATION 14
cheat You have undertaken to c. me LITIGATION 7
cheated of their right and reduced to beggary
LAWYERS (CON) 9
check immediate c. is required to save the
FREEDOM OF SPEECH 10
so it may be a c. upon both, as both
SEPARATION OF POWERS 2
the only c. upon our own exercise of
JUDICIAL REVIEW 32

which shall be denominated a c. action
CODIFICATION 1
civilians Republics abound in young c. who believe
LEGISLATION 11
civilization cannot tolerate their being ignored
WAR CRIMES 1
I do not suppose that c. will come to an   CASES 6
needs of life in a developing c.   PRODUCTS LIABILITY 4
real complaining party at your bar is C.
WAR CRIMES 6
represents the pathology of c.   CRIMINAL LAW 15
Since the general c. of mankind, I   FREEDOM 1
test of the quality of a c. is its
CRIMINAL PROCEDURE 28
civilized customs and usages of c. nations
INTERNATIONAL LAW 10
first principles is the mark of a c. man   HOLMES 21
I get c. society for it   TAXATION 32
man's struggle to make himself c.   FIFTH AMEND 8
no longer morally tolerable in our c.
CAPITAL PUNISHMENT 30
people do not allow unregulated access   OBSCENITY 26
Taxes are what we pay for c. society   TAXATION 28
whole law does so as soon as it is c.   DISTINCTIONS 5
civilizing small price to pay for the c. hand of   LAW 86
civilly in the eye of the law, c. dead   WOMEN'S RIGHTS 5
claim none of the rights and privileges which
SLAVERY 14
receives earnings under a c. of right   TAXATION 33
the broad, undifferentiated c. of public   PRESIDENT 17
claiming they have a propensity for c. everything
ADVOCACY 18
clamours deaf as an adder to the c. of the   LAW 6
clarity proved with clear and convincing c.
LEGAL WRITING 24
class if the c.-suit device had been left
CIVIL PROCEDURE 17
provide for first and second c. citizens
CIVIL RIGHTS 17
the only c. of society specially adapted   JUDGES 27
while there is a lower c., I am in it   TRIALS, FAMOUS 11
classes knows nor tolerates c. among citizens
SEGREGATION 8
narrowly limited c. of speech   FREEDOM OF SPEECH 26
classification problem of legislative c. is a perennial
EQUAL PROTECTION 12
The c. is for advantage of the lawyers   MURDER 4
the c. must be reasonable, not arbitrary
EQUAL PROTECTION 6
to justify the use of a suspect c., a
EQUAL PROTECTION 19
classifications based upon sex, like classifications
SEX DISCRIMINATION 10
by gender must serve important
SEX DISCRIMINATION 12
classified If these doctrines could be so c. and
CASE SYSTEM 2
when everything is c., then nothing is
FREEDOM OF THE PRESS 40
classify to select, c., and arrange all the cases
CASE SYSTEM 3
clause no c. in the Constitution purports to
CONFLICT OF LAWS 10
that's what they call a sanity c.   CONTRACTS 21
clauses the great c. of the Constitution must be
ORIGINAL INTENTION 8
clavicle just as the c. in the cat only tells of

clear a c. field for future effort, unhampered
BANKRUPTCY 5
and imminent danger that it will bring
FREEDOM OF SPEECH 11
create a c. and present danger that they
FREEDOM OF SPEECH 8
proved with c. and convincing clarity
LEGAL WRITING 24
The power of c. statement is the great   ADVOCACY 8
to draw a c. line of separation between
FREEDOM OF THE PRESS 14
clearly A finding is "c. erroneous" when   APPEALS 12
speaking more c. than you think   ADVOCACY 28
cleric paces of the cloistered c.   NEGLIGENCE 17
clerks confirm the appointment of law c.
SUPREME COURT 33
client A c. is a fact, and a true lawyer hates   CLIENT 17
I am convinced my c. was incapable of   ETHICS 28
Just get yourself a corporation for a c.
CORPORATIONS 21
may be a pleasant paunch upon your c.
LAWYERS (CON) 41
My c.'s conscience, and my own, are   ETHICS 4
n. A person who has made the customary   CLIENT 6
own conscience and not that of his c.   ETHICS 14
The ideal c. is the very wealthy man in   CLIENT 9
will often have a fool for his c.   CLIENT 1
clients I would rather have c. than be   CLIENT 4
telling would-be c. that they are damned   CLIENT 15
utter captives and choreboys of their c.   LAWYERS 53
cliff a busload of lawyers to go over a c.
LAWYER JOKES 5
cloaked arrogance c. as humility
ORIGINAL INTENTION 15
clocks Like c., they must be occasionally   LAW 29
clog and embarrass its execution   GOVERNMENT 10
cloistered paces of the c. cleric   NEGLIGENCE 17
This is no life of c. ease to which you   LAWYERS 42
close connection between crime and progress
CRIMINAL 5
We are not to c. our eyes as judges to   JUDGES 28
clothed Property does become c. with a public
PROPERTY 15
clothes only an ordinary guess in evening c.   EXPERTS 3
clown The antics of the c. are not the paces
NEGLIGENCE 17
coach lawyers use to c. their clients so that   ETHICS 34
coachman The c. was tipsy, the chariot drove Home
APPEALS 4
coarse Constitution protects c. expression as
CENSORSHIP 16
It is a c. tool and not a mathematical   LAW 39
Coase The C. theorem . . . asserts that under
LAW AND ECONOMICS 2
cock-sure We have been c. of many things that were
CERTAINTY 2
code a living growth, not a changeless c.
LAW, GROWTH 1
In the new C. of Laws which I suppose it
WOMEN'S RIGHTS 1
partake of the prolixity of a legal c.   CONSTITUTION 17
codes their eyes, their laws, and their c.   RAPE 4
co-equal all the departments c. and co-sovereign
JUDICIAL REVIEW 16
coercion Words uttered under c. are proof of
FIRST AMEND 17

455

The matter of the boat's c. JUDGES 18

condone "good trusts" and condemn "bad" ones ANTITRUST 26

conduces Nothing c. to brevity like a caving in HOLMES 35

conduct if his c. is within the rules MORALITY 3
Many forms of c. permissible in a TRUSTS 5
rules which are to govern the c. of men LAWYERS (PRO) 6

Speech is c., and actions speak FREEDOM OF SPEECH 41

Standards of prudent c. are declared at NEGLIGENCE 20

This is c. that shocks the conscience SEARCHES AND SEIZ 41

which would not be blameworthy in the PUNISHMENT 11

confederation without them it is a c. FEDERALISM 22

conferred They c., as against the Government, the PRIVACY 3

confess I c. that I have not yet written the SEGREGATION 21

confessing once let the cat out of the bag by c. CONFESSIONS 3

confession suicide is c. CONFESSIONS 1
There is no refuge from c. but suicide CONFESSIONS 1

confided the fewer laws, and the less c. power GOVERNMENT 15

confidence a society's lack of c. in itself CENSORSHIP 16
let no more be said of c. in man, but CONSTITUTION 12
property may be denied but the c. cannot TRADEMARKS 4

confidentiality explicit reference to a privilege of c. PRESIDENT 18
only on the generalized interest in c. PRESIDENT 19
public interest in the c. of such PRESIDENT 17

confine the notion of "laws" to what is found STATUTES 10

confined from molar to molecular motions JUDICIAL LEGISLATION 2
must be c. to the interpretation which ORIGINAL INTENTION 8
taken out of jail when c. for the wrong CRIMINAL PROCEDURE 10

confirm the appointment of law clerks SUPREME COURT 33

confirmation bother about c. of Justices but ought to SUPREME COURT 33

conflict such laws as c., in any way, with the WOMEN'S RIGHTS 6

conform must follow, and c. to, the progress of LAW, GROWTH 3

conformity only to induce external c. to rule CRIMINAL LAW 7

confrontation a c. with other values arises PRESIDENT 17

confused leaving this area of the law more c. ABORTION 9

confusion When the risk of c. is so great as to EVIDENCE 11

Congress has no power to declare substantive CONFLICT OF LAWS 10
instead of by psychoanalysis of C. LEGISLATIVE HISTORY 5
made Women humans by Act of C.

now for C. and ultimately the American WOMEN'S RIGHTS 13
 IMPEACHMENT 5

Congressional President endorses the whole C. Record LEGISLATIVE HISTORY 3

connection if there be no rational c. between the STATUTES 11
the close c. between crime and progress CRIMINAL 5

connections No C., Interests, or Intercessions MILITARY JUSTICE 1

conscience an aroused popular c. that sears the VOTING 10
formula through which the c. of equity TRUSTS 4
his lack of c. is what makes him a ETHICS 19
his own c. and not that of his client ETHICS 14
I cannot and will not cut my c. to fit FIFTH AMEND 5
in the vaguer sanctions of c. MORALITY 7
made binding upon the c. by a penalty WITNESSES 3
My client's c., and my own, are distinct ETHICS 4
sears the c. of the people's VOTING 10
This is conduct that shocks the c. SEARCHES AND SEIZ 41

conscious a c. process of intimidation by which RAPE 2
if a judge reads his c. or unconscious JUDGES 21
live our lives in c. submission to rules LITIGATION 15

consciously why I should be c. wrong today because PRECEDENT 48

consciousness It was under a solemn c. of the dangers FREEDOM OF RELIGION 21

consecrated He is to draw his inspiration from c. JUDGES 31

consensus are unable to arrive at any c. ABORTION 4

consent based upon the c. of the governed, and INTERNATIONAL LAW 14
imposed on them, but with their own c. TAXATION 2
in advance, c. to be a knave ETHICS 6
whispering 'I will ne'er c.,'—consented FREEDOM OF RELIGION 43

consented whispering 'I will ne'er consent,'—c. FREEDOM OF RELIGION 43

consenting if 60,000 fully c. adults crowded into OBSCENITY 30

consequence The only universal c. of a legally DAMAGES 2

conservatism one of the last citadels of wavering c. LAW PRACTICE 21

conservative the man of forms, the c.—is a tame man LAW 24
timid habits and more c. inclinations in LAWYERS 11

conservatizing law has always been a narrow, c. JUDGES 19

consider The more I c. the independence of the FREEDOM OF THE PRESS 22

consideration for the feelings of a poor orphan SENTENCING 1
is as much a form as a seal CONTRACTS 8
would constitute a valuable c. CONTRACTS 3

considerations of analogy, of convenience, of policy NEGLIGENCE 8

consist Constitutions should c. only of general CONSTITUTION 5

consistency always approaching and never reaching c. LAW, GROWTH 4
approaching, and never reaching, c. LAW, GROWTH 5
law constantly is tending towards c. LAW 44
not Truth, but c. or a consistent LAWYERS (CON) 11

consistent become entirely c. only when it ceases

what was actually d. in the earlier   LEGAL REALISM 6
decides when a man d. that he is not God   HOLMES 15
decision broad enough to encompass a woman's d.
                                           ABORTION 1
cooking up a d. in Caucus and delivering
                                           SUPREME COURT 4
factors that govern the abortion d.   ABORTION 2
I never bow to a d. iv a judge unless
                                           OBEDIENCE TO LAW 20
John Marshall has made his d.: now let
                                           SUPREME COURT 7
of the Legislature must be accepted   DISTINCTIONS 9
privacy includes the abortion d., but   ABORTION 3
rules of d. in trials at common law in
                                           CONFLICT OF LAWS 1
the d. whether to bear or beget a child   PRIVACY 15
The d. will depend on a judgment or   CASES 5
We must know what a d. means before the
                                           ADMINISTRATIVE LAW 7
which is the law and not the d. of the   CONST LAW 30
decisionmaking new currency of this Court's d.
                                           PRECEDENT 60
decisions by which they had arrived at their d.
                                           LEGAL REALISM 6
contended that the d. of Courts   CONFLICT OF LAWS 5
Few d. are more personal and intimate   ABORTION 17
important d. of the Supreme Court are
                                           SUPREME COURT 40
the multitude of little d. made daily by
                                           LAW, DEFINITIONS 5
declare if we lost our power to d. an Act of
                                           JUDICIAL REVIEW 29
the Law is what the judges d.   LAW, DEFINITIONS 3
declared are d. at times by courts, but they are
                                           NEGLIGENCE 20
When the laws have d. and enforced all   LAW 12
decline the exercise of jurisdiction which is
                                           JURISDICTION 5
decrees Judicial d. may not change the heart
                                           MORALITY 18
deef Blind she is, an' deef an' dumb an' has   JUSTICE 18
deem I know of no title that I d. more
                                           HARVARD LAW SCHOOL 5
deeply no matter how d. I may cherish them or
                                           CONST LAW 43
deep-seated D. preferences can not be argued about
                                           NATURAL LAW 14
defaulted America has d. on this promissory note
                                           CIVIL RIGHTS 26
defeat sanguinary laws d. their own purpose by
                                           PUNISHMENT 5
defeating agency for d. justice that human wisdom
                                           JURY 21
defect the product of a mental disease or d.
                                           INSANITY 14
defects arise from the d. of language   LANGUAGE 2
defend specially adapted to d. themselves   JUDGES 27
defendant every d. stands equal before the law
                                           CRIMINAL PROCEDURE 30
defendants We find the d. incredibly guilty   GUILT 4
defender The D. of the Damned   DARROW 1
defenders task of their protection a body of d.
                                           JUDICIAL REVIEW 30
defense nor any d. except such as I believe to
                                           ETHICS 17
deference calls for great d. from the courts
                                           PRESIDENT 17

defiance may set that law at d. with impunity
                                           GOVERNMENT 18
deficient Who was sadly d. in sex   LAWYER JOKES 7
define If you can't d. it, you can't prosecute
                                           OBSCENITY 29
they will d. and define freedom out of
                                           FREEDOM OF SPEECH 7
definite does not exist without some d. authority
                                           LAW 61
The controversy must be d. and concrete   CASES 7
definition the very d. of tyranny
                                           SEPARATION OF POWERS 4
degenerating preventing law from d. into justice
                                           JURY 35
degrade Your laws d., rather than exalt woman
                                           WOMEN'S RIGHTS 10
degree difference is one of d.   DISTINCTIONS 3
difference is only one of d.   DISTINCTIONS 2
estimates it, some matter of d.   DISTINCTIONS 4
my view depends on differences of d.   DISTINCTIONS 5
Some d. of abuse is inseparable from the
                                           FREEDOM OF THE PRESS 12
delay further analysis for fifty years   WORDS 6
To d. justice, is injustice   JUSTICE 3
delegation not a forbidden d. of legislative power
                                           SEPARATION OF POWERS 15
This is d. running riot   SEPARATION OF POWERS 17
deliberate with all d. speed the parties to these
                                           SEGREGATION 17
deliberately Our country has d. undertaken a great
                                           INTOXICATION 5
deliberating a whole People d. calmly on what form of
                                           CONST CONVENTION 16
deliberative the d. forces should prevail over the
                                           FREEDOM OF SPEECH 20
delicate Its d. and difficult office is to
                                           JUDICIAL REVIEW 31
very d., plenary and exclusive power of   PRESIDENT 8
deliver stop reading dirty books and d. the mail
                                           CENSORSHIP 13
delusive exactness is a source of fallacy   ERROR 2
demand Equity does not d. that its suitors   EQUITY 5
New times d. new measures and new men
                                           LAW, GROWTH 2
There is in all men a d. for the   INTOXICATION 3
demanded Obedience to the law is d. as a right
                                           OBEDIENCE TO LAW 19
demean should d. themselves as good citizens
                                           FREEDOM OF RELIGION 18
demented a few d. judges expect anything better
                                           JUSTICE 44
demigods It is really an assembly of d.
                                           CONST CONVENTION 11
democracy great postulate of our d.
                                           FREEDOM OF SPEECH 32
proclaimed the United States to be a d.
                                           DEMOCRACY 6
democrat person called himself or herself a d.
                                           DEMOCRACY 6
democratic counterpoise to the d. element   LAWYERS 13
essential part of the d. process   LAW 72
It is a d. institution, representative   JURY 60
to the processes of d. government
                                           JUDICIAL REVIEW 32
demonstrable a textually d. constitutional commitment
                                           SEPARATION OF POWERS 22
pretend that d. differences between men

469

embalmed legal literature . . . is regularly e.
LAW REVIEWS 4

embarrass clog and e. its execution   GOVERNMENT 10

embedded those so e. in the hearts of men that
CONSTITUTION 47

embodies The law e. the story of a nation's   LAW 35

embody A constitution is not intended to e. a
DUE PROCESS 15

right of a majority to e. their opinions
DUE PROCESS 13

embrace the exhilarating opportunity of   COURTS 29

embraced scarcely be e. by the human mind
CONSTITUTION 17

emergency may furnish the occasion for the
DUE PROCESS 29

While e. does not create power   DUE PROCESS 29

emetic reader undoubtedly is somewhat e.
OBSCENITY 5

eminence some counsel whose e. makes their
LAWYERS 27

eminent An e. lawyer cannot be a dishonest man
ETHICS 5

into the hands of that e. tribunal   JUDICIAL REVIEW 22

emotional ninety percent of any decision is e.
SUPREME COURT 27

emperor big stealin' dey makes you E. and puts
CRIME 5

emphasis changes in e. and arrangement without
CONSTITUTION 46

emphatically has been e. termed a government of laws
OBEDIENCE TO LAW 5

It is e. the province and duty of the
JUDICIAL REVIEW 9

empire Law's e. is defined by attitude, not
LAW, DEFINITIONS 10

employees discharge or retain e. at will for good
LABOR LAW 2

employer the e.'s choice between unions may have
LABOR LAW 18

employment never fails of e. in it   LAW PRACTICE 1

empty go over a cliff with three e. seats
LAWYER JOKES 5

seems to me an e. hum-bug   HOLMES 22

that right to remain an e. promise
SEARCHES AND SEIZ 48

vessels into which he can pour nearly   CONST LAW 33

enact Fourteenth Amendment does not e. Mr.
DUE PROCESS 14

We e. many laws that manufacture   CRIMINAL 2

enclaves sanctuaries or e. where no majority can
PROPERTY 28

encompass broad enough to e. a woman's decision
ABORTION 1

encroachment every e. upon rights expressly
BILL OF RIGHTS 7

encroachments gradual and silent e. of those in power
FREEDOM 1

encysted ideas become e. in phrases   WORDS 9

end a lot of law at the e. of a nightstick
LAW ENFORCEMENT 9

Even patent litigation must e. somewhere   PATENTS 14

Freedom of the press . . . is not an e. in
FREEDOM OF THE PRESS 32

It the e. be clearly comprehended within
GOVERNMENT 5

Justice is the e. of government   JUSTICE 8

Let the e. be legitimate, let it be   GOVERNMENT 12

Life is an e. in itself, and the only   HOLMES 10

no e. to the laws and no beginning to
LAW ENFORCEMENT 3

The chief e. of man is to frame general   HOLMES 23

The very aim and e. of our institutions
FREEDOM OF EXPRESS 6

we'll add it to the e.   LEGAL WRITING 20

endangered can never be e. from that quarter
JUDICIARY 5

little sympathy even as an e. species
LEGAL WRITING 26

endeavor I am handicapped in that weird e.
LEGISLATIVE HISTORY 5

endeavors he uses his best e. to secure the
SEPARATION OF POWERS 12

endless writing so that e. others of his craft
LEGAL WRITING 11

endorses the President e. the whole Congressional
LEGISLATIVE HISTORY 3

ends attainment of the e. of such power
GOVERNMENT 4

philosophy that the e. justify the means
LAW ENFORCEMENT 14

endure constitution intended to e. for ages to
CONSTITUTION 19

enemy We think of the law as an e.
LAW ENFORCEMENT 12

enforce made his decision: now let him e. it
SUPREME COURT 7

this is all the laws should e. on him   LAW 12

to e. a law not supported by the people
LAW ENFORCEMENT 13

enforcing never succeed in e. the criminal law at
PROSECUTION 8

engine the greatest legal e. ever invented for
CROSS-EXAMINATION 2

engineers make the pie grow larger, lawyers only
LAWYERS (CON) 61

English constitutional documents of E.-speaking
SEARCHES AND SEIZ 35

in the mouth of a normal speaker of E.   WORDS 5

sheer torture of the E. language
SEARCHES AND SEIZ 57

should be written in the E. language
LEGAL WRITING 22

the E. teacher emphasizes what the judge
LEGAL EDUCATION 27

the opinions of the E. judges are a mine
QUOTATIONS 3

they ought to teach E. as a Second   LEGAL WRITING 31

engraved The law must be e. in our hearts and
COURTROOM SCENES 7

engulf tides and currents which e. the rest of
JUDGES 33

enhance in order to e. the relative voice of
FREEDOM OF SPEECH 46

enigmatic as e. as the dreams Joseph was called
ORIGINAL INTENTION 9

enjoins It e. upon its branches separateness but
SEPARATION OF POWERS 20

enjoy abolished while th' people e. it so much
CAPITAL PUNISHMENT 6

in order to e. the inestimable benefits
FREEDOM OF THE PRESS 21

No rogue should e. his ill-gotten   FRAUD 3

enjoyment preference to its inhabitants in the e.
COMMERCE CLAUSE 10

This is of the very e. of judicial duty
PROCEDURE 7

to restrain, is of their very e.
JUDICIAL REVIEW 9

very e. of a scheme of ordered liberty
ANTITRUST 14

essential It is e. to the idea of a law, that it
FOURTEENTH AMEND 10

no greater than is e. to the furtherance
GOVERNMENT 1

one of the most e. branches of English
FIRST AMEND 42

peculiarly e. in a limited constitution
SEARCHES AND SEIZ 3

establish the first to e. so just a rule
JUDICIARY 6

established what government is the e. one in a State
PRECEDENT 6

establishment support of no dogma, the e. of no sect
GOVERNMENT 16

The "e. of religion" clause of the First
FREEDOM OF RELIGION 22

esteem We are superstitious, and e. the statute
FREEDOM OF RELIGION 40

estimating man's fate depends on his e. rightly
STATUTES 1

eternal the common law, in its e. youth, grows
DISTINCTIONS 4

eternally vigilant against attempts to check the
PRIVACY 1

ethical considerations can no more be excluded
FREEDOM OF SPEECH 10

ethics law floats in a sea of e.
MORALITY 4

pure e. and sound logic are also parts
ETHICS 35

Why should you expect the e. of the game
COMMON LAW 6

evanescent refined, and, sometimes, almost e.
LEGAL REALISM 8

evaporate The First Amendment does not e. with the
COPYRIGHT 2

even a dog distinguishes between being
MILITARY JUSTICE 13

patent litigation must end somewhere
INTENT 2

there are some things e. rats won't do
PATENTS 14

evening only an ordinary guess in e. clothes
LAWYER JOKES 10

everlasting the interpreters of the e. laws which
EXPERTS 3

every agreement concerning trade, every
LAWYERS 21

American ought to have the right to be
ANTITRUST 14

calling is great when greatly pursued
CIVIL RIGHTS 24

direct authority known to us is against
LAWYERS (PRO) 4

judge is a culprit, every law an abuse
PRECEDENT 13

Not e. push or shove, even if it may
CRIMINAL 1

one is personally interested in
DUE PROCESS 52

person of good moral character, being a
OBEDIENCE TO LAW 7

unpunished murder takes away something
LAW PRACTICE 7

everybody is a potential murderer
MURDER 1

I've noticed that e. that is for
MURDER 5

every-day intended for e. work
ABORTION 13

everyone a wicked law, like cholera, destroys e.
LAW 39

everything I like to do is either illegal, immoral
COURTROOM SCENES 17

may make anything mean e. or nothing
ILLEGALITY 2

they have a propensity for claiming e.
STATUTORY CONSTRUC 1

ADVOCACY 18

worth saying shall be said
FIRST AMEND 21

evidence have the whole e. against him to pick
CRIMINAL PROCEDURE 13

If the e. is against you, talk about the
ADVOCACY 22

only e. of what the laws are; and are
CONFLICT OF LAWS 5

Some circumstantial e. is very strong
EVIDENCE 3

statement he does make may be used as e.
CONFESSIONS 9

suppression by the prosecution of e.
CRIMINAL PROCEDURE 31

Tell me not of technical rules of e.
EVIDENCE 4

the jury would never hear the e.
COURTS 33

which reasonable men draw from e.
SEARCHES AND SEIZ 32

evidential in this twilight zone the e. force of
EXPERTS 1

evil fitting remedy for e. counsels is good
FREEDOM OF SPEECH 21

gravity of the "e.," discounted by its
FREEDOM OF SPEECH 31

I think it a less e. that some criminals
SEARCHES AND SEIZ 26

it is a self-imposed e., and, secondly
OBEDIENCE TO LAW 8

keeping of the law the instrument of e.
LAW 77

Law cannot restrain e.; for the freedom
LAW 77

the remedy is worse than the e.
CIVIL DISOBEDIENCE 5

with an e. eye and an unequal hand
EQUAL PROTECTION 2

evils certain substantive e. that the United
FREEDOM OF SPEECH 11

submit to the inevitable e. which it
FREEDOM OF THE PRESS 21

evolving the e. standards of decency that mark
PUNISHMENT 19

ex Judge-made law is e. post facto law, and
COMMON LAW 10

unlimited and unchecked e. parte
GRAND JURY 2

what laws I consider e. post facto laws
LEGISLATION 8

exact Equal and e. justice to all men, of
RIGHTS 7

exactions taxes are enforced e., not voluntary
TAXATION 46

exactness Delusive e. is a source of fallacy
ERROR 2

examination law student who marks his own e. papers
JUDGES 25

unlimited and unchecked ex parte e.
GRAND JURY 2

examine When I e. a question, I go from headland
MARSHALL 8

example it teaches the whole people by its e.
GOVERNMENT 23

So long as governments set the e. of
CAPITAL PUNISHMENT 7

whose eminence makes their e. important
LAWYERS 27

exceed the lawful rapes e. the unlawful ones a
RAPE 1

excellence peculiar boast and e. of the common law
COMMON LAW 13

peculiar boast and e. of the common law
COMMON LAW 14

excellent Should the States reject this e.
CONST CONVENTION 13

except death and taxes
TAXATION 6

exceptions artificial islands of e., created from
RULES 3

These e. certainly go as far as the
JURISDICTION 1

excesses prepared to curb the e. of either, able
LAWYERS (CON) 22

extremest take the e. view in favor of free speech
　　　　　　　　　　　　　　FREEDOM OF SPEECH 14
eye an e. to every side and angle of　　　LAWYERS 22
　with an evil e. and an unequal hand
　　　　　　　　　　　　　　EQUAL PROTECTION 2
eyes being set vertically rather than on an
　　　　　　　　　　　　　　LEGAL WRITING 25
　dance before my e. in a meaningless
　　　　　　　　　　　　　　LEGAL WRITING 16
　existence except to the e. of faith　　LEGAL REALISM 14
　They rape us with their e., their laws　　　RAPE 4
　this majestic theme, my e. dazzle　　　　LAW 40
　We are not to close our e. as judges to　　JUDGES 28
　we can never see them with any e. except　JUDGES 29
eye-witnesses In the absence of e. there's always a
　　　　　　　　　　　　　　GUILT 3

face carry its death warrant upon its f.　DAMAGES 3
　essence is to take them at their f.　　　WORDS 18
　her hood the inexorable f. of death　　　LAW 43
　they ain't took the black off of your f.　CIVIL RIGHTS 22
facetious ordered liberty" is, at best, f.　　SEX 8
fact A client is a f., and a true lawyer　CLIENT 17
　"strict" in theory and fatal in f.
　　　　　　　　　　　　　　EQUAL PROTECTION 16
　The blunt, inexcusable f. is that this　　LAW 99
　The very f. that no sabotage has taken
　　　　　　　　　　　　　　CIVIL RIGHTS 13
　unable to show a f. that no one doubted　PROOF 1
　what the courts will do in f., and　LAW, DEFINITIONS 2
factions The most common and durable source of f.
　　　　　　　　　　　　　　PROPERTY 3
facts a true lawyer hates f.　　　　　CLIENT 17
　forced to retreat from the world of f.　　LAW 66
　let F. be submitted to a candid world　ENGLISH LAW 4
　Let me find the f. for the people of my
　　　　　　　　　　　　　　ADMINISTRATIVE LAW 5
　point to specific and articulable f.
　　　　　　　　　　　　　　SEARCHES AND SEIZ 59
　sunshine of actual f.　　　　　　　EVIDENCE 7
　the f. and circumstances within their
　　　　　　　　　　　　　　SEARCHES AND SEIZ 19
　they are taken over from the f. of life　NEGLIGENCE 20
faculties all the f. by which man is likest to a　LAW 41
faculty an academic f. which pins its reputation
　　　　　　　　　　　　　　LAW REVIEWS 2
faggots The f. must be put together and rebound
　　　　　　　　　　　　　　PROPERTY 24
failure The f. of the modern American law school
　　　　　　　　　　　　　　LAW SCHOOL 4
　to observe that fundamental fairness
　　　　　　　　　　　　　　CRIMINAL PROCEDURE 20
fair a f. and substantial relation to the
　　　　　　　　　　　　　　EQUAL PROTECTION 6
　and enlightened system of justice would
　　　　　　　　　　　　　　FOURTEENTH AMEND 10
　and reasonable criticism　　　　　COPYRIGHT 3
　combatants, manfully standing to their　LAW 43
　fundamental and essential to f. trials
　　　　　　　　　　　　　　CRIMINAL PROCEDURE 29
　judge of it by the f. meaning of the　CONST LAW 13
　many things in life that are not f.　ABORTION 11
　rudimentary requirements of f. play
　　　　　　　　　　　　　　ADMINISTRATIVE LAW 11
　the instinct of giving the game f. play　EVIDENCE 6
　Though the law itself be f. on its face
　　　　　　　　　　　　　　EQUAL PROTECTION 2

to achieve a f. trial anywhere in the　　TRIALS 6
　traditional notions of f. play and　JURISDICTION 25
　use may be defined as a privilege in　COPYRIGHT 22
　warning should be given to the world in
　　　　　　　　　　　　　　CRIMINAL LAW 11
　when Truth and Error have f. Play, the
　　　　　　　　　　　　　　FREEDOM OF SPEECH 1
fairly A reviewer may f. cite largely from the
　　　　　　　　　　　　　　COPYRIGHT 3
fairness failure to observe that fundamental f.
　　　　　　　　　　　　　　CRIMINAL PROCEDURE 20
　The concept of f. must not be strained
　　　　　　　　　　　　　　CRIMINAL LAW 12
faith a priesthood that had lost their f. and
　　　　　　　　　　　　　　CRITICAL LEGAL STUD 5
　existence except to the eyes of f.　LEGAL REALISM 14
　guaranty in the f. of the people　　LIBERTY 5
　If that f. should be lost, five or nine　LIBERTY 5
　the f. is true and adorable which leads　HOLMES 8
　The great act of f. is when a man　　HOLMES 15
faithful secure the f. execution of the laws
　　　　　　　　　　　　　　SEPARATION OF POWERS 12
faiths judicially examining other people's f.
　　　　　　　　　　　　　　FREEDOM OF RELIGION 39
　time has upset many fighting f., they
　　　　　　　　　　　　　　FREEDOM OF SPEECH 13
fall Never let your correspondence f. behind
　　　　　　　　　　　　　　LAW PRACTICE 4
　than to f. in love with novelties　　JUDGES 16
　The f. of a citadel is a dramatic moment
　　　　　　　　　　　　　　PRODUCTS LIABILITY 7
fallacy Delusive exactness is a source of f.　ERROR 2
Fallopian enough to cover cutting the F. tubes
　　　　　　　　　　　　　　HOLMES 27
falls loss from accident must lie where it f.　TORTS 1
　when I pull a thread, my sleeve f. off　ABORTION 21
　when our arrow f. to earth it is in　HOLMES 38
false there is no such thing as a f. idea　LIBEL 12
　These are f. hopes, believe me, these　LIBERTY 6
falsehood we protect some f. in order to protect
　　　　　　　　　　　　　　LIBEL 13
fame stem the turbulent current for bubble f.
　　　　　　　　　　　　　　NEGLIGENCE 22
familiar accepts what has been f. and accepted by
　　　　　　　　　　　　　　NATURAL LAW 13
family constitution of the f. organization　WOMEN 3
far make me believe that we are that f. gone
　　　　　　　　　　　　　　IMMIGRATION 4
　so f. and so fast as its means allow
　　　　　　　　　　　　　　EQUAL PROTECTION 7
　There is f. too much law for those who　LAW 98
　too little for those who cannot　　　LAW 98
farce a Prologue to a F. or a Tragedy; or
　　　　　　　　　　　　　　FREEDOM OF THE PRESS 19
fascinating just one f. moment after another　DARROW 3
fascism we are the first victims of American F.
　　　　　　　　　　　　　　TRIALS, FAMOUS 20
fashion law for the litigants before him　PRECEDENT 21
　of wearing jewels in this country　WILLS, FAMOUS 1
fashionable to resist the f. opinions of the day
　　　　　　　　　　　　　　JUDICIARY 13
　we are to yield to f. conventions　　HOLMES 28
fashions cut my conscience to fit this year's f.
　　　　　　　　　　　　　　FIFTH AMEND 5
　finally f. it to suit its own purposes　LAWYERS 15
fast A F.-Fish belongs to the party fast to　ADMIRALTY 5
　Stealing too f.　　　　　　　　SECURITIES LAW 5

fitted new reasons more f. to the time have
PRECEDENT 10
old glasses f., as it were, for the SUPREME COURT 21
the coat which f. him when a boy CONSTITUTION 15
fitting the f. remedy for evil counsels is good
FREEDOM OF SPEECH 21
five I'll take f. and ten in Woolworth SENTENCING 5
or nine men in Washington could not long LIBERTY 5
fix they f. too for the people the CONSTITUTION 13
to my man and they can f. it up
JUSTICE DEPARTMENT 2
fixed a criminal whose counsel has f. the jury
INNOCENCE 2
by decisions that this or that concrete RIGHTS 12
is to be irrevocably f. by decisions of
JUDICIAL REVIEW 22
never will be a body of f. and LEGAL REALISM 5
star in our constitutional constellation
FREEDOM OF RELIGION 36
technical conception with a f. content
DUE PROCESS 41
This opinion was at that time f. and SLAVERY 15
where all words have a f., precisely LANGUAGE 4
fixing the outside border of reasonable
JUDICIAL REVIEW 25
fixity laws have no f., but shift from
LAW, DEFINITIONS 1
flag because the f. involved is our own FREEDOM 3
in the festivities with f.-waving fervor
CONSTITUTION 52
no better way to counter a f.-burner's FIRST AMEND 51
th' constitution follows th' f. or not
SUPREME COURT 11
The Constitution follows the f. CONSTITUTION 41
The f. is but a bunting to one who MARSHALL 10
The f. is the symbol of our national GOVERNMENT 26
the f. protects those who hold it in FIRST AMEND 52
flame a single, flickering f. ABORTION 22
Otis was a f. of fire!—with a SEARCHES AND SEIZ 7
the f. has grown bright ABORTION 22
flames our arrow falls to earth it is in f. HOLMES 38
flash must reveal the f. of creative genius PATENTS 17
there was "a f. of thought" by which PATENTS 9
Flavius you have confessedly violated the
SEARCHES AND SEIZ 29
flavor necessary to turn a f. into a poison FRAUD 5
flawless No prosecution is tried with f. PROSECUTION 8
flexibility The f. and capacity for growth and
COMMON LAW 14
This f. and capacity for growth and COMMON LAW 13
fling The world has its f. at lawyers LAWYERS (PRO) 3
flitting bats of the law, f. in the twilight EVIDENCE 7
floats law f. in a sea of ethics ETHICS 35
flock much people f. thither LAW 3
flourish according to the zeal of its adherents
FREEDOM OF RELIGION 52
not apt to f. where its advocates are CRIMINAL 6
not apt to f. where its advocates are
SEARCHES AND SEIZ 44
patriotism will not f. if patriotic FREEDOM 3
fly with safety or to disable his assailant
CRIMINAL LAW 9
flying backward because it didn't care where it
PRECEDENT 38
with f. banners and beating drums we are
FIRST AMEND 7
foggy it was as f. as the statute the Attorney ERROR 4

foible The footnote f. breeds nothing but
LEGAL WRITING 15
follow Legislation and adjudication must f.
LAW, GROWTH 3
never felt constrained to f. precedent PRECEDENT 42
Quote Learned, and f. "Gus" JUDGES, INDIVIDUAL 10
follows supreme coort f. th' iliction returns
SUPREME COURT 11
th' constitution f. th' flag or not SUPREME COURT 11
The Constitution f. the flag CONSTITUTION 41
folly To many this is, and always will be, f.
FREEDOM OF EXPRESS 17
foment we are determined to f. a Rebellion, and
WOMEN'S RIGHTS 1
fool A f. who having property of his own PROPERTY 20
Court F., n. The plaintiff LITIGATION 11
if a man is a f., the best thing to do
FREEDOM OF SPEECH 15
The wisest thing to do with a f. is to
FREEDOM OF SPEECH 6
will often have a f. for his client CLIENT 1
You can't f. me CONTRACTS 21
your f. ideas that no intelligent RELIGION 6
foolish legislation is a rope of sand which
LEGISLATION 11
fools I would rather talk to the damned f.
JUDICIAL APPOINT 5
only f., children, left-wing Democrats JUSTICE 44
they are damned f. and should stop CLIENT 15
foot Whose f. is to be the measure to which
CENSORSHIP 2
footnote a fat f. is a mother lode, a vein of
LEGAL WRITING 17
The f. foible breeds nothing but sloppy
LEGAL WRITING 15
forbad condemn "bad" ones; it f. all ANTITRUST 26
forbidden not a f. delegation of legislative power
SEPARATION OF POWERS 15
not f. by any particular provision of GOVERNMENT 5
forbidding all l. consists in f. men to do some LAW 58
forbids It merely f. discrimination SEGREGATION 13
force a counter-majoritarian f. in our system
JUDICIAL REVIEW 35
attached by the mere f. of law to CONTRACTS 11
avoid an encounter with the public f. MORALITY 5
Constitution does not f. a lawyer upon a
CRIMINAL PROCEDURE 21
Fraud is the homage that f. pays to FRAUD 6
have neither F. nor Will, but merely JUDICIARY 3
the overthrow of the government by f.
FREEDOM OF EXPRESS 10
the public f. will be brought to bear RIGHTS 14
what open f. would not dare attempt JUDICIARY 15
forces I have spoken of the f. of which judges
LEGAL REALISM 3
which singly or in combination shape the
LAW, GROWTH 7
forcible and compulsory extortion of a man's own
SEARCHES AND SEIZ 9
foreign The language of the law must not be f.
LANGUAGE 6
The Law is carried on in a f. language LANGUAGE 7
wholly f. to the First Amendment FIRST AMEND 47
wholly f. to the First Amendment
FREEDOM OF SPEECH 46
forfeited Liberty is too priceless to be f. LIBERTY 8
forget we must never f. that it is a CONSTITUTION 18

forgets immediately f. that he was ever a lawyer
JUDICIAL APPOINT 9
form a party which is but little feared and LAWYERS 15
Consideration is as much a f. as a seal CONTRACTS 8
Fourth Amendment to a f. of words
SEARCHES AND SEIZ 12
one f. of action, for the enforcement or
CODIFICATION 1
one f. of action to be known as "civil
CIVIL PROCEDURE 10
one f. of civil action and procedure for
CIVIL PROCEDURE 8
the f. of justice will be without JUSTICE 24
through f. that all organization is PROCEDURE 1
will only be two lines on the tax f. TAXATION 55
forma pauperis (Latin). In the character of a
LITIGATION 12
formal cuts through f. concepts and transitory LAW 70
formalism absurd f., which even yet at times JURY 40
Law reaches past f. FREEDOM OF RELIGION 74
What we need to fear is the archaic f.
CRIMINAL PROCEDURE 12
formalities justice lies chiefly in outward f. JUSTICE 12
former when convinced of f. error, this Court
PRECEDENT 42
formidable inestimable to them and f. to tyrants
ENGLISH LAW 4
the majority raises f. barriers around
FREEDOM OF EXPRESS 4
they would cease to be f. from their CASE SYSTEM 2
forms a people so choked and stultified by f. LAW 27
punished without the f. of law than that
CRIMINAL PROCEDURE 6
the f. of business shall be cast in CONTRACTS 20
the man of f., the conservative—is a LAW 24
We adore the f. of law, instead of LAW 27
formula has not been reduced to any f.
DUE PROCESS 46
peace of mind in the word, the f., the WORDS 13
To rest upon a f. is a slumber that HOLMES 20
formulas mathematical f. having their essence in
CONST LAW 26
fortress not to make a f. out of the dictionary
WORDS 20
forts small movable f. and magazines, at the
CIVIL DISOBEDIENCE 3
fortunes numbers of f. in the State would shrink
TAXATION 24
forum plaintiff's choice of f. should rarely
CIVIL PROCEDURE 15
forward to go f. with the haste of the mob
CRIMINAL PROCEDURE 16
foster Government should not itself f. and pay
SEARCHES AND SEIZ 27
fought I f. the law, and the law won LAW 83
foul he is not at liberty to strike f. ones PROSECUTION 7
found I most always f. principles suited to my
JUDGES 6
resulting product is not f., but made
JUDICIAL LEGISLATION 6
found that ever was f. in an English law-book
SEARCHES AND SEIZ 1
foundation The f. of jurisdiction is physical power
JURISDICTION 18
the very f. of individuality PROPERTY 27
upon which our governmental structure
FIRST AMEND 14

founders The F. gave no such amending power to
CONST AMENDMENT 9
fountain And some with a f. pen CRIMINAL 7
four a world founded upon f. essential human
FIRST AMEND 13
fourteenth Amendment does not enact Mr. Herbert
DUE PROCESS 14
Amendment is not a pedagogical
FOURTEENTH AMEND 6
Amendment prohibits only racial
FOURTEENTH AMEND 14
Amendment was designed to protect
FOURTEENTH AMEND 14
liberty guaranteed by the F. Amendment
FREEDOM OF SPEECH 17
more varied use than the F. Amendment
FOURTEENTH AMEND 15
scope given to the F. Amendment in DUE PROCESS 25
strong case for the F. Amendment to DUE PROCESS 20
the F. Amendment guarantees a right of JURY 68
The F. Amendment, itself a historical DUE PROCESS 20
the word liberty in the F. Amendment
DUE PROCESS 16
use of the F. Amendment beyond the DUE PROCESS 19
fourth a veritable f. branch of the Government
ADMINISTRATIVE LAW 19
Amendment protects people, not places
SEARCHES AND SEIZ 54
and Fifth Amendments run almost into
SEARCHES AND SEIZ 9
point of the F. Amendment is not that it
SEARCHES AND SEIZ 32
reduces the F. Amendment to a form of
SEARCHES AND SEIZ 12
They constitute a headless "f. branch"
ADMINISTRATIVE LAW 10
foxholes signs on the f. or graveyards of battle
CIVIL RIGHTS 25
frame as durable as the f. of human society JUSTICE 11
The chief end of man is to f. general HOLMES 23
framed in the condition of the men who f. that
ORIGINAL INTENTION 6
framers how the "F." would have answered the
ORIGINAL INTENTION 10
The F. of the Constitution knew human
FREEDOM OF EXPRESS 20
The f. of this great provision builded
FOURTEENTH AMEND 2
when it came from the hands of its f.
ORIGINAL INTENTION 5
the f.' intentions . . . are the sole
ORIGINAL INTENTION 13
frames of preference among which he must choose
JUDGES 54
framework The Roe f., then, is clearly on a
ABORTION 15
Frankenstein Such is the F. monster which States have
CORPORATIONS 17
fraud is the homage that force pays to reason FRAUD 6
the details of predatory f., either in LAWYERS (CON) 19
free A f. press stands as one of the great
FREEDOM OF THE PRESS 30
all men shall be f. to profess, and by
FREEDOM OF RELIGION 9
appeal of our institutions to f. minds FREEDOM 3
as the air to common use COPYRIGHT 15
ceases to be f. for irreligion it will

479

frittered They are not to be f. away to please the
CONST LAW 15

frontier a world which is like a f. town, without
INTERNATIONAL LAW 20

frozen more water is added—and f.   LAWYERS (CON) 33

fruit a f. of the poisonous tree   SEARCHES AND SEIZ 28

fruits are attributed to a different tree from
TAXATION 30

when they are the f. of hope as when   CONFESSIONS 2

fuck once you use them they f. everything up
LAWYERS (CON) 62

fuel The patent system added the f. of   PATENTS 7

fugitive to meet the f. exigencies of the hour
STATUTES 7

full Never in our f. life could we hope to do
TRIALS, FAMOUS 14

participation of women in the economic   ABORTION 18

full-blossomed We do not pick our rules of law f. from
JUDICIAL LEGISLATION 5

fun That's the only f. in law anyway   LAW PRACTICE 20

function judicial f. is that of interpretation
CONST LAW 39

of the citizen to keep the Government   CENSORSHIP 8

operation is essentially a public f.   PROPERTY 25

The f. of the lawyer is to preserve a   LAWYERS 57

To live is to f.   HOLMES 34

usurps the f. of both judge and jury   ETHICS 8

functions It is usurping the f. of a legislator
CONST LAW 14

fundamental category of rights deemed to be f.
CONST LAW 62

failure to observe that f. fairness
CRIMINAL PROCEDURE 20

It is poignant but f. that the flag   FIRST AMEND 52

the f. personal rights and "liberties"
FOURTEENTH AMEND 7

The number of f. legal doctrines is much
CASE SYSTEM 2

this is not a matter of f. principle but
AFFIRMATIVE ACTION 5

what interests are so f. as to be   DUE PROCESS 38

fundamentally made for people of f. differing views
DUE PROCESS 15

furnish they f. a text to which those who are
CONSTITUTION 13

furniture My intellectual f. consists of an   HOLMES 13

furthered suitably f. by the differential
EQUAL PROTECTION 17

future a clear field for f. effort, unhampered
BANKRUPTCY 5

I am pleading for the f.   CAPITAL PUNISHMENT 17

Now we must deny it a f.   RAPE 3

of the Republic, to a great extent   ETHICS 13

The dissenter speaks to the f., and his   DISSENT 7

The f. is their care and provision for   CONST LAW 24

the f. of the republic depends upon our   ETHICS 12

the man of the f. is the man of   LAW AND ECONOMICS 1

tie which the f. has to the past   PRECEDENT 50

to the intelligence of a f. day, when a   DISSENT 5

fuzzed ideas all f. along their edges
LEGAL EDUCATION 23

fuzzy Dealing in long, vague, f.-meaning words
WORDS 16

gained I have g. my Suit; but he was stark
LITIGATION 1

the knowledge I have g. in the work of a

gallop A man can never g. over the fields of   LAWYERS 4

gallows The g. has long been the penalty of
CAPITAL PUNISHMENT 2

game a g. at which only one (the professor)
CASE SYSTEM 13

different from the g. itself   LEGAL REALISM 8

expect the ethics of the g. to be   LEGAL REALISM 8

My job is to play the g. according to   HOLMES 37

not a chart to govern conduct but a g.   PRECEDENT 43

practical ends, not a g. of chess   LITIGATION 20

ganglion A great man represents a great g. in the
HOLMES 11

gaps but often there are no g.   LITIGATION 15

right to legislate within g., but often   LITIGATION 15

garment tied in a single g. of destiny   INJUSTICE 4

gashing the g. there brings sight   LEGAL EDUCATION 26

gate expression at the schoolhouse g.   EDUCATION 8

gears the nation simply changes g. and takes   WAR 8

gender classifications by g. must serve
SEX DISCRIMINATION 12

general A g. law, which bears the name of   JUSTICE 10

all matters of g. knowledge   PRECEDENT 15

chief end of man is to frame g. ideas   HOLMES 23

Constitutions should consist only of g.
CONSTITUTION 5

expressions, in every opinion, are to be   PRECEDENT 1

foreseeable future—gain g. assent   CONST LAW 51

I care little who lays down the g.
ADMINISTRATIVE LAW 5

is the law so g. a study   LAWYERS 2

law which is couched in g. words   STATUTES 4

no g. idea is worth a straw   HOLMES 23

no g. proposition is worth a damn   HOLMES 13

Nor is the concept of g. welfare static   LEGISLATION 38

propositions do not decide concrete   CASES 5

Since the g. civilization of mankind   FREEDOM 1

standards of g. application   NEGLIGENCE 2

The prize of the g. is not a bigger tent   HOLMES 17

The remoter and more g. aspects of the
LAW PRACTICE 11

There is no federal g. common law
CONFLICT OF LAWS 9

generalities a throng of glittering g., like a swarm
LEGAL EDUCATION 19

The great g. of the constitution have a   CONST LAW 28

generality patterns of increasing g. will fit
COPYRIGHT 17

the Act has a g. and adaptability   ANTITRUST 18

generalize to g. is to omit   CORPORATIONS 9

generalized based only on the g. interest in
PRESIDENT 19

The g. assertion of privilege must yield   PRESIDENT 19

generals that's not against the law for g.
MILITARY JUSTICE 12

generation check of a preceding g. on the present
COURTS 27

Each g. . . . [has] a right to   CONSTITUTION 16

earth belongs always to the living g.   CONSTITUTION 8

every g. must work out for itself   REGULATION 9

for the needs of another g.   SUPREME COURT 21

never been seen by this g.   ILLEGALITY 5

not merely for the g. which then existed
CONSTITUTION 28

generations Three g. of imbeciles are enough
HOLMES 27

generous you are very g. to the Ladies, for

WOMEN'S RIGHTS 4

genitalia Man's discovery that his g. could serve   RAPE 2

genitals to display their g. to one another, even
OBSCENITY 30

genius must reveal the flash of creative g.   PATENTS 17

the fuel of interest to the fire of g.   PATENTS 7

the g. of the Constitution rests not in
ORIGINAL INTENTION 16

genocide By "g." we mean the destruction of a
INTERNATIONAL LAW 17

Gentile as judges we are neither Jew nor G.
FREEDOM OF RELIGION 33

gentle Laws too g. are seldom obeyed; too
LEGISLATION 4

gentlemen the opinions of half-a-dozen old g.
SUPREME COURT 12

There's sort of a g.'s agreement   CIVIL RIGHTS 18

geometric portions of property in g. progression
TAXATION 5

germ the g. of some wider theory, and   CASES 2

The g. of the dissolution of our federal   JUDICIARY 12

German translated from the G. by someone with a
LAW REVIEWS 6

get Just g. yourself a corporation for a
CORPORATIONS 21

takes a hundred years to g. rid of it   LEGISLATION 15

to g. beyond racism, we must first take
AFFIRMATIVE ACTION 7

gets right after the highway patrol g. here
NEGLIGENCE 26

ghost haunted by the g. of the innocent man
CRIMINAL PROCEDURE 12

gift My g. of John Marshall to the people of
MARSHALL 3

girdled laws are g. too tight   LIBERTY 2

give but one law firm to g. to my country   LAW FIRMS 3

I g., devise and bequeath to the United   HOLMES 39

I g. up. Now I realize what Mark Twain
SECURITIES LAW 3

something that does g. a little   JURY 55

given to love and to be wise, is not g. to men
TAXATION 3

whatever is g. for the love of God, or
WILLS, FAMOUS 2

gladiator he is the g. making a last stand against
DISSENT 6

gladiators a contest between two legal g. with
CIVIL PROCEDURE 19

glasses old g. fitted, as it were, for the needs
SUPREME COURT 21

glittering a throng of g. generalities, like a
LEGAL EDUCATION 19

glory The g. of lawyers, like that of men of   LAWYERS 28

gloss an ominous g. on freedom of the press
CENSORSHIP 18

disregard the g. which life has written   CONST LAW 48

disregard the g. which life has written   STATUTES 10

go ahead, make my day   TAXATION 56

telling you to g. plumb straight to Hell   LAW SCHOOL 6

you might as well g. to law with the   ADMIRALTY 3

you wanted to g. home early Sunday night
LAW FIRMS 4

gob a g. of spit in the face of Art, a kick   OBSCENITY 7

god Almighty G. hath created the mind free
FREEDOM OF RELIGION 8

attempt to see men as G. sees them, for
NEGLIGENCE 2

faculties by which man is likest to a g.   LAW 41

I don't believe in G. because I don't   DARROW 5

If we only had some G. in the country's   RELIGION 2

In the name of G., do your duty   JURY 65

is any respecter of persons   TRIALS, FAMOUS 7

It is by the goodness of G. that in our   FIRST AMEND 5

relation to G. involving duties superior
FREEDOM OF RELIGION 29

save the United States and this   SUPREME COURT 43

that which no reasonable G. would do   CONTRACTS 30

The laws of nature are the laws of G.   NATURAL LAW 1

to limit or defeat a law of G.   RELIGION 5

to say there are twenty gods, or no g.
FREEDOM OF RELIGION 13

was left out of the Constitution but was
FREEDOM OF RELIGION 25

whatever is given for the love of G., or
WILLS, FAMOUS 2

when a man decides that he is not G.   HOLMES 15

works wonders now and then; Behold! a
LAWYERS (CON) 2

godlike not the least g. of man's activities is
LAW PRACTICE 9

gods come, like kissing, by favor of the g.
LEGAL EDUCATION 22

to say there are twenty g., or no god
FREEDOM OF RELIGION 13

going I thought of after g. to bed that night
ADVOCACY 20

gold has proved an "apple of g." to us   LIBERTY 3

golf out of the American people than G. has
TAXATION 26

good A g. beginning   LAWYER JOKES 14

a g. lawyer seldom is a good neighbor   ETHICS 3

Absolute g. faith with the enemy must be   WAR 6

An Act to encourage g. shooting   CRIMINAL LAW 3

because you did not have a good l. and
WEALTH AND POVERTY 6

Every person of g. moral character   LAW PRACTICE 7

fitting remedy for evil counsels is g.
FREEDOM OF SPEECH 21

I am as desirous of being a g. neighbor
CIVIL DISOBEDIENCE 7

Loyalty comes from love of g. government
FIRST AMEND 29

men must not obey the laws too well
OBEDIENCE TO LAW 13

publishing the truth, from g. motives
FREEDOM OF THE PRESS 15

should demean themselves as g. citizens
FREEDOM OF RELIGION 18

The best use of g. laws is to teach men   RIGHTS 9

the firmest pillar of G. Government   JUDICIARY 7

The g. lawyer is not the man who has an   LAWYERS 22

The g. society must have its hiding   PRIVACY 13

They're only g. in their silos   LAWYERS (CON) 62

where g. laws are, much people flock   LAW 3

goodness It is by the g. of God that in our
FIRST AMEND 5

goofs a mutineer or one of the dumbest g. in
MILITARY JUSTICE 7

goose I don't believe in Mother G.   DARROW 5

Gordian The G. Knot of the Constitution seems to
CONFLICT OF LAWS 3

gored only a matter of whose ox is g.
AFFIRMATIVE ACTION 5

gotten we have always g. the pick of the Bar

cases like hard cases make bad law CASES 4
causes are never tried on their merits TRIALS 2
constitutional provisions must be CONST LAW 19
do not let so g. an achievement suffer ILLEGALITY 1
Every calling is g. when greatly pursued
LAWYERS (PRO) 4
fewer instances of truly g. judges, than JUDGES 8
grand manner, and to make g. lawyers LAW SCHOOL 2
he is ugly, but feeling that he is g.
JUDGES, INDIVIDUAL 5
is Justice JUSTICE 13
is Law—great are the old few landmarks LAW 30
It is of g. importance in a republic
SEPARATION OF POWERS 7
Justice, Sir, is the g. interest of man JUSTICE 11
nations, like great men, should keep
AMERICAN INDIAN LAW 11
not by what are called g. questions and CASES 2
nothing on the face of the g. charter of SLAVERY 20
one of the g. bulwarks of liberty
FREEDOM OF THE PRESS 3
one of the g. landmarks in man's FIFTH AMEND 7
one of the g. landmarks in man's FIFTH AMEND 8
principle of constitutional law is not CONST LAW 36
stuff out of which g. and shining truths
PRECEDENT 24
The g. act of faith is when a man HOLMES 15
the g. body of property is socially WORDS 10
the g. clauses of the Constitution must
ORIGINAL INTENTION 8
The G. Dissenter HOLMES 1
The g. generalities of the constitution CONST LAW 28
The g. object of my fear is the federal JUDICIARY 11
the g. power at the bar ADVOCACY 8
The g. tides and currents which engulf JUDGES 33
The Law of a g. nation means the SUPREME COURT 12
the very wealthy man in very g. trouble CLIENT 9
weight has always been attached, and
LEGISLATIVE HISTORY 1
greater its symmetry, to many, g. than before
DOUBLE JEOPARDY 4
greatest It's the g. murder trial of the century TRIALS 5
perhaps the g. place that ever was MARSHALL 9
The g. dangers to liberty lurk in GOVERNMENT 22
the g. freedom of speech was the
FREEDOM OF SPEECH 15
the g. legal engine ever invented for
CROSS-EXAMINATION 2
The g. scourge an angry Heaven ever JUDICIARY 17
you're going to see the g. miracle take NEGLIGENCE 24
greatly a man may live g. in the law as well as
LAW PRACTICE 9
A man may live g. in the law as well as
LAWYERS (PRO) 5
Every calling is great when g. pursued
LAWYERS (PRO) 4
greatness part of his g. consists in his being
HOLMES 11
greedy relief not for the needy but for the g.
TAXATION 45
grind The mills of the law g. slowly—but not
CONTEMPT 3
which g. exceedingly small and sure CONTEMPT 3
grist Hubris is g. for other mills, which CONTEMPT 3
groom The g. and bride each comes within JURY 31
grosser religion does not furnish g. bigots than
JUDGES 4

ground fiction always is a poor g. for RIGHTS 11
These two provisions cover the whole g.
FEDERALISM 22
grounds decisions reached on other g., then the
LEGAL REALISM 13
his g. are just as good as ours NATURAL LAW 14
It is difficult to imagine any g., other DUE PROCESS 33
group ride rough-shod over others simply
FREEDOM OF RELIGION 35
groups a callous indifference to religious g.
FREEDOM OF RELIGION 53
grow consistent only when it ceases to g.
LAW, GROWTH 4
consistent only when it ceases to g. LAW, GROWTH 5
plants that will g. in any soil that is LAWYERS (CON) 6
growed Our Administrative Law has largely "g."
ADMINISTRATIVE LAW 13
growing too short and too tight for g. humankind
LAW 71
growth It must have a principle of g. LAW, GROWTH 9
Modification implies g. PRECEDENT 28
must be found in a principle of g. CERTAINTY 3
The g. of enormously rich and powerful LAWYERS 27
The g. of law is very apt to take place DISTINCTIONS 1
The law is a living g., not a changeless
LAW, GROWTH 1
This flexibility and capacity for g. and
COMMON LAW 13
grub man, like the grub that prepares a HOLMES 19
guarantee minimum g. of the First Amendment
FIRST AMEND 38
guaranteed Freedom of the press is g. only to those
FREEDOM OF THE PRESS 33
guarantees I view the g. of the First Amendment
FIRST AMEND 14
which must be written are less secure
CONSTITUTION 47
guaranty ultimate g. in the faith of the people
LIBERTY 5
guard most on our g. to protect liberty when
GOVERNMENT 22
to g. one part of the society against
SEPARATION OF POWERS 7
guardian Justice the G. of Liberty SUPREME COURT 45
guardians legislatures are ultimate g. of the
CONST LAW 19
the g. of those rights; they will be an
BILL OF RIGHTS 7
to be ruled by a bevy of Platonic G. GOVERNMENT 29
guardianship public authority from assuming a g. of
FIRST AMEND 18
guards property g. the troubled boundary PROPERTY 27
guess Expert opinion . . . is only an ordinary g.
EXPERTS 3
to g. what it would have intended on a
STATUTORY CONSTRUC 7
guide If we would g. by the light of reason
DUE PROCESS 28
guides step by step, the accredited g.
STATUTORY CONSTRUC 16
guiding He requires the g. hand of counsel at
CRIMINAL PROCEDURE 17
guilt find fatally easy the assumption of g. GUILT 5
the actual g. of the party concerned is MORALITY 2
guilty But the g. never escape unscathed FEES 10
even a g. person should be punished
CRIMINAL PROCEDURE 6

the release of countless g. criminals
SEARCHES AND SEIZ 61
We find the defendants incredibly g. GUILT 4
guise Under the g. of interpreting the CONST LAW 21
gun Some will rob you with a six g. CRIMINAL 7
guns don't die, people die CRIME 13
don't kill people, people kill people CRIME 12
only outlaws will have g. CRIME 11
people with sneakers, g., dope, lust, or
YALE LAW SCHOOL 5
Send lawyers, g. and money, the shit has LAWYERS 58
steal more than a hundred men with g.
LAWYERS (CON) 52
When g. are outlawed, only outlaws will CRIME 11
Gus Quote Learned, and follow "G."
JUDGES, INDIVIDUAL 10
gymnastic mental g. which is beyond, not only
EVIDENCE 10

habeas corpus. A writ by which a man may be
CRIMINAL PROCEDURE 10
corpus cuts through all forms and goes
CRIMINAL PROCEDURE 11
habit the h. of assent, not to a factitious
OBEDIENCE TO LAW 21
Hades passage aboard the hand basket to H. CLIENT 22
hain't I got the power LAWLESSNESS 9
hair Who has put pubic h. on my Coke
JUDICIAL APPOINT 14
half a man who takes h. a page to say what
LEGAL WRITING 5
About h. the practice of a decent lawyer CLIENT 15
believed by h. his fellow men to be JUDGES 21
One-h. the doubts in life arise from the LANGUAGE 2
the opinions of h.-a-dozen old gentlemen
SUPREME COURT 12
to represent nearly h. a lifetime CASES 1
to three-quarters of them would be in
MILITARY JUSTICE 12
hall puts you in de H. o' Fame when you CRIME 5
hallmark litigation will remain the h. of a free
LITIGATION 30
hallowed The Place of Justice is a H. Place
JUSTICE DEPARTMENT 1
halls place you see the justice, is in the h. JUSTICE 43
Hamlets We have all become H. in our country
COURTROOM SCENES 19
hamper free from the h. he puts upon himself
CONTRACTS 16
hand failed to specify which h. he blew it JUDGES 13
failed to stretch forth a saving h. FIRST AMEND 9
He requires the guiding h. of counsel at
CRIMINAL PROCEDURE 17
I'd rather have my h. cut off than CLIENT 19
passage aboard the h. basket to Hades CLIENT 22
handed you h. it to me upside down
JUDGES, INDIVIDUAL 8
handicap used so as to h. religions than it is to
FREEDOM OF RELIGION 42
handicapped I am h. in that weird endeavor
LEGISLATIVE HISTORY 5
hands a lawyer should have his h. in his own
LAWYERS (CON) 14
cultivated by the h. of others LAWYERS (CON) 6
in helpless submission, the h. of their PRECEDENT 27
keep one's h. off the beastly drains LAWYERS 56
liberty of every man in the h. of every

SEARCHES AND SEIZ 2
hang Are you going to h. him anyhow—and try
LAWLESSNESS 8
hang the panel than to h. the traitor JURY 18
he would h. a man for blowing his nose JUDGES 13
more ready to h. the panel than to hang JURY 18
You may h. these boys; you may hang them
CAPITAL PUNISHMENT 16
hanging the h. of a murderer restores his victim
PUNISHMENT 7
happier the sheep are h. of themselves, than LAW 10
happiness I am sure from having known many
LAW PRACTICE 10
they find it inconsistent with their h. CONSTITUTION 4
happy It is one of the h. incidents of the
DUE PROCESS 28
The h. Union of these States is a wonder
FEDERALISM 19
hard Great cases like h. cases make bad law CASES 4
patently offensive "h. core" materials OBSCENITY 26
while he may strike h. blows, he is not
PROSECUTION 7
hard-core limited to h. pornography OBSCENITY 14
hardening of the judicial arteries SUPREME COURT 22
hardest The h. case we ever heard of lived in
SENTENCING 1
hardships the balance of h. tips decidedly towards
INJUNCTIONS 4
harm criminal law does not do more h. than LAW 45
harmless whose h. private pleasures the
CENSORSHIP 19
harmonizes best h. with the nature and objects
CONST LAW 12
harmony in national life is a resultant of the
FREEDOM OF EXPRESS 9
harpy bands of lawyers, sharpers, technical TRIALS 4
Harvard that of Professor of the H. Law School
HARVARD LAW SCHOOL 5
haste to go forward with the h. of the mob
CRIMINAL PROCEDURE 16
hastily a h. drafted document upon which little
FIRST AMEND 43
hasty my judgment was too h. LAW SCHOOL 6
Perhaps I've been too h. LAW SCHOOL 9
hat retire to the jury room and pass the h. DAMAGES 6
hatched more of them h. than come to perfection
LAWYERS (CON) 3
hate freedom for the thought that we h.
FREEDOM OF EXPRESS 12
he said: "I h. justice," which he didn't HOLMES 37
I do not believe in the law of h. CIVIL RIGHTS 12
I h. justice, which means that I know if JUSTICE 34
I h. wurruk JUDGES 17
I may h. the sin but never the sinner DARROW 6
likely to h. at sight any analysis to JUDGES 16
must be accorded to the ideas we h. or
FIRST AMEND 34
hates a true lawyer h. facts CLIENT 17
have The lawyers h. us and mean to keep us
LAWYERS (CON) 31
haven a general h. for reform movements
SUPREME COURT 39
havens of refuge for those who might otherwise
DUE PROCESS 36
head go to him as openly and break his h.
FREEDOM OF THE PRESS 7
judges who possess both h. and a heart JUDGES 53

485

headland I go from h. to headland, from case to
MARSHALL 8
headless They constitute a h. "fourth branch" of
ADMINISTRATIVE LAW 10
heads serve the state chiefly with their h.
CIVIL DISOBEDIENCE 4
health of whose h. thieves asked before they
LAWYERS, INDIVIDUAL 2
hear I wish I may never h. of the United   TREASON 2
not h. a damned word he says   MARSHALL 6
The court does not wish to h. argument
FOURTEENTH AMEND 3
the jury would never h. the evidence   COURTS 33
we never h. of after the work is done   FEES 5
you never h. the name of the United   TREASON 2
heard given a meaningful opportunity to be h.
DUE PROCESS 51
The right to be h. would be, in many
CRIMINAL PROCEDURE 17
hears a law which h. before it condemns   LAW 13
hearsay is merely a legal term for unconfirmed
EVIDENCE 13
hearse Why does a h. horse snicker   LAWYERS (CON) 36
heart a lawyer who does not believe in his h.
ADVOCACY 5
A man may have as bad a h. as he   MORALITY 3
have not the h. for so great a struggle   LAW 41
judges who possess both head and a h.   JUDGES 53
Judicial decrees may not change the h.   MORALITY 18
mind's opportunity in the h.'s revenge
CRITICAL LEGAL STUD 5
the law is not in his h.,—is not the   ETHICS 5
the rats devoured my h.   LAWYERS (CON) 34
heartless but they can restrain the h.   MORALITY 18
hearts Liberty lies in the h. of men and women
LIBERTY 6
may affect their h. and minds in a way
SEGREGATION 12
our h. were touched with fire   HOLMES 5
The law must be engraved in our h. and
COURTROOM SCENES 7
those so embedded in the h. of men that
CONSTITUTION 47
heaven In H. there will be no law, and the lion   LAW 92
its blue our h.   MARSHALL 10
The greatest scourge an angry H. ever   JUDICIARY 17
heavenly Like the course of the h. bodies
FREEDOM OF EXPRESS 9
heaviest the h. concentration of lawyers on Earth
LAWYERS (CON) 59
hedged as it is h. in by laws, is the living   FREEDOM 5
heights aloof on these chill and distant h.   JUDGES 33
heirs toils for h. he knows not who   WILLS 1
hell if my fellow citizens want to go to H. I   HOLMES 25
In H. there will be nothing but law, and   LAW 92
"May he rot in h.," David said   CASE SYSTEM 11
telling you to go plumb straight to H.   LAW SCHOOL 6
hell-bent a society h. for absolutes   LAWYERS 57
help want to go to Hell I will h. them   HOLMES 25
helpless ought not to tie, in h. submission, the
PRECEDENT 27
Henry amoral a human being as H. Miller
OBSCENITY 18
it was laid down in the time of H. IV   HISTORY 3
Miller who shuns a bath of clean words   OBSCENITY 19
here comes the judge   JUDGES 61
I'm h. as the lawyer   LAWYERS 62

lies a lawyer and an honest man   LAWYER JOKES 2
heresy The law knows no h., and is committed to
FREEDOM OF RELIGION 22
heroin unregulated access to h. because it is a
OBSCENITY 26
hesitate I should not h. a moment to prefer the
FREEDOM OF THE PRESS 5
should make us h. to correct   COURTS 23
they sometimes would h. where now they
LEGAL EDUCATION 20
heterosexual Some men are h. and some men are
LAWYERS (CON) 54
hide a certain toughening of the mental h. is   TORTS 8
No, I'm doing my best to h. it   CONTEMPT 2
hierophant He has laid aside the role of the h.
DISSENT 6
higgling In the heels of the h. lawyers, Bob
LAWYERS (CON) 37
high I have a h. opinion of lawyers   LAWYERS (PRO) 14
murdered a judge downtown at h. noon, in   ETHICS 37
narrow, and not of a h. order   LEGAL EDUCATION 11
so h. that he is above the law   GOVERNMENT 18
the h. price it extracts from society
SEARCHES AND SEIZ 61
the h. quality of early opinions   LAW BOOKS 9
higher there is a h. law than the Constitution
NATURAL LAW 8
highest but it is not the h.   OBEDIENCE TO LAW 6
I have the h. regard for the courts   JUDICIARY 18
mercy is the h. attribute of man
CAPITAL PUNISHMENT 17
Only those interests of the h. order and
FREEDOM OF RELIGION 68
professions this has the h. standards   LAWYERS (PRO) 3
The h. morality almost always is the   MORALITY 19
high-priced You must think I am a h. man   FEES 8
high-tech it is a h. lynching for uppity blacks
JUDICIAL APPOINT 15
high-toned in which a h. morality is more   ETHICS 7
highway right after the h. patrol gets here
NEGLIGENCE 26
himself a contract to which he is h. a party
OBEDIENCE TO LAW 7
Hinnissy A law, H., that might look like a wall
LAWYERS 33
hint a h. of the universal law   LAW PRACTICE 11
hips Read my h.   TAXATION 61
hire encourage him to h. a hall and discourse
FREEDOM OF SPEECH 6
I h. him to tell me how to do what I   CLIENT 5
hiring prima facie a h. at will, and if the   LABOR LAW 1
his lips are moving   LAWYER JOKES 9
historic continuity with the past is not a duty
HISTORY 1
history a strategic point in the campaign of h.
HOLMES 11
altered the course of h. to the   TREASON 3
at a given moment in h.   IMPEACHMENT 4
did not destroy h. for the States   DUE PROCESS 20
enshrined in the h. and the basic
SEARCHES AND SEIZ 35
I can give it as the condensed h. of   LAWYERS 17
is a part of the rational study [of law]   HISTORY 2
most complete personality in the h. of   HOLMES 40
no small measure, the h. of procedure   PROCEDURE 5
page of h. is worth a volume of logic   HISTORY 5
The h. of American freedom is, in no   PROCEDURE 5

The h. of liberty has largely been the   PROCEDURE 4
the h. of the destruction of liberty
                          CRIMINAL PROCEDURE 35
the record on which h. will judge us   WAR CRIMES 3
the sediment of h. which is law, and, as
                              SUPREME COURT 38
within the limits of its h.   HISTORY 4
hit If you want to h. a bird on the wing   HOLMES 9
hobo of the mind, that licentious nomad OBSCENITY 19
hold to h. the government back to the time of
                              CONST LAW 23
holds the law h. fast the thief and murderer
                          CIVIL DISOBEDIENCE 8
holy party prejudices into a h. field
                          FREEDOM OF RELIGION 50
homage by trifling favors, but by lavish h.   LAW 16
Fraud is the h. that force pays to   FRAUD 6
home because we deal with it otherwise at h.
                          CONFLICT OF LAWS 7
comes h. in its effects to every man's   JUDICIARY 16
reach into the privacy of one's own h.   OBSCENITY 22
The timorous may stay at h.   NEGLIGENCE 17
This h. iv opporchunity where ivry man   LAW 50
you wanted to go h. early Sunday night LAW FIRMS 4
homeopathic as thin as the h. soup that was made by
                              SLAVERY 19
Homer thinking that for once H. nodded   HOLMES 41
homicidal cross-examinations are suicidal than h.
                          CROSS-EXAMINATION 3
homicide n. The slaying of one human being by
                              MURDER 4
homme French would call l'h. moyen sensuel
                              OBSCENITY 4
honest a standard to which the wise and the h.
                          CONST CONVENTION 12
Behold! a Lawyer, an h. Man!   LAWYERS (CON) 2
citizen may be relieved from the burden
                              BANKRUPTCY 2
Here lies a lawyer and an h. man   LAWYER JOKES 2
make a lawyer h. by an act of the   ETHICS 19
men have shaped their conduct upon the
                              PRECEDENT 32
Our judges are as h. as other men, and
                          JUDICIAL REVIEW 16
resolve to be h. at all events; and if   ETHICS 6
to live outside the law, you must be h.
                              LAWLESSNESS 14
you cannot be an h. lawyer, resolve to   ETHICS 6
honestly debatable under the law of the land ETHICS 17
honesty Not h. alone, but the punctilio of a TRUSTS 5
honeycombed our society is h. with disputes
                          LEGAL REALISM 7
honor and courage written down on every page
                              HOLMES 31
I h. the man who is willing to sink
                          FREEDOM OF EXPRESS 5
Style is thus a form of h. and courage   HOLMES 31
the Court should lose the h. of being   PRECEDENT 6
honorable I know of no title that I deem more h.
                          HARVARD LAW SCHOOL 5
in some h. walk in life that wuz once
                          LAWYERS (CON) 39
save the United States and this h. Court
                              SUPREME COURT 43
hood beneath her h. the inexorable face of   LAW 43
Hoosierdome consenting adults crowded into the H. to
                              OBSCENITY 30

hope a trembling h. that one has come near to
                              HOLMES 29
still the h. of mankind across the globe
                              FIRST AMEND 46
The h. is an illusion   WORDS 13
though I h. I would die for it   FREEDOM OF SPEECH 14
when they are the fruits of h. as when CONFESSIONS 2
hopes not realized and promises not fulfilled
                              CONSTITUTION 52
These are false h., believe me, these   LIBERTY 6
whether we do not rest our h. too much   LIBERTY 6
horizontal rather than on an inefficient h. plane
                          LEGAL WRITING 25
horse Kemp-Roth was always a Trojan h. to
                              TAXATION 53
relegated to the h.-and-buggy definition
                          COMMERCE CLAUSE 13
This is a h. soon curried   JURISDICTION 26
Why does a hearse h. snicker   LAWYERS (CON) 36
horses back to the time of h. and wagons
                              CONST LAW 23
hostility toward religion or toward prayer
                          FREEDOM OF RELIGION 58
hour meet the fugitive exigencies of the h.   STATUTES 7
such a constitution to live an h.   SLAVERY 2
The law knows no finer h. than when it   LAW 70
yield nothing, and talk by the h.   CONGRESS 2
house a majority of the H. of Representatives
                              IMPEACHMENT 4
A man's h. is his castle; and while he
                          SEARCHES AND SEIZ 3
a man's own h. is a monopoly   PATENTS 5
a small part of his environment, his h.   PRIVACY 4
get a Lawyer within ten miles of your h.   WILLS 12
houses invading the h., hearts, and minds of   SEX 6
how But h. and in what balance weigh John
                          TRIALS, FAMOUS 15
can we adjudge to summary and shameful
                              INNOCENCE 1
can you tell if a lawyer is lying   LAWYER JOKES 9
could mere justice cope with poetry?   ADVOCACY 26
I dislike writing opinions   SUPREME COURT 16
I hire him to tell me h. to do what I   CLIENT 5
much do you want it to be   LAWYER JOKES 6
much is two times two   LAWYER JOKES 6
much justice can you afford WEALTH AND POVERTY 16
says now, h. are you feeling   CROSS-EXAMINATION 11
will the judges act   JUDGES 14
hubris is grist for other mills, which grind   CONTEMPT 3
huckster against a squalid h. of bad liquor may
                          SEARCHES AND SEIZ 23
huddled An opinion is h. up in conclave, perhaps
                              MARSHALL 2
Hughes once cut off an attorney in the middle
                              ADVOCACY 23
human beings are not stationary existences
                              PUNISHMENT 9
conception of h. rights enshrined in the
                          SEARCHES AND SEIZ 35
Every h. being of adult years and sound
                          MEDICAL JURISPRUD 1
every h. being with an aspiration and a
                          CAPITAL PUNISHMENT 16
founded upon four essential h. freedoms
                              FIRST AMEND 13
innate h. dignity and sense of worth   DUE PROCESS 53
mean the perpetuation of h. slavery   LAW 51

imaginations the trackless field of their own i.
COMMON LAW 8

imbeciles Three generations of i. are enough
HOLMES 27

imbibe it at every pore; we meet it when we
COMMON LAW 5

imitation the rule simply persists from blind i.
HISTORY 3

immediate check is required to save the country
FREEDOM OF SPEECH 10

transcending the i. result that is   CONST LAW 50

immediately Appeal i.   APPEALS 9

The illegal we do i.   ILLEGALITY 4

immemorially they have i. been held in trust for the
FIRST AMEND 10

immense it is of i. social value   LEGAL REALISM 4

immigration Now they have i. laws   IMMIGRATION 1

imminent clear and i. danger that it will bring
FREEDOM OF SPEECH 11

inciting or producing i. lawless action
FREEDOM OF EXPRESS 25

the danger apprehended is i.   FREEDOM OF SPEECH 22

imminently threaten immediate interference with the
FREEDOM OF SPEECH 10

immoral either i., illegal, or fattening   ILLEGALITY 3

either illegal, i. or fattening   ILLEGALITY 2

immortal An i. right to bring an eternally   RIGHTS 13

that suits may not be i., while men are   LITIGATION 4

immortality designed to approach i. as nearly as
CONSTITUTION 21

immunities that are valid as against the federal
FOURTEENTH AMEND 9

immunity for every possible use of language
FREEDOM OF SPEECH 9

from competition is a narcotic, and   ANTITRUST 26

of the press from previous restraint in
FREEDOM OF THE PRESS 29

impact it has a racially disproportionate i.
CIVIL RIGHTS 41

impair alert not to i. the ancient landmarks
BILL OF RIGHTS 14

impairment Fourteenth Amendment from i. by the
FOURTEENTH AMEND 7

impartial fair on its face and i. in appearance
EQUAL PROTECTION 2

interpretation of the laws, and   JUDGES 1

impartially cannot administer a wicked law i.
COURTROOM SCENES 17

whose obligation to govern i. is as   PROSECUTION 6

impeachable An i. offense is whatever a majority of
IMPEACHMENT 4

impeachment I suppose it is not a basis for i.
LAW REVIEWS 1

is scarcely a scare-crow   JUDICIARY 12

impenetrable they will be an i. bulwark against every
BILL OF RIGHTS 7

imperative There are precautions so i. that even
NEGLIGENCE 19

imperfect it is still a struggling and i. thing
WAR CRIMES 6

It's a very i. mechanism   JUSTICE 40

One receives only i. justice in this   JUSTICE 44

imperfection its only i.; its want of resemblance
ADVOCACY 1

imperiled I do think the Union would be i. if we
JUDICIAL REVIEW 29

imperishable shall be cast in i. moulds   CONTRACTS 20

impetuosity carried away by the i. of their ideas
LAWYERS 14

implement Law is an i. of society which is   LAW 39

implicit in the concept of ordered liberty
FOURTEENTH AMEND 9

in the history of the First Amendment is   OBSCENITY 9

import Their true i., as far as respects   TREATIES 1

we do not i. into the discussion our own
CONST LAW 21

importance It is of great i. in a republic, not
SEPARATION OF POWERS 7

important execution of the laws is more i. than   JURY 4

I think that's pretty i.   MORALITY 17

lawyers could be an i. source of protein
LAWYER JOKES 16

Legally, this was an i. victory   MORALITY 22

more i. that the applicable rule of law   PRECEDENT 35

most i. thing we do is not doing   SUPREME COURT 26

imports if they were intended to affect i. and
INTERNATIONAL LAW 18

imposed they are i. upon the community as Law
STATUTORY CONSTRUC 6

imposing a more i. judicial power was never
SUPREME COURT 8

impregnable That wall must be kept high and i.
FREEDOM OF RELIGION 41

impressions light i. which may fairly be supposed
JURY 6

strong and deep i. which will close the   JURY 6

imprison He is not required to i. himself in an
IMMIGRATION 2

imprisons Under a government which i. any unjustly
CIVIL DISOBEDIENCE 6

improbability discounted by its i., justifies such
FREEDOM OF SPEECH 31

improbable always probable that something i. will
COURTS 10

impropriety even the appearance of professional i.
ETHICS 43

improve Who shall i., on what they did
CONST AMENDMENT 3

imprudent ever composed of ı. or bad men, the
SUPREME COURT 9

impulse an irresistible and uncontrollable i.   INSANITY 1

The pupil of i., it forc'd him along   APPEALS 4

in no such thing as justice—i. or out of   JUSTICE 35

inborn sporting instinct of Anglo-Normandom
EVIDENCE 6

incapable my client was i. of committing the crime
ETHICS 28

the law is i. of calibrating anything so   GUILT 6

incidents It is one of the happy i. of the federal
DUE PROCESS 28

incitement Every idea is an i.   FREEDOM OF SPEECH 19

incitements to acts of violence and the overthrow by
FREEDOM OF THE PRESS 26

inciting or producing imminent lawless action and
FREEDOM OF EXPRESS 25

inclination the swerve, or the i. of the soul   GUILT 6

included I have finally been i. in "We, the
CIVIL RIGHTS 38

I was not i. in that "We, the people."   CIVIL RIGHTS 38

under the word "citizens" in the   SLAVERY 14

inclusion "pricked out" by a process of i. and
DUE PROCESS 24

incoherent so i. that they cannot be understood
LEGISLATION 6

income all i. from whatever source derived
TAXATION 48
having an i. of fifty thousand dollars
LAW PRACTICE 10
The I. Tax has made more Liars out of TAXATION 26
incommensurables preference, or choice between i.
NEGLIGENCE 21
inconsistent they find it i. with their happiness
CONSTITUTION 4
with the conception of human rights
SEARCHES AND SEIZ 35
increase in proportion to the power of the people
LAWYERS 10
not even a patriotic duty to i. one's TAXATION 39
increased The labor of judges would be i. almost
PRECEDENT 25
incredible accumulating with an almost i. rapidity
LAW BOOKS 5
incredibly We find the defendants i. guilty GUILT 4
independence State is bound to respect the i. of
INTERNATIONAL LAW 8
The complete i. of the courts of justice JUDICIARY 6
The more I consider the i. of the press
FREEDOM OF THE PRESS 22
Then and there the child I. was born
SEARCHES AND SEIZ 7
Those who won our i. believed that the
FREEDOM OF SPEECH 20
Those who won our i. believed . . . that
FREEDOM OF SPEECH 21
Those who won our i. by revolution were
FREEDOM OF SPEECH 23
independent A judiciary i. of a king or executive
JUDICIARY 8
professional judgment on behalf of a ETHICS 40
tribunals of justice will consider BILL OF RIGHTS 7
indestructible all its provisions, looks to an i. Union
CONSTITUTION 38
Union, composed of i. States CONSTITUTION 38
indeterminate liability in an i. amount for an
NEGLIGENCE 18
time to an indeterminate class NEGLIGENCE 18
index man who had the best card i. of the
PRECEDENT 21
indexes one of the surest i. of a mature and WORDS 20
india if they were not made of i.-rubber REGULATION 1
indication a disturbing and confirming i. that such
CIVIL RIGHTS 13
indictment drawing up an i. against an whole people
CRIMINAL LAW 2
indifference the government show a callous i. to
FREEDOM OF RELIGION 53
indignant as fine a lot iv cross an' i. men as
JUDICIARY 19
indignation the burning i. that fills woman's soul
WOMEN'S RIGHTS 8
indispensable it is the matrix, the i. condition, of
FREEDOM OF EXPRESS 13
latter are not i. parties CIVIL PROCEDURE 1
individual an i. who breaks a law that conscience
CIVIL DISOBEDIENCE 11
if the i. is no longer to be sovereign
SEARCHES AND SEIZ 56
Jury competence is an i. rather than a JURY 59
legislatures may curtail i. freedom in DUE PROCESS 33
premise of i. dignity and choice upon
FREEDOM OF EXPRESS 26

profit without individual responsibility
CORPORATIONS 12
protection of the humblest i. CONST LAW 8
right of the i., married or single, to PRIVACY 15
the right of the i. to contract DUE PROCESS 21
who considers himself injured JUDICIAL REVIEW 6
individualism We can have intellectual i. and the rich
FREEDOM 4
individuality the very foundation of i. PROPERTY 27
induce only to i. external conformity to rule
CRIMINAL LAW 7
industrial dispense his own brand of i. justice
LABOR LAW 22
inefficient rather than on an i. horizontal plane
LEGAL WRITING 25
inequality no greater i. than the equal treatment
JUSTICE 38
silently lessening the i. of property TAXATION 5
inestimable in order to enjoy the i. benefits which
FREEDOM OF THE PRESS 21
inevitable submit to the i. evils which it creates
FREEDOM OF THE PRESS 21
inexorable beneath her hood the i. face of death
LAW 43
But it is not a universal, i. command PRECEDENT 29
it is i. to the cries and lamentations LAW 6
infallibility doubt a little of his own i., and, to
CONST CONVENTION 9
infallible we are i. only because we are final
APPEALS 13
We are not final because we are i., but APPEALS 13
you needed only an i. memory for names LAWYERS 49
infamy protect the accused against i. as well
FIFTH AMEND 9
infected any law touching communication is i.
FREEDOM OF SPEECH 29
the absence of that fairness fatally i.
CRIMINAL PROCEDURE 20
infectious akin to entanglement with an i. disease
FREEDOM OF RELIGION 73
inference death of the cook, that being only an i.
LIBEL 7
government should refuse, or rest on i.
BILL OF RIGHTS 2
inferences usual i. which reasonable men draw from
SEARCHES AND SEIZ 32
inferior If one race be i. to the other socially
SEGREGATION 5
inferred from the nature of the instrument
CONSTITUTION 17
infinite catch an echo of the i., a glimpse of
LAW PRACTICE 11
the i. variety of cases and facets to
CAPITAL PUNISHMENT 25
varieties of temperament, intellect, and NEGLIGENCE 2
We aim at the i. and when our arrow HOLMES 38
inflexible division into i. compartments
DISTINCTIONS 6
inflicted an angry Heaven ever i. upon an JUDICIARY 17
influence if the i. of lawyers in public business
LAWYERS 10
the almost invisible i. of their legal LAWYERS 14
influences a thousand i. gained only from life
COURTS 21
information A popular Government, without popular i.
FREEDOM OF THE PRESS 19
The special i. which lawyers derive from LAWYERS 9

My i. furniture consists of an   HOLMES 13
We can have i. individualism and the   FREEDOM 4
intelligence jury system puts a ban upon i. and   JURY 23
    put a premium on i. and character   JURY 24
    to the i. of a future day, when a later   DISSENT 5
intelligent fool ideas that no i. Christian on earth
                                     RELIGION 6
    that's the first i. thing you've said   LAW SCHOOL 9
    waiver of the right to counsel must
                      CRIMINAL PROCEDURE 19
intelligible an i. principle to which the person or
                     SEPARATION OF POWERS 15
intend I i. to prove that Mr. Kringle is Santa
                      COURTROOM SCENES 8
intended guess what it would have i. on a point
                      STATUTORY CONSTRUC 7
intensifier of economic advantage and disadvantage
                      CONTRACTS 26
intent Budd's i. or non-intent is nothing to
                      MILITARY JUSTICE 4
    can make infringement of what otherwise   PATENTS 19
    personal, or individual, i. of the   CONTRACTS 11
intention If a judge abandons i. as his guide
                     ORIGINAL INTENTION 17
    Is it your i. to overthrow the   IMMIGRATION 6
    The i. of the law-giver is the law   INTENT 1
    the i. of the people to the intention of
                     JUDICIAL REVIEW 2
intentional A waiver is ordinarily an i.
                     CRIMINAL PROCEDURE 19
    infliction of temporal damage is a   TORTS 5
intentions the framers' i. . . . are the sole
                     ORIGINAL INTENTION 13
intercourse something more: it is i.
                     COMMERCE CLAUSE 1
interdependence separateness but i., autonomy but
                     SEPARATION OF POWERS 20
    that type of i. between religion and
                     FREEDOM OF RELIGION 61
interest a man rightly prefers his own i. to
                     LEGISLATION 17
    appropriate governmental i. suitably
                     EQUAL PROTECTION 17
    clothed with a public i. when used in a   PROPERTY 15
    Justice, Sir, is the great i. of man on   JUSTICE 11
    My keenest i. is excited, not by what   CASES 2
    proper for the i. and liberty of the   JURISDICTION 1
    The patent system added the fuel of i.   PATENTS 7
interested every one is personally i. in enforcing
                     OBEDIENCE TO LAW 7
    was mightily i. in where it had been   PRECEDENT 38
interests considered against important state i.
                     ABORTION 3
    have ever formed distinct i. in society   PROPERTY 3
    Only those i. of the highest order and
                     FREEDOM OF RELIGION 68
interfered Had I i. in the manner, which I admit
                     TRIALS, FAMOUS 6
    had I so i. in behalf of any of the rich
                     TRIALS, FAMOUS 6
interference threaten immediate i. with the lawful
                     FREEDOM OF SPEECH 10
international law is part of our law, and must be
                     INTERNATIONAL LAW 10
interposing justify the State in . . . i. its authority
                     DUE PROCESS 10
interpret absolute authority to i. any written or

STATUTORY CONSTRUC 5
    smart man could i. every law there is
                     LAWYERS (CON) 42
    statutes do not i. themselves   STATUTORY CONSTRUC 6
    to i. a statute out of existence as to
                     STATUTORY CONSTRUC 8
interpretation constitutional i. is not the business of
                     CONST LAW 61
    it is disgraceful for an i. of the   CONST LAW 56
    It must leave i. to others, principally
                     STATUTORY CONSTRUC 19
    Legal i. takes place in a field of pain
                     INTERPRETATION 3
    power of amendment under the guise of i.
                     CONST LAW 39
    safest rule of i. after all will be   CONST LAW 16
    The difficulties of so-called i. arise
                     STATUTORY CONSTRUC 7
    The i. of the laws is the proper and
                     JUDICIAL REVIEW 2
    The judicial function is that of i.   CONST LAW 39
interpreter not the only i. of the Constitution
                     CONST LAW 61
interpreters If they were the i. of the everlasting
                     LAWYERS 21
    one of the great i. between the
                     FREEDOM OF THE PRESS 30
interpreting Under the guise of i. the Constitution
                     CONST LAW 21
interpretive entirely obscured by its i. barnacles
                     PROCEDURE 8
interrogation By custodial i., we mean questioning
                     CONFESSIONS 8
    stemming from custodial i. of the   CONFESSIONS 8
interstate horse-and-buggy definition of i.
                     COMMERCE CLAUSE 13
    If it is i. commerce that feels the
                     COMMERCE CLAUSE 15
    in some way obstructed i. commerce   SEX 1
interstitially they can do so only i.
                     JUDICIAL LEGISLATION 2
interval the shortest i. of time known to man
                     JUDICIAL APPOINT 9
intimidate to i. women into continuing pregnancies
                     ABORTION 16
intimidation a conscious process of i. by which all
                     RAPE 2
intonation the mere i. of interests such as
                     MILITARY JUSTICE 13
intricacies depend upon the i. of the law of sales
                     PRODUCTS LIABILITY 1
intruder regarded by the other as an alien i.
                     ADMINISTRATIVE LAW 12
intrusion In justifying the particular i. the
                     SEARCHES AND SEIZ 59
    unwarranted governmental i. into matters   PRIVACY 15
invaded courts have i. rights which in our
                     CONFLICT OF LAWS 10
invading the houses, hearts, and minds of   SEX 6
invalidity infected with presumptive i.
                     FREEDOM OF SPEECH 29
invasion of his indefeasible right of personal
                     SEARCHES AND SEIZ 9
invasions resist i. of it in the case of others
                     FREEDOM OF RELIGION 20
invented the greatest legal engine ever i. for
                     CROSS-EXAMINATION 2

the m. of forms, the conservative—is a   LAW 24
the relationship between m. and religion
    FREEDOM OF RELIGION 65
The wisdom of m. never yet contrived a   TAXATION 9
Till the m. in the moon will allow it's   ADVOCACY 6
We ask no m.'s permission when we
    OBEDIENCE TO LAW 18
what has m. done?—and not what has the
    CIVIL RIGHTS 12
when a m. decides that he is not God   HOLMES 15
Whenever you put a m. on the Supreme
    JUDICIAL APPOINT 6
with all his wisdom, toils for heirs he   WILLS 1
management Spoliation is not m.
    AMERICAN INDIAN LAW 8
mandate "discover" a constitutional m. to have
    CRIMINAL PROCEDURE 34
Mandrake everybody in M. Falls is pixilated
    COURTROOM SCENES 1
manhood moral and physical fibre of its m. and
    LEGISLATION 36
manifest there is a m. necessity for the act   JURY 7
mankind Adjudicated quarrels of m.   LAW LIBRARIES 4
has worked and fought its way from   LAW 42
Property is surely a right of m. as   PROPERTY 2
Since the general civilization of m., I   FREEDOM 1
sustained by the organized opinion of m.
    INTERNATIONAL LAW 14
than most other varieties of m.   LAWYERS (PRO) 14
manner It is to teach law in the grand m., and
    LAW SCHOOL 2
manual would have to turn to m. labor
    LAWYERS (CON) 42
manufacture Commerce succeeds to m., and is not a
    COMMERCE CLAUSE 6
We enact many laws that m. criminals   CRIMINAL 2
many are the crimes committed in its name
    CRIMINAL PROCEDURE 26
marble Palace   SUPREME COURT 36
marching we are m. backward to the glorious ages
    FIRST AMEND 7
marital sacred precincts of m. bedrooms for   PRIVACY 9
maritime comprehends all m. contracts, torts, and
    ADMIRALTY 2
mark evolving standards of decency that m.
    PUNISHMENT 19
His m. is his authentic seal; by it he   TRADEMARKS 6
Now I realize what M. Twain meant when
    SECURITIES LAW 3
The m. of a master is, that facts which
    LEGAL EDUCATION 18
market accepted in the competition of the m.
    FREEDOM OF SPEECH 13
stricter than the morals of the m. place   TRUSTS 5
marketplace In today's m. of ideas, the public
    FIRST AMEND 54
The theory of the truth of the m.
    FREEDOM OF SPEECH 45
marks A law student who m. his own examination
    JUDGES 25
There are skid m. leading up to the   LAWYER JOKES 11
marriage is a coming together for better or worse
    MARRIAGE 10
married A m. woman has the same right to control
    RAPE 5
whether they are m. and, if so, to whom   MARRIAGE 8
marry The freedom to m. has long been   MARRIAGE 11

Marshall has a compass, puts out to sea, and goes
    MARSHALL 8
John M. has made his decision: now let
    SUPREME COURT 7
My gift of John M. to the people of the   MARSHALL 3
There fell to M. perhaps the greatest   MARSHALL 9
martial law operating through us   MILITARY JUSTICE 3
martyr if you are a Crook or a M.   TAXATION 26
One who is a m. to a principle
    FREEDOM OF RELIGION 31
martyrdom does not prove by his m. that he has
    FREEDOM OF RELIGION 31
mask another can use it only as a m.   TRADEMARKS 6
mass a cumulative and m. effect; these, after
    LEGAL WRITING 10
at last into one consolidated m.   JUDICIARY 9
The m. of the law is, to be sure   LAW BOOKS 5
massive a m. diversion of exceptional talent
    LAWYERS (CON) 60
master The mark of a m. is, that facts which
    LEGAL EDUCATION 18
The prairie-lawyer, m. of us all
    LAWYERS, INDIVIDUAL 3
therefore the real m. of society   JURY 9
you must m. those which lie next to it
    LEGAL EDUCATION 17
masters are fast becoming the people's m.
    CORPORATIONS 6
subdue our M. and without violence throw
    WOMEN'S RIGHTS 4
match the colors of the case at hand against
    PRECEDENT 21
material It is difficult to make our m. condition
    LEGISLATION 24
mathematical a coarse tool and not a m. instrument
    LAW 39
formulas having their essence in their   CONST LAW 26
mathematics axioms and corollaries of a book of m.
    LAW 35
matrix it is the m., the indispensable
    FREEDOM OF EXPRESS 13
matter No m. whether th' constitution follows
    SUPREME COURT 11
of constitutional law, not of   FEDERALISM 37
only a m. of whose ox is gored   AFFIRMATIVE ACTION 5
The m. of the boat's condition   JUDGES 18
matters in order to protect speech that m.   LIBEL 13
judicial cognizance of all m. of general   PRECEDENT 15
mature one of the surest indexes of a m. and
    WORDS 20
maturing that mark the progress of a m. society
    PUNISHMENT 19
maximum his authority is at its m., for it
    PRESIDENT 10
maze We shall be lost in a m. if we put that
    JURISDICTION 22
me don't tax m., tax that fellow behind   TAXATION 50
mean I understand it to m. what the words say
    FIRST AMEND 35
People say law, but they m. wealth
    WEALTH AND POVERTY 4
pretentious, are what I m. by the law
    LAW, DEFINITIONS 2
The lawyers have us and m. to keep us
    LAWYERS (CON) 31
they do not always m. what they say   STATUTES 2
what those words would m. in the mouth   WORDS 5

DUE PROCESS 35

minority most vilified and persecuted m. in
FREEDOM OF RELIGION 33

The m. are right   TRIALS, FAMOUS 10

the m. may shortly rally the majority to
OBEDIENCE TO LAW 7

the m. possess their equal rights, which   RIGHTS 6

minuet jungle warfare is a stately m. LAWYERS (CON) 50

minute The m. you read something and you can't
LEGAL WRITING 12

minutiae whose m. contract and distract the mind
LAW 11

miracle a small daily m. of democracy in action LAW 81

the true m. was not the birth of the   CONSTITUTION 52

you're going to see the greatest m. take
NEGLIGENCE 24

miracles union has been prolonged thus far by m.
CONSTITUTION 23

mirror The Law, wherein, as in a magic m., we LAW 40

misapprehend no more likely way to m. the meaning
LANGUAGE 10

mischief wider application than the m. which gave
CONST LAW 24

miserable a small and usually m. minority of men
JUSTICE 25

how to remove the life of one m.   MILITARY JUSTICE 6

misfortune his m. to live in a dark age that knew
INSANITY 5

misgovernment They augur m. at a distance, and snuff
LAWYERS (PRO) 1

misinterpreted If judges have wofully m. the mores of
PRECEDENT 27

misread There is no surer way to m. any document
STATUTORY CONSTRUC 18

mistake It is a great m. to be frightened by the
LEGAL RESEARCH 2

the m. I made in the Court below   ADVOCACY 16

When I make a m., it's a beaut   JUDICIAL APPOINT 3

mistaken a current m. view of the Constitution
SUPREME COURT 39

think that ye may be m.   COURTS 32

mistakes only profession which records its m.
PRECEDENT 56

yet does not identify them as m.   PRECEDENT 56

mister Oh, M. President, do not let so great an
ILLEGALITY 1

mistress it is a jealous m., and requires a long LAW 16

to speak of the law as our m., we who   LAW 41

mnemonic poetic or m. devices for formulating
LEGAL REALISM 13

the m. power of alliteration and   LEGAL WRITING 8

mob elected by a m. intent on death
CRIMINAL PROCEDURE 11

law does not become due process of law
CRIMINAL PROCEDURE 11

to go forward with the haste of the m.
CRIMINAL PROCEDURE 16

mockery constitution itself becomes a solemn m.
COURTS 3

equal protection becomes a m.
WEALTH AND POVERTY 15

mode that m. of attacking or defending a man
LAWYERS 21

there is a m. prescribed in the   ORIGINAL INTENTION 4

moderation the spirit of m. is gone, no court can
COURTS 28

moderator the judge is not a mere m., but is the

JURY 47

modern law school belongs in the m. university
LAW SCHOOL 3

the problems that arise in a m. society
ORIGINAL INTENTION 10

modification implies growth   PRECEDENT 28

molar confined from m. to molecular motions
JUDICIAL LEGISLATION 2

molecular confined from molar to m. motions
JUDICIAL LEGISLATION 2

molested on account of his mode of worship or
FREEDOM OF RELIGION 17

moment An alert lawyer will make that m. his
LAWYERS (CON) 51

considers [it] to be at a given m. in   IMPEACHMENT 4

That last m. belongs to us—that agony
TRIALS, FAMOUS 14

There is a magic m. during which a man
LAWYERS (CON) 51

momentum for respect lacking when appeal is made
DUE PROCESS 38

money a litigant without m. for lawyers is
LITIGATION 12

depends on the amount of m. he has
EQUAL PROTECTION 13

Send lawyers, guns and m., the shit has   LAWYERS 58

supplied by a spirit of . . . m. catching
LAW PRACTICE 2

vile thing to plead for m. or reward   FEES 2

you did not have enough m. to pay a good
WEALTH AND POVERTY 6

money-getting learned profession, not a mere m. trade
ETHICS 30

monopoly a man's own house is a m.   PATENTS 5

an inventor to his invention is no m.   PATENTS 5

for every trifling device, every shadow   PATENTS 11

may have been thrust upon it   ANTITRUST 28

use of m. power, however lawfully   ANTITRUST 30

Where a trust becomes a m. the State has
ANTITRUST 6

monotonous strange to think of that m. series as a
LAW BOOKS 6

monster Such is the Frankenstein m. which States
CORPORATIONS 17

monstrous There is something m. in commands
LANGUAGE 6

monument for the little known and unremembered
LAWYERS (PRO) 10

monuments let them stand undisturbed as m. of the
FREEDOM OF SPEECH 4

moon Till the man in the m. will allow it's a
ADVOCACY 6

moral A m. tone ought to be infused into the
LITIGATION 6

an abiding conviction, to a m. certainty   JURY 15

compendiously described as "m. character   ETHICS 33

Every person of good m. character, being
LAW PRACTICE 7

external deposit of our m. life   MORALITY 6

if every word of m. significance could   MORALITY 9

If the m. and physical fibre of its   LEGISLATION 36

mandates into mere m. reflections   CONST LAW 39

one has a m. responsibility to disobey
CIVIL DISOBEDIENCE 10

the m. judgment that the community has
LEGISLATION 31

With purely m. obligations the law does

I may hate the sin but n. the sinner   CONST CONVENTION 6
                       DARROW 6
I n. ask a question unless I know
                CROSS-EXAMINATION 4
I n. bow to a decision iv a judge onless
                OBEDIENCE TO LAW 20
I n. take a case unless I am convinced   ETHICS 28
I wish I may n. hear of the United   TREASON 2
in our full life could we hope to do
                 TRIALS, FAMOUS 14
Law n. made men a whit more just; and   INJUSTICE 1
N., never, never, on cross-examination
                CROSS-EXAMINATION 7
stir up litigation   LITIGATION 6
tell her you'll n. be a lawyer   LAW SCHOOL 9
The law will n. make men free; it is men   LAW 25
using two words where one will do
                LEGAL EDUCATION 1
you n. hear the name of the United   TREASON 2
never-never the n. land of abstract principles and
                LAW 66
new a constant infusion of n. blood in the
                SUPREME COURT 21
a n. opportunity in life and a clear   BANKRUPTCY 5
a n. world of law, where the strong are
                INTERNATIONAL LAW 21
a n. world order—a world where the rule
                INTERNATIONAL LAW 24
a n. world order, where diverse nations
                INTERNATIONAL LAW 25
one old law is worth two n. ones   NATURAL LAW 6
read my lips, no n. taxes   TAXATION 58
this Constitution that is absolutely n.
                CONSTITUTION 40
times demand new measures and new men
                LAW, GROWTH 2
tolerable in Las Vegas, or New York City
                OBSCENITY 25
We must create a n. property   PROPERTY 28
what the N. York courts would think the
                CONFLICT OF LAWS 13
newspapers a government without n., or newspapers
                FREEDOM OF THE PRESS 5
or n. without a government, I should not
                FREEDOM OF THE PRESS 5
next the n. will be drawn in blood
                CONST CONVENTION 13
you must master those which lie n. to it
                LEGAL EDUCATION 17
nexus The n. demanded of federal taxpayers has
                STANDING 3
nibble Can a mouse n. at it   LAWYERS (CON) 37
nice controversies involving not very n.   LIBERTY 9
hold the balance n., clear and true
                CRIMINAL PROCEDURE 14
in the n. balance of a jeweler's scale
                FREEDOM OF EXPRESS 11
indulge in n. calculations as to the
                CRIMINAL PROCEDURE 22
night and day, childhood and maturity, or any
                DISTINCTIONS 9
nightgown Here I am an old man in a long n. making
                JUDGES 58
nightmare our long national n. is over
                CONSTITUTION 51
nightstick There's a lot of law at the end of a n.

nincompoop juror is not some kind of a dithering n.
                LAW ENFORCEMENT 9
                JURY 70
nine tenths of you are in jail because you
                WEALTH AND POVERTY 6
The N. Old Men   SUPREME COURT 19
the n. old men of the Supreme Court are
                SUPREME COURT 17
The switch in time that saved the N.
                SUPREME COURT 24
nineteen naturally expires at the end of 19 years
                CONSTITUTION 8
Section 1979 should be read against   CIVIL RIGHTS 19
nineteenth more than the N. Amendment to convince
                SEX DISCRIMINATION 3
The N. Amendment—I think that's the one
                WOMEN'S RIGHTS 13
ninety percent of any decision is emotional
                SUPREME COURT 27
percent of our lawyers serve 10 percent
                LAWYERS (CON) 59
niver I n. bow to a decision iv a judge onless
                OBEDIENCE TO LAW 20
Nixon pardon unto Richard N. for all offenses
                PARDONS 3
no general proposition is worth a damn   HOLMES 13
government ought to be without censors
                FREEDOM OF THE PRESS 10
I read "n. law . . . abridging" to mean no
                FIRST AMEND 27
law, as among the savage Americans, or   LAW 10
law can be sacred to me but that of my
                NATURAL LAW 7
man has a natural right to commit   LAW 12
man is above it, and no man is below it
                OBEDIENCE TO LAW 17
man is above the law and no man is below
                OBEDIENCE TO LAW 19
man's life, liberty or property are safe   LEGISLATION 16
read my lips, n. new taxes   TAXATION 58
set of legal institutions or   LAW 100
there is n. end to the laws and no
                LAW ENFORCEMENT 3
There is n. such thing as justice—in or   JUSTICE 35
noble social and economic experiment, n. in
                INTOXICATION 5
nobles In America, there are no n. or literary
                LAWYERS 12
noblest the n. of human productions—knowledge
                COPYRIGHT 15
nodded thinking that for once Homer n.   HOLMES 41
noiseless advancing its n. step like a thief, over
                JUDICIARY 12
the n., and therefore unalarming   SUPREME COURT 5
with n. foot, and unalarming advance   JUDICIARY 11
noises making muffled n. at people who may be
                JUDGES 58
nominal the n. politics of the man has nothing
                JUDICIAL APPOINT 2
non-conforming victims of prejudice and public
                DUE PROCESS 36
non-conformity is not an outstanding characteristic of
                EDUCATION 4
none can make a law of nations   INTERNATIONAL LAW 2
nonmarital a contract between n. partners is   SEX 2
nonpersons imbeciles, and other classes of legal n.

odds with the betting o. in favor of Judas   COURTS 19
ode compose anew Keats's O. on a Grecian Urn
          COPYRIGHT 18
odium to bring courts of justice into o.; and   COURTS 5
offense An impeachable o. is whatever a majority
          IMPEACHMENT 4
  making temporary insanity a capital o.   INSANITY 2
offered no one having o. them a fee for
          LAWYERS (CON) 25
office The o. of a lawyer is too delicate
          LEGAL PROFESSION 3
officer in the hands of every petty o.
          SEARCHES AND SEIZ 2
  No o. of the law may set that law at   GOVERNMENT 18
officers All the o. of the government, from the
          GOVERNMENT 18
offices noble and benign o. of wife and mother
          WOMEN 3
official compose o. prayers for any group of the
          FREEDOM OF RELIGION 57
  law, then, always lags somewhat behind   LAW 74
  no o., high or petty, can prescribe what
          FREEDOM OF RELIGION 36
  spokesmen have all the loud-speakers   CENSORSHIP 14
  When there is o. censorship it is a sign
          CENSORSHIP 14
officials What these o. do about disputes is, to
          LEGAL REALISM 7
officiated unsuccessful case, and I have o. at many
          LAWYERS (PRO) 9
offspring or product of mental disease   INSANITY 4
often so o. announced, so confidently relied
          PRECEDENT 55
old cat versus bird is as o. as time   LEGISLATION 39
  glasses fitted, as it were, for the   SUPREME COURT 21
  gradually changing its o. channels and
          COMMON LAW 7
  Here I am an o. man in a long nightgown   JUDGES 58
  I am an o. country lawyer and I don't
          CROSS-EXAMINATION 10
  much that is as o. as Magna Charta   CONSTITUTION 40
  one o. law is worth two new ones   NATURAL LAW 6
  opinions of half-a-dozen old gentlemen
          SUPREME COURT 12
  The Fifth Amendment is an o. friend and
          FIFTH AMEND 7
  The Nine O. Men   SUPREME COURT 19
  the nine o. men of the Supreme Court are
          SUPREME COURT 17
omission First the o. of a bill of rights
          BILL OF RIGHTS 1
omit to generalize is to o.   CORPORATIONS 9
omitted crime or vice was accidentally o.   CRIME 3
omnipresence common law is not a brooding o. in the
          COMMON LAW 15
once loosed, the idea of Equality is not   CIVIL RIGHTS 33
one a game at which only o. (the professor)
          CASE SYSTEM 13
  arrow, if fatal, is fatal enough   CIVIL PROCEDURE 18
  at least o. member, more ready to hang   JURY 18
  country, one constitution, one destiny
          CONSTITUTION 26
  Even o. day in prison would be a cruel
          PUNISHMENT 20
  form of action, for the enforcement or
          CODIFICATION 1
  form of action to be known as "civil

CIVIL PROCEDURE 10
  form of civil action and procedure for
          CIVIL PROCEDURE 8
  has a moral responsibility to disobey
          CIVIL DISOBEDIENCE 10
  he's not just breaking o. law but all   LAWLESSNESS 12
  I regret that I have but o. law firm to   LAW FIRMS 3
  man's vulgarity is another's lyric
          FREEDOM OF SPEECH 43
  may do what he will with his own   TRUSTS 1
  not be finished in the first o. hundred
          INTERNATIONAL LAW 21
  Nothing is illegal if o. hundred   ILLEGALITY 6
  of you three won't be here next year   LAW SCHOOL 5
  old law is worth two new ones   NATURAL LAW 6
  one country, o. constitution, one   CONSTITUTION 26
  only o. thing—one person, one vote   VOTING 11
  the people send 150. lawyers, whose   CONGRESS 2
  thing when applied to one individual and
          AFFIRMATIVE ACTION 12
  who belongs to the most vilified and
          FREEDOM OF RELIGION 33
  with the law is a majority   LAW 55
  That a body containing 100 lawyers in it   CONGRESS 1
  That 150. lawyers should do business   CONGRESS 2
only Lawyer: The o. man in whom ignorance of
          LAWYERS (CON) 24
  outlaws will have guns   CRIME 11
  That's the o. fun in law anyway   LAW PRACTICE 20
  the little people pay taxes   TAXATION 60
  the o. class of society specially   JUDGES 27
  The o. prize much cared for by the   HOLMES 17
  The o. question for the lawyer is, how   JUDGES 14
  The o. tool of the lawyer is words   WORDS 25
  the o. way that we can: as Twentieth
          ORIGINAL INTENTION 16
open a gratuitous public school, ever o., in   JURY 10
  indispensable conditions of an o. as   DUE PROCESS 38
  not extended to the o. fields   SEARCHES AND SEIZ 15
  what o. force would not dare attempt   JUDICIARY 15
operate taxation that would o. with perfect   TAXATION 9
operation narrower scope for o. of the presumption
          DUE PROCESS 35
opinion An o. is huddled up in conclave, perhaps
          MARSHALL 2
  barriers around the liberty of o.
          FREEDOM OF EXPRESS 4
  Compulsory unification of o. achieves   DISSENT 8
  Expert o. . . . is only an ordinary guess in   EXPERTS 3
  I have a high o. of lawyers   LAWYERS (PRO) 14
  I have not yet written the o.   SEGREGATION 21
  natural outcome of a dominant o.   DUE PROCESS 16
  public o. which is the final source of
          FREEDOM OF EXPRESS 8
  sustained by the organized o. of mankind
          INTERNATIONAL LAW 14
  This o. was at that time fixed and   SLAVERY 15
  We are all of o. that it does   FOURTEENTH AMEND 3
opinions copyright in the written o. delivered by
          COPYRIGHT 1
  How I dislike writing o.   SUPREME COURT 16
  quotes the o. of others, and how little   LAWYERS 11
  the high quality of early o.   LAW BOOKS 9
  The Law of a great nation means the o.
          SUPREME COURT 12
  The o. of men are not the subject of
          FREEDOM OF RELIGION 10

515

men are least willing to p. the taxes TAXATION 32
Only the little people p. taxes TAXATION 10
Taxes are what we p. for civilized TAXATION 60
the dues that we p. for the privileges TAXATION 28
we get our satisfactions and our p. TAXATION 41
wonder vaguely whether law and order p. LAWYERS 52
SUPREME COURT 14
paycheck relationship to the size of his p.
WEALTH AND POVERTY 14
paying constitutional way of p. for the change
EMINENT DOMAIN 6
so used to p. taxes that it would just TAXATION 27
peace We seek to find p. of mind in the word
WORDS 13
peace-maker As a p. the lawyer has a superior
LITIGATION 5
pebbles Words are not p. in alien juxtaposition
WORDS 17
Pecos The Law West of the P. JUDGES, INDIVIDUAL 2
peculiar boast and excellence of the common law
COMMON LAW 13
boast and excellence of the common law
COMMON LAW 14
Our p. security is in the possession of CONST LAW 1
pedagogical requirement of the impracticable
FOURTEENTH AMEND 6
pedestal put women, not on a p., but in a cage
SEX DISCRIMINATION 9
The p. upon which women have been placed
WOMEN 6
peer The humblest is the p. of the most
SEGREGATION 8
Pegasus gallop over the fields of law on P., nor
LAWYERS 4
pen And some with a fountain p. CRIMINAL 7
penal as to the meaning of p. statutes CRIMINAL LAW 14
penalty a p. or punishment for disobedience
GOVERNMENT 1
made binding upon the conscience by a p.
WITNESSES 3
The p. for laughing in the courtroom is COURTS 33
The p. of death differs from all other
CAPITAL PUNISHMENT 28
The p. of death is qualitatively
CAPITAL PUNISHMENT 31
the smaller the p. the fewer the crimes
CAPITAL PUNISHMENT 5
pencil With a p. dipped in the most vivid ADVOCACY 1
pennyworth a p. of content is most frequently
LAW REVIEWS 4
penumbra a line drawn somewhere in the p. between
DISTINCTIONS 1
find in the vague p. of a statute some
STATUTORY CONSTRUC 17
First Amendment has a p. where privacy PRIVACY 8
never touches the border land, the p. LAW 57
the law allows a p. to be embraced that
DISTINCTIONS 8
to end in a p. or debatable land NEGLIGENCE 3
penumbras guarantees in the Bill of Rights have p.
BILL OF RIGHTS 16
people A bill of rights is what the p. are
BILL OF RIGHTS 2
a p. so choked and stultified by forms LAW 27
an indictment against an whole p. CRIMINAL LAW 2
and not in the government over the p. CENSORSHIP 1

are fast becoming the p.'s masters CORPORATIONS 6
controversies involving not very nice p. LIBERTY 9
far too little of the "p.'s lawyer" LAWYERS (CON) 22
for the interest and liberty of the p. JURISDICTION 1
Fourth Amendment protects p., not places
SEARCHES AND SEIZ 54
Guns don't die, p. die CRIME 13
Guns don't kill p., people kill people CRIME 12
hate taxes the way children hate TAXATION 63
Here the p. rule CONSTITUTION 51
in proportion to the power of the p. LAWYERS 10
In war, we are one p. In making peace
GOVERNMENT 14
It is, Sir, the p.'s Constitution, the DEMOCRACY 1
leave the p.'s homes secure only in the
SEARCHES AND SEIZ 34
Legislators represent p., not trees or VOTING 15
made for the p., made by the people, and
DEMOCRACY 1
much p. flock thither LAW 3
of Maine or Mississippi accept public OBSCENITY 25
Only the little p. pay taxes TAXATION 60
power was never constituted by any p.
SUPREME COURT 8
say law, but they mean wealth
WEALTH AND POVERTY 4
Spectacle of a whole P. deliberating
CONST CONVENTION 16
take government off the backs of p. and
GOVERNMENT 32
the only p. in Washington who do their
SUPREME COURT 25
The p. made the constitution, and the
CONSTITUTION 22
The p. make them, the people adopt them
CONSTITUTION 24
the p. must resort to the polls, not to
JUDICIAL REVIEW 23
the P. should obey the magistrate
OBEDIENCE TO LAW 1
the p. will have ceased, to be their own
JUDICIAL REVIEW 22
the power of the p. is superior to both
JUDICIAL REVIEW 3
The P.'s Attorney JUDGES, INDIVIDUAL 3
the right of the p. to alter or abolish CONSTITUTION 4
They are ordained by the will of the p. CONST LAW 15
to enforce a law not supported by the p.
LAW ENFORCEMENT 13
truly, a government of the p. GOVERNMENT 8
unfounded assumptions about how p. live
CONST LAW 56
"We the p." It is a very eloquent CIVIL RIGHTS 38
When a p. lose respect for one bad law
LEGISLATION 35
with sneakers, guns, dope, lust, or
YALE LAW SCHOOL 5
peoples of the several states must sink or swim
FEDERALISM 32
pepper A cent or a p. corn, in legal estimation
CONTRACTS 3
per se unreasonable under the Fourth
SEARCHES AND SEIZ 55
perfect can a p. production be expected?
CONST CONVENTION 8
discontent at the remoteness of p. law LAW 84
operate with p. equality TAXATION 9

GOVERNMENT 29

Respect for judicial p. is a small price   LAW 86
the p. and proceedings of the courts of
       DUE PROCESS 4
the p. in its highest reaches is not   JUDGES 32
through the p. of amendment   CIVIL RIGHTS 38
procession before my eyes in a meaningless p.
       LEGAL WRITING 16
produced fewer instances of truly great judges
       JUDGES 8
producers prefer a system of small p., each
       ANTITRUST 27
product offspring or p. of mental disease   INSANITY 4
the p. of a mental disease or defect   INSANITY 14
profess all men shall be free to p., and by
       FREEDOM OF RELIGION 9
profession a learned p., not a mere money-getting
       ETHICS 30
a p. as distinguished from a business is ANTITRUST 32
a p. whose general principles enlighten   LAW 11
always been a narrow, conservatizing p.   JUDGES 19
And what a p. it is!   LAWYERS (PRO) 4
no p., after that of the sacred ministry   ETHICS 7
the only p. which records its mistakes   PRECEDENT 56
professional an expert, a p. liar, to show him new
       WITNESSES 5
even the appearance of p. impropriety   ETHICS 43
independent p. judgment on behalf of a   ETHICS 40
"No," said his wife, "just p. courtesy."
       LAWYER JOKES 3
professions of all secular p. this has the highest
       LAWYERS (PRO) 3
one of the last of the unpredictable p.   ADVOCACY 24
professor that of P. of the Harvard Law School
       HARVARD LAW SCHOOL 5
the American p. explains what the judge
       LEGAL EDUCATION 27
profit individual p. without individual
       CORPORATIONS 12
profited I have never p., never profited from
       PRESIDENT 15
profound background of a p. national commitment
       LIBEL 9
debates that ushered our Federal   FEDERALISM 35
some p. interstitial change in the very   CASES 2
program Oh, that was our summer p.   LAW FIRMS 7
progress close connection between crime and p.
       CRIMINAL 5
follow, and conform to, the p. of   LAW, GROWTH 3
hand in hand with the p. of the human
       CONSTITUTION 15
must be by analogy to what is already   PRECEDENT 2
shape the p. of the law   LAW, GROWTH 7
that mark the p. of a maturing society
       PUNISHMENT 19
prohibit did not p. the most ingenious and
       AFFIRMATIVE ACTION 10
prohibited acts p. and acts allowed, are of equal
       CONSTITUTION 14
prohibition of the Equal Protection Clause goes no
       EQUAL PROTECTION 12
only drives drunkenness behind doors
       INTOXICATION 1
prohibitions meant their p. to be "absolutes"
       BILL OF RIGHTS 15
proletarian beliefs expressed in p. dictatorship are
       FREEDOM OF SPEECH 19
prolixity partake of the p. of a legal code

       CONSTITUTION 17
prologue a P. to a Farce or a Tragedy; or perhaps
       FREEDOM OF THE PRESS 19
prolonged a slumber that, p., means death   HOLMES 20
union has been p. thus far by miracles
       CONSTITUTION 23
prominent on the surface of any case held to
       SEPARATION OF POWERS 22
promise A p. may be lacking, and yet the whole
       CONTRACTS 13
a p. that a certain private sphere of   PRIVACY 18
a p. to the ear to be broken to the hope
       FOURTEENTH AMEND 11
consequence of a legally binding p. is   DAMAGES 2
that right to remain an empty p.
       SEARCHES AND SEIZ 48
the Thirteenth Amendment made a p. the
       CIVIL RIGHTS 36
promised if the p. event does not come to pass
       DAMAGES 2
promises commercial age, is made up largely of p.
       COMMERCIAL LAW 3
hopes not realized and p. not fulfilled
       CONSTITUTION 52
the law must keep its p.   CAPITAL PUNISHMENT 20
promisor the law makes the p. pay damages if the
       DAMAGES 2
promissory they were signing a p. note to which
       CIVIL RIGHTS 26
pronouncing a statute to be unconstitutional, forms
       JUDICIAL REVIEW 21
propensities oppose their aristocratic p. to the
       LAWYERS 14
proper always a p. subject for adjudication
       HUMAN RIGHTS 1
for the interest and liberty of the   JURISDICTION 1
inseparable from the p. use of
       FREEDOM OF THE PRESS 12
property ability to buy p. turn on the color of
       CIVIL RIGHTS 35
about human rights than about p. rights   PROPERTY 21
does become clothed with a public   PROPERTY 15
equally said to have a p. in his rights   PROPERTY 5
every man holds his p. subject to the   REGULATION 7
guards the troubled boundary between   PROPERTY 27
in whatever manner, the laws of p.   PROPERTY 10
is an instrument of humanity   PROPERTY 21
is surely a right of mankind as really   PROPERTY 2
man is said to have a right to his p.   PROPERTY 5
may be denied but the confidence cannot
       TRADEMARKS 4
more like "p." than a "gratuity"   PROPERTY 29
Neither p. rights nor contract rights   DUE PROCESS 30
only liberty to acquire and enjoy p.
       FREEDOM OF SPEECH 17
the great body of p. is socially   WORDS 10
the love of p. more active and more   PROPERTY 10
The personal right to acquire p., which   PROPERTY 8
the right of p. in a slave is distinctly   SLAVERY 16
The word p. as applied to trade-marks   TRADEMARKS 4
various and unequal distribution of p.   PROPERTY 3
We must create a new p.   PROPERTY 28
with socialized p. we should have women   HOLMES 22
prophecies The p. of what the courts will do in
       LAW, DEFINITIONS 2
prophecy a right is only the hypostasis of a p.
       RIGHTS 14

silence beyond the r. of government   FIFTH AMEND 10
we do not think they r. into the privacy   OBSCENITY 22
reached that the community has already r.
LEGISLATION 31
reaching approaching and never r. consistency
LAW, GROWTH 4
read as though every i has to be dotted and
STATUTORY CONSTRUC 23
get the books, and r., and study them
LEGAL EDUCATION 15
I never r. or see the materials coming   CENSORSHIP 17
I r. "no law . . . abridging" to mean no law
FIRST AMEND 27
in what order the books are to be r.   LAW LIBRARIES 1
in what order to r. them   LEGAL EDUCATION 2
it, Judge? I can't even lift it   LEGAL WRITING 18
minute you r. something and you can't
LEGAL WRITING 12
misread any document than to r. it
STATUTORY CONSTRUC 18
my hips   TAXATION 61
my lips, no new taxes   TAXATION 58
We current Justices r. the Constitution
ORIGINAL INTENTION 16
we r. its words, not as we read   CONST LAW 42
what books he may r. or what films he   OBSCENITY 22
what books to r., and in what order to
LEGAL EDUCATION 2
who don't know anything and can't r.   JURY 20
reading get satisfaction r. the obituary notices
MURDER 5
stop r. dirty books and deliver the mail
CENSORSHIP 13
reads he r. the books for himself without an
LEGAL EDUCATION 14
if a judge r. his conscious or   JUDGES 21
ready like the traveler, must be r. for the
LAW, GROWTH 9
real and substantial relation to the object
DUE PROCESS 31
His r. politics are all important   JUDICIAL APPOINT 2
if we are to keep to the r. and the true   WORDS 7
The r. complaining party at your bar is   WAR CRIMES 6
therefore the r. master of society   JURY 9
realistic in a commonsense and r. fashion
SEARCHES AND SEIZ 51
realities should yield to the logic of r.   WORDS 14
reality it is a living, working r.   JURY 65
realize we are obligated—to r. those rights   RIGHTS 21
realized hopes not r. and promises not fulfilled
CONSTITUTION 52
reason And thus there seems a r. in all things
ADMIRALTY 8
Eloquence may set fire to r.   FREEDOM OF SPEECH 19
It is revolting to have no better r. for   HISTORY 3
overwhelmed the r., conscience, and   INSANITY 1
Power, not r., is the new currency of   PRECEDENT 60
power should answer to r. none the less
SUPREME COURT 30
the homage that force pays to r.   FRAUD 6
the perfect r. of the State   LAWYERS (PRO) 2
The r. the public thinks so much of the
SUPREME COURT 25
through r. called law   JUDGES 50
tributes that Power ever has paid to R.   WAR CRIMES 1
where r. is left free to combat it
FREEDOM OF SPEECH 4

worth as much as it weighs in r. and   PRECEDENT 20
would never fully triumph; but there was   LAW 103
reasonable classification must be r., not arbitrary
EQUAL PROTECTION 6
doubt . . . is a term often used, probably   JURY 15
not immunity from r. regulations and   CONTRACTS 12
outside border of r. legislative action
JUDICIAL REVIEW 25
proof beyond a r. doubt of every fact
CRIMINAL PROCEDURE 33
society is prepared to recognize as "r."   PRIVACY 14
that which no r. God would do   CONTRACTS 30
to warrant a man of r. caution in the
SEARCHES AND SEIZ 19
truth of the fact to a r. and moral   PROOF 2
very wide of any r. mark   DISTINCTIONS 9
reasonably electric chair should be r. accurate
COURTROOM SCENES 14
expect to induce action or forbearance   CONTRACTS 19
related in scope to the circumstances
SEARCHES AND SEIZ 58
they had r. trustworthy information
SEARCHES AND SEIZ 19
reasoning an artificial system of r., exclusively
JUSTICE 9
reasons unless there are r. for a difference
LANGUAGE 12
rebellion are shortly in r. against all law
LEGISLATION 35
in cases of R. or Invasion, involving   WAR 3
we are determined to foment a R., and
WOMEN'S RIGHTS 1
rebound put together and r. from time to time
PROPERTY 24
recalled The past cannot be r. by the most
CONTRACTS 1
receive the right to r. publications is such a
FIRST AMEND 40
reciprocity autonomy but r.   SEPARATION OF POWERS 20
reconstruct We could r. the corpus from them if all
LEGAL RESEARCH 2
record endorses the whole Congressional R.
LEGISLATIVE HISTORY 3
the r. on which we judge these   WAR CRIMES 3
records only profession which r. its mistakes
PRECEDENT 56
recruiting actual obstruction to its r. service or
FREEDOM OF THE PRESS 26
recurrence is not therefore an inevitable badge of
COPYRIGHT 21
red its r. is our lifeblood, its stars our   MARSHALL 10
justice requires me to cut r. tape and
TRIALS, FAMOUS 12
redeeming even the slightest r. social importance
OBSCENITY 9
utterly without r. social importance   OBSCENITY 9
utterly without r. social value   OBSCENITY 15
redressed poor Men are r.—till they're undone
WEALTH AND POVERTY 1
reduce would r. the Amendment to a nullity and
SEARCHES AND SEIZ 34
reduced cheated of their right and r. to beggary
LAWYERS (CON) 9
reduces the Fourth Amendment to a form of words
SEARCHES AND SEIZ 12
reexamine power to r. the basis of   PRECEDENT 42
reflect on which I r. with more pleasure   MARSHALL 3

The more we r. upon all that occurs in　　LAWYERS 13
Words are chameleons, which r. the color　　WORDS 21
reflection　Detached r. cannot be demanded in the
　　CRIMINAL LAW 9
reforged　must be r. in men's hearts every day　　LAW 81
reform　a general haven for r. movements
　　SUPREME COURT 39
refreshed　my retainer has not been renewed, or r.
　　FEES 4
refuge　havens of r. for those who might
　　DUE PROCESS 36
Liberty finds no r. in a jurisprudence　　ABORTION 24
There is no r. from confession but　　CONFESSIONS 1
refuse　When I r. to obey an unjust law, I do
　　CIVIL DISOBEDIENCE 1
refusing　to laugh at jokes　　CRITICAL LEGAL STUD 1
to obey it as a political rule　　SLAVERY 18
refutation　the statement carries its own r.
　　ORIGINAL INTENTION 8
refute　To state the proposition is to r. it
　　COMMERCE CLAUSE 9
regards　he r. it as a contract to which he
　　OBEDIENCE TO LAW 7
regret　I r. that I have but one law firm to　　LAW FIRMS 3
regulate　power to r. is not a power to destroy
　　REGULATION 2
right of the community to r. its use to　　REGULATION 7
that which it subsidizes　　REGULATION 12
the abortion procedure in ways that are　　ABORTION 5
regulation　a government r. is sufficiently
　　FIRST AMEND 42
if r. goes too far it will be recognized
　　EMINENT DOMAIN 6
is the substitution of error for chance　REGULATION 15
it is subject to state r.　　PROPERTY 25
sufficiently compelling to sustain r. of　　ABORTION 2
regulations　not immunity from reasonable r. and
　　CONTRACTS 12
rehearings　were not matters of right, but were
　　ADMINISTRATIVE LAW 14
reign　the r. of law, based upon the consent of
　　INTERNATIONAL LAW 14
reject　one ought not to r. it merely because it
　　PRECEDENT 53
Should the States r. this excellent
　　CONST CONVENTION 13
rejection　its r. by contemporary society is
　　CAPITAL PUNISHMENT 26
related　reasonably r. in scope to the
　　SEARCHES AND SEIZ 58
than they were before　　JURY 31
relations　Life has r. not capable always of
　　DISTINCTIONS 6
one's views of his r. to his Creator　　RELIGION 3
to enter into most of the r. of life　　CONTRACTS 16
relationship　In the r. between man and religion, the
　　FREEDOM OF RELIGION 65
relative　Of r. justice law may know something
　　JUSTICE 16
relatively　Injustice is r. easy to bear; what　　JUSTICE 28
relativism　this total r.—cannot be the theory of
　　FREEDOM OF SPEECH 45
to preserve a skeptical r. in a society　　LAWYERS 57
release　consider liberty a r. from all law, from
　　LIBERTY 4
relegated　We have been r. to the horse-and-buggy
　　COMMERCE CLAUSE 13

relevancy　the r. of color to a legitimate
　　AFFIRMATIVE ACTION 1
relevant　nothing that is logically r. should be
　　STATUTORY CONSTRUC 21
reliable　Covert tools are never r. tools
　　COMMERCIAL LAW 4
relic　it too is a r. of slavery　　CIVIL RIGHTS 35
relief　a tax r. bill providing relief not for　　TAXATION 45
must come through an aroused popular　　VOTING 10
providing r. not for the needy but for　　TAXATION 45
The cry of distress is the summons to r.
　　NEGLIGENCE 9
relieve　we r. stress; we correct mistakes; we
　　LAWYERS (PRO) 11
religion　and law were almost identical, and in
　　RELIGION 1
does not furnish grosser bigots than law　　JUDGES 4
entanglement with r. as something akin
　　FREEDOM OF RELIGION 73
In the relationship between man and r.
　　FREEDOM OF RELIGION 65
it will cease to be free for r.—except
　　FREEDOM OF RELIGION 54
laws which aid one r., aid all religions
　　FREEDOM OF RELIGION 40
neither advances nor inhibits r.
　　FREEDOM OF RELIGION 67
no r. in the world that has any other　　EVIDENCE 8
The essence of r. is belief in a
　　FREEDOM OF RELIGION 29
The "establishment of r." clause of the
　　FREEDOM OF RELIGION 40
The term "r." has reference to one's　　RELIGION 3
religious　follower and the atheist are no longer
　　FREEDOM OF RELIGION 49
no more dependence on our r. opinions
　　FREEDOM OF RELIGION 8
participate in the affairs of any r.
　　FREEDOM OF RELIGION 40
show a callous indifference to r. groups
　　FREEDOM OF RELIGION 53
symbolism is even used by some with the
　　FREEDOM OF RELIGION 38
We are a r. people whose institutions
　　FREEDOM OF RELIGION 52
religiously　they should be r. observed
　　OBEDIENCE TO LAW 12
relinquishment　intentional r. or abandonment of a
known　　CRIMINAL PROCEDURE 19
relying　too much on speech-making　　ADVOCACY 9
remain　he has the right to r. silent　　CONFESSIONS 12
warned that he has a right to r. silent　　CONFESSIONS 9
You have a right to r. silent　　CONFESSIONS 14
remainder　Whether a r. is vested or contingent　WILLS 4
remedies　The r. of injured consumers ought not to
　　PRODUCTS LIABILITY 1
remedy　but one r. exists to deter violations of
　　SEARCHES AND SEIZ 39
if the laws furnish no r. for the　OBEDIENCE TO LAW 5
judicial r. for every political mischief　　COURTS 36
laws of his country for a r.　　JUDICIAL REVIEW 6
Publicity is justly commended as a r.　LEGISLATION 30
the fitting r. for evil counsels is good
　　FREEDOM OF SPEECH 21
the r. is worse than the evil　CIVIL DISOBEDIENCE 5
the R., Justice, is worse than Injustice　　JUSTICE 6
the r. to be applied is more speech, not

To r. upon a formula is a slumber that   HOLMES 20
whether we do not r. our hopes too much   LIBERTY 6
restate it from the present point of view
    LEGAL RESEARCH 2
restitution The "r. interest," involving a   DAMAGES 4
restore the First Amendment liberties to the
    FIRST AMEND 24
restrain all from which the laws ought to r. him
    LAW 12
but they can r. the heartless   MORALITY 18
Law cannot r. evil; for the freedom of   LAW 77
restrains every regulation of trade, r.   ANTITRUST 14
restraint immunity of the press from previous r.
    FREEDOM OF THE PRESS 29
not merely freedom from bodily r. but
    DUE PROCESS 21
see how there could be any other r.   CONST LAW 37
some form of r. upon commercial   ANTITRUST 23
whether the r. imposed is such as merely
    ANTITRUST 15
restraints cannot exist without wholesome r.   LAW 14
The r. of rhyme or metre, the exigencies   JUSTICE 30
the r. on which the people must often
    COMMERCE CLAUSE 4
those wise r. that make men free
    HARVARD LAW SCHOOL 7
restrict government has no power to r. expression
    FIRST AMEND 45
the speech of some elements of our
    FREEDOM OF SPEECH 46
restricted railroad ticket, good for this day and
    PRECEDENT 44
restrictions All legal r. which curtail the civil
    EQUAL PROTECTION 8
restrictive unreasonably r. of competitive   ANTITRUST 10
result out to sea, and goes directly to his r.
    MARSHALL 8
transcending the immediate r. that is   CONST LAW 50
results its r. tend to favor those who can
    WEALTH AND POVERTY 9
prevent certain external r.   LAW 47
retail mere r. stuff compared with the   COMMON LAW 3
retained always been r. on the side of power   LAW 17
retainer my r. has not been renewed, or refreshed
    FEES 4
retaining an absolute power over Wives
    WOMEN'S RIGHTS 4
give up his skin for the hope of r. his   LITIGATION 13
retaliation constant dread of r.   PROSECUTION 9
retire You may r. to the jury room and pass the
    DAMAGES 6
retired virtually r. from the field and given up
    ADMINISTRATIVE LAW 3
retouching on which some strokes only want r.
    CONSTITUTION 6
retribution would bring terrible r.   GOVERNMENT 23
returns supreme coort follows th' iliction r.
    SUPREME COURT 11
revelation not as the priests of a completed r.
    JUDGES 24
the r. of the great purposes which were   CONST LAW 42
revenge all R. is Crime   CAPITAL PUNISHMENT 3
reverence constitutions with sanctimonious r.
    CONSTITUTION 15
I contemplate with sovereign r. that act
    FREEDOM OF RELIGION 19
Let r. for the laws, be breathed by   LAW 21

reverse the Supreme Court of the United States
    LAW REVIEWS 12
review when the lads on the Law R. say I'm
    LAW REVIEWS 3
reviews except in the American law r.   LAW REVIEWS 2
in the law r. that the most highly   LAW REVIEWS 4
revision our constitution for its r. at stated
    CONSTITUTION 16
revival the r. of claims that have been allowed
    CIVIL PROCEDURE 12
revolting private pleasures the busybodies find r.
    CENSORSHIP 19
to have no better reason for a rule of   HISTORY 3
revolution a "right of r." is a contradiction in
    REVOLUTION 3
in a moral point of view, justify r.   REVOLUTION 1
swear by the blood of the R., never to
    OBEDIENCE TO LAW 11
Teaching and espousing r.   REVOLUTION 4
This country is the product of r.   REVOLUTION 4
revolutionary a single r. spark may kindle a fire that
    FREEDOM OF EXPRESS 11
the Constitution is the most r. document
    CONSTITUTION 48
their r. right to dismember, or   REVOLUTION 2
revolutions are often "right," but a "right of
    REVOLUTION 3
reward act worthy of r. rather than punishment
    TRIALS, FAMOUS 6
for his allegiance, taxes and personal   JUSTICE 22
vile thing to plead for money or r.   FEES 2
Rex There was a young lawyer named R.
    LAWYER JOKES 7
rhetoric a lot of archaic and high-flown r. if we   LAW 81
rich a different law for the r. and the poor
    WEALTH AND POVERTY 18
interfered in behalf of any of the r.   TRIALS, FAMOUS 6
the poor man nor yet of the r. man
    OBEDIENCE TO LAW 18
rid takes a hundred years to get r. of it   LEGISLATION 15
riddle supply the answer to the r.   DISTINCTIONS 11
riders The r. in a race do not stop short when
    HOLMES 34
ridiculous you would accept the most r. fictions
    LEGAL FICTIONS 3
right a man is said to have a r. to his   PROPERTY 5
A nuisance may be merely a r. thing in   TORTS 6
a r. is only the hypostasis of a   RIGHTS 14
a "r. of revolution" is a contradiction   REVOLUTION 3
a r. which must be made available to all   EDUCATION 7
A woman's r. to make that choice freely   ABORTION 17
abandonment of a known r. or privilege
    CRIMINAL PROCEDURE 19
An immortal r. to bring an eternally   RIGHTS 13
An unconditional r. to say what one   FIRST AMEND 38
An unlimited r. to tax, implies a right   TAXATION 8
any clearly written constitutional r.   REVOLUTION 1
be settled than that it be settled r.   PRECEDENT 35
Citizenship is man's basic r. for it is   IMMIGRATION 5
conclusions are more likely to be
    FREEDOM OF EXPRESS 17
Constitution places the r. of silence   FIFTH AMEND 10
each party has an equal r. to judge for   FEDERALISM 7
First Amendment r. to broadcast
    COMMUNICATIONS LAW 2
for the law, so much as for the r.
    CIVIL DISOBEDIENCE 2

robbery absolutely necessary is legalized r.
　　　　　　　　　　　　　　TAXATION 38
none the less a r. because it is done　　TAXATION 13
robed the r. buffoon who makes merry at his
　　　　　　　　　　　　　　JUDGES 49
Robert Bork's America is a land in which women
　　　　　　　　　　　JUDICIAL APPOINT 12
giving R. some legal experience as
　　　　　　　　JUSTICE DEPARTMENT 5
robust uninhibited, r., and wide-open　　LIBEL 9
rock Laws are sand, customs are r.　LEGISLATION 25
Rockefeller makes a pauper the equal of a R.
　　　　　　　　　　　　　　COURTS 35
Roe The R. framework, then, is clearly on a
　　　　　　　　　　　　　　ABORTION 15
rogue No r. should enjoy his ill-gotten　FRAUD 3
romantic an attitude of "r. paternalism" which
　　　　　　　　　　SEX DISCRIMINATION 9
room There is always r. at the top　LAW PRACTICE 8
there'd be r. for two men in that one　LAWYER JOKES 2
rootless Homestead Act for r. twentieth century
　　　　　　　　　　　　　　PROPERTY 28
rope foolish legislation is a r. of sand　LEGISLATION 11
rot "May he r. in hell," David said　CASE SYSTEM 11
rough a r. sense of justice, the law　NEGLIGENCE 13
Constitution is going to have a r. time
　　　　　　　　　　　　　CONSTITUTION 34
The Constitution was built for r. as　　WAR 8
Trial by jury is a r. scales at best　　JURY 48
roving Here in effect is a r. commission to
　　　　　　　　　SEPARATION OF POWERS 17
Liar, n. A lawyer with a r. commission
　　　　　　　　　　　LAWYERS (CON) 27
royal I don't believe there is any r. road to　JUSTICE 36
There are two r. fish so styled by the　ADMIRALTY 8
rubber if they were not made of india-r., would
　　　　　　　　　　　　　REGULATION 1
merely as a r. stamp for the police
　　　　　　　　　SEARCHES AND SEIZ 52
rubbish pay for, a good deal of r.
　　　　　　　　　FREEDOM OF RELIGION 39
ruin I will r. you　　　　　LITIGATION 7
it is easy enough to r. it by bad laws　LEGISLATION 24
rule a r. becomes entirely obscured by its
　　　　　　　　　　　　　PROCEDURE 8
A r. protective of law-abiding citizens　CRIMINAL 6
law is the r. for simple and untaught
　　　　　　　　　　LEGAL PROFESSION 4
means of teaching it how to r. well　JURY 11
only to induce external conformity to r.
　　　　　　　　　　　CRIMINAL LAW 7
refusing to obey it as a political r.　SLAVERY 18
the first to establish so just a r.　PRECEDENT 6
The r. in Shelley's Case, the Don　PROPERTY 19
The r. of joy and the law of duty seem　HOLMES 9
the r. simply persists from blind　HISTORY 3
ruled most irksome to be r. by a bevy of
　　　　　　　　　　　　　GOVERNMENT 29
rulers law for r. and people, equally in war
　　　　　　　　　　　　CONSTITUTION 36
will have ceased, to be their own r.
　　　　　　　　　　JUDICIAL REVIEW 22
rules fixed and predetermined r. for all
　　　　　　　　　　　LEGAL REALISM 5
guide, but they do not control decision
　　　　　　　　　　　LEGAL REALISM 8
if his conduct is within the r.　MORALITY 3

of decision in trials at common law in
　　　　　　　　　CONFLICT OF LAWS 1
of law that will enable individuals to　MARRIAGE 8
play the game according to the r.　HOLMES 37
since they didn't make the r., the rules　WOMEN 8
state not r. for the passing hour, but　CONST LAW 29
the r. have nothing to do with them　WOMEN 8
We do not pick our r. of law　JUDICIAL LEGISLATION 5
which are to govern the conduct of men
　　　　　　　　　　LAWYERS (PRO) 6
rulings interpretations and opinions of the
　　　　　　　　　ADMINISTRATIVE LAW 15
rummage to r. at will among his papers in search
　　　　　　　　　SEARCHES AND SEIZ 23
run Fourth and Fifth Amendments r. almost
　　　　　　　　　SEARCHES AND SEIZ 9
running Judges are not given the task of r. the
　　　　　　　　　MILITARY JUSTICE 10
Russia and Geneva have equal rights
　　　　　　　　　INTERNATIONAL LAW 2
go to law with the Czar of R.　ADMIRALTY 3
ruthless Absolute discretion is a r. master
　　　　　　　　　ADMINISTRATIVE LAW 17

sabotage The very fact that no s. has taken place
　　　　　　　　　　　CIVIL RIGHTS 13
Sacco S.'s name will live in the hearts of the
　　　　　　　　　　TRIALS, FAMOUS 13
sacrament get pregnant, abortion would be a s.
　　　　　　　　　　　　ABORTION 8
sacred literary property will be as s. as　COPYRIGHT 7
No law can be s. to me but that of my
　　　　　　　　　　NATURAL LAW 7
steal into the s. area of religious
　　　　　　　　FREEDOM OF RELIGION 50
sacredly obligatory upon all　CONSTITUTION 10
sacrifice ever admitted that it could not s.　HOLMES 2
unceasingly upon its altars　LAW 21
who know too much to s. good sense to a
　　　　　　　　　　　PRECEDENT 10
sacrificing his will and his welfare to that of the
　　　　　　　　　　　　HOLMES 2
thus absurdly s. the end to the means
　　　　　　　　　OBEDIENCE TO LAW 6
saddest For the s. epitaph which can be carved
　　　　　　　　　　FIRST AMEND 9
safe drunken man is as much entitled to a s.
　　　　　　　　　　NEGLIGENCE 1
every man able to read, all is s.
　　　　　　　FREEDOM OF THE PRESS 18
This is Choate, who made it s. to murder
　　　　　　　LAWYERS, INDIVIDUAL 2
while the Legislature is in session　LEGISLATION 16
safeguards history of observance of procedural s.
　　　　　　　　　　　PROCEDURE 4
The s. of liberty have frequently been　LIBERTY 9
safety monuments of the s. with which error of
　　　　　　　　　FREEDOM OF SPEECH 4
no right to strike against the public s.　LABOR LAW 6
said everything worth saying shall be s.
　　　　　　　　　　FIRST AMEND 21
making every other word a "s." or　LEGAL WRITING 1
sail Your constitution is all s. and no　CONSTITUTION 30
sailing publication of s. dates of transports or
　　　　　　　FREEDOM OF THE PRESS 26
saints it is not the s. of the world who
　　　　　　　　　SEX DISCRIMINATION 1

533

men don't think about sex at all, you
LAWYERS (CON) 54
there are s. things even rats won't do
LAWYER JOKES 10
will rob you with a six gun   CRIMINAL 7
somebody rather have clients than be s.'s lawyer
CLIENT 4
to let off s. else who broke something
SEARCHES AND SEIZ 29
someone looks like s. designed it on purpose
TAXATION 51
something to let off somebody else who broke s.
SEARCHES AND SEIZ 29
son because he was a dumb s. of a bitch
MILITARY JUSTICE 12
You're a s. of a bitch, Kingsfield
LAW SCHOOL 9
sophisticated nullifies s. as well as simple-minded
VOTING 5
sophisticates who s. the law to his mind, by the turn
MARSHALL 2
sordid The s. controversies of litigants are
PRECEDENT 24
sorry I am s. that I have lived so long
CAPITAL PUNISHMENT 12
soul All I want in exchange is your s.
LAWYER JOKES 17
its protected crannies for the s.   PRIVACY 13
Liberty is the s.'s right to breathe   LIBERTY 2
The s. of one man cannot by human law be
SLAVERY 3
the swerve, or the inclination of the s.   GUILT 6
while there is a s. in prison, I am not
TRIALS, FAMOUS 11
sound first requirement of a s. body of law is   LAW 38
pure ethics and s. logic are also parts COMMON LAW 6
The s. of tireless voices is the price
FREEDOM OF SPEECH 40
soup as thin as the homeopathic s. that was
SLAVERY 19
source all income from whatever s. derived
TAXATION 48
lawyers could be an important s. of LAWYER JOKES 16
strangle the free mind at its s. and   EDUCATION 3
We have put its s. in the law   PRODUCTS LIABILITY 3
We have put the s. of the obligation
PRODUCTS LIABILITY 3
sovereign articulate voice of some s. or
COMMON LAW 15
Every s. State is bound to respect the
INTERNATIONAL LAW 8
I contemplate with s. reverence that act
FREEDOM OF RELIGION 19
is exempt from suit, not because of any
SOVEREIGN IMMUNITY 1
one of the s. prerogatives of   SEGREGATION 22
the precise word was the s. talisman   CONTRACTS 13
sovereignty appeal from the s. of the people to the
CIVIL DISOBEDIENCE 1
he be said . . . to personify the federal s.
PRESIDENT 10
people to the s. of mankind   CIVIL DISOBEDIENCE 1
the doctrine of the s. of the people
FREEDOM OF THE PRESS 20
Soviet enforced by S. procedural practices
PROCEDURE 10
live under S. substantive law applied in
PROCEDURE 10

space freedoms need breathing s. to survive
FIRST AMEND 36
The lawyer's vacation is the s. between   LAWYERS 20
the s. between men, as it is hedged in   FREEDOM 5
spare me quotations, which, though learn'd
QUOTATIONS 1
spark a single revolutionary s. may kindle a
FREEDOM OF EXPRESS 11
speak as I am when I s. in court   ADVOCACY 7
Freedom to s. and write about public   FIRST AMEND 14
Speech is conduct, and actions s.
FREEDOM OF SPEECH 41
They are to s. in the same voice now   CONST LAW 15
to s. of the law as our mistress, we who   LAW 41
speaker mean in the mouth of a normal s. of WORDS 5
speaking by s. and writing Truth   TRIALS, FAMOUS 3
Extemporaneous s. should be practised   ADVOCACY 9
more clearly than you think   ADVOCACY 28
speaks The dissenter s. to the future, and his
DISSENT 7
special any value the Constitution marks as s.
ABORTION 7
The s. information which lawyers derive   LAWYERS 9
specific goes beyond the s. guarantees to protect
FIRST AMEND 40
point to s. and articulable facts which
SEARCHES AND SEIZ 59
the s. content of the utterer's mind at   LANGUAGE 11
spectacle the Novel and astonishing Spectacle of a
CONST CONVENTION 16
speech agree with the common s., unless there
LANGUAGE 12
Free s. carries with it some freedom to
FREEDOM OF SPEECH 48
freedom of s. and expression—everywhere
FIRST AMEND 13
Freedom of s. and of the press . . . are
FOURTEENTH AMEND 7
freedom of s., freedom of conscience   FIRST AMEND 5
freedom of s. or expression at the   EDUCATION 8
in order to protect s. that matters   LIBEL 13
is conduct, and actions speak FREEDOM OF SPEECH 41
is often provocative and challenging
FREEDOM OF SPEECH 38
it is a sign that s. is serious   CENSORSHIP 14
no coherent theory of free s.   FIRST AMEND 43
restrict the s. of some elements of our
FREEDOM OF SPEECH 46
such invasion of free s. as is necessary
FREEDOM OF SPEECH 31
the extremest view in favor of free s.
FREEDOM OF SPEECH 14
the greatest freedom of s. was the
FREEDOM OF SPEECH 15
the remedy to be applied is more s., not
FREEDOM OF SPEECH 23
when s. is caught upon the wing and   LIBEL 8
speech-making relying too much on s.   ADVOCACY 9
speed with all deliberate s. the parties to
SEGREGATION 17
Spencer does not enact Mr. Herbert S.'s Social
DUE PROCESS 14
spend Than s. the Whole, entangled in the Laws
LITIGATION 2
sphere a certain private s. of individual   PRIVACY 18
spine he has not, but O, a beak he has
LAWYERS (CON) 41

it is a rising and not a setting s.
CONST CONVENTION 10
Sunday you wanted to go home early S. night
LAW FIRMS 4
sunlight is said to be the best of disinfectants
LEGISLATION 30
sunshine disappearing in the s. of actual facts
EVIDENCE 7
super a s. board of education for every school
EDUCATION 6
tribunal, not a s.-legal-aid bureau   SUPREME COURT 31
We do not sit as a s.-legislature to
JUDICIAL REVIEW 37
superficial engage in gestures of s. equality
EQUAL PROTECTION 21
superfluous to many people the s. is the necessary
HOLMES 28
superior a s. opportunity of being a good man
LITIGATION 5
duties s. to those arising from any
FREEDOM OF RELIGION 29
no s., dominant, ruling class of   SEGREGATION 8
that which has the s. obligation and
JUDICIAL REVIEW 2
the power of the people is s. to both
JUDICIAL REVIEW 3
this is "s. in obligation to any other"
WOMEN'S RIGHTS 6
superiority This notion of their s. perpetually
LAWYERS 9
superlative There is in all men a demand for the s.
INTOXICATION 3
supernatural entities which do not have a verifiable
LEGAL REALISM 14
supersede not to criticize, but to s. the use of
COPYRIGHT 3
superstitious their s. attachment to what is old to
LAWYERS 14
We are s., and esteem the statute   STATUTES 1
supper Isn't it time we wint to s.   JURY 32
supplies The rational part of us s. the reasons
SUPREME COURT 27
supply could not long s. its want   LIBERTY 5
Life in all its fullness must s. the   DISTINCTIONS 11
support committed to the s. of no dogma
FREEDOM OF RELIGION 22
supported and still be s. by an array of cases
PRECEDENT 14
to enforce a law not s. by the people
LAW ENFORCEMENT 13
suppose I s. it is not a basis for impeachment
LAW REVIEWS 1
suppress a government determined to s. political
SEARCHES AND SEIZ 23
suppression in s. lies ordinarily the greatest peril
FREEDOM OF EXPRESS 9
the s. by the prosecution of evidence
CRIMINAL PROCEDURE 31
unrelated to the s. of free expression   FIRST AMEND 42
supreme coort follows th' iliction returns
SUPREME COURT 11
Court seemed too anemic to endure a long
SUPREME COURT 28
does not establish a s. law of the land   CONST LAW 60
fixed by decisions of the S. Court   JUDICIAL REVIEW 22
If the S. Court is ever composed of   SUPREME COURT 9
In a government acknowledgedly s.   FEDERALISM 15

in the last resort, to one s. tribunal   SUPREME COURT 1
institutions presuppose a S. Being
FREEDOM OF RELIGION 52
so much of the Justices of the S. Court
SUPREME COURT 25
The Constitution is s.   FEDERALISM 31
the nine old men of the S. Court are
SUPREME COURT 17
the organization of the S. Court, and
SUPREME COURT 8
The Tenth Justice of the S. Court
JUDGES, INDIVIDUAL 4
they are both sitting on the S. Court
JUDICIAL APPOINT 10
Whenever you put a man on the S. Court
JUDICIAL APPOINT 6
within its sphere of action   FEDERALISM 12
sure that it was drawn up by a lawyer
LEGAL WRITING 12
the spirit which is not too s. that it   LIBERTY 7
where many ignorant men are s.; that is   DARROW 4
surer There is no s. way to misread any
STATUTORY CONSTRUC 18
surest one of the s. indexes of a mature and   WORDS 20
the s. way to lose their essence is to   WORDS 18
surgeon condemn the s. who bled a man in the
STATUTORY CONSTRUC 14
surprises preventing s. through the revival of
CIVIL PROCEDURE 12
surprising ignorance of the purpose of litigation
WILLS 7
surrendering former views to a better considered
ERROR 4
surrogate serve as the Founders' s. for the
ORIGINAL INTENTION 12
survival the s. of life after death is the   WILLS 13
survive it cannot s. their being repeated   WAR CRIMES 1
survived long s. every cause that gave it birth
PROPERTY 19
susceptible not s. of comprehensive statement in an
CONST LAW 36
suspect inherently s., and must therefore be
SEX DISCRIMINATION 10
justify the use of a s. classification
EQUAL PROTECTION 19
single racial group are immediately s.   CIVIL RIGHTS 14
single racial group are immediately s.
EQUAL PROTECTION 8
suspended any of its provisions can be s. during
CONSTITUTION 36
sustain sufficiently compelling to s. regulation
ABORTION 2
swayed Juries are not leaves s. by every breath   JURY 39
swear by the blood of the Revolution, never to
OBEDIENCE TO LAW 11
sweep a man may s. juries before him, command
LAWYERS 32
away all opposition   FREEDOM OF SPEECH 12
swerve the s., or the inclination of the soul   GUILT 6
swift justice demands more than just swiftness
CRIMINAL PROCEDURE 27
v. Tyson shall now be disapproved
CONFLICT OF LAWS 8
swiftness swift justice demands more than just s.
CRIMINAL PROCEDURE 27
swim several states must sink or s. together
FEDERALISM 32

and unchecked ex parte examination   GRAND JURY 2
Do not put such u. power into the hands
    WOMEN'S RIGHTS 1
undefined, u., permanent and perpetual
    CONSTITUTION 28
unmitigated practicing lawyers know to be u. fiction
    JURY 62
unofficial always lags somewhat behind u. law   LAW 74
unorthodoxy Mere u. or dissent from the prevailing
    FREEDOM OF EXPRESS 23
unpopular protect u. citizens against   LAW 70
unpredictable one of the last of the u. professions
    ADVOCACY 24
unpunished Every u. murder takes away something
    MURDER 1
unqualified this right is not u. and must be
    ABORTION 3
unreal It is an u. dream   CRIMINAL PROCEDURE 12
unreasonable not all searches and seizures, but u.
    SEARCHES AND SEIZ 45
per se u. under the Fourth Amendment
    SEARCHES AND SEIZ 55
secure from all u. searches, and   SEARCHES AND SEIZ 5
shall not be u., arbitrary or capricious
    DUE PROCESS 31
unreasonably restrictive of competitive conditions
    ANTITRUST 10
unredressed better to leave u. the wrongs done by
    PROSECUTION 9
unsettled will not be u. overnight, for certainty
    PRECEDENT 32
unspeakably those three u. precious things
    FIRST AMEND 5
unsullied our maintenance of Justice pure and u.
    ETHICS 13
the shrine of justice pure and u.   ETHICS 12
unusual nor cruel and u. punishments inflicted
    PUNISHMENT 2
unusualness Formally to detain one accused of u.
    CRIMINAL LAW 8
unwarranted governmental intrusion into matters so
    PRIVACY 15
unwise whether we think this law is u., or even
    PRIVACY 11
uplifted demanded in the presence of an u. knife
    CRIMINAL LAW 9
uppity it is a high-tech lynching for u. blacks
    JUDICIAL APPOINT 15
upside you handed it to me u. down
    JUDGES, INDIVIDUAL 8
usages customs and u. of civilized nations
    INTERNATIONAL LAW 10
settled u. and modes of proceeding   DUE PROCESS 7
use free as the air to common u.   COPYRIGHT 15
once you u. them they fuck everything up
    LAWYERS (CON) 62
The u. of the due process clause to   DUE PROCESS 37
used anything he says can be u. against him
    CONFESSIONS 12
can and will be u. against you in court
    CONFESSIONS 14
so u. to paying taxes that it would just   TAXATION 27
useful It qualifies a man to be u. to himself
    LEGAL EDUCATION 3
other u. agencies of civilized life   LAW BOOKS 8
usefulness no taint of u., for other than the
    LAWYERS (CON) 18

useless I think it u. and undesirable, as a rule
    DISSENT 4
There is a u. lawsuit in every useless
    LEGAL WRITING 4
usual meaning which the law imposes upon them
    CONTRACTS 11
usually it u. takes a hundred years to get rid
    LEGISLATION 15
usurping It is u. the functions of a legislator
    CONST LAW 14
usurps the function of both judge and jury   ETHICS 8
utter captives and choreboys of their clients
    LAWYERS 53
The best description of "u. waste" would
    LAWYER JOKES 5
utterance the "meaning" of an u. is exhausted by
    LANGUAGE 11
utterances such u. are no essential part of any
    FREEDOM OF SPEECH 26
whether their u. transcend the bounds of
    FIRST AMEND 8
utterly at a loss to decide upon the statute's
    LANGUAGE 3
the u. devastating argument that I   ADVOCACY 20
without redeeming social importance   OBSCENITY 9
without redeeming social value   OBSCENITY 15

vacated Not lightly v. is the verdict of   HISTORY 6
vacation The lawyer's v. is the space between the
    LAWYERS 20
vagrant Discretion is not unconfined and v.
    SEPARATION OF POWERS 16
It is unconfined and v.   SEPARATION OF POWERS 17
vague The v. contours of the Due Process
    DUE PROCESS 43
When twenty years ago a v. terror went   HOLMES 18
vaguer in the v. sanctions of conscience   MORALITY 7
valid contrary to the constitution can be v.
    JUDICIAL REVIEW 1
validity no right to question the v. of a law
    JUDICIAL REVIEW 5
valuable All that is v. in the United States
    CONSTITUTION 33
value any v. the Constitution marks as special
    ABORTION 7
it is of immense social v.   LEGAL REALISM 4
no subordinate v. can be protected
    FREEDOM OF SPEECH 33
this is the ultimate v. of any society
    FREEDOM OF SPEECH 33
utterly without redeeming social v.   OBSCENITY 15
valued They v. liberty both as an end and as a
    FREEDOM OF SPEECH 20
values tramples the v. that the Fourteenth
    FOURTEENTH AMEND 14
vanished carved in memory of a v. liberty is that
    FIRST AMEND 9
varieties infinite v. of temperament, intellect
    NEGLIGENCE 2
than most other v. of mankind   LAWYERS (PRO) 14
vary significance that v. from age to age   CONST LAW 28
varying emphasis, tacit assumptions, unwritten
    COURTS 21
Vegas found tolerable in Las V., or New York
    OBSCENITY 25
vegetable they will extinguish every other v. that
    LAWYERS (CON) 6

553

comment upon the w. of courts, who are   COURTS 26
constitutions are the w. of time and not
   CONSTITUTION 20
I hate w.   JUDGES 17
It isn't w. for me; just one fascinating   DARROW 3
people in Washington who do their own w.
   SUPREME COURT 25
right to w. for a living in the common
   EQUAL PROTECTION 5
such a w. could not fail to be of   CASE SYSTEM 3
the knowledge I have gained in the w. of
   TRIALS, FAMOUS 8
the w. never is done while the power to   HOLMES 34
the w. of a judge is an art   JUDGES 54
They are better to w. with or play with
   LAWYERS (PRO) 14
Upon any w., and especially upon a play
   COPYRIGHT 17
upon the w. of undergraduate students
   LAW REVIEWS 2
W., work, work, is the main thing
   LEGAL EDUCATION 15
workable dispersed powers into a w. government
   SEPARATION OF POWERS 20
worked Only when you have w. alone, . . . then only
   HOLMES 7
workman without books would be like a w. without
   LAW BOOKS 1
works God w. wonders now and then; Behold! a
   LAWYERS (CON) 2
world a new w. order—a world where the rule
   INTERNATIONAL LAW 24
a new w. order, where diverse nations
   INTERNATIONAL LAW 25
a w. founded upon four essential human
   FIRST AMEND 13
a w. in which we live   LAW 100
In no country in the w. is the love of   PROPERTY 10
in the w. an academic faculty which pins
   LAW REVIEWS 2
it is not the saints of the w. who
   SEX DISCRIMINATION 1
let Facts be submitted to a candid w.   ENGLISH LAW 4
only imperfect justice in this w.   JUSTICE 44
The w. has its fling at lawyers   LAWYERS (PRO) 3
The w., my fellow citizens, has produced   JUDGES 8
The w.'s law was no law for her mind   LAWLESSNESS 5
This w. has been one long slaughterhouse
   CAPITAL PUNISHMENT 11
whether the w. would be any the worse
   CIVIL PROCEDURE 17
worlds the choice between the two w. will be
   ABORTION 23
worse A w. man can scarcely be found than one
   LITIGATION 6
it is w. to be entirely without it   LAW 15
making the w. argument appear the   ADVOCACY 29
the remedy is w. than the evil   CIVIL DISOBEDIENCE 5
whether the world would be any the w.
   CIVIL PROCEDURE 17
Your crime is w. than murder   TREASON 3
worship freedom of every person to w. God in his
   FIRST AMEND 13
worst absurdity to put the w. to death
   CAPITAL PUNISHMENT 4
it should banish an alien from our w.   IMMIGRATION 3
the w. instrument of arbitrary power

   SEARCHES AND SEIZ 1
worth A decided case is w. as much as it
   PRECEDENT 20
A verbal contract isn't w. the paper   CONTRACTS 22
any lawyer w. his salt will tell the   CONFESSIONS 4
everything w. saying shall be said   FIRST AMEND 21
no general proposition is w. a damn   HOLMES 13
question as to whether it is w. living   HOLMES 10
subjects that are not w. the bother of   LAW REVIEWS 8
What it is w. when it arrives, is for   JURY 28
wound up, and set to true time   LAW 29
wreak he may w. himself upon life, may drink
   LAWYERS (PRO) 5
wreck an answer that might w. your case
   CROSS-EXAMINATION 7
write I w. for that man   HOLMES 36
it in the books of law   CIVIL RIGHTS 23
time now to w. the next chapter, and to
   CIVIL RIGHTS 23
writes Everytime a lawyer w. something, he is
   LEGAL WRITING 11
woman moulds the lawgiver and w. the law   WOMEN 2
writing by speaking and w. Truth   TRIALS, FAMOUS 3
How I dislike w. opinions   SUPREME COURT 16
Legal w. is one of those rare creatures
   LEGAL WRITING 26
so that endless others of his craft can
   LEGAL WRITING 11
things wrong with almost all legal w.
   LEGAL WRITING 13
writs of assistance and general warrants are
   SEARCHES AND SEIZ 25
written A strict observance of the w. laws is
   OBEDIENCE TO LAW 6
Briefs should be w. in the English   LEGAL WRITING 22
constitutions may be violated in moments
   CONSTITUTION 13
does to the w. word what the Cuisinart
   LAW REVIEWS 15
guarantees which must be w. are less
   CONSTITUTION 47
I have not yet w. the opinion   SEGREGATION 21
in the possession of a w. Constitution   CONST LAW 1
isn't worth the paper it's w. on   CONTRACTS 22
Our Constitution was not w. in the sands
   CONST LAW 54
over the portals of every church, every   COURTS 32
primarily in order that they may be w.
   LAW REVIEWS 10
rules of government ever w.   CONSTITUTION 45
that they need not be w.   CONSTITUTION 47
the Constitution is a w. document is a   CONST LAW 34
the constitution is w.   CONSTITUTION 14
wrong As it is now they are trying the w. man
   ETHICS 25
atone for the w. this day done   SEGREGATION 10
because I was unconsciously w. yesterday
   PRECEDENT 48
directions which do not put the traveler   ERROR 1
I found out the w. guy was on trial
   MILITARY JUSTICE 9
I see nothing w. with giving Robert some
   JUSTICE DEPARTMENT 5
merely a right thing in the w. place   TORTS 6
the lads on the Law Review say I'm w.
   LAW REVIEWS 3
There are two things w. with almost all

Index by Author

CRIME 7
CRIMINAL 5
JURY 38, 53
LAW 63
LAW PRACTICE 15
LAWYERS 41
LEGAL WRITING 6
Traver, Robert (pseudonym of John D. Voelker 1903–
1991), *writer and judge*
ADVOCACY 24
CLIENT 18
DEFENSE 2
ETHICS 34
JUDGES 53
LAW 80, 81, 82
LAW PRACTICE 21
MURDER 6
Traynor, Roger J. (1900–1983), *judge*
CONTRACTS 24
CUSTODY 2
PRODUCTS LIABILITY 5
Tribe, Laurence H. (b. 1941),
Chinese-born American legal scholar
JUDICIARY 21
Trillin, Calvin (b. 1935), *author*
LAW PRACTICE 22
SECURITIES LAW 5
Trotti, Lamar (1900–1952), *author*
LAWLESSNESS 12
Truman, Harry S. (1884–1972),
president of the United States
FIRST AMENDMENT 26
INTERNATIONAL LAW 19
JUDICIAL APPOINTMENTS 6
MILITARY JUSTICE 12
Tucker, Benjamin R. (1854–1939), *anarchist*
CRIMINAL 2
Tucker, Gideon J. (fl. 1870), *judge*
LEGISLATION 16
Tullock, Gordon (b. 1922), *economist*
EVIDENCE 15
Turow, Scott (b. 1949), *writer*
CASE SYSTEM 11
LAW 103
LEGAL FICTIONS 3
TORTS 14
Tussman, Joseph (b. 1914), *philosopher*
EQUAL PROTECTION 11
Twain, Mark (pseudonym of Samuel Langhorne Clemens
1835–1910), *writer*
ADVOCACY 13
CLIENT 3
COPYRIGHT 7, 11, 12
COURTS 13
DEMOCRACY 3
ETHICS 11
FIRST AMENDMENT 5
FREEDOM OF RELIGION 24, 25
FREEDOM OF THE PRESS 23
GOVERNMENT 17
INSANITY 3, 5, 6, 7, 8, 9
INTOXICATION 1
JURY 20, 21, 22, 23, 24, 25, 26
JUSTICE 14
LAW ENFORCEMENT 3, 4
LAWLESSNESS 8
LAWYERS (CON) 13, 14, 16, 17

LEGAL EDUCATION 16
LEGISLATION 19, 25
MURDER 3
NATURAL LAW 11, 12
OBEDIENCE TO LAW 16
PARDONS 2
PUNISHMENT 13
RELIGION 2, 5
STATUTORY CONSTRUCTION 2
SUPREME COURT 10
TAXATION 11, 20, 21, 22
WILLS 6
Tweed, Harrison (1885–1969), *lawyer*
LAW FIRMS 4
LAWYERS (PRO) 14

Uelmen, Gerald F. (b. 1940), *legal scholar*
DEFENSE 5
Underwood, Oscar W. (1862–1929), *political leader*
LEGISLATION 35
Unger, Roberto Mangabeira (b. 1947), *legal scholar*
CRITICAL LEGAL STUDIES 4, 5
United States Army
WAR CRIMES 10
United States War Department
WAR 6
Untermeyer, Louis (1885–1977), *author and editor*
JUDGES 26

Van Buren, Martin (1782–1862),
president of the United States
CONSTITUTION 20
Van Orsdel, Josiah A. (1860–1937), *judge*
EXPERTS 1
Vanderbilt, Arthur T. (1898–1957),
judge and legal scholar
CIVIL PROCEDURE 19
Vanderbilt, Cornelius (1794–1877), *capitalist*
LAWLESSNESS 9
LITIGATION 7
Vann, Irving G. (1842–1921), *judge*
TRUSTS 3
Vanzetti, Bartolomeo (1888–1927), *political radical*
TRIALS, FAMOUS 13, 14
Veblen, Thorstein (1857–1929), *economist*
LAW 54
LAWYERS (CON) 18, 19
LITIGATION 18
LAW SCHOOL 3
Veeck, Bill (1914–1986), *baseball team owner*
LAWYERS (CON) 50
SPORTS 2
Vest, George Graham (1830–1904), *political leader*
ADVOCACY 12
Vidal, Gore (b. 1925), *author*
OBSCENITY 23
REGULATION 13
Vinson, Fred M. (1890–1953),
judge and government official
FREEDOM OF SPEECH 33
TAXATION 47
Vlasic, Ivan A. (b. 1926), *author*
LITIGATION 26
Voelker, John D. (Robert Traver 1903–1991),
writer and judge
ADVOCACY 24
CLIENT 18